ISC Exams 2026

AF819605

All in One®

Mathematics

Class 12

Simplified Theory

Topic & Chapter Exercises

Exam Pattern Questions

Specimen & Sample Papers

Authors
Laxman Prasad,
Brijesh Dwivedi

arihant
SUCCESS AND NOTHING LESS

arihant
SUCCESS AND NOTHING LESS

ARIHANT PRAKASHAN
(School Division Series)

卐 ADMINISTRATIVE & PRODUCTION OFFICES

Regd. Office

'Ramchhaya' 4577/15, Agarwal Road, Darya Ganj, New Delhi -110002
Tele: 011- 47630600, 43518550; Fax: 011- 23280316

卐 *Head Office*

Kalindi, TP Nagar, Meerut (UP) - 250002, Tel: 0121-7156203, 7156204

卐 SALES & SUPPORT OFFICES

Agra, Ahmedabad, Bengaluru, Bareilly, Chennai, Delhi, Guwahati, Hyderabad, Jaipur, Jhansi, Kolkata, Lucknow, Nagpur & Pune.

PO No : TXT-XX-XXXXXXX-X-XX

Published By Arihant Publications (India) Ltd.

For further information about the books published by Arihant, log on to www.arihantbooks.com or e-mail at info@arihantbooks.com

Follow us on

卐 PRICE ₹635.00

PRODUCTION TEAM

Publishing Managers	Cover Designer	Inner Designer
Mahendra Singh Rawat & Keshav Mohan	Salman Shaikh	Ankit Tyagi
Project Head	*Page Layouting*	*Proof Reader*
Ashwani	Shivam Prajapati	Manish Kumar

Index *cum* Study Planner

One Book- Endless Features

to Help you Succeed

In this Chapter

At the start of each chapter, all the topics of the chapter have been listed, so that students may know what they are going to study.

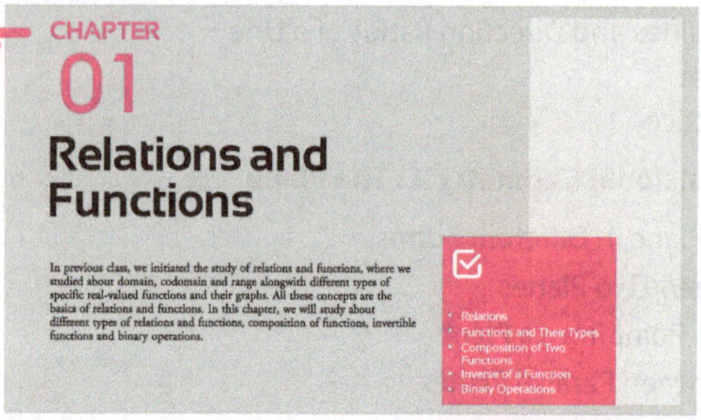
CHAPTER 01

Relations and Functions

In previous class, we initiated the study of relations and functions, where we studied about domain, codomain and range alongwith different types of specific real-valued functions and their graphs. All these concepts are the basics of relations and functions. In this chapter, we will study about different types of relations and functions, composition of functions, invertible functions and binary operations.

- Relations
- Functions and Their Types
- Composition of Two Functions
- Inverse of a Function
- Binary Operations

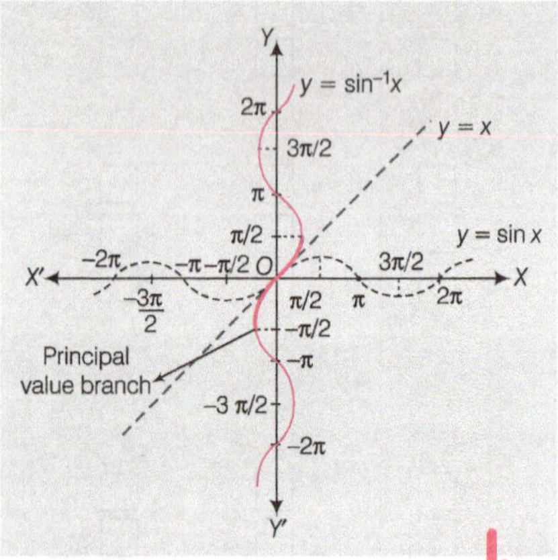

Complete Theory in Each Chapter

Each chapter has Complete, Easy to Understand and Simplified theory covering latest syllabus and latest NCERT Textbook. Theory is developed in such a way that it is Suitable for all typer of learners.

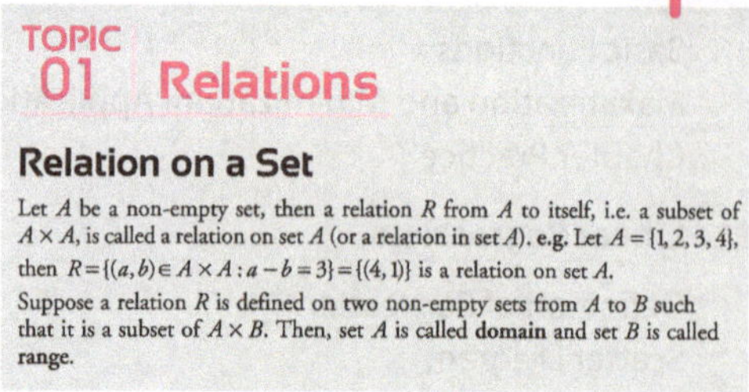
TOPIC 01 Relations

Relation on a Set

Let A be a non-empty set, then a relation R from A to itself, i.e. a subset of $A \times A$, is called a relation on set A (or a relation in set A). e.g. Let $A = \{1, 2, 3, 4\}$, then $R = \{(a, b) \in A \times A : a - b = 3\} = \{(4, 1)\}$ is a relation on set A.

Suppose a relation R is defined on two non-empty sets from A to B such that it is a subset of $A \times B$. Then, set A is called **domain** and set B is called **range**.

Illustrative Figures

To make the concepts completely visible, illustrative diagrams have been given at various place.

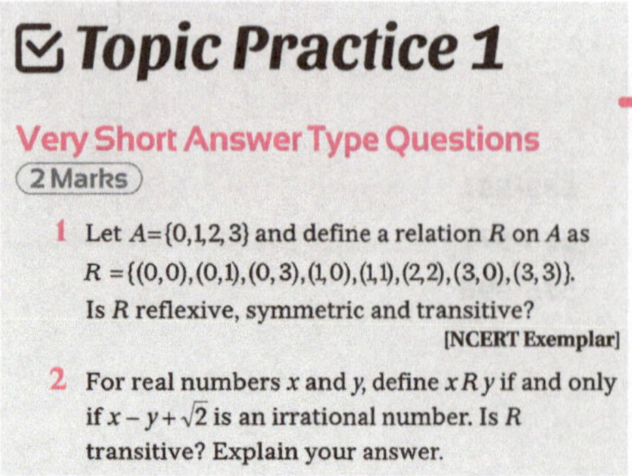
Topic Practice 1

Very Short Answer Type Questions (2 Marks)

1 Let $A=\{0,1,2,3\}$ and define a relation R on A as $R=\{(0,0),(0,1),(0,3),(1,0),(1,1),(2,2),(3,0),(3,3)\}$. Is R reflexive, symmetric and transitive? **[NCERT Exemplar]**

2 For real numbers x and y, define $x R y$ if and only if $x - y + \sqrt{2}$ is an irrational number. Is R transitive? Explain your answer.

Topical Exercises

To make students understand the chapter in a smooth part-by-part manner, Topical Exercises have been given in each chapter. These Exercises help students to assess the understanding of related concepts at regular interval.

One Book- Endless Features

to Help you Succeed

Chapter Practice

The students can check their understanding of the chapter through Chapter Practice given at the end of each chapter.

Chapter Practice

Very Short Answer Type Questions (2 Marks)

1. Check whether the relation R, defined in the set $\{1, 2, 3, 4, 5, 6\}$ as $R = \{(a, b) : b = a + 1\}$, is reflexive, symmetric or transitive. [NCERT]
2. Let N be the set of natural numbers and relation R on N be defined by $R = \{(x, y) : x, y \in N, x + y = 10\}$. Then, check whether R is reflexive, symmetric and transitive.
3. Show that the function $f : R \to R$, $f(x) = x^4$ is many-one and into.
4. Show that the function $f : Z \to Z$ defined by $f(x) = x^2 + x$, is a many-one function.
5. Show that signum function is neither one-one nor onto.
6. If $f(x) = \frac{1}{x}$ and $g(x) = 0$, then show that fog is not defined.

Short Answer Type Questions (4 Marks)

11. If $A = \{1, 2, 3, 4\}$, define relations on A which have properties of being
    (i) reflexive, transitive but not symmetric.
    (ii) symmetric but neither reflexive nor transitive. [NCERT Exemplar]
12. Show that relation R in the set of real numbers, defined as $R = \{(a, b) : a \le b^2\}$ is neither reflexive nor symmetric nor transitive. [NCERT]
13. Check whether the relation R defined in the set A of human beings in a city at particular time as $R = \{(x, y) : x$ is wife of $y\}$, is reflexive, symmetric and transitive. [NCERT]
14. Let S be the set of all real numbers and R be the relation on S defined by $R = \{(a, b) : |a| \le b\}$. Show that R is neither reflexive nor symmetric but transitive.
15. Let n be a fixed ositive inte er. Define a

ISC Examination Paper 2025

A Highly Simulated Sample Question Paper for ISC Class XII

MATHEMATICS (Fully Solved)

GENERAL INSTRUCTIONS

1. The Question Paper consists of three sections A, B and C.
2. Candidates are required to attempt all questions from *Section A* and all questions either from *Section B* or *Section C*.
3. *Section A*: Internal choice has been provided in two questions of two marks each, two questions of four marks each and two questions of six marks each.
4. *Section B*: Internal choice has been provided in one question of two marks and one question of four marks.
5. *Section C*: Internal choice has been provided in one question of two marks and one question of four marks.
6. All working, including rough work, should be done on the same sheet as, and adjacent to the rest of the answer.
7. The intended marks for questions or parts of questions are given in brackets [ ].
8. Mathematical tables and graph papers are provided.

Time : 3 Hours *Max. Marks : 80*

Section A (65 Marks)

1. In subparts (i) to (xi), choose the correct options and in subparts (xii) to (xv), answer the questions as instructed.
   (i) If $A = \begin{bmatrix} 0 & a \\ 0 & 0 \end{bmatrix}$ then A^{16} is
   (a) unit matrix (b) null matrix
   (c) diagonal matrix (d) skew-symmetric matrix
   (ii) Which of the following is a homogeneous differential equation?
   (a) $(4x^2 + 6y + 5)\,dy - (3y^2 + 2x + 4)\,dx = 0$
   (b) $(xy)\,dx - (x^3 + y^3)\,dy = 0$
   (c) $(x^3 + 2y^2)\,dx + 2xy\,dy = 0$
   (d) $y^2 dx + (x^2 - xy - y^2)\,dy = 0$
   (iii) Consider the graph of the function $f(x)$ shown below

Sample Question Papers & Latest ISC Specimen Paper

Chapterwise study is not the only feature of this book, after the Chapterwise Study it has a supplement of **3 Sample Question Papers** and **Latest ISC Specimen Paper.**

Exam Papers

For complete practice, there is Solved Paper 2025 also given at the end of the book.

SAMPLE QUESTION PAPER 1

A Highly Simulated Sample Question Paper for ISC Class XII

MATHEMATICS (Unsolved)

General Instructions

1. This Question Paper consists of three sections A, B and C.
2. Candidates are required to attempt all questions from Section A and all questions either from Section B Or Section C.
3. Section A Internal choice has been provided in two questions of 2 marks each, two questions of 4 marks each and two questions of 6 marks each.
4. Section B Internal choice has been provided in one question of 2 marks and one question of 4 marks.
5. Section C Internal choice has been provided in one question of 2 marks and one question of 4 marks.
6. All working, including rough work, should be done on the same sheet as and adjacent to the rest of the answer.
7. The intended marks for questions or parts of questions are given in brackets [].
8. Mathematical tables and graph papers are provided.

Time : 3 Hrs.
Max. Marks : 80

Section A (65 Marks)

1. In sub-parts (i) to (xi) choose the correct option and in sub-parts (xii) to (xv), answer the questions as instructed.
   (i) Let $A = \{3, 5\}$. Then, number of reflexive relations on A is • *Understanding*
   (a) 2 (b) 4 (c) 0 (d) 8
   (ii) **Statement I** If $y = \sin(x^2 + 5)$, then the value of $\frac{dy}{dx}$ is $2x\cos(x^2 + 5)$.
   Statement II If $y = \log x + \frac{1}{x}$, then the value of $\frac{dy}{dx}$ is $\frac{1}{x} + \frac{1}{x^2}$. • *Analysis*
   (a) Statement I is true and Statement II is false.
   (b) Statement II is true and Statement I is false.
   (c) Both the statement are true.
   (d) Both the statement are false.
   (iii) **Assertion** (A) The function $f : R \to R$ given by $f(x) = x^3$ is injective.
   Reason (R) The function $f : X \to Y$ is injective, if $f(x) = f(y) \Rightarrow x = y$ for all $x, y \in X$. • *Analysis*
   (a) Both Assertion and Reason are true and Reason is the correct explanation for Assertion.
   (b) Both Assertion and Reason are true but Reason is not the correct explanation for Assertion.
   (c) Assertion is true and Reason is false.
   (d) Assertion is false and Reason is true.

Latest Course Structure

There will be two papers in the subject :

Paper I : Theory (3 hours) 80 Marks

Paper II : Project work 20 Marks

Paper I : Theory 80 Marks

The syllabus is divided into three sections A, B and C.

Section A is compulsory for all candidates. Candidates will have a choice of attempting questions from **EITHER** Section B **OR** Section C.

DISTRIBUTION OF MARKS FOR THE THEORY PAPER.

S.No.	Unit Name	Total Weightage
	Section A : 65 Marks	
1.	Relations and Functions	10 Marks
2.	Algebra	10 Marks
3.	Calculus	32 Marks
4.	Probability	13 Marks
	Section B : 15 Marks	
5.	Vectors	5 Marks
6.	Three-Dimensional Geometry	6 Marks
7.	Applications of Integrals	4 Marks
	OR Section C : 15 Marks	
8.	Applications of Calculus	5 Marks
9.	Linear Regression	6 Marks
10.	Linear Programming	4 Marks
	Total	**80 Marks**

SECTION A

1. Relations and Functions

(i) Types of relations: reflexive, symmetric, transitive and equivalence relations. One to one and onto functions, inverse of a function.

- **Relations as**
  - Relation on a set A
  - Identity relation, empty relation, universal relation.
  - Types of Relations: reflexive, symmetric, transitive and equivalence relation.
- **Functions**
  - As special relations, concept of writing "y is a function of x" as $y = f(x)$.
  - Types: one to one, many to one, into, onto.
  - Real Valued function.
  - Domain and range of a function.
  - Conditions of invertibility.
  - Invertible functions (algebraic functions only).

(ii) Inverse Trigonometric Functions

Definition, domain, range, principal value branch. Elementary properties of inverse trigonometric functions.

- Principal values.
- $\sin^{-1} x, \cos^{-1} x, \tan^{-1} x$, etc.
- $\sin^{-1} x = \cos^{-1}\sqrt{1-x^2} = \tan^{-1}\dfrac{x}{\sqrt{1-x^2}}$
- $\sin^{-1} x = \operatorname{cosec}^{-1}\dfrac{1}{x}$; $\sin^{-1} x + \cos^{-1} x = \dfrac{\pi}{2}$ and similar relations for $\cot^{-1} x, \tan^{-1} x$, etc.

$$\sin^{-1} x \pm \sin^{-1} y = \sin^{-1}\left(x\sqrt{1-y^2} \pm y\sqrt{1-x^2}\right)$$

$$\cos^{-1} x \pm \cos^{-1} y = \cos^{-1}\left(xy \mp \sqrt{1-y^2}\sqrt{1-x^2}\right)$$

Similarly,

$$\tan^{-1} x + \tan^{-1} y = \tan^{-1}\frac{x+y}{1-xy}, xy < 1,$$

$$\tan^{-1} x - \tan^{-1} y = \tan^{-1}\frac{x-y}{1+xy}, xy > -1$$

Formulae for $2\sin^{-1}x$, $2\cos^{-1}x$, $2\tan^{-1}x$, $3\tan^{-1}x$ etc. and application of these formulae.

2. Algebra

Matrices and Determinants

(i) Matrices

Concept, notation, order, equality, types of matrices, zero and identity matrix, transpose of a matrix, symmetric and skew-symmetric matrices. Operation on matrices: Addition and multiplication and multiplication with a scalar. Simple properties of addition, multiplication and scalar multiplication. Non-commutativity of multiplication of matrices and existence of non-zero matrices whose product is the zero matrix (restrict to square matrices of order upto 3). Invertible matrices and proof of the uniqueness of inverse, if it exists (here all matrices will have real entries).

(ii) Determinants

Determinant of a square matrix (up to 3 x 3 matrices), properties of determinants, minors, co-factors and applications of determinants in finding the area of a triangle. Adjoint and inverse of a square matrix. Consistency, inconsistency and number of solutions of system of linear equation by examples. Solving system of linear equations in two or three variables (having unique solution) using inverse of a matrix.

- Types of matrices ($m \times n$; $m, n \leq 3$), order; Identity matrix, Diagonal matrix.
- Symmetric, Skew-symmetric.
- Operation – addition, subtraction, multiplication of a matrix with scalar, multiplication of two matrices (the compatibility).

e.g. $\begin{bmatrix} 1 & 1 \\ 0 & 2 \\ 1 & 1 \end{bmatrix}\begin{bmatrix} 1 & 2 \\ 2 & 2 \end{bmatrix} = AB$ (say) but BA is not possible.

– Singular and non-singular matrices.
– Existence of two non-zero matrices whose product is a zero matrix.

Inverse $(2 \times 2, 3 \times 3)$ $A^{-1} = \dfrac{\text{adj}\, A}{|A|}$

- *Martin's Rule (i.e. using matrices)*

$a_1x + b_1y + c_1z = d_1$
$a_2x + b_2y + c_2z = d_2$
$a_3x + b_3y + c_3z = d_3$

$$A = \begin{bmatrix} a_1 & b_1 & c_1 \\ a_2 & b_2 & c_2 \\ a_3 & b_3 & c_3 \end{bmatrix}, B = \begin{bmatrix} d_1 \\ d_2 \\ d_3 \end{bmatrix}, X = \begin{bmatrix} x \\ y \\ z \end{bmatrix}$$

$$AX = B \Rightarrow X = A^{-1}B$$

Problems based on above.

Note : *The conditions for consistency of equations in two and three variables using matrices are to be covered.*

- *Determinants*
  – *Order.*
  – *Minors.*
  – *Cofactors.*
  – *Expansion.*
  – *Application of determinants is finding the area or triangle and collinearity.*
  – *Properties of determinants. Problems based on properties of determinants.*

3. Calculus

(viii) Continuity, Differentiability and Differentiation. Continuity and differentiability, derivative of composite functions, chain rule, derivatives of inverse trigonometric functions, derivative of implicit functions. Concept of exponential and logarithmic functions.

Derivatives of logarithmic and exponential functions. Logarithmic differentiation, derivative of functions expressed in parametric forms. Second order derivatives.

- *Continuity*
  – *Continuity of a function at a point $x = a$.*
  – *Continuity of a function in an interval.*
  – *Algebra of continuous function.*
  – *Removable discontinuity.*
- *Differentiation*
  – *Concept of continuity and differentiability of $|x|$, $[x]$, etc.*
  – *Derivatives of trigonometric functions.*
  – *Derivatives of exponential functions.*
  – *Derivatives of logarithmic functions.*
  – *Derivatives of inverse trigonometric functions - differentiation by means of substitution.*
  – *Derivatives of implicit functions and chain rule for composite functions.*
  – *Derivatives of Parametric functions.*
  – *Differentiation of a function with respect to another function e.g. differentiation of $\sin x^3$ with respect to x^3.*
  – *Logarithmic Differentiation - Finding dy/dx when $y = x^{x^x}$*
  – *Successive differentiation upto 2nd order.*

Note : *Derivatives of composite functions using chain rule.*

(ii) Applications of Derivatives

Applications of derivatives: rate of change of bodies, increasing/decreasing functions, tangents and normals, maxima and minima (first derivative test motivated geometrically and second derivative test given as a provable tool). Simple problems (that illustrate basic principles and understanding of the subject as well as real-life situations).

- *Equation of Tangent and Normal.*
- *Rate measure.*
- *Increasing and decreasing functions.*
- *Maxima and minima*
  – *Stationary/turning points.*
  – *Absolute maxima/minima.*
  – *Local maxima/minima.*
  – *First derivatives test and second derivatives test.*
  – *Application problems based on maxima and minima.*

(iii) Integrals

Integration as inverse process of differentiation. Integration of a variety of functions by substitution, by partial fractions and by parts, Evaluation of simple integrals of the following types and problems based on them.

Fundamental Theorem of Calculus (without proof). Basic properties of definite integrals and evaluation of definite integrals.

- *Indefinite integral*
  – *Integration as the inverse of differentiation.*
  – *Anti-derivatives of polynomials and functions $(ax + b)^n$, $\sin x$, $\cos x$, $\sec^2 x$, $\text{cosec}^2 x$ etc .*
  – *Integrals of the type $\sin^2 x$, $\sin^3 x$, $\sin^4 x$, $\cos^2 x$, $\cos^3 x$, $\cos^4 x$.*
  – *Integration of $1/x$, e^x.*
  – *Integration by substitution.*
  – *Integrals of the type $f'(x)\,[f(x)]^n$, $\dfrac{f'(x)}{f(x)}$*
  – *Integration of $\tan x$, $\cot x$, $\sec x$, $\text{cosec}\, x$.*
  – *Integration by parts.*
  – *Integration using partial fractions.*

Expressions of the form $\dfrac{f(x)}{g(x)}$, when, degree of $f(x) <$ degree of $g(x)$.

e.g. $\dfrac{x+2}{(x-3)(x+1)} = \dfrac{A}{x-3} + \dfrac{B}{x+1}$,

$$\frac{x+2}{(x-2)(x-1)^2} = \frac{A}{x-1} + \frac{B}{(x-1)^2} + \frac{C}{x-2}$$

$$\frac{x+1}{(x^2+3)(x-1)} = \frac{Ax+B}{x^2+3} + \frac{C}{x-1}$$

When degree of $f(x) \geq$ degree of $g(x)$,

e.g. $\dfrac{x^2+1}{x^2+3x+2} = 1 - \left(\dfrac{3x+1}{x^2+3x+2}\right)$.

Integrals of the type :

$$\int \frac{dx}{x^2 \pm a^2}, \int \frac{dx}{\sqrt{x^2 \pm a^2}}, \int \frac{px+q}{ax^2+bx+c}\,dx,$$

$$\int \frac{px+q}{\sqrt{ax^2+bx+c}}\,dx \text{ and } \int \sqrt{a^2 \pm x^2}\,dx, \int \sqrt{x^2 - a^2}\,dx,$$

$$\int (px+q)\sqrt{ax^2+bx+c}\,dx \quad \int \sqrt{ax^2+bx+c}\,dx,$$

integrations reducible to the above forms.

- Integrals of the form

$$\int \frac{dx}{a\cos x + b\sin x}, \int \frac{dx}{a + b\cos x}, \int \frac{dx}{a + b\sin x},$$

$$\int \frac{dx}{a\cos x + b\sin x + c}, \int \frac{(a\cos x + b\sin x)}{c\cos x + d\sin x}\,dx,$$

$$\int \frac{dx}{a\cos^2 x + b\sin^2 x + c}, \int \frac{1 \pm x^2}{1 + x^4}\,dx, \int \frac{dx}{1 + x^4},$$

$$\int \sqrt{\tan x}\,dx, \int \sqrt{\cot x}\,dx \text{ etc.}$$

- Definite integral
  - Fundamental theorem of calculus (without proof).
  - Properties of definite integrals.

Problems based on the following properties of definite integrals are to be covered.

$$\int_a^b f(x)\,dx = \int_a^b f(t)\,dt$$

$$\int_a^b f(x)\,dx = -\int_b^a f(x)\,dx$$

$$\int_a^b f(x)\,dx = \int_a^c f(x)\,dx + \int_c^b f(x)\,dx, \text{ where } a < c < b$$

$$\int_a^b f(x)\,dx = \int_a^b f(a + b - x)\,dx$$

$$\int_0^a f(x)\,dx = \int_0^a f(a - x)\,dx$$

$$\int_0^{2a} f(x)\,dx = \begin{cases} 2\int_0^a f(x)\,dx, & \text{if } f(2a - x) = f(x) \\ 0, & \text{if } f(2a - x) = -f(x) \end{cases}$$

$$\int_{-a}^a f(x)\,dx = \begin{cases} 2\int_0^a f(x)\,dx, & \text{if } f \text{ is an even function} \\ 0, & \text{if } f \text{ is an odd function} \end{cases}$$

(iv) Differential Equations

Definition, order and degree, general and particular solutions of a differential equation. Solution of differential equations by method of separation of variables solutions of homogeneous differential equations of first order and first degree.

Solutions of linear differential equation of the type: $\frac{dy}{dx} + py = q$, where p and q are functions of x or constants. $\frac{dx}{dy} + px = q$, where p and q are functions of y or constants.

- Differential equations, order and degree.
- Formation of differential equation by eleminating arbitrary constant (s).
- Solution of differential equations.
- Variable separable.
- Homogeneous equations.
- Linear form $\frac{dy}{dx} + Py = Q$, where P and Q are functions.

of x only. Similarly for dx/dy.

Note 1 : Equations reducible to variable separable type are included.

Note 2 : The second order differential equations are excluded.

4. Probability

Conditional probability, multiplication theorem on probability, independent events, total probability, Bayes' theorem, Random variable and its probability distribution, mean and variance of random variable.

- Independent and dependent events, conditional events.
- Laws of probability, addition theorem, multiplication theorem, conditional probability.
- Theorem of Total Probability.
- Baye's theorem.
- Theoretical probability distribution, probability distribution function; mean of random variable.

SECTION B

5. Vectors

Vectors and scalars, magnitude and direction of a vector. Direction cosines and direction ratios of a vector. Types of vectors (equal, unit, zero, parallel and collinear vectors), position vector of a point, negative of a vector, components of a vector, addition of vectors, multiplication of a vector by a scalar, position vector of a point dividing a line segment in a given ratio. Definition, Geometrical Interpretation, properties and application of scalar (dot) product of vectors, vector (cross) product of vectors.

- *As directed line segments.*
- *Magnitude and direction of a vector.*
- *Types: equal vectors, unit vectors, zero vector.*
- *Position vector.*
- *Components of a vector.*
- *Vectors in two and three dimensions.*
- *i, j, k as unit vectors along the X, Y and Z-axes; expressing a vector in terms of the unit vectors.*
- *Operations: Sum and Difference of vectors; scalar multiplication of a vector.*
- *Section formulae.*
- *Scalar (dot) product of vectors and its geometrical significance.*
- *Cross product - its properties - area of a triangle, area of parallelogram, collinear vectors.*

Note *Proofs of geometrical theorems by using Vector algebra are excluded.*

6. Three Dimensional Geometry

Direction cosines and direction ratios of a line joining two points. Cartesian equation and vector equation of a line, coplanar and skew lines, shortest distance between two lines. Cartesian and vector equation of a plane. Angle between (i) two lines, (ii) two planes, (iii) a line and a plane. Distance of a point from a plane.

- *Equation of X-axis, Y-axis, Z-axis and lines parallel to them.*
- *Equation of XY-plane, YZ-plane, ZX-plane.*
- *Direction cosines, direction ratios.*
- *Angle between two lines in terms of direction cosines /direction ratios.*
- *Condition for lines to be perpendicular/ parallel.*

- ***Lines***
  - *Cartesian and vector equations of a line through one and two points.*
  - *Coplanar and skew lines.*
  - *Conditions for intersection of two lines.*
  - *Distance of a point from a line.*
  - *Shortest distance between two lines.*

- ***Planes***
  - *Cartesian and vector equation of a plane.*
  - *Direction ratios of the normal to the plane.*
  - *One point form.*
  - *Normal form.*
  - *Intercept form.*
  - *Distance of a point from a plane.*
  - *Intersection of the line and plane.*
  - *Angle between two planes, a line and a plane.*

7. Application of Integrals

Application in finding the area bounded by simple curves and coordinate axes. Area enclosed between two curves.

- *Application of definite integrals - area bounded by curves, lines and coordinate axes is required to be covered.*
- *Simple curves: lines, circles/ parabolas/ ellipses, (only standard forms), simple polynomial functions, modulus function.*

SECTION C

8. Application of Calculus

Application of Calculus in Commerce and Economics in the following:

- *Cost function,*
- *average cost,*
- *marginal cost and its interpretation*
- *demand function,*
- *revenue function,*
- *marginal revenue function and its interpretation,*
- *Profit function and breakeven point.*
- *Rough sketching of the following curves: AR, MR, R, C, AC, MC and their mathematical interpretation using the concept of maxima & minima and increasing- decreasing functions.*
- *Self-explanatory*

Note : *Application involving differentiation, increasing and decreasing function and maxima and minima to be covered.*

9. Linear Regression

- *Lines of regression of x on y and y on x.*
- *Scatter diagrams*
- *The method of least squares.*
- *Lines of best fit.*
- *Regression coefficient of x on y and y on x.*
- $b_{xy} \times b_{yx} = r^2,\ 0 \le b_{xy} \times b_{yx} \le 1$
- *Identification of regression equations*
- *Properties of regression lines.*
- *Estimation of the value of one variable using the value of other variable from appropriate line of regression.*
- *Self-explanatory*

10. Linear Programming

Introduction, related terminology such as constraints, objective function, optimization, different types of Linear Programming (LP) problems, mathematical formulation of LP problems, graphical method of solution for problems in two variables, feasible and infeasible regions (bounded and unbounded), feasible and infeasible solutions, optimal feasible solutions (up to three non-trivial constraints).

Introduction, definition of related terminology such as constraints, objective function, optimization, advantages of linear programming; limitations of linear programming; application areas of linear programming; different types of Linear Programming (LP) problems, mathematical formulation of LP problems, graphical method of solution for problems in two variables, feasible and infeasible regions, feasible and infeasible solutions, optimum feasible solution.

CHAPTER

01

Relations and Functions

In previous class, we initiated the study of relations and functions, where we studied about domain, codomain and range alongwith different types of specific real-valued functions and their graphs. All these concepts are the basics of relations and functions. In this chapter, we will study about different types of relations and functions, composition of functions, invertible functions and binary operations.

- Relations
- Functions and Their Types
- Inverse of a Function

TOPIC 01 Relations

Relation on a Set

Let A be a non-empty set, then a relation R from A to itself, i.e. a subset of $A \times A$, is called a relation on set A (or a relation in set A). **e.g.** Let $A = \{1, 2, 3, 4\}$, then $R = \{(a, b) \in A \times A : a - b = 3\} = \{(4, 1)\}$ is a relation on set A.

Suppose a relation R is defined on two non-empty sets from A to B such that it is a subset of $A \times B$. Then, set A is called **domain** and set B is called **range.**

Some Basic Relations on Set

There are three basic relations which are given below

Empty or Void Relation

Relation R on a set A is called an empty relation, if no element of A is related to any element of A, i.e. $R = \phi \subset A \times A$.

e.g. Let set $A = \{1, 2, 3, 8, 10, 11\}$ and R be a relation on A, given by $R = \{(a, b) : a - b = 4\}$. Then, R is an empty relation. Since, no element $(a, b) \in A \times A$ satisfy the property $a - b = 4$.

Note Empty relation is always a smallest relation on set A.

Universal Relation

Relation R on a set A is called a universal relation, if each element of A is related to every element of A, i.e. $R = A \times A$.

e.g. Let set $A = \{1, 2, 3, 4\}$ and relation R is given by $R = \{(a, b) : |a - b| \geq 0\}$. Then, R is a universal relation. Since, all ordered pairs $(a, b) \in A \times A$ satisfy the property $|a - b| \geq 0$.

Note (i) A Universal relation is always a largest relation on set A.

(ii) Both the relations empty and universal are sometimes known as **trivial relations.**

Identity Relation

Relation R on a set A is called an identity relation, if each element of A is related to itself only and it is denoted by I_A, i.e. $I_A = R = \{(a, a) : a \in A\}$.

e.g. Let set $A = \{1, 2\}$, then the identity relation R on A is given by $R = \{(1, 1), (2, 2)\}$. But the relation $R_1 = \{(1, 1), (2, 2), (1, 2)\}$ is not an identity relation on A, because element 1 is related to elements 1 and 2.

Types of Relations

There are three types of relations, which are given below

Reflexive Relation

Relation R on a set A is called reflexive relation, if $(a, a) \in R$, for every $a \in A$, i.e. $aRa, \forall a \in A$. **e.g.**

(i) Let $A = \{11, 12, 15\}$ and relation R on it is defined as $R = \{(11, 11), (12, 12), (11, 12), (15, 15), (11, 15), (12, 15)\}$. Then, R is a reflexive relation.
Since, for every element 11, 12 and 15 of A, $(11, 11), (12, 12)$ and $(15, 15) \in R$.

(ii) Let A be the set of real numbers and relation R on it is defined as $R = \{(x, y) : x + y \in A\}$. Then, R is a reflexive relation.
Since, sum of two real numbers is also a real number, therefore $R = A \times A$. Hence, R is reflexive, as $(a, a) \in R$, for every $a \in A$.

Symmetric Relation

Relation R on a set A is called symmetric relation, if $(a, b) \in R \Rightarrow (b, a) \in R$, for every $a, b \in A$.
i.e. $aRb \Rightarrow bRa, \forall a, b \in A$.

e.g. (i) Let $A = \{11, 12, 13\}$ and relation R on it is defined as $R = \{(11, 11), (11, 12), (12, 12), (12, 11)\}$.
Then, R is a symmetric relation.
Since, $(11, 12) \in R \Rightarrow (12, 11) \in R$

(ii) Let A be the set of even natural numbers and relation R on it is defined as
$$R = \{(x, y) : x + y \text{ is divisible by } 2\}.$$
Then, it is a symmetric relation.
Since, sum of two even natural numbers is always even and hence divisible by 2, therefore $R = A \times A$.
Thus, $(a, b) \in R \Rightarrow (b, a) \in R$, for every $a, b \in A$.

Transitive Relation

Relation R on a set A is called transitive relation, if $(a, b) \in R$ and $(b, c) \in R \Rightarrow (a, c) \in R, \forall a, b, c \in A$,
i.e. aRb and $bRc \Rightarrow aRc, \forall a, b, c \in A$.

e.g. (i) Let $A = \{11, 12, 14\}$ and relation R on it is defined as $R = \{(11, 11), (11, 12), (12, 14), (12, 12), (11, 14)\}$.
Then, it is a transitive relation.
Since, $(11, 12) \in R$ and $(12, 14) \in R \Rightarrow (11, 14) \in R$.

(ii) Let A be the set of positive integers and relation R on it is defined as $R = \{(x, y) : x < y, \forall x, y \in A\}$.
Then, it is a transitive relation.
Since, $x < y$ and $y < z$
$\Rightarrow x < z$, for every $x, y, z \in A$.
Thus, $(x, y) \in R$ and $(y, z) \in R \Rightarrow (x, z) \in R$, for every $x, y, z \in A$.

Note (i) A relation R on set A is not reflexive, if there exists an element $a \in A$ such that $(a, a) \notin R$.

e.g. Let $A = \{4, 5, 7\}$ and $R = \{(4, 4), (4, 5), (7, 7)\}$, then R is not reflexive. Since, $5 \in A$ but $(5, 5) \notin R$.

(ii) If R does not have any element of the type (a, b), where $a \neq b$, then R is symmetric. Also, if R does not have elements of the type (a, b) and (b, c), then R is transitive.

e.g. Let $A = \{1, 2, 3\}$ and $R = \{(1, 1), (2, 2)\}$, then R is symmetric and transitive.

(iii) Identity relation is always reflexive, symmetric and transitive.

Method to Solve the Problems Based on Types of Relations

In these types of problems, a set and a relation defined on that set is given to us and we have to check or show that given relation is reflexive or symmetric or transitive. For this, first we denote the given set as A and the given relation as R. Then, check the given relation is reflexive or symmetric or transitive as follows

For Reflexive We have to show that for all $a \in A$, $(a, a) \in R$. For this, we will take an arbitrary element of set A in the form of a variable (say x) and then check whether (x, x) satisfy the given condition of R or not (i.e. $(x, x) \in R$ or not). If it satisfy the given condition, then R is reflexive otherwise not.

For Symmetric We have to show that if $(a, b) \in R$, then $(b, a) \in R$, where $a, b \in A$. For this, we will take two arbitrary elements of set A in the form of two variables (say x and y) such that $(x, y) \in R$ and then check (y, x) satisfy the given condition of R or not (i.e. $(y, x) \in R$ or not). If they satisfy the given condition, then R is symmetric otherwise not.

For Transitive We have to show that if $(a, b) \in R$ and $(b, c) \in R$, then $(a, c) \in R$, where $a, b, c \in A$. For this, we will take three arbitrary elements of set A in the form of three variables (say x, y and z) such that $(x, y) \in R$ and $(y, z) \in R$ and then check whether (x, z) satisfy the given condition of R or not (i.e. $(x, z) \in R$ or not). If they satisfy the given condition, then R is transitive otherwise not.

Note Generally, whenever we have to prove or show that given relation is reflexive, symmetric or transitive, then we take variables and when we have to show that given relation is not reflexive or symmetric or transitive, then we take elements of set to justify.

Example 1 Show that the relation R on the set $\{1, 2, 3\}$ given by $R = \{(1, 1), (2, 2), (3, 3), (1, 2), (2, 3)\}$ is reflexive but neither symmetric nor transitive.

Sol. Let the given set be $A = \{1, 2, 3\}$

and $R = \{(1, 1), (2, 2), (3, 3), (1, 2), (2, 3)\}$

Reflexive Here, $1, 2, 3 \in A$ and $(1, 1), (2, 2), (3, 3) \in R$ i.e. for all $a \in A$, $(a, a) \in R$. So, R is reflexive.

Symmetric Here, $(1, 2) \in R$ but $(2, 1) \notin R$.

So, R is not symmetric.

Transitive Here, $(1, 2) \in R$ and $(2, 3) \in R$ but $(1, 3) \notin R$.

So, R is not transitive.

Example 2 Check whether the relation R defined on set $A = \{1, 2, 3, \ldots, 13, 14\}$ as $R = \{(x, y): 3x - y = 0\}$ is reflexive, symmetric and transitive.

Sol. Given, $A = \{1, 2, 3, \ldots, 13, 14\}$

and $R = \{(x, y): 3x - y = 0\} = \{(x, y): y = 3x\}$

Clearly, $R = \{(1, 3), (2, 6), (3, 9), (4, 12)\}$.

Now, let us check the reflexivity, symmetricity and transitivity of R.

Reflexive Here, $2 \in A$ but $(2, 2) \notin R$, therefore R is not reflexive.

Symmetric Here, $(1, 3) \in R$ but $(3, 1) \notin R$, therefore R is not symmetric.

Transitive Here, $(1, 3) \in R$ and $(3, 9) \in R$ but $(1, 9) \notin R$, therefore R is not transitive. Hence, R is neither reflexive nor symmetric nor transitive.

Example 3 Give an example of a relation, which is

(i) symmetric but neither reflexive nor transitive.

(ii) transitive but neither reflexive nor symmetric.

(iii) reflexive and symmetric but not transitive.

(iv) reflexive and transitive but not symmetric.

(v) symmetric and transitive but not reflexive. **[NCERT]**

Sol. (i) Let $A = \{1, 2, 3\}$ and defined a relation R on A as $R = \{(1, 2), (2, 1)\}$.

Then, R is symmetric, as $(1, 2) \in R \Rightarrow (2, 1) \in R$.

R is not reflexive, as $1 \in A$ but $(1, 1) \notin R$.

R is not transitive, as $(1, 2) \in R$ and $(2, 1) \in R$ but $(1, 1) \notin R$.

(ii) Let $A = \{1, 2, 3\}$ and defined a relation R on A as $R = \{(1, 2), (2, 2)\}$.

Then, R is transitive, as $(1, 2) \in R$ and $(2, 2) \in R$ $\Rightarrow (1, 2) \in R$

R is not reflexive, as $1 \in A$ but $(1, 1) \notin R$.

R is not symmetric, as $(1, 2) \in R$ but $(2, 1) \notin R$.

(iii) Let $A = \{1, 2, 3\}$ and defined a relation R on A, as $R = \{(1, 1), (2, 2), (3, 3), (1, 2), (2, 1), (2, 3), (3, 2)\}$

Then, R is reflexive, as for each $a \in A$, $(a, a) \in R$.

R is symmetric, as $(1, 2) \in R \Rightarrow (2, 1) \in R$ and $(2, 3) \in R \Rightarrow (3, 2) \in R$.

R is not transitive, as $(1, 2) \in R$ and $(2, 3) \in R$ but $(1, 3) \notin R$.

(iv) Let $A = \{1, 2, 3\}$ and defined a relation R on A as $R = \{(1, 1), (2, 2), (3, 3), (1, 2)\}$

Then, R is reflexive, as for each $a \in A$, $(a, a) \in R$.

R is transitive, as $(1, 1) \in R$ and $(1, 2) \in R \Rightarrow (1, 2) \in R$ and $(1, 2) \in R$, $(2, 2) \in R \Rightarrow (1, 2) \in R$.

R is not symmetric, as $(1, 2) \in R$ but $(2, 1) \notin R$.

(v) Let $A = \{1, 2, 3\}$ and defined a relation R on A as $R = \{(2, 2), (3, 3)\}$.

Then, R is symmetric, as R does not have any element of the type (a, b), where $a \neq b$.

R is transitive, as R does not have elements of the type (a, b) and (b, c).

R is not reflexive, as $1 \in A$ but $(1, 1) \notin R$.

Example 4 Check whether the relation R defined in the set $A = \{1, 2, 3, 4, 5, 6\}$ as $R = \{(x, y) : y$ is divisible by $x\}$ is reflexive, symmetric and transitive. **[NCERT]**

For reflexive, show for all $x \in A$, $(x, x) \in R$. For symmetric, show $(x, y) \in R \Rightarrow (y, x) \in R$, $x, y \in A$. For transitive, show $(x, y) \in R$ and $(y, z) \in R \Rightarrow (x, z) \in R$, $x, y, z \in A$.

Sol. Given, $R = \{(x, y): y$ is divisible by $x\}$

and $A = \{1, 2, 3, 4, 5, 6\}$

Reflexive Let $x \in A$ be any arbitrary element.

Then, x is divisible by x.

[$\because$ every real number except zero is divisible by itself]

$\Rightarrow \quad (x, x) \in R$

Since, $x \in A$ was arbitrary element, therefore $(x, x) \in R$, $\forall\ x \in A$. So, R is reflexive.

Symmetric Clearly, $2, 4 \in A$ and 4 is divisible by 2, but 2 is not divisible by 4.

$\therefore \quad (2, 4) \in R$ but $(4, 2) \notin R$

So, R is not symmetric.

Transitive Let $x, y, z \in A$ such that $(x, y) \in R$ and $(y, z) \in R$.

Now, as $(x, y) \in R$, therefore y is divisible by x.

i.e. $\frac{y}{x} = k_1$(say) ...(i)

where, k_1 is a natural number

and as $(y, z) \in R$, therefore z is divisible by y.

i.e. $\frac{z}{y} = k_2$ (say) ...(ii)

where, k_2 is a natural number.

On multiplying Eqs. (i) and (ii), we get

$$\frac{y}{x} \times \frac{z}{y} = k_1 k_2 \Rightarrow \frac{z}{x} = k_1 k_2$$

where, $k_1 k_2$ is a natural number.

$\therefore$ z is divisible by x.

Thus, $(x, z) \in R$, for $(x, y), (y, z) \in R$,

i.e. $(x, y) \in R, (y, z) \in R \Rightarrow (x, z) \in R$

Hence, R is transitive.

Example 5 Let a relation R on the set N of natural number be define as $R = \{(x, y) : 3x^2 - 7xy + 4y^2 = 0; x, y \in N\}$. Then, show that relation R is reflexive but neither symmetric nor transitive.

Sol. Given, $R = \{(x, y): 3x^2 - 7xy + 4y^2 = 0; x, y \in N\}$

$= \{(x, y): 3x^2 - 3xy - 4xy + 4y^2 = 0; x, y \in N\}$

$= \{(x, y): 3x(x - y) - 4y(x - y) = 0; x, y \in N\}$

$= \{(x, y): (x - y)(3x - 4y) = 0; x, y \in N\}$

Here, we will get those ordered pairs (x, y) which satisfy the equation defined in R.

Reflexive Since, $xRx \Rightarrow (x - x)(3x - 4x) = 0$

$\Rightarrow 0 = 0$, which is true, so R is reflexive.

Symmetric Here, $xRy \Rightarrow (x - y)(3x - 4y) = 0$

and $yRx \Rightarrow (y - x)(3y - 4x) = 0$

Clearly, $xRy \neq yRx$

e.g. $4R3$ as $(4 - 3)(3 \times 4 - 4 \times 3) = 0$

but $3 \not{R} 4$ as $(3 - 4)(3 \times 3 - 4 \times 4) \neq 0$

So, R is not symmetric.

Transitive Here, $xRy \Rightarrow (x - y)(3x - 4y) = 0$

$yRz \Rightarrow (y - z)(3y - 4z) = 0$

and $xRz \Rightarrow (x - z)(3x - 4z) = 0$

Clearly, $(x - y)(3x - 4y) = 0$ and $(y - z)(3y - 4z) = 0$

$\not\Rightarrow$ $(x - z)(3x - 4z) = 0$

e.g. $16R12$ and $12R9$ but $16 \not{R} 9$.

So, R is not transitive.

Equivalence Relation

A relation R on a set A is said to be an equivalence relation iff it is

(i) **reflexive** i.e. aRa or $(a, a) \in R, \forall a \in A$.

(ii) **symmetric** i.e. $aRb \Rightarrow bRa$ or $(a, b) \in R \Rightarrow (b, a) \in R$, where $a, b \in A$.

(iii) **transitive** i.e. if aRb and bRc, then aRc or $(a, b) \in R$ and $(b, c) \in R \Rightarrow (a, c) \in R$, where $a, b, c \in A$.

Note Identity relation on a non-empty set is always an equivalence relation.

Example 6 Let T be the set of all triangles in a plane with R is a relation on T given by $R = \{(T_1, T_2): T_1$ is congruent to T_2 and $T_1, T_2 \in T\}$. Show that R is an equivalence relation.

Or

Show that the relation 'is congruent to' on the set of all triangles in a plane is an equivalence relation.

Sol. Given, T = Set of all triangles in a plane

and $R = \{(T_1, T_2): T_1$ is congruent to T_2 and $T_1, T_2 \in T\}$

We know that two triangles are said to be congruent, if they have same shape and same size.

Reflexive Let $T_1 \in T$ be any arbitrary element. We know that, every triangle is congruent to itself. So, $T_1 R T_1$, i.e. $(T_1, T_1) \in R$. Now, as T_1 was arbitrary element of T, therefore R is reflexive.

Symmetric Let $T_1, T_2 \in T$, such that

$(T_1, T_2) \in R \Rightarrow T_1$ is congruent to T_2.

$\Rightarrow$ T_2 is congruent to T_1.

[$\because$ if a triangle is congruent to another triangle, then they are congruent to each other]

$\Rightarrow$ $(T_2, T_1) \in R$

$\therefore$ R is symmetric.

Transitive Let $T_1, T_2, T_3 \in T$, such that $(T_1, T_2) \in R$ and $(T_2, T_3) \in R$.

$\Rightarrow$ T_1 is congruent to T_2 and T_2 is congruent to T_3.

$\Rightarrow$ T_1 is congruent to T_3

$\Rightarrow$ $(T_1, T_3) \in R$

$\therefore$ R is transitive.

Thus, the relation R is reflexive, symmetric and transitive. Hence, R is an equivalence relation.

Example 7 Given a non-empty set X. Consider $P(X)$, which is the set of all subset of X. Defined the relation R in $P(X)$ as follows.

For subsets A and B in $P(X)$, ARB if and only if $A \subseteq B$

Is R an equivalence relation on $P(X)$? Justify your answer. **[NCERT]**

Sol. Given, $R = \{(A, B): A \subseteq B$ and $A, B \in P(X)\}$.

Reflexive We know that every set is a subset of itself, therefore $ARA, \forall A \in P(X)$.

So, R is reflexive.

Symmetric Let $A, B \in P(X)$ such that $ARB \Rightarrow A \subseteq B$

This may not be implied that $B \subseteq A$.

For instance, if $A = \{1, 2\}$ and $B = \{1, 2, 3\}$, then A is related to B as $A \subseteq B$ but it cannot be implied that B is related to A as $B \subseteq A$.
So, R is not symmetric.
Hence, R is not an equivalence relation on $P(X)$, since it is not symmetric.

Equivalence Classes

Consider an equivalence relation R on a set A and let $a \in A$. Then, the set of all those elements of A which are related to a, is called the equivalence class of R determined by a; and it is denoted by $[a]$. Thus, $[a] = \{b \in A : (a, b) \in R\}$.

e.g. Let R be the equivalence relation on the set $A = \{0, 1, 2, 3, 4, 5\}$ given by $R = \{(a, b) : 2 \text{ divides } (a - b)\}$. Then, equivalence class of 0, i.e. $[0]$ is

$$\{b \in A : (0, b) \in R\} = \{b \in A : 2 \text{ divides } (0 - b)\}$$
$$= \{b \in A : 2 \text{ divides } (-b)\}.$$

So, b can be 0, 2, 4.
Hence, equivalence class $[0] = \{0, 2, 4\}$.

Now, by finding the classes determined by the elements of A, we can write A as union of disjoint classes. We call these classes as equivalence classes of R. Thus, R divides A into mutually disjoint equivalence classes.

In other words, **if R is an equivalence relation on a set A, then R divides A into mutually disjoint subsets A_i called partitions or sub-divisions of A, satisfying**

(i) **for each i; all elements of A_i are related to each other.**

(ii) **no element of A_i is related to any element of $A_j, i \neq j$.**

(iii) **$\cup A_i = A$ and $A_i \cap A_j = \phi, i \neq j$.**

Here, subsets A_i are called equivalence classes of R.

e.g. Consider a equivalence relation R on the set Z of all integers defined as $R = \{(a, b) : a, b \in Z, a - b \text{ is divisible by } 2\}$, then $Z = [0] \cup [1]$, i.e. R divides Z into mutually disjoint equivalence classes, $[0]$ and $[1]$.

Justification We know that

(i) if both a and b are even or odd integer, then $a - b$ is divisible by 2.

(ii) if one of a and b is an odd integer and other is an even integer, then $a - b$ is not divisible by 2.

So, $(a, b) \in R$ iff both a and b are even or odd integers.

Now, clearly all even integers including 0 are related to 0, because $(0, 0)$, $(0, \pm 2)$, $(0, \pm 4)$, etc., lie in R. Also, all odd integers including 1 are related to 1, because $(1, \pm 1)$, $(1, \pm 3)$, etc., lie in R.

Thus, all even integers belongs to the class determined by 0 (i.e. denoted by $[0]$) and all odd integers belongs to the class determined by 1 (i.e. denoted by $[1]$). Also, we know that the set Z is the union of set of even integers and set of odd integers. Hence, $Z = [0] \cup [1]$.

Note Converse of above situation is also true, i.e. for given partition of a set A, there exists an equivalence relation on A for which given partition are distinct equivalence classes.

e.g. Let $Z = A_1 \cup A_2 \cup A_3$, where

$A_1 = \{\ldots, -6, -3, 0, 3, 6, \ldots\}$
$A_2 = \{\ldots, -5, -2, 1, 4, 7, \ldots\}$
$A_3 = \{\ldots, -4, -1, 2, 5, 8, \ldots\}$

Then, A_1, A_2 and A_3 forms a partition of Z.

Now, we can define a relation R on Z as $R = \{(a, b) : 3 \text{ divides } a - b\}$, which will be an equivalence relation and $[0] = A_1$, $[1] = A_2$ and $[2] = A_3$.

Example 8 Show that the relation R on the set $A = \{1, 2, 3, 4, 5\}$ given by $R = \{(a, b) : |a - b| \text{ is divisible by } 2\} = \{(a, b) : |a - b| \text{ is a multiple of } 2\}$ is an equivalence relation. Write all the equivalence classes of R.

Sol. We have a relation R on set $A = \{1, 2, 3, 4, 5\}$ defined as

$$R = \{(a, b) : |a - b| \text{ is divisible by } 2\}$$

Clearly, $R = \{(1, 1), (1, 3), (1, 5), (2, 2), (2, 4), (3, 1), (3, 3), (3, 5), (4, 2), (4, 4), (5, 1), (5, 3), (5, 5)\}$

Reflexive For any $a \in A$, we have $|a - a| = 0$, which is divisible by 2.

$\Rightarrow (a, a) \in R, \forall\ a \in A$

Thus, R is reflexive.

Symmetric Let $a, b \in A$, such that $(a, b) \in R$

$\Rightarrow |a - b|$ is divisible by 2
$\Rightarrow |a - b| = 2\lambda$ for some $\lambda \in N$
$\Rightarrow |b - a| = 2\lambda$ for some $\lambda \in N$ $\quad [\because |a - b| = |b - a|]$
$\Rightarrow |b - a|$ is divisible by 2 $\Rightarrow (b, a) \in R$

Thus, R is symmetric.

Transitive Let $a, b, c \in A$, such that $(a, b) \in R$ and $(b, c) \in R$

$\Rightarrow |a - b|$ is divisible by 2 and $|b - c|$ is divisible by 2.
$\Rightarrow |a - b| = 2\lambda$ and $|b - c| = 2\mu$, for some $\lambda, \mu \in N$
$\Rightarrow (a - b) = \pm 2\lambda$ and $(b - c) = \pm 2\mu$

Now, $|a - c| = |(a - b) + (b - c)| = |\pm 2\lambda + (\pm 2\mu)|$
$= |\pm 2\lambda \pm 2\mu| = 2|\pm \lambda \pm \mu|$
$= 2$ (some positive number)

$\Rightarrow |a - c|$ is divisible by 2 $\Rightarrow (a, c) \in R$

Thus, R is transitive.

Hence, R is an equivalence relation.

Now, $[a] = \{x \in A : (a, x) \in R\}$

$\therefore$ Equivalence class $[1] = \{1, 3, 5\}$, $[2] = \{2, 4\}$, $[3] = \{1, 3, 5\}$, $[4] = \{2, 4\}$ and $[5] = \{1, 3, 5\}$

Hence, $[1] = [3] = [5] = \{1, 3, 5\}$ and $[2] = [4] = \{2, 4\}$

Example 9 Let L be the set of all lines in XY-plane and R be the relation on L defined as

$$R = \{(l_1, l_2) : l_1 \text{ is parallel to } l_2\}.$$

Show that R is an equivalence relation. Find the set of all lines related to the line $y = 2x + 4$. **[NCERT]**

Sol. Given, $R = \{(l_1, l_2) : l_1 \text{ is parallel to } l_2\}$.

Reflexive Clearly, R is reflexive as every line is parallel to itself and so $(l, l) \in R$, $\forall\ l \in L$.

Symmetric Let $(l_1, l_2) \in R$

$\Rightarrow$ l_1 is parallel to $l_2 \Rightarrow l_2$ is parallel to l_1

$\Rightarrow$ $(l_2, l_1) \in R$

So, R is symmetric.

Transitive Let $(l_1, l_2), (l_2, l_3) \in R$

Then, l_1 is parallel to l_2 and l_2 is parallel to l_3.

$\Rightarrow$ l_1 is parallel to l_3. $\Rightarrow (l_1, l_3) \in R$.

So, R is transitive.

Hence, R is an equivalence relation.

The set of all lines related to the line $y = 2x + 4$ is the set of all lines that are parallel to the line $y = 2x + 4$.

Slope of line, $y = 2x + 4$ is $m = 2$.

It is known that parallel lines have the same slope.

So, the line parallel to the given line will be of the form $y = 2x + c$, where $c \in R$.

Hence, the set of all lines related to the given line is given by $y = 2x + c$, where $c \in R$.

Example 10 Let $A = \{1, 2, 3, \ldots, 9\}$ and R be the relation on $A \times A$ defined by $(a, b) R (c, d)$, if $a + d = b + c$ for (a, b), (c, d) in $A \times A$. Prove that R is an equivalence relation and also obtain the equivalence class $[(2, 5)]$. **[NCERT Exemplar]**

Sol. Given a relation R on $A \times A$, defined as

$$R = \{((a, b), (c, d)) : a + d = b + c\}$$

or $(a, b)\ R\ (c, d)$, if $a + d = b + c$, where $A = \{1, 2, 3, \ldots, 9\}$

Reflexive Let (a, b) be any arbitrary element of $A \times A$.

Clearly, $a + b = b + a$ [$\because$ addition is commutative on the set of natural numbers]

$\therefore$ $(a, b)R(a, b)$

So, R is reflexive.

Symmetric Let $(a, b), (c, d) \in A \times A$, such that $(a, b)R(c, d)$, then $a + d = b + c$

$\Rightarrow$ $b + c = a + d \Rightarrow c + b = d + a \Rightarrow (c, d)R(a, b)$

So, R is symmetric.

Transitive Let $(a, b), (c, d), (e, f) \in A \times A$ such that $(a, b)R(c, d)$ and $(c, d)R(e, f)$.

Then, $a + d = b + c$ and $c + f = d + e$

On adding LHS to LHS terms and RHS to RHS terms, we get

$$a + d + c + f = b + c + d + e$$

$\Rightarrow$ $a + f = b + e \Rightarrow (a, b)R(e, f)$

So, R is transitive.

Thus, R is reflexive, symmetric and transitive. Hence, R is an equivalence relation.

Now, equivalence class containing an element x of A is given by $\{y : xRy\}$. Here, $(a, b)R(c, d)$

$\Rightarrow$ $a + d = b + c$

So, for $(2, 5)$, we will find (c, d) such that $2 + d = 5 + c$ where $c, d \in A$.

Clearly, $(2, 5)R(1, 4)$ as $2 + 4 = 5 + 1$

$(2, 5)R(2, 5)$ as $2 + 5 = 5 + 2$

$(2, 5)R(3, 6)$ as $2 + 6 = 5 + 3$

$(2, 5)R(4, 7)$ as $2 + 7 = 5 + 4$

$(2, 5)R(5, 8)$ as $2 + 8 = 5 + 5$

and $(2, 5)R(6, 9)$ as $2 + 9 = 5 + 6$

Hence, equivalence class $[(2, 5)] = \{(1, 4), (2, 5), (3, 6), (4, 7), (5, 8), (6, 9)\}$.

Topic Practice 1

Very Short Answer Type Questions

(2 Marks)

1 Let $A = \{0, 1, 2, 3\}$ and define a relation R on A as $R = \{(0,0), (0,1), (0,3), (1,0), (1,1), (2,2), (3,0), (3,3)\}$. Is R reflexive, symmetric and transitive? **[NCERT Exemplar]**

2 For real numbers x and y, define xRy if and only if $x - y + \sqrt{2}$ is an irrational number. Is R transitive? Explain your answer.

3 Let $A = \{a, b, c\}$ and the relation R be defined on A as $R = \{(a,a), (b,c), (a,b)\}$. Then, write minimum number of ordered pairs to be added in R to make R reflexive and transitive.

Short Answer Type Questions

(4 Marks)

4 Let $A = \{1, 2, 3\}$. Then, show that the number of relations containing (1, 2) and (2, 3) which are reflexive and transitive but not symmetric is three.

5 Show that the relation R in the set A of real numbers defined as $R = \{(a, b) : a \le b\}$ is reflexive and transitive but not symmetric. **[NCERT]**

6 Let a relation R on the set A of real numbers be defined as $(a, b) \in R \Rightarrow 1 + ab > 0, \forall\, a, b \in A$. Show that R is reflexive and symmetric but not transitive.

7 Show that the relation S in the set R of real numbers defined as $S = \{(a, b) : a, b \in R$ and $a \le b^3\}$ is neither reflexive nor symmetric nor transitive.

8 Let N be the set of all natural numbers and let R be a relation in N, defined by

$$R = \{(a, b) : a \text{ is a multiple of } b\}.$$

Show that R is reflexive and transitive but not symmetric.

9 Let A be the set of all points in a plane and R be a relation on A defined as $R = \{(P, Q)$: distance between P and Q is less than 2 units$\}$. Show that R is reflexive and symmetric but not transitive.

10 Let R be a relation defined on the set of natural numbers N as $R = \{(x, y): x \in N, y \in N$ and $2x + y = 24\}$. Then, find the domain and range of the relation R. Also, find whether R is an equivalence relation or not.

11 Let $A = \{1, 2, 3\}$. Then, find the number of equivalence relations containing (1, 2).

12 Show that the relation R in the set Z of integers given by $R = \{(a, b) : a \equiv b \bmod 2\}$ is an equivalence relation.

[**Hint** x is said to be congruent to y modulo m, written as $x \equiv y \pmod m$ iff m divides $(x - y)$]

13 Let R be a relation on the set A of ordered pairs of positive integers defined by $(x, y)\ R\ (u, v)$ if and only if $xv = yu$. Show that R is an equivalence relation. **[NCERT]**

14 Show that the relation R defined by $(a, b)\ R\ (c, d) \Rightarrow a + d = b + c$ on the set $N \times N$ is an equivalence relation.

Long Answer Type Questions

6 Marks

15 If N denotes the set of all natural numbers and R is the relation on $N \times N$ defined by $(a, b)\ R\ (c, d)$, if $ad(b + c) = bc(a + d)$. Show that R is an equivalence relation.

16 Show that the relation R in the set $A = \{1, 2, 3, 4, 5\}$ given by $R = \{(a, b) : |a - b|$ is even$\}$ is an equivalence relation. Also, show that all elements of $\{1, 3, 5\}$ are related to each other and all the elements of $\{2, 4\}$ are related to each other, but no element of $\{1, 3, 5\}$ is related to any element of $\{2, 4\}$. **[NCERT]**

17 Show that the relation R in the set A of points in a plane given by $R = \{(P, Q)$: distance of the point P from the origin is same as the distance of the point Q from the origin$\}$ is an equivalence relation. Further, show that the set of all points related to a point $P \neq (0,0)$ is the circle passing through P with origin as centre. **[NCERT]**

18 In the set of natural numbers N, define a relation R as follows $\forall\ n, m \in N, nRm$, if on division by 5 each of the integers n and m leaves the same remainder less than 5, i.e. one of numbers 0, 1, 2, 3 and 4. Show that R is an equivalence relation. Also, obtain the pairwise disjoint subset determined by R. **[NCERT Exemplar]**

Hints & Solutions

1. **Hint** (i) R is reflexive, as $(a, a) \in R, \forall a \in A$.

(ii) R is symmetric, as $(0, 1) \in R \Rightarrow (1, 0) \in R$ and $(0, 3) \in R \Rightarrow (3, 0) \in R$.

(iii) R is not transitive, as $(3, 0), (0, 1) \in R \not\Rightarrow (3, 1) \in R$.

[**Ans.** Reflexive, symmetric and not transitive]

2. **Hint** Consider $(x, y) = (1, \sqrt{3})$ and $(y, z) = (\sqrt{3}, \sqrt{2})$

[**Ans.** No]

3. For R to be reflexive, (b, b) and (c, c) should belong to R and for R to be transitive (a, c) should belong to R, as $(a, b) \in R$ and $(b, c) \in R$. Hence, minimum number of ordered pairs to be added in R is 3. [2]

4. The smallest relation R containing (1, 2) and (2, 3), which is reflexive and transitive but not symmetric is $\{(1, 1), (2, 2), (3, 3), (1, 2), (2, 3), (1, 3)\}$. [1]

Now, we are left with three pairs, (2, 1), (3, 1) and (3, 2). If we add the ordered pair (2, 1) to R, then we get the relation say R_1. [1]

It can be observed that, the relation R_1 will be reflexive, transitive but not symmetric. Similarly, if we add the ordered pair (3, 2) to R, then we get the relation say R_2, which will be reflexive, transitive but not symmetric. [1]

But if we add two ordered pairs (2, 1), (3, 2) or single ordered pair (3, 1) to R at a time, then we have to add some other ordered pair to maintain the condition of transitivity, but in this process the relation become symmetric also which is not required.

Hence, the total number of desired relations is three. [1]

5. Given, A = Set of real numbers and $R = \{(a, b) : a \leq b\}$.

Reflexive Let $a \in A$ be any arbitrary real number.

We know that every real number is equal to itself, therefore $a = a$.

Also, we can write it as $a \leq a \Rightarrow (a, a) \in R$

So, R is reflexive. [1]

Symmetric Let $(a, b) \in R$, then $a < b$ or $a = b$

If $a = b$, then $b = a$

But if we consider $a < b$, then $b \not< a \Rightarrow (b, a) \notin R$.

e.g. $4 < 5$ but $5 \not< 4$

So, R is not symmetric. [1½]

Transitive Let $(a, b), (b, c) \in R$, then

$$(a, b) \in R \Rightarrow a \leq b \quad \text{...(i)}$$

$$(b, c) \in R \Rightarrow b \leq c \quad \text{...(ii)}$$

From Eqs. (i) and (ii), we get $a \leq c \Rightarrow (a, c) \in R$

So, R is transitive. [1½]

6. Given, A = Set of real numbers and $R = \{(a, b): 1 + ab > 0\}$.

Reflexive Let a be any real number.

Then, $1 + aa = 1 + a^2 > 0 \quad [\because a^2 \geq 0, \forall a \in A]$

$\Rightarrow (a, a) \in R, \forall a \in A$

So, R is reflexive. [1]

Symmetric Let $(a, b) \in R$, then

$(1 + ab) > 0 \Rightarrow 1 + ba > 0$ $[\because ab = ba, \forall\ a, b \in A]$

$\Rightarrow (b, a) \in R$

Thus, $(a, b) \in R \Rightarrow (b, a) \in R, \forall\ a, b \in A$

So, R is symmetric. [1½]

Transitive We observe that $\left(1, \frac{1}{2}\right) \in R$ as

$1 + 1 \cdot \frac{1}{2} = 1 + \frac{1}{2} > 0$

and $\left(\frac{1}{2}, -1\right) \in R$ as $1 + (-1)\left(\frac{1}{2}\right) = 1 - \frac{1}{2} > 0$

But $(1, -1) \notin R$

Because $1 + 1 \times (-1) = 0 \not> 0$

So, R is not transitive. [1½]

7. **Hint Reflexive** Take $a = \frac{1}{2}$, then $(a, a) \notin R$

Symmetric Take $a = 1$ and $b = 2$, then $(a, b) \in R$ but $(b, a) \notin R$

Transitive Take $a = 10$, $b = 4$ and $c = 2$, then $(a, b), (b, c) \in R$ but $(a, c) \notin R$.

8. Similar as Example 4.

9. Given, A = Set of all points in a plane.

$R = \{(P, Q)$: Distance between P and Q is less than 2 units$\}$ [1/2]

Reflexive Let $P \in A$ be any arbitrary point. Then, distance between P and P is 0, which is less than 2 units.

$\Rightarrow (P, P) \in R$

Thus, $(P, P) \in R, \forall\ P \in A$

So, R is reflexive. [1]

Symmetric Let $P, Q \in A$ such that $(P, Q) \in R$, i.e. distance between P and Q is less than 2 units.

$\Rightarrow$ Distance between Q and P is less than 2 units.

$\Rightarrow (Q, P) \in R$

So, R is symmetric. [1]

Transitive Consider the points P, Q and S having coordinates $(0, 0)$, $(1, 0)$ and $(2, 0)$, respectively. We can observe that, the distance between P and Q is 1 unit, which is less than 2 units and also the distance between Q and S is 1 unit.

But the distance between P and S is 2 units, which is not less than 2 units. Thus, $(P, Q) \in R, (Q, S) \in R$ but $(P, S) \notin R$.

So, R is not transitive. [1½]

10. Given, $R = \{(x, y) : x \in N, y \in N$ and $2x + y = 24\}$

Here if $x = 1$, then $y = 22$

$[\because$ put $x = 1$ in $2x + y = 24$, we get $y = 22]$

If $x = 2$, then $y = 20$; If $x = 3$, then $y = 18$;
If $x = 4$, then $y = 16$; If $x = 5$, then $y = 14$;
If $x = 6$, then $y = 12$; If $x = 7$, then $y = 10$;
If $x = 8$, then $y = 8$; If $x = 9$, then $y = 6$;
If $x = 10$, then $y = 4$; If $x = 11$, then $y = 2$; [1]

$\therefore R = \{(1, 22), (2, 20), (3, 18), (4, 16), (5, 14), (6, 12), (7, 10), (8, 8), (9, 6), (10, 4), (11, 2)\}$ [1]

Hence, the domain $= \{1, 2, 3, 4, 5, 6, 7, 8, 9, 10, 11\}$

and range $= \{22, 20, 18, 16, 14, 12, 10, 8, 6, 4, 2\}$. [1]

Reflexive Clearly, $1 \in N$ but $(1, 1) \notin R$, so R is not reflexive.

Hence, R is not an equivalence relation. [1]

11. It is given that, $A = \{1, 2, 3\}$ and we know, an equivalence relation is reflexive, symmetric and transitive.

The smallest equivalence relation containing $(1, 2)$ is given by

$R_1 = \{(1, 1), (2, 2), (3, 3), (1, 2), (2, 1)\}$ [1]

Now, we are left with only four pairs, $(2, 3)$, $(3, 2)$, $(1, 3)$ and $(3, 1)$. If we add any one pair [say $(2, 3)$] to R_1, then for symmetry, we must add $(3, 2)$. [1]

Also, for transitivity, we are required to add $(1, 3)$ and $(3, 1)$.

Hence, the only equivalence relation (bigger than R_1) is the universal relation. [1]

This shows that, the total number of equivalence relations containing $(1, 2)$ is two. [1]

12. Given, $R = \{(a, b) : 2$ divides $(a - b)\}$

and Z = Set of integers

Reflexive Let $a \in Z$ be any arbitrary element. Now, if $(a, a) \in R$ then 2 divides $a - a$, which is true.

So, R is reflexive. [1]

Symmetric Let $a, b \in Z$, such that

$(a, b) \in R \Rightarrow 2$ divides $(a - b)$

$\Rightarrow (a - b) = 2m$ for some $m \in Z$

$\Rightarrow b - a = 2(-m)$, where $(-m) \in Z$

$\Rightarrow 2$ divides $(b - a) \Rightarrow (b, a) \in R$

So, R is symmetric. [1]

Transitive Let $a, b, c \in Z$, such that $(a, b) \in R$ and $(b, c) \in R$

$\Rightarrow a - b$ and $b - c$ both are divisible by 2.

$\Rightarrow a - b + b - c$ is divisible by 2.

$\Rightarrow (a - c)$ is divisible by 2 $\Rightarrow (a, c) \in R$

So, R is transitive. [1]

Thus, R is reflexive, symmetric and transitive.

Hence, R is an equivalence relation. [1]

13. Given, $A = N \times N$ and a relation R on A, defined as $(x, y) R (u, v)$, iff $xv = yu$.

Reflexive Let $(x, y) \in A$ be any arbitrary element.

Now, we have to show that $(x, y) R (x, y)$.

Clearly, $xy = yx \Rightarrow (x, y) R (x, y)$

$\because (x, y) \in A$ was arbitrary.

$\therefore (x, y) R (x, y), \forall\ (x, y) \in A$ [1]

So, R is reflexive.

Symmetric Let (x, y) and $(u, v) \in A$ such that $(x, y) R (u, v)$.

Now, we have to show that $(u, v) R (x, y)$, i.e. $uy = vx$.

$\because \quad (x, y) R (u, v)$

$\Rightarrow \quad xv = yu \Rightarrow yu = xv$

$\Rightarrow \quad uy = vx \Rightarrow (u, v) R (x, y)$

So, R is symmetric. [1½]

Transitive Let (x, y), (u, v) and $(a, b) \in A$, such that $(x, y) R (u, v)$ and $(u, v) R (a, b)$

Now, we have to show that $(x, y) R (a, b)$, i.e. $xb = ya$.

$\because \quad (x, y) R (u, v) \Rightarrow xv = yu$ ...(i)

and $\quad (u, v) R (a, b) \Rightarrow ub = va$ ...(ii)

Now, multiplying both sides of Eq. (i) by $\frac{a}{u}$, we get

$$xv\left(\frac{a}{u}\right) = yu\left(\frac{a}{u}\right)$$

$\Rightarrow \quad xv\left(\frac{b}{v}\right) = yu\left(\frac{a}{u}\right)$ [using Eq. (ii)]

$\Rightarrow \quad xb = ya$

$\Rightarrow \quad (x, y) R (a, b)$

So, R is transitive.

Hence, R is an equivalence relation. [1½]

14. Similar as Example 10.

15. We have a relation R on $N \times N$ defined by $(a, b) R (c, d)$, if $ad(b + c) = bc(a + d)$ [1/2]

Reflexive Let $(a, b) \in N \times N$ be any arbitrary element. We have to show that $(a, b) R (a, b)$, i.e. $ab(b + a) = ba(a + b)$, which is always true, as natural numbers are commutative under usual multiplication and addition.

Since, $(a, b) \in N \times N$ was arbitrary, so R is reflexive. [1]

Symmetric Let $(a, b), (c, d) \in N \times N$ such that $(a, b) R (c, d)$, i.e. $ad(b + c) = bc(a + d)$ ...(i)

We have to show that $(c, d) R (a, b)$, i.e. $cb(d + a) = da(c + b)$

From Eq. (i), we have $ad(b + c) = bc(a + d)$

$\Rightarrow \quad da(c + b) = cb(d + a)$

[$\because$ natural numbers are commutative under usual addition and multiplication] [1]

$\Rightarrow \quad cb(d + a) = da(c + b)$

$\Rightarrow \quad (c, d) R (a, b)$

So, R is symmetric. [1]

Transitive Let (a, b), (c, d) and $(e, f) \in N \times N$ such that $(a, b) R (c, d)$ and $(c, d) R (e, f)$.

$\because \quad (a, b) R (c, d) \Rightarrow ad(b + c) = bc(a + d)$

$\Rightarrow \quad \frac{b + c}{bc} = \frac{a + d}{ad}$

$\Rightarrow \quad \frac{1}{c} + \frac{1}{b} = \frac{1}{d} + \frac{1}{a}$ ...(ii)

and $(c, d) R (e, f) \Rightarrow cf(d + e) = de(c + f)$

$\Rightarrow \quad \frac{d + e}{de} = \frac{c + f}{cf}$

$\Rightarrow \quad \frac{1}{e} + \frac{1}{d} = \frac{1}{f} + \frac{1}{c}$ ...(iii) [1]

Now, on adding Eqs. (ii) and (iii), we get

$$\left(\frac{1}{c} + \frac{1}{b}\right) + \left(\frac{1}{e} + \frac{1}{d}\right) = \left(\frac{1}{d} + \frac{1}{a}\right) + \left(\frac{1}{f} + \frac{1}{c}\right)$$ [1/2]

$\Rightarrow \quad \frac{1}{b} + \frac{1}{e} = \frac{1}{a} + \frac{1}{f} \Rightarrow \frac{e + b}{be} = \frac{f + a}{af}$

$\Rightarrow \quad af(e + b) = be(f + a)$

$\Rightarrow \quad af(b + e) = be(a + f)$

$\Rightarrow \quad (a, b) R (e, f)$

So, R is transitive.

Hence, R is an equivalence relation. [1]

16. Given, $A = \{1, 2, 3, 4, 5\}$ and $R = \{(a, b) : |a - b| \text{ is even}\}$.

Reflexive For any $a \in A$, we have $|a - a| = 0$, which is even.

Thus, $(a, a) \in R, \forall a \in A$

So, R is reflexive. [1]

Symmetric Let $a, b \in A$ such that $(a, b) \in R \Rightarrow |a - b|$ is even.

$\Rightarrow \quad |-(b - a)|$ is even.

$\Rightarrow \quad |b - a|$ is even.

$\Rightarrow \quad (b, a) \in R$.

So, R is symmetric. [1]

Transitive Let $a, b, c \in A$ such that $(a, b) \in R$ and $(b, c) \in R$

$\Rightarrow \quad |a - b|$ is even and $|b - c|$ is even.

$\Rightarrow$ (a and b both are even or both are odd) and (b and c both are even or both are odd)

***Case* I** *When b is even.*

In this case, a is even and c is even

$\Rightarrow |a - c|$ is even $\Rightarrow (a, c) \in R$.

***Case* II** *When b is odd.*

In this case, a is odd and c is odd

$\Rightarrow |a - c|$ is even $\Rightarrow (a, c) \in R$

Thus, $(a, b) \in R, (b, c) \in R \Rightarrow (a, c) \in R$

So, R is transitive.

Hence, R is an equivalence relation. [1]

Now, all elements of the set {1, 3, 5} are related to each other as all the elements of this set are odd and so the modulus of the difference between any two elements will be even. [1]

Similarly, all elements of the set {2, 4} are related to each other as all the elements of this set are even and so the modulus of the difference between any two elements will be even. [1]

But no element of the set {1, 3, 5} can be related to any element of {2, 4} as all the elements of set {1, 3, 5} are odd and all the elements of set {2, 4} are even.

So, the modulus of the difference between the two elements each from these two subsets [e.g. $3 - 2 = 1$ not even, $5 - 2 = 3$ not even, etc.] will not be even. [1]

17. Given, A = {all points in a plane} and
$R = \{(P, Q)$: distance of the point P from the origin is the same as the distance of the point Q from the origin} [1/2]

Reflexive Let $P \in A$ be any arbitrary point. Then, distance of a point P from the origin is always same.

$\therefore \quad (P, P) \in R$

So, R is reflexive. [1]

Symmetric Let $(P, Q) \in R$, where $P, Q \in A$.

$\Rightarrow$ The distance of point P from the origin is same as the distance of point Q from the origin.

$\Rightarrow$ The distance of point Q from the origin is same as the distance of point P from the origin.

$\Rightarrow \quad (Q, P) \in R$

Thus, $(P, Q) \in R \Rightarrow (Q, P) \in R$, where $P, Q \in A$.

So, R is symmetric. [1]

Transitive Let $(P, Q), (Q, S) \in R$, where $P, Q, S \in A$.

$$\left.\begin{aligned} \Rightarrow \quad OP &= OQ \\ \text{and} \quad OQ &= OS \end{aligned}\right\} \Rightarrow OP = OS$$

i.e. the distance of points P and S from the origin is same.

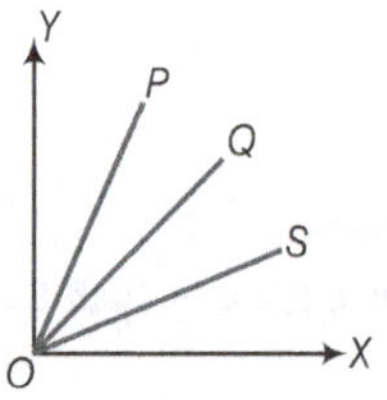

[1]

$\Rightarrow \quad (P, S) \in R$

So, R is transitive.

Hence, R is an equivalence relation on A. [1]

Let $P \neq (0, 0)$ be a fixed point in the plane and $Q(x, y)$ be any point in the plane related to P.

Then, $\quad OP = OQ = k$ (say) [1/2]

$\because \quad OQ = \sqrt{(x-0)^2 + (y-0)^2}$

$\therefore \quad k = \sqrt{x^2 + y^2} \Rightarrow x^2 + y^2 = k^2$

This is an equation of the circle with centre (0, 0) and radius k (distance of point P from origin). Thus, all the points related to P satisfy this equation. Hence, the set of all points related to a point $P \neq (0, 0)$ is the circle passing through P with origin as centre. [1]

18. R is reflexive, since for each $a \in N$, aRa. [1/2]

R is symmetric, since if aRb, then bRa for $a, b \in N$. [1]

Also, R is transitive, since for $a, b, c \in N$, if aRb and bRc, then aRc. [1]

Hence, R is an equivalence relation in N which will partition the set N into the pairwise disjoint subsets. [1]

The equivalence classes are as mentioned below

A_0 = {Set of numbers, which leaves remainder 0}
$= \{5, 10, 15, 20, \ldots\}$

A_1 = {Set of numbers, which leaves remainder 1}
$= \{1, 6, 11, 16, 21, \ldots\}$

A_2 = {Set of numbers, which leaves remainder 2}
$= \{2, 7, 12, 17, 22, \ldots\}$

A_3 = {Set of numbers, which leaves remainder 3}
$= \{3, 8, 13, 18, 23, \ldots\}$

A_4 = {Set of numbers, which leaves remainder 4}
$= \{4, 9, 14, 19, 24, \ldots\}$ [2]

It is evident that the above five sets are pairwise disjoint and $A_0 \cup A_1 \cup A_2 \cup A_3 \cup A_4 = \bigcup_{i=0}^{4} A_i = N$. [1/2]

TOPIC 02 Functions and Their Types

Function as a Special Relation

Let A and B be two non-empty sets. A function from set A to set B is a relation from A to B (denoted by f) satisfying the following conditions

(i) For each $a \in A$, there exists $b \in B$ such that $(a, b) \in f$.

(ii) no two distinct ordered pairs in f have the same first element.

e.g. If $A = \{1, 2, 3\}$ and $B = \{4, 5\}$, then $f = \{(1, 4), (2, 5), (3, 4)\}$ is a function but $f = \{(1, 4), (1, 5), (2, 4), (3, 5)\}$ is not a function, because the ordered pairs (1, 4) and (1, 5) have the same first element.

If f is a function from A to B and $(a, b) \in f$, then we can write $f(a) = b$, where b is called the **image** of a under f and a is called the **pre-image** of b under f.

Note Every function is a relation but converse is not always true. e.g. If $A = \{1, 2, 3\}$ and $B = \{1, 4\}$, then $R = \{(1, 1), (1, 4), (2, 4)\}$ is a relation but not a function.

Function as a Rule

For any two non-empty sets A and B, a function f from A to B is a rule which associates each element of set A to a unique element of set B. It is represented by

$$f : A \to B \text{ or } A \xrightarrow{f} B.$$

In other words, if A and B are two non-empty sets, then a subset f of $A \times B$ is called a **function** (or mapping or map) from A to B if and only if for every $x \in A$, there exists a unique $y \in B$ such that $(x, y) \in f$.

e.g. $f : N \to N$ define as $f(x) = x^2$ is a function, because f associate each element of N to a unique element in N as shown in figure.

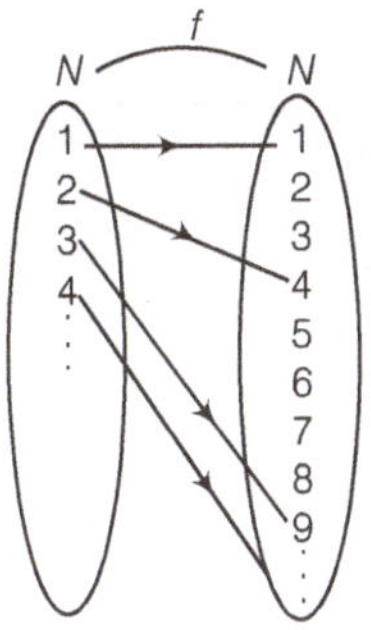

The Notation $y = f(x)$

Let $x \in A$ is associated to $y \in B$ under the function $f : A \to B$. Then, the value of y depends upon the choice of x. So we can say that y is a function of x. We write it as $y = f(x)$.

The value of y is called the **f-image** of x or **image of x under f** or the value of the function at x, where x is called the **pre-image** of y under the function f. The rotation can be shown by the following figure.

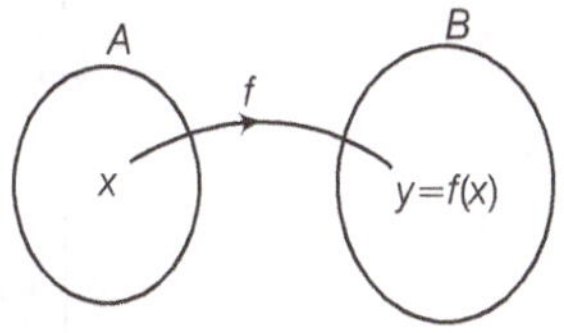

Note If $n(A) = p$ and $n(B) = q$, then the **number of functions** defined from A to B is q^p.

Domain, Codomain and Range of a Function

Consider a function $f : A \to B$, then elements of set A are called **domain** of f and elements of set B are called **codomain** of f, and the set of all f-images obtained in set B corresponding to each element belongs to set A is called **range** of f.

e.g. Let $f : A \to B$ be a function represented by the following diagram.

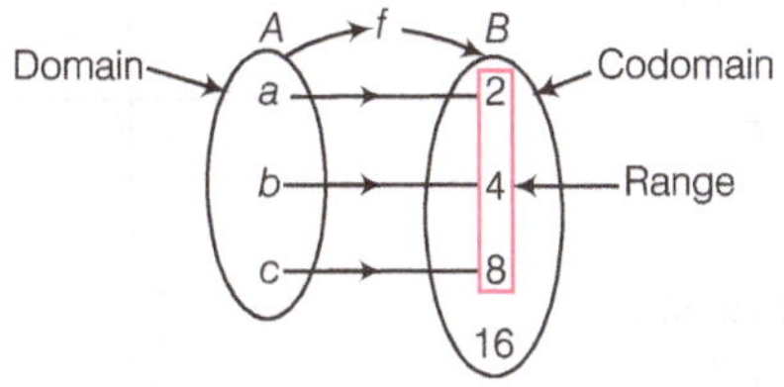

Then, domain $= \{a, b, c\}$, codomain $= \{2, 4, 8, 16\}$
and range $= \{2, 4, 8\}$.

Example 1 Let $A = \{1, 2, 3\}$ and $B = \{2, 4, 6, 8\}$. Consider the rule $f : A \to B$, defined as $f(x) = 2x$, $\forall\ x \in A$. Find the domain, codomain and range of f.

Find the image of 1, 2, 3 using definition of f.

Sol. Given, $f(x) = 2x$, $\forall\ x \in A$

Value of function at $x = 1$, $f(1) = 2(1) = 2$

Value of function at $x = 2$, $f(2) = 2(2) = 4$

Value of function at $x = 3$, $f(3) = 2(3) = 6$

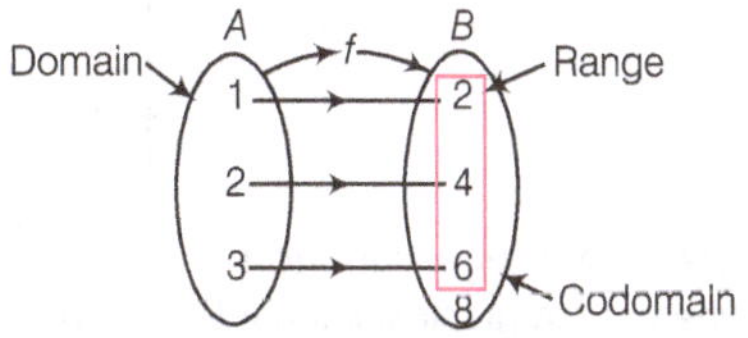

We can write it as $f = \{(1, 2), (2, 4), (3, 6)\}$

$\therefore$ Domain of $f = \{1, 2, 3\}$, Codomain of $f = \{2, 4, 6, 8\}$

and range of $f = \{2, 4, 6\}$

Real Valued Function

A function, whose codomain is a set (or a subset) of real numbers, is known as **real-valued function** and a function whose domain and codomain both are the sets (or subsets) of real numbers, is known as **real function**. Note that every real function is a real-valued function, but converse may not be true.

e.g. $f : C \to R$ is a real-valued function but not real function, where C is a set of complex numbers.

Note Domain of a real function is the set of all possible real numbers x for which $f(x)$ is a real number.

Some Special Real Functions

Some special real functions and their domain, range and graphs are given below

Function	Graph

Identity function

$f(x) = x, \forall x \in R$

Domain $\to R$

Range $\to R$

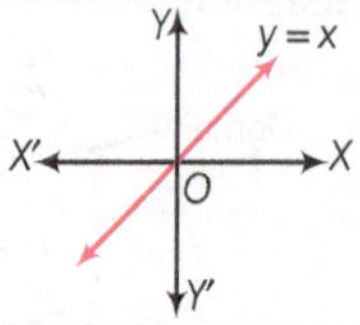

Constant function

$f(x) = c, \forall x \in R$

Domain $\to R$

Range $\to \{c\}$

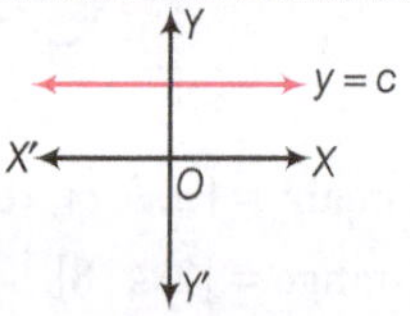

Reciprocal function

$f(x) = \frac{1}{x}, \forall x \in R - \{0\}$

Domain $\to R - \{0\}$

Range $\to R - \{0\}$

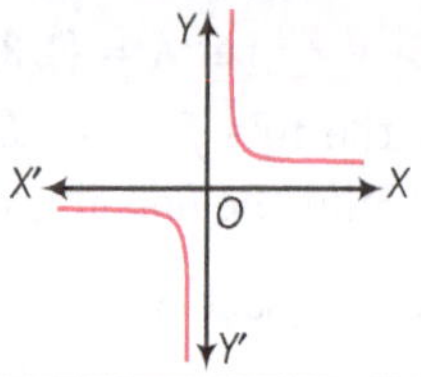

Greatest integer function

$f(x) = [x], \forall x \in R$

Domain $\to R$

Range $\to I$

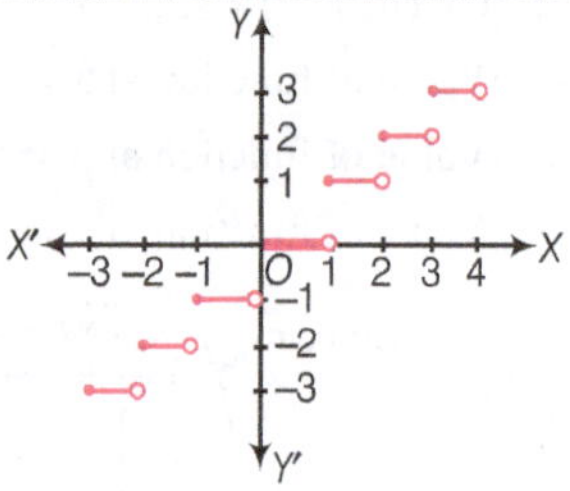

Properties of greatest integer function

If $n < x < n + 1$, where n is a greatest integer less than x and x is a real number, then

- $[x] = n$
- $[-x] = -[x] - 1$
- $[x + m] = [x] + m$, for any integer m.

Modulus function

$f(x) = |x|, \forall x \in R = \begin{cases} x, & \text{if } x \ge 0 \\ -x, & \text{if } x < 0 \end{cases}$

Domain $\to R$

Range $\to [0, \infty)$

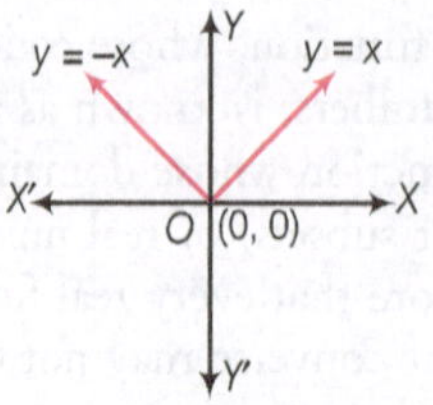

Properties of modulus function

Let $x, y \in R$ (set of real numbers). Then,

- $\sqrt{x^2} = |x|$
- $x^2 \le a^2 \Leftrightarrow |x| \le a \Leftrightarrow -a \le x \le a$
- $x^2 \ge a^2 \Leftrightarrow |x| \ge a \Leftrightarrow x \le -a$ or $x \ge a$
- $|x \pm y| \le |x| + |y|$
- $|x \pm y| \ge ||x| - |y||$

Function	Graph

Signum function

$f(x) = \text{sgn}(x) = \frac{|x|}{x}$

or $f(x) = \begin{cases} -1, & \text{for } x < 0 \\ 0, & \text{for } x = 0 \\ 1, & \text{for } x > 0 \end{cases}$

Domain $\to R$

Range $\to \{-1, 0, 1\}$

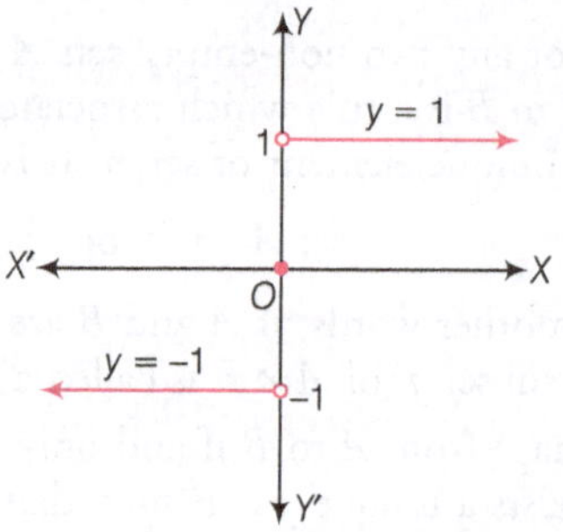

Exponential function

$f(x) = a^x$, where $a > 0$ and $a \ne 1, \forall x \in R$

***Case* I** When $a > 1$,

$f(x) = a^x \to \begin{cases} < 1, & \text{for } x < 0 \\ = 1, & \text{for } x = 0 \\ > 1, & \text{for } x > 0 \end{cases}$

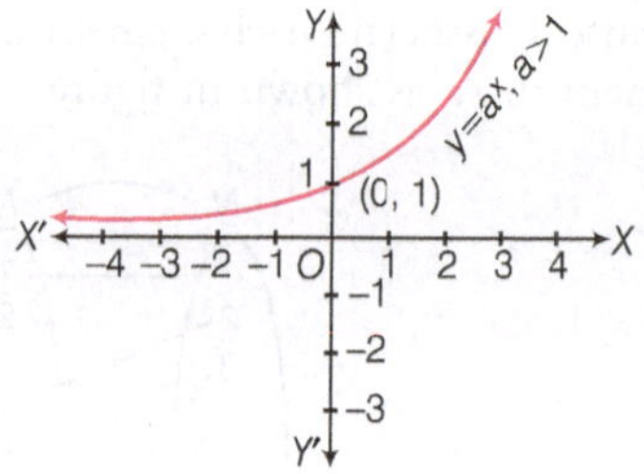

***Case* II** When $0 < a < 1$,

$f(x) = a^x \to \begin{cases} > 1, & \text{for } x < 0 \\ = 1, & \text{for } x = 0 \\ < 1, & \text{for } x > 0 \end{cases}$

Domain $\to R$

Range $\to (0, \infty)$

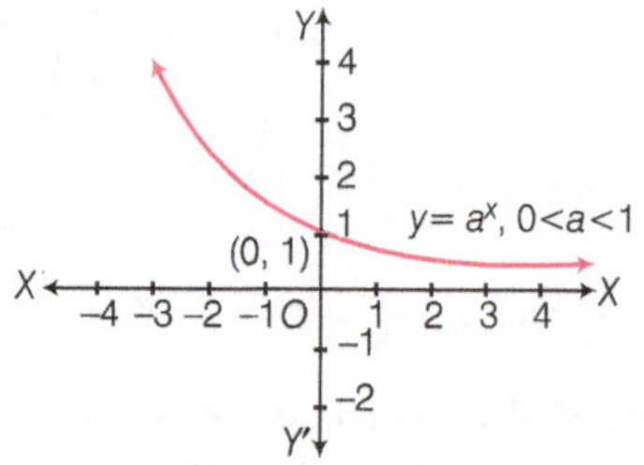

Logarithmic function

$f(x) = \log_a x, \forall x > 0$, where $a > 0$ and $a \ne 1$

***Case* I** When $a > 1$,

$f(x) \to \begin{cases} < 0, & \text{for } 0 < x < 1 \\ = 0, & \text{for } x = 1 \\ > 0, & \text{for } x > 1 \end{cases}$

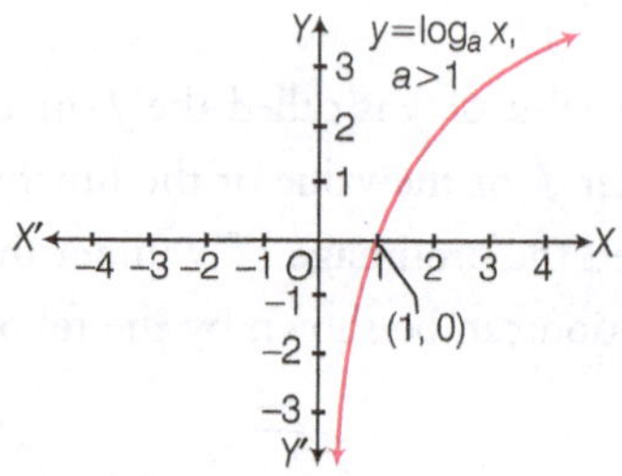

***Case* II** When $0 < a < 1$,

$f(x) \to \begin{cases} > 0, & \text{for } 0 < x < 1 \\ = 0, & \text{for } x = 1 \\ < 0, & \text{for } x > 1 \end{cases}$

Domain $\to R^+$

Range $\to R$

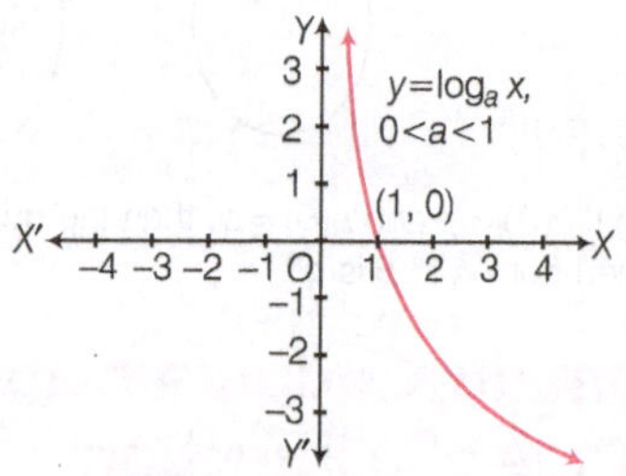

Types of Functions

As we know that if $f: A \to B$ is a function, then f associates all the elements of set A to the elements in set B such that an element of set A is associated to a unique element of set B.

But there are some more possibilities, which may occur in a function, such as

(i) more than one elements of A may have same image in B.
(ii) each elements of B is image of some elements of A.
(iii) there may be some elements in B, which are not the images of any element of A.

Corresponding to these possibilities, we define the following types of functions.

One-One (Injective) Function

A function $f: A \to B$ is called a one-one or injective function, if distinct elements of A have distinct images in B, i.e. for every $a_1, a_2 \in A$, if $a_1 \neq a_2$, then $f(a_1) \neq f(a_2)$ and if $f(a_1) = f(a_2)$, then $a_1 = a_2$.

e.g. Let $f: A \to B$ be a function represented by the following diagram.

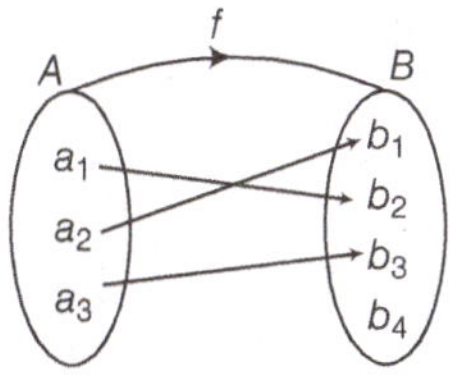

Here, f is a one-one function, because each element have distinct image.

Many-One Function

A function $f: A \to B$ is called a many-one function, if there exist atleast two distinct elements in A, whose images are same in B, i.e. if there exist $a_1, a_2 \in A$, such that $a_1 \neq a_2$ and $f(a_1) = f(a_2)$, then f is many-one.

In other words, a function $f: A \to B$ is called a many-one function, if it is not one-one. **e.g.** Let $f: A \to B$ be a function represented by the following diagram.

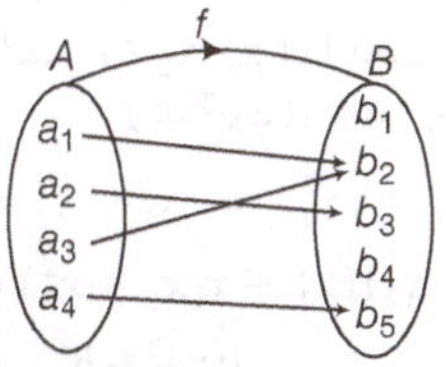

Here, f is many-one function, because a_1 and a_3 have same image b_2.

Methods to Check Whether a Function is One-One or Many-One

Sometimes, a function is given to us and we have to check whether this function is one-one or many-one.

Method I In this we use the following steps

I. First, consider any two arbitrary elements, say $a_1, a_2 \in$ (domain of function).
II. Put $f(a_1) = f(a_2)$ and simplify the equation.
III. If we get $a_1 = a_2$, then f is one-one, otherwise f is many-one.

Method II (Horizontal line test) If a horizontal line intersects the graph of function more than once, then f is not one-one.

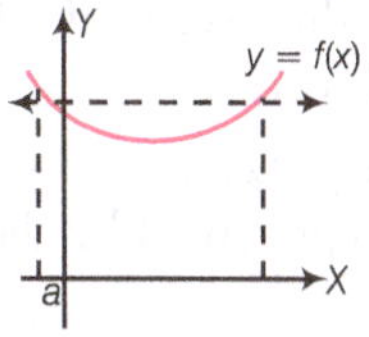

Example 2 Determine whether the function $f: A \to B$ defined by $f(x) = 4x + 7$, $x \in A$ is one-one.

Sol. Given, $f: A \to B$ defined by $f(x) = 4x + 7$, $x \in A$

Let $x_1, x_2 \in A$, such that $f(x_1) = f(x_2)$

$\Rightarrow 4x_1 + 7 = 4x_2 + 7 \Rightarrow 4x_1 = 4x_2 \Rightarrow x_1 = x_2$

So, f is one-one function.

Example 3 Show that the signum function $f: R \to R$, given by $f(x) = \begin{cases} 1, & \text{if } x > 0 \\ 0, & \text{if } x = 0 \\ -1, & \text{if } x < 0 \end{cases}$ is many-one.

Sol. Given, $f: R \to R$ defined by $f(x) = \begin{cases} 1, & \text{if } x > 0 \\ 0, & \text{if } x = 0 \\ -1, & \text{if } x < 0 \end{cases}$

Clearly, $f(1) = f(2) = f(3) = \dots = 1$,

$f(0) = 0$,

and $f(-1) = f(-2) = f(-3) = \dots = -1$.

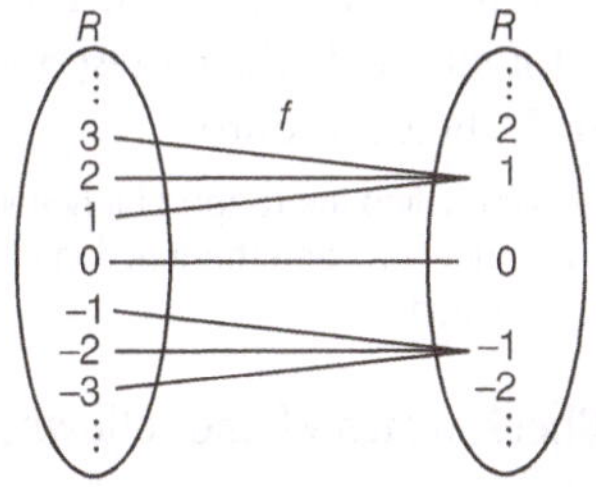

We can observe that all positive real numbers have same image 1 and all negative real numbers have same image -1.

Hence, it is a many-one function.

Note In order to prove f is not one-one, it is sufficient to show that $f(1) = 1$ and $f(2) = 1$.

Onto (Surjective) and Into Function

A function $f: A \rightarrow B$ is said to be **onto** (or surjective), if every element of B is the image of at least one element of A under f, i.e. for every $b \in B$, there exists an element a in A such that $f(a) = b$.

In other words, $f: A \rightarrow B$ is onto if and only if

Range of $f = B$ i.e. Range = Codomain

A function $g: X \rightarrow Y$ is an **into function**, if there exists one element in Y, which have no pre-image in X. In other words, if a function is not onto, then it is an into function.

e.g. Let $f: A \rightarrow B$ and $g: X \rightarrow Y$ be two functions represented by the following diagrams.

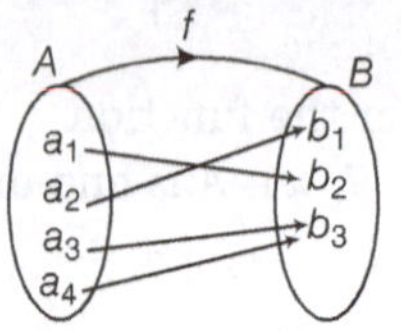

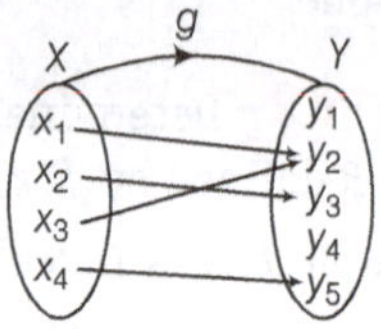

Here, f is an onto function and g is an into function because y_1 and y_4 are elements of Y, which do not have pre-image in X.

Method to Check Whether the Function is Onto or Into

Sometimes, a function is given to us and we have to check whether this function is onto or into. For this, we use the following steps

I. Let $f: A \rightarrow B$ be the given function, then first consider y be an arbitrary element of B.

II. Put $y = f(x)$ and simplify it to obtain x in terms of y.

III. Now, if for any $y \in B$, the corresponding value of x does not belongs to A, then f is not onto, i.e. f is into but if for all $y \in B$, the corresponding value of x belongs to A, then f is onto.

Note Sometimes, we simply find the range of function. If range of function = Codomain of function, then the function is onto, otherwise it is an into function.

Example 4 Check which of the following function is onto or into.

(i) $f: A \rightarrow B$, given by $f(x) = 3x$, where $A = \{0, 1, 2\}$ and $B = \{0, 3, 6\}$.

(ii) $f: Z \rightarrow Z$, given by $f(x) = 3x + 2$, where Z = set of integers.

Sol. (i) We have a function, $f: A \rightarrow B$, given by $f(x) = 3x$, where $A = \{0, 1, 2\}$ and $B = \{0, 3, 6\}$.

Let $y \in B$ be any arbitrary element.

Then, $y = f(x) \Rightarrow y = 3x \Rightarrow x = \dfrac{y}{3}$

Now, at $y = 0$, $x = \dfrac{0}{3} = 0 \in A$

At $y = 3$, $x = \dfrac{3}{3} = 1 \in A$; At $y = 6$, $x = \dfrac{6}{3} = 2 \in A$

Thus, for each element y of B, there is a pre-image in A.

So, $f: A \rightarrow B$ is an onto function.

(ii) We have a function, $f: Z \rightarrow Z$, given by $f(x) = 3x + 2$.

Let $y \in Z$, (codomain of f) be any arbitrary element.

Then, $y = f(x) \Rightarrow y = 3x + 2 \Rightarrow x = \dfrac{y-2}{3}$

Now, when $y = 0$, then $x = \dfrac{0-2}{3} = \dfrac{-2}{3} \notin Z$

Thus, $y = 0 \in Z$ (codomain of f) does not has pre-image in Z(domain). Hence, f is not an onto function, i.e. it is an into function.

Bijective (One-to-One Correspondence)

A function $f: A \rightarrow B$ is said to be **bijective**, if f is both one-one and onto, i.e. all elements of A have distinct images in B and every element of B is the image of some elements of A. **e.g.** Let $f: A \rightarrow B$ be a function represented by the following diagram.

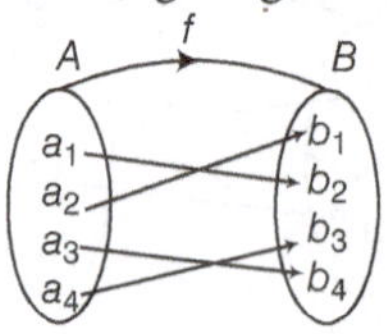

Here, f is bijective function because each element have distinct image and every element of B have pre-image.

Note If A and B are finite sets having the same number of elements are n. Then, number of bijections from A and B is $n!$.

Example 5 If $f: R \rightarrow R$ is the function defined by $f(x) = 4x^3 + 7$, then show that f is a bijection.

Sol. The given function is $f: R \rightarrow R$ such that

$$f(x) = 4x^3 + 7$$

To show f is bijective, we have to show that f is one-one and onto.

One-one function Let $x_1, x_2 \in R$ such that $f(x_1) = f(x_2)$.

$$\Rightarrow \quad 4x_1^3 + 7 = 4x_2^3 + 7$$

$$\Rightarrow \quad 4x_1^3 = 4x_2^3 \Rightarrow x_1^3 - x_2^3 = 0$$

$$\Rightarrow \quad (x_1 - x_2)(x_1^2 + x_1 x_2 + x_2^2) = 0$$

$$[\because a^3 - b^3 = (a-b)(a^2 + ab + b^2)]$$

$$\Rightarrow \quad (x_1 - x_2)\left[\left(x_1 + \frac{x_2}{2}\right)^2 + \frac{3}{4}x_2^2\right] = 0$$

$\Rightarrow$ Either $x_1 - x_2 = 0$ ...(i)

or $\left(x_1 + \frac{x_2}{2}\right)^2 + \frac{3}{4}x_2^2 = 0$ ...(ii)

But Eq. (ii) is not possible as $x_1, x_2 \in R$.

$\therefore$ $x_1 - x_2 = 0 \Rightarrow x_1 = x_2$

Thus, $f(x_1) = f(x_2) \Rightarrow x_1 = x_2, \forall x_1, x_2 \in R$

Therefore, $f(x)$ is a one-one function.

Onto function Let $y \in R$ (codomain) be any arbitrary number.

Then, $f(x) = y \Rightarrow 4x^3 + 7 = y \Rightarrow 4x^3 = y - 7$

$$\Rightarrow x^3 = \frac{y-7}{4} \Rightarrow x = \left(\frac{y-7}{4}\right)^{1/3}$$

which is a real number. $[\because y \in R]$

Thus, for every $y \in R$ (codomain), there exists

$$x = \left(\frac{y-7}{4}\right)^{1/3} \in R \text{ (domain) such that}$$

$$f(x) = f\left[\left(\frac{y-7}{4}\right)^{1/3}\right] = 4\left[\left(\frac{y-7}{4}\right)^{1/3}\right]^3 + 7$$

$$= 4\left(\frac{y-7}{4}\right) + 7 = y - 7 + 7 = y$$

$\Rightarrow f(x)$ is an onto function.

Since, $f(x)$ is both one-one and onto, so it is a bijective.

Example 6 If $f : R \to R$ is defined by $f(x) = \frac{2x-7}{4}$, show that $f(x)$ is one-one and onto. **[ISC 2024]**

Sol. A mapping $f : R \longrightarrow R$ is defined by $f(x) = \frac{2x-7}{4}$

Let $x_1, x_2 \in R$, then for one-one

$$f(x_1) = f(x_2)$$

$$\Rightarrow \frac{2x_1 - 7}{4} = \frac{2x_2 - 7}{4}$$

$$\Rightarrow 2x_1 - 7 = 2x_2 - 7 \Rightarrow x_1 = x_2$$

Thus, f is one-one.

Now, let $y = \frac{2x-7}{4}$

Then, $4y = 2x - 7$

$\Rightarrow$ $2x = 4y + 7$

$$x = \frac{4y+7}{2} = f(y)$$

Clearly, for each $y \in R$, there exists

$$x = \frac{4y+7}{2} \in R \text{ such that}$$

$$f(x) = f\left(\frac{4y+7}{2}\right) = \frac{1}{4}\left[2\left(\frac{4y+7}{2}\right) - 7\right]$$

$$= \frac{1}{4}[4y + 7 - 7] = y$$

$\Rightarrow f$ is onto.

Hence, f is one-one and onto i.e. f is bijective.

Example 7 Show that the function $f : R \to R$ defined as $f(x) = x^2$ is neither one-one nor onto.

Sol. Given, a function $f : R \to R$ defined as $f(x) = x^2$

One-One Clearly, at $x = 1, f(1) = 1$

and at $x = -1, f(-1) = (-1)^2 = 1$

Thus, $f(1) = f(-1) = 1$, but $1 \neq -1$

So, f is not one-one.

Onto Let $y \in R$ (codomain) be any arbitrary element.

Then, $y = f(x) \Rightarrow y = x^2$

$\Rightarrow$ $x = \pm\sqrt{y}$

Now, for $y = -2 \in R, x = \pm\sqrt{-2} \notin R$ (domain)

So, f is not onto.

Hence, given function is neither one-one nor onto.

Example 8 Show that the function $f : N \to N$, given by $f(x) = 2x$ is one-one but not onto.

Sol. Given a function $f : N \to N$, defined by $f(x) = 2x$

For one-one Let $x_1, x_2 \in N$, such that $f(x_1) = f(x_2)$

$\Rightarrow$ $2x_1 = 2x_2 \Rightarrow x_1 = x_2$

So, f is one-one.

For onto Let $y \in N$ (codomain) be any arbitrary element.

Then, $y = f(x)$

$$\Rightarrow y = 2x \Rightarrow x = \frac{y}{2}$$

Now, for $y = 1, x = \frac{1}{2} \notin N$ (domain)

Thus, $y = 1 \in N$ (codomain) does not have a pre-image in domain (N). So, f is not onto.

Example 9 Show that the function $f: N \to N$, given by $f(1) = f(2) = 1$ and $f(x) = x - 1$ for every $x > 2$, is onto but not one-one.

Sol. We have a function $f : N \to N$, defined as

$$f(1) = f(2) = 1 \text{ and } f(x) = x - 1, \text{ for every } x > 2$$

One-One Since, $f(1) = f(2) = 1$, therefore 1 and 2 have same image, namely 1. So, f is not one-one.

Onto Note that $y = 1$ has two pre-images, namely 1 and 2. Now, let $y \in N$ (codomain), $y \neq 1$ be any arbitrary element.

Then, $y = f(x) \Rightarrow y = x - 1$

$\Rightarrow$ $x = y + 1 > 2$ for every $y \in N, y \neq 1$.

Thus, for every $y \in N, y \neq 1$, there exists $x = y + 1$ such that

$$f(x) = f(y+1)$$
$$= y + 1 - 1 = y$$

Hence, f is onto.

Topic Practice 2

Very Short Answer Type Questions

(2 Marks)

1 Is $g = \{(1, 1), (2, 3), (3, 5), (4, 7)\}$ a function? If g is described by $g(x) = \alpha x + \beta$. Then, what value should be assigned to α and β? **[NCERT Exemplar]**

2 Let $f : R \to R$ be defined by $f(x) = x^2 + 1$. Then, find pre-images of 17 and – 3.

3 Find whether the function $f : Z \to Z$, defined by $f(x) = x^2 + 5, \forall x \in Z$ is one-one or not.

4 State whether the function $f : R \to R$, defined by $f(x) = 3 - 4x$ is onto or not.

5 Check the injectivity of the function $f : R \to R$ given by $f(x) = x^3$. **[NCERT]**

6 Prove that the greatest integer function $f : R \to R$, given by $f(x) = [x]$ is neither one-one nor onto, where $[x]$ denotes the greatest integer less than or equal to x.

7 Show that the function $f : R \to R$, given by $f(x) = \cos x, \forall x \in R$ is neither one-one nor onto.

8 Let C be the set of complex numbers. Prove that the mapping $f : C \to R$ given by $f(z) = |z|, z \in C$, is neither one-one nor onto. **[NCERT Exemplar]**

Short Answer Type Questions

(4 Marks)

9 Consider a function $f : [0, \pi/2] \to R$, given by $f(x) = \sin x$ and $g : [0, \pi/2] \to R$, given by $g(x) = \cos x$. Show that f and g are one-one, but $f + g$ is not one-one. **[NCERT]**

10 Let $f : N \to N$ be defined by

$$f(n) = \begin{cases} \dfrac{n+1}{2}, & \text{if } n \text{ is odd} \\ \dfrac{n}{2}, & \text{if } n \text{ is even} \end{cases}.$$

Show that f is many-one and onto function. **[NCERT]**

11 Let A and B be sets. Show that $f : A \times B \to B \times A$, such that $f(a, b) = (b, a)$ is bijective function. **[NCERT]**

Long Answer Type Questions

(6 Marks)

12 With the help of following graph, find the equation of function. Also, check whether the function is many-one or not. **[NCERT]**

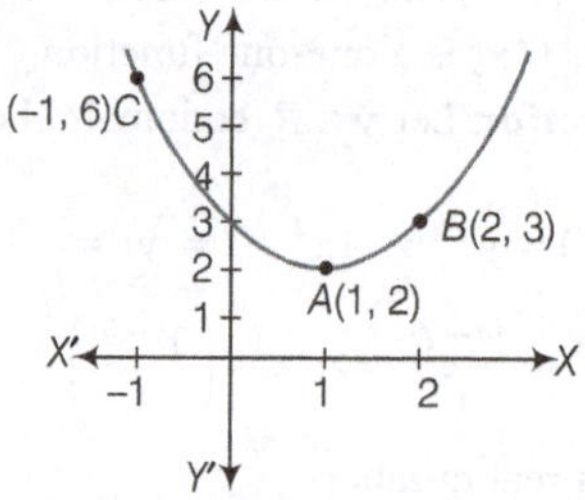

13 Show that the function $f : R \to R$, defined by $f(x) = \dfrac{x}{x^2 + 1}, \forall x \in R$ is neither one-one nor onto. **[NCERT Exemplar]**

14 Show that $f : N \to N$, given by

$$f(x) = \begin{cases} x + 1, & \text{if } x \text{ is odd} \\ x - 1, & \text{if } x \text{ is even} \end{cases}$$ is bijective (both one-one and onto).

15 Show that the function $f : R \to \{x \in R : -1 < x < 1\}$ defined by $f(x) = \dfrac{x}{1 + |x|}, x \in R$ is one-one and onto function. **[NCERT]**

Hints & Solutions

1. **Hint** According to the given information, we can have $1 = \alpha + \beta$ and $3 = 2\alpha + \beta$. [**Ans.** Yes; $\alpha = 2$ and $\beta = -1$]

2. To find the pre-images, consider $x^2 + 1 = 17$ and $x^2 + 1 = -3$
$\Rightarrow \quad x^2 = 16$ and $x^2 = -4$, which is not possible. [1]
$\Rightarrow \quad x = \pm 4$
Hence, pre-images of 17 are ± 4 and pre-image(s) of -3 does not exist. [1]

3. Let $x_1, x_2 \in Z$, such that $f(x_1) = f(x_2)$
$\Rightarrow \quad x_1^2 + 5 = x_2^2 + 5 \Rightarrow x_1^2 = x_2^2 \Rightarrow x_1 = \pm x_2$ [1]
Clearly, f is not a one-one function, as if we take $x_1 = 1$ and $x_2 = -1$, then $f(1) = 6 = f(-1)$, but $1 \neq -1$. [1]

4. Let $y \in R$ (codomain) be any real number and let $f(x) = y$.
Then, $y = 3 - 4x \Rightarrow 4x = 3 - y$
$\Rightarrow \quad x = \dfrac{3 - y}{4}$, which will be a real number for each $y \in R$
[write x in terms of y] [1]

So, for any real number $y \in R$ (codomain), there exists $\frac{3-y}{4}$ in R (domain), such that

$$f\left(\frac{3-y}{4}\right) = 3 - 4\left(\frac{3-y}{4}\right) = 3 - 3 + y = y$$

Hence, f is onto. [1]

5. Similar as Example 3.

6. Given, $f : R \to R$, defined as $f(x) = [x]$.

$\because$ $f(1.2) = [1.2] = 1$; $f(1.9) = [1.9] = 1$

$\therefore$ $f(1.2) = f(1.9)$, but $1.2 \neq 1.9$

So, f is not one-one. [1]

We known that $f(x) = [x]$ is always an integer.

$\therefore$ For $0.7 \in R$ (codomain) there does not exist any element $x \in R$ (domain of f), such that $f(x) = 0.7$.

Thus, f is not onto.

Hence, the greatest integer function is neither one-one nor onto. [1]

7. We have a function $f : R \to R$, defined by

$f(x) = \cos x \Rightarrow f(0) = \cos 0 = 1$ and $f(2\pi) = \cos 2\pi = 1$

So, f is not one-one. [1]

Also, range $f = [-1, 1] \neq R$ (codomain)

So, f is not onto. [1]

Hence, $f(x)$ is neither one-one nor onto.

8. **Hint**

(i) For one-one consider, $z_1 = 3 + 4i$ and $z_2 = 4 + 3i$, as $z_1 \neq z_2$ but we get $f(z_1) = f(z_2) \Rightarrow f$ is not one-one.

(ii) Since, for all $z \in C, |z| \geq 0$. Therefore, range of $f = [0, \infty)$, which is not equal to R (codomain).

9. Let $x_1, x_2 \in \left[0, \frac{\pi}{2}\right]$, such that $x_1 \neq x_2$.

Then, $\sin x_1 \neq \sin x_2$ and $\cos x_1 \neq \cos x_2$

[$\because$ for any two distinct values of x in $\left[0, \frac{\pi}{2}\right]$, sine function cannot give same value. This is also true for cosine function]

Hence, f and g must be one-one.

[$\because a_1 \neq a_2 \Rightarrow f(a_1) \neq f(a_2)$] [1]

But $(f + g)(0) = \sin 0 + \cos 0 = 1$ [1]

and $(f+g)\left(\frac{\pi}{2}\right) = \sin\frac{\pi}{2} + \cos\frac{\pi}{2} = 1$

$\therefore f + g$ is not one-one. [2]

10. Given, $f : N \to N$, defined by

$$f(n) = \begin{cases} \frac{n+1}{2}, & \text{if } n \text{ is odd} \\ \frac{n}{2}, & \text{if } n \text{ is even} \end{cases}$$

For one-one

Here, $f(1) = \frac{1+1}{2} = 1$ and $f(2) = \frac{2}{2} = 1$

Since, at two distinct values of domain (N), $f(x)$ has same image.

So, f is not one-one, i.e. f is many-one. [1]

For onto

Now, consider a natural number m in codomain N.

Case I *Let* $m = f(n) = \frac{n+1}{2} \Rightarrow 2m = n + 1$

$\Rightarrow n = 2m - 1$, which is odd for each $m \in N$.

Thus, for each $m \in N$ (codomain), there exists

$n = 2m - 1 \in N$, such that $f(2m-1) = \frac{2m-1+1}{2} = m$ [1]

Case II *Let* $m = f(n) = n/2$

$\Rightarrow n = 2m$, which is even for each $m \in N$.

Thus, for each $m \in N$ (codomain), there exists $n = 2m \in N$, such that $f(2m) = \frac{2m}{2} = m$. [1]

Since, from both cases, we have pre-images. So, we can choose either of the cases to get the pre-images.

Therefore, f is onto.

Hence, f is many-one and onto function. [1]

11. We have a mapping $f : A \times B \to B \times A$, defined as

$$f(a, b) = (b, a)$$

For one-one Let (a_1, b_1) and $(a_2, b_2) \in A \times B$, such that $f(a_1, b_1) = f(a_2, b_2) \Rightarrow (b_1, a_1) = (b_2, a_2)$ [1]

$\Rightarrow$ $b_1 = b_2$ and $a_1 = a_2 \Rightarrow (a_1, b_1) = (a_2, b_2)$

So, f is one-one. [1]

For onto Let $(b', a') \in B \times A$ be any arbitrary element, then there exists $(a', b') \in A \times B$, such that

$$f(a', b') = (b', a')$$ [1]

Since, (b', a') was arbitrary, so f is onto.

Hence, f is bijective function. [1]

12. Since, the given graph is representing a parabolic curve. So, let the equation of the curve is

$$y = ax^2 + bx + c \quad \text{...(i)}$$ [1]

Points on the curve are $A(1, 2)$, $B(2, 3)$ and $C(-1, 6)$.

On putting the points $A(1, 2)$, $B(2, 3)$ and $C(-1, 6)$ in the Eq. (i) one-by-one, we get

$2 = a(1)^2 + b(1) + c \Rightarrow 2 = a + b + c$ ...(ii)

$3 = a(2)^2 + 2b + c \Rightarrow 3 = 4a + 2b + c$ ...(iii)

$6 = a(-1)^2 + b(-1) + c \Rightarrow 6 = a - b + c$ ...(iv) [1]

On solving Eqs. (ii), (iii) and (iv), we get

$$a = 1, b = -2 \text{ and } c = 3$$ [1]

On putting the values of a, b and c in Eq. (i), we get

$$y = x^2 - 2x + 3$$ [1/2]

$\therefore$ Required equation of function is

$$f(x) = y = x^2 - 2x + 3 = (x-1)^2 + 2$$ [1]

Here, we can see that for two different values of domain (i.e. $x = 0, 2$), function have same image (i.e. $y = 3$). [1]

Hence, $f(x)$ is many-one function. [1/2]

13. Given, $f : R \to R$, defined by $f(x) = \frac{x}{x^2+1}, \forall x \in R$

For one-one Let $x_1, x_2 \in R$ such that $f(x_1) = f(x_2)$

$\Rightarrow$ $\frac{x_1}{x_1^2+1} = \frac{x_2}{x_2^2+1}$ [1/2]

$\Rightarrow$ $x_1 x_2^2 + x_1 = x_2 x_1^2 + x_2$

$\Rightarrow \quad x_1x_2^2 - x_2x_1^2 + x_1 - x_2 = 0$ [1/2]

$\Rightarrow x_1x_2(x_2 - x_1) - 1(x_2 - x_1) = 0$

$\Rightarrow \quad (x_2 - x_1)(x_1x_2 - 1) = 0$

$\Rightarrow \quad x_2 = x_1$ or $x_1x_2 = 1$

$\Rightarrow \quad x_1 = x_2$ or $x_1 = \dfrac{1}{x_2}$ [1]

$\therefore f$ is not one-one, as if we take $x_1 = 3$ and $x_2 = \dfrac{1}{3}$,

because $f(3) = \dfrac{3}{10} = f\left(\dfrac{1}{3}\right)$ but $3 \neq \dfrac{1}{3}$ [1]

For onto Let $k \in R$ be any arbitrary element and let $f(x) = k$

$\Rightarrow \quad \dfrac{x}{x^2+1} = k \quad \left[\because f(x) = \dfrac{x}{x^2+1}\right]$ [1/2]

$\Rightarrow \quad kx^2 + k = x \Rightarrow kx^2 - x + k = 0$ [1/2]

$\Rightarrow \quad x = \dfrac{1 \pm \sqrt{1-4k^2}}{2k} \notin R$, if $1 - 4k^2 < 0$

or $(1-2k)(1+2k) < 0$, i.e. $k > 1/2$ or $k < -1/2$ [1]

So, f is not onto. [1/2]

Hence, f is neither one-one nor onto. [1/2]

14. Given, $f: N \to N$, defined by $f(x) = \begin{cases} x+1, & \text{if } x \text{ is odd} \\ x-1, & \text{if } x \text{ is even} \end{cases}$

For one-one Let $x_1, x_2 \in N$ (domain) such that $f(x_1) = f(x_2)$. [1/2]

Now, following cases arise

Case I *When both x_1 and x_2 are odd*

In this case, $f(x_1) = f(x_2) \Rightarrow x_1 + 1 = x_2 + 1 \Rightarrow x_1 = x_2$ [1]

Case II *When both x_1 and x_2 are even*

In this case, $f(x_1) = f(x_2) \Rightarrow x_1 - 1 = x_2 - 1 \Rightarrow x_1 = x_2$ [1]

Case III *When one of them is odd and other is even*

Let x_1 is odd and x_2 is even. Then,

$f(x_1) = f(x_2) \Rightarrow x_1 + 1 = x_2 - 1$

$\Rightarrow$ even integer = odd integer, which is false.

So, $f(x_1) \neq f(x_2)$

Thus, $x_1 \neq x_2 \Rightarrow f(x_1) \neq f(x_2)$. [1]

From above three cases, it follows that f is one-one. [1/2]

For onto Let $y \in N$ (codomain) be any arbitrary element. Clearly, when y is odd then there exist $y+1$, which is even and belongs to N (domain), such that

$f((y+1)) = (y+1) - 1 = y$

and when y is even then there exist $y-1$, which is odd and belongs to N (domain), such that

$f((y-1)) = (y-1) + 1 = y$ [1]

Thus, from both cases we find that every element in the codomain of f has its pre-image in the domain of $f \Rightarrow f$ is onto.

Hence, the given function is bijective. [1]

15. We have a function $f: R \to \{x \in R: -1 < x < 1\}$, defined as

$$f(x) = \frac{x}{1+|x|} = \begin{cases} \dfrac{x}{1+x}, & \text{if } x \geq 0 \\ \dfrac{x}{1-x}, & \text{if } x < 0 \end{cases}$$

For one-one Let $x_1, x_2 \in R$ such that

$f(x_1) = f(x_2)$.

Now, the following cases arise

Case I *When both are less than 0*

In this case, $f(x_1) = f(x_2)$

$\Rightarrow \quad \dfrac{x_1}{1-x_1} = \dfrac{x_2}{1-x_2} \Rightarrow x_1 - x_1x_2 = x_2 - x_1x_2$

$\Rightarrow \quad x_1 = x_2$ [1]

Case II *When both are greater than or equal to 0*

In this case, $f(x_1) = f(x_2)$

$\Rightarrow \quad \dfrac{x_1}{1+x_1} = \dfrac{x_2}{1+x_2} \Rightarrow x_1 + x_1x_2 = x_2 + x_1x_2$

$\Rightarrow \quad x_1 = x_2$ [1]

Case III *When one is non-negative and other is negative*

Let $x_1 \geq 0$ and $x_2 < 0$.

Then, $f(x_1) = f(x_2) \Rightarrow \dfrac{x_1}{1+x_1} = \dfrac{x_2}{1-x_2}$

$\Rightarrow x_1 - x_1x_2 = x_2 + x_1x_2$

$\Rightarrow \quad x_1 - x_2 = 2x_1x_2$, which is not possible as LHS > 0 and RHS ≤ 0. Thus, $x_1 \neq x_2 \Rightarrow f(x_1) \neq f(x_2)$

From cases I, II and III, we get f is one-one. [1]

For onto Let $y \in (-1, 1)$ be any arbitrary element. Then, the following cases arise :

Case I *When $y \geq 0$, i.e. $0 \leq y < 1$*

Consider, $y = f(x) = \dfrac{x}{1+x} \quad \left[\because f(x) = \dfrac{x}{1+x} \geq 0\right]$

$\Rightarrow \quad y + yx = x \Rightarrow y = x - yx$

$\Rightarrow \quad x = \dfrac{y}{1-y} \geq 0$, for $0 \leq y < 1$ [1½]

Thus, for each $y \in [0, 1)$, there exists $x = \dfrac{y}{1-y} \in R$ such that $f(x) = y$.

Case II *When $y < 0$, i.e. $-1 < y < 0$*

Consider, $y = f(x) = \dfrac{x}{1-x} \quad \left[\because f(x) = \dfrac{x}{1-x} < 0\right]$

$\Rightarrow \quad y - yx = x \Rightarrow y = yx + x = x(y+1)$

$\Rightarrow \quad x = \dfrac{y}{y+1} < 0$, for $-1 < y < 0$

Thus, for each $y \in (-1, 0)$, there exist $x = \dfrac{y}{y+1} \in R$ such that $f(x) = y$. From cases I and II, we get f is onto. [1½]

TOPIC 03

Inverse of a Function

Invertible Functions

A function $f: A \to B$ is defined to be invertible, if there exists a function $g: B \to A$, such that $gof = I_A$ and $fog = I_B$. Here, the function g is called the **inverse of** f and denoted by f^{-1}.

A function whose inverse exists, is called **an invertible function** or **inversible.**

(i) Domain (f^{-1}) = Range (f)

(ii) Range (f^{-1}) = Domain (f)

(iii) If $f(x) = y$, then $f^{-1}(y) = x$ and *vice-versa.*

e.g. Suppose $f(x) = 4x + 5$, then $g(x) = \dfrac{x-5}{4}$ is the inverse of $f(x)$,

as $$fog(x) = f(g(x)) = f\left(\frac{x-5}{4}\right) = 4\left(\frac{x-5}{4}\right) + 5$$
$$= \frac{4x - 20 + 20}{4} = \frac{4x}{4} = x = I(x)$$

and $$gof(x) = g(f(x)) = g(4x+5) = \left(\frac{4x+5-5}{4}\right)$$
$$= \frac{4x}{4} = x = I(x)$$

i.e. $fog = I = gof$.

Example 1 Find the inverse of the invertible function $f(x) = (x-3)^3$.

Sol. Let $y = (x-3)^3$.

On taking cube roots both sides, we get

$$(y)^{1/3} = ((x-3)^3)^{1/3} \Rightarrow y^{1/3} = x - 3 \Rightarrow x = 3 + y^{1/3}$$

$\therefore$ $f^{-1}(y) = 3 + y^{1/3}$ $\quad [\because y = f(x) \Rightarrow x = f^{-1}(y)]$

or $f^{-1}(x) = 3 + x^{1/3}$

Hence, the inverse of $f(x)$ is $3 + x^{1/3}$.

Method to Show that Given Function is Invertible

Suppose we need to show a function $f: X \to Y$ given by $f(x)$ = any algebraic expression in x, is invertible. Then, we can show this by using following steps

I. Take an arbitrary element, say $y \in Y$ and assume that $y = f(x)$. Simplify it to get x in terms of y.

II. Define a new function $g: Y \to X$, given by $g(y)$ = value of x obtained in Step I.

III. Find gof and fog.

IV. Now, f is invertible, if $gof = I_{X\,(\text{domain of } f)}$ and $fog = I_{Y\,(\text{domain of } g)}$, otherwise not.

V. If f is invertible, then g gives inverse of f.

This process can be understand with the help of following examples.

Example 2 Let $f: N \to Y$ be a function defined as $f(x) = 10x + 3$, where $Y = \{y \in N : y = 10x + 3$ for some $x \in N\}$. Show that f is invertible. Also, find the inverse.

Sol. Given, $f: N \to Y$ defined as $f(x) = 10x + 3$, where

$Y = \{y \in N : y = 10x + 3,\ x \in N\}$.

Consider an arbitrary element $y \in Y$.

Then, $y = 10x + 3$, for some $x \in N$

$$\Rightarrow \quad y - 3 = 10x \Rightarrow x = \frac{y-3}{10}$$

Now, let us define a function $g: Y \to N$ by $g(y) = \dfrac{y-3}{10}$

Clearly, $gof(x) = g\{f(x)\} = g(10x+3) = \dfrac{10x+3-3}{10} = x$

and $fog(y) = f\{g(y)\} = f\left(\dfrac{y-3}{10}\right) = 10\left(\dfrac{y-3}{10}\right) + 3 = y$

Since, $gof(x) = x, \forall x \in N$, therefore $gof = I_N$

and $fog(y) = y, \forall\ y \in Y$; therefore $fog = I_Y$

Thus, f is invertible and $f^{-1} = g$,

i.e. $f^{-1}(y) = \dfrac{y-3}{10}$ or $f^{-1}(x) = \dfrac{x-3}{10}$

Example 3 Let $Y = \{n^2 : n \in N\} \subset N$. Consider $f: N \to Y$ as $f(n) = n^2$. Show that f is invertible. Also, find the inverse of f. **[NCERT]**

Sol. Given, $f: N \to Y$, defined as $f(n) = n^2$

where, $Y = \{n^2 : n \in N\}$.

Let $y \in Y$, then $y = n^2$ for some n in N.

$\Rightarrow$ $n = \sqrt{y}$ $\quad [\because n > 0]$

Now, let us define a function $g: Y \to N$ by $g(y) = \sqrt{y}$.

Clearly, $gof(n) = g(f(n)) = g(n^2) = \sqrt{n^2} = n$

and $fog(y) = f(g(y)) = f(\sqrt{y}) = (\sqrt{y})^2 = y$

Since, $gof(n) = n, \forall\ n \in N$ (domain of f)

$\therefore$ $gof = I_N$ and $fog(y) = y, \forall\ y \in Y$ (domain of g)

$\therefore$ $fog = I_Y$

Thus, f is invertible and its inverse is $f^{-1} = g$,

i.e. $f^{-1}(y) = \sqrt{y}$ or $f^{-1}(n) = \sqrt{n}$

Conditions of Invertibility

A function f is **invertible**, if and only if f is one-one and onto. So, we can show given function is invertible by using following steps

I. **Show that f is one-one** For this, choose any two arbitrary elements say x_1 and x_2 belongs to domain such that $f(x_1) = f(x_2)$ and show that $x_1 = x_2$.

II. **Show that f is onto** For this, suppose $y = f(x)$ and express x in terms of y, then check whether $x \in$ domain or not, for each value of y.

III. If f is one-one and onto both, then it is invertible and value of x in terms of y gives its inverse.
This process can be understand with the help of following examples.

Example 4 Let $S = \{1, 2, 3\}$. Determine whether the functions $f : S \to S$ defined as below have inverses. Find f^{-1}, if it exists.

(i) $f = \{(1, 1), (2, 2), (3, 3)\}$
(ii) $f = \{(1, 2), (2, 1), (3, 1)\}$
(iii) $f = \{(1, 3), (3, 2), (2, 1)\}$

Sol. Given, $f : S \to S, S = \{1, 2, 3\}$, defined as

(i) $f = \{(1, 1), (2, 2), (3, 3)\}$
As distinct elements have distinct images and each element of codomain have a pre-image in domain, therefore f is one-one and onto.

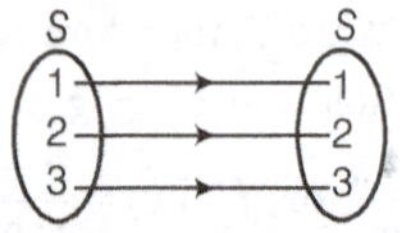

So, f is invertible and
$$f^{-1} = \{(1, 1), (2, 2), (3, 3)\} = f$$

(ii) $f = \{(1, 2), (2, 1), (3, 1)\}$. Here, $f(2) = f(3) = 1$
$\therefore$ f is not one-one.

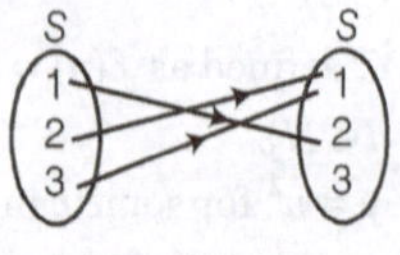

So, f is not invertible.

(iii) $f = \{(1, 3), (3, 2), (2, 1)\}$
As distinct elements have distinct images and each element of codomain have a pre-image in domain, therefore f is one-one and onto. So, f is invertible and

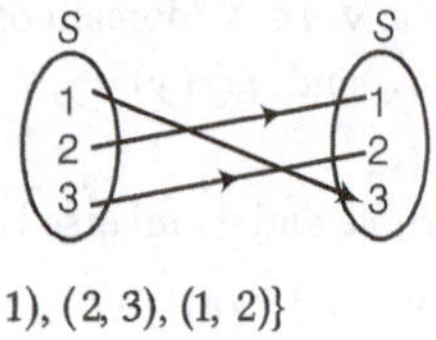

$$f^{-1} = \{(3, 1), (2, 3), (1, 2)\}$$

Note The components of the ordered pairs of a function are interchanged in the inverse function.

Example 5 If $f : A \to A$ and $A = R - \left\{\frac{8}{5}\right\}$, show that the function $f(x) = \frac{8x + 3}{5x - 8}$ is one-one onto, then find f^{-1}.

[ISC 2019]

Sol. We have, $f : A \to A$, $A = R - \frac{8}{5}$

and $f(x) = \frac{8x + 3}{5x - 8}$

For one-one Let $x_1, x_2 \in A$ such that $f(x_1) = f(x_2)$

$$\Rightarrow \quad \frac{8x_1 + 3}{5x_1 - 8} = \frac{8x_2 + 3}{5x_2 - 8}$$

$$\Rightarrow (8x_1 + 3)(5x_2 - 8) = (5x_1 - 8)(8x_2 + 3)$$
$$= 40x_1x_2 - 64x_1 + 15x_2 - 24$$
$$= 40xx_1 + 15x_1 - 64x_2 - 24$$
$$\Rightarrow \quad 15x_1 + 64x_1 = 15x_2 + 64x_2$$
$$\Rightarrow \quad 79x_1 = 79x_2$$
$$\Rightarrow \quad x_1 = x_2$$

$\therefore$ $f(x)$ is one-one function.

For onto Let y be an arbitrary element of A (codomain). Then, $f(x) = y$

$$\Rightarrow \quad \frac{8x + 3}{5x - 8} = y$$
$$\Rightarrow \quad 5xy - 8y = 8x + 3$$
$$\Rightarrow \quad x(5y - 8) = 3 + 8y$$
$$\Rightarrow \quad x = \frac{8y + 3}{5y - 8}, \; y \neq \frac{8}{5} \qquad \text{...(i)}$$

Clearly, $x = \frac{8y + 3}{5y - 8}$ is a real number for all $y \neq \frac{8}{5}$.

Thus, for every $y \in A$ (Codomain) there exists,

$$x = \frac{8y + 3}{5y - 8} \in A \text{ (domain) such that}$$

$$f(x) = f\left[\frac{8y + 3}{5y - 8}\right] = \frac{8\left(\frac{8y + 3}{5y - 8}\right) + 3}{5\left(\frac{8y + 3}{5y - 8}\right) - 8}$$

$$= \frac{64y + 24 + 15y - 24}{40y + 15 - 40y + 64} = \frac{79y}{79} = y$$

$\Rightarrow f(x)$ is onto function.

Since, $f(x)$ is a bijective function, so its inverse exists.

From Eq. (i), we get

$$x = \frac{8y + 3}{5y - 8}$$

$$\Rightarrow f^{-1}(y) = \frac{8y + 3}{5y - 8} \qquad [\because y = f(x) \Rightarrow x = f^{-1}(y)]$$

$$\therefore \; f^{-1}(x) = \frac{8x + 3}{5x - 8}, \; x \neq \frac{8}{5}$$

Example 6 Show that the function $f : R \to R$, $f(x) = 2x + 3$ is invertible and find f^{-1}.

To show f is invertible, prove that f is one-one and onto. Then, find the value of x in terms of y to get f^{-1}.

Sol. Given, $f: R \to R$, such that $f(x) = 2x + 3$

For one-one Let x_1 and x_2 be any two elements of R, such that $f(x_1) = f(x_2)$

On putting the values of $f(x_1)$ and $f(x_2)$, we get

$$2x_1 + 3 = 2x_2 + 3$$

$$\Rightarrow \quad 2x_1 = 2x_2 \Rightarrow x_1 = x_2$$

So, f is one-one.

For onto Let $y = f(x)$.

Then, $\quad y = 2x + 3$

$$\Rightarrow \quad x = \frac{y-3}{2} \quad \text{[expressing } x \text{ in terms of } y] \quad \ldots(i)$$

Clearly, for every value of y, $x \in R$ (domain)

So, for each $y \in R$ (codomain), there exists

$$x = \frac{y-3}{2} \in R \text{ (domain), such that}$$

$$f(x) = f\left(\frac{y-3}{2}\right) = 2\left(\frac{y-3}{2}\right) + 3$$

$$= y - 3 + 3 = y$$

$\Rightarrow f$ is onto. Thus, f is one-one and onto.

Hence, f is invertible and from Eq. (i) its inverse $f^{-1}: R \to R$ is given by $f^{-1}(x) = \frac{x-3}{2}$.

$$[\because y = f(x) \Rightarrow x = f^{-1}(y)]$$

Properties of Inverse Functions

(i) The inverse of a invertible function is unique.

(ii) The inverse of a bijective function is also a bijective function.

(iii) If f is an invertible function, then $(f^{-1})^{-1} = f$.

(iv) If $f : A \to B$ is bijective, then $f^{-1} of = I_A$ and $fof^{-1} = I_B$.

(v) If f is invertible, then the graph of f^{-1} is the mirror image of $y = f(x)$ about the line $y = x$.

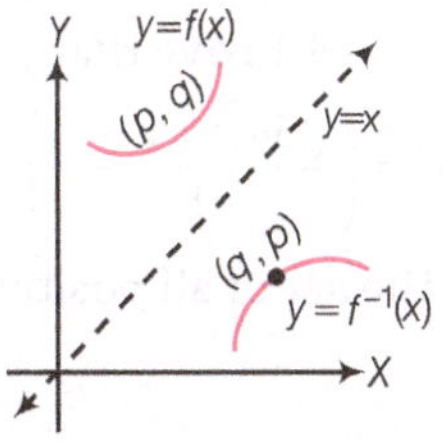

(vi) If $f : X \to Y$ and $g : Y \to Z$ are two invertible functions. Then, $gof : X \to Z$ is also invertible with $(gof)^{-1} = f^{-1}og^{-1}$.

Example 7 Consider $f = \{1, 2, 3\} \to \{2, 4, 6\}$ defined as $f(1) = 2$, $f(2) = 4$ and $f(3) = 6$. Find the inverse f^{-1}. Also, show that $(f^{-1})^{-1} = f$.

Sol. Given, $f = \{1, 2, 3\} \to \{2, 4, 6\}$

and $f(1) = 2$, $f(2) = 4$ and $f(3) = 6$

$\therefore \quad f = \{(1, 2), (2, 4), (3, 6)\}$

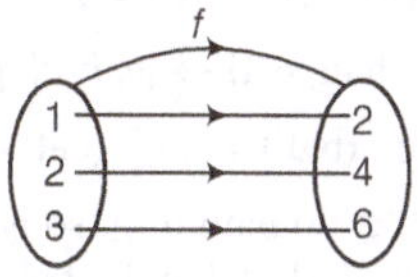

It is clear that f is one-one and onto, so its inverse f^{-1} exists.

To find the inverse of f, we have to change the components of the ordered pairs of function f.

Therefore, $f^{-1} = \{(2, 1), (4, 2), (6, 3)\}$.

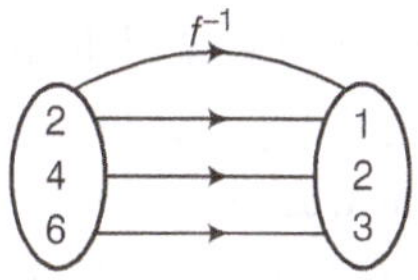

It is clear that f^{-1} is one-one and onto, so its inverse $(f^{-1})^{-1}$ exist.

To find the inverse again, we change the order of the components in the ordered pairs of function f^{-1}.

Therefore, $(f^{-1})^{-1} = \{(1, 2), (2, 4), (3, 6)\} = f$

Example 8 If $f(x) = [4 - (x-7)^3]^{\frac{1}{5}}$ is a real invertible function, then find $f^{-1}(x)$. **[ISC 2023]**

Sol. We have, $f(x) = [4 - (x-7)^3]^{1/5}$

We know that $f(f^{-1}(x)) = x$

$$\therefore \quad f(f^{-1}(x)) = [4 - (f^{-1}(x) - 7)^3]^{1/5}$$

$$\Rightarrow \quad x = [4 - (f^{-1}(x) - 7)^3]^{1/5}$$

$$\Rightarrow \quad x^5 = 4 - (f^{-1}(x) - 7)^3$$

$$\Rightarrow \quad (f^{-1}(x) - 7)^3 = 4 - x^5$$

$$\Rightarrow \quad f^{-1}(x) - 7 = (4 - x^5)^{1/3}$$

$$\Rightarrow \quad f^{-1}(x) = 7 + (4 - x^5)^{1/3}$$

Example 9 Consider $f : \{1, 2, 3\} \to \{a, b, c\}$ and $g : \{a, b, c\} \to$ {apple, ball, cat}, defined as $f(1) = a$, $f(2) = b$, $f(3) = c$, $g(a) =$ apple, $g(b) =$ ball and $g(c) =$ cat. Show that f, g and gof are invertible. Find out f^{-1}, g^{-1} and $(gof)^{-1}$. Show that $(gof)^{-1} = f^{-1}og^{-1}$.

Sol. Given, $f : \{1, 2, 3\} \to \{a, b, c\}$

and $\quad g : \{a, b, c\} \to$ {apple, ball, cat}

defined as $f(1) = a, f(2) = b, f(3) = c,$

$g(a) = \text{apple}, g(b) = \text{ball}, g(c) = \text{cat}$

As distinct elements have distinct images and each element of codomain have a pre-image in domain, therefore f and g are bijective functions.

So, both are invertible.

Now, clearly $f^{-1} : \{a, b, c\} \to \{1, 2, 3\}$, given by

$f^{-1}(a) = 1, f^{-1}(b) = 2, f^{-1}(c) = 3$

and $g^{-1} : \{\text{apple, ball, cat}\} \to \{a, b, c\}$, given by

$g^{-1}(\text{apple}) = a, g^{-1}(\text{ball}) = b, g^{-1}(\text{cat}) = c$

Since, range $(f) \subseteq$ domain of g, so gof is defined and therefore $gof : \{1, 2, 3\} \to \{\text{apple, ball, cat}\}$ with $gof(1) = \text{apple}, gof(2) = \text{ball}, gof(3) = \text{cat}$

Now, as distinct elements have distinct images and each element of codomain have a pre-image in domain, therefore gof is invertible and

$$(gof)^{-1} : \{\text{apple, ball, cat}\} \to \{1, 2, 3\}$$

with $(gof)^{-1}(\text{apple}) = 1, (gof)^{-1}(\text{ball}) = 2, gof^{-1}(\text{cat}) = 3,$

Now, as range of $g^{-1} \subseteq$ domain of f^{-1}, therefore $f^{-1}og^{-1}$ is defined and given by

$$f^{-1}og^{-1}(\text{apple}) = f^{-1}\{g^{-1}(\text{apple})\} = f^{-1}(a) = 1$$

$$f^{-1}og^{-1}(\text{ball}) = f^{-1}\{g^{-1}(\text{ball})\} = f^{-1}(b) = 2$$

and $$f^{-1}og^{-1}(\text{cat}) = f^{-1}\{g^{-1}(\text{cat})\} = f^{-1}(c) = 3$$

Hence, $$(gof)^{-1} = f^{-1}og^{-1}$$

Topic Practice 3

Very Short Answer Type Questions

(2 Marks)

1 Find the inverse of the following invertible functions.

(i) $y = x$ (ii) $y = x + 1$

2 Let $f(x) = \{4 - (x-7)^3\}$ is an invertible function, then find $f^{-1}(x)$.

3 If $f : [1, \infty) \to [2, \infty)$ is defined by $f(x) = x + \frac{1}{x}$, then find $f^{-1}(x)$.

4 Consider $f : \{1, 2, 3\} \to \{a, b, c\}$ given by $f(1) = a$, $f(2) = b, f(3) = c$. Find f^{-1}. Show that $(f^{-1})^{-1} = f$.

Short Answer Type Questions

(4 Marks)

5 If the function $f(x) = \sqrt{2x-3}$ is invertible, then find its inverse. Hence prove that $(fof^{-1})(x) = x$. **[ISC 2018]**

6 Let $f : R \to R$ be defined by $f(x) = 3x - 7$. Show that f is invertible. Find f^{-1}.

7 Let $f: W \to W$ be defined as $f(x) = x - 1$, if x is odd and $f(x) = x + 1$, if x is even, then show that f is invertible. Also, find the inverse of f, where W is the set of all whole numbers.

8 Show that $f : [-1, 1] \to R$, given by $f(x) = \frac{x}{x+2}$ is one-one. Find the inverse of the function $f : [-1, 1] \to \text{Range}(f)$. **[NCERT]**

9 Let f be an invertible function. Then, prove that $(f^{-1})^{-1} = f$.

Long Answer Type Questions

(6 Marks)

10 Let $f : R - \left\{-\frac{4}{3}\right\} \to R$ be a function defined as $f(x) = \frac{4x}{3x+4}$. Show that f is a one-one function. Also check whether f is an onto function or not. Hence, find f^{-1} in (Range of f) $\to R - \left\{-\frac{4}{3}\right\}$.

11 Consider $f : R - \left\{-\frac{4}{3}\right\} \to R - \left\{\frac{4}{3}\right\}$ given by $f(x) = \frac{4x+3}{3x+4}$. Show that f is bijective. Find the inverse of f and hence find $f^{-1}(0)$ and x such that $f^{-1}(x) = 2$.

12 Consider $f : R^+ \to (-9, \infty)$ given by $f(x) = 5x^2 + 6x - 9$. Prove that f is invertible with

$$f^{-1}(y) = \left(\frac{\sqrt{54+5y}-3}{5}\right)$$

where, R^+ is the set of all positive real numbers.

Hints & Solutions

1. Similar as Example 1. [**Ans.** (i) x (ii) $x-1$]
2. Similar as Example 1. [**Ans.** $7+(4-x)^{1/3}$]
3. Given, a function $f:[1,\infty)\to[2,\infty)$ defined by

$$f(x)=x+\frac{1}{x}$$

Now, let $y=f(x) \Rightarrow y=x+\frac{1}{x}$

$$\Rightarrow y=\frac{x^2+1}{x} \Rightarrow xy=x^2+1$$

$$\Rightarrow x^2-xy+1=0$$

$$\Rightarrow x=\frac{y\pm\sqrt{y^2-4}}{2}$$

$$\Rightarrow x=\frac{y+\sqrt{y^2-4}}{2}$$ [1]

$$\left[\text{neglecting } x=\frac{y-\sqrt{y^2-4}}{2} \because \text{For } y=3\in[2,\infty),\right.$$

$$\left. x=\frac{3-\sqrt{9-4}}{2}=\frac{3-\sqrt{5}}{2}=\frac{3-2.23}{2}=\frac{0.77}{2}\notin[1,\infty)\right]$$

$$\Rightarrow f^{-1}(y)=\frac{y+\sqrt{y^2-4}}{2} \quad [\because y=f(x)\Rightarrow x=f^{-1}(y)]$$

or $$f^{-1}(x)=\frac{x+\sqrt{x^2-4}}{2}$$ [1]

4. We have, $f:\{1,2,3\}\to\{a,b,c\}$, given by

$$f(1)=a,\ f(2)=b \text{ and } f(3)=c$$

i.e. $f=\{(1,a),(2,b),(3,c)\}$ ...(i)

Clearly, $f^{-1}=\{(a,1),(b,2),(c,3)\}$ [1]

and $(f^{-1})^{-1}=\{(1,a),(2,b),(3,c)\}$ ...(ii)

From Eqs. (i) and (ii), we get

$(f^{-1})^{-1}=f$ [1]

5. Let $f(x)=\sqrt{2x-3}$ is invertible function.

Then, $f(x)=y$

$\Rightarrow f^{-1}(y)=x$ and $y=\sqrt{2x-3}$ [1]

$$\Rightarrow y^2=2x-3$$

$$\Rightarrow x=\frac{y^2+3}{2}$$

$$\Rightarrow f^{-1}(y)=\frac{y^2+3}{2}$$

or $$f^{-1}(x)=\frac{x^2+3}{2}$$

$\therefore$ Inverse of $f(x)$ is $\frac{x^2+3}{2}$. [1]

Now, $(fof^{-1})(x)=f(f^{-1}(x))=f\left(\frac{x^2+3}{2}\right)$ [1]

$$=\sqrt{\frac{2(x^2+3)}{2}-3} \quad [\because f(x)=\sqrt{2x-3}]$$

$$=\sqrt{x^2+3-3}$$

$$=\sqrt{x^2}=x$$

$\therefore (fof^{-1})(x)=x$ **Hence proved.** [1]

6. Similar as Example 6. $\left[\textbf{Ans. } f^{-1}=\frac{x+7}{3}\right]$
7. **Hint**

(i) In order to prove that f is invertible, we have prove f is one-one and onto function.

(ii) For inverse function let $f^{-1}(x)$ be inverse of $f(x)$.

$\therefore$ $fof^{-1}=I$

$\Rightarrow$ $fof^{-1}(x)=I(x)$

$\Rightarrow$ $f\{f^{-1}(x)\}=x$ $[\because I(x)=x]$

$\Rightarrow$ $f^{-1}(x)-1=x$, if $f^{-1}(x)$ is odd

and $f^{-1}(x)+1=x$, if $f^{-1}(x)$ is even

$\Rightarrow$ $f^{-1}(x)=x+1$ if x is even

and $f^{-1}(x)=x-1$, if x is odd

i.e. $f^{-1}=f$

8. **Hint**

(i) Show $f:[-1,1]\to R$ is one-one.

(ii) Then, $f:[-1,1]\to$ Range(f) is one-one and onto, as $f:[-1,1]\to R$ is one-one and codomain = range(f)

(iii) Find f^{-1}. $\left[\textbf{Ans. } f^{-1}(y)=\frac{2y}{1-y}, y\neq 1\right]$

9. Let $f:X\to Y$ be an invertible function.

Then, there exists a function $g:Y\to X$ such that $gof=I_X$ and $fog=I_Y$. [1]

Here, $f^{-1}=g$ [1]

$\therefore$ $gof=I_X$ and $fog=I_Y$.

$\Rightarrow f^{-1}of=I_X$ and $fof^{-1}=I_Y$. [1]

$\Rightarrow f^{-1}:Y\to X$ is invertible and f is the inverse of f^{-1}.

i.e. $(f^{-1})^{-1}=f$. [1]

10. We have, $f(x)=\frac{4x}{3x+4}$

One-one Let $x_1, x_2\in R-\left\{-\frac{4}{3}\right\}$ such that

$$f(x_1)=f(x_2)$$ [1/2]

$$\Rightarrow \frac{4x_1}{3x_1+4}=\frac{4x_2}{3x_2+4}$$ [1/2]

$\Rightarrow \quad 12x_1x_2 + 16x_1 = 12x_1x_2 + 16x_2$

$\Rightarrow \quad 16x_1 = 16x_2$

$\Rightarrow \quad x_1 = x_2$

$\Rightarrow f$ is one-one. [1]

Onto Let $y \in R$ be any arbitrary element.

Consider, $y = f(x)$

$\Rightarrow \quad y = \dfrac{4x}{3x+4}$

$\Rightarrow \quad 3xy + 4y = 4x$

$\Rightarrow \quad x(3y-4) = -4y$

$\Rightarrow \quad x = \dfrac{4y}{4-3y}$ ...(i) [1]

Clearly for $y = \dfrac{4}{3}, x \notin R - \{-4/3\}$

Thus, $y = \dfrac{4}{3}$ does not have a pre-image.

So, f is not onto. [1]

Also, f is invertible when $f : R - \{-4/3\} \to \text{Range}(f)$

i.e. when $f : R - \{-4/3\} \to R - \{4/3\}$

[$\because$ Range $(f) = R - \{4/3\}$, using Eq. (i)] [1]

Now, from Eq. (i), we get

$f^{-1}(y) = \dfrac{4y}{4-3y}$ or $f^{-1}(x) = \dfrac{4x}{4-3x}$ [1/2]

Thus, $f^{-1} : R - \{4/3\} \to R - \{-4/3\}$

given by $f^{-1}(x) = \dfrac{4x}{4-3x}, \forall\, x \in R - \{4/3\}$ [1/2]

11. Hint

(i) Similar as Example 5.

(ii) $f^{-1}(x) = \dfrac{4x-3}{4-3x} \Rightarrow f^{-1}(0) = \dfrac{0-3}{4-0} = \dfrac{-3}{4}$ and also

$f^{-1}(x) = 2 \Rightarrow \dfrac{4x-3}{4-3x} = 2 \Rightarrow x = \dfrac{11}{10}$

12. We have a mapping $f : R^+ \to (-9, \infty)$

given by $f(x) = 5x^2 + 6x - 9$

For one-one Let $x_1, x_2 \in R^+$ be any arbitrary elements, such that

$$f(x_1) = f(x_2)$$

$\Rightarrow \quad 5x_1^2 + 6x_1 - 9 = 5x_2^2 + 6x_2 - 9$ [1]

$\Rightarrow \quad 5(x_1^2 - x_2^2) + 6(x_1 - x_2) = 0$

$\Rightarrow \quad 5(x_1 + x_2)(x_1 - x_2) + 6(x_1 - x_2) = 0$

$\Rightarrow \quad (x_1 - x_2)[5(x_1 + x_2) + 6] = 0$

$\Rightarrow \quad x_1 - x_2 = 0$ or $5x_1 + 5x_2 + 6 = 0$

$\Rightarrow \quad x_1 - x_2 = 0$ [$\because 5x_1 + 5x_2 + 6 \neq 0$ as $x_1, x_2 \in R^+$]

$\Rightarrow \quad x_1 = x_2$

So, f is one-one. [1]

For onto Let $y \in (-9, \infty)$ be any arbitrary element and $y = f(x)$.

Then, $y = 5x^2 + 6x - 9$

$\Rightarrow \quad 5x^2 + 6x - 9 - y = 0$

$\Rightarrow \quad x = \dfrac{-6 \pm \sqrt{36 + 4 \times 5(9+y)}}{10}$

$\left[\because x = \dfrac{-b \pm \sqrt{b^2 - 4ac}}{2a}\right]$ [1]

$\Rightarrow \quad x = \dfrac{-6 \pm \sqrt{216 + 20y}}{10}$

$\Rightarrow \quad x = \dfrac{-6 \pm 2\sqrt{54 + 5y}}{10}$

$\Rightarrow \quad x = \dfrac{-3 + \sqrt{54 + 5y}}{5}$

or $\quad x = \dfrac{-3 - \sqrt{54 + 5y}}{5}$ [1]

$\because \quad x \in R^+$, therefore $x \neq \dfrac{-3 - \sqrt{54 + 5y}}{5}$

Now, $\quad x = \dfrac{-3 + \sqrt{54 + 5y}}{5} \in R^+$ for each $y \in (-9, \infty)$

$\because \quad -9 < y < \infty$

$\Rightarrow \quad -45 < 5y < \infty$ [multiply each term by 5]

$\Rightarrow \quad 54 - 45 < 54 + 5y < \infty$ [add 54 in each term]

$\Rightarrow \quad 9 < 54 + 5y < \infty$

$\Rightarrow \quad 3 < \sqrt{54 + 5y} < \infty$ [taking square root]

$\Rightarrow \quad -3 + 3 < -3 + \sqrt{54 + 5y} < \infty$ [subtract −3 in each term]

$\Rightarrow \quad -3 + \sqrt{54 + 5y} > 0$

Thus, for each $y \in (-9, \infty)$, there exists

$$x = \frac{-3 + \sqrt{54 + 5y}}{5} \in R^+ \text{ such that } f(x) = y$$

So, f is onto. [1]

$\Rightarrow f$ is invertible and inverse of f is given by

$f^{-1} : (-9, \infty) \to R^+$, defined as

$$f^{-1}(y) = \frac{-3 + \sqrt{54 + 5y}}{5}$$ [1]

Chapter Practice

Multiple Choice Type Questions

(1 Mark)

1 Let L be a set of all straight lines in a plane. The relation R on L defined as 'perpendicular to' is [ISC 2024]

(a) symmetric and transitive
(b) transitive
(c) symmetric
(d) equivalence

2 Let A be a non-empty set.

Statement I Identity relation on A is reflexive.

Statement II Every reflexive relation on A is an identity relation. [ISC 2024]

(a) Both the statements are true.
(b) Both the statements are false.
(c) Statement I is true and Statement II is false.
(d) Statement I is false and Statement II is true.

3 A relation R on $\{1, 2, 3\}$ is given by $R = \{(1, 1), (2, 2), (1, 2), (3, 3), (2, 3)\}$. Then, the relation R is [ISC 2023]

(a) reflexive
(b) symmetric
(c) transitive
(d) symmetric and transitive

4 Let $f(x) = x^3$ be a function with domain $\{0, 1, 2, 3\}$. Then, the domain of f^{-1} is [ISC 2023]

(a) $\{3, 2, 1, 0\}$ (b) $\{0, -1, -2, -3\}$
(c) $\{0, 1, 8, 27\}$ (d) $\{0, -1, -8, -27\}$

Assertion-Reason Type Questions

(1 Mark)

Directions (Q. Nos. 5-8) *In the questions given below are two statements labelled as Assertion (A) and Reason (R). In the context of the two statements, which one of the following is correct?*

(a) Both A and R are correct; R is the correct explanation of A
(b) Both A and R are correct; R is not the correct explanation of A
(c) A is correct; R is incorrect
(d) R is correct; A is incorrect

5 **Assertion (A)** The relation R in the set $A = \{1, 2, 3, 4, 5, 6\}$ defined as $R = \{(x, y) : y$ is divisible by $x\}$ is not an equivalence relation.

Reason (R) The relation R will be an equivalence relation, if it is reflexive, symmetric and transitive.

6 **Assertion (A)** Let $f : X \to Y$ be a function. Define a relation R on X given by $R = \{(a, b) : f(a) = f(b)\}$. Then, R is equivalence relation.

Reason (R) R is not symmetric.

7 **Assertion (A)** The $f : R \to R$ given by $f(x) = |x| + x$ is one-one onto.

Reason (R) A function is said to be one-one and onto, if each element has unique image and range of $f(x)$ is equal to codomain of $f(x)$.

8 **Assertion (A)** The function $f : R \to R$ given by $f(x) = x^3$ is injective.

Reason (R) The function $f : X \to Y$ is injective, if $f(x) = f(y) \Rightarrow x = y, \forall\, x, y \in X$.

Very Short Answer Type Questions

(2 Marks)

9 Check whether the relation R, defined in the set $\{1, 2, 3, 4, 5, 6\}$ as $R = \{(a, b) : b = a + 1\}$, is reflexive, symmetric or transitive. [NCERT]

10 Let N be the set of natural numbers and relation R on N be defined by $R = \{(x, y) : x, y \in N, x + y = 10\}$. Then, check whether R is reflexive, symmetric and transitive.

11 Show that the function $f : R \to R$, $f(x) = x^4$ is many-one and into.

12 Show that the function $f : Z \to Z$ defined by $f(x) = x^2 + x$, is a many-one function.

13 Show that signum function is neither one-one nor onto.

Short Answer Type Questions

4 Marks

14 If $A = \{1, 2, 3, 4\}$, define relations on A which have properties of being

(i) reflexive, transitive but not symmetric.

(ii) symmetric but neither reflexive nor transitive. **[NCERT Exemplar]**

15 Show that relation R in the set of real numbers, defined as $R = \{(a, b) : a \le b^2\}$ is neither reflexive nor symmetric nor transitive. **[NCERT]**

16 Check whether the relation R defined in the set A of human beings in a city at particular time as $R = \{(x, y) : x \text{ is wife of } y\}$, is reflexive, symmetric and transitive. **[NCERT]**

17 Let S be the set of all real numbers and R be the relation on S defined by $R = \{(a, b) : |a| \le b\}$. Show that R is neither reflexive nor symmetric but transitive.

18 Let n be a fixed positive integer. Define a relation R in Z for all $a, b \in Z$, aRb, if and only if $a - b$ is divisible by n. Show that R is an equivalence relation. **[NCERT Exemplar]**

19 Show that the logarithmic function $f : R^+ \to R^+$, defined by $f(x) = \log_a x (a > 0, a \ne 1)$ is a bijection, where R^+ is the set all positive real numbers.

20 Prove that the function $f : N \to N$ defined by $f(x) = x^2 + x + 1$ is one-one but not onto.

Long Answer Type Questions

6 Marks

21 Show that the relation R, defined in the set A of all triangles as $R = \{(T_1, T_2) : T_1 \text{ is similar to } T_2\}$, is equivalence relation. Consider three right angle triangles T_1 with sides 3, 4, 5; T_2 with sides 5, 12, 13 and T_3 with sides 6, 8, 10, which triangle among T_1, T_2 and T_3 are related? **[NCERT]**

22 Let $A = [-1, 1]$, then discuss whether the following functions defined on A are one-one and onto or bijective.

(i) $f(x) = x/2$ (ii) $g(x) = |x|$

(iii) $h(x) = x|x|$ (iv) $k(x) = x^2$

[NCERT Exemplar]

Case-Based Type Question

6 Marks

23 In a school, madam Sunita take lecture in Class XII. In this class, students divided into two groups A and B. Group A has 20 students and group B has 25 students.

Group A Group B

The relation between students of these groups are defined as R : group $A \to$ group B or $R : A \to B$ $R = [(x, y) : x \in A \text{ and } y \in B]$.

(i) Find the number of elements in codomain of $R : A \to B$.

(ii) Find the set of all identity elements.

(iii) Find the total number of relations that can be formed from set A to B.

(iv) Suppose the relation defined from set A to set B is $R_1 = \{(a_1, b_1), (a_2, b_3), (a_3, b_4)\}$, then find the inverse relation.

Answers

1. (c) **2.** (c) **3.** (a) **4.** (c) **5.** (a) **6.** (c)

7. (a) **8.** (a) **9.** Neither reflexive nor symmetric nor transitive.

10. Symmetric but neither reflexive nor transitive. **14.** (i) $\{(1, 1), (1, 2), (2, 3), (2, 2), (1, 3), (3, 3), (4, 4)\}$ (ii) $\{(2, 2), (1, 2), (2, 1)\}$

16. Transitive but neither reflexive nor symmetric. **21.** T_1 and T_3

22. (i) f is one-one but not onto (ii) g is neither one-one nor onto (iii) h is bijective (iv) k is neither one-one nor onto

23. (i) 25 (ii) equivalence (iii) 2^{500} (iv) $\{(b_1, a_1), (b_3, a_2), (b_4, a_3)\}$

CHAPTER

02

Inverse Trigonometric Functions

In previous chapter, we have studied about the existence of inverse of a function. In this chapter, we will study about the restrictions on domains of trigonometric functions, which ensure the existence of their inverse.

- Definitions and Some Basic Concepts
- Elementary Properties of Inverse Trigonometric Functions

TOPIC 01 Definitions and Some Basic Concepts

Inverse of a Function

We know that if a function is one-one and onto, then it is an invertible function. Suppose $f: X \to Y$ such that $f(x) = y$ is one-one and onto, then we can define a unique function $g: Y \to X$ such that $g(y) = x$, where $x \in X$ and $y \in Y$. Here, g is called the inverse of f and it is denoted by 'f^{-1}'. Thus, $g = f^{-1}: Y \to X$.

Note (i) Domain of f^{-1} = range of f and range of f^{-1} = domain of f.

(ii) $f^{-1}(y) = x$ if and only if $f(x) = y$.

Inverse Trigonometric Functions

To study the inverse of trigonometric function, we should know the domain and range of trigonometric function, which are shown below

Function	Domain	Range
sin	R	$[-1, 1]$
cos	R	$[-1, 1]$
tan	$R - \left\{x : x = (2n+1)\frac{\pi}{2}, n \in Z\right\}$	R
cot	$R - \{x : x = n\pi, n \in Z\}$	R
sec	$R - \left\{x : x = (2n+1)\frac{\pi}{2}, n \in Z\right\}$	$R - (-1, 1)$
cosec	$R - \{x : x = n\pi, n \in Z\}$	$R - (-1, 1)$

As we know that **trigonometric functions are periodic functions, so these functions cannot be one-one over their whole domains and hence their inverse does not exist. But if we restrict their domain then their inverse may exists.**

Domain and Range of Inverse Trigonometric Functions

The range of trigonometric functions becomes the **domain** of **inverse trigonometric functions** and restricted domain of trigonometric functions becomes **range** of inverse trigonometric functions.

e.g. Consider the sine function, i.e. sine : $R \to [-1, 1]$.

Since, $\sin\left(\frac{\pi}{6}\right) = \sin\left(\frac{5\pi}{6}\right) = \frac{1}{2}$, $\sin\left(\frac{\pi}{3}\right) = \sin\left(\frac{2\pi}{3}\right) = \frac{\sqrt{3}}{2}$, etc.

Therefore, it is not one-one function and hence its inverse does not exist. But, if we restrict its domains to anyone of the intervals $\left[\frac{-3\pi}{2}, \frac{-\pi}{2}\right], \left[\frac{-\pi}{2}, \frac{\pi}{2}\right], \left[\frac{\pi}{2}, \frac{3\pi}{2}\right]$, etc. then it becomes one-one and onto and hence invertible.

The inverse of sine function is denoted by $\sin^{-1}$ (also written as arc sine).

Thus, $\sin^{-1}$ is a function whose domain is $[-1, 1]$ and range may be any of the intervals $\left[\frac{-3\pi}{2}, \frac{-\pi}{2}\right], \left[\frac{-\pi}{2}, \frac{\pi}{2}\right], \left[\frac{\pi}{2}, \frac{3\pi}{2}\right]$ and so on.

Function $\sin^{-1} x$, with domain $[-1, 1]$ and range $\left[\frac{-\pi}{2}, \frac{\pi}{2}\right]$, is written as $\sin^{-1} : [-1, 1] \to \left[\frac{-\pi}{2}, \frac{\pi}{2}\right]$.

Principal Values of Inverse Trigonometric Functions

The least numerical value i.e. the value irrespective of signs, of an inverse trigonometric function is called the **principal value of the function.**

e.g. The values belonging to $\left[-\frac{\pi}{2}, \frac{\pi}{2}\right]$ are called the principal values of $\sin^{-1} x$.

Principal Value Branch

Let us understand this by considering inverse function of sine.

Here, we have seen that the range of $\sin^{-1}$ may be any of the intervals $\left[-\frac{3\pi}{2}, -\frac{\pi}{2}\right], \left[-\frac{\pi}{2}, \frac{\pi}{2}\right], \left[\frac{\pi}{2}, \frac{3\pi}{2}\right]$ and so on.

The branch with range $\left[-\frac{\pi}{2}, \frac{\pi}{2}\right]$ is called **principal value branch.**

In other words, the branch in which principal values of inverse trigonometric function lies is called **principal value branch.**

Domain, Range and Principal Value Branch of Inverse Trigonometric Functions

Function	Domain	Range	Principal value branch
$y = \sin^{-1} x$	$[-1, 1]$	$\left[\frac{-3\pi}{2}, \frac{-\pi}{2}\right], \left[-\frac{\pi}{2}, \frac{\pi}{2}\right], \left[\frac{\pi}{2}, \frac{3\pi}{2}\right]$, etc.	$\left[-\frac{\pi}{2}, \frac{\pi}{2}\right]$
$y = \cos^{-1} x$	$[-1, 1]$	$[-\pi, 0], [0, \pi], [\pi, 2\pi]$, etc.	$[0, \pi]$
$y = \tan^{-1} x$	R	$\left(\frac{-3\pi}{2}, \frac{-\pi}{2}\right), \left(-\frac{\pi}{2}, \frac{\pi}{2}\right), \left(\frac{\pi}{2}, \frac{3\pi}{2}\right)$ etc.	$\left(-\frac{\pi}{2}, \frac{\pi}{2}\right)$
$y = \sec^{-1} x$	$R - (-1, 1)$	$[-\pi, 0] - \left\{-\frac{\pi}{2}\right\}$, $[0, \pi] - \left\{\frac{\pi}{2}\right\}$, $[\pi, 2\pi] - \left\{\frac{3\pi}{2}\right\}$, etc.	$[0, \pi] - \left\{\frac{\pi}{2}\right\}$
$y = \operatorname{cosec}^{-1} x$	$R - (-1, 1)$	$\left[\frac{-3\pi}{2}, \frac{-\pi}{2}\right] - \{-\pi\}$, $\left[\frac{-\pi}{2}, \frac{\pi}{2}\right] - \{0\}$, $\left[\frac{\pi}{2}, \frac{3\pi}{2}\right] - \{\pi\}$, etc.	$\left[\frac{-\pi}{2}, \frac{\pi}{2}\right] - \{0\}$
$y = \cot^{-1} x$	R	$(-\pi, 0), (0, \pi), (\pi, 2\pi)$, etc.	$(0, \pi)$

Important Points Related to Inverse Trigonometric Functions

(i) $\sin^{-1} y \neq (\sin y)^{-1}$, $\sin^{-1} y \neq \sin\left(\frac{1}{y}\right)$,

$\sin^{-1} y \neq \frac{1}{\sin y}$. Similarly, for other inverse trigonometric functions.

(ii) Whenever no branch of an inverse trigonometric function is mentioned, we consider the principal value branch of that function.

(iii) $\sin^{-1} x = y \Leftrightarrow x = \sin y$, where x is the element of domain and y is the element of range $\sin^{-1} x$. Same is true for other five inverse trigonometric functions as well.

Problems Based on Principal Value Branch of Inverse Trigonometric Functions

There are mainly two types of problems. In first type of problem, we have to find the principal value of given inverse trigonometric function and in second type of problem, we have to find the value of two or more than two inverse trigonometric functions, which are connecting with operations '+' or '–'.

For solving such problems, we take value of each inverse trigonometric function in its principal value branch.

Example 1 Check whether the following functions are defined or not at the indicated point.

(i) $\tan^{-1} x$ at $x = 1$

(ii) $\sec^{-1} x$ at $x = \frac{1}{2}$

(iii) $\cos^{-1} x$ at $x = -\frac{5}{2}$

Sol. (i) $\tan^{-1}(1)$ is defined, since the domain of $\tan^{-1} x$ is R and $1 \in R$.

(ii) $\sec^{-1}\left(\frac{1}{2}\right)$ is not defined, since the domain of $\sec^{-1} x$ is $R-(-1,1)$ and $\frac{1}{2} \notin R-(-1, 1)$.

(iii) $\cos^{-1}\left(-\frac{5}{2}\right)$ is not defined, since the domain of $\cos^{-1} x$ is $[-1, 1]$ and $-\frac{5}{2} \notin [-1, 1]$.

Example 2 Find the domain of the following functions.

(i) $\cos^{-1}(5x - 2)$ (ii) $\sec^{-1}(3 - 2x)$

Sol. (i) For $\cos^{-1}(5x - 2)$ to be defined,

$$-1 \leq 5x - 2 \leq 1 \quad [\because \text{domain of } \cos^{-1} x \text{ is } [-1, 1]]$$

$$\Rightarrow \quad 2 - 1 \leq (5x - 2) + 2 \leq 1 + 2$$

$$\Rightarrow \quad 1 \leq 5x \leq 3 \Rightarrow \frac{1}{5} \leq x \leq \frac{3}{5}$$

So, the domain of $\cos^{-1}(5x - 2)$ is $\left[\frac{1}{5}, \frac{3}{5}\right]$.

(ii) For $\sec^{-1}(3 - 2x)$ to be defined,

$$|3 - 2x| \geq 1 \quad [\because \text{domain of } \sec^{-1} \text{ is } R - (-1, 1)]$$

i.e. $3 - 2x \geq 1$ or $3 - 2x \leq -1$

i.e. $-2x \geq -2$ or $-2x \leq -4$

i.e. $x \leq 1$ or $x \geq 2$

So, the domain of $\sec^{-1}(3 - 2x)$ is $(-\infty, 1] \cup [2, \infty)$.

Example 3 Find the principal value of the following.

(i) $\sin^{-1}\left(\frac{1}{\sqrt{2}}\right)$ (ii) $\sin^{-1}\left(-\frac{1}{2}\right)$

(iii) $\cot^{-1}\left(\frac{-1}{\sqrt{3}}\right)$ [NCERT]

Sol. (i) Let $y = \sin^{-1}\left(\frac{1}{\sqrt{2}}\right)$

$$\Rightarrow \quad \sin y = \frac{1}{\sqrt{2}} = \sin\left(\frac{\pi}{4}\right) \quad \left[\because \sin\frac{\pi}{4} = \frac{1}{\sqrt{2}}\right]$$

We know that the principal value branch of $\sin^{-1}$ is $\left[-\frac{\pi}{2}, \frac{\pi}{2}\right]$ and $y = \frac{\pi}{4} \in \left[-\frac{\pi}{2}, \frac{\pi}{2}\right]$.

$\therefore$ The principal value of $\sin^{-1}\left(\frac{1}{\sqrt{2}}\right)$ is $\frac{\pi}{4}$.

(ii) Let $\sin^{-1}\left(-\frac{1}{2}\right) = \theta \Rightarrow \sin\theta = -\frac{1}{2}$

$$\therefore \sin\theta = -\frac{1}{2} = -\sin\frac{\pi}{6} = \sin\left(-\frac{\pi}{6}\right)$$

$$[\because \sin(-\theta) = -\sin\theta]$$

We know that the principal value branch of $\sin^{-1}$ is $\left[-\frac{\pi}{2}, \frac{\pi}{2}\right]$ and $\theta = -\frac{\pi}{6} \in \left[-\frac{\pi}{2}, \frac{\pi}{2}\right]$.

$\therefore$ The principal value of $\sin^{-1}\left(-\frac{1}{2}\right)$ is $-\frac{\pi}{6}$.

(iii) Let $y = \cot^{-1}\left(\frac{-1}{\sqrt{3}}\right) \Rightarrow \cot y = \frac{-1}{\sqrt{3}}$

$\Rightarrow \cot y = -\cot\frac{\pi}{3} = \cot\left(\pi - \frac{\pi}{3}\right)$

$[\because \cot(\pi - \theta) = -\cot\theta]$

$\Rightarrow \cot y = \cot\left(\frac{2\pi}{3}\right)$

We know that the principal value branch of $\cot^{-1}$ is $(0, \pi)$ and $y = \frac{2\pi}{3} \in (0, \pi)$.

$\therefore$ The principal value of $\cot^{-1}\left(-\frac{1}{3}\right)$ is $\frac{2\pi}{3}$.

Example 4 Find the value of $\tan^{-1}(-1)$ in the interval $\left(\frac{\pi}{2}, \frac{3\pi}{2}\right)$.

Sol. Let $y = \tan^{-1}(-1) \Rightarrow \tan y = -1$

$= -\tan\left(\frac{\pi}{4}\right) = \tan\left(\pi - \frac{\pi}{4}\right)$ $[\because \tan(\pi - \theta) = -\tan\theta]$

$\Rightarrow \quad \tan y = \tan\frac{3\pi}{4}$

Since, $y = \frac{3\pi}{4} \in \left(\frac{\pi}{2}, \frac{3\pi}{2}\right)$, therefore the required value of $\tan^{-1}(-1)$ is $\frac{3\pi}{4}$.

Example 5 Find the value of $\sin^{-1}\left(\frac{\sqrt{3}}{2}\right) + \tan^{-1}(\sqrt{3})$.

Sol. For principal value of $\sin^{-1}\left(\frac{\sqrt{3}}{2}\right)$.

Let $x = \sin^{-1}\frac{\sqrt{3}}{2} \Rightarrow \sin x = \frac{\sqrt{3}}{2}$

$\Rightarrow \quad \sin x = \sin\frac{\pi}{3}$ $\left[\because \sin\frac{\pi}{3} = \frac{\sqrt{3}}{2}\right]$

Since, the principal value branch of $\sin^{-1}$ is $\left[\frac{-\pi}{2}, \frac{\pi}{2}\right]$ and $x = \frac{\pi}{3} \in \left[-\frac{\pi}{2}, \frac{\pi}{2}\right]$.

So, the principal value of $\sin^{-1}\left(\frac{\sqrt{3}}{2}\right)$ is $\frac{\pi}{3}$.

For principal value of $\tan^{-1}(\sqrt{3})$, consider

$y = \tan^{-1}(\sqrt{3}) \Rightarrow \tan y = \sqrt{3}$

$\Rightarrow \quad \tan y = \tan\left(\frac{\pi}{3}\right)$ $\left[\because \tan\frac{\pi}{3} = \sqrt{3}\right]$

Since, the principal value branch of $\tan^{-1}$ is $\left(\frac{-\pi}{2}, \frac{\pi}{2}\right)$ and $y = \frac{\pi}{3} \in \left(-\frac{\pi}{2}, \frac{\pi}{2}\right)$.

So, the principal value of $\tan^{-1}(\sqrt{3})$ is $\frac{\pi}{3}$.

Hence, $\sin^{-1}\left(\frac{\sqrt{3}}{2}\right) + \tan^{-1}(\sqrt{3}) = \frac{\pi}{3} + \frac{\pi}{3} = \frac{2\pi}{3}$

Example 6 Evaluate $\cos^{-1}\left(\frac{1}{2}\right) + 2\sin^{-1}\left(\frac{1}{2}\right)$. **[NCERT]**

Sol. Let $\cos^{-1}\left(\frac{1}{2}\right) = x$

$\Rightarrow \quad \cos x = \frac{1}{2} = \cos\frac{\pi}{3}$

Since, the principal value branch of $\cos^{-1}$ is $[0, \pi]$ and $x = \frac{\pi}{6} \in [0, \pi]$.

So, the principal value of $\cos^{-1}\left(\frac{1}{2}\right)$ is $\frac{\pi}{3}$.

Again, let $\sin^{-1}\left(\frac{1}{2}\right) = y$

$\Rightarrow \quad \sin y = \frac{1}{2} = \sin\frac{\pi}{6}$

Since, the principal value branch of $\sin^{-1}$ is $\left[-\frac{\pi}{2}, \frac{\pi}{2}\right]$ and $y = \frac{\pi}{6} \in \left[-\frac{\pi}{2}, \frac{\pi}{2}\right]$.

So, the principal value of $\sin^{-1}\left(\frac{1}{2}\right)$ is $\frac{\pi}{6}$.

Hence, $\cos^{-1}\left(\frac{1}{2}\right) + 2\sin^{-1}\left(\frac{1}{2}\right) = \frac{\pi}{3} + 2\cdot\frac{\pi}{6}$

$= \frac{\pi}{3} + \frac{\pi}{3} = \frac{2\pi}{3}$

Example 7 Find the value of

$$\cos^{-1}\left(-\frac{1}{2}\right) + \tan^{-1}(-\sqrt{3}) - \operatorname{cosec}^{-1}(2).$$

Sol. Let $x = \cos^{-1}\left(-\frac{1}{2}\right)$

$\Rightarrow \cos x = \frac{-1}{2} = -\cos\frac{\pi}{3}$

$= \cos\left(\pi - \frac{\pi}{3}\right)$ $[\because \cos(\pi - \theta) = -\cos\theta]$

$\Rightarrow \cos x = \cos\left(\frac{2\pi}{3}\right)$

Since, the principal value branch of $\cos^{-1}$ is $[0, \pi]$ and $x = \frac{2\pi}{3} \in [0, \pi]$.

So, the principal value of $\cos^{-1}\left(-\frac{1}{2}\right)$ is $\frac{2\pi}{3}$.

Now, find the principal value of $\tan^{-1}(-\sqrt{3})$.

Let $y = \tan^{-1}(-\sqrt{3})$

$\Rightarrow \quad \tan y = -\sqrt{3} = -\tan\frac{\pi}{3} \quad \left[\because \tan\frac{\pi}{3} = \sqrt{3}\right]$

$\Rightarrow \quad \tan y = \tan\left(\frac{-\pi}{3}\right) \quad [\because \tan(-\theta) = -\tan\theta]$

Since, the principal value branch of $\tan^{-1}$ is $\left(\frac{-\pi}{2}, \frac{\pi}{2}\right)$

and $y = -\frac{\pi}{3} \in \left(\frac{-\pi}{2}, \frac{\pi}{2}\right)$.

So, the principal value of $\tan^{-1}(-\sqrt{3})$ is $\left(-\frac{\pi}{3}\right)$.

Now, find the principal value of $\operatorname{cosec}^{-1}(2)$.

Let $\quad z = \operatorname{cosec}^{-1}(2)$

$\Rightarrow \quad \operatorname{cosec} z = 2 = \operatorname{cosec}\frac{\pi}{6}$

Since, the principal value branch of $\operatorname{cosec}^{-1}$ is

$\left[\frac{-\pi}{2}, \frac{\pi}{2}\right] - \{0\}$ and $z = \frac{\pi}{6} \in \left[\frac{-\pi}{2}, \frac{\pi}{2}\right] - \{0\}$.

So, the principal value of $\operatorname{cosec}^{-1}(2)$ is $\frac{\pi}{6}$.

Hence, $\cos^{-1}\left(-\frac{1}{2}\right) + \tan^{-1}(-\sqrt{3}) - \operatorname{cosec}^{-1}(2)$

$$= \frac{2\pi}{3} - \frac{\pi}{3} - \frac{\pi}{6}$$

$$= \frac{(4-2-1)\pi}{6} = \frac{\pi}{6}$$

Topic Practice 1

Very Short Answer Type Questions

(2 Marks)

1 Find which of the following functions are not defined and also write the reason

(i) $\cot^{-1}(7)$ (ii) $\sin^{-1}(1, 2)$ (iii) $\cos^{-1}\left(-\frac{1}{2}\right)$

2 Find the domain of the function defined by $f(x) = \sin^{-1}\sqrt{x-1}$. **[NCERT Exemplar]**

3 Find the principal value of the following.

(i) $\cos^{-1}\left(\frac{\sqrt{3}}{2}\right)$ (ii) $\operatorname{cosec}^{-1}(-\sqrt{2})$

4 Write two branches other than the principal value branch of $\tan^{-1} x$.

5 Find the value of $\tan^{-1}(\sqrt{3}) - \sec^{-1}(-2)$. **[NCERT]**

6 Find the principal value of $\tan^{-1}(\sqrt{3}) - \cot^{-1}(-\sqrt{3})$.

7 Write the principal value of

$$\left[\cos^{-1}\left(\frac{\sqrt{3}}{2}\right) + \cos^{-1}\left(\frac{-1}{2}\right)\right].$$

8 Find the value of $2\sec^{-1}2 + \sin^{-1}\left(\frac{1}{2}\right)$. **[NCERT Exemplar]**

9 Write the value of $\cos^{-1}\left(-\frac{1}{2}\right) + 2\sin^{-1}\left(\frac{1}{2}\right)$.

10 Write the value of $\cos^{-1}\left(\frac{1}{2}\right) - 2\sin^{-1}\left(\frac{-1}{2}\right)$.

11 Find the value of $\tan^{-1}(1) + \cos^{-1}\left(\frac{-1}{2}\right) + \sin^{-1}\left(\frac{-1}{2}\right)$. **[NCERT]**

Hints & Solutions

1. (i) We know that $\cot^{-1} x$ is defined for all real values of x except $x = 0$.

$\therefore$ $\cot^{-1}(7)$ is defined.

(ii) We know that $\sin^{-1} x$ is defined in the interval $[-1, 1]$.

$\therefore$ $\sin^{-1}(1, 2)$ is not defined, because $1 \cdot 2 \notin [-1, 1]$. [1/2]

(iii) We know that $\cos^{-1} x$ is defined in the interval $[-1, 1]$.

$\therefore$ $\cos^{-1}\left(-\frac{1}{2}\right)$ is defined. [1]

2. Given function, $f(x) = \sin^{-1}\sqrt{x-1}$

For domain of $f(x)$, $0 \le \sqrt{x-1} \le 1$ [1]

$[\because$ domain of $\sin^{-1} x$ is $[-1, 1]$ and $\sqrt{x-1} \ge 0]$

$\Rightarrow \quad 0 \le x-1 \le 1$

$\Rightarrow \quad 1 \le x \le 2$

$\therefore$ Required domain is $[1, 2]$. [1]

3. Similar as Example 3.

$\left[\textbf{Ans. } (i) \frac{\pi}{6} \ (ii) -\frac{\pi}{4}\right]$

4. Principal value branch of $\tan^{-1} x$ is $\left(-\frac{\pi}{2}, \frac{\pi}{2}\right)$.

The branches of $\tan^{-1} x$ other than principal values are $\left(-\frac{3\pi}{2}, -\frac{\pi}{2}\right)$ and $\left(\frac{\pi}{2}, \frac{3\pi}{2}\right)$ [2]

5. Let $\tan^{-1}\sqrt{3} = x, -\frac{\pi}{2} < x < \frac{\pi}{2}$

$\left[\because \text{principal value branch of } \tan^{-1} \text{ is } \left(-\frac{\pi}{2}, \frac{\pi}{2}\right)\right]$

$\Rightarrow \tan x = \sqrt{3} = \tan\frac{\pi}{3}$ $\left[\because \tan\frac{\pi}{3} = \sqrt{3}\right]$

$\Rightarrow x = \frac{\pi}{3} \in \left(-\frac{\pi}{2}, \frac{\pi}{2}\right)$ [1]

Again, let $\sec^{-1}(-2) = y, y \in [0, \pi] - \{\pi/2\}$

$\left[\because \text{principal value branch of } \sec^{-1} \text{ is } [0, \pi] - \left\{\frac{\pi}{2}\right\}\right]$

$\Rightarrow \sec y = -2 = -\sec\frac{\pi}{3}$

$\Rightarrow \sec y = \sec\left(\pi - \frac{\pi}{3}\right)$ $[\because \sec(\pi - \theta) = -\sec\theta]$

$\Rightarrow \sec y = \sec\frac{2\pi}{3}$

$\Rightarrow y = \frac{2\pi}{3} \in [0, \pi] - \left\{\frac{\pi}{2}\right\}$

$\therefore \tan^{-1}(\sqrt{3}) - \sec^{-1}(-2) = \frac{\pi}{3} - \frac{2\pi}{3} = -\frac{\pi}{3}$ [1]

6. Similar as Question 5. $\left[\textbf{Ans. } -\frac{\pi}{2}\right]$

7. Similar as Question 5. $\left[\textbf{Ans. } \frac{5\pi}{6}\right]$

8. Similar as Example 6. $\left[\textbf{Ans. } \frac{5\pi}{6}\right]$

9. Similar as Example 6. [**Ans.** π]

10. Similar as Example 6. $\left[\textbf{Ans. } \frac{2\pi}{3}\right]$

11. Similar as Example 7. $\left[\textbf{Ans. } \frac{3\pi}{4}\right]$

TOPIC 02 Elementary Properties of Inverse Trigonometric Functions

Elementary properties of inverse trigonometric functions are valid within the principal value branches of the corresponding inverse trigonometric function and wherever they are defined.

PROPERTY I (Self-Adjusting Property)

(i) $\sin^{-1}(\sin\theta) = \theta, \theta \in \left[-\frac{\pi}{2}, \frac{\pi}{2}\right]$

(ii) $\cos^{-1}(\cos\theta) = \theta, \theta \in [0, \pi]$

(iii) $\tan^{-1}(\tan\theta) = \theta, \theta \in \left(-\frac{\pi}{2}, \frac{\pi}{2}\right)$

(iv) $\cot^{-1}(\cot\theta) = \theta, \theta \in (0, \pi)$

(v) $\text{cosec}^{-1}(\text{cosec}\,\theta) = \theta, \theta \in \left[-\frac{\pi}{2}, \frac{\pi}{2}\right] - \{0\}$

(vi) $\sec^{-1}(\sec\theta) = \theta, \theta \in [0, \pi] - \left\{\frac{\pi}{2}\right\}$

(vii) $\sin(\sin^{-1} x) = x, x \in [-1, 1]$

(viii) $\cos(\cos^{-1} x) = x, x \in [-1, 1]$

(ix) $\tan(\tan^{-1} x) = x, x \in R$

(x) $\cot(\cot^{-1} x) = x, x \in R$

(xi) $\text{cosec}(\text{cosec}^{-1} x) = x, x \in (-\infty, -1] \cup [1, \infty)$ or $|x| \geq 1$

(xii) $\sec(\sec^{-1} x) = x, x \in (-\infty, -1] \cup [1, \infty)$ or $|x| \geq 1$

Proof of part (i)

Let $\sin\theta = x$. Then, $\theta = \sin^{-1} x$

$\Rightarrow \theta = \sin^{-1}(\sin\theta)$ $[\because x = \sin\theta]$

Thus, $\sin^{-1}(\sin\theta) = \theta, \theta \in \left[-\frac{\pi}{2}, \frac{\pi}{2}\right]$

Similarly, we can prove other parts.

Note It should be noted that $\sin^{-1}(\sin\theta) \neq \theta$, if $\theta \notin [-\pi/2, \pi/2]$, $\cot^{-1}(\cot\theta) \neq \theta$ if $\theta \notin (0, \pi)$, etc.

So, students should remember the restrictions specified against each formula.

Example 1 Evaluate each of the following.

(i) $\cos\left(\cos^{-1}\frac{1}{2}\right)$ (ii) $\tan^{-1}\left(\tan\frac{\pi}{4}\right)$

(iii) $\sin^{-1}\left(\sin\frac{2\pi}{3}\right)$ (iv) $\cos^{-1}\left(\cos\frac{7\pi}{6}\right)$

Sol. (i) We know that, $\cos(\cos^{-1} x) = x, x \in [-1, 1]$.

Here, we have $\cos\left(\cos^{-1}\frac{1}{2}\right)$.

Since, $\frac{1}{2} \in [-1, 1]$, therefore $\cos\left(\cos^{-1}\frac{1}{2}\right) = \frac{1}{2}$.

(ii) $\tan^{-1}\left(\tan\frac{\pi}{4}\right)=\frac{\pi}{4}$ $\left[\because \frac{\pi}{4}\in\left(\frac{-\pi}{2},\frac{\pi}{2}\right)\right]$

(iii) $\sin^{-1}\left(\sin\frac{2\pi}{3}\right)=\sin^{-1}\left\{\sin\left(\pi-\frac{\pi}{3}\right)\right\}$

$\left[\because \frac{2\pi}{3}\notin\left[\frac{-\pi}{2},\frac{\pi}{2}\right], \text{ so we write } \frac{2\pi}{3} \text{ as } \left(\pi-\frac{\pi}{3}\right)\right]$

$=\sin^{-1}\left(\sin\frac{\pi}{3}\right)$ $[\because \sin(\pi-\theta)=\sin\theta]$

$=\frac{\pi}{3}$ $\left[\because \frac{\pi}{3}\in\left[\frac{-\pi}{2},\frac{\pi}{2}\right]\right]$

(iv) $\cos^{-1}\left(\cos\frac{7\pi}{6}\right)=\cos^{-1}\left\{\cos\left(2\pi-\frac{5\pi}{6}\right)\right\}$

$\left[\because \frac{7\pi}{6}\notin[0,\pi], \text{ so we write } \frac{7\pi}{6} \text{ as } \left(2\pi-\frac{5\pi}{6}\right)\right]$

$=\cos^{-1}\left(\cos\frac{5\pi}{6}\right)$

$[\because \cos(2\pi-\theta)=\cos\theta]$

$=\frac{5\pi}{6}$ $\left[\because \frac{5\pi}{6}\in[0,\pi]\right]$

Example 2 What is the principal value of $\cos^{-1}\left(\cos\frac{2\pi}{3}\right)+\sin^{-1}\left(\sin\frac{2\pi}{3}\right)$?

Sol. We know that the principal value branch of $\cos^{-1}$ is $[0,\pi]$ and for $\sin^{-1}$ is $\left[-\frac{\pi}{2},\frac{\pi}{2}\right]$.

$\therefore \cos^{-1}\left(\cos\frac{2\pi}{3}\right)+\sin^{-1}\left(\sin\frac{2\pi}{3}\right)$

$=\frac{2\pi}{3}+\sin^{-1}\left[\sin\left(\pi-\frac{\pi}{3}\right)\right]$ $\left[\because \frac{2\pi}{3}\in[0,\pi]\right]$

$=\frac{2\pi}{3}+\sin^{-1}\left(\sin\frac{\pi}{3}\right)$ $[\because \sin(\pi-\theta)=\sin\theta]$

$=\frac{2\pi}{3}+\frac{\pi}{3}=\frac{3\pi}{3}=\pi$ $\left[\because \frac{\pi}{3}\in\left[-\frac{\pi}{2},\frac{\pi}{2}\right]\right]$

PROPERTY II (Reciprocal Property)

(i) $\operatorname{cosec}^{-1}x=\sin^{-1}\frac{1}{x}, |x|\geq 1$

(ii) $\sec^{-1}x=\cos^{-1}\frac{1}{x}, |x|\geq 1$

(iii) $\cot^{-1}x=\begin{cases}\tan^{-1}\frac{1}{x}, & x>0\\ \pi+\tan^{-1}\frac{1}{x}, & x<0\end{cases}$

Proof of part (i)

Let $y=\operatorname{cosec}^{-1}x$, where $\frac{-\pi}{2}\leq y\leq\frac{\pi}{2}, y\neq 0$

Then, $x=\operatorname{cosec} y \Rightarrow \frac{1}{x}=\frac{1}{\operatorname{cosec} y}$

$\Rightarrow \frac{1}{x}=\sin y$

$\Rightarrow y=\sin^{-1}\frac{1}{x}$ $\left[\because \frac{-\pi}{2}\leq y\leq\frac{\pi}{2}, y\neq 0\right]$

Thus, $\operatorname{cosec}^{-1}x=\sin^{-1}\frac{1}{x}, |x|\geq 1$

Similarly, we can prove (ii) and (iii) parts.

Example 3 Simplify $\operatorname{cosec}\left(\sin^{-1}\frac{1}{5}\right)+\sec\left(\cos^{-1}\frac{1}{3}\right)$.

Sol. We have, $\operatorname{cosec}\left(\sin^{-1}\frac{1}{5}\right)+\sec\left(\cos^{-1}\frac{1}{3}\right)$

$=\operatorname{cosec}(\operatorname{cosec}^{-1}5)+\sec(\sec^{-1}3)$

$\left[\because \sin^{-1}\frac{1}{x}=\operatorname{cosec}^{-1}x \text{ and } \cos^{-1}\frac{1}{x}=\sec^{-1}x, \forall |x|\geq 1\right]$

$=5+3=8$

$[\because \operatorname{cosec}(\operatorname{cosec}^{-1}x)=x \text{ and } \sec(\sec^{-1}x)=x, \forall |x|\geq 1]$

PROPERTY III

(i) $\sin^{-1}(-x)=-\sin^{-1}x, x\in[-1,1]$

(ii) $\cos^{-1}(-x)=\pi-\cos^{-1}x, x\in[-1,1]$

(iii) $\tan^{-1}(-x)=-\tan^{-1}x, x\in R$

(iv) $\cot^{-1}(-x)=\pi-\cot^{-1}x, x\in R$

(v) $\operatorname{cosec}^{-1}(-x)=-\operatorname{cosec}^{-1}x, |x|\geq 1$ or $x\in(-\infty,-1]\cup[1,\infty)$

(vi) $\sec^{-1}(-x)=\pi-\sec^{-1}x, |x|\geq 1$ or $x\in(-\infty,-1]\cup[1,\infty)$

Proof of part (i)

Let $y=\sin^{-1}(-x), -\frac{\pi}{2}\leq y\leq\frac{\pi}{2}$.

Then, $\sin y=-x \Rightarrow -\sin y=x$

$\Rightarrow \sin(-y)=x$ $[\because \sin(-\theta)=-\sin\theta]$

$\Rightarrow -y=\sin^{-1}x \Rightarrow y=-\sin^{-1}x$

$\left[\because -\frac{\pi}{2}\leq -y\leq\frac{\pi}{2}\right]$

Thus, $\sin^{-1}(-x)=-\sin^{-1}x, x\in[-1,1]$

Proof of part (ii)

Let $y = \cos^{-1}(-x), 0 \le y \le \pi$. Then, $\cos y = -x$

$\Rightarrow \quad -\cos y = x$

$\Rightarrow \quad \cos(\pi - y) = x \quad [\because (-\cos\theta) = \cos(\pi - \theta)]$

$\Rightarrow \quad \pi - y = \cos^{-1} x$

$[\because 0 \le y \le \pi \Rightarrow -\pi \le -y \le 0 \Rightarrow \pi - y \le \pi]$

$\Rightarrow \quad y = \pi - \cos^{-1} x$

Thus, $\cos^{-1}(-x) = \pi - \cos^{-1} x, x \in [-1, 1]$

Similarly, we can prove other parts.

Example 4 Evaluate $\sin\left[\frac{\pi}{3} - \sin^{-1}\left(-\frac{1}{2}\right)\right]$. **[NCERT]**

Sol. We have, $\sin\left[\frac{\pi}{3} - \sin^{-1}\left(-\frac{1}{2}\right)\right]$

$= \sin\left[\frac{\pi}{3} + \sin^{-1}\left(\frac{1}{2}\right)\right]$

$[\because \sin^{-1}(-x) = -\sin^{-1} x, x \in [-1, 1]]$

$= \sin\left[\frac{\pi}{3} + \sin^{-1}\left(\sin\frac{\pi}{6}\right)\right] \quad \left[\because \sin\frac{\pi}{6} = \frac{1}{2}\right]$

$= \sin\left(\frac{\pi}{3} + \frac{\pi}{6}\right) \quad \left[\because \sin^{-1}(\sin\theta) = \theta, \forall\theta \in \left[-\frac{\pi}{2}, \frac{\pi}{2}\right]\right]$

$= \sin\left[\frac{2\pi + \pi}{6}\right] = \sin\frac{3\pi}{6} = \sin\frac{\pi}{2} = 1$

Example 5 Evaluate $\cos\left[\cos^{-1}\left(\frac{-\sqrt{3}}{2}\right) + \frac{\pi}{6}\right]$.

Sol. We have,

$\cos\left[\cos^{-1}\left(\frac{-\sqrt{3}}{2}\right) + \frac{\pi}{6}\right] = \cos\left[\pi - \cos^{-1}\frac{\sqrt{3}}{2} + \frac{\pi}{6}\right]$

$[\because \cos^{-1}(-x) = \pi - \cos^{-1} x, x \in [-1,1]]$

$= \cos\left[\pi - \cos^{-1}\left(\cos\frac{\pi}{6}\right) + \frac{\pi}{6}\right] \quad \left[\because \cos\frac{\pi}{6} = \frac{\sqrt{3}}{2}\right]$

$= \cos\left[\pi - \frac{\pi}{6} + \frac{\pi}{6}\right] [\because \cos^{-1}(\cos\theta) = \theta, \forall\theta \in [0, \pi]]$

$= \cos\pi = -1$

PROPERTY IV (Complementary Property)

(i) $\sin^{-1} x + \cos^{-1} x = \frac{\pi}{2}, x \in [-1, 1]$

(ii) $\tan^{-1} x + \cot^{-1} x = \frac{\pi}{2}, x \in R$

(iii) $\operatorname{cosec}^{-1} x + \sec^{-1} x = \frac{\pi}{2}, \; x \in (-\infty, -1] \cup [1, \infty)$

Proof of part (i)

Let $y = \sin^{-1} x, -\frac{\pi}{2} \le y \le \frac{\pi}{2}$ ...(i)

Then, $\sin y = x$

$\Rightarrow \quad x = \cos\left(\frac{\pi}{2} - y\right) \quad \left[\because \cos\left(\frac{\pi}{2} - \theta\right) = \sin\theta\right]$

$\Rightarrow \quad \cos^{-1} x = \frac{\pi}{2} - y \Rightarrow y = \frac{\pi}{2} - \cos^{-1} x$ ...(ii)

$\left[\because -\frac{\pi}{2} \le y \le \frac{\pi}{2} \Rightarrow -\frac{\pi}{2} \le -y \le \frac{\pi}{2} \Rightarrow 0 \le \frac{\pi}{2} - y \le \pi\right]$

From Eqs. (i) and (ii), we get

$\sin^{-1} x = \frac{\pi}{2} - \cos^{-1} x \Rightarrow \sin^{-1} x + \cos^{-1} x = \frac{\pi}{2}$

Similarly, we can prove the other parts.

Example 6 Evaluate $\cot(\tan^{-1} a + \cot^{-1} a)$. **[NCERT]**

Sol. $\cot(\tan^{-1} a + \cot^{-1} a)$

$= \cot\left(\frac{\pi}{2}\right) = 0 \quad \left[\because \tan^{-1} x + \cot^{-1} x = \frac{\pi}{2}, \forall x \in R\right]$

PROPERTY V (Conversion Property)

(i) $\sin^{-1} x = \cos^{-1}\sqrt{1 - x^2} = \tan^{-1}\left(\frac{x}{\sqrt{1 - x^2}}\right)$, $0 \le x \le 1$

(ii) $\cos^{-1} x = \sin^{-1}\sqrt{1 - x^2} = \tan^{-1}\left(\frac{\sqrt{1 - x^2}}{x}\right)$, $0 \le x \le 1$

(iii) $\tan^{-1} x = \sin^{-1}\left(\frac{x}{\sqrt{1 + x^2}}\right) = \cos^{-1}\left(\frac{1}{\sqrt{1 + x^2}}\right), x \ge 0$

Proof of part (i)

Let $\sin^{-1} x = \theta$, then $x = \sin\theta$

Since, $0 \le x \le 1$, therefore $0 \le \theta \le \frac{\pi}{2}$.

Now, $\cos\theta = \sqrt{1 - \sin^2\theta} = \sqrt{1 - x^2}$

$\Rightarrow \quad \theta = \cos^{-1}(\sqrt{1 - x^2}) \quad \left[\because \theta \in \left[0, \frac{\pi}{2}\right] \subset [0, \pi]\right]$

Also, $\tan\theta = \frac{\sin\theta}{\cos\theta} = \frac{x}{\sqrt{1 - x^2}} \Rightarrow \theta = \tan^{-1}\left(\frac{x}{\sqrt{1 - x^2}}\right)$

$\therefore$ Equating the values of θ, we get

$\sin^{-1} x = \cos^{-1}\sqrt{1 - x^2} = \tan^{-1}\left(\frac{x}{\sqrt{1 - x^2}}\right)$

Similarly, we can prove the parts (ii) and (iii).

Example 6 Evaluate $\cos\left(\tan^{-1}\dfrac{3}{4}\right)$.

Sol. We have, $\cos\left(\tan^{-1}\dfrac{3}{4}\right)$

Clearly, $\tan^{-1}\dfrac{3}{4} = \cos^{-1}\left(\dfrac{1}{\sqrt{1+(3/4)^2}}\right)$

$$\left[\because \tan^{-1}x = \cos^{-1}\left(\frac{1}{\sqrt{1+x^2}}\right), x \geq 0\right]$$

$$= \cos^{-1}\left(\frac{1}{\sqrt{25/16}}\right) = \cos^{-1}\left(\frac{4}{5}\right)$$

$$\therefore \cos\left(\tan^{-1}\frac{3}{4}\right) = \cos\left(\cos^{-1}\frac{4}{5}\right) = \frac{4}{5}$$

$$[\because \cos(\cos^{-1}x) = x, \forall\, x \in [-1,1]]$$

Example 8 Evaluate $\cos(2\cos^{-1}x + \sin^{-1}x)$ at $x = \dfrac{1}{5}$, where $0 \leq \cos^{-1}x \leq \pi$ and $-\dfrac{\pi}{2} \leq \sin^{-1}x \leq \dfrac{\pi}{2}$.

Sol. We have, $\cos(2\cos^{-1}x + \sin^{-1}x)$

$$= \cos(\cos^{-1}x + \cos^{-1}x + \sin^{-1}x)$$

$$= \cos\left(\frac{\pi}{2} + \cos^{-1}x\right) \qquad \left[\because \sin^{-1}x + \cos^{-1}x = \frac{\pi}{2}\right]$$

$$= -\sin(\cos^{-1}x) \qquad \left[\because \cos\left(\frac{\pi}{2}+\theta\right) = -\sin\theta\right]$$

$$= -\sin[\sin^{-1}(\sqrt{1-x^2})], \text{ for } 0 \leq x \leq 1$$

$$= -(\sqrt{1-x^2}), \text{ for } 0 \leq x \leq 1$$

$$[\because \sin(\sin^{-1}x) = x, \forall x \in [-1,1] \text{ and here } 0 \leq x \leq 1$$
$$\Rightarrow 0 \leq x^2 \leq 1 \Rightarrow -1 \leq -x^2 \leq 0 \Rightarrow 0 \leq 1-x^2 \leq 1$$
$$\Rightarrow 0 \leq \sqrt{1-x^2} \leq 1]$$

On putting $x = 1/5$, we get

$$\cos(2\cos^{-1}x + \sin^{-1}x) = -\sqrt{1-\left(\frac{1}{5}\right)^2} = -\sqrt{\frac{24}{25}} = -\frac{2\sqrt{6}}{5}$$

PROPERTY VI

(i) $\tan^{-1}x + \tan^{-1}y$

$$= \begin{cases} \tan^{-1}\left(\dfrac{x+y}{1-xy}\right), xy < 1 \\ \pi + \tan^{-1}\dfrac{x+y}{1-xy}; xy > 1, x, y > 0 \\ -\pi + \tan^{-1}\dfrac{x+y}{1-xy}; xy > 1, x, y < 0 \end{cases}$$

(ii) $\tan^{-1}x - \tan^{-1}y$

$$= \begin{cases} \tan^{-1}\left(\dfrac{x-y}{1+xy}\right), xy > -1 \\ \pi + \tan^{-1}\left(\dfrac{x-y}{1+xy}\right); x > 0, y < 0 \text{ and } xy < -1 \\ -\pi + \tan^{-1}\dfrac{x-y}{1+xy}; x < 0, y > 0 \text{ and } xy = -1 \end{cases}$$

Proof of part (i)

Let $\tan^{-1}x = \theta$ and $\tan^{-1}y = \phi$.

Then, $x = \tan\theta$ and $y = \tan\phi$

I. We know that $\tan(\theta+\phi) = \dfrac{\tan\theta + \tan\phi}{1-\tan\theta\tan\phi} = \dfrac{x+y}{1-xy}$

$$\Rightarrow \qquad \theta + \phi = \tan^{-1}\left(\frac{x+y}{1-xy}\right)$$

$$\Rightarrow \qquad \tan^{-1}x + \tan^{-1}y = \tan^{-1}\left(\frac{x+y}{1-xy}\right)$$

Explanation of Restriction

***Case* 1** *When* $x > 0,\ y > 0$

In this case, LHS > 0 but RHS will be positive if and only if $xy < 1$.

***Case* 2** *When* $x < 0,\ y < 0$

In this case, LHS < 0 but RHS will be negative if and only if $xy < 1$.

***Case* 3** *When* $x < 0, y > 0$ *(or* $x > 0,\ y < 0$*)*

Consider, $x < 0$, $y > 0$, then $xy < 0$, i.e. $xy < 1$.

II. When $x > 0$, $y > 0$ and $xy > 1$

$$\Rightarrow \quad \frac{1}{x} > 0, \frac{1}{y} > 0 \text{ and } \frac{1}{x} < 1$$

From I, $\tan^{-1}\dfrac{1}{x} + \tan^{-1}\dfrac{1}{y} = \tan^{-1}\left(\dfrac{\dfrac{1}{x}+\dfrac{1}{y}}{1-\dfrac{1}{x}\times\dfrac{1}{y}}\right)$

$$\Rightarrow \quad \cot^{-1}x + \cot^{-1}y = \tan^{-1}\left(\frac{y+x}{xy-1}\right)$$

$$\Rightarrow \quad \frac{\pi}{2} - \tan^{-1}x + \frac{\pi}{2} - \tan^{-1}y = \tan^{-1}\left(-\frac{x+y}{1-xy}\right)$$

$$\Rightarrow \quad \pi - (\tan^{-1}x + \tan^{-1}y) = -\tan^{-1}\left(\frac{x+y}{1-xy}\right)$$

$$\Rightarrow \quad \tan^{-1}x + \tan^{-1}y = \pi + \tan^{-1}\left(\frac{x+y}{1-xy}\right)$$

III. When, $x<0$, $y<0$ and $xy>1$

$$\Rightarrow -x>0, -y>0 \text{ and } \left(-\frac{1}{x}\right)\left(-\frac{1}{y}\right)<1$$

From I,

$$\tan^{-1}\left(-\frac{1}{x}\right)+\tan^{-1}\left(-\frac{1}{y}\right)=\tan^{-1}\frac{\left(-\frac{1}{x}+\left(-\frac{1}{y}\right)\right)}{1-\left(-\frac{1}{x}\right)\left(-\frac{1}{y}\right)}$$

$$\Rightarrow \cot^{-1}(-x)+\cot^{-1}(-y)=\tan^{-1}\left(\frac{x+y}{1-xy}\right)$$

$$\Rightarrow \frac{\pi}{2}-\tan^{-1}(-x)+\frac{\pi}{2}-\tan^{-1}(-y)=\tan^{-1}\left(\frac{x+y}{1-xy}\right)$$

$$\Rightarrow \pi-(-\tan^{-1}x-\tan^{-1}y)=\tan^{-1}\left(\frac{x+y}{1-xy}\right)$$

$$\Rightarrow \tan^{-1}x+\tan^{-1}y=-\pi+\tan^{-1}\left(\frac{x+y}{1-xy}\right)$$

Similarly, we can prove the part (ii) by replacing y by $(-y)$.

Example 9 Prove that $\tan^{-1}\frac{2}{11}+\tan^{-1}\frac{7}{24}=\tan^{-1}\frac{1}{2}$.

Sol. LHS $=\tan^{-1}\frac{2}{11}+\tan^{-1}\frac{7}{24}=\tan^{-1}\left\{\frac{\frac{2}{11}+\frac{7}{24}}{1-\frac{2}{11}\times\frac{7}{24}}\right\}$

$$\left[\because \tan^{-1}x+\tan^{-1}y=\tan^{-1}\left(\frac{x+y}{1-xy}\right), \text{ if } xy<1\right]$$

$$=\tan^{-1}\left\{\frac{48+77}{264-14}\right\}$$

$$=\tan^{-1}\left\{\frac{125}{250}\right\}$$

$$=\tan^{-1}\left\{\frac{1}{2}\right\}=\text{RHS}$$

Hence proved.

Example 10 Evaluate $\tan\left(\sin^{-1}\frac{3}{5}+\cot^{-1}\frac{3}{2}\right)$. **[NCERT]**

Sol. $\tan\left(\sin^{-1}\frac{3}{5}+\cot^{-1}\frac{3}{2}\right)=\tan\left[\tan^{-1}\frac{3}{4}+\tan^{-1}\frac{2}{3}\right]$

$$\left[\because \sin^{-1}x=\tan^{-1}\left(\frac{x}{\sqrt{1-x^2}}\right) \text{for } 0\le x\le 1 \text{ and } \cot^{-1}x=\tan^{-1}\frac{1}{x}, x>0\right]$$

$$=\tan\left[\tan^{-1}\left(\frac{\frac{3}{4}+\frac{2}{3}}{1-\frac{3}{4}\times\frac{2}{3}}\right)\right]=\tan\left[\tan^{-1}\frac{\frac{17}{12}}{\frac{1}{2}}\right]$$

$$\left[\because \tan^{-1}x+\tan^{-1}y=\tan^{-1}\left(\frac{x+y}{1-xy}\right), \text{ if } xy<1\right]$$

$$=\tan\left[\tan^{-1}\frac{17}{6}\right]=\frac{17}{6} \qquad [\because \tan(\tan^{-1}x)=x, \forall x\in R]$$

Example 11 If $\tan^{-1}\left(\frac{x-1}{x+1}\right)+\tan^{-1}\left(\frac{2x-1}{2x+1}\right)=\tan^{-1}\left(\frac{23}{36}\right)$, then prove that $24x^2-23x-12=0$. **[ISC 2023]**

Sol. We have, $\tan^{-1}\left(\frac{x-1}{x+1}\right)+\tan^{-1}\left(\frac{2x-1}{2x+1}\right)=\tan^{-1}\left(\frac{23}{36}\right)$

$$\Rightarrow \tan^{-1}\left[\frac{\frac{x-1}{x+1}+\frac{2x-1}{2x+1}}{1-\frac{(x-1)(2x-1)}{(x+1)(2x+1)}}\right]=\tan^{-1}\left[\frac{23}{36}\right]$$

$$\left[\therefore \tan^{-1}x+\tan^{-1}y=\tan^{-1}\left(\frac{x+y}{1-xy}\right)\right]$$

$$\Rightarrow \frac{(x-1)(2x+1)+(2x-1)(x+1)}{(x+1)(2x+1)-(x-1)(2x-1)}=\frac{23}{36}$$

$$\Rightarrow \frac{2x^2-x-1+2x^2+x-1}{2x^2+3x+1-2x^2+3x-1}=\frac{23}{36}$$

$$\Rightarrow \frac{4x^2-2}{6x}=\frac{23}{36} \Rightarrow \frac{2(2x^2-1)}{6x}=\frac{23}{36}$$

$$\Rightarrow 24x^2-23x-12=0$$

Example 12 Prove that

$$\sin^{-1}\frac{x}{\sqrt{1+x^2}}+\cos^{-1}\frac{x+1}{\sqrt{x^2+2x+2}}=\tan^{-1}(x^2+x+1).$$ **[ISC 2000]**

Sol. LHS $=\sin^{-1}\frac{x}{\sqrt{1+x^2}}+\cos^{-1}\frac{x+1}{\sqrt{x^2+2x+2}}$

$$=\tan^{-1}x+\tan^{-1}\left(\frac{\sqrt{1-\frac{x^2+2x+1}{x^2+2x+2}}}{\frac{x+1}{\sqrt{x^2+2x+2}}}\right)$$

$$\left[\because \tan^{-1}x=\sin^{-1}\left(\frac{x}{\sqrt{1+x^2}}\right) \text{ and } \cos^{-1}x=\tan^{-1}\frac{\sqrt{1-x^2}}{x}\right]$$

$$= \tan^{-1} x + \tan^{-1}\left(\frac{\sqrt{1}}{\sqrt{x^2+2x+2}} \times \frac{\sqrt{x^2+2x+2}}{x+1}\right)$$

$$= \tan^{-1} x + \tan^{-1}\frac{1}{x+1}$$

$$= \tan^{-1}\left(\frac{x+\frac{1}{x+1}}{1-\frac{x}{x+1}}\right)$$

$$\left[\because \tan^{-1} x + \tan^{-1} y = \tan^{-1}\left(\frac{x+y}{1-xy}\right), \text{ if } xy<1 \text{ and here } \frac{x}{1+x}<1\right]$$

$$= \tan^{-1}\left(\frac{x^2+x+1}{x+1} \times \frac{x+1}{1}\right)$$

$$= \tan^{-1}\left(\frac{x^2+x+1}{1}\right)$$

$$= \tan^{-1}(x^2+x+1)$$

= RHS **Hence proved.**

PROPERTY VII

(i) $2\tan^{-1} x = \sin^{-1}\left(\frac{2x}{1+x^2}\right), |x| \le 1$ or $-1 \le x \le 1$

(ii) $2\tan^{-1} x = \cos^{-1}\left(\frac{1-x^2}{1+x^2}\right), 0 \le x \le 1$

(iii) $2\tan^{-1} x = \tan^{-1}\left(\frac{2x}{1-x^2}\right), -1 < x < 1$

Proof of part (i)

Let $\tan^{-1} x = y$, then $x = \tan y$.

Since, $|x| \le 1$, therefore $-\frac{\pi}{4} \le y \le \frac{\pi}{4}$.

Now, $\sin^{-1}\left(\frac{2x}{1+x^2}\right) = \sin^{-1}\left(\frac{2\tan y}{1+\tan^2 y}\right)$

$$= \sin^{-1}(\sin 2y) \qquad \left[\because \sin 2\theta = \frac{2\tan\theta}{1+\tan^2\theta}\right]$$

$$= 2y = 2\tan^{-1} x$$

$$\left[\because -\frac{\pi}{4} \le y \le \frac{\pi}{4} \Rightarrow -\frac{\pi}{2} \le 2y \le \frac{\pi}{2}\right]$$

Similarly, we can prove the other parts.

Example 13 Evaluate $\tan\left[2\tan^{-1}\frac{1}{2} - \cot^{-1} 3\right]$.

[ISC 2014]

Sol. We have, $\tan\left[2\tan^{-1}\frac{1}{2} - \cot^{-1} 3\right]$

$$= \tan\left[\tan^{-1}\frac{2\left(\frac{1}{2}\right)}{1-\left(\frac{1}{2}\right)^2} - \tan^{-1}\frac{1}{3}\right]$$

$$\left[\because 2\tan^{-1} x = \tan^{-1}\frac{2x}{1-x^2}, -1<x<1 \text{ and } \cot^{-1} x = \tan^{-1}\frac{1}{x}, x>0\right]$$

$$= \tan\left[\tan^{-1}\frac{1}{\frac{3}{4}} - \tan^{-1}\frac{1}{3}\right] = \tan\left[\tan^{-1}\frac{4}{3} - \tan^{-1}\frac{1}{3}\right]$$

$$= \tan\left[\tan^{-1}\frac{\frac{4}{3}-\frac{1}{3}}{1+\frac{4}{3}\cdot\frac{1}{3}}\right]$$

$$\left[\because \tan^{-1} x - \tan^{-1} y = \tan^{-1}\left(\frac{x-y}{1+xy}\right), xy>-1\right]$$

$$= \tan\left[\tan^{-1}\left(\frac{\frac{4-1}{3}}{\frac{9+4}{9}}\right)\right] = \frac{3}{3}\cdot\frac{9}{13} = \frac{9}{13}$$

$$[\because \tan(\tan^{-1} x) = x, \forall x \in R]$$

Example 14 Find the value of

$$\tan\frac{1}{2}\left[\sin^{-1}\frac{2x}{1+x^2} + \cos^{-1}\frac{1-y^2}{1+y^2}\right],$$

where $|x| < 1$, $y > 0$ and $xy < 1$.

Sol. We have, $\tan\frac{1}{2}\left(\sin^{-1}\frac{2x}{1+x^2} + \cos^{-1}\frac{1-y^2}{1+y^2}\right)$

$$= \tan\frac{1}{2}(2\tan^{-1} x + 2\tan^{-1} y)$$

$$\left[\because 2\tan^{-1} x = \begin{cases} \sin^{-1}\left(\frac{2x}{1+x^2}\right), & -1 \le x \le 1 \\ \cos^{-1}\left(\frac{1-x^2}{1+x^2}\right), & x \ge 0 \end{cases}\right]$$

$$= \tan\frac{1}{2} \times 2(\tan^{-1} x + \tan^{-1} y)$$

$$= \tan\left[\tan^{-1}\left(\frac{x+y}{1-xy}\right)\right]$$

$$= \frac{x+y}{1-xy} \qquad \left[\because \tan^{-1} x + \tan^{-1} y = \tan^{-1}\left(\frac{x+y}{1-xy}\right), xy<1 \text{ and } \tan(\tan^{-1} x) = x, \forall x \in R\right]$$

Example 15 Show that

$$\tan^{-1}\sqrt{x} = \frac{1}{2}\cos^{-1}\left(\frac{1-x}{1+x}\right), x \in [0, 1].$$ [ISC 2017]

Sol. LHS $= \tan^{-1}\sqrt{x} = \frac{1}{2}(2\tan^{-1}\sqrt{x})$

[multiply and divide by 2]

$$= \frac{1}{2}\cos^{-1}\left\{\frac{1-(\sqrt{x})^2}{1+(\sqrt{x})^2}\right\}$$

$$\left[\because 2\tan^{-1}x = \cos^{-1}\left(\frac{1-x^2}{1+x^2}\right), 0 \le x \le 1\right]$$

$$= \frac{1}{2}\cos^{-1}\left(\frac{1-x}{1+x}\right) = \text{RHS}$$

Example 16 Prove that

$$2\tan^{-1}\frac{1}{5} + \cos^{-1}\frac{7}{5\sqrt{2}} + 2\tan^{-1}\frac{1}{8} = \frac{\pi}{4}.$$ [ISC 2011]

Sol. LHS $= 2\tan^{-1}\frac{1}{5} + \cos^{-1}\frac{7}{5\sqrt{2}} + 2\tan^{-1}\frac{1}{8}$

$$= \tan^{-1}\left(\frac{2\cdot\frac{1}{5}}{1-\frac{1}{25}}\right) + \tan^{-1}\left(\frac{\sqrt{1-\frac{49}{50}}}{\frac{7}{5\sqrt{2}}}\right) + \tan^{-1}\left(\frac{2\cdot\frac{1}{8}}{1-\frac{1}{64}}\right)$$

$$\left[\because 2\tan^{-1}x = \tan^{-1}\left(\frac{2x}{1-x^2}\right), -1 < x < 1\right.$$

$$\left.\text{and } \cos^{-1}x = \tan^{-1}\left(\frac{\sqrt{1-x^2}}{x}\right), 0 \le x \le 1\right]$$

$$= \tan^{-1}\left(\frac{2}{5}\times\frac{25}{24}\right) + \tan^{-1}\left(\frac{1}{5\sqrt{2}}\times\frac{5\sqrt{2}}{7}\right) + \tan^{-1}\left(\frac{1}{4}\times\frac{64}{63}\right)$$

$$= \tan^{-1}\left(\frac{5}{12}\right) + \tan^{-1}\left(\frac{1}{7}\right) + \tan^{-1}\left(\frac{16}{63}\right)$$

$$= \tan^{-1}\left(\frac{5}{12}\right) + \tan^{-1}\left(\frac{\frac{1}{7}+\frac{16}{63}}{1-\frac{1}{7}\times\frac{16}{63}}\right)$$

$$\left[\because \tan^{-1}x + \tan^{-1}y = \tan^{-1}\left(\frac{x+y}{1-xy}\right), xy < 1\right]$$

$$= \tan^{-1}\left(\frac{5}{12}\right) + \tan^{-1}\left(\frac{63+112}{441-16}\right) = \tan^{-1}\frac{5}{12} + \tan^{-1}\frac{175}{425}$$

$$= \tan^{-1}\frac{5}{12} + \tan^{-1}\frac{7}{17} = \tan^{-1}\left(\frac{\frac{5}{12}+\frac{7}{17}}{1-\frac{5}{12}\cdot\frac{7}{17}}\right)$$

$$\left[\because \tan^{-1}x + \tan^{-1}y = \tan^{-1}\left(\frac{x+y}{1-xy}\right), xy < 1\right]$$

$$= \tan^{-1}\left(\frac{85+84}{204-35}\right)$$

$$= \tan^{-1}\left(\frac{169}{169}\right) = \tan^{-1}(1) \qquad \left[\because \tan\frac{\pi}{4} = 1\right]$$

$$= \frac{\pi}{4} = \text{RHS}$$

Hence proved.

PROPERTY VIII

(i) $2\sin^{-1}x = \sin^{-1}(2x\sqrt{1-x^2})$, if $x \in \left[-\frac{1}{\sqrt{2}}, \frac{1}{\sqrt{2}}\right]$

(ii) $2\cos^{-1}x = \cos^{-1}(2x^2-1)$, if $x \in [0, 1]$

(iii) $3\sin^{-1}x = \sin^{-1}(3x-4x^3)$, if $x \in \left[-\frac{1}{2}, \frac{1}{2}\right]$

(iv) $3\cos^{-1}x = \cos^{-1}(4x^3-3x)$, if $x \in \left[\frac{1}{2}, 1\right]$

(v) $3\tan^{-1}x = \tan^{-1}\left(\frac{3x-x^3}{1-3x^2}\right)$, if $x \in \left(-\frac{1}{\sqrt{3}}, \frac{1}{\sqrt{3}}\right)$

Proof of part (i)

Let $\sin^{-1}x = y$, then $x = \sin y$.

Since, $-\frac{1}{\sqrt{2}} \le x \le \frac{1}{\sqrt{2}}$, therefore $-\frac{\pi}{4} \le y \le \frac{\pi}{4}$

Now, $\sin 2y = 2\sin y\cos y$

$$= 2\sin y\sqrt{1-\sin^2 y} = 2x\sqrt{1-x^2}$$

$$\left[\because \cos y > 0 \text{ for } y \in \left[-\frac{\pi}{4}, \frac{\pi}{4}\right]\right]$$

$$\Rightarrow \quad 2y = \sin^{-1}(2x\sqrt{1-x^2}) \qquad \left[\because -\frac{\pi}{2} \le 2y \le \frac{\pi}{2}\right]$$

$$\Rightarrow 2\sin^{-1}x = \sin^{-1}(2x\sqrt{1-x^2})$$

Similarly, we can prove the part (ii).

Proof of part (iii)

Let $\sin^{-1}x = \theta$, then $x = \sin\theta$.

Since, $x \in \left[-\frac{1}{2}, \frac{1}{2}\right]$, therefore $\theta \in \left[-\frac{\pi}{6}, \frac{\pi}{6}\right]$.

Now, $\sin 3\theta = 3\sin\theta - 4\sin^3\theta$

$$\Rightarrow \quad 3\theta = \sin^{-1}(3\sin\theta - 4\sin^3\theta)$$

$$\left[\because 3\theta \in \left[-\frac{\pi}{2}, \frac{\pi}{2}\right]\right]$$

$$= \sin^{-1}(3x-4x^3)$$

Similarly, we can prove the parts (iv) and (v).

Example 17 Find the value of $\sin\left[3\sin^{-1}\left(\frac{1}{5}\right)\right]$.

Sol. $\sin\left[3\sin^{-1}\left(\frac{1}{5}\right)\right]=\sin\left[\sin^{-1}\left\{3\left(\frac{1}{5}\right)-4\left(\frac{1}{5}\right)^3\right\}\right]$

$[\because 3\sin^{-1}x=\sin^{-1}(3x-4x^3)]$

$=\sin\left[\sin^{-1}\left(\frac{3}{5}-\frac{4}{125}\right)\right]=\sin\left[\sin^{-1}\left(\frac{71}{125}\right)\right]$

$=\frac{71}{125}$ $\quad[\because \sin(\sin^{-1}x)=x,\ x\in[-1,1]]$

PROPERTY IX

(i) $\sin^{-1}x\pm\sin^{-1}y=\sin^{-1}(x\sqrt{1-y^2}\pm y\sqrt{1-x^2})$,

if $|x|,|y|\le 1$ and $x^2+y^2\le 1$

(ii) $\cos^{-1}x+\cos^{-1}y=\cos^{-1}(xy-\sqrt{1-y^2}\sqrt{1-x^2})$,

if $|x|,|y|\le 1$ and $x+y\ge 0$.

(iii) $\cos^{-1}x-\cos^{-1}y=\cos^{-1}\{xy+\sqrt{1-x^2}\sqrt{1-y^2}\}$,

$|x|,|y|\le 1$ and $x\le y$.

Proof of part (i)

Let $\sin^{-1}x=\theta_1$ and $\sin^{-1}y=\theta_2$

$\Rightarrow\quad x=\sin\theta_1$ and $y=\sin\theta_2$

Now, $\sin(\theta_1\pm\theta_2)=\sin\theta_1\cos\theta_2\pm\cos\theta_1\sin\theta_2$

$=\sin\theta_1\sqrt{1-\sin^2\theta_2}\pm\sqrt{1-\sin^2\theta_1}\cdot\sin\theta_2$

$\left[\because \theta_1,\theta_2\in\left[-\frac{\pi}{2},\frac{\pi}{2}\right]\text{, therefore }\cos\theta_1,\cos\theta_2\ge 0\right]$

$=x\sqrt{1-y^2}\pm\sqrt{1-x^2}\cdot y$

$\Rightarrow \theta_1+\theta_2=\sin^{-1}(x\sqrt{1-y^2}\pm y\sqrt{1-x^2})$

$[\because x^2+y^2\le 1\Rightarrow 1-x^2\ge y^2$ and $1-y^2\ge x^2$

$\Rightarrow (1-x^2)(1-y^2)\ge x^2y^2\Rightarrow \sqrt{1-x^2}\sqrt{1-y^2}\ge xy$

$\Rightarrow\quad \sqrt{1-x^2}\sqrt{1-y^2}-xy\ge 0$

$\Rightarrow\quad \sqrt{1-\sin^2\theta_1}\sqrt{1-\sin^2\theta_2}-\sin\theta_1\sin\theta_2\ge 0$

$\Rightarrow\quad \cos\theta_1\cos\theta_2-\sin\theta_1\sin\theta_2\ge 0$

$\Rightarrow\quad \cos(\theta_1+\theta_2)\ge 0\Rightarrow(\theta_1+\theta_2)\in\left[-\frac{\pi}{2},\frac{\pi}{2}\right]]$

$\Rightarrow \sin^{-1}x\pm\sin^{-1}y=\sin^{-1}(x\sqrt{1-y^2}\pm y\sqrt{1-x^2})$

Similarly, we can prove the other parts.

Example 18 Find the value of

$$\sin^{-1}\left(\frac{1}{\sqrt5}\right)+\sin^{-1}\left(\frac{2}{\sqrt5}\right).$$

Sol. We have, $\sin^{-1}\left(\frac{1}{\sqrt5}\right)+\sin^{-1}\left(\frac{2}{\sqrt5}\right)$

We know that,

$\sin^{-1}x+\sin^{-1}y=\sin^{-1}(x\sqrt{1-y^2}\pm y\sqrt{1-x^2})$,

if $|x|,|y|\le 1$ and $x^2+y^2\le 1$

Here, $\quad x=\frac{1}{\sqrt5}\Rightarrow |x|\le 1$

and $\quad y=\frac{2}{\sqrt5}\Rightarrow |y|\le 1.$

and also, $x^2+y^2=\frac{1}{5}+\frac{4}{5}=1$

Now, $\sin^{-1}\left(\frac{1}{\sqrt5}\right)+\sin^{-1}\left(\frac{2}{\sqrt5}\right)$

$=\sin^{-1}\left[\frac{1}{\sqrt5}\sqrt{1-\left(\frac{2}{\sqrt5}\right)^2}+\frac{2}{\sqrt5}\sqrt{1-\left(\frac{1}{\sqrt5}\right)^2}\right]$

$=\sin^{-1}\left[\frac{1}{\sqrt5}\sqrt{\frac{5-4}{5}}+\frac{2}{\sqrt5}\sqrt{\frac{5-1}{5}}\right]$

$=\sin^{-1}\left[\frac{1}{\sqrt5}\cdot\frac{1}{\sqrt5}+\frac{2}{\sqrt5}\cdot\frac{2}{\sqrt5}\right]$

$=\sin^{-1}\left[\frac{1}{5}+\frac{4}{5}\right]=\sin^{-1}(1)=\frac{\pi}{2}$

Example 19 Prove that

$$\cos^{-1}\frac{63}{65}+2\tan^{-1}\frac{1}{5}=\sin^{-1}\frac{3}{5}.$$ **[ISC 2012]**

Sol. LHS $=\cos^{-1}\left(\frac{63}{65}\right)+2\tan^{-1}\left(\frac{1}{5}\right)$

$=\sin^{-1}\sqrt{1-\left(\frac{63}{65}\right)^2}+\sin^{-1}\left[\frac{2\times\frac{1}{5}}{1+\left(\frac{1}{5}\right)^2}\right]$

$\left[\because \cos^{-1}x=\sin^{-1}\sqrt{1-x^2},\ 0\le x\le 1\right.$

$\left.\text{and } 2\tan^{-1}x=\sin^{-1}\frac{2x}{1+x^2},-1\le x\le 1\right]$

$=\sin^{-1}\sqrt{\frac{(65)^2-(63)^2}{(65)^2}}+\sin^{-1}\left(\frac{\frac{2}{5}}{\frac{25+1}{25}}\right)$

$=\sin^{-1}\sqrt{\frac{(65-63)(65+63)}{(65)^2}}+\sin^{-1}\left(\frac{2}{5}\times\frac{25}{26}\right)$

$[\because a^2-b^2=(a-b)(a+b)]$

$$= \sin^{-1}\sqrt{\frac{2\times128}{(65)^2}} + \sin^{-1}\left(\frac{5}{13}\right)$$

$$= \sin^{-1}\sqrt{\frac{256}{(65)^2}} + \sin^{-1}\left(\frac{5}{13}\right) = \sin^{-1}\left(\frac{16}{65}\right) + \sin^{-1}\left(\frac{5}{13}\right)$$

$$= \sin^{-1}\left[\frac{16}{65}\sqrt{1-\left(\frac{5}{13}\right)^2} + \frac{5}{13}\sqrt{1-\left(\frac{16}{65}\right)^2}\right]$$

$$[\because \sin^{-1} A + \sin^{-1} B = \sin^{-1}(A\sqrt{1-B^2}) + B\sqrt{1-A^2})]$$

$$= \sin^{-1}\left[\frac{16}{65}\sqrt{\frac{13^2-5^2}{13^2}} + \frac{5}{13}\sqrt{\frac{65^2-16^2}{65^2}}\right]$$

$$= \sin^{-1}\left[\frac{16}{65}\sqrt{\frac{(13-5)(13+5)}{(13)^2}}\right] + \frac{5}{13}\sqrt{\frac{(65-16)(65+16)}{(65)^2}}$$

$$= \sin^{-1}\left[\frac{16}{65}\sqrt{\frac{8\times18}{(13)^2}} + \frac{5}{13}\sqrt{\frac{49\times81}{(65)^2}}\right]$$

$$= \sin^{-1}\left[\frac{16\times4\times3}{13\times65} + \frac{5}{13}\times\frac{7\times9}{65}\right]$$

$$= \sin^{-1}\left[\frac{192+315}{65\times13}\right] = \sin^{-1}\left(\frac{507}{65\times13}\right) = \sin^{-1}\left(\frac{3}{5}\right)$$

= RHS **Hence proved.**

Example 20 Prove that

$$\sin\left[2\tan^{-1}\frac{3}{5} - \sin^{-1}\frac{7}{25}\right] = \frac{304}{425}.$$ **[ISC 2010]**

Sol. We have to prove,

$$\sin\left[2\tan^{-1}\frac{3}{5} - \sin^{-1}\frac{7}{25}\right] = \frac{304}{425}$$

i.e. $2\tan^{-1}\frac{3}{5} - \sin^{-1}\frac{7}{25} = \sin^{-1}\frac{304}{425}$

Now, $\text{LHS} = 2\tan^{-1}\frac{3}{5} - \sin^{-1}\frac{7}{25}$

$$= \sin^{-1}\left(\frac{2\cdot\frac{3}{5}}{1+\frac{9}{25}}\right) - \sin^{-1}\frac{7}{25}$$

$$\left[\because 2\tan^{-1} x = \sin^{-1}\frac{2x}{1+x^2}, -1 \le x \le 1\right]$$

$$= \sin^{-1}\left(\frac{6/5}{34/25}\right) - \sin^{-1}\frac{7}{25}$$

$$= \sin^{-1}\frac{30}{34} - \sin^{-1}\frac{7}{25}$$

$$= \sin^{-1}\left[\frac{30}{34}\sqrt{1-\frac{49}{625}} - \frac{7}{25}\sqrt{1-\frac{900}{1156}}\right]$$

$$[\because \sin^{-1} x - \sin^{-1} y = \sin^{-1}(x\sqrt{1-y^2} - y\sqrt{1-x^2})$$
$$\text{if } |x|, |y| \le 1 \text{ and } x^2 + y^2 \le 1]$$

$$= \sin^{-1}\left[\frac{30}{34}\cdot\frac{24}{25} - \frac{7}{25}\cdot\frac{16}{34}\right]$$

$$= \sin^{-1}\left[\frac{720-112}{850}\right] = \sin^{-1}\frac{608}{850}$$

$$= \sin^{-1}\frac{304}{425} = \text{RHS}$$ **Hence proved.**

Example 21 If $\sin^{-1} x + \sin^{-1} y + \sin^{-1} z = \pi$, then prove that $x^2 - y^2 - z^2 + 2yz\sqrt{1-x^2} = 0$. **[ISC 2024, 09]**

Sol. Given, $\sin^{-1} x + \sin^{-1} y + \sin^{-1} z = \pi$

$$\Rightarrow \sin^{-1} x + \sin^{-1} y = \pi - \sin^{-1} z$$

$$\Rightarrow \sin^{-1}[x\sqrt{1-y^2} + y\sqrt{1-x^2}] = \pi - \sin^{-1} z$$

$$\Rightarrow x\sqrt{1-y^2} + y\sqrt{1-x^2} = \sin(\pi - \sin^{-1} z)$$

$$\Rightarrow x\sqrt{1-y^2} + y\sqrt{1-x^2} = \sin(\sin^{-1} z)$$

$$[\because \sin(\pi - \theta) = \sin\theta]$$

$$\Rightarrow x\sqrt{1-y^2} + y\sqrt{1-x^2} = z$$

$$\Rightarrow x\sqrt{1-y^2} = z - y\sqrt{1-x^2}$$

On squaring both sides, we get

$$x^2(1-y^2) = z^2 + y^2(1-x^2) - 2zy\sqrt{1-x^2}$$

$$\Rightarrow x^2 - x^2y^2 = z^2 + y^2 - x^2y^2 - 2zy\sqrt{1-x^2}$$

$$\therefore x^2 - y^2 - z^2 + 2zy\sqrt{1-x^2} = 0$$ **Hence proved.**

Different Problems Related to Inverse Trigonometric Functions

There are many problems, which are related to inverse trigonometric functions. Some of them can be divide in the following three types.

1. Problems Based on Simplest Form

In this type of problem, we have to write given inverse trigonometric function or expression in the simplest form. For this, we use some substitutions or trigonometric formulae and then apply properties of inverse trigonometric functions.

Trigonometric Substitution in Algebraic Expressions

S. No.	Expression	Substitution
1.	$\sqrt{1+x^2}$	$x=\tan\theta$ or $x=\cot\theta$
2.	$\sqrt{a^2+x^2}$	$x=a\tan\theta$ or $x=a\cot\theta$
3.	$\sqrt{1-x^2}$	$x=\sin\theta$ or $x=\cos\theta$
4.	$\sqrt{a^2-x^2}$	$x=a\sin\theta$ or $x=a\cos\theta$
5.	$\sqrt{x^2-1}$	$x=\sec\theta$ or $x=\operatorname{cosec}\theta$
6.	$\sqrt{x^2-a^2}$	$x=a\sec\theta$ or $x=a\operatorname{cosec}\theta$
7.	$\sqrt{1+x^2}\pm\sqrt{1-x^2}, \sqrt{\frac{1+x^2}{1-x^2}}, \sqrt{\frac{1-x^2}{1+x^2}}$	$x^2=\cos 2\theta$
8.	$\sqrt{a^2+x^2}\pm\sqrt{a^2-x^2}, \sqrt{\frac{a^2+x^2}{a^2-x^2}}, \sqrt{\frac{a^2-x^2}{a^2+x^2}}$	$x^2=a^2\cos 2\theta$
9.	$\sqrt{1+x}\pm\sqrt{1-x}, \sqrt{\frac{1+x}{1-x}}, \sqrt{\frac{1-x}{1+x}}$	$x=\cos 2\theta$
10.	$\sqrt{a+x}\pm\sqrt{a-x}, \sqrt{\frac{a+x}{a-x}}, \sqrt{\frac{a-x}{a+x}}$	$x=a\cos 2\theta$

Important Formulae Related to Trigonometric Functions

(i) $\sin^2\theta+\cos^2\theta=1$

(ii) $1+\tan^2\theta=\sec^2\theta$

(iii) $1+\cot^2\theta=\operatorname{cosec}^2\theta$

(iv) $\sin 2\theta=2\sin\theta\cos\theta$

(v) $\cos 2\theta=\cos^2\theta-\sin^2\theta=1-2\sin^2\theta=2\cos^2\theta-1$

(vi) $\tan 2\theta=\dfrac{2\tan\theta}{1-\tan^2\theta}$

(vii) $1+\cos 2\theta=2\cos^2\theta$, $1-\cos 2\theta=2\sin^2\theta$

(viii) $1\pm\sin 2\theta=(\cos\theta\pm\sin\theta)^2$

(ix) $\sin 2\theta=\dfrac{2\tan\theta}{1+\tan^2\theta}$, $\cos 2\theta=\dfrac{1-\tan^2\theta}{1+\tan^2\theta}$

(x) $\sin 3\theta=3\sin\theta-4\sin^3\theta$, $\cos 3\theta=4\cos^3\theta-3\cos\theta$

(xi) $\tan 3\theta=\dfrac{3\tan\theta-\tan^3\theta}{1-3\tan^2\theta}$

Example 22 Express the expression in simplest form $\tan^{-1}\left[\dfrac{x}{a+\sqrt{a^2-x^2}}\right]$.

Sol. Let $y=\tan^{-1}\left[\dfrac{x}{a+\sqrt{a^2-x^2}}\right]$

Put $x=a\sin\theta$, then $\theta=\sin^{-1}\left(\dfrac{x}{a}\right)$

Now, $y=\tan^{-1}\left[\dfrac{a\sin\theta}{a+\sqrt{a^2-a^2\sin^2\theta}}\right]$

$=\tan^{-1}\left[\dfrac{a\sin\theta}{a+a\sqrt{1-\sin^2\theta}}\right]$

$=\tan^{-1}\left[\dfrac{a\sin\theta}{a(1+\cos\theta)}\right]$

$[\because \sqrt{1-\sin^2\theta}=\sqrt{\cos^2\theta}=\cos\theta]$

$=\tan^{-1}\left[\dfrac{2\sin\frac{\theta}{2}\cos\frac{\theta}{2}}{2\cos^2\frac{\theta}{2}}\right]$

$[\because \sin 2\theta=2\sin\theta\cos\theta \text{ and } 1+\cos 2\theta=2\cos^2\theta]$

$=\tan^{-1}\left(\tan\dfrac{\theta}{2}\right)$

$=\dfrac{\theta}{2}=\dfrac{1}{2}\sin^{-1}\left(\dfrac{x}{a}\right)$ [substituting the value of θ]

Example 23 Write in simplest form

$\tan^{-1}\left[\dfrac{3a^2x-x^3}{a^3-3ax^2}\right]$, $a>0-\dfrac{a}{\sqrt{3}}<x<\dfrac{a}{\sqrt{3}}$. **[NCERT]**

Sol. Let $y=\tan^{-1}\left[\dfrac{3a^2x-x^3}{a^3-3ax^2}\right]$

$=\tan^{-1}\left[\dfrac{3\left(\frac{x}{a}\right)-\left(\frac{x}{a}\right)^3}{1-3\left(\frac{x}{a}\right)^2}\right]$

[dividing numerator and denominator by a^3]

Put $\dfrac{x}{a}=\tan\theta$, then $\theta=\tan^{-1}\left(\dfrac{x}{a}\right)$

Now, $y=\tan^{-1}\left[\dfrac{3\tan\theta-\tan^3\theta}{1-3\tan^2\theta}\right]=\tan^{-1}(\tan 3\theta)$

$\left[\because \tan 3\theta=\dfrac{3\tan\theta-\tan^3\theta}{1-3\tan^2\theta}\right]$

$$= 3\theta \left[\because -\frac{1}{\sqrt{3}} < \frac{x}{a} < \frac{1}{\sqrt{3}} \Rightarrow -\frac{\pi}{6} < \theta < \frac{\pi}{6} \Rightarrow -\frac{\pi}{2} < 3\theta < \frac{\pi}{2}\right]$$

$$= 3\tan^{-1}\left(\frac{x}{a}\right) \quad \text{[substituting the value of } \theta]$$

2. Problems Based on Proving/Showing the Given Result

In this type of problem, we have to prove/show the given result. For this, we take LHS (or sometime RHS) of given equation and simplify it by using properties of inverse trigonometric functions or by using trigonometric formulae or by using substitution to get value equal to RHS (or sometime LHS).

Example 24 Prove that

$$\cos^{-1}(x) + \cos^{-1}\left\{\frac{x}{2} + \frac{\sqrt{3-3x^2}}{2}\right\} = \frac{\pi}{3},\ x \in \left[\frac{1}{2}, 1\right].$$

Sol. LHS $= \cos^{-1}(x) + \cos^{-1}\left\{\frac{x}{2} + \frac{\sqrt{3-3x^2}}{2}\right\}$

Let $\cos^{-1}x = \alpha \Rightarrow x = \cos\alpha$

Then, LHS $= \alpha + \cos^{-1}\left[\cos\alpha \cdot \cos\frac{\pi}{3} + \frac{\sqrt{3}}{2}\sqrt{1-\cos^2\alpha}\right]$

$$= \alpha + \cos^{-1}\left[\cos\frac{\pi}{3}\cos\alpha + \sin\frac{\pi}{3}\sin\alpha\right]$$

$$\left[\because \sin\alpha = \sqrt{1-\cos^2\alpha} \text{ and } \sin\frac{\pi}{3} = \frac{\sqrt{3}}{2}\right]$$

$$= \alpha + \cos^{-1}\left[\cos\left(\frac{\pi}{3} - \alpha\right)\right]$$

$$[\because \cos(A-B) = \cos A\cos B + \sin A\sin B]$$

$$= \alpha + \frac{\pi}{3} - \alpha$$

$$\left[\because \frac{1}{2} \le x \le 1 \Rightarrow 0 \le \alpha \le \frac{\pi}{3} \Rightarrow 0 \le \frac{\pi}{3} - \alpha \le \frac{\pi}{3}\right]$$

$$= \frac{\pi}{3} = \text{RHS}$$

Hence proved.

Example 25 Prove that

$$\cot^{-1}\left[\frac{\sqrt{1+\sin x} + \sqrt{1-\sin x}}{\sqrt{1+\sin x} - \sqrt{1-\sin x}}\right] = \frac{x}{2},\ x \in \left(0, \frac{\pi}{4}\right).$$

[NCERT]

Sol. LHS $= \cot^{-1}\left[\frac{\sqrt{1+\sin x} + \sqrt{1-\sin x}}{\sqrt{1+\sin x} - \sqrt{1-\sin x}}\right]$

Consider, $\sqrt{1+\sin x} = \sqrt{\cos^2\frac{x}{2} + \sin^2\frac{x}{2} + 2\sin\frac{x}{2}\cos\frac{x}{2}}$

$$= \sqrt{\left(\cos\frac{x}{2} + \sin\frac{x}{2}\right)^2} = \cos\frac{x}{2} + \sin\frac{x}{2}$$

Similarly, $\sqrt{1-\sin x} = \sqrt{\cos^2\frac{x}{2} + \sin^2\frac{x}{2} - 2\sin\frac{x}{2}\cos\frac{x}{2}}$

$$= \sqrt{\left(\cos\frac{x}{2} - \sin\frac{x}{2}\right)^2} = \cos\frac{x}{2} - \sin\frac{x}{2}$$

$$\left[\because x \in \left(0, \frac{\pi}{4}\right), \text{ therefore } \cos\frac{x}{2} > \sin\frac{x}{2} \text{ and so } \sqrt{\left(\cos\frac{x}{2} - \sin\frac{x}{2}\right)^2} = \cos\frac{x}{2} - \sin\frac{x}{2}\right]$$

Now, LHS $= \cot^{-1}\left[\frac{\sqrt{1+\sin x} + \sqrt{1-\sin x}}{\sqrt{1+\sin x} - \sqrt{1-\sin x}}\right]$

$$= \cot^{-1}\left[\frac{\left(\cos\frac{x}{2} + \sin\frac{x}{2}\right) + \left(\cos\frac{x}{2} - \sin\frac{x}{2}\right)}{\left(\cos\frac{x}{2} + \sin\frac{x}{2}\right) - \left(\cos\frac{x}{2} - \sin\frac{x}{2}\right)}\right]$$

$$= \cot^{-1}\left[\frac{2\cos\frac{x}{2}}{2\sin\frac{x}{2}}\right] = \cot^{-1}\left[\cot\frac{x}{2}\right] = \frac{x}{2} = \text{RHS}$$

Hence proved.

Note For $x \in \left[0, \frac{\pi}{2}\right]$, $\sqrt{\left(\cos\frac{x}{2} - \sin\frac{x}{2}\right)^2} = \cos\frac{x}{2} - \sin\frac{x}{2}$

and for $x \in \left[\frac{\pi}{2}, \pi\right]$, $\sqrt{\left(\cos\frac{x}{2} - \sin\frac{x}{2}\right)^2} = -\left(\cos\frac{x}{2} - \sin\frac{x}{2}\right)$.

3. Problems Based on Finding the Value of *x*

In this type of problem an equation in *x*, formed by inverse trigonometric functions, is given to us and we have to solve it to find the value of *x*.

Example 26 If $\sin\left(\sin^{-1}\frac{1}{5} + \cos^{-1}x\right) = 1$, then find the value of *x*. **[NCERT]**

Sol. We have, $\sin\left(\sin^{-1}\frac{1}{5} + \cos^{-1}x\right) = 1$

$$\Rightarrow \sin^{-1}\frac{1}{5} + \cos^{-1}x = \sin^{-1}(1)$$

$$[\because \sin\theta = x \Rightarrow \theta = \sin^{-1}x]$$

$$\Rightarrow \sin^{-1}\frac{1}{5} + \cos^{-1}x = \sin^{-1}\left(\sin\frac{\pi}{2}\right) \quad \left[\because \sin\frac{\pi}{2} = 1\right]$$

$$\Rightarrow \sin^{-1}\frac{1}{5} + \cos^{-1}x = \frac{\pi}{2} \quad [\because \sin^{-1}(\sin\theta) = \theta]$$

But we know that, $\sin^{-1}x + \cos^{-1}x = \frac{\pi}{2},\ x \in [-1, 1]$

$$\therefore \quad \sin^{-1}\frac{1}{5} = \sin^{-1}x \Rightarrow x = \frac{1}{5}$$

Example 27 Solve the following equation.

$$\cos(\tan^{-1}x) = \sin\left(\cot^{-1}\frac{3}{4}\right)$$ **[NCERT Exemplar]**

Sol. Given, $\cos(\tan^{-1}x) = \sin\left(\cot^{-1}\frac{3}{4}\right)$

$\Rightarrow \sin\left\{\frac{\pi}{2} - \tan^{-1}x\right\} = \sin\left(\cot^{-1}\frac{3}{4}\right)$

$\left[\because \sin\left(\frac{\pi}{2} - \theta\right) = \cos\theta\right]$

On comparing both sides, we get

$\frac{\pi}{2} - \tan^{-1}x = \cot^{-1}\frac{3}{4}$

$\Rightarrow \cot^{-1}x = \cot^{-1}\frac{3}{4}$ $\left[\because \tan^{-1}x + \cot^{-1}x = \frac{\pi}{2}\right]$

Again, comparing both sides, we get $x = \frac{3}{4}$

Example 28 Solve for x : $5\tan^{-1}x + 3\cot^{-1}x = 2\pi$. **[ISC 2023]**

Sol. Given, $5\tan^{-1}x + 3\cot^{-1}x = 2\pi$

$\Rightarrow 2\tan^{-1}x + 3(\tan^{-1}x + \cot^{-1}x) = 2\pi$

$\Rightarrow 2\tan^{-1}x + 3\left(\frac{\pi}{2}\right) = 2\pi$

$\left[\because \tan^{-1}\theta + \cot^{-1}\theta = \frac{\pi}{2}\right]$

$\Rightarrow 2\tan^{-1}x = 2\pi - \frac{3\pi}{2}$

$\Rightarrow 2\tan^{-1}x = \frac{\pi}{2}$

$\Rightarrow \tan^{-1}x = \frac{\pi}{4} \Rightarrow x = \tan\frac{\pi}{4} = 1$

Example 29 If $\sin^{-1}x + \tan^{-1}x = \frac{\pi}{2}$, then prove that $2x^2 + 1 = \sqrt{5}$. **[ISC 2016]**

Sol. Given, $\sin^{-1}x + \tan^{-1}x = \frac{\pi}{2}$

$\Rightarrow \tan^{-1}x = \left(\frac{\pi}{2} - \sin^{-1}x\right)$

$\Rightarrow \tan^{-1}x = \cos^{-1}x$ $\left[\because \cos^{-1}x + \sin^{-1}x = \frac{\pi}{2}\right]$

$\Rightarrow \tan^{-1}x = \tan^{-1}\frac{\sqrt{1-x^2}}{x}$

$\left[\because \cos^{-1}x = \tan^{-1}\frac{\sqrt{1-x^2}}{x}\right]$

$\Rightarrow x = \tan\left(\tan^{-1}\frac{\sqrt{1-x^2}}{x}\right)$

$\Rightarrow x = \frac{\sqrt{1-x^2}}{x}$ $[\because \tan(\tan^{-1}x) = x]$

$\Rightarrow x^2 = \sqrt{1-x^2}$

$\Rightarrow (x^2)^2 = 1 - x^2$ [squaring on both sides]

$\Rightarrow x^4 = 1 - x^2$

$\Rightarrow x^4 + x^2 - 1 = 0$

$\therefore x^2 = \frac{-1 \pm \sqrt{5}}{2}$ $\left[\because x = \frac{-b \pm \sqrt{b^2 - 4ac}}{2a}\right]$

$\Rightarrow 2x^2 + 1 = \pm\sqrt{5}$

$\Rightarrow 2x^2 + 1 = \sqrt{5}$

$[\because 2x^2 + 1 > 0 \Rightarrow 2x^2 + 1 = -\sqrt{5}$, which is not possible$]$

Hence proved.

Example 30 Find the minimum value of n for which $\tan^{-1}\left(\frac{n}{\pi}\right) > \frac{\pi}{4}$, $n \in N$ is valid. **[NCERT Exemplar]**

Sol. Given, $\tan^{-1}\left(\frac{n}{\pi}\right) > \frac{\pi}{4}$

$\Rightarrow \frac{n}{\pi} > \tan\frac{\pi}{4}$ $[\because \tan^{-1}\theta > \phi \Rightarrow \theta > \tan\phi]$

$\Rightarrow \frac{n}{\pi} > 1 \Rightarrow n > \pi$

$\Rightarrow n > 3.14$ $[\because \pi \approx 3.14]$

Hence, the minimum value of n is 4.

Example 31 Find the number of real solutions of the equation $\sqrt{1 + \cos 2x} = \sqrt{2}\cos^{-1}(\cos x)$ in $\left[\frac{\pi}{2}, \pi\right]$. **[NCERT Exemplar]**

Sol. Given, $\sqrt{1 + \cos 2x} = \sqrt{2}\cos^{-1}(\cos x)$, $\left[\frac{\pi}{2}, \pi\right]$

$\therefore \sqrt{1 + 2\cos^2 x - 1} = \sqrt{2}\cos^{-1}(\cos x)$

$\Rightarrow -\sqrt{2}\cos x = \sqrt{2}\cos^{-1}(\cos x)$

$\left[\because \cos x < 0 \text{ for } x \in \left[\frac{\pi}{2}, \pi\right]\right]$

$\Rightarrow -\cos x = x$ $[\because \cos^{-1}(\cos x) = x, \forall x \in [0, \pi]]$

which is not true for any $x \in \left[\frac{\pi}{2}, \pi\right]$.

Hence, no real solution exists in the given interval.

Topic Practice 2

Very Short Answer Type Questions

2 Marks

1 Evaluate the following.

(i) $\sin^{-1}\left(\sin\frac{\pi}{3}\right)$ (ii) $\cos^{-1}\left(\cos\frac{2\pi}{3}\right)$

(iii) $\tan^{-1}\left(\tan\frac{\pi}{8}\right)$ (iv) $\sec(\sec^{-1}2)$

2 Show that $\sin^{-1}\frac{\sqrt{3}}{2}+2\tan^{-1}\frac{1}{\sqrt{3}}=\frac{2\pi}{3}$. **[ISC 2002]**

3 Find the value of $\sin^{-1}\left[\cos\left(\frac{33\pi}{5}\right)\right]$.

4 Solve $3\tan^{-1}x+\cot^{-1}x=\pi$. **[ISC 2018]**

5 Evaluate $\cot\left[\cos^{-1}\left(\frac{7}{25}\right)\right]$. **[NCERT Exemplar]**

6 Prove that $\tan^{-1}x+\tan^{-1}\left(\frac{2x}{1-x^2}\right)$

$=\tan^{-1}\left(\frac{3x-x^3}{1-3x^2}\right), |x|<\frac{1}{\sqrt{3}}$. **[NCERT]**

7 Evaluate $\tan\left(2\tan^{-1}\frac{1}{3}\right)$.

8 Find the value of $\cot\left(\frac{\pi}{2}-2\cot^{-1}\sqrt{3}\right)$.

9 Write $\cot^{-1}\left(\frac{1}{\sqrt{x^2-1}}\right), x>1$ in simplest form.

10 Simplify $\tan^{-1}\left[\sqrt{\frac{1-\cos x}{1+\cos x}}\right], 0<x<\pi$. **[NCERT]**

11 Write $\tan^{-1}\left(\frac{\cos x-\sin x}{\cos x+\sin x}\right), -\frac{\pi}{4}<x<\frac{3\pi}{4}$ in the simplest form. **[NCERT]**

12 Prove that $\tan^2(\sec^{-1}2)+\cot^2(\text{cosec}^{-1}3)=11$. **[ISC 2020]**

13 Solve for x, $\sin(2\tan^{-1}x)=1$. **[ISC 2019, 11]**

Short Answer Type Questions

4 Marks

14 If $\cos^{-1}\alpha+\cos^{-1}\beta+\cos^{-1}\gamma=3\pi$, then find $\alpha(\beta+\gamma)+\beta(\gamma+\alpha)+\gamma(\alpha+\beta)$. **[NCERT Exemplar]**

15 Prove that $\frac{9\pi}{8}-\frac{9}{4}\sin^{-1}\left(\frac{1}{3}\right)=\frac{9}{4}\sin^{-1}\left(\frac{2\sqrt{2}}{3}\right)$. **[NCERT]**

16 Prove that $\tan^{-1}\frac{1}{2}+\tan^{-1}\frac{1}{5}+\tan^{-1}\frac{1}{8}=\frac{\pi}{4}$.

17 Prove that $\cot^{-1}7+\cot^{-1}8+\cot^{-1}18=\cot^{-1}3$.

18 If $\tan^{-1}x+\tan^{-1}y=\frac{\pi}{4}$; $xy<1$, then write the value of $x+y+xy$.

19 Prove that $\tan^{-1}\left(\frac{1}{4}\right)+\tan^{-1}\left(\frac{2}{9}\right)=\frac{1}{2}\tan^{-1}\left(\frac{4}{3}\right)$.

20 Prove that $\tan^{-1}\frac{1}{4}+\tan^{-1}\frac{2}{9}=\frac{1}{2}\sin^{-1}\frac{4}{5}$. **[ISC 2013]**

21 Find the value of the expression $\sin\left(2\tan^{-1}\frac{1}{3}\right)+\cos(\tan^{-1}2\sqrt{2})$. **[NCERT Exemplar]**

22 Prove that $2\tan^{-1}\left(\frac{1}{2}\right)+\tan^{-1}\left(\frac{1}{7}\right)=\tan^{-1}\left(\frac{31}{17}\right)$.

23 Prove that $2\tan^{-1}\left(\frac{3}{4}\right)-\tan^{-1}\left(\frac{17}{31}\right)=\frac{\pi}{4}$.

24 Prove that $2\sin^{-1}\left(\frac{3}{5}\right)-\tan^{-1}\left(\frac{17}{31}\right)=\frac{\pi}{4}$.

25 Show that $\sin^{-1}\left(\frac{8}{17}\right)+\sin^{-1}\left(\frac{3}{5}\right)=\cos^{-1}\left(\frac{36}{85}\right)$.

26 Show that $\sin^{-1}\left(\frac{3}{5}\right)-\sin^{-1}\left(\frac{8}{17}\right)=\cos^{-1}\left(\frac{84}{85}\right)$. **[NCERT]**

27 Show that $\tan\left(\frac{1}{2}\sin^{-1}\frac{3}{4}\right)=\frac{4-\sqrt{7}}{3}$. **[NCERT Exemplar]**

28 Prove that $\cot\left(\frac{\pi}{4}-2\cot^{-1}3\right)=7$. **[ISC 2005]**

29 Prove that $\tan^{-1}\left(\frac{\sqrt{1+x^2}+\sqrt{1-x^2}}{\sqrt{1+x^2}-\sqrt{1-x^2}}\right)=\frac{\pi}{4}+\frac{1}{2}\cos^{-1}x^2$. **[NCERT Exemplar]**

30 Prove that $\tan^{-1}\left(\frac{\sqrt{1+x}-\sqrt{1-x}}{\sqrt{1+x}+\sqrt{1-x}}\right)=\frac{\pi}{4}-\frac{1}{2}\cos^{-1}x$, where $-\frac{1}{\sqrt{2}}\le x\le 1$.

31 Solve $\cos^{-1}[\sin(\cos^{-1}x)]=\frac{\pi}{3}$. **[ISC 2010]**

32 Solve for x, $\cos(2\sin^{-1}x)=\frac{1}{9}, x>0$.

33 Solve for x,

$\tan^{-1}\left(\frac{2x}{1-x^2}\right)+\cot^{-1}\left(\frac{1-x^2}{2x}\right)=\frac{\pi}{3}, -1<x<1$.

34 If $\sin^{-1}(1-x) - 2\sin^{-1}x = \frac{\pi}{2}$, then find the value of x. **[NCERT]**

35 Solve for x, $\sin^{-1}\left(\frac{x}{2}\right) + \cos^{-1}x = \frac{\pi}{6}$. **[ISC 2024]**

36 If $\sin[\cot^{-1}(x+1)] = \cos(\tan^{-1}x)$, then find x.

37 If $\tan^{-1}\left(\frac{x-2}{x-4}\right) + \tan^{-1}\left(\frac{x+2}{x+4}\right) = \frac{\pi}{4}$, then find the value of x.

38 If $\tan^{-1}\left(\frac{x-2}{x-1}\right) + \tan^{-1}\left(\frac{x+2}{x+1}\right) = \frac{\pi}{4}$, then find the value of x.

39 Solve for x, $2\tan^{-1}(\cos x) = \tan^{-1}(2\operatorname{cosec} x)$. **[NCERT]**

40 Solve for x, $2\tan^{-1}(\sin x) = \tan^{-1}(2\sec x), x \neq \frac{\pi}{2}$.

41 Solve following equation for x.

$$\tan^{-1}\left(\frac{1-x}{1+x}\right) = \frac{1}{2}\tan^{-1}x, x > 0$$

Long Answer Type Questions

6 Marks

42 Find the value of x, satisfying

$$\sin^{-1}\left(\frac{2a}{1+a^2}\right) + \cos^{-1}\left(\frac{1-a^2}{1+a^2}\right) = \tan^{-1}\left(\frac{2x}{1-x^2}\right).$$

[NCERT Exemplar]

43 Prove that

$$2\tan^{-1}\left(\frac{1}{5}\right) + \sec^{-1}\left(\frac{5\sqrt{2}}{7}\right) + 2\tan^{-1}\left(\frac{1}{8}\right) = \frac{\pi}{4}.$$

44 If $\cos^{-1}x + \cos^{-1}y + \cos^{-1}z = \pi$, then show that $x^2 + y^2 + z^2 + 2xyz = 1$. **[ISC 2014]**

45 If $\cos^{-1}\frac{x}{a} + \cos^{-1}\frac{y}{b} = \theta$, then prove that

$$\frac{x^2}{a^2} - \frac{2xy}{ab}\cos\theta + \frac{y^2}{b^2} = \sin^2\theta.$$

46 Solve for x, $\tan^{-1}(x-1) + \tan^{-1}x + \tan^{-1}(x+1) = \tan^{-1}3x$. **[ISC 2008]**

47 Solve for x, $\sin^{-1}x + \sin^{-1}(1-x) = \cos^{-1}x$. **[ISC 2017, 2013]**

Hints & Solutions

1. (i) $\sin^{-1}\left(\sin\frac{\pi}{3}\right) = \frac{\pi}{3}$, as $\frac{\pi}{3} \in \left[-\frac{\pi}{2}, \frac{\pi}{2}\right]$ [1/2]

(ii) $\cos^{-1}\left(\cos\frac{2\pi}{2}\right) = \frac{2\pi}{3}$, as $\frac{2\pi}{3} \in [0, \pi]$ [1/2]

(iii) $\tan^{-1}\left(\tan\frac{\pi}{8}\right) = \frac{\pi}{8}$, as $\frac{\pi}{8} \in \left(-\frac{\pi}{2}, \frac{\pi}{2}\right)$ [1/2]

(iv) $\sec(\sec^{-1}2) = 2$, as $2 \in (-\infty, \infty) - (-1, 1)$ [1/2]

2. LHS $= \sin^{-1}\frac{\sqrt{3}}{2} + 2\tan^{-1}\frac{1}{\sqrt{3}}$

$= \sin^{-1}\left(\sin\frac{\pi}{3}\right) + 2\tan^{-1}\left(\tan\frac{\pi}{6}\right)$

$\left[\because \sin\frac{\pi}{3} = \frac{\sqrt{3}}{2} \text{ and } \tan\frac{\pi}{6} = \frac{1}{\sqrt{3}}\right]$ [1]

$= \frac{\pi}{3} + 2\cdot\frac{\pi}{6} = \frac{\pi}{3} + \frac{\pi}{3}$

$\left[\because \sin^{-1}(\sin\theta) = \theta \text{ and } \tan^{-1}(\tan\theta) = \theta, \forall\theta \in \left(-\frac{\pi}{2}, \frac{\pi}{2}\right)\right]$

$= \frac{2\pi}{3} =$ RHS **Hence proved.** [1]

3. $\sin^{-1}\left[\cos\left(\frac{33\pi}{5}\right)\right] = \sin^{-1}\left[\cos\left(6\pi + \frac{3\pi}{5}\right)\right]$

$= \sin^{-1}\left[\cos\frac{3\pi}{5}\right]$ $[\because \cos(2n\pi + \theta) = \cos\theta]$

$= \sin^{-1}\left[\cos\left(\frac{\pi}{2} + \frac{\pi}{10}\right)\right]$

$= \sin^{-1}\left[-\sin\left(\frac{\pi}{10}\right)\right]$ [1]

$= -\sin^{-1}\left(\sin\frac{\pi}{10}\right)$ $[\because \sin^{-1}(-x) = -\sin^{-1}x]$

$= -\frac{\pi}{10}$ $\left[\because \sin^{-1}(\sin\theta) = \theta, \theta \in \left[-\frac{\pi}{2}, \frac{\pi}{2}\right]\right]$ [1]

4. We have, $3\tan^{-1}x + \cot^{-1}x = \pi$

$\Rightarrow 3\tan^{-1}x + \frac{\pi}{2} - \tan^{-1}x = \pi$

$\left[\because \tan^{-1}x + \cot^{-1}x = \frac{\pi}{2}\right]$ [1]

$\Rightarrow 2\tan^{-1}x = \frac{\pi}{2} \Rightarrow \tan^{-1}x = \frac{\pi}{4}$

$\Rightarrow x = \tan\frac{\pi}{4}$

$\Rightarrow x = 1$ [1]

5. Clearly, $\cot\left[\cos^{-1}\left(\frac{7}{25}\right)\right] = \cot\left[\tan^{-1}\left(\frac{\sqrt{1-(7/25)^2}}{7/25}\right)\right]$

$\left[\because \cos^{-1}x = \tan^{-1}\frac{\sqrt{1-x^2}}{x}, 0 \le x \le 1\right]$ [1]

$= \cot\left[\cot^{-1}\left(\frac{7/25}{\sqrt{1-(7/25)^2}}\right)\right]$ [1/2]

$= \frac{7/25}{24/25} = \frac{7}{24}$ [1/2]

6. LHS $= \tan^{-1}x + \tan^{-1}\left(\frac{2x}{1-x^2}\right) = \tan^{-1}\left[\frac{x+\frac{2x}{1-x^2}}{1-x\left(\frac{2x}{1-x^2}\right)}\right]$

$\left[\because \tan^{-1}x + \tan^{-1}y = \tan^{-1}\left(\frac{x+y}{1-xy}\right), \text{ if } xy < 1 \right.$
$\left. \text{and here } |x| < \frac{1}{\sqrt{3}} \Rightarrow x^2 < \frac{1}{3} \Rightarrow 2x^2 < \frac{2}{3} \text{ and } 1 - x^2 > \frac{2}{3}\right]$ [1]

$= \tan^{-1}\left[\frac{\left(\frac{x - x^3 + 2x}{1-x^2}\right)}{\left(\frac{1-x^2-2x^2}{1-x^2}\right)}\right]$

$= \tan^{-1}\left[\frac{3x - x^3}{1-3x^2}\right]$ = RHS **Hence proved.** [1]

7. Use the formula $2kn^{-1}x = kn^{-1}\left(\frac{2x}{1-x^2}\right)$ $\left[\textbf{Ans. } \frac{3}{4}\right]$

8. $\cot\left(\frac{\pi}{2} - 2\cot^{-1}\sqrt{3}\right) = \tan(2\cot^{-1}\sqrt{3})$ [1/2]

$= \tan\left(2\tan^{-1}\frac{1}{\sqrt{3}}\right) = \tan\left[\tan^{-1}\frac{2\times\frac{1}{\sqrt{3}}}{1-\left(\frac{1}{\sqrt{3}}\right)^2}\right]$ [1]

$\left[\because 2\tan^{-1}x = \tan^{-1}\left(\frac{2x}{1-x^2}\right), -1 < x < 1\right]$

$= \tan\left[\tan^{-1}\left(\frac{2/\sqrt{3}}{1-(1/3)}\right)\right] = \tan[\tan^{-1}(\sqrt{3})] = \sqrt{3}$ [1/2]

9. Put $x = \sec\theta$, then $\theta = \sec^{-1}x$.

Also, as $x > 1$, therefore $\theta \in \left(0, \frac{\pi}{2}\right)$. [1]

Now, $\cot^{-1}\left(\frac{1}{\sqrt{x^2-1}}\right) = \cot^{-1}\left(\frac{1}{\sqrt{\sec^2\theta - 1}}\right) = \cot^{-1}\left(\frac{1}{|\tan\theta|}\right)$

$= \cot^{-1}\left(\frac{1}{\tan\theta}\right)$ $\left[\because \tan\theta > 0 \text{ for } \theta \in \left(0, \frac{\pi}{2}\right)\right]$

$= \cot^{-1}(\cot\theta) = \theta = \sec^{-1}x$ [1]

10. We have, $\tan^{-1}\left[\sqrt{\frac{1-\cos x}{1+\cos x}}\right] = \tan^{-1}\left[\sqrt{\frac{2\sin^2 x/2}{2\cos^2 x/2}}\right]$

$\left[\because 1 - \cos\theta = 2\sin^2\frac{\theta}{2}, 1 + \cos\theta = 2\cos^2\frac{\theta}{2}\right]$

$= \tan^{-1}[\sqrt{\tan^2 x/2}]$ [1]

$= \tan^{-1}\left(\left|\tan\frac{x}{2}\right|\right) = \tan^{-1}\left(\tan\frac{x}{2}\right)$

$\left[\because 0 < x < \pi \Rightarrow 0 < \frac{x}{2} < \frac{\pi}{2} \text{ and thus } \tan\frac{x}{2} > 0\right]$

$= \frac{x}{2}$ [1]

11. Let $y = \tan^{-1}\left(\frac{\cos x - \sin x}{\cos x + \sin x}\right)$

On dividing numerator and denominator by $\cos x$ inside the bracket, we get

$y = \tan^{-1}\left[\frac{\frac{\cos x}{\cos x} - \frac{\sin x}{\cos x}}{\frac{\cos x}{\cos x} + \frac{\sin x}{\cos x}}\right] = \tan^{-1}\left(\frac{1-\tan x}{1+\tan x}\right)$ [1]

$= \tan^{-1}\left[\tan\left(\frac{\pi}{4} - x\right)\right]$ $\left[\because \tan\left(\frac{\pi}{4} - x\right) = \frac{1-\tan x}{1+\tan x}\right]$

$= \frac{\pi}{4} - x$ $\left[\begin{array}{l}\because \tan^{-1}(\tan\theta), \forall \theta \in \left(-\frac{\pi}{2}, \frac{\pi}{2}\right) \\ \text{and here } -\frac{\pi}{4} < x < \frac{3\pi}{4} \\ \Rightarrow -\frac{3\pi}{4} < -x < \frac{\pi}{4} \Rightarrow -\frac{\pi}{2} < \frac{\pi}{4} - x < \frac{\pi}{2}\end{array}\right]$ [1]

12. We have,

LHS $= \tan^2(\sec^{-1}2) + \cot^2(\text{cosec}^{-1}3)$

$= (\sec(\sec^{-1}2))^2 - 1 + (\text{cosec}(\text{cosec}^{-1}3))^2 - 1$

$[\because \tan^2\theta = \sec^2\theta - 1 \text{ and } \cot^2\theta = \text{cosec}^2\theta - 1]$

$= (2)^2 - 1 + (3)^2 - 1$

$[\because \sec(\sec^{-1}\theta) = \theta \text{ and cosec}(\text{cosec}^{-1}\theta) = \theta]$

$= 4 - 1 + 9 - 1$

$= 11 =$ RHS **Hence proved.**

13. Given, $\sin(2\tan^{-1}x) = 1$

$\Rightarrow \sin(2\tan^{-1}x) = \sin\frac{\pi}{2}$ [1]

$\Rightarrow 2\tan^{-1}x = \frac{\pi}{2} \Rightarrow \tan^{-1}x = \frac{\pi}{4}$

$\therefore x = \tan\frac{\pi}{4} = 1$ [1]

14. Hint $0 \le \cos^{-1}x \le \pi$

Also, $\cos^{-1}\alpha + \cos^{-1}\beta + \cos^{-1}\gamma = 3\pi$

$\therefore \cos^{-1}\alpha = \cos^{-1}\beta = \cos^{-1}\gamma = \pi$

$\Rightarrow \alpha = \beta = \gamma = 1$ [**Ans.** 6]

15. $\text{LHS} = \frac{9\pi}{8} - \frac{9}{4}\sin^{-1}\left(\frac{1}{3}\right) = \frac{9}{4}\left[\frac{\pi}{2} - \sin^{-1}\left(\frac{1}{3}\right)\right]$ [1]

$= \frac{9}{4}\left[\cos^{-1}\left(\frac{1}{3}\right)\right]$ $\left[\because \sin^{-1}x + \cos^{-1}x = \frac{\pi}{2}\right]$ [1]

$= \frac{9}{4}\sin^{-1}\sqrt{1-\left(\frac{1}{3}\right)^2}$ [1]

$[\because \cos^{-1}x = \sin^{-1}\sqrt{1-x^2}, 0 \le x \le 1]$

$= \frac{9}{4}\sin^{-1}\sqrt{1-\frac{1}{9}}$

$= \frac{9}{4}\sin^{-1}\frac{2\sqrt{2}}{3} = \text{RHS}$ **Hence proved.** [1]

16. $\text{LHS} = \left(\tan^{-1}\frac{1}{2} + \tan^{-1}\frac{1}{5}\right) + \tan^{-1}\frac{1}{8}$

$= \tan^{-1}\left(\frac{\frac{1}{2}+\frac{1}{5}}{1-\left(\frac{1}{2}\times\frac{1}{5}\right)}\right) + \tan^{-1}\frac{1}{8}$ [1]

$= \tan^{-1}\left(\frac{7/10}{9/10}\right) + \tan^{-1}\frac{1}{8}$

$= \tan^{-1}\left(\frac{7}{9}\right) + \tan^{-1}\left(\frac{1}{8}\right)$ [1]

$= \tan^{-1}\left(\frac{\frac{7}{9}+\frac{1}{8}}{1-\frac{7}{9}\times\frac{1}{8}}\right) = \tan^{-1}\left(\frac{56+9}{72-7}\right)$

$= \tan^{-1}\left(\frac{65}{65}\right) = \tan^{-1}(1)$

$= \tan^{-1}\left(\tan\frac{\pi}{4}\right) = \frac{\pi}{4}$ [2]

17. **Hint** $\cot^{-1}7 + \cot^{-1}8 + \cot^{-1}18$

$= \tan^{-1}\frac{1}{7} + \tan^{-1}\frac{1}{8} + \tan^{-1}\frac{1}{18}$

$\left[\because \cot^{-1}x = \tan^{-1}\left(\frac{1}{x}\right), x > 0\right]$

Now, solve as Question 16.

18. **Hint** $\tan^{-1}x + \tan^{-1}y = \tan^{-1}\left(\frac{x+y}{1-xy}\right)$. [**Ans.** 1]

19. To prove, $\tan^{-1}\left(\frac{1}{4}\right) + \tan^{-1}\left(\frac{2}{9}\right) = \left(\frac{1}{2}\right)\tan^{-1}\left(\frac{4}{3}\right)$

Above equation can be rewritten as

$2\tan^{-1}\left(\frac{1}{4}\right) + 2\tan^{-1}\left(\frac{2}{9}\right) = \tan^{-1}\left(\frac{4}{3}\right)$ [1]

Now, $\text{LHS} = 2\tan^{-1}\left(\frac{1}{4}\right) + 2\tan^{-1}\left(\frac{2}{9}\right)$

$= 2\left[\tan^{-1}\left(\frac{1}{4}\right) + \tan^{-1}\left(\frac{2}{9}\right)\right]$ [1]

$= 2\tan^{-1}\left(\frac{\frac{1}{4}+\frac{2}{9}}{1-\frac{1}{4}\times\frac{2}{9}}\right)$

$= 2\tan^{-1}\left(\frac{17}{34}\right) = 2\tan^{-1}\left(\frac{1}{2}\right)$ [1]

$= \tan^{-1}\left(\frac{2\cdot\frac{1}{2}}{1-\left(\frac{1}{2}\right)^2}\right)$

$= \tan^{-1}\left(\frac{4}{3}\right) = \text{RHS}$ **Hence proved.** [1]

20. $\text{LHS} = \tan^{-1}\frac{1}{4} + \tan^{-1}\frac{2}{9}$

$= \tan^{-1}\left(\frac{\frac{1}{4}+\frac{2}{9}}{1-\frac{1}{4}\cdot\frac{2}{9}}\right) = \tan^{-1}\left(\frac{\frac{9+8}{36}}{\frac{36-2}{36}}\right)$

$\left[\because \tan^{-1}x + \tan^{-1}y = \tan^{-1}\left(\frac{x+y}{1-xy}\right), xy < 1\right]$ [1]

$= \tan^{-1}\left(\frac{\frac{17}{36}}{\frac{34}{36}}\right) = \tan^{-1}\frac{17}{34} = \tan^{-1}\frac{1}{2}$ [1]

$= \frac{1}{2}(2\cdot\tan^{-1}x) = \frac{1}{2}\sin^{-1}\left[\frac{2\times\frac{1}{2}}{1+\left(\frac{1}{2}\right)^2}\right]$

$\left[\because 2\tan^{-1}x = \sin^{-1}\left(\frac{2x}{1+x^2}\right), -1 \le x \le 1\right]$ [1]

$= \frac{1}{2}\sin^{-1}\left(\frac{1}{\frac{1+4}{4}}\right) = \frac{1}{2}\sin^{-1}\left(\frac{4}{5}\right)$

$= \text{RHS}$ **Hence proved.** [1]

21. Let $E = \sin\left(2\tan^{-1}\frac{1}{3}\right) + \cos(\tan^{-1}2\sqrt{2})$

Now, $2\tan^{-1}\left(\frac{1}{3}\right) = \sin^{-1}\left(\frac{2\times\frac{1}{3}}{1+\left(\frac{1}{3}\right)^2}\right)$

$\left[\because 2\tan^{-1}x = \sin^{-1}\left(\frac{2x}{1+x^2}\right), -1 \le x \le 1\right]$

$\Rightarrow\ 2\tan^{-1}\left(\frac{1}{3}\right) = \sin^{-1}\left(\frac{2/3}{10/9}\right) = \sin^{-1}\left(\frac{3}{5}\right)$ [1]

and $\tan^{-1}2\sqrt{2} = \cos^{-1}\left(\frac{1}{\sqrt{1+(2\sqrt{2})^2}}\right) = \cos^{-1}\left(\frac{1}{3}\right)$ [1]

$\therefore\ E = \sin\left(2\tan^{-1}\frac{1}{3}\right) + \cos(\tan^{-1} 2\sqrt{2})$

$= \sin\left(\sin^{-1}\frac{3}{5}\right) + \cos\left(\cos^{-1}\frac{1}{3}\right)$

$= \frac{3}{5} + \frac{1}{3} = \frac{9+5}{15} = \frac{14}{15}$ [2]

22. **Hint** Firstly, use the identity $2\tan^{-1} x = \tan^{-1}\frac{2x}{1-x^2}$ and then similar as Example 9.

23. **Hint** Firstly, use the identity $2\tan^{-1} x = \tan^{-1}\frac{2x}{1-x^2}$ and then use $\tan^{-1} x - \tan^{-1} y = \tan^{-1}\left(\frac{x-y}{1+xy}\right)$

24. **Hint** Firstly, convert $\sin^{-1}$ in terms of $\tan^{-1}$ and then use the identity $2\tan^{-1} x = \tan^{-1}\left(\frac{2x}{1-x^2}\right)$.

Further, use the identity $\tan^{-1} x - \tan^{-1} y = \tan^{-1}\left(\frac{x-y}{1+xy}\right)$

25. To prove, $\sin^{-1}\left(\frac{8}{17}\right) + \sin^{-1}\left(\frac{3}{5}\right) = \cos^{-1}\left(\frac{36}{85}\right)$

We know that,

$\sin^{-1} x + \sin^{-1} y = \sin^{-1}\{x\sqrt{1-y^2} + y\sqrt{1-x^2}\}$, if $|x|, |y| \le 1$ and $x^2 + y^2 \le 1$

$\therefore \sin^{-1}\left(\frac{8}{17}\right) + \sin^{-1}\left(\frac{3}{5}\right)$

$= \sin^{-1}\left\{\frac{8}{17}\sqrt{1-\left(\frac{3}{5}\right)^2} + \frac{3}{5}\sqrt{1-\left(\frac{8}{17}\right)^2}\right\}$ [1]

$= \sin^{-1}\left\{\frac{8}{17}\sqrt{\frac{16}{25}} + \frac{3}{5}\sqrt{\frac{225}{289}}\right\}$

$= \sin^{-1}\left\{\frac{8}{17}\times\frac{4}{5} + \frac{3}{5}\times\frac{15}{17}\right\} = \sin^{-1}\left\{\frac{32}{85} + \frac{45}{85}\right\}$ [1]

$= \sin^{-1}\left\{\frac{77}{85}\right\} = \cos^{-1}\sqrt{1-\left(\frac{77}{85}\right)^2}$ [1]

$[\because \sin^{-1} x = \cos^{-1}\sqrt{1-x^2}, 0 \le x \le 1]$

$= \cos^{-1}\sqrt{\frac{7225-5929}{7225}} = \cos^{-1}\sqrt{\frac{1296}{7225}}$

$= \cos^{-1}\left(\frac{36}{85}\right)$ **Hence proved.** [1]

26. Solve as Question 25.

27. LHS $= \tan\left(\frac{1}{2}\sin^{-1}\frac{3}{4}\right)$ ...(i)

Put $\frac{1}{2}\sin^{-1}\left(\frac{3}{4}\right) = \theta$ ...(ii)

$\Rightarrow \sin^{-1}\left(\frac{3}{4}\right) = 2\theta$

$\Rightarrow \sin 2\theta = \frac{3}{4}$ and $0 < 2\theta < \frac{\pi}{2}$ [1]

$\Rightarrow \frac{2\tan\theta}{1+\tan^2\theta} = \frac{3}{4}$ $\left[\because \sin 2\theta = \frac{2\tan\theta}{1+\tan^2\theta}\right]$

$\Rightarrow 8\tan\theta = 3 + 3\tan^2\theta$

$\Rightarrow 3\tan^2\theta - 8\tan\theta + 3 = 0$ [1]

By using Sridharacharya's rule,

$\tan\theta = \frac{8 \pm \sqrt{64-36}}{2\times 3} = \frac{8\pm\sqrt{28}}{6} = \frac{4\pm\sqrt{7}}{3}$

$\Rightarrow \tan\theta = \frac{4-\sqrt{7}}{3}$ $\left[\because 0 < \theta < \frac{\pi}{4} \Rightarrow 0 < \tan\theta < 1\right]$ [1]

$\Rightarrow \theta = \tan^{-1}\left(\frac{4-\sqrt{7}}{3}\right)$

$\Rightarrow \frac{1}{2}\sin^{-1}\left(\frac{3}{4}\right) = \tan^{-1}\left(\frac{4-\sqrt{7}}{3}\right)$ [from Eq. (ii)]

$\Rightarrow \tan\left(\frac{1}{2}\sin^{-1}\frac{3}{4}\right) = \frac{4-\sqrt{7}}{3}$

$\therefore$ LHS = RHS **Hence proved.** [1]

28. LHS $= \cot\left(\frac{\pi}{4} - 2\cot^{-1} 3\right) = \cot\left(\frac{\pi}{4} - 2\tan^{-1}\frac{1}{3}\right)$

$\left[\because \cot^{-1} x = \tan^{-1}\frac{1}{x}, x > 0\right]$ [1/2]

Let $\theta = \tan^{-1}\frac{1}{3}$.

Then, LHS $= \frac{1}{\tan\left(\frac{\pi}{4} - 2\theta\right)} = \frac{1 + \tan\frac{\pi}{4}\cdot\tan 2\theta}{\tan\frac{\pi}{4} - \tan 2\theta}$

$\left[\because \tan(A-B) = \frac{\tan A - \tan B}{1 + \tan A\cdot\tan B}\right]$ [1]

$= \frac{1+\tan 2\theta}{1-\tan 2\theta} = \frac{1 + \frac{2\tan\theta}{1-\tan^2\theta}}{1 - \frac{2\tan\theta}{1-\tan^2\theta}}$

$\left[\because \tan\frac{\pi}{4} = 1 \text{ and } \tan 2A = \frac{2\tan A}{1-\tan^2 A}\right]$ [1]

$= \frac{1 + \frac{2\cdot(1/3)}{1-(1/9)}}{1 - \frac{2\cdot(1/3)}{1-(1/9)}}$ $\left[\because \tan(\tan^{-1} x) = x, \forall x \in R \text{ and } \theta = \tan^{-1}(1/3)\right]$

$= \frac{1 + \frac{2}{3}\cdot\frac{9}{8}}{1 - \frac{2}{3}\cdot\frac{9}{8}} = \frac{1+\frac{3}{4}}{1-\frac{3}{4}} = \frac{7}{1}$

$= 7 =$ RHS **Hence proved.** [1]

29. LHS $= \tan^{-1}\left(\dfrac{\sqrt{1+x^2}+\sqrt{1-x^2}}{\sqrt{1+x^2}-\sqrt{1-x^2}}\right)$

Put $x^2 = \cos 2\theta$, then

$$\text{LHS} = \tan^{-1}\left(\frac{\sqrt{1+\cos 2\theta}+\sqrt{1-\cos 2\theta}}{\sqrt{1+\cos 2\theta}-\sqrt{1-\cos 2\theta}}\right) \quad [1]$$

$$= \tan^{-1}\left(\frac{\sqrt{2}\cos\theta+\sqrt{2}\sin\theta}{\sqrt{2}\cos\theta-\sqrt{2}\sin\theta}\right)$$

$[\because 1+\cos 2\theta = 2\cos^2\theta \text{ and } 1-\cos 2\theta = 2\sin^2\theta]$

$$= \tan^{-1}\left(\frac{\cos\theta+\sin\theta}{\cos\theta-\sin\theta}\right) = \tan^{-1}\left(\frac{1+\tan\theta}{1-\tan\theta}\right) \quad [1]$$

[divide numerator and denominator inside the bracket by $\cos\theta$]

$$= \tan^{-1}\left(\frac{\tan\frac{\pi}{4}+\tan\theta}{1-\left(\tan\frac{\pi}{4}\right)(\tan\theta)}\right) \quad \left[\because \tan\frac{\pi}{4}=1\right] \ [1]$$

$\left[\because \tan(\theta+\phi) = \dfrac{\tan\theta+\tan\phi}{1-\tan\theta\tan\phi}\right]$

$$= \tan^{-1}\left[\tan\left(\frac{\pi}{4}+\theta\right)\right]$$

$$= \frac{\pi}{4}+\theta = \frac{\pi}{4}+\frac{1}{2}\cos^{-1}x^2$$

$\left[\because x^2 = \cos 2\theta \Rightarrow \theta = \dfrac{1}{2}\cos^{-1}x^2\right]$

$\therefore$ LHS = RHS **Hence proved.** [1]

30. Solve as Question 29.

Hint Put $x = \cos\theta$ then $\theta = \cos^{-1}x$

Also as $-\dfrac{1}{\sqrt{2}} \le x \le 1$, therefore $\theta \in \left[0, \dfrac{3\pi}{4}\right]$.

31. Given, $\cos^{-1}[\sin(\cos^{-1}x)] = \dfrac{\pi}{3}$

$\Rightarrow \sin(\cos^{-1}x) = \cos\dfrac{\pi}{3}$

$\Rightarrow \sin(\cos^{-1}x) = \dfrac{1}{2}$ [1]

$\Rightarrow \cos^{-1}x = \sin^{-1}\dfrac{1}{2}$ [1]

$\Rightarrow \cos^{-1}x = \sin^{-1}\left[\sin\left(\dfrac{\pi}{6}\right)\right] \quad \left[\because \sin\dfrac{\pi}{6} = \dfrac{1}{2}\right]$

$\Rightarrow \cos^{-1}x = \dfrac{\pi}{6} \quad \left[\because \sin^{-1}(\sin\theta) = \theta, \forall\theta \in \left[-\dfrac{\pi}{2}, \dfrac{\pi}{2}\right]\right]$ [1]

$\therefore x = \cos\dfrac{\pi}{6} = \dfrac{\sqrt{3}}{2}$ [1]

32. Hint Firstly, put $\sin^{-1}x = \theta \Rightarrow x = \sin\theta$

$\therefore \cos 2\theta = \dfrac{1}{9} \Rightarrow 1-2\sin^2\theta = \dfrac{1}{9}$

$\Rightarrow 1-2x^2 = \dfrac{1}{9} \quad \left[\textbf{Ans. } \dfrac{2}{3}\right]$

33. Hint $\tan^{-1}\left(\dfrac{2x}{1-x^2}\right) + \cot^{-1}\left(\dfrac{1-x^2}{2x}\right) = \dfrac{\pi}{3}$

$\Rightarrow \tan^{-1}\left(\dfrac{2x}{1-x^2}\right) + \tan^{-1}\left(\dfrac{2x}{1-x^2}\right) = \dfrac{\pi}{3}$

$\Rightarrow 2\tan^{-1}\left(\dfrac{2x}{1-x^2}\right) = \dfrac{\pi}{3} \Rightarrow \dfrac{2x}{1-x^2} = \tan\left(\dfrac{\pi}{6}\right)$

[**Ans.** $2-\sqrt{3}$]

34. Given equation is $\sin^{-1}(1-x) - 2\sin^{-1}x = \dfrac{\pi}{2}$.

$\Rightarrow -2\sin^{-1}x = \dfrac{\pi}{2} - \sin^{-1}(1-x)$

$\Rightarrow -2\sin^{-1}x = \cos^{-1}(1-x)$ [1]

$\left[\because \sin^{-1}x + \cos^{-1}x = \dfrac{\pi}{2}\right]$

$\Rightarrow \cos(-2\sin^{-1}x) = (1-x)$

$\Rightarrow \cos[2\sin^{-1}(-x)] = 1-x \quad [\because -\sin^{-1}x = \sin^{-1}(-x)]$

$\Rightarrow [1-2\sin^2\{\sin^{-1}(-x)\}] = 1-x \quad [\because \cos 2\theta = 1-2\sin^2\theta]$ [1]

$\Rightarrow [1-2\{\sin(\sin^{-1}(-x)\}^2] = 1-x \quad [\because \sin^2 x = (\sin x)^2]$

$\Rightarrow 1-2(-x)^2 = 1-x$

$\Rightarrow 2x^2 - x = 0 \Rightarrow x(2x-1) = 0$

$\Rightarrow x = 0, \dfrac{1}{2}$ [1]

But $x = \dfrac{1}{2}$ does not satisfy the given equation.

$\left[\because \sin^{-1}\left(1-\dfrac{1}{2}\right) - 2\sin^{-1}\left(\dfrac{1}{2}\right) = \dfrac{\pi}{6} - 2\times\dfrac{\pi}{6} \ne \dfrac{\pi}{2}\right]$

Hence, $x = 0$ is the required solution. [1]

Note Sometimes, it may be possible that resulting values of x does not satisfy the given equation.

35. Given, $\sin^{-1}\left(\dfrac{x}{2}\right) + \cos^{-1}x = \dfrac{\pi}{6}$.

$\Rightarrow \sin^{-1}\left(\dfrac{x}{2}\right) = \dfrac{\pi}{6} - \cos^{-1}x$

$\Rightarrow \dfrac{x}{2} = \sin\left(\dfrac{\pi}{6} - \cos^{-1}x\right)$ [1]

$\Rightarrow \dfrac{x}{2} = \sin\dfrac{\pi}{6}\cos(\cos^{-1}x) - \cos\dfrac{\pi}{6}\sin(\cos^{-1}x)$

$\Rightarrow \dfrac{x}{2} = \dfrac{1}{2}\cdot x - \dfrac{\sqrt{3}}{2}\sin(\sin^{-1}\sqrt{1-x^2}), 0 \le x \le 1$ [1]

$\Rightarrow \dfrac{x}{2} = \dfrac{x}{2} - \dfrac{\sqrt{3}}{2}\sqrt{1-x^2}$

$\Rightarrow -\dfrac{\sqrt{3}}{2}\sqrt{1-x^2} = 0$ [1]

$\Rightarrow \quad \sqrt{1-x^2} = 0$

$\Rightarrow \quad 1-x^2 = 0$

$\Rightarrow \quad x = \pm 1$

But $0 \le x \le 1$, therefore $x = 1$ is the only solution. [1]

36. Given, $\sin[\cot^{-1}(x+1)] = \cos(\tan^{-1} x)$ ...(i)

Let $\cot^{-1}(x+1) = \theta \Rightarrow \cot\theta = x+1$

$$\Rightarrow \quad \sin\theta = \frac{1}{\sqrt{x^2+2x+2}}$$ [1/2]

$$\Rightarrow \quad \theta = \sin^{-1}\left(\frac{1}{\sqrt{x^2+2x+2}}\right)$$

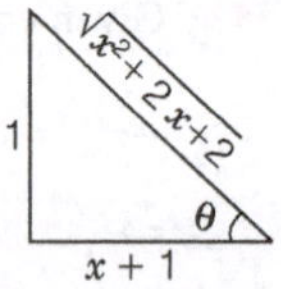

$$\Rightarrow \cot^{-1}(x+1) = \sin^{-1}\left(\frac{1}{\sqrt{x^2+2x+2}}\right)$$

and we know that, $\tan^{-1} x = \cos^{-1}\left(\frac{1}{\sqrt{x^2+1}}\right)$ [1] [1]

$\therefore$ From Eq. (i), we get

$$\sin\left[\sin^{-1}\left(\frac{1}{\sqrt{x^2+2x+2}}\right)\right] = \cos\left[\cos^{-1}\left(\frac{1}{\sqrt{1+x^2}}\right)\right]$$

$$\Rightarrow \quad \frac{1}{\sqrt{x^2+2x+2}} = \frac{1}{\sqrt{1+x^2}}$$ [1/2]

$\Rightarrow \quad \sqrt{x^2+2x+2} = \sqrt{1+x^2}$

$\Rightarrow \quad x^2+2x+2 = 1+x^2$

$\Rightarrow \quad 2x+2 = 1 \Rightarrow 2x = -1$

$$\Rightarrow \quad x = -\frac{1}{2}$$ [1]

37. Given, $\tan^{-1}\left(\frac{x-2}{x-4}\right) + \tan^{-1}\left(\frac{x+2}{x+4}\right) = \frac{\pi}{4}$

$$\Rightarrow \tan^{-1}\left[\frac{\frac{x-2}{x-4}+\frac{x+2}{x+4}}{1-\left(\frac{x-2}{x-4}\right)\left(\frac{x+2}{x+4}\right)}\right] = \frac{\pi}{4}, \frac{(x-2)(x+2)}{(x-4)(x+4)} < 1$$

$\left[\because \tan^{-1} x + \tan^{-1} y = \tan^{-1}\left(\frac{x+y}{1-xy}\right) \text{if } xy < 1\right]$ [1]

$$\Rightarrow \quad \tan^{-1}\left[\frac{\frac{(x-2)(x+4)+(x+2)(x-4)}{(x-4)(x+4)}}{\frac{(x-4)(x+4)-(x-2)(x+2)}{(x-4)(x+4)}}\right] = \frac{\pi}{4}, \frac{x^2-4}{x^2-16} < 1$$

$$\Rightarrow \quad \frac{x^2-2x+4x-8+x^2-4x+2x-8}{(x^2-16)-(x^2-4)} = \tan\frac{\pi}{4}, \frac{x^2-4}{x^2-16} - 1 < 0$$ [1]

$$\Rightarrow \quad \frac{2x^2-16}{-12} = 1 \Rightarrow 2x^2-16 = -12, \frac{12}{x^2-16} < 0$$

$\Rightarrow \quad 2x^2 = -12+16, x^2-16 < 0$

$\Rightarrow \quad 2x^2 = 4 \Rightarrow x^2 = 2, (x-4)(x+4) < 0$

$\therefore \quad x = \pm\sqrt{2}, -4 < x < 4$ [1]

Since, both values of x satisfy $-4 < x < 4$, therefore $\sqrt{2}$ and $-\sqrt{2}$ are the required values of x. [1]

38. Solve as Question 37. $\left[\textbf{Ans. } x = \pm\sqrt{\frac{7}{2}}\right]$

39. Given, $2\tan^{-1}(\cos x) = \tan^{-1}(2\operatorname{cosec} x)$

$$\Rightarrow \quad \tan^{-1}\left(\frac{2\cos x}{1-\cos^2 x}\right) = \tan^{-1}\left(\frac{2}{\sin x}\right)$$ [1]

$\left[\because 2\tan^{-1} x = \tan^{-1}\left(\frac{2x}{1-x^2}\right), -1 < x < 1\right]$

$$\Rightarrow \quad \frac{2\cos x}{1-\cos^2 x} = \frac{2}{\sin x}$$ [1]

$$\Rightarrow \quad \frac{2\cos x}{\sin^2 x} = \frac{2}{\sin x}$$ [1]

$$\Rightarrow \quad \cot x = 1 \Rightarrow x = \frac{\pi}{4}$$ [1]

40. Solve as Question 39. $\left[\textbf{Ans. } x = \frac{\pi}{4}\right]$

41. We have, $\tan^{-1}\left(\frac{1-x}{1+x}\right) = \frac{1}{2}\tan^{-1} x, x > 0$

$$\Rightarrow \quad 2\tan^{-1}\left(\frac{1-x}{1+x}\right) = \tan^{-1} x$$

$$\Rightarrow \quad \tan^{-1}\left[\frac{2\left(\frac{1-x}{1+x}\right)}{1-\left(\frac{1-x}{1+x}\right)^2}\right] = \tan^{-1} x$$

$\left[\because 2\tan^{-1} x = \tan^{-1}\left(\frac{2x}{1-x^2}\right)\right]$ [1]

$$\Rightarrow \quad \tan^{-1}\left[\frac{2(1-x)(1+x)}{(1+x)^2-(1-x)^2}\right] = \tan^{-1} x$$

$$\Rightarrow \quad \tan^{-1}\left(\frac{2-2x^2}{4x}\right) = \tan^{-1} x$$

$[\because a^2-b^2 = (a-b)(a+b)]$ [1]

$$\Rightarrow \quad \frac{1-x^2}{2x} = x \Rightarrow 1-x^2 = 2x^2 \Rightarrow 3x^2 = 1$$

$$\Rightarrow \quad x^2 = \frac{1}{3} \Rightarrow x = \pm\frac{1}{\sqrt{3}}$$ [1]

But it is given that, $x > 0$

$$\therefore \quad x = \frac{1}{\sqrt{3}}$$ [1]

42. We have, $\sin^{-1}\left(\frac{2a}{1+a^2}\right)+\cos^{-1}\left(\frac{1-a^2}{1+a^2}\right)$

$$= \tan^{-1}\left(\frac{2x}{1-x^2}\right)$$

$\therefore\ 2\tan^{-1}a + 2\tan^{-1}a = 2\tan^{-1}x$, where $0 \le a \le 1$ and $-1 < x < 1$ [2]

$$\left[\because 2\tan^{-1}x = \begin{cases} \tan^{-1}\left(\frac{2x}{1-x^2}\right), & -1<x<1 \\ \cos^{-1}\left(\frac{1-x^2}{1+x^2}\right), & 0\le x\le 1 \\ \sin^{-1}\left(\frac{2x}{1+x^2}\right), & -1\le x\le 1 \end{cases}\right]$$

$\Rightarrow \quad 2\tan^{-1}a = \tan^{-1}x$

$\Rightarrow \quad \tan^{-1}x = \tan^{-1}\left(\frac{2a}{1-a^2}\right), 0 \le a < 1$ [1]

$\Rightarrow \quad x = \tan\left(\tan^{-1}\left(\frac{2a}{1-a^2}\right)\right), 0 \le a < 1$

$\Rightarrow \quad x = \frac{2a}{1-a^2}, 0 \le a < 1$

$[\because \tan(\tan^{-1}x) = x, \forall x \in R]$ [1]

43. LHS $= 2\tan^{-1}\left(\frac{1}{5}\right)+\sec^{-1}\left(\frac{5\sqrt{2}}{7}\right)+2\tan^{-1}\left(\frac{1}{8}\right)$

$$= 2\left(\tan^{-1}\frac{1}{5}+\tan^{-1}\frac{1}{8}\right)+\sec^{-1}\left(\frac{5\sqrt{2}}{7}\right)$$

$$= 2\tan^{-1}\left[\frac{\frac{1}{5}+\frac{1}{8}}{1-\frac{1}{5}\times\frac{1}{8}}\right]+\cos^{-1}\left(\frac{7}{5\sqrt{2}}\right)$$ [1]

$$= 2\tan^{-1}\left[\frac{13/40}{39/40}\right]+\tan^{-1}\left(\frac{\sqrt{1-(7/5\sqrt{2})^2}}{7/5\sqrt{2}}\right)$$

$$\left[\because \cos^{-1}x = \tan^{-1}\left(\frac{\sqrt{1-x^2}}{x}\right), 0 \le x \le 1\right]$$ [1½]

$$= 2\tan^{-1}\frac{13}{39}+\tan^{-1}\left(\frac{1}{5\sqrt{2}}\times\frac{5\sqrt{2}}{7}\right)$$

$$= 2\tan^{-1}\frac{1}{3}+\tan^{-1}\frac{1}{7}$$

$$= \tan^{-1}\left\{\frac{2\times\frac{1}{3}}{1-\left(\frac{1}{3}\right)^2}\right\}+\tan^{-1}\frac{1}{7}$$

$$\left[\because 2\tan^{-1}x = \tan^{-1}\left\{\frac{2x}{1-x^2}\right\}, -1<x<1\right]$$ [1½]

$$= \tan^{-1}\frac{3}{4}+\tan^{-1}\frac{1}{7}$$

$$= \tan^{-1}\left(\frac{\frac{3}{4}+\frac{1}{7}}{1-\left(\frac{3}{4}\times\frac{1}{7}\right)}\right)$$

$$= \tan^{-1}\left(\frac{21+4}{28-3}\right)$$

$$= \tan^{-1}(1)$$

$$= \tan^{-1}\left(\tan\frac{\pi}{4}\right)$$

$= \frac{\pi}{4} =$ RHS $[\because \tan^{-1}(\tan\theta) = \theta]$ **Hence proved.** [2]

44. Similar as Example 21.

45. Given, $\cos^{-1}\frac{x}{a}+\cos^{-1}\frac{y}{b} = \theta$

$\Rightarrow \quad \cos^{-1}\frac{x}{a} = \theta - \cos^{-1}\frac{y}{b}$

$\Rightarrow \quad \frac{x}{a} = \cos\left(\theta - \cos^{-1}\frac{y}{b}\right)$ [1]

$\Rightarrow \frac{x}{a} = \cos\theta\left[\cos\left(\cos^{-1}\frac{y}{b}\right)\right]+\sin\theta\left[\sin\left(\cos^{-1}\frac{y}{b}\right)\right]$ [1]

$[\because \cos(A-B) = \cos A\cos B + \sin A \sin B]$

$\Rightarrow \quad \frac{x}{a} = \frac{y}{b}\cos\theta + \sin\theta\left[\sin\left(\sin^{-1}\sqrt{1-\frac{y^2}{b^2}}\right)\right]$ [1]

$[\because \cos^{-1}x = \sin^{-1}\sqrt{1-x^2}]$

$\Rightarrow \quad \frac{x}{a}-\frac{y}{b}\cos\theta = \sin\theta\sqrt{1-\frac{y^2}{b^2}}$ [1]

On squaring both sides, we get

$$\frac{x^2}{a^2}+\frac{y^2}{b^2}\cos^2\theta - \frac{2xy}{ab}\cos\theta = \sin^2\theta\left(1-\frac{y^2}{b^2}\right)$$

$\Rightarrow \frac{x^2}{a^2}-\frac{2xy}{ab}\cos\theta+\frac{y^2}{b^2}\cos^2\theta = \sin^2\theta-(\sin^2\theta)\frac{y^2}{b^2}$ [1]

$\Rightarrow \quad \frac{x^2}{a^2}-\frac{2xy}{ab}\cos\theta+\frac{y^2}{b^2}(\cos^2\theta+\sin^2\theta) = \sin^2\theta$

$\Rightarrow \quad \frac{x^2}{a^2}-\frac{2xy}{ab}\cos\theta+\frac{y^2}{b^2} = \sin^2\theta \quad [\because \cos^2\theta+\sin^2\theta = 1]$

Hence proved. [1]

46. Given, $\tan^{-1}(x-1)+\tan^{-1}(x+1) = \tan^{-1}3x - \tan^{-1}x$

$\Rightarrow \quad \tan^{-1}\left[\frac{x-1+x+1}{1-(x-1)(x+1)}\right] = \tan^{-1}\left[\frac{3x-x}{1+3x\cdot x}\right],$

provided $(x+1)(x-1) < 1$ [1]

$$\left[\begin{array}{l} \because \tan^{-1}A+\tan^{-1}B = \tan^{-1}\left(\frac{A+B}{1-AB}\right) \text{if } AB<1 \\ \text{and } \tan^{-1}A-\tan^{-1}B = \tan^{-1}\left(\frac{A-B}{1+AB}\right) \text{if } AB>-1 \end{array}\right]$$

$\Rightarrow \tan^{-1}\left[\dfrac{2x}{1-(x^2-1)}\right] = \tan^{-1}\left[\dfrac{2x}{1+3x^2}\right], x^2-1<1$ [2]

$\Rightarrow \dfrac{2x}{2-x^2} = \dfrac{2x}{1+3x^2}, x^2 < 2$

$\Rightarrow 2x(1+3x^2) = 2x(2-x^2), |x| < \sqrt{2}$ [1]

$\Rightarrow 2x(1+3x^2-2+x^2) = 0$

$\Rightarrow 2x(4x^2-1) = 0, |x| < 2$

$\Rightarrow (2x+1)(2x-1) = 0$

or $x = 0, |x| < \sqrt{2}$

$\Rightarrow x = \pm\dfrac{1}{2}, 0, |x| < \sqrt{2}$

Since, all values of x satisfying $|x| < \sqrt{2}$, therefore the solutions are $x = 0, \dfrac{1}{2}, -\dfrac{1}{2}$ [2]

47. Given, $\sin^{-1} x + \sin^{-1}(1-x) = \cos^{-1} x$

$\therefore \sin^{-1}[x\sqrt{1-(1-x)^2} + (1-x)\sqrt{1-x^2}] = \cos^{-1} x$

$[\because \sin^{-1} A + \sin^{-1} B = \sin^{-1}(A\sqrt{1-B^2} + B\sqrt{1-A^2})]$ [1]

$\Rightarrow \sin^{-1}[x\sqrt{1-(1+x^2-2x)} + (1-x)\sqrt{1-x^2}]$
$= \sin^{-1}\sqrt{1-x^2}$ [1]

$[\because \cos^{-1} A = \sin^{-1}\sqrt{1-A^2}]$

$\Rightarrow x\sqrt{2x-x^2} + (1-x)\sqrt{1-x^2} = \sqrt{1-x^2}$ [1]

$\Rightarrow x\sqrt{2x-x^2} = (1-1+x)\sqrt{1-x^2}$

$\Rightarrow x\sqrt{2x-x^2} = x\sqrt{1-x^2}$

$\Rightarrow x\sqrt{2x-x^2} - x\sqrt{1-x^2} = 0$

$\Rightarrow x[\sqrt{2x-x^2} - \sqrt{1-x^2}] = 0 \Rightarrow x = 0$

or $\sqrt{2x-x^2} - \sqrt{1-x^2} = 0$ [1]

Now, $\sqrt{2x-x^2} - \sqrt{1-x^2} = 0$

$\Rightarrow \sqrt{2x-x^2} = \sqrt{1-x^2}$

On squaring both sides, we get

$2x - x^2 = 1 - x^2 \Rightarrow 2x = 1 \Rightarrow x = \dfrac{1}{2}$ [1]

Note that both values of x satisfy the given equation.

Hence, $x = 0, \dfrac{1}{2}$. [1]

Chapter Practice

Multiple Choice Type Questions

1 Mark

1 If $\sin^{-1}x+\sin^{-1}y+\sin^{-1}z=\frac{3\pi}{2}$, then the value of $x^{100}+y^{100}+z^{100}-\frac{9}{x^{101}+y^{101}+z^{101}}$ is

(a) 0 (b) 1 (c) 2 (d) 3

2 The value of

$$\sin^{-1}\left\{\cot\left(\sin^{-1}\frac{\sqrt{2-\sqrt{3}}}{2}+\cos^{-1}\frac{\sqrt{12}}{4}+\sec^{-1}\sqrt{2}\right)\right\}$$

is

(a) 0 (b) $\frac{\pi}{2}$ (c) $\frac{\pi}{3}$ (d) $\frac{\pi}{4}$

3 $\sin^{-1}(1-x)-2\sin^{-1}x=\frac{\pi}{2}$, then x is equal to

(a) $0, \frac{1}{2}$ (b) $1, \frac{1}{2}$ (c) 0 (d) $\frac{1}{2}$

4 The value of $\sin\left[\frac{\pi}{3}+\sin^{-1}\left(\frac{1}{2}\right)\right]$ is

(a) 1 (b) $\frac{1}{2}$ (c) $\frac{1}{3}$ (d) $\frac{1}{4}$

5 The value of $\text{cosec}\left(\sin^{-1}\left(\frac{-1}{2}\right)\right)-\sec\left(\cos^{-1}\left(\frac{-1}{2}\right)\right)$ is equal to **[ISC 2024]**

(a) -4 (b) 0 (c) -1 (d) 4

Assertion-Reason Type Questions

1 Mark

Directions (Q. Nos. 6-10) *In the questions given below are two statements labelled as Assertion (A) and Reason (R). In the context of the two statements, which one of the following is correct?*

(a) Both A and R are correct; R is the correct explanation of A
(b) Both A and R are correct; R is not the correct explanation of A
(c) A is correct; R is incorrect
(d) R is correct; A is incorrect

6 **Assertion** (A) The value of $\sin\left(\tan^{-1}(-\sqrt{3})+\cos^{-1}\left(-\frac{\sqrt{3}}{2}\right)\right)$ is 1.

Reason (R) $\tan^{-1}(-x)=\tan^{-1}x$ and $\cos^{-1}(-x)=\cos^{-1}x$.

7 **Assertion** (A) The value of $\sin^{-1}\left(\cos\frac{33\pi}{5}\right)$ is $-\frac{\pi}{10}$.

Reason (R) The principal value branch of $\sin^{-1}x$ is $[0, \pi]$.

8 **Assertion** (A) The range of the function $f(x)=2\sin^{-1}x+\frac{3\pi}{2}$, where $x\in[-1,1]$ is $\left[\frac{\pi}{2},\frac{5\pi}{2}\right]$.

Reason (R) The range of the principal value branch of $\sin^{-1}x$ is $\sin^{-1}x$ is $[0, \pi]$.

9 **Assertion** (A) Maximum value of $(\cos^{-1}x)^2$ is π^2.

Reason (R) The principal value branch of $\cos^{-1}x$ is $\left[\frac{-\pi}{2},\frac{\pi}{2}\right]$.

10 **Assertion** (A) All trigonometric functions have their inverses over their respective domains.

Reason (R) The inverse of $\tan^{-1}x$ exists for some $x\in R$.

Very Short Answer Type Questions

2 Marks

11 Find the domain of the function $\cos^{-1}(2x-1)$. **[NCERT Exemplar]**

12 Write the value of the following.

(i) $\sin^{-1}(\sin 1550°)$. (ii) $\tan^{-1}\left[\tan\left(\frac{15\pi}{4}\right)\right]$.

13 If $\tan^{-1}x+\tan^{-1}y=\frac{4\pi}{5}$, then find $\cot^{-1}x+\cot^{-1}y$. **[NCERT Exemplar]**

14 If $\tan^{-1}x-\tan^{-1}y=\frac{\pi}{4}$, where $xy>-1$, then find the value of $x-y-xy$.

15 Simplify $2\tan^{-1}x+\sin^{-1}\left(\frac{2x}{1+x^2}\right)$ in terms of $\tan^{-1}x$. **[NCERT Exemplar]**

16 If $\tan^{-1}(\sqrt{3})+\cot^{-1}x=\frac{\pi}{2}$, then find x.

17 Solve for x, if $\tan(\cos^{-1}x)=\frac{2}{\sqrt{5}}$. **[ISC 2016]**

18 Solve for x, $\cos^{-1}\{\sin(\cos^{-1}x)\}=\frac{\pi}{6}$. **[ISC 2015]**

Short Answer Type Questions

4 Marks

19 Find the value of $\sin[\cot^{-1}\{\tan(\cos^{-1}x)\}]$.

20 Solve for x, $\sin^{-1}\left(\frac{2\alpha}{1+\alpha^2}\right)+\sin^{-1}\left(\frac{2\beta}{1+\beta^2}\right)=2\tan^{-1}x$.

21 Solve the equation for x, $\sin^{-1}\frac{5}{x}+\sin^{-1}\frac{12}{x}=\frac{\pi}{2}$, $x\neq 0$ **[ISC 2015]**

Directions (Q. Nos. 12-23) *Prove the following.*

22 $\cos[\tan^{-1}\{\sin(\cot^{-1}x)\}]=\sqrt{\frac{x^2+1}{x^2+2}}$

23 $\left(\tan^{-1}\frac{1}{3}+\tan^{-1}\frac{1}{5}\right)+\left(\tan^{-1}\frac{1}{7}+\tan^{-1}\frac{1}{8}\right)=\frac{\pi}{4}$ **[NCERT]**

24 $\tan^{-1}\frac{1}{4}+\tan^{-1}\frac{2}{9}=\frac{1}{2}\cos^{-1}\frac{3}{5}$

25 $\tan^{-1}\left(\frac{1-x}{1+x}\right)-\tan^{-1}\left(\frac{1-y}{1+y}\right)=\sin^{-1}\left(\frac{y-x}{\sqrt{1+x^2}\sqrt{1+y^2}}\right)$

26 $\tan^{-1}\frac{yz}{xr}+\tan^{-1}\frac{zx}{yr}+\tan^{-1}\frac{xy}{zr}=\frac{\pi}{2}$, where $x^2+y^2+z^2=r^2$.

27 $2\tan^{-1}\frac{1}{2}+\tan^{-1}\frac{1}{7}=\sin^{-1}\left(\frac{31}{25\sqrt{2}}\right)$

28 $2\tan^{-1}\frac{1}{3}+\cot^{-1}4=\tan^{-1}\frac{16}{13}$. **[ISC 2007]**

29 $\cos\left(2\tan^{-1}\frac{1}{7}\right)=\sin\left(4\tan^{-1}\frac{1}{3}\right)$ **[NCERT Exemplar]**

30 $\tan^{-1}\left(\frac{\sqrt{1+\cos x}+\sqrt{1-\cos x}}{\sqrt{1+\cos x}-\sqrt{1-\cos x}}\right)=\frac{\pi}{4}-\frac{x}{2}$, where $\pi<x<\frac{3\pi}{2}$

31 Simplify $\tan^{-1}\left[\frac{x}{\sqrt{a^2-x^2}}\right]$, $|x|<a$.

[Hint Put $x=a\sin\theta$**]**

Long Answer Type Questions

6 Marks

32 Find the value of $\tan^{-1}\left(\tan\frac{5\pi}{6}\right)+\cos^{-1}\left(\cos\frac{13\pi}{6}\right)$. **[NCERT Exemplar]**

33 Show that $2\tan^{-1}\left\{\tan\frac{\alpha}{2}\tan\left(\frac{\pi}{4}-\frac{\beta}{2}\right)\right\}=\tan^{-1}\left(\frac{\sin\alpha\cos\beta}{\cos\alpha+\sin\beta}\right)$. **[NCERT Exemplar]**

34 Find the value of $4\tan^{-1}\frac{1}{5}-\tan^{-1}\frac{1}{239}$. **[NCERT Exemplar]**

35 Prove that $\tan^{-1}\left[\frac{\cos x}{1+\sin x}\right]=\frac{\pi}{4}-\frac{x}{2}$, $x\in\left[\frac{-\pi}{2},\frac{\pi}{2}\right]$.

Directions (Q. Nos. 36) *Solve the following equations.*

36 $\cos(\tan^{-1}x)=\sin\left(\cot^{-1}\frac{3}{4}\right)$.

Answers

1. (a) **2.** (a) **3.** (c) **4.** (a) **5.** (b) **6.** (c)
7. (c) **8.** (c) **9.** (c) **10.** (c)
11. $x\in[0,1]$ **12.** (i) 70° (ii) $\frac{-\pi}{4}$ **13.** $\frac{\pi}{5}$ **14.** 1 **15.** $4\tan^{-1}x$ **16.** $\sqrt{3}$
17. $\pm\frac{\sqrt{5}}{3}$ **18.** $\frac{1}{2}$ **19.** x **20.** $\frac{\alpha+\beta}{1-\alpha\beta}$ **21.** 13 **31.** $\sin^{-1}\left(\frac{x}{a}\right)$
32. 0 **33.** $\frac{\pi}{4}$ **36.** $x=\pm\frac{3}{4}$

CHAPTER

03

Matrices

The evolution of concept of matrices is the results of an attempt to obtain compact and simple method of solving system of linear equations. Matrix notation and operations are used in electronic spreadsheet, advanced statistics, etc. In this chapter, we shall study about fundamentals of matrix and matrix algebra.

- Basic Concepts of Matrix and Its Types
- Addition and Scalar Multiplication of Matrices
- Multiplication of Matrices
- Transpose of a Matrix, Symmetric and Skew-symmetric Matrices

TOPIC 01 Basic Concepts of Matrix and Its Types

Matrix

A matrix is an ordered **rectangular array** of numbers or functions arranged in **rows** and **columns**, and enclosed by [ ] or ( ). Matrix is represented by a single **capital letter** like A, B, X, Y, etc., and elements of a matrix are represented by the small letters $a, b, c, \ldots$ etc.

The numbers (real or complex) or functions are called the **elements** or the **entries** of the matrix. In a matrix, horizontal lines are called **rows** and vertical lines are called **columns**.

e.g. $$A = \begin{bmatrix} 2 & -5 \\ 7 & 0 \\ \sqrt{5} & 3 \end{bmatrix} \begin{matrix} \rightarrow \text{First row } (R_1) \\ \rightarrow \text{Second row } (R_2) \\ \rightarrow \text{Third row } (R_3) \end{matrix}$$

$\downarrow$ First column (C_1) $\quad$ $\downarrow$ Second column (C_2)

Note In this chapter, we will consider only those matrices whose elements or entries are real numbers or functions taking real values.

Order of a Matrix

Suppose a matrix have m **rows** and n **columns**, then order of matrix is written as $m \times n$, where m represents number of rows and n represents number of columns, and read as m by n matrix.

In general, $m \times n$ matrix has the following rectangular array

$$A=\begin{bmatrix} a_{11} & a_{12} & \cdots & a_{1n} \\ a_{21} & a_{22} & \cdots & a_{2n} \\ \vdots & \vdots & \vdots & \vdots \\ a_{m1} & a_{m2} & \cdots & a_{mn} \end{bmatrix}_{m\times n}$$

In notation form, it can be rewritten as $A=[a_{ij}]_{m\times n}$, where $1\le i\le m$, $1\le j\le n$ and $i, j\in N$.

Here, the ith row consists of the elements a_{i1}, a_{i2}, $a_{i3}, \ldots, a_{in}$, while jth column consists of the elements a_{1j}, a_{2j}, $a_{3j}, \ldots, a_{mj}$.

In general, a_{ij} is an element lying in the ith row and jth column. We can also call it as (i, j)th element of matrix A. The number of elements in $m \times n$ matrix will be equal to mn.

e.g. $A=\begin{bmatrix} 2 & 0 \\ 4 & -3 \\ -7 & 1 \end{bmatrix}$

Here, A has 3 rows and 2 columns. So, the order of matrix is 3×2 and it has $3\times 2=6$ elements.

Example 1 In the matrix $A=\begin{bmatrix} 2 & 5 & 19 & -7 \\ 35 & -2 & \frac{5}{2} & 12 \\ \sqrt{3} & 1 & -5 & 17 \end{bmatrix}$,

(i) write the order of the matrix.

(ii) write the value of elements a_{13}, a_{21}, a_{23} and a_{33}.

[NCERT]

Sol. (i) Here, matrix A has 3 rows and 4 columns, so the order of the matrix is 3×4.

(ii) Since, a_{ij} represents the element in ith row and jth column.

$\therefore$ a_{13} = Element in first row and third column $=19$

Similarly, $a_{21}=35$, $a_{23}=\frac{5}{2}$ and $a_{33}=-5$

Method to Find the Order of a Matrix When Number of Elements is Given

Suppose number of elements (say P) of a matrix is given, then to find the possible orders of matrix, we use the following steps

I. As matrix of order $m\times n$ has mn elements. So, firstly put mn = number of elements, say P.

II. Find all possible factors of P.

III. Now, form all possible ordered pairs with the help of these factors such that the product of elements of each ordered pair is P. These ordered pairs gives the possible orders of given matrix.

Example 2 If a matrix has 16 elements, then what are the possible orders it can have?

Sol. Given number of elements, $mn=16$

All factors of 16 are 1, 2, 4, 8 and 16.

Possible ordered pairs, whose element's product is 16, are (1, 16), (2, 8), (4, 4), (8, 2) and (16, 1).

Hence, the possible orders of matrix are

1×16, 2×8, 4×4, 8×2 and 16×1.

Formation of a Matrix

Sometimes, a relation between the elements and its position is given to us. Then, to form a matrix, whose elements satisfies this relation, we put different values of i and j according to given order to find all elements and then write the matrix of given order.

Example 3 Construct a matrix of order 3×2, whose elements are determined by $a_{ij}=\frac{2i-j}{3}$.

Sol. Let A be a matrix of order 3×2.

Then, $A=[a_{ij}]_{3\times 2}=\begin{bmatrix} a_{11} & a_{12} \\ a_{21} & a_{22} \\ a_{31} & a_{32} \end{bmatrix}$ ...(i)

Given, $a_{ij}=\frac{2i-j}{3}$

$\therefore$ $a_{11}=\frac{2(1)-1}{3}=\frac{1}{3}$, $a_{12}=\frac{2(1)-2}{3}=0$,

$a_{21}=\frac{2(2)-1}{3}=1$, $a_{22}=\frac{2(2)-2}{3}=\frac{2}{3}$,

$a_{31}=\frac{2(3)-1}{3}=\frac{5}{3}$, $a_{32}=\frac{2(3)-2}{3}=\frac{4}{3}$

On putting all above values in Eq. (i), we get

$$A=\begin{bmatrix} \frac{1}{3} & 0 \\ 1 & \frac{2}{3} \\ \frac{5}{3} & \frac{4}{3} \end{bmatrix}$$

which is the required 3×2 order matrix.

Types of Matrices

There are various types of matrices, which are given below

(i) **Row Matrix** A matrix having only one row is called a row matrix.

e.g. $A=[1 \quad 2 \quad 3]_{1\times 3}$ [one row and three columns]

In general, row matrix $A=[a_{ij}]_{1\times n}$

where, n is number of columns.

(ii) **Column Matrix** A matrix having only one column is called a column matrix.

e.g. $B = \begin{bmatrix} 1 \\ 2 \\ 3 \end{bmatrix}_{3 \times 1}$ [one column and three rows]

In general, column matrix $B = [b_{ij}]_{m \times 1}$

where, m is number of rows.

(iii) **Zero or Null Matrix** If all the elements of a matrix are zero, then it is called a zero or null matrix. It is denoted by letter O.

e.g. $O = \begin{bmatrix} 0 & 0 & 0 \\ 0 & 0 & 0 \end{bmatrix}_{2 \times 3}$ $[a_{ij} = 0, \forall\, i \text{ and } j]$

(iv) **Square Matrix** A matrix in which number of rows and number of columns are equal, is called a square matrix.

e.g. $A = \begin{bmatrix} a & b \\ c & d \end{bmatrix}_{2 \times 2}$ [order is 2×2]

In general, square matrix $A = [a_{ij}]_{m \times m}$ or $[a_{ij}]_{n \times n}$

where, number of rows = number of columns = m or n.

Note

(i) A matrix of order $n \times n$ is also known as a **square matrix** of order 'n'.

(ii) If $A = [a_{ij}]$ is any square matrix of order n, then the elements $a_{11}, a_{22}, a_{33}, \ldots, a_{nn}$ are said to constitute the diagonal of the matrix A. We call these elements as **diagonal elements** and the line in which these elements lie, is called the **principal diagonal** or **diagonal** of the matrix.

(v) **Diagonal Matrix** A square matrix $A = [a_{ij}]_{m \times m}$ is said to be a diagonal matrix, if all the elements lying outside the diagonal elements are zero.

e.g. $A = \begin{bmatrix} a & 0 & 0 \\ 0 & b & 0 \\ 0 & 0 & c \end{bmatrix}_{3 \times 3}$ $[a_{ij} = 0, \text{ for } i \neq j]$

In above, A can be written as $A = \text{diag}\,[a, b, c]$.

A diagonal matrix of order $m \times m$ having $a_{11}, a_{22}, \ldots, a_{mm}$ as diagonal elements is denoted by $\text{diag}[a_{11}, a_{22}, \ldots, a_{mm}]$.

(vi) **Scalar Matrix** A diagonal matrix in which all diagonal elements are equal, is called a scalar matrix. In other words, a square matrix $A = [a_{ij}]_{m \times m}$ is said to be scalar, if

$$a_{ij} = \begin{cases} 0, & \text{for } i \neq j \\ \text{constant}\, k, & \text{for } i = j \end{cases}.$$

e.g. $A = \begin{bmatrix} 2 & 0 & 0 \\ 0 & 2 & 0 \\ 0 & 0 & 2 \end{bmatrix}_{3 \times 3}$

$[a_{ij} = 2, \text{ when } i = j \text{ and } a_{ij} = 0, \text{ when } i \neq j]$

Note A scalar matrix is a diagonal matrix but a diagonal matrix may or may not be a scalar matrix.

(vii) **Unit or Identity Matrix** A square matrix in which all diagonals elements are 1 and rest are 0, is called an identity matrix. In other words, a square matrix $A = [a_{ij}]_{n \times n}$ is an identity matrix, if

$$a_{ij} = \begin{cases} 1, & \text{for } i = j \\ 0, & \text{for } i \neq j \end{cases}.$$

Identity matrix of order n is denoted by I_n or simply I (when order is clear from context).

e.g. $A = \begin{bmatrix} 1 & 0 \\ 0 & 1 \end{bmatrix}_{2 \times 2}$

$[a_{ij} = 1, \text{ when } i = j \text{ and } a_{ij} = 0, \text{ when } i \neq j]$

Note A scalar matrix is an identity matrix, when $k = 1$ and every identity matrix is always a scalar matrix.

(viii) **Triangular Matrices** In a square matrix, if $a_{ij} = 0, \forall\, i > j$, i.e. all the elements below the diagonal are zero then it is called an **upper triangular matrix** and if $a_{ij} = 0, \forall\, i < j$, i.e. all the elements upper the diagonal are zero, then it is called a **lower triangular matrix.**

A matrix, in upper or lower triangular, is called a **triangular matrix.** A triangular matrix $A = [a_{ij}]_{n \times n}$ is called **strictly** triangular, if $a_{ii} = 0, \forall\, 1 \leq i \leq n$.

e.g. $\begin{bmatrix} 3 & 1 & 2 \\ 0 & 6 & -1 \\ 0 & 0 & 2 \end{bmatrix}$ Upper triangular matrix, $\begin{bmatrix} 1 & 0 & 0 \\ 2 & 1 & 0 \\ 1 & 1 & 1 \end{bmatrix}$ Lower triangular matrix

Example 4 Identify the following types of matrices.

(i) $[1 \;\; 4 \;\; 5]$

(ii) $\begin{bmatrix} 1 & 2 \\ 4 & 6 \end{bmatrix}$

(iii) $\begin{bmatrix} 3 & 0 & 0 \\ 0 & 3 & 0 \\ 0 & 0 & 3 \end{bmatrix}$

(iv) $\begin{bmatrix} 1 & 0 & 0 \\ 0 & 4 & 0 \\ 0 & 0 & 2 \end{bmatrix}$

Sol. (i) We have, $[1 \;\; 4 \;\; 5]$. Here, we see that matrix has only one row and three columns, so it is a row matrix.

(ii) We have, $\begin{bmatrix} 1 & 2 \\ 4 & 6 \end{bmatrix}$. Here, we see that matrix has two rows and two columns. So, it is a square matrix.

(iii) We have, $\begin{bmatrix} 3 & 0 & 0 \\ 0 & 3 & 0 \\ 0 & 0 & 3 \end{bmatrix}$. Here, we see that all diagonal elements of square matrix are equal but different from one and non-diagonal elements are zero. So, it is a scalar matrix.

(iv) We have, $\begin{bmatrix} 1 & 0 & 0 \\ 0 & 4 & 0 \\ 0 & 0 & 2 \end{bmatrix}$. Here, we see that diagonal elements are not equal and non-diagonal elements are zero. So, it is a diagonal matrix.

Comparable Matrices

Two matrices A and B are said to be comparable, if they have same order.

e.g. $\begin{bmatrix} 3 & 1 \\ 2 & -4 \\ 5 & 0 \end{bmatrix}$ and $\begin{bmatrix} 8 & -5 \\ 4 & 7 \\ 3 & 2 \end{bmatrix}$ are comparable matrices, since each of them have order 3×2.

Equality of Matrices

Two matrices, say $A = [a_{ij}]$ and $B = [b_{ij}]$, are said to be equal, if their order are same and their corresponding elements are also equal, i.e. $a_{ij} = b_{ij}, \forall\, i$ and j. Symbolically, if two matrices A and B are equal, then we write $A = B$.

e.g. $\begin{bmatrix} 1 & 2 \\ 0 & 4 \end{bmatrix}$ and $\begin{bmatrix} 1 & 2 \\ 0 & 4 \end{bmatrix}$ are equal matrices, but $\begin{bmatrix} 1 & 2 \\ 0 & 4 \end{bmatrix}$ and $\begin{bmatrix} 2 & 1 \\ 4 & 0 \end{bmatrix}$ are not equal matrices because corresponding elements are not equal.

Example 5 Find the values of a, b and c, when $\begin{bmatrix} a & 3 \\ 2 & c \end{bmatrix} = \begin{bmatrix} 1 & b \\ 2 & 2 \end{bmatrix}$.

Sol. Given, $\begin{bmatrix} a & 3 \\ 2 & c \end{bmatrix} = \begin{bmatrix} 1 & b \\ 2 & 2 \end{bmatrix}$

Here, both matrices are equal, so we equate the corresponding elements.

Now, $a = 1$, $3 = b$ and $c = 2$

i.e. $a = 1$, $b = 3$ and $c = 2$

Example 6 If $\begin{bmatrix} x - y & 2x + z \\ 2x - y & 3z + w \end{bmatrix} = \begin{bmatrix} -1 & 5 \\ 0 & 13 \end{bmatrix}$, then find x, y, z and w.

Sol. Given, $\begin{bmatrix} x - y & 2x + z \\ 2x - y & 3z + w \end{bmatrix} = \begin{bmatrix} -1 & 5 \\ 0 & 13 \end{bmatrix}$

Here, both matrices are equal, so we equate the corresponding elements

Now, $x - y = -1$ ...(i)

$2x + z = 5$ ...(ii)

$2x - y = 0$ ...(iii)

and $3z + w = 13$ ...(iv)

On solving Eqs. (i) and (iii), we get

$x = 1$ and $y = 2$

On putting the value of x in Eq. (ii), we get

$2 \times 1 + z = 5 \Rightarrow z = 5 - 2 = 3$

On putting the value of z in Eq. (iv), we get

$3 \times 3 + w = 13 \Rightarrow w = 13 - 9 = 4$

Hence, $x = 1$, $y = 2$, $z = 3$ and $w = 4$.

Topic Practice 1

Very Short Answer Type Questions

(2 Marks)

1 The sale figure of three car dealers during March 2015 showed that dealer A solds 6 deluxe, 4 premium and 5 standard cars, dealer B solds 8 deluxe, 3 premium and 4 standard cars and dealer C solds 4 deluxe, 2 premium and 3 standard cars. Write 3×3 matrices summarising sales data for March.

2 In the matrix, $A = \begin{bmatrix} a & 1 & x \\ 2 & \sqrt{3} & x^2 - y \\ 0 & 5 & -2/5 \end{bmatrix}$. Write

(i) the order of the matrix A.

(ii) the number of elements.

(iii) the value of elements a_{23}, a_{31} and a_{12}. **[NCERT Exemplar]**

3 Write the number of all possible matrices of order 2×2 with each entry 1, 2 or 3.

4 If a matrix has 24 elements, then what are the possible orders it can have? What if it has 13 elements? **[NCERT]**

5 If matrix $A = [a_{ij}]_{2 \times 2}$, where $a_{ij} = \begin{cases} 2, & i \neq j \\ 0, & i = j \end{cases}$, then write the matrix A.

6 Construct a 3×4 matrix, whose elements are given by $a_{ij} = \frac{1}{2}|-3i + j|$. **[NCERT]**

7 Construct a 3×2 matrix, whose elements are given by $a_{ij} = e^{ix} \sin jx$. **[NCERT Exemplar]**

8 Identify the following types of matrices.

(i) $\begin{bmatrix}1 & 0\\0 & 1\end{bmatrix}$ (ii) $\begin{bmatrix}1\\2\\-3\\4\end{bmatrix}$

(iii) $\begin{bmatrix}1 & -1 & 0\\2 & -3 & 4\\5 & -6 & 7\end{bmatrix}$ (iv) $\begin{bmatrix}1 & 0 & 0\\0 & 4 & 0\\0 & 0 & 9\end{bmatrix}$

9 If $\begin{bmatrix}a+4 & 3b\\8 & -6\end{bmatrix}=\begin{bmatrix}2a+2 & b+2\\8 & a-8b\end{bmatrix}$, then write the value of $a-2b$.

10 A is a matrix of order 2×6 and R is a row of A, then write the type of R as a matrix.

11 Find the values of a, b, c and d from the equation

$$\begin{bmatrix}2a+b & a-2b\\5c-d & 4c+3d\end{bmatrix}=\begin{bmatrix}4 & -3\\11 & 24\end{bmatrix}.$$ [NCERT]

12 Find the values of x, y and z, if $\begin{bmatrix}x+y+z\\x+z\\y+z\end{bmatrix}=\begin{bmatrix}9\\5\\7\end{bmatrix}$. [NCERT]

Short Answer Type Questions

4 Marks

13 For what values of x and y are the following matrices equal?

$A=\begin{bmatrix}2x+1 & 3y\\0 & y^2-5y\end{bmatrix}$ and $B=\begin{bmatrix}x+3 & y^2+2\\0 & -6\end{bmatrix}$

14 If $\begin{bmatrix}x+y & 2\\5 & xy\end{bmatrix}=\begin{bmatrix}6 & 2\\5 & 8\end{bmatrix}$, then find the values of x and y.

Hints & Solutions

1. In table form, the given information can be written as

	Deluxe	Premium	Standard
A	6	4	5
B	8	3	4
C	4	2	3

[1]

Here, we see that above table has 3 rows and 3 columns, so the given information in matrix form can be written as

$$\begin{array}{c} \\ A\\ B\\ C\end{array}\begin{array}{c}\text{Deluxe} \quad \text{Premium} \quad \text{Standard}\\ \begin{bmatrix}6 & 4 & 5\\8 & 3 & 4\\4 & 2 & 3\end{bmatrix}\end{array}$$ [1]

2. Similar as Example 1.

[**Ans.** (i) 3×3 (ii) 9 (iii) $a_{23}=x^2-y$, $a_{31}=0$, $a_{12}=1$]

3. We know that a matrix of order 2×2 has 4 entries. Since, each entry has 3 choices, namely 1, 2 or 3, therefore number of required matrices

$$=3\times3\times3\times3=3^4=81$$ [2]

4. The possible orders of a matrix having 24 elements are 1×24, 24×1, 2×12, 12×2, 3×8, 8×3, 4×6 and 6×4. [1]

The possible orders of a matrix having 13 elements are 1×13 and 13×1. [1]

5. Clearly, $A=\begin{bmatrix}a_{11} & a_{12}\\a_{21} & a_{22}\end{bmatrix}$

Now, $a_{11}=0$, $a_{12}=2$, $a_{21}=2$ and $a_{22}=0$

$\left[\because a_{ij}=\begin{cases}2, & \text{for } i\neq j\\0, & \text{for } i=j\end{cases}\right]$

$\therefore \quad A=\begin{bmatrix}0 & 2\\2 & 0\end{bmatrix}$ [2]

6. Let A be a 3×4 matrix.

Then, $A=\begin{bmatrix}a_{11} & a_{12} & a_{13} & a_{14}\\a_{21} & a_{22} & a_{23} & a_{24}\\a_{31} & a_{32} & a_{33} & a_{34}\end{bmatrix}_{3\times4}$ ...(i)

Here, $a_{ij}=\frac{1}{2}|-3i+j|$

$\therefore \quad a_{11}=\frac{1}{2}|-3+1|=1$, $a_{12}=\frac{1}{2}|-3+2|=\frac{1}{2}$,

$a_{13}=\frac{1}{2}|-3+3|=0$, $a_{14}=\frac{1}{2}|-3+4|=\frac{1}{2}$,

$a_{21}=\frac{1}{2}|-6+1|=\frac{5}{2}$, $a_{22}=\frac{1}{2}|-6+2|=2$,

$a_{23}=\frac{1}{2}|-6+3|=\frac{3}{2}$, $a_{24}=\frac{1}{2}|-6+4|=1$, [1]

$a_{31}=\frac{1}{2}|-9+1|=4$, $a_{32}=\frac{1}{2}|-9+2|=\frac{7}{2}$,

$a_{33}=\frac{1}{2}|-9+3|=3$ and $a_{34}=\frac{1}{2}|-9+4|=\frac{5}{2}$

On putting the values in Eq. (i), we get the required matrix, i.e. $A=\begin{bmatrix}1 & 1/2 & 0 & 1/2\\5/2 & 2 & 3/2 & 1\\4 & 7/2 & 3 & 5/2\end{bmatrix}_{3\times4}$ [1]

7. Similar as Question 6. $\left[\textbf{Ans.} \begin{bmatrix}e^x\sin x & e^x\sin 2x\\e^{2x}\sin x & e^{2x}\sin 2x\\e^{3x}\sin x & e^{3x}\sin 2x\end{bmatrix}\right]$

8. Similar as Example 4.

[**Ans.** (i) Identity matrix (ii) Column matrix (iii) Square matrix (iv) Diagonal matrix]

9. Similar as Example 6. [**Ans.** 0]

10. Given order of matrix A is 2×6.,

Clearly, each row of A contains 6 elements. [1]

Therefore, R is a row matrix of type 1×6. [1]

11. Similar as Example 6.

[**Ans.** $a=1$, $b=2$, $c=3$ and $d=4$]

12. Here, two matrices are equal. Therefore, equating the corresponding elements of two matrices, we get

$$x + y + z = 9 \quad \text{...(i)}$$
$$x + z = 5 \quad \text{...(ii)}$$
and $$y + z = 7 \quad \text{...(iii)}$$

On solving Eqs. (i) and (ii), we get

$$y = 9 - 5 = 4 \quad [1]$$

On putting $y = 4$ in Eq. (iii), we get

$$4 + z = 7 \Rightarrow z = 7 - 4 = 3$$

On putting $z = 3$ in Eq. (ii), we get

$$x + 3 = 5 \Rightarrow x = 5 - 3 = 2$$

Hence, $x = 2$, $y = 4$ and $z = 3$. [1]

13. Consider, $A = B$, then

$$\begin{bmatrix} 2x+1 & 3y \\ 0 & y^2-5y \end{bmatrix} = \begin{bmatrix} x+3 & y^2+2 \\ 0 & -6 \end{bmatrix}$$

$$\Rightarrow \quad 2x+1 = x+3 \quad \text{...(i)}$$
$$3y = y^2 + 2 \quad \text{...(ii)}$$
and $$y^2 - 5y = -6 \quad \text{...(iii)}$$

[$\because$ corresponding elements of two equal matrices are equal] [1]

Now, from Eq. (i), we get

$$2x + 1 = x + 3 \Rightarrow 2x - x = 3 - 1$$
$$\Rightarrow \quad x = 2 \quad [1]$$

Now, from Eq. (ii), we get

$$y^2 - 3y + 2 = 0 \Rightarrow (y-1)(y-2) = 0$$
$$\Rightarrow \quad y = 1 \text{ or } y = 2 \quad [1]$$

Now, from Eq. (iii), we get

$$y^2 - 5y + 6 = 0 \Rightarrow (y-2)(y-3) = 0$$
$$\Rightarrow \quad y = 2 \text{ or } y = 3$$

Hence, $x = 2$ and $y = 2$. [$\because y = 1, 2$ and $y = 2, 3 \Rightarrow y = 2$] [1]

14. **Hint** Use the identity, $(x-y)^2 = (x+y)^2 - 4xy$.

[**Ans.** $x = 4$, $y = 2$ or $x = 2$, $y = 4$]

TOPIC 02 Addition and Scalar Multiplication of Matrices

Here, we will discuss certain **operations** on matrices namely, addition of matrices, multiplication of a matrix by a scalar and difference of matrices.

Addition of Matrices

The sum of matrices A and B is a matrix whose elements are obtained by adding the corresponding elements of A and B. Let $A = [a_{ij}]$ and $B = [b_{ij}]$ be the two matrices of the same order, say $m \times n$. Then, the sum of two matrices A and B is defined as a matrix $C = [c_{ij}]_{m \times n}$, where $c_{ij} = a_{ij} + b_{ij}$ for all possible values of i and j.

e.g. $$\begin{bmatrix} 2 & 3 \\ 0 & -1 \end{bmatrix} + \begin{bmatrix} 6 & 9 \\ -4 & 1 \end{bmatrix} = \begin{bmatrix} 2+6 & 3+9 \\ 0+(-4) & -1+1 \end{bmatrix} = \begin{bmatrix} 8 & 12 \\ -4 & 0 \end{bmatrix}$$

Note

(i) If A and B are not of the same order, then $A + B$ is not defined and we say that both matrices are not compatiable for the sum $(A + B)$.

e.g. If $A = \begin{bmatrix} 2 & 3 \\ 1 & 0 \end{bmatrix}$ and $B = \begin{bmatrix} 1 & 2 & 3 \\ 1 & 0 & 1 \end{bmatrix}$, then $A + B$ is not defined.

(ii) Addition of matrices is an example of binary operation on the set of matrices of the same order.

Example 1 Find the sum of two matrices A and B, if

$$A = \begin{bmatrix} 1 & \sqrt{2} \\ 3 & 2 \end{bmatrix} \text{ and } B = \begin{bmatrix} 3 & -\sqrt{2} \\ 4 & 1 \end{bmatrix}.$$

Sol. Given matrices are $A = \begin{bmatrix} 1 & \sqrt{2} \\ 3 & 2 \end{bmatrix}$ and $B = \begin{bmatrix} 3 & -\sqrt{2} \\ 4 & 1 \end{bmatrix}$

Here, we see that both matrices are of same order, therefore sum of A and B is defined.

$$\text{Now, } A + B = \begin{bmatrix} 1 & \sqrt{2} \\ 3 & 2 \end{bmatrix} + \begin{bmatrix} 3 & -\sqrt{2} \\ 4 & 1 \end{bmatrix}$$
$$= \begin{bmatrix} 1+3 & \sqrt{2}-\sqrt{2} \\ 3+4 & 2+1 \end{bmatrix} \quad \left[\because \text{adding corresponding elements of } A \text{ and } B\right]$$
$$= \begin{bmatrix} 4 & 0 \\ 7 & 3 \end{bmatrix}$$

Negative of a Matrix

If $A = [a_{ij}]_{m \times n}$ is a matrix, then $-A = [-a_{ij}]_{m \times n}$ is called the **negative** of matrix A. In negative of A, each element is multiply by (-1).

e.g. Let $A = \begin{bmatrix} 1 & 3 \\ -2 & 4 \end{bmatrix}$, then $-A = (-1)A = \begin{bmatrix} -1 & -3 \\ 2 & -4 \end{bmatrix}$

Difference (or Subtraction) of Matrices

Difference of two matrices is equal to the addition of negative of a matrix to other matrix.

Difference of two matrices A and B,

i.e. $\quad B - A = B + (-A)$.

Let $A=[a_{ij}]$ and $B=[b_{ij}]$ be the two matrices of the same order (say $m \times n$), then the difference of these matrices, $A-B$ is defined as a matrix $D=[d_{ij}]$, where $d_{ij}=a_{ij}-b_{ij}$ for all values of i and j.

e.g. Let $A=\begin{bmatrix} a & b \\ c & d \end{bmatrix}$ and $B=\begin{bmatrix} e & f \\ g & h \end{bmatrix}$

Then, $A-B=A+(-1)B=\begin{bmatrix} a & b \\ c & d \end{bmatrix}+(-1)\begin{bmatrix} e & f \\ g & h \end{bmatrix}$

$$=\begin{bmatrix} a & b \\ c & d \end{bmatrix}+\begin{bmatrix} -e & -f \\ -g & -h \end{bmatrix}$$

$$=\begin{bmatrix} a-e & b-f \\ c-g & d-h \end{bmatrix}$$

Example 2 If $A=\begin{bmatrix} 4 & 4 \\ 2 & 7 \end{bmatrix}$, $B=\begin{bmatrix} 1 & 2 \\ -1 & 3 \end{bmatrix}$ and $C=\begin{bmatrix} 1 & 4 \\ 3 & -5 \end{bmatrix}$, then find $A-B-C$.

Sol. Here, A, B, C are the three matrices of same order 2×2.

Now, $A-B-C=A+(-1)B+(-1)C$

$$=\begin{bmatrix} 4 & 4 \\ 2 & 7 \end{bmatrix}+(-1)\begin{bmatrix} 1 & 2 \\ -1 & 3 \end{bmatrix}+(-1)\begin{bmatrix} 1 & 4 \\ 3 & -5 \end{bmatrix}$$

$$=\begin{bmatrix} 4 & 4 \\ 2 & 7 \end{bmatrix}+\begin{bmatrix} -1 & -2 \\ 1 & -3 \end{bmatrix}+\begin{bmatrix} -1 & -4 \\ -3 & 5 \end{bmatrix}$$

$$=\begin{bmatrix} 4-1-1 & 4-2-4 \\ 2+1-3 & 7-3+5 \end{bmatrix}=\begin{bmatrix} 2 & -2 \\ 0 & 9 \end{bmatrix}$$

Example 3 Two farmers Ramkishan and Gurucharan Singh cultivates only three varieties of rice namely Basmati, Permal and Naura. The sales (in ₹) of these varieties of rice by both the farmers in the months of September and October are given by the matrices A and B.

September sales (in ₹)

$$\begin{array}{cccc} & \text{Basmati} & \text{Permal} & \text{Naura} \end{array}$$
$$A=\begin{bmatrix} 10000 & 20000 & 30000 \\ 50000 & 30000 & 10000 \end{bmatrix}\begin{array}{l}\text{Ramkishan} \\ \text{Gurucharan Singh}\end{array}$$

October sales (in ₹)

$$\begin{array}{cccc} & \text{Basmati} & \text{Permal} & \text{Naura} \end{array}$$
$$B=\begin{bmatrix} 5000 & 10000 & 6000 \\ 20000 & 10000 & 10000 \end{bmatrix}\begin{array}{l}\text{Ramkishan} \\ \text{Gurucharan Singh}\end{array}$$

(i) Find the combined sales in September and October for each farmer in each variety.

(ii) Find the decrease in sales from September to October.

(iii) If both farmers receive 2% profit on gross sales, then compute the profit for each farmer and for each variety sold in October.

Sol. (i) Combined sales in September and October for each farmer in each variety is given by

$$A+B=\begin{bmatrix} 10000 & 20000 & 30000 \\ 50000 & 30000 & 10000 \end{bmatrix}+\begin{bmatrix} 5000 & 10000 & 6000 \\ 20000 & 10000 & 10000 \end{bmatrix}$$

$$\begin{array}{cccc} & \text{Basmati} & \text{Permal} & \text{Naura} \end{array}$$
$$=\begin{bmatrix} 15000 & 30000 & 36000 \\ 70000 & 40000 & 20000 \end{bmatrix}\begin{array}{l}\text{Ramkishan} \\ \text{Gurucharan Singh}\end{array}$$

(ii) Changes in sales from September to October is given by

$$A-B=\begin{bmatrix} 10000 & 20000 & 30000 \\ 50000 & 30000 & 10000 \end{bmatrix}-\begin{bmatrix} 5000 & 10000 & 6000 \\ 20000 & 10000 & 10000 \end{bmatrix}$$

$$\begin{array}{cccc} & \text{Basmati} & \text{Permal} & \text{Naura} \end{array}$$
$$=\begin{bmatrix} 5000 & 10000 & 24000 \\ 30000 & 20000 & 0 \end{bmatrix}\begin{array}{l}\text{Ramkishan} \\ \text{Gurucharan Singh}\end{array}$$

(iii) 2% of $B=\frac{2}{100}\times B=0.02\times B$

$$\begin{array}{cccc} & \text{Basmati} & \text{Permal} & \text{Naura} \end{array}$$
$$=0.02\begin{bmatrix} 5000 & 10000 & 6000 \\ 20000 & 10000 & 10000 \end{bmatrix}\begin{array}{l}\text{Ramkishan} \\ \text{Gurucharan Singh}\end{array}$$

$$\begin{array}{cccc} & \text{Basmati} & \text{Permal} & \text{Naura} \end{array}$$
$$=\begin{bmatrix} 100 & 200 & 120 \\ 400 & 200 & 200 \end{bmatrix}\begin{array}{l}\text{Ramkishan} \\ \text{Gurucharan Singh}\end{array}$$

[multiply each element by 0.02]

Hence, the profits earn by Ramkishan in the sale of each variety of rice are ₹ 100, ₹ 200, ₹ 120 respectively and profits earn by Gurucharan Singh in the sale of each variety of rice are ₹ 400, ₹ 200, ₹ 200 respectively.

Properties of Matrix Addition

Let $A=[a_{ij}]$, $B=[b_{ij}]$ and $C=[c_{ij}]$ be any three matrices of the same order $m \times n$. Then, we have the following properties

(i) **Commutative Law** Matrix addition is commutative,

i.e. $A+B=[a_{ij}]+[b_{ij}]=[a_{ij}+b_{ij}]=[b_{ij}+a_{ij}]$
$=[b_{ij}]+[a_{ij}]=B+A$

(ii) **Associative Law** Matrix addition is associative,

i.e. $A+(B+C)=[a_{ij}]+([b_{ij}]+[c_{ij}])$
$=a_{ij}+(b_{ij}+c_{ij})=[a_{ij}+b_{ij}]+c_{ij}$
$=([a_{ij}]+[b_{ij}])+[c_{ij}]=(A+B)+C$

(iii) **Existence of Additive Identity** Let O be a zero matrix of order $m \times n$, then $A+O=O+A=A$. So, O is the additive identity for matrix addition.

(iv) **Existence of Additive Inverse** Let A be a matrix, then $(-A)$ is another matrix of same order $m \times n$, such that $A+(-A)=O=(-A)+A$.
So, $(-A)$ or negative of A is the additive inverse of A.

Example 4 If $A=\begin{bmatrix}2 & 2\\ -3 & 1\\ 4 & 0\end{bmatrix}$, $B=\begin{bmatrix}6 & 2\\ 1 & 3\\ 0 & 4\end{bmatrix}$ and $C=\begin{bmatrix}-8 & -4\\ 2 & -4\\ -4 & -4\end{bmatrix}$, then

(i) verify the commutative law with respect to addition, i.e. verify $A+B=B+A$.
(ii) verify the associative law with respect to addition, i.e. verify $A+(B+C)=(A+B)+C$.
(iii) find the additive inverse of matrix A.

Sol. Given matrices are $A=\begin{bmatrix}2 & 2\\ -3 & 1\\ 4 & 0\end{bmatrix}$, $B=\begin{bmatrix}6 & 2\\ 1 & 3\\ 0 & 4\end{bmatrix}$ and $C=\begin{bmatrix}-8 & -4\\ 2 & -4\\ -4 & -4\end{bmatrix}$.

Now,

(i) $$A+B=\begin{bmatrix}2 & 2\\ -3 & 1\\ 4 & 0\end{bmatrix}+\begin{bmatrix}6 & 2\\ 1 & 3\\ 0 & 4\end{bmatrix}=\begin{bmatrix}2+6 & 2+2\\ -3+1 & 1+3\\ 4+0 & 0+4\end{bmatrix}$$
$$=\begin{bmatrix}8 & 4\\ -2 & 4\\ 4 & 4\end{bmatrix} \quad \text{...(i)}$$
and $$B+A=\begin{bmatrix}6 & 2\\ 1 & 3\\ 0 & 4\end{bmatrix}+\begin{bmatrix}2 & 2\\ -3 & 1\\ 4 & 0\end{bmatrix}$$
$$=\begin{bmatrix}6+2 & 2+2\\ 1-3 & 3+1\\ 0+4 & 4+0\end{bmatrix}=\begin{bmatrix}8 & 4\\ -2 & 4\\ 4 & 4\end{bmatrix}$$

Thus, $A+B=B+A$.
Hence, commutative law is verified.

(ii) $$A+(B+C)=\begin{bmatrix}2 & 2\\ -3 & 1\\ 4 & 0\end{bmatrix}+\left(\begin{bmatrix}6 & 2\\ 1 & 3\\ 0 & 4\end{bmatrix}+\begin{bmatrix}-8 & -4\\ 2 & -4\\ -4 & -4\end{bmatrix}\right)$$
$$=\begin{bmatrix}2 & 2\\ -3 & 1\\ 4 & 0\end{bmatrix}+\begin{bmatrix}6-8 & 2-4\\ 1+2 & 3-4\\ 0-4 & 4-4\end{bmatrix}$$
$$=\begin{bmatrix}2 & 2\\ -3 & 1\\ 4 & 0\end{bmatrix}+\begin{bmatrix}-2 & -2\\ 3 & -1\\ -4 & 0\end{bmatrix}$$
$$=\begin{bmatrix}2-2 & 2-2\\ -3+3 & 1-1\\ 4-4 & 0+0\end{bmatrix}=\begin{bmatrix}0 & 0\\ 0 & 0\\ 0 & 0\end{bmatrix}$$

and $$(A+B)+C=\begin{bmatrix}8 & 4\\ -2 & 4\\ 4 & 4\end{bmatrix}+\begin{bmatrix}-8 & -4\\ 2 & -4\\ -4 & -4\end{bmatrix} \quad \text{[from Eq. (i)]}$$
$$=\begin{bmatrix}8-8 & 4-4\\ -2+2 & 4-4\\ 4-4 & 4-4\end{bmatrix}=\begin{bmatrix}0 & 0\\ 0 & 0\\ 0 & 0\end{bmatrix}$$

Thus, $A+(B+C)=(A+B)+C$.
Hence, associative law is verified.

(iii) We know that additive inverse of A is $(-1)A$.

$$\therefore \quad (-1)A=(-1)\begin{bmatrix}2 & 2\\ -3 & 1\\ 4 & 0\end{bmatrix}=\begin{bmatrix}-2 & -2\\ 3 & -1\\ -4 & 0\end{bmatrix}$$
[multiplying each element by (−1)]

Multiplication of a Matrix by a Scalar (or a Number)

Let $A=[a_{ij}]_{m\times n}$ be a matrix and k be a scalar, then kA is a another matrix which is obtained by multiplying each element of A by the scalar k.

If $A=\begin{bmatrix}a & b\\ c & d\end{bmatrix}$, then $kA=k\begin{bmatrix}a & b\\ c & d\end{bmatrix}=\begin{bmatrix}ka & kb\\ kc & kd\end{bmatrix}$.

Thus, $kA=k[a_{ij}]_{m\times n}=[k(a_{ij})]_{m\times n}$, i.e. (i, j)th element of kA is ka_{ij} for all possible values of i and j.

e.g. If $A=\begin{bmatrix}7 & 18\\ -1 & 3\end{bmatrix}$ and $k=3$.

Then, $$kA=3A=3\begin{bmatrix}7 & 18\\ -1 & 3\end{bmatrix}$$
$$=\begin{bmatrix}3\times 7 & 3\times 18\\ 3\times(-1) & 3\times 3\end{bmatrix}=\begin{bmatrix}21 & 54\\ -3 & 9\end{bmatrix}$$

Example 5 If $A=\begin{bmatrix}1 & 0 & 0\\ 0 & -1 & 0\\ 0 & 0 & 2\end{bmatrix}$ and $B=\begin{bmatrix}2 & 0 & 0\\ 0 & 3 & 0\\ 0 & 0 & -1\end{bmatrix}$, then find $3A+4B$.

Sol. We have, $A=\begin{bmatrix}1 & 0 & 0\\ 0 & -1 & 0\\ 0 & 0 & 2\end{bmatrix}$ and $B=\begin{bmatrix}2 & 0 & 0\\ 0 & 3 & 0\\ 0 & 0 & -1\end{bmatrix}$

Now, $$3A+4B=3\begin{bmatrix}1 & 0 & 0\\ 0 & -1 & 0\\ 0 & 0 & 2\end{bmatrix}+4\begin{bmatrix}2 & 0 & 0\\ 0 & 3 & 0\\ 0 & 0 & -1\end{bmatrix}$$
$$=\begin{bmatrix}3 & 0 & 0\\ 0 & -3 & 0\\ 0 & 0 & 6\end{bmatrix}+\begin{bmatrix}8 & 0 & 0\\ 0 & 12 & 0\\ 0 & 0 & -4\end{bmatrix}$$
$$=\begin{bmatrix}3+8 & 0 & 0\\ 0 & -3+12 & 0\\ 0 & 0 & 6-4\end{bmatrix}=\begin{bmatrix}11 & 0 & 0\\ 0 & 9 & 0\\ 0 & 0 & 2\end{bmatrix}$$

Example 6 If $2\begin{bmatrix}1 & 3\\ 0 & x\end{bmatrix}+\begin{bmatrix}y & 0\\ 1 & 2\end{bmatrix}=\begin{bmatrix}5 & 6\\ 1 & 8\end{bmatrix}$, then find the value of $(x+y)$.

Sol. Given, $2\begin{bmatrix}1 & 3\\ 0 & x\end{bmatrix}+\begin{bmatrix}y & 0\\ 1 & 2\end{bmatrix}=\begin{bmatrix}5 & 6\\ 1 & 8\end{bmatrix}$

$$\Rightarrow \begin{bmatrix}2 & 6\\ 0 & 2x\end{bmatrix}+\begin{bmatrix}y & 0\\ 1 & 2\end{bmatrix}=\begin{bmatrix}5 & 6\\ 1 & 8\end{bmatrix}$$

$$\Rightarrow \begin{bmatrix}2+y & 6+0\\ 0+1 & 2x+2\end{bmatrix}=\begin{bmatrix}5 & 6\\ 1 & 8\end{bmatrix}$$

Comparing the corresponding elements, we get

$$2+y=5 \text{ and } 2x+2=8$$

$$\Rightarrow y=5-2=3 \text{ and } 2x=8-2$$

$$\Rightarrow y=3 \text{ and } x=\frac{6}{2}=3$$

$$\therefore x+y=6$$

Properties of Scalar Multiplication

Let $A=[a_{ij}]$ and $B=[b_{ij}]$ be the two matrices of same order $m\times n$. Then,

(i) $k(A+B)=kA+kB$, where k is a scalar.

(ii) $(k_1+k_2)A=k_1A+k_2A$, where k_1 and k_2 are scalars.

(iii) $(kl)A=k(lA)=l(kA)$, where l and k are scalars.

(iv) $1A=A$

(v) $(-1)A=-A$

Example 7 Let A and B be two matrices such that $A=\begin{bmatrix}2 & 1\\ -1 & 0\\ 2 & 5\end{bmatrix}$ and $B=\begin{bmatrix}-1 & 2\\ 0 & -1\\ 3 & 2\end{bmatrix}$, then verify the following results.

(i) $3(A+B)=3A+3B$

(ii) $(5+7)A=5A+7A$

Sol. Given matrices are $A=\begin{bmatrix}2 & 1\\ -1 & 0\\ 2 & 5\end{bmatrix}$ and $B=\begin{bmatrix}-1 & 2\\ 0 & -1\\ 3 & 2\end{bmatrix}$.

(i) $\text{LHS}=3(A+B)=3\left(\begin{bmatrix}2 & 1\\ -1 & 0\\ 2 & 5\end{bmatrix}+\begin{bmatrix}-1 & 2\\ 0 & -1\\ 3 & 2\end{bmatrix}\right)$

$$=3\begin{bmatrix}2-1 & 1+2\\ -1+0 & 0-1\\ 2+3 & 5+2\end{bmatrix}=3\begin{bmatrix}1 & 3\\ -1 & -1\\ 5 & 7\end{bmatrix}=\begin{bmatrix}3 & 9\\ -3 & -3\\ 15 & 21\end{bmatrix}$$

[multiplying each element by 3]

and $\text{RHS}=3A+3B$

$$=3\begin{bmatrix}2 & 1\\ -1 & 0\\ 2 & 5\end{bmatrix}+3\begin{bmatrix}-1 & 2\\ 0 & -1\\ 3 & 2\end{bmatrix}$$

$$=\begin{bmatrix}6 & 3\\ -3 & 0\\ 6 & 15\end{bmatrix}+\begin{bmatrix}-3 & 6\\ 0 & -3\\ 9 & 6\end{bmatrix}$$

[multiplying each element by 3]

$$=\begin{bmatrix}6-3 & 3+6\\ -3+0 & 0-3\\ 6+9 & 15+6\end{bmatrix}=\begin{bmatrix}3 & 9\\ -3 & -3\\ 15 & 21\end{bmatrix}$$

Thus, LHS = RHS **Hence verified.**

(ii) $\text{LHS}=(5+7)A=12A$

$$=12\begin{bmatrix}2 & 1\\ -1 & 0\\ 2 & 5\end{bmatrix}=\begin{bmatrix}24 & 12\\ -12 & 0\\ 24 & 60\end{bmatrix}$$

[multiplying each element by 12]

and $\text{RHS}=5A+7A$

$$=5\begin{bmatrix}2 & 1\\ -1 & 0\\ 2 & 5\end{bmatrix}+7\begin{bmatrix}2 & 1\\ -1 & 0\\ 2 & 5\end{bmatrix}$$

$$=\begin{bmatrix}10 & 5\\ -5 & 0\\ 10 & 25\end{bmatrix}+\begin{bmatrix}14 & 7\\ -7 & 0\\ 14 & 35\end{bmatrix}$$

$$=\begin{bmatrix}10+14 & 5+7\\ -5-7 & 0\\ 10+14 & 25+35\end{bmatrix}=\begin{bmatrix}24 & 12\\ -12 & 0\\ 24 & 60\end{bmatrix}$$

Thus, LHS = RHS **Hence verified.**

Example 8 If $A=\begin{bmatrix}8 & 0\\ 4 & -2\\ 3 & 6\end{bmatrix}$ and $B=\begin{bmatrix}2 & -2\\ 4 & 2\\ -5 & 1\end{bmatrix}$, then find the matrix X, such that $2A+3X=5B$.

Sol. Given, $A=\begin{bmatrix}8 & 0\\ 4 & -2\\ 3 & 6\end{bmatrix}$ and $B=\begin{bmatrix}2 & -2\\ 4 & 2\\ -5 & 1\end{bmatrix}$

Also given, $2A+3X=5B \Rightarrow 3X=5B-2A$

$$\Rightarrow X=\frac{1}{3}[5B-2A]=\frac{1}{3}\left\{5\begin{bmatrix}2 & -2\\ 4 & 2\\ -5 & 1\end{bmatrix}-2\begin{bmatrix}8 & 0\\ 4 & -2\\ 3 & 6\end{bmatrix}\right\}$$

$$=\frac{1}{3}\left\{\begin{bmatrix}10 & -10\\ 20 & 10\\ -25 & 5\end{bmatrix}+\begin{bmatrix}-16 & 0\\ -8 & 4\\ -6 & -12\end{bmatrix}\right\}$$

$$=\frac{1}{3}\begin{bmatrix}10-16 & -10+0\\ 20-8 & 10+4\\ -25-6 & 5-12\end{bmatrix}=\frac{1}{3}\begin{bmatrix}-6 & -10\\ 12 & 14\\ -31 & -7\end{bmatrix}$$

$$\Rightarrow X=\begin{bmatrix}-2 & -\frac{10}{3}\\ 4 & \frac{14}{3}\\ -\frac{31}{3} & -\frac{7}{3}\end{bmatrix}$$, which is the required matrix X.

Example 9 Find X and Y, if $X+Y=\begin{bmatrix}7&0\\2&5\end{bmatrix}$ and $X-Y=\begin{bmatrix}3&0\\0&3\end{bmatrix}$. **[ISC 2008]**

Sol. Given, $X+Y=\begin{bmatrix}7&0\\2&5\end{bmatrix}$ ...(i)

and $X-Y=\begin{bmatrix}3&0\\0&3\end{bmatrix}$ ...(ii)

On adding Eqs. (i) and (ii), we get

$$2X=\begin{bmatrix}7&0\\2&5\end{bmatrix}+\begin{bmatrix}3&0\\0&3\end{bmatrix}$$

$$\Rightarrow\quad 2X=\begin{bmatrix}7+3&0\\2&5+3\end{bmatrix}$$

$$\Rightarrow\quad X=\frac{1}{2}\begin{bmatrix}10&0\\2&8\end{bmatrix}\Rightarrow X=\begin{bmatrix}5&0\\1&4\end{bmatrix}$$

On putting the value of X in Eq. (i), we get

$$\begin{bmatrix}5&0\\1&4\end{bmatrix}+Y=\begin{bmatrix}7&0\\2&5\end{bmatrix}$$

$$\Rightarrow\quad Y=\begin{bmatrix}7&0\\2&5\end{bmatrix}-\begin{bmatrix}5&0\\1&4\end{bmatrix}$$

$$=\begin{bmatrix}7-5&0\\2-1&5-4\end{bmatrix}=\begin{bmatrix}2&0\\1&1\end{bmatrix}$$

Topic Practice 2

Very Short Answer Type Questions

(2 Marks)

1 If $X+\begin{bmatrix}1&3\\-1&2\end{bmatrix}=\begin{bmatrix}4&-1\\6&2\end{bmatrix}$, then find matrix X of order 2 by 2.

2 Simplify $4\begin{bmatrix}1&3\\1&-4\end{bmatrix}-\frac{1}{2}\begin{bmatrix}8&4\\4&8\end{bmatrix}$.

3 If $2\begin{bmatrix}3&4\\5&x\end{bmatrix}+\begin{bmatrix}1&y\\0&1\end{bmatrix}=\begin{bmatrix}7&0\\10&5\end{bmatrix}$, then find $(x-y)$.

4 If $A=\begin{bmatrix}2&3\\1&2\end{bmatrix}$, $B=\begin{bmatrix}1&3&2\\4&3&1\end{bmatrix}$, $C=\begin{bmatrix}1\\2\end{bmatrix}$ and $D=\begin{bmatrix}4&6&8\\5&7&9\end{bmatrix}$, then which of the sum $A+B$, $B+C$, $C+D$ and $B+D$ is defined?

5 Find x, y, z and t, if $2\begin{bmatrix}x&z\\y&t\end{bmatrix}+3\begin{bmatrix}1&-1\\0&2\end{bmatrix}=3\begin{bmatrix}3&5\\4&6\end{bmatrix}$. **[NCERT]**

6 Simplify $\cos\theta\begin{bmatrix}\cos\theta&\sin\theta\\-\sin\theta&\cos\theta\end{bmatrix}+\sin\theta\begin{bmatrix}\sin\theta&-\cos\theta\\\cos\theta&\sin\theta\end{bmatrix}$. **[NCERT]**

7 If $A=\frac{1}{\pi}\begin{bmatrix}\sin^{-1}(x\pi)&\tan^{-1}\left(\frac{x}{\pi}\right)\\\sin^{-1}\left(\frac{x}{\pi}\right)&\cot^{-1}(\pi x)\end{bmatrix}$ and $B=\frac{1}{\pi}\begin{bmatrix}-\cos^{-1}(\pi x)&\tan^{-1}\left(\frac{x}{\pi}\right)\\\sin^{-1}\left(\frac{x}{\pi}\right)&-\tan^{-1}(\pi x)\end{bmatrix}$, then find $(A-B)$. **[NCERT Exemplar]**

8 If $X=\begin{bmatrix}3&1&-1\\5&-2&-3\end{bmatrix}$ and $Y=\begin{bmatrix}2&1&-1\\7&2&4\end{bmatrix}$, then find matrix Z, such that $X+Y+Z$ is a zero matrix.

Short Answer Type Questions

(4 Marks)

9 Solve for x and y, if $\begin{bmatrix}x^2\\y^2\end{bmatrix}+2\begin{bmatrix}2x\\3y\end{bmatrix}=3\begin{bmatrix}7\\-3\end{bmatrix}$. **[ISC 2012; 2006]**

10 If $\begin{bmatrix}x^2&3&4\\1&9&8\end{bmatrix}+\begin{bmatrix}-3x&1&-5\\-3&-2&-6\end{bmatrix}=\begin{bmatrix}4&4&1\\-2&7&2\end{bmatrix}$, then find the value of x. **[ISC 2003]**

11 Find X and Y, if

$$2X+3Y=\begin{bmatrix}2&3\\4&0\end{bmatrix} \text{ and } 3X+2Y=\begin{bmatrix}2&-2\\-1&5\end{bmatrix}.$$ **[NCERT]**

Hints & Solutions

1. Hint $X=\begin{bmatrix}4&-1\\6&2\end{bmatrix}-\begin{bmatrix}1&3\\-1&2\end{bmatrix}$ **Ans.** $\begin{bmatrix}3&-4\\7&0\end{bmatrix}$

2. Given, $4\begin{bmatrix}1&3\\1&-4\end{bmatrix}-\frac{1}{2}\begin{bmatrix}8&4\\4&8\end{bmatrix}$

$$=\begin{bmatrix}4&12\\4&-16\end{bmatrix}-\begin{bmatrix}4&2\\2&4\end{bmatrix}=\begin{bmatrix}0&10\\2&-20\end{bmatrix}$$ [2]

3. Given, $2\begin{bmatrix}3&4\\5&x\end{bmatrix}+\begin{bmatrix}1&y\\0&1\end{bmatrix}=\begin{bmatrix}7&0\\10&5\end{bmatrix}$

$$\Rightarrow\quad \begin{bmatrix}6&8\\10&2x\end{bmatrix}+\begin{bmatrix}1&y\\0&1\end{bmatrix}=\begin{bmatrix}7&0\\10&5\end{bmatrix}$$

$$\Rightarrow\quad \begin{bmatrix}7&8+y\\10&2x+1\end{bmatrix}=\begin{bmatrix}7&0\\10&5\end{bmatrix}$$ [1]

On comparing the corresponding elements, we get

$$8+y=0 \text{ and } 2x+1=5$$

$$\Rightarrow\quad y=-8 \text{ and } x=\frac{5-1}{2}=2$$

$$\therefore\quad x-y=2-(-8)=10$$ [1]

4. Here, we see that order of A is 2×2, order of B is 2×3, order of C is 2×1 and order of D is 2×3.

We know that addition of two matrices is defined only when both of them have the same order. So, only $B+D$ is defined. [2]

5. Similar as Example 6.

[**Ans.** $x = 3$, $y = 6$, $z = 9$ and $t = 6$]

6. Consider,

$$\cos\theta\begin{bmatrix}\cos\theta & \sin\theta\\ -\sin\theta & \cos\theta\end{bmatrix}+\sin\theta\begin{bmatrix}\sin\theta & -\cos\theta\\ \cos\theta & \sin\theta\end{bmatrix}$$

$$=\begin{bmatrix}\cos^2\theta & \sin\theta\cos\theta\\ -\sin\theta\cos\theta & \cos^2\theta\end{bmatrix}+\begin{bmatrix}\sin^2\theta & -\sin\theta\cos\theta\\ \sin\theta\cos\theta & \sin^2\theta\end{bmatrix}$$

$$=\begin{bmatrix}\cos^2\theta+\sin^2\theta & \sin\theta\cos\theta-\sin\theta\cos\theta\\ -\sin\theta\cos\theta+\sin\theta\cos\theta & \cos^2\theta+\sin^2\theta\end{bmatrix}$$ [1]

$$=\begin{bmatrix}1 & 0\\ 0 & 1\end{bmatrix}=I \qquad [\because \sin^2\theta+\cos^2\theta=1]$$ [1]

7. Now,

$$A-B=\frac{1}{\pi}\begin{bmatrix}\sin^{-1}(\pi x)+\cos^{-1}(\pi x) & 0\\ 0 & \cot^{-1}(\pi x)+\tan^{-1}(\pi x)\end{bmatrix}$$ [1]

$$=\frac{1}{\pi}\begin{bmatrix}\frac{\pi}{2} & 0\\ 0 & \frac{\pi}{2}\end{bmatrix}=\frac{1}{\pi}\times\frac{\pi}{2}I=\frac{1}{2}I$$ [1]

8. Hint $X+Y+Z=O \Rightarrow Z=-(X+Y)$

$\left[\textbf{Ans.}\begin{bmatrix}-5 & -2 & 2\\ -12 & 0 & -1\end{bmatrix}\right]$

9. Given matrix equation can be rewritten as

$$\begin{bmatrix}x^2\\ y^2\end{bmatrix}+\begin{bmatrix}4x\\ 6y\end{bmatrix}=\begin{bmatrix}21\\ -9\end{bmatrix}$$

$$\Rightarrow \begin{bmatrix}x^2+4x\\ y^2+6y\end{bmatrix}=\begin{bmatrix}21\\ -9\end{bmatrix}$$ [2]

On equating the corresponding elements, we get

$x^2+4x=21$	$y^2+6y=-9$
$x^2+4x-21=0$	$y^2+6y+9=0$
$x^2+7x-3x-21=0$	$(y+3)^2=0$
$x(x+7)-3(x+7)=0$	$(y+3)(y+3)=0$
$(x-3)(x+7)=0$	$y=-3,-3$
$x=3,-7$	

Hence, x can be 3 or -7 and y is -3. [2]

10. Given, $\begin{bmatrix}x^2 & 3 & 4\\ 1 & 9 & 8\end{bmatrix}+\begin{bmatrix}-3x & 1 & -5\\ -3 & -2 & -6\end{bmatrix}=\begin{bmatrix}4 & 4 & -1\\ -2 & 7 & 2\end{bmatrix}$

$$\Rightarrow \begin{bmatrix}x^2-3x & 3+1 & 4-5\\ 1-3 & 9-2 & 8-6\end{bmatrix}=\begin{bmatrix}4 & 4 & -1\\ -2 & 7 & 2\end{bmatrix}$$

$$\Rightarrow \begin{bmatrix}x^2-3x & 4 & -1\\ -2 & 7 & 2\end{bmatrix}=\begin{bmatrix}4 & 4 & -1\\ -2 & 7 & 2\end{bmatrix}$$

[by additive property] [2]

On equating the corresponding elements, we get

$$x^2-3x=4$$
$$\Rightarrow x^2-3x-4=0$$
$$\Rightarrow x^2-4x+x-4=0$$
$$\Rightarrow x(x-4)+1(x-4)=0$$
$$\Rightarrow (x+1)(x-4)=0$$
$$\therefore x=-1 \text{ or } 4$$ [2]

11. We have, $2X+3Y=\begin{bmatrix}2 & 3\\ 4 & 0\end{bmatrix}$ ...(i)

and $3X+2Y=\begin{bmatrix}2 & -2\\ -1 & 5\end{bmatrix}$ ...(ii)

On multiplying Eq. (i) by 2 and Eq. (ii) by 3, we get

$$4X+6Y=\begin{bmatrix}4 & 6\\ 8 & 0\end{bmatrix}$$ ...(iii)

and $9X+6Y=\begin{bmatrix}6 & -6\\ -3 & 15\end{bmatrix}$ ...(iv) [1]

On subtracting Eq. (iii) from Eq. (iv), we get

$$(9X+6Y)-(4X+6Y)=\begin{bmatrix}6 & -6\\ -3 & 15\end{bmatrix}-\begin{bmatrix}4 & 6\\ 8 & 0\end{bmatrix}$$

$$\Rightarrow 9X+6Y-4X-6Y=\begin{bmatrix}6-4 & -6-6\\ -3-8 & 15-0\end{bmatrix}=\begin{bmatrix}2 & -12\\ -11 & 15\end{bmatrix}$$

$$\Rightarrow X=\frac{1}{5}\begin{bmatrix}2 & -12\\ -11 & 15\end{bmatrix}=\begin{bmatrix}\frac{2}{5} & \frac{-12}{5}\\ \frac{-11}{5} & 3\end{bmatrix}$$ [1]

On substituting the value of X in Eq. (i), we get

$$2\begin{bmatrix}\frac{2}{5} & \frac{-12}{5}\\ \frac{-11}{5} & 3\end{bmatrix}+3Y=\begin{bmatrix}2 & 3\\ 4 & 0\end{bmatrix}$$ [1/2]

$$\Rightarrow \begin{bmatrix}\frac{4}{5} & \frac{-24}{5}\\ \frac{-22}{5} & 6\end{bmatrix}+3Y=\begin{bmatrix}2 & 3\\ 4 & 0\end{bmatrix}$$

$$\Rightarrow 3Y=\begin{bmatrix}2 & 3\\ 4 & 0\end{bmatrix}-\begin{bmatrix}\frac{4}{5} & \frac{-24}{5}\\ \frac{-22}{5} & 6\end{bmatrix}$$ [1/2]

$$\Rightarrow Y=\frac{1}{3}\begin{bmatrix}2-\frac{4}{5} & 3+\frac{24}{5}\\ 4+\frac{22}{5} & 0-6\end{bmatrix}$$

$$\Rightarrow Y=\frac{1}{3}\begin{bmatrix}\frac{6}{5} & \frac{39}{5}\\ \frac{42}{5} & -6\end{bmatrix}=\begin{bmatrix}\frac{2}{5} & \frac{13}{5}\\ \frac{14}{5} & -2\end{bmatrix}$$ [1]

TOPIC 03 Multiplication of Matrices

The product AB of two matrices A and B is defined, if the **number of columns of A is equal to the number of rows of B** and we say, both matrices are compatiable or conformable for the product AB.

Let $A=[a_{ij}]$ be the $m\times n$ matrix and $B=[b_{jk}]$ be the $n\times p$ matrix. Then, the product AB of the matrices A and B is matrix C of order $m\times p$.

Thus, $C=[c_{ik}]_{m\times p}=AB=[a_{ij}]_{m\times n}\;[b_{jk}]_{n\times p}$

(Same number: n and n; Order of resulting matrix: $m\times p$)

To get the (i,k)th element c_{ik} of the matrix C, we take the ith row of A and kth column of B, multiply them elementwise and take the sum of all these products.

e.g. $$[1\;\;4]\begin{bmatrix}3\\2\end{bmatrix}=[(1\times3)+(4\times2)]=[3+8]=[11]$$

[multiplying row by column]

Method of Multiplying Two Matrices

Let A and B be two matrices of order 2×3 and 3×2, respectively. Then, the simplest way to remember the multiplication of matrices as

$$AB=\begin{bmatrix}\text{First row}\times\text{First column} & \text{First row}\times\text{Second column}\\ \text{Second row}\times\text{First column} & \text{Second row}\times\text{Second column}\end{bmatrix}$$

Multiplication of two matrices can be understood through the following example

e.g. Suppose we have two matrices

$$A=\begin{bmatrix}3&4&-5\\5&7&9\end{bmatrix}_{2\times3}\text{ and }B=\begin{bmatrix}4&5\\2&3\\-2&5\end{bmatrix}_{3\times2}$$

Now, we have to multiplied two matrices A and B by using row-by-column method. In this method, we use the following steps.

***Step* I** *Multiply first row of matrix A by both the columns of matrix B*

Multiply each element of the first row of matrix A to the corresponding element of first column of matrix B and then add all these products.

Similarly, each element of first row of matrix A to the corresponding element of second column of matrix B and then add all these products.

$$\begin{bmatrix}3&4&-5\\5&7&9\end{bmatrix}_{2\times3}\begin{bmatrix}4&5\\2&3\\-2&5\end{bmatrix}_{3\times2}$$

$$=\begin{bmatrix}3\times4+4\times2+(-5)\times(-2) & 3\times5+4\times3+(-5)\times5\\ \square & \square\end{bmatrix}$$

$$=\begin{bmatrix}12+8+10 & 15+12-25\\ \square & \square\end{bmatrix}=\begin{bmatrix}30 & 2\\ \square & \square\end{bmatrix}$$

***Step* II** *Multiply second row of matrix A by both the columns of matrix B* Multiply each element of second row by matrix A to the corresponding element of first column of matrix B and then add all these products.

Similarly, each element of second row of matrix A to the corresponding element of second column of matrix B and then add all these products.

$$\begin{bmatrix}3&4&-5\\5&7&9\end{bmatrix}\begin{bmatrix}4&5\\2&3\\-2&5\end{bmatrix}$$

$$=\begin{bmatrix}\square & \square\\ 5\times4+7\times2+9\times-2 & 5\times5+7\times3+9\times5\end{bmatrix}$$

$$=\begin{bmatrix}\square & \square\\ 20+14-18 & 25+21+45\end{bmatrix}=\begin{bmatrix}\square & \square\\ 16 & 91\end{bmatrix}$$

***Step* III** Now, combined Steps I and II, then we get the required product of both the matrices A and B as

$$AB=\begin{bmatrix}30&2\\16&91\end{bmatrix}$$

Example 1 Find AB, if $A=\begin{bmatrix}6&9\\2&3\end{bmatrix}$ and $B=\begin{bmatrix}2&6&0\\7&9&8\end{bmatrix}$.

Sol. We have, $A=\begin{bmatrix}6&9\\2&3\end{bmatrix}_{2\times2}$ and $B=\begin{bmatrix}2&6&0\\7&9&8\end{bmatrix}_{2\times3}$

Here, number of columns of A = number of rows of B = 2.

So, product AB of matrices A and B is possible and its order will be 2×3. Now, let us multiply Ist and IInd row of A with Ist, IInd and IIIrd column of B.

Clearly, multiplication of Ist row of $A(R_1)$ with Ist column of $B(C_1)=R_1C_1=[6\;\;9]\begin{bmatrix}2\\7\end{bmatrix}=6\times2+9\times7$

Multiplication of Ist row of $A(R_1)$ with IInd column of $B(C_2) = R_1C_2 = [6 \quad 9]\begin{bmatrix}6\\9\end{bmatrix} = 6\times6+9\times9$

Multiplication of Ist row of $A(R_1)$ with IIIrd column of $B(C_3) = R_1C_3 = [6 \quad 9]\begin{bmatrix}0\\8\end{bmatrix} = 6\times0+9\times8$

Multiplication of IInd row of $A(R_2)$ with Ist column of $B(C_1) = R_2C_1 = [2 \quad 3]\begin{bmatrix}2\\7\end{bmatrix} = 2\times2+3\times7$

Multiplication of IInd row of $A(R_2)$ with IInd column of $B(C_2) = R_2C_2 = [2 \quad 3]\begin{bmatrix}6\\9\end{bmatrix} = 2\times6+3\times9$

Multiplication of IInd row of $A(R_2)$ with IIIrd column of $B(C_3) = R_2C_3 = [2 \quad 3]\begin{bmatrix}0\\8\end{bmatrix} = 2\times0+3\times8$

Thus, we have

$$C_{11} = R_1C_1 = 6\times2+9\times7 = 12+63 = 75$$
$$C_{12} = R_1C_2 = 6\times6+9\times9 = 36+81 = 117$$
$$C_{13} = R_1C_3 = 6\times0+9\times8 = 0+72 = 72$$
$$C_{21} = R_2C_1 = 2\times2+3\times7 = 4+21 = 25$$
$$C_{22} = R_2C_2 = 2\times6+3\times9 = 12+27 = 39$$

and $C_{23} = R_2C_3 = 2\times0+3\times8 = 0+24 = 24$

Hence, $C = AB = \begin{bmatrix}C_{11} & C_{12} & C_{13}\\ C_{21} & C_{22} & C_{23}\end{bmatrix} = \begin{bmatrix}75 & 117 & 72\\ 25 & 39 & 24\end{bmatrix}_{2\times3}$

which is the required product, i.e. AB.

Note

(i) In the product AB, the matrix A is called the **pre-factor** and the matrix B is called the **post-factor**. Also, we can say that matrix A has been **post-multiplied** by matrix and the matrix B has been **pre-multiplied** by matrix A.

(ii) If AB is defined, then BA need not be defined. Let $A = [a_{ij}]_{2\times3}$ and $B = [b_{jk}]_{3\times3}$, then $AB = [a_{ij}b_{jk}]_{2\times3}$ is defined but BA is not defined, since B has 3 columns while A has 2 rows.

(iii) If A is a matrix of order $m\times n$ and B is a matrix of order $k\times l$, then both AB and BA will be defined, if and only if $n = k$ and $l = m$. In particular, if both A and B are square matrices of the same order, then AB and BA both are defined.

Example 2 Compute the product of $\begin{bmatrix}2 & 3 & 4\\ 3 & 4 & 5\\ 4 & 5 & 6\end{bmatrix}$ and $\begin{bmatrix}1 & -3 & 5\\ 0 & 2 & 4\\ 3 & 0 & 5\end{bmatrix}$. **[NCERT]**

Sol. Let $A = \begin{bmatrix}2 & 3 & 4\\ 3 & 4 & 5\\ 4 & 5 & 6\end{bmatrix}$ and $B = \begin{bmatrix}1 & -3 & 5\\ 0 & 2 & 4\\ 3 & 0 & 5\end{bmatrix}$. Here, number of columns of A = number of rows of $B = 3$, so AB is defined.

Now, $AB = \begin{bmatrix}2 & 3 & 4\\ 3 & 4 & 5\\ 4 & 5 & 6\end{bmatrix}\begin{bmatrix}1 & -3 & 5\\ 0 & 2 & 4\\ 3 & 0 & 5\end{bmatrix}$

Here, $C_{11} = R_1C_1 = [2\ 3\ 4]\begin{bmatrix}1\\0\\3\end{bmatrix} = 2+0+12 = 14$

$$C_{12} = R_1C_2 = [2\ 3\ 4]\begin{bmatrix}-3\\2\\0\end{bmatrix} = -6+6+0 = 0$$

$$C_{13} = R_1C_3 = [2\ 3\ 4]\begin{bmatrix}5\\4\\5\end{bmatrix} = 10+12+20 = 42$$

$$C_{21} = R_2C_1 = [3\ 4\ 5]\begin{bmatrix}1\\0\\3\end{bmatrix} = 3+0+15 = 18$$

$$C_{22} = R_2C_2 = [3\ 4\ 5]\begin{bmatrix}-3\\2\\0\end{bmatrix} = -9+8+0 = -1$$

$$C_{23} = R_2C_3 = [3\ 4\ 5]\begin{bmatrix}5\\4\\5\end{bmatrix} = 15+16+25 = 56$$

$$C_{31} = R_3C_1 = [4\ 5\ 6]\begin{bmatrix}1\\0\\3\end{bmatrix} = 4+0+18 = 22$$

$$C_{32} = R_3C_2 = [4\ 5\ 6]\begin{bmatrix}-3\\2\\0\end{bmatrix} = -12+10+0 = -2$$

and $C_{33} = R_3C_3 = [4\ 5\ 6]\begin{bmatrix}5\\4\\5\end{bmatrix} = 20+20+30 = 70$

Hence, $C = AB = \begin{bmatrix}C_{11} & C_{12} & C_{13}\\ C_{21} & C_{22} & C_{23}\\ C_{31} & C_{32} & C_{33}\end{bmatrix} = \begin{bmatrix}14 & 0 & 42\\ 18 & -1 & 56\\ 22 & -2 & 70\end{bmatrix}$.

Example 3 Use matrix multiplication to divide ₹30000 in two parts such that the total annual interest at 9% on the first part and 11% on the second part amounts ₹3060. **[NCERT Exemplar]**

Sol. Let the first part be ₹x and the second part be ₹$(30000-x)$. Let A be the 1×2 matrix representing these two parts and B be the 2×1 matrix representing the annual interest rates on two parts.

i.e. $A = \overset{\text{Part I}}{[x} \quad \overset{\text{Part II}}{30000-x]}$ and $B = \begin{bmatrix}0.09\\0.11\end{bmatrix}\begin{matrix}\text{Part I}\\ \text{Part II}\end{matrix}$

Clearly, the total interest is given by the matrix AB,

i.e. $AB = [x \quad 30000-x]\begin{bmatrix}0.09\\0.11\end{bmatrix}$

$$= [x\times0.09+(30000-x)\times0.11]$$
$$= [0.09x+3300-0.11x] = [3300-0.02x]$$

Thus, $3300-0.02x = 3060$ [$\because$ total interest = ₹3060]

$\Rightarrow \quad 0.02x = 240 \Rightarrow x = 12000$

Hence, two parts are ₹12000 and ₹18000, respectively.

Example 4 If $M(\theta) = \begin{bmatrix} \cos\theta & \sin\theta \\ -\sin\theta & \cos\theta \end{bmatrix}$, then show that $M(x)\,M(y) = M(x+y)$. **[ISC 2009]**

Sol. Given, $M(\theta) = \begin{bmatrix} \cos\theta & \sin\theta \\ -\sin\theta & \cos\theta \end{bmatrix}$

$$\text{LHS} = M(x)\,M(y)$$

$$= \begin{bmatrix} \cos x & \sin x \\ -\sin x & \cos x \end{bmatrix} \begin{bmatrix} \cos y & \sin y \\ -\sin y & \cos y \end{bmatrix}$$

$$= \begin{bmatrix} \cos x \cos y - \sin x \sin y & \cos x \sin y + \sin x \cos y \\ -\sin x \cos y - \cos x \sin y & -\sin x \sin y + \cos x \cos y \end{bmatrix}$$

[by multiplication property]

$$= \begin{bmatrix} \cos(x+y) & \sin(x+y) \\ -\sin(x+y) & \cos(x+y) \end{bmatrix}$$

[by trigonometric formulae]

$$= M(x+y) = \text{RHS}$$

Properties of Multiplication of Matrices

Multiplication of matrices have following properties

(i) **Associative Law** Matrix multiplication is associative, i.e. if A, B and C are three matrices, then
$A(BC) = (AB)C$, whenever both sides are defined.

(ii) **Distributive Law** Matrix multiplication is distributive over matrix addition, if A, B and C are three matrices, then
$A(B+C) = AB + AC$ or $(A+B)C = AC + BC$
whenever both sides are defined.

(iii) **Existence of Multiplicative Identity** For every square matrix A, there exists an identity matrix I of same order such that $AI = A = IA$. So, I is the multiplicative identity for every square matrix A.

(iv) **Non-commutativity** Generally, matrix multiplication is not commutative, i.e. if A and B are two matrices and AB, BA both exists, then it is not necessary that $AB = BA$.

(v) **Zero Matrix as the Product of Two Non-zero Matrices** If the product of two matrices is a zero matrix, then it is not necessary that one of the matrices is zero matrix.

e.g. Let $A = \begin{bmatrix} 0 & -1 \\ 0 & 2 \end{bmatrix}$ and $B = \begin{bmatrix} 3 & 5 \\ 0 & 0 \end{bmatrix}$.

Then, $AB = \begin{bmatrix} 0 & -1 \\ 0 & 2 \end{bmatrix} \begin{bmatrix} 3 & 5 \\ 0 & 0 \end{bmatrix} = \begin{bmatrix} 0 & 0 \\ 0 & 0 \end{bmatrix} = O.$

But, here $A \neq O$ and $B \neq O$.

Note

(i) Multiplication of diagonal matrices of same order will be commutative.

(ii) If A is an $n \times n$ matrix and I be an $n \times n$ matrix, then $AI_n = I_n A = A$

Example 5 If $A = \begin{bmatrix} 1 & -2 & 3 \\ -4 & 2 & 5 \end{bmatrix}$ and $B = \begin{bmatrix} 2 & 3 \\ 4 & 5 \\ 2 & 1 \end{bmatrix}$, then find AB and BA. Show that A and B are not commutative, i.e. $AB \neq BA$.

Sol. Here, order of matrix A is 2×3 and order of matrix B is 3×2. So, AB will be of order 2×2 and BA will be of order 3×3.

Now, $AB = \begin{bmatrix} 1 & -2 & 3 \\ -4 & 2 & 5 \end{bmatrix} \begin{bmatrix} 2 & 3 \\ 4 & 5 \\ 2 & 1 \end{bmatrix}$

$$= \begin{bmatrix} 2-8+6 & 3-10+3 \\ -8+8+10 & -12+10+5 \end{bmatrix}$$

[multiplying rows by columns]

$$AB = \begin{bmatrix} 0 & -4 \\ 10 & 3 \end{bmatrix} \text{ and } BA = \begin{bmatrix} 2 & 3 \\ 4 & 5 \\ 2 & 1 \end{bmatrix} \begin{bmatrix} 1 & -2 & 3 \\ -4 & 2 & 5 \end{bmatrix}$$

$$= \begin{bmatrix} 2-12 & -4+6 & 6+15 \\ 4-20 & -8+10 & 12+25 \\ 2-4 & -4+2 & 6+5 \end{bmatrix}$$

[multiplying rows by columns]

$$= \begin{bmatrix} -10 & 2 & 21 \\ -16 & 2 & 37 \\ -2 & -2 & 11 \end{bmatrix}$$

Clearly, $AB \neq BA$.

Example 6 Three matrices A, B and C defined as $A = \begin{bmatrix} 1 & 2 \\ -1 & 3 \end{bmatrix}$, $B = \begin{bmatrix} 4 & 0 \\ 1 & 5 \end{bmatrix}$ and $C = \begin{bmatrix} 2 & 0 \\ 1 & -2 \end{bmatrix}$, then show that matrices A, B and C satisfy

(i) the property of associativity with respect to multiplication, i.e. $A(BC) = (AB)C$.

(ii) the property of distributivity with respect to addition, i.e. $A(B+C) = AB + AC$. **[NCERT Exemplar]**

Sol. Given, $A = \begin{bmatrix} 1 & 2 \\ -1 & 3 \end{bmatrix}$, $B = \begin{bmatrix} 4 & 0 \\ 1 & 5 \end{bmatrix}$ and $C = \begin{bmatrix} 2 & 0 \\ 1 & -2 \end{bmatrix}$

(i) Here, $BC = \begin{bmatrix} 4 & 0 \\ 1 & 5 \end{bmatrix} \begin{bmatrix} 2 & 0 \\ 1 & -2 \end{bmatrix} = \begin{bmatrix} 8+0 & 0+0 \\ 2+5 & 0-10 \end{bmatrix}$

[multiplying rows by columns]

$$= \begin{bmatrix} 8 & 0 \\ 7 & -10 \end{bmatrix} \quad \text{...(i)}$$

$$\therefore \text{LHS} = A(BC) = \begin{bmatrix} 1 & 2 \\ -1 & 3 \end{bmatrix} \begin{bmatrix} 8 & 0 \\ 7 & -10 \end{bmatrix} \quad \text{[using Eq. (i)]}$$

$$= \begin{bmatrix} 8+14 & 0-20 \\ -8+21 & 0-30 \end{bmatrix} = \begin{bmatrix} 22 & -20 \\ 13 & -30 \end{bmatrix}$$

[multiplying rows by columns]

and $AB = \begin{bmatrix} 1 & 2 \\ -1 & 3 \end{bmatrix}\begin{bmatrix} 4 & 0 \\ 1 & 5 \end{bmatrix} = \begin{bmatrix} 4+2 & 0+10 \\ -4+3 & 0+15 \end{bmatrix}$ [multiplying rows by columns]

$= \begin{bmatrix} 6 & 10 \\ -1 & 15 \end{bmatrix}$ ...(ii)

$\therefore$ RHS $= (AB)C = \begin{bmatrix} 6 & 10 \\ -1 & 15 \end{bmatrix}\begin{bmatrix} 2 & 0 \\ 1 & -2 \end{bmatrix}$ [using Eq. (ii)]

$= \begin{bmatrix} 12+10 & 0-20 \\ -2+15 & 0-30 \end{bmatrix}$ [multiplying rows by columns]

$= \begin{bmatrix} 22 & -20 \\ 13 & -30 \end{bmatrix}$

Thus, LHS = RHS

(ii) Here, $B + C = \begin{bmatrix} 4 & 0 \\ 1 & 5 \end{bmatrix} + \begin{bmatrix} 2 & 0 \\ 1 & -2 \end{bmatrix}$

$= \begin{bmatrix} 4+2 & 0 \\ 1+1 & 5-2 \end{bmatrix} = \begin{bmatrix} 6 & 0 \\ 2 & 3 \end{bmatrix}$ ...(iii)

and $AC = \begin{bmatrix} 1 & 2 \\ -1 & 3 \end{bmatrix}\begin{bmatrix} 2 & 0 \\ 1 & -2 \end{bmatrix} = \begin{bmatrix} 2+2 & 0-4 \\ -2+3 & 0-6 \end{bmatrix}$

$= \begin{bmatrix} 4 & -4 \\ 1 & -6 \end{bmatrix}$ ...(iv)

[multiplying rows by columns]

LHS $= A(B+C) = \begin{bmatrix} 1 & 2 \\ -1 & 3 \end{bmatrix}\begin{bmatrix} 6 & 0 \\ 2 & 3 \end{bmatrix}$ [using Eq. (iii)]

$= \begin{bmatrix} 6+4 & 0+6 \\ -6+6 & 0+9 \end{bmatrix}$ [multiplying rows by columns]

$= \begin{bmatrix} 10 & 6 \\ 0 & 9 \end{bmatrix}$

and RHS $= AB + AC = \begin{bmatrix} 6 & 10 \\ -1 & 15 \end{bmatrix} + \begin{bmatrix} 4 & -4 \\ 1 & -6 \end{bmatrix} = \begin{bmatrix} 10 & 6 \\ 0 & 9 \end{bmatrix}$

[using Eqs. (ii) and (iv)]

Thus, LHS = RHS

Positive Integral Powers of a Square Matrix

If we multiply the square matrix by itself, then it will give the positive integral powers of the square matrix.

i.e. For any square matrix, say A, we define

$A^1 = A,\ A^2 = A \cdot A,\ A^3 = A^2 \cdot A,\ A^4 = A^3 \cdot A, \ldots,$

$A^n = A^{n-1} \cdot A$, where n is a positive integer.

Note $I^n = I$ for any positive integer n, where I is the identity matrix.

Example 7 If $A = \begin{bmatrix} 3 & 1 \\ 7 & 5 \end{bmatrix}$, then find the values of x and y, such that $A^2 + xI_2 = yA$. **[ISC 2014]**

Sol. Given, $A = \begin{bmatrix} 3 & 1 \\ 7 & 5 \end{bmatrix}$

Now, $A^2 = A \cdot A = \begin{bmatrix} 3 & 1 \\ 7 & 5 \end{bmatrix}\begin{bmatrix} 3 & 1 \\ 7 & 5 \end{bmatrix}$

$= \begin{bmatrix} 9+7 & 3+5 \\ 21+35 & 7+25 \end{bmatrix} = \begin{bmatrix} 16 & 8 \\ 56 & 32 \end{bmatrix}$

Also given, $A^2 + xI_2 = yA$

$\therefore \begin{bmatrix} 16 & 8 \\ 56 & 32 \end{bmatrix} + x\begin{bmatrix} 1 & 0 \\ 0 & 1 \end{bmatrix} = y\begin{bmatrix} 3 & 1 \\ 7 & 5 \end{bmatrix}$

$\Rightarrow \begin{bmatrix} 16 & 8 \\ 56 & 32 \end{bmatrix} + \begin{bmatrix} x & 0 \\ 0 & x \end{bmatrix} = \begin{bmatrix} 3y & y \\ 7y & 5y \end{bmatrix}$

$\Rightarrow \begin{bmatrix} 16+x & 8 \\ 56 & 32+x \end{bmatrix} = \begin{bmatrix} 3y & y \\ 7y & 5y \end{bmatrix}$

[by addition property]

On equating the corresponding elements, we get

$y = 8$ and $32 + x = 5y$

$\Rightarrow 32 + x = 5 \times 8 \Rightarrow 32 + x = 40 \Rightarrow x = 40 - 32 = 8$

Hence, $x = 8$ and $y = 8$.

Example 8 If A is a square matrix such that $A^2 = I$, then find the simplified value of $(A - I)^3 + (A + I)^3 - 7A$.

Sol. Given, $A^2 = I$ ...(i)

Now, $(A - I)^3 + (A + I)^3 - 7A = (A^3 - 3A^2I + 3AI^2 - I^3) + (A^3 + 3A^2 I + 3AI^2 + I^3) - 7A$

$= (A^3 - 3A^2 + 3AI - I) + (A^3 + 3A^2 + 3AI + I) - 7A$

$[\because A^2I = A^2$ and $I^3 = I^2 = I]$

$= 2A^3 + 6AI - 7A$

$= 2A^2A + 6A - 7A$ $[\because AI = A]$

$= 2\,IA - A$ [from Eq. (i)]

$= 2A - A = A$ $[\because IA = A]$

Problems on nth Power of a Matrix (To be Solved using Principle of Mathematical Induction)

In this type of problems, a matrix (say A) is given to us and an equation involving nth power of A is given to us. We have to show/prove that the given equation is true. For proving/showing such problems, we use the concept of mathematical induction, which is given below.

Suppose there is a statement $P(n)$ involving the natural number n such that

(i) $P(1)$ is true, i.e. statement is true for $n = 1$.

(ii) Truth of $P(k)$ implies the truth of $P(k+1)$, i.e. if the statement is true for $n = k$ (k is positive integer), then statement is also true for $n = k + 1$.

Then, by principal of mathematical induction, $P(n)$ is true for all natural numbers n.

Example 9 If $A = \begin{bmatrix} \cos\theta & \sin\theta \\ -\sin\theta & \cos\theta \end{bmatrix}$, then prove that

$$A^n = \begin{bmatrix} \cos n\theta & \sin n\theta \\ -\sin n\theta & \cos n\theta \end{bmatrix}, n \in N.$$

Sol. Let given statement be $P(n)$,

i.e. $P(n)$: If $A = \begin{bmatrix} \cos\theta & \sin\theta \\ -\sin\theta & \cos\theta \end{bmatrix}$, then

$$A^n = \begin{bmatrix} \cos n\theta & \sin n\theta \\ -\sin n\theta & \cos n\theta \end{bmatrix}, n \in N$$

For $n = 1$, $A^1 = A = \begin{bmatrix} \cos\theta & \sin\theta \\ -\sin\theta & \cos\theta \end{bmatrix}$

$\therefore$ $P(1)$ is true.

Let $P(n)$ be true for $n = k$, so

$$P(k): A^k = \begin{bmatrix} \cos k\theta & \sin k\theta \\ -\sin k\theta & \cos k\theta \end{bmatrix}$$

Now, we have to prove the statement for $n = k+1$.

Consider,

$$A^{k+1} = A^k \cdot A = \begin{bmatrix} \cos k\theta & \sin k\theta \\ -\sin k\theta & \cos k\theta \end{bmatrix}\begin{bmatrix} \cos\theta & \sin\theta \\ -\sin\theta & \cos\theta \end{bmatrix}$$

$$= \begin{bmatrix} \cos k\theta\cos\theta - \sin k\theta\sin\theta & \cos k\theta\sin\theta + \sin k\theta\cos\theta \\ -\sin k\theta\cos\theta - \cos k\theta\sin\theta & -\sin k\theta\sin\theta + \cos k\theta\cos\theta \end{bmatrix}$$

$$= \begin{bmatrix} \cos(k\theta+\theta) & \sin(k\theta+\theta) \\ -\sin(k\theta+\theta) & \cos(k\theta+\theta) \end{bmatrix}$$

$$= \begin{bmatrix} \cos(k+1)\theta & \sin(k+1)\theta \\ -\sin(k+1)\theta & \cos(k+1)\theta \end{bmatrix}$$

Thus, the statement is true for $n = k+1$.

Hence, by principal of mathematical induction,

$$A^n = \begin{bmatrix} \cos n\theta & \sin n\theta \\ -\sin n\theta & \cos n\theta \end{bmatrix}, \forall n \in N. \quad \textbf{Hence proved.}$$

Matrix Polynomial

Let $f(x) = a_0 x^n + a_1 x^{n-1} + a_2 x^{n-2} + \ldots + a_{n-1} x + a_n$ be a polynomial in x and A be a square matrix.

Then, $f(A) = a_0 A^n + a_1 A^{n-1} + a_2 A^{n-2} + \ldots + a_{n-1} A + a_n I$ is called a matrix polynomial, where I is the identity matrix of order of A.

Method to Solve Problems Based on Matrix Polynomial

Sometimes, a square matrix (say A) is given to us and we have to find the value of a polynomial in which variable is a matrix. (e.g. $A^3 - 23A - 40I$). For this, firstly we find the value of each term having power of A by multiplying A by itself as many times as power and then put these values in given expression to find the required value.

Example 10 Let $A = \begin{bmatrix} 0 & 1 \\ 1 & 2 \end{bmatrix}$ and $f(x) = x^2 + x - 1$, then find $f(A)$.

Sol. We have, $A = \begin{bmatrix} 0 & 1 \\ 1 & 2 \end{bmatrix}$

$$\therefore A^2 = A \cdot A = \begin{bmatrix} 0 & 1 \\ 1 & 2 \end{bmatrix}\begin{bmatrix} 0 & 1 \\ 1 & 2 \end{bmatrix} = \begin{bmatrix} 0+1 & 0+2 \\ 0+2 & 1+4 \end{bmatrix}$$

$$= \begin{bmatrix} 1 & 2 \\ 2 & 5 \end{bmatrix} \quad \text{[multiplying rows by columns]}$$

Now, $f(A) = A^2 + A - I = \begin{bmatrix} 1 & 2 \\ 2 & 5 \end{bmatrix} + \begin{bmatrix} 0 & 1 \\ 1 & 2 \end{bmatrix} - \begin{bmatrix} 1 & 0 \\ 0 & 1 \end{bmatrix}$

$$= \begin{bmatrix} 1+0-1 & 2+1-0 \\ 2+1-0 & 5+2-1 \end{bmatrix} = \begin{bmatrix} 0 & 3 \\ 3 & 6 \end{bmatrix}$$

Example 11 If $A = \begin{bmatrix} 1 & 0 & 2 \\ 0 & 2 & 1 \\ 2 & 0 & 3 \end{bmatrix}$ and $A^3 - 6A^2 + 7A + kI_3 = O$, find k.

Sol. Given, $A = \begin{bmatrix} 1 & 0 & 2 \\ 0 & 2 & 1 \\ 2 & 0 & 3 \end{bmatrix}$

Now, $A^2 = \begin{bmatrix} 1 & 0 & 2 \\ 0 & 2 & 1 \\ 2 & 0 & 3 \end{bmatrix}\begin{bmatrix} 1 & 0 & 2 \\ 0 & 2 & 1 \\ 2 & 0 & 3 \end{bmatrix}$

$$= \begin{bmatrix} 1+0+4 & 0+0+0 & 2+0+6 \\ 0+0+2 & 0+4+0 & 0+2+3 \\ 2+0+6 & 0+0+0 & 4+0+9 \end{bmatrix} = \begin{bmatrix} 5 & 0 & 8 \\ 2 & 4 & 5 \\ 8 & 0 & 13 \end{bmatrix}$$

and $A^3 = A \cdot A^2 = \begin{bmatrix} 1 & 0 & 2 \\ 0 & 2 & 1 \\ 2 & 0 & 3 \end{bmatrix}\begin{bmatrix} 5 & 0 & 8 \\ 2 & 4 & 5 \\ 8 & 0 & 13 \end{bmatrix}$

$$= \begin{bmatrix} 5+0+16 & 0+0+0 & 8+0+26 \\ 0+4+8 & 0+8+0 & 0+10+13 \\ 10+0+24 & 0+0+0 & 16+0+39 \end{bmatrix}$$

$$= \begin{bmatrix} 21 & 0 & 34 \\ 12 & 8 & 23 \\ 34 & 0 & 55 \end{bmatrix}$$

Since, $A^3 - 6A^2 + 7A + kI_3 = O$

$$\therefore \begin{bmatrix} 21 & 0 & 34 \\ 12 & 8 & 23 \\ 34 & 0 & 55 \end{bmatrix} - 6\begin{bmatrix} 5 & 0 & 8 \\ 2 & 4 & 5 \\ 8 & 0 & 13 \end{bmatrix} + 7\begin{bmatrix} 1 & 0 & 2 \\ 0 & 2 & 1 \\ 2 & 0 & 3 \end{bmatrix} + k\begin{bmatrix} 1 & 0 & 0 \\ 0 & 1 & 0 \\ 0 & 0 & 1 \end{bmatrix} = \begin{bmatrix} 0 & 0 & 0 \\ 0 & 0 & 0 \\ 0 & 0 & 0 \end{bmatrix}$$

$$\Rightarrow \begin{bmatrix} 21 & 0 & 34 \\ 12 & 8 & 23 \\ 34 & 0 & 55 \end{bmatrix} - \begin{bmatrix} 30 & 0 & 48 \\ 12 & 24 & 30 \\ 48 & 0 & 78 \end{bmatrix} + \begin{bmatrix} 7 & 0 & 14 \\ 0 & 14 & 7 \\ 14 & 0 & 21 \end{bmatrix} + \begin{bmatrix} k & 0 & 0 \\ 0 & k & 0 \\ 0 & 0 & k \end{bmatrix} = \begin{bmatrix} 0 & 0 & 0 \\ 0 & 0 & 0 \\ 0 & 0 & 0 \end{bmatrix}$$

$$\Rightarrow \begin{bmatrix} 21-30+7+k & 0-0+0+0 & 34-48+14+0 \\ 12-12+0+0 & 8-24+14+k & 23-30+7+0 \\ 34-48+14+0 & 0-0+0+0 & 55-78+21+k \end{bmatrix} = \begin{bmatrix} 0 & 0 & 0 \\ 0 & 0 & 0 \\ 0 & 0 & 0 \end{bmatrix}$$

$$\Rightarrow \begin{bmatrix} -2+k & 0 & 0 \\ 0 & -2+k & 0 \\ 0 & 0 & -2+k \end{bmatrix} = \begin{bmatrix} 0 & 0 & 0 \\ 0 & 0 & 0 \\ 0 & 0 & 0 \end{bmatrix}$$

On equating the corresponding elements, we get

$$-2+k=0$$

$$\therefore \quad k = 2$$

Topic Practice 3

Very Short Answer Type Questions

(2 Marks)

1 Identify whether the multiplication of following matrices are possible, if possible find the multiplication AB.

(i) $A = \begin{bmatrix} 1 & 2 & 3 \\ 4 & 5 & 6 \end{bmatrix}_{2\times 3}$ and $B = \begin{bmatrix} 4 & 5 & 6 \\ 7 & 8 & 9 \end{bmatrix}_{2\times 3}$

(ii) $A = \begin{bmatrix} 2 & 4 & -1 \\ -1 & 0 & 2 \end{bmatrix}_{2\times 3}$ and $B = \begin{bmatrix} 3 & 4 \\ -1 & 2 \\ 2 & 1 \end{bmatrix}_{3\times 2}$

2 Find the product AB of the following matrices.

(i) $A = \begin{bmatrix} 1 & -2 \\ 2 & 3 \end{bmatrix}, B = \begin{bmatrix} 1 & 2 & 3 \\ 2 & 3 & 1 \end{bmatrix}$

(ii) $A = \begin{bmatrix} 3 & -1 & 3 \\ -1 & 0 & 2 \end{bmatrix}, B = \begin{bmatrix} 2 & -3 \\ 1 & 0 \\ 3 & 1 \end{bmatrix}$

3 Show that if A and B are square matrices such that $AB = BA$, then $(A+B)^2 = A^2 + 2AB + B^2$. **[NCERT Exemplar]**

4 If A is a square matrix such that $A^2 = A$, then write the value of $7A - (I + A)^3$, where I is an identity matrix. **[NCERT Exemplar]**

5 If $[2x \;\; 3]\begin{bmatrix} 1 & 2 \\ -3 & 0 \end{bmatrix}\begin{bmatrix} x \\ 8 \end{bmatrix} = O$, then find the value of x. **[NCERT Exemplar]**

6 If $X_{m\times 3}\, Y_{p\times 4} = Z_{2\times b}$, for three matrices X, Y and Z, then find the values of m, p and b.

7 If $A = \begin{bmatrix} x & 0 \\ 1 & 1 \end{bmatrix}$ and $B = \begin{bmatrix} 1 & 0 \\ 5 & 1 \end{bmatrix}$, then find the value of x for which $A^2 = B$.

8 If $A = \begin{bmatrix} 1 & 2 \\ 2 & 1 \end{bmatrix}$, then show that $A^2 - 3I = 2A$. **[ISC 2007]**

9 Find the value of x such that

$$[1 \;\; x \;\; 1]\begin{bmatrix} 1 & 3 & 2 \\ 2 & 5 & 1 \\ 15 & 3 & 2 \end{bmatrix}\begin{bmatrix} 1 \\ 2 \\ x \end{bmatrix} = O.$$

Short Answer Type Questions

(4 Marks)

10 If $A = \begin{bmatrix} 1 & 3 & -1 \\ 2 & 4 & -5 \\ 6 & 7 & 3 \end{bmatrix}$ and $B = \begin{bmatrix} 2 & 4 & -1 \\ 5 & -7 & 6 \\ 4 & 2 & 1 \end{bmatrix}$, then show that $AB \neq BA$.

11 If $A = \begin{bmatrix} 1 & 0 \\ 1 & 1 \end{bmatrix}, B = \begin{bmatrix} 2 & 0 \\ 1 & 1 \end{bmatrix}$ and $C = \begin{bmatrix} -1 & 2 \\ 3 & 1 \end{bmatrix}$, then show that $(AB)C = A(BC)$.

12 If $A = \begin{bmatrix} 1 & -1 \\ 2 & 1 \end{bmatrix}, B = \begin{bmatrix} 1 & 0 \\ -1 & 3 \end{bmatrix}$ and $C = \begin{bmatrix} 3 & 4 \\ -1 & 2 \end{bmatrix}$, then show that $A(B+C) = AB + AC$.

13 Find the matrix A such that

$$A\begin{bmatrix} 1 & 2 & 3 \\ 4 & 5 & 6 \end{bmatrix} = \begin{bmatrix} -7 & -8 & -9 \\ 2 & 4 & 6 \end{bmatrix}.$$

14 If $f(x) = \begin{bmatrix} \cos x & -\sin x & 0 \\ \sin x & \cos x & 0 \\ 0 & 0 & 1 \end{bmatrix}$, then show that $f(x)\cdot f(y) = f(x+y)$. **[NCERT]**

15 If $A = \begin{bmatrix} 1 & -1 \\ 2 & -1 \end{bmatrix}, B = \begin{bmatrix} a & 1 \\ b & -1 \end{bmatrix}$ and $(A+B)^2 = A^2 + B^2$, then find the values of a and b.

16 If $A = \begin{bmatrix} 0 & 1 \\ -1 & 0 \end{bmatrix}$, then find the real values x and y such that $(xI + yA)^2 = A$.

17 If $A = \begin{bmatrix} 0 & -\tan\alpha/2 \\ \tan\alpha/2 & 0 \end{bmatrix}$ and I is the identity matrix of order 2, then show that

$$I + A = (I - A)\begin{bmatrix} \cos\alpha & -\sin\alpha \\ \sin\alpha & \cos\alpha \end{bmatrix}.$$ **[NCERT]**

18 Find the value of k, if $M = \begin{bmatrix} 1 & 2 \\ 2 & 3 \end{bmatrix}$ and $M^2 - kM - I_2 = O$. **[ISC 2015]**

Long Answer Type Questions

6 Marks

19 If $A=\begin{bmatrix}1 & 3 & 2\\ 2 & 0 & -1\\ 1 & 2 & 3\end{bmatrix}$, then show that $A^3-4A^2-3A+11I=O$.

20 If $A=\begin{bmatrix}1 & 0 & -2\\ -2 & -1 & 2\\ 3 & 4 & 1\end{bmatrix}$, then show that $A^3-A^2-3A-I_3=O$.

Hints & Solutions

1. (i) Given order of A is 2×3 and order B is 2×3. Here, we see that number of columns in A is not equal to number of rows in B. So multiplication of A and B is not possible. [1]

(ii) Given order of A is 2×3 and order B is 3×2. Here, we see that number of columns in A is equal to number of rows in B. So multiplicaiton of A and B is possible.

$$\therefore AB=\begin{bmatrix}2 & 4 & -1\\ -1 & 0 & 2\end{bmatrix}\begin{bmatrix}3 & 4\\ -1 & 2\\ 2 & 1\end{bmatrix}=\begin{bmatrix}0 & -15\\ 1 & -2\end{bmatrix}$$ [1]

2. Similar as Example 1.

$$\left[\textbf{Ans.}\ \text{(i)}\begin{bmatrix}-3 & -4 & 1\\ 8 & 13 & 9\end{bmatrix}\ \text{(ii)}\begin{bmatrix}14 & -6\\ 4 & 5\end{bmatrix}\right]$$

3. Given, $AB=BA$

Now, $(A+B)^2=(A+B)\cdot(A+B)$

$=A\cdot(A+B)+B\cdot(A+B)$ [1]

$=A^2+AB+BA+B^2$

$=A^2+AB+AB+B^2$ [$\because BA=AB$, given]

$=A^2+2AB+B^2$ [1]

4. We have, $A^2=A$

Now, $7A-(I+A)^3=7A-[I^3+A^3+3IA(I+A)]$

[$\because (x+y)^3=x^3+y^3+3xy(x+y)$]

$=7A-[I+A^2\cdot A+3A(I+A)]$ [$\because IA=A$ and $I^3=I$] [1]

$=7A-[I+A\cdot A+3AI+3A^2]$ [$\because A^2=A$]

$=7A-[I+A+3A+3A]$ [$\because A^2=A$]

$=7A-[I+7A]=-I$ [1]

5. Given matrix equation is

$$[2x\ \ 3]\begin{bmatrix}1 & 2\\ -3 & 0\end{bmatrix}\begin{bmatrix}x\\ 8\end{bmatrix}=O$$

$$\Rightarrow\quad [2x\ \ 3]\left[\begin{bmatrix}1 & 2\\ -3 & 0\end{bmatrix}\begin{bmatrix}x\\ 8\end{bmatrix}\right]=O$$ [1]

[by associative law of multiplication]

$$\Rightarrow\quad [2x\ \ 3]\begin{bmatrix}x+16\\ -3x\end{bmatrix}=O$$

$\Rightarrow\quad [2x(x+16)-9x]=[0]$

$\Rightarrow\quad 2x^2+32x-9x=0$

$\Rightarrow\quad 2x^2+23x=0$

$\Rightarrow\quad x(2x+23)=0$

$\Rightarrow\quad x=0$ and $x=-23/2$ [1]

6. Given, $X_{m\times3}Y_{p\times4}=Z_{2\times b}$ ...(i)

XY is defined only, when $p=3$. [1]

Now, Eq. (i) will be of the form $Z_{m\times4}=Z_{2\times b}$, which is possible only, when $m=2$ and $b=4$.

$\therefore\quad m=2,\ p=3$ and $b=4$ [1]

7. We have, $\begin{bmatrix}x & 0\\ 1 & 1\end{bmatrix}\begin{bmatrix}x & 0\\ 1 & 1\end{bmatrix}=\begin{bmatrix}1 & 0\\ 5 & 1\end{bmatrix}$

$$\Rightarrow\quad \begin{bmatrix}x^2 & 0\\ x+1 & 1\end{bmatrix}=\begin{bmatrix}1 & 0\\ 5 & 1\end{bmatrix}$$

$\Rightarrow\quad x^2=1$ ...(i)

and $\quad x+1=5$ ...(ii) [1]

From Eq. (ii), we get $x=4$, which does not satisfy Eq. (i). So, no value of x exist. [1]

8. Given, $A=\begin{bmatrix}1 & 2\\ 2 & 1\end{bmatrix}$

Now, $A^2=A\cdot A=\begin{bmatrix}1 & 2\\ 2 & 1\end{bmatrix}\begin{bmatrix}1 & 2\\ 2 & 1\end{bmatrix}$

$$=\begin{bmatrix}1+4 & 2+2\\ 2+2 & 4+1\end{bmatrix}=\begin{bmatrix}5 & 4\\ 4 & 5\end{bmatrix}$$ [1]

Taking LHS $=A^2-3I=\begin{bmatrix}5 & 4\\ 4 & 5\end{bmatrix}-3\begin{bmatrix}1 & 0\\ 0 & 1\end{bmatrix}$

$$=\begin{bmatrix}5 & 4\\ 4 & 5\end{bmatrix}-\begin{bmatrix}3 & 0\\ 0 & 3\end{bmatrix}=\begin{bmatrix}5-3 & 4-0\\ 4-0 & 5-3\end{bmatrix}$$

$$=\begin{bmatrix}2 & 4\\ 4 & 2\end{bmatrix}=2\begin{bmatrix}1 & 2\\ 2 & 1\end{bmatrix}$$

$=2A=$ RHS **Hence proved.** [1]

9. We have, $[1\ \ x\ \ 1]\begin{bmatrix}1 & 3 & 2\\ 2 & 5 & 1\\ 15 & 3 & 2\end{bmatrix}\begin{bmatrix}1\\ 2\\ x\end{bmatrix}=O$

$$\Rightarrow\quad [1\ \ x\ \ 1]\begin{bmatrix}1+6+2x\\ 2+10+x\\ 15+6+2x\end{bmatrix}=O$$

$$\Rightarrow\quad [1\ \ x\ \ 1]\begin{bmatrix}7+2x\\ 12+x\\ 21+2x\end{bmatrix}=O$$ [1]

$\Rightarrow\quad [7+2x+x(12+x)+21+2x]=[0]$

$\Rightarrow\quad x^2+16x+28=0$

$\Rightarrow\quad (x+14)(x+2)=0$

$\Rightarrow\quad x=-14$ or $x=-2$ [1]

10. Similar as Example 5.

11. Similar as Example 6 (i).

12. Similar as Example 6 (ii).

13. The right side of given matrix equation is of order 2×3, so left side of the given matrix equation should be of order 2×3. It is clear that, the product of A with 2×3 matrix is a 2×3 matrix, therefore A is a 2×2 matrix.

Let $A=\begin{bmatrix} u & v \\ w & x \end{bmatrix}$. Then, [1]

$$\text{LHS}=\begin{bmatrix} u & v \\ w & x \end{bmatrix}\begin{bmatrix} 1 & 2 & 3 \\ 4 & 5 & 6 \end{bmatrix}$$

$$=\begin{bmatrix} u+4v & 2u+5v & 3u+6v \\ w+4x & 2w+5x & 3w+6x \end{bmatrix}$$

$$\therefore \begin{bmatrix} u+4v & 2u+5v & 3u+6v \\ w+4x & 2w+5x & 3w+6x \end{bmatrix}=\begin{bmatrix} -7 & -8 & -9 \\ 2 & 4 & 6 \end{bmatrix}$$ [1]

On comparing the elements from both sides, we get

$$u+4v=-7,\ 2u+5v=-8,\ 3u+6v=-9,$$

$$w+4x=2,\ 2w+5x=4 \text{ and } 3w+6x=6$$ [1]

On solving, we get $u=1$, $v=-2$, $w=2$ and $x=0$

$$\therefore \quad A=\begin{bmatrix} 1 & -2 \\ 2 & 0 \end{bmatrix}$$ [1]

14. Given, $f(x)=\begin{bmatrix} \cos x & -\sin x & 0 \\ \sin x & \cos x & 0 \\ 0 & 0 & 1 \end{bmatrix}$

To prove, $f(x)\cdot f(y)=f(x+y)$.

For $f(y)$, replace x with y, so that $f(x)$ becomes $f(y)$.

LHS $=f(x)\cdot f(y)$

$$=\begin{bmatrix} \cos x & -\sin x & 0 \\ \sin x & \cos x & 0 \\ 0 & 0 & 1 \end{bmatrix}\begin{bmatrix} \cos y & -\sin y & 0 \\ \sin y & \cos y & 0 \\ 0 & 0 & 1 \end{bmatrix}$$ [1]

$$=\begin{bmatrix} \cos x\cos y-\sin x\sin y+0 & -\cos x\sin y-\sin x\cos y+0 & 0+0+0 \\ \sin x\cos y+\cos x\sin y+0 & -\sin x\sin y+\cos x\cos y+0 & 0+0+0 \\ 0+0+0 & 0+0+0 & 0+0+1 \end{bmatrix}$$ [2]

[multiplying rows by columns]

$$=\begin{bmatrix} \cos(x+y) & -\sin(x+y) & 0 \\ \sin(x+y) & \cos(x+y) & 0 \\ 0 & 0 & 1 \end{bmatrix}$$

$$\left[\begin{array}{l} \because \cos(A+B)=\cos A\cos B-\sin A\sin B \\ \text{and } \sin(A+B)=\sin A\cos B+\cos A\sin B \end{array}\right]$$

$=f(x+y)=\text{RHS}$ [1]

15. Given, $A=\begin{bmatrix} 1 & -1 \\ 2 & -1 \end{bmatrix}$ and $B=\begin{bmatrix} a & 1 \\ b & -1 \end{bmatrix}$

Clearly, $A+B=\begin{bmatrix} 1 & -1 \\ 2 & -1 \end{bmatrix}+\begin{bmatrix} a & 1 \\ b & -1 \end{bmatrix}=\begin{bmatrix} 1+a & -1+1 \\ 2+b & -1-1 \end{bmatrix}$

$$=\begin{bmatrix} 1+a & 0 \\ 2+b & -2 \end{bmatrix}$$ [1/2]

$$\Rightarrow \quad (A+B)^2=\begin{bmatrix} 1+a & 0 \\ 2+b & -2 \end{bmatrix}\cdot\begin{bmatrix} 1+a & 0 \\ 2+b & -2 \end{bmatrix}$$

$$=\begin{bmatrix} 1+a^2+2a & 0 \\ 2+2a+b+ab-4-2b & 4 \end{bmatrix}$$

$$=\begin{bmatrix} a^2+2a+1 & 0 \\ 2a-b+ab-2 & 4 \end{bmatrix}$$ [1]

Now, $A^2+B^2=\begin{bmatrix} 1 & -1 \\ 2 & -1 \end{bmatrix}\cdot\begin{bmatrix} 1 & -1 \\ 2 & -1 \end{bmatrix}+\begin{bmatrix} a & 1 \\ b & -1 \end{bmatrix}\cdot\begin{bmatrix} a & 1 \\ b & -1 \end{bmatrix}$

$$=\begin{bmatrix} -1 & 0 \\ 0 & -1 \end{bmatrix}+\begin{bmatrix} a^2+b & a-1 \\ ab-b & b+1 \end{bmatrix}$$

$$=\begin{bmatrix} a^2+b-1 & a-1 \\ ab-b & b \end{bmatrix}$$ [1]

Since, $(A+B)^2=A^2+B^2$

$$\therefore \begin{bmatrix} a^2+2a+1 & 0 \\ 2a-b+ab-2 & 4 \end{bmatrix}=\begin{bmatrix} a^2+b-1 & a-1 \\ ab-b & b \end{bmatrix}$$ [1/2]

On equating the corresponding elements, we get

$$a^2+2a+1=a^2+b-1$$

$$\Rightarrow \quad 2a-b=-2, \quad \text{...(i)}$$

$$a-1=0$$

$$\Rightarrow \quad a=1, \quad \text{...(ii)}$$

$$2a-b+ab-2=ab-b$$

$$\Rightarrow \quad 2a-2=0$$

$$\Rightarrow \quad a=1 \quad \text{...(iii)}$$

$$\text{and} \quad b=4 \quad \text{...(iv)}$$

Since, $a=1$, $b=4$ satisfy all four Eqs. (i), (ii), (iii) and (iv), therefore

$$a=1 \text{ and } b=4$$ [1]

16. We have, $A=\begin{bmatrix} 0 & 1 \\ -1 & 0 \end{bmatrix}$

$$\Rightarrow \quad xI+yA=x\begin{bmatrix} 1 & 0 \\ 0 & 1 \end{bmatrix}+y\begin{bmatrix} 0 & 1 \\ -1 & 0 \end{bmatrix}$$

$$=\begin{bmatrix} x & 0 \\ 0 & x \end{bmatrix}+\begin{bmatrix} 0 & y \\ -y & 0 \end{bmatrix}=\begin{bmatrix} x & y \\ -y & x \end{bmatrix}$$ [1]

Now, $(xI+yA)^2=\begin{bmatrix} x & y \\ -y & x \end{bmatrix}^2=\begin{bmatrix} x & y \\ -y & x \end{bmatrix}\begin{bmatrix} x & y \\ -y & x \end{bmatrix}$

$$=\begin{bmatrix} x^2-y^2 & 2xy \\ -2xy & x^2-y^2 \end{bmatrix}$$ [1]

Since, $(xI+yA)^2=A$, therefore

$$\begin{bmatrix} x^2-y^2 & 2xy \\ -2xy & x^2-y^2 \end{bmatrix}=\begin{bmatrix} 0 & 1 \\ -1 & 0 \end{bmatrix}$$

$$\Rightarrow \quad x^2-y^2=0,\ 2xy=1,\ -2xy=-1 \text{ and } x^2-y^2=0$$

$$\Rightarrow \quad x^2-y^2=0 \text{ and } 2xy=1$$

$$\Rightarrow \quad x=\pm y \text{ and } 2xy=1$$ [1]

***Case* I** When $x=y$ and $2xy=1$.

In this case, $2x^2=1 \Rightarrow x=\pm\dfrac{1}{\sqrt{2}}$

Thus, $\left(x=\dfrac{1}{\sqrt{2}} \text{ and } y=\dfrac{1}{\sqrt{2}}\right)$

or $\left(x = -\frac{1}{\sqrt{2}} \text{ and } y = -\frac{1}{\sqrt{2}}\right)$

***Case* II** *When $x = -y$ and $2xy = 1$.*

In this case, $x^2 = \frac{-1}{2}$

$\Rightarrow x = \pm\frac{i}{\sqrt{2}}$, which is imaginary.

Hence, only real values of x and y are

$$x = \frac{1}{\sqrt{2}}, y = \frac{1}{\sqrt{2}}$$

or $$x = -\frac{1}{\sqrt{2}}, y = -\frac{1}{\sqrt{2}}$$ [1]

17. LHS $= I + A$

$$= \begin{bmatrix} 1 & 0 \\ 0 & 1 \end{bmatrix} + \begin{bmatrix} 0 & -\tan\frac{\alpha}{2} \\ \tan\frac{\alpha}{2} & 0 \end{bmatrix}$$

$$= \begin{bmatrix} 1 & -\tan\frac{\alpha}{2} \\ \tan\frac{\alpha}{2} & 1 \end{bmatrix}$$ [1/2]

$$\text{RHS} = (I - A)\begin{bmatrix} \cos\alpha & -\sin\alpha \\ \sin\alpha & \cos\alpha \end{bmatrix}$$

$$= \left\{\begin{bmatrix} 1 & 0 \\ 0 & 1 \end{bmatrix} - \begin{bmatrix} 0 & -\tan\alpha/2 \\ \tan\alpha/2 & 0 \end{bmatrix}\right\}\begin{bmatrix} \cos\alpha & -\sin\alpha \\ \sin\alpha & \cos\alpha \end{bmatrix}$$

$$= \begin{bmatrix} 1-0 & 0+\tan\alpha/2 \\ 0-\tan\alpha/2 & 1-0 \end{bmatrix}\begin{bmatrix} \cos\alpha & -\sin\alpha \\ \sin\alpha & \cos\alpha \end{bmatrix}$$

$$= \begin{bmatrix} 1 & \tan\alpha/2 \\ -\tan\alpha/2 & 1 \end{bmatrix}\begin{bmatrix} \cos\alpha & -\sin\alpha \\ \sin\alpha & \cos\alpha \end{bmatrix}$$ [1]

$$= \begin{bmatrix} \cos\alpha + \tan\frac{\alpha}{2}\sin\alpha & -\sin\alpha + \tan\frac{\alpha}{2}\cos\alpha \\ -\tan\frac{\alpha}{2}\cos\alpha + \sin\alpha & \tan\frac{\alpha}{2}\sin\alpha + \cos\alpha \end{bmatrix}$$ [1/2]

[multiplying rows by columns]

$$= \begin{bmatrix} \dfrac{\cos\alpha\cos\frac{\alpha}{2} + \sin\frac{\alpha}{2}\sin\alpha}{\cos\frac{\alpha}{2}} & \dfrac{-\sin\alpha\cos\frac{\alpha}{2} + \sin\frac{\alpha}{2}\cos\alpha}{\cos\frac{\alpha}{2}} \\ \dfrac{-\sin\frac{\alpha}{2}\cos\alpha + \sin\alpha\cos\frac{\alpha}{2}}{\cos\frac{\alpha}{2}} & \dfrac{\sin\frac{\alpha}{2}\sin\alpha + \cos\alpha\cos\frac{\alpha}{2}}{\cos\frac{\alpha}{2}} \end{bmatrix}$$

$$= \begin{bmatrix} \dfrac{\cos\left(\alpha - \frac{\alpha}{2}\right)}{\cos(\alpha/2)} & \dfrac{\sin\left(\frac{\alpha}{2} - \alpha\right)}{\cos(\alpha/2)} \\ \dfrac{\sin\left(\alpha - \frac{\alpha}{2}\right)}{\cos\frac{\alpha}{2}} & \dfrac{\cos\left(\alpha - \frac{\alpha}{2}\right)}{\cos\frac{\alpha}{2}} \end{bmatrix}$$ [1]

$$\left[\begin{array}{l} \because \cos(A-B) = \cos A\cos B + \sin A\sin B \\ \text{and } \sin(A-B) = \sin A\cos B - \cos A\sin B \end{array}\right]$$

$$= \begin{bmatrix} \dfrac{\cos\frac{\alpha}{2}}{\cos\frac{\alpha}{2}} & \dfrac{-\sin\frac{\alpha}{2}}{\cos\frac{\alpha}{2}} \\ \dfrac{\sin\frac{\alpha}{2}}{\cos\frac{\alpha}{2}} & \dfrac{\cos\frac{\alpha}{2}}{\cos\frac{\alpha}{2}} \end{bmatrix} = \begin{bmatrix} 1 & -\tan\frac{\alpha}{2} \\ \tan\frac{\alpha}{2} & 1 \end{bmatrix} = \text{LHS}$$

Hence proved. [1]

18. Given, $M = \begin{bmatrix} 1 & 2 \\ 2 & 3 \end{bmatrix}$ and $M^2 - kM - I_2 = O$

Now, $M^2 = \begin{bmatrix} 1 & 2 \\ 2 & 3 \end{bmatrix}\begin{bmatrix} 1 & 2 \\ 2 & 3 \end{bmatrix} = \begin{bmatrix} 1+4 & 2+6 \\ 2+6 & 4+9 \end{bmatrix}$

[multiplying row-by-column]

$$= \begin{bmatrix} 5 & 8 \\ 8 & 13 \end{bmatrix}$$ [1]

$\because$ $M^2 - kM - I_2 = O$

$\therefore$ $\begin{bmatrix} 5 & 8 \\ 8 & 13 \end{bmatrix} - k\begin{bmatrix} 1 & 2 \\ 2 & 3 \end{bmatrix} - \begin{bmatrix} 1 & 0 \\ 0 & 1 \end{bmatrix} = O$ $\left[\because I_2 = \begin{bmatrix} 1 & 0 \\ 0 & 1 \end{bmatrix}\right]$ [1]

$\Rightarrow \begin{bmatrix} 5 & 8 \\ 8 & 13 \end{bmatrix} - \begin{bmatrix} k & 2k \\ 2k & 3k \end{bmatrix} - \begin{bmatrix} 1 & 0 \\ 0 & 1 \end{bmatrix} = \begin{bmatrix} 0 & 0 \\ 0 & 0 \end{bmatrix}$

$\Rightarrow \begin{bmatrix} 5-k-1 & 8-2k-0 \\ 8-2k-0 & 13-3k-1 \end{bmatrix} = \begin{bmatrix} 0 & 0 \\ 0 & 0 \end{bmatrix}$

$\Rightarrow \begin{bmatrix} 4-k & 8-2k \\ 8-2k & 12-3k \end{bmatrix} = \begin{bmatrix} 0 & 0 \\ 0 & 0 \end{bmatrix}$ [1]

On equating the corresponding elements, we get

$$4 - k = 0, 8 - 2k = 0, 12 - 3k = 0$$

$\therefore$ $k = 4$ [1]

19. Hint $A^2 = A \cdot A = \begin{bmatrix} 9 & 7 & 5 \\ 1 & 4 & 1 \\ 8 & 9 & 9 \end{bmatrix}$

and $A^3 = A^2 \cdot A = \begin{bmatrix} 28 & 37 & 26 \\ 10 & 5 & 1 \\ 35 & 42 & 34 \end{bmatrix}$

Now, consider LHS $= A^3 - 4A^2 - 3A + 11I$

$$= \begin{bmatrix} 28 & 37 & 26 \\ 10 & 5 & 1 \\ 35 & 42 & 34 \end{bmatrix} - 4\begin{bmatrix} 9 & 7 & 5 \\ 1 & 4 & 1 \\ 8 & 9 & 9 \end{bmatrix} - 3\begin{bmatrix} 1 & 3 & 2 \\ 2 & 0 & -1 \\ 1 & 2 & 3 \end{bmatrix} + 11\begin{bmatrix} 1 & 0 & 0 \\ 0 & 1 & 0 \\ 0 & 0 & 1 \end{bmatrix}$$

$$= \begin{bmatrix} 0 & 0 & 0 \\ 0 & 0 & 0 \\ 0 & 0 & 0 \end{bmatrix} = 0 = \text{RHS}$$

20. Similar as Question 19.

TOPIC 04 Transpose of a Matrix, Symmetric and Skew-symmetric Matrices

Transpose of a Matrix

The matrix obtained by interchanging the rows and columns of matrix A is called the **transpose of matrix** A and the transpose of matrix A is represented by A' or A^c or A^T.

In other words, if $A=[a_{ij}]$ is $m \times n$ matrix.

Then $A^T=[a_{ji}]_{n\times m}$.

e.g. Let $A=\begin{bmatrix} 1 & 5 \\ \sqrt{2} & 1 \\ -1/5 & 0 \end{bmatrix}_{3\times 2}$.

Then, $A'=\begin{bmatrix} 1 & \sqrt{2} & -1/5 \\ 5 & 1 & 0 \end{bmatrix}_{2\times 3}$

Example 1 Find the transpose of the matrix $\begin{bmatrix} 4 & 3 & 1 \\ 1 & -2 & 3 \\ 4 & 5 & -1 \end{bmatrix}$.

Sol. Let $A=\begin{bmatrix} 4 & 3 & 1 \\ 1 & -2 & 3 \\ 4 & 5 & -1 \end{bmatrix}$.

Then, $A'=\begin{bmatrix} 4 & 3 & 1 \\ 1 & -2 & 3 \\ 4 & 5 & -1 \end{bmatrix}'=\begin{bmatrix} 4 & 1 & 4 \\ 3 & -2 & 5 \\ 1 & 3 & -1 \end{bmatrix}$

[interchanging the elements of rows and columns]

Properties of Transpose of Matrices

For any matrices A and B of suitable orders, we have

(i) $(A')'=A$

(ii) $(A\pm B)'=A'\pm B'$

(iii) $(kA)'=kA'$, where k is any constant.

(iv) $(-A)'=-A'$

(v) $(AB)'=B'A'$ [reversal law]

Note $(A^n)^T=(A^T)^n$, where n is a positive integer.

Example 2 If $A=\begin{bmatrix} 3 & \sqrt{3} & 2 \\ 4 & 2 & 0 \end{bmatrix}$ and $B=\begin{bmatrix} 2 & -1 & 2 \\ 1 & 2 & 4 \end{bmatrix}$, then verify that

(i) $(A')'=A$

(ii) $(A+B)'=A'+B'$

(iii) $(kB)'=kB'$, where k is any constant.

Sol. We have, $A=\begin{bmatrix} 3 & \sqrt{3} & 2 \\ 4 & 2 & 0 \end{bmatrix}'$ and $B=\begin{bmatrix} 2 & -1 & 2 \\ 1 & 2 & 4 \end{bmatrix}$, then

$$A'=\begin{bmatrix} 3 & 4 \\ \sqrt{3} & 2 \\ 2 & 0 \end{bmatrix} \text{ and } B'=\begin{bmatrix} 2 & 1 \\ -1 & 2 \\ 2 & 4 \end{bmatrix}$$

[interchanging the elements of rows and columns]

(i) $(A')'=\begin{bmatrix} 3 & 4 \\ \sqrt{3} & 2 \\ 2 & 0 \end{bmatrix}'=\begin{bmatrix} 3 & \sqrt{3} & 2 \\ 4 & 2 & 0 \end{bmatrix}=A$

[interchanging the elements of rows and columns]

(ii) $A+B=\begin{bmatrix} 3 & \sqrt{3} & 2 \\ 4 & 2 & 0 \end{bmatrix}+\begin{bmatrix} 2 & -1 & 2 \\ 1 & 2 & 4 \end{bmatrix}$

$$=\begin{bmatrix} 3+2 & \sqrt{3}-1 & 2+2 \\ 4+1 & 2+2 & 0+4 \end{bmatrix}$$

$$=\begin{bmatrix} 5 & \sqrt{3}-1 & 4 \\ 5 & 4 & 4 \end{bmatrix}$$

$$\therefore (A+B)'=\begin{bmatrix} 5 & \sqrt{3}-1 & 4 \\ 5 & 4 & 4 \end{bmatrix}'=\begin{bmatrix} 5 & 5 \\ \sqrt{3}-1 & 4 \\ 4 & 4 \end{bmatrix} \quad ...(i)$$

[interchanging the elements of rows and columns]

and $A'+B'=\begin{bmatrix} 3 & 4 \\ \sqrt{3} & 2 \\ 2 & 0 \end{bmatrix}+\begin{bmatrix} 2 & 1 \\ -1 & 2 \\ 2 & 4 \end{bmatrix}$

$$=\begin{bmatrix} 3+2 & 4+1 \\ \sqrt{3}-1 & 2+2 \\ 2+2 & 0+4 \end{bmatrix}$$

$$=\begin{bmatrix} 5 & 5 \\ \sqrt{3}-1 & 4 \\ 4 & 4 \end{bmatrix} \quad ...(ii)$$

Thus, $(A+B)'=A'+B'$ [from Eqs. (i) and (ii)]

(iii) $kB=k\begin{bmatrix} 2 & -1 & 2 \\ 1 & 2 & 4 \end{bmatrix}=\begin{bmatrix} 2k & -k & 2k \\ k & 2k & 4k \end{bmatrix}$

and $(kB)'=\begin{bmatrix} 2k & -k & 2k \\ k & 2k & 4k \end{bmatrix}'=\begin{bmatrix} 2k & k \\ -k & 2k \\ 2k & 4k \end{bmatrix}$

$$=k\begin{bmatrix} 2 & 1 \\ -1 & 2 \\ 2 & 4 \end{bmatrix}=kB'$$

Thus, $(kB)'=kB'$

Example 3 For the matrices A and B, verify that $(AB)' = B'A'$, where $A = \begin{bmatrix} 1 \\ -4 \\ 3 \end{bmatrix}$ and $B = [-1 \ \ 2 \ \ 1]$. **[NCERT]**

Sol. Given, $A = \begin{bmatrix} 1 \\ -4 \\ 3 \end{bmatrix}_{3\times 1}$ and $B = [-1 \ \ 2 \ \ 1]_{1\times 3}$

$\therefore \quad A' = [1 \ \ -4 \ \ 3]_{1\times 3}$

[interchanging the elements of rows and columns]

and $B' = \begin{bmatrix} -1 \\ 2 \\ 1 \end{bmatrix}_{3\times 1}$

[interchanging the elements of rows and columns]

Now, $AB = \begin{bmatrix} 1 \\ -4 \\ 3 \end{bmatrix}_{3\times 1} [-1 \ \ 2 \ \ 1]_{1\times 3}$

Since, number of columns in A is equal to the number of rows in B. So, AB exists.

Thus, $AB = \begin{bmatrix} -1 & 2 & 1 \\ 4 & -8 & -4 \\ -3 & 6 & 3 \end{bmatrix}_{3\times 3}$

[multiplying rows by columns]

$\Rightarrow (AB)' = \begin{bmatrix} -1 & 4 & -3 \\ 2 & -8 & 6 \\ 1 & -4 & 3 \end{bmatrix}_{3\times 3}$ ...(i)

[interchanging the elements of rows and columns]

Now, $B'A' = \begin{bmatrix} -1 \\ 2 \\ 1 \end{bmatrix}_{3\times 1} [1 \ \ -4 \ \ 3]_{1\times 3}$

$= \begin{bmatrix} -1 & 4 & -3 \\ 2 & -8 & 6 \\ 1 & -4 & 3 \end{bmatrix}_{3\times 3}$ ...(ii)

[multiplying rows by columns]

From Eqs. (i) and (ii), we get $(AB)' = B'A'$

Hence verified.

Symmetric Matrix

A square matrix A is called a **symmetric matrix**, if the transpose of matrix A is equal to the matrix A, i.e. $A' = A$. In other words, let $A = [a_{ij}]_{n\times n}$, then A is said to be **symmetric matrix**, if $[a_{ij}] = [a_{ji}]$, for all possible values of i and j, i.e. $a_{12} = a_{21}, a_{13} = a_{31}, a_{23} = a_{32}$, etc.

e.g. Let $A = \begin{bmatrix} 2 & 1 & 5 \\ 1 & 2 & 7 \\ 5 & 7 & 3 \end{bmatrix}$.

Then, $A' = \begin{bmatrix} 2 & 1 & 5 \\ 1 & 2 & 7 \\ 5 & 7 & 3 \end{bmatrix}' = \begin{bmatrix} 2 & 1 & 5 \\ 1 & 2 & 7 \\ 5 & 7 & 3 \end{bmatrix} = A$

[interchanging the elements of rows and columns]

Hence, A is a symmetric matrix. $[\because A' = A]$

Example 4 If the matrix $\begin{bmatrix} 6 & -x^2 \\ 2x-15 & 10 \end{bmatrix}$ is symmetric, then find the value of x. **[ISC 2017]**

Sol. Let $A = \begin{bmatrix} 6 & -x^2 \\ 2x-15 & 10 \end{bmatrix}$

Given, matrix A is symmetric.

$\therefore \quad A = A'$ [here, A' is transpose of matrix A] ...(i)

Clearly, $A' = \begin{bmatrix} 6 & 2x-15 \\ -x^2 & 10 \end{bmatrix}$

From Eq. (i), we get

$$\begin{bmatrix} 6 & -x^2 \\ 2x-15 & 10 \end{bmatrix} = \begin{bmatrix} 6 & 2x-15 \\ -x^2 & 10 \end{bmatrix}$$

$\because$ Both the matrices are equal.

$\therefore \quad -x^2 = 2x - 15$

$\Rightarrow \quad x^2 + 2x - 15 = 0$

$\Rightarrow \quad x^2 + 5x - 3x - 15 = 0$

$\Rightarrow \quad x(x+5) - 3(x+5) = 0$

$\Rightarrow \quad (x+5)(x-3) = 0$

$\therefore \quad x = -5$ or $x = 3$

Example 5 Show that all positive integral powers of a symmetric matrix are symmetric.

Sol. Let A be a symmetric matrix and $n \in N$.

Then, $(A^n)^T = [A \cdot A \cdot A \ldots n \text{ times}]^T$

$= [A^T \cdot A^T \ldots n \text{ times}] \quad [\because (AB)^T = B^T A^T]$

$= [A\ A \ldots n \text{ times}] = (A)^n$

$[\because A$ is symmetric, therefore $A^T = A]$

Example 6 Show that $(A + A')$ is symmetric matrix, if $A = \begin{bmatrix} 2 & 4 \\ 3 & 5 \end{bmatrix}$. **[ISC 2019]**

Sol. We have, $A = \begin{bmatrix} 2 & 4 \\ 3 & 5 \end{bmatrix}$

Now, $A + A' = \begin{bmatrix} 2 & 4 \\ 3 & 5 \end{bmatrix} + \begin{bmatrix} 2 & 3 \\ 4 & 5 \end{bmatrix} = \begin{bmatrix} 4 & 7 \\ 7 & 10 \end{bmatrix}$

$\therefore (A + A')' = \begin{bmatrix} 4 & 7 \\ 7 & 10 \end{bmatrix}' = \begin{bmatrix} 4 & 7 \\ 7 & 10 \end{bmatrix} = A + A'$

Hence, $(A + A')$ is symmetric matrix.

Skew-Symmetric Matrix

A square matrix A is said to be **skew-symmetric matrix**, if the transpose of matrix A is equal to the negative of matrix A, i.e. $A' = -A$.

In other words, let $A = [a_{ij}]_{n \times n}$, then A is said to be **skew-symmetric matrix**, if $[a_{ji}] = -[a_{ij}]$, for all values of i and j, i.e. $a_{12} = -a_{21}$, $a_{13} = -a_{31}$, $a_{23} = -a_{32}$, etc.

e.g. Let $A = \begin{bmatrix} 0 & 1 & 2 \\ -1 & 0 & 5 \\ -2 & -5 & 0 \end{bmatrix}$.

Then, $A' = \begin{bmatrix} 0 & -1 & -2 \\ 1 & 0 & -5 \\ 2 & 5 & 0 \end{bmatrix}$

[interchanging the elements of rows and columns]

$$= -\begin{bmatrix} 0 & 1 & 2 \\ -1 & 0 & 5 \\ -2 & -5 & 0 \end{bmatrix}$$

[taking (−1) common from the matrix]

$\Rightarrow \quad A' = -A$

Note

(i) The principal diagonal elements of a skew-symmetric matrix are always zero, because if we put $i = j$ in $a_{ji} = -a_{ij}$, then $a_{ii} = -a_{ii}$.
$\therefore\ 2a_{ii} = 0 \Rightarrow a_{ii} = 0,\ \forall\ i$.

(ii) Only zero matrix is both symmetric and skew-symmetric matrix.

Example 7 For what value of k, the matrix $\begin{bmatrix} 0 & k \\ -6 & 0 \end{bmatrix}$ is a skew-symmetric matrix? **[ISC 2023]**

Sol. Given, $\begin{bmatrix} 0 & k \\ -6 & 0 \end{bmatrix}$ is skew-symmetric matrix.

Since, A is skew-symmetric matrix.

$\therefore\ A = -A'$

$\therefore\ k = -(-6) = 6$

Example 8 Show that matrix $B = \begin{bmatrix} 0 & 3 & -4 \\ -3 & 0 & 2 \\ 4 & -2 & 0 \end{bmatrix}$ is skew-symmetric matrix.

Sol. Given, $B = \begin{bmatrix} 0 & 3 & -4 \\ -3 & 0 & 2 \\ 4 & -2 & 0 \end{bmatrix}$

Now, $B' = \begin{bmatrix} 0 & 3 & -4 \\ -3 & 0 & 2 \\ 4 & -2 & 0 \end{bmatrix}' = \begin{bmatrix} 0 & -3 & 4 \\ 3 & 0 & -2 \\ -4 & 2 & 0 \end{bmatrix}$

[interchanging the elements of rows and columns]

$$= -\begin{bmatrix} 0 & 3 & -4 \\ -3 & 0 & 2 \\ 4 & -2 & 0 \end{bmatrix}$$

[taking (−1) common from the matrix]

$\therefore \quad B' = -B$

Hence, B is skew-symmetric matrix.

Some Important Theorems

Theorem 1. For a square matrix A with real number entries, $A + A'$ is a symmetric and $A - A'$ is a skew-symmetric matrix.

Theorem 2. A square matrix A can be expressed as the sum of a symmetric and skew-symmetric matrices.

i.e. $\quad A = \frac{1}{2}(A + A') + \frac{1}{2}(A - A')$, where $\frac{1}{2}(A + A')$ is symmetric and $\frac{1}{2}(A - A')$ is skew-symmetric.

Example 9 Prove that the square matrix $\begin{bmatrix} 5 & 2 \\ 3 & -6 \end{bmatrix}$ can be expressed as a sum of symmetric and skew-symmetric matrices.

Sol. Let $A = \begin{bmatrix} 5 & 2 \\ 3 & -6 \end{bmatrix}$. Then, $A' = \begin{bmatrix} 5 & 3 \\ 2 & -6 \end{bmatrix}$

[interchanging the elements of rows and columns]

Now, $A + A' = \begin{bmatrix} 5 & 2 \\ 3 & -6 \end{bmatrix} + \begin{bmatrix} 5 & 3 \\ 2 & -6 \end{bmatrix}$

$\Rightarrow \quad A + A' = \begin{bmatrix} 5+5 & 2+3 \\ 3+2 & -6-6 \end{bmatrix} = \begin{bmatrix} 10 & 5 \\ 5 & -12 \end{bmatrix}$

$\Rightarrow \frac{1}{2}(A + A') = \frac{1}{2}\begin{bmatrix} 10 & 5 \\ 5 & -12 \end{bmatrix}$, which is symmetric. ...(i)

Also, $A - A' = \begin{bmatrix} 5 & 2 \\ 3 & -6 \end{bmatrix} - \begin{bmatrix} 5 & 3 \\ 2 & -6 \end{bmatrix}$

$= \begin{bmatrix} 5-5 & 2-3 \\ 3-2 & -6+6 \end{bmatrix} = \begin{bmatrix} 0 & -1 \\ 1 & 0 \end{bmatrix}$

$\Rightarrow \frac{1}{2}(A - A') = \frac{1}{2}\begin{bmatrix} 0 & -1 \\ 1 & 0 \end{bmatrix}$,

which is skew-symmetric. ...(ii)

On adding Eqs. (i) and (ii), we get

$\frac{1}{2}(A + A') + \frac{1}{2}(A - A')$

$= \frac{1}{2}\begin{bmatrix} 10 & 5 \\ 5 & -12 \end{bmatrix} + \frac{1}{2}\begin{bmatrix} 0 & -1 \\ 1 & 0 \end{bmatrix}$

$= \frac{1}{2}\begin{bmatrix} 10+0 & 5-1 \\ 5+1 & -12+0 \end{bmatrix}$

$= \frac{1}{2}\begin{bmatrix} 10 & 4 \\ 6 & -12 \end{bmatrix}$

$= \begin{bmatrix} 5 & 2 \\ 3 & -6 \end{bmatrix} = A$ **Hence proved.**

Invertible Matrix

A square matrix A of order m is said to be **invertible** (or inversible), if there exists another square matrix B of same order m, such that $AB = BA = I$, where I is a unit matrix of same order m. The matrix B, is called the **inverse of matrix** A and is denoted by A^{-1}.

e.g. Let $A = \begin{bmatrix} 3 & 10 \\ 2 & 7 \end{bmatrix}$ and $B = \begin{bmatrix} 7 & -10 \\ -2 & 3 \end{bmatrix}$ be two square matrices of order 2.

Then, $AB = \begin{bmatrix} 3 & 10 \\ 2 & 7 \end{bmatrix}\begin{bmatrix} 7 & -10 \\ -2 & 3 \end{bmatrix}$

$= \begin{bmatrix} 21-20 & -30+30 \\ 14-14 & -20+21 \end{bmatrix} = \begin{bmatrix} 1 & 0 \\ 0 & 1 \end{bmatrix}$

$= I$, which is of order 2.

Also, $BA = \begin{bmatrix} 7 & -10 \\ -2 & 3 \end{bmatrix}\begin{bmatrix} 3 & 10 \\ 2 & 7 \end{bmatrix}$

$= \begin{bmatrix} 21-20 & 70-70 \\ -6+6 & -20+21 \end{bmatrix} = \begin{bmatrix} 1 & 0 \\ 0 & 1 \end{bmatrix}$

$= I$, which is of order 2.

Thus, $AB = BA = I$.

Hence, A is invertible and $A^{-1} = B$.

Note

(i) A rectangular matrix does not possess inverse matrix. Since, for the products BA and AB to be defined and to be equal, it is necessary that matrices A and B are square matrices of the same order.

(ii) If B is the inverse of A, then A is also the inverse of B.

Some Important Theorems

Theorem 1. (*Uniqueness of Inverse*) Inverse of a square matrix, if it exists, is unique.

Proof Let A be a square matrix such that its inverse exists.

If possible, let B and C be two inverses of A.

Then, we need to show $B = C$.

Since, B is the inverse of A.

$\therefore \quad AB = BA = I \quad \ldots$(i)

Also, C is the inverse of A.

$\therefore \quad AC = CA = I \quad \ldots$(ii)

Now, we can write $B = BI$

$= B(AC)$ [using Eq. (ii)]

$= (BA)C$

[by associative law of matrix multiplication]

$= IC$ [using Eq. (i)]

$= C$ **Hence proved.**

Theorem 2. If A and B are invertible matrices of the same order, then $(AB)^{-1} = B^{-1}A^{-1}$.

Proof By definition of inverse, we have

$(AB)(AB)^{-1} = I$

$\Rightarrow \quad A^{-1}(AB)(AB)^{-1} = A^{-1}I$

[pre-multiplying both sides by A^{-1}]

$\Rightarrow \quad (A^{-1}A)B(AB)^{-1} = A^{-1}$

[by associative law of matrix multiplication and by using $AI = A = IA$]

$\Rightarrow \quad IB(AB)^{-1} = A^{-1}$ [$\because AA^{-1} = I = A^{-1}A$]

$\Rightarrow \quad B(AB)^{-1} = A^{-1}$

$\Rightarrow \quad B^{-1}B(AB)^{-1} = B^{-1}A^{-1}$

[pre-multiplying both sides by B^{-1}]

$\Rightarrow \quad I(AB)^{-1} = B^{-1}A^{-1}$

$\Rightarrow \quad (AB)^{-1} = B^{-1}A^{-1}$ **Hence proved.**

Example 10 If $(AB)^{-1} = A^{-1}B^{-1}$, then prove that A^{-1} and B^{-1} satisfy commutative property with respect to multiplication. **[NCERT Exemplar]**

Sol. Given, $(AB)^{-1} = A^{-1}B^{-1}$ ...(i)

Now as, $(AB)^{-1} = B^{-1}A^{-1}$ [by theorem 2]

$\therefore \quad A^{-1}B^{-1} = B^{-1}A^{-1}$ [from Eq. (i)]

Here, we see that A^{-1} and B^{-1} satisfy the property of commutative with respect to multiplication.

Topic Practice 4

Very Short Answer Type Questions

2 Marks

1 Find the transpose of the following matrices.

(i) $A = \begin{bmatrix} 3 & 4 & 6 \\ -2 & 5 & 2 \\ 1 & -1 & 2 \end{bmatrix}$ (ii) $B = \begin{bmatrix} \sin\theta & \cos\theta & -\sin\theta \\ \cos\theta & -\sin\theta & 3 \\ 4 & -\tan\theta & 2 \end{bmatrix}$

2 If $A = \begin{bmatrix} 1 & 2 \\ 3 & 4 \end{bmatrix}$, $B = \begin{bmatrix} 4 & 6 \\ 7 & 8 \end{bmatrix}$, then find $(A+B)'$.

3 If $P = \begin{bmatrix} 1 & 3 & 4 \\ 2 & 5 & 6 \\ 3 & 2 & 1 \end{bmatrix}$ and $Q = \begin{bmatrix} 4 & 6 & 7 \\ 3 & 2 & -1 \\ 5 & 2 & 6 \end{bmatrix}$, then find $(P-Q)'$.

4 If $A=\begin{bmatrix}\cos\alpha & \sin\alpha\\ -\sin\alpha & \cos\alpha\end{bmatrix}$, then find the value of $A'A$. [NCERT]

5 If $A=\begin{bmatrix}\cos\alpha & \sin\alpha\\ -\sin\alpha & \cos\alpha\end{bmatrix}$, then find α satisfying $0<\alpha<\frac{\pi}{2}$ when $A+A^T=\sqrt{2}\,I_2$, where A^T is transpose of A.

6 If $A=\begin{bmatrix}5 & a\\ b & 0\end{bmatrix}$ and A is symmetric matrix, show that $a=b$. [ISC 2018]

7 Matrix $A=\begin{bmatrix}0 & 2b & -2\\ 3 & 1 & 3\\ 3a & 3 & -1\end{bmatrix}$ is given to be symmetric, then find the values of a and b.

8 If $A'=\begin{bmatrix}-2 & 3\\ 1 & 2\end{bmatrix}$ and $B=\begin{bmatrix}-1 & 0\\ 1 & 2\end{bmatrix}$, then find $(A+2B)'$. [NCERT]

9 Show that $A'A$ and AA' are both symmetric matrices for any matrix A. [NCERT Exemplar]

10 If A and B are symmetric matrices, then prove that $AB+BA$ is a symmetric matrix.

11 If A and B are symmetric matrices of the same order, then prove that following matrices are skew-symmetric matrix.

(i) $AB'-BA'$ (ii) $AB-BA$ [NCERT]

12 If matrix $\begin{bmatrix}0 & a & 3\\ 2 & b & -1\\ c & 1 & 0\end{bmatrix}$ is a skew-symmetric matrix, then find the values of a, b and c.

Short Answer Type Questions

4 Marks

13 If $A=\begin{bmatrix}1 & 2\\ 4 & 1\\ 5 & 6\end{bmatrix}$ and $B=\begin{bmatrix}1 & 2\\ 6 & 4\\ 7 & 3\end{bmatrix}$, then verify that $(2A+B)'=2A'+B'$. [NCERT Exemplar]

14 If $A=\begin{bmatrix}1 & 2 & 2\\ 2 & 1 & -2\\ x & 2 & y\end{bmatrix}$ is a matrix satisfying $AA'=9I$, then find the values of x and y.

15 For the matrix $A=\begin{bmatrix}1 & 5\\ 6 & 7\end{bmatrix}$, verify that

(i) $(A+A')$ is a symmetric matrix.

(ii) $(A-A')$ is a skew-symmetric matrix. [NCERT]

16 Express the matrix $A=\begin{bmatrix}2 & 4 & -6\\ 7 & 3 & 5\\ 1 & -2 & 4\end{bmatrix}$ as the sum of a symmetric and a skew-symmetric matrices. [NCERT Exemplar]

Hints & Solutions

1. Similar as Example 1.

$$\left[\textbf{Ans.}\text{(i)}\begin{bmatrix}3 & -2 & 1\\ 4 & 5 & -1\\ 6 & 2 & 2\end{bmatrix}\text{(ii)}\begin{bmatrix}\sin\theta & \cos\theta & 4\\ \cos\theta & -\sin\theta & -\tan\theta\\ -\sin\theta & 3 & 2\end{bmatrix}\right]$$

2. Now, $A+B=\begin{bmatrix}1 & 2\\ 3 & 4\end{bmatrix}+\begin{bmatrix}4 & 6\\ 7 & 8\end{bmatrix}=\begin{bmatrix}5 & 8\\ 10 & 12\end{bmatrix}$

$\therefore\quad (A+B)'=\begin{bmatrix}5 & 10\\ 8 & 12\end{bmatrix}$

3. Similar as Question 2.

$$\left[\textbf{Ans.}\begin{bmatrix}-3 & -1 & -2\\ -3 & 3 & 0\\ -3 & 7 & -5\end{bmatrix}\right]$$

4. We have, $A=\begin{bmatrix}\cos\alpha & \sin\alpha\\ -\sin\alpha & \cos\alpha\end{bmatrix}$

$\therefore\quad A'=\begin{bmatrix}\cos\alpha & -\sin\alpha\\ \sin\alpha & \cos\alpha\end{bmatrix}$

[interchanging the elements of rows and columns]

Now, $A'A=\begin{bmatrix}\cos\alpha & -\sin\alpha\\ \sin\alpha & \cos\alpha\end{bmatrix}\begin{bmatrix}\cos\alpha & \sin\alpha\\ -\sin\alpha & \cos\alpha\end{bmatrix}$ [1]

$$=\begin{bmatrix}\cos^2\alpha+\sin^2\alpha & \cos\alpha\sin\alpha-\sin\alpha\cos\alpha\\ \sin\alpha\cos\alpha-\sin\alpha\cos\alpha & \sin^2\alpha+\cos^2\alpha\end{bmatrix}$$

[multiplying rows by columns]

$=\begin{bmatrix}1 & 0\\ 0 & 1\end{bmatrix}$ [$\because\ \cos^2\theta+\sin^2\theta=1$] [1]

5. Given, $A=\begin{bmatrix}\cos\alpha & \sin\alpha\\ -\sin\alpha & \cos\alpha\end{bmatrix}$

Also, given $A+A^T=\sqrt{2}\,I_2$

$\therefore\quad \begin{bmatrix}\cos\alpha & \sin\alpha\\ -\sin\alpha & \cos\alpha\end{bmatrix}+\begin{bmatrix}\cos\alpha & \sin\alpha\\ -\sin\alpha & \cos\alpha\end{bmatrix}^T=\sqrt{2}\begin{bmatrix}1 & 0\\ 0 & 1\end{bmatrix}$

$\Rightarrow\quad \begin{bmatrix}\cos\alpha & \sin\alpha\\ -\sin\alpha & \cos\alpha\end{bmatrix}+\begin{bmatrix}\cos\alpha & -\sin\alpha\\ \sin\alpha & \cos\alpha\end{bmatrix}=\begin{bmatrix}\sqrt{2} & 0\\ 0 & \sqrt{2}\end{bmatrix}$

[1]

$\Rightarrow\quad \begin{bmatrix}\cos\alpha+\cos\alpha & \sin\alpha-\sin\alpha\\ -\sin\alpha+\sin\alpha & \cos\alpha+\cos\alpha\end{bmatrix}=\begin{bmatrix}\sqrt{2} & 0\\ 0 & \sqrt{2}\end{bmatrix}$

$\Rightarrow\quad \begin{bmatrix}2\cos\alpha & 0\\ 0 & 2\cos\alpha\end{bmatrix}=\begin{bmatrix}\sqrt{2} & 0\\ 0 & \sqrt{2}\end{bmatrix}$

$\Rightarrow\quad 2\cos\alpha=\sqrt{2}$

$$\Rightarrow \quad \cos\alpha = \frac{1}{\sqrt{2}}$$

$$\Rightarrow \quad \alpha = \frac{\pi}{4}$$ [1]

6. Given, $A = \begin{bmatrix} 5 & a \\ b & 0 \end{bmatrix}$

$\therefore \quad A' = \begin{bmatrix} 5 & b \\ a & 0 \end{bmatrix}$ [1]

$\because$ A is a symmetric matrix.

$\therefore \quad A = A'$

$$\Rightarrow \begin{bmatrix} 5 & a \\ b & 0 \end{bmatrix} = \begin{bmatrix} 5 & b \\ a & 0 \end{bmatrix}$$

On comparing the corresponding element, we get $a = b$.

Hence proved. [1]

7. Given, $A = \begin{bmatrix} 0 & 2b & -2 \\ 3 & 1 & 3 \\ 3a & 3 & -1 \end{bmatrix}$ is a symmetric matrix.

We know that a matrix A is symmetric, if $A' = A$.

$$\therefore \text{ We have, } \begin{bmatrix} 0 & 2b & -2 \\ 3 & 1 & 3 \\ 3a & 3 & -1 \end{bmatrix}' = \begin{bmatrix} 0 & 2b & -2 \\ 3 & 1 & 3 \\ 3a & 3 & -1 \end{bmatrix}$$

$$\Rightarrow \begin{bmatrix} 0 & 3 & 3a \\ 2b & 1 & 3 \\ -2 & 3 & -1 \end{bmatrix} = \begin{bmatrix} 0 & 2b & -2 \\ 3 & 1 & 3 \\ 3a & 3 & -1 \end{bmatrix}$$ [1]

On equating the corresponding elements, we get

$$3 = 2b \text{ and } 3a = -2$$

$$\therefore \quad b = \frac{3}{2} \text{ and } a = -\frac{2}{3}$$ [1]

8. We have, $A' = \begin{bmatrix} -2 & 3 \\ 1 & 2 \end{bmatrix}$ and $B = \begin{bmatrix} -1 & 0 \\ 1 & 2 \end{bmatrix}$

$$\therefore \quad A = (A')' = \begin{bmatrix} -2 & 3 \\ 1 & 2 \end{bmatrix}' = \begin{bmatrix} -2 & 1 \\ 3 & 2 \end{bmatrix}$$

[interchanging the elements of rows and columns] [1]

$$\text{Now, } A + 2B = \begin{bmatrix} -2 & 1 \\ 3 & 2 \end{bmatrix} + 2\begin{bmatrix} -1 & 0 \\ 1 & 2 \end{bmatrix}$$

$$= \begin{bmatrix} -2 & 1 \\ 3 & 2 \end{bmatrix} + \begin{bmatrix} -2 & 0 \\ 2 & 4 \end{bmatrix}$$

$$= \begin{bmatrix} -2-2 & 1+0 \\ 3+2 & 2+4 \end{bmatrix}$$

$$= \begin{bmatrix} -4 & 1 \\ 5 & 6 \end{bmatrix}$$

$$\Rightarrow \quad (A + 2B)' = \begin{bmatrix} -4 & 1 \\ 5 & 6 \end{bmatrix}' = \begin{bmatrix} -4 & 5 \\ 1 & 6 \end{bmatrix}$$

[interchanging the elements of rows and columns] [1]

9. Consider, $(A'A)' = (A)'(A')'$ $\quad [\because (AB)' = B'A']$

$= A' \cdot A$ $\quad [\because (A')' = A]$

Hence, $A'A$ is symmetric matrix for any matrix A. [1]

Now, $(AA')' = (A')'(A)' = AA'$ $\quad [\because (AB)' = B'A']$

Hence, AA' is also symmetric matrix for any matrix A. [1]

10. Given, A and B are symmetric matrices.

$\therefore \quad A' = A$ and $B' = B$

Now, $(AB + BA)' = (AB)' + (BA)'$ $\quad [\because (A + B)' = A' + B']$

$= B'A' + A'B'$ $\quad [\because (AB)' = B'A']$ [1]

$= BA + AB$ $\quad [\because A' = A \text{ and } B' = B]$

$= AB + BA$ $\quad$ [$\because$ matrix addition is commutative]

Hence, $AB + BA$ is a symmetric matrix. [1]

11. (i) Consider $(AB' - BA')' = [AB' + (-BA')]'$

$= (AB')' + (-BA')'$ $\quad [\because (A + B)' = A' + B']$

$= (AB')' - (BA')'$ $\quad [\because (kA)' = kA']$

$= (B')'A' - (A')'B'$ $\quad [(CD)' = D'C']$

$= BA' - AB'$ $\quad [\because (C^T)^T = C]$

$= -(AB' - BA')$

Hence, $(AB' - BA')$ is a skew-symmetric matrix. [1]

(ii) Similar as part (i). [1]

12. Similar as Example 7.

[**Ans.** $a = -2, b = 0$ and $c = -3$]

13. Similar as Example 2 (ii).

14. Given, $A = \begin{bmatrix} 1 & 2 & 2 \\ 2 & 1 & -2 \\ x & 2 & y \end{bmatrix}$

$$\therefore \quad A' = \begin{bmatrix} 1 & 2 & x \\ 2 & 1 & 2 \\ 2 & -2 & y \end{bmatrix}$$

[interchanging the elements of rows and columns]

Since, $\quad AA' = 9I$

$$\begin{bmatrix} 1 & 2 & 2 \\ 2 & 1 & -2 \\ x & 2 & y \end{bmatrix} \begin{bmatrix} 1 & 2 & x \\ 2 & 1 & 2 \\ 2 & -2 & y \end{bmatrix} = 9\begin{bmatrix} 1 & 0 & 0 \\ 0 & 1 & 0 \\ 0 & 0 & 1 \end{bmatrix}$$ [1]

$$\Rightarrow \begin{bmatrix} 1+4+4 & 2+2-4 & x+4+2y \\ 2+2-4 & 4+1+4 & 2x+2-2y \\ x+4+2y & 2x+2-2y & x^2+4+y^2 \end{bmatrix} = \begin{bmatrix} 9 & 0 & 0 \\ 0 & 9 & 0 \\ 0 & 0 & 9 \end{bmatrix}$$

[multiplying rows by columns]

$$\Rightarrow \begin{bmatrix} 9 & 0 & x+4+2y \\ 0 & 9 & 2x+2-2y \\ x+4+2y & 2x+2-2y & x^2+4+y^2 \end{bmatrix} = \begin{bmatrix} 9 & 0 & 0 \\ 0 & 9 & 0 \\ 0 & 0 & 9 \end{bmatrix}$$

[1]

On equating the corresponding elements, we get

$x + 4 + 2y = 0 \Rightarrow x + 2y = -4$ ...(i)

$2x + 2 - 2y = 0 \Rightarrow x - y = -1$ ...(ii)

and $\quad x^2 + y^2 + 4 = 9 \Rightarrow x^2 + y^2 = 5$ ...(iii) [1]

On subtracting Eq. (ii) from Eq. (i), we get

$$3y = -3 \Rightarrow y = -1$$

On putting $y = -1$ in Eq. (ii), we get

$$x + 1 = -1 \Rightarrow x = -2$$

Thus, $x = -2$ and $y = -1$, which also satisfy Eq. (iii).

Hence, $x = -2$ and $y = -1$. [1]

15. (i) Here, $A + A' = \begin{bmatrix} 1 & 5 \\ 6 & 7 \end{bmatrix} + \begin{bmatrix} 1 & 5 \\ 6 & 7 \end{bmatrix}'$

$$= \begin{bmatrix} 1 & 5 \\ 6 & 7 \end{bmatrix} + \begin{bmatrix} 1 & 6 \\ 5 & 7 \end{bmatrix} = \begin{bmatrix} 2 & 11 \\ 11 & 14 \end{bmatrix}$$ [1]

and $(A + A')' = \begin{bmatrix} 2 & 11 \\ 11 & 14 \end{bmatrix} = A + A'$

$\therefore (A + A')$ is a symmetric matrix. [1]

(ii) Here, $A - A' = \begin{bmatrix} 1 & 5 \\ 6 & 7 \end{bmatrix} - \begin{bmatrix} 1 & 5 \\ 6 & 7 \end{bmatrix}'$

$$= \begin{bmatrix} 1 & 5 \\ 6 & 7 \end{bmatrix} - \begin{bmatrix} 1 & 6 \\ 5 & 7 \end{bmatrix} = \begin{bmatrix} 0 & -1 \\ 1 & 0 \end{bmatrix}$$ [1]

and $(A - A')' = \begin{bmatrix} 0 & 1 \\ -1 & 0 \end{bmatrix} = -\begin{bmatrix} 0 & -1 \\ 1 & 0 \end{bmatrix} = -(A - A')$

$\therefore$ $(A - A')$ is a skew-symmetric matrix. [1]

16. We have, $A = \begin{bmatrix} 2 & 4 & -6 \\ 7 & 3 & 5 \\ 1 & -2 & 4 \end{bmatrix}$.

$$\Rightarrow \quad A' = \begin{bmatrix} 2 & 7 & 1 \\ 4 & 3 & -2 \\ -6 & 5 & 4 \end{bmatrix}$$ [1/2]

Let $P = \frac{1}{2}(A + A') = \frac{1}{2}\left\{\begin{bmatrix} 2 & 4 & -6 \\ 7 & 3 & 5 \\ 1 & -2 & 4 \end{bmatrix} + \begin{bmatrix} 2 & 7 & 1 \\ 4 & 3 & -2 \\ -6 & 5 & 4 \end{bmatrix}\right\}$

$$= \frac{1}{2}\begin{bmatrix} 4 & 11 & -5 \\ 11 & 6 & 3 \\ -5 & 3 & 8 \end{bmatrix} = \begin{bmatrix} 2 & \frac{11}{2} & -\frac{5}{2} \\ \frac{11}{2} & 3 & \frac{3}{2} \\ -\frac{5}{2} & \frac{3}{2} & 4 \end{bmatrix},$$

which is symmetric matrix. [1]

and $Q = \frac{1}{2}(A - A') = \frac{1}{2}\left\{\begin{bmatrix} 2 & 4 & -6 \\ 7 & 3 & 5 \\ 1 & -2 & 4 \end{bmatrix} - \begin{bmatrix} 2 & 7 & 1 \\ 4 & 3 & -2 \\ -6 & 5 & 4 \end{bmatrix}\right\}$

$$= \frac{1}{2}\begin{bmatrix} 0 & -3 & -7 \\ 3 & 0 & 7 \\ 7 & -7 & 0 \end{bmatrix} = \begin{bmatrix} 0 & -\frac{3}{2} & -\frac{7}{2} \\ \frac{3}{2} & 0 & \frac{7}{2} \\ \frac{7}{2} & -\frac{7}{2} & 0 \end{bmatrix},$$

which is skew-symmetric matrix. [1]

Now, $P + Q = \frac{1}{2}(A + A') + \frac{1}{2}(A - A')$

$$= \begin{bmatrix} 2 & \frac{11}{2} & -\frac{5}{2} \\ \frac{11}{2} & 3 & \frac{3}{2} \\ -\frac{5}{2} & \frac{3}{2} & 4 \end{bmatrix} + \begin{bmatrix} 0 & -\frac{3}{2} & -\frac{7}{2} \\ \frac{3}{2} & 0 & \frac{7}{2} \\ \frac{7}{2} & -\frac{7}{2} & 0 \end{bmatrix}$$

$$= \begin{bmatrix} 2 & 4 & -6 \\ 7 & 3 & 5 \\ 1 & -2 & 4 \end{bmatrix} = A$$ [1]

Hence, A is represented as sum of symmetric and skew-symmetric matrix. [1/2]

Chapter Practice

Multiple Choice Type Questions

1 Mark

1 If A and B are symmetric matrices of the same order, then $AB - BA$ is **[ISC 2024]**

(a) Skew-symmetric matrix
(b) Symmetric matrix
(c) Diagonal matrix
(d) Identity matrix

2 If for a square matrix A, $A^2 - 3A + I = 0$ and $A^{-1} = xA + yI$, then the value of $x + y$ is

(a) -2 (b) 2
(c) 3 (d) -3

3 If $A = \begin{bmatrix} 3 & 4 \\ 5 & 2 \end{bmatrix}$ and $2A + B$ is a null matrix, then B is equal to

(a) $\begin{bmatrix} 6 & 8 \\ 10 & 4 \end{bmatrix}$ (b) $\begin{bmatrix} -6 & -8 \\ -10 & -4 \end{bmatrix}$
(c) $\begin{bmatrix} 5 & 8 \\ 10 & 3 \end{bmatrix}$ (d) $\begin{bmatrix} -5 & -8 \\ -10 & -3 \end{bmatrix}$

4 If $\begin{bmatrix} 2x + y & 4x \\ 5x - 7 & 4x \end{bmatrix} = \begin{bmatrix} 7 & 7y - 13 \\ y & x + 6 \end{bmatrix}$, then

(a) $x = 3, y = 1$
(b) $x = 2, y = 3$
(c) $x = 2, y = 4$
(d) $x = 3, y = 3$

5 If A is a square matrix and $A^2 = A$, then $(I + A)^2 - 3A$ is equal to

(a) I (b) A
(c) $2A$ (d) $3I$

6 If $A = \begin{bmatrix} 0 & 1 \\ 0 & 0 \end{bmatrix}$, then A^{2023} is equal to

(a) $\begin{bmatrix} 0 & 1 \\ 0 & 0 \end{bmatrix}$ (b) $\begin{bmatrix} 0 & 2023 \\ 0 & 0 \end{bmatrix}$
(c) $\begin{bmatrix} 0 & 0 \\ 0 & 0 \end{bmatrix}$ (d) $\begin{bmatrix} 2023 & 0 \\ 0 & 2023 \end{bmatrix}$

7 A and B are skew-symmetric matrices of same order. AB is symmetric, if

(a) $AB = 0$ (b) $AB = -BA$
(c) $AB = BA$ (d) $BA = 0$

Assertion-Reason Type Questions

1 Mark

Directions (Q. Nos. 8-11) *In the questions given below are two statements labelled as Assertion (A) and Reason (R). In the context of the two statements, which one of the following is correct?*

(a) Both A and R are correct; R is the correct explanation of A
(b) Both A and R are correct; R is not the correct explanation of A
(c) A is correct; R is incorrect
(d) R is correct; A is incorrect

8 **Assertion (A)** Matrix $\begin{bmatrix} 1 & 0 & 0 \\ 0 & 3 & 0 \\ 0 & 0 & 4 \end{bmatrix}$ is a diagonal matrix.

Reason (R) Identity matrix of order 3 is a diagonal matrix.

9 **Assertion (A)** The product of two matrices $\begin{bmatrix} 1 & 3 & 4 \\ -1 & 2 & 0 \\ 1 & 3 & 2 \end{bmatrix}$ and $\begin{bmatrix} -1 & 2 \\ 3 & 4 \\ -1 & 2 \end{bmatrix}$ is $\begin{bmatrix} 4 & 22 \\ 7 & 6 \\ 6 & 18 \end{bmatrix}$.

Reason (R) The product of two matrices A and B is defined, if the number of columns of A is equal to the number of rows of B.

10 **Assertion (A)** Let the matrices $A = \begin{pmatrix} -3 & 2 \\ -5 & 4 \end{pmatrix}$ and $B = \begin{pmatrix} 4 & -2 \\ 5 & -3 \end{pmatrix}$ be such that $A^{100}B = BA^{100}$.

Reason (R) $AB = BA$ implies $A^nB = BA^n$ for all positive integers n. **[ISC 2024]**

11. **Assertion (A)** Matrix $A = \begin{bmatrix} 1 & 2 & 4 \\ 2 & 3 & -1 \\ 4 & -1 & 5 \end{bmatrix}$ is symmetric matrix.

Reason (R) Matrix $B = \begin{bmatrix} 0 & 1 & -2 \\ -1 & 0 & 3 \\ 2 & -3 & 0 \end{bmatrix}$ is a skew-symmetric matrix.

Very Short Answer Type Questions

(2 Marks)

12 Find non-zero values of x satisfying the matrix equation $x\begin{bmatrix} 2x & 2 \\ 3 & x \end{bmatrix} + 2\begin{bmatrix} 8 & 5x \\ 4 & 4x \end{bmatrix} = 2\begin{bmatrix} x^2+8 & 24 \\ 10 & 6x \end{bmatrix}$. [NCERT Exemplar]

13 If $\begin{bmatrix} 9 & -1 & 4 \\ -2 & 1 & 3 \end{bmatrix} = A + \begin{bmatrix} 1 & 2 & -1 \\ 0 & 4 & 9 \end{bmatrix}$, then find the matrix A.

14 Let $A = [a_{ij}]_{n \times n}$ be a diagonal matrix whose diagonal elements are different and $B = [b_{ij}]_{n \times n}$ is some another matrix. If $AB = [c_{ij}]_{n \times n}$, then find c_{ij}.

15 If $\begin{bmatrix} 1 & 0 & 0 \\ 0 & y & 0 \\ 0 & 0 & 1 \end{bmatrix}\begin{bmatrix} x \\ -1 \\ z \end{bmatrix} = \begin{bmatrix} 1 \\ 2 \\ 1 \end{bmatrix}$, then find $x + y + z$.

16 If matrix $A = \begin{bmatrix} 1 & -1 \\ -1 & 1 \end{bmatrix}$ and $A^2 = kA$, then write the value of k.

17 Show by an example that for $A \neq O$, $B \neq O$ and $AB = O$. [NCERT Exemplar]

18 If $A = \begin{bmatrix} \cos\alpha & -\sin\alpha \\ \sin\alpha & \cos\alpha \end{bmatrix}$, then for what value of α, A is an identity matrix?

19 If $\begin{bmatrix} x+3 & z+4 & 2y-7 \\ -6 & a-1 & 0 \\ b-3 & -21 & 0 \end{bmatrix} = \begin{bmatrix} 0 & 6 & 3y-2 \\ -6 & -3 & 2c+2 \\ 2b+4 & -21 & 0 \end{bmatrix}$, then find the values of a, b, c and z. [NCERT]

20 Assume Y, W and P are the matrices of orders $3 \times k$, $n \times 3$ and $p \times k$. Find the restrictions on n, k and p, so that $PY + WY$ will be defined. [NCERT]

21 Find the symmetric and skew-symmetric matrices of matrix $A = \begin{bmatrix} 0 & -2 & 4 \\ 2 & 0 & -1 \\ -4 & 1 & 0 \end{bmatrix}$.

22 If A and B are symmetric matrices, then prove that $BA - 2AB$ is neither a symmetric matrix nor skew-symmetric matrix. [NCERT Exemplar]

Short Answer Type Questions

(4 Marks)

23 Prove by mathematical induction that $(A')^n = (A^n)'$, where $n \in N$ for any square matrix A. [NCERT Exemplar]

24 If $A = \begin{bmatrix} 3 & -4 \\ 1 & 1 \\ 2 & 0 \end{bmatrix}$ and $B = \begin{bmatrix} 2 & 1 & 2 \\ 1 & 2 & 4 \end{bmatrix}$, then verify that $(BA)^2 \neq B^2A^2$. [NCERT Exemplar]

25 Solve the matrix $[x \quad -5 \quad -1]\begin{bmatrix} 1 & 0 & 2 \\ 0 & 2 & 1 \\ 2 & 0 & 3 \end{bmatrix}\begin{bmatrix} x \\ 4 \\ 1 \end{bmatrix} = O$. [NCERT]

26 If $A_\alpha = \begin{bmatrix} \cos\alpha & \sin\alpha \\ -\sin\alpha & \cos\alpha \end{bmatrix}$, then prove that $A_\alpha A_\beta = A_{\alpha+\beta}$.

27 Find the matrix A satisfying the matrix equation $\begin{bmatrix} 2 & 1 \\ 3 & 2 \end{bmatrix} A \begin{bmatrix} -3 & 2 \\ 5 & -3 \end{bmatrix} = \begin{bmatrix} 1 & 0 \\ 0 & 1 \end{bmatrix}$. [NCERT Exemplar]

28 If $(A-2I)(A-3I) = O$, where $A = \begin{bmatrix} 4 & 2 \\ -1 & x \end{bmatrix}$ and $I = \begin{bmatrix} 1 & 0 \\ 0 & 1 \end{bmatrix}$, then find the value of x. [ISC 2013]

29 If $A = \begin{bmatrix} 4 & 0 \\ 2k & 5k \end{bmatrix}$ and $B = \begin{bmatrix} k & 0 \\ 3 & -1 \end{bmatrix}$, such that $AB = BA$. Then, show that $2k^2 + 17k - 12 = 0$.

30 A manufacturer sells the products x, y and z in two markets. Annual sales are indicated below

Market	Products		
	x	y	z
I	10000	2000	18000
II	6000	20000	8000

(i) If unit sale prices of x, y and z are ₹ 2.50, ₹ 1.50 and ₹ 1.00 respectively, then find the total revenue in each market with the help of matrix algebra.

(ii) If the unit costs of the above three commodities are ₹ 2.00, ₹ 1.00 and 50 paise, respectively. Find the gross profit.

[**Hint** Profit = Revenue – Cost] [NCERT]

31 If $AB = BA$ for any two square matrices, then prove by mathematical induction that $(AB)^n = A^n B^n$. **[NCERT Exemplar]**

32 If $A = \begin{bmatrix} -1 & 2 & 3 \\ 5 & 7 & 9 \\ -2 & 1 & 1 \end{bmatrix}$ and $B = \begin{bmatrix} -4 & 1 & -5 \\ 1 & 2 & 0 \\ 1 & 3 & 1 \end{bmatrix}$, then verify that

(i) $(A + B)' = A' + B'$

(ii) $(A - B)' = A' - B'$ **[NCERT]**

33 Show that the matrix $B^T AB$ is symmetric or skew-symmetric, according as A is symmetric or skew-symmetric. **[NCERT]**

Long Answer Type Questions

6 Marks

34 If $A = \begin{bmatrix} 1 & 0 & 2 \\ 0 & 2 & 1 \\ 2 & 0 & 3 \end{bmatrix}$, then prove that A is a root of the polynomial $f(x) = x^3 - 6x^2 + 7x + 2$. **[NCERT]**

[**Hint** Prove that $f(A) = O$]

Case-Based Type Questions

6 Marks

35 Two classes, Class 1 and Class 2 are raising fund for charity. They sold burger and maggi during a funfair. The details of their business on the funfair is given below

	Burger	Maggi
Class 1	27	14
Class 2	32	21

They sold each unit of burger at ₹ 90 and each maggi at ₹ 50. It cost them ₹ 70 per unit to buy burger and ₹ 35 to buy one maggi.

Given that $Q = \begin{bmatrix} 27 & 14 \\ 32 & 21 \end{bmatrix}$, $C = \begin{bmatrix} 70 \\ 35 \end{bmatrix}$

and $S = \begin{bmatrix} 90 \\ 50 \end{bmatrix}$.

(i) Find QC.

(ii) Find $S - C$.

(iii) Find $Q(S - C)$.

36 Three brands of cat food are sold at two stores. The following tables show the price of each brand at each store.

The prices are given in cents per 100 g. Data is given for the months May and June.

	Store 1	Store 2
Brand A	9.4	9.6
Brand B	10.2	9.4
Brand C	11.4	11.0

May

	Store 1	Store 2
Brand A	9.8	10.0
Brand B	10.2	10.2
Brand C	12.0	12.0

June

It is given that $X = \begin{bmatrix} 9.4 & 9.6 \\ 10.2 & 9.4 \\ 11.4 & 11.0 \end{bmatrix}$

and $Y = \begin{bmatrix} 9.8 & 10.0 \\ 10.2 & 10.2 \\ 12.0 & 12.0 \end{bmatrix}$

(i) (a) Evaluate $Y - X$.

(b) Explain what the numbers is your answer represent.

(ii) The cat food is sold in tins containing 500 g. Write down the matrix M such that the product XM will shown for each brand, the total cost, in cents, to buying ten tins at both stores during May.

Answers

1. (a) 2. (b) 3. (b) 4. (b) 5. (a) 6. (c)

7. (c) 8. (b) 9. (a) 10. (a) 11. (b) 12. $x = 4$

13. $\begin{bmatrix} 8 & -3 & 5 \\ -2 & -3 & -6 \end{bmatrix}$ 14. $a_{ii}\ b_{ij}$ 15. 0 16. $k = 2$ 18. $\alpha = 0°$

19. $a = -2,\ b = -7,\ c = -1$ and $z = 2$ 20. $k = 3,\ p = n$ 21. $\begin{bmatrix} 0 & 0 & 0 \\ 0 & 0 & 0 \\ 0 & 0 & 0 \end{bmatrix}; \begin{bmatrix} 0 & -2 & 4 \\ 2 & 0 & -1 \\ -4 & 1 & 0 \end{bmatrix}$

25. $x = \pm 4\sqrt{3}$ 27. $\begin{bmatrix} 1 & 1 \\ 1 & 0 \end{bmatrix}$ 28. 1

30. (i) Total revenue in market I is ₹ 46000 and market II is ₹ 53000. (ii) Gross profit = ₹ 32000

35. (i) $QC = \begin{bmatrix} 2380 \\ 2975 \end{bmatrix}$

The cost to buy burger and maggi for Class 1 and Class 2 are ₹ 2380 and ₹ 2975 respectively.

(ii) $S - C = \begin{bmatrix} 20 \\ 15 \end{bmatrix}$

The profit on burger is ₹ 20 and the profit on maggi is ₹ 15 each.

(iii) $Q(S - C) = \begin{bmatrix} 750 \\ 955 \end{bmatrix}$

Class 1 made a total profit of ₹ 750 while Class 2 made a total profit of ₹ 955.

36. (i) (a) $Y - X = \begin{bmatrix} 0.4 & 0.4 \\ 0 & 0.8 \\ 0.6 & 1 \end{bmatrix}$

(b) They represent the difference in price between May and June in each store for the 3 different brands.

(ii) $XM = \begin{bmatrix} 9.4 & 9.6 \\ 10.2 & 9.4 \\ 11.4 & 11.0 \end{bmatrix} \begin{bmatrix} 50 \\ 50 \end{bmatrix};\ M = \begin{bmatrix} 50 \\ 50 \end{bmatrix}$

CHAPTER

04

Determinants

A number that determine whether the system of linear equations, like $a_1x+b_1y=c_1$, $a_2x+b_2y=c_2$ has a unique solution or not, is called determinant.

In the previous chapter, we study about matrices and algebra of matrices. Here, we will study determinants, its properties and various applications.

- Determinant and Its Properties
- Minors, Cofactors and Applications of Determinants in Coordinate Geometry
- Adjoint and Inverse of a Matrix
- Applications of Determinants and Matrices

TOPIC 01 Determinant and Its Properties

Let us consider linear equation in two variables $a_1x+b_1y=c_1$ and $a_2x+b_2y=c_2$, which can be represented in matrix form as $\begin{bmatrix} a_1 & b_1 \\ a_2 & b_2 \end{bmatrix}\begin{bmatrix} x \\ y \end{bmatrix}=\begin{bmatrix} c_1 \\ c_2 \end{bmatrix}$. The pair of liner equations is consistent or inconsistent can be decided by the number $(a_1b_2-a_1b_1)$, which is called the **determinant** of $\begin{bmatrix} a_1 & b_1 \\ a_2 & b_2 \end{bmatrix}$ and represented as $\begin{vmatrix} a_1 & b_1 \\ a_2 & b_2 \end{vmatrix}$.

Definition of Determinant

To every square matrix $A=[a_{ij}]$ of order n, a unique number (real or complex) can be associated, which is called **determinant of the square matrix.**

In other words, we can say that if M is the set of square matrices, K is the set of numbers (real or complex) and $f: M \to K$ is defined by $f(A)=k$, where $A \in M$ and $k \in K$, then $f(A)$ is called the determinant of A. It is denoted by Δ (read as delta) or det (A) or $|A|$.

i.e. if $A=[a_{ij}]_{n\times n}$, then $|A|=\begin{vmatrix} a_{11} & a_{12} & \cdots & a_{1n} \\ a_{21} & a_{22} & \cdots & a_{2n} \\ \vdots & \vdots & \vdots & \vdots \\ a_{n1} & a_{n2} & \cdots & a_{nn} \end{vmatrix}$.

Note
(i) For any matrix A, $|A|$ is read as determinant of A and not read as modulus of A.
(ii) Only square matrix has determinant.
(iii) In determinant we can determine the value but in matrix we cannot determine the value.
(iv) Here, we will study determinants upto order three only with real entries.

Determinants of Matrix of Different Orders and Their Expansions

Determinant of a Matrix of Order 1

Let $A=[a]$ be a square matrix of order 1, then $|A|=|a|=a$, i.e. element itself a determinant. e.g. $|3|=3$

Note A determinant of order 1 should not be confused with the absolute value of a real (or complex) number.

Determinant of a Matrix of Order 2

Let $A=\begin{vmatrix} a_{11} & a_{12} \\ a_{21} & a_{22} \end{vmatrix}$ be a square matrix of order 2×2.

Then, det (A) or $|A|=\begin{vmatrix} a_{11} & a_{12} \\ a_{21} & a_{22} \end{vmatrix}=a_{11}a_{22}-a_{21}a_{12}$,

where $a_{11}, a_{12}, a_{21}, a_{22}$ are called the **elements of the determinant.**

The determinant of order 2 is equal to the product of diagonal elements minus the product of non-diagonal elements. e.g. $\begin{vmatrix} 2 & 3 \\ 0 & -1 \end{vmatrix}=2\times(-1)-0\times 3=-2$

Example 1 Evaluate the following determinant.

(i) $|-12|$ (ii) $\begin{vmatrix} 3 & 5 \\ -2 & 4 \end{vmatrix}$

(iii) $\begin{vmatrix} x-1 & 1 \\ x^3 & x^2+x+1 \end{vmatrix}$ (iv) $\begin{vmatrix} \cos\theta & -\sin\theta \\ \sin\theta & \cos\theta \end{vmatrix}$

Sol. (i) Clearly, $|-12|=-12$ $[\because |-a|=-a]$

(ii) We have, $\begin{vmatrix} 3 & 5 \\ -2 & 4 \end{vmatrix}=3\times 4-(-2)\times 5$

$\left[\because \begin{vmatrix} a_{11} & a_{12} \\ a_{21} & a_{22} \end{vmatrix}=a_{11}a_{22}-a_{21}a_{12}\right]$

$=12+10=22$

(iii) We have, $\begin{vmatrix} x-1 & 1 \\ x^3 & x^2+x+1 \end{vmatrix}=(x-1)(x^2+x+1)-x^3$

$\left[\because \begin{vmatrix} a_{11} & a_{12} \\ a_{21} & a_{22} \end{vmatrix}=a_{11}a_{22}-a_{21}a_{12}\right]$

$=(x^3-1)-x^3$ $[\because (a-b)(a^2+ab+b^2)=a^3-b^3]$

$=-1$

(iv) We have,

$\begin{vmatrix} \cos\theta & -\sin\theta \\ \sin\theta & \cos\theta \end{vmatrix}=\cos\theta\times\cos\theta-(\sin\theta)(-\sin\theta)$

$\left[\because \begin{vmatrix} a_{11} & a_{12} \\ a_{21} & a_{22} \end{vmatrix}=a_{11}a_{22}-a_{21}a_{12}\right]$

$=\cos^2\theta+\sin^2\theta=1$ $[\because \cos^2 x+\sin^2 x=1]$

Example 2 Evaluate x if $\begin{vmatrix} 2 & 4 \\ 5 & 1 \end{vmatrix}=\begin{vmatrix} 2x & 4 \\ 6 & x \end{vmatrix}$.

Sol. Given, $\begin{vmatrix} 2 & 4 \\ 5 & 1 \end{vmatrix}=\begin{vmatrix} 2x & 4 \\ 6 & x \end{vmatrix}$

$\Rightarrow$ $2\times 1-5\times 4=2x\times x-6\times 4$

$\Rightarrow$ $2-20=2x^2-24 \Rightarrow -18=2x^2-24$

$\Rightarrow$ $2x^2=6 \Rightarrow x^2=3$

$\therefore$ $x=\pm\sqrt{3}$ [taking square root]

Determinant of Matrix of Order 3

(Expansion along Row or Column Step-by-Step)

Determinant of a matrix of order three can be determined by expressing it in terms of second order determinants.

This is known as expansion of a determinant along a row or a column. There are six ways of expanding a determinant of order 3, corresponding to each of three rows R_1, R_2, R_3 and three columns C_1, C_2, C_3 giving the same value. Let $A=[a_{ij}]_{3\times 3}$ be a square matrix of order 3, then

$$|A|=\begin{vmatrix} a_{11} & a_{12} & a_{13} \\ a_{21} & a_{22} & a_{23} \\ a_{31} & a_{32} & a_{33} \end{vmatrix}$$

Expansion along First Row (R_1) For expanding the determinant of A along first row,

$$|A|=(-1)^{1+1}a_{11}\begin{vmatrix} a_{22} & a_{23} \\ a_{32} & a_{33} \end{vmatrix}+(-1)^{1+2}a_{12}\begin{vmatrix} a_{21} & a_{23} \\ a_{31} & a_{33} \end{vmatrix}+(-1)^{1+3}a_{13}\begin{vmatrix} a_{21} & a_{22} \\ a_{31} & a_{32} \end{vmatrix}$$

or $|A|=a_{11}(a_{22}a_{33}-a_{32}a_{23})$
$-a_{12}(a_{21}a_{33}-a_{31}a_{23})+a_{13}(a_{21}a_{32}-a_{31}a_{22})$
$=a_{11}a_{22}a_{33}-a_{11}a_{23}a_{32}-a_{12}a_{21}a_{33}$
$+a_{12}a_{23}a_{31}+a_{13}a_{21}a_{32}-a_{13}a_{22}a_{31}$

Example 3 Evaluate the determinant of matrix

$$\begin{bmatrix} 3 & -4 & 5 \\ 1 & 1 & -2 \\ 2 & 3 & 1 \end{bmatrix}.$$

Sol. Let $A = \begin{bmatrix} 3 & -4 & 5 \\ 1 & 1 & -2 \\ 2 & 3 & 1 \end{bmatrix}$, then $|A| = \begin{vmatrix} 3 & -4 & 5 \\ 1 & 1 & -2 \\ 2 & 3 & 1 \end{vmatrix}$

$$= (-1)^{1+1}(3)\begin{vmatrix} 1 & -2 \\ 3 & 1 \end{vmatrix} + (-1)^{1+2}(-4)\begin{vmatrix} 1 & -2 \\ 2 & 1 \end{vmatrix} + (-1)^{1+3}(5)\begin{vmatrix} 1 & 1 \\ 2 & 3 \end{vmatrix}$$

[expanding along R_1]

$$= (-1)^2 3\,[1\times1 - 3\times(-2)] + (-1)^3(-4)[1\times1 - 2\times(-2)] + (-1)^4 5(3-2)$$

$$= 3(1+6) + 4(1+4) + 5(1) = 21 + 20 + 5 = 46$$

Expansion along First Column (C_1) On expanding the determinant of A along first column (C_1), we get

$$|A| = (-1)^{1+1} a_{11}\begin{vmatrix} a_{22} & a_{23} \\ a_{32} & a_{33} \end{vmatrix} + (-1)^{2+1} a_{21}\begin{vmatrix} a_{12} & a_{13} \\ a_{32} & a_{33} \end{vmatrix} + (-1)^{3+1} a_{31}\begin{vmatrix} a_{12} & a_{13} \\ a_{22} & a_{23} \end{vmatrix}$$

$$= a_{11}(a_{22}a_{33} - a_{23}a_{32}) - a_{21}(a_{12}a_{33} - a_{13}a_{32}) + a_{31}(a_{12}a_{23} - a_{13}a_{22}) \quad \ldots(i)$$

or $|A| = a_{11}a_{22}a_{33} - a_{11}a_{23}a_{32} - a_{21}a_{12}a_{33} + a_{21}a_{13}a_{32} + a_{31}a_{12}a_{23} - a_{31}a_{13}a_{22}$

or $|A| = a_{11}a_{22}a_{33} - a_{11}a_{23}a_{32} - a_{12}a_{21}a_{33} + a_{12}a_{23}a_{31} + a_{13}a_{21}a_{32} - a_{13}a_{22}a_{31} \quad \ldots(ii)$

Clearly, the values of $|A|$ from Eqs. (i) and (ii) are equal. Hence, expanding a determinant along any row or column gives same value.

Similarly, we can expand along R_2, R_3, C_2 and C_3 step-by-step.

Note

(i) For easier calculations, we shall expand the determinant along that row or column which contains maximum number of zeroes.

(ii) While expanding, instead of multiplying by $(-1)^{i+j}$, we can multiply by +1 or –1 according to $(i + j)$ is even or odd.

Or While expanding the determinant, we can attach the following '+' and '–' signs.

$$\begin{vmatrix} + & - & + \\ - & + & - \\ + & - & + \end{vmatrix}$$

Example 4 Evaluate the determinant

$$\Delta = \begin{vmatrix} 0 & \sin\alpha & -\cos\alpha \\ -\sin\alpha & 0 & \sin\beta \\ \cos\alpha & -\sin\beta & 0 \end{vmatrix}.$$

Sol. Given, $\Delta = \begin{vmatrix} 0 & \sin\alpha & -\cos\alpha \\ -\sin\alpha & 0 & \sin\beta \\ \cos\alpha & -\sin\beta & 0 \end{vmatrix}$

$$= 0\cdot[0 - (-\sin\beta)(\sin\beta)] - (-\sin\alpha)(\sin\alpha\cdot 0 - \cos\alpha\sin\beta) + \cos\alpha(\sin\alpha\sin\beta - 0)$$ [expanding along C_1]

$$= 0 + \sin\alpha(-\cos\alpha\sin\beta) + \cos\alpha\sin\alpha\sin\beta$$

$$= -\sin\alpha\cos\alpha\sin\beta + \sin\alpha\cos\alpha\sin\beta = 0$$

Properties of Determinants

Given below are the properties of the determinant which simplifies its evaluation by obtaining maximum number of zeroes in a row or column.

These properties are true for determinants of any order. But, here we will study the properties of determinants upto order 3.

Property 1. If all the elements of any row or column of a determinant are zero, then the value of such determinant becomes zero.

e.g. $\begin{vmatrix} 0 & 3 & 2 \\ 0 & 4 & 5 \\ 0 & 6 & 7 \end{vmatrix} = 0$

Property 2. If rows and columns of a determinant are interchanged, then the value of determinant remains unchanged.

For interchanging of rows and columns, we will symbolically write $C_i \leftrightarrow R_i$, where R_i = ith row and C_i = ith column.

e.g. $\begin{vmatrix} 1 & 2 & 3 \\ 3 & 2 & 1 \\ 2 & 3 & 1 \end{vmatrix} = \begin{vmatrix} 1 & 3 & 2 \\ 2 & 2 & 3 \\ 3 & 1 & 1 \end{vmatrix}$

It is clear from this property that if A is a square matrix, then $\det(A) = \det(A')$, where A' = transpose of A.

Property 3. If any two rows or columns of a determinant are interchanged, then the value of such determinant becomes negative of itself.

We denote the interchange of rows by $R_i \leftrightarrow R_j$ and interchange of columns by $C_i \leftrightarrow C_j$.

e.g. $\begin{vmatrix} a & b & c \\ d & e & f \\ g & h & i \end{vmatrix} = -\begin{vmatrix} d & e & f \\ a & b & c \\ g & h & i \end{vmatrix}$ [here, $R_1 \leftrightarrow R_2$]

Note If any row (or column) of a determinant (Δ) be passed (jumped) over n rows (or columns), then the resulting determinant $\Delta_1 = (-1)^n \Delta$.

e.g. $\begin{vmatrix} a & b & c \\ d & e & f \\ g & h & i \end{vmatrix} = (-1)^2 \begin{vmatrix} d & e & f \\ g & h & i \\ a & b & c \end{vmatrix}$

Property 4. If all the elements of any two rows or columns of a determinant are identical or proportional, then the value of such determinant becomes zero.

e.g. $\begin{vmatrix} 1 & 2 & 3 \\ 1 & 2 & 3 \\ 4 & 5 & 6 \end{vmatrix} = 0$, because rows R_1 and R_2 are identical.

Property 5. If every element of any row or column of a determinant is multiplied by a constant k, then the value of new determinant is k times the value of original determinant.

e.g. $\begin{vmatrix} ka_{11} & ka_{12} & ka_{13} \\ a_{21} & a_{22} & a_{23} \\ a_{31} & a_{32} & a_{33} \end{vmatrix} = k \begin{vmatrix} a_{11} & a_{12} & a_{13} \\ a_{21} & a_{22} & a_{23} \\ a_{31} & a_{32} & a_{33} \end{vmatrix}$

Note

(i) By this property, we can take out any common factor from any one row or column of a given determinant.

(ii) If B is a square matrix of order n, then

$|kB| = k^n |B|$, where $n = 1, 2, 3, \ldots$

(iii) If two parallel lines (rows or columns) of a determinant are such that the elements of a line are equi-multiples of the elements of other line, then the value of determinant is zero.

Property 6. If some or all elements of any row or column of a determinant are expressed as a sum of two or more terms, then such determinant can be expressed as sum of two or more determinants of the same order.

e.g. $\begin{vmatrix} a & b & c \\ d+e & f+g & h+i \\ j & k & l \end{vmatrix} = \begin{vmatrix} a & b & c \\ d & f & h \\ j & k & l \end{vmatrix} + \begin{vmatrix} a & b & c \\ e & g & i \\ j & k & l \end{vmatrix}$

Property 7. If all the elements of any two rows or columns of a determinant are proportional, then the value of such determinant becomes zero.

e.g. $\begin{vmatrix} a_{11} & a_{12} & a_{13} \\ ka_{11} & ka_{12} & ka_{13} \\ a_{31} & a_{32} & a_{33} \end{vmatrix} = k \begin{vmatrix} a_{11} & a_{12} & a_{13} \\ a_{11} & a_{12} & a_{13} \\ a_{31} & a_{32} & a_{33} \end{vmatrix} = 0$

[here R_1 and R_2 are equal]

Property 8. The value of any determinant of upper/lower triangular matrix is the product of its diagonal elements.

e.g. $\begin{vmatrix} a_{11} & 0 & 0 \\ a_{21} & a_{22} & 0 \\ a_{31} & a_{32} & a_{33} \end{vmatrix} = a_{11}\, a_{12}\, a_{13}$

Property 9. Product of two determinants

Let two determinants be

$$\Delta_1 = \begin{vmatrix} a_1 & b_1 & c_1 \\ a_2 & b_2 & c_2 \\ a_3 & b_3 & c_3 \end{vmatrix} \text{ and } \Delta_2 = \begin{vmatrix} \alpha_1 & \beta_1 & \gamma_1 \\ \alpha_2 & \beta_2 & \gamma_2 \\ \alpha_3 & \beta_3 & \gamma_3 \end{vmatrix}, \text{ then}$$

$$\Delta_1 \times \Delta_2 = \begin{vmatrix} a_1 & b_1 & c_1 \\ a_2 & b_2 & c_2 \\ a_3 & b_3 & c_3 \end{vmatrix} \times \begin{vmatrix} \alpha_1 & \beta_1 & \gamma_1 \\ \alpha_2 & \beta_2 & \gamma_2 \\ \alpha_3 & \beta_3 & \gamma_3 \end{vmatrix}$$

$$= \begin{vmatrix} a_1\alpha_1 + b_1\beta_1 + c_1\gamma_1 & a_1\alpha_2 + b_1\beta_2 + c_1\gamma_2 & a_1\alpha_3 + b_1\beta_3 + c_1\gamma_3 \\ a_2\alpha_1 + b_2\beta_1 + c_2\gamma_1 & a_2\alpha_2 + b_2\beta_2 + c_2\gamma_2 & a_2\alpha_3 + b_2\beta_3 + c_2\gamma_3 \\ a_3\alpha_1 + b_3\beta_1 + c_3\gamma_1 & a_3\alpha_2 + b_3\beta_2 + c_3\gamma_2 & a_3\alpha_3 + b_3\beta_3 + c_3\gamma_3 \end{vmatrix}$$

Example 5 Without expanding, show that

(i) $\begin{vmatrix} 102 & 1 & 17 \\ 18 & 3 & 3 \\ 36 & 4 & 6 \end{vmatrix} = 0$ (ii) $\begin{vmatrix} x & a & x+a \\ y & b & y+b \\ z & c & z+c \end{vmatrix} = 0$

Sol. (i) Let $\Delta = \begin{vmatrix} 102 & 1 & 17 \\ 18 & 3 & 3 \\ 36 & 4 & 6 \end{vmatrix}$

$= \begin{vmatrix} 6(17) & 1 & 17 \\ 6(3) & 3 & 3 \\ 6(6) & 4 & 6 \end{vmatrix} = 6 \begin{vmatrix} 17 & 1 & 17 \\ 3 & 3 & 3 \\ 6 & 4 & 6 \end{vmatrix}$

[taking 6 common from C_1]

$= 6 \times 0$ [$\because C_1$ and C_3 are identical]

$= 0$

(ii) Let $\Delta = \begin{vmatrix} x & a & x+a \\ y & b & y+b \\ z & c & z+c \end{vmatrix} = \begin{vmatrix} x & a & x \\ y & b & y \\ z & c & z \end{vmatrix} + \begin{vmatrix} x & a & a \\ y & b & b \\ z & c & c \end{vmatrix}$

[using property 6]

$= 0 + 0$ [$\because$ in first determinant, C_1 and C_3 are identical and in second determinant, C_2 and C_3 are identical]

$= 0$

Topic Practice 1

Very Short Answer Type Questions

2 Marks

1 Evaluate the following determinant.

(i) $\begin{vmatrix} 2 & 4 \\ -5 & -1 \end{vmatrix}$ (ii) $\begin{vmatrix} 1 & 2 \\ 4 & 2 \end{vmatrix}$

2 Without expanding the determinants, show that

(i) $\begin{vmatrix} 42 & 1 & 6 \\ 28 & 7 & 4 \\ 14 & 3 & 2 \end{vmatrix} = 0$ (ii) $\begin{vmatrix} 5 & 15 & -25 \\ 7 & 21 & 30 \\ 8 & 24 & 42 \end{vmatrix} = 0.$

3 Evaluate

(i) $\begin{vmatrix} \sec\theta & -\tan\theta \\ -\tan\theta & \sec\theta \end{vmatrix}$. [NCERT]

(ii) $\begin{vmatrix} \cos 15^\circ & \sin 15^\circ \\ \sin 75^\circ & \cos 75^\circ \end{vmatrix}$.

4 (i) If $\begin{vmatrix} 2x & x+3 \\ 2(x+1) & x+1 \end{vmatrix} = \begin{vmatrix} 1 & 5 \\ 3 & 3 \end{vmatrix}$, then find the value of x.

(ii) If $A = \begin{bmatrix} 1 & 2 \\ 3 & -1 \end{bmatrix}$ and $B = \begin{bmatrix} 1 & 3 \\ -1 & 1 \end{bmatrix}$, then write the value of $|AB|$.

5 (i) If A is a 3×3 matrix, $|A| \neq 0$ and $|3A| = k|A|$, then find the value of k.

(ii) Let A be a square matrix of order 3×3, then write the value of $|2A|$, where $|A| = 4$.

6 If there are two values of a which makes determinant, $\Delta = \begin{vmatrix} 1 & -2 & 5 \\ 2 & a & -1 \\ 0 & 4 & 2a \end{vmatrix} = 86$, then find the sum of these numbers. **[NCERT Exemplar]**

7 Show that $\begin{vmatrix} a & b & c \\ a+2x & b+2y & c+2z \\ x & y & z \end{vmatrix} = 0.$

Short Answer Type Questions

4 Marks

8 If $\cos 2\theta = 0$, then simplify $\begin{vmatrix} 0 & \cos\theta & \sin\theta \\ \cos\theta & \sin\theta & 0 \\ \sin\theta & 0 & \cos\theta \end{vmatrix}^2$. **[NCERT Exemplar]**

9 If x, y and z are different and

$$\Delta = \begin{vmatrix} x & x^2 & 1+x^3 \\ y & y^2 & 1+y^3 \\ z & z^2 & 1+z^3 \end{vmatrix} = 0, \text{ then show that } 1 + xyz = 0.$$ **[NCERT]**

Hints & Solutions

1. Similar as Example 1.
Ans. (i) 18 (ii) -6

2. **Hint** By using the properties of determinants.

3. (i) We have, $\begin{vmatrix} \sec\theta & -\tan\theta \\ -\tan\theta & \sec\theta \end{vmatrix}$

$= \sec\theta \times \sec\theta - (-\tan\theta) \times (-\tan\theta)$ [1/2]

$= \sec^2\theta - \tan^2\theta = 1$ $\quad [\because \sec^2\theta - \tan^2\theta = 1]$ [1/2]

(ii) We have, $\begin{vmatrix} \cos 15^\circ & \sin 15^\circ \\ \sin 75^\circ & \cos 75^\circ \end{vmatrix}$

$= \cos 15^\circ \cos 75^\circ - \sin 15^\circ \sin 75^\circ$ [1/2]

$= \cos(15^\circ + 75^\circ)$

$[\because \cos A \cos B - \sin A \sin B = \cos(A+B)]$

$= \cos 90^\circ = 0$ [1/2]

4. (i) We have, $\begin{vmatrix} 2x & x+3 \\ 2(x+1) & x+1 \end{vmatrix} = \begin{vmatrix} 1 & 5 \\ 3 & 3 \end{vmatrix}$

$\Rightarrow 2x(x+1) - 2(x+1)(x+3) = 3 - 15$

$\Rightarrow 2x^2 + 2x - 2(x^2 + 3x + x + 3) = -12$ [1/2]

$\Rightarrow 2x^2 + 2x - 2x^2 - 6x - 2x - 6 = -12$

$\Rightarrow -6x - 6 = -12$

$\Rightarrow -6x = -12 + 6 = -6 \Rightarrow x = 1$ [1/2]

(ii) We have, $A = \begin{bmatrix} 1 & 2 \\ 3 & -1 \end{bmatrix}$ and $B = \begin{bmatrix} 1 & 3 \\ -1 & 1 \end{bmatrix}$

Now, $AB = \begin{bmatrix} 1 & 2 \\ 3 & -1 \end{bmatrix}\begin{bmatrix} 1 & 3 \\ -1 & 1 \end{bmatrix} = \begin{bmatrix} 1-2 & 3+2 \\ 3+1 & 9-1 \end{bmatrix}$

$= \begin{bmatrix} -1 & 5 \\ 4 & 8 \end{bmatrix}$ [1/2]

$\Rightarrow |AB| = \begin{vmatrix} -1 & 5 \\ 4 & 8 \end{vmatrix} = -8 - 20 = -28$ [1/2]

Alternate method

$|AB| = |A||B| = \begin{vmatrix} 1 & 2 \\ 3 & -1 \end{vmatrix}\begin{vmatrix} 1 & 3 \\ -1 & 1 \end{vmatrix}$ [1]

$= (-1-6)(1+3)$

$= -7 \times 4 = -28$ [1]

5. (i) Consider, $|3A| = 3^3|A|$

[if A is a square matrix of order n, then $|kA| = k^n|A|$] [1/2]

$\therefore \quad k = 3^3 = 27$ [1/2]

(ii) Similar as part (i). [**Ans.** 32]

6. We have, $\Delta = \begin{vmatrix} 1 & -2 & 5 \\ 2 & a & -1 \\ 0 & 4 & 2a \end{vmatrix} = 86$

$\Rightarrow 1(2a^2 + 4) - 2(-4a - 20) + 0 = 86$

[expanding along first column]

$\Rightarrow 2a^2 + 4 + 8a + 40 = 86$ [1]

$\Rightarrow 2a^2 + 8a + 44 - 86 = 0$

$\Rightarrow a^2 + 4a - 21 = 0$

$\Rightarrow a^2 + 7a - 3a - 21 = 0$

$\Rightarrow (a+7)(a-3) = 0$

$\Rightarrow a = -7$ and 3

$\therefore$ Required sum $= -7 + 3 = -4$ [1]

7. Let $\Delta = \begin{vmatrix} a & b & c \\ a+2x & b+2y & c+2z \\ x & y & z \end{vmatrix}$

$= \begin{vmatrix} a & b & c \\ a & b & c \\ x & y & z \end{vmatrix} + \begin{vmatrix} a & b & c \\ 2x & 2y & 2z \\ x & y & z \end{vmatrix}$

$$= 0 + 2\begin{vmatrix} a & b & c \\ x & y & z \\ x & y & z \end{vmatrix}$$ [1]

[$\because$ in first determinant, R_1 and R_2 are identical and taking common 2 from R_2 of second determinant]

$= 0 + 2 \times 0$ [$\because$ R_2 and R_3 are identical]

$= 0$ [1]

8. Since, $\cos 2\theta = 0$

$\Rightarrow \quad \cos 2\theta = \cos \frac{\pi}{2} \Rightarrow 2\theta = \frac{\pi}{2} \Rightarrow \theta = \frac{\pi}{4}$ [1]

$\therefore \quad \sin \frac{\pi}{4} = \frac{1}{\sqrt{2}}$ and $\cos \frac{\pi}{4} = \frac{1}{\sqrt{2}}$ [1]

$$\therefore \Delta = \begin{vmatrix} 0 & \cos\theta & \sin\theta \\ \cos\theta & \sin\theta & 0 \\ \sin\theta & 0 & \cos\theta \end{vmatrix}^2 = \begin{vmatrix} 0 & \frac{1}{\sqrt{2}} & \frac{1}{\sqrt{2}} \\ \frac{1}{\sqrt{2}} & \frac{1}{\sqrt{2}} & 0 \\ \frac{1}{\sqrt{2}} & 0 & \frac{1}{\sqrt{2}} \end{vmatrix}^2$$ [1]

Expanding along R_1, we get

$$\Delta = \left[0 - \frac{1}{\sqrt{2}}\left(\frac{1}{2}\right) + \frac{1}{\sqrt{2}}\left(-\frac{1}{2}\right)\right]^2$$

$$= \left[\frac{-2}{2\sqrt{2}}\right]^2 = \left(\frac{-1}{\sqrt{2}}\right)^2 = \frac{1}{2}$$ [1]

9. **Hint** $\Delta = \begin{vmatrix} x & x^2 & 1 \\ y & y^2 & 1 \\ z & z^2 & 1 \end{vmatrix} + \begin{vmatrix} x & x^2 & x^3 \\ y & y^2 & y^3 \\ z & z^2 & z^3 \end{vmatrix}$

$$= \begin{vmatrix} x & x^2 & 1 \\ y & y^2 & 1 \\ z & z^2 & 1 \end{vmatrix} + xyz\begin{vmatrix} 1 & x & x^2 \\ 1 & y & y^2 \\ 1 & z & z^2 \end{vmatrix}$$

$$= \begin{vmatrix} 1 & x & x^2 \\ 1 & y & y^2 \\ 1 & z & z^2 \end{vmatrix}(1 + xyz)$$

$$= (x - y)(y - z)(z - x)(1 + xyz)$$

Now, $\Delta = 0$

$\Rightarrow \quad 1 + xyz = 0$ [$\because$ x, y and z are different]

TOPIC 02 Minors, Cofactors and Applications of Determinants in Coordinate Geometry

Here, we will study how to write the expansion of a determinant in compact form using minors and cofactors.

Minor

Let determinant, $\Delta = \begin{vmatrix} a_{11} & a_{12} & a_{13} \\ a_{21} & a_{22} & a_{23} \\ a_{31} & a_{32} & a_{33} \end{vmatrix}$. If we delete ith row and jth column passing through the element a_{ij}, then the second order determinant is obtained and it is called the **minor** of the element a_{ij}.

In other words, minor of an element a_{ij} of a determinant is the determinant obtained by deleting ith row and jth column. It is denoted by M_{ij}.

e.g. Let $\Delta = \begin{vmatrix} 2 & 0 & 3 \\ 1 & -3 & 4 \\ 7 & 6 & 5 \end{vmatrix}$. Then, minor of a_{11}, i.e. minor of 2, is the determinant obtained by deleting first row and first column,

i.e. $M_{11} = \begin{vmatrix} -3 & 4 \\ 6 & 5 \end{vmatrix} = -15 - 24 = -39$

Note Minor of an element a_{ij} of a determinant of order n ($n \geq 2$) has order ($n - 1$).

Expansion of Determinant in Terms of Minor

The determinant, $\Delta = \begin{vmatrix} a_{11} & a_{12} & a_{13} \\ a_{21} & a_{22} & a_{23} \\ a_{31} & a_{32} & a_{33} \end{vmatrix}$ can be written in terms of minor as along first row

$$\Delta = (-1)^{1+1} a_{11}M_{11} + (-1)^{1+2} a_{12}M_{12} + (-1)^{1+3} a_{13}M_{13}$$

$$= a_{11}M_{11} - a_{12}M_{12} + a_{13}M_{13}$$

Similarly, as along first column.

$$\Delta = a_{11}M_{11} - a_{21}M_{21} + a_{31}M_{31}$$

Cofactor

If M_{ij} is the minor of an element a_{ij}, then the **cofactor** of a_{ij} is denoted by C_{ij} or A_{ij} and defined as

$$C_{ij} \text{ or } A_{ij} = (-1)^{i+j} M_{ij}.$$

e.g. Let $\Delta = \begin{vmatrix} 2 & 0 & 3 \\ 1 & -3 & 4 \\ 7 & 6 & 5 \end{vmatrix}$.

Then, cofactor of a_{11},

i.e. cofactor of 2 $=(-1)^{1+1}$ minor of a_{11}

i.e. $C_{11}=(-1)^{1+1}(-39)=-39$

Note if $i+j$ is even, then $C_{ij}=M_{ij}$ and if $i+j$ is odd, then $C_{ij}=-M_{ij}$.

Expansion of Determinant in Terms of Cofactors

The determinant, $\Delta=\begin{vmatrix} a_{11} & a_{12} & a_{13} \\ a_{21} & a_{22} & a_{23} \\ a_{31} & a_{32} & a_{33} \end{vmatrix}$ can be written in terms of cofactors as $a_{11}C_{11}+a_{12}C_{12}+a_{13}C_{13}$

or $a_{21}C_{21}+a_{22}C_{22}+a_{23}C_{23}$

or $a_{31}C_{31}+a_{32}C_{32}+a_{33}C_{33}$.

i.e. Δ = **Sum of product of elements of a row with their corresponding cofactors.**

We can also write $\Delta=a_{11}C_{11}+a_{21}C_{21}+a_{31}C_{31}$

or $a_{12}C_{12}+a_{22}C_{22}+a_{32}C_{32}$ etc.

i.e. Δ = Sum of product of elements of a column with their corresponding cofactors.

If elements of a row or column are multiplied with cofactors of any other row or column, then their sum is zero.

e.g. $a_{11}C_{21}+a_{12}C_{22}+a_{13}C_{23}$

$$=a_{11}(-1)^{2+1}\begin{vmatrix} a_{12} & a_{13} \\ a_{32} & a_{33} \end{vmatrix}+a_{12}(-1)^{2+2}\begin{vmatrix} a_{11} & a_{13} \\ a_{31} & a_{33} \end{vmatrix}+a_{13}(-1)^{2+3}\begin{vmatrix} a_{11} & a_{12} \\ a_{31} & a_{32} \end{vmatrix}$$

$$=-a_{11}(a_{12}a_{33}-a_{13}a_{32})+a_{12}(a_{11}a_{33}-a_{31}a_{13})-a_{13}(a_{11}a_{32}-a_{31}a_{12})$$

$$=-a_{11}a_{12}a_{33}+a_{11}a_{13}a_{32}+a_{12}a_{11}a_{33}-a_{12}a_{31}a_{13}-a_{13}a_{11}a_{32}+a_{13}a_{31}a_{12}=0$$

Example 1 If $\Delta=\begin{vmatrix} 5 & 6 & -3 \\ -4 & 3 & 2 \\ -4 & -7 & 3 \end{vmatrix}$, then write the cofactor of the element a_{21}.

Sol. Given, $\Delta=\begin{vmatrix} 5 & 6 & -3 \\ -4 & 3 & 2 \\ -4 & -7 & 3 \end{vmatrix}$

Now, cofactors of $a_{21}=(-1)^{2+1}\begin{vmatrix} 6 & -3 \\ -7 & 3 \end{vmatrix}=-(18-21)=3$

Example 2 Find minors and cofactors of all the elements of the determinant $\begin{vmatrix} 2 & -1 \\ 3 & 5 \end{vmatrix}$.

Sol. Minors of elements of determinant $\begin{vmatrix} 2 & -1 \\ 3 & 5 \end{vmatrix}$ are

$M_{11}=5$ [minor of an element a_{11}, i.e. 2]

$M_{12}=3$ [minor of an element a_{12}, i.e. −1]

$M_{21}=-1$ [minor of an element a_{21}, i.e. 3]

and $M_{22}=2$ [minor of an element a_{22}, i.e. 5]

Cofactors of elements of determinant $\begin{vmatrix} 2 & -1 \\ 3 & 5 \end{vmatrix}$ are

$C_{11}=(-1)^{1+1}M_{11}=(-1)^2\times 5=5$ [cofactor of element a_{11}, i.e. 2]

$C_{12}=(-1)^{1+2}M_{12}=(-1)^3\times 3=-3$ [cofactor of element a_{12}, i.e. −1]

$C_{21}=(-1)^{2+1}M_{21}=(-1)^3\times(-1)=1$ [cofactor of element a_{21}, i.e. 3]

$C_{22}=(-1)^{2+2}M_{22}=(-1)^4\times 2=2$ [cofactor of element a_{22}, i.e. 5]

Example 3 Find the minors and cofactors of the elements of first row of determinant $\begin{vmatrix} 1 & 2 & 0 \\ 3 & 5 & -1 \\ 4 & 7 & 8 \end{vmatrix}$.

Sol. The minors and cofactors of the elements of first row of the determinant $\begin{vmatrix} 1 & 2 & 0 \\ 3 & 5. & -1 \\ 4 & 7 & 8 \end{vmatrix}$ are given below

$M_{11}=\begin{vmatrix} 5 & -1 \\ 7 & 8 \end{vmatrix}=40+7=47$ [minor of an element a_{11}, i.e. 1]

$M_{12}=\begin{vmatrix} 3 & -1 \\ 4 & 8 \end{vmatrix}=24+4=28$ [minor of an element a_{12}, i.e. 2]

$M_{13}=\begin{vmatrix} 3 & 5 \\ 4 & 7 \end{vmatrix}=21-20=1$ [minor of an element a_{13}, i.e. 0]

$C_{11}=(-1)^{1+1}M_{11}=(-1)^2\times 47=47$ [cofactor of an element a_{11}, i.e. 1]

$C_{12}=(-1)^{1+2}M_{12}=(-1)^3\times 28=-28$ [cofactor of an element a_{12}, i.e. 2]

$C_{13}=(-1)^{1+3}M_{13}=(-1)^4\times 1=1$ [cofactor of an element a_{13}, i.e. 0]

Applications of Determinants in Coordinate Geometry

We can use determinants in geometry also. Here, we will use determinant to find the area of triangle and to find equation of line.

Area of a Triangle

Let the vertices of a ΔABC be $A(x_1, y_1)$, $B(x_2, y_2)$ and $C(x_3, y_3)$. Then, in the form of determinant,

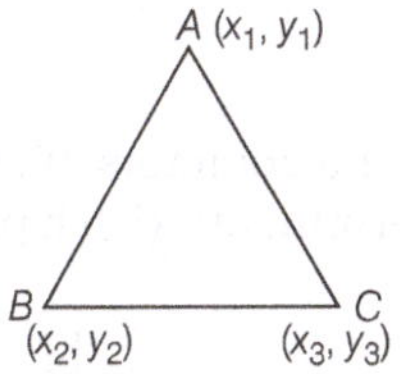

$$\text{Area of } \Delta ABC = \frac{1}{2}\begin{vmatrix} x_1 & y_1 & 1 \\ x_2 & y_2 & 1 \\ x_3 & y_3 & 1 \end{vmatrix}$$

$$= \frac{1}{2}[x_1(y_2 - y_3) + x_2(y_3 - y_1) + x_3(y_1 - y_2)]$$

Note

(i) Area is a positive quantity, so we take the absolute value of determinant.

(ii) If area is given, then take both negative and positive values of determinant for calculation.

Example 4 Find the area of the triangle, whose vertices are (3, 8), (– 4, 2) and (5, 1).

Sol. Given vertices of a triangle are (3, 8), (– 4, 2) and (5, 1).

Let $(x_1, y_1) = (3, 8)$, $(x_2, y_2) = (-4, 2)$ and $(x_3, y_3) = (5, 1)$

$$\text{Then, the area of triangle} = \frac{1}{2}\begin{vmatrix} x_1 & y_1 & 1 \\ x_2 & y_2 & 1 \\ x_3 & y_3 & 1 \end{vmatrix}$$

$$= \frac{1}{2}\begin{vmatrix} 3 & 8 & 1 \\ -4 & 2 & 1 \\ 5 & 1 & 1 \end{vmatrix}$$

$$= \frac{1}{2}\left[3\begin{vmatrix} 2 & 1 \\ 1 & 1 \end{vmatrix} - 8\begin{vmatrix} -4 & 1 \\ 5 & 1 \end{vmatrix} + 1\begin{vmatrix} -4 & 2 \\ 5 & 1 \end{vmatrix}\right]$$

$$= \frac{1}{2}[3(2-1) - 8(-4-5) + 1(-4-10)]$$

$$= \frac{1}{2}[3 + 72 - 14]$$

$$= \frac{61}{2} \text{ sq units}$$

Example 5 If the area of a triangle with vertices (–3, 0), (3, 0) and (0, k) is 9 sq units, then find the value of k.

Sol. Given area of a triangle with vertices (–3, 0), (3, 0) and (0, k) is 9 sq units.

$$\text{We have, } \frac{1}{2}\begin{vmatrix} -3 & 0 & 1 \\ 3 & 0 & 1 \\ 0 & k & 1 \end{vmatrix} = \pm 9$$

$$\Rightarrow \begin{vmatrix} -3 & 0 & 1 \\ 3 & 0 & 1 \\ 0 & k & 1 \end{vmatrix} = \pm 18$$

$$\Rightarrow -3(0-k) - 0 + 1(3k - 0) = \pm 18$$

$$\Rightarrow 3k + 3k = \pm 18$$

$$\Rightarrow 6k = \pm 18$$

$$\Rightarrow k = \pm 3$$

Condition of Collinearity for Three Points

Three points $A(x_1, y_1)$, $B(x_2, y_2)$ and $C(x_3, y_3)$ are collinear if and only if the area of triangle formed by these three points is zero,

$$\text{i.e.} \quad \begin{vmatrix} x_1 & y_1 & 1 \\ x_2 & y_2 & 1 \\ x_3 & y_3 & 1 \end{vmatrix} = 0.$$

Example 6 If the points (2, – 3), (λ, – 1) and (0, 4) are collinear, then find the value of λ.

Sol. Given points (2, – 3), (λ, – 1) and (0, 4) are collinear.

So, area of triangle formed by these three points will be zero.

$$\therefore \begin{vmatrix} 2 & -3 & 1 \\ \lambda & -1 & 1 \\ 0 & 4 & 1 \end{vmatrix} = 0$$

Now, on expanding along R_1, we get

$$2(-1-4) + 3(\lambda - 0) + 1(4\lambda - 0) = 0$$

$$-10 + 3\lambda + 4\lambda = 0$$

$$7\lambda = 10$$

$$\lambda = \frac{10}{7}$$

Equation of Line through Two Points

Let $A(x_1, y_1)$ and $B(x_2, y_2)$ be two given points, then the line joining A and B is given by considering any point $P(x, y)$ on the line, so that the points P, A and B are collinear.

Thus, we have

$$\frac{1}{2}\begin{vmatrix} x & y & 1 \\ x_1 & y_1 & 1 \\ x_2 & y_2 & 1 \end{vmatrix} = 0 \text{ or } \begin{vmatrix} x & y & 1 \\ x_1 & y_1 & 1 \\ x_2 & y_2 & 1 \end{vmatrix} = 0$$

which gives the required equation of line.

Example 7 Find the equation of line joining (2, 3) and (–1, 2) using determinants.

Sol. Equation of line is given by $\begin{vmatrix} x & y & 1 \\ x_1 & y_1 & 1 \\ x_2 & y_2 & 1 \end{vmatrix} = 0$

Consider, $(x_1, y_1) = (2, 3)$ and $(x_2, y_2) = (-1, 2)$

$$\therefore \begin{vmatrix} x & y & 1 \\ 2 & 3 & 1 \\ -1 & 2 & 1 \end{vmatrix} = 0$$

$$\Rightarrow x(3-2) - y(2+1) + 1(4+3) = 0 \text{ [expanding along } R_1]$$

$$\Rightarrow x - 3y + 7 = 0$$

Example 8 Find the equation of line joining $P(11, 7)$ and $Q(5, 5)$ using determinants. Also, find the value of k, if $R(-1, k)$ is the point such that area of ΔPQR is 9 sq m.

Sol. The equation of line joining points $P(11, 7)$ and $Q(5, 5)$ in given by

$$\begin{vmatrix} 11 & 7 & 1 \\ 5 & 5 & 1 \\ x & y & 1 \end{vmatrix} = 0$$

On expanding along R_1, we get

$$11(5-y) - 7(5-x) + 1(5y - 5x) = 0$$

$$\Rightarrow 55 - 11y - 35 + 7x + 5y - 5x = 0$$

$$\Rightarrow 2x - 6y + 20 = 0$$

$$\Rightarrow x - 3y + 10 = 0 \quad \text{[dividing by 2]}$$

which is the required equation of line joining points P and Q.

According to the question,

Area of $\Delta PQR = 9$ sq m

$$\therefore \frac{1}{2}\begin{vmatrix} 11 & 7 & 1 \\ 5 & 5 & 1 \\ -1 & k & 1 \end{vmatrix} = \pm 9$$

$$\left[\because \text{ area of a triangle with vertices } (x_1, y_1), (x_2, y_2) \text{ and } (x_3, y_3) = \frac{1}{2}\begin{vmatrix} x_1 & y_1 & 1 \\ x_2 & y_2 & 1 \\ x_3 & y_3 & 1 \end{vmatrix}\right]$$

On expanding along R_1, we get

$$\frac{1}{2}[11(5-k) - 7(5+1) + 1(5k+5)] = \pm 9$$

$$\frac{1}{2}[55 - 11k - 42 + 5k + 5] = \pm 9$$

$$\frac{1}{2}[18 - 6k] = \pm 9$$

$$\Rightarrow (-6k + 18) = \pm 18 \Rightarrow -6k = -18 \pm 18$$

For positive sign, $k = \dfrac{-18+18}{-6} = 0$

and for negative sign, $k = \dfrac{-18-18}{-6} = 6$

Hence, the required values of k are 0 and 6.

Topic Practice 2

Very Short Answer Type Questions

2 Marks

1 Write minors and cofactors of elements of following determinants. (Each part carries 2 Marks)

(i) $\begin{vmatrix} 2 & -4 \\ 0 & 3 \end{vmatrix}$ (ii) $\begin{vmatrix} a & c \\ b & d \end{vmatrix}$ [NCERT]

2 Find the minors of the diagonal elements of the determinant $\begin{vmatrix} 1 & i & -i \\ -i & 1 & i \\ 1 & -i & i \end{vmatrix}$.

3 Using cofactors of elements of third row, evaluate $\Delta = \begin{vmatrix} 1 & x & y+z \\ 1 & y & z+x \\ 1 & z & x+y \end{vmatrix}$.

4 Using cofactors of elements of third column, evaluate $\Delta = \begin{vmatrix} 1 & x & yz \\ 1 & y & zx \\ 1 & z & xy \end{vmatrix}$ [NCERT]

5 If the points (a_1, b_1), (a_2, b_2) and $(a_1 + a_2, b_1 + b_2)$ are collinear, then show that $a_1b_2 = a_2b_1$.

6 If area of a triangle is 35 sq units with vertices $(2, -6)$, $(5, 4)$ and $(k, 4)$, then find the values of k. [NCERT]

7 Find the value of k, if the points $(k+1, 1)$, $(2k+1, 3)$ and $(2k+2, 2k)$ are collinear.

Short Answer Type Questions

4 Marks

8 Using cofactor of third row, evaluate

$$\Delta = \begin{vmatrix} \sqrt{23}+\sqrt{3} & \sqrt{5} & \sqrt{5} \\ \sqrt{15}+\sqrt{46} & 5 & \sqrt{10} \\ 3+\sqrt{115} & \sqrt{15} & 5 \end{vmatrix}.$$

9 Find minors and cofactors of the elements of the determinant $\begin{vmatrix} 2 & -3 & 5 \\ 6 & 0 & 4 \\ 1 & 5 & -7 \end{vmatrix}$ and verify that $a_{11}C_{31} + a_{12}C_{32} + a_{13}C_{33} = 0$. [NCERT]

10 Find the equation of the line joining $A(1, 3)$ and $B(0, 0)$ using determinants and find k, if $D(k, 0)$ is a point such that area of ΔABD is 3 sq units. **[NCERT]**

Hints & Solutions

1. (i) Similar as Example 2. [**Ans.** $M_{11}=3, M_{12}=0, M_{21}=-4$ and $M_{22}=2$, $C_{11}=3$, $C_{12}=0$, $C_{21}=4$ and $C_{22}=2$]

(ii) Given determinant is $\begin{vmatrix} a & c \\ b & d \end{vmatrix}$.

$\therefore$ Minors, $M_{11}=d$, $M_{12}=b$, $M_{21}=c$ and $M_{22}=a$ [1]

Also, cofactors are $A_{11}=(-1)^{1+1}M_{11}=1\times d=d$

$$A_{12}=(-1)^{1+2}M_{12}=(-1)\times b=-b$$

$$A_{21}=(-1)^{2+1}M_{21}=(-1)\times c=-c$$

and $\quad A_{22}=(-1)^{2+2}M_{22}=1\times a=a$ [1]

2. The minors of the diagonal elements of the determinant $\begin{vmatrix} 1 & i & -i \\ -i & 1 & i \\ 1 & -i & i \end{vmatrix}$ are given below

$$M_{11}=\begin{vmatrix} 1 & i \\ -i & i \end{vmatrix}=i+i^2=i-1 \quad [\because i^2=-1] \; [1]$$

$$M_{22}=\begin{vmatrix} 1 & -i \\ 1 & i \end{vmatrix}=i+i=2i$$

and $\quad M_{33}=\begin{vmatrix} 1 & i \\ -i & 1 \end{vmatrix}=1+i^2=1-1=0$ [1]

3. Given, $\Delta=\begin{vmatrix} 1 & x & y+z \\ 1 & y & z+x \\ 1 & z & x+y \end{vmatrix}$

Using cofactors of elements of third row, we have

$$\Delta=a_{31}C_{31}+a_{32}C_{32}+a_{33}C_{33}=(-1)^{3+1}\cdot 1\begin{vmatrix} x & y+z \\ y & z+x \end{vmatrix}$$

$$+(-1)^{3+2}\cdot z\begin{vmatrix} 1 & y+z \\ 1 & z+x \end{vmatrix}+(-1)^{3+3}\cdot(x+y)\begin{vmatrix} 1 & x \\ 1 & y \end{vmatrix} \; [1]$$

$[\because$ cofactor $A_{ij}=(-1)^{i+j}M_{ij}]$

$$=1(zx+x^2-y^2-yz)-z(z+x-y-z)+(x+y)(y-x)$$

$$=zx+x^2-y^2-yz-zx+yz+y^2-x^2=0 \quad [1]$$

4. **Hint** $\Delta=a_{13}C_{13}+a_{23}C_{23}+a_{33}C_{33}$

[**Ans.** $(x-y)(y-z)(z-x)$]

5. If the given points are collinear, then

$$\begin{vmatrix} a_1 & b_1 & 1 \\ a_2 & b_2 & 1 \\ a_1+a_2 & b_1+b_2 & 1 \end{vmatrix}=0$$

On expanding along R_1, we get

$$a_1(b_2-b_1-b_2)-b_1(a_2-a_1-a_2)+1[a_2(b_1+b_2)-b_2(a_1+a_2)]=0$$

$$-a_1b_1+b_1a_1+a_2b_1+a_2b_2-b_2a_1-b_2a_2=0$$

$$\Rightarrow \quad -a_1b_2+a_2b_1=0$$

$$\Rightarrow \quad a_1b_2=a_2b_1$$

Hence proved. [1]

6. Given, $\dfrac{1}{2}\begin{vmatrix} 2 & -6 & 1 \\ 5 & 4 & 1 \\ k & 4 & 1 \end{vmatrix}=\pm 35$

$$\Rightarrow \quad 2(4-4)+6(5-k)+1(20-4k)=\pm 70$$

$$\Rightarrow \quad 0+30-6k+20-4k=\pm 70 \quad [1]$$

On taking positive sign, we get

$$-10k+50=70$$

$$\Rightarrow \quad -10k=20$$

$$\Rightarrow \quad k=-2$$

On taking negative sign, we get

$$-10k+50=-70$$

$$\Rightarrow \quad -10k=-120$$

$$\Rightarrow \quad k=12$$

Hence, the values of k are 12 and -2. [1]

7. Since, the given points are collinear.

$$\therefore \quad \begin{vmatrix} k+1 & 1 & 1 \\ 2k+1 & 3 & 1 \\ 2k+2 & 2k & 1 \end{vmatrix}=0$$

$\left[\because \text{ if the points } (x_1, y_1), (x_2, y_2) \text{ and } (x_3, y_3) \text{ are collinear, then } \begin{vmatrix} x_1 & y_1 & 1 \\ x_2 & y_2 & 1 \\ x_3 & y_3 & 1 \end{vmatrix}=0\right]$

On expanding along R_1, we get

$$(kH)[(3-2k)-1(2k+1-2k-2)+1(2k(2k+1)-3(2k+2)]=0$$

$$3k+3-2k^2-2k+1+(4k^2+2k-6k-6)=0$$

$$\Rightarrow \quad 2k^2-3k-2=0$$

$$\Rightarrow \quad 2k^2-4k+k-2=0$$

$$\Rightarrow \quad 2k(k-2)+1(k-2)=0$$

$$\Rightarrow \quad (k-2)(2k+1)=0$$

$$\Rightarrow \quad k-2=0 \text{ or } 2k+1=0$$

$$\therefore \quad k=2 \text{ or } k=-\frac{1}{2} \quad [1]$$

8. Given, $\Delta=\begin{vmatrix} \sqrt{23}+\sqrt{3} & \sqrt{5} & \sqrt{5} \\ \sqrt{15}+\sqrt{46} & 5 & \sqrt{10} \\ 3+\sqrt{115} & \sqrt{15} & 5 \end{vmatrix}$

Using cofactors of elements of third row, we have

$$\Delta=a_{31}C_{31}+a_{32}C_{32}+a_{33}C_{33}$$

$= (3+\sqrt{115})(-1)^{3+1}\begin{vmatrix}\sqrt{5} & \sqrt{5}\\ 5 & \sqrt{10}\end{vmatrix}$

$+\sqrt{15}(-1)^{3+2}\begin{vmatrix}\sqrt{23}+\sqrt{3} & \sqrt{5}\\ \sqrt{15}+\sqrt{46} & \sqrt{10}\end{vmatrix}$

$+5(-1)^{3+3}\begin{vmatrix}\sqrt{23}+\sqrt{3} & \sqrt{5}\\ \sqrt{15}+\sqrt{46} & 5\end{vmatrix}$ [1]

$= (3+\sqrt{23}\sqrt{5})(\sqrt{5}\sqrt{10}-5\sqrt{5})$

$-\sqrt{15}(\sqrt{10}\sqrt{23}+\sqrt{10}\sqrt{3}-\sqrt{5}\sqrt{15}-\sqrt{5}\sqrt{46})$

$+5(5\sqrt{23}+5\sqrt{3}-\sqrt{5}\sqrt{15}-\sqrt{5}\sqrt{46})$ [1]

$= (3+\sqrt{23}\sqrt{5})(5\sqrt{2}-5\sqrt{5})$

$-\sqrt{15}(\sqrt{10}\sqrt{23}+\sqrt{10}\sqrt{3}-5\sqrt{3}-\sqrt{5}\sqrt{46})$

$+5(5\sqrt{23}+5\sqrt{3}-5\sqrt{3}-\sqrt{5}\sqrt{46})$ [1/2]

$= 15\sqrt{2}-15\sqrt{5}+5\sqrt{23}\sqrt{10}-25\sqrt{23}$

$-\sqrt{15}\sqrt{10}\sqrt{23}-\sqrt{15}\sqrt{10}\sqrt{3}+\sqrt{15}\,5\sqrt{3}$

$+\sqrt{15}\sqrt{5}\sqrt{46}+25\sqrt{23}-5\sqrt{5}\sqrt{46}$ [1/2]

$= 15\sqrt{2}-15\sqrt{5}+5\sqrt{23}\sqrt{10}-\sqrt{15}\sqrt{5}\sqrt{46}-15\sqrt{2}$

$+15\sqrt{5}+\sqrt{15}\sqrt{5}\sqrt{46}-5\sqrt{10}\sqrt{23}$ [1]

$= 0$

9. Given, determinant $= \begin{vmatrix}2 & -3 & 5\\ 6 & 0 & 4\\ 1 & 5 & -7\end{vmatrix}$.

We have, $M_{11} = \begin{vmatrix}0 & 4\\ 5 & -7\end{vmatrix} = 0-20 = -20;$

$C_{11} = (-1)^{1+1}M_{11} = (-20) = -20;$

$[\because \text{cofactor } C_{ij} = (-1)^{i+j}M_{ij}]$

$M_{12} = \begin{vmatrix}6 & 4\\ 1 & -7\end{vmatrix} = -42-4 = -46;$

$C_{12} = (-1)^{1+2}M_{12} = -(-46) = 46;$

$M_{13} = \begin{vmatrix}6 & 0\\ 1 & 5\end{vmatrix} = 30-0 = 30;$

$C_{13} = (-1)^{1+3}M_{13} = (30) = 30;$ [1]

$M_{21} = \begin{vmatrix}-3 & 5\\ 5 & -7\end{vmatrix} = 21-25 = -4;$

$C_{21} = (-1)^{2+1}M_{21} = -(-4) = 4;$

$M_{22} = \begin{vmatrix}2 & 5\\ 1 & -7\end{vmatrix} = -14-5 = -19;$

$C_{22} = (-1)^{2+2}M_{22} = (-19) = -19$

$M_{23} = \begin{vmatrix}2 & -3\\ 1 & 5\end{vmatrix} = 10+3 = 13;$

$C_{23} = (-1)^{2+3}M_{23} = -(13) = -13;$ [1]

$M_{31} = \begin{vmatrix}-3 & 5\\ 0 & 4\end{vmatrix} = -12-0 = -12;$

$C_{31} = (-1)^{3+1}M_{31} = (-12) = -12;$

$M_{32} = \begin{vmatrix}2 & 5\\ 6 & 4\end{vmatrix} = 8-30 = -22;$

$C_{32} = (-1)^{3+2}M_{32} = -(-22) = 22;$

$M_{33} = \begin{vmatrix}2 & -3\\ 6 & 0\end{vmatrix} = 0+18 = 18;$

$C_{33} = (-1)^{3+3}M_{33} = (18) = 18$ [1]

We have, $a_{11} = 2, a_{12} = -3, a_{13} = 5, C_{31} = -12,$

$C_{32} = 22, C_{33} = 18$

$\therefore\ a_{11}C_{31} + a_{12}C_{32} + a_{13}C_{33}$

$= (2)(-12) + (-3)(22) + (5)(18)$

$= -24-66+90 = -90+90 = 0$ [1]

10. Similar as Example 8.

[**Ans.** $y = 3x$ and $k = \pm 2$]

TOPIC 03 Adjoint and Inverse of a Matrix

Singular and Non-Singular Matrices

A square matrix A is said to be a **singular matrix**, if $|A| = 0$ and if $|A| \neq 0$, then matrix A is said to be **non-singular matrix.**

e.g. Let $A = \begin{bmatrix}2 & 1\\ 6 & 3\end{bmatrix}$. Then, $|A| = 6-6 = 0$

So, the matrix A is a singular matrix.

Example 1 Check whether the matrix $\begin{bmatrix}2 & 1 & 3\\ 4 & -1 & 0\\ -7 & 2 & 1\end{bmatrix}$ is singular or not.

Sol. Let $A = \begin{bmatrix}2 & 1 & 3\\ 4 & -1 & 0\\ -7 & 2 & 1\end{bmatrix}$.

Now, $|A| = \begin{vmatrix}2 & 1 & 3\\ 4 & -1 & 0\\ -7 & 2 & 1\end{vmatrix}$

$$= 2(-1-0) - 1(4-0) + 3(8-7)$$
$$= -2 - 4 + 3$$
$$= -6 + 3$$
$$= -3 \neq 0$$

Hence, A is a non-singular matrix.

Example 2 If the matrix $A = \begin{bmatrix} 6 & x & 2 \\ 2 & -1 & 2 \\ -10 & 5 & 2 \end{bmatrix}$ is a singular matrix, then find the value of x. **[ISC 2010]**

Sol. Given, $A = \begin{bmatrix} 6 & x & 2 \\ 2 & -1 & 2 \\ -10 & 5 & 2 \end{bmatrix}$

Since, A is a singular matrix. Therefore, it means $|A| = 0$

i.e. $\begin{vmatrix} 6 & x & 2 \\ 2 & -1 & 2 \\ -10 & 5 & 2 \end{vmatrix} = 0$ [given]

On expanding LHS along R_1, we get

$$6[-2-10] - x[4+20] + 2[10-10] = 0$$
$$\Rightarrow \quad -72 - 24x + 0 = 0$$
$$\Rightarrow \quad 24x = -72$$
$$\Rightarrow \quad x = \frac{-72}{24} = -3$$

Adjoint of a Matrix

The adjoint of a square matrix $A = [a_{ij}]_{n \times n}$ is defined as the transpose of the matrix formed by cofactors of the elements a_{ij} and it is denoted by adj (A).

e.g. If $A = \begin{bmatrix} a_{11} & a_{12} & a_{13} \\ a_{21} & a_{22} & a_{23} \\ a_{31} & a_{32} & a_{33} \end{bmatrix}$.

Then, adj (A) = Transpose of $\begin{bmatrix} C_{11} & C_{12} & C_{13} \\ C_{21} & C_{22} & C_{23} \\ C_{31} & C_{32} & C_{33} \end{bmatrix}$

or $\quad$ adj $(A) = \begin{bmatrix} C_{11} & C_{21} & C_{31} \\ C_{12} & C_{22} & C_{32} \\ C_{13} & C_{23} & C_{33} \end{bmatrix}$

where, C_{ij} is the cofactor of element a_{ij}.

Note For a square matrix of order 2 given by $A = \begin{bmatrix} a_{11} & a_{12} \\ a_{21} & a_{22} \end{bmatrix}$, adj (A) can also be obtained by interchanging a_{11} and a_{22} and by changing signs of a_{12} and a_{21},

i.e. adj $(A) = \begin{bmatrix} a_{22} & -a_{12} \\ -a_{21} & a_{11} \end{bmatrix}$.

Example 3 Find the adjoint of the matrix

(i) $\begin{bmatrix} 1 & 2 \\ 3 & 4 \end{bmatrix}$. (ii) $\begin{bmatrix} 1 & -1 & 2 \\ 2 & 3 & 5 \\ -2 & 0 & 1 \end{bmatrix}$. **[NCERT]**

Sol. (i) Let $A = \begin{bmatrix} 1 & 2 \\ 3 & 4 \end{bmatrix}$, then $|A| = \begin{vmatrix} 1 & 2 \\ 3 & 4 \end{vmatrix}$.

Now, cofactors of elements of $|A|$ are

$C_{11} = (-1)^{1+1}4 = 4$, $C_{12} = (-1)^{1+2}(3) = -3$,

$C_{21} = (-1)^{2+1}(2) = -2$ and $C_{22} = (-1)^{2+2}(1) = 1$

Now, $\quad$ adj $(A) = \begin{bmatrix} C_{11} & C_{12} \\ C_{21} & C_{22} \end{bmatrix}^T$

$$= \begin{bmatrix} 4 & -3 \\ -2 & 1 \end{bmatrix}^T = \begin{bmatrix} 4 & -2 \\ -3 & 1 \end{bmatrix}$$

(ii) Let $A = \begin{bmatrix} 1 & -1 & 2 \\ 2 & 3 & 5 \\ -2 & 0 & 1 \end{bmatrix}$

Cofactors of elements of first row of $|A|$ are

$$A_{11} = (-1)^{1+1}\begin{vmatrix} 3 & 5 \\ 0 & 1 \end{vmatrix} = 3 - 0 = 3,$$

$$A_{12} = (-1)^{1+2}\begin{vmatrix} 2 & 5 \\ -2 & 1 \end{vmatrix} = -(2+10) = -12$$

and $\quad A_{13} = (-1)^{1+3}\begin{vmatrix} 2 & 3 \\ -2 & 0 \end{vmatrix} = 0 - (-6) = 6$

Cofactors of elements of second row are

$$A_{21} = (-1)^{2+1}\begin{vmatrix} -1 & 2 \\ 0 & 1 \end{vmatrix} = -(-1-0) = 1,$$

$$A_{22} = (-1)^{2+2}\begin{vmatrix} 1 & 2 \\ -2 & 1 \end{vmatrix} = 1 + 4 = 5$$

and $\quad A_{23} = (-1)^{2+3}\begin{vmatrix} 1 & -1 \\ -2 & 0 \end{vmatrix} = -(0-2) = 2$

Cofactors of elements of third row are

$$A_{31} = (-1)^{3+1}\begin{vmatrix} -1 & 2 \\ 3 & 5 \end{vmatrix} = -5 - 6 = -11,$$

$$A_{32} = (-1)^{3+2}\begin{vmatrix} 1 & 2 \\ 2 & 5 \end{vmatrix} = -(5-4) = -1$$

and $\quad A_{33} = (-1)^{3+3}\begin{vmatrix} 1 & -1 \\ 2 & 3 \end{vmatrix} = 3 + 2 = 5$

Hence, adj $(A) = \begin{bmatrix} A_{11} & A_{12} & A_{13} \\ A_{21} & A_{22} & A_{23} \\ A_{31} & A_{32} & A_{33} \end{bmatrix}^T$

$$= \begin{bmatrix} 3 & -12 & 6 \\ 1 & 5 & 2 \\ -11 & -1 & 5 \end{bmatrix}^T$$

$$= \begin{bmatrix} 3 & 1 & -11 \\ -12 & 5 & -1 \\ 6 & 2 & 5 \end{bmatrix}$$

Some Important Theorems

Theorem 1. If A is any given square matrix of order n, then $A(\text{adj } A) = (\text{adj } A)A = |A| I_n$, where I is the identity matrix of order n. Thus, for a square matrix A of order 2 and 3, we can write respectively,

$$A(\text{adj } A) = (\text{adj } A)\, A = |A| I_2$$

and $$A(\text{adj } A) = (\text{adj } A)\, A = |A| I_3$$

Theorem 2. If A and B are non-singular matrices of the same order, then AB and BA are also non-singular matrices of the same order.

Theorem 3. The determinant of the product of matrices is equal to the product of their respective determinants, i.e. $|AB| = |A||B|$

where, A and B are square matrices of the same order.

Example 4 Find the adjoint of the matrix

$$A = \begin{bmatrix} -1 & -2 & -2 \\ 2 & 1 & -2 \\ 2 & -2 & 1 \end{bmatrix}$$ and hence show that

$A(\text{adj } A) = |A| I_3$.

Sol. We have, $A = \begin{bmatrix} -1 & -2 & -2 \\ 2 & 1 & -2 \\ 2 & -2 & 1 \end{bmatrix}$.

Let C_{ij} be the cofactor of the element a_{ij} of $|A|$.

Now, cofactors of $|A|$ are

$$C_{11} = (-1)^{1+1} \begin{vmatrix} 1 & -2 \\ -2 & 1 \end{vmatrix} = 1 - 4 = -3$$

$$C_{12} = (-1)^{1+2} \begin{vmatrix} 2 & -2 \\ 2 & 1 \end{vmatrix} = -(2+4) = -6$$

$$C_{13} = (-1)^{1+3} \begin{vmatrix} 2 & 1 \\ 2 & -2 \end{vmatrix} = -4 - 2 = -6$$

$$C_{21} = (-1)^{2+1} \begin{vmatrix} -2 & -2 \\ -2 & 1 \end{vmatrix} = -(-2-4) = 6$$

$$C_{22} = (-1)^{2+2} \begin{vmatrix} -1 & -2 \\ 2 & 1 \end{vmatrix} = -1 + 4 = 3$$

$$C_{23} = (-1)^{2+3} \begin{vmatrix} -1 & -2 \\ 2 & -2 \end{vmatrix} = -(2+4) = -6$$

$$C_{31} = (-1)^{3+1} \begin{vmatrix} -2 & -2 \\ 1 & -2 \end{vmatrix} = 4 + 2 = 6$$

$$C_{32} = (-1)^{3+2} \begin{vmatrix} -1 & -2 \\ 2 & -2 \end{vmatrix} = -(2+4) = -6$$

$$C_{33} = (-1)^{3+3} \begin{vmatrix} -1 & -2 \\ 2 & 1 \end{vmatrix} = -1 + 4 = 3$$

Now, the adjoint of the matrix A is given by

$$\text{adj}(A) = \begin{bmatrix} C_{11} & C_{21} & C_{31} \\ C_{12} & C_{22} & C_{32} \\ C_{13} & C_{23} & C_{33} \end{bmatrix} = \begin{bmatrix} -3 & 6 & 6 \\ -6 & 3 & -6 \\ -6 & -6 & 3 \end{bmatrix}$$

Now, $|A| = \begin{vmatrix} -1 & -2 & -2 \\ 2 & 1 & -2 \\ 2 & -2 & 1 \end{vmatrix}$

$$= -1(1-4) + 2(2+4) - 2(-4-2)$$
$$= -1(-3) + 2(6) - 2(-6) = 3 + 12 + 12 = 27$$

and $$A \cdot (\text{adj } A) = \begin{bmatrix} -1 & -2 & -2 \\ 2 & 1 & -2 \\ 2 & -2 & 1 \end{bmatrix} \begin{bmatrix} -3 & 6 & 6 \\ -6 & 3 & -6 \\ -6 & -6 & 3 \end{bmatrix}$$

$$= \begin{bmatrix} 3+12+12 & -6-6+12 & -6+12-6 \\ -6-6+12 & 12+3+12 & 12-6-6 \\ -6+12-6 & 12-6-6 & 12+12+3 \end{bmatrix}$$

$$= \begin{bmatrix} 27 & 0 & 0 \\ 0 & 27 & 0 \\ 0 & 0 & 27 \end{bmatrix} = 27 \begin{bmatrix} 1 & 0 & 0 \\ 0 & 1 & 0 \\ 0 & 0 & 1 \end{bmatrix}$$

$$= 27 I_3 = |A| I_3$$

Example 5 If $A = \begin{bmatrix} \cos x & \sin x \\ -\sin x & \cos x \end{bmatrix}$ and $A \cdot (\text{adj}A) = k \begin{bmatrix} 1 & 0 \\ 0 & 1 \end{bmatrix}$, then find the value of k. **[ISC 2005]**

Sol. Given, $A = \begin{bmatrix} \cos x & \sin x \\ -\sin x & \cos x \end{bmatrix}$

Now, cofactors of $|A|$ are

$$A_{11} = (-1)^{1+1} \cos x = \cos x,$$
$$A_{12} = (-1)^{1+2} (-\sin x) = \sin x,$$
$$A_{21} = (-1)^{2+1} \sin x = -\sin x$$

and $$A_{22} = (-1)^{2+2} \cos x = \cos x$$

$\therefore$ $$\text{adj}(A) = \begin{bmatrix} A_{11} & A_{21} \\ A_{12} & A_{22} \end{bmatrix} = \begin{bmatrix} \cos x & -\sin x \\ \sin x & \cos x \end{bmatrix}$$

Now, $$A \cdot (\text{adj}A) = \begin{bmatrix} \cos x & \sin x \\ -\sin x & \cos x \end{bmatrix} \begin{bmatrix} \cos x & -\sin x \\ \sin x & \cos x \end{bmatrix}$$

$$= \begin{bmatrix} \cos x^2 + \sin^2 x & -\sin x \cos x + \cos x \sin x \\ -\sin x \cos x + \cos x \sin x & \sin^2 x + \cos^2 x \end{bmatrix}$$ [by product rule]

$$= \begin{bmatrix} 1 & 0 \\ 0 & 1 \end{bmatrix}$$ $[\because \sin^2 A + \cos^2 A = 1]$ ...(i)

Also given, $A \cdot (\text{adj}A) = k \begin{bmatrix} 1 & 0 \\ 0 & 1 \end{bmatrix}$ [given]

$$\Rightarrow \begin{bmatrix} 1 & 0 \\ 0 & 1 \end{bmatrix} = k \begin{bmatrix} 1 & 0 \\ 0 & 1 \end{bmatrix}$$

$$\Rightarrow \begin{bmatrix} 1 & 0 \\ 0 & 1 \end{bmatrix} = \begin{bmatrix} k & 0 \\ 0 & k \end{bmatrix}$$ [from Eq. (i)]

$\therefore$ $k = 1$

Properties of Adjoint of a Matrix

Suppose A and B are two non-singular matrices of same order n. Then,

(i) $\text{adj}\,(A^T) = [\text{adj}\,(A)]^T$

(ii) $\text{adj}\,(kA) = k^{n-1}\,(\text{adj}\,A), k \in R$

(iii) $\text{adj}\,(AB) = [\text{adj}\,(B)][\text{adj}\,(A)]$

(iv) $|\text{adj}\,A| = |A|^{n-1}$

(v) $|\text{adj}\,[\text{adj}\,(A)]| = |A|^{(n-1)^2}$

(vi) $\text{adj}\,(\text{adj}\,A) = |A|^{n-2} \cdot A$

Example 6 Let A be the non-singular square matrix of order 3×3, then prove that $|\text{adj}\,(A)| = |A|^2$. **[NCERT]**

Sol. We know that $[\text{adj}\,(A)] \cdot A = |A| I$

$$= |A| \begin{bmatrix} 1 & 0 & 0 \\ 0 & 1 & 0 \\ 0 & 0 & 1 \end{bmatrix} = \begin{bmatrix} |A| & 0 & 0 \\ 0 & |A| & 0 \\ 0 & 0 & |A| \end{bmatrix}$$

On taking determinant both sides, we get

$$|(\text{adj}\,A) \cdot (A)| = \begin{vmatrix} |A| & 0 & 0 \\ 0 & |A| & 0 \\ 0 & 0 & |A| \end{vmatrix}$$

$$\Rightarrow \quad |(\text{adj}\,A)A| = |A|^3 \begin{vmatrix} 1 & 0 & 0 \\ 0 & 1 & 0 \\ 0 & 0 & 1 \end{vmatrix}$$

$$= |A|^3 |I| = |A|^3 \qquad [\because |I| = 1]$$

$$\Rightarrow \quad |\text{adj}\,(A)| |A| = |A|^3 \qquad [\because |AB| = |A| \cdot |B|]$$

$$\therefore \quad |\text{adj}\,(A)| = |A|^2 \qquad [\because |A| \neq 0]$$

Hence proved.

Example 7 If $A = \begin{bmatrix} 1 & 2 \\ 3 & 4 \end{bmatrix}$, then verify the following results.

(i) $|\text{adj}\,A| = |A|$ (ii) $\text{adj}\,(A^T) = (\text{adj}\,A)^T$

(iii) $|\text{adj}\,(\text{adj}\,A)| = |A|$

Sol. Let $A = \begin{bmatrix} 1 & 2 \\ 3 & 4 \end{bmatrix}$, then $|A| = \begin{vmatrix} 1 & 2 \\ 3 & 4 \end{vmatrix}$.

Now, cofactors of elements of $|A|$ are

$A_{11} = 4, A_{12} = -3, A_{21} = -2$ and $A_{22} = 1$

$$\therefore \text{adj}\,A = \begin{bmatrix} A_{11} & A_{12} \\ A_{21} & A_{22} \end{bmatrix}^T = \begin{bmatrix} 4 & -3 \\ -2 & 1 \end{bmatrix}^T = \begin{bmatrix} 4 & -2 \\ -3 & 1 \end{bmatrix} \qquad \text{...(i)}$$

(i) Now, $|A| = \begin{vmatrix} 1 & 2 \\ 3 & 4 \end{vmatrix} = 4 - 6 = -2$ ...(ii)

and $|\text{adj}(A)| = \begin{vmatrix} 4 & -2 \\ -3 & 1 \end{vmatrix} = 4 - 6 = -2$ ...(iii)

$$\therefore \quad |\text{adj}\,(A)| = |A| \qquad \text{[from Eqs. (ii) and (iii)]}$$

(ii) We have, $A = \begin{bmatrix} 1 & 2 \\ 3 & 4 \end{bmatrix}$

$$\therefore \quad A^T = \begin{bmatrix} 1 & 3 \\ 2 & 4 \end{bmatrix} \text{ and } |A^T| = \begin{vmatrix} 1 & 3 \\ 2 & 4 \end{vmatrix}$$

Now, cofactors of elements of $|A^T|$ are $C_{11} = 4$, $C_{12} = -2$, $C_{21} = -3$, $C_{22} = 1$.

$$\therefore \text{adj}\,(A^T) = \begin{bmatrix} C_{11} & C_{12} \\ C_{21} & C_{22} \end{bmatrix}^T$$

$$= \begin{bmatrix} 4 & -2 \\ -3 & 1 \end{bmatrix}^T = \begin{bmatrix} 4 & -3 \\ -2 & 1 \end{bmatrix} \qquad \text{...(iv)}$$

From Eq. (i), we get

$$(\text{adj}\,A)^T = \begin{bmatrix} 4 & -2 \\ -3 & 1 \end{bmatrix}^T = \begin{bmatrix} 4 & -3 \\ -2 & 1 \end{bmatrix}$$

$$\Rightarrow \quad (\text{adj}\,A)^T = \text{adj}\,(A^T) \qquad \text{[from Eq. (iv)]}$$

(iii) We have, $(\text{adj}\,A) = \begin{bmatrix} 4 & -2 \\ -3 & 1 \end{bmatrix}$

$$\therefore \quad \text{adj}\,A| = \begin{vmatrix} 4 & -2 \\ -3 & 1 \end{vmatrix}$$

Now, cofactors of elements of $|\text{adj}\,A|$ are

$C_{11} = 1, C_{12} = 3, C_{21} = 2$ and $C_{22} = 4$.

$$\therefore \quad \text{adj}\,(\text{adj}\,A) = \begin{bmatrix} C_{11} & C_{12} \\ C_{21} & C_{22} \end{bmatrix}^T = \begin{bmatrix} 1 & 3 \\ 2 & 4 \end{bmatrix}^T = \begin{bmatrix} 1 & 2 \\ 3 & 4 \end{bmatrix}$$

$$\Rightarrow \quad |\text{adj}\,(\text{adj}\,A)| = \begin{vmatrix} 1 & 2 \\ 3 & 4 \end{vmatrix} = 4 - 6 = -2$$

$= |A|$ [from Eq. (ii)] **Hence verified.**

Inverse of a Matrix

Suppose A is a non-zero square matrix of order n and there exists matrix B of same order n such that $AB = BA = I_n$, then such matrix B is called an inverse of matrix A. It is denoted by A^{-1}.

> **Theorem 3.** A square matrix A is invertible if and only if A is non-singular matrix.

Proof Let A be an invertible matrix of order n and I be an identity matrix of same order n. Then, there exists a square matrix B of same order n such that

$$AB = BA = I$$

Now, $\quad AB = I$

$$\therefore \quad |AB| = |I| \Rightarrow |AB| = 1 \qquad [\because |I| = 1]$$

$$\Rightarrow \quad |A||B| = 1$$

$$\Rightarrow \quad |A| \neq 0$$

Hence, A is non-singular matrix.

Now, conversely let A be non-singular matrix, then $|A| \neq 0$. By theorem 1, we have

$$A(\text{adj } A) = (\text{adj } A)A = |A|\, I$$

$$\Rightarrow \quad A\left(\frac{1}{|A|}\text{adj } A\right) = \left(\frac{1}{|A|}\text{adj } A\right)A = I$$

$$\Rightarrow \quad AB = BA = I$$

where, $B = \dfrac{1}{|A|}\text{adj }(A)$

Thus, A is invertible and $A^{-1} = \dfrac{1}{|A|}\text{adj }(A)$.

Note If A is a square matrix of order n and there exists a square matrix B of order n such that $AB = BA = I_n \Rightarrow B = A^{-1}$ and $A = B^{-1}$.

Theorem 4. If A, B and C are all square matrices of order n and A is non-singular, then

(i) $AB = AC \Rightarrow B = C$ [left cancellation law]

(ii) $BA = CA \Rightarrow B = C$ [right cancellation law]

Proof of part (i)

Since, $AB = AC$

$$\Rightarrow \quad A^{-1}(AB) = A^{-1}(AC)$$

[$\because A$ is non-singular $\Rightarrow A^{-1}$ exists]

$$\Rightarrow \quad (A^{-1}A)B = (A^{-1}A)C$$

$$\Rightarrow \quad I_nB = I_nC \Rightarrow B = C \qquad [\because A^{-1}A = I]$$

Note $AB = AC \Rightarrow B = C$ is true only when $|A| \neq 0$. Otherwise, there exist matrices A, B, C such that $AB = AC$ but $B \neq C$.

Properties of Inverse of a Matrix

Let A and B be two square invertible matrices of same order. Then,

(i) $(A^{-1})^{-1} = A$

(ii) $(AB)^{-1} = B^{-1}A^{-1}$ [reversal law]

(iii) $(A^T)^{-1} = (A^{-1})^T$

(iv) $|A^{-1}| = |A|^{-1}$

(v) $AA^{-1} = A^{-1}A = I$

(vi) $(kA)^{-1} = \dfrac{1}{k}A^{-1}, k \neq 0$

Note

(i) Only square matrices have adjoint or inverse.

(ii) $(AA)^{-1} = A^{-1}A^{-1} \Rightarrow (A^2)^{-1} = (A^{-1})^2$

(iii) If A, B and C are invertible matrices of the same order, then $(ABC)^{-1} = C^{-1}B^{-1}A^{-1}$.

Method of Finding the Inverse of a Matrix

Suppose a square matrix A of order n is given. Sometimes, we have to find inverse of A by using formula and sometimes an algebraic equation in A is given to us and we have to find inverse of A by using this equation.

| TYPE I |
Inverse of Matrix by using the Formula

I. Let the given matrix be A. Then, find $|A|$ and check whether it is singular or non-singular matrix. If A is singular, i.e. $|A| = 0$, then inverse of A does not exists and if A is non-singular, i.e. $|A| \neq 0$, then inverse of A exists, so go to next step.

II. Find the cofactors corresponding to each element of $|A|$.

III. Find adj (A), i.e. write the matrix of cofactors and then find transpose of this cofactors matrix, to get adj (A).

IV. Now, put the value of $|A|$ and adj (A) in the formula $A^{-1} = \dfrac{1}{|A|}\text{adj }(A)$ to get required inverse of matrix A.

Example 8 Find the inverse of following matrices.

(i) $\begin{bmatrix} -1 & 5 \\ -3 & 2 \end{bmatrix}$ (ii) $\begin{bmatrix} 1 & -1 & 1 \\ 2 & -1 & 0 \\ 1 & 0 & 0 \end{bmatrix}$ [NCERT]

Sol. (i) Let $A = \begin{bmatrix} -1 & 5 \\ -3 & 2 \end{bmatrix}$, then $|A| = \begin{vmatrix} -1 & 5 \\ -3 & 2 \end{vmatrix} = -2 + 15 = 13 \neq 0$

So, A is non-singular matrix and therefore A^{-1} exists.

Now, cofactors of each element of $|A|$ are

$A_{11} = (-1)^{1+1}(2) = 2$, $A_{12} = (-1)^{1+2}(-3) = 3$,

$A_{21} = (-1)^{2+1}(5) = -5$ and $A_{22} = (-1)^{2+2}(-1) = -1$

Thus, matrix of cofactors $= \begin{bmatrix} A_{11} & A_{12} \\ A_{21} & A_{22} \end{bmatrix} = \begin{bmatrix} 2 & 3 \\ -5 & -1 \end{bmatrix}$

and $\text{adj}(A) = \begin{bmatrix} 2 & 3 \\ -5 & -1 \end{bmatrix}^T = \begin{bmatrix} 2 & -5 \\ 3 & -1 \end{bmatrix}$

Now, $A^{-1} = \dfrac{1}{|A|}\cdot \text{adj} A = \dfrac{1}{13}\begin{bmatrix} 2 & -5 \\ 3 & -1 \end{bmatrix}$

which is the required inverse of given matrix A.

(ii) Let $A = \begin{bmatrix} 1 & -1 & 1 \\ 2 & -1 & 0 \\ 1 & 0 & 0 \end{bmatrix}$

Then, $|A| = 1\begin{vmatrix} -1 & 0 \\ 0 & 0 \end{vmatrix} - 2\begin{vmatrix} -1 & 1 \\ 0 & 0 \end{vmatrix} + 1\begin{vmatrix} -1 & 1 \\ -1 & 0 \end{vmatrix}$

[expanding along C_1]

$= 1(0) - 2(0) + 1(0 + 1) = 1 \neq 0$

Thus, A is a non-singular matrix, so A^{-1} exists.

Now, cofactors corresponding to each element of determinant A are

$$C_{11} = (-1)^{1+1}\begin{vmatrix} -1 & 0 \\ 0 & 0 \end{vmatrix} = 1(-0-0) = 0$$

$[\because C_{ij} = (-1)^{i+j} M_{ij}]$

$$C_{12} = (-1)^{1+2}\begin{vmatrix} 2 & 0 \\ 1 & 0 \end{vmatrix} = -1(0-0) = 0$$

$$C_{13} = (-1)^{1+3}\begin{vmatrix} 2 & -1 \\ 1 & 0 \end{vmatrix} = 1(0+1) = 1$$

$$C_{21} = (-1)^{2+1}\begin{vmatrix} -1 & 1 \\ 0 & 0 \end{vmatrix} = -1(0-0) = 0$$

$$C_{22} = (-1)^{2+2}\begin{vmatrix} 1 & 1 \\ 1 & 0 \end{vmatrix} = 1(0-1) = -1$$

$$C_{23} = (-1)^{2+3}\begin{vmatrix} 1 & -1 \\ 1 & 0 \end{vmatrix} = -1(0+1) = -1$$

$$C_{31} = (-1)^{3+1}\begin{vmatrix} -1 & 1 \\ -1 & 0 \end{vmatrix} = 1(0+1) = 1$$

$$C_{32} = (-1)^{3+2}\begin{vmatrix} 1 & 1 \\ 2 & 0 \end{vmatrix} = -1(0-2) = 2$$

$$C_{33} = (-1)^{3+3}\begin{vmatrix} 1 & -1 \\ 2 & -1 \end{vmatrix} = 1(-1+2) = 1$$

Thus, the matrix of cofactors

$$= \begin{bmatrix} C_{11} & C_{12} & C_{13} \\ C_{21} & C_{22} & C_{23} \\ C_{31} & C_{32} & C_{33} \end{bmatrix} = \begin{bmatrix} 0 & 0 & 1 \\ 0 & -1 & -1 \\ 1 & 2 & 1 \end{bmatrix}$$

and $\text{adj}(A) = \begin{bmatrix} 0 & 0 & 1 \\ 0 & -1 & -1 \\ 1 & 2 & 1 \end{bmatrix}^T = \begin{bmatrix} 0 & 0 & 1 \\ 0 & -1 & 2 \\ 1 & -1 & 1 \end{bmatrix}$

[interchange rows and columns]

Now, $A^{-1} = \dfrac{1}{|A|}\text{adj}(A) = \dfrac{1}{1}\begin{bmatrix} 0 & 0 & 1 \\ 0 & -1 & 2 \\ 1 & -1 & 1 \end{bmatrix}$

$\Rightarrow \quad A^{-1} = \begin{bmatrix} 0 & 0 & 1 \\ 0 & -1 & 2 \\ 1 & -1 & 1 \end{bmatrix}$

which is the required inverse of given matrix A.

Example 9 If $A = \begin{bmatrix} 2 & 3 \\ 1 & -4 \end{bmatrix}$ and $B = \begin{bmatrix} 1 & -2 \\ -1 & 3 \end{bmatrix}$, then verify that

(i) $(AB)^{-1} = B^{-1}A^{-1}$

(ii) $AA^{-1} = I$

(iii) $|A^{-1}| = |A|^{-1}$.

Sol. (i) Given, $A = \begin{bmatrix} 2 & 3 \\ 1 & -4 \end{bmatrix}$ and $B = \begin{bmatrix} 1 & -2 \\ -1 & 3 \end{bmatrix}$, then

$$AB = \begin{bmatrix} 2 & 3 \\ 1 & -4 \end{bmatrix}\begin{bmatrix} 1 & -2 \\ -1 & 3 \end{bmatrix} = \begin{bmatrix} 2-3 & -4+9 \\ 1+4 & -2-12 \end{bmatrix} = \begin{bmatrix} -1 & 5 \\ 5 & -14 \end{bmatrix}$$

Now, $|A| = \begin{vmatrix} 2 & 3 \\ 1 & -4 \end{vmatrix} = -8-3 = -11 \neq 0$

and $|B| = \begin{vmatrix} 1 & -2 \\ -1 & 3 \end{vmatrix} = 3-2 = 1 \neq 0$

Now, $AB = \begin{bmatrix} 2 & 3 \\ 1 & -4 \end{bmatrix}\begin{bmatrix} 1 & -2 \\ -1 & 3 \end{bmatrix}$

$$= \begin{bmatrix} 2-3 & -4+9 \\ 1+4 & -2-12 \end{bmatrix} = \begin{bmatrix} -1 & 5 \\ 5 & -14 \end{bmatrix}$$

$\therefore \quad |AB| = \begin{vmatrix} -1 & 5 \\ 5 & -14 \end{vmatrix} = 14 - 25 = -11 \neq 0$

Thus A, B and AB are non-singular matrices, so their inverse exists.

Now, $\text{adj}(A) = \begin{bmatrix} -4 & -3 \\ -1 & 2 \end{bmatrix}$, $\left[\because \text{adj}\begin{bmatrix} a & b \\ c & d \end{bmatrix} = \begin{bmatrix} d & -b \\ -c & a \end{bmatrix}\right]$

$\text{adj}(B) = \begin{bmatrix} 3 & 2 \\ 1 & 1 \end{bmatrix}$ and $\text{adj}(AB) = \begin{bmatrix} -14 & -5 \\ -5 & -1 \end{bmatrix}$

$$\therefore \quad (AB)^{-1} = \frac{1}{|AB|}\text{adj}(AB) = \frac{1}{-11}\begin{bmatrix} -14 & -5 \\ -5 & -1 \end{bmatrix}$$

$$= \frac{1}{11}\begin{bmatrix} 14 & 5 \\ 5 & 1 \end{bmatrix} \quad \text{...(i)}$$

$$A^{-1} = \frac{1}{|A|}\text{adj}(A) = \frac{1}{-11}\begin{bmatrix} -4 & -3 \\ -1 & 2 \end{bmatrix} = \frac{1}{11}\begin{bmatrix} 4 & 3 \\ 1 & -2 \end{bmatrix}$$

and $B^{-1} = \dfrac{1}{|B|}\text{adj}(B) = \dfrac{1}{1}\begin{bmatrix} 3 & 2 \\ 1 & 1 \end{bmatrix} = \begin{bmatrix} 3 & 2 \\ 1 & 1 \end{bmatrix}$

Now, $B^{-1}A^{-1} = \begin{bmatrix} 3 & 2 \\ 1 & 1 \end{bmatrix}\dfrac{1}{11}\begin{bmatrix} 4 & 3 \\ 1 & -2 \end{bmatrix} = \dfrac{1}{11}\begin{bmatrix} 3 & 2 \\ 1 & 1 \end{bmatrix}\begin{bmatrix} 4 & 3 \\ 1 & -2 \end{bmatrix}$

$$= \frac{1}{11}\begin{bmatrix} 12+2 & 9-4 \\ 4+1 & 3-2 \end{bmatrix} = \frac{1}{11}\begin{bmatrix} 14 & 5 \\ 5 & 1 \end{bmatrix}$$

$= (AB)^{-1}$ [from Eq. (i)]

$\therefore \quad (AB)^{-1} = B^{-1}A^{-1}$ **Hence verified.**

(ii) $AA^{-1} = \begin{bmatrix} 2 & 3 \\ 1 & -4 \end{bmatrix}\dfrac{1}{11}\begin{bmatrix} 4 & 3 \\ 1 & -2 \end{bmatrix}$

$$= \frac{1}{11}\begin{bmatrix} 2 & 3 \\ 1 & -4 \end{bmatrix}\begin{bmatrix} 4 & 3 \\ 1 & -2 \end{bmatrix} = \frac{1}{11}\begin{bmatrix} 8+3 & 6-6 \\ 4-4 & 3+8 \end{bmatrix}$$

$= \dfrac{1}{11}\begin{bmatrix} 11 & 0 \\ 0 & 11 \end{bmatrix} = \begin{bmatrix} 1 & 0 \\ 0 & 1 \end{bmatrix} = I$ **Hence verified.**

(iii) $|A^{-1}| = \left(\dfrac{1}{11}\right)^2 \begin{vmatrix} 4 & 3 \\ 1 & -2 \end{vmatrix}$

[$\because$ if A is a matrix of order 2×2, then $|kA| = k^2|A|$]

$$= \frac{1}{(11)^2}[-8-3] = \frac{-11}{(11)^2} = -\frac{1}{11}$$

and $|A|^{-1} = (-11)^{-1} = -\dfrac{1}{11}$

$\therefore \quad |A^{-1}| = |A|^{-1}$ **Hence verified.**

Example 10 Find the matrix X for which

$$\begin{bmatrix} 5 & 4 \\ 1 & 1 \end{bmatrix} X = \begin{bmatrix} 1 & -2 \\ 1 & 3 \end{bmatrix}.$$

[ISC 2016]

Sol. Given, $\begin{bmatrix} 5 & 4 \\ 1 & 1 \end{bmatrix} X = \begin{bmatrix} 1 & -2 \\ 1 & 3 \end{bmatrix}$

Let $A=\begin{bmatrix}5 & 4\\1 & 1\end{bmatrix}$ and $B=\begin{bmatrix}1 & -2\\1 & 3\end{bmatrix}$

Then, $|A|=\begin{vmatrix}5 & 4\\1 & 1\end{vmatrix}=(5\times1)-(1\times4)=5-4=1\neq0$

So, A^{-1} exists.

Now, cofactors of elements of determinant A are given below

$$A_{11}=1, A_{12}=-1, A_{21}=-4 \text{ and } A_{22}=5$$

Now, $\text{adj}(A)=\begin{bmatrix}1 & -1\\-4 & 5\end{bmatrix}^T=\begin{bmatrix}1 & -4\\-1 & 5\end{bmatrix}$

$\therefore\ A^{-1}=\dfrac{1}{|A|}\text{adj } A=\dfrac{1}{1}\begin{bmatrix}1 & -4\\-1 & 5\end{bmatrix}\Rightarrow A^{-1}=\begin{bmatrix}1 & -4\\-1 & 5\end{bmatrix}$

So, the given matrix equation is

$$AX=B\Rightarrow A^{-1}(AX)=A^{-1}B$$

$$\Rightarrow (A^{-1}A)X=A^{-1}B\Rightarrow IX=A^{-1}B\Rightarrow X=A^{-1}B$$

$$\Rightarrow\quad X=\begin{bmatrix}1 & -4\\-1 & 5\end{bmatrix}\begin{bmatrix}1 & -2\\1 & 3\end{bmatrix}$$

$$\Rightarrow\quad X=\begin{bmatrix}1\times1+(-4)\times1 & 1\times(-2)+(-4)\times3\\-1\times1+5\times1 & (-1)\times(-2)+5\times3\end{bmatrix}$$

$$=\begin{bmatrix}1-4 & -2-12\\-1+5 & 2+15\end{bmatrix}=\begin{bmatrix}-3 & -14\\4 & 17\end{bmatrix}$$

| TYPE II |

Inverse of Matrix by using Algebraic Equation

Sometimes, a matrix (say A) and algebraic equation in matrix A is given to us and we have to show that A satisfies this algebraic equation and then find inverse of A by using this equation.

For this, we use the following steps

I. Firstly, we show that matrix A satisfies given algebraic equation in A and for this

(i) Find the value of all terms having power of A by multiplying A itself (as $A^2=A\cdot A$, $A^3=A\cdot A^2$).

(ii) Put the values of I, A, A^2, A^3, etc., in given algebraic equation and show that LHS = RHS.

II. Now, pre-multiply or post-multiply both sides in given algebraic equation by A^{-1}.

III. Simplify the equation obtained in Step II by using properties of inverse, as $AA^{-1}=I$, $A^2A^{-1}=A$, $IA^{-1}=A^{-1}$, etc., and then take A^{-1} in LHS and other terms in RHS.

IV. Now, put the values of I, A, A^2, A^3, etc., in RHS of equation obtained in Step III and find required value of inverse of A.

Note If a matrix A and an algebraic equation in variable x is given to us and we have to show that matrix A satisfies this equation in x, then we replace x by A in the given equation and then solve by using above method.

Example 11 If $A=\begin{bmatrix}2 & -1\\-1 & 2\end{bmatrix}$ and I is the identity matrix of order 2, then show that $A^2=4A-3I$. Hence find A^{-1}.

Sol. Here, $A=\begin{bmatrix}2 & -1\\-1 & 2\end{bmatrix}$.

Now, $A^2=A\cdot A=\begin{bmatrix}2 & -1\\-1 & 2\end{bmatrix}\begin{bmatrix}2 & -1\\-1 & 2\end{bmatrix}$

$$=\begin{bmatrix}4+1 & -2-2\\-2-2 & 1+4\end{bmatrix}=\begin{bmatrix}5 & -4\\-4 & 5\end{bmatrix}$$

[multiplying row by column]...(i)

Also, $4A-3I=4\begin{bmatrix}2 & -1\\-1 & 2\end{bmatrix}-3\begin{bmatrix}1 & 0\\0 & 1\end{bmatrix}$

$$=\begin{bmatrix}8 & -4\\-4 & 8\end{bmatrix}-\begin{bmatrix}3 & 0\\0 & 3\end{bmatrix}=\begin{bmatrix}5 & -4\\-4 & 5\end{bmatrix} \quad ...(ii)$$

From Eqs. (i) and (ii), we get

$$A^2=4A-3I \quad ...(iii)$$

Now, $|A|=\begin{vmatrix}2 & -1\\-1 & 2\end{vmatrix}=4-1=3\neq0$

$\therefore\ A^{-1}$ exists.

Now, pre-multiplying both sides of Eq. (iii) by A^{-1}, we get

$$A^{-1}\cdot A^2=A^{-1}\cdot(4A-3I)$$

$$\Rightarrow (A^{-1}\cdot A)\cdot A=4A^{-1}\cdot A-3A^{-1}\cdot I$$

$$\Rightarrow\quad IA=4I-3A^{-1}$$

$[\because A\cdot A^{-1}=I=A^{-1}A \text{ and } A^{-1}\cdot I=A^{-1}]$

$$\Rightarrow\quad A=4I-3A^{-1} \quad [\because IA=A=AI]$$

$$\Rightarrow\quad 3A^{-1}=4I-A$$

$$\therefore\quad A^{-1}=\frac{1}{3}\left(4\begin{bmatrix}1 & 0\\0 & 1\end{bmatrix}-\begin{bmatrix}2 & -1\\-1 & 2\end{bmatrix}\right)$$

$$=\frac{1}{3}\left(\begin{bmatrix}4 & 0\\0 & 4\end{bmatrix}-\begin{bmatrix}2 & -1\\-1 & 2\end{bmatrix}\right)$$

$$=\frac{1}{3}\begin{bmatrix}2 & 1\\1 & 2\end{bmatrix}=\begin{bmatrix}2/3 & 1/3\\1/3 & 2/3\end{bmatrix}$$

Topic Practice 3

Very Short Answer Type Questions

2 Marks

1 Check whether following matrix is singular or non-singular.

(i) $\begin{bmatrix} 6 & 2 \\ 12 & 4 \end{bmatrix}$ (ii) $\begin{bmatrix} \sec\theta & \operatorname{cosec}\theta \\ \sin\theta & \cos\theta \end{bmatrix}$

(iii) $\begin{bmatrix} 1 & 2 & 4 \\ 1 & 3 & 9 \\ 1 & 4 & 16 \end{bmatrix}$

2 Find the adjoint of the following matrices.

(i) $A = \begin{bmatrix} -1 & 2 \\ 8 & 4 \end{bmatrix}$ (ii) $P = \begin{bmatrix} 5 & -3 \\ 2 & -4 \end{bmatrix}$

3 (i) If for any 2×2 square matrix A,

$A(\operatorname{adj} A) = \begin{bmatrix} 8 & 0 \\ 0 & 8 \end{bmatrix}$, then write the value of $|A|$.

(ii) If A and B are matrix of order 3 and $|A| = 5$, $|B| = 3$, then find the value of $|3AB|$. [NCERT Exemplar]

4 (i) If A is matrix of order 3 and $|A| = 4$, then find the value of $|\operatorname{adj}(A)|$.

(ii) If A is a square matrix of order 3 such that $|\operatorname{adj}(A)| = 64$, then find $|A|$.

5 Find the inverse of the matrix $\begin{bmatrix} 2 & -2 \\ 4 & 3 \end{bmatrix}$. [NCERT]

6 If $A = \begin{bmatrix} 2 & \lambda & -3 \\ 0 & 2 & 5 \\ 1 & 1 & 3 \end{bmatrix}$, then A^{-1} exist for which value of λ? [NCERT Exemplar]

7 Find the inverse of the matrix $\begin{bmatrix} \cos\theta & \sin\theta \\ -\sin\theta & \cos\theta \end{bmatrix}$.

8 If A is a matrix of order 2×2, then find the value of $(A^3)^{-1}$. [NCERT Exemplar]

9 If A and B are invertible matrices, then which of the following is incorrect?

(i) $\operatorname{adj}(A) = |A| A^{-1}$ (ii) $(A + B)^{-1} = B^{-1} + A^{-1}$

(iii) $\det(A^{-1}) \cdot [\det(A)] = 1$ [NCERT]

10 In the interval $\frac{\pi}{2} < x < \pi$, find the value of x for which the matrix $\begin{bmatrix} 2\sin x & 3 \\ 1 & 2\sin x \end{bmatrix}$ is singular.

Short Answer Type Questions

4 Marks

11 Find the adjoint of the matrix $\begin{bmatrix} 1 & 2 & 5 \\ 2 & 3 & 1 \\ -1 & 1 & 1 \end{bmatrix}$. [NCERT]

12 Find the adjoint of the matrix $A = \begin{bmatrix} 1 & 2 \\ 3 & 4 \end{bmatrix}$ and verify that $A[\operatorname{adj}(A)] = |A| I$.

13 Given $A = \begin{bmatrix} 2 & -3 \\ -4 & 7 \end{bmatrix}$, then compute A^{-1} and show that $2A^{-1} = 9I - A$.

14 If $A = \begin{bmatrix} 1 & \tan x \\ -\tan x & 1 \end{bmatrix}$, then show that $A^T A^{-1} = \begin{bmatrix} \cos 2x & -\sin 2x \\ \sin 2x & \cos 2x \end{bmatrix}$.

Directions (Q. Nos. 15-16) *Find the inverse of the following matrices.*

15 $\begin{bmatrix} 1 & 0 & 0 \\ 3 & 3 & 0 \\ 5 & 2 & -1 \end{bmatrix}$

16 $\begin{bmatrix} 1 & 0 & 0 \\ 0 & \cos\alpha & \sin\alpha \\ 0 & \sin\alpha & -\cos\alpha \end{bmatrix}$

17 Let $A = \begin{bmatrix} 3 & 7 \\ 2 & 5 \end{bmatrix}$ and $B = \begin{bmatrix} 6 & 8 \\ 7 & 9 \end{bmatrix}$, then verify that $(AB)^{-1} = B^{-1}A^{-1}$. [NCERT]

18 If $A = \begin{bmatrix} 1 & -1 & 1 \\ 2 & -1 & 0 \\ 1 & 0 & 0 \end{bmatrix}$, then show that $A^{-1} = A^2$.

19 Find A^{-1}, if $A = \begin{bmatrix} 0 & 1 & 1 \\ 1 & 0 & 1 \\ 1 & 1 & 0 \end{bmatrix}$ and show that $A^{-1} = \frac{A^2 - 3I}{2}$. [NCERT Exemplar]

20 If $A = \begin{bmatrix} 1 & -2 & 3 \\ 0 & -1 & 4 \\ -2 & 2 & 1 \end{bmatrix}$, then find $(A')^{-1}$.

21 Compute $(AB)^{-1}$,

if $A = \begin{bmatrix} 1 & 1 & 2 \\ 0 & 2 & -3 \\ 3 & -2 & 4 \end{bmatrix}$ and $B^{-1} = \begin{bmatrix} 1 & 2 & 0 \\ 0 & 3 & -1 \\ 1 & 0 & 2 \end{bmatrix}$. [NCERT]

22 Suppose a matrix B of order 2×2 such that $B\begin{bmatrix}1 & -2\\1 & 4\end{bmatrix}=\begin{bmatrix}6 & 0\\0 & 6\end{bmatrix}$. Find matrix B by using the inverse of matrix method.

23 Show that the matrix $A=\begin{bmatrix}3 & 1\\-1 & 2\end{bmatrix}$ satisfies the equation $A^2-5A+7I=O$. Hence find A^{-1}. **[NCERT]**

24 Show that $A=\begin{bmatrix}2 & -3\\3 & 4\end{bmatrix}$ satisfies the equation $x^2-6x+17=0$. Hence find A^{-1}.

25 For the matrix $A=\begin{bmatrix}3 & 1\\7 & 5\end{bmatrix}$, find x and y, so that $A^2+xI=yA$. Hence find A^{-1}.

Long Answer Type Questions

6 Marks

26 If $A=\begin{bmatrix}3 & -2\\4 & -2\end{bmatrix}$, then find x such that $A^2=xA-2I$. Then, find A^{-1}. **[ISC 2011]**

27 If $A=\begin{bmatrix}1 & 2 & 2\\2 & 1 & 2\\2 & 2 & 1\end{bmatrix}$, then prove that $A^2-4A-5I=O$. Hence find A^{-1}.

28 If $A=\begin{bmatrix}2 & -1 & 1\\-1 & 2 & -1\\1 & -1 & 2\end{bmatrix}$, then verify that $A^3-6A^2+9A-4I=O$ and hence find A^{-1}. **[NCERT]**

Hints & Solutions

1. Similar as Example 1.
[**Ans.** (i) Singular (ii) Singular (iii) Non-singular]

2. Similar as Example 3 (i).
$\left[\textbf{Ans.} \text{(i)} \begin{bmatrix}4 & -2\\-8 & -1\end{bmatrix} \quad \text{(ii)} \begin{bmatrix}-4 & 3\\-2 & 5\end{bmatrix}\right]$

3. (i) **Hint** Use $A(\text{adj } A)=|A|I$ [**Ans.** $|A|=8$]

(ii) Clearly, $|3AB|=3^3\,|A|\,|B|=27\times5\times3=405$

[$\because$ if matrix A is of order $n\times n$, then $|kA|=k^n|A|$ and $|AB|=|A|\,|B|$] [1]

4. (i) Given, $|A|=4$

Clearly, $|\text{adj}(A)|=|A|^{3-1}=|A|^2=4^2=16$ [1]

(ii) We know that for a non-singular square matrix of order n, $|\text{adj}(A)|=|A|^{n-1}$.

Here, $n=3$.

$\therefore \quad |\text{adj}(A)|=|A|^{3-1}=|A|^2$ [1/2]

Given, $|\text{adj } A|=64$

$\Rightarrow \quad 64=|A|^2 \Rightarrow (8)^2=|A|^2$

$\Rightarrow \quad |A|=\pm 8$ [taking square root] [1/2]

5. Similar as Example 8 (i).
$\left[\textbf{Ans. } A^{-1}=\frac{1}{14}\begin{bmatrix}3 & 2\\-4 & 2\end{bmatrix}\right]$

6. **Hint** A^{-1} exists, if $|A|\neq 0 \Rightarrow \lambda \neq -\frac{8}{5}$

$\left[\textbf{Ans. } \lambda \in R-\left\{\frac{-8}{5}\right\}\right]$

7. Let $A=\begin{bmatrix}\cos\theta & \sin\theta\\-\sin\theta & \cos\theta\end{bmatrix}$, then

$|A|=\begin{vmatrix}\cos\theta & \sin\theta\\-\sin\theta & \cos\theta\end{vmatrix}=\cos^2\theta+\sin^2\theta=1\neq 0$

$\therefore \; A^{-1}$ exists. [1]

Also, $\text{adj}(A)=\begin{bmatrix}\cos\theta & -\sin\theta\\\sin\theta & \cos\theta\end{bmatrix}$

$\left[\because \text{adj}\begin{bmatrix}a & b\\c & d\end{bmatrix}=\begin{bmatrix}d & -b\\-c & a\end{bmatrix}\right]$

Now, $A^{-1}=\frac{1}{|A|}\text{adj}(A)=\begin{bmatrix}\cos\theta & -\sin\theta\\\sin\theta & \cos\theta\end{bmatrix}$ [1]

8. $(A^3)^{-1}=(AAA)^{-1}$

$=A^{-1}A^{-1}A^{-1}=(A^{-1})^3$

[$\because (ABC)^{-1}=C^{-1}B^{-1}A^{-1}$] [2]

9. Since, A is an invertible matrix, therefore we have

(i) $A^{-1}=\frac{1}{|A|}\text{adj}(A) \Rightarrow \text{adj}(A)=|A|\cdot A^{-1}$,

which is correct. [1/2]

(ii) $\because (A+B)^{-1}\neq B^{-1}+A^{-1}$, so given result is incorrect. [1/2]

(iii) $\because \det(A^{-1})=(\det(A))^{-1} \Rightarrow \det(A^{-1})=\frac{1}{\det(A)}$

$\Rightarrow \det(A)\cdot\det(A^{-1})=1$, which is correct. [1]

10. Let $A=\begin{bmatrix}2\sin x & 3\\1 & 2\sin x\end{bmatrix}$

$\because$ A is a singular matrix. [1/2]

$\therefore \quad |A|=0 \Rightarrow \begin{vmatrix}2\sin x & 3\\1 & 2\sin x\end{vmatrix}=0$

$\Rightarrow \quad 4\sin^2 x-3=0 \Rightarrow \sin^2 x=\frac{3}{4}$

$\Rightarrow \quad \sin x=\frac{\sqrt{3}}{2}$ $\left[\because \frac{\pi}{2}<x<\pi\right]$ [1]

$\Rightarrow \quad x=\frac{2\pi}{3}$ [1/2]

11. Similar as Example 3 (ii). $\left[\textbf{Ans.} \begin{bmatrix} 2 & 3 & -13 \\ -3 & 6 & 9 \\ 5 & -3 & -1 \end{bmatrix}\right]$

12. We have, $A = \begin{bmatrix} 1 & 2 \\ 3 & 4 \end{bmatrix}$, therefore $|A| = \begin{vmatrix} 1 & 2 \\ 3 & 4 \end{vmatrix}$

Now, cofactors of elements of $|A|$ are

$C_{11} = (-1)^{1+1} \times 4 = 4;\ C_{12} = (-1)^{1+2} \times 3 = -3;$

$C_{21} = (-1)^{2+1} \times 2 = -2$ and $C_{22} = (-1)^{2+2} \times 1 = 1$ [1]

$\therefore\ \text{adj}(A) = \begin{bmatrix} C_{11} & C_{12} \\ C_{21} & C_{22} \end{bmatrix}^T = \begin{bmatrix} 4 & -3 \\ -2 & 1 \end{bmatrix}^T = \begin{bmatrix} 4 & -2 \\ -3 & 1 \end{bmatrix}$ [1]

Now, $|A| = \begin{vmatrix} 1 & 2 \\ 3 & 4 \end{vmatrix} = 4 - 6 = -2$ ...(i) [1/2]

and $A[\text{adj}(A)] = \begin{bmatrix} 1 & 2 \\ 3 & 4 \end{bmatrix}\begin{bmatrix} 4 & -2 \\ -3 & 1 \end{bmatrix} = \begin{bmatrix} 4-6 & -2+2 \\ 12-12 & -6+4 \end{bmatrix}$ [1]

$= \begin{bmatrix} -2 & 0 \\ 0 & -2 \end{bmatrix} = -2\begin{bmatrix} 1 & 0 \\ 0 & 1 \end{bmatrix} = |A|\, I$

[from Eq. (i)]

Hence, $A[\text{adj}(A)] = |A|\, I.$ [1/2]

13. Hint

(i) Compute A^{-1}, $2A^{-1}$ and $9I - A$.

(ii) Prove LHS = RHS $\left[\textbf{Ans. } A^{-1} = \frac{1}{2}\begin{bmatrix} 7 & 3 \\ 4 & 2 \end{bmatrix}\right]$

14. Given, $A = \begin{bmatrix} 1 & \tan x \\ -\tan x & 1 \end{bmatrix}$

Now, $|A| = \begin{vmatrix} 1 & \tan x \\ -\tan x & 1 \end{vmatrix} = 1 + \tan^2 x \neq 0$ [1/2]

$\therefore\ A^{-1}$ exists. Let C_{ij} be the cofactor of a_{ij} in $|A|$. Then,

$C_{11} = (-1)^{1+1}1 = 1;\ C_{12} = (-1)^{1+2}(-\tan x) = \tan x;$

$C_{21} = (-1)^{2+1}\tan x = -\tan x$ and $C_{22} = (-1)^{2+2}1 = 1$ [1]

$\therefore \text{adj}(A) = \begin{bmatrix} C_{11} & C_{12} \\ C_{21} & C_{22} \end{bmatrix}^T$

$= \begin{bmatrix} 1 & \tan x \\ -\tan x & 1 \end{bmatrix}^T$

$= \begin{bmatrix} 1 & -\tan x \\ \tan x & 1 \end{bmatrix}$ [1/2]

$\because\ A^{-1} = \frac{1}{|A|}\text{adj}(A)$

$\therefore\ A^{-1} = \frac{1}{1+\tan^2 x}\begin{bmatrix} 1 & -\tan x \\ \tan x & 1 \end{bmatrix}$

$= \begin{bmatrix} \frac{1}{1+\tan^2 x} & \frac{-\tan x}{1+\tan^2 x} \\ \frac{\tan x}{1+\tan^2 x} & \frac{1}{1+\tan^2 x} \end{bmatrix}$ [1]

Now, $A^T A^{-1} = \begin{bmatrix} 1 & -\tan x \\ \tan x & 1 \end{bmatrix}\begin{bmatrix} \frac{1}{1+\tan^2 x} & \frac{-\tan x}{1+\tan^2 x} \\ \frac{\tan x}{1+\tan^2 x} & \frac{1}{1+\tan^2 x} \end{bmatrix}$

$= \begin{bmatrix} \frac{1}{1+\tan^2 x} - \frac{\tan^2 x}{1+\tan^2 x} & -\frac{\tan x}{1+\tan^2 x} - \frac{\tan x}{1+\tan^2 x} \\ \frac{\tan x}{1+\tan^2 x} + \frac{\tan x}{1+\tan^2 x} & -\frac{\tan^2 x}{1+\tan^2 x} + \frac{1}{1+\tan^2 x} \end{bmatrix}$

[multiplying rows by columns]

$= \begin{bmatrix} \frac{1-\tan^2 x}{1+\tan^2 x} & -\frac{2\tan x}{1+\tan^2 x} \\ \frac{2\tan x}{1+\tan^2 x} & \frac{1-\tan^2 x}{1+\tan^2 x} \end{bmatrix}$

$= \begin{bmatrix} \cos 2x & -\sin 2x \\ \sin 2x & \cos 2x \end{bmatrix}$ **Hence verified.** [1]

15. Similar as Example 8 (ii). $\left[\textbf{Ans. } \frac{-1}{3}\begin{bmatrix} -3 & 0 & 0 \\ 3 & -1 & 0 \\ -9 & -2 & 3 \end{bmatrix}\right]$

16. Let $A = \begin{bmatrix} 1 & 0 & 0 \\ 0 & \cos\alpha & \sin\alpha \\ 0 & \sin\alpha & -\cos\alpha \end{bmatrix}$.

Then, $|A| = \begin{vmatrix} 1 & 0 & 0 \\ 0 & \cos\alpha & \sin\alpha \\ 0 & \sin\alpha & -\cos\alpha \end{vmatrix}$

$= 1(-\cos^2\alpha - \sin^2\alpha)$

$= -(\cos^2\alpha + \sin^2\alpha)$

$= -(1) = -1 \neq 0$ [1/2]

$\therefore\ A^{-1}$ exists.

Now, cofactors of elements of $|A|$ are

$C_{11} = (-1)^{1+1}\begin{vmatrix} \cos\alpha & \sin\alpha \\ \sin\alpha & -\cos\alpha \end{vmatrix}$

$= (-\cos^2\alpha - \sin^2\alpha) = -1$ $[\because \cos^2\theta + \sin^2\theta = 1]$

$C_{12} = (-1)^{1+2}\begin{vmatrix} 0 & \sin\alpha \\ 0 & -\cos\alpha \end{vmatrix} = -(0) = 0$

$C_{13} = (-1)^{1+3}\begin{vmatrix} 0 & \cos\alpha \\ 0 & \sin\alpha \end{vmatrix} = 1(0) = 0$

$C_{21} = (-1)^{2+1}\begin{vmatrix} 0 & 0 \\ \sin\alpha & -\cos\alpha \end{vmatrix} = -1(0) = 0$

$C_{22} = (-1)^{2+2}\begin{vmatrix} 1 & 0 \\ 0 & -\cos\alpha \end{vmatrix} = (-\cos\alpha - 0) = -\cos\alpha$

$C_{23} = (-1)^{2+3}\begin{vmatrix} 1 & 0 \\ 0 & \sin\alpha \end{vmatrix} = -(\sin\alpha) = -\sin\alpha$

$C_{31} = (-1)^{3+1}\begin{vmatrix} 0 & 0 \\ \cos\alpha & \sin\alpha \end{vmatrix} = 0$

$$C_{32} = (-1)^{3+2}\begin{vmatrix}1 & 0\\ 0 & \sin\alpha\end{vmatrix} = -(\sin\alpha - 0) = -\sin\alpha$$

$$C_{33} = (-1)^{3+3}\begin{vmatrix}1 & 0\\ 0 & \cos\alpha\end{vmatrix} = (\cos\alpha - 0) = \cos\alpha$$ [1½]

$$\therefore \text{adj}(A) = \begin{bmatrix}C_{11} & C_{12} & C_{13}\\ C_{21} & C_{22} & C_{23}\\ C_{31} & C_{32} & C_{33}\end{bmatrix}^T$$

$$= \begin{bmatrix}-1 & 0 & 0\\ 0 & -\cos\alpha & -\sin\alpha\\ 0 & -\sin\alpha & \cos\alpha\end{bmatrix}^T$$

$$= \begin{bmatrix}-1 & 0 & 0\\ 0 & -\cos\alpha & -\sin\alpha\\ 0 & -\sin\alpha & \cos\alpha\end{bmatrix}$$ [1]

and $A^{-1} = \frac{1}{|A|}[\text{adj}(A)]$

$$= \frac{1}{-1}\begin{bmatrix}-1 & 0 & 0\\ 0 & -\cos\alpha & -\sin\alpha\\ 0 & -\sin\alpha & \cos\alpha\end{bmatrix}$$

$$= \begin{bmatrix}1 & 0 & 0\\ 0 & \cos\alpha & \sin\alpha\\ 0 & \sin\alpha & -\cos\alpha\end{bmatrix}$$ [1]

17. Similar as Example 9 (i).

18. **Hint** Compute A^{-1} and A^2 and prove the result.

19. We have, $A = \begin{bmatrix}0 & 1 & 1\\ 1 & 0 & 1\\ 1 & 1 & 0\end{bmatrix}$

Now, cofactors of elements of $|A|$ are

$C_{11} = -1, C_{12} = 1, C_{13} = 1, C_{21} = 1, C_{22} = -1,$
$C_{23} = 1, C_{31} = 1, C_{32} = 1$ and $C_{33} = -1$ [1]

$$\therefore \text{adj}(A) = \begin{bmatrix}-1 & 1 & 1\\ 1 & -1 & 1\\ 1 & 1 & -1\end{bmatrix}^T = \begin{bmatrix}-1 & 1 & 1\\ 1 & -1 & 1\\ 1 & 1 & -1\end{bmatrix}$$ [1/2]

Also, $|A| = -1(-1) + 1\cdot 1 = 2$ [1/2]

$$\text{Now, } A^{-1} = \frac{\text{adj}(A)}{|A|} = \frac{1}{2}\begin{bmatrix}-1 & 1 & 1\\ 1 & -1 & 1\\ 1 & 1 & -1\end{bmatrix} \quad ...(i)$$

$$\text{and } A^2 = \begin{bmatrix}0 & 1 & 1\\ 1 & 0 & 1\\ 1 & 1 & 0\end{bmatrix}\cdot\begin{bmatrix}0 & 1 & 1\\ 1 & 0 & 1\\ 1 & 1 & 0\end{bmatrix} = \begin{bmatrix}2 & 1 & 1\\ 1 & 2 & 1\\ 1 & 1 & 2\end{bmatrix} \quad ...(ii)$$ [1]

$$\therefore \frac{A^2 - 3I}{2} = \frac{1}{2}\left\{\begin{bmatrix}2 & 1 & 1\\ 1 & 2 & 1\\ 1 & 1 & 2\end{bmatrix} - \begin{bmatrix}3 & 0 & 0\\ 0 & 3 & 0\\ 0 & 0 & 3\end{bmatrix}\right\}$$

$$= \frac{1}{2}\begin{bmatrix}-1 & 1 & 1\\ 1 & -1 & 1\\ 1 & 1 & -1\end{bmatrix} = A^{-1}$$ [using Eq. (i)]

Hence proved. [1]

20. We have, $A = \begin{bmatrix}1 & -2 & 3\\ 0 & -1 & 4\\ -2 & 2 & 1\end{bmatrix}$.

$$\text{Now, } |A| = \begin{vmatrix}1 & -2 & 3\\ 0 & -1 & 4\\ -2 & 2 & 1\end{vmatrix} = 1(-1-8) + 2(0+8) + 3(0-2)$$

[expanding along R_1]

$= -9 + 16 - 6 = 1 \neq 0$

$\therefore A^{-1}$ exists. [1/2]

Cofactors of elements of $|A|$ are

$$C_{11} = (-1)^{1+1}\begin{vmatrix}-1 & 4\\ 2 & 1\end{vmatrix} = (-1-8) = -9$$

$$C_{12} = (-1)^{1+2}\begin{vmatrix}0 & 4\\ -2 & 1\end{vmatrix} = -(0+8) = -8$$

$$C_{13} = (-1)^{1+3}\begin{vmatrix}0 & -1\\ -2 & 2\end{vmatrix} = (0-2) = -2$$

$$C_{21} = (-1)^{2+1}\begin{vmatrix}-2 & 3\\ 2 & 1\end{vmatrix} = -(-2-6) = 8$$

$$C_{22} = (-1)^{2+2}\begin{vmatrix}1 & 3\\ -2 & 1\end{vmatrix} = (1+6) = 7$$

$$C_{23} = (-1)^{2+3}\begin{vmatrix}1 & -2\\ -2 & 2\end{vmatrix} = -(2-4) = 2$$

$$C_{31} = (-1)^{3+1}\begin{vmatrix}-2 & 3\\ -1 & 4\end{vmatrix} = (-8+3) = -5$$

$$C_{32} = (-1)^{3+2}\begin{vmatrix}1 & 3\\ 0 & 4\end{vmatrix} = -(4-0) = -4$$

$$C_{33} = (-1)^{3+3}\begin{vmatrix}1 & -2\\ 0 & -1\end{vmatrix} = (-1-0) = -1$$ [1½]

$$\text{Thus, adj}(A) = \begin{bmatrix}C_{11} & C_{21} & C_{31}\\ C_{12} & C_{22} & C_{32}\\ C_{13} & C_{23} & C_{33}\end{bmatrix} = \begin{bmatrix}-9 & 8 & -5\\ -8 & 7 & -4\\ -2 & 2 & -1\end{bmatrix}$$

$$\therefore \quad A^{-1} = \frac{1}{|A|}\text{adj}(A) = \frac{1}{1}\begin{bmatrix}-9 & 8 & -5\\ -8 & 7 & -4\\ -2 & 2 & -1\end{bmatrix}$$ [1]

$$\text{Now, } (A')^{-1} = (A^{-1})' = \begin{bmatrix}-9 & 8 & -5\\ -8 & 7 & -4\\ -2 & 2 & -1\end{bmatrix}'$$

$$= \begin{bmatrix}-9 & -8 & -2\\ 8 & 7 & 2\\ -5 & -4 & -1\end{bmatrix}$$ [1]

21. We have, $A = \begin{bmatrix}1 & 1 & 2\\ 0 & 2 & -3\\ 3 & -2 & 4\end{bmatrix}$.

$$\text{Now, } |A| = \begin{vmatrix}1 & 1 & 2\\ 0 & 2 & -3\\ 3 & -2 & 4\end{vmatrix} = 1(8-6) - 0 + 3(-3-4)$$

[expanding along C_1]

$= 2 - 21 = -19 \neq 0$

$\therefore A^{-1}$ exists. [1/2]

Now, cofactors of elements of $|A|$ are

$$C_{11}=(-1)^{1+1}\begin{vmatrix}2&-3\\-2&4\end{vmatrix}=8-6=2$$

$$C_{12}=(-1)^{1+2}\begin{vmatrix}0&-3\\3&4\end{vmatrix}=-(0+9)=-9$$

$$C_{13}=(-1)^{1+3}\begin{vmatrix}0&2\\3&-2\end{vmatrix}=0-6=-6$$

$$C_{21}=(-1)^{2+1}\begin{vmatrix}1&2\\-2&4\end{vmatrix}=-(4+4)=-8$$

$$C_{22}=(-1)^{2+2}\begin{vmatrix}1&2\\3&4\end{vmatrix}=4-6=-2$$

$$C_{23}=(-1)^{2+3}\begin{vmatrix}1&1\\3&-2\end{vmatrix}=-(-2-3)=5$$

$$C_{31}=(-1)^{3+1}\begin{vmatrix}1&2\\2&-3\end{vmatrix}=-3-4=-7$$

$$C_{32}=(-1)^{3+2}\begin{vmatrix}1&2\\0&-3\end{vmatrix}=-(-3-0)=3$$

$$C_{33}=(-1)^{3+3}\begin{vmatrix}1&1\\0&2\end{vmatrix}=2-0=2$$ [1½]

$$\therefore \quad \text{adj}(A)=\begin{bmatrix}C_{11}&C_{12}&C_{13}\\C_{21}&C_{22}&C_{23}\\C_{31}&C_{32}&C_{33}\end{bmatrix}^T$$

$$=\begin{bmatrix}2&-9&-6\\-8&-2&5\\-7&3&2\end{bmatrix}^T=\begin{bmatrix}2&-8&-7\\-9&-2&3\\-6&5&2\end{bmatrix}$$

and $$A^{-1}=\frac{1}{|A|}\text{adj}(A)=\frac{-1}{19}\begin{bmatrix}2&-8&-7\\-9&-2&3\\-6&5&2\end{bmatrix}$$ [1]

Now, $(AB)^{-1}=B^{-1}A^{-1}$

$$=\begin{bmatrix}1&2&0\\0&3&-1\\1&0&2\end{bmatrix}\cdot\frac{-1}{19}\begin{bmatrix}2&-8&-7\\-9&-2&3\\-6&5&2\end{bmatrix}$$

[$\because (AB)^{-1}=B^{-1}A^{-1}$]

$$=\frac{-1}{19}\begin{bmatrix}2-18-0&-8-4+0&-7+6+0\\0-27+6&0-6-5&0+9-2\\2+0-12&-8+0+10&-7+0+4\end{bmatrix}$$

[multiplying row by column]

$$=\frac{-1}{19}\begin{bmatrix}-16&-12&-1\\-21&-11&7\\-10&2&-3\end{bmatrix}=\begin{bmatrix}\frac{16}{19}&\frac{12}{19}&\frac{1}{19}\\\frac{21}{19}&\frac{11}{19}&\frac{-7}{19}\\\frac{10}{19}&\frac{-2}{19}&\frac{3}{19}\end{bmatrix}$$ [1]

22. Given, $B\begin{bmatrix}1&-2\\1&4\end{bmatrix}=\begin{bmatrix}6&0\\0&6\end{bmatrix}$ ...(i)

Let $A=\begin{bmatrix}1&-2\\1&4\end{bmatrix}$ and $C=\begin{bmatrix}6&0\\0&6\end{bmatrix}$.

Then, Eq. (i) becomes $BA=C\Rightarrow(BA)A^{-1}=CA^{-1}$

[post-multiplying both sides by A^{-1}, as $|A|=\begin{vmatrix}1&-2\\1&4\end{vmatrix}=4+2=6\neq 0$]

$\Rightarrow B(AA^{-1})=CA^{-1}$ [$\because AA^{-1}=I$]

$\Rightarrow \quad B(I)=CA^{-1}\Rightarrow B=CA^{-1}$ ...(ii)

Let C_{ij} be the cofactors of a_{ij} in $|A|$. [1]

Then, $C_{11}=(-1)^{1+1}4=4, C_{12}=(-1)^{1+2}1=-1,$

$C_{21}=(-1)^{2+1}(-2)=2$ and $C_{22}=(-1)^{2+2}1=1$

$$\therefore \quad \text{adj}(A)=\begin{bmatrix}C_{11}&C_{12}\\C_{21}&C_{22}\end{bmatrix}^T$$

$$=\begin{bmatrix}4&-1\\2&1\end{bmatrix}^T=\begin{bmatrix}4&2\\-1&1\end{bmatrix}$$ [1]

and $$A^{-1}=\frac{1}{|A|}\text{adj}(A)=\frac{1}{6}\begin{bmatrix}4&2\\-1&1\end{bmatrix}$$ [1]

$\therefore$ From Eq. (ii), we get

$$B=\begin{bmatrix}6&0\\0&6\end{bmatrix}\frac{1}{6}\begin{bmatrix}4&2\\-1&1\end{bmatrix}=\frac{1}{6}\begin{bmatrix}6&0\\0&6\end{bmatrix}\begin{bmatrix}4&2\\-1&1\end{bmatrix}$$

$$=\frac{1}{6}\begin{bmatrix}24+0&12+0\\0-6&0+6\end{bmatrix}$$ [multiplying row by column]

$$=\frac{1}{6}\begin{bmatrix}24&12\\-6&6\end{bmatrix}=\begin{bmatrix}4&2\\-1&1\end{bmatrix}$$ [1]

23. Similar as Example 11. $\left[\textbf{Ans. } A^{-1}=\frac{1}{7}\begin{bmatrix}2&-1\\1&3\end{bmatrix}\right]$

24. **Hint** (i) To show $A^2-6A+17I_2=O$

(ii) Use above result to find A^{-1}.

$\left[\textbf{Ans. } A^{-1}=\frac{1}{17}\begin{bmatrix}4&3\\-3&2\end{bmatrix}\right]$

25. **Hint** (i) First, find A^2.

(ii) Then, put the values of A^2 and A in the given equation $A^2+xI=yA$. Also, solve it to find x and y.

(iii) Now, use the above result to find A^{-1}, as in Example 11.

$\left[\textbf{Ans. } x=8,\ y=8,\ A^{-1}=\frac{1}{8}\begin{bmatrix}5&-1\\-7&3\end{bmatrix}\right]$

26. Given, $A=\begin{bmatrix}3&-2\\4&-2\end{bmatrix}$

Now, $A^2=A\cdot A$

$$=\begin{bmatrix}3&-2\\4&-2\end{bmatrix}\begin{bmatrix}3&-2\\4&-2\end{bmatrix}$$

$$=\begin{bmatrix}9-8&-6+4\\12-8&-8+4\end{bmatrix}$$

[by multiplication property]

$$=\begin{bmatrix}1&-2\\4&-4\end{bmatrix}$$ ...(i) [1]

Now, $xA = x\begin{bmatrix} 3 & -2 \\ 4 & -2 \end{bmatrix} = \begin{bmatrix} 3x & -2x \\ 4x & -2x \end{bmatrix}$ ...(ii)

$-2I = -2\begin{bmatrix} 1 & 0 \\ 0 & 1 \end{bmatrix} = \begin{bmatrix} -2 & 0 \\ 0 & -2 \end{bmatrix}$ ...(iii) [1]

Also given, $A^2 = xA - 2I$

or $A^2 = xA + (-2I)$

$\Rightarrow \begin{bmatrix} 1 & -2 \\ 4 & -4 \end{bmatrix} = \begin{bmatrix} 3x & -2x \\ 4x & -2x \end{bmatrix} + \begin{bmatrix} -2 & 0 \\ 0 & -2 \end{bmatrix}$

[using Eqs. (i), (ii) and (iii)]

$\Rightarrow \begin{bmatrix} 1 & -2 \\ 4 & -4 \end{bmatrix} = \begin{bmatrix} 3x-2 & -2x \\ 4x & -2x-2 \end{bmatrix}$ [1]

On equating the corresponding elements, we get

$3x - 2 = 1 \Rightarrow 3x = 3 \Rightarrow x = 1$

$\because$ $A^2 = xA - 2I$ [given]

$\therefore$ $A^2 = A - 2I$ [$\because x = 1$]

$\Rightarrow$ $A^2 - A + 2I = O$ ...(iv) [1]

On multiplying both sides by A^{-1} in Eq. (iv), we get

$A^{-1} \cdot A^2 - A^{-1} \cdot A + 2A^{-1} \cdot I = A^{-1} \cdot O$

$\Rightarrow$ $(A^{-1} \cdot A)A - I + 2A^{-1} = O$

[$\because A^{-1}A = I$ and $A^{-1}I = A^{-1}$]

$\Rightarrow$ $I \cdot A - I + 2A^{-1} = O$ [1]

$\Rightarrow$ $2A^{-1} = I - A$ [$\because I \cdot A = A$]

$\Rightarrow$ $2A^{-1} = \begin{bmatrix} 1 & 0 \\ 0 & 1 \end{bmatrix} - \begin{bmatrix} 3 & -2 \\ 4 & -2 \end{bmatrix}$

$\Rightarrow$ $2A^{-1} = \begin{bmatrix} 1-3 & 0+2 \\ 0-4 & 1+2 \end{bmatrix} = \begin{bmatrix} -2 & 2 \\ -4 & 3 \end{bmatrix}$

[by subtraction property]

$\therefore$ $A^{-1} = \frac{1}{2}\begin{bmatrix} -2 & 2 \\ -4 & 3 \end{bmatrix} = \begin{bmatrix} -1 & 1 \\ -2 & 3/2 \end{bmatrix}$ [1]

27. $A^2 = A \cdot A = \begin{bmatrix} 1 & 2 & 2 \\ 2 & 1 & 2 \\ 2 & 2 & 1 \end{bmatrix}\begin{bmatrix} 1 & 2 & 2 \\ 2 & 1 & 2 \\ 2 & 2 & 1 \end{bmatrix}$

$= \begin{bmatrix} 1+4+4 & 2+2+4 & 2+4+2 \\ 2+2+4 & 4+1+4 & 4+2+2 \\ 2+4+2 & 4+2+2 & 4+4+1 \end{bmatrix} = \begin{bmatrix} 9 & 8 & 8 \\ 8 & 9 & 8 \\ 8 & 8 & 9 \end{bmatrix}$

[multiplying rows by columns] [1]

Now, $A^2 - 4A - 5I = \begin{bmatrix} 9 & 8 & 8 \\ 8 & 9 & 8 \\ 8 & 8 & 9 \end{bmatrix} - 4\begin{bmatrix} 1 & 2 & 2 \\ 2 & 1 & 2 \\ 2 & 2 & 1 \end{bmatrix} - 5\begin{bmatrix} 1 & 0 & 0 \\ 0 & 1 & 0 \\ 0 & 0 & 1 \end{bmatrix}$

$= \begin{bmatrix} 9 & 8 & 8 \\ 8 & 9 & 8 \\ 8 & 8 & 9 \end{bmatrix} - \begin{bmatrix} 4 & 8 & 8 \\ 8 & 4 & 8 \\ 8 & 8 & 4 \end{bmatrix} - \begin{bmatrix} 5 & 0 & 0 \\ 0 & 5 & 0 \\ 0 & 0 & 5 \end{bmatrix}$

$= \begin{bmatrix} 9-4-5 & 8-8-0 & 8-8-0 \\ 8-8-0 & 9-4-5 & 8-8-0 \\ 8-8-0 & 8-8-0 & 9-4-5 \end{bmatrix}$

$= \begin{bmatrix} 0 & 0 & 0 \\ 0 & 0 & 0 \\ 0 & 0 & 0 \end{bmatrix}$

$\Rightarrow A^2 - 4A - 5I = O$ [1]

Now, $|A| = \begin{vmatrix} 1 & 2 & 2 \\ 2 & 1 & 2 \\ 2 & 2 & 1 \end{vmatrix} = 1(1-4) - 2(2-4) + 2(4-2)$

[expanding along R_1]

$= -3 + 4 + 4 = 5 \neq 0$

$\therefore$ A^{-1} exists. [1]

$\because$ $A^2 - 4A - 5I = O$

$\therefore$ On pre-multiplying both sides by A^{-1}, we get

$A^{-1}A^2 - 4A^{-1}A - 5A^{-1}I = A^{-1}O$

$\Rightarrow$ $IA - 4I - 5A^{-1} = O$ [$\because A^{-1}I = A^{-1}$ and $A \cdot A^{-1} = I$]

$\Rightarrow$ $5A^{-1} = A - 4I$

$\Rightarrow$ $A^{-1} = \frac{1}{5}(A - 4I)$ [1½]

$\Rightarrow$ $A^{-1} = \frac{1}{5}\left(\begin{bmatrix} 1 & 2 & 2 \\ 2 & 1 & 2 \\ 2 & 2 & 1 \end{bmatrix} - 4\begin{bmatrix} 1 & 0 & 0 \\ 0 & 1 & 0 \\ 0 & 0 & 1 \end{bmatrix}\right)$

$= \frac{1}{5}\begin{bmatrix} 1-4 & 2-0 & 2-0 \\ 2-0 & 1-4 & 2-0 \\ 2-0 & 2-0 & 1-4 \end{bmatrix}$

$\Rightarrow$ $A^{-1} = \frac{1}{5}\begin{bmatrix} -3 & 2 & 2 \\ 2 & -3 & 2 \\ 2 & 2 & -3 \end{bmatrix}$ [1½]

28. Solve as Question 27.

$\left[\textbf{Ans. } A^{-1} = \frac{1}{4}\begin{bmatrix} 3 & 1 & -1 \\ 1 & 3 & 1 \\ -1 & 1 & 3 \end{bmatrix}\right]$

TOPIC 04 Applications of Determinants and Matrices

Determinants and matrices can be used for solving the system of linear equations in two or three variables and for checking the consistency of the system of linear equations.

Consistent and Inconsistent System

A system of equations is said to be **consistent**, if its solution (one or more) exists and a system of equations is said to be **inconsistent**, if its solution does not exist, i.e. no solution exist.

Solution of System of Linear Equations using Inverse of a Matrix (Martin's Rule)

1. When System of Equations is Non-Homogeneous

Let the system of linear equations in three variables are

$$a_1x + b_1y + c_1z = d_1,\ a_2x + b_2y + c_2z = d_2$$

and $\quad a_3x + b_3y + c_3z = d_3.$

Now, let $A = \begin{bmatrix} a_1 & b_1 & c_1 \\ a_2 & b_2 & c_2 \\ a_3 & b_3 & c_3 \end{bmatrix}$, $X = \begin{bmatrix} x \\ y \\ z \end{bmatrix}$ and $B = \begin{bmatrix} d_1 \\ d_2 \\ d_3 \end{bmatrix}$,

where A, X and B are known as **coefficient matrix, variable matrix** and **constant matrix** respectively.

Then, the matrix representation of above system of linear equations is

$$AX = B \qquad \text{...(i)}$$

Case I *If A is a non-singular matrix*

Here, A is a non-singular matrix, i.e. $|A| \neq 0$, therefore inverse of A exists.

Now, pre-multiplying Eq. (i) by A^{-1}, we get

$$A^{-1}(AX) = A^{-1}B$$

$$\Rightarrow \quad (A^{-1}A)X = A^{-1}B \quad \text{[by associative property]}$$

$$\Rightarrow \quad IX = A^{-1}B$$

$$\Rightarrow \quad X = A^{-1}B \quad [\because IX = X]$$

This method of solving system of equations is known as **Matrix method** or **Martin's Rule**. As we know that inverse of a matrix is unique, so we get **unique solution** for the given system of equations and this system of equations is consistent.

Case II *If A is a singular matrix*

Here, A is a singular matrix, i.e. $|A| = 0$, therefore its inverse does not exist. In this case, we calculate (adj A)B. Then, we have two conditions

(i) If (adj A)$B \neq O$ (where O being zero matrix), then solution does not exist and the system of equations is **inconsistent**.

(ii) If (adj A) $B = O$, then system of equations may be either consistent or inconsistent, according as system have **either infinitely many solutions** or **no solution**.

In the form of diagram, above cases can be represented as

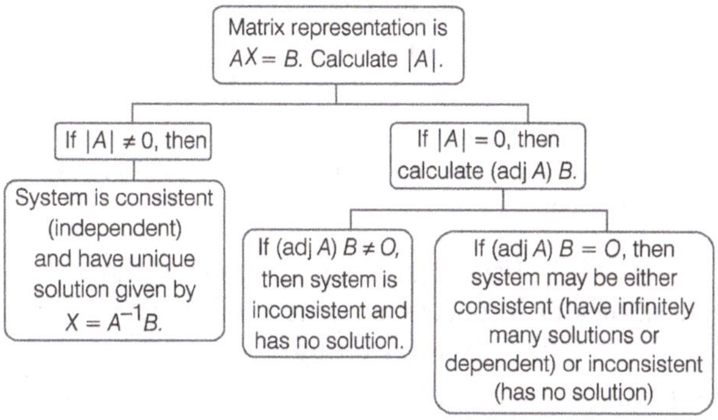

2. When System of Equations is Homogeneous

If the system of linear equations, written in matrix form as $AX = O$, then the given system of equations is called homogeneous system of linear equations. In that case, if

(i) A is non-singular matrix, then A^{-1} exists. So, it has unique solution, i.e. $x_1 = x_2 = \ldots = x_n = 0$, which is also called as **trivial solution**.

(ii) A is singular matrix, i.e $|A| = 0$, then the given system of equations is consistent (or dependent) and it has infinitely many solutions.

Example 1 Examine the consistency of the system of equations $x + 2y = 2$ and $2x + 3y = 3$. **[NCERT]**

Sol. The given system of equations can be written in matrix form as

$$AX = B,$$

where $A = \begin{bmatrix} 1 & 2 \\ 2 & 3 \end{bmatrix}$, $X = \begin{bmatrix} x \\ y \end{bmatrix}$ and $B = \begin{bmatrix} 2 \\ 3 \end{bmatrix}$

Now, $|A| = \begin{vmatrix} 1 & 2 \\ 2 & 3 \end{vmatrix} = 1(3) - 2(2) = 3 - 4 = -1 \neq 0$

Since, A is non-singular, so A^{-1} exists.

Hence, the given system of equations is consistent.

Example 2 Test the consistency of the system of equations $3x - y = 5$ and $6x - 2y = 3$.

Sol. Given system of equations is $3x - y = 5$ ...(i)

and $6x - 2y = 3$ ...(ii)

Given equations can be written in matrix form as

$$AX = B,$$

where $A = \begin{bmatrix} 3 & -1 \\ 6 & -2 \end{bmatrix}, X = \begin{bmatrix} x \\ y \end{bmatrix}$ and $B = \begin{bmatrix} 5 \\ 3 \end{bmatrix}$

Now, $|A| = \begin{vmatrix} 3 & -1 \\ 6 & -2 \end{vmatrix} = -6 + 6 = 0$

$\therefore A^{-1}$ does not exist.

Now, $\text{adj}(A) = \begin{bmatrix} -2 & 1 \\ -6 & 3 \end{bmatrix}$ $\left[\because \text{adj}\begin{bmatrix} a & b \\ c & d \end{bmatrix} = \begin{bmatrix} d & -b \\ -c & a \end{bmatrix}\right]$

$\therefore \quad \text{adj}(A)B = \begin{bmatrix} -2 & 1 \\ -6 & 3 \end{bmatrix}\begin{bmatrix} 5 \\ 3 \end{bmatrix}$

$= \begin{bmatrix} -10 + 3 \\ -30 + 9 \end{bmatrix} = \begin{bmatrix} -7 \\ -21 \end{bmatrix}$

$\Rightarrow \text{adj}(A)B \neq O$

Hence, the equations are inconsistent and have no solution.

Example 3 Using Martin's rule, examine the consistency or inconsistency of the following

$2x + 3y = 5, 4x + 6y = 10$

Sol. Given system of equations is

$2x + 3y = 5$ ...(i)

$4x + 6y = 10$ ... (ii)

In matrix form, it may be represented as

$$AX = B,$$

where $A = \begin{bmatrix} 2 & 3 \\ 4 & 6 \end{bmatrix}, X = \begin{bmatrix} x \\ y \end{bmatrix}$ and $B = \begin{bmatrix} 5 \\ 10 \end{bmatrix}$

Now, $|A| = \begin{vmatrix} 2 & 3 \\ 4 & 6 \end{vmatrix} = -12 - 12 = 0$

$\Rightarrow A^{-1}$ does not exist.

Now, $\text{adj}(A) = \begin{bmatrix} 6 & -3 \\ -4 & 2 \end{bmatrix}$

$\therefore \text{adj}(A)B = \begin{bmatrix} 6 & -3 \\ -4 & 2 \end{bmatrix}\begin{bmatrix} 5 \\ 10 \end{bmatrix} = \begin{bmatrix} 30 - 30 \\ -20 + 20 \end{bmatrix} = \begin{bmatrix} 0 \\ 0 \end{bmatrix} = O$

Since, $\text{adj}(A)B = O$, therefore the given system of equations has infinite number of solutions or no solution.

On putting $y = k$ in Eq. (i), we get

$2x + 3k = 5$

$\Rightarrow \quad 2x = 5 - 3k \Rightarrow x = \frac{1}{2}(5 - 3k)$

Again, on putting $y = k$ in Eq. (ii), we get

$4x + 6k = 10 \Rightarrow 2x + 3k = 5$

$\Rightarrow \quad x = \frac{1}{2}(5 - 3k)$

Here, we get same value of x from both equations, if on putting $y = k$ in both the given equations, therefore the given system of equations has infinite many solutions. Hence, the given system of equation is consistent.

Example 4 Using the matrices, determine whether the following of equations is consistent or inconsistent.

(i) $5x - y + 4z = 5, 2x + 3y + 5z = 2, 5x - 2y + 6z = -1$

(ii) $3x - y - 2z = 2, 2y - z = -1, 3x - 5y = 3$ [NCERT]

Sol. (i) The given system of equations is $5x - y + 4z = 5$, $2x + 3y + 5z = 2$ and $5x - 2y + 6z = -1$

In matrix form, it may be represented as $AX = B$,

where $A = \begin{bmatrix} 5 & -1 & 4 \\ 2 & 3 & 5 \\ 5 & -2 & 6 \end{bmatrix}, X = \begin{bmatrix} x \\ y \\ z \end{bmatrix}$ and $B = \begin{bmatrix} 5 \\ 2 \\ -1 \end{bmatrix}$

Now $|A| = \begin{vmatrix} 5 & -1 & 4 \\ 2 & 3 & 5 \\ 5 & -2 & 6 \end{vmatrix}$

$= 5(18 + 10) - (-1)(12 - 25) + 4(-4 - 15)$

$= 140 - 13 - 76 = 51 \neq 0$ [expanding along R_1]

Thus, A is a non-singular matrix.

$\therefore A^{-1}$ exists and the given system has a unique solution.

Hence, the given system is consistent.

(ii) The given system of equations is $3x - y - 2z = 2$, $2y - z = -1$ and $3x - 5y = 3$.

In matrix form, it may be represented as $AX = B$,

where $A = \begin{bmatrix} 3 & -1 & -2 \\ 0 & 2 & -1 \\ 3 & -5 & 0 \end{bmatrix}, X = \begin{bmatrix} x \\ y \\ z \end{bmatrix}$ and $B = \begin{bmatrix} 2 \\ -1 \\ 3 \end{bmatrix}$

Now, $|A| = \begin{vmatrix} 3 & -1 & -2 \\ 0 & 2 & -1 \\ 3 & -5 & 0 \end{vmatrix}$

$= 3(0 - 5) + 3(1 + 4)$ [expanding along C_1]

$= -15 + 15 = 0$

Now, we calculate $(\text{adj}A)B$.

Here, $C_{11} = (-1)^{1+1}\begin{vmatrix} 2 & -1 \\ -5 & 0 \end{vmatrix} = -5,$

$C_{12} = (-1)^{1+2}\begin{vmatrix} 0 & -1 \\ 3 & 0 \end{vmatrix} = -3,$

$C_{13} = (-1)^{1+3}\begin{vmatrix} 0 & 2 \\ 3 & -5 \end{vmatrix} = -6;$

$$C_{21} = (-1)^{2+1} \begin{vmatrix} -1 & -2 \\ -5 & 0 \end{vmatrix} = 10,$$

$$C_{22} = (-1)^{2+2} \begin{vmatrix} 3 & -2 \\ 3 & 0 \end{vmatrix} = 6,$$

$$C_{23} = (-1)^{2+3} \begin{vmatrix} 3 & -1 \\ 3 & -5 \end{vmatrix} = 12;$$

$$C_{31} = (-1)^{3+1} \begin{vmatrix} -1 & -2 \\ 2 & -1 \end{vmatrix} = 5,$$

$$C_{32} = (-1)^{3+2} \begin{vmatrix} 3 & -2 \\ 0 & -1 \end{vmatrix} = 3,$$

and $C_{33} = (-1)^{3+3} \begin{vmatrix} 3 & -1 \\ 0 & 2 \end{vmatrix} = 6,$

$$\therefore \text{adj}(A) = \begin{bmatrix} C_{11} & C_{12} & C_{13} \\ C_{21} & C_{22} & C_{23} \\ C_{31} & C_{32} & C_{33} \end{bmatrix}^T = \begin{bmatrix} -5 & -3 & -6 \\ 10 & 6 & 12 \\ 5 & 3 & 6 \end{bmatrix}^T$$

$$= \begin{bmatrix} -5 & 10 & 5 \\ -3 & 6 & 3 \\ -6 & 12 & 6 \end{bmatrix}$$

$$\therefore \text{adj } A) B = \begin{bmatrix} -5 & 10 & 5 \\ -3 & 6 & 3 \\ -6 & 12 & 6 \end{bmatrix} \begin{bmatrix} 2 \\ -1 \\ 3 \end{bmatrix}$$

$$= \begin{bmatrix} -10-10+15 \\ -6-6+9 \\ -12-12+18 \end{bmatrix} = \begin{bmatrix} -5 \\ -3 \\ -6 \end{bmatrix} \neq O$$

Hence, the given system is inconsistent.

Example 5 Show that the following equations is consistent.

$x - y + z = 3$, $2x + y - z = 2$ and $-x - 2y + 2z = 1$

Sol. The given system of equation is

$$x - y + z = 3 \quad \text{... (i)}$$

$$2x + y - z = 2 \quad \text{... (ii)}$$

and $$-x - 2y + 2z = 1 \quad \text{... (iii)}$$

In matrix form, it may be represented as

$$AX = B,$$

where $A = \begin{bmatrix} 1 & -1 & 1 \\ 2 & 1 & -1 \\ -1 & -2 & 2 \end{bmatrix}, X = \begin{bmatrix} x \\ y \\ z \end{bmatrix}, B = \begin{bmatrix} 3 \\ 2 \\ 1 \end{bmatrix}$

Now, $|A| = \begin{vmatrix} 1 & -1 & 1 \\ 2 & 1 & -1 \\ -1 & -2 & 2 \end{vmatrix}$

$$= 1(2-2) + 1(4-1) + 1(-4+1) = 0 + 3 - 3 = 0$$

Hence, the given system of equation has either no solution or infinitely many solutions.

According $(\text{adj}A)B = O$ or $(\text{adj}A)\, B \neq O$, the given system of equations will be consistent or inconsistent.

Cofactors of elements of $|A|$ are

$$C_{11} = (-1)^{1+1} \begin{vmatrix} 1 & -1 \\ -2 & 2 \end{vmatrix} = 2 - 2 = 0$$

$$C_{12} = (-1)^{1+2} \begin{vmatrix} 2 & -1 \\ -1 & 2 \end{vmatrix} = -(4-1) = -3$$

$$C_{13} = (-1)^{1+3} \begin{vmatrix} 2 & 1 \\ -1 & -2 \end{vmatrix} = -4 + 1 = -3$$

$$C_{21} = (-1)^{2+1} \begin{vmatrix} -1 & 1 \\ -2 & 2 \end{vmatrix} = -(-2+2) = 0$$

$$C_{22} = (-1)^{2+2} \begin{vmatrix} 1 & 1 \\ -1 & 2 \end{vmatrix} = 2 + 1 = 3$$

$$C_{23} = (-1)^{2+3} \begin{vmatrix} 1 & -1 \\ -1 & -2 \end{vmatrix} = -(-2-1) = 3$$

$$C_{31} = (-1)^{3+1} \begin{vmatrix} -1 & 1 \\ 1 & -1 \end{vmatrix} = (1-1) = 0$$

$$C_{32} = (-1)^{3+2} \begin{vmatrix} 1 & 1 \\ 2 & -1 \end{vmatrix} = -(-1-2) = 3$$

and $C_{33} = (-1)^{3+3} \begin{vmatrix} 1 & -1 \\ 2 & 1 \end{vmatrix} = (1+2) = 3$

$$\therefore \quad \text{adj}(A) = \begin{bmatrix} C_{11} & C_{12} & C_{13} \\ C_{21} & C_{22} & C_{23} \\ C_{31} & C_{32} & C_{33} \end{bmatrix}^T$$

$$= \begin{bmatrix} 0 & -3 & -3 \\ 0 & 3 & 3 \\ 0 & 3 & 3 \end{bmatrix}^T = \begin{bmatrix} 0 & 0 & 0 \\ -3 & 3 & 3 \\ -3 & 3 & 3 \end{bmatrix}$$

Now, $(\text{adj } A)\, B = \begin{bmatrix} 0 & 0 & 0 \\ -3 & 3 & 3 \\ -3 & 3 & 3 \end{bmatrix} \begin{bmatrix} 3 \\ 2 \\ 1 \end{bmatrix}$

$$= \begin{bmatrix} 0 \\ -9+6+3 \\ -9+6+3 \end{bmatrix} = \begin{bmatrix} 0 \\ 0 \\ 0 \end{bmatrix} = O$$

Since, $(\text{adj}A)B = O$

$\therefore$ The given system of equation may be either consistent (have infinitely many solutions) or inconsistent (has no solution).

On putting $z = t$ in Eqs. (i) and (ii), we get

$$x - y = 3 - t \quad \text{...(iv)}$$

and $$2x + y = 2 + t \quad \text{...(v)}$$

On solving Eqs. (iv) and (v), we get $x = \frac{5}{3}$, $y = -\frac{4}{3} + t$

Now, on substituting the values of x, y and z in Eq. (iii), we get

$$-\frac{5}{3} - 2\left(-\frac{4}{3} + t\right) + 2t = 1$$

$$\Rightarrow \quad -\frac{5}{3} + \frac{8}{3} - 2t + 2t = 1$$

$$\Rightarrow \quad 1 = 1$$

which is true and satisfies the third equation.

Thus, the given system of equations has infinite.

Hence, the number of solutions are given by

$x = \frac{5}{3}$, $y = \frac{-4}{3} + t$, $y = t$, where t is any real number.

Method to Solve the System of Equations by Matrix Method

To solve the system of equations by matrix method, we use the following steps

I. First, write the given system of linear equations in matrix form as $AX = B$. ...(i)
If linear equations are not given, then first form them by using given conditions and then write in matrix form as Eq. (i).

II. Calculate $|A|$. If $|A| \neq 0$, then go to next step.

III. Find the inverse of A, i.e. A^{-1}. For this, firstly find adj (A) and then use formula $A^{-1} = \frac{1}{|A|}$ adj (A).

IV. The solution of Eq. (i) is given by
$$X = A^{-1}B \quad ...(ii)$$
So, put the values of A^{-1} and B in RHS of Eq. (ii) and simplify it.

V. Now, compare the LHS of Eq. (ii) with simplified RHS obtained in step IV and get the required values of x, y and z, etc. (variables in X).

Note Matrix method is applicable only, when the number of variables and number of linear equations is same.

Example 6 Solve the system of linear equations by using matrices $4x - 3y = 3$ and $3x - 5y = 7$.

Sol. The given system of linear equations can be written in matrix form as $AX = B$,

where $A = \begin{bmatrix} 4 & -3 \\ 3 & -5 \end{bmatrix}$, $X = \begin{bmatrix} x \\ y \end{bmatrix}$ and $B = \begin{bmatrix} 3 \\ 7 \end{bmatrix}$

Now, $|A| = \begin{vmatrix} 4 & -3 \\ 3 & -5 \end{vmatrix} = -20 + 9 = -11 \neq 0$

So, A^{-1} exists and it is given by

$$A^{-1} = \frac{1}{|A|} \text{adj } (A) = \frac{1}{-11}\begin{bmatrix} -5 & 3 \\ -3 & 4 \end{bmatrix} = \frac{1}{11}\begin{bmatrix} 5 & -3 \\ 3 & -4 \end{bmatrix}$$

$$\left[\because \text{adj}\begin{bmatrix} a & b \\ c & d \end{bmatrix} = \begin{bmatrix} d & -b \\ -c & a \end{bmatrix}\right]$$

$\because \quad X = A^{-1}B$

$$\therefore \quad X = \frac{1}{11}\begin{bmatrix} 5 & -3 \\ 3 & -4 \end{bmatrix}\begin{bmatrix} 3 \\ 7 \end{bmatrix} = \frac{1}{11}\begin{bmatrix} 15 - 21 \\ 9 - 28 \end{bmatrix} = \frac{1}{11}\begin{bmatrix} -6 \\ -19 \end{bmatrix}$$

$$\Rightarrow \quad \begin{bmatrix} x \\ y \end{bmatrix} = \begin{bmatrix} -6/11 \\ -19/11 \end{bmatrix}$$

Now, on comparing the corresponding elements, we get

$$x = \frac{-6}{11} \text{ and } y = \frac{-19}{11}.$$

Example 7 Solve the following system of linear equations using matrices.

$$x - 2y = 10,\ 2x - y - z = 8,\ -2y + z = 7 \quad \textbf{[ISC 2020]}$$

Sol. Given system of equations

$$x - 2y = 10,\ 2x - y - z = 8,\ -2y + z = 7$$

The given system of equations can also be written in matrix form as

$$\begin{bmatrix} 1 & -2 & 0 \\ 2 & -1 & -1 \\ 0 & -2 & 1 \end{bmatrix}\begin{bmatrix} x \\ y \\ z \end{bmatrix} = \begin{bmatrix} 10 \\ 8 \\ 7 \end{bmatrix}$$

i.e. $AX = B \Rightarrow X = A^{-1}B$,

where $A = \begin{bmatrix} 1 & -2 & 0 \\ 2 & -1 & -1 \\ 0 & -2 & 1 \end{bmatrix}$, $X = \begin{bmatrix} x \\ y \\ z \end{bmatrix}$, $B = \begin{bmatrix} 10 \\ 8 \\ 7 \end{bmatrix}$

Now, $|A| = \begin{vmatrix} 1 & -2 & 0 \\ 2 & -1 & -1 \\ 0 & -2 & 1 \end{vmatrix} = 1(-1-2) + 2(2-0) = 1 \neq 0$

Since, A is non-singular matrix, so the system of equation has unique solution.

Now, cofactors of A are

$$A_{11} = -3, A_{12} = -2, A_{13} = -4,$$
$$A_{21} = 2, A_{22} = 1, A_{23} = 2,$$
$$A_{31} = 2, A_{32} = 1, A_{33} = 3$$

Now, $\text{adj } (A) = \begin{bmatrix} A_{11} & A_{21} & A_{31} \\ A_{12} & A_{22} & A_{32} \\ A_{13} & A_{23} & A_{33} \end{bmatrix} = \begin{bmatrix} -3 & 2 & 2 \\ -2 & 1 & 1 \\ -4 & 2 & 3 \end{bmatrix}$

$$A^{-1} = \frac{1}{|A|} \text{adj } (A) = \begin{bmatrix} -3 & 2 & 2 \\ -2 & 1 & 1 \\ -4 & 2 & 3 \end{bmatrix}$$

$$X = A^{-1}B = \begin{bmatrix} -3 & 2 & 2 \\ -2 & 1 & 1 \\ -4 & 2 & 3 \end{bmatrix}\begin{bmatrix} 10 \\ 8 \\ 7 \end{bmatrix}$$

$$= \begin{bmatrix} -30 + 16 + 14 \\ -20 + 8 + 7 \\ -40 + 16 + 21 \end{bmatrix} = \begin{bmatrix} 0 \\ -5 \\ -3 \end{bmatrix}$$

$\therefore \quad x = 0,\ y = -5$ and $z = -3$

Example 8 Find A^{-1}, where $A = \begin{bmatrix} 4 & 2 & 3 \\ 1 & 1 & 1 \\ 3 & 1 & -2 \end{bmatrix}$. Then, solve the following system of linear equations.

$$4x + 2y + 3z = 2,\ x + y + z = 1 \text{ and } 3x + y - 2z = 5$$

[ISC 2013]

Sol. Given system of equations, $4x + 2y + 3z = 2$,
$x + y + z = 1$ and $3x + y - 2z = 5$.

The given system of equations can also be written in matrix form as

$$\begin{bmatrix} 4 & 2 & 3 \\ 1 & 1 & 1 \\ 3 & 1 & -2 \end{bmatrix} \begin{bmatrix} x \\ y \\ z \end{bmatrix} = \begin{bmatrix} 2 \\ 1 \\ 5 \end{bmatrix}$$

i.e. $AX = B$

$\Rightarrow$ $X = A^{-1}B,$

where $A = \begin{bmatrix} 4 & 2 & 3 \\ 1 & 1 & 1 \\ 3 & 1 & -2 \end{bmatrix}, X = \begin{bmatrix} x \\ y \\ z \end{bmatrix}$ and $B = \begin{bmatrix} 2 \\ 1 \\ 5 \end{bmatrix}$

Now, $|A| = \begin{vmatrix} 4 & 2 & 3 \\ 1 & 1 & 1 \\ 3 & 1 & -2 \end{vmatrix}$

$= 4[-2-1] - 2[-2-3] + 3[1-3]$

$= 4[-3] + 2[5] + 3[-2]$

$= -12 + 10 - 6 = -8 \neq 0$

Since, A is a non-singular matrix, so the system of equations has unique solution.

Now, cofactors of $|A|$ are

$$C_{11} = (-1)^{1+1} \begin{vmatrix} 1 & 1 \\ 1 & -2 \end{vmatrix} = [-2-1] = -3$$

$$C_{12} = (-1)^{1+2} \begin{vmatrix} 1 & 1 \\ 3 & -2 \end{vmatrix} = -[-2-3] = 5$$

$$C_{13} = (-1)^{1+3} \begin{vmatrix} 1 & 1 \\ 3 & 1 \end{vmatrix} = [1-3] = -2$$

$$C_{21} = (-1)^{2+1} \begin{vmatrix} 2 & 3 \\ 1 & -2 \end{vmatrix} = -[-4-3] = 7$$

$$C_{22} = (-1)^{2+2} \begin{vmatrix} 4 & 3 \\ 3 & -2 \end{vmatrix} = [-8-9] = -17$$

$$C_{23} = (-1)^{2+3} \begin{vmatrix} 4 & 2 \\ 3 & 1 \end{vmatrix} = -[4-6] = 2$$

$$C_{31} = (-1)^{3+1} \begin{vmatrix} 2 & 3 \\ 1 & 1 \end{vmatrix} = [2-3] = -1$$

$$C_{32} = (-1)^{3+2} \begin{vmatrix} 4 & 3 \\ 1 & 1 \end{vmatrix} = -[4-3] = -1$$

and $C_{33} = (-1)^{3+3} \begin{vmatrix} 4 & 2 \\ 1 & 1 \end{vmatrix} = [4-2] = 2$

Now, $\text{adj}(A) = \begin{bmatrix} C_{11} & C_{21} & C_{31} \\ C_{12} & C_{22} & C_{32} \\ C_{13} & C_{23} & C_{33} \end{bmatrix} = \begin{bmatrix} -3 & 7 & -1 \\ 5 & -17 & -1 \\ -2 & 2 & 2 \end{bmatrix}$

$\therefore$ $A^{-1} = \frac{1}{|A|}\text{adj}(A) = \frac{1}{-8}\begin{bmatrix} -3 & 7 & -1 \\ 5 & -17 & -1 \\ -2 & 2 & 2 \end{bmatrix}$

$X = A^{-1}B$

$\Rightarrow$ $\begin{bmatrix} x \\ y \\ z \end{bmatrix} = \frac{1}{-8}\begin{bmatrix} -3 & 7 & -1 \\ 5 & -17 & -1 \\ -2 & 2 & 2 \end{bmatrix}\begin{bmatrix} 2 \\ 1 \\ 5 \end{bmatrix}$

[by multiplication property]

$$= \frac{1}{-8}\begin{bmatrix} -6+7-5 \\ 10-17-5 \\ -4+2+10 \end{bmatrix} = \frac{1}{-8}\begin{bmatrix} -4 \\ -12 \\ 8 \end{bmatrix}$$

$\Rightarrow$ $\begin{bmatrix} x \\ y \\ z \end{bmatrix} = \begin{bmatrix} 1/2 \\ 3/2 \\ -1 \end{bmatrix}$

Hence, $x = \frac{1}{2}$, $y = \frac{3}{2}$ and $z = -1$.

Example 9 The sum of three numbers is 6. If we multiply third number by 3 and add second number to it, we get 11. By adding first and third numbers, we get double of the second number. Represent it algebraically and find the numbers using matrix method.

Sol. Let first, second and third numbers be denoted by x, y and z, respectively.

Then, according to the question, we get

$$x + y + z = 6,\ y + 3z = 11$$

and $x + z = 2y \Rightarrow x - 2y + z = 0$

In matrix form, this system of equations can be written as

$AX = B,$ ...(i)

where $A = \begin{bmatrix} 1 & 1 & 1 \\ 0 & 1 & 3 \\ 1 & -2 & 1 \end{bmatrix}, X = \begin{bmatrix} x \\ y \\ z \end{bmatrix}$ and $B = \begin{bmatrix} 6 \\ 11 \\ 0 \end{bmatrix}$

Here, $|A| = \begin{vmatrix} 1 & 1 & 1 \\ 0 & 1 & 3 \\ 1 & -2 & 1 \end{vmatrix} = 1(1+6) - 1(0-3) + 1(0-1)$

[expanding along R_1]

$= 7 + 3 - 1 = 9 \neq 0$

Since, $|A| \neq 0$, so the inverse of A exists.

Now, cofactors corresponding to each element of $|A|$ are

$$C_{11} = (-1)^{1+1} \begin{vmatrix} 1 & 3 \\ -2 & 1 \end{vmatrix} = (1+6) = 7$$

$$C_{12} = (-1)^{1+2} \begin{vmatrix} 0 & 3 \\ 1 & 1 \end{vmatrix} = -(0-3) = 3$$

$$C_{13} = (-1)^{1+3} \begin{vmatrix} 0 & 1 \\ 1 & -2 \end{vmatrix} = (0-1) = -1$$

$$C_{21} = (-1)^{2+1} \begin{vmatrix} 1 & 1 \\ -2 & 1 \end{vmatrix} = -(1+2) = -3$$

$$C_{22} = (-1)^{2+2} \begin{vmatrix} 1 & 1 \\ 1 & 1 \end{vmatrix} = (1-1) = 0$$

$$C_{23} = (-1)^{2+3} \begin{vmatrix} 1 & 1 \\ 1 & -2 \end{vmatrix} = -(-2-1) = 3$$

$$C_{31} = (-1)^{3+1} \begin{vmatrix} 1 & 1 \\ 1 & 3 \end{vmatrix} = (3-1) = 2$$

$$C_{32} = (-1)^{3+2} \begin{vmatrix} 1 & 1 \\ 0 & 3 \end{vmatrix} = -(3-0) = -3$$

and $C_{33} = (-1)^{3+3} \begin{vmatrix} 1 & 1 \\ 0 & 1 \end{vmatrix} = (1-0) = 1$

Then, $\text{adj}(A) = \begin{bmatrix} 7 & 3 & -1 \\ -3 & 0 & 3 \\ 2 & -3 & 1 \end{bmatrix}^T = \begin{bmatrix} 7 & -3 & 2 \\ 3 & 0 & -3 \\ -1 & 3 & 1 \end{bmatrix}$

Thus, $A^{-1} = \frac{1}{|A|}\text{adj}(A)$

$$= \frac{1}{9}\begin{bmatrix} 7 & -3 & 2 \\ 3 & 0 & -3 \\ -1 & 3 & 1 \end{bmatrix}$$

Now, the solution of Eq. (i) is given by

$$X = A^{-1}B \quad \text{...(ii)}$$

On putting the values of A^{-1} and B in RHS of Eq. (ii), we get

$$X = \frac{1}{9}\begin{bmatrix} 7 & -3 & 2 \\ 3 & 0 & -3 \\ -1 & 3 & 1 \end{bmatrix}\begin{bmatrix} 6 \\ 11 \\ 0 \end{bmatrix}$$

$$= \frac{1}{9}\begin{bmatrix} 7\times6-3\times11+2\times0 \\ 3\times6+0\times11-3\times0 \\ -1\times6+3\times11+1\times0 \end{bmatrix}$$

$$= \frac{1}{9}\begin{bmatrix} 42-33+0 \\ 18+0-0 \\ -6+33+0 \end{bmatrix}$$

$$= \frac{1}{9}\begin{bmatrix} 9 \\ 18 \\ 27 \end{bmatrix} = \begin{bmatrix} 9/9 \\ 18/9 \\ 27/9 \end{bmatrix} = \begin{bmatrix} 1 \\ 2 \\ 3 \end{bmatrix}$$

$$\Rightarrow \begin{bmatrix} x \\ y \\ z \end{bmatrix} = \begin{bmatrix} 1 \\ 2 \\ 3 \end{bmatrix}$$

On comparing both sides, we get

$$x = 1, y = 2 \text{ and } z = 3$$

which are the required numbers.

Example 10 Given that $A = \begin{bmatrix} 1 & -1 & 0 \\ 2 & 3 & 4 \\ 0 & 1 & 2 \end{bmatrix}$ and $B = \begin{bmatrix} 2 & 2 & -4 \\ -4 & 2 & -4 \\ 2 & -1 & 5 \end{bmatrix}$, find AB. Using this result, solve the system of equations $x - y = 3$, $2x + 3y + 4z = 17$ and $y + 2z = 7$. **[ISC 2017]**

Sol. Given, $A = \begin{bmatrix} 1 & -1 & 0 \\ 2 & 3 & 4 \\ 0 & 1 & 2 \end{bmatrix}$ and $B = \begin{bmatrix} 2 & 2 & -4 \\ -4 & 2 & -4 \\ 2 & -1 & 5 \end{bmatrix}$

$$\therefore AB = \begin{bmatrix} 1 & -1 & 0 \\ 2 & 3 & 4 \\ 0 & 1 & 2 \end{bmatrix}\begin{bmatrix} 2 & 2 & -4 \\ -4 & 2 & -4 \\ 2 & -1 & 5 \end{bmatrix}$$

$$= \begin{bmatrix} 2+4+0 & 2-2+0 & -4+4+0 \\ 4-12+8 & 4+6-4 & -8-12+20 \\ 0-4+4 & 0+2-2 & 0-4+10 \end{bmatrix}$$

[by multiplication property]

$$\Rightarrow AB = \begin{bmatrix} 6 & 0 & 0 \\ 0 & 6 & 0 \\ 0 & 0 & 6 \end{bmatrix} = 6I_3 \quad \text{...(i)}$$

Now, the given system of equations can be written in matrix form as

$$\begin{bmatrix} 1 & -1 & 0 \\ 2 & 3 & 4 \\ 0 & 1 & 2 \end{bmatrix}\begin{bmatrix} x \\ y \\ z \end{bmatrix} = \begin{bmatrix} 3 \\ 17 \\ 7 \end{bmatrix}$$

i.e. $AX = C \Rightarrow X = A^{-1}C$, ...(ii)

where $A = \begin{bmatrix} 1 & -1 & 0 \\ 2 & 3 & 4 \\ 0 & 1 & 2 \end{bmatrix}$, $X = \begin{bmatrix} x \\ y \\ z \end{bmatrix}$ and $C = \begin{bmatrix} 3 \\ 17 \\ 7 \end{bmatrix}$

From Eq. (i), we get

$$AB = 6I_3$$

$$\Rightarrow A\left(\frac{B}{6}\right) = I_3 \Rightarrow A^{-1} = \frac{1}{6}B$$

$$\Rightarrow A^{-1} = \frac{1}{6}\begin{bmatrix} 2 & 2 & -4 \\ -4 & 2 & -4 \\ 2 & -1 & 5 \end{bmatrix}$$

On putting value of A^{-1} in Eq. (ii), we get

$$X = \frac{1}{6}\begin{bmatrix} 2 & 2 & -4 \\ -4 & 2 & -4 \\ 2 & -1 & 5 \end{bmatrix}\begin{bmatrix} 3 \\ 17 \\ 7 \end{bmatrix}$$

$$= \frac{1}{6}\begin{bmatrix} 6+34-28 \\ -12+34-28 \\ 6-17+35 \end{bmatrix} = \frac{1}{6}\begin{bmatrix} 12 \\ -6 \\ 24 \end{bmatrix} = \begin{bmatrix} 2 \\ -1 \\ 4 \end{bmatrix}$$

$$\Rightarrow \begin{bmatrix} x \\ y \\ z \end{bmatrix} = \begin{bmatrix} 2 \\ -1 \\ 4 \end{bmatrix}$$

$$\therefore \quad x = 2, \ y = -1 \text{ and } z = 4$$

Example 11 Solve the following system of homogeneous linear equations.

$$3x + y - 2z = 0, \ x + y + z = 0 \text{ and } x - 2y + z = 0$$

Sol. The given system of equations can be written in matrix form as

$$AX = O,$$

where $A = \begin{bmatrix} 3 & 1 & -2 \\ 1 & 1 & 1 \\ 1 & -2 & 1 \end{bmatrix}$, $X = \begin{bmatrix} x \\ y \\ z \end{bmatrix}$, $O = \begin{bmatrix} 0 \\ 0 \\ 0 \end{bmatrix}$

Now, $|A| = \begin{vmatrix} 3 & 1 & -2 \\ 1 & 1 & 1 \\ 1 & -2 & 1 \end{vmatrix}$

$$= 3(1+2) - 1(1-1) - 2(-2+1)$$

$$= 3(3) - 2(-3)$$

$$= 15 \neq 0$$

$\therefore A$ is non-singular matrix, i.e. A^{-1} exists.

Thus, the given system of equations has trivial solution.

Hence, $x = 0$, $y = 0$ and $z = 0$.

Example 12 Using matrices, solve the following system of homogeneous linear equations.

$x + y + z = 0,\ x - y - 5z = 0$ and $x + 2y + 4z = 0$

Sol. The given system of equations can be written in matrix form as $AX = O$,

where $A = \begin{bmatrix} 1 & 1 & 1 \\ 1 & -1 & -5 \\ 1 & 2 & 4 \end{bmatrix}$, $X = \begin{bmatrix} x \\ y \\ z \end{bmatrix}$, $O = \begin{bmatrix} 0 \\ 0 \\ 0 \end{bmatrix}$

Now, $|A| = \begin{vmatrix} 1 & 1 & 1 \\ 1 & -1 & -5 \\ 1 & 2 & 4 \end{vmatrix}$

$= 1(-4 + 10) - 1(4 + 5) + 1(2 + 1)$

$= 6 - 9 + 3 = 0$

Thus, the given system of equation has infinitely many solutions.

On putting $z = t$ in given first two equations, we get

$$x + y = -t,\ x - y = 5t$$

On solving these equations, we get $x = 2t,\ y = -3t$

On putting the values of x and y in given equation

$x + 2y + 4z = 0$, we get

$$2t + 2(-3t) + 4t = 0$$

$\Rightarrow \quad 2t - 6t + 4t = 0$

$\Rightarrow \quad 0 = 0$, which is true.

So, the values of x and y satisfies third equation.

Hence, the solutions of the given system of equations are $x = 2t,\ y = -3t$ and $z = t$, where t is any real number.

Topic Practice 4

Very Short Answer Type Questions

(2 Marks)

Directions (Q. Nos. 1-2) *Examine the consistency of the system of equations.*

1 (i) $2x - y = 5$ and $x + y = 4$ **[NCERT]**

(ii) $x + 3y = 5$ and $2x + 6y = 8$ **[NCERT]**

2 $x + y + z = 1, 2x + 3y + 2z = 2$ and $bx + by + 2bz = 4$. **[NCERT]**

3 For what values of k, the system of linear equations $x + y + z = 2, 2x + y - z = 3$ and $3x + 2y + kz = 4$ has a unique solution?

4 Solve the system of linear equations using matrix method.

(i) $2x - y = -2$ and $3x + 4y = 3$.

(ii) $5x + 2y = 4$ and $7x + 3y = 5$.

Short Answer Type Questions

(4 Marks)

Directions (Q. Nos. 5-8) *Solve the following system of equations by matrix method.*

5 $3x + y + z = 1, 2x + 2z = 0, 5x + y + 2z = 2$ **[ISC 2016]**

6 $x - 2y = 10, 2x + y + 3z = 8$ and $-2y + z = 7$ **[ISC 2014]**

7 $x + y + z = 9, 2x + 5y + 7z = 52$ and $2x + y - z = 0$ **[ISC 2009]**

8 $x + y + z = 6, x - y + z = 2$ and $2x + y - z = 1$. **[ISC 2007]**

Long Answer Type Questions

(6 Marks)

9 Using matrices, solve the following system of equations.

$2x - 3y + 5z = 11, 3x + 2y - 4z = -5$

and $x + y - 2z = -3$ **[ISC 2018]**

10 Using matrix method, solve the following system of equations.

$\frac{2}{x} + \frac{3}{y} + \frac{10}{z} = 4,\ \frac{4}{x} - \frac{6}{y} + \frac{5}{z} = 1$ and $\frac{6}{x} + \frac{9}{y} - \frac{20}{z} = 2,$

where x, y and $z \neq 0$ **[ISC 2023]**

11 An amount of ₹ 5000 is put into three investments at the rate of interest of 6%, 7% and 8% per annum, respectively. The total annual income is ₹ 358. If the combined income from the first two investments is ₹ 70 more than the income from the third, then find the amount of each investment by matrix method.

12 Find A^{-1}, where $A = \begin{bmatrix} 1 & 2 & -3 \\ 2 & 3 & 2 \\ 3 & -3 & -4 \end{bmatrix}$. Hence solve the system of equations $x + 2y - 3z = -4$, $2x + 3y + 2z = 2$ and $3x - 3y - 4z = 11$. **[ISC 2008]**

13 If $A = \begin{bmatrix} 1 & 2 & 1 \\ -1 & 1 & 1 \\ 1 & -3 & 1 \end{bmatrix}$, then find A^{-1} and hence solve the system of equations $x + 2y + z = 4$, $-x + y + z = 0$ and $x - 3y + z = 4$.

14 If $A=\begin{bmatrix}1 & 2 & 0\\ -2 & -1 & -2\\ 0 & -1 & 1\end{bmatrix}$, then find A^{-1}. Using A^{-1}, solve the system of linear equations $x-2y=10$, $2x-y-z=8$ and $-2y+z=7$. **[NCERT Exemplar]**

15 If $A=\begin{bmatrix}2 & 3 & 10\\ 4 & -6 & 5\\ 6 & 9 & -20\end{bmatrix}$, then find A^{-1}. Using A^{-1}, solve the system of equations $\frac{2}{x}+\frac{3}{y}+\frac{10}{z}=2$, and $\frac{6}{x}+\frac{9}{y}-\frac{20}{z}=-4$.

16 Determine the product of $\begin{bmatrix}-4 & 4 & 4\\ -7 & 1 & 3\\ 5 & -3 & -1\end{bmatrix}\begin{bmatrix}1 & -1 & 1\\ 1 & -2 & -2\\ 2 & 1 & 3\end{bmatrix}$ and then use to solve the system of equations $x-y+z=4$, $x-2y-2z=9$ and $2x+y+3z=1$.

17 An automobile company uses three types of steels S_1, S_2 and S_3 for producing three types of cars C_1, C_2 and C_3. Steel requirements (in tonne) for each type of cars are given below

Steel/Car	C_1	C_2	C_3
S_1	2	3	4
S_2	1	1	2
S_3	3	2	1

Find the number of cars of each type which can be produced using 29, 13 and 16 tonne of steel of three types, respectively.

Hints & Solutions

1. (i) Similar as Example 1. [**Ans.** Consistent]
(ii) Similar as Example 2. [**Ans.** Inconsistent]

2. Given system of linear equations is
$x+y+z=1$, $2x+3y+2z=2$ and $bx+by+2bz=4$
It can be written in matrix form as $AX=B$,
where $A=\begin{bmatrix}1 & 1 & 1\\ 2 & 3 & 2\\ b & b & 2b\end{bmatrix}$, $X=\begin{bmatrix}x\\ y\\ z\end{bmatrix}$ and $B=\begin{bmatrix}1\\ 2\\ 4\end{bmatrix}$ [1]

Here, $|A|=\begin{vmatrix}1 & 1 & 1\\ 2 & 3 & 2\\ b & b & 2b\end{vmatrix}$
$=1[6b-2b]-1[4b-2b]+1[2b-3b]$ [1/2]
$=4b-2b-b=b\neq 0$
Since, A is non-singular. So, A^{-1} exists.
Hence, the given system of equations is consistent. [1/2]

3. **Hint** For unique solution, $\begin{vmatrix}1 & 1 & 1\\ 2 & 1 & -1\\ 3 & 2 & k\end{vmatrix}\neq 0$ [**Ans.** $k\neq 0$]

4. Similar as Example 6. [**Ans.** (i) $x=\frac{-5}{11}$ and $y=\frac{12}{11}$ (ii) $x=2$ and $y=-3$]

Solutions (Q. Nos. 5-8) Similar as Example 7.

5. $x=1$, $y=-1$ and $z=-1$

6. $x=4$, $y=-3$ and $z=1$

7. $x=1$, $y=3$, $z=5$

8. $x=1$, $y=2$, $z=3$

9. Similar as Example 7.
[**Ans.** $x=1$, $y=2$, $z=3$]

10. The given system of equations is
$$\frac{2}{x}+\frac{3}{y}+\frac{10}{z}=4,\ \frac{4}{x}-\frac{6}{y}+\frac{5}{z}=1$$
and $$\frac{6}{x}+\frac{9}{y}-\frac{20}{z}=2;\ x,y,z\neq 0$$
Let $\frac{1}{x}=u$, $\frac{1}{y}=v$ and $\frac{1}{z}=w$, then the system of equations can be written as
$$\left.\begin{aligned}2u+3v+10w&=4\\ 4u-6v+5w&=1\\ 6u+9v-20w&=2\end{aligned}\right\}\quad \text{...(i)}$$
Above system of Eq. (i) can be written in matrix form as $AX=B$, where
$$A=\begin{bmatrix}2 & 3 & 10\\ 4 & -6 & 5\\ 6 & 9 & -20\end{bmatrix},\ B=\begin{bmatrix}4\\ 1\\ 2\end{bmatrix} \text{ and } X=\begin{bmatrix}u\\ v\\ w\end{bmatrix}.$$
Its solution is given by
$$X=A^{-1}B \quad \text{...(ii) [1]}$$
Here, $|A|=2(120-45)-3(-80-30)+10(36+36)$
$=2(75)-3(-110)+10(72)$
$=150+330+720=1200$
$\Rightarrow |A|=1200$ [1/2]
Since, $|A|\neq 0$, so unique solution exists.
Now, cofactors of elements of $|A|$ are
$$C_{11}=(-1)^2\begin{vmatrix}-6 & 5\\ 9 & -20\end{vmatrix}=1(120-45)=75$$
$$C_{12}=(-1)^3\begin{vmatrix}4 & 5\\ 6 & -20\end{vmatrix}=-1(-80-30)=110$$
$$C_{13}=(-1)^4\begin{vmatrix}4 & -6\\ 6 & 9\end{vmatrix}=1(36+36)=72$$
$$C_{21}=(-1)^3\begin{vmatrix}3 & 10\\ 9 & -20\end{vmatrix}=-1(-60-90)=150$$
$$C_{22}=(-1)^4\begin{vmatrix}2 & 10\\ 6 & -20\end{vmatrix}=1(-40-60)=-100$$

$$C_{23}=(-1)^5\begin{vmatrix}2&3\\6&9\end{vmatrix}=-1(18-18)=0$$

$$C_{31}=(-1)^4\begin{vmatrix}3&10\\-6&5\end{vmatrix}=1(15+60)=75$$

$$C_{32}=(-1)^5\begin{vmatrix}2&10\\4&5\end{vmatrix}=-1(10-40)=30$$

and $C_{33}=(-1)^6\begin{vmatrix}2&3\\4&-6\end{vmatrix}=1(-12-12)=-24$ [1]

$$\therefore\ \text{adj}(A)=\begin{bmatrix}C_{11}&C_{12}&C_{13}\\C_{21}&C_{22}&C_{23}\\C_{31}&C_{32}&C_{33}\end{bmatrix}^T=\begin{bmatrix}75&110&72\\150&-100&0\\75&30&-24\end{bmatrix}^T$$

$$=\begin{bmatrix}75&150&75\\110&-100&30\\72&0&-24\end{bmatrix}$$ [1]

and $A^{-1}=\dfrac{\text{adj}(A)}{|A|}$

$$=\frac{1}{1200}\begin{bmatrix}75&150&75\\110&-100&30\\72&0&-24\end{bmatrix}$$ [1/2]

On putting the values X, A^{-1} and B in Eq. (ii), we get

$$\begin{bmatrix}u\\v\\w\end{bmatrix}=\frac{1}{1200}\begin{bmatrix}75&150&75\\110&-100&30\\72&0&-24\end{bmatrix}\begin{bmatrix}4\\1\\2\end{bmatrix}$$

$$=\frac{1}{1200}\begin{bmatrix}300+150+150\\440-100+60\\288+0-48\end{bmatrix}$$

$$\Rightarrow\ \begin{bmatrix}u\\v\\w\end{bmatrix}=\frac{1}{1200}\begin{bmatrix}600\\400\\240\end{bmatrix}$$

On comparing corresponding elements, we get

$$u=\frac{600}{1200},\ v=\frac{400}{1200},\ w=\frac{240}{1200}$$

$\therefore\quad u=\dfrac{1}{2},\ v=\dfrac{1}{3}$ and $w=\dfrac{1}{5}$ [1]

But $\quad\dfrac{1}{x}=u,\ \dfrac{1}{y}=v$ and $\dfrac{1}{z}=w$

$\Rightarrow\quad\dfrac{1}{x}=\dfrac{1}{2},\ \dfrac{1}{y}=\dfrac{1}{3}$ and $\dfrac{1}{z}=\dfrac{1}{5}$

$\therefore\quad x=2,\ y=3$ and $z=5$ [1]

11. Hint The system of equations is $x+y+z=5000$,

$\dfrac{6x}{100}+\dfrac{7y}{100}+\dfrac{8z}{100}=358$ and $\dfrac{6x}{100}+\dfrac{7y}{100}=70+\dfrac{8z}{100}$

Then, further solve as Question 10.

[**Ans.** ₹1000, ₹2200 and ₹1800]

12. Given, $A=\begin{bmatrix}1&2&-3\\2&3&2\\3&-3&-4\end{bmatrix}$

$$|A|=1(-12+6)-2(-8-6)-3(-6-9)$$
$$=-6+28+45=67\neq 0$$

Thus, A^{-1} exists. [1/2]

Now, cofactors of elements of $|A|$ are

$$C_{11}=(-1)^{1+1}\begin{vmatrix}3&2\\-3&-4\end{vmatrix}=-12+6=-6$$

$$C_{12}=(-1)^{1+2}\begin{vmatrix}2&2\\3&-4\end{vmatrix}=-(-8-6)=14$$

$$C_{13}=(-1)^{1+3}\begin{vmatrix}2&3\\3&-3\end{vmatrix}=(-6-9)=-15$$

$$C_{21}=(-1)^{2+1}\begin{vmatrix}2&-3\\-3&-4\end{vmatrix}=-(-8-9)=17$$

$$C_{22}=(-1)^{2+2}\begin{vmatrix}1&-3\\3&-4\end{vmatrix}=(-4+9)=5$$

$$C_{23}=(-1)^{2+3}\begin{vmatrix}1&2\\3&-3\end{vmatrix}=-(-3-6)=9$$

$$C_{31}=(-1)^{3+1}\begin{vmatrix}2&-3\\3&2\end{vmatrix}=(4+9)=13$$

$$C_{32}=(-1)^{3+2}\begin{vmatrix}1&-3\\2&2\end{vmatrix}=-(2+6)=-8$$

and $\quad C_{33}=(-1)^{3+3}\begin{vmatrix}1&2\\2&3\end{vmatrix}=(3-4)=-1$ [1½]

$$\therefore\quad\text{adj}(A)=\begin{bmatrix}C_{11}&C_{12}&C_{13}\\C_{21}&C_{22}&C_{23}\\C_{31}&C_{32}&C_{33}\end{bmatrix}^T=\begin{bmatrix}-6&14&-15\\17&5&9\\13&-8&-1\end{bmatrix}^T$$

$$=\begin{bmatrix}-6&17&13\\14&5&-8\\-15&9&-1\end{bmatrix}$$ [1]

$\because\quad A^{-1}=\dfrac{1}{|A|}\cdot\text{adj}(A)$

$$\Rightarrow\quad A^{-1}=\frac{1}{67}\begin{bmatrix}-6&17&13\\14&5&-8\\-15&9&-1\end{bmatrix}$$ [1]

Given system of equations can be written in matrix form as

$$AX=B\Rightarrow X=A^{-1}B,$$

where $\quad B=\begin{bmatrix}-4\\2\\11\end{bmatrix}$ and $X=\begin{bmatrix}x\\y\\z\end{bmatrix}$ [1]

$$\therefore\ X=A^{-1}B=\frac{1}{67}\begin{bmatrix}-6&17&13\\14&5&-8\\-15&9&-1\end{bmatrix}\begin{bmatrix}-4\\2\\11\end{bmatrix}$$

$$=\frac{1}{67}\begin{bmatrix}24+34+143\\-56+10-88\\60+18-11\end{bmatrix}$$

$$\Rightarrow \begin{bmatrix} x \\ y \\ z \end{bmatrix} = \frac{1}{67}\begin{bmatrix} 201 \\ -134 \\ 67 \end{bmatrix} = \begin{bmatrix} 3 \\ -2 \\ 1 \end{bmatrix}$$

On comparing corresponding elements, we get

$x = 3,\ y = -2$ and $z = 1$. [1]

13. Solve as Question 12.

[**Ans.** $A^{-1} = \frac{1}{10}\begin{bmatrix} 4 & -5 & 1 \\ 2 & 0 & -2 \\ 2 & 5 & 3 \end{bmatrix}$; $x = 2,\ y = 0,\ z = 2$]

14. **Hint** (i) Find A^{-1}.

(ii) Given system of equations can be written in matrix form as $\begin{bmatrix} 1 & -2 & 0 \\ 2 & -1 & -1 \\ 0 & -2 & 1 \end{bmatrix}\begin{bmatrix} x \\ y \\ z \end{bmatrix} = \begin{bmatrix} 10 \\ 8 \\ 7 \end{bmatrix}$

i.e. $A^T \cdot X = B$, where $X = \begin{bmatrix} x \\ y \\ z \end{bmatrix}$ and $B = \begin{bmatrix} 10 \\ 8 \\ 7 \end{bmatrix}$

$$\Rightarrow \quad X = (A^T)^{-1} \cdot B \quad \text{...(i)}$$

(iii) We know that $(A^T)^{-1} = (A^{-1})^T$, so find transpose of A^{-1} and substitute in Eq. (i), to get the required values of x, y and z.

[**Ans.** $A^{-1} = \begin{bmatrix} -3 & -2 & -4 \\ 2 & 1 & 2 \\ 2 & 1 & 3 \end{bmatrix}$; $x = 0,\ y = -5$ and $z = -3$]

15. **Hint** (i) Find A^{-1}.

(ii) Write the given system of equations in matrix form as

$AX = B$, where $X = \begin{bmatrix} 1/x \\ 1/y \\ 1/z \end{bmatrix}$ and $B = \begin{bmatrix} 2 \\ 5 \\ -4 \end{bmatrix}$.

(iii) Required solution is given by $X = A^{-1}B$.

[**Ans.** $A^{-1} = \frac{1}{1200}\begin{bmatrix} 75 & 150 & 75 \\ 110 & -100 & 30 \\ 72 & 0 & -24 \end{bmatrix}$; $x = 2,\ y = -3,\ z = 5$]

16. Let $B = \begin{bmatrix} -4 & 4 & 4 \\ -7 & 1 & 3 \\ 5 & -3 & -1 \end{bmatrix}$ and $A = \begin{bmatrix} 1 & -1 & 1 \\ 1 & -2 & -2 \\ 2 & 1 & 3 \end{bmatrix}$

$$\therefore BA = \begin{bmatrix} -4 & 4 & 4 \\ -7 & 1 & 3 \\ 5 & -3 & -1 \end{bmatrix}\begin{bmatrix} 1 & -1 & 1 \\ 1 & -2 & -2 \\ 2 & 1 & 3 \end{bmatrix}$$

$$= \begin{bmatrix} -4+4+8 & 4-8+4 & -4-8+12 \\ -7+1+6 & 7-2+3 & -7-2+9 \\ 5-3-2 & -5+6-1 & 5+6-3 \end{bmatrix}$$

$$= \begin{bmatrix} 8 & 0 & 0 \\ 0 & 8 & 0 \\ 0 & 0 & 8 \end{bmatrix} = 8\begin{bmatrix} 1 & 0 & 0 \\ 0 & 1 & 0 \\ 0 & 0 & 1 \end{bmatrix} = 8I$$

[1½]

$\Rightarrow BA = 8I \Rightarrow B(AA^{-1}) = 8IA^{-1}$

[post-multiplying both sides by A^{-1}]

$\Rightarrow \quad B = 8A^{-1}$ [$\because AA^{-1} = I$]

$$\therefore A^{-1} = \frac{1}{8}\begin{bmatrix} -4 & 4 & 4 \\ -7 & 1 & 3 \\ 5 & -3 & -1 \end{bmatrix}$$ [1]

Given system of equations can be written in matrix form as

$AX = C \Rightarrow X = A^{-1}C$, [1]

where $A = \begin{bmatrix} 1 & -1 & 1 \\ 1 & -2 & -2 \\ 2 & 1 & 3 \end{bmatrix}$, $C = \begin{bmatrix} 4 \\ 9 \\ 1 \end{bmatrix}$ and $X = \begin{bmatrix} x \\ y \\ z \end{bmatrix}$ [1/2]

$$\therefore \quad X = \frac{1}{8}\begin{bmatrix} -4 & 4 & 4 \\ -7 & 1 & 3 \\ 5 & -3 & -1 \end{bmatrix}\begin{bmatrix} 4 \\ 9 \\ 1 \end{bmatrix}$$

$$\Rightarrow \begin{bmatrix} x \\ y \\ z \end{bmatrix} = \frac{1}{8}\begin{bmatrix} -16+36+4 \\ -28+9+3 \\ 20-27-1 \end{bmatrix} = \frac{1}{8}\begin{bmatrix} 24 \\ -16 \\ -8 \end{bmatrix} = \begin{bmatrix} 3 \\ -2 \\ -1 \end{bmatrix}$$ [1]

On comparing corresponding elements, we get

$x = 3,\ y = -2$ and $z = -1$ [1]

17. **Hint** Let x be the number of C_1 cars produced, y be the number of C_2 cars produced and z be the number of C_3 cars produced.

Now, according to the given conditions, we have

$2x + 3y + 4z = 29,\ x + y + 2z = 13$ and $3x + 2y + z = 16$

Then, similar as Example 7.

[**Ans.** $x = 2,\ y = 3$ and $z = 4$]

Chapter Practice

Multiple Choice Type Questions

(1 Mark)

1 If $\begin{vmatrix} \alpha & 3 & 4 \\ 1 & 2 & 1 \\ 1 & 4 & 1 \end{vmatrix} = 0$, then the value of α is

(a) 1 (b) 2 (c) 3 (d) 4

2 $\begin{vmatrix} 2 & 3 & 4 \\ 5 & 6 & 8 \\ 6x & 9x & 12x \end{vmatrix}$ is equal to

(a) 0 (b) $3x$
(c) $9x^2$ (d) None of these

3 If A is a square matrix such that $|A| = 2$, then $|AA^T|$ is equal to

(a) 2 (b) 4
(c) 8 (d) 16

4 If A is a square matrix of order 3, then $|2A|$ is equal to **[ISC 2023]**

(a) $2|A|$ (b) $4|A|$
(c) $8|A|$ (d) $6|A|$

5 The adjoint of the matrix $A = \begin{bmatrix} 1 & 2 \\ 3 & 4 \end{bmatrix}$ is

(a) $\begin{bmatrix} 4 & 2 \\ 3 & 1 \end{bmatrix}$ (b) $\begin{bmatrix} -4 & 2 \\ 3 & -1 \end{bmatrix}$

(c) $\begin{bmatrix} 4 & -2 \\ -3 & 1 \end{bmatrix}$ (d) $\begin{bmatrix} 1 & -2 \\ -3 & 4 \end{bmatrix}$

6 Let A be a 3×3 matrix such that $|\text{adj} A| = 64$. Then, $|A|$ is equal to

(a) 8 only (b) -8 only
(c) 64 (d) 8 or -8

7 If $A = \begin{bmatrix} a & 0 & 0 \\ 0 & a & 0 \\ 0 & 0 & a \end{bmatrix}$, then $|A|$ is equal to

(a) a^{27} (b) a^9
(c) a^6 (d) a^2

8 If $\begin{bmatrix} 1 & 1 & 1 \\ 0 & 1 & 1 \\ 0 & 0 & 1 \end{bmatrix} \begin{bmatrix} x \\ y \\ z \end{bmatrix} = \begin{bmatrix} 6 \\ 3 \\ 2 \end{bmatrix}$, then the value of $(2x + y - z)$ is

(a) 1 (b) 2
(c) 3 (d) 5

Assertion-Reason Type Questions

(1 Mark)

Directions (Q. Nos. 9-12) *In the questions given below are two statements labelled as Assertion (A) and Reason (R). In the context of the two statements, which one of the following is correct?*

(a) Both A and R are correct and R is the correct explanation of A
(b) Both A and R are correct but R is not the correct explanation of A
(c) A is correct but R is incorrect
(d) R is correct but A is incorrect

9 **Assertion (A)** $\begin{vmatrix} 0 & -1 & 2 \\ 1 & 0 & 3 \\ -2 & -3 & 0 \end{vmatrix} = 0$

Reason (R) Determinant of odd ordered skew-symmetric is zero.

10 **Assertion (A)** $\text{adj}(\text{adj} A) = |A|^{n-2} \cdot A$

Reason (R) $|\text{adj } A| = |A|^{n-1}$.

11 **Assertion (A)** If $|A| = 4$, then $|A^{-1}| = -4$.

Reason (R) $|A^{-1}| = \dfrac{1}{|A|}$

12 **Assertion (A)** If A is a non-singular matrix, then A^{-1} exist.

Reason (R) Determinant of a non-singular matrix is zero.

Very Short Answer Type Questions

(2 Marks)

13 (i) If $\begin{vmatrix} x+1 & x-1 \\ x-3 & x+2 \end{vmatrix} = \begin{vmatrix} 4 & -1 \\ 1 & 3 \end{vmatrix}$, then write the value of x.

(ii) If $x \in N$ and $\begin{vmatrix} x+3 & -2 \\ -3x & 2x \end{vmatrix} = 8$, then find the value of x.

14 (i) If $A = \begin{bmatrix} 1 & 2 \\ 4 & 2 \end{bmatrix}$, then show that $|2A| = 4|A|$. **[NCERT]**

(ii) If the determinant of matrix A of order 3×3 is of value 4, then write the value of $|3A|$.

15 (i) If A is a 3×3 invertiable matrix, then what will be the value of k, if $\det(A^{-1}) = (\det A)^k$?

(ii) If A is an invertible matrix of order 2 and $\det(A) = 4$, then write the value of $\det(A^{-1})$.

16 If A is skew-symmetric matrix of order 3, then prove that $\det(A) = 0$.

17 If $f(x) = \begin{vmatrix} 0 & x-a & x-b \\ x+a & 0 & x-c \\ x+b & x+c & 0 \end{vmatrix}$, then show that $f(0) = 0$. **[NCERT Exemplar]**

18 If $f(x) = \begin{vmatrix} (1+x)^{17} & (1+x)^{19} & (1+x)^{23} \\ (1+x)^{23} & (1+x)^{29} & (1+x)^{34} \\ (1+x)^{41} & (1+x)^{43} & (1+x)^{47} \end{vmatrix}$

$= A + Bx + Cx^2 + \dots$, then find the value of A. **[NCERT Exemplar]**

19 Show that the points $(a+5, a-4)$, $(a-2, a+3)$ and (a, a) do not lie on a straight line for any value of a. **[NCERT Exemplar]**

[**Hint** Show that the given points are not collinear for any value of a]

20 If the value of a third order determinant is 12, then find the value of the determinant formed by replacing each element by its cofactor. **[NCERT Exemplar]**

21 If for the non-singular matrix A, $A^2 = I$, then find A^{-1}.

22 If A is a non-singular symmetric matrix, then write whether A^{-1} is symmetric or skew-symmetric.

Short Answer Type Questions

4 Marks

23 If $a_1, a_2, a_3, \dots, a_r$ are in GP, then prove that the determinant $\begin{vmatrix} a_{r+1} & a_{r+5} & a_{r+9} \\ a_{r+7} & a_{r+11} & a_{r+15} \\ a_{r+11} & a_{r+17} & a_{r+21} \end{vmatrix}$ is independent of r. **[NCERT Exemplar]**

24 By using the properties of determinant, prove that the determinant $\begin{vmatrix} a & \sin x & \cos x \\ -\sin x & -a & 1 \\ \cos x & 1 & a \end{vmatrix}$ is independent of x. **[ISC 2010, NCERT]**

25 Using properties of determinants, evaluate $\begin{vmatrix} 0 & ab^2 & ac^2 \\ a^2b & 0 & bc^2 \\ a^2c & cb^2 & 0 \end{vmatrix}$. **[ISC 2017]**

26 Prove that $\begin{vmatrix} -a^2 & ab & ac \\ ba & -b^2 & bc \\ ca & cb & -c^2 \end{vmatrix} = 4a^2b^2c^2$.

[**Hint** Take a, b and c common from R_1, R_2 and R_3] **[NCERT]**

27 Find the values of k, if the area of triangle is 4 sq units and vertices are $(-2, 0)$, $(0, 4)$, $(0, k)$. **[NCERT]**

28 Show that the points $A(a, b+c)$, $B(b, c+a)$ and $C(c, a+b)$ are collinear. **[NCERT]**

29 If $A = \begin{bmatrix} 3 & -2 \\ 4 & -2 \end{bmatrix}$, then find the value of λ so that $A^2 = \lambda A - 2I$. Hence find A^{-1}.

30 For the matrix $A = \begin{bmatrix} 1 & 1 & 1 \\ 1 & 2 & -3 \\ 2 & -1 & 3 \end{bmatrix}$, show that $A^3 - 6A^2 + 5A + 11I = O$. Then, find A^{-1}. **[NCERT]**

31 If $x + y + z = 0$, then prove that $\begin{vmatrix} xa & yb & zc \\ yc & za & xb \\ zb & xc & ya \end{vmatrix} = xyz \begin{vmatrix} a & b & c \\ c & a & b \\ b & c & a \end{vmatrix}$. **[NCERT Exemplar]**

32 Let $A = \begin{bmatrix} 1 & \sin\theta & 1 \\ -\sin\theta & 1 & \sin\theta \\ -1 & -\sin\theta & 1 \end{bmatrix}$, where $0 \le \theta \le 2\pi$, then prove that $\det(A) \in [2, 4]$. **[NCERT Exemplar]**

33 If $f(t) = \begin{vmatrix} \cos t & t & 1 \\ 2\sin t & t & 2t \\ \sin t & t & t \end{vmatrix}$, then find $\lim_{t \to 0} \frac{f(t)}{t^2}$. **[NCERT Exemplar]**

34 Find the value of θ satisfying $\begin{vmatrix} 1 & 1 & \sin 3\theta \\ -4 & 3 & \cos 2\theta \\ 7 & -7 & -2 \end{vmatrix} = 0$. **[NCERT Exemplar]**

35 If A, B and C are angles of a triangle, then find the determinant $\begin{vmatrix} -1 & \cos C & \cos B \\ \cos C & -1 & \cos A \\ \cos B & \cos A & -1 \end{vmatrix}$. **[NCERT Exemplar]**

36 Find the number of distinct real roots of $\begin{vmatrix} \sin x & \cos x & \cos x \\ \cos x & \sin x & \cos x \\ \cos x & \cos x & \sin x \end{vmatrix} = 0$ in the interval $-\frac{\pi}{4} \le x \le \frac{\pi}{4}$. **[NCERT Exemplar]**

37 Find the adjoint of the matrix $A = \begin{bmatrix} 1 & 0 & -1 \\ 3 & 4 & 5 \\ 0 & -6 & -7 \end{bmatrix}$, then find A^{-1}. **[ISC 2006]**

38 Given the matrix, $A = \begin{bmatrix} 1 & 0 & 2 \\ -2 & 1 & 0 \\ 0 & -1 & 2 \end{bmatrix}$, then find A^{-1}. **[ISC 2005]**

Long Answer Type Questions

6 Marks

39 A triangle has its three sides equal to a, b and c. If the coordinates of its vertices are $A(x_1, y_1)$, $B(x_2, y_2)$ and $C(x_3, y_3)$, then show that

$$\begin{vmatrix} x_1 & y_1 & 2 \\ x_2 & y_2 & 2 \\ x_3 & y_3 & 2 \end{vmatrix}^2 = (a+b+c)(b+c-a)(c+a-b)(a+b-c).$$ **[NCERT Exemplar]**

40 If $A = \begin{bmatrix} 1 & 3 & 3 \\ 1 & 4 & 3 \\ 1 & 3 & 4 \end{bmatrix}$, then verify that $A \cdot \text{adj}(A) = |A| I$.

Also, find A^{-1}. **[NCERT]**

41 Find the inverse of the matrix $A = \begin{bmatrix} a & b \\ c & \frac{1+bc}{a} \end{bmatrix}$ and show that $aA^{-1} = (a^2 + bc + 1)I - aA$.

42 Suppose $A = \begin{bmatrix} 2 & 2 & 1 \\ -2 & 1 & 2 \\ 1 & -2 & 2 \end{bmatrix}$ and $B = \begin{bmatrix} 1 & 3 & 2 \\ 1 & 1 & 1 \\ 2 & -3 & 1 \end{bmatrix}$, verify that $(AB)^{-1} = B^{-1}A^{-1}$. **[NCERT]**

43 Let $A = \begin{bmatrix} 1 & -2 & 1 \\ -2 & 3 & 1 \\ 1 & 1 & 5 \end{bmatrix}$, then verify that $[\text{adj} A]^{-1} = \text{adj}(A^{-1})$. **[NCERT]**

44 Using matrices, solve the system of equations $4x + 3y + 2z = 60$, $x + 2y + 3z = 45$ and $6x + 2y + 3z = 70$

45 Using the matrices solve the following equations.

$5x + 3y + z = 16$, $2x + y + 3z = 19$ and $x + 2y + 4z = 25$. **[ISC 2010]**

46 If $A = \begin{bmatrix} 3 & -4 & 2 \\ 2 & 3 & 5 \\ 1 & 0 & 1 \end{bmatrix}$, then find A^{-1} and hence solve the following system of equations.

$3x - 4y + 2z = -1$, $2x + 3y + 5z = 7$ and $x + z = 2$

47 Solve the following system of equations using matrix method.

$\frac{2}{x} + \frac{3}{y} + \frac{10}{z} = 4$, $\frac{4}{x} - \frac{6}{y} + \frac{5}{z} = 1$ and $\frac{6}{x} + \frac{9}{y} - \frac{20}{z} = 2$ **[ISC 2011]**

48 If $\begin{bmatrix} 1 & 2 & -3 \\ 2 & 3 & 2 \\ 3 & -3 & 4 \end{bmatrix}$, then find A^{-1} and solve the following system of linear equations.

$x + 2y - 3z = -4$, $2x + 3y + 2z = 2$ and $3x - 3y - 4z = 11$.

Case-Based Type Questions

6 Marks

49 Consider a matrix A of order 3×3 such that $|A| = 5$.

On the basis of above information, answer the following questions.

(i) Find the value of $|\text{adj} A|$.

(ii) Find the value of $|\text{adj}(\text{adj} A)|$.

(iii) Find the value of $|5A^{-1}|$.

50 Two factories decided to award their employees for three values of (a) adaptable to new techniques, (b) careful and alert in difficult situations and (c) keeping calm in tense situations, at the rate of ₹ x, ₹ y and ₹ z per person respectively. The first factory decided to honour respectively 2, 4 and 3 employees with a total prize money of ₹ 29000. The second factory decided to honour respectively 5, 2 and 3 employees with the prize money of ₹ 30500. If the three prizes per person together cost ₹ 9500.

The above situation is expressed by a matrix equation as below

$$AX = B,$$

where A is 3×3 matrix and X and B are 3×1 matrix.

On the basis of above information, answer the following questions.

(i) Find the matrix A.

(ii) Find the inverse of matrix A.

(iii) Find the value of x.

(iv) Find the value of y.

51 A furniture factory uses three types of wood namely, teakwood, rosewood and satinwood for manufacturing three types of furniture, that are table, chair and cot.

The wood requirements (in tonnes) for each type of furniture are given below

	Table	Chair	Cot
Teakwood	2	3	4
Rosewood	1	1	2
Satinwood	3	2	1

It is found that 29 tonnes of teakwood, 13 tonnes of rosewood and 16 tonnes of satinwood are available to make all three types of furniture.

Using the above information, answer the following questions:

(i) Express the data given in the table above in the form of a set of simultaneous equations.

(ii) Solve the set of simultaneous equations formed in subpart (i) by matrix method.

(iii) Hence, find the number of table(s), chair(s) and cot(s) produced.

Answers

1. (d) **2.** (a) **3.** (b) **4.** (c) **5.** (c)

6. (d) **7.** (c) **8.** (d) **9.** (a) **10.** (c)

11. (d) **12.** (c) **13.** (i) $x = 2$ (ii) $x = 2$ **14.** (ii) 108 **15.** (i) $k = -1$ (ii) $\frac{1}{4}$

18. $A = 0$ **20.** 144 **21.** A **22.** Symmetric **25.** $2a^3b^3c^3$

27. $k = 0, 8$ **29.** $\lambda = 1$; $A^{-1} = \begin{bmatrix} -1 & 1 \\ -2 & 3/2 \end{bmatrix}$ **30.** $A^{-1} = \frac{1}{11}\begin{bmatrix} -3 & 4 & 5 \\ 9 & -1 & -4 \\ 5 & -3 & -1 \end{bmatrix}$ **33.** 0 **34.** $n\pi$ or $n\pi + (-1)^n \frac{\pi}{6}$

35. 0 **36.** 1 **37.** $\text{adj}(A) = \begin{bmatrix} 2 & 6 & 4 \\ 21 & -7 & -8 \\ -18 & 6 & 4 \end{bmatrix}$; $A^{-1} = \frac{1}{20}\begin{bmatrix} 2 & 6 & 4 \\ 21 & -7 & -8 \\ -18 & 6 & 4 \end{bmatrix}$

38. $\frac{1}{6}\begin{bmatrix} 2 & -2 & -2 \\ 4 & 2 & -4 \\ 2 & 1 & 1 \end{bmatrix}$ **40.** $A^{-1} = \begin{bmatrix} 7 & -3 & -3 \\ -1 & 1 & 0 \\ -1 & 0 & 1 \end{bmatrix}$ **41.** $\begin{bmatrix} \frac{1+bc}{a} & -b \\ -c & a \end{bmatrix}$ **44.** $x = 5, y = 8$ and $z = 8$

45. $x = 1, y = 2, z = 5$ **46.** $A^{-1} = \frac{-1}{9}\begin{bmatrix} 3 & 4 & -26 \\ 3 & 1 & -11 \\ -3 & -4 & 17 \end{bmatrix}$; $x = 3, y = 2$ and $z = -1$ **47.** $x = 2, y = 3$ and $z = 5$

48. $\frac{1}{59}\begin{bmatrix} 18 & 1 & 13 \\ -2 & 13 & -8 \\ -15 & 9 & -1 \end{bmatrix}$ $x = 3, y = -2$ and $z = 1$

49. (i) 25 (ii) 625 (iii) 25

50. (i) $\begin{bmatrix} 2 & 4 & 3 \\ 5 & 2 & 3 \\ 1 & 1 & 1 \end{bmatrix}$ (ii) $\begin{bmatrix} 1 & 1 & -6 \\ 2 & 1 & -9 \\ -3 & -2 & 16 \end{bmatrix}$ (iii) 2500 (iv) 3000

51. (i) $2x + 3y + 4z = 29$

$x + y + 2z = 13$

$3x + 2y + z = 16$

(ii) $x = 2, y = 3, z = 4$

(iii) Tables = 2, Chairs = 3 and Cots = 4

CHAPTER

05

Continuity and Differentiability

In class XI, we have studied about the concept of limit, i.e. left hand and right hand limits of polynomials, rational and trigonometric functions.

In this chapter, we will introduce the very important concepts of continuity, differentiability and relations between them. We will also illustrate certain geometrical obvious conditions through differential calculus.

- Continuity
- Properties of Continuous Functions
- Differentiability

TOPIC 01 Continuity

If we can draw the graph of a function around the given fixed point without lifting the pen from the plane of paper, then the function is said to be **continuous** at that point.

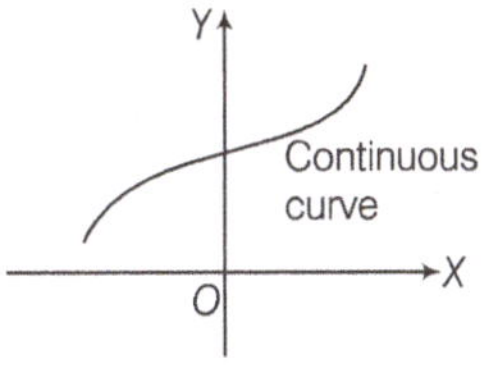

Continuity of a Real Function at a Point

A function $f(x)$ is said to be **continuous** at $x = c$, if

$$\lim_{x \to c^-} f(x) = \lim_{x \to c^+} f(x) = f(c).$$

In other words, a function $f(x)$ is said to be **continuous** at $x = c$, if

(i) $f(x)$ is defined at $x = c$. (ii) $\lim_{x \to c} f(x)$ exists. (iii) $\lim_{x \to c} f(x) = f(c)$,

i.e. left hand limit, right hand limit and the value of the function at $x = c$ coincide.

Note (i) A function $f(x)$ is said to be **left continuous** or **continuous at $x = c$ from left**, if $\lim_{x \to c^-} f(x) = f(c)$.

(ii) A function $f(x)$ is said to be **right continuous** or **continuous at $x = c$ from right**, if $\lim_{x \to c^+} f(x) = f(c)$.

Working Rule to Check Continuity of a Function at Given Point

Suppose a function and a point is given to us and we have to check/examine/discuss the continuity of function at this point.

For this, we use the following steps

I. Write the given function say $f(x)$ and given point say $x = c$, at which we have to check continuity.

II. Find the value of $f(x)$ at $x = c$.

III. Find LHL (Left Hand Limit) of $f(x)$ at $x = c$.

IV. Find RHL (Right Hand Limit) of $f(x)$ at $x = c$.

V. Now, if LHL = RHL = $f(c)$. Then, f is continuous at $x = c$, otherwise not continuous.

Note (i) If a function is not continuous at $x = c$, then it is said to be **discontinuous** at c and c is called the point of discontinuity of the function.

(ii) $f(x)$ is discontinuous at $x = c$, if any one of the following cases arise.

(a) $f(c)$ is not defined. (b) $\lim_{x \to c} f(x)$ does not exist.

(c) $\lim_{x \to c} f(x) \neq f(c)$.

Some Standard Results Based on Limits

(i) $\lim_{x \to a} \frac{x^n - a^n}{x - a} = na^{n-1}$ (ii) $\lim_{x \to 0} \frac{\sin x}{x} = 1$

(iii) $\lim_{x \to 0} \frac{\tan x}{x} = 1$ (iv) $\lim_{x \to 0} \frac{\sin^{-1} x}{x} = 1$

(v) $\lim_{x \to 0} \frac{\tan^{-1} x}{x} = 1$ (vi) $\lim_{x \to 0} \frac{e^x - 1}{x} = 1$

(vii) $\lim_{x \to 0} \frac{a^x - 1}{x} = \log_e a$ (viii) $\lim_{x \to 0} \frac{\log(1 + x)}{x} = 1$

(ix) $\lim_{x \to 0} (1 + x)^{1/x} = e$ (x) $\lim_{x \to \infty} \left(1 + \frac{1}{x}\right)^x = e$

(xi) $\lim_{x \to \infty} \frac{\sin x}{x} = \lim_{x \to \infty} \frac{\cos x}{x} = 0$

Example 1 Examine the continuity of the following functions at given points.

(i) $f(x) = x^2$ at $x = -2$ (ii) $f(x) = 2x^2 - 1$ at $x = 3$

(iii) $f(x) = |x - 5|$ at $x = 5$ **[NCERT]**

Sol. (i) Given, $f(x) = x^2$

At point $x = -2$, $f(x) = (-2)^2 = 4$, i.e. $f(-2) = 4$

and $\lim_{x \to -2} f(x) = \lim_{x \to -2} x^2 = (-2)^2 = 4$

$\because \quad f(-2) = \lim_{x \to -2} f(x)$

$\therefore f(x)$ is continuous at $x = -2$.

(ii) Given, $f(x) = 2x^2 - 1$

At point $x = 3$, $f(x) = 2(3)^2 - 1 = 2(9) - 1 = 17$, i.e. $f(3) = 17$

and $\lim_{x \to 3} f(x) = \lim_{x \to 3} (2x^2 - 1) = 2(3)^2 - 1 = 17$

$\because \quad f(3) = \lim_{x \to 3} f(x)$

$\therefore f(x)$ is continuous at $x = 3$.

(iii) Given, $f(x) = |x - 5| = \begin{cases} x - 5, & \text{if } x \geq 5 \\ 5 - x, & \text{if } x < 5 \end{cases}$

At point $x = 5$, $f(x) = |5 - 5| = 0$, i.e. $f(5) = 0$

Also, LHL $= \lim_{x \to 5^-} f(x) = \lim_{x \to 5^-} (5 - x) = 0$

$[\because$ for $x < 5$, $f(x) = 5 - x]$

and RHL $= \lim_{x \to 5^+} f(x) = \lim_{x \to 5^+} (x - 5) = 0$

$[\because$ for $x > 5$, $f(x) = x - 5]$

$\because \quad$ LHL = RHL = $f(5) = 0$

$\therefore f(x)$ is continuous at $x = 5$.

Example 2 Discuss the continuity of the function

$$f(x) = \begin{cases} \frac{\sin 5x}{x}, & \text{if } x \neq 0 \\ 5, & \text{if } x = 0 \end{cases} \text{ at } x = 0.$$

Sol. We have, $f(x) = \begin{cases} \frac{\sin 5x}{x}, & \text{if } x \neq 0 \\ 5, & \text{if } x = 0 \end{cases}$

At $x = 0$, $\lim_{x \to 0} f(x) = \lim_{x \to 0} \frac{\sin 5x}{x}$

On multiplying numerator and denominator by 5 and then using result $\lim_{x \to 0} \frac{\sin x}{x} = 1$, we get

$$\lim_{x \to 0} f(x) = \lim_{x \to 0} \frac{5 \sin 5x}{5x} = 5 \times 1 = 5$$

Also, at $x = 0$, $f(x) = 5$, i.e. $f(0) = 5$

$\because \quad \lim_{x \to 0} f(x) = f(0)$

$\therefore f(x)$ is continuous at $x = 0$.

Example 3 $f(x) = \frac{x^2 - 9}{x - 3}$ is not defined at $x = 3$.

What value should be assigned to $f(3)$ for continuity of $f(x)$ at $x = 3$? **[ISC 2019]**

Sol. We have, $f(x) = \frac{x^2 - 9}{x - 3}$

Now, RHL $= \lim_{x \to 3^+} f(x) = \lim_{x \to 3^+} \frac{x^2 - 9}{x - 3}$

$$= \lim_{h \to 0} \frac{(3 + h)^2 - 9}{3 + h - 3}$$

On putting $x = 3 + h$ as $x \to 3^+$ when $h \to 0$

$$= \lim_{h \to 0} \frac{9 + h^2 + 6h - 9}{h}$$

$$= \lim_{h \to 0} (6 + h) = 6$$

and $\quad \text{LHL} = \lim_{x \to 3^-} f(x) = \lim_{x \to 3^-} \frac{x^2 - 9}{x - 3}$

$$= \lim_{h \to 0} \frac{(3 - h)^2 - 9}{3 - h - 3}$$

On putting $x = 3 - h$ as $x \to 3^-$ when $h \to 0$

$$= \lim_{h \to 0} \frac{(9 + h^2 - 6h) - 9}{-h}$$

$$= \lim_{h \to 0} (6 - h) = 6$$

To make $f(x)$ continuous, $f(3)$ should be equal to 6.

Removable Discontinuity

When $\lim_{x \to a} f(x)$ exists but either $f(a)$ does not exist or $\lim_{x \to a} f(x) \neq f(a)$, then f has a removable discontinuity at $x = a$, otherwise f has non-removable discontinuity at $x = a$.

Example 4 Find whether the given function has removable or non-removable discontinuity at $x = -2$,

$$f(x) = \begin{cases} \dfrac{x^2 - x - 6}{x + 2}, & \text{if } x \neq -2 \\ 8, & \text{if } x = -2 \end{cases}.$$

Sol. We have, $f(x) = \begin{cases} \dfrac{x^2 - x - 6}{x + 2}, & \text{if } x \neq -2 \\ 8, & \text{if } x = -2 \end{cases}$

At $x = -2$, $\lim_{x \to -2} f(x) = \lim_{x \to -2} \dfrac{x^2 - x - 6}{x + 2}$ ...(i)

Now, factorising the numerator, we get

$$\lim_{x \to -2} f(x) = \lim_{x \to -2} \frac{(x - 3)(x + 2)}{(x + 2)}$$

$$= \lim_{x \to -2} (x - 3) = -2 - 3 = -5$$

and at $x = -2$, $f(x) = 8$ i.e. $f(-2) = 8$

$\because \quad \lim_{x \to -2} f(x) \neq f(-2)$

$\therefore$ $f(x)$ is discontinuous at $x = -2$.

This discontinuity can be removed by redefining $f(x)$ as

$$f(x) = \begin{cases} \dfrac{x^2 - x - 6}{x + 2}, & \text{if } x \neq -2 \\ -5, & \text{if } x = -2 \end{cases}$$

So, $f(x)$ has removable discontinuity at $x = -2$.

Example 5 Find whether the given function has removable or non-removable discontinuity at $x = 0$,

$$f(x) = \begin{cases} \dfrac{|x|}{x}, & \text{if } x \neq 0 \\ 0, & \text{if } x = 0 \end{cases}.$$

Sol. We have, $f(x) = \begin{cases} \dfrac{|x|}{x}, & \text{if } x \neq 0 \\ 0, & \text{if } x = 0 \end{cases}$

At $x = 0$, $\text{LHL} = \lim_{x \to 0^-} f(x) = \lim_{x \to 0^-} \dfrac{|x|}{x}$

$$= \lim_{x \to 0^-} \frac{-x}{x} \qquad [\because |x| = -x \text{ for } x < 0]$$

$$= \lim_{x \to 0^-} (-1) = -1$$

and $\text{RHL} = \lim_{x \to 0^+} f(x)$

$$= \lim_{x \to 0^+} \frac{|x|}{x} = \lim_{x \to 0^+} \frac{x}{x} \qquad [\because |x| = x, \text{ for } x \geq 0]$$

$$= \lim_{x \to 0^+} (1) = 1$$

$\because \quad \text{LHL} \neq \text{RHL}.$

$\therefore$ $f(x)$ is not continuous at $x = 0$, i.e. $f(x)$ is discontinuous at $x = 0$.

Also, no choice of $f(0)$ can make the function continuous at $x = 0$, therefore f has non-removable discontinuity at $x = 0$.

Example 6 Discuss the removable or non-removable discontinuity of the function $f(x)$ at $x = 1/2$, when $f(x)$ is defined as follows.

$$f(x) = \begin{cases} 1/2 + x, & \text{if } 0 \leq x < 1/2 \\ 1, & \text{if } x = 1/2 \\ 3/2 + x, & \text{if } 1/2 < x \leq 1 \end{cases}.$$

Sol. The given function is $f(x) = \begin{cases} \dfrac{1}{2} + x, & \text{if } 0 \leq x < \dfrac{1}{2} \\ 1, & \text{if } x = \dfrac{1}{2} \\ \dfrac{3}{2} + x, & \text{if } \dfrac{1}{2} < x \leq 1 \end{cases}$

At $x = \dfrac{1}{2}$, $\text{LHL} = \lim_{x \to \frac{1}{2}^-} f(x) = \lim_{x \to \frac{1}{2}^-} \left(\dfrac{1}{2} + x\right) = 1$

$$\left[\because \text{for } x < \frac{1}{2}, f(x) = \frac{1}{2} + x\right]$$

$$\text{RHL} = \lim_{x \to \frac{1}{2}^+} f(x) = \lim_{x \to \frac{1}{2}^+} \left(\frac{3}{2} + x\right) = 2$$

$$\left[\because \text{for } x > \frac{1}{2}, f(x) = \frac{3}{2} + x\right]$$

Here, $\text{LHL} \neq \text{RHL}$

$\therefore$ $f(x)$ is discontinuous at $x = 1/2$.

Also, no choice of $f(1/2)$ can make the function continuous at $x = 1/2$, therefore f has non-removable discontinuity at $x = 1/2$.

Continuous Function

A function f is said to be **continuous**, if it is continuous at every point of its domain.

Note

(i) The domain of continuous function may be a proper subset of domain of the function.

(ii) The set of all points where the function is continuous is called its **domain of continuity**.

Continuity of a Function in an Interval

(i) A function $f(x)$ is said to be **continuous in open interval** (a, b), if it is continuous for every value of x in the interval (a, b).

(ii) A function $f(x)$ is said to be **continuous in closed interval** $[a, b]$, if

(a) it is continuous for every value of x in the open interval (a, b).

(b) $f(x)$ is continuous at $x = a$ from right,

i.e. $\lim_{x \to a^+} f(x) = f(a)$.

(c) $f(x)$ is continuous at $x = b$ from left,

i.e. $\lim_{x \to b^-} f(x) = f(b)$.

Note (i) If the domain of function f is a singleton set, i.e. it is defined only at one point, then it is a continuous function.

(ii) A continuous function in an interval has a least and greatest value.

Example 7 Discuss the continuity of the function f given by $f(x) = x^3 + x^2 - 1$.

Sol. Given, $f(x) = x^3 + x^2 - 1$.

Here, $f(x)$ is always defined in R, so domain of $f = R$.

Now, we need to check the continuity at every point of R.

Let c be any real number, i.e. $c \in R$.

Then, at $x = c$, $f(x) = c^3 + c^2 - 1$,

i.e. $f(c) = c^3 + c^2 - 1$

and $\lim_{x \to c} f(x) = \lim_{x \to c} (x^3 + x^2 - 1)$

$= c^3 + c^2 - 1$

$\because \quad f(c) = \lim_{x \to c} f(x)$

So, $f(x)$ is continuous at $x = c$.

But $c \in R$ was arbitrary, therefore f is continuous for every real values of x.

Example 8 Discuss the continuity of the function f, where f is defined by

$$f(x) = \begin{cases} -2, & \text{if } x \le -1 \\ 2x, & \text{if } -1 < x \le 1. \\ 2, & \text{if } x > 1 \end{cases}$$

[NCERT]

Sol. We have, $f(x) = \begin{cases} -2, & \text{if } x \le -1 \\ 2x, & \text{if } -1 < x \le 1. \\ 2, & \text{if } x > 1 \end{cases}$

Graphically, $f(x)$ can be plotted as shown in the following figure.

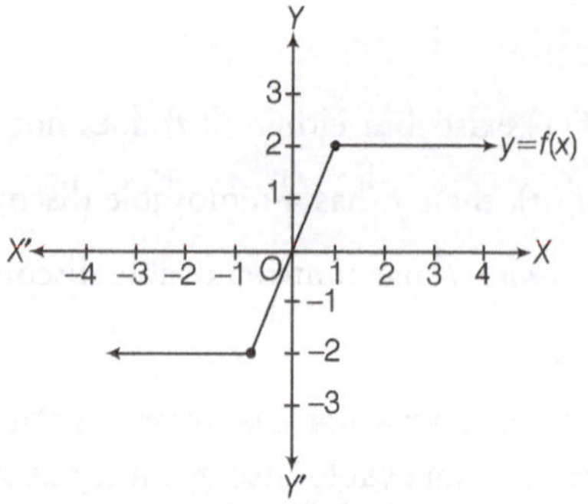

Note that to draw the graph of this function there is no need to lift the pen from the plane of the paper. So, we can say $f(x)$ is continuous everywhere.

Topic Practice 1

Very Short Answer Type Questions

2 Marks

1 Examine the continuity of the following functions at the given point. **[NCERT]**

(i) $f(x) = 5x - 3$ at $x = -3$

(ii) $f(x) = x^2 + 3x + 4$ at $x = 1$

2 Show that the function $f(x) = 2x - |x|$ is continuous at $x = 0$.

3 Show that the function

$$f(x) = \begin{cases} \dfrac{\sin x}{x} + \cos x, & \text{if } x \ne 0 \\ 2, & \text{if } x = 0 \end{cases}$$

is continuous at $x = 0$.

Short Answer Type Questions

(4 Marks)

4 Is the function f defined by $f(x)=\begin{cases}x, & \text{if } x\le 1\\ 5, & \text{if } x>1\end{cases}$ continuous at $x=0$, at $x=1$ and at $x=2$? **[NCERT]**

5 Discuss the continuity of the following function at $x=0$.

$$f(x)=\begin{cases}\dfrac{x^4+2x^3+x^2}{\tan^{-1}x}, & \text{if } x\neq 0\\ 0, & \text{if } x=0\end{cases}$$

6 Is the function $f(x)=\dfrac{3x+4\tan x}{x}$ continuous at $x=0$? If not, then how may the function be defined to make it continuous at this point?

7 If $f(x)=\dfrac{\sqrt{2}\cos x-1}{\cot x-1}, x\neq\dfrac{\pi}{4}$. Then, find the value of $f(\pi/4)$, so that $f(x)$ becomes continuous at $x=\pi/4$. **[NCERT Exemplar]**

8 Show that the function defined by $g(x)=x-[x]$ is discontinuous at all integral points. Here, $[x]$ denotes the greatest integer less than or equal to x. **[NCERT]**

9 Examine the continuity of a function

$$f(x)=\begin{cases}|x|\cos\dfrac{1}{x}, & \text{if } x\neq 0\\ 0, & \text{if } x=0\end{cases} \text{ at } x=0.$$ **[NCERT Exemplar]**

10 Show that the function

$$f(x)=\begin{cases}\dfrac{e^{1/x}-1}{e^{1/x}+1}, & \text{when } x\neq 0\\ 0, & \text{when } x=0\end{cases}$$

has non-removable discontinuity at $x=0$. **[NCERT Exemplar]**

11 Show that the function $f(x)=\begin{cases}\dfrac{e^{1/x}}{1+e^{1/x}}, & \text{if } x\neq 0\\ 0, & \text{if } x=0\end{cases}$ is discontinuous at $x=0$. **[NCERT Exemplar]**

12 Examine the function $f(x)=\begin{cases}x-1, & x<0\\ 1/4, & x=0\\ x^2-1, & x>0\end{cases}$

Discuss the continuity and if discontinuous remove the discontinuity.

Hints & Solutions

1. Similar as Example 1.

[**Ans.** (i) Continuous (ii) Continuous]

2. The given function is $f(x)=2x-|x|$.

$\therefore\ f(x)=\begin{cases}2x-x, & \text{if } x\ge 0\\ 2x-(-x), & \text{if } x<0\end{cases}\left[\because |x|=\begin{cases}x, & \text{if } x\ge 0\\ -x, & \text{if } x<0\end{cases}\right]$

i.e. $f(x)=\begin{cases}x, & \text{if } x\ge 0\\ 3x, & \text{if } x<0\end{cases}$ [1/2]

At $x=0$, LHL $=\lim\limits_{x\to 0^-}f(x)=\lim\limits_{x\to 0^-}3x=3\times 0=0$ [1/2]

and RHL $=\lim\limits_{x\to 0^+}f(x)=\lim\limits_{x\to 0^+}x=0$

Also, $f(0)=0$ [1/2]

Thus, LHL = RHL = $f(0)$

Hence, $f(x)$ is continuous function at $x=0$. [1/2]

3. We have, $f(x)=\begin{cases}\dfrac{\sin x}{x}+\cos x, & x\neq 0\\ 2, & x=0\end{cases}$

Here, $\lim\limits_{x\to 0}f(x)=\lim\limits_{x\to 0}\left[\dfrac{\sin x}{x}+\cos x\right]$

$=\lim\limits_{x\to 0}\dfrac{\sin x}{x}+\lim\limits_{x\to 0}\cos x$

$=1+1=2\quad\left[\because \lim\limits_{x\to 0}\dfrac{\sin x}{x}=1 \text{ and } \cos 0=1\right]$ [1]

and $f(0)=2$

$\therefore\ \lim\limits_{x\to 0}f(x)=f(0)$

Hence, $f(x)$ is continuous at $x=0$. [1]

4. We have, $f(x)=\begin{cases}x, & \text{if } x\le 1\\ 5, & \text{if } x>1\end{cases}$

At $x=0$, $\lim\limits_{x\to 0}f(x)=\lim\limits_{x\to 0}x$ [$\because$ in the neighbourhood of 0, $f(x)=x$]

$=0$

and $f(0)=0$

$\because\ f(0)=\lim\limits_{x\to 0}f(x)$

$\therefore f$ is continuous at $x=0$. [1]

At $x=1$,

LHL $=\lim\limits_{x\to 1^-}f(x)=\lim\limits_{x\to 1^-}x$ [$\because$ for $x<1$, $f(x)=x$]

$=1$

RHL $=\lim\limits_{x\to 1^+}f(x)=\lim\limits_{x\to 1^+}5$ [$\because$ for $x>1$, $f(x)=5$]

$=5$

and $f(1)=1$

$\because$ LHL $\neq$ RHL

$\therefore\ f$ is not continuous at $x=1$. [2]

At $x=2$, $\lim\limits_{x\to 2}f(x)=\lim\limits_{x\to 2}5$ [$\because$ in the neighbourhood of 2, $f(x)=5$]

$=5$

and $f(2)=5$

$\because\ f(2)=\lim\limits_{x\to 2}f(x)$

$\therefore\ f$ is continuous at $x=2$. [1]

Hence, f is continuous at $x=0$ and $x=2$ but not at $x=1$.

5. **Hint** $\lim_{x\to 0} f(x) = \lim_{x\to 0}\left(\frac{x^4+2x^3+x^2}{\tan^{-1}x}\right) = \lim_{x\to 0}\frac{x^2(x+1)^2}{\tan^{-1}x}$

$$= \lim_{x\to 0} x(x+1)^2 = 0 \quad \left[\because \lim_{x\to 0}\frac{\tan^{-1}x}{x} = 1\right]$$

[**Ans.** $f(x)$ is continuous at $x = 0$]

6. **Hint** $\lim_{x\to 0} f(x) = \lim_{x\to 0}\left(\frac{3x+4\tan x}{x}\right)$

$$= \lim_{x\to 0}\left(\frac{3x}{x}+\frac{4\tan x}{x}\right) = 3+4 = 7 \neq f(0)$$

Thus, for f to be continuous $f(0)$ should be 7.

$$\left[\textbf{Ans. } f(x) = \begin{cases}\dfrac{3x+4\tan x}{x}, & \text{when } x\neq 0\\ 7, & \text{when } x = 0\end{cases}\right]$$

7. For $f(x)$ to be continuous at $x = \frac{\pi}{4}$,

$$\lim_{x\to\pi/4} f(x) = f\left(\frac{\pi}{4}\right) \quad [1/2]$$

Consider, $\lim_{x\to\frac{\pi}{4}}\frac{\sqrt{2}\cos x - 1}{\cot x - 1} = \lim_{x\to\frac{\pi}{4}}\frac{(\sqrt{2}\cos x - 1)\sin x}{(\cos x - \sin x)}$

$$= \lim_{x\to\frac{\pi}{4}}\left[\frac{(\sqrt{2}\cos x - 1)(\sqrt{2}\cos x + 1)}{(\sqrt{2}\cos x + 1)}\cdot\frac{\sin x}{(\cos x - \sin x)}\cdot\frac{(\cos x + \sin x)}{(\cos x + \sin x)}\right] \quad [1]$$

$$= \lim_{x\to\frac{\pi}{4}}\left[\frac{(\sqrt{2}\cos x)^2 - 1}{\sqrt{2}\cos x + 1}\cdot\frac{\sin x}{(\cos^2 x - \sin^2 x)}\cdot(\cos x + \sin x)\right] \quad [1]$$

$$= \lim_{x\to\frac{\pi}{4}}\left[\frac{2\cos^2 x - 1}{\sqrt{2}\cos x + 1}\cdot\frac{\sin x}{\cos 2x}\cdot(\cos x + \sin x)\right]$$

$$= \lim_{x\to\frac{\pi}{4}}\frac{\cos 2x}{\cos 2x}\cdot\lim_{x\to\frac{\pi}{4}}\frac{\sin x(\cos x + \sin x)}{\sqrt{2}\cos x + 1} \quad [1/2]$$

$$= 1\times\frac{\frac{1}{\sqrt{2}}\left(\frac{1}{\sqrt{2}}+\frac{1}{\sqrt{2}}\right)}{\sqrt{2}\times\frac{1}{\sqrt{2}}+1} = \frac{1}{2} \quad [1]$$

8. Here, $g(x) = x - [x]$

Let a be an integer and h is very small, $h > 0$, then

$$[a-h] = a-1,\ [a+h] = a \text{ and } [a] = a. \quad [1]$$

At $x = a$, LHL $= \lim_{x\to a^-} g(x) = \lim_{x\to a^-}(x - [x])$ [1/2]

Put $x = a - h$; when $x\to a^-$, then $h\to 0^+$

LHL $= \lim_{h\to 0^+}(a - h - [a-h])$

$$= \lim_{h\to 0^+}(a - h - (a-1)) \quad [\because [a-h] = a-1]$$

$$= \lim_{h\to 0^+}(-h+1) = 1 \quad [1/2]$$

RHL $= \lim_{x\to a^+} g(x) = \lim_{x\to a^+}(x - [x])$

Put $x = a + h$; when $x\to a^+$, then $h\to 0^+$ [1]

RHL $= \lim_{h\to 0^+}(a + h - [a+h]) = \lim_{h\to 0^+}(a + h - a)$

$$= \lim_{h\to 0^+} h = 0 \quad [\because [a+h] = a]$$

$\because$ LHL $\neq$ RHL

$\therefore g(x)$ is discontinuous at all integral points. [1]

9. Given, $f(x) = \begin{cases}|x|\cos\frac{1}{x}, & \text{if } x\neq 0\\ 0, & \text{if } x = 0\end{cases}$

At $x = 0$,

LHL $= \lim_{x\to 0^-} f(x) = \lim_{x\to 0^-}|x|\cos\frac{1}{x} = \lim_{x\to 0^-}(-x)\cos\frac{1}{x}$

$= 0\times$ (An oscillating value lie between -1 and 1)

$= 0$ $\quad[\because \cos\theta$ lies between -1 to 1$]$ [1½]

RHL $= \lim_{x\to 0^+} f(x) = \lim_{x\to 0^+}|x|\cos\frac{1}{x} = \lim_{x\to 0^+} x\cos\frac{1}{x}$

$= 0\times$ (An oscillating value lie between -1 and 1)

$= 0$ [1½]

and $f(0) = 0$

$\because$ LHL = RHL = $f(0)$

$\therefore f(x)$ is continuous at $x = 0$. [1]

10. We have, $\begin{cases}\dfrac{e^{1/x}-1}{e^{1/x}+1}, & \text{when } x\neq 0\\ 0, & \text{when } x = 0\end{cases}$

At $x = 0$, $f(0) = 0$

LHL $= \lim_{x\to 0^-} f(x) = \lim_{x\to 0^-}\frac{(e^{1/x}-1)}{(e^{1/x}+1)}$ [1]

$$= \frac{0-1}{0+1} = -1 \quad \left[\because x\to 0^- \Rightarrow \frac{1}{x}\to -\infty \Rightarrow e^{-\infty}\to 0\right] \quad [1]$$

and RHL $= \lim_{x\to 0^+} f(x) = \lim_{x\to 0^+}\frac{e^{1/x}-1}{e^{1/x}+1}$

On dividing numerator and denominator by $e^{1/x}$, we get

$$\text{RHL} = \lim_{x\to 0^+}\frac{\left(1-\frac{1}{e^{1/x}}\right)}{\left(1+\frac{1}{e^{1/x}}\right)} = \lim_{x\to 0^+}\frac{(1-e^{-1/x})}{(1+e^{-1/x})} = \frac{1-0}{1+0} = 1 \quad [1]$$

$$\left[\because x\to 0^+ \Rightarrow \frac{1}{x}\to\infty \Rightarrow e^{1/x}\to\infty \Rightarrow e^{-1/x}\to 0\right]$$

$\because$ LHL $\neq$ RHL

$\therefore f(x)$ has non-removable discontinuity. [1]

11. Solve as Question 10.

12. Graphically, $f(x)$ can be plotted as shown in the following figure

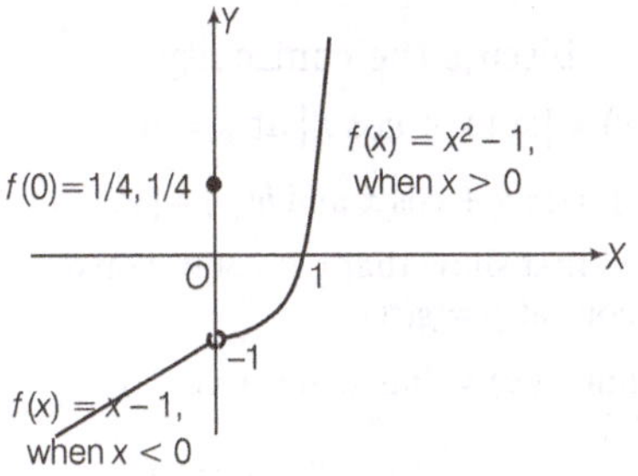

Clearly, $f(x)$ is continuous everywhere except at $x=0$.
Also, $\lim_{x\to 0^-} f(x) = \lim_{x\to 0^+} f(x) = -1$, but $f(0)=1/4$

So, $f(x)$ has removable discontinuity at $x=0$ and $f(x)$ could be made continuous by taking $f(0)=-1$

$$\Rightarrow \quad f(x)=\begin{cases} x-1, & x<0 \\ -1, & x=0 \\ x^2-1, & x>0 \end{cases}$$

TOPIC 02 Properties of Continuous Functions

There are some functions which are always continuous in their respective domain.

e.g.

(i) Constant function is continuous everywhere.

(ii) Identity function is continuous everywhere.

(iii) Polynomial function is continuous everywhere.

(iv) Rational function is continuous at every point of its domain.

(v) Modulus (or absolute) function $f(x)=|x|$ is continuous everywhere.

(vi) All trigonometric functions are continuous at every point of their respective domain of definition.

(vii) The greatest integer function is continuous everywhere except at integers.

(viii) The basic inverse trigonometric functions are continuous at every point of their respective domain of definition.

Algebra of Continuous Functions

We know that continuity of a function at a point is entirely dictated by the limit of the function at that point, so it is reasonable to expect results similar to the case of limits.

Theorem 1. Let f and g be two real functions continuous at a real number c, then

(i) $(f+g)$ is continuous at $x=c$.

(ii) $(f-g)$ is continuous at $x=c$.

(iii) fg is continuous at $x=c$.

(iv) f/g is continuous at $x=c$, provided that $g(c)\neq 0$.

(v) αf is continuous at $x=c$, for all $\alpha\in R$.

Proof Given, f and g are continuous at $x=c$.

So, $\lim_{x\to c} f(x)=f(c)$ and $\lim_{x\to c} g(x)=g(c)$

Now, $\lim_{x\to c}(f+g)x = \lim_{x\to c}[f(x)+g(x)]$

$$= \lim_{x\to c} f(x)+\lim_{x\to c} g(x)$$
$$= f(c)+g(c)$$
$$= (f+g)(c)$$

Hence, $(f+g)$ is continuous at $x=c$.
Similarly, we can prove other parts.

Note

(i) In particular, if $\alpha=-1$, then $-f$ is continuous at $x=c$. Thus, if f is continuous, then $-f$ is also continuous.

(ii) In part (iv) of given theorem, if we take f = constant function say λ, then $\frac{\lambda}{g}$ is continuous at $x=c$, provided $g(c)\neq 0$.

In particular, if $\lambda=1$, then $\frac{1}{g}$ is continuous at $x=c$. Thus, if g is continuous, then $\frac{1}{g}$ is also continuous provided that $g\neq 0$.

(iii) f^n is continuous at $x=c$ for all $n\in N$.

Theorem 2. Let D_1 and D_2 be the domains of continuity of the functions f and g respectively, then

(i) αf is continuous on D_1 for all $\alpha\in R$.

(ii) $f+g$, $f-g$ and fg are continuous on $D_1\cap D_2$.

(iii) f/g is also continuous on $D_1\cap D_2$ except those points, where $g(x)=0$.

(iv) f^n is continuous on D_1 for all $n\in N$.

(v) $\frac{1}{f}$ is continuous on D_1 except at those points where $f(x)=0$.

Theorem 3. *The composition of two continuous function is continuous* Suppose f and g are real valued functions such that (fog) is defined at c. If g is continuous at c and if f is continuous at $g(c)$, then (fog) is continuous at c.

Note If f and g are two real valued functions, then $(fog)(x) = f(g(x))$ is defined, whenever the range of g is a subset of domain of f.

Example 1 Discuss the continuity of sine function. **[NCERT]**

Sol. We know that, $f(x) = \sin x$ is defined for every real number. So, we need to show $f(x)$ is continuous for every real number.

Let c be any real number.

Then, $\lim_{x \to c} f(x) = \lim_{x \to c} \sin x = \lim_{h \to 0} \sin(c + h)$

[put $x = c + h$; when $x \to c$, then $h \to 0$]

$$= \lim_{h \to 0} [\sin c \cos h + \cos c \sin h]$$

$$= \lim_{h \to 0} (\sin c \cos h) + \lim_{h \to 0} (\cos c \sin h)$$

$$= \sin c \lim_{h \to 0} \cos h + \cos c \lim_{h \to 0} \sin h$$

$$= \sin c \times 1 + \cos c \times 0$$

$\left[\because \lim_{x \to 0} \cos x = 1 \text{ and } \lim_{x \to 0} \sin x = 0\right]$

$$= \sin c = f(c)$$

But c was arbitrary real number.

$\therefore$ f is a continuous function.

Example 2 A function $f(x)$ is defined below

$$f(x) = \begin{vmatrix} 1 & \cos x & 1 - \cos x \\ 1 + \sin x & \cos x & 1 + \sin x - \cos x \\ \sin x & \sin x & 1 \end{vmatrix}$$

Determine $f(x)$ and check continuity of $f(x)$, $\forall x \in R$.

Sol. Given, $f(x) = \begin{vmatrix} 1 & \cos x & 1 - \cos x \\ 1 + \sin x & \cos x & 1 + \sin x - \cos x \\ \sin x & \sin x & 1 \end{vmatrix}$

On applying $C_3 \to C_3 + C_2 - C_1$, we get

$$f(x) = \begin{vmatrix} 1 & \cos x & 0 \\ 1 + \sin x & \cos x & 0 \\ \sin x & \sin x & 1 \end{vmatrix}$$

On expanding along C_3, we get

$$f(x) = 0 + 0 + 1[\cos x - \cos x(1 + \sin x)]$$

$$= \cos x - \cos x - \cos x \sin x$$

$$= -\frac{1}{2}(2\sin x \cos x)$$

$= -\frac{1}{2}\sin 2x$, which is continuous everywhere.

[$\because$ $\sin x$ is continuous everywhere, so $\lambda \sin x$ is also continuous for any constant value λ]

Example 3 Discuss the continuity of

$$f(x) = |\sin x + \cos x| \text{ at } x = \pi.$$

Sol. Let $g(x) = \sin x + \cos x$ and $h(y) = |y|$

We shall first show that g is continuous at $x = \pi$ and h is continuous at $y = g(\pi)$.

Now, $\lim_{x \to \pi} g(x) = \lim_{x \to \pi} (\sin x + \cos x)$

$$= \sin \pi + \cos \pi = -1$$

Also, $g(\pi) = \sin \pi + \cos \pi = -1$

$\Rightarrow$ $\lim_{x \to \pi} g(x) = g(\pi)$

So, g is continuous at $x = \pi$.

Since, $g(\pi) = -1$

$\therefore$ $h[g(\pi)] = h(-1) = |-1| = 1$

Also, $\lim_{y \to (-1)^+} h(y) = \lim_{y \to (-1)^+} |y| = \lim_{y \to -1^+} (-y) = 1$

[$\because$ for $y < 0$, $|y| = -y$]

and $\lim_{y \to (-1)^-} h(y) = \lim_{y \to (-1)^-} |y| = \lim_{y \to (-1)^-} (-y) = 1$

$\therefore$ $h[g(\pi)] = \lim_{y \to g(\pi)} h(y)$

This shows that h is continuous at $g(\pi)$.

Consequently, (hog) is continuous at $x = \pi$.

But $hog(x) = h[g(x)] = h(\sin x + \cos x)$

$$= |\sin x + \cos x| = f(x)$$

Hence, $f(x)$ is continuous at $x = \pi$.

Example 4 Show that the function defined by $f(x) = \sin(x^2)$ is a continuous function. **[NCERT]**

Sol. Given, $f(x) = \sin(x^2)$

It is defined for every real number.

Suppose $g(x) = \sin x$ and $h(x) = x^2$, then $f(x) = goh(x)$

Since, both $g(x)$ and $h(x)$ are continuous functions.

So, their composition is also continuous function.

Hence, $f(x) = \sin(x^2)$ is a continuous function.

Problems Based on Continuity

There are many problems which are based on continuity. Some of them with their method of solving are given below.

|TYPE I|

Problems Based on Finding Unknown Constant in Continuous Function

Suppose a function having one or two unknown constants is given to us. Also, suppose function is continuous at some point say $x = c$, then for finding the value of unknown or unknowns, we use the following steps

I. First, write the given function having unknown constants and the point say $x = c$ at which it is continuous.
II. Find the value of function at $x = c$, which may or may not be in terms of unknown.
III. Find LHL at $x = c$, which may or may not be in terms of unknown.
IV. Find RHL at $x = c$, which may or may not be in terms of unknown.
V. Use the condition of continuity,
i.e. $f(c) = \text{LHL} = \text{RHL}$
and simplify them by taking two terms at a time to get values of unknown.

Example 5 Find the value of a, so that

$$f(x) = \begin{cases} ax + 5, & \text{if } x \le 2 \\ x - 1, & \text{if } x > 2 \end{cases}$$ is continuous at $x = 2$.

Sol. Given, $f(x) = \begin{cases} ax + 5, & \text{if } x \le 2 \\ x - 1, & \text{if } x > 2 \end{cases}$

and at $x = 2$, $f(x)$ is continuous.

$\therefore \quad x = c = 2$

Here, a is an unknown constant.

At $x = 2$, $f(x) = a(2) + 5 = 2a + 5$, i.e. $f(2) = 2a + 5$

$$\text{LHL} = \lim_{x \to 2^-} f(x) = \lim_{x \to 2^-} (ax + 5) = 2a + 5$$

and $$\text{RHL} = \lim_{x \to 2^+} f(x) = \lim_{x \to 2^+} (x - 1) = 1$$

Since, $f(x)$ is continuous at $x = 2$.

$\therefore \quad \text{LHL} = \text{RHL} = f(2)$

$\Rightarrow \quad 2a + 5 = 1 = 2a + 5 \Rightarrow 2a + 5 = 1$

$\Rightarrow \quad 2a = -4 \Rightarrow a = -2$

Hence, the required value of a is -2 for which $f(x)$ is continuous at $x = 2$.

Example 6 Find the relationship between a and b so that the function f defined by $f(x) = \begin{cases} ax + 1, & \text{if } x \le 3 \\ bx + 3, & \text{if } x > 3 \end{cases}$ is continuous at $x = 3$. **[NCERT]**

Sol. Given, $f(x) = \begin{cases} ax + 1, & \text{if } x \le 3 \\ bx + 3, & \text{if } x > 3 \end{cases}$

and $f(x)$ is continuous at $x = 3$.

Here, a and b are two unknowns.

Now, at $x = 3$, $f(3) = a(3) + 1 = 3a + 1$, i.e. $f(3) = 3a + 1$

$$\text{LHL} = \lim_{x \to 3^-} f(x) = \lim_{x \to 3^-} (ax + 1) = 3a + 1$$

and $$\text{RHL} = \lim_{x \to 3^+} f(x) = \lim_{x \to 3^+} \{bx + 3\} = 3b + 3$$

Since, $f(x)$ is continuous at $x = 3$.

$\therefore \quad f(3) = \text{LHL} = \text{RHL}.$

$\Rightarrow \quad 3a + 1 = 3a + 1 = 3b + 3$

$\Rightarrow \quad 3a + 1 = 3b + 3 \Rightarrow 3a = 3b + 3 - 1$

$\Rightarrow \quad a = \dfrac{(3b + 2)}{3} \Rightarrow a = b + \dfrac{2}{3}$

which is the required relation between a and b.

|TYPE III|

Problems Based on Finding Points of Discontinuity of a Function

Suppose a function $f(x)$ is given to us and we have to find points of discontinuity, then we use following steps

I. First, find all possible points of given domain at which we have doubt for continuity of $f(x)$, say it is $x = a$. (here, more than one point is also possible)
II. Now, find LHL and RHL of $f(x)$ at $x = a$, if
(i) $f(x)$ is continuous at $x = a$, so there is no point of discontinuity.
(ii) $f(x)$ is not continuous at $x = a$, then $x = a$, is the required point of discontinuity.

Example 7 Discuss the continuity of the function f defined by $f(x) = \begin{cases} x + 2, & \text{if } x \le 1 \\ x - 2, & \text{if } x > 1 \end{cases}$.

Sol. Given, $f(x) = \begin{cases} x + 2, & \text{if } x \le 1 \\ x - 2, & \text{if } x > 1 \end{cases}$

When $x < 1$, we have $f(x) = x + 2$, which is a polynomial function, so it is continuous for each $x < 1$.

Also, when $x > 1$, we have $f(x) = x - 2$, which is a polynomial function, so it is continuous for each point $x > 1$.

Now, we have to check the continuity at $x = 1$.

$$\text{LHL} = \lim_{x \to 1^-} f(x) = \lim_{x \to 1^-} (x + 2) = 3$$

and $$\text{RHL} = \lim_{x \to 1^+} f(x) = \lim_{x \to 1^+} (x - 2) = -1$$

$\because \quad \text{LHL} \ne \text{RHL}$ at $x = 1$.

So, $f(x)$ is not continuous at $x = 1$.

Hence, $x = 1$ is the only point of discontinuity of f.

Example 8 Find all points of discontinuity of f, where f is defined by $f(x) = \begin{cases} |x| + 3, & \text{if } x \le -3 \\ -2x, & \text{if } -3 < x < 3 \\ 6x + 2, & \text{if } x \ge 3 \end{cases}$. **[NCERT]**

Sol. Given, $f(x)=\begin{cases}|x|+3, & \text{if } x\le -3\\ -2x, & \text{if } -3<x<3\\ 6x+2, & \text{if } x\ge 3\end{cases}$

$=\begin{cases}-x+3, & \text{if } x\le -3\\ -2x, & \text{if } -3<x<3\\ 6x+2, & \text{if } x\ge 3\end{cases}$

Here, we have to check the continuity only at points $x=-3$ and $x=3$.

[$\because$ functions defined in each interval is a polynomial, so it is continuous at every point except possibly at $x=-3$ and $x=3$]

At $x=-3$, LHL $=\lim_{x\to -3^-} f(x)=\lim_{x\to -3^-}\{-x+3\}=6$

RHL $=\lim_{x\to -3^+} f(x)=\lim_{x\to -3^+}(-2x)=6$

and $f(-3)=-(-3)+3=6$

$\because$ $f(-3)=$ LHL $=$ RHL.

So, $f(x)$ is continuous at $x=-3$.

At $x=3$,

LHL $=\lim_{x\to 3^-} f(x)=\lim_{x\to 3^-}(-2x)=-6$

RHL $=\lim_{x\to 3^+} f(x)=\lim_{x\to 3^+}(6x+2)=20$

$\because$ LHL $\ne$ RHL.

So, $f(x)$ is not continuous at $x=3$.

Hence, point of discontinuity is $x=3$.

Topic Practice 2

Very Short Answer Type Questions

(2 Marks)

1 Examine the following functions for continuity.

(i) $f(x)=\dfrac{1}{x-5}, x\ne 5$ **[NCERT]**

(ii) $f(x)=\dfrac{1}{x+3}, x\in R$

(iii) $f(x)=\dfrac{x^2-25}{x+5}, x\ne -5$ **[NCERT]**

2 Show that the function defined by $f(x)=\cos x^2$ is a continuous function. **[NCERT]**

3 Examine that $\sin|x|$ is a continuous function.

4 Show that the function $f(x)=\cos|x|$ is continuous.

5 Determine the value of 'k' for which the following function is continuous at $x=3$.

$f(x)=\begin{cases}\dfrac{(x+3)^2-36}{x-3}, & x\ne 3\\ k, & x=3\end{cases}$ **[ISC 2024]**

6 Find the value of constant 'k', so that the function f defined as

$f(x)=\begin{cases}\dfrac{x^2-2x-3}{x+1}, & \text{if } x\ne -1\\ k, & \text{if } x=-1\end{cases}$

is continuous at $x=-1$. **[ISC 2018]**

7 Find the value of k for which the function

$f(x)=\begin{cases}\dfrac{x^2+3x-10}{x-2}, & x\ne 2\\ k, & x=2\end{cases}$ is continuous at $x=2$.

8 For what value of k, the function

$f(x)=\begin{cases}\dfrac{\tan 2x}{x}, & \text{if } x\ne 0\\ k, & \text{if } x=0\end{cases}$ is continuous at $x=0$?

9 If the function $f(x)=\begin{cases}\dfrac{\sin x}{x}+\cos x, & \text{if } x\ne 0\\ k, & \text{if } x=0\end{cases}$ is continuous at $x=0$, then find the value of k. **[NCERT Exemplar]**

10 Find the value of a, so that the function $f(x)$ is defined by $f(x)=\begin{cases}\dfrac{\sin^2 ax}{x^2}, & x\ne 0\\ 1, & x=0\end{cases}$ may be continuous at $x=0$.

11 Find the value of p for which the function

$f(x)=\begin{cases}\dfrac{1-\cos 4x}{x^2}, & x\ne 0\\ p, & x=0\end{cases}$ is continuous at $x=0$.

Short Answer Type Questions

(4 Marks)

12 Show that tangent function is continuous in their domain.

13 Show that the function f defined by $f(x)=|1-x+|x||$, where x is any real number is a continuous function. **[NCERT]**

14 Find the value of k for which the function

$f(x)=\begin{cases}\dfrac{\sin x-\cos x}{4x-\pi}, & x\ne \dfrac{\pi}{4}\\ k, & x=\dfrac{\pi}{4}\end{cases}$ is continuous at $x=\dfrac{\pi}{4}$.

15 Find the value of m, such that the function

$$f(x)=\begin{cases} m(x^2-2x), & \text{if } x<0 \\ \cos x, & \text{if } x\ge 0\end{cases}$$ is continuous at $x=0$.

16 Find the value of k, so that the function defined by $f(x)=\begin{cases} kx+1, & \text{if } x\le \pi \\ \cos x, & \text{if } x>\pi\end{cases}$ is continuous at $x=\pi$.

17 For what value of λ is the function

$$f(x)=\begin{cases} \lambda(x^2-2x), & \text{if } x\le 0 \\ 4x+1, & \text{if } x>0\end{cases}$$ continuous at $x=0$?

What about continuity at $x=1$?

18 Prove that the function

$$f(x)=\begin{cases} \dfrac{x}{|x|+2x^2}, & \text{if } x\ne 0 \\ k, & \text{if } x=0\end{cases}$$ is continuous at $x=0$

regardless of the value of k.

19 If $f(x)=\begin{cases} \dfrac{\cos^2 x-\sin^2 x-1}{\sqrt{x^2+1}-1}, & \text{if } x\ne 0 \\ k, & \text{if } x=0\end{cases}$ is continuous at $x=0$, then find k.

20 Discuss the continuity of function f defined by

$$f(x)=\begin{cases} \dfrac{1}{2}-x, & \text{if } 0\le x<\dfrac{1}{2} \\ 1, & \text{if } x=\dfrac{1}{2} \\ \dfrac{3}{2}-x, & \text{if } \dfrac{1}{2}<x\le 1\end{cases}.$$

21 Given, $f(x)=\dfrac{1}{x-1}$. Find the point(s) of discontinuity of composite function $y=f\{f(x)\}$.

Long Answer Type Questions

6 Marks

22 Find the values of a and b such that the function defined by

$$f(x)=\begin{cases} 5, & \text{if } x\le 2 \\ ax+b, & \text{if } 2<x<10 \\ 21, & \text{if } x\ge 10\end{cases}$$

is a continuous function. **[NCERT]**

23 Let $f(x)=\begin{cases} \dfrac{1-\cos 4x}{x^2}, & \text{if } x<0 \\ a, & \text{if } x=0 \\ \dfrac{\sqrt{x}}{\sqrt{16+\sqrt{x}}-4}, & \text{if } x>0\end{cases}$ for what value of a, f is continuous at $x=0$? **[NCERT Exemplar]**

Hints & Solutions

1. (i) Here, $f(x)=\dfrac{1}{x-5}$ is a rational function $\left[\text{i.e. } \dfrac{p(x)}{q(x)}\right]$.

So, $f(x)$ is continuous for all values of x except $x=5$. [1/2]

(ii) Solve as part (i). [**Ans.** $f(x)$ is continuous everywhere except at $x=-3$] [1/2]

(iii) Here, $f(x)=\dfrac{x^2-25}{x+5}, x\ne -5$

$$=\frac{(x-5)(x+5)}{x+5}, x\ne -5 = x-5$$

$\therefore f(x)=x-5$, $x\ne -5$ is a polynomial function, hence $f(x)$ is continuous at all values of x, $x\ne -5$. [1]

Note In a rational function $f(x)=\dfrac{p(x)}{q(x)}$, if $q(x)$ is zero at any value of x, then $f(x)$ is not continuous at that point.

2. Solve as Example 4.

3. Let $g(x)=|x|$ and $h(x)=\sin x$

Then, $hog(x)=h[g(x)]=h(|x|)=\sin|x|=f(x)$ [1]

Since, $g(x)$ and $h(x)$ are both continuous function for all $x\in R$, so composition of $g(x)$ and $h(x)$ is also a continuous function for all $x\in R$.

Hence, $f(x)=\sin|x|$ is a continuous function. [1]

4. Solve as Question 3.

5. Given, $f(x)=\begin{cases} \dfrac{(x+3)^2-36}{x-3}, & x\ne 3 \\ k, & x=3\end{cases}$

Let $f(x)$ is continuous at $x=3$.

Then, $\lim_{x\to 3} f(x)=f(3)$

$$\Rightarrow \lim_{x\to 3}\frac{(x+3)^2-36}{x-3}=k$$

$$\Rightarrow \lim_{x\to 3}\frac{(x+3)^2-6^2}{x-3}=k \quad [1]$$

$$\Rightarrow \lim_{x\to 3}\frac{(x+3-6)(x+3+6)}{x-3}=k$$

$[\because a^2-b^2=(a-b)(a+b)]$

$$\Rightarrow \lim_{x\to 3}\frac{(x-3)(x+9)}{(x-3)}=k \Rightarrow \lim_{x\to 3}(x+9)=k$$

$\Rightarrow 3+9=k \Rightarrow k=12$, which is the required value of k. [1]

6. Given, $f(x)=\begin{cases} \dfrac{x^2-2x-3}{x+1}, & \text{if } x\ne -1 \\ k, & \text{if } x=-1\end{cases}$

Let $f(x)$ is continuous at $x=-1$. Then,

$$\lim_{x\to -1} f(x)=f(-1) \quad [1/2]$$

$$\Rightarrow \lim_{x\to -1}\frac{x^2-2x-3}{x+1}=k$$

$$\Rightarrow \lim_{x\to -1} \frac{(x+1)(x-3)}{(x+1)} = k$$ [1]

$$\Rightarrow \lim_{x\to -1} (x-3) = k \Rightarrow k = -4$$

which is the required value of k. [1/2]

7. Solve as Question 6. [**Ans.** $k = 7$]

8. We have, $f(x) = \begin{cases} \dfrac{\tan 2x}{x}, & \text{if } x \neq 0 \\ k, & \text{if } x = 0 \end{cases}$

Let $f(x)$ is continuous at $x = 0$.

Then, $\lim_{x\to 0} f(x) = f(0)$ [1/2]

$$\Rightarrow \lim_{x\to 0} \frac{\tan 2x}{x} = k \quad [\because f(0) = k]$$

$$\Rightarrow \lim_{x\to 0} \frac{\tan 2x}{x} \times \frac{2}{2} = k \Rightarrow \lim_{x\to 0} \frac{2\tan 2x}{2x} = k$$ [1]

$$\Rightarrow 2\lim_{x\to 0} \frac{\tan 2x}{2x} = k$$

$$\Rightarrow k = 2 \quad \left[\because \lim_{x\to 0} \frac{\tan x}{x} = 1\right]$$

Hence, for $k = 2$, the given function $f(x)$ is continuous at $x = 0$. [1/2]

9. Hint $\lim_{x\to 0} f(x) = f(0)$

$$\Rightarrow \lim_{x\to 0} \frac{\sin x}{x} + \lim_{x\to 0} \cos x = k$$

$$\Rightarrow 1 + 1 = k \quad [\textbf{Ans. } k = 2]$$

10. Hint $\lim_{x\to 0} f(x) = f(0)$

$$\Rightarrow a^2 \lim_{x\to 0} \left(\frac{\sin ax}{ax}\right)^2 = 1 \quad [\textbf{Ans. } a = \pm 1]$$

11. Hint $\lim_{x\to 0} f(x) = f(0)$

$$\Rightarrow \lim_{x\to 0} \frac{2\sin^2 2x}{x^2} = p$$

$$\Rightarrow 8 \lim_{x\to 0} \left(\frac{\sin 2x}{2x}\right)^2 = p \quad [\textbf{Ans. } p = 8]$$

12. Let $f(x) = \tan x$, then domain of $f(x)$ be

$R - \left\{(2n+1)\frac{\pi}{2}, n \in I\right\}$.

Let $c \in R - \left\{(2n+1)\frac{\pi}{2}, n \in I\right\}$.

Then, $\lim_{x\to c} \tan x = \lim_{x\to c} \dfrac{\sin x}{\cos x} = \dfrac{\lim_{h\to 0} \sin(c+h)}{\lim_{h\to 0} \cos(c+h)}$

[put $x = c + h$; when $x \to c$, then $h \to 0$]

$$= \frac{\lim_{h\to 0}(\sin c \cos h + \cos c \sin h)}{\lim_{h\to 0}(\cos c \cos h - \sin c \sin h)}$$ [1]

$$= \frac{\sin c \times \cos 0 + \cos c \times \sin 0}{\cos c \times \cos 0 - \sin c \times \sin 0}$$ [1]

$$= \frac{\sin c \times 1 + \cos c \times 0}{\cos c \times 1 - \sin c \times 0}$$

$$= \frac{\sin c + 0}{\cos c - 0} = \tan c$$ [1]

Thus, $\tan x$ is continuous for all

$c \in R - \left\{(2n+1)\frac{\pi}{2} : n \in I\right\}$.

Hence, $f(x)$ is continuous in their domain. [1]

13. Let $g(x) = 1 - x + |x|$ and $h(x) = |x|$ be two functions defined on R. [1]

Then, $(hog)(x) = h(g(x)) = h(1 - x + |x|)$

$= |1 - x + |x|| = f(x), \forall x \in R$.

Since, $(1 - x)$ is a polynomial function and $|x|$ is a modulus function, so both are continuous function on R. [1]

Therefore, $g(x) = 1 - x + |x|$ is continuous function on R. Also, $h(x) = |x|$ is continuous function on R.

Hence, $f = hog$ is continuous for all real numbers. [2]

14. Hint $\lim_{x\to \pi/4} f(x) = f(\pi/4)$

$$\Rightarrow \lim_{x\to \pi/4} \frac{\sqrt{2}\left(\frac{1}{\sqrt{2}}\sin x - \cos x \cdot \frac{1}{\sqrt{2}}\right)}{4\left(x - \frac{\pi}{4}\right)} = k$$

$$\Rightarrow \frac{1}{2\sqrt{2}} \lim_{x\to \pi/4} \frac{\sin\left(x - \frac{\pi}{4}\right)}{\left(x - \frac{\pi}{4}\right)} = k \quad \left[\textbf{Ans. } k = \frac{1}{2\sqrt{2}}\right]$$

15. We have, $f(x) = \begin{cases} m(x^2 - 2x), & \text{if } x < 0 \\ \cos x, & \text{if } x \geq 0 \end{cases}$

Let $f(x)$ is continuous at $x = 0$.

Then, LHL = RHL = $f(0)$

$$\Rightarrow \lim_{x\to 0^-} f(x) = \lim_{x\to 0^+} f(x) = f(0)$$ [1]

$$\Rightarrow \lim_{x\to 0^-} m(x^2 - 2x) = \lim_{x\to 0^+} (\cos x) = \cos 0$$ [1]

$$\Rightarrow m(0 - 0) = \cos 0 = \cos 0 \Rightarrow 0 = 1 = 1$$ [1]

which is not possible.

So, the value of m cannot be determined. [1]

16. Solve as Question 15. $\left[\textbf{Ans. } k = \frac{-2}{\pi}\right]$

17. Here, $f(x) = \begin{cases} \lambda(x^2 - 2x), & \text{if } x \leq 0 \\ 4x + 1, & \text{if } x > 0 \end{cases}$

At $x = 0$, LHL $= \lim_{x\to 0^-} f(x) = \lim_{x\to 0^-} \lambda(x^2 - 2x) = 0$ [1]

RHL $= \lim_{x\to 0^+} f(x) = \lim_{x\to 0^+} (4x + 1) = 1$

$\because$ LHL $\neq$ RHL

$\therefore f(x)$ is not continuous at $x=0$ for any value of λ. [1]

At $x=1$,

$$\text{LHL} = \lim_{x\to 1^-} f(x) = \lim_{x\to 1^-}(4x+1) = 5$$

$$\text{RHL} = \lim_{x\to 1^+} f(x) = \lim_{x\to 1^+}(4x+1) = 5 \quad [1]$$

Also, $f(1) = 4\times 1+1 = 5$ $[\because f(x) = 4x+1]$

Thus, $f(x)$ is continuous at $x=1$ for all values of λ. [1]

18. Hint $f(x) = \begin{cases} \dfrac{x}{|x|+2x^2}, & x\neq 0 \\ k, & x=0 \end{cases}$

$$\Rightarrow \quad f(x) = \begin{cases} \dfrac{1}{2x-1}, & x<0 \\ k, & x=0 \\ \dfrac{1}{2x+1}, & x>0 \end{cases}$$

Here, $\lim\limits_{x\to 0^-} f(x) = \lim\limits_{x\to 0^-} \dfrac{1}{2x-1} = -1$

and $\lim\limits_{x\to 0^+} f(x) = \lim\limits_{x\to 0^+} \dfrac{1}{2x+1} = 1$

$\because \lim\limits_{x\to 0^-} f(x) \neq \lim\limits_{x\to 0^+} f(x)$

$\therefore f(x)$ is discontinuous at $x=0$.

[**Ans.** $f(x)$ is not continuous for any value of k]

19. Hint $\lim\limits_{x\to 0} f(x) = f(0)$

$$\Rightarrow \lim_{x\to 0} \frac{\cos 2x - 1}{\sqrt{x^2+1}-1} \times \frac{\sqrt{x^2+1}+1}{\sqrt{x^2+1}+1} = k$$

$$\Rightarrow \lim_{x\to 0} \frac{\cos 2x - 1}{x^2} \cdot \lim_{x\to 0}\left(\sqrt{x^2+1}+1\right) = k \quad [\textbf{Ans. } k = -4]$$

20. We have, $f(x) = \begin{cases} \dfrac{1}{2} - x, & 0\le x < \dfrac{1}{2} \\ 1, & x = \dfrac{1}{2} \\ \dfrac{3}{2} - x, & \dfrac{1}{2} < x \le 1 \end{cases}$

Here, given function is a polynomial function in the given intervals, so it is continuous everywhere except possible at $x = \dfrac{1}{2}$. [1]

Now, we have to check the continuity at $x = \dfrac{1}{2}$.

$$\text{LHL} = \lim_{x\to \frac{1}{2}^-} f(x) = \lim_{x\to \frac{1}{2}^-} \left(\frac{1}{2} - x\right) = 0 \quad [1]$$

and $$\text{RHL} = \lim_{x\to \frac{1}{2}^+} f(x) = \lim_{x\to \frac{1}{2}^+} \left(\frac{3}{2} - x\right) = 1 \quad [1]$$

$\because$ LHL $\neq$ RHL

$\therefore f(x)$ is not continuous at $x = \dfrac{1}{2}$. [1]

21. Hint We have, $f(x) = \dfrac{1}{x-1}$, which is not defined at $x=1$.

Also, $y = f\{f(x)\} = \dfrac{1}{f(x)-1} = \dfrac{1}{\dfrac{1}{x-1} - 1}$

$$= \frac{x-1}{1-x+1} = \frac{x-1}{2-x}$$

which is not defined at $x=2$ [**Ans.** 1, 2]

22. Here, $f(x) = \begin{cases} 5, & \text{if } x\le 2 \\ ax+b, & \text{if } 2<x<10 \\ 21, & \text{if } x\ge 10 \end{cases}$

Since, $f(x)$ is continuous function, therefore it will be continuous at $x=2$ and $x=10$ also.

At $x=2$, LHL $= \lim\limits_{x\to 2^-} f(x) = \lim\limits_{x\to 2^-} (5) = 5$ [1]

$$\text{RHL} = \lim_{x\to 2^+} f(x) = \lim_{x\to 2^+} (ax+b) = 2a+b$$

and $f(2) = 5$ [1]

Since, $f(x)$ is continuous at $x=2$.

$\therefore$ LHL = RHL = $f(2) \Rightarrow 2a+b=5$ ...(i) [1]

Now, at $x=10$,

$$\text{LHL} = \lim_{x\to 10^-} f(x) = \lim_{x\to 10^-} (ax+b) = 10a+b \quad [1]$$

$$\text{RHL} = \lim_{x\to 10^+} f(x) = \lim_{x\to 10^+} (21) = 21$$

and $f(10) = 21$.

Since, $f(x)$ is continuous at $x=10$.

$\therefore$ LHL = RHL = $f(10)$

$\Rightarrow 10a+b = 21$ ...(ii) [1]

On subtracting Eq. (i) from Eq. (ii), we get

$$8a = 16 \Rightarrow a = 2$$

On putting $a=2$ in Eq. (i), we get $2\times 2 + b = 5 \Rightarrow b = 1$

Hence, the values of a and b are 2 and 1, respectively. [1]

23. Hint At $x=0$, we have $f(0) = a$.

$$\text{LHL} = \lim_{x\to 0^-} f(x)$$

$$= \lim_{x\to 0^-} \frac{4\cdot 2\sin^2 2x}{4\cdot x^2}$$

$$= \lim_{x\to 0^-} 8\left(\frac{\sin^2 2x}{2x}\right)^2 \quad \left[\because \lim_{x\to 0} \frac{\sin x}{x} = 1\right]$$

$$\text{RHL} = \lim_{x\to 0^+} f(x)$$

$$= \lim_{x\to 0^+} \frac{\sqrt{x}}{\sqrt{16+\sqrt{x}}-4} \times \frac{\sqrt{16+\sqrt{x}}+4}{\sqrt{16+\sqrt{x}}+4}$$

$$= \lim_{x\to 0^+} \frac{\sqrt{x}\,[\sqrt{16+\sqrt{x}}+4]}{16+\sqrt{x}-16} = 4+4 = 8$$

$\Rightarrow$ LHL = RHL = $f(0)$ [**Ans.** $a = 8$]

TOPIC 03 Differentiability

Differentiability or Derivability

A real function f is said to be **derivable** or **differentiable** at a point c in its domain, if $\lim_{x\to c}\frac{f(x)-f(c)}{x-c}$ exist or $\lim_{h\to 0}\frac{f(c+h)-f(c)}{h}$ exist or its **left hand** and **right hand derivatives** at c exist (i.e. finite and unique) and are equal, i.e. $Lf'(c)=Rf'(c)$.

Here, at $x=c$ left hand derivative,

$$\text{LHD}=\lim_{x\to c^-}\frac{f(x)-f(c)}{x-c}$$

$$=\lim_{h\to 0^-}\frac{f(c-h)-f(c)}{-h}=Lf'(c)$$

and right hand derivative,

$$\text{RHD}=\lim_{x\to c^+}\frac{f(x)-f(c)}{x-c}$$

$$=\lim_{h\to 0^+}\frac{f(c+h)-f(c)}{h}=Rf'(c).$$

The same value of $Lf'(c)$ and $Rf'(c)$ is known as **derivative or differential coefficient of** $f(x)$ at $x=c$ and it is denoted by $\frac{d}{dx}(f(x))|_c$ or $f'(c)$.

Thus, $f'(c)=\lim_{x\to c}\frac{f(x)-f(c)}{x-c}$

$$=\lim_{h\to 0}\frac{f(c+h)-f(c)}{h}, \text{ provided it exist.}$$

Working Rule to Show Differentiability of a Function at a Point

Suppose a function $f(x)$ is given to us and we have to check its differentiability at point $x=c$ in its domain. Then, we use the following steps

I. First, write the given function say $f(x)$ and the point say $x=c$ at which we have to check differentiability.

II. Find Left Hand Derivative (LHD) at $x=c$ by using the formula, LHD $=\lim_{h\to 0^-}\frac{f(c-h)-f(c)}{-h}$.

III. Find Right Hand Derivative (RHD) at $x=c$ by using the formula, RHD $=\lim_{h\to 0^+}\frac{f(c+h)-f(c)}{h}$.

IV. If LHD = RHD at $x=c$, then $f(x)$ is differentiable at $x=c$, otherwise $f(x)$ is not differentiable at $x=c$.

Differentiable Function

A function f is said to be a **differentiable function** iff it is differentiable at every point of its domain.

A function is said to be **differentiable in an interval** (a, b), if it is differentiable at every point of (a,b).

Similarly, a function is said to be differentiable in an interval $[a,b]$, if it is **differentiable at every point of** $[a,b]$.

Note As in case of continuity we will take right hand derivative at a and left hand derivative at b.

Example 1 Discuss the differentiability of $f(x)=x^2$ at $x=1$.

Sol. We have, $f(x)=x^2$

Test for differentiability at $x=1$,

Here, $f'(1)=\lim_{h\to 0}\frac{f(1+h)-f(1)}{h}=\lim_{h\to 0}\frac{(1+h)^2-1}{h}$

$$=\lim_{h\to 0}\frac{h^2+2h+1-1}{h}$$

$$=\lim_{h\to 0}(h+2)=2, \text{ which is finite}$$

$\therefore$ $f(x)$ is differentiable at $x=1$.

Example 2 Prove that $f(x)=|x|$ is not differentiable at $x=0$.

Sol. We have, $f(x)=|x|$.

Test for differentiability at $x=0$,

$$Lf'(0)=\lim_{h\to 0^-}\frac{f(0-h)-f(0)}{-h}=\lim_{h\to 0^-}\frac{f(-h)-f(0)}{-h}$$

$$=\lim_{h\to 0^-}\frac{|-h|-|0|}{-h} \quad [\because f(x)=|x|]$$

$$=\lim_{h\to 0^-}\frac{h}{-h}=\lim_{h\to 0^-}(-1)=-1$$

and $Rf'(0)=\lim_{h\to 0^+}\frac{f(0+h)-f(0)}{h}=\lim_{h\to 0^+}\frac{f(h)-f(0)}{h}$

$$= \lim_{h \to 0^+} \frac{|h| - |0|}{h}$$

$$= \lim_{h \to 0^+} \left(\frac{h}{h}\right) = \lim_{h \to 0^+} (1) = 1$$

$\because \quad Lf'(0) \neq Rf'(0)$

Hence, f is not differentiable at $x = 0$.

Example 3 Examine the following function $f(x)$ for continuity at $x = 1$ and differentiability at $x = 2$.

$$f(x) = \begin{cases} 5x - 4, & \text{if } 0 < x < 1 \\ 4x^2 - 3x, & \text{if } 1 \leq x < 2 \\ 3x + 4, & \text{if } x \geq 2 \end{cases}$$

Sol. We have, $f(x) = \begin{cases} 5x - 4, & \text{if } 0 < x < 1 \\ 4x^2 - 3x, & \text{if } 1 \leq x < 2 \\ 3x + 4, & \text{if } x \geq 2 \end{cases}$

For continuity, at $x = 1$

$$\text{LHL} = \lim_{x \to 1^-} f(x) = \lim_{x \to 1^-} (5x - 4) = 1$$

$$\text{RHL} = \lim_{x \to 1^+} f(x) = \lim_{x \to 1^+} (4x^2 - 3x) = 1$$

Also, $f(1) = 4(1)^2 - 3(1) = 1$.

$\because \quad \text{LHL} = \text{RHL} = f(1)$.

$\therefore f(x)$ is continuous at $x = 1$.

For differentiability at $x = 2$,

$$\text{LHD} = \lim_{h \to 0^-} \frac{f(2 - h) - f(2)}{-h}$$

$$= \lim_{h \to 0^-} \frac{\{4(2 - h)^2 - 3(2 - h)\} - \{3(2) + 4\}}{-h}$$

$$= \lim_{h \to 0^-} \frac{\{4(4 - 4h + h^2) - 6 + 3h\} - \{6 + 4\}}{-h}$$

$$= \lim_{h \to 0^-} \frac{16 - 16h + 4h^2 - 6 + 3h - 10}{-h}$$

$$= \lim_{h \to 0^-} \frac{4h^2 - 13h}{-h} = \lim_{h \to 0^-} (-4h + 13) = 13$$

$$\text{RHD} = \lim_{h \to 0^+} \frac{f(2 + h) - f(2)}{h}$$

$$= \lim_{h \to 0^+} \frac{3(2 + h) + 4 - (3 \times 2 + 4)}{h}$$

$$= \lim_{h \to 0^+} \frac{(6 + 3h + 4 - 10)}{h}$$

$$= \lim_{h \to 0^+} \left(\frac{3h}{h}\right) = \lim_{h \to 0^+} (3) = 3$$

Since, LHD $\neq$ RHD

$\therefore f$ is not differentiable at $x = 2$.

Some Basic Differentiable Functions

There are some functions which are differentiable in their respective domain.

(i) Every polynomial function is differentiable at each $x \in R$.

(ii) The exponential function a^x, $a > 0$ is differentiable at each $x \in R$.

(iii) Every constant function is differentiable at each $x \in R$.

(iv) The logarithmic function is differentiable at each point in its domain.

(v) The trigonometric and inverse trigonometric functions are differentiable in their respective domains.

(vi) The sum, difference, product and quotient of two differentiable functions is differentiable.

(vii) The composition of differentiable functions is a differentiable function.

Note The function $f(x) = |x - a_1| + |x - a_2| + |x - a_3| + \ldots + |x - a_n|$ is not differentiable at $x = a_1, a_2, a_3, \ldots, a_n$.

Relation between Differentiability and Continuity

Theorem If a function is differentiable at any point, it is necessarily continuous at that point.

Proof Let a function f be differentiable at $x = a$, then by definition, $\lim_{h \to 0} \frac{f(a + h) - f(a)}{h}$ exists.

and $\quad f'(a) = \lim_{h \to 0} \frac{f(a + h) - f(a)}{h}$

Now, $\quad f(a + h) - f(a) = \frac{f(a + h) - f(a)}{h} \cdot h \quad [\because h \neq 0]$

$$\Rightarrow \lim_{h \to 0} (f(a + h) - f(a)) = \lim_{h \to 0} \left(\frac{f(a + h) - f(a)}{h} \cdot h\right)$$

$$\Rightarrow \lim_{h \to 0} f(a + h) - \lim_{h \to 0} f(a) = \lim_{h \to 0} \frac{f(a + h) - f(a)}{h} \cdot \lim_{h \to 0} h$$

$$\Rightarrow \quad \lim_{h \to 0} f(a + h) - f(a) = f'(a) \cdot 0 = 0$$

$$\Rightarrow \quad \lim_{h \to 0} f(a + h) = f(a)$$

$$\Rightarrow \quad \lim_{x \to a} f(x) = f(a) \quad [\text{putting } x = a + h]$$

Hence, f is continuous at $x = a$.

Note The converse of the above theorem may not be true, i.e. a function may be continuous at a point but may not be derivable at that point, e.g. $f(x) = |x|$.

Example 4 Examine the function 'f' for differentiability and continuity at $x = 0$, where

$$f(x) = \begin{cases} 1 - x^2, & x \le 0 \\ 1 + x^2, & x > 0 \end{cases}$$

Sol. Given, $f(x) = \begin{cases} 1 - x^2, & x \le 0 \\ 1 + x^2, & x > 0 \end{cases}$

Here, $\text{LHD} = \lim_{h \to 0^-} \dfrac{f(0-h) - f(0)}{-h}$

$= \lim_{h \to 0^-} \dfrac{f(-h) - f(0)}{-h}$

$= \lim_{h \to 0^-} \dfrac{(1-(-h)^2) - (1-0^2)}{-h}$

$= \lim_{h \to 0^-} \dfrac{1 - h^2 - 1}{-h}$

$= \lim_{h \to 0^-} \dfrac{-h^2}{-h} = \lim_{h \to 0} h$

$= 0$

and $\text{RHD} = \lim_{h \to 0^+} \dfrac{f(0+h) - f(0)}{h}$

$= \lim_{h \to 0^+} \dfrac{(1+h^2) - (1-0^2)}{h}$

$= \lim_{h \to 0^+} \dfrac{1 + h^2 - 1}{h}$

$= \lim_{h \to 0^+} \dfrac{h^2}{h} = 0$

$\because$ LHD = RHD

$\therefore f(x)$ is differentiable at $x = 0$

Now, as we know that every differentiable function is necessarily continuous at that point.

$\therefore f(x)$ is continuous at $x = 0$.

Example 5 Show that the function $f(x) = |x - 4|$, $x \in R$ is continuous but not differentiable at $x = 4$. **[ISC 2019]**

Sol. We have, $f(x) = |x - 4| = \begin{cases} x - 4, & x \ge 4 \\ 4 - x, & x < 4 \end{cases}$

Check continuity at x = 4

$\text{LHL} = \lim_{x \to 4^-} f(x) = \lim_{h \to 0} f(4 - h)$

$= \lim_{h \to 0} [4 - (4 - h)] = \lim_{h \to 0} h = 0$

$\text{RHL} = \lim_{x \to 4^+} f(x) = \lim_{h \to 0} f(4 + h)$

$= \lim_{h \to 0} \{(4 + h) - 4\} = \lim_{h \to 0} h = 0$

and $f(4) = 4 - 4 = 0$

Here, LHL = RHL = $f(4) = 4$

Hence, $f(x)$ is continuous at $x = 4$.

Check differentiability at x = 4

$\text{LHD} = \lim_{h \to 0^-} \dfrac{f(4-h) - f(4)}{-h}$

$= \lim_{h \to 0} \dfrac{4 - (4 - h) - (4 - 4)}{-h}$

$= \lim_{h \to 0} \left(-\dfrac{h}{h}\right) = -1$

$\text{RHD} = \lim_{h \to 0^+} \dfrac{f(4+h) - f(4)}{h}$

$= \lim_{h \to 0} \dfrac{(4 + h - 4) - (4 - 4)}{h}$

$= \lim_{h \to 0} \dfrac{h}{h} = 1$

Here, LHD $\ne$ RHD

Hence, $f(x)$ is not differentiable at $x = 4$.

Topic Practice 3

Very Short Answer Type Questions

(2 Marks)

1 Examine the differentiability of $f(x) = x + 1$ at $x = 2$.

2 Check the differentiability of $f(x) = \log x$ at $x = 2$.

3 Prove that the greatest integer function defined by $f(x) = [x], 0 < x < 3$ is not differentiable at $x = 1$.

4 Examine the differentiability of the function $f(x) = \begin{cases} x[x], & \text{if } 0 \le x < 2 \\ (x-1)x, & \text{if } 2 \le x < 3 \end{cases}$ at $x = 2$. **[NCERT Exemplar]**

5 Examine the differentiability of $f(x) = \begin{cases} 1 + x, & \text{if } x \le 2 \\ 5 - x, & \text{if } x > 2 \end{cases}$ at $x = 2$.

Short Answer Type Questions

(4 Marks)

6 Prove that the function f given by $f(x) = |x - 1|$, $x \in R$ is not differentiable at $x = 1$. **[NCERT]**

7 Show that the function $f(x) = |x - 1| + |x + 1|, \forall$ $x \in R$ is not differentiable at the points $x = -1$ and $x = 1$.

8 A function $f(x)$ is defined as follows

$$f(x)=\begin{cases} x^2 \sin \dfrac{1}{x}, & \text{if } x \neq 0 \\ 0, & \text{if } x = 0 \end{cases}.$$

Show that $f(x)$ is differentiable at $x = 0$.

[NCERT Exemplar]

9 Let $f(x) = x|x|, \forall\ x \in R$. Discuss the derivability of $f(x)$ at $x = 0$. **[NCERT Exemplar]**

10 Show that the function $f(x) = |x - 5|$ is continuous but not differentiable at $x = 5$.

[NCERT Exemplar]

11 Show that the function $f(x)=\begin{cases} x^2, & \text{if } x \leq 1 \\ \dfrac{1}{x}, & \text{if } x > 1 \end{cases}$ is continuous at $x = 1$ but not differentiable.

[ISC 2018]

Hints & Solutions

1. Similar as Example 1. [**Ans.** Differentiable]

2. We have, $f(x) = \log x$

$$\text{LHD} = \lim_{h \to 0} \frac{f(2-h) - f(2)}{-h}$$

$$= \lim_{h \to 0} \frac{\log(2-h) - \log 2}{-h}$$

$$= \lim_{h \to 0} \frac{\log\left(1 - \dfrac{h}{2}\right)}{-h} \quad [1]$$

$$= \lim_{h \to 0} \frac{-\left[\dfrac{h}{2} + \dfrac{1}{2}\left(\dfrac{h}{2}\right)^2 + \ldots\right]}{-h}$$

$$= \lim_{h \to 0} \frac{-h\left[\dfrac{1}{2} + \dfrac{1}{2} \times \dfrac{h}{4} + \ldots\right]}{-h} = \frac{1}{2} \quad [1]$$

3. Here, $f(x) = [x], 0 < x < 3$

For differentiability at $x = 1$,

$$\text{LHD} = \lim_{h \to 0^-} \frac{f(1-h) - f(1)}{-h}$$

$$= \lim_{h \to 0^-} \frac{[1-h] - [1]}{-h} \quad [\because [1-h] = 0 \text{ and } [1] = 1]$$

$$= \lim_{h \to 0^-} \frac{0-1}{-h} \quad [1]$$

$$= \lim_{h \to 0} \frac{1}{h}, \text{ which does not exist.}$$

Hence, $f(x)$ is not differentiable at $x = 1$. [1]

4. Given, $f(x)=\begin{cases} x[x], & \text{if } 0 \leq x < 2 \\ (x-1)x, & \text{if } 2 \leq x < 3 \end{cases}$

$$\text{At } x = 2,\ \text{LHD} = \lim_{h \to 0^-} \frac{f(2-h) - f(2)}{2-h-2}$$

$$= \lim_{h \to 0^-} \frac{(2-h)[2-h] - (2-1)2}{-h}$$

[$\because$ $[a-h] = a-1$, where a is any positive number]

$$= \lim_{h \to 0^-} \frac{(2-h)(1) - 2}{-h} = \lim_{h \to 0^-} \frac{-h}{-h} = 1 \quad [1]$$

$$\text{and}\quad \text{RHD} = \lim_{h \to 0^+} \frac{f(2+h) - f(2)}{2+h-2}$$

$$= \lim_{h \to 0^+} \frac{(2+h-1)(2+h) - (2-1)\cdot 2}{h}$$

$$= \lim_{h \to 0^+} \frac{(1+h)(2+h) - 2}{h}$$

$$= \lim_{h \to 0^+} \frac{h(h+3)}{h} = 3$$

$\because$ LHD $\neq$ RHD

Hence, $f(x)$ is not differentiable at $x = 2$. [1]

5. We have, $f(x)=\begin{cases} 1+x, & \text{if } x \leq 2 \\ 5-x, & \text{if } x > 2 \end{cases}$ at $x = 2$.

For differentiability at $x = 2$,

$$Lf'(2) = \lim_{x \to 2^-} \frac{f(x) - f(2)}{x-2}$$

$$= \lim_{x \to 2^-} \frac{(1+x) - (1+2)}{x-2}$$

$$= \lim_{x \to 2^-} \frac{x-2}{x-2} = \lim_{x \to 2^-} (1) = 1 \quad [1/2]$$

$$Rf'(2) = \lim_{x \to 2^+} \frac{f(x) - f(2)}{x-2} = \lim_{x \to 2^+} \frac{(5-x) - 3}{x-2}$$

$$= \lim_{x \to 2^+} \frac{2-x}{x-2} = \lim_{x \to 2^+} (-1) = -1 \quad [1/2]$$

$\because$ $Lf'(2) \neq Rf'(2)$

So, $f(x)$ is not differentiable at $x = 2$. [1]

6. Similar as Example 2.

7. Hint Given, $f(x) = |x-1| + |x+1|$

Put $x - 1 = 0$ and $x + 1 = 0$

$\Rightarrow$ $x = 1$ and $x = -1$

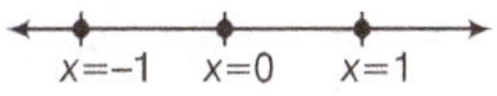

***Case* I** *When* $x < -1$

In this case $x - 1 < 0$ and $x + 1 < 0$

$\Rightarrow$ $|x-1| = -(x-1)$ and $|x+1| = -(x+1)$

$$\therefore \quad f(x) = -(x-1) + \{-(x+1)\}$$

$$= -x + 1 - x - 1$$

$$\Rightarrow \quad f(x) = -2x$$

Case* II *When $-1 \le x < 1$

In this case $x-1<0$ and $x+1 \ge 0$

$\Rightarrow |x-1| = -(x-1)$ and $|x+1| = x+1$

$\therefore \quad f(x) = -(x-1)+(x+1)$

$= -x+1+x+1 = 2$

Case* III *When $x \ge 1$

In this case $x-1 \ge 0$ and $x+1 \ge 0$

$\Rightarrow |x-1| = x-1$ and $|x+1| = x+1$

$\therefore \quad f(x) = (x-1)+(x+1) = 2x$

Thus, $f(x) = \begin{cases} -2x, & \text{if } x < -1 \\ 2, & \text{if } -1 \le x < 1 \\ 2x, & \text{if } x \ge 1 \end{cases}$

In the intervals $(-\infty, -1), (-1, 1)$ and $(1, \infty)$, $f(x)$ is a polynomial differentiable everywhere except possibly at $x=1$ and $x=-1$.

Now, examine the differentiability of the function $f(x)$, at $x=-1$ and $x=1$.

8. Given, $f(x) = \begin{cases} x^2 \sin \frac{1}{x}, & \text{if } x \ne 0 \\ 0, & \text{if } x = 0 \end{cases}$

Here, $f'(0) = \lim_{h \to 0} \frac{f(0+h)-f(0)}{h}$

$= \lim_{h \to 0} \frac{f(h)-f(0)}{h} = \lim_{h \to 0} \frac{h^2 \sin \frac{1}{h} - 0}{h}$ [1]

$= \lim_{h \to 0} \frac{h^2 \sin \frac{1}{h}}{h} = \lim_{h \to 0} h \sin\left(\frac{1}{h}\right)$ [1]

$= 0 \times$ (An oscillating value between -1 and 1)

$= 0$, which is finite [1½]

Hence, $f(x)$ is differentiable at $x=0$. [1/2]

9. **Hint** $f(x) = \begin{cases} -x^2, & x < 0 \\ 0, & x = 0 \\ x^2, & x > 0 \end{cases}$, then similar as Example 3.

[**Ans.** Derivable at $x=0$].

10. Given $f(x) = |x-5|$

$\therefore \quad f(x) = \begin{cases} -(x-5), & \text{if } x < 5 \\ x-5, & \text{if } x \ge 5 \end{cases}$

For continuity at $x=5$,

$\text{LHL} = \lim_{x \to 5^-} |x-5| = \lim_{x \to 5^-} [-(x-5)] = 0$ [1]

$\text{RHL} = \lim_{x \to 5^+} (x-5) = 0$

and $f(5) = 5-5 = 0$

$\because \quad \text{LHL} = \text{RHL} = f(5)$

$\therefore f(x)$ is continuous at $x=5$. [1]

For differentiability at $x=5$,

$\text{LHD} = \lim_{x \to 5^-} \frac{f(x)-f(5)}{x-5}$

$= \lim_{x \to 5^-} \frac{-x+5-0}{x-5}$

$= \lim_{x \to 5^-} \frac{-(x-5)}{x-5} = -1$

and $\text{RHD} = \lim_{x \to 5^+} \frac{f(x)-f(5)}{x-5}$ [1]

$= \lim_{x \to 5^+} \frac{x-5-0}{x-5} = 1$

$\because \quad \text{LHD} \ne \text{RHD}$

$\therefore f(x) = |x-5|$ is not differentiable at $x=5$. [1]

11. Given, $f(x) = \begin{cases} x^2, & \text{if } x \le 1 \\ \frac{1}{x}, & \text{if } x > 1 \end{cases}$

For continuity at $x=1$

$\text{LHL} = \lim_{x \to 1^-} f(x) = \lim_{x \to 1^-} (x^2) = 1$

$\text{RHL} = \lim_{x \to 1^+} f(x) = \lim_{x \to 1^+} \left(\frac{1}{x}\right) = 1$

and $f(1) = 1$

$\because \quad \text{LHL} = \text{RHL} = f(1)$ [1]

$\therefore$ The given function $f(x)$ is continuous at $x=1$.

For differentiability at $x=1$

$Lf'(1) = \lim_{h \to 0^+} \frac{f(1-h)-f(1)}{-h}$ [1]

$= \lim_{h \to 0^+} \frac{(1-h)^2-(1)^2}{-h}$

$= \lim_{h \to 0^+} \frac{1+h^2-2h-1}{-h}$

$= \lim_{h \to 0^+} \left(\frac{h^2-2h}{-h}\right)$

$= \lim_{h \to 0^+} (2-h) = 2$

and $Rf'(1) = \lim_{h \to 0^+} \frac{f(1+h)-f(1)}{h}$ [1]

$= \lim_{h \to 0^+} \left(\frac{\frac{1}{1+h}-1}{h}\right)$

$= \lim_{h \to 0^+} \left(\frac{-h}{h(1+h)}\right)$

$= \lim_{h \to 0^+} \left(\frac{-1}{1+h}\right) = -1$

$\because \quad Lf'(1) \ne Rf'(1)$

$\therefore f(x)$ is not differentiable at $x=1$. [1]

Chapter Practice

Multiple Choice Type Questions

1 Mark

1 If the following function is continuous at $x = 2$, then the value of k will be

$$f(x) = \begin{cases} 2x+1, & \text{if } x<2 \\ k, & \text{if } x=2 \\ 3x-1, & \text{if } x>2 \end{cases}$$ **[ISC 2023]**

(a) 2 (b) 3 (c) 5 (d) -1

2 The graph of the function f is shown below

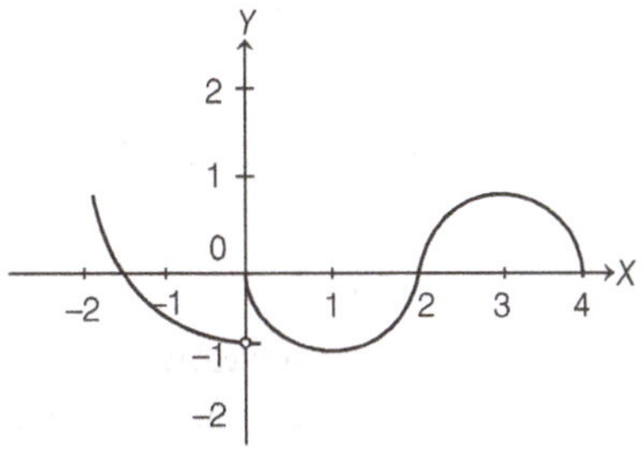

Of the following options, at what values of x is the function f not differentiable? **[ISC 2024]**

(a) At $x = 0$ and $x = 2$
(b) At $x = 1$ and $x = 3$
(c) At $x = -1$ and $x = 1$
(d) At $x = -1.5$ and $x = 1.5$

3 If $f(x) = |\cos x|$, then

(a) f is everywhere differentiable
(b) f is everywhere continuous but not differentiable at $x = n\pi, n \in Z$
(c) f is everywhere continuous but not differentiable at $x = (2n+1)\frac{\pi}{2}, n \in Z$
(d) None of the above

4 The value of k for which function

$f(x) = \begin{cases} x^2, & x \ge 0 \\ kx, & x < 0 \end{cases}$ is differentiable at $x = 0$, is

(a) 1 (b) 2
(c) any real number (d) 0

Assertion-Reason Type Questions

1 Mark

Directions (Q. Nos. 5-8) *In the questions given below are two statements labelled as Assertion (A) and Reason (R). In the context of the two statements, which one of the following is correct?*

(a) Both A and R are correct; R is the correct explanation of A
(b) Both A and R are correct; R is not the correct explanation of A
(c) A is correct; R is incorrect
(d) R is correct; A is incorrect

5 **Assertion (A)** $\sin^{-1} x$ is continuous on $[-1, 1]$.

Reason (R) $\cos x^2$ is discontinuous on $x \in R$.

6 **Assertion (A)** The function $f(x) = \frac{|x|}{x}$ is continuous at $x = 0$.

Reason (R) The left-hand limit and right-hand limit of the function $f(x) = \frac{|x|}{x}$ are not equal at $x = 0$.

7 **Assertion (A)** $f(x) = |x-1| + |x-2|$ is continuous but not differentiable at $x = 1, 2$.

Reason (R) Every differentiable function is continuous.

8 **Assertion (A)** $f(x) = [x]$ greatest integer function is not differentiable at $x = 2$.

Reason (R) The greatest integer function is not continuous at any integer.

Very Short Answer Type Questions

2 Marks

9 Show that the function $f(x) = \begin{cases} \frac{|x-a|}{x-a}, & x \ne a \\ 1, & x = a \end{cases}$ is discontinuous at $x = a$. **[NCERT]**

13 Determine the value of constant 'k', so that function $f(x)=\begin{cases}\dfrac{kx}{|x|}, & \text{if } x<0\\ 3, & \text{if } x\geq 0\end{cases}$ is continuous at $x=0$.

14 If a function f is differentiable at a point c, then prove that it is also continuous at that point.

Short Answer Type Questions

4 Marks

15 Examine the continuity of the function

$$f(x)=\begin{cases}\dfrac{|\sin x|}{x}, & x\neq 0\\ 1, & x=0\end{cases} \text{ at } x=0.$$

16 Discuss the continuity of the function

$$f(x)=\begin{cases}\dfrac{x}{|x|+2x^2}, & x\neq 0\\ 2, & x=0\end{cases} \text{ at } x=0.$$

17 If the function $f(x)=\begin{cases}3ax+b, & \text{if } x>1\\ 11, & \text{if } x=1\\ 5ax-2b, & \text{if } x<1\end{cases}$

is continuous at $x=1$, then find the values of a and b.

18 Find the value of k, if the function,

$f(x)=\begin{cases}\dfrac{1-\sin x}{(\pi-2x)^2}, & x\neq \pi/2\\ k, & x=\pi/2\end{cases}$ is continuous at $x=\pi/2$.

19 Find the value of k, so that the function f is continuous at $x=\pi/2$, $f(x)=\begin{cases}\dfrac{k\cos x}{\pi-2x}, & \text{if } x\neq \dfrac{\pi}{2}\\ 3, & \text{if } x=\dfrac{\pi}{2}\end{cases}$.

20 Find the point of discontinuity, if any of the function $f(x)=\begin{cases}x^{10}-1, & \text{if } x\leq 1\\ x^2, & \text{if } x>1\end{cases}$. [NCERT]

21 Show that the function $f(x)=|x-3|$, $x\in R$ is continuous but not differentiable at $x=3$.

22 Prove that the function $f(x)=\begin{cases}\dfrac{x}{|x|}, & x\neq 0\\ 1, & x=0\end{cases}$ is not differentiable at $x=0$.

Case-Based Type Question

6 Marks

23 Let $f(x)$ be a function defined in $1\leq x<\infty$ by

$$f(x)=\begin{cases}2-x & \text{for } 1\leq x\leq 2\\ 3x-x^2 & \text{for } x \quad 2\end{cases}.$$

Answer the following questions.

(i) Is the function at $x=2$ continuous or not?

(ii) Find the left hand derivative of $f(x)$ at $x=1.5$.

(iii) Find the right hand derivative of $f(x)$ at $x=1.5$.

(iv) What is the differential coefficient of $f(x)$ at $x=3$?

Answers

1. (c) 2. (a) 3. (c) 4. (d) 5. (c) 6. (d)

7. (b) 8. (a) 10. 8 11. Continuous everywhere except $x=(2n+1)\dfrac{\pi}{2}, n\in I$.

12. $\dfrac{2}{3}$ 13. $k=-3$ 15. Discontinuous at $x=0$

16. Discontinuous at $x=0$ 17. $a=3, b=2$ 18. $k=\dfrac{1}{8}$ 19. $k=6$

20. $f(x)$ is discontinuous at $x=1$.

23. (i) The function is polynomial, so it is continuous at $x\in[1,\infty)-\{2\}$.

(ii) -1 (iii) -1 (iv) -3

CHAPTER

06

Differentiation

In class XI, we have learnt about derivative as rate of change. We have also studied how to differentiate simple algebraic and trigonometric functions. In this chapter, we will introduce differentiations of some more functions like inverse trigonometric, exponential, logarithmic, implicit and composite functions, etc.

- Derivatives of Composite and Trigonometric Functions
- Differentiation of Exponential, Logarithmic and Implicit Functions
- Derivatives of Inverse Trigonometric Functions
- Differentiation of Parametric Functions
- Differentiation of a Function w.r.t. Another Function
- Logarithmic Differentiation and Derivatives of Infinite Series
- Successive Differentiation

TOPIC 01 Derivatives of Composite and Trigonometric Functions

Quick Review of Derivatives

- **Derivative or Differential Coefficient** Let f be a real valued function and c be a point in its domain, then derivative of f at c is given by

$$f'(c) = \lim_{h \to 0} \frac{f(c+h) - f(c)}{h}.$$

The derivative is defined, whenever the limit exists.

In general, the derivative of f at x is given by

$$f'(x) = \lim_{h \to 0} \frac{f(x+h) - f(x)}{h}, \text{ provided limit exists.}$$

(i) The derivative of $f(x)$ is denoted by $f'(x)$ or $\frac{d}{dx} f(x)$.

(ii) If $y = f(x)$, then derivative or the differential coefficient of f w.r.t. x is denoted by $\frac{dy}{dx}$ or y' or $f'(x)$ or $Df(x)$.

- Differentiation is the process of finding the derivative of a function.
- **Sum and Difference Rule** Let u and v be the two functions of x.

Then, $\frac{d}{dx}(u \pm v) = \frac{du}{dx} \pm \frac{dv}{dx}$.

- **Product or Leibnitz Rule** Derivative of product of two functions is given as
$$\frac{d}{dx}(uv) = u\frac{dv}{dx} + v\frac{du}{dx}$$
i.e. Derivative of the product of two functions
= (First function × Derivative of second function) + (Second function × Derivative of first function)

- **Quotient Rule** Derivative of quotient of two functions is given as
$$\frac{d}{dx}\left(\frac{u}{v}\right) = \frac{\left[v\frac{du}{dx} - u\frac{dv}{dx}\right]}{v^2}$$
$$= \frac{\left[\text{Denominator} \times \frac{d}{dx}(\text{Numerator}) - \text{Numerator} \times \frac{d}{dx}(\text{Denominator})\right]}{(\text{Denominator})^2}$$

- **Derivatives of Some Standard Functions** Derivatives of some standard functions are given below
  (i) $\frac{d}{dx}(\text{constant}) = 0$
  (ii) $\frac{d}{dx}(x^n) = nx^{n-1}$
  (iii) $\frac{d}{dx}(cx^n) = cnx^{n-1}$
  (iv) $\frac{d}{dx}(ax+b)^n = n \cdot (ax+b)^{n-1} \cdot a$
  (v) $\frac{d}{dx}|x| = \frac{x}{|x|}, x \neq 0$

Derivatives of Composite Functions

Derivative of a composite function can be found out by chain rule.

Chain Rule

Chain rule is applied when the given function is the function of function, i.e. when function is in the form of $fog(x)$ or $f[g(x)]$.

Let y be a real valued function which is a composite of two functions, say $y = f(u)$, where $u = g(x)$.

Then, $\frac{dy}{dx} = \frac{dy}{du} \cdot \frac{du}{dx} = f'(u) \cdot g'(x)$

i.e. $\frac{d}{dx}[f\{g(x)\}] = f'\{g(x)\} \cdot g'(x)$

Extension of Chain Rule

Chain rule is also applicable when the given function (say y) is a composite of three or more functions.

e.g. If $y = f(u)$, $u = g(v)$ and $v = h(x)$, then
$$\frac{dy}{dx} = \frac{dy}{du} \cdot \frac{du}{dv} \cdot \frac{dv}{dx} = f'(u) \cdot g'(v) \cdot h'(x)$$
i.e. $\frac{d}{dx}[f(g(h(x)))] = f'[g(h(x)]. g'(h(x)) \cdot h'(x)$.

Note (i) $\frac{dy}{dx} = \frac{dy/dt}{dx/dt}$ (ii) $\frac{dy}{dx} = \frac{1}{dx/dy}$ (iii) $\frac{dy}{dx} \cdot \frac{dx}{dy} = 1$

Example 1 Differentiate each of the following w.r.t. 'x'.

(i) $(ax^2 + bx + c)^n$ (ii) $\sqrt{1+x^2}$

Sol. (i) Let $y = u^n$, where $u = ax^2 + bx + c$

Using chain rule, $\frac{dy}{dx} = \frac{dy}{du}\frac{du}{dx} = nu^{n-1}\frac{du}{dx}$
$$= n(ax^2+bx+c)^{n-1} \cdot \frac{d}{dx}(ax^2+bx+c)$$
$$= n(ax^2+bx+c)^{n-1} \cdot (2ax+b)$$
$$= n(2ax+b)(ax^2+bx+c)^{n-1},$$
which is the required differentiation.

(ii) Let $y = \sqrt{u}$, where $u = 1 + x^2$

Using chain rule,
$$\frac{dy}{dx} = \frac{dy}{du} \cdot \frac{du}{dx} = \frac{d}{du}(u)^{1/2}\frac{du}{dx} = \frac{1}{2}u^{-1/2}\frac{d}{dx}(1+x^2)$$
$$= \frac{1}{2\sqrt{u}} \cdot 2x = \frac{x}{\sqrt{u}} = \frac{x}{\sqrt{1+x^2}}$$
which is the required differentiation.

Outer-Inner Rule

If $y = f(g(x))$, then its derivative involves the following steps

(a) Find the derivative of outer function f.
(b) Find the derivative of inner function g.
(c) Product the derivatives obtained in (a) and (b).

Example 2 If $y = (x + \sqrt{x^2-1})^m$, then prove that $(x^2-1)\left(\frac{dy}{dx}\right)^2 = m^2y^2$.

Sol. Given, $y = (x + \sqrt{x^2-1})^m$

On differentiating y w.r.t. 'x', we get
$$\frac{dy}{dx} = m(x+\sqrt{x^2-1})^{m-1}\frac{d}{dx}(x+\sqrt{x^2-1})$$
[by chain rule]
$$= m(x+\sqrt{x^2-1})^{m-1}\left[1 + \frac{1}{2}(x^2-1)^{-1/2}\frac{d}{dx}x^2\right]$$

$$= m(x+\sqrt{x^2-1})^{m-1}\left[1+\frac{1}{2\sqrt{x^2-1}}\cdot 2x\right]$$

$$= m(x+\sqrt{x^2-1})^{m-1}\left[\frac{\sqrt{x^2-1}+x}{\sqrt{x^2-1}}\right]$$

$$\Rightarrow \frac{dy}{du} = \frac{m(x+\sqrt{x^2-1})^m}{\sqrt{x^2-1}}$$

$$\Rightarrow \sqrt{x^2-1}\frac{dy}{dx} = my \quad [\because \text{given, } y=(x+\sqrt{x^2-1})^m]$$

$$\Rightarrow (x^2-1)\left(\frac{dy}{dx}\right)^2 = m^2y^2 \quad \text{[squaring on both sides]}$$

Hence proved.

Derivatives of Absolute Value Function

If $y=|x|=\sqrt{x^2}$, then on differentiating y w.r.t. 'x', we get

$$\frac{dy}{dx} = \frac{1}{2}(x^2)^{-1/2}\frac{d}{dx}(x^2)$$

$$= \frac{1}{2}\times\frac{1}{\sqrt{x^2}}\times 2x = \frac{x}{|x|},\ x\neq 0 \quad [\because |x|=\sqrt{x^2}]$$

Example 3 Differentiate $|x^2-5|$ w.r.t. x.

Sol. Let $y=|x^2-5|$

On differentiating both sides w.r.t. x, we get

$$\frac{dy}{dx} = \frac{d}{dx}(|x^2-5|)$$

$$= \frac{x^2-5}{|x^2-5|}\cdot\frac{d}{dx}(x^2-5),\ x\neq\pm\sqrt{5}$$

$$\left[\because \frac{d}{dx}(|x|) = \frac{x}{|x|},\ x\neq 0\right]$$

$$= \frac{(x^2-5)}{|x^2-5|}\cdot 2x,\ x\neq\pm\sqrt{5}$$

Derivatives of Trigonometric Functions

Derivatives of standard trigonometric functions are given below

(i) $\frac{d}{dx}(\sin x) = \cos x$ (ii) $\frac{d}{dx}(\cos x) = -\sin x$

(iii) $\frac{d}{dx}(\tan x) = \sec^2 x$

(iv) $\frac{d}{dx}(\operatorname{cosec} x) = -\operatorname{cosec} x \cot x$

(v) $\frac{d}{dx}(\sec x) = \sec x \tan x$

(vi) $\frac{d}{dx}(\cot x) = -\operatorname{cosec}^2 x$

Example 4 Differentiate $\sin(x^2+5)$ w.r.t. x. **[NCERT]**

Sol. Let $y=\sin u$, where $u=x^2+5$.

Using chain rule,

$$\frac{dy}{dx} = \frac{dy}{du}\cdot\frac{du}{dx} = \cos u\cdot\frac{du}{dx}$$

$$= \cos(x^2+5)\frac{d}{dx}(x^2+5)$$

$$= \cos(x^2+5)\cdot(2x) = 2x\cdot\cos(x^2+5)$$

Example 5 Differentiate $\sin^2(3x+1)$ w.r.t. x.

Sol. Let $y=\sin^2(3x+1)$

Here, y is a composite of three functions.

Let $y=t^2$, where $t=\sin u$ and $u=3x+1$.

Then, $\frac{dy}{dx} = \frac{dy}{dt}\cdot\frac{dt}{du}\cdot\frac{du}{dx}$ [by chain rule]

$$= \frac{d}{dt}[t^2]\cdot\frac{d}{du}(\sin u)\cdot\frac{d}{dx}(3x+1)$$

$$= 2t(\cos u)\cdot 3 = 6t\cos u$$

$$= 6\sin u\cos u \quad [\because t=\sin u]$$

$$= 3\sin 2u \quad [\because 2\sin\theta\cos\theta = \sin 2\theta]$$

$$= 3\sin 2(3x+1) \quad [\text{put } u=3x+1]$$

$$= 3\sin(6x+2)$$

Example 6 Differentiate $\sin 5x\cdot\cos 7x$ w.r.t. x.

Sol. Let $y=\sin 5x\cdot\cos 7x = \frac{1}{2}[2\sin 5x\cdot\cos 7x]$

$$= \frac{1}{2}[\sin(5x+7x)+\sin(5x-7x)]$$

$$[\because 2\sin A\cos B = \sin(A+B)+\sin(A-B)]$$

$$= \frac{1}{2}[\sin 12x - \sin 2x]$$

$$\Rightarrow y = \frac{1}{2}\sin 12x - \frac{1}{2}\sin 2x$$

On differentiating both sides w.r.t. x, we get

$$\frac{dy}{dx} = \frac{1}{2}\cdot\frac{d}{dx}(\sin 12x) - \frac{1}{2}\cdot\frac{d}{dx}(\sin 2x) \text{ [by difference rule]}$$

$$= \frac{1}{2}\cos 12x\frac{d}{dx}(12x) - \frac{1}{2}\cos 2x\frac{d}{dx}(2x)$$

$$= \frac{1}{2}\cos 12x\cdot 12 - \frac{1}{2}\cos 2x\cdot 2$$

$$= 6\cos 12x - \cos 2x$$

Example 7 Differentiate $2\sqrt{\cot(x^2)}$ w.r.t. x. [NCERT]

Sol. Let $y = 2\sqrt{\cot(x^2)}$

On differentiating both sides w.r.t. x, we get

$$\frac{dy}{dx} = \frac{d}{dx} 2(\cot x^2)^{1/2} = 2 \cdot \frac{1}{2} \{\cot(x^2)\}^{\frac{1}{2}-1} \cdot \frac{d}{dx}\cot(x^2)$$

$$\left[\text{using chain rule, } \frac{d}{dx}[f(g(x))] = f'\{g(x)\}\frac{d}{dx}g(x)\right]$$

$$= \frac{1}{\sqrt{\cot(x^2)}}[-\operatorname{cosec}^2 x^2]\frac{d}{dx}(x^2) \text{ [using chain rule]}$$

$$= -\frac{\operatorname{cosec}^2(x^2)\, 2x}{\sqrt{\cot(x^2)}} = \frac{-2x\operatorname{cosec}^2(x^2)}{\sqrt{\cot(x^2)}}$$

Example 8 If $\sin y = x\cos(a+y)$, then show that $\frac{dy}{dx} = \frac{\cos^2(a+y)}{\cos a}$. Also, show that $\frac{dy}{dx} = \cos a$, when $x = 0$.

Sol. We have, $\sin y = x\cos(a+y)$

$$\Rightarrow x = \frac{\sin y}{\cos(a+y)}$$

On differentiating both sides w.r.t. y, we get

$$\frac{dx}{dy} = \frac{\left[\cos(a+y)\frac{d}{dy}\sin y - \sin y\frac{d}{dy}\cos(a+y)\right]}{[\cos(a+y)]^2}$$

[by quotient rule of derivative]

$$= \frac{\cos(a+y)\cos y - \sin y[-\sin(a+y)\cdot 1]}{\cos^2(a+y)}$$

$$= \frac{\cos(a+y)\cos y + \sin y\sin(a+y)}{\cos^2(a+y)}$$

$$= \frac{\cos(a+y-y)}{\cos^2(a+y)}$$

$[\because \cos A\cos B + \sin A\sin B = \cos(A-B)]$

$$= \frac{\cos a}{\cos^2(a+y)}$$

$$\Rightarrow \frac{dy}{dx} = \frac{\cos^2(a+y)}{\cos a} \quad \left[\text{using } \frac{dy}{dx} = \frac{1}{(dx/dy)}\right]$$

Given, $\sin y = x\cos(a+y)$

When $x = 0$, then $\sin y = 0 \Rightarrow y = n\pi, n \in I$.

$\therefore$ At $x = 0$,

$$\frac{dy}{dx} = \frac{\cos^2(a+n\pi)}{\cos a} = \frac{\cos^2 a}{\cos a} = \cos a$$

$[\because \cos^2(n\pi+\theta) = \cos^2\theta]$

Hence proved.

Topic Practice 1

Very Short Answer Type Questions

2 Marks

1 If $x^{2/3} + y^{2/3} = a^{2/3}$, then find $\frac{dy}{dx}$.

Directions (Q. Nos. 2-8) *Differentiate the following functions.*

2 $\tan(x^2+5)$

3 $\cos(x^2+5)$

4 $\sin(x^3-3)$

5 $\tan(\sin x)$

6 $\operatorname{cosec}(\sqrt{x^2+2})$

7 $\sec\left(\frac{5}{x}\right)$

8 $\sqrt{\frac{1-\cos x}{1+\cos x}}$ **[ISC 2008]**

9 If $f(x) = \sin 2x - \cos 2x$, then find $f'\left(\frac{\pi}{6}\right)$.

10 If $f(x) = |\cos x|$, then find $f'\left(\frac{3\pi}{4}\right)$. **[NCERT Exemplar]**

11 If $f(x) = |\cos x - \sin x|$, then find $f'\left(\frac{\pi}{6}\right)$.

12 Differentiate $\sqrt{\tan\sqrt{x}}$ w.r.t. x. **[NCERT Exemplar]**

13 Differentiate $\cos x^3 \cdot \sin^2(x^5)$ w.r.t. x. **[NCERT]**

Short Answer Type Questions

4 Marks

14 If $y = [x + \sqrt{x^2+a^2}]^n$, then prove that $\frac{dy}{dx} = \frac{ny}{\sqrt{x^2+a^2}}$.

15 If $y = \sin^3\sqrt{ax^2+bx+c}$, then find $\frac{dy}{dx}$.

16 If $y = \sqrt{\frac{1-\sin 2x}{1+\sin 2x}}$, then show that $\frac{dy}{dx} + \sec^2\left(\frac{\pi}{4}-x\right) = 0, x \in \left[0, \frac{\pi}{4}\right]$.

Long Answer Type Questions

6 Marks

17 Differentiate $\sqrt{\frac{a^2 - x^2}{a^2 + x^2}}$.

18 Find the derivative of $y = \frac{\sqrt{a+x} - \sqrt{a-x}}{\sqrt{a+x} + \sqrt{a-x}}$.

19 If $f(x) = \sqrt{\frac{\sec x - 1}{\sec x + 1}}$, then find the derivative of $f(x)$ at $x = \frac{\pi}{3}$.

20 If $\sin y = x \sin(a + y)$, then show that $\frac{dy}{dx} = \frac{\sin^2(a+y)}{\sin a}$. **[ISC 2007]**

Hints & Solutions

1. We have, $x^{2/3} + y^{2/3} = a^{2/3}$

On differentiating both sides w.r.t. x, we get

$$\frac{d}{dx}(x^{2/3} + y^{2/3}) = \frac{d}{dx}(a^{2/3})$$

$$\Rightarrow \frac{d}{dx}(x^{2/3}) + \frac{d}{dx}(y^{2/3}) = 0$$

$$\Rightarrow \frac{2}{3}x^{\frac{2}{3}-1} + \frac{2}{3}y^{\frac{2}{3}-1}\frac{dy}{dx} = 0 \quad [1]$$

$$\Rightarrow x^{-1/3} + y^{-1/3}\frac{dy}{dx} = 0$$

$$\Rightarrow y^{-1/3}\frac{dy}{dx} = -x^{-1/3}$$

$$\Rightarrow \frac{dy}{dx} = \frac{-x^{-1/3}}{y^{-1/3}} = -\left(\frac{y}{x}\right)^{1/3} \quad [1]$$

2. Let $y = \tan u$, where $u = x^2 + 5$

By using chain rule of derivative, we get

$$\frac{dy}{dx} = \frac{dy}{du} \times \frac{du}{dx} \quad [1]$$

$$\frac{dy}{dx} = \frac{d}{du}(\tan u) \times \frac{d}{dx}(x^2 + 5)$$

$$= \sec^2 u \times 2x = 2x\sec^2(x^2 + 5)$$

[put $u = x^2 + 5$] [1]

3. Solve as Question 2. [**Ans.** $-2x\sin(x^2 + 5)$]

4. Solve as Question 2. [**Ans.** $3x^2 \cos(x^3 - 3)$]

5. Solve as Question 2. [**Ans.** $\sec^2(\sin x) \cdot \cos x$]

6. Let $y = \operatorname{cosec} u$, where $u = \sqrt{v}$ and $v = x^2 + 2$

By using chain rule of derivative, we get

$$\frac{dy}{dx} = \frac{dy}{du} \times \frac{du}{dv} \times \frac{dv}{dx}$$

$$\Rightarrow \frac{dy}{dx} = \frac{d}{du}(\operatorname{cosec} u) \times \frac{d}{dv}(\sqrt{v}) \times \frac{d}{dx}(x^2 + 2) \quad [1]$$

$$= -\operatorname{cosec} u \cot u \times \frac{1}{2}v^{-1/2} \times 2x$$

$$= -\operatorname{cosec}\sqrt{v}\cot\sqrt{v} \times \frac{1}{\sqrt{v}} \times x \quad [\text{put } u = \sqrt{v}]$$

$$= -\operatorname{cosec}\sqrt{x^2+2}\cot\sqrt{x^2+2} \times \frac{x}{\sqrt{x^2+2}}$$

[put $v = x^2 + 2$] [1]

7. Solve as Question 6. $\left[\textbf{Ans. } \sec\left(\frac{5}{x}\right)\tan\left(\frac{5}{x}\right) \times \frac{-5}{x^2}\right]$

8. Let $y = \sqrt{\frac{1 - \cos x}{1 + \cos x}} = \sqrt{\frac{2\sin^2 x/2}{2\cos^2 x/2}} = \sqrt{\tan^2 x/2}$

$$y = \tan\frac{x}{2} \quad [1]$$

On differentiating both sides wr.t. x, we get

$$\frac{dy}{dx} = \sec^2\frac{x}{2}\frac{d}{dx}\left(\frac{x}{2}\right) \quad [\text{by chain rule}]$$

$$\Rightarrow \frac{dy}{dx} = \sec^2\frac{x}{2}\left(\frac{1}{2}\right) = \frac{1}{2}\sec^2\frac{x}{2} \quad [1]$$

9. We have, $f(x) = \sin 2x - \cos 2x$

$$\therefore \quad f'(x) = 2\cos 2x + 2\sin 2x \quad [1]$$

Now, $f'\left(\frac{\pi}{6}\right) = 2\left[\cos\frac{\pi}{3} + \sin\frac{\pi}{3}\right] = 1 + \sqrt{3}$ [1]

10. We have, $f(x) = |\cos x|$

$$\therefore \quad f'(x) = \frac{\cos x}{|\cos x|} \cdot \frac{d}{dx}(\cos x) = \frac{\cos x}{|\cos x|} \cdot (-\sin x) \quad [1]$$

Now, $$f'\left(\frac{3\pi}{4}\right) = \frac{\cos\frac{3\pi}{4}}{\left|\cos\frac{3\pi}{4}\right|}\left(-\sin\frac{3\pi}{4}\right)$$

$$= \frac{\left(-\frac{1}{\sqrt{2}}\right)}{\left|-\frac{1}{\sqrt{2}}\right|}\left(-\frac{1}{\sqrt{2}}\right) = \frac{1}{\sqrt{2}} \quad [1]$$

$$\left[\begin{array}{l} \because \cos\left(\frac{3\pi}{4}\right) = \cos\left(\pi - \frac{\pi}{4}\right) = -\cos\frac{\pi}{4} = -\frac{1}{\sqrt{2}} \\ \text{and } \sin\left(\frac{3\pi}{4}\right) = \sin\left(\pi - \frac{\pi}{4}\right) = \sin\frac{\pi}{4} = \frac{1}{\sqrt{2}} \end{array}\right]$$

11. **Hint** $f'(x) = \frac{\cos x - \sin x}{|\cos x - \sin x|} \cdot \frac{d}{dx}(\cos x - \sin x)$

$\left[\textbf{Ans. } -\frac{1}{2}(1 + \sqrt{3})\right]$

12. Similar as Example 7. $\left[\textbf{Ans. } \frac{\sec^2(\sqrt{x})}{4\sqrt{x}\sqrt{\tan\sqrt{x}}}\right]$

13. **Hint** Apply product and chain rule.

[**Ans.** $10x^4 \sin x^5 \cos x^5 \cos x^3 - 3x^2 \sin x^3 \sin^2 x^5$]

14. Similar as Example 2.

15. **Hint** $\frac{dy}{dx} = 3\sin^2 \sqrt{ax^2+bx+c} \cdot \frac{d}{dx}(\sin\sqrt{ax^2+bx+c})$

$$= 3\sin^2 \sqrt{ax^2+bx+c} \cdot \cos\sqrt{ax^2+bx+c} \cdot \frac{d}{dx}(\sqrt{ax^2+bx+c})$$

$$\left[\textbf{Ans. } \frac{3}{2}\sin^2\sqrt{ax^2+bx+c} \cdot \cos\sqrt{ax^2+bx+c} \cdot \frac{(2ax+b)}{\sqrt{ax^2+bx+c}}\right]$$

16. We have, $y = \sqrt{\frac{1-\sin 2x}{1+\sin 2x}}$

$$= \sqrt{\frac{\sin^2 x + \cos^2 x - 2\sin x \cos x}{\sin^2 x + \cos^2 x + 2\sin x \cos x}}$$

$[\because \sin^2 x + \cos^2 x = 1 \text{ and } \sin 2x = 2\sin x \cos x]$ [1]

$$= \sqrt{\frac{(\cos x - \sin x)^2}{(\cos x + \sin x)^2}}$$

$\left[\because \text{for } x \in \left[0, \frac{\pi}{4}\right], \cos x \ge \sin x, \text{ therefore we take } (\cos x - \sin x)^2 \text{ instead of } (\sin x - \cos x)^2\right]$ [1]

$$= \frac{\cos x - \sin x}{\cos x + \sin x} = \frac{1-\tan x}{1+\tan x}$$

[dividing numerator and denominator by cos x]

$\Rightarrow y = \tan\left(\frac{\pi}{4} - x\right) \left[\because \tan(x-y) = \frac{\tan x - \tan y}{1 + \tan x \tan y}\right]$ [1]

On differentiating both sides w.r.t. x, we get

$$\frac{dy}{dx} = \sec^2\left(\frac{\pi}{4} - x\right)\frac{d}{dx}\left(\frac{\pi}{4} - x\right)$$

[by chain rule of derivative]

$$= \sec^2\left(\frac{\pi}{4} - x\right)(-1) = -\sec^2\left(\frac{\pi}{4} - x\right)$$

$\Rightarrow \frac{dy}{dx} + \sec^2\left(\frac{\pi}{4} - x\right) = 0$ **Hence proved.** [1]

17. Let $y = \sqrt{\frac{a^2-x^2}{a^2+x^2}} \Rightarrow y = \left(\frac{a^2-x^2}{a^2+x^2}\right)^{1/2}$ [1]

On differentiating y w.r.t. 'x', we get

$$\frac{dy}{dx} = \frac{1}{2}\left(\frac{a^2-x^2}{a^2+x^2}\right)^{\frac{1}{2}-1} \frac{d}{dx}\left(\frac{a^2-x^2}{a^2+x^2}\right)$$ [1]

$$= \frac{1}{2}\left(\frac{a^2-x^2}{a^2+x^2}\right)^{-1/2}$$

$$\left[\frac{(a^2+x^2)\frac{d}{dx}(a^2-x^2) - (a^2-x^2)\frac{d}{dx}(a^2+x^2)}{(a^2+x^2)^2}\right]$$ [1]

$$= \frac{1}{2}\sqrt{\frac{a^2+x^2}{a^2-x^2}}\left[\frac{(a^2+x^2)(0-2x) - (a^2-x^2)(0+2x)}{(a^2+x^2)^2}\right]$$

$$= \frac{1}{2}\sqrt{\frac{a^2+x^2}{a^2-x^2}}\left[\frac{-(a^2+x^2)\times 2x - (a^2-x^2)\times 2x}{(a^2+x^2)^2}\right]$$ [1]

$$= \frac{1}{2}\sqrt{\frac{a^2+x^2}{a^2-x^2}}\left[\frac{-2x[a^2+x^2+a^2-x^2]}{(a^2+x^2)^2}\right]$$

$$= \frac{1}{2}\sqrt{\frac{a^2+x^2}{a^2-x^2}}\left[\frac{-4xa^2}{(a^2+x^2)^2}\right]$$ [1]

$$= \frac{-2xa^2}{(a^2+x^2)^2}\sqrt{\frac{a^2+x^2}{a^2-x^2}} = \frac{-2xa^2}{\sqrt{a^2-x^2}\,(a^2+x^2)^{3/2}}$$ [1]

18. Given, $y = \frac{\sqrt{a+x} - \sqrt{a-x}}{\sqrt{a+x} + \sqrt{a-x}}$

$$y = \frac{(\sqrt{a+x} - \sqrt{a-x})(\sqrt{a+x} - \sqrt{a-x})}{(\sqrt{a+x} + \sqrt{a-x})(\sqrt{a+x} - \sqrt{a-x})}$$

[rationalising]

$$= \frac{(\sqrt{a+x} - \sqrt{a-x})^2}{(\sqrt{a-x})^2 - (\sqrt{a-x})^2}$$ [1]

$$= \frac{a+x+a-x-2\sqrt{a+x}\,\sqrt{a-x}}{a+x-(a-x)}$$

$$= \frac{2a - 2\sqrt{(a+x)(a-x)}}{a+x-a+x}$$ [1]

$$= \frac{2[a-\sqrt{a^2-x^2})}{2x}$$

$\Rightarrow y = \frac{a-\sqrt{a^2-x^2}}{x}$ [1]

On differentiating y w.r.t. 'x', we get

$$\frac{dy}{dx} = \frac{x\frac{dy}{dx}(a-\sqrt{a^2-x^2}) - (a-\sqrt{a^2-x^2})\frac{d}{dx}x}{x^2}$$

$$= \frac{x\left[-\frac{1}{2}(a^2-x^2)^{-1/2}(-2x)\right] - (a-\sqrt{a^2-x^2})1}{x^2}$$ [1]

$$= \frac{\frac{x^2}{\sqrt{a^2-x^2}} - (a-\sqrt{a^2-x^2})}{x^2}$$

$$= \frac{x^2 - (a-\sqrt{a^2-x^2})(\sqrt{a^2-x^2})}{x^2\sqrt{a^2-x^2}}$$ [1]

$$= \frac{x^2 - a\sqrt{a^2-x^2} + a^2 - x^2}{x^2\sqrt{a^2-x^2}} = \frac{a^2 - a\sqrt{a^2-x^2}}{x^2\sqrt{a^2-x^2}}$$

$$= \frac{a(a-\sqrt{a^2-x^2})}{x^2\sqrt{a^2-x^2}}$$ [1]

19. Given, $f(x)=\sqrt{\dfrac{\sec x-1}{\sec x+1}}=\sqrt{\dfrac{(\sec x-1)(\sec x-1)}{(\sec x+1)(\sec x-1)}}$ [rationalising]

$$=\sqrt{\frac{(\sec x-1)^2}{\sec^2 x-1}}=\frac{\sec x-1}{\sqrt{\tan^2 x}}=\frac{\sec x-1}{\tan x} \quad [1]$$

$$=\frac{\dfrac{1}{\cos x}-1}{\dfrac{\sin x}{\cos x}}$$

$$f(x)=\frac{1-\cos x}{\sin x} \quad [1]$$

On differentiating both sides w.r.t. 'x', we get

$$f'(x)=\frac{\sin x\dfrac{d}{dx}(1-\cos x)-(1-\cos x)\dfrac{d}{dx}\sin x}{\sin^2 x}$$

$$=\frac{\sin x(0+\sin x)-(1-\cos x)\cos x}{\sin^2 x} \quad [1]$$

$$=\frac{\sin^2 x-\cos x+\cos^2 x}{\sin^2 x}$$

$$=\frac{1-\cos x}{\sin^2 x}=\frac{1-\cos x}{1-\cos^2 x} \quad [1]$$

$$=\frac{(1-\cos x)}{(1-\cos x)(1+\cos x)}$$

$[\because a^2-b^2=(a-b)(a+b)]$ [1/2]

$$=\frac{1}{1+\cos x} \quad [1/2]$$

$$\therefore \quad f\left(\frac{\pi}{3}\right)=\frac{1}{1+\cos\left(\dfrac{\pi}{3}\right)}=\frac{1}{1+\dfrac{1}{2}}=\frac{2}{3} \quad [1]$$

20. Similar as Example 8.

TOPIC 02 Differentiation of Exponential, Logarithmic and Implicit Functions

Exponential Function

The function defined as $y=f(x)=b^x$ with positive base $b>0,\ b\neq 1$ is called the **general exponential function.**

(i) If the base of an exponential function is e, i.e. $b=e$, then it is called **natural exponential function.**

(ii) If the base of an exponential function is 10, i.e. $b=10$, then it is called the **common exponential function.**

The graph of $y=b^x$ is as shown in the following figure

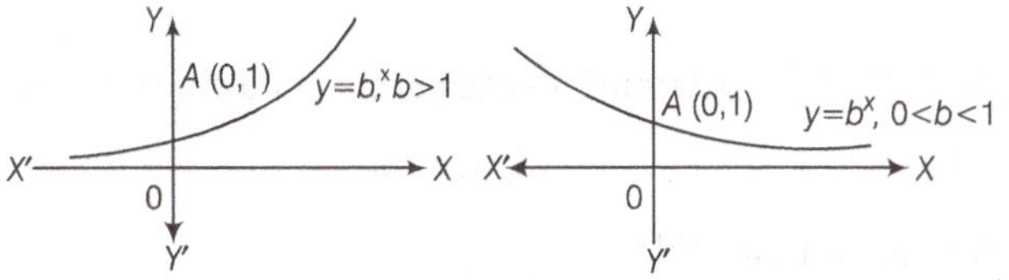

Main Features of Exponential Function

(i) The domain of exponential function is R, i.e. the set of all real numbers.

(ii) The range of exponential function is R^+, i.e. the set of all positive real numbers.

(iii) The point (0,1) always lies on the graph of exponential function.

(iv) For large negative values of x and $b>1$, the exponential function is very close to 0, i.e. it tends to zero.

(v) Exponential function having base greater than 1 is always increasing, i.e. as we move from left to right, the graph rises above.

Note The important property of the natural exponential function in differential calculus is that it does not change during the process of differentiation. In this chapter, if base is not mentioned consider it as 'e'.

Logarithmic Function

Let b be a positive real number such that $b>0, b\neq 1$, then the function $\log_b : R^+ \to R$ defined as $\log_b(x)=y$, if $b^y=x$, is called the **logarithmic function.**

If base $b=10$, then it is called **common logarithm** and if $b=e$, then it is called **natural logarithm.**

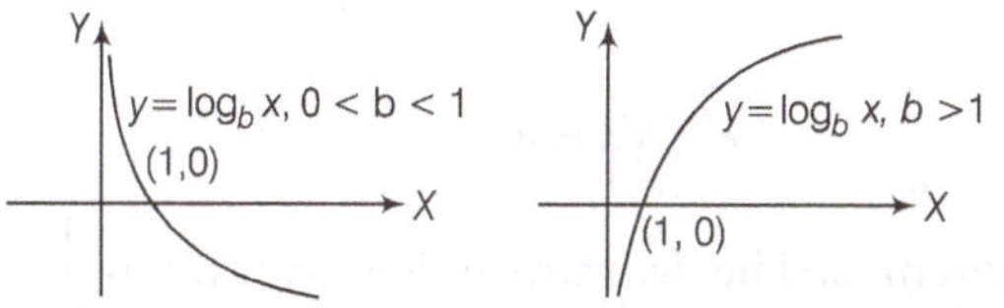

Note Logarithm of a to base b is x if $b^x=-a$, i.e. $\log_b a=x$, if $b^x=a$.

Main Features of Logarithmic Function

(i) The domain of logarithmic function is R^+, because logarithm of non-positive numbers cannot be defined meaningfully.
(ii) The range of logarithmic function is the set of all real numbers.
(iii) The logarithmic function having base greater than 1 is always increasing, i.e. as we move from left to right, the graph rises above.
(iv) For x, which is very near to zero and $b > 1$, the value of $\log_b x$ can be made lesser than any given real number.
(v) The point (1, 0) always lies on the graph of logarithmic function.
(vi) The graph of functions $f(x) = e^x$ and $f(x) = \ln(x)$ are mirror images of each other w.r.t. the line $y = x$.

Note When the base of a logarithmic function is not mentioned, then consider it as 'e'.

Basic Properties of Logarithms

(i) $\log_a (mn) = \log_a m + \log_a n$,
$m > 0, n > 0, a > 0, a \neq 1$
(ii) $\log_a x = \log_a e \log_e x, a > 0, a \neq 1, x > 0$
(iii) $\log_a \dfrac{m}{n} = \log_a m - \log_a n$,
$m > 0, n > 0, \ a > 0, a \neq 1$
(iv) $\log_a m^n = n \log_a m, m > 0, a > 0, \ a \neq 1$
(v) $e^{\log_e x} = x, x > 0$
(vi) $\log_a x = \dfrac{\log x}{\log a}, a > 0, a \neq 1, x > 0$
(vii) $\log_n m = \dfrac{1}{\log_m n}, m, n > 0$ and $m, n \neq 1$
(viii) $\log_{10} 10 = 1, \log_e e = 1$ and $\log_a 1 = 0, a > 0, a \neq 1$

Important Theorems

Theorem 1. The derivative of e^x w.r.t. x is e^x, for all $x \in R$.

i.e. $\dfrac{d}{dx}(e^x) = e^x, \forall x \in R$

Theorem 2. The derivative of $\log x$ w.r.t. x is $\dfrac{1}{x}$, where $x > 0$

i.e. $\dfrac{d}{dx}(\log x) = \dfrac{1}{x}, \forall x > 0$

Note (i) $\dfrac{d}{dx}(a^x) = \dfrac{d}{dx}(e^{\log a^x}) = \dfrac{d}{dx}(e^{x\log a}) = e^{x\log a} \cdot \dfrac{d}{dx}(x\log a)$

$= a^x \cdot \log a \cdot \dfrac{d}{dx}(x) = a^x \log a, a > 0, a \neq 1$

(ii) $\dfrac{d}{dx}(\log_a x) = \dfrac{d}{dx}\left(\dfrac{\log x}{\log a}\right) = \dfrac{1}{\log a}\dfrac{d}{dx}(\log x)$

$= \dfrac{1}{\log a} \cdot \dfrac{1}{x}, x > 0, a > 0, a \neq 1$

(iii) $\dfrac{d}{dx}(\log |x|) = \dfrac{1}{|x|} \cdot \dfrac{d}{dx}(|x|) = \dfrac{1}{|x|} \cdot \dfrac{x}{|x|} = \dfrac{x}{|x|^2} = \dfrac{x}{x^2} = \dfrac{1}{x}, x \neq 0$

(iv) $\dfrac{d}{dx}(\log_a |x|) = \dfrac{d}{dx}\left(\dfrac{\log |x|}{\log a}\right) = \dfrac{1}{\log a}\dfrac{d}{dx}(\log |x|)$

$= \dfrac{1}{\log a} \cdot \dfrac{1}{x}, x \neq 0, a > 0, a \neq 1$

Example 1 Differentiate the following w.r.t. x.

(i) e^{x^3} (ii) $\log(\cos e^x)$ **[NCERT]**

Sol. (i) Let $y = e^{x^3}$

On differentiating both sides w.r.t. x, we get

$\dfrac{dy}{dx} = e^{x^3} \dfrac{d}{dx}(x^3)$ [by chain rule of derivative]

$= e^{x^3} \cdot 3x^2 = 3x^2 e^{x^3}$

(ii) Let $y = \log(\cos e^x)$

On differentiating both sides w.r.t. x, we get

$\dfrac{dy}{dx} = \dfrac{1}{\cos e^x} \cdot \dfrac{d}{dx}(\cos e^x)$

$\left[\text{by chain rule of derivative and } \dfrac{d}{dt}(\log t) = \dfrac{1}{t}\right]$

$= \dfrac{1}{\cos e^x}(-\sin e^x)\dfrac{d}{dx}(e^x)$

[again by chain rule of derivative]

$= -\tan e^x \times e^x = -e^x \tan e^x$

Example 2 Differentiate each of the following w.r.t. x.

(i) $e^{\sqrt{\cot x}}$ (ii) $\log \tan \dfrac{x}{2}$

Sol. (i) Let $y = e^{\sqrt{\cot x}}$

On differentiating both sides w.r.t. x, we get

$\dfrac{dy}{dx} = e^{\sqrt{\cot x}} \cdot \dfrac{d}{dx}(\sqrt{\cot x})$ [by chain rule]

$= e^{\sqrt{\cot x}} \cdot \dfrac{1}{2}(\cot x)^{\frac{1}{2}-1} \cdot \dfrac{d}{dx}(\cot x)$ [by chain rule]

$= \dfrac{1}{2}e^{\sqrt{\cot x}} \cdot \dfrac{1}{\sqrt{\cot x}}(-\operatorname{cosec}^2 x)$

$= -e^{\sqrt{\cot x}} \cdot \dfrac{\operatorname{cosec}^2 x}{2\sqrt{\cot x}}$

(ii) Let $y = \log \tan \frac{x}{2}$

On differentiating both sides w.r.t. x, we get

$$\frac{dy}{dx} = \frac{1}{\tan \frac{x}{2}} \frac{d}{dx}\left(\tan \frac{x}{2}\right)$$

$$= \frac{1}{\tan \frac{x}{2}} \times \sec^2 \frac{x}{2} \times \frac{d}{dx}\left(\frac{x}{2}\right)$$

$$= \frac{\cos \frac{x}{2}}{\sin \frac{x}{2}} \times \frac{1}{\cos^2 \frac{x}{2}} \times \frac{1}{2} = \frac{1}{2\sin \frac{x}{2} \cos \frac{x}{2}}$$

$$\Rightarrow \quad \frac{dy}{dx} = \frac{1}{\sin x} = \operatorname{cosec} x$$

Example 3 Find the derivative of $y = \log x + \frac{1}{x}$ with respect to x. **[ISC 2024]**

Sol. We have,

$$y = \log x + \frac{1}{x}$$

On differentiating w.r.t. x, we get

$$\frac{dy}{dx} = \frac{d}{dx}(\log x) + \frac{d}{dx}\left(\frac{1}{x}\right)$$

$$= \frac{1}{x} - \frac{1}{x^2}$$

Derivatives of Implicit Functions

If the variables x and y are connected by a relation $f(x, y) = 0$ and it is not possible to express y as a function of x or in the form $y = \phi(x)$, then y is said to be **an implicit function of x.**

e.g. $x^2 + y^2 = xy$, $\cos(x + y) = \log(x \cdot y)$

Working Rule to Find dy/dx of Implicit Functions

Following steps are used to find dy / dx of implicit functions.

I. Write the given equation in x and y and then differentiate both sides of the given equation w.r.t. x.

II. Take all terms involving $\frac{dy}{dx}$ on LHS and transfer the remaining terms on RHS to get an equation of the form of $\frac{dy}{dx} f(x, y) = g(x, y)$.

III. Now, find $\frac{dy}{dx}$, i.e. $\frac{dy}{dx} = \frac{g(x, y)}{f(x, y)}$.

Example 4 If $x^3 + y^3 = 3axy$, then find $\frac{dy}{dx}$. **[ISC 2020]**

Sol. Given, $x^3 + y^3 = 3axy$

On differentiating both sides w.r.t. x, we get

$$3x^2 + 3y^2 \frac{dy}{dx} = 3a \frac{d}{dx}(xy)$$

$$\Rightarrow \quad x^2 + y^2 \frac{dy}{dx} = a\left(1 \cdot y + x \frac{dy}{dx}\right)$$

[by product rule of derivative]

$$\Rightarrow \quad x^2 + y^2 \frac{dy}{dx} = ay + ax \frac{dy}{dx}$$

$$\Rightarrow \quad y^2 \frac{dy}{dx} - ax \frac{dy}{dx} = ay - x^2$$

[taking terms involving dy/dx in LHS]

$$\Rightarrow \quad (y^2 - ax) \frac{dy}{dx} = (ay - x^2)$$

$$\Rightarrow \quad \frac{dy}{dx} = \frac{ay - x^2}{y^2 - ax}$$

Example 5 Find $\frac{dy}{dx}$ for the equation

$$x^3 + y^3 = \sin(x + y).$$

Sol. We have,

$$x^3 + y^3 = \sin(x + y)$$

On differentiating both sides w.r.t. x, we get

$$3x^2 + 3y^2 \cdot \frac{dy}{dx} = \cos(x + y) \frac{d}{dx}(x + y)$$

[by chain rule of derivative]

$$\Rightarrow \quad 3x^2 + 3y^2 \frac{dy}{dx} = \cos(x + y)\left(1 + \frac{dy}{dx}\right)$$

$$\Rightarrow \quad 3x^2 + 3y^2 \frac{dy}{dx} = \cos(x + y) + \cos(x + y) \cdot \frac{dy}{dx}$$

$$\Rightarrow \quad 3y^2 \frac{dy}{dx} - \cos(x + y) \frac{dy}{dx} = \cos(x + y) - 3x^2$$

$\left[\text{taking terms involving } \frac{dy}{dx} \text{ in LHS}\right]$

$$\Rightarrow \quad \frac{dy}{dx}[3y^2 - \cos(x + y)] = \cos(x + y) - 3x^2$$

$$\Rightarrow \quad \frac{dy}{dx} = \frac{\cos(x + y) - 3x^2}{3y^2 - \cos(x + y)}$$

Topic Practice 2

Very Short Answer Type Questions

(2 Marks)

1 Differentiate $e^{\sin 2x}$ w.r.t. x.

2 If $y = \frac{\log x}{x}$, then find $\frac{dy}{dx}$.

3 Differentiate $\log(\log x), x > 1$ w.r.t. 'x'.

4 If $f(x) = x\cos x + e^x$, then find $f'(0)$.

5 Find the derivative of $xe^x \sin x$ w.r.t. 'x'.

6 Find the derivative of $\log[\log(\log x^5)]$ w.r.t. 'x'.

7 Find the derivative of $xy + y^2 = \tan x + y$ **[NCERT]**

8 If $y = \tan(x+y)$, then find $\frac{dy}{dx}$ **[NCERT Exemplar]**

Short Answer Type Questions

(4 Marks)

9 If $y = e^{\sin x^2}$, then find dy/dx **[ISC 2006]**

10 If $y = e^x \log(\tan 2x)$, then find dy/dx **[ISC 2002]**

11 If $y = \log\sqrt{\frac{1-\cos x}{1+\cos x}}$, then find $\frac{dy}{dx}$ **[ISC 2000]**

12 If $x\sqrt{1+y} + y\sqrt{1+x} = 0, x \pm y$, then prove that $\frac{dy}{dx} = -\frac{1}{(1+x)^2}$.

13 Find $\frac{dy}{dx}$ for the following equation.

$$x^2 - y^2 = \cos(x+y)$$

14 If $\sin(xy) + \cos(xy) = 1$ and $\tan(xy) \neq 1$, then show that $\frac{dy}{dx} = \frac{-y}{x}$. **[ISC 2005]**

Hints & Solutions

1. Let $y = e^{\sin 2x}$

On differentiating both sides w.r.t. 'x', we get

$$\frac{dy}{dx} = e^{\sin 2x}\frac{d}{dx}(\sin 2x) \quad \text{[by chain rule] [1]}$$

$$= e^{\sin 2x}\cos 2x \frac{d}{dx}(2x) \quad \text{[again, by chain rule]}$$

$$= e^{\sin 2x}\cos 2x \cdot 2 = 2\cos 2x\, e^{\sin 2x} \quad [1]$$

2. We have, $y = \frac{\log x}{x}$

On differentiating both sides w.r.t. x, we get

$$\frac{dy}{dx} = \frac{\left(x\frac{d}{dx}(\log x) - \log x \frac{d}{dx}(x)\right)}{x^2} \quad [1]$$

[by quotient rule of derivative]

$$= \frac{\left(x \times \frac{1}{x} - \log x\right)}{x^2} = \frac{1-\log x}{x^2} \quad [1]$$

3. Similar as Example 2 (ii). $\left[\textbf{Ans. } \frac{1}{x\log x}\right]$

4. We have, $f(x) = x\cos x + e^x$

On differentiating both sides w.r.t. x, we get

$$f'(x) = \frac{d}{dx}(x\cos x) + \frac{d}{dx}(e^x)$$

$$\Rightarrow f'(x) = x\frac{d}{dx}(\cos x) + \cos x\frac{d}{dx}(x) + \frac{d}{dx}(e^x) \quad [1]$$

$$= -x\sin x + \cos x + e^x$$

At $x = 0$,

$$f'(0) = -(0)\sin 0 + \cos 0 + e^0 = 0 + 1 + 1 = 2 \quad [1]$$

5. **Hint** Use product rule of derivative.

[**Ans.** $xe^x\cos x + (x+1)e^x \sin x$]

6. **Hint** Use chain rule of derivative.

$\left[\textbf{Ans. } \frac{5}{x\log(x^5)\log\log(x^5)}\right]$

7. Similar as Example 4. $\left[\textbf{Ans. } \frac{\sec^2 x - y}{x+2y-1}\right]$

8. Similar as Example 5. [**Ans.** $-\text{cosec}^2(x+y)$]

9. Given, $y = e^{\sin x^2}$

Let $y = e^z$, where $z = \sin t$ and $t = x^2$ [1]

On differentiating both sides of t w.r.t. x, we get

$$\frac{dt}{dx} = 2x \quad \text{...(i)}$$

On differentiating both sides of z w.r.t. t, we get

$$\frac{dz}{dt} = \cos t \quad \text{...(ii) [1]}$$

On differentiating both sides of y w.r.t. z, we get

$$\frac{dy}{dz} = e^z \quad \text{...(iii) [1]}$$

Using chain rule of derivative, $\frac{dy}{dx}$

$$= \frac{dy}{dz} \times \frac{dz}{dt} \times \frac{dt}{dx} = e^z \times \cos t \times 2x$$

[from Eqs. (i), (ii) and (iii)]

$$= 2x\, e^{\sin t}\cos t = 2x\, e^{\sin x^2}\cos x^2 \quad [1]$$

10. Given, $y = e^x \log \tan 2x$

On differentiating both sides w.r.t. x, we get

$$\frac{dy}{dx} = e^x \cdot \frac{d}{dx}(\log \tan 2x) + \log \tan 2x \, \frac{d(e^x)}{dx}$$

[product rule of derivative] [1]

$$= e^x \frac{d(\log \tan 2x)}{d(\tan 2x)} \times \frac{d(\tan 2x)}{d(2x)} \times \frac{d(2x)}{dx}$$

$+ e^x \log \tan 2x$ [by chain rule of derivative]

$$= \frac{2e^x \sec^2 2x}{\tan 2x} + e^x \log \tan 2x \quad [1]$$

$$= \frac{2e^x}{\sin 2x \cos 2x} + e^x \log \tan 2x$$

$$= \frac{2 \times 2e^x}{2 \sin 2x \cos 2x} + e^x \log \tan 2x$$

$$= \frac{4e^x}{\sin 4x} + e^x \log \tan 2x \quad [1]$$

$[\because \sin 2x = 2 \sin x \cos x]$

$$= 4e^x \operatorname{cosec} 4x + e^x \log \tan 2x$$

$$= e^x \{4 \operatorname{cosec} 4x + \log(\tan 2x)\} \quad [1]$$

11. Given, $y = \log \sqrt{\frac{1 - \cos x}{1 + \cos x}}$

$$\Rightarrow \quad y = \frac{1}{2} \log \left(\frac{1 - \cos x}{1 + \cos x} \right)$$

$$\Rightarrow \quad y = \frac{1}{2} [\log(1 - \cos x) - \log(1 + \cos x)]$$

$[\because \log m^n = n \log m \text{ and } \log \frac{m}{n} = \log m - \log n]$ [1]

On differentiating both sides w.r.t. x, we get

$$y = \frac{1}{2} \left[\frac{1}{(1 - \cos x)} \times \frac{d}{dx}(1 - \cos x) - \frac{1}{1 + \cos x} \times \frac{d}{dx}(1 + \cos x) \right] \quad [1]$$

$$\Rightarrow \quad \frac{dy}{dx} = \frac{1}{2} \left[\frac{-(-\sin x)}{1 - \cos x} - \frac{(-\sin x)}{1 + \cos x} \right]$$

$$= \frac{1}{2} \left[\frac{\sin x (1 + \cos x + 1 - \cos x)}{1 - \cos^2 x} \right] \quad [1]$$

$$= \frac{1}{2} \left(\frac{2 \sin x}{\sin^2 x} \right) \quad [\because \sin^2 x + \cos^2 x = 1]$$

$$= \frac{1}{\sin x} = \operatorname{cosec} x \quad [1]$$

12. We have, $x\sqrt{1+y} + y\sqrt{1+x} = 0$ ...(i)

$$\Rightarrow \quad x\sqrt{1+y} = -y\sqrt{1+x}$$

$$\Rightarrow \quad x^2(1+y) = y^2(1+x) \quad \text{[square both sides]}$$

$$\Rightarrow \quad x^2 + x^2 y = y^2 + y^2 x \quad [1]$$

$$\Rightarrow \quad x^2 y - xy^2 + x^2 - y^2 = 0$$

$$\Rightarrow \quad xy(x - y) + (x - y)(x + y) = 0$$

$$\Rightarrow \quad (x - y)(xy + x + y) = 0$$

$$\Rightarrow \quad x - y = 0 \text{ or } xy + x + y = 0$$

$$\Rightarrow \quad x = y \text{ or } xy + x + y = 0 \quad [1]$$

Suppose, if we put $x = y$ in Eq. (i) it does not satisfy it.

Now, consider $xy + x + y = 0$

$$\Rightarrow \quad y(x+1) + x = 0$$

$$\Rightarrow \quad y = -\frac{x}{1+x} \quad [1]$$

On differentiating both sides w.r.t. x, we get

$$\frac{dy}{dx} = -\frac{(1+x)(1) - x(1)}{(1+x)^2}$$

$$= -\frac{1}{(1+x)^2}$$

Hence proved. [1]

13. Similar as Example 5.

$$\left[\textbf{Ans. } \frac{\sin(x+y) + 2x}{2y - \sin(x+y)} \right]$$

14. Given, $\sin(xy) + \cos(xy) = 1$

On differentiating both sides w.r.t. x, we get

$$\frac{d}{dx}[\sin(xy) + \cos(xy)] = \frac{d(1)}{dx}$$

$$\Rightarrow \quad \frac{d}{d(xy)}(\sin xy) \frac{d}{dx}(xy) + \frac{d}{d(xy)}(\cos xy) \frac{d}{dx}(xy) = 0 \quad [1]$$

$$\Rightarrow \quad \frac{d}{d(xy)}[\sin(xy) + \cos(xy)] \times \frac{d(xy)}{dx} = 0$$

$$\Rightarrow \quad \left[\frac{d \sin(xy)}{d(xy)} + \frac{d \cos(xy)}{d(xy)} \right] \times \left(x\frac{dy}{dx} + y\frac{dx}{dx} \right) = 0$$

$$\left[\because \frac{d}{dx}\{f(x) \cdot g(x)\} = f(x) \cdot \frac{d}{dx} \cdot \{g(x)\} + g(x) \frac{d}{dx}\{f(x)\} \right] \quad [1]$$

$$\Rightarrow \quad (\cos(xy) - \sin(xy)) \left(x\frac{dy}{dx} + y \right) = 0$$

$$\Rightarrow \quad \left(1 - \frac{\sin xy}{\cos xy} \right) \left(x\frac{dy}{dx} + y \right) = 0$$

[divide by $\cos xy$] [1]

$$\Rightarrow \quad (1 - \tan xy) \left(x\frac{dy}{dx} + y \right) = 0$$

$$\Rightarrow \quad x\frac{dy}{dx} + y = 0 \quad [\because \tan xy \neq 1, \text{ given}]$$

$$\therefore \quad x\frac{dy}{dx} = -y$$

$$\Rightarrow \quad \frac{dy}{dx} = -y/x$$

Hence proved. [1]

TOPIC 03 Derivatives of Inverse Trigonometric Functions

Derivatives of standard inverse trigonometric functions are given below

(i) $\frac{d}{dx}(\sin^{-1} x) = \frac{1}{\sqrt{1-x^2}}, |x|<1$

(ii) $\frac{d}{dx}(\cos^{-1} x) = \frac{-1}{\sqrt{1-x^2}}, |x|<1$

(iii) $\frac{d}{dx}(\tan^{-1} x) = \frac{1}{1+x^2}, x \in R$

(iv) $\frac{d}{dx}(\cot^{-1} x) = \frac{-1}{1+x^2}, x \in R$

(v) $\frac{d}{dx}(\sec^{-1} x) = \frac{1}{|x|\sqrt{x^2-1}}, |x|>1$

(vi) $\frac{d}{dx}(\text{cosec}^{-1} x) = \frac{-1}{|x|\sqrt{x^2-1}}, |x|>1$

Proof (i) $\frac{d}{dx}(\sin^{-1} x) = \frac{1}{\sqrt{1-x^2}}, |x|<1$

Let $y = \sin^{-1} x \Rightarrow x = \sin y$

On differentiating both sides w.r.t. y, we get

$$\frac{dx}{dy} = \cos y > 0$$

$$\left[\because |x|<1 \Rightarrow y \in \left(\frac{-\pi}{2}, \frac{\pi}{2}\right) \Rightarrow \cos y > 0\right]$$

$$\Rightarrow \quad \frac{dx}{dy} = \sqrt{1-\sin^2 y} = \sqrt{1-x^2}$$

$$\Rightarrow \quad \frac{dy}{dx} = \frac{1}{\sqrt{1-x^2}}$$

Hence, $\frac{d}{dx}(\sin^{-1} x) = \frac{1}{\sqrt{1-x^2}}$

Similarly, we can prove other parts.

Note (i) For $x > 1$, $\frac{d}{dx}(\sec^{-1} x) = \frac{1}{x\sqrt{x^2-1}}$

and $\frac{d}{dx}(\text{cosec}^{-1} x) = \frac{-1}{x\sqrt{x^2-1}}$

(ii) In practice, we use the formulae mentioned in note (i) and in such circumstances it is understood that $x > 1$.

Example 1 Differentiate $\cos^{-1}(5x^2+4)$ w.r.t. x.

Sol. Let $y = \cos^{-1}(5x^2+4)$. Put $z = 5x^2+4$. Then, $y = \cos^{-1} z$.

On differentiating both sides w.r.t. x, we get

$$\frac{dy}{dx} = \frac{d}{dx}(\cos^{-1} z) = \frac{d}{dz}(\cos^{-1} z)\frac{dz}{dx} \quad \text{[by chain rule]}$$

$$= \frac{-1}{\sqrt{1-z^2}} \frac{d}{dx}(5x^2+4) \quad [\because z = 5x^2+4]$$

$$= -\frac{1}{\sqrt{1-(5x^2+4)^2}} \times [5 \times 2x + 0] \quad [\text{put } z = 5x^2+4]$$

$$= -\frac{10x}{\sqrt{1-(5x^2+4)^2}}$$

Example 2 Differentiate $\cot^{-1}\left(\frac{1-x}{1+x}\right)$ w.r.t. x.

Sol. Let $y = \cot^{-1}\left(\frac{1-x}{1+x}\right)$.

Put $\frac{1-x}{1+x} = u$ ...(i)

Then, $y = \cot^{-1} u$ ...(ii)

Thus, y is a composite function, so we use chain rule of derivative.

Now, $\frac{dy}{dx} = \frac{dy}{du} \cdot \frac{du}{dx}$ ...(iii)

On differentiating Eq. (i) w.r.t. x, we get

$$\frac{du}{dx} = \frac{d}{dx}\left(\frac{1-x}{1+x}\right)$$

$$= \frac{(1+x)(-1)-(1-x)(1)}{(1+x)^2}$$

[by quotient rule of derivative]

$$= \frac{-1-x-1+x}{(1+x)^2} = \frac{-2}{(1+x)^2}$$

On differentiating both sides of Eq. (ii) w.r.t. u, we get

$$\frac{dy}{du} = \frac{-1}{1+u^2} = \frac{-1}{1+\left(\frac{1-x}{1+x}\right)^2} \quad \text{[from Eq. (i)]}$$

$$\Rightarrow \quad \frac{dy}{du} = \frac{-(1+x)^2}{(1+x)^2+(1-x)^2} = \frac{-(1+x)^2}{2(1+x^2)}$$

On putting the values of $\frac{du}{dx}$ and $\frac{dy}{du}$ in Eq. (iii), we get

$$\frac{dy}{dx} = \frac{-(1+x)^2}{2(1+x^2)} \cdot \frac{-2}{(1+x)^2} \Rightarrow \frac{dy}{dx} = \frac{1}{1+x^2}$$

Example 3 If $y = \dfrac{x \sin^{-1} x}{\sqrt{1-x^2}}$, then prove that

$$(1-x^2)\frac{dy}{dx} = x + \frac{y}{x}.$$ **[ISC 2014]**

Sol. Given, $y = \dfrac{x \sin^{-1} x}{\sqrt{1-x^2}}$

On differentiating both sides w.r.t. x, we get

$$\frac{dy}{dx} = \frac{\sqrt{1-x^2}\frac{d}{dx}(x\sin^{-1}x) - (x\sin^{-1}x)\frac{d}{dx}(\sqrt{1-x^2})}{(\sqrt{1-x^2})^2}$$

$$\left[\text{using quotient rule of deriative, i.e. } \frac{d}{dx}\left(\frac{f(x)}{g(x)}\right) = \frac{g(x)\frac{d}{dx}f(x) - f(x)\frac{d}{dx}g(x)}{[g(x)]^2}\right]$$

$$= \frac{\left\{\sqrt{1-x^2}\left[\sin^{-1}x\frac{d}{dx}(x) + x\frac{d}{dx}(\sin^{-1}x)\right] - (x\sin^{-1}x)\left[\frac{\frac{d}{dx}(1-x^2)}{2\sqrt{1-x^2}}\right]\right\}}{(\sqrt{1-x^2})^2}$$

$$\frac{dy}{dx} = \frac{\sqrt{1-x^2}\left\{\sin^{-1}x + \frac{x}{\sqrt{1-x^2}}\right\} - \frac{(x\sin^{-1}x)(-2x)}{2\sqrt{1-x^2}}}{(1-x^2)}$$

$$\Rightarrow (1-x^2)\frac{dy}{dx} = \sqrt{1-x^2}\sin^{-1}x + x + \frac{x^2\sin^{-1}x}{\sqrt{1-x^2}}$$

$$= x + \left[\frac{(1-x^2)\sin^{-1}x + x^2\sin^{-1}x}{\sqrt{1-x^2}}\right]$$

$$= x + \frac{\sin^{-1}x}{\sqrt{1-x^2}}$$

$$= x + \frac{y}{x} \qquad \left[\because y = \frac{x\sin^{-1}x}{\sqrt{1-x^2}}\right]$$

Hence proved.

Derivatives of Inverse Trigonometric Functions by Trigonometrical Transformations

Sometimes differentiation of inverse trigonometric functions becomes difficult by chain rule. In that case, we can differentiate them easily by using trigonometrical transformations.

Generally, we use the following trigonometric and inverse trigonometric formulae

(i) $\sin 2x = 2\sin x \cos x = \dfrac{2\tan x}{1+\tan^2 x}$

(ii) $\cos 2x = \cos^2 x - \sin^2 x = 2\cos^2 x - 1 = 1 - 2\sin^2 x = \dfrac{1-\tan^2 x}{1+\tan^2 x}$

(iii) $\tan 2x = \dfrac{2\tan x}{1-\tan^2 x}$

(iv) $\tan(x \pm y) = \dfrac{\tan x \pm \tan y}{1 \mp \tan x \tan y}$

(v) $\sin^{-1}(-x) = -\sin^{-1}(x)$, $\cos^{-1}(-x) = \pi - \cos^{-1}x$, $\tan^{-1}(-x) = -\tan^{-1}x$

(vi) $\sin^{-1}(\sin\theta) = \theta$; $\cos^{-1}(\cos\theta) = \theta$, $\tan^{-1}(\tan\theta) = \theta$

(vii) $\sin^{-1}x + \cos^{-1}x = \dfrac{\pi}{2}$, $\tan^{-1}x + \cot^{-1}x = \dfrac{\pi}{2}$, $\sec^{-1}x + \text{cosec}^{-1}x = \dfrac{\pi}{2}$

(viii) $\sin^{-1}(\sqrt{1-x^2}) = \cos^{-1}x$, $\cos^{-1}(\sqrt{1-x^2}) = \sin^{-1}x$

(ix) $\sin^{-1}x \pm \sin^{-1}y = \sin^{-1}\{x\sqrt{1-y^2} \pm y\sqrt{1-x^2}\}$

$\cos^{-1}x \pm \cos^{-1}y = \cos^{-1}\{xy \mp \sqrt{1-x^2}\sqrt{1-y^2}\}$

(x) $\tan^{-1}x \pm \tan^{-1}y = \tan^{-1}\left(\dfrac{x \pm y}{1 \mp xy}\right)$

Some Important Substitutions

S.No.	Expression	Substitution
(i)	$a^2 - x^2$	$x = a\cos\theta$ or $x = a\sin\theta$
(ii)	$a^2 + x^2$	$x = a\tan\theta$ or $x = a\cot\theta$
(iii)	$x^2 - a^2$	$x = a\sec\theta$ or $x = a\,\text{cosec}\,\theta$
(iv)	$\sqrt{\frac{a+x}{a-x}}$ or $\sqrt{\frac{a-x}{a+x}}$	$x = a\cos 2\theta$
(v)	$\sqrt{\frac{a^2-x^2}{a^2+x^2}}$ or $\sqrt{\frac{a^2+x^2}{a^2-x^2}}$	$x^2 = a^2\cos 2\theta$

Working Rule

To find the derivative of given inverse trigonometric function by trigonometrical transformation, we use the following steps

I. First, put the given inverse function equal to y, say $y = f^{-1}(x)$.

II. Convert $f^{-1}(x)$ to simplest form by using suitable trigonometric formulae or substitution.

III. Now, differentiate y with respect to x to get required dy/dx.

Example 4 Differentiate $\tan^{-1}(\sec x+\tan x)$ w.r.t. x.

Sol. Let $y=\tan^{-1}(\sec x+\tan x)=\tan^{-1}\left(\frac{1}{\cos x}+\frac{\sin x}{\cos x}\right)$

$$\Rightarrow\quad y=\tan^{-1}\left(\frac{1+\sin x}{\cos x}\right)=\tan^{-1}\left[\frac{1-\cos\left(\frac{\pi}{2}+x\right)}{\sin\left(\frac{\pi}{2}+x\right)}\right]$$

$$\left[\because \cos\left(\frac{\pi}{2}+x\right)=-\sin x \text{ and } \sin\left(\frac{\pi}{2}+x\right)=\cos x\right]$$

$$\Rightarrow\quad y=\tan^{-1}\left[\frac{2\sin^2\left(\frac{\pi}{4}+\frac{x}{2}\right)}{2\sin\left(\frac{\pi}{4}+\frac{x}{2}\right)\cdot\cos\left(\frac{\pi}{4}+\frac{x}{2}\right)}\right]$$

$$\left[\begin{array}{l}\because \cos\theta=1-2\sin^2\frac{\theta}{2}\Rightarrow 2\sin^2\frac{\theta}{2}=1-\cos\theta\\ \text{and } \sin\theta=2\sin\frac{\theta}{2}\cos\frac{\theta}{2}\end{array}\right]$$

$$\Rightarrow\quad y=\tan^{-1}\left[\tan\left(\frac{\pi}{4}+\frac{x}{2}\right)\right]\Rightarrow y=\frac{\pi}{4}+\frac{x}{2}$$

On differentiating both sides w.r.t. x, we get

$$\frac{dy}{dx}=0+\frac{1}{2}\Rightarrow\frac{dy}{dx}=\frac{1}{2}$$

Example 5 If $y=\sec^{-1}\left(\frac{x^2+1}{x^2-1}\right)$, then find $\frac{dy}{dx}$.

Sol. We have, $y=\sec^{-1}\left(\frac{x^2+1}{x^2-1}\right)$.

Here, put $x=\tan\theta$, we get $y=\sec^{-1}\left(\frac{\tan^2\theta+1}{\tan^2\theta-1}\right)$

$$\Rightarrow\quad y=\cos^{-1}\left(\frac{\tan^2\theta-1}{\tan^2\theta+1}\right)\qquad\left[\because \sec^{-1}\theta=\cos^{-1}\left(\frac{1}{\theta}\right)\right]$$

$$\Rightarrow\quad y=\cos^{-1}\left[-\left(\frac{1-\tan^2\theta}{1+\tan^2\theta}\right)\right]$$

$$\Rightarrow\quad y=\cos^{-1}[-\cos 2\theta]\qquad\left[\because \cos 2\theta=\frac{1-\tan^2\theta}{1+\tan^2\theta}\right]$$

$$\Rightarrow\quad y=\pi-\cos^{-1}(\cos 2\theta)\ [\because \cos^{-1}(-x)=\pi-\cos^{-1}x]$$

$$\Rightarrow\quad y=\pi-2\theta\qquad[\because \cos^{-1}(\cos x)=x]$$

$$\Rightarrow\quad y=\pi-2\tan^{-1}x\ [\because \tan\theta=x\Rightarrow\theta=\tan^{-1}x]\ \ldots\text{(i)}$$

On differentiating both sides of Eq. (i) w.r.t. x, we get

$$\frac{dy}{dx}=0-\frac{2}{1+x^2}\Rightarrow\frac{dy}{dx}=\frac{-2}{1+x^2}$$

Example 6 Using a suitable substitution, find the derivative of $\tan^{-1}\sqrt{\frac{a-x}{a+x}}$ with respect to x. **[ISC 2010]**

Sol. Given, $y=\tan^{-1}\sqrt{\frac{a-x}{a+x}}$

Put $x=a\cos 2\theta$, we get

$$y=\tan^{-1}\sqrt{\frac{a-a\cos 2\theta}{a+a\cos 2\theta}}=\tan^{-1}\sqrt{\frac{a(1-\cos 2\theta)}{a(1+\cos 2\theta)}}$$

$$\left[\begin{array}{l}\because \cos 2x=2\cos^2 x-1\Rightarrow 1+\cos 2x=2\cos^2 x\\ \text{and } \cos 2x=1-2\sin^2 x\Rightarrow 1-\cos 2x=2\sin^2 x\end{array}\right]$$

$$=\tan^{-1}\sqrt{\frac{2\sin^2\theta}{2\cos^2\theta}}=\tan^{-1}\sqrt{\tan^2\theta}$$

$$=\tan^{-1}\tan\theta=\theta\qquad[\because \tan^{-1}(\tan x)=x]$$

$$=\frac{1}{2}\cos^{-1}\frac{x}{a}\qquad\left[\because x=a\cos 2\theta\Rightarrow 2\theta=\cos^{-1}\frac{x}{a}\right]$$

On differentiating both sides w.r.t. x, we get

$$\frac{dy}{dx}=\frac{1}{2}\cdot\frac{-1}{\sqrt{1-\frac{x^2}{a^2}}}\cdot\frac{1}{a}=\frac{-1}{2\sqrt{a^2-x^2}}$$

Example 7 Find $\frac{dy}{dx}$, if $y=\sin^{-1}\left(\frac{5x+12\sqrt{1-x^2}}{13}\right)$.

Sol. Given, $y=\sin^{-1}\left(\frac{5x+12\sqrt{1-x^2}}{13}\right)$

$$=\sin^{-1}\left(x\cdot\frac{5}{13}+\frac{12}{13}\sqrt{1-x^2}\right)$$

$$=\sin^{-1}\left(x\cdot\sqrt{1-\left(\frac{12}{13}\right)^2}+\frac{12}{13}\sqrt{1-x^2}\right)$$

$$=\sin^{-1}x+\sin^{-1}\frac{12}{13}$$

$$[\because \sin^{-1}x+\sin^{-1}y=\sin^{-1}(x\sqrt{1-y^2}+y\sqrt{1-x^2})]$$

Now, on differentiating both sides w.r.t. x, we get

$$\frac{dy}{dx}=\frac{1}{\sqrt{1-x^2}}+0\qquad\left[\because \sin^{-1}\frac{12}{13}\text{ is a constant}\right]$$

$$=\frac{1}{\sqrt{1-x^2}}$$

Example 8 Differentiate $\tan^{-1}\left(\frac{a\cos x-b\sin x}{b\cos x+a\sin x}\right)$, $-\frac{\pi}{2}<x<\frac{\pi}{2}$ and $\frac{a}{b}\tan x>-1$. **[NCERT Exemplar]**

Sol. Let $y=\tan^{-1}\left(\frac{a\cos x-b\sin x}{b\cos x+a\sin x}\right)$

$$\Rightarrow\quad y=\tan^{-1}\left[\frac{\left(\frac{a\cos x-b\sin x}{b\cos x}\right)}{\left(\frac{b\cos x+a\sin x}{b\cos x}\right)}\right]$$

[dividing the numerator and denominator by $b\cos x$]

$$\Rightarrow \quad y = \tan^{-1}\left[\frac{\left(\frac{a}{b} - \tan x\right)}{\left(1 + \frac{a}{b}\tan x\right)}\right]$$

Put $\frac{a}{b} = \tan\alpha \Rightarrow \alpha = \tan^{-1}\left(\frac{a}{b}\right)$

Then, $y = \tan^{-1}\left[\frac{\tan\alpha - \tan x}{1 + \tan\alpha \cdot \tan x}\right]$

$$\Rightarrow \quad y = \tan^{-1}[\tan(\alpha - x)] \quad \left[\because \tan(x - y) = \frac{\tan x - \tan y}{1 + \tan x \cdot \tan y}\right]$$

$$\Rightarrow \quad y = \alpha - x \quad [\because \tan^{-1}(\tan\theta) = \theta]$$

$$\Rightarrow \quad y = \tan^{-1}\left(\frac{a}{b}\right) - x \quad \left[\because \alpha = \tan^{-1}\left(\frac{a}{b}\right)\right]$$

On differentiating both sides w.r.t. x, we get

$$\frac{dy}{dx} = 0 - 1 = -1$$

☑ Topic Practice 3

Very Short Answer Type Questions

(2 Marks)

1 Differentiate the following functions. (Each part carries 2 Marks)

(i) $\sin^{-1}(1-2x^2)$ (ii) $\cos^{-1}(2x-1)$

(iii) $\tan^{-1}(1-3x^4)$

2 If $y = \frac{\sin^{-1}x}{\sqrt{1-x^2}}$, then prove that $(1-x^2)\frac{dy}{dx} - xy = 1$. **[ISC 2006]**

3 If $y = \sin^{-1}\left(\frac{2x}{1+x^2}\right)$, then find $\frac{dy}{dx}$. **[NCERT]**

4 Differentiate $\cos^{-1}\left(\frac{1-x^2}{1+x^2}\right)$ w. r. t. x. **[NCERT]**

5 If $y = \tan^{-1}\left(\frac{2x}{1-x^2}\right)$, then prove that $\frac{dy}{dx} = \frac{2}{1+x^2}$. **[ISC 2003]**

6 Differentiate $\tan^{-1}\left[\frac{\sqrt{x}+\sqrt{a}}{1-\sqrt{ax}}\right]$ w.r.t. x.

7 If $y = \sin^{-1}(6x\sqrt{1-9x^2})$, $-\frac{1}{3\sqrt{2}} < x < \frac{1}{3\sqrt{2}}$, then find $\frac{dy}{dx}$.

8 If $y = \sin^{-1}(2x\sqrt{1-x^2})$, $-\frac{1}{\sqrt{2}} < x < \frac{1}{\sqrt{2}}$, then find $\frac{dy}{dx}$. **[NCERT]**

9 Find $\frac{dy}{dx}$, if $y = \tan^{-1}\left(\frac{3x-x^3}{1-3x^2}\right)$, $-\frac{1}{\sqrt{3}} < x < \frac{1}{\sqrt{3}}$. **[NCERT Exemplar]**

10 Find $\frac{dy}{dx}$, if $y = \tan^{-1}\left[\frac{\sqrt{1+x^2}-1}{x}\right]$. **[ISC 2008]**

Short Answer Type Questions

(4 Marks)

11 Using a suitable substitution, find the derivative of $\tan^{-1}\frac{4\sqrt{x}}{1-4x}$ with respect to x. **[ISC 2009]**

12 Find the derivative of $\tan^{-1}\left(\frac{\cos x}{1+\sin x}\right)$ w.r.t. x.

13 If $y = \cot^{-1}\left[\frac{\sqrt{1+\sin x}+\sqrt{1-\sin x}}{\sqrt{1+\sin x}-\sqrt{1-\sin x}}\right]$, $0 < x < \frac{\pi}{2}$, then find dy/dx. **[NCERT]**

14 Find the derivative of $\cos^{-1}\left(\frac{3\cos x - 4\sin x}{5}\right)$ w. r. t. x.

15 If $y = \sin^{-1}[x\sqrt{1-x} - \sqrt{x}\sqrt{1-x^2}]$ and $0 < x < 1$, then find dy/dx.

16 If $y = \tan^{-1}\left[\frac{\sqrt{1+x^2}+\sqrt{1-x^2}}{\sqrt{1+x^2}-\sqrt{1-x^2}}\right]$, $-1 < x < 1$, then find the derivative of y. **[NCERT Exemplar]**

17 Find the derivative of

$$\tan^{-1}\left(\frac{3a^2x - x^3}{a^3 - 3ax^2}\right), -\frac{1}{\sqrt{3}} < \frac{x}{a} < \frac{1}{\sqrt{3}}.$$

[NCERT Exemplar]

Hints & Solutions

1. (i) Let $y = \sin^{-1}(1-2x^2)$

On differentiating both sides w.r.t. x, we get

$$\frac{dy}{dx} = \frac{1}{\sqrt{1-(1-2x^2)^2}}\frac{d}{dx}(1-2x^2) \quad [1]$$

$$= \frac{-4x}{\sqrt{1-(1+4x^4-4x^2)}} = -\frac{4x}{\sqrt{4x^2-4x^4}} \quad [1]$$

(ii) Similar as part (i) $\left[\textbf{Ans.} \frac{-2}{\sqrt{4x-4x^2}}\right]$

(iii) Similar as part (i) $\left[\textbf{Ans.} \frac{-12x^3}{2+9x^8-6x^4}\right]$

2. Given, $y = \dfrac{\sin^{-1} x}{\sqrt{1-x^2}}$ ...(i)

On differentiating both sides w.r.t. x, we get

$$\frac{dy}{dx} = \frac{\sqrt{1-x^2}\frac{d}{dx}(\sin^{-1} x) - (\sin^{-1} x)\frac{d}{dx}\sqrt{1-x^2}}{(\sqrt{1-x^2})^2}$$

$$\left[\because \frac{d}{dx}\left\{\frac{f(x)}{g(x)}\right\} = \frac{g(x)\,f'(x) - f(x)\,g'(x)}{\{g(x)^2\}}\right] \text{[1]}$$

$$\frac{dy}{dx} = \frac{\sqrt{1-x^2} \times \frac{1}{\sqrt{1-x^2}} - \sin^{-1} x \times \frac{-2x}{2\sqrt{1-x^2}}}{(1-x^2)}$$

$$\left[\because \frac{d}{dx}\sin^{-1} x = \frac{1}{\sqrt{1-x^2}}\right]$$

$$\Rightarrow (1-x^2)\frac{dy}{dx} = 1 + \frac{x\sin^{-1} x}{\sqrt{1-x^2}} \Rightarrow (1-x^2)\frac{dy}{dx} = 1 + xy$$

[from Eq. (i)]

$$\Rightarrow (1-x^2)\frac{dy}{dx} - xy = 1$$ **Hence proved.** [1]

3. We have, $y = \sin^{-1}\left(\dfrac{2x}{1+x^2}\right)$

Put $x = \tan\theta \Rightarrow \theta = \tan^{-1} x$

$$\therefore \quad y = \sin^{-1}\left(\frac{2\tan\theta}{1+\tan^2\theta}\right) = \sin^{-1}(\sin 2\theta) = 2\theta$$

$$\left[\because \sin 2\theta = \frac{2\tan\theta}{1+\tan^2\theta}\right] \text{[1]}$$

$$\Rightarrow \quad y = 2\tan^{-1} x \qquad [\because \theta = \tan^{-1} x]$$

On differentiating both sides w.r.t. x, we get

$$\frac{dy}{dx} = 2 \times \frac{1}{1+x^2} = \frac{2}{1+x^2}$$ [1]

4. Let $y = \cos^{-1}\left(\dfrac{1-x^2}{1+x^2}\right)$

Put $x = \tan\theta \Rightarrow \theta = \tan^{-1} x$

$$\therefore \quad y = \cos^{-1}\left(\frac{1-\tan^2\theta}{1+\tan^2\theta}\right)$$ [1]

$$= \cos^{-1}(\cos 2\theta) = 2\theta \qquad \left[\because \cos 2\theta = \frac{1-\tan^2\theta}{1+\tan^2\theta}\right]$$

$$\Rightarrow \quad y = 2\tan^{-1} x \qquad [\because \theta = \tan^{-1} x]$$

On differentiating both sides w.r.t. x, we get

$$\frac{dy}{dx} = 2 \times \frac{1}{1+x^2} = \frac{2}{1+x^2}$$ [1]

5. Let $y = \tan^{-1}\left(\dfrac{2x}{1-x^2}\right)$

Put $x = \tan\theta$, then

$$y = \tan^{-1}\left(\frac{2\tan\theta}{1-\tan^2\theta}\right)$$

$$= \tan^{-1}(\tan 2\theta) \qquad \left[\because \tan 2\theta = \frac{2\tan\theta}{1-\tan^2\theta}\right] \text{[1]}$$

$$= 2\theta \qquad [\because \tan^{-1}(\tan\theta) = \theta]$$

$$\Rightarrow \quad y = 2\tan^{-1} x \qquad [\because x = \tan\theta \Rightarrow \theta = \tan^{-1} x]$$

On differentiating both sides w.r.t. x, we get

$$\frac{dy}{dx} = 2\frac{d}{dx}(\tan^{-1} x) = \frac{2}{1+x^2}$$ **Hence proved.** [1]

6. Let $y = \tan^{-1}\left[\dfrac{\sqrt{x}+\sqrt{a}}{1-\sqrt{ax}}\right] = \tan^{-1}\left[\dfrac{\sqrt{x}+\sqrt{a}}{1-\sqrt{a}\sqrt{x}}\right]$

$$\Rightarrow y = \tan^{-1}\sqrt{x} + \tan^{-1}\sqrt{a}$$ [1]

$$\left[\because \tan^{-1} x + \tan^{-1} y = \tan^{-1}\left(\frac{x+y}{1-xy}\right)\right]$$

On differentiating both sides w.r.t. x, we get

$$\frac{dy}{dx} = \frac{1}{1+(\sqrt{x})^2}\frac{d}{dx}(\sqrt{x}) + 0 \qquad [\because \tan^{-1}\sqrt{a} = \text{constant}]$$

$$= \frac{1}{(1+x)} \times \frac{1}{2}x^{-1/2} = \frac{1}{2(1+x)\sqrt{x}}$$ [1]

7. Given, $y = \sin^{-1}(6x\sqrt{1-9x^2}) \Rightarrow y = \sin^{-1}(2\cdot 3x\sqrt{1-(3x)^2})$

Put $3x = \sin\theta$. Then, $y = \sin^{-1}(2\sin\theta \cdot \cos\theta)$

$$\Rightarrow \quad y = \sin^{-1}(\sin 2\theta)$$

$$\Rightarrow \quad y = 2\theta \Rightarrow y = 2\sin^{-1}(3x)$$ [1]

$$\therefore \quad \frac{dy}{dx} = \frac{2}{\sqrt{1-9x^2}}(3) = \frac{6}{\sqrt{1-9x^2}}$$ [1]

8. Solve as Question 7. $\left[\textbf{Ans. } \dfrac{2}{\sqrt{1-x^2}}\right]$

9. Hint Put $x = \tan\theta$. $\left[\textbf{Ans. } \dfrac{3}{1+x^2}\right]$

10. Hint Put $x = \tan\theta$. $\left[\textbf{Ans. } \dfrac{1}{2(1+x^2)}\right]$

11. Given, $y = \tan^{-1}\dfrac{4\sqrt{x}}{1-4x}$

Put $x = \dfrac{1}{4}\tan^2\theta$, we get

$$y = \tan^{-1}\left(\frac{4 \times \frac{\tan\theta}{2}}{1 - 4 \times \frac{1}{4}\tan^2\theta}\right)$$ [1]

$$= \tan^{-1}\left(\frac{2\tan\theta}{1-\tan^2\theta}\right)$$

$$= \tan^{-1}(\tan 2\theta) \qquad \left[\because \tan 2\theta = \frac{2\tan\theta}{1-\tan^2\theta}\right]$$

$$= 2\theta = 2 \times \tan^{-1} 2\sqrt{x}$$ [1]

$$\left[\because x = \frac{1}{4}\tan^2\theta \Rightarrow 2\sqrt{x} = \tan\theta \Rightarrow \theta = \tan^{-1} 2\sqrt{x}\right]$$

On differentiating both sides w.r.t. x, we get

$$\frac{dy}{dx}=2\frac{d}{dx}(\tan^{-1}2\sqrt{x}) \quad [1]$$

$$=2\frac{d(\tan^{-1}2\sqrt{x})}{d(2\sqrt{x})}\times\frac{d(2\sqrt{x})}{dx}$$

$$=2\times\frac{1}{1+4x}\times\frac{2}{2\sqrt{x}}\left[\because \frac{d}{dx}(\tan^{-1}x)=\frac{1}{1+x^2}\right]$$

$$=\frac{2}{\sqrt{x}(1+4x)} \quad [1]$$

12. Let $y=\tan^{-1}\left(\frac{\cos x}{1+\sin x}\right)=\tan^{-1}\left[\frac{\sin\left(\frac{\pi}{2}-x\right)}{1+\cos\left(\frac{\pi}{2}-x\right)}\right]$

$$\left[\because \cos x=\sin\left(\frac{\pi}{2}-x\right)\text{ and }\sin x=\cos\left(\frac{\pi}{2}-x\right)\right] \quad [1]$$

$$=\tan^{-1}\left[\frac{2\sin\left(\frac{\pi}{4}-\frac{x}{2}\right)\cdot\cos\left(\frac{\pi}{4}-\frac{x}{2}\right)}{2\cos^2\left(\frac{\pi}{4}-\frac{x}{2}\right)}\right] \quad [1]$$

$$\left[\because \sin\theta=2\sin\frac{\theta}{2}\cos\frac{\theta}{2}\text{ and }1+\cos\theta=2\cos^2\frac{\theta}{2}\right]$$

$$\Rightarrow\quad y=\tan^{-1}\left[\tan\left(\frac{\pi}{4}-\frac{x}{2}\right)\right]$$

$$\Rightarrow\quad y=\frac{\pi}{4}-\frac{x}{2} \quad [\because \tan^{-1}(\tan\theta)=\theta] \quad [1]$$

On differentiating both sides w.r.t. x, we get

$$\frac{dy}{dx}=-\frac{1}{2} \quad [1]$$

13. Let $y=\cot^{-1}\left[\frac{\sqrt{1+\sin x}+\sqrt{1-\sin x}}{\sqrt{1+\sin x}-\sqrt{1-\sin x}}\right]$

$$=\cot^{-1}\left[\frac{\left(\sin\frac{x}{2}+\cos\frac{x}{2}\right)+\left(\cos\frac{x}{2}-\sin\frac{x}{2}\right)}{\left(\sin\frac{x}{2}+\cos\frac{x}{2}\right)-\left(\cos\frac{x}{2}-\sin\frac{x}{2}\right)}\right] \quad [2]$$

$$\left[\begin{array}{l}\because 1+\sin x=\sin^2\frac{x}{2}+\cos^2\frac{x}{2}+2\sin\frac{x}{2}.\cos\frac{x}{2}\\ =\left(\sin\frac{x}{2}+\cos\frac{x}{2}\right)^2\text{ and }1-\sin x=\sin^2\frac{x}{2}+\cos^2\frac{x}{2}\\ -2\sin\frac{x}{2}\cos\frac{x}{2}=\left(\cos\frac{x}{2}-\sin\frac{x}{2}\right)^2\text{ as }0<\frac{x}{2}<\frac{\pi}{4}.\end{array}\right]$$

$$=\cot^{-1}\left[\frac{2\cos(x/2)}{2\sin(x/2)}\right]=\cot^{-1}\left[\cot\left(\frac{x}{2}\right)\right]=\frac{x}{2} \quad [1]$$

$$\Rightarrow\frac{dy}{dx}=\frac{1}{2} \quad [1]$$

14. Let $y=\cos^{-1}\left(\frac{3\cos x-4\sin x}{5}\right)$

$$\Rightarrow\quad y=\cos^{-1}\left(\frac{3}{5}\cos x-\frac{4}{5}\sin x\right) \quad ...(i)$$

Let $\frac{3}{5}=r\cos\alpha$ ...(ii)

and $\frac{4}{5}=r\sin\alpha$ ...(iii)

On squaring and adding Eqs. (ii) and (iii), we get

$$r^2\cos^2\alpha+r^2\sin^2\alpha=\frac{9}{25}+\frac{16}{25}=\frac{25}{25}=1 \quad [1]$$

$$\Rightarrow\quad r^2(\cos^2\alpha+\sin^2\alpha)=1\Rightarrow r^2=1\Rightarrow r=1$$

$$\therefore\quad \frac{3}{5}=\cos\alpha\text{ and }\frac{4}{5}=\sin\alpha$$

$$\Rightarrow\quad \frac{\sin\alpha}{\cos\alpha}=\frac{4/5}{3/5}=\frac{4}{3}$$

$$\Rightarrow\quad \tan\alpha=\frac{4}{3}\Rightarrow\alpha=\tan^{-1}\left(\frac{4}{3}\right) \quad [1]$$

Now, from Eq. (i), we get

$$y=\cos^{-1}(\cos\alpha\cos x-\sin\alpha\sin x)$$

$$\Rightarrow\quad y=\cos^{-1}[\cos(\alpha+x)]$$

$$[\because \cos(A+B)=\cos A\cos B-\sin A\sin B]$$

$$\Rightarrow\quad y=\alpha+x\Rightarrow y=\tan^{-1}\frac{4}{3}+x \quad [1]$$

On differentiating both sides w.r.t. x, we get

$$\frac{dy}{dx}=0+1=1 \quad [1]$$

15. Let $y=\sin^{-1}[x\sqrt{1-x}-\sqrt{x}\sqrt{1-x^2}]$

$$=\sin^{-1}\{x\sqrt{1-(\sqrt{x})^2}-\sqrt{x}\sqrt{1-x^2}\} \quad [1]$$

$$\Rightarrow\quad y=\sin^{-1}x-\sin^{-1}\sqrt{x} \quad ...(i)\ [1]$$

$$[\because \sin^{-1}x+\sin^{-1}y=\sin^{-1}[x\sqrt{1-y^2}+y\sqrt{1-x^2}]]$$

On differentiating both sides of Eq. (i) w.r.t. x, we get

$$\frac{dy}{dx}=\frac{1}{\sqrt{1-x^2}}-\frac{1}{\sqrt{1-(\sqrt{x})^2}}\frac{d}{dx}(\sqrt{x}) \quad [1]$$

[by chain rule of derivative]

$$=\frac{1}{\sqrt{1-x^2}}-\frac{1}{\sqrt{1-x}}\cdot\frac{1}{2}x^{-1/2}$$

$$=\frac{1}{\sqrt{1-x^2}}-\frac{1}{2\sqrt{x}\sqrt{1-x}}$$

$$=\frac{1}{\sqrt{1-x^2}}-\frac{1}{2\sqrt{x-x^2}} \quad [1]$$

16. **Hint** Put $x^2=\cos 2\theta$ and then use the formulae $1-\cos 2\theta=2\sin^2\theta$ and $1+\cos 2\theta=2\cos^2\theta$

$$\left[\textbf{Ans. }\frac{-x}{\sqrt{1-x^4}}\right]$$

17. **Hint** Put $\frac{x}{a}=\tan\theta$. $\left[\textbf{Ans. }\frac{3a}{a^2+x^2}\right]$

TOPIC 04 Differentiation of Parametric Functions

If the variables x and y are explicity expressed in terms of a third variable say $x = \phi(t)$ and $y = \psi(t)$, then x and y are called **parametric functions** or **parametric equations** and t is called the **parameter.**

To find the derivatives of parametric functions, we use following steps

I. First, write the given parametric functions, say $x = f(t)$ and $y = g(t)$, where t is a parameter.

II. Differentiate both functions separately with respect to parameter t, i.e. find $\frac{dx}{dt}$ and $\frac{dy}{dt}$.

III. Then, $\frac{dy}{dx} = \frac{dy/dt}{dx/dt} = \frac{g'(t)}{f'(t)}$, where $f'(t) \neq 0$.

Note $\frac{dy}{dx}$ is expressed in terms of parameter only.

Example 1 If $x = a\sin^3 t$ and $y = a\cos^3 t$, then find dy/dx. **[ISC 2004]**

Sol. Given, $x = a\sin^3 t$ and $y = a\cos^3 t$

On differentiating both sides of x w.r.t. t, we get

$$\frac{dx}{dt} = a\frac{d}{dt}(\sin^3 t)$$

$$= a\frac{d(\sin^3 t)}{d(\sin t)} \times \frac{d(\sin t)}{dt}$$

$$= a \times 3\sin^2 t \times \cos t$$

$$= 3a\sin^2 t\cos t \quad \text{...(i)}$$

Now, differentiating both sides of y w.r.t. t, we get

$$\frac{dy}{dt} = a\frac{d(\cos^3 t)}{dt}$$

$$= a\frac{d(\cos^3 t)}{d(\cos t)} \times \frac{d(\cos t)}{dt}$$

$$= a \times 3\cos^2 t \times (-\sin t)$$

$$= -3a\sin t\cos^2 t \quad \text{...(ii)}$$

Now, $\frac{dy}{dx} = \frac{dy}{dt} \times \frac{dt}{dx}$

$$= \frac{-3a\sin t\cos^2 t}{3a\sin^2 t\cos t} \quad \text{[from Eqs. (i) and (ii)]}$$

$$= \frac{-\cos t}{\sin t} = -\cot t$$

Example 2 If $y = e^{\sin^{-1} x}$ and $z = e^{-\cos^{-1} x}$, then prove that $\frac{dy}{dz} = e^{\pi/2}$. **[ISC 2019]**

Sol. We have, $y = e^{\sin^{-1} x}$ and $z = e^{-\cos^{-1} x}$

On differentiating both sides w.r.t. x, we get

$$\frac{dy}{dx} = e^{\sin^{-1} x}\frac{d}{dx}(\sin^{-1} x)$$

and $$\frac{dz}{dx} = e^{-\cos^{-1} x}\frac{d}{dx}(-\cos^{-1} x)$$

[using chain rule of derivative]

$\therefore$ $$\frac{dy}{dx} = e^{\sin^{-1} x} \times \frac{1}{\sqrt{1-x^2}}$$

and $$\frac{dz}{dx} = e^{-\cos^{-1} x} \times \left(-\frac{-1}{\sqrt{1-x^2}}\right)$$

$$= e^{-\cos^{-1} x} \times \frac{1}{\sqrt{1-x^2}}$$

$\therefore$ $$\frac{dy}{dz} = \frac{\frac{dy}{dx}}{\frac{dz}{dx}} = \frac{e^{\sin^{-1} x} \times \frac{1}{\sqrt{1-x^2}}}{e^{-\cos^{-1} x} \times \frac{1}{\sqrt{1-x^2}}}$$

$\Rightarrow$ $$\frac{dy}{dz} = e^{\sin^{-1} x + \cos^{-1} x} = e^{\frac{\pi}{2}}$$

$$\left[\because \sin^{-1} x + \cos^{-1} x = \frac{\pi}{2}\right]$$

Example 3 If $x = \cos\theta - \cos 2\theta$ and $y = \sin\theta - \sin 2\theta$, then find $\frac{dy}{dx}$. **[NCERT]**

Sol. We have, $x = \cos\theta - \cos 2\theta$

On differentiating both sides w.r.t. θ, we get

$$\frac{dx}{d\theta} = -\sin\theta + \sin 2\theta \cdot 2$$

$\Rightarrow$ $$\frac{dx}{d\theta} = 2\sin 2\theta - \sin\theta$$

Also, we have $y = \sin\theta - \sin 2\theta$

On differentiating both sides w.r.t. θ, we get

$$\frac{dy}{d\theta} = \cos\theta - 2\cos 2\theta$$

Now, $$\frac{dy}{dx} = \frac{dy/d\theta}{dx/d\theta} = \frac{\cos\theta - 2\cos 2\theta}{2\sin 2\theta - \sin\theta}$$

Example 4 If $x = ae^t (\sin t + \cos t)$ and $y = ae^t(\sin t - \cos t)$, then prove that $\frac{dy}{dx} = \frac{x+y}{x-y}$.

Sol. Given, $x = ae^t (\sin t + \cos t)$

On differentiating x both sides w.r.t. t, we get

$$\frac{dx}{dt} = ae^t \frac{d}{dt}(\sin t + \cos t) + (\sin t + \cos t)\frac{d}{dt}(ae^t)$$

$$\Rightarrow \frac{dx}{dt} = ae^t (\cos t - \sin t) + ae^t(\sin t + \cos t)$$

$$= -ae^t (\sin t - \cos t) + ae^t(\sin t + \cos t)$$

$$\Rightarrow \frac{dx}{dt} = -y + x$$

Also, we have $y = ae^t(\sin t - \cos t)$

On differentiating y both sides w.r.t. t, we get

$$\frac{dy}{dt} = ae^t \frac{d}{dt}(\sin t - \cos t) + (\sin t - \cos t)\frac{d}{dt}(ae^t)$$

$$\Rightarrow \frac{dy}{dt} = ae^t(\cos t + \sin t) + ae^t(\sin t - \cos t)$$

$$\Rightarrow \frac{dy}{dt} = ae^t(\sin t + \cos t) + ae^t(\sin t - \cos t) = x + y$$

Now, $\frac{dy}{dx} = \frac{dy/dt}{dx/dt} = \frac{x+y}{-y+x} = \frac{x+y}{x-y}$ **Hence proved.**

Topic Practice 4

Very Short Answer Type Questions

(2 Marks)

1 Find dy/dx, when $x = \cos^2\theta$ and $y = \sin^2\theta$.

2 If $x = a \sec^3\theta$ and $y = a \tan^3\theta$, then find $\frac{dy}{dx}$ at $\theta = \frac{\pi}{3}$. **[NCERT Exemplar]**

3 Find dy/dx, if $x = a(\theta - \sin\theta)$ and $y = a(1 + \cos\theta)$. **[NCERT]**

4 If $x = t + \frac{1}{t}$ and $y = t - \frac{1}{t}$, then find $\frac{dy}{dx}$.

Short Answer Type Questions

(4 Marks)

5 If $x = 2\cos\theta - \cos 2\theta$ and $y = 2\sin\theta - \sin 2\theta$, then prove that $\frac{dy}{dx} = \tan\left(\frac{3\theta}{2}\right)$.

6 Find the value of $\frac{dy}{dx}$ at $\theta = \frac{\pi}{4}$, if $x = ae^\theta(\sin\theta - \cos\theta)$ and $y = ae^\theta(\sin\theta + \cos\theta)$.

7 If $x = \cos t(3 - 2\cos^2 t)$ and $y = \sin t(3 - 2\sin^2 t)$, then find the value of $\frac{dy}{dx}$ at $x = \frac{\pi}{4}$.

8 If $x = e^\theta\left(\theta + \frac{1}{\theta}\right)$, $y = e^{-\theta}\left(\theta - \frac{1}{\theta}\right)$, then find $\frac{dy}{dx}$.

9 If $x = \sqrt{a^{\sin^{-1} t}}$, $y = \sqrt{a^{\cos^{-1} t}}$, then show that $\frac{dy}{dx} = -\frac{y}{x}$. **[NCERT]**

10 If $x = e^{\cos 2t}$ and $y = e^{\sin 2t}$, then prove that $\frac{dy}{dx} = \frac{-y \log x}{x \log y}$.

11 If $x = \frac{\sin^3 t}{\sqrt{\cos 2t}}$ and $y = \frac{\cos^3 t}{\sqrt{\cos 2t}}$, then find $\frac{dy}{dx}$. **[NCERT]**

Hints & Solutions

1. We have, $x = \cos^2\theta$ and $y = \sin^2\theta$

On differentiating x and y w.r.t. θ, we get

$$\frac{dx}{d\theta} = 2\cos\theta \frac{d}{d\theta}(\cos\theta) = 2\cos\theta(-\sin\theta)$$

$$= -2\sin\theta\cos\theta = -\sin 2\theta \quad [1]$$

and $\frac{dy}{d\theta} = 2\sin\theta \frac{d}{d\theta}(\sin\theta) = 2\sin\theta\cos\theta = \sin 2\theta$ [1/2]

Now, $\frac{dy}{dx} = \left(\frac{dy}{d\theta}\right) \times \left(\frac{d\theta}{dx}\right) = \frac{\sin 2\theta}{-\sin 2\theta} = -1$ [1/2]

2. Similar as Question 1. $\left[\textbf{Ans. } \frac{\sqrt{3}}{2}\right]$

3. We have, $x = a(\theta - \sin\theta)$ and $y = a(1 + \cos\theta)$

On differentiating x and y w.r.t. θ, we get

$\frac{dx}{d\theta} = a(1 - \cos\theta)$ [1/2]

and $\frac{dy}{d\theta} = a(0 - \sin\theta) = -a\sin\theta$ [1/2]

Now, $\frac{dy}{dx} = \left(\frac{dy}{d\theta}\right) \times \left(\frac{d\theta}{dx}\right) = \frac{-a\sin\theta}{a(1-\cos\theta)}$

$$= \frac{\left(-2\sin\frac{\theta}{2}\cos\frac{\theta}{2}\right)}{2\sin^2\frac{\theta}{2}} \quad [1/2]$$

$\left[\because \sin\theta = 2\sin\frac{\theta}{2}\cos\frac{\theta}{2} \text{ and } 1 - \cos\theta = 2\sin^2\frac{\theta}{2}\right]$

$= -\cot\left(\frac{\theta}{2}\right)$ [1/2]

4. **Hint** $\frac{dx}{dt}=1-\frac{1}{t^2}$ and $\frac{dy}{dt}=1+\frac{1}{t^2}\left[\textbf{Ans. } \frac{t^2+1}{t^2-1}\right]$

5. Similar as Example 3.

6. Similar as Example 4.

Hint $\frac{dx}{d\theta}=2ae^{\theta}\sin\theta$ and $\frac{dy}{d\theta}=2ae^{\theta}\cos\theta$

$\therefore \quad \frac{dy}{dx}=\cot\theta$ [**Ans.** 1]

7. Similar as Example 3. $\left[\textbf{Ans. } \frac{dy}{dx}=0\right]$

8. Similar as Example 4. $\left[\textbf{Ans. } e^{-2\theta}\left(\frac{-\theta^3+\theta^2+\theta+1}{\theta^3+\theta^2+\theta-1}\right)\right]$

9. Given, $x=\sqrt{a^{\sin^{-1}t}}$

Taking log on both sides, we get

$$\log x=\log(a^{\sin^{-1}t})^{1/2} \Rightarrow \log x=\frac{1}{2}\log a^{\sin^{-1}t}$$

$$\Rightarrow \log x=\frac{1}{2}\sin^{-1}t\log a \Rightarrow \log x=\frac{1}{2}\log a\sin^{-1}t \quad [1/2]$$

On differentiating both sides w.r.t. t, we get

$$\frac{1}{x}\cdot\frac{dx}{dt}=\frac{1}{2}\log a\frac{d}{dt}(\sin^{-1}t)=\frac{1}{2}\log a\frac{1}{\sqrt{1-t^2}}$$

$$\Rightarrow \frac{dx}{dt}=\frac{x\log a}{2}\cdot\frac{1}{\sqrt{1-t^2}} \quad [1]$$

Also, we have $y=\sqrt{a^{\cos^{-1}t}}$

Taking log on both sides, we get

$$\log y=\log(a^{\cos^{-1}t})^{1/2}$$

$$\Rightarrow \log y=\frac{1}{2}\log a^{\cos^{-1}t}$$

$$\Rightarrow \log y=\frac{1}{2}\cos^{-1}t\log a \quad [1/2]$$

On differentiating both sides w.r.t. t, we get

$$\frac{1}{y}\cdot\frac{dy}{dt}=\frac{1}{2}\log a\cdot\left[\frac{-1}{\sqrt{1-t^2}}\right]$$

$$\Rightarrow \frac{dy}{dt}=\frac{y\log a}{2}\cdot\frac{-1}{\sqrt{1-t^2}} \quad [1]$$

Now, $\frac{dy}{dx}=\left(\frac{dy}{dt}\right)\cdot\left(\frac{dt}{dx}\right)$

$$\Rightarrow \frac{dy}{dx}=\frac{-y\log a}{2}\cdot\frac{1}{\sqrt{1-t^2}}\cdot\frac{2\cdot\sqrt{1-t^2}}{x\log a}$$

$$\Rightarrow \frac{dy}{dx}=\frac{-y}{x} \quad [1]$$

10. **Hint** $\frac{dx}{dt}=e^{\cos 2t}(-\sin 2t)\cdot 2$ and $\frac{dy}{dt}=e^{\sin 2t}(\cos 2t)\cdot 2$

11. Given, $x=\frac{\sin^3 t}{\sqrt{\cos 2t}}$, $y=\frac{\cos^3 t}{\sqrt{\cos 2t}}$.

On differentiating x and y w.r.t. t, we get

$$\frac{dx}{dt}=\frac{d}{dt}\left(\frac{\sin^3 t}{\sqrt{\cos 2t}}\right)$$

$$=\frac{\sqrt{\cos 2t}(3\sin^2 t\cos t)-\sin^3 t\left(\frac{-2\sin 2t}{2\sqrt{\cos 2t}}\right)}{(\sqrt{\cos 2t})^2}$$

[using quotient rule of derivative]

$$=\frac{3(\cos 2t)\sin^2 t\cos t+\sin 2t\sin^3 t}{\cos 2t\sqrt{\cos 2t}}$$

$$=\frac{3(1-2\sin^2 t)\sin^2 t\cos t+(2\sin t\cos t)\sin^3 t}{\cos 2t\sqrt{\cos 2t}}$$

$[\because \cos 2t=1-2\sin^2 t \text{ and } \sin 2t=2\sin t\cos t]$

$$=\frac{3\sin^2 t\cos t-4\sin^4 t\cos t}{\cos 2t\sqrt{\cos 2t}} \quad [1½]$$

and $\frac{dy}{dt}=\frac{d}{dt}\left(\frac{\cos^3 t}{\sqrt{\cos 2t}}\right)$

$$=\frac{\sqrt{\cos 2t}(-3\cos^2 t\sin t)-\cos^3 t\left(\frac{-2\sin 2t}{2\sqrt{\cos 2t}}\right)}{(\sqrt{\cos 2t})^2}$$

[using quotient rule of derivative]

$$=\frac{-3(\cos 2t)\cos^2 t\sin t+\sin 2t\cos^3 t}{\cos 2t\sqrt{\cos 2t}}$$

$$=\frac{-3(2\cos^2 t-1)\cos^2 t\sin t+\cos^3 t(2\sin t\cos t)}{\cos 2t\sqrt{\cos 2t}}$$

$$=\frac{3\cos^2 t\sin t-4\cos^4 t\sin t}{\cos 2t\sqrt{\cos 2t}} \quad [1½]$$

Now, $\frac{dy}{dx}=\frac{dy}{dt}\times\frac{dt}{dx}=\frac{3\cos^2 t\sin t-4\cos^4 t\sin t}{3\sin^2 t\cos t-4\sin^4 t\cos t}$

$$=\frac{\cos^2 t\sin t(3-4\cos^2 t)}{\sin^2 t\cos t(3-4\sin^2 t)}=\frac{\cos t(3-4\cos^2 t)}{\sin t(3-4\sin^2 t)}$$

$$=\frac{3\cos t-4\cos^3 t}{3\sin t-4\sin^3 t}$$

$$=\frac{-\cos 3t}{\sin 3t}=-\cot 3t$$

$[\because \cos 3t=4\cos^3 t-3\cos t \text{ and } \sin 3t=3\sin t-4\sin^3 t]$

[1]

TOPIC 05 Differentiation of a Function w.r.t. Another Function

Suppose it is required to differentiate a function $f(x)$ with respect to another function $g(x)$. Let $y = f(x)$ and $z = g(x)$.

Here, both functions are different but both are in same variable x. Then, to find the derivative of $f(x)$ with respect to $g(x)$ or derivative of $g(x)$ with respect to $f(x)$, i.e. to find $\frac{dy}{dz}$ or $\frac{dz}{dy}$. We first differentiate both functions $f(x)$ and $g(x)$ with respect to x separately and then put these values in the following formulae

$$\frac{dy}{dz} = \frac{dy/dx}{dz/dx} \text{ or } \frac{dz}{dy} = \frac{dz/dx}{dy/dx}$$

Example 1 Find the derivative of $\sin x^2$ with respect to x^3. **[ISC 2009]**

Sol. Let $u = \sin x^2$ and $v = x^3$

To find the value of $\frac{du}{dv}$.

Consider, $u = \sin x^2$

On differentiating both sides w.r.t. x, we get

$$\frac{du}{dx} = \frac{d}{dx}(\sin x^2) = \frac{d(\sin x^2)}{d(x^2)} \times \frac{d(x^2)}{dx}$$

$$= 2x \cos x^2 \quad \text{...(i)}$$

Now, consider $v = x^3$

On differentiating both sides w.r.t. x, we get

$$\frac{dv}{dx} = \frac{d(x^3)}{dx} = 3x^2 \quad \text{...(ii)}$$

$$\therefore \quad \frac{du}{dv} = \frac{du}{dx} \times \frac{dx}{dv} = \frac{2x \cos x^2}{3x^2} = \frac{2 \cos x^2}{3x}$$

[from Eqs. (i) and (ii)]

Example 2 Differentiate x^6 w.r.t. $\frac{1}{\sqrt{x}}$.

Sol. Let $f = x^6$ and $g = \frac{1}{\sqrt{x}} = x^{-1/2}$

Then, $\frac{df}{dx} = 6x^5$ and $\frac{dg}{dx} = -\frac{1}{2} x^{-\frac{1}{2}-1} = -\frac{1}{2} x^{-\frac{3}{2}}$

$$\therefore \quad \frac{df}{dg} = \frac{6x^5}{-\frac{1}{2} x^{-\frac{3}{2}}} = -12\, x^{5+\frac{3}{2}} = -12\, x^{\frac{13}{2}}$$

Example 3 Differentiate $\sin^2 x$ w.r.t. $e^{\cos x}$. **[NCERT]**

Sol. Let $y = \sin^2 x$ and $z = e^{\cos x}$.

On differentiating y and z w.r.t. x, we get

$$\frac{dy}{dx} = 2 \sin x \cos x$$

and $$\frac{dz}{dx} = e^{\cos x}(-\sin x) = -(\sin x)\, e^{\cos x}$$

Now, $$\frac{dy}{dz} = \frac{dy/dx}{dz/dx}$$

$$= \frac{2 \sin x \cos x}{-(\sin x)\, e^{\cos x}} = \frac{-2 \cos x}{e^{\cos x}}$$

Example 4 Differentiate $\log(1 + x^2)$ w.r.t. $\tan^{-1} x$.

Sol. Let $y = \log(1 + x^2)$.

On differentiating both sides w.r.t. x, we get

$$\frac{dy}{dx} = \frac{1}{1 + x^2} \frac{d}{dx}(1 + x^2)$$

$$\left[\text{by chain rule of derivative and } \frac{d}{dx}(\log x) = \frac{1}{x}\right]$$

$$\Rightarrow \quad \frac{dy}{dx} = \frac{2x}{(1 + x^2)}$$

Again, let $z = \tan^{-1} x$

On differentiating both sides w.r.t. x, we get

$$\frac{dz}{dx} = \frac{1}{1 + x^2} \quad \left[\because \frac{d}{dx}(\tan^{-1} x) = \frac{1}{1 + x^2}\right]$$

Now, $$\frac{dy}{dz} = \frac{(dy/dx)}{(dz/dx)} = \frac{\left(\frac{2x}{1 + x^2}\right)}{\left(\frac{1}{1 + x^2}\right)} = 2x$$

Example 5 Find derivative of $\sin^{-1} x$ w.r.t. $\tan^{-1} x$.

Sol. Let $f(x) = \sin^{-1} x$ and $g(x) = \tan^{-1} x$

On differentiating $f(x)$ and $g(x)$ w.r.t. x, we get

$$\frac{df}{dx} = \frac{1}{\sqrt{1 - x^2}} \text{ and } \frac{dg}{dx} = \frac{1}{1 + x^2}$$

Now, $$\frac{df}{dg} = \frac{df}{dx} \times \frac{dx}{dg} = \frac{1}{\sqrt{1 - x^2}} \times (1 + x^2)$$

$$= \frac{1 + x^2}{\sqrt{1 - x^2}}$$

Topic Practice 5

Very Short Answer Type Questions

2 Marks

1 Differentiate $\sin x^2$ w.r.t. x^2.

2 Differentiate $\tan e^x$ w.r.t. e^x.

3 Differentiate $\log x \cdot \log \sin x$ w.r.t. $\sin x$.

Short Answer Type Questions

4 Marks

4 Differentiate $\tan^{-1}\left(\frac{\sqrt{1-x^2}}{x}\right)$ w.r.t. $\cos^{-1}(2x\sqrt{1-x^2})$, when $x \neq 0$.

5 Find the derivative of $\tan^{-1}\left[\frac{\sqrt{1+x^2}-1}{x}\right]$ w.r.t. $\tan^{-1}\frac{2x}{1-x^2}$.

6 Find the derivative of $\sec^{-1}\left(\frac{1}{2x^2-1}\right)$ w.r.t. $\sqrt{1-x^2}$ at $x=\frac{1}{2}$.

7 Differentiate $\tan^{-1}\left(\frac{\sqrt{1+x^2}-1}{x}\right)$ w.r.t. $\tan^{-1}x$, when $x \neq 0$. **[NCERT Exemplar]**

8 Differentiate $\tan^{-1}\left(\frac{\sqrt{1+x^2}-1}{x}\right)$ w.r.t. $\sin^{-1}\left(\frac{2x}{1+x^2}\right)$, when $x \neq 0$.

Hints & Solutions

1. Similar as Example 1. [**Ans.** $\cos x^2$]

2. Similar as Example 1. [**Ans.** $\sec^2 e^x$]

3. **Hint** $u = \log x \log \sin x$

$$\Rightarrow \frac{du}{dx} = \frac{\log x}{\sin x} \times \cos x + \frac{\log \sin x}{x}$$

$$\Rightarrow \frac{du}{dx} = \left[\cot x \log x + \frac{\log \sin x}{x}\right]$$

$$\left[\textbf{Ans. } \frac{\left[\cot x \log x + \frac{\log \sin x}{x}\right]}{\cos x}\right]$$

4. Let $u = \tan^{-1}\left[\frac{\sqrt{1-x^2}}{x}\right]$.

Put $x = \cos\theta \Rightarrow \theta = \cos^{-1}x$

$$\therefore u = \tan^{-1}\left[\frac{\sqrt{1-\cos^2\theta}}{\cos\theta}\right] = \tan^{-1}\left[\frac{\sqrt{\sin^2\theta}}{\cos\theta}\right] = \tan^{-1}\left[\frac{\sin\theta}{\cos\theta}\right] = \tan^{-1}[\tan\theta] = \theta$$

$\Rightarrow u = \cos^{-1}x$ **[1]**

On differentiating both sides w.r.t. x, we get

$$\frac{du}{dx} = -\frac{1}{\sqrt{1-x^2}}$$ **[1/2]**

Again, let $v = \cos^{-1}(2x\sqrt{1-x^2})$

Put $x = \cos\theta \Rightarrow \theta = \cos^{-1}x$

$$\therefore v = \cos^{-1}[2\cos\theta\sqrt{1-\cos^2\theta}]$$

$$= \cos^{-1}[2\cos\theta\sin\theta]$$

$[\because \cos^2\theta + \sin^2\theta = 1 \Rightarrow \sin\theta = \sqrt{1-\cos^2\theta}]$

$$= \cos^{-1}[\sin 2\theta]$$

$$= \cos^{-1}\left[\cos\left(\frac{\pi}{2}-2\theta\right)\right] \quad \left[\because \sin\theta = \cos\left(\frac{\pi}{2}-\theta\right)\right]$$

$$= \frac{\pi}{2} - 2\theta = \frac{\pi}{2} - 2\cos^{-1}x$$ **[1]**

On differentiating both sides, w.r.t. x, we get

$$\frac{dv}{dx} = \frac{2}{\sqrt{1-x^2}}$$ **[1/2]**

Now, $$\frac{du}{dv} = \left(\frac{du}{dx}\right) \times \left(\frac{dx}{dv}\right) = -\frac{1}{\sqrt{1-x^2}} \times \frac{\sqrt{1-x^2}}{2} = -\frac{1}{2}$$ **[1]**

5. Let $u = \tan^{-1}\left[\frac{\sqrt{1+x^2}-1}{x}\right]$.

Put $x = \tan\theta \Rightarrow \theta = \tan^{-1}x$

$$\therefore u = \tan^{-1}\left[\frac{\sqrt{1+\tan^2\theta}-1}{\tan\theta}\right] = \tan^{-1}\left[\frac{\sec\theta - 1}{\tan\theta}\right]$$

$[\because \sec^2\theta = 1 + \tan^2\theta]$ **[1/2]**

$$= \tan^{-1}\left[\frac{\frac{1}{\cos\theta} - 1}{\frac{\sin\theta}{\cos\theta}}\right]$$

$$= \tan^{-1}\left[\frac{1-\cos\theta}{\cos\theta}\times\frac{\cos\theta}{\sin\theta}\right]$$

$$= \tan^{-1}\left[\frac{1-\cos\theta}{\sin\theta}\right] = \tan^{-1}\left[\frac{2\sin^2\frac{\theta}{2}}{2\sin\frac{\theta}{2}\cos\frac{\theta}{2}}\right]$$

$$\left[\because \sin\theta = 2\sin\frac{\theta}{2}\cos\frac{\theta}{2} \text{ and } 1-\cos\theta = 2\sin^2\frac{\theta}{2}\right]$$ [1]

$$= \tan^{-1}\left[\tan\frac{\theta}{2}\right] = \frac{\theta}{2} \qquad \left[\because \tan^{-1}\left(\tan\frac{\theta}{2}\right) = \frac{\theta}{2}\right]$$

$$\Rightarrow u = \frac{1}{2}\tan^{-1}x \qquad [\because \theta = \tan^{-1}x]$$

On differentiating both sides w.r.t. x, we get

$$\frac{du}{dx} = \frac{1}{2}\times\frac{1}{1+x^2} = \frac{1}{2(1+x^2)}$$ [1½]

Again, let $v = \tan^{-1}\left(\frac{2x}{1-x^2}\right) = 2\tan^{-1}x$

On differentiating both sides w.r.t. x, we get

$$\frac{dv}{dx} = 2\times\frac{1}{1+x^2}$$

Now, $$\frac{du}{dv} = \frac{du}{dx}\times\frac{dx}{dv}$$

$$= \frac{1}{2(1+x^2)}\times\frac{(1+x^2)}{2} = \frac{1}{4}$$ [1]

6. **Hint** Put $x = \cos\theta$ in first function [**Ans.** 4]

7. Solve as Question 5. $\left[\textbf{Ans. } \frac{1}{2}\right]$

8. Solve as Question 5. $\left[\textbf{Ans. } \frac{1}{4}\right]$

TOPIC 06 Logarithmic Differentiation and Derivatives of Infinite Series

Logarithmic Differentiation

Logarithmic differentiation is a powerful technique to differentiate functions of the form $y = [u(x)]^{v(x)}$. In this process

I. Take log on both sides and use suitable property of logarithm to convert it into simplest form for differentiation,

i.e. $\log y = v(x)\log u(x)$ ...(i)

II. Differentiate Eq. (i) obtained in step II with respect to x by using suitable formula,

i.e. $\frac{1}{y}\frac{dy}{dx} = v(x)\frac{1}{u(x)}\cdot u'(x) + v'(x)\log u(x)$ ...(ii)

III. Now, transfer (or shift) the terms other than dy/dx from LHS to RHS and put the value of y. Then, we get the required answer.

Note Here, functions should always be positive otherwise their logarithms are not defined.

Example 1 Differentiate a^x w.r.t. x, where a is a positive constant. [NCERT]

Sol. Let $y = a^x$.

Taking log on both sides, we get $\log y = x\log a$

On differentiating both sides w.r.t. x, we get

$$\frac{1}{y}\frac{dy}{dx} = \log a \Rightarrow \frac{dy}{dx} = y\log a$$

Thus, $\frac{d}{dx}(a^x) = a^x\log a$.

Example 2 If $y = (\cos x)^x + \sin^{-1}\sqrt{3x}$, find $\frac{dy}{dx}$.

Sol. Let $y = (\cos x)^x + \sin^{-1}\sqrt{3x}$

Again, let $u = (\cos x)^x$, $v = \sin^{-1}\sqrt{3x}$

$\therefore \quad y = u + v$

On differentiating both sides w.r.t. x, we get

$$\frac{dy}{dx} = \frac{du}{dx} + \frac{dv}{dx} \quad \text{...(i)}$$

Now, $u = (\cos x)^x$

Taking log on both sides, we get

$$\log u = \log(\cos x)^x = x\log(\cos x)$$

On differentiating both sides w.r.t. x, we get

$$\frac{1}{u}\frac{du}{dx} = x\frac{d}{dx}\log(\cos x) + \log(\cos x)\frac{d}{dx}(x)$$

$$= \frac{x}{\cos x}(-\sin x) + \log(\cos x)$$

$$\Rightarrow \frac{du}{dx} = u[-x\tan x + \log\cos x]$$

$$\Rightarrow \quad \frac{du}{dx} = (\cos x)^x [-x \tan x + \log \cos x]$$

Again, $v = \sin^{-1}\sqrt{3x}$

$$\frac{dv}{dx} = \frac{1}{\sqrt{1-(\sqrt{3x})^2}} \frac{d}{dx}[(3x)^{1/2}]$$

$$\Rightarrow \quad \frac{dv}{dx} = \frac{1}{\sqrt{1-3x}} \frac{1}{2}(3x)^{-1/2} \times 3$$

$$\Rightarrow \quad \frac{dv}{dx} = \frac{1}{\sqrt{1-3x}} \times \frac{3}{2\sqrt{3x}}$$

$$\Rightarrow \quad \frac{dv}{dx} = \frac{3}{2\sqrt{3x}\sqrt{1-3x}}$$

$$\Rightarrow \quad \frac{dv}{dx} = \frac{\sqrt{3}}{2\sqrt{x-3x^2}}$$

On putting the values of $\frac{du}{dx}$ and $\frac{dv}{dx}$ in Eq. (i), we get

$$\frac{dy}{dx} = (\cos x)^x [-x \tan x + \log \cos x] + \frac{\sqrt{3}}{2\sqrt{x-3x^2}}$$

Example 3 If $y = x^{x^x}$, then find $\frac{dy}{dx}$.

Sol. Given, $y = x^{x^x}$ ...(i)

Taking log on both sides, we get

$$\log y = \log x^{x^x} \quad \text{...(ii)}$$

$$\Rightarrow \quad \log y = x^x \log x \quad [\because \log m^n = n \log m]$$

Again, taking log on both sides, we get

$$\log \log y = \log (x^x \log x)$$

$$\Rightarrow \quad \log \log y = \log x^x + \log \log x$$

$$[\because \log (mn) = \log m + \log n]$$

$$\Rightarrow \quad \log \log y = x \log x + \log \log x$$

On differentiating both sides w.r.t. x, we get

$$\frac{1}{\log y} \cdot \frac{d}{dx}(\log y) = \left[x \frac{d}{dx}(\log x) + \log x \frac{d}{dx}(x)\right] + \left[\frac{1}{\log x} \cdot \frac{d}{dx}(\log x)\right]$$

[by product rule and chain rule of derivative]

$$\Rightarrow \quad \frac{1}{\log y} \cdot \frac{1}{y} \cdot \frac{dy}{dx} = \left[x \cdot \frac{1}{x} + \log x \cdot 1\right] + \left[\frac{1}{\log x} \cdot \frac{1}{x}\right]$$

$$\Rightarrow \quad \frac{1}{y \log y} \cdot \frac{dy}{dx} = 1 + \log x + \frac{1}{x \log x}$$

$$\Rightarrow \quad \frac{dy}{dx} = y \log y \left[1 + \log x + \frac{1}{x \log x}\right]$$

$$= x^{x^x} \log x^{x^x} \left[1 + \log x + \frac{1}{x \log x}\right]$$

[from Eqs. (i) and (ii)]

Example 4 Differentiate $\sqrt{\frac{(x-3)(x^2+4)}{3x^2+4x+5}}$ with respect to x. **[NCERT]**

Sol. Let given function be $y = \sqrt{\frac{(x-3)(x^2+4)}{3x^2+4x+5}}$

$$\Rightarrow \quad y = \left\{\frac{(x-3)(x^2+4)}{3x^2+4x+5}\right\}^{1/2}$$

Taking log on both sides, we get

$$\log y = \log \left\{\frac{(x-3)(x^2+4)}{3x^2+4x+5}\right\}^{1/2}$$

$$= \frac{1}{2} \log \left\{\frac{(x-3)(x^2+4)}{3x^2+4x+5}\right\} \quad [\because \log m^n = n \log m]$$

$$= \frac{1}{2} [\log (x-3)(x^2+4) - \log (3x^2+4x+5)]$$

$$[\because \log (m/n) = \log m - \log n]$$

$$= \frac{1}{2} [\log (x-3) + \log (x^2+4) - \log (3x^2+4x+5)] \quad \text{...(i)}$$

$$[\because \log mn = \log m + \log n]$$

On differentiating both sides of Eq. (i) w.r.t. x, we get

$$\frac{1}{y}\frac{dy}{dx} = \frac{1}{2}\left[\frac{1}{(x-3)}\frac{d}{dx}(x-3) + \frac{1}{(x^2+4)}\frac{d}{dx}(x^2+4) - \frac{1}{(3x^2+4x+5)}\frac{d}{dx}(3x^2+4x+5)\right]$$

[by chain rule of derivative]

$$= \frac{1}{2}\left[\frac{1}{x-3} + \frac{2x}{x^2+4} - \frac{6x+4}{3x^2+4x+5}\right]$$

$$\Rightarrow \quad \frac{dy}{dx} = \frac{y}{2}\left[\frac{1}{x-3} + \frac{2x}{x^2+4} - \frac{6x+4}{3x^2+4x+5}\right]$$

$$= \frac{1}{2}\sqrt{\frac{(x-3)(x^2+4)}{3x^2+4x+5}}\left[\frac{1}{x-3} + \frac{2x}{x^2+4} - \frac{6x+4}{3x^2+4x+5}\right]$$

Note In order to find the derivative of a product of a number of functions or a quotient of a number of functions, we may take logarithm on both sides and then differentiate.

Differentiation of Infinite Series

When the value of y is given as an infinite series, then the process of finding the derivative of such infinite series is called **the differentiation of infinite series.**

In such cases, we use the fact that, if one term is deleted from an infinite series, it remains unaffected, so we can replace all terms except first term by y. Thus, we convert it into a finite series or function. Then, we differentiate it to find required value.

Example 5 If $y=\sqrt{\log x+\sqrt{\log x+\sqrt{\log x+\ldots+\infty}}}$, then find $\frac{dy}{dx}$.

Sol. We have, $y=\sqrt{\log x+\sqrt{\log x+\sqrt{\log x+\ldots+\infty}}}$

Then, $y=\sqrt{\log x+y}$

$\Rightarrow \quad y^2=\log x+y$ [squaring on both sides]

On differentiating both sides w.r.t. x, we get

$$2y\cdot\frac{dy}{dx}=\frac{1}{x}+\frac{dy}{dx}$$

$$\Rightarrow \quad 2y\frac{dy}{dx}-\frac{dy}{dx}=\frac{1}{x}\Rightarrow\frac{dy}{dx}(2y-1)=\frac{1}{x}$$

$$\Rightarrow \quad \frac{dy}{dx}=\frac{1}{x(2y-1)}$$

Example 6 If $y=(\sin x)^{(\sin x)^{(\sin x)\ldots\infty}}$, then prove that $\frac{dy}{dx}=\frac{y^2\cos x}{1-y\log\sin x}$.

Sol. We have, $y=(\sin x)^{(\sin x)^{(\sin x)\ldots\infty}}$. Then, $y=(\sin x)^y$

Taking log on both sides, we get

$\log y=y\log\sin x$

On differentiating both sides w.r.t. x, we get

$$\frac{1}{y}\frac{dy}{dx}=y\frac{d}{dx}(\log\sin x)+\log\sin x\frac{d}{dx}(y)$$

$$\Rightarrow \quad \frac{1}{y}\frac{dy}{dx}=y\cdot\frac{1}{\sin x}\cdot\cos x+\log\sin x\cdot\frac{dy}{dx}$$

$$\Rightarrow \quad \frac{dy}{dx}\left(\frac{1}{y}-\log\sin x\right)=y\cot x$$

$$\Rightarrow \quad \frac{dy}{dx}\left(\frac{1-y\log\sin x}{y}\right)=y\cot x$$

$$\therefore \quad \frac{dy}{dx}=\frac{y^2\cot x}{1-y\log\sin x}$$ **Hence proved.**

Topic Practice 6

Very Short Answer Type Questions

2 Marks

1 Find the derivative of $y=a^{\sin x}$.

2 Differentiate $(\sin x)^{\log x}$ w.r.t. x.

3 If $e^{x+y}=xy$, then show that $\frac{dy}{dx}=\frac{y(1-x)}{x(y-1)}$ [ISC 2007]

4 Find the derivative of $\left(\frac{1}{x}\right)^x$.

5 If $y=\sqrt{\sin x+\sqrt{\sin x+\sqrt{\sin x+\ldots+\infty}}}$, then find $\frac{dy}{dx}$.

Short Answer Type Questions

4 Marks

6 If $(x-y)\cdot e^{\frac{x}{x-y}}=a$, then prove that $y\frac{dy}{dx}+x=2y$.

7 If $y^x=e^{y-x}$, then prove that $\frac{dy}{dx}=\frac{(1+\log y)^2}{\log y}$.

8 If $y^x=x^y$, then find $\frac{dy}{dx}$. [NCERT]

9 If $(\cos x)^y=(\cos y)^x$, then find $\frac{dy}{dx}$.

10 If $x^p y^q=(x+y)^{p+q}$, then prove that $\frac{dy}{dx}=\frac{y}{x}$. [ISC 2005]

11 If u, v and w are functions of x, then show that
$$\frac{d}{dx}(u\cdot v\cdot w)=\frac{du}{dx}v\cdot w+u\cdot\frac{dv}{dx}\cdot w+u\cdot v\frac{dw}{dx}.$$
In two ways, first by repeated application of product rule, second by logarithmic differentiation. [NCERT]

12 Find the derivative of $y=(x+3)^2(x+4)^3(x+5)^4$. [NCERT]

13 Find the derivative of the function given by $f(x)=(1+x)(1+x^2)(1+x^4)(1+x^8)$ and hence find $f'(1)$. [NCERT]

14 Differentiate $\cos x\cos 2x\cos 3x$ w.r.t. x. [NCERT]

15 If $x^y+y^x=a^b$, then find $\frac{dy}{dx}$.

16 Differentiate the following function w.r.t. x, $(\log x)^x+x^{\log x}$.

17 If $y=x^{\sin x}+(\sin x)^{\cos x}$, then find $\frac{dy}{dx}$. [NCERT]

18 If $e^x+e^y=e^{x+y}$, then prove that $\frac{dy}{dx}+\frac{e^x(e^y-1)}{e^y(e^x-1)}=0$.

Or If $e^x+e^y=e^{x+y}$, then prove that $\frac{dy}{dx}+e^{y-x}=0$.

19 If $y=x^{x^{x\ldots\infty}}$, then show that $\frac{dy}{dx}=\frac{y^2}{x(1-y\log x)}$.

20 If $y=e^{x+e^{x+e^{x+e^{x+\ldots+\infty}}}}$, then find $\frac{dy}{dx}$.

21 If $y = x + \cfrac{1}{x + \cfrac{1}{x + \cfrac{1}{x + \ldots + \infty}}}$, then find $\frac{dy}{dx}$.

22 If $y = 1 + x + \frac{x^2}{2!} + \frac{x^3}{3!} + \ldots + \frac{x^n}{n!}$, then show that

$$\frac{dy}{dx} - y + \frac{x^n}{n!} = 0.$$

23 If $y = (\cos x)^{(\cos x)^{(\cos x)^{\ldots\infty}}}$, then show that

$$\frac{dy}{dx} = \frac{y^2 \tan x}{y \log \cos x - 1}.$$ **[NCERT Exemplar]**

Hints & Solutions

1. Similar as Example 1. [**Ans.** $\cos x\, a^{\sin x} \log a$]

2. Let $y = (\sin x)^{\log x}$

On taking log both sides, we get

$$\log y = \log (\sin x)^{\log x}$$

$$\Rightarrow \quad \log y = \log x \log (\sin x)$$

On differentiating both sides w.r.t. 'x', we get

$$\frac{1}{y}\frac{dy}{dx} = \log x \frac{d}{dx}\log(\sin x) + \log(\sin x)\frac{d}{dx}(\log x) \quad [1]$$

$$\Rightarrow \frac{1}{y}\frac{dy}{dx} = \log x \frac{1}{\sin x}\frac{d}{dx}\sin x + \log(\sin x)\frac{1}{x}$$

$$= \log x \frac{1}{\sin x}\cos x + \frac{1}{x}\log(\sin x)$$

$$= \cot x \log x + \frac{\log(\sin x)}{x}$$

$$\Rightarrow \frac{dy}{dx} = y\left[\cot x \log x + \frac{\log(\sin x)}{x}\right]$$

$$= (\sin x)^{\log x}\left[\cot x \cdot \log x + \frac{\log(\sin x)}{x}\right] \quad [1]$$

3. Given, $e^{x+y} = xy$

Taking logarithm on both sides, we get

$$x + y = \log_e(xy) = \log_e x + \log_e y$$

$$\left[\because \begin{array}{l}\log_e x^y = y \log_e x \\ \log_e xy = \log_e x + \log_e y\end{array}\right] \quad [1/2]$$

On differentiating both sides w.r.t. x, we get

$$1 + \frac{dy}{dx} = \frac{d}{dx}(\log_e x) + \frac{d}{dx}(\log_e y)$$

$$\Rightarrow 1 + \frac{dy}{dx} = \frac{1}{x} + \frac{d(\log_e y)}{d(y)} \cdot \frac{dy}{dx}$$

$$\Rightarrow 1 + \frac{dy}{dx} = \frac{1}{x} + \frac{1}{y} \cdot \frac{dy}{dx} \quad [1]$$

$$\Rightarrow \left(1 - \frac{1}{y}\right)\frac{dy}{dx} = \frac{1}{x} - 1$$

$$\Rightarrow \frac{(y-1)}{y}\frac{dy}{dx} = \frac{1-x}{x}$$

$$\therefore \frac{dy}{dx} = \frac{y(1-x)}{x(y-1)}$$ **Hence proved.** [1/2]

4. Let $y = \left(\frac{1}{x}\right)^x$

Taking log on both sides, we get

$$\log y = \log\left(\frac{1}{x}\right)^x$$

$$\Rightarrow \log y = x \log\left(\frac{1}{x}\right) = x \log x^{-1}$$

$$\Rightarrow \log y = -x \log x \quad [1]$$

On differentiating both sides w.r.t. 'x', we get

$$\frac{1}{y}\frac{dy}{dx} = -\left[x \cdot \frac{1}{x} + 1 \cdot \log x\right] = -[1 + \log x]$$

$$\Rightarrow \frac{dy}{dx} = -y[1 + \log x]$$

$$\Rightarrow \frac{dy}{dx} = -\left(\frac{1}{x}\right)^x [1 + \log x] \quad [1]$$

5. We have, $y = \sqrt{\sin x + \sqrt{\sin x + \sqrt{\sin x + \ldots + \infty}}}$

$$\therefore \quad y = \sqrt{\sin x + y}$$

$$\Rightarrow \quad y^2 = \sin x + y \quad \text{[squaring on both sides]} \quad [1]$$

On differentiating both sides w.r.t. x, we get

$$2y\frac{dy}{dx} = \cos x + \frac{dy}{dx}$$

$$\Rightarrow 2y\frac{dy}{dx} - \frac{dy}{dx} = \cos x$$

$$\Rightarrow \frac{dy}{dx}(2y - 1) = \cos x \Rightarrow \frac{dy}{dx} = \frac{\cos x}{2y - 1} \quad [1]$$

6. Given, $(x - y) \cdot e^{\frac{x}{x-y}} = a$

Taking log on both sides, we get

$$\log(x - y) + \log e^{\frac{x}{x-y}} = \log a$$

$$\Rightarrow \log(x - y) + \frac{x}{x - y} = \log a \quad \ldots \text{(i)}$$

$$\Rightarrow (x - y)\log(x - y) + x = (x - y)\log a \quad [1]$$

On differentiating both sides w.r.t. y, we get

$$\left(\frac{dx}{dy} - 1\right)\log(x - y) + (x - y) \times \frac{1}{x - y} \times \left(\frac{dx}{dy} - 1\right) + \frac{dx}{dy} = \left(\frac{dx}{dy} - 1\right)\log a \quad [1]$$

$$\Rightarrow \left(\frac{dx}{dy}-1\right)\log(x-y)+2\frac{dx}{dy}-1$$

$$=\left(\frac{dx}{dy}-1\right)\left[\log(x-y)+\frac{x}{x-y}\right] \text{[from Eq. (i)]}$$

$$\Rightarrow \quad 2\frac{dx}{dy}-1=\left(\frac{dx}{dy}-1\right)\left(\frac{x}{x-y}\right)$$

$$\Rightarrow \quad \frac{dx}{dy}\left(2-\frac{x}{x-y}\right)=-\frac{x}{x-y}+1$$

$$\Rightarrow \quad \frac{dx}{dy}\left(\frac{x-2y}{x-y}\right)=-\frac{y}{x-y}$$ [1]

$$\Rightarrow \quad \frac{dx}{dy}(x-2y)=-y$$

$$\Rightarrow \quad \frac{ydy}{dx}+x=2y$$ **Hence proved.** [1]

7. We have, $y^x = e^{y-x}$

Taking log on both sides, we get

$$x\log y=(y-x) \Rightarrow x\log y+x=y$$

$$\Rightarrow \quad x=\frac{y}{1+\log y}$$ [1]

On differentiating both sides w.r.t. x, we get

$$1=\frac{(1+\log y)\frac{dy}{dx}-y\left(0+\frac{1}{y}\right)\frac{dy}{dx}}{(1+\log y)^2}$$ [1]

$$\Rightarrow \quad 1=\frac{(1+\log y)-(1)}{(1+\log y)^2}\times\frac{dy}{dx}$$

$$\Rightarrow \quad \frac{dy}{dx}=\frac{(1+\log y)^2}{\log y}$$ **Hence proved.** [2]

8. We have, $y^x = x^y$

Taking log on both sides, we get

$$\log y^x = \log x^y$$

$$\Rightarrow \quad x\log y = y\log x$$ [1]

On differentiating both sides w.r.t. x, we get

$$x\frac{d}{dx}(\log y)+\log y\frac{d}{dx}(x)=y\frac{d}{dx}(\log x)+\log x\frac{d}{dx}(y)$$

[by product rule of derivative]

$$\Rightarrow \quad x\frac{1}{y}\cdot\frac{dy}{dx}+\log y=y\times\frac{1}{x}+\log x\times\frac{dy}{dx}$$ [1]

$$\Rightarrow \quad \frac{x}{y}\frac{dy}{dx}-\log x\frac{dy}{dx}=\frac{y}{x}-\log y$$

$$\Rightarrow \quad \frac{dy}{dx}\left[\frac{x}{y}-\log x\right]=\frac{y}{x}-\log y$$

$$\Rightarrow \quad \frac{dy}{dx}\left[\frac{x-y\log x}{y}\right]=\left[\frac{y-x\log y}{x}\right]$$ [1]

$$\Rightarrow \quad \frac{dy}{dx}=\frac{y}{x}\left[\frac{y-x\log y}{x-y\log x}\right]$$ [1]

9. Given, $(\cos x)^y = (\cos y)^x$

Taking log on both sides, we get

$$\log(\cos x)^y = \log(\cos y)^x$$

$$\therefore \quad y\log(\cos x)=x\log(\cos y)$$ [1]

On differentiating both sides w.r.t. x, we get

$$y\cdot\frac{d}{dx}\log(\cos x)+\log(\cos x)\cdot\frac{d}{dx}(y)$$

$$=x\frac{d}{dx}\log(\cos y)+\log(\cos y)\frac{d}{dx}(x)$$

$$\left[\because \frac{d}{dx}(uv)=u\frac{dv}{dx}+v\frac{du}{dx}\right]$$ [1]

$$\Rightarrow \quad y\cdot\frac{1}{\cos x}\frac{d}{dx}(\cos x)+\log(\cos x)\frac{dy}{dx}$$

$$=x\cdot\frac{1}{\cos y}\frac{d}{dx}(\cos y)+\log(\cos y)\cdot 1$$

$$\Rightarrow \quad y.\frac{1}{\cos x}(-\sin x)+\log(\cos x)\cdot\frac{dy}{dx}$$

$$=x\frac{1}{\cos y}(-\sin y)\cdot\frac{dy}{dx}+\log(\cos y)\cdot 1$$ [1]

$$\Rightarrow \quad -y\tan x+\log(\cos x)\frac{dy}{dx}=-x\tan y\frac{dy}{dx}+\log(\cos y)$$

$$\Rightarrow \quad [x\tan y+\log(\cos x)]\frac{dy}{dx}=\log(\cos y)+y\tan x$$

$$\therefore \quad \frac{dy}{dx}=\frac{\log(\cos y)+y\tan x}{x\tan y+\log(\cos x)}$$ [1]

10. We have, $x^p y^q = (x+y)^{p+q}$

Taking log on both sides, we get

$$\log x^p + \log y^q = \log(x+y)^{p+q}$$

$$\Rightarrow p\log x+q\log y=(p+q)\log(x+y)$$ [1]

On differentiating both sides w.r.t. x, we get

$$p\frac{1}{x}+q\frac{1}{y}\cdot\frac{dy}{dx}=(p+q)\frac{1}{(x+y)}\cdot\frac{d}{dx}(x+y)$$

$$\Rightarrow \quad \frac{p}{x}+\frac{q}{y}\cdot\frac{dy}{dx}=\left(\frac{p+q}{x+y}\right)\left[1+\frac{dy}{dx}\right]$$ [1]

$$\Rightarrow \quad \frac{p}{x}+\frac{q}{y}\frac{dy}{dx}=\frac{p+q}{x+y}+\left(\frac{p+q}{x+y}\right)\frac{dy}{dx}$$

$$\Rightarrow \quad \frac{q}{y}\frac{dy}{dx}-\left(\frac{p+q}{x+y}\right)\frac{dy}{dx}=\frac{p+q}{x+y}-\frac{p}{x}$$ [1]

$$\Rightarrow \quad \frac{dy}{dx}\left[\frac{qx+qy-py-qy}{y(x+y)}\right]=\frac{px+qx-px-py}{(x+y)x}$$

$$\Rightarrow \quad \frac{dy}{dx}\left[\frac{qx-py}{y(x+y)}\right]=\frac{(qx-py)}{x(x+y)}$$

$$\Rightarrow \quad \frac{dy}{dx}=\frac{(qx-py)}{(x+y)x}\cdot\frac{y(x+y)}{(qx-py)}$$

$$\Rightarrow \quad \frac{dy}{dx}=\frac{y}{x}$$ **Hence proved.** [1]

11. First, we use product rule and find that

$$\frac{d}{dx}(uvw) = \frac{d}{dx}[(uv)\,w]$$

$$= (uv)\frac{dw}{dx} + w\frac{d}{dx}(uv)$$

[consider here uv as one function and w as another function]

$$= uv\frac{dw}{dx} + w\left(u\frac{dv}{dx} + v\frac{du}{dx}\right)$$

$$= uv\frac{dw}{dx} + wu\frac{dv}{dx} + wv\frac{du}{dx} \quad \text{...(i) [1]}$$

Next, we use the logarithmic differentiation to obtain $d(uvw)/dx$.

Let $y = uvw$

Taking log on both sides, we get

$$\log y = \log(uvw) \quad [1]$$

$$\Rightarrow \log y = \log u + \log v + \log w$$

On differentiating both sides w.r.t. x, we get

$$\frac{1}{y}\frac{dy}{dx} = \frac{1}{u}\frac{du}{dx} + \frac{1}{v}\frac{dv}{dx} + \frac{1}{w}\frac{dw}{dx} \quad [1]$$

$$\Rightarrow \frac{dy}{dx} = y\left\{\frac{1}{u}\frac{du}{dx} + \frac{1}{v}\frac{dv}{dx} + \frac{1}{w}\frac{dw}{dx}\right\}$$

$$= (uvw)\left\{\frac{1}{u}\frac{du}{dx} + \frac{1}{v}\frac{dv}{dx} + \frac{1}{w}\frac{dw}{dx}\right\}$$

$$= (vw)\frac{du}{dx} + (uw)\frac{dv}{dx} + (uv)\frac{dw}{dx}$$

$$= (uv)\frac{dw}{dx} + wu\frac{dv}{dx} + wv\frac{du}{dx} \quad \text{...(ii)}$$

From Eqs. (i) and (ii), we find that the result obtained is same in the two cases. [1]

12. **Hint** Taking log on both sides and then differentiate it.

[**Ans.** $(x+3)(x+4)^2(x+5)^3\,[9x^2+70x+133]$]

13. Given, $f(x) = (1+x)(1+x^2)(1+x^4)(1+x^8)$

Taking log on both sides, we get

$$\log\{f(x)\} = \log\{(1+x)(1+x^2)(1+x^4)(1+x^8)\}$$

$$\Rightarrow \log\{f(x)\} = \log(1+x) + \log(1+x^2) + \log(1+x^4) + \log(1+x^8)$$

On differentiating both sides w.r.t. x, we get

$$\frac{d}{dx}\log\{f(x)\} = \frac{d}{dx}\log(1+x) + \frac{d}{dx}\log(1+x^2) + \frac{d}{dx}\log(1+x^4) + \frac{d}{dx}\log(1+x^8) \quad [1]$$

$$\Rightarrow \frac{1}{f(x)}f'(x) = \frac{1}{1+x}(0+1) + \frac{1}{1+x^2}(0+2x) + \frac{1}{1+x^4}(0+4x^3) + \frac{1}{1+x^8}(0+8x^7) \quad [1]$$

$$\Rightarrow f'(x) = f(x)\left\{\frac{1}{1+x} + \frac{2x}{1+x^2} + \frac{4x^3}{1+x^4} + \frac{8x^7}{1+x^8}\right\}$$

$$= (1+x)(1+x^2)(1+x^4)(1+x^8)\left\{\frac{1}{1+x} + \frac{2x}{1+x^2} + \frac{4x^3}{1+x^4} + \frac{8x^7}{1+x^8}\right\} \quad [1]$$

$$\therefore f'(1) = (1+1)(1+1)(1+1)(1+1)\left\{\frac{1}{1+1} + \frac{2}{1+1} + \frac{4}{1+1} + \frac{8}{1+1}\right\}$$

$$= 2^4\left\{\frac{1}{2} + 1 + 2 + 4\right\} = 16\left(\frac{15}{2}\right) = 120 \quad [1]$$

14. Let $y = \cos x \cos 2x \cos 3x$. ...(i)

Taking log on both sides, we get

$$\log y = \log(\cos x \cdot \cos 2x \cdot \cos 3x)$$

$$\Rightarrow \log y = \log\cos x + \log\cos 2x + \log\cos 3x \quad [1]$$

[$\because \log(mnp) = \log m + \log n + \log p$]

On differentiating both sides w.r.t. x, we get

$$\frac{1}{y}\cdot\frac{dy}{dx} = \frac{1}{\cos x}\cdot\frac{d}{dx}(\cos x) + \frac{1}{\cos 2x}\cdot\frac{d}{dx}(\cos 2x) + \frac{1}{\cos 3x}\cdot\frac{d}{dx}(\cos 3x)$$

[by chain rule of derivative] [1]

$$\Rightarrow \frac{dy}{dx} = y\left[\frac{1}{\cos x}(-\sin x) + \frac{1}{\cos 2x}(-\sin 2x)\frac{d}{dx}(2x) + \frac{1}{\cos 3x}(-\sin 3x)\frac{d}{dx}(3x)\right]$$

[by chain rule of derivative]

$$= y[-\tan x - 2\tan 2x - 3\tan 3x] \quad [1]$$

$$= -\cos x\cos 2x\cos 3x\,[\tan x + 2\tan 2x + 3\tan 3x]$$

[from Eq. (i)] [1]

15. Given, $x^y + y^x = a^b$ ...(i)

Let $x^y = v$ and $y^x = u$ ...(ii)

On putting these values in Eq. (i), we get

$$v + u = a^b$$

On differentiating both sides w.r.t. x, we get

$$\frac{dv}{dx} + \frac{du}{dx} = 0 \quad \text{...(iii) [1/2]}$$

Now, $x^y = v$ [from Eq. (ii)]

Taking log on both sides, we get

$$\log x^y = \log v$$

$$\Rightarrow y\log x = \log v \quad [1/2]$$

On differentiating both sides w.r.t. x, we get

$$y\cdot\frac{1}{x} + \log x\cdot\frac{dy}{dx} = \frac{1}{v}\frac{dv}{dx}$$

$$\Rightarrow v\left(\frac{y}{x} + \log x\cdot\frac{dy}{dx}\right) = \frac{dv}{dx}$$

$\Rightarrow \quad \frac{dv}{dx} = x^y\left(\frac{y}{x} + \log x \cdot \frac{dy}{dx}\right)$ ...(iv) [1/2]

[from Eq. (ii)]

and $\quad y^x = u$ [from Eq. (ii)]

Taking log on both sides, we get

$\log y^x = \log u \Rightarrow x \log y = \log u$ [1/2]

On differentiating both sides w.r.t. x, we get

$x \cdot \frac{1}{y}\frac{dy}{dx} + 1 \cdot \log y = \frac{1}{u}\frac{du}{dx}$

$\Rightarrow \quad \frac{x}{y}\frac{dy}{dx} + \log y = \frac{1}{u}\frac{du}{dx}$

$\Rightarrow \quad u\left[\frac{x}{y}\frac{dy}{dx} + \log y\right] = \frac{du}{dx}$

$\Rightarrow \quad y^x\left[\frac{x}{y}\frac{dy}{dx} + \log y\right] = \frac{du}{dx}$ [from Eq. (ii)] ...(v) [1/2]

On putting the values of $\frac{dv}{dx}$ and $\frac{du}{dx}$ from Eqs. (iv) and (v) respectively in Eq. (iii), we get

$x^y\left(\frac{y}{x} + \log x \cdot \frac{dy}{dx}\right) + y^x\left(\frac{x}{y}\frac{dy}{dx} + \log y\right) = 0$ [1/2]

$\Rightarrow \quad x^y\frac{y}{x} + x^y \log x \cdot \frac{dy}{dx} + y^x \cdot \frac{x}{y}\frac{dy}{dx} + y^x \log y = 0$

$\Rightarrow \quad x^y \log x \cdot \frac{dy}{dx} + y^x \frac{x}{y} \cdot \frac{dy}{dx} = -x^y \frac{y}{x} - y^x \log y$

$\Rightarrow \quad \frac{dy}{dx}\left[x^y \log x + y^x \cdot \frac{x}{y}\right] = -x^y \cdot \frac{y}{x} - y^x \log y$

$\therefore \quad \frac{dy}{dx} = \frac{-x^{y-1} \cdot y - y^x \log y}{x^y \log x + y^{x-1} \cdot x}$ [1]

16. Let $y = (\log x)^x + x^{\log x}$ and $u = (\log x)^x$ and $v = x^{\log x}$.

Then, $y = u + v$.

On differentiating both sides w.r.t. x, we get

$\frac{dy}{dx} = \frac{du}{dx} + \frac{dv}{dx}$ ...(i) [1/2]

Now, $\quad u = (\log x)^x$

Taking log on both sides, we get

$\log u = \log(\log x)^x$

$\Rightarrow \quad \log u = x \log(\log x)$ [1/2]

On differentiating both sides w.r.t. x, we get

$\frac{1}{u} \cdot \frac{du}{dx} = x\frac{d}{dx}\log(\log x) + \log(\log x)\frac{d}{dx}(x)$ [1/2]

[by chain rule of derivative]

$\Rightarrow \quad \frac{1}{u} \cdot \frac{du}{dx} = \frac{x}{\log x} \times \frac{1}{x} + \log(\log x)$

$\Rightarrow \quad \frac{du}{dx} = u\left[\frac{1}{\log x} + \log(\log x)\right]$

$\Rightarrow \quad \frac{du}{dx} = (\log x)^x\left[\frac{1}{\log x} + \log(\log x)\right]$ [1/2]

Again, $v = x^{\log x}$

Taking log on both sides, we get

$\log v = \log x^{\log x} \Rightarrow \log v = (\log x)(\log x)$

$\Rightarrow \quad \log v = (\log x)^2$ [1/2]

On differentiating both sides w.r.t. x, we get

$\frac{1}{v} \cdot \frac{dv}{dx} = 2\log x \frac{d}{dx}(\log x) = 2\log x \times \frac{1}{x}$ [1/2]

$\Rightarrow \quad \frac{dv}{dx} = v\left[\frac{2\log x}{x}\right]$

$\Rightarrow \quad \frac{dv}{dx} = x^{\log x}\left[\frac{2\log x}{x}\right]$

Now, putting the values of $\frac{du}{dx}$ and $\frac{dv}{dx}$ in Eq. (i), we get

$\frac{dy}{dx} = (\log x)^x\left[\frac{1}{\log x} + \log(\log x)\right] + x^{\log x}\left[\frac{2\log x}{x}\right]$

$= (\log x)^{x-1}[1 + \log x \log(\log x)] + 2x^{\log x - 1} \cdot \log x$ [1]

17. We have, $y = x^{\sin x} + (\sin x)^{\cos x}$

Let $u = x^{\sin x}$ and $v = (\sin x)^{\cos x}$

Then, $y = u + v$

$\therefore \quad \frac{dy}{dx} = \frac{du}{dx} + \frac{dv}{dx}$ [differentiate both sides] ...(i) [1/2]

Now, $u = x^{\sin x}$

Taking log on both sides, we get

$\log u = \log x^{\sin x}$

$\Rightarrow \log u = \sin x \log x$

On differentiating both sides w.r.t. x, we get

$\frac{1}{u} \cdot \frac{du}{dx} = \sin x \frac{d}{dx}(\log x) + \log x \frac{d}{dx}(\sin x)$ [1/2]

[by product rule of derivative]

$\Rightarrow \quad \frac{1}{u} \cdot \frac{du}{dx} = \frac{1}{x}\sin x + \log x \cdot \cos x$

$\Rightarrow \quad \frac{du}{dx} = u\left[\frac{\sin x}{x} + \log x \cdot \cos x\right]$

$= x^{\sin x}\left[\frac{\sin x}{x} + \cos x \log x\right]$ ...(ii) [1/2]

Also, $v = (\sin x)^{\cos x}$.

Taking log on both sides, we get

$\log v = \log(\sin x)^{\cos x}$

$\Rightarrow \quad \log v = \cos x \log(\sin x)$

On differentiating both sides w.r.t. x, we get

$\frac{1}{v}\frac{dv}{dx} = \cos x \frac{d}{dx}[\log(\sin x)] + \log \sin x \frac{d}{dx}(\cos x)$ [1/2]

[by product rule of derivative]

$$\Rightarrow \frac{1}{v}\frac{dv}{dx} = \cos x \times \frac{1}{\sin x}\cdot \cos x + \log \sin x\,(-\sin x)$$

$$\Rightarrow \frac{dv}{dx} = v\,[\cos x \cdot \cot x - \sin x \log \sin x]$$

$$\Rightarrow \frac{dv}{dx} = (\sin x)^{\cos x}\,[\cos x \cot x - \sin x \log \sin x] \quad ...(iii)$$

[1]

On adding Eqs. (ii) and (iii), we get

$$\frac{du}{dx} + \frac{dv}{dx} = x^{\sin x}\left[\frac{\sin x}{x} + \cos x \log x\right] + (\sin x)^{\cos x}\,[\cos x \cot x - \sin x \log \sin x]$$

$$\therefore \quad \frac{dy}{dx} = x^{\sin x}\left[\frac{\sin x}{x} + \cos x \log x\right] + (\sin x)^{\cos x}\,[\cos x \cot x - \sin x \log \sin x]$$

[from Eq. (i)] [1]

18. We have, $e^x + e^y = e^{x+y}$.

On differentiating both sides w.r.t. x, we get

$$e^x + e^y \frac{dy}{dx} = e^{x+y}\frac{d}{dx}(x+y)$$

[by chain rule of derivative] [1]

$$\Rightarrow e^x + e^y \frac{dy}{dx} = e^{x+y}\left[1 + \frac{dy}{dx}\right]$$

$$\Rightarrow e^x + e^y \frac{dy}{dx} = e^{x+y} + e^{x+y}\frac{dy}{dx}$$

$$\Rightarrow e^y \frac{dy}{dx} - e^{x+y}\frac{dy}{dx} = e^{x+y} - e^x \quad [1]$$

$$\Rightarrow -e^y \frac{dy}{dx}(e^x - 1) = e^x(e^y - 1) \Rightarrow \frac{dy}{dx} = \frac{-e^x(e^y-1)}{e^y(e^x-1)}$$

$$\Rightarrow \frac{dy}{dx} + \frac{e^x(e^y-1)}{e^y(e^x-1)} = 0 \quad [1]$$

$$\text{or} \quad \frac{dy}{dx} = \frac{-e^{x+y}+e^x}{e^{x+y}-e^y} = \frac{-e^x - e^y + e^x}{e^x + e^y - e^y} \quad \text{[given]}$$

$$\Rightarrow \frac{dy}{dx} = \frac{-e^y}{e^x} = -e^{y-x}$$

$$\Rightarrow \frac{dy}{dx} + e^{y-x} = 0$$

Hence proved. [1]

19. We have, $y = x^{x^{x\ldots\infty}}$.

Then, $y = x^y$. [1]

Taking log on both sides, we get

$$\log y = \log x^y \Rightarrow \log y = y \log x \quad [1/2]$$

On differentiating both sides w.r.t. x, we get

$$\frac{1}{y}\frac{dy}{dx} = y\frac{d}{dx}\log x + \log x \frac{d}{dx}(y) \quad [1]$$

[by product rule of derivative]

$$\Rightarrow \frac{1}{y}\frac{dy}{dx} = y\cdot\frac{1}{x} + \log x \frac{dy}{dx}$$

$$\Rightarrow \frac{1}{y}\frac{dy}{dx} - \log x \frac{dy}{dx} = \frac{y}{x} \quad [1/2]$$

$$\Rightarrow \frac{dy}{dx}\left(\frac{1}{y} - \log x\right) = \frac{y}{x}$$

$$\Rightarrow \frac{dy}{dx}\left(\frac{1 - y\log x}{y}\right) = \frac{y}{x}$$

$$\Rightarrow \frac{dy}{dx} = \frac{y^2}{x(1 - y\log x)} \quad [1]$$

20. We have, $y = e^{x + e^{x + e^{x+\ldots\infty}}}$.

Then, $\quad y = e^{x+y}$ [1]

Taking log on both sides, we get

$$\log y = \log e^{(x+y)}$$

$$\Rightarrow \log y = (x+y)\log e \Rightarrow \log y = (x+y)$$

$[\because \log e = 1]$ [1]

On differentiating both sides w.r.t. x, we get

$$\frac{1}{y}\frac{dy}{dx} = 1 + \frac{dy}{dx} \Rightarrow \frac{1}{y}\frac{dy}{dx} - \frac{dy}{dx} = 1$$

$$\Rightarrow \frac{dy}{dx}\left(\frac{1}{y} - 1\right) = 1 \quad [1]$$

$$\Rightarrow \frac{dy}{dx}\left(\frac{1-y}{y}\right) = 1 \Rightarrow \frac{dy}{dx} = \frac{y}{1-y} \quad [1]$$

21. We have, $y = x + \cfrac{1}{x + \cfrac{1}{x + \cfrac{1}{x + \ldots + \infty}}}$

$$\therefore \quad y = x + \frac{1}{y} \Rightarrow y = \frac{xy+1}{y} \quad [2]$$

$$\Rightarrow y^2 = xy + 1$$

On differentiating both sides w.r.t. x, we get

$$2y\frac{dy}{dx} = x\frac{dy}{dx} + y\cdot 1 + 0 \quad [1]$$

[by product rule of derivative]

$$\Rightarrow 2y\frac{dy}{dx} - x\frac{dy}{dx} = y$$

$$\Rightarrow (2y - x)\frac{dy}{dx} = y$$

$$\Rightarrow \frac{dy}{dx} = \frac{y}{2y - x} \quad [1]$$

22. **Hint** Find $\frac{dy}{dx}$, then substitute this value in the LHS of shown result.

23. Similar as Example 6.

TOPIC 07 | Successive Differentiation and Derivatives of Determinants

Successive Differentiation upto Second Order (Second Order Derivative)

Second order derivative of a function is the derivative of the **first order derivative** of the function.

Let $\quad y = f(x) \qquad \ldots$(i)

Then, $\dfrac{dy}{dx} = f'(x)$ is called the first derivative of y or $f(x)$. It can also be written as y' or y_1.

If $f'(x)$ is differentiable, then derivative of dy/dx exists.

Again, differentiating Eq. (i) both sides w.r.t. x, we get

$$\frac{d}{dx}\left(\frac{dy}{dx}\right) = \frac{d}{dx}[f'(x)]$$

$$\Rightarrow \quad \frac{d^2y}{dx^2} = f''(x)$$

where, $\dfrac{d}{dx}\left(\dfrac{dy}{dx}\right)$ is called the **second order derivative** of y w.r.t. x and is denoted by $\dfrac{d^2y}{dx^2}$ or $f''(x)$ or y'' or D^2y or y_2.

Similarly, $\dfrac{d}{dx}\left(\dfrac{d^2y}{dx^2}\right) = \dfrac{d}{dx}\{f''(x)\}$

$$\Rightarrow \quad \frac{d^3y}{dx^3} = f'''(x)$$

is called the **third order derivative** of y w.r.t. x and is denoted by $\dfrac{d^3y}{dx^3}$ or $f'''(x)$ or y''' or D^3y or y_3.

In general, $\dfrac{d^ny}{dx^n} = f^n(x)$ is called the ***n*th order derivative** of y w.r.t. x and is denoted by $\dfrac{d^ny}{dx^n}$ or $f^n(x)$ or $y^{'''\ldots n}$ or D^ny or y_n.

Problems Based on Second Order Derivative

There are many problems in which we have to find second order derivative. Some of them are given below

| TYPE I |

Problems Based on Finding the Second Order Derivative

In this type of problems, a function say $y = f(x)$ is given to us and we have to find its second order derivative. For this, we differentiate $y = f(x)$ two times w.r.t. x by using suitable formula.

Example 1 Find the second order derivative of

(i) $x^4 + \cot x$ (ii) $\sin(\log x)$

Sol. (i) Let $y = x^4 + \cot x$.

On differentiating both sides w.r.t. x, we get

$$\frac{dy}{dx} = 4x^3 - \operatorname{cosec}^2 x$$

Again, differentiating both sides w.r.t. x, we get

$$\frac{d}{dx}\left(\frac{dy}{dx}\right) = 12x^2 - 2\operatorname{cosec} x\,(-\operatorname{cosec} x \cdot \cot x)$$

$$\Rightarrow \quad \frac{d^2y}{dx^2} = 12x^2 + 2\operatorname{cosec}^2 x \cdot \cot x$$

(ii) Let $y = \sin(\log x)$

On differentiating both sides w.r.t. x, we get

$$\frac{dy}{dx} = \cos(\log x)\frac{d}{dx}(\log x)$$

$$\Rightarrow \quad \frac{dy}{dx} = \cos(\log x)\cdot\frac{1}{x}$$

$$\Rightarrow \quad x.\frac{dy}{dx} = \cos(\log x) \qquad \ldots\text{(i)}$$

Again, differentiating both sides w.r.t. x, we get

$$x\cdot\frac{d^2y}{dx^2} + \frac{dy}{dx} = -\frac{\sin(\log x)}{x}$$

$$\Rightarrow \quad x^2\frac{d^2y}{dx^2} + x\frac{dy}{dx} = -\sin(\log x)$$

$$\Rightarrow x^2\frac{d^2y}{dx^2} + \cos(\log x) = -\sin(\log x) \quad \text{[from Eq. (i)]}$$

$$\Rightarrow \quad x^2\frac{d^2y}{dx^2} = -\sin(\log x) - \cos(\log x)$$

$$\Rightarrow \quad \frac{d^2y}{dx^2} = -\frac{1}{x^2}[\sin(\log x) + \cos(\log x)]$$

Example 2 If $y = e^x \sin 5x$, then find $\dfrac{d^2y}{dx^2}$. [NCERT]

Sol. We have, $y = e^x \sin 5x$.

On differentiating both sides w.r.t. x, we get

$$\frac{dy}{dx} = e^x \cdot \frac{d}{dx} \sin 5x + \sin 5x \cdot \frac{d}{dx} e^x$$

[by product rule of derivative]

$$= e^x \cdot \cos 5x \cdot \frac{d}{dx}(5x) + \sin 5x \cdot e^x$$

[by chain rule of derivative]

$$= e^x \cdot \cos 5x \cdot 5 + e^x \sin 5x$$

$$\Rightarrow \frac{dy}{dx} = e^x (5 \cos 5x + \sin 5x)$$

Again, differentiating both sides w.r.t. x, we get

$$\frac{d^2y}{dx^2} = e^x \cdot \frac{d}{dx}[5 \cos 5x + \sin 5x] + [5 \cos 5x + \sin 5x]\frac{d}{dx} \cdot (e^x)$$

[by product rule of derivative]

$$= e^x \left[5(-\sin 5x) \cdot \frac{d}{dx}(5x) + \cos 5x \cdot \frac{d}{dx}(5x)\right] + [5 \cos 5x + \sin 5x] \cdot e^x$$ [by chain rule of derivative]

$$= e^x [5(-\sin 5x)5 + \cos 5x(5)] + [5 \cos 5x + \sin 5x] e^x$$

$$= e^x [-25 \sin 5x + 5 \cos 5x + 5 \cos 5x + \sin 5x]$$

$$= e^x [10 \cos 5x - 24 \sin 5x]$$

$$\therefore \frac{d^2y}{dx^2} = 2e^x [5 \cos 5x - 12 \sin 5x]$$

Example 3 A curve has the equation $y = \dfrac{x+6}{2x-3}$, when $x \neq \dfrac{3}{2}$.

(i) Show that the derivative of the curve can be expressed as $\dfrac{k}{(2x-3)^2}$, where k is a constant.

(ii) Find the value of x for which $\dfrac{d^2y}{dx^2} = \dfrac{12}{25}$.

Sol. (i) Given equation of curve is $y = \dfrac{x+6}{2x-3}$.

On differentiating both sides w.r.t. x, we get

$$\frac{dy}{dx} = \frac{(2x-3)\frac{d}{dx}(x+6) - (x+6)\frac{d}{dx}(2x-3)}{(2x-3)^2}$$

$$= \frac{(2x-3)(1) - (x+6)(2)}{(2x-3)^2}$$

$$\Rightarrow \frac{dy}{dx} = \frac{-15}{(2x-3)^2} \text{ is of the form of } \frac{k}{(2x-3)^2} \quad \text{...(i)}$$

(ii) Again, differentiating both sides of Eq. (i) w.r.t. x,

we get $\dfrac{d^2y}{dx^2} = -15 \dfrac{d}{dx}(2x-3)^{-2}$

$$= -15 \times (-2)(2x-3)^{-2-1} \times \frac{d}{dx}(2x-3)$$

$$= 30(2x-3)^{-3} \times 2 = \frac{60}{(2x-3)^3}$$

Also, given $\dfrac{d^2y}{dx^2} = \dfrac{12}{25}$

$$\Rightarrow \frac{12}{25} = \frac{60}{(2x-3)^3}$$

$$\Rightarrow (2x-3)^3 = (5)^3$$

$$\Rightarrow 2x - 3 = 5 \quad \text{[taking cube root]}$$

$$\Rightarrow 2x = 8 \Rightarrow x = 4$$

| TYPE II |

Problems Based on Finding Second Order Derivatives of Parametric Functions

Suppose two parametric functions, say $y = f(t)$ and $x = g(t)$, are given to us and we have to find their second order derivative, i.e. $\dfrac{d^2y}{dx^2}$, then we use the following steps

I. First, write the given functions and differentiate them with respect to parameters.
i.e. let $y = f(t)$ and $x = f(t)$, then find $\dfrac{dy}{dt}$ and $\dfrac{dx}{dt}$.

II. Divide derivative of first function by derivative of second function, i.e. put the values of $\dfrac{dy}{dt}$ and $\dfrac{dx}{dt}$ in the formula

$$\frac{dy}{dx} = \frac{dy/dt}{dx/dt} \quad \text{...(i)}$$

III. Now, differentiate Eq. (i) w.r.t. x to get required second order derivative,

i.e. $\dfrac{d}{dx}\left(\dfrac{dy}{dx}\right) = \dfrac{d}{dx}\left(\dfrac{dy/dt}{dx/dt}\right)$

$$\Rightarrow \frac{d^2y}{dx^2} = \frac{d}{dt}\left(\frac{dy/dt}{dx/dt}\right)\frac{dt}{dx} \text{ and simplify it.}$$

Example 4 If $x = a(\theta + \sin\theta)$ and $y = a(1 - \cos\theta)$, then find $\dfrac{d^2y}{dx^2}$ at $\theta = \dfrac{\pi}{2}$.

Sol. We have, $x = a(\theta + \sin\theta)$ ...(i)

and $y = a(1 - \cos\theta)$ ...(ii)

where, θ is a parameter.

On differentiating Eqs. (i) and (ii), respectively w.r.t. θ, we get

$$\frac{dx}{d\theta} = \frac{d}{d\theta}[a(\theta + \sin\theta)] = a(1 + \cos\theta) \quad ...(iii)$$

and $$\frac{dy}{d\theta} = \frac{d}{d\theta}[a(1 - \cos\theta)] = a(0 + \sin\theta) = a\sin\theta \quad ...(iv)$$

On putting the values from Eqs. (iii) and (iv) in the formula $\frac{dy}{dx} = \frac{dy/d\theta}{dx/d\theta}$, we get

$$\frac{dy}{dx} = \frac{a\sin\theta}{a(1 + \cos\theta)}$$

$$= \frac{\sin\theta}{1 + \cos\theta} = \frac{2\sin\left(\frac{\theta}{2}\right)\cos\left(\frac{\theta}{2}\right)}{2\cos^2\left(\frac{\theta}{2}\right)} = \tan\frac{\theta}{2}$$

Now, differentiating both sides w.r.t. x, we get

$$\frac{d^2y}{dx^2} = \frac{d}{dx}\left(\tan\frac{\theta}{2}\right) = \frac{d}{d\theta}\left(\tan\frac{\theta}{2}\right)\cdot\frac{d\theta}{dx}$$

$$= \frac{1}{2}\sec^2\frac{\theta}{2}\cdot\frac{1}{a(1 + \cos\theta)} \quad \text{[from Eq. (iii)]}$$

$$= \frac{\sec^2\frac{\theta}{2}}{2a(1 + \cos\theta)}$$

Now, at $\theta = \frac{\pi}{2}$, $\frac{d^2y}{dx^2} = \frac{\sec^2\frac{\pi}{4}}{2a\left(1 + \cos\frac{\pi}{2}\right)} = \frac{2}{2a(1+0)} = \frac{1}{a}$

|TYPE III|

Problems Based on Proving the Result/Equation

Sometimes a function, say $y = f(x)$, is given to us and we have to show/prove that given equation having first and second order derivatives of y is satisfied or not. For this, we use following steps

I. First, write the given function say $y = f(x)$.

II. Differentiate it w.r.t. x, i.e. find first derivative of function, i.e. $\frac{dy}{dx}$.

III. Find second derivative of function, i.e. $\frac{d^2y}{dx^2}$.

IV. Put the values of y, first derivative and second derivative in LHS of given equation and check whether LHS = RHS or not, for proving the given equation.

Note Sometimes, we differentiate given function two times to get required equation.

Example 5 If $y = x^x$, then prove that

$$\frac{d^2y}{dx^2} - \frac{1}{y}\left(\frac{dy}{dx}\right)^2 - \frac{y}{x} = 0.$$

[ISC 2011]

Sol. We have, $y = x^x$

Taking log on both sides, we get

$$\log y = \log x^x \Rightarrow \log y = x\log x$$

On differentiating both sides w.r.t. x, we get

$$\frac{1}{y}\frac{dy}{dx} = x\frac{d}{dx}(\log x) + \log x\frac{d}{dx}(x)$$

$$\Rightarrow \frac{1}{y}\frac{dy}{dx} = x \times \frac{1}{x} + \log x$$

$$\Rightarrow \frac{dy}{dx} = y(1 + \log x) \quad ...(i)$$

Again, differentiating both sides of Eq. (i) w.r.t. x, we get

$$\frac{d^2y}{dx^2} = y\frac{d}{dx}(1 + \log x) + (1 + \log x)\frac{dy}{dx}$$

$$= y \times \frac{1}{x} + (1 + \log x)\frac{dy}{dx}$$

$$\Rightarrow \frac{d^2y}{dx^2} = \frac{y}{x} + (1 + \log x)\frac{dy}{dx} \quad ...(ii)$$

Now, LHS $= \frac{d^2y}{dx^2} - \frac{1}{y}\left(\frac{dy}{dx}\right)^2 - \frac{y}{x}$

On putting the values of $\frac{d^2y}{dx^2}$ and $\frac{dy}{dx}$ from Eqs. (i) and (ii), we get

$$\text{LHS} = \frac{y}{x} + (1 + \log x)\, y(1 + \log x) - \frac{1}{y}[y^2(1 + \log x)^2] - \frac{y}{x}$$

$$= y(1 + \log x)^2 - y(1 + \log x)^2 = 0 = \text{RHS}$$

Hence proved.

Example 6 If $y = \sin^{-1} x$, then show that

$$(1 - x^2)\frac{d^2y}{dx^2} - x\frac{dy}{dx} = 0.$$

Sol. We have, $y = \sin^{-1} x$

On differentiating both sides w.r.t. x, we get

$$\frac{dy}{dx} = \frac{1}{\sqrt{1 - x^2}}$$

$$\Rightarrow \sqrt{1 - x^2}\frac{dy}{dx} = 1$$

On squaring both sides, we get

$$(1 - x^2)\left(\frac{dy}{dx}\right)^2 = 1$$

Again, differentiating both sides w.r.t. x, we get

$$\frac{d}{dx}\left[(1-x^2)\left(\frac{dy}{dx}\right)^2\right]=\frac{d}{dx}(1) \quad \text{...(i)}$$

$$\Rightarrow (1-x^2)\frac{d}{dx}\left(\frac{dy}{dx}\right)^2+\left(\frac{dy}{dx}\right)^2\frac{d}{dx}(1-x^2)=0$$

$$\Rightarrow \quad (1-x^2)2\frac{dy}{dx}\cdot\frac{d^2y}{dx^2}+\left(\frac{dy}{dx}\right)^2(0-2x)=0$$

$$\Rightarrow \quad \frac{2dy}{dx}\left[(1-x^2)\frac{d^2y}{dx^2}-x\frac{dy}{dx}\right]=0$$

$$\Rightarrow \quad (1-x^2)\frac{d^2y}{dx^2}-x\frac{dy}{dx}=0$$

Example 7 If $y=3\cos(\log x)+4\sin(\log x)$, show that $x^2\frac{d^2y}{dx^2}+x\frac{dy}{dx}+y=0.$ **[ISC 2024]**

Sol. We have, $y=3\cos(\log x)+4\sin(\log x)$ ...(i)

On differentating w.r.t 'x', we get

$$\frac{dy}{dx}=\frac{-3}{x}\sin(\log x)+\frac{4}{x}\cos(\log x) \quad \text{...(ii)}$$

On multiplying by 'x' both sides, we get

$$x\frac{dy}{dx}=-3\sin(\log x)+4\cos(\log x) \quad \text{...(iii)}$$

Again, on differentating Eq. (ii) w.r.t x, we get

$$\frac{d^2y}{dx^2}=\frac{3}{x^2}\sin(\log x)-\frac{3}{x^2}\cos(\log x)$$
$$-\frac{4}{x^2}\cos(\log x)-\frac{4}{x^2}\sin(\log x)$$

On multiplying x^2 both sides, we get

$$x^2\frac{d^2y}{dx^2}=3\sin(\log x)-3\cos(\log x)$$
$$-4\cos(\log x)-4\sin(\log x)$$
$$=-[-3\sin(\log x)+4\cos(\log x)]$$
$$-[3\cos(\log x)+4\sin(\log x)]$$

$$\Rightarrow \quad x^2\frac{d^2y}{dx^2}=-x\frac{dy}{dx}-y \quad \text{[using Eqs. (i) and (iii)]}$$

$$\Rightarrow \quad x^2\frac{d^2y}{dx^2}+x\frac{dy}{dx}+y=0$$ **Hence proved.**

Topic Practice 7

Very Short Answer Type Questions

(2 Marks)

1 Find the second derivative of the following functions. (Each part carries 2 Marks)
(i) $y=\log(\log x)$ (ii) $x^3\log x$ (iii) $e^{6x}\cos 3x$ **[NCERT]**

2 If $y=x^x$, then find $\frac{d^2y}{dx^2}$.

3 If $f(x)=\tan^{-1}x$, then find $f''(x)$. **[NCERT]**

4 If $y=A\sin x+B\cos x$, then prove that $\frac{d^2y}{dx^2}+y=0$. **[NCERT]**

5 If $\log y=\tan^{-1}x$, then prove that $(1+x^2)\frac{d^2y}{dx^2}+(2x-1)\frac{dy}{dx}=0$ **[ISC 2016]**

Short Answer Type Questions

(4 Marks)

6 If $y=3e^{2x}+2e^{3x}$, then prove that $\frac{d^2y}{dx^2}-5\frac{dy}{dx}+6y=0$. **[NCERT]**

7 If $y=500e^{7x}+600e^{-7x}$, then show that $\frac{d^2y}{dx^2}=49y$. **[NCERT]**

8 If $y=\tan x+\sec x$, then prove that $\frac{d^2y}{dx^2}=\frac{\cos x}{(1-\sin x)^2}$. **[NCERT Exemplar]**

9 If $y=\cos(\sin x)$, then show that $\frac{d^2y}{dx^2}+\tan x\frac{dy}{dx}+y\cos^2 x=0$. **[ISC 2017]**

10 If $x=\tan\left(\frac{1}{a}\log y\right)$, then prove that $(1+x^2)\frac{d^2y}{dx^2}+(2x-a)\frac{dy}{dx}=0$. **[ISC 2018]**

11 If $x\cos(a+y)=\cos y$, then prove that $\frac{dy}{dx}=\frac{\cos^2(a+y)}{\sin a}$. Hence show that $\sin a\frac{d^2y}{dx^2}+\sin 2(a+y)\frac{dy}{dx}=0$.

12 If $e^y(x+1)=1$, then show that $\frac{d^2y}{dx^2}=\left(\frac{dy}{dx}\right)^2$. **[ISC 2012]**

13 If $y=(\cot^{-1}x)^2$, then show that
$$(1+x^2)^2\frac{d^2y}{dx^2}+2x(1+x^2)\frac{dy}{dx}=2$$ **[ISC 2013]**

14 If $y=e^{a\cos^{-1}3x}$, then prove that
$$(1-9x^2)\frac{d^2y}{dx^2}-9x\frac{dy}{dx}-9a^2y=0.$$

15 If $y=x^3\log\left(\frac{1}{x}\right)$, then prove that
$$x\frac{d^2y}{dx^2}-2\frac{dy}{dx}+3x^2=0.$$

16 If $y=e^{ax}\cdot\cos bx$, then prove that
$$\frac{d^2y}{dx^2}-2a\frac{dy}{dx}+(a^2+b^2)y=0.$$ **[ISC 2023]**

17 If $y=\sqrt{x+1}-\sqrt{x-1}$, then prove that
$$(x^2-1)\frac{d^2y}{dx^2}+x\frac{dy}{dx}-\frac{1}{4}y=0.$$

18 If $x^m y^n=(x+y)^{m+n}$, then prove that $\frac{d^2y}{dx^2}=0$.

19 If $y=3\cos(\log x)+4\sin(\log x)$, then show that $x^2y_2+xy_1+y=0$. **[NCERT]**

20 If $(x-a)^2+(y-b)^2=c^2$, then prove that
$$\frac{\left[1+\left(\frac{dy}{dx}\right)^2\right]^{3/2}}{\frac{d^2y}{dx^2}}$$
is a constant and independent of a and b. **[NCERT]**

21 If $f(x)=|x|^3$, then show that $f''(x)$ exists for all real x and find it. **[NCERT]**

22 If $x=\sin t$ and $y=\sin pt$, then prove that
$$(1-x^2)\frac{d^2y}{dx^2}-x\frac{dy}{dx}+p^2y=0.$$ **[NCERT Exemplar]**

23 If $x=3\cos t-2\cos^3 t$ and $y=3\sin t-2\sin^3 t$, then find $\frac{d^2y}{dx^2}$.

24 If $x=a\sec^3\theta$, $y=a\tan^3\theta$, then find $\frac{d^2y}{dx^2}$ at $\theta=\frac{\pi}{4}$.

25 If $x=a(\cos t+t\sin t)$ and $y=a(\sin t-t\cos t)$, then find $\frac{d^2y}{dx^2}$ at $t=\frac{\pi}{4}$.

Hints & Solutions

1. (i) **Hint** $\frac{dy}{dx}=\frac{1}{\log x}\cdot\frac{1}{x}=(x\cdot\log x)^{-1}$

and $\frac{d^2y}{dx^2}=(-1)(x\log x)^{-2}\cdot\left(x\cdot\frac{1}{x}+\log x\right)$

$\left[\textbf{Ans. } \frac{-(1+\log x)}{(x\log x)^2}\right]$

(ii) Let $y=x^3\log x$.

On differentiating both sides w.r.t. x, we get
$$\frac{dy}{dx}=\frac{d}{dx}(x^3\log x)=x^3\frac{d}{dx}(\log x)+\log x\frac{d}{dx}(x^3)$$
[by product rule of derivative]
$$=x^3\left(\frac{1}{x}\right)+(\log x)(3x^2)=x^2(1+3\log x)$$ [1]

Again, differentiating both sides w.r.t. x, we get
$$\frac{d^2y}{dx^2}=x^2\frac{d}{dx}(1+3\log x)+\frac{d}{dx}(x^2)\cdot(1+3\log x)$$
$$=x^2\left(0+\frac{3}{x}\right)+(1+3\log x)(2x)$$
$$=3x+2x(1+3\log x)=x(5+6\log x)$$ [1]

(iii) Similar as Example 2. [**Ans.** $9e^{6x}(3\cos 3x-4\sin 3x)$]

2. Similar as Example 5. $\left[\textbf{Ans. } x^x\left\{(1+\log x)^2+\frac{1}{x}\right\}\right]$

3. We have, $f(x)=\tan^{-1}x$

On differentiating both sides w.r.t. x, we get
$$f'(x)=\frac{1}{1+x^2}=(1+x^2)^{-1}$$ [1]

Again, differentiating both sides w.r.t. x, we get
$$f''(x)=-1(1+x^2)^{-2}\frac{d}{dx}(1+x^2)$$
[by chain rule of derivative]
$$=\frac{-1}{(1+x^2)^2}\times(0+2x)=\frac{-2x}{(1+x^2)^2}$$ [1]

4. **Hint** $\frac{dy}{dx} = A\cos x + B(-\sin x) = A\cos x - B\sin x$

$$\frac{d^2y}{dx^2} = A(-\sin x) - B\cos x = -A\sin x - B\cos x$$

5. Given, $\log y = \tan^{-1} x$

On differentiating both sides w.r.t. x, we get

$$\frac{1}{y}\cdot\frac{dy}{dx} = \frac{1}{1+x^2}$$

$$\Rightarrow \frac{dy}{dx} = \frac{y}{1+x^2} \Rightarrow (1+x^2)\frac{dy}{dx} = y \quad [1]$$

Again differentiating w.r.t. x, we get

$$(1+x^2)\frac{d^2y}{dx^2} + \frac{dy}{dx}(2x) = \frac{dy}{dx}$$

$$\Rightarrow (1+x^2)\frac{d^2y}{dx^2} + (2x-1)\frac{dy}{dx} = 0$$ **Hence proved.** [1]

6. We have, $y = 3e^{2x} + 2e^{3x}$

On differentiating both sides w.r.t. x, we get

$$\frac{dy}{dx} = 3e^{2x}\frac{d}{dx}(2x) + 2e^{3x}\frac{d}{dx}(3x)$$

[by chain rule of derivative]

$$\Rightarrow \frac{dy}{dx} = 3e^{2x}\cdot 2 + 2e^{3x}\cdot 3 = 6e^{2x} + 6e^{3x} \quad [1]$$

Again, differentiating both sides w.r.t. x, we get

$$\frac{d^2y}{dx^2} = 6e^{2x}\frac{d}{dx}(2x) + 6e^{3x}\frac{d}{dx}(3x)$$

[by chain rule of derivative]

$$\Rightarrow \frac{d^2y}{dx^2} = 6e^{2x}\cdot 2 + 6e^{3x}\cdot 3 = 12e^{2x} + 18e^{3x} \quad [1]$$

Now, $\text{LHS} = \frac{d^2y}{dx^2} - 5\frac{dy}{dx} + 6y$

On putting the values of $\frac{d^2y}{dx^2}, \frac{dy}{dx}$ and y, we get

$$\text{LHS} = (12e^{2x} + 18e^{3x}) - 5(6e^{2x} + 6e^{3x}) + 6(3e^{2x} + 2e^{3x})$$

$$= 12e^{2x} - 30e^{2x} + 18e^{2x} + 18e^{3x} - 30e^{3x} + 12e^{3x} \quad [1]$$

$$= 30e^{2x} - 30e^{2x} + 30e^{3x} - 30e^{3x} = 0$$

$$\therefore \frac{d^2y}{dx^2} - 5\frac{dy}{dx} + 6y = 0 = \text{RHS}$$ **Hence proved.** [1]

7. Solve as Question 6.

8. Given, $y = \tan x + \sec x$

$$\Rightarrow y = \frac{1+\sin x}{\cos x} \quad [1/2]$$

On differentiating both sides w.r.t. x, we get

$$\frac{dy}{dx} = \frac{\cos x\cdot\cos x - (1+\sin x)(-\sin x)}{\cos^2 x} \quad [1]$$

[by quotient rule of derivative]

$$\Rightarrow \frac{dy}{dx} = \frac{\cos^2 x + \sin x + \sin^2 x}{\cos^2 x} = \frac{1+\sin x}{1-\sin^2 x} \quad [1]$$

$$\Rightarrow \frac{dy}{dx} = \frac{1+\sin x}{(1+\sin x)(1-\sin x)} = \frac{1}{1-\sin x} \quad [1/2]$$

Again, differentiating both sides w.r.t. x, we get

$$\frac{d^2y}{dx^2} = -(1-\sin x)^{-2}\frac{d}{dx}(1-\sin x) = \frac{\cos x}{(1-\sin x)^2}$$

Hence proved. [1]

9. Given, $y = \cos(\sin x)$ ...(i)

On differentiating both sides w.r.t. x, we get

$$\frac{dy}{dx} = \frac{d}{dx}\cos(\sin x) = \frac{d\{\cos(\sin x)\}}{d(\sin x)} \times \frac{d(\sin x)}{dx}$$

$$= -\sin(\sin x) \times \cos x \quad \text{...(ii) [1]}$$

On differentiating again w.r.t. x, we get

$$\frac{d^2y}{dx^2} = \frac{d}{dx}\{-\sin(\sin x)\cos x\}$$

$$= \cos x\frac{d\{-\sin(\sin x)\}}{d(\sin x)} \times \frac{d(\sin x)}{dx} + \{-\sin(\sin x)\}\frac{d(\cos x)}{dx}$$

$$= \cos x\{-\cos(\sin x) \times \cos x\} - \sin(\sin x)(-\sin x) \quad [1]$$

$$= -\cos^2 x\cos(\sin x) + \sin x\cdot\sin(\sin x) \quad \text{...(iii)}$$

$$= -\cos^2 x\cdot y - \sin x\frac{1}{\cos x}\frac{dy}{dx}$$

[using Eqs. (i) and (ii)]

$$= -y\cos^2 x - \tan x\frac{dy}{dx} \quad [1]$$

$$\Rightarrow \frac{d^2y}{dx^2} + \tan x\cdot\frac{dy}{dx} + y\cos^2 x = 0 \quad [1]$$

10. We have, $x = \tan\left(\frac{1}{a}\log y\right)$

$$\Rightarrow \log y = a\tan^{-1} x \quad [1]$$

On differentiating w.r.t. x, we get

$$\frac{1}{y}\frac{dy}{dx} = \frac{a}{1+x^2}$$

$$\Rightarrow (1+x^2)\frac{dy}{dx} = ay \quad [1]$$

Again differentiating w.r.t. x, we get

$$(1+x^2)\frac{d^2y}{dx^2} + 2x\frac{dy}{dx} = a\frac{dy}{dx} \quad [1]$$

$$\Rightarrow (1+x^2)\frac{d^2y}{dx^2} + (2x-a)\frac{dy}{dx} = 0 \quad [1]$$

11. Given, $x\cos(a+y) = \cos y$

$$\Rightarrow x = \frac{\cos y}{\cos(a+y)}$$

On differentiating both sides w.r.t. y, we get

$$\frac{dx}{dy}=\frac{\cos(a+y)\frac{d}{dy}(\cos y)-\cos y\frac{d}{dy}(\cos(a+y))}{\cos^2(a+y)}$$

[by using quotient rule of derivative]

$$=\frac{\cos(a+y)\cdot(-\sin y)+\cos y\cdot\sin(a+y)}{\cos^2(a+y)}$$ [1]

$$=\frac{\sin(a+y)\cos y-\cos(a+y)\sin y}{\cos^2(a+y)}$$

$$\Rightarrow\quad \frac{dx}{dy}=\frac{\sin(a+y-y)}{\cos^2(a+y)}=\frac{\sin a}{\cos^2(a+y)}$$

[$\because \sin A\cos B-\cos A\sin B=\sin(A-B)$]

$$\Rightarrow\quad \frac{dy}{dx}=\frac{\cos^2(a+y)}{\sin a}\quad \text{...(i)}$$ [1]

On differentiating both sides of Eq. (i) w.r.t. x, we get

$$\frac{d^2y}{dx^2}=\frac{1}{\sin a}\frac{d}{dx}[\cos^2(a+y)]$$

$$=\frac{1}{\sin a}\times\frac{d}{dy}[\cos^2(a+y)]\times\frac{dy}{dx}$$ [1]

$$=\frac{1}{\sin a}\times 2\cos(a+y)[-\sin(a+y)]\times\frac{dy}{dx}$$

$$=-\frac{2\sin(a+y)\cos(a+y)}{\sin a}\times\frac{dy}{dx}$$

$$\Rightarrow\quad \frac{d^2y}{dx^2}=-\frac{\sin 2(a+y)}{\sin a}\frac{dy}{dx}\qquad [\because 2\sin\theta\cos\theta=\sin 2\theta]$$

$$\Rightarrow\quad \sin a\frac{d^2y}{dx^2}+\sin 2(a+y)\frac{dy}{dx}=0$$ **Hence proved.** [1]

12. Given, $e^y(x+1)=1$

Taking log on both sides, we get

$$\log[e^y(x+1)]=\log 1$$

$$\Rightarrow\quad \log e^y+\log(x+1)=\log 1$$

$$\Rightarrow\quad y+\log(x+1)=\log 1$$ [1]

On differentiating both sides w.r.t. x, we get

$$\frac{dy}{dx}+\frac{1}{x+1}=0\quad \text{...(i)}$$ [1]

Again, differentiating both sides w.r.t. x, we get

$$\frac{d^2y}{dx^2}-\frac{1}{(x+1)^2}=0$$ [1]

$$\Rightarrow\quad \frac{d^2y}{dx^2}-\left(-\frac{dy}{dx}\right)^2=0\qquad \text{[from Eq. (i)]}$$

$$\Rightarrow\quad \frac{d^2y}{dx^2}-\left(\frac{dy}{dx}\right)^2=0$$

$$\Rightarrow\quad \frac{d^2y}{dx^2}=\left(\frac{dy}{dx}\right)^2$$ [1]

13. Given, $y=(\cot^{-1}x)^2$

On differentiating both sides w.r.t. x, we get

$$\frac{dy}{dx}=2(\cot^{-1}x)^{2-1}\frac{d}{dx}(\cot^{-1}x)$$ [1]

[using chain rule of derivative]

$$\Rightarrow\quad \frac{dy}{dx}=2\cot^{-1}x\times\left(\frac{-1}{1+x^2}\right)$$

$$\Rightarrow\quad (1+x^2)\frac{dy}{dx}=-2\cot^{-1}x$$ [1]

Again, differentiating w.r.t. x, we get

$$(1+x^2)\frac{d^2y}{dx^2}+2x\frac{dy}{dx}=-2\times\left(\frac{-1}{1+x^2}\right)$$ [1]

$$\Rightarrow\quad (1+x^2)^2\frac{d^2y}{dx^2}+2x(1+x^2)\frac{dy}{dx}=2$$ **Hence proved.** [1]

14. We have, $y=e^{a\cos^{-1}3x}$ ...(i)

$$\Rightarrow\quad \frac{dy}{dx}=e^{a\cos^{-1}3x}\cdot\left(a\cdot\frac{-1}{\sqrt{1-(3x)^2}}\cdot 3\right)$$

$$\Rightarrow\quad \frac{dy}{dx}=\frac{-3ay}{\sqrt{1-9x^2}}\qquad \text{[using Eq. (i)]}$$ [1]

$$\Rightarrow\quad \sqrt{1-9x^2}\frac{dy}{dx}=-3ay$$

$$\Rightarrow\quad (1-9x^2)\left(\frac{dy}{dx}\right)^2=9a^2y^2\qquad \text{[squaring both sides]}$$ [1]

On differentiating both sides, we get

$$(1-9x^2)2\left(\frac{dy}{dx}\right)\frac{d^2y}{dx^2}+\left(\frac{dy}{dx}\right)^2(-18x)=18a^2y\frac{dy}{dx}$$ [1]

On dividing both sides by $2\frac{dy}{dx}$, we get

$$(1-9x^2)\frac{d^2y}{dx^2}-9x\frac{dy}{dx}=9a^2y$$

$$\Rightarrow\quad (1-9x^2)\frac{d^2y}{dx^2}-9x\frac{dy}{dx}-9a^2y=0$$ **Hence proved.** [1]

15. **Hint** $y=x^3(\log 1-\log x)=-x^3\log x$

$$\Rightarrow\quad \frac{dy}{dx}=-x^3\cdot\frac{1}{x}+\log x(-3x^2)=-x^2(1+3\log x)$$

$$\Rightarrow\quad \frac{d^2y}{dx^2}=-x^2\cdot\frac{3}{x}+(1+3\log x)(-2x)$$

$$=-3x-2x(1+3\log x)=-5x-6x\log x$$

On substituting these values in LHS, we get RHS.

16. Similar as Example 2.

17. Given, $y=\sqrt{x+1}-\sqrt{x-1}$

On differentiating both sides w.r.t. x, we get

$$\frac{dy}{dx}=\frac{1}{2\sqrt{x+1}}-\frac{1}{2\sqrt{x-1}}$$

$$=\frac{1}{2}\left[\frac{\sqrt{x-1}-\sqrt{x+1}}{\sqrt{x^2-1}}\right]$$

$$\Rightarrow \quad 2\sqrt{x^2-1}\cdot\frac{dy}{dx}=-y$$ [1]

Now, squaring both sides, we get $4(x^2-1)\left(\frac{dy}{dx}\right)^2=y^2$ [1]

Again, differentiating both sides w.r.t. x, we get

$$4(x^2-1)\,2\frac{dy}{dx}\cdot\frac{d^2y}{dx^2}+\left(\frac{dy}{dx}\right)^2\cdot 8x=2y\left(\frac{dy}{dx}\right)$$ [1]

On dividing both sides by $2\frac{dy}{dx}$, we get

$$4(x^2-1)\frac{d^2y}{dx^2}+4x\frac{dy}{dx}-y=0$$

$$\therefore \quad (x^2-1)\frac{d^2y}{dx^2}+x\frac{dy}{dx}-\frac{y}{4}=0$$ **Hence proved.** [1]

18. We have, $x^m y^n=(x+y)^{m+n}$

Taking log on both sides, we get

$$\log(x^m y^n)=\log(x+y)^{m+n}$$

$$\Rightarrow \quad \log x^m+\log y^n=\log(x+y)^{m+n}$$

$$\Rightarrow \quad m\log x+n\log y=(m+n)\log(x+y)$$ [1]

On differentiating both sides w.r.t. x, we get

$$\frac{m}{x}+\frac{n}{y}\cdot\frac{dy}{dx}=\frac{(m+n)}{x+y}\cdot\left(1+\frac{dy}{dx}\right)$$

$$\Rightarrow \quad \frac{dy}{dx}\left(\frac{n}{y}-\frac{m+n}{x+y}\right)=\frac{m+n}{x+y}-\frac{m}{x}$$ [1]

$$\Rightarrow \frac{dy}{dx}\left(\frac{nx+ny-my-ny}{y(x+y)}\right)=\left(\frac{mx+nx-mx-my}{x(x+y)}\right)$$

$$\Rightarrow \frac{dy}{dx}\left(\frac{nx-my}{y(x+y)}\right)=\left(\frac{nx-my}{x(x+y)}\right) \Rightarrow \frac{dy}{dx}=\frac{y}{x}$$ ... (i) [1]

Again, differentiating both sides w.r.t. x, we get

$$\frac{d^2y}{dx^2}=\frac{x\cdot\frac{dy}{dx}-y\cdot 1}{x^2}=\frac{x\left(\frac{y}{x}\right)-y}{x^2}$$ [from Eq. (i)]

$$=\frac{y-y}{x^2}=0$$ **Hence proved.** [1]

19. Given, $y=3\cos(\log x)+4\sin(\log x)$ ...(i)

On differentiating both sides w.r.t. x, we get

$$\frac{dy}{dx}=y_1=-3\sin(\log x)\frac{d}{dx}(\log x)+4\cos(\log x)\frac{d}{dx}(\log x)$$

[by chain rule of derivative]

$$\Rightarrow \quad y_1=-3\sin(\log x)\times\frac{1}{x}+4\cos(\log x)\times\frac{1}{x}$$ [1]

$$\Rightarrow x\,y_1=-3\sin(\log x)+4\cos(\log x)$$

[multiplying both sides by x]

Again, differentiating both sides w.r.t. x, we get

$$x\frac{d}{dx}(y_1)+y_1\times\frac{d}{dx}(x)=-3\cos(\log x)\frac{d}{dx}(\log x)$$

$$-4\sin(\log x)\frac{d}{dx}(\log x)$$ [by chain rule of derivative] [1]

$$\Rightarrow x\,y_2+y_1=-3\cos(\log x)\times\frac{1}{x}-4\sin(\log x)\times\frac{1}{x}$$ [1]

$$\Rightarrow \quad x^2y_2+x\,y_1=-3\cos(\log x)-4\sin(\log x)$$

[multiplying both sides by x]

$$\Rightarrow \quad x^2y_2+x\,y_1=-[3\cos(\log x)+4\sin(\log x)]$$

$$\Rightarrow \quad x^2y_2+x\,y_1=-y$$ [from Eq. (i)]

$$\Rightarrow x^2y_2+x\,y_1+y=0$$ [1]

20. Given, $(x-a)^2+(y-b)^2=c^2$ ...(i)

On differentiating both sides w.r.t. x, we get

$$2(x-a)+2(y-b)\frac{dy}{dx}=0$$

$$\Rightarrow \quad (x-a)+(y-b)\frac{dy}{dx}=0$$ [dividing both sides by 2]

$$\Rightarrow \quad \frac{dy}{dx}=-\left(\frac{x-a}{y-b}\right)$$ ...(ii) [1]

$$\Rightarrow \quad \frac{d^2y}{dx^2}=-\left[\frac{(y-b)\cdot 1-(x-a)\frac{dy}{dx}}{(y-b)^2}\right]$$

[by quotient rule of derivative]

$$\Rightarrow \quad \frac{d^2y}{dx^2}=-\left[\frac{(y-b)+\frac{(x-a)^2}{(y-b)}}{(y-b)^2}\right]$$ [using Eq. (ii)]

$$\Rightarrow \quad \frac{d^2y}{dx^2}=-\left[\frac{(y-b)^2+(x-a)^2}{(y-b)^3}\right]$$ [1]

$$\Rightarrow \quad \frac{d^2y}{dx^2}=-\frac{c^2}{(y-b)^3}$$ [using Eq. (i)] ...(iii) [1/2]

Now, consider $\dfrac{\left[1+\left(\frac{dy}{dx}\right)^2\right]^{3/2}}{\frac{d^2y}{dx^2}}$

$$=-\frac{\left[1+\frac{(x-a)^2}{(y-b)^2}\right]^{3/2}}{\frac{c^2}{(y-b)^3}}$$

[using Eqs. (ii) and (iii)]

$$=-\frac{\left(\frac{c^2}{(y-b)^2}\right)^{3/2}}{\frac{c^2}{(y-b)^3}}$$ [using Eq. (i)] [1]

$$=-\frac{c^3}{(y-b)^3}\times\frac{(y-b)^3}{c^2}=-c,$$

which is constant and independent of a and b.

Hence proved. [1/2]

21. We have, $f(x)=|x|^3=\begin{cases} x^3, & \text{if } x\ge 0 \\ -x^3, & \text{if } x<0\end{cases}$

Clearly $f''(x)$ exist for all $x \in R$ except possibly at $x = 0$.

[$\because f(x)$ is an polynomial function for $(-\infty, 0)\cup(0,\infty)$] [1]

Now, $Lf'(0)=\lim_{h\to 0}\frac{f(0-h)-f(0)}{-h}=\lim_{h\to 0}\frac{f(-h)-f(0)}{-h}$

$=\lim_{h\to 0}\frac{-(-h)^3-0}{-h}=\lim_{h\to 0-}\frac{h^3}{h}=\lim_{h\to 0}-h^2=0$

and $Rf'(0)=\lim_{h\to 0}\frac{f(0+h)-f(0)}{h}=\lim_{h\to 0}\frac{f(h)-f(0)}{h}$

$=\lim_{h\to 0}\frac{h^3-0}{h}=\lim_{h\to 0}h^2=0$ [1]

$\because \quad Lf'(0)=Rf'(0)$

$\therefore f(x)$ is differentiable at $x = 0$, i.e. $f'(x)$ exist at $x = 0$ also.

Thus, $f'(x)=\begin{cases} 3x^2, & \text{if } x\ge 0 \\ -3x^2, & \text{if } x<0\end{cases}$ [1/2]

Now, $Lf''(0)=\lim_{h\to 0}\frac{f'(0-h)-f'(0)}{-h}$

$=\lim_{h\to 0}\frac{f'(-h)-f(0)}{-h}$

$=\lim_{h\to 0}\frac{-3(-h)^2-0}{-h}=\lim_{h\to 0}3h=0$

and $Rf''(0)=\lim_{h\to 0}\frac{f'(0+h)-f'(0)}{h}$

$=\lim_{h\to 0}\frac{f'(h)-f'(0)}{h}$

$=\lim_{h\to 0}\frac{3h^2-0}{h}=\lim_{h\to 0}3h=0$

$\because \quad Lf''=Rf''(0)$ [1]

$\therefore f'(x)$ is differentiable at $x = 0$, i.e, $f''(x)$ exist at $x = 0$ also.

Hence, $f''(x)=\begin{cases} 6x, & \text{if } x\ge 0 \\ -6x, & \text{if } x<0\end{cases}$ [1/2]

22. Similar as Example 7.

23. We have, $x=3\cos t-2\cos^3 t$ and $y=3\sin t-2\sin^3 t$

Now, $\frac{dx}{dt}=-3\sin t+6\cos^2 t\sin t=3\sin t(2\cos^2 t-1)$

$=3\sin t\cdot\cos 2t$ ...(i)

and $\frac{dy}{dt}=3\cos t-6\sin^2 t\cos t$

$=3\cos t(1-2\sin^2 t)$

$=3\cos t\cdot\cos 2t$ ...(ii) [1]

$\therefore \quad \frac{dy}{dx}=\frac{dy/dt}{dx/dt}=\frac{3\cos t\cos 2t}{3\sin t\cos 2t}$

[using Eqs. (i) and (ii)] [1]

$=\cot t$

$\Rightarrow \quad \frac{d^2y}{dx^2}=-\operatorname{cosec}^2 t\cdot\frac{dt}{dx}$

$=-\operatorname{cosec}^2 t\cdot\frac{1}{3\sin t\cos 2t}$ [using Eq. (i)]

$=\frac{-1}{3\sin^3 t\cos 2t}$ [2]

24. Hint $\frac{dx}{d\theta}=3a\sec^2\theta\cdot\sec\theta\tan\theta$

and $\frac{dy}{d\theta}=3a\tan^2\theta\cdot\sec^2\theta$ $\left[\textbf{Ans. } \frac{1}{12a}\right]$

25. Given, $x=a(\cos t+t\sin t)$ and $y=a(\sin t-t\cos t)$

On differentiating x and y w.r.t. t, we get

$\frac{dx}{dt}=a\left[\frac{d}{dt}(\cos t)+\left(t\frac{d}{dt}(\sin t)+\sin t\frac{d}{dt}(t)\right)\right]$

$\left[\because \frac{d}{dx}(u\cdot v)=u\frac{dv}{dx}+v\frac{du}{dx}\right]$

$\therefore \quad \frac{dx}{dt}=a\{-\sin t+(t\cos t+\sin t\cdot 1)\}=at\cos t$ [1]

and $\frac{dy}{dt}=a\left[\frac{d}{dt}(\sin t)-\left(t\frac{d}{dt}(\cos t)+\cos t\frac{d}{dt}(t)\right)\right]$

$\Rightarrow \quad \frac{dy}{dt}=a\{\cos t-t(-\sin t)-\cos t\cdot 1\}=at\sin t$ [1]

Now, $\frac{dy}{dx}=\frac{dy/dt}{dx/dt}$

$=\frac{at\sin t}{at\cos t}=\tan t$ [1/2]

Again, differentiating both sides w.r.t. x, we get

$\frac{d^2y}{dx^2}=\frac{d}{dx}(\tan t)$

$=\frac{d}{dt}(\tan t)\frac{dt}{dx}=\frac{\sec^2 t}{at\cos t}$

$=\frac{1}{at}\sec^3 t$ $\left[\because \frac{dx}{dt}=at\cos t\right]$ [1/2]

At $t=\frac{\pi}{4}$, $\frac{d^2y}{dx^2}=\frac{1}{a\times\frac{\pi}{4}}\sec^3\left(\frac{\pi}{4}\right)$

$=\frac{4}{a\pi}(\sqrt{2})^3=\frac{8\sqrt{2}}{a\pi}$ [1]

Chapter Practice

Multiple Choice Type Questions

(1 Mark)

1 If $x^a y^b = (x+y)^{(a+b)}$, then $\frac{dy}{dx}$ is

(a) xy (b) $\frac{y}{x}$ (c) $\frac{x}{y}$ (d) xy^2

2 The derivative of $\log x$ with respect to $\frac{1}{x}$ is

(a) $\frac{1}{x}$ (b) $\frac{-1}{x^3}$ (c) $\frac{-1}{x}$ (d) $-x$

3 If $y = \log(\sin e^x)$, then $\frac{dy}{dx}$ is

(a) $\cot e^x$ (b) $\operatorname{cosec} e^x$
(c) $e^x \cot e^x$ (d) $e^x \operatorname{cosec} e^x$

4 If $y = x\cos x$, then $\frac{d^2y}{dx^2}$ is

(a) $-x\cos x - 2\sin x$ (b) $x\cos x + 2\sin x$
(c) $x\sin x + \cos x$ (d) None of these

5 If $y^{\frac{1}{m}} + y^{-\frac{1}{m}} = 2x$, then $(x^2-1)\,y_2 + xy_1$ is equal to

(a) $\pm m^2 y$ (b) $m^2 y$ (c) $-m^2 y$ (d) $-my$

Assertion-Reason Type Questions

(1 Mark)*

Directions (Q. Nos. 6-9) *In the questions given below are two statements labelled as Assertion (A) and Reason (R). In the context of the two statements, which one of the following is correct?*

(a) Both A and R are correct; R is the correct explanation of A
(b) Both A and R are correct; R is not the correct explanation of A
(c) A is correct; R is incorrect
(d) R is correct; A is incorrect

6 **Assertion (A)** If $f(x)$ is an odd function, then $f'(x)$ is an even function.

Reason (R) If $u = f(x)$, $v = g(x)$, then the derivative of f with respect to g is $\frac{du}{dv} = \frac{du/dx}{dv/dx}$.

7 **Assertion (A)** If $e^{xy} + \log(xy) + \cos(xy) + 4 = 0$, then $\frac{dy}{dx} = -\frac{y}{x}$.

Reason (R) $\frac{d}{dx}(xy) = 0 \Rightarrow \frac{dy}{dx} = -\frac{y}{x}$

8 **Assertion (A)** If $f(x) = \sqrt{1+\cos^2(x^2)}$, then $f'\left(\frac{\sqrt{\pi}}{2}\right)$ is $\frac{\pi}{3}$.

Reason (R) If $f(x) = e^x$, $g(x) = \sin^{-1} x$ and $h(x) = f(g(x))$, then $\frac{h'(x)}{h(x)}$ is $\frac{1}{\sqrt{1-x^2}}$.

9 **Assertion (A)** If $y = \cos^2 x^2$, then $\frac{dy}{dx} = -4x \cos x^2 \sin x^2$.

Reason (R) For the curve $\sqrt{x} + \sqrt{y} = 1$, $\frac{dy}{dx}$ at $\left(\frac{1}{4}, \frac{1}{4}\right)$ is -1.

Very Short Answer Type Questions

(2 Marks)

10 Find the derivative of $\cos(\sqrt{x})$. **[NCERT]**

11 Differentiate $\sin[\cos(x^2)]$ w.r.t. x. **[NCERT]**

12 Find the derivative of $\log \sin x$ w.r.t. x.

13 Differentiate $e^{\sqrt{x}}$ w.r.t. x.

14 Differentiate $e^{3x} \cdot \cos 2x$ w.r.t. x.

15 Find $\frac{dy}{dx}$, when $2x + 3y = \sin y$.

16 Find the second derivative of $\log x$. **[NCERT]**

17 Find the derivative of $\sin(\tan^{-1} x)$ w.r.t. x.

18 If $x = a\cos\theta$ and $y = b\cos\theta$, then find $\frac{dy}{dx}$. **[NCERT]**

19 Differentiate $x^{\cos x}$ w.r.t. x. **[NCERT]**

Short Answer Type Questions

(4 Marks)

20 If $y = \dfrac{\sin(ax+b)}{\cos(cx+d)}$, then find $\dfrac{dy}{dx}$. [NCERT]

21 Find the derivative of $\dfrac{x+\sin x}{x+\cos x}$ w.r.t. x.

22 Differentiate w.r.t. x, $\sin^{-1}\left[\dfrac{2^{x+1}\cdot 3^x}{1+(36)^x}\right]$.

23 If $y = \tan^{-1}\left(\dfrac{a}{x}\right) + \log\sqrt{\dfrac{x-a}{x+a}}$, then prove that $\dfrac{dy}{dx} = \dfrac{2a^3}{x^4-a^4}$. [NCERT]

24 If $y = (\sin x - \cos x)^{(\sin x - \cos x)}$, $\dfrac{\pi}{4} < x < \dfrac{3\pi}{4}$, then find $\dfrac{dy}{dx}$.

25 Find the derivative of the following function w.r.t. x at $x = 1$.

$$\cos^{-1}\left[\sin\sqrt{\frac{1+x}{2}}\right] + x^x$$

26 Find $\dfrac{dy}{dx}$, if $y = (\cos x)^x + (\sin x)^{1/x}$.

27 If $y = (\sin x)^x + \sin^{-1}\sqrt{x}$, then find $\dfrac{dy}{dx}$.

28 If $y = x^{\sin x - \cos x} + \dfrac{x^2-1}{x^2+1}$, then find $\dfrac{dy}{dx}$.

29 Find $\dfrac{dy}{dx}$, when $y = x^{\cot x} + \dfrac{2x^2-3}{x^2+x+2}$.

30 Differentiate $x^{x\cos x} + \dfrac{x^2+1}{x^2-1}$ w.r.t. x.

31 Find $\dfrac{dy}{dx}$, if $y^x + x^y + x^x = a^b$.

32 If $x = a\left(\dfrac{1+t^2}{1-t^2}\right)$ and $y = \dfrac{2t}{1-t^2}$, then find $\dfrac{dy}{dx}$.

33 If $x = a\left(\cos\theta + \log\tan\dfrac{\theta}{2}\right)$ and $y = a\sin\theta$, then find the value of $\dfrac{dy}{dx}$ at $\theta = \dfrac{\pi}{4}$.

Case-Based Type Question

(6 Marks)

34 Consider function $u = e^x\sin x$ and $v = e^x\cos x$. Answer the following questions.

(i) Find the value of $\dfrac{du}{dx}$.

(ii) Find the value of $\dfrac{du}{dx} + \dfrac{dv}{dx}$.

(iii) Find the value of $v\dfrac{du}{dx} - u\dfrac{dv}{dx}$.

(iv) Find the value of $\dfrac{d^2u}{dx^2}$.

Answers

1. (b) 2. (d) 3. (a) 4. (c) 5. (b) 6. (b) 7. (a) 8. (d)

9. (b) 10. $-\dfrac{\sin\sqrt{x}}{2\sqrt{x}}$ 11. $-2x\cos x(\cos x^2)\sin x^2$ 12. $\cot x$ 13. $\dfrac{e^{\sqrt{x}}}{2\sqrt{x}}$ 14. $e^{3x}(-2\sin 2x + 3\cos 2x)$

15. $\dfrac{2}{\cos y - 3}$ 16. $-\dfrac{1}{x^2}$ 17. $\dfrac{\cos(\tan^{-1}x)}{1+x^2}$ 18. $\dfrac{b}{a}$ 19. $x^{\cos x}\left[\dfrac{\cos x}{x} - (\log x)\sin x\right]$

20. $\dfrac{[a\cos(cx+d)\cos(ax+b) + c\sin(ax+b)\sin(cx+d)]}{\cos^2(cx+d)}$ 21. $\dfrac{x(\cos x+\sin x)+\cos x-\sin x+1}{(x+\cos x)^2}$

22. $\left[\dfrac{2^{x+1}\cdot 3^x}{1+(36)^x}\right]\log 6$ 24. $(\sin x-\cos x)^{(\sin x - \cos x)}\times(\cos x+\sin x)[1+\log(\sin x-\cos x)]$ 25. $\dfrac{3}{4}$

26. $(\cos x)^x[-x\tan x+\log\cos x] + (\sin x)^{1/x}\left[\dfrac{\cot x}{x} - \dfrac{\log(\sin x)}{x^2}\right]$

27. $(\sin x)^x[x\cot x+\log\sin x] + \dfrac{1}{\sqrt{1-x}}\cdot\dfrac{1}{2\sqrt{x}}$ 28. $x^{\sin x-\cos x}\left[\dfrac{\sin x-\cos x}{x} + (\cos x+\sin x)\log x\right] + \dfrac{4x}{(x^2+1)^2}$

29. $x^{\cot x}\left(\dfrac{\cot x}{x} - \operatorname{cosec}^2 x\cdot\log x\right) + \dfrac{2x^2+14x+3}{(x^2+x+2)^2}$ 30. $x^{x\cos x}[\cos x - x\sin x\log x + \cos x\log x] - \dfrac{4x}{(x^2-1)^2}$

31. $\dfrac{-[y^x\log y + y\cdot x^{y-1} + x^x(1+\log x)]}{x\cdot y^{x-1} + x^y\log x}$ 32. $\dfrac{1+t^2}{2at}$ 33. 1 34. (i) $e^x(\sin x+\cos x)$ (ii) $e^x(2\cos x)$ (iii) u^2+v^2 (iv) $2v$

CHAPTER

07

Application of Derivatives

In this chapter, we will study the use of derivatives

(i) to find the equation of tangents and normal to a curve at a point.
(ii) to find approximate value of a certain quantities.
(iii) to determine rate of change of quantities.
(iv) to find interval on which a given function is increasing or decreasing.
(v) to find turning points on the graph of a function which in turn will help us to locate points at which largest or smallest value of a function occurs.
(vi) to find maximum and minimum values of a function.

TOPIC 01 Tangents and Normals

A **tangent** is a straight line, which touches the curve $y = f(x)$ at a point.

A **normal** is a straight line perpendicular to a tangent to the curve $y = f(x)$ intersecting at the point of contact.

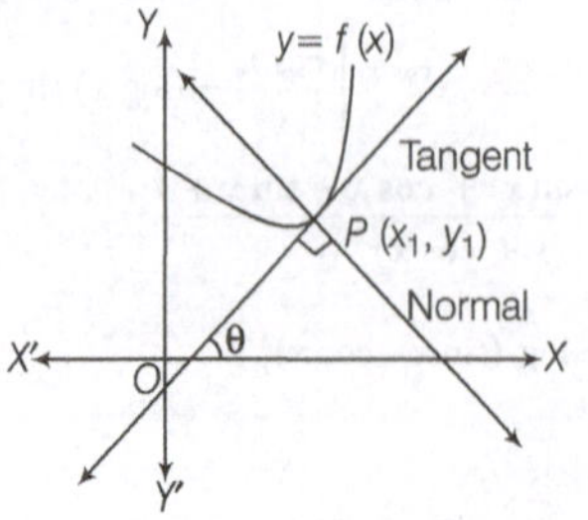

Slope of Tangent and Normal

Suppose the given curve is $y = f(x)$. Then, the slope (or gradient) of tangent to this curve at point (x_1, y_1) is given by $\left(\frac{dy}{dx}\right)_{(x_1, y_1)}$ or $f'(x_1)$.

Also, slope of the normal to the curve (i), i.e. at point (x_1, y_1)

$$= \frac{-1}{\text{slope of tangent}}, \text{ i.e. } \frac{-1}{\left(\frac{dy}{dx}\right)_{(x_1, y_1)}}.$$

Geometrical Interpretation of *dy/dx*

Since, dy/dx represents the slope of the tangent (m) to the continuous curve $y = f(x)$ at any point $P(x_1, y_1)$ on the curve.

Also, from the principles of coordinate geometry, slope of any line (m) is $\tan\theta$. Where θ is the angle made by the line with the positive direction of X-axis.

$\therefore$ Slope of the tangent at point $P(x_1, y_1) = dy/dx = \tan\theta$.

Particular Cases

Case I If slope of the tangent line is zero, i.e. $dy/dx = 0$ $\Rightarrow \tan\theta = 0 \Rightarrow \theta = 0$, then it means the **tangent line** is **parallel to X-axis.**

Case II If $\theta \to \frac{\pi}{2}$, then $\frac{dy}{dx} = \tan\theta \to \infty$, which means the **tangent line is perpendicular to X-axis**, i.e. **parallel to Y-axis.**

Equations of Tangents and Normals

Let $y = f(x)$ be a curve and $P(x_1, y_1)$ be a point on curve. Then, the equations of tangent and normal at P according to slope are given below

(i) **When slope is m**

If the slope of tangent is $m = dy/dx$ at point (x_1, y_1), then

(a) the equation of tangent is $(y - y_1) = m(x - x_1)$.

(b) the equation of normal is $y - y_1 = m_1 (x - x_1)$ where, $m_1 = -1/m$.

(ii) **When slope is zero**

If the slope of tangent is $dy/dx = 0$, i.e. $\theta = 0$, then

(a) the equation of tangent is $y = y_1$.

(b) the equation of normal is $x = x_1$.

(iii) **When slope is tends to infinity.**

If the slope of tangent is $dy/dx \to \infty$, i.e. $\theta \to \pi/2$, then

(a) the equation of tangent is $x = x_1$.

(b) the equation of normal is $y = y_1$.

Different Problems Related to Tangents and Normals

There are many problems related to tangents and normals in which we have to find slope/point/equation of tangent or normal, etc. Some problems with their solving methods are given below

| TYPE I |

Problems Based on Finding the Slope

Suppose a curve $y = f(x)$ is given to us and we have to calculate the slope at a point.

First, we find dy/dx and then put the given point in the value of dy/dx to get the required slope.

Example 1 Find the slope of the tangent and normal to the following curve.

(i) $y = 2x^2 + 3\sin x$ at $x = 0$.

(ii) $y = (\sin 2x + \cot x + 2)^2$ at $x = \frac{\pi}{2}$

Sol. (i) We have, $y = 2x^2 + 3\sin x$

On differentiating both sides w.r.t. x, we get

$$\frac{dy}{dx} = 4x + 3\cos x$$

$$\therefore \text{ Slope of tangent } \left(\frac{dy}{dx}\right)_{\text{at } x=0} = 4 \times 0 + 3\cos 0 = 3$$

$$\therefore \text{ Slope of normal} = -\frac{1}{\left(\frac{dy}{dx}\right)_{\text{at } x=0}} = -\frac{1}{3}$$

(ii) We have, $y = (\sin 2x + \cot x + 2)^2$

On differentiating both sides w.r.t. x, we get

$$\frac{dy}{dx} = 2(\sin 2x + \cot x + 2)\frac{d}{dx}(\sin 2x + \cot x + 2)$$

[by chain rule of derivative]

$$= 2(\sin 2x + \cot x + 2)(2\cos 2x - \operatorname{cosec}^2 x)$$

$$\therefore \left(\frac{dy}{dx}\right)_{\text{at } x=\frac{\pi}{2}} = 2\left[\sin\pi + \cot\frac{\pi}{2} + 2\right]\left[2\cos\pi - \operatorname{cosec}^2\frac{\pi}{2}\right]$$

$$= 2[0 + 0 + 2][-2 - 1] = -12$$

$\therefore$ Slope of tangent $= -12$

$$\text{and slope of normal} = -\frac{1}{\left(\frac{dy}{dx}\right)_{\text{at } x=\frac{\pi}{2}}} = -\frac{1}{-12} = \frac{1}{12}$$

Example 2 The equation of tangent at (2, 3) on the curve $y^2 = px^3 + q$ is $y = 4x - 7$. Find the values of p and q. **[ISC 2020]**

Sol. Given curve

$$y^2 = px^3 + q$$

Since, it passes through (2, 3).

$$\therefore \quad (3)^2 = p(2)^3 + q$$

$$\Rightarrow \quad 8p + q = 9 \quad \text{... (i)}$$

Now, $\quad y^2 = px^3 + q$

$$\Rightarrow \quad 2y\frac{dy}{dx} = 3px^2 \Rightarrow \frac{dy}{dx} = \frac{3px^2}{2y}$$

$$\Rightarrow \left(\frac{dy}{dx}\right)_{(2,3)} = \frac{3p(2)^2}{2(3)} = 2p$$

Equation of tangent of curve $y^2 = px^3 + q$ is

$$y = 4x - 7$$

$$\therefore \quad \frac{dy}{dx} = 4 = 2p$$

$$\Rightarrow \quad p = 2$$

Now, putting the value of p in Eq. (i), we get

$$8(2) + q = 9$$

$$\Rightarrow \quad q = 9 - 16 = -7$$

$$\therefore \quad p = 2 \text{ and } q = -7$$

| TYPE II |

Problems Based on Finding the Point at which Tangent/Normal satisfy the Given Condition

Suppose a curve $y = f(x)$ is given and we have to find that point at which tangent/normal is parallel to axis/chord or tangent passes through origin or equation of tangent is given, etc. First, find the slope of tangent to the given curve at a point, [say (x_1, y_1)] and then put this slope equal to the slope of line/axis given in condition to calculate the value of x_1. Now, find the value of y_1 by using the value of x_1 and given curve. Hence, (x_1, y_1) gives the required point.

Example 3 Find points on the curve $\frac{x^2}{4} + \frac{y^2}{25} = 1$ at which the tangents are **[NCERT]**

(i) parallel to X-axis. (ii) parallel to Y-axis.

Sol. Given curve is $\frac{x^2}{4} + \frac{y^2}{25} = 1$ ...(i)

Let (x_1, y_1) be a point on the given curve.

$$\therefore \quad \frac{x_1^2}{4} + \frac{y_1^2}{25} = 1 \quad \text{...(ii)}$$

On differentiating both sides of Eq. (i) w.r.t. x, we get

$$\frac{2x}{4} + \frac{2y}{25}\frac{dy}{dx} = 0 \Rightarrow \frac{x}{2} + \frac{2y}{25}\frac{dy}{dx} = 0$$

$$\Rightarrow \quad \frac{2y}{25}\frac{dy}{dx} = \frac{-x}{2} \Rightarrow \frac{dy}{dx} = \frac{-25}{2y} \cdot \frac{x}{2}$$

$$\Rightarrow \quad \frac{dy}{dx} = \frac{-25x}{4y}$$

$$\therefore \quad \left(\frac{dy}{dx}\right)_{(x_1, y_1)} = \frac{-25x_1}{4y_1}$$

(i) Now, at point (x_1, y_1), tangent is parallel to X-axis.
So, slope of tangent = 0

$$\therefore \quad \frac{-25x_1}{4y_1} = 0$$

[if a line is parallel to X-axis, then its slope is zero]

$$\Rightarrow \quad -25x_1 = 0 \Rightarrow x_1 = 0$$

On putting $x_1 = 0$ in Eq. (ii), we get

$$\frac{0}{4} + \frac{y_1^2}{25} = 1 \Rightarrow y_1^2 = 25 \Rightarrow y_1 = \pm 5$$

Thus, the points at which the tangent is parallel to the X-axis are (0, 5) and (0, – 5).

(ii) Now, at point (x_1, y_1), tangent is parallel to Y-axis.
We know that, slope of Y-axis $= \infty = 1/0$.
$\therefore$ Slope of tangent = Slope of Y-axis

$$\Rightarrow \quad \frac{-25x_1}{4y_1} = \frac{1}{0} \Rightarrow 4y_1 = 0 \Rightarrow y_1 = 0$$

On putting $y_1 = 0$ in Eq. (ii), we get

$$\frac{x_1^2}{4} + \frac{0}{25} = 1 \Rightarrow x_1^2 = 4 \Rightarrow x_1 = \pm 2$$

Thus, the points at which the tangent is parallel to the Y-axis are (2, 0) and (– 2, 0).

| TYPE III |

Problems Based on Finding the Equation of Tangent and Normal

Suppose a curve $y = f(x)$ is given and we have to find the equation of tangent or normal when point or slope or any other condition is given. Then, we use the following steps

I. First, write the given curve and find $\frac{dy}{dx}$.

II. (i) If point is given at which we have to find tangent/normal, then find slope at this point.

(ii) If point is not given, then we find that point by using given conditions.

(iii) If the slope of tangent line is given, then put $\frac{dy}{dx}$ = slope and find the point.

III. Now, find the required equation of tangent/normal at point (obtained in step II) by using suitable formula. Equation of tangent is $y - y_0 = m(x - x_0)$ and equation of normal is $y - y_0 = m_1(x - x_0)$, where (x_0, y_0) is the point, m and m_1 i.e. $m_1 = -\frac{1}{m}$ are slopes of tangent and normal lines.

Note A tangent line can be drawn to every point of a curve using its gradient value.

Example 4 Find the equations of the tangent and normal to the curve $x^{2/3} + y^{2/3} = 2$ at (1, 1). **[NCERT]**

Sol. Given curve is $x^{2/3} + y^{2/3} = 2$

On differentiating both sides w.r.t. x, we get

$$\frac{2}{3}x^{-1/3} + \frac{2}{3}y^{-1/3}\frac{dy}{dx} = 0 \Rightarrow \frac{1}{x^{1/3}} + \frac{1}{y^{1/3}}\frac{dy}{dx} = 0$$

$$\Rightarrow \frac{dy}{dx} = -\frac{y^{1/3}}{x^{1/3}} \Rightarrow \frac{dy}{dx} = -\left(\frac{y}{x}\right)^{1/3}$$

At point (1, 1), slope of tangent,

$$m = \left(\frac{dy}{dx}\right)_{(1,1)} = -\left(\frac{1}{1}\right)^{1/3} = -1$$

and slope of normal, $m_1 = \dfrac{-1}{\left(\frac{dy}{dx}\right)_{(1,1)}} = \dfrac{-1}{-1} = 1$

Now, the equation of tangent at (1, 1) is

$$y - 1 = -1(x - 1) \quad [\because y - y_1 = m(x - x_1)]$$

$$\Rightarrow y - 1 = -x + 1 \Rightarrow y + x - 2 = 0$$

and equation of normal at (1, 1) is

$$y - 1 = 1(x - 1) \quad [\because y - y_1 = m_1(x - x_1)]$$

$$\Rightarrow y - 1 = x - 1 \Rightarrow y - x = 0$$

Hence, the required equation of tangent and normal are $y + x - 2 = 0$ and $y - x = 0$, respectively.

Example 5 The tangent to the curve $y = 2x^2 - 7x + 3$ at certain point is parallel to the straight line $y = x + 2$. Find the equation of this tangent and the point, where it cuts Y-axis.

Sol. Given equation of curve is $y = 2x^2 - 7x + 3$ ...(i)

On differentiating both sides w.r.t. x, we get

$$\frac{dy}{dx} = 4x - 7$$

Slope of tangent, $m_1 = 4x - 7$

and given equation of line is $y = x + 2$

On comparing with $y = m_2x + c$, we get $m_2 = 1$

Since, the tangent is parallel to the line.

$$\therefore \quad m_1 = m_2 \Rightarrow 4x - 7 = 1$$

$$\Rightarrow \quad 4x = 8 \Rightarrow x = 2$$

On substituting the value $x = 2$ in Eq. (i), we get

$$y = 2(2)^2 - 7(2) + 3 = 8 - 14 + 3 = -3$$

$\therefore$ Point on curve $(x_1, y_1) = (2, -3)$

Now, equation of tangent at (x_1, y_1) i.e. $(2, -3)$ is

$$y + 3 = 1(x - 2) \quad [\because y - y_1 = m_1(x - x_1)]$$

$$\Rightarrow \quad x - y = 5 \quad \text{...(ii)}$$

Also, the tangent cut Y-axis, so put $x = 0$ in Eq. (ii), we get

$$0 - y = 5 \Rightarrow y = -5$$

Hence, the required equation of tangent is $x - y = 5$ and the point, where it cuts the Y-axis is $(0, -5)$.

Note If two lines are parallel and their slopes are m_1 and m_2 respectively, then $m_1 = m_2$.

Angle between Intersection of Two Curves

Angle between the intersection of two curves is equal to an angle between their tangents at the point of intersection.

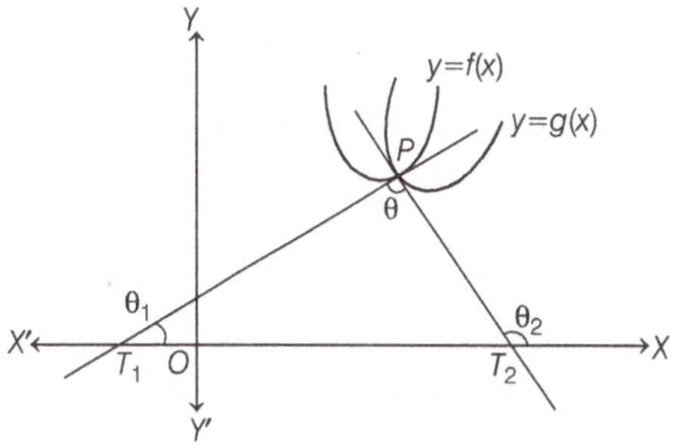

Let $y = f(x)$ and $y = g(x)$ be two curves and let PT_1 and PT_2 be two tangents at their point of intersection (P). Let slope of tangents of two curves at any point P are m_1, m_2 and θ be the angle between the two curves at any point P. Then, the angle between two curves is given by

$$\tan\theta = \left|\frac{m_1 - m_2}{1 - m_1 m_2}\right|$$

(i) Tangents are parallel, if $m_1 = m_2$.

(ii) Tangents are perpendicular (orthogonally), if $m_1 m_2 = -1$.

Note Angle between intersection of the curves is defined as acute angle between their tangents.

Example 6 Prove that the curve $x = y^2$ and $xy = k$ cuts at right angles, if $8k^2 = 1$. **[NCERT]**

Sol. Given curves are $x = y^2$ ...(i)

and $xy = k$ ...(ii)

On putting the value of x from Eq. (i) in Eq. (ii), we get

$$y^2 \cdot y = k \Rightarrow y^3 = k$$

$$\Rightarrow \quad y = (k)^{1/3}$$

On putting the value of y in Eq. (i), we get

$$x = (k^{1/3})^2 = k^{2/3}$$

$\therefore$ Point of intersection is $(k^{2/3}, k^{1/3})$.

On differentiating both sides of Eq. (i) w.r.t. x, we get

$$1 = 2y\frac{dy}{dx} \Rightarrow \frac{dy}{dx} = \frac{1}{2y}$$

Then, m_1 = Slope of tangent at $(k^{2/3}, k^{1/3})$

$$= \left[\frac{dy}{dx}\right]_{(k^{2/3}, k^{1/3})} = \frac{1}{2k^{1/3}}$$

On differentiating both sides of Eq. (ii) w.r.t. x, we get

$$x\frac{dy}{dx} + y \cdot 1 = 0$$

$$\Rightarrow \quad \frac{dy}{dx} = \frac{-y}{x}$$

Then, m_2 = Slope of tangent at $(k^{2/3}, k^{1/3})$

$$= -\frac{k^{1/3}}{k^{2/3}} = -\frac{1}{k^{1/3}}$$

Since, the curves (i) and (ii) cut at right angles.

$$\therefore \quad m_1 m_2 = -1$$

$$\Rightarrow \quad \frac{1}{2k^{1/3}}\left(-\frac{1}{k^{1/3}}\right) = -1$$

$$\Rightarrow \quad 2k^{2/3} = 1$$

$$\Rightarrow \quad (2k^{2/3})^3 = 1 \quad \text{[cubing on both sides]}$$

$$\therefore \quad 8k^2 = 1$$

Hence proved.

Topic Practice 1

Very Short Answer Type Questions

2 Marks

1 (i) Find the slope of the tangent to the curve $y = x^3 - 3x + 2$ at the point, whose x-coordinate is 3. **[NCERT]**

(ii) Write the equation of tangent drawn to the curve $y = \sin x$ at the point (0, 0).

2 Find the slope of the normal to the curve $x = a\cos^3\theta$ and $y = a\sin^3\theta$ at $\theta = \frac{\pi}{4}$. **[NCERT]**

3 Find the point at which the tangent to the curve $y = \sqrt{4x-3} - 1$ has its slope $\frac{2}{3}$. **[NCERT]**

4 Find the equations of all lines having slope 0, which are tangent to the curve $y = \frac{1}{x^2 - 2x + 3}$. **[NCERT]**

5 Find the equation of normal at the point (am^2, am^3) for the curve $ay^2 = x^3$. **[NCERT]**

Short Answer Type Questions

4 Marks

6 Find the equation of tangent to the curve $4x^2 + 9y^2 = 36$ at the point $(3\cos\theta, 2\sin\theta)$.

7 Find points on the curve $\frac{x^2}{9} + \frac{y^2}{16} = 1$ at which the tangents are

(i) parallel to X-axis.

(ii) parallel to Y-axis. **[NCERT]**

8 Find a point on the curve $y = (x-2)^2$ at which the tangent is parallel to the chord joining the points (2, 0) and (4, 4). **[ISC 2024]**

9 Find the points on the curve $4x^2 + 9y^2 = 1$, where the tangents are perpendicular to the line $2y + x = 0$.

10 Find the equation of the tangent and normal to the curve $\frac{x^2}{a^2} - \frac{y^2}{b^2} = 1$ at the point $(\sqrt{2}a, b)$.

11 The equation of tangent at (2, 3) on the curve $y^2 = ax^3 + b$ is $y = 4x - 5$. Find the values of a and b.

12 Find the equations of the normal to the curve $y = x^3 + 2x + 6$, which are parallel to line $x + 14y + 4 = 0$. **[NCERT]**

13 Find the equations of the tangent to the curve $y = x^2 - 2x + 7$, which is

(i) parallel to the line $2x - y + 9 = 0$.

(ii) perpendicular to the line $5y - 15x = 13$.

14 Find the equations of the tangent and the normal to the curve $y = \frac{x-7}{(x-2)(x-3)}$ at the point, where it cuts the X-axis. **[NCERT]**

15 Find the equation of tangents to the curve $y = (x^2 - 1)(x - 1)$ at the points, where the curve cuts the X-axis.

16 Find the equation of the normal to the curve $y = e^{2x} + x^2$ at $x = 0$. Also, find the distance from origin to the line.

17 For the curve $y = 4x^3 - 2x^5$, find all the points on the curve at which the tangent passes through the origin.

Long Answer Type Questions

6 Marks

18 Find the coordinates of the point on the curve $\sqrt{x} + \sqrt{y} = 4$ at which tangent is equally inclined to the axes. **[NCERT Exemplar]**

19 Find the point on the curve $9y^2 = x^3$, where the normal to the curve makes equal intercepts on the axes.

20 Find the equation of tangent to the curve $x = a\cos\theta + a\theta\sin\theta$, $y = a\sin\theta - a\theta\cos\theta$ at any point θ of the curve. Also, show that at any point θ of the curve the normal is at a constant distance from origin.

21 Find the equation of the normal at a point on the curve $x^2 = 4y$, which passes through the point (1, 2). Also, find the equation of the corresponding tangent.

Hints & Solutions

1. (i) Given curve is $y = x^3 - 3x + 2$

On differentiating both sides w.r.t. x, we get

$$\frac{dy}{dx} = 3x^2 - 3$$

Now, at $x = 3$,

$$m = \left(\frac{dy}{dx}\right)_{x=3} = 3(3)^2 - 3 = 27 - 3 = 24$$

Hence, the required slope of the tangent is 24. [1]

(ii) Given, $y = \sin x$

Here, $\frac{dy}{dx} = \cos x$

$\therefore$ Slope of tangent at $(0, 0) = 1$

Hence, the equation of tangent is $y = x$. [1]

2. Given, $x = a\cos^3\theta$ and $y = a\sin^3\theta$

On differentiating both sides w.r.t. θ, we get

$$\frac{dx}{d\theta} = 3a\cos^2\theta \frac{d}{d\theta}(\cos\theta)$$

[by chain rule of derivative]

$$= 3a\cos^2\theta(-\sin\theta) = -3a\sin\theta\cos^2\theta$$

and $\frac{dy}{d\theta} = 3a\sin^2\theta \frac{d}{d\theta}(\sin\theta) = 3a\sin^2\theta\cos\theta$ [1]

[by chain rule of derivative]

Then, $\frac{dy}{dx} = \frac{dy/d\theta}{dx/d\theta} = \frac{3a\sin^2\theta\cos\theta}{-3a\sin\theta\cos^2\theta} = -\tan\theta$

Now, at $\theta = \frac{\pi}{4}$,

Slope of normal $= \frac{-1}{\left(\frac{dy}{dx}\right)_{\theta=\frac{\pi}{4}}} = \frac{-1}{-\tan\frac{\pi}{4}} = 1$ [1]

3. **Hint** Put $\frac{dy}{dx} = \frac{2}{3}$ [**Ans.** (3, 2)]

4. **Hint** Put $\frac{dy}{dx} = 0$ and get the point, then find the equation of tangent. $\left[\textbf{Ans. } y = \frac{1}{2}\right]$

5. Similar as Example 4.
[**Ans.** $2x + 3my - am^2(3m^2 + 2) = 0$]

6. Similar as Example 4. [**Ans.** $2x\cos\theta + 3y\sin\theta - 6 = 0$]

7. Given curve is $\frac{x^2}{9} + \frac{y^2}{16} = 1$ ...(i)

On differentiating both sides w.r.t. x, we get

$$\frac{2x}{9} + \frac{2y}{16}\frac{dy}{dx} = 0$$

$\Rightarrow$ $\frac{2y}{16}\frac{dy}{dx} = \frac{-2x}{9} \Rightarrow \frac{dy}{dx} = \frac{-16x}{9y}$ [1]

(i) Since, the tangents are parallel to X-axis.

$\therefore$ $\frac{dy}{dx} = 0 \Rightarrow \frac{-16x}{9y} = 0 \Rightarrow x = 0$ [1/2]

On putting $x = 0$ in Eq. (i), we get

$$0 + \frac{y^2}{16} = 1 \Rightarrow y^2 = 16 \Rightarrow y = \pm 4$$

Hence, the required points are (0, 4) and (0, −4). [1]

(ii) Since, the tangents are parallel to Y-axis.

$\therefore$ $\frac{dx}{dy} = 0 \Rightarrow \frac{9y}{-16x} = 0 \Rightarrow y = 0$ [1/2]

On putting $y = 0$ in Eq. (i), we get

$$\frac{x^2}{9} + 0 = 1 \Rightarrow x^2 = 9 \Rightarrow x = \pm 3$$

Hence, required points are (3, 0) and (− 3, 0). [1]

8. Given curve is $y = (x - 2)^2$ ...(i)

On differentiating both sides w.r.t. x, we get

$\frac{dy}{dx} = 2(x - 2)$ [1]

Slope of the chord joining the points (2, 0) and (4, 4)

$= \frac{4-0}{4-2} = \frac{4}{2} = 2$ $\left[\because \text{slope} = \frac{y_2 - y_1}{x_2 - x_1}\right]$ ...(ii) [1]

According to the question, the tangent is parallel to the chord joining the points.

$\therefore$ $\frac{dy}{dx}$ = Slope of the chords [1]

$\Rightarrow \quad 2(x-2)=2 \Rightarrow x-2=1 \Rightarrow x=3$

On putting $x=3$ in Eq. (i), we get

$$y=(3-2)^2=1$$

Hence, the required point is (3, 1). [1]

9. Given curve is $4x^2+9y^2=1$. ...(i)

On differentiating both sides w.r.t. x, we get

$$8x+18y\frac{dy}{dx}=0 \Rightarrow 18y\frac{dy}{dx}=-8x$$

$$\Rightarrow \frac{dy}{dx}=\frac{-8x}{18y} \Rightarrow \frac{dy}{dx}=\frac{-4x}{9y}$$

Slope of the tangent at (x, y), $m_1=\frac{-4x}{9y}$ [1]

Also, given line is $2y+x=0$. ...(ii)

Slope of line, $m_2=-\frac{1}{2}$ $\left[\because m_2=-\frac{\text{Coefficient of } x}{\text{Coefficient of } y}\right]$

Since, tangent at (x, y) is perpendicular to the line (ii).

$$\therefore \quad m_1\cdot m_2=-1 \Rightarrow \frac{-4x}{9y}\times\left(-\frac{1}{2}\right)=-1$$

$$\Rightarrow \quad 2x=-9y \Rightarrow y=\frac{-2x}{9} \quad \text{...(iii) [1]}$$

On putting the value of y in Eq. (i), we get

$$4x^2+9\left(\frac{-2x}{9}\right)^2=1 \Rightarrow 4x^2+9\left(\frac{4x^2}{81}\right)=1$$

$$\Rightarrow \quad 4x^2+\frac{4x^2}{9}=1 \Rightarrow \frac{40}{9}x^2=1$$

$$\Rightarrow \quad x^2=\frac{9}{40} \Rightarrow x=\pm\frac{3}{2\sqrt{10}} \quad [1]$$

When $x=\frac{3}{2\sqrt{10}}$, then from Eq. (iii), we get

$$y=\frac{-2x}{9}=\frac{-2}{9}\times\frac{3}{2\sqrt{10}}=\frac{-1}{3\sqrt{10}}$$

When $x=-\frac{3}{2\sqrt{10}}$, then from Eq. (iii), we get

$$y=\frac{-2}{9}\times\frac{-3}{2\sqrt{10}}=\frac{1}{3\sqrt{10}}$$

Hence, the required points are $\left(\frac{3}{2\sqrt{10}}, \frac{-1}{3\sqrt{10}}\right)$ and $\left(\frac{-3}{2\sqrt{10}}, \frac{1}{3\sqrt{10}}\right)$. [1]

10. Given equation of curve is $\frac{x^2}{a^2}-\frac{y^2}{b^2}=1$

On differentiating both sides w.r.t. x, we get

$$\frac{2x}{a^2}-\frac{2y}{b^2}\frac{dy}{dx}=0 \Rightarrow \frac{dy}{dx}=\frac{b^2x}{a^2y}$$

$\therefore$ Slope of the tangent at point $(\sqrt{2}a, b)$

$$=\left(\frac{dy}{dx}\right)_{(\sqrt{2}a,\, b)}=\frac{\sqrt{2}ab^2}{ba^2}=\frac{\sqrt{2}b}{a} \quad [1]$$

Hence, the required equation of the tangent at point $(\sqrt{2}a, b)$ is

$$y-b=\frac{\sqrt{2}b}{a}(x-\sqrt{2}a)$$

$$\Rightarrow \quad a(y-b)=\sqrt{2}b(x-\sqrt{2}a)$$

$$\Rightarrow \quad ay-ab=\sqrt{2}bx-2ab$$

$$\Rightarrow \sqrt{2}bx-ay-ab=0 \quad [1]$$

Now, slope of the normal at point $(\sqrt{2}a, b)$

$$=\frac{-1}{\text{Slope of tangent}}=-\frac{a}{\sqrt{2}b} \quad [1]$$

Hence, the required equation of the normal at point $(\sqrt{2}a, b)$ is

$$(y-b)=-\frac{a}{\sqrt{2}b}(x-\sqrt{2}a)$$

$$\Rightarrow \quad \sqrt{2}b(y-b)=-a(x-\sqrt{2}a)$$

$$\Rightarrow \sqrt{2}by-\sqrt{2}b^2=-ax+\sqrt{2}a^2$$

$$\Rightarrow \quad ax+\sqrt{2}by-\sqrt{2}(a^2+b^2)=0 \quad [1]$$

11. Given equation of curve is $y^2=ax^3+b$.

On differentiating both sides w.r.t. x, we get

$$2y\frac{dy}{dx}=3ax^2 \Rightarrow \frac{dy}{dx}=\frac{3ax^2}{2y}$$

$$\Rightarrow \text{Slope of tangent at (2, 3)}=\frac{3a(2)^2}{2(3)}=2a \quad \text{...(i) [1]}$$

Since, equation of tangent to the curve is $y=4x-5$

$\therefore$ Slope of tangent $=4$ ...(ii)

From Eqs. (i) and (ii), we get

$$2a=4 \Rightarrow a=2 \quad [1]$$

Now, as the curve passes through the point (2, 3), therefore we get [1]

$$9=8a+b \Rightarrow b=9-8a$$

$$\Rightarrow \quad b=9-16 \Rightarrow b=-7$$

Hence, the required value of a and b are 2 and -7 respectively. [1]

12. Given equation of curve is

$$y=x^3+2x+6 \quad \text{...(i)}$$

and equation of line is

$$x+14y+4=0 \quad \text{...(ii)}$$

On differentiating both sides of Eq. (i) w.r.t. x, we get

$$\frac{dy}{dx}=3x^2+2$$

$$\therefore \text{Slope of normal}=\frac{-1}{\left(\frac{dy}{dx}\right)}=\frac{-1}{3x^2+2} \quad [1]$$

Also, slope of the line $x+14y+4=0$ is $-\frac{1}{14}$.

$\left[\because \text{slope of the line } Ax+By+C=0 \text{ is } \left(-\frac{A}{B}\right)\right]$

Since, the normal to the curve is parallel to the line.

$\therefore$ Slope of line = Slope of normal

$$\Rightarrow \quad \frac{-1}{14}=\frac{-1}{3x^2+2} \Rightarrow 3x^2+2=14$$

$\Rightarrow \quad 3x^2 = 12 \Rightarrow x^2 = 4 \Rightarrow x = \pm 2$ [1/2]

From Eq. (i), at $x = 2$, we get

$$y = (2)^3 + 2(2) + 6 = 8 + 4 + 6 = 18$$

and at $x = -2$, we get

$$y = (-2)^3 + 2(-2) + 6 = -8 - 4 + 6 = -6$$ [1/2]

$\therefore$ Normal passes through the points $(2, 18)$ and $(-2, -6)$.

Also, slope of normal $= \frac{-1}{14}$

Hence, equation of normal at point $(2, 18)$ is

$$y - y_1 = \text{Slope of normal} \times (x - x_1)$$

$$\Rightarrow \quad y - 18 = \frac{-1}{14}(x - 2)$$

$$\Rightarrow \quad 14y - 252 = -x + 2 \Rightarrow x + 14y = 254$$ [1]

and equation of normal at point $(-2, -6)$ is

$$y + 6 = -\frac{1}{14}(x + 2)$$

$$\Rightarrow \quad 14y + 84 = -x - 2 \Rightarrow x + 14y = -86$$

Hence, the two equations of normal are $x + 14y = 254$ and $x + 14y = -86$. [1]

13. Given equation of curve is $y = x^2 - 2x + 7$ ...(i)

On differentiating both sides w.r.t. x, we get

$$\frac{dy}{dx} = 2x - 2$$

(i) The equation of the given line is $2x - y + 9 = 0$.

$\Rightarrow \quad y = 2x + 9$

which is in the form of $y = mx + c$.

$\therefore$ Slope of the line is $m = 2$.

If a tangent is parallel to the line, then slope of tangent is equal to the slope of the line.

$$\therefore \quad \frac{dy}{dx} = m \Rightarrow 2x - 2 = 2 \Rightarrow x = 2$$

When $x = 2$, then from Eq. (i), we get

$$y = 2^2 - 2 \times 2 + 7 \Rightarrow y = 7$$ [1]

The point on the given curve at which tangent is parallel to given line is $(2, 7)$ and the equation of the tangent is

$$y - 7 = 2(x - 2) \Rightarrow y - 2x - 3 = 0$$

Hence, the equation of the tangent line to the given curve which is parallel to line $2x - y + 9 = 0$ is $y - 2x - 3 = 0$. [1]

(ii) The equation of the given line is $5y - 15x = 13$

$$\Rightarrow \quad y = \frac{15x + 13}{5} = 3x + \frac{13}{5}$$

which is in the form of $y = mx + c$.

$\therefore$ Slope of the given line is $m = 3$.

If a tangent is perpendicular to the line $5y - 15x = 13$

Then, the slope of the tangent $= \frac{-1}{m} = -\frac{1}{3}$

$$\Rightarrow \quad \frac{dy}{dx} = -\frac{1}{3} \Rightarrow 2x - 2 = \frac{-1}{3} \Rightarrow x = \frac{5}{6}$$

When $x = \frac{5}{6}$, then from Eq. (i), we get

$$y = \left(\frac{5}{6}\right)^2 - 2\left(\frac{5}{6}\right) + 7 \Rightarrow y = \frac{217}{36}$$ [1]

$\therefore$ The point on the given curve at which tangent is perpendicular to the given line is $\left(\frac{5}{6}, \frac{217}{36}\right)$ and the equation of the tangent is

$$y - \frac{217}{36} = \frac{-1}{3}\left(x - \frac{5}{6}\right) \Rightarrow \frac{36y - 217}{36} = \frac{-x}{3} + \frac{5}{18}$$

$$\Rightarrow \quad 12x + 36y - 227 = 0$$

Hence, the equation of the tangent line to the given curve which is perpendicular to the line $5y - 15x = 13$ is $36y + 12x - 227 = 0$. [1]

14. **Hint** Put $y = 0$, we get $x = 7$. Then, find the equation of tangent and normal at point $(7, 0)$.

[**Ans.** Equation of tangent is $x - 20y - 7 = 0$. Equation of normal is $20x + y - 140 = 0$]

15. **Hint** Put $y = 0$, we get $x = 1$ and -1.

Then, find the equation of tangents at $(1, 0)$ and $(-1, 0)$.

[**Ans.** $y = 0$ and $4x - y + 4 = 0$]

16. Given equation of curve is $y = e^{2x} + x^2$ ....(i)

Then, at $x = 0$, $y = e^0 + 0 = 1$ [1/2]

On differentiating both sides of Eq. (i) w.r.t. x, we get

$$\frac{dy}{dx} = 2e^{2x} + 2x$$ [1/2]

Now, slope of normal at point $(0, 1) = -\frac{1}{\left(\frac{dy}{dx}\right)_{(0,1)}}$

$$= -\frac{1}{2e^{2\times 0} + 2 \times 0} = -\frac{1}{2 \times 1 + 0} = -\frac{1}{2}$$ [1]

$\therefore$ Equation of normal at point $(0, 1)$ is

$$y - 1 = -\frac{1}{2}(x - 0) \Rightarrow y - 1 = -\frac{x}{2} \Rightarrow 2y + x - 2 = 0$$

which is the required equation of normal. [1]

Now, required distance

= Perpendicular distance from $(0, 0)$ to the above line

$$= \frac{|2 \times 0 + 0 - 2|}{\sqrt{(2)^2 + (1)^2}}$$

$\left[\because \text{perpendicular distance from } x_1, y_1 \quad \frac{ax \quad by \quad c}{\sqrt{a^2 + b^2}}\right]$

$$= \frac{|-2|}{\sqrt{4 + 1}} = \frac{2}{\sqrt{5}}$$ [1]

17. **Hint** $\frac{dy}{dx} = 12x^2 - 10x^4$

Equation of tangent at (x_1, y_1) is

$$y - y_1 = (12x_1^2 - 10x_1^4)(x - x_1)$$

$\Rightarrow y - (4x_1^3 - 2x_1^5) = (12x_1^2 - 10x_1^4)(x - x_1)$ passes through the point $(0, 0)$

$$\Rightarrow 0 - (4x_1^3 - 2x_1^5) = (12x_1^2 - 10x_1^4)(0 - x_1)$$

$$\Rightarrow \quad x_1 = 0, x_1 = \pm 1$$

[**Ans.** $(0, 0)$, $(1, 2)$ and $(-1, -2)$]

18. **Hint** For equally inclined, consider $\frac{dy}{dx} = \pm 1$. [**Ans.** (4,4)]

19. Given curve is $9y^2 = x^3$ ...(i)

On differentiating both sides w.r.t. x, we get

$$9 \times 2y\frac{dy}{dx} = 3x^2 \Rightarrow \frac{dy}{dx} = \frac{3x^2}{18y} = \frac{x^2}{6y}$$

Let (x_1, y_1) be the required point on the curve (i).

$\therefore$ Slope of tangent to the curve (i) at point (x_1, y_1),

$$\frac{dy}{dx} = \frac{x_1^2}{6y_1}$$ [1]

$\Rightarrow$ Slope of normal to the curve (i) at point (x_1, y_1)

$$= -\frac{1}{dy/dx} = \frac{-6y_1}{x_1^2} \quad ...(ii)$$

Since, normal makes equal intercept on the axes.

$\therefore$ Slope of normal $= \tan\frac{\pi}{4}$ or $\tan\frac{3\pi}{4} = \pm 1$ [1]

Hence, $\frac{-6y_1}{x_1^2} = \pm 1$ [from Eq. (ii)]

$\Rightarrow \quad y_1 = \pm\frac{x_1^2}{6}$

Again, the point (x_1, y_1) lies on curve (i). ...(iii)

$\therefore \quad 9y_1^2 = x_1^3$

$\Rightarrow \quad 9\left(\pm\frac{x_1^2}{6}\right)^2 = x_1^3$ [using Eq. (iii)] [1]

$\Rightarrow \quad \frac{9x_1^4}{36} = x_1^3 \Rightarrow \frac{x_1}{4} = 1 \Rightarrow x_1 = 4$

$\therefore \quad y_1 = \pm\frac{x_1^2}{6} = \pm\frac{16}{6} = \pm\frac{8}{3}$

Hence, the required points are $\left(4, \frac{8}{3}\right)$ and $\left(4, \frac{-8}{3}\right)$. [1]

20. Given equation of curve is

$$x = a\cos\theta + a\theta\sin\theta,\ y = a\sin\theta - a\theta\cos\theta$$

Now, $\frac{dx}{d\theta} = -a\sin\theta + a\sin\theta + a\theta\cos\theta = a\theta\cos\theta$

and $\frac{dy}{d\theta} = a\cos\theta - a\cos\theta + a\theta\sin\theta = a\theta\sin\theta$ [1]

$\Rightarrow \frac{dy}{dx} = \frac{a\theta\sin\theta}{a\theta\cos\theta} = \tan\theta$

$\therefore$ Equation of tangent at any point θ is

$y - (a\sin\theta - a\theta\cos\theta)$

$= \tan\theta\,[x - (a\cos\theta + a\theta\sin\theta)]$ [1]

$\Rightarrow y\cos\theta - \cos\theta(a\sin\theta - a\theta\cos\theta)$

$= \sin\theta(x - a\cos\theta - a\theta\sin\theta)$

$\Rightarrow y\cos\theta - a\cos\theta\sin\theta + a\theta\cos^2\theta$

$= x\sin\theta - a\sin\theta\cos\theta - a\theta\sin^2\theta$

$\Rightarrow x\sin\theta - y\cos\theta = a\theta(\sin^2\theta + \cos^2\theta)$

$\Rightarrow x\sin\theta - y\cos\theta = a\theta$ [1]

and equation of normal at any point θ is

$y - (a\sin\theta - a\theta\cos\theta)$

$= -\cot\theta\,[x - (a\cos\theta + a\theta\sin\theta)]$

$\Rightarrow y - a\sin\theta + a\theta\cos\theta$

$= -\frac{\cos\theta}{\sin\theta}[x - a\cos\theta - a\theta\sin\theta]$ [1]

$\Rightarrow y\sin\theta - a\sin^2\theta + a\theta\sin\theta\cos\theta$

$= -x\cos\theta + a\cos^2\theta + a\theta\sin\theta\cos\theta$

$\Rightarrow y\sin\theta + x\cos\theta = a$ [1]

Now, distance of normal from origin

$$= \frac{|0\cdot\sin\theta + 0\cdot\cos\theta - a|}{\sqrt{\sin^2\theta + \cos^2\theta}} = |a| = \text{Constant}$$

Hence proved. [1]

21. Given curve is $x^2 = 4y$

On differentiating both sides w.r.t. x, we get

$$2x = 4\frac{dy}{dx} \Rightarrow \frac{dy}{dx} = \frac{x}{2}$$ [1]

Let (h, k) be the coordinates of the point of contact of the normal to the curve $x^2 = 4y$.

Now, slope of the tangent at (h, k) is given by

$$\left[\frac{dy}{dx}\right]_{(h,k)} = \frac{h}{2}$$ [1]

Therefore, slope of the normal at $(h, k) = \frac{-2}{h}$

$\left[\because \text{slope of normal} = \frac{-1}{\text{slope of tangent}}\right]$

Now, the equation of normal at (h, k) is

$$y - k = \frac{-2}{h}(x - h) \quad ...(i)$$ [1]

$\left[\because \text{equation of normal in slope form is } y - y_1 = -\frac{1}{m}(x - x_1)\right]$

Since, the normal passes through the point (1, 2), So putting $x = 1$, $y = 2$ in Eq. (i), we get

$$2 - k = \frac{-2}{h}(1 - h) \Rightarrow k = 2 + \frac{2}{h}(1 - h) \quad ...(ii)$$ [1]

Also, (h, k) lies on the curve $x^2 = 4y$.

$\therefore \quad h^2 = 4k$ ...(iii)

On solving Eqs. (ii) and (iii), we get $h = 2$ and $k = 1$.

On substituting the values of h and k in Eq. (i), we get

$$y - 1 = \frac{-2}{2}(x - 2) \Rightarrow x + y = 3$$

which is the required equation of normal. [1]

Now, the equation of tangent at (h, k) is

$$y - k = \frac{h}{2}(x - h)$$

On putting $h = 2$ and $k = 1$, we get

$$y - 1 = \frac{2}{2}(x - 2) \Rightarrow y - 1 = x - 2 \Rightarrow y = x - 1$$

which is the required equation of tangent. [1]

TOPIC 02 Rate of Change of Quantities (Rate Measure)

By the derivative ds/dt, we mean the rate of change of distance s with respect to time t. Here, s is dependent quantity and t is independent quantity. So, we can say that the rate of change of a quantity is the derivative of this dependent quantity with respect to that quantity at which it depends.

Suppose one quantity y (dependent quantity) varies with another quantity, say x (independent) satisfying some rule $y = f(x)$, then $\frac{dy}{dx}$ **or** $f'(x)$ **represents the rate of change of** y **with respect to** x.

Rate of Change of a Quantity at a Point

Suppose quantity y varies with another quantity x, then rate of change of y with respect to x at point $x = x_0$ is given by $\left(\frac{dy}{dx}\right)_{x=x_0}$ or $f'(x_0)$, i.e. firstly, find the derivative of y with respect to x and then put x_0 in place of x in $\frac{dy}{dx}$.

Rate of Change of Two Variables

Suppose two variables are varying with respect to another variable t, i.e. $y = f(t)$ and $x = g(t)$. Then, rate of change of y with respect to x is given by

$$\frac{dy}{dx} = \frac{dy/dt}{dx/dt}, \text{ provided that } \frac{dx}{dt} \neq 0 \text{ or } \frac{dy}{dx} = \frac{dy}{dt} \cdot \frac{dt}{dx}.$$

[by chain rule of derivative]

Thus, the rate of change of y with respect to x can be calculated using the rate of change of y and that of x both with respect to t.

Another method by chain rule, $\frac{dy}{dx} = \frac{dy/dt}{dx/dt}$

$$\Rightarrow \quad \frac{dy}{dt} = \frac{dy}{dx} \cdot \frac{dx}{dt}$$

$\Rightarrow$ **Rate of change of** $y = \frac{dy}{dx} \times$ **Rate of change of** x.

Note

(i) The term 'rate of change' means the instantaneous rate of change.

(ii) $\frac{dy}{dx}$ is positive, if y increases as x increases and is negative, if y decreases as x increases.

(iii) For rate of change of shadow, use the concept of similar triangles to establish the relationship between the variables.

Method of Finding the Rate of Change

To find the rate of change, we generally use the following steps

I. First, identify the quantity for which we have to find rate of change, i.e. dependent quantity, generally this quantity is given as area or volume of geometrical figure, etc.

II. Identify that quantity at which quantity obtained in step I is depend, i.e. independent quantity as radius, side, etc.

III. Differentiate the quantity obtained in step I with respect to quantity obtained in step II and find required rate of change.

IV. If we have to calculate rate of change at a particular value of quantity obtained in step II, then put that particular value in rate of change obtained in step III and get required answer.

Note Sometimes, rate of change of independent quantity is given, then we find the rate of change of dependent quantity with respect to that quantity at which independent quantity depend.

Some Useful Results

(i) Area of a square $= x^2$ and perimeter $= 4x$ where, x is the side of the square.

(ii) Area of a rectangle $= xy$ and perimeter $= 2(x + y)$ where, x and y are length and breadth of rectangle.

(iii) Area of a trapezium $= \frac{1}{2} \times$ Sum of parallel sides $\times$ Perpendicular distance between them

(iv) Area of a circle $= \pi r^2$ and circumference of a circle $= 2\pi r$ where, r is the radius of a circle.

(v) Volume of a sphere $= \frac{4}{3}\pi r^3$ and surface area $= 4\pi r^2$ where, r is the radius of sphere.

(vi) Total surface area of a right circular cylinder $= 2\pi rh + 2\pi r^2$. Curved surface area of a right circular cylinder $= 2\pi rh$ and volume $= \pi r^2 h$, where r is the radius and h is the height of the cylinder.

(vii) Volume of a right circular cone $= \frac{1}{3}\pi r^2 h$

Curved surface area $= \pi rl$

and total surface area $= \pi r^2 + \pi rl$

where, r is the radius, h is the height and l is the slant height of the cone.

(viii) Volume of a parallelopiped (cuboid) $= xyz$ and surface area $= 2(xy + yz + zx)$, where x, y and z are the dimensions of a parallelopiped.

(ix) Volume of a cube $= x^3$ and surface area $= 6x^2$ where, x is the side of the cube.

(x) Area of an equilateral triangle $= \frac{\sqrt{3}}{4}(\text{Side})^2$

Example 1 A balloon which always remains spherical has a variable radius, find the rate at which its volume is increasing with respect to its radius, when the radius is 7 cm.

Sol. Here, we have to find rate of change of volume with respect to radius, so volume is dependent quantity and radius is independent quantity.

Let r be the radius and V be the volume of spherical balloon, then $V = \frac{4}{3}\pi r^3$.

On differentiating both sides w.r.t. r, we get

$$\frac{dV}{dr} = \frac{4}{3}\pi(3r^2) = 4\pi r^2 \quad \text{...(i)}$$

Now, we have to find rate of change of volume, when radius is 7 cm. So, putting $r = 7$ in Eq. (i), we get

$$\left(\frac{dV}{dr}\right)_{r=7} = 4\pi(7)^2 = 4\pi(49) = 196\pi \text{ cm}^3/\text{cm}$$

Hence, the volume is increasing with respect to its radius at the rate of 196π cm^3/cm, when the radius is 7 cm.

Example 2 The radius of a circle increases at a rate of 0.2 cm/s. Calculate the rate of the increase of the area, when the radius is 5 cm.

Sol. Here, we have to calculate rate of change of area with respect to radius.

So, let x be the radius and y be the area of circle. Then,

$$y = \pi x^2 \quad \text{...(i)}$$

Also, rate of change of radius with respect to time is 0.2 cm/s.

$$\therefore \quad dx/dt = 0.2 \quad \text{...(ii)}$$

[$\because$ radius changing with time, so area depends on time]

Now, differentiating both sides of Eq. (i) w.r.t. t, we get

$$\frac{dy}{dt} = \pi \cdot 2x \cdot \frac{dx}{dt} \quad \text{[by chain rule]}$$

$$= 2\pi x(0.2) = 0.4\pi x \quad \text{[using Eq. (ii)]}$$

When radius $x = 5$ cm, then

$$\left(\frac{dy}{dt}\right) = 0.4\,\pi \times 5 = 2\pi \text{ cm}^2/\text{s}$$

Hence, the required rate of increase of the area is 2π cm^2/s.

Example 3 The volume of a sphere is increasing at the rate of 3 cm^3/s. Find the rate of increase of its surface area, when the radius is 2 cm.

Sol. Let r be the radius of sphere and V be its volume.

Then, $V = \frac{4}{3}\pi r^3$

$$\Rightarrow \quad \frac{dV}{dt} = \frac{4}{3}\pi(3r^2)\frac{dr}{dt} \quad \text{...(i)}$$

Given, $\frac{dV}{dt} = 3 \text{ cm}^3/\text{s}$ ...(ii)

From Eqs. (i) and (ii), we get

$$3 = \frac{4}{3}(3\pi r^2)\frac{dr}{dt} \Rightarrow \frac{dr}{dt} = \frac{3}{4\pi r^2} \quad \text{... (iii)}$$

Now, let S be the surface area of sphere, then

$$S = 4\pi r^2$$

$$\Rightarrow \quad \frac{dS}{dt} = 4\pi(2r)\frac{dr}{dt}$$

$$\Rightarrow \quad \frac{dS}{dt} = 8\pi r\left(\frac{3}{4\pi r^2}\right) = \frac{6}{r} \quad \text{[using Eq. (iii)]}$$

When $r = 2$, then

$$\frac{dS}{dt} = \frac{6}{2} = 3 \text{ cm}^2/\text{s}$$

Example 4 The radius r of a right circular cone is decreasing at the rate of 3 cm/min and the height h is increasing at the rate of 2 cm/min. When $r = 9$ cm and $h = 6$ cm, find the rate of change of its volume.

Sol. We have, $\frac{dr}{dt} = -3$ cm/min ...(i)

and $\frac{dh}{dt} = 2$ cm/min ...(ii)

Let V be the volume of a cone.

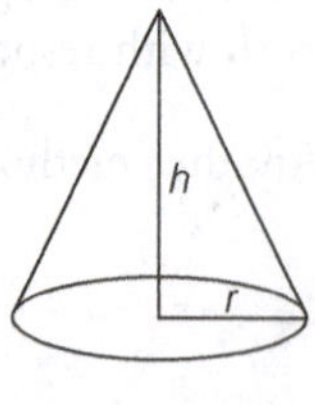

Then, $V = \frac{1}{3}\pi r^2 h$

$$\Rightarrow \quad \frac{dV}{dt} = \frac{1}{3}\pi\left(r^2 \cdot \frac{dh}{dt} + h \cdot 2r\frac{dr}{dt}\right)$$

$$\Rightarrow \quad \frac{dV}{dt} = \frac{1}{3}\pi\,[2r^2 + 2rh(-3)]$$

[using Eqs. (i) and (ii)]

Now, $\frac{dV}{dt}$ when $r = 9$ and $h = 6$, is given by

$$\left(\frac{dV}{dt}\right)_{\text{at } r=9,\, h=6} = \frac{1}{3}\pi[2(9)^2 - 6(9)(6)] = \frac{1}{3}\pi(162 - 324)$$

$$= \frac{1}{3}\pi(-162) = -54\pi \text{ cm}^3/\text{min}$$

Thus, the volume is decreasing at the rate 54π cm^3/min.

Example 5 The edge of a variable cube is increasing at the rate of 10 cm/s. How fast is the volume of the cube increasing when the edge is 5 cm long? **[ISC 2020]**

Sol. Let x be the edge of cube and V be its volume

Given, $\frac{dx}{dt} = 10$ cm/s

Now, $V = x^3$

$$\Rightarrow \frac{dV}{dt} = 3x^2\frac{dx}{dt}$$

Now, $\frac{dV}{dt}$ when $x = 5$ is given by

$$\left(\frac{dV}{dt}\right)_{x=5} = 3(5)^2(10) \qquad \left[\because \frac{dx}{dt} = 10 \text{ cm/s}\right]$$

$$\Rightarrow \frac{dV}{dt} = 750 \text{ cm}^3/\text{s}$$

Thus, the volume of cube is increasing at the rate of 750 cm^3/s.

Example 6 A 13 m long ladder is leaning against a wall, touching the wall at a certain height from the ground level. The bottom of the ladder is pulled away from the wall, along the ground, at the rate of 2 m/s. How fast is the height on the wall decreasing when the foot of the ladder is 5 m away from the wall? **[ISC 2019]**

Sol. Let $AC = 13$ m be the length of ladder and AB be the distance of the ladder from the wall at any time t, such that $AB = x$ and $BC = y$.

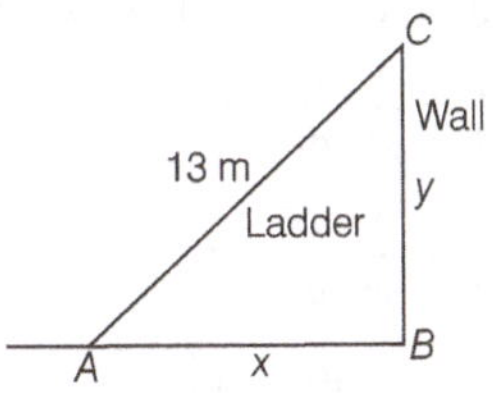

Given, $x = 5$ m and $\frac{dx}{dt} = 2$ m/s

In right angled ΔABC, we get

$$AB^2 + BC^2 = AC^2 \quad \text{[by Pythagoras theorem]}$$

$$\therefore \quad x^2 + y^2 = (13)^2$$

$$\Rightarrow \quad x^2 + y^2 = 169 \quad \text{...(i)}$$

When $x = 5$, then

$$5^2 + y^2 = 169$$

$$\Rightarrow \quad y^2 = 169 - 25 = 144 \Rightarrow y = 12$$

On differentiating Eq. (i) w.r.t. t, we get

$$2x\frac{dx}{dt} + 2y\frac{dy}{dt} = 0 \Rightarrow x\frac{dx}{dt} + y\frac{dy}{dt} = 0$$

$$\Rightarrow \quad 5 \times 2 + 12 \times \frac{dy}{dt} = 0 \Rightarrow \frac{dy}{dt} = \frac{-10}{12} = -\frac{5}{6} \text{ m/s}$$

Hence, the height of ladder on the wall is decreasing at the rate of $\frac{5}{6}$ m/s, when ladder is 5 m away from the wall.

Example 7 Water is dripping out from a conical funnel of semi-verticle angle $\pi/4$ at the uniform rate of 2 cm^2/s in the surface, through a tiny hole at the vertex of the bottom. When the slant height of the water level is 4 cm, find the rate of decrease of the slant height of the water. **[ISC 2018]**

Sol. Let r be the radius, l be the slant height, α be the semi-vertical angle of the cone and S be the curved surface area of cone.

Given, $\frac{dS}{dt} = -2$ cm^2/s, $l = 4$ and $\alpha = \frac{\pi}{4}$

In ΔOAB, $\sin\alpha = \frac{r}{l} \Rightarrow \sin\frac{\pi}{4} = \frac{r}{l} \Rightarrow r = l\sqrt{2}$

Curved surface area of cone $= \pi rl$

i.e. $S = \pi rl = \sqrt{2}\pi l^2 \quad [\because r = l\sqrt{2}]$

On differentiating w.r.t. t, we get

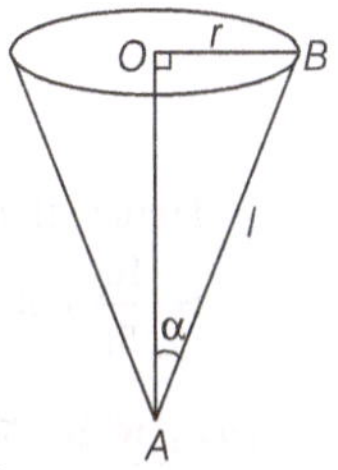

$$\frac{dS}{dt} = 2\sqrt{2}\pi l\frac{dl}{dt}$$

$$\Rightarrow \quad -2 = 2\sqrt{2}\pi(4)\frac{dl}{dt}$$

$$\Rightarrow \quad \frac{dl}{dt} = \frac{-1}{4\sqrt{2}\pi} \text{ cm/s}$$

Hence, the rate at which the water level decreasing is $\frac{1}{4\sqrt{2}\pi}$ cm/s.

Example 8 Water is leaking from a conical funnel at the rate of 5 cm^3/s. If the radius of the base of funnel is 5 cm and height is 10 cm, then find the rate at which the water level is dropping when it is 2.5 cm from the top.

Sol. Let r be the radius of base, h be the height at any stage and V be the volume of water in conical funnel.

Here, the radius of base of the conical funnel is 5 cm and height of the conical funnel is 10 cm.

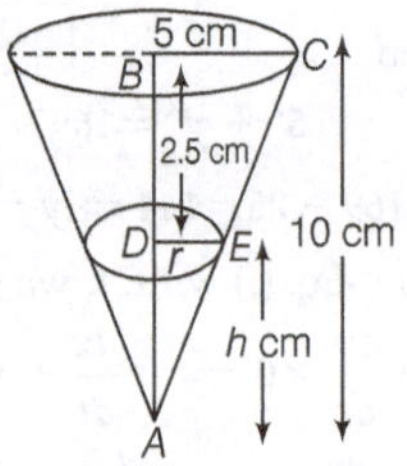

$\therefore \quad \frac{dV}{dt} = -5 \text{ cm}^3\text{/s}$

[here, negative (−) sign taken for leaking of water]

and $\quad h = 10 - 2.5 = 7.5$ cm

Since, $\Delta ABC \sim \Delta ADE$

$\therefore \quad \frac{AB}{AD} = \frac{BC}{DE}$ [by property of similar triangles]

$\Rightarrow \quad \frac{10}{h} = \frac{5}{r} \Rightarrow 10r = 5h \Rightarrow r = h/2$

We know that,

Volume of cone $= \frac{1}{3}\pi r^2 h$

$\therefore$ Volume of water in conical funnel,

$$V = \frac{1}{3}\pi\left(\frac{h}{2}\right)^2 \cdot h = \frac{\pi}{12}h^3$$

On differentiating both sides w.r.t. t, we get

$$\frac{dV}{dt} = \frac{\pi}{12} \times 3h^2 \times \frac{dh}{dt} = \frac{\pi}{4}h^2\frac{dh}{dt}$$

$$\Rightarrow \quad -5 = \frac{\pi}{4} \times (7.5)^2 \frac{dh}{dt}$$

$$\Rightarrow \quad \frac{dh}{dt} = -5 \times \frac{4}{\pi} \times \frac{1}{56.25}$$

$$\Rightarrow \quad \frac{dh}{dt} = \frac{-20 \times 100}{\pi \times 5625} = \frac{-20 \times 4}{\pi \times 225} = \frac{-16}{45\pi} \text{ cm/s}$$

Hence, the rate at which the water level dropping is $\frac{16}{45\pi}$ cm/s.

Example 9 Two men A and B start with velocities v at the same time from the junction of two roads inclined at 45° to each other. If they travel by different roads, then find the rate at which they are being separated.

[NCERT Exemplar]

Sol. Let two men start from the point C with velocity v each at the same time.

Also, $\angle BCA = 45°$

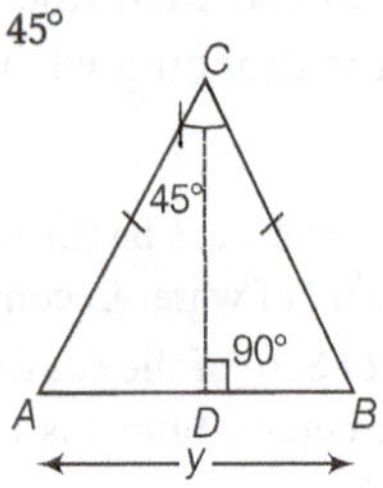

Since, A and B are moving with same velocity v, so they will cover same distance in same time.

Therefore, ΔABC is an isosceles triangle with $AC = BC$.

Now, draw $CD \perp AB$.

Let at any instant t, the distance between them is AB.

Let $AC = BC = x$ and $AB = y$

In ΔACD and ΔDCB, we get

$\angle CAD = \angle CBD \quad [\because BC = AC \Rightarrow \angle A = \angle B]$

$\angle CDA = \angle CDB = 90°$

$\therefore \quad \angle ACD = \angle DCB$

or $\quad \angle ACD = \frac{1}{2} \times \angle ACB$

$\Rightarrow \quad \angle ACD = \frac{1}{2} \times 45° \Rightarrow \angle ACD = 22.5°$

$\therefore \quad \sin 22.5° = \frac{AD}{AC}$

$\Rightarrow \quad \sin 22.5° = \frac{y/2}{x} \Rightarrow \frac{y}{2} = x \sin 22.5°$

$\Rightarrow \quad y = 2x \cdot \sin 22.5°$

On differentiating both sides w.r.t. t, we get

$$\frac{dy}{dt} = 2 \cdot \sin 22.5° \frac{dx}{dt} = 2 \cdot \sin 22.5° \, v \quad \left[\because v = \frac{dx}{dt}\right]$$

$$= 2v \cdot \frac{\sqrt{2-\sqrt{2}}}{2} = v\sqrt{2-\sqrt{2}} \quad \left[\because \sin 22.5° = \frac{\sqrt{2-\sqrt{2}}}{2}\right]$$

which is the required rate at which A and B are being separated.

Example 10 Given that $\frac{1}{y} + \frac{1}{x} = \frac{1}{12}$ and y decreases at a rate of 1 cms^{-1}, find the rate of change of x when $x = 5$ cm and $y = 1$ cm. **[ISC 2024]**

Sol. We have,

$$\frac{1}{y} + \frac{1}{x} = \frac{1}{12} \quad \text{...(i)}$$

and $\quad \frac{dy}{dt} = -1$ cm/s

On differentiating Eq. (i) w.r.t. 't', we get

$$-\frac{1}{y^2}\frac{dy}{dt} - \frac{1}{x^2}\frac{dx}{dt} = 0$$

$$\Rightarrow \quad \frac{1}{y^2} - \frac{1}{x^2}\frac{dx}{dt} = 0 \quad \left[\because \frac{dy}{dt} = -1\right]$$

$$\Rightarrow \quad \frac{dx}{dt} = \frac{x^2}{y^2}$$

When $x = 5$ cm and $y = 1$ cm, then

$$\frac{dx}{dt} = \frac{5^2}{1^2} = 25 \text{ cm/s}$$

Hence, the rate of change of x i.e. $\frac{dx}{dt}$ is 25 cm/s.

Topic Practice 3

Very Short Answer Type Questions

(2 Marks)

1 (i) The radius of an air bubble is increasing at the rate of $\frac{1}{2}$ cm/s. At what rate is the volume of bubble increasing, when the radius is 1 cm? [NCERT[

(ii) Find an angle θ, where $0 < \theta < \frac{\pi}{2}$, which increases twice as fast as its sine.

2 (i) The sides of an equilateral triangle are increasing at the rate of 2 cm/s. Find the rate at which the area increases, when the side is 10 cm.

(ii) A balloon which always remains spherical on inflation is being inflated by pumping in 900 cu cm of gas per second. Find the rate at which the radius of the balloon increases, when the radius is 15 cm. [NCERT]

3 If the area of a circle increase at a uniform rate, then prove that perimeter varies inversely as the radius. [NCERT Exemplar]

4 The volume of a cube is increasing at a rate of 9 cm^3/s. How fast is the surface area increasing when the length of an edge is 10 cm?

5 The volume of a cube increases at a constant rate. Prove that the increase in its surface area varies inversely as the length of the side. [NCERT Exemplar]

6 For the curve $y = 5x - 2x^3$, if x increase at the rate of 2 units/s, then find the rate of change of the slope of curve changing when $x = 3$. [NCERT Exemplar]

7 The radius r of a right circular cylinder is increasing at the rate of 5 cm/min and its height h, is decreasing at the rate of 4 cm/min. Find the rate of change of volume when its $r = 8$ cm and $h = 6$ cm.

8 A balloon which always remains spherical has a variable diameter $\frac{3}{2}(2x+1)$. Then, find the rate of change of its volume with respect to x.

9 A spherical ball of salt is dissolving in water in such a manner that the rate of decreasing of the volume at any instant is proportional to the surface. Prove that the radius is decreasing at a constant rate. [NCERT Exemplar]

Short Answer Type Questions

(4 Marks)

10 The length x of a rectangle is decreasing at the rate of 5 cm/min and the width y is increasing at the rate of 4 cm/min. When $x = 8$ cm and $y = 6$ cm, find the rate of change of

(i) the perimeter.

(ii) the area of the rectangle. [NCERT]

11 A man 2 m tall, walks at a uniform speed of 6 km/h away from a lamp post 6 m high. Find the rate at which the length of his shadow increases.

12 A man is moving away from a tower 41.6 m high at the rate of 2 m/s. Find the rate at which the angle of elevation of the top of the tower is changing when he is at a distance of 30 m from the foot of the tower. Assume that the eye level of the man is 1.6 m from the ground.

13 A swimming pool is to be drained for cleaning. If L represents the number of litres of water in the pool t seconds after the pool has been plugged off to drain and $L = 200(10 - t)^2$. How fast is the water running out at the end of 5 s and what is the average rate at which the water flows out during the first 5 s? [NCERT Exemplar]

Long Answer Type Questions

(6 Marks)

14 Sand is pouring from a pipe at the rate of 12 cm^3/s. The falling sand form a cone on the ground in such a way that the height of the cone is always one-sixth of the radius of the base. How fast is the height of the sand cone increasing when the height is 4 cm?

15 Water is running into a conical vessel, 15 cm deep and 5 cm in radius at the rate of 0.1 cm^3/s, when the water is 6 cm deep. Find at what rate is

(i) the water level rising?

(ii) the water surface area increasing?

(iii) the wetted surface of the vessel increasing?

16 Water is dripping out at a steady rate of 1 cm^3/s through a tiny hole at the vertex of the conical vessel, whose axis is vertical. When the slant height of water in the vessel is 4 cm, find the rate of decrease of slant height, where the semi-vertical angle of the conical vessel is $\frac{\pi}{6}$.

17 A kite is moving horizontally at a height of 151.5 m. If the speed of kite is 10 m/s, then how fast is the string being let out, when the kite is 250 m away from the boy who is flying the kite, if the height of boy is 1.5 m? **[NCERT Exemplar]**

Hints & Solutions

1. (i) Let r be the radius and V be the volume of the air bubble.

Given, $r = 1$ cm, $\frac{dr}{dt} = \frac{1}{2}$ cm/s ...(i)

Volume of air bubble, $V = \frac{4}{3}\pi r^3$ [1/2]

On differentiating both sides w.r.t. t, we get

$$\frac{dV}{dt} = \frac{4}{3}\pi(3r^2)\frac{dr}{dt} = 4\pi r^2\frac{dr}{dt}$$ [1/2]

$$\Rightarrow \frac{dV}{dt} = 4\pi(1^2)\frac{1}{2}$$

$$\Rightarrow \frac{dV}{dt} = 2\pi \text{ cm}^3/\text{s}$$ [from Eq. (i)]

Hence, the volume of bubble is increasing at the rate of 2π cm^3/s, when the radius is 1cm. [1]

(ii) Suppose θ increases twice as fast as its sine.

$\therefore \quad \theta = 2\sin\theta$

Now, differentiating both sides w.r.t. t, we get

$$\frac{d\theta}{dt} = 2\cdot\cos\theta\cdot\frac{d\theta}{dt}$$ [1]

$$\Rightarrow 1 = 2\cos\theta \Rightarrow \frac{1}{2} = \cos\theta$$

$$\Rightarrow \cos\theta = \cos\frac{\pi}{3} \Rightarrow \theta = \frac{\pi}{3}$$

So, the required angle is $\frac{\pi}{3}$. [1]

2. (i) Let the side of triangle be a.

Given, $\frac{da}{dt} = 2$ cm/s

Now, area of equilateral triangle having side a is given by

$$A = \frac{\sqrt{3}a^2}{4}$$ [1]

On differentiating both sides w.r.t. t, we get

$$\frac{dA}{dt} = \frac{\sqrt{3}}{4}\cdot(2a)\frac{da}{dt}$$ [1/2]

On putting $\frac{da}{dt} = 2$ cm/s and $a = 10$ cm, we get

$$\frac{dA}{dt} = \frac{\sqrt{3}}{4}\times 2\times 10\times 2 = 10\sqrt{3} \text{ cm}^2/\text{s}$$ [1/2]

(ii) **Hint** $\frac{dV}{dt} = 900 \text{cm}^3/\text{s}$

$$\Rightarrow \frac{d}{dt}\left(\frac{4}{3}\pi r^3\right) = 900 \Rightarrow 4\pi r^2\frac{dr}{dt} = 900$$

$$\Rightarrow \frac{dr}{dt} = \frac{900}{4\pi r^2}\left[\textbf{Ans. } \frac{1}{\pi}\text{cm/s}\right]$$

3. Let r be the radius, A be the area and P be the perimeter.

Then, we have $\frac{dA}{dt} = \text{constant} = k$ (say)

$$\Rightarrow \frac{d}{dt}(\pi r^2) = k \Rightarrow 2\pi r\frac{dr}{dt} = k$$

$$\Rightarrow \frac{dr}{dt} = \frac{k}{2\pi r}$$ ...(i) [1]

Now, $\frac{dp}{dt} = \frac{d}{dt}(2\pi r) = 2\pi\frac{dr}{dt}$

$$= 2\pi\times\frac{k}{2\pi r} = \frac{k}{r}$$ [from Eq. (i)]

Thus, $\frac{dp}{dt} \propto \frac{1}{r}$ **Hence proved.** [1]

4. Let the volume of a cube be V cm^3.

Then, we have

$$\frac{dV}{dt} = 9 \text{ cm}^3/\text{s}$$

and edge of cube, $x = 10$ cm

$\because \quad V = x^3$

On differentiating both sides w.r.t. t, we get

$$\frac{dV}{dt} = 3x^2\frac{dx}{dt}$$

$$\Rightarrow 9 = 3x^2\frac{dx}{dt} \Rightarrow \frac{dx}{dt} = \frac{3}{x^2}$$ [1]

Also, surface area of a cube, $S = 6x^2$

On differentiating both sides w.r.t. t, we get

$$\frac{dS}{dt} = 12x\frac{dx}{dt} = 12\times x\times\frac{3}{x^2}$$

$$= 12\times 10\times\frac{3}{10\times 10} = 3.6 \text{ cm}^2/\text{s}$$ [1]

5. **Hint** $\frac{dV}{dt} = k$ (constant)

$$\Rightarrow 3a^2\frac{da}{dt} = k \Rightarrow \frac{da}{dt} = \frac{k}{3a^2}$$ [$\because V = a^3$]

Now, $\frac{dS}{dt} = \frac{d}{dt}(6a^2) = 12a\frac{da}{dt}$

$$= 12a\cdot\frac{k}{3a^2} = 4\frac{k}{a} \Rightarrow \frac{dS}{dt} \propto \frac{1}{a}$$

6. Given curve is $y = 5x - 2x^3$ and $\frac{dx}{dt} = 2$ units/s ...(i)

Now, slope of the curve $\frac{dy}{dx} = 5 - 6x^2 = M$ (say)

Rate of change of the slope,

$$\frac{dM}{dt} = -6\frac{d}{dt}(x^2)$$ [1]

$$\Rightarrow \frac{dM}{dt} = -12x\frac{dx}{dt}$$

When $x = 3$, then

$$\frac{dM}{dt} = -12 \times 3 \times 2 = -72 \text{ unit/s}$$

Thus, the slope of decreasing at a rate of 72 units/s. [1]

7. Similar as Example 4. [**Ans.** $224\pi \text{ cm}^3/\text{s}$]

8. Given, diameter of the balloon $= \frac{3}{2}(2x+1)$

$\therefore$ Radius of the balloon $= \frac{\text{Diameter}}{2}$

$$= \frac{1}{2}\left[\frac{3}{2}(2x+1)\right] = \frac{3}{4}(2x+1)$$

For the volume V, the balloon is given by

$$V = \frac{4}{3}\pi(\text{radius})^3 = \frac{4}{3}\pi\left[\frac{3}{4}(2x+1)\right]^3 = \frac{9\pi}{16}(2x+1)^3$$ [1]

For the rate of change of volume, differentiate w.r.t. x, we get

$$\frac{dV}{dx} = \frac{9\pi}{16} \times 3(2x+1)^2 \times 2 = \frac{27\pi}{8}(2x+1)^2$$

Thus, the rate of change of volume is $\frac{27\pi}{8}(2x+1)^2$. [1]

9. Let the radius of spherical ball of the salt be r.

$\therefore$ Volume of the ball, $V = \frac{4}{3}\pi r^3$

and surface area, $S = 4\pi r^2$

$$\therefore \quad \frac{dV}{dt} = \frac{d}{dt}\left(\frac{4}{3}\pi r^3\right) = -\frac{4}{3}\pi \cdot 3r^2\frac{dr}{dt} = -4\pi r^2\frac{dr}{dt}$$ [1]

[here, we take negative sign because salt is dissolving]

According to the given condition,

$\frac{dV}{dt} \propto S \Rightarrow \frac{dV}{dt} = kS$, where k is proportionality constant.

$$\Rightarrow \quad -4\pi r^2\frac{dr}{dt} = k \cdot 4\pi r^2 \Rightarrow \frac{dr}{dt} = -k$$

Hence, the radius of ball is decreasing at constant rate. [1]

10. Let P be the perimeter and A be the area of the rectangle of length x and width y.

Given, $\frac{dx}{dt} = -5$ cm/min,

[negative (−) sign for decreasing rate]

$x = 8$ cm, $\frac{dy}{dt} = 4$ cm/min and $y = 6$ cm [1]

(i) Perimeter of the rectangle, $P = 2(x+y)$

On differentiating both sides w.r.t. t, we get

$$\frac{dP}{dt} = 2\left(\frac{dx}{dt} + \frac{dy}{dt}\right)$$ [1/2]

$$= 2(-5+4)$$
$$= -2 \text{ cm/min}$$

So, perimeter decreases at the rate of 2 cm/min. [1]

(ii) Area of the rectangle, $A = xy$

On differentiating both sides w.r.t. t, we get

$$\frac{dA}{dt} = x\frac{dy}{dt} + y\frac{dx}{dt}$$ [1/2]

$$= 8 \times 4 + 6 \times (-5)$$
$$= 32 - 30 = 2 \text{ cm}^2/\text{min}$$

Hence, area increases at the rate of $2 \text{ cm}^2/\text{min}$. [1]

11. Let AB be the lamp post and a man CD be at a distance x from the lamp post and let $CE = y$ be his shadow.

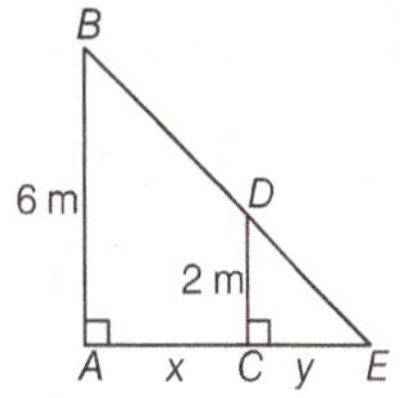

Given that, $\frac{dx}{dt} = 6$ km / h, $AB = 6 \text{ m} = \frac{6}{1000}$ km and

$CD = 2 \text{ m} = \frac{2}{1000}$ km [$\because$ 1 km = 1000 m] [1]

Here, $\Delta BAE \sim \Delta DCE$

$$\therefore \quad \frac{AB}{CD} = \frac{AE}{CE} \quad \text{[by property of similar triangles]}$$

$$\Rightarrow \quad \frac{\frac{6}{1000}}{\frac{2}{1000}} = \frac{x+y}{y} \Rightarrow 3 = \frac{x+y}{y}$$ [1]

$$\Rightarrow \quad 3y = x + y$$

$$\Rightarrow \quad 3y - y = x \Rightarrow 2y = x$$ [1/2]

On differentiating both sides w.r.t. t, we get

$$2\frac{dy}{dt} = \frac{dx}{dt}$$

$$\Rightarrow \quad 2\frac{dy}{dt} = 6 \quad \left[\because \frac{dx}{dt} = 6\right]$$ [1/2]

$$\Rightarrow \quad \frac{dy}{dt} = \frac{6}{2} = 3 \text{ km/h}$$

Hence, the shadow increases at the rate of 3 km/h. [1]

12. Let θ and x as shown in the figure below.

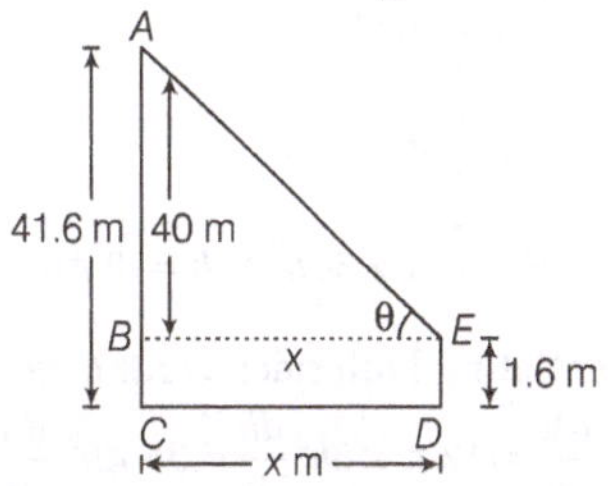

Then, we have

$$\frac{dx}{dt} = 2 \text{ m/s}$$ [1]

$$\therefore \text{ In } \Delta ABE, \tan\theta = \frac{40}{x} \quad ...(i)$$

$\Rightarrow \quad x = 40\cot\theta$ [1]

$\Rightarrow \quad \dfrac{dx}{dt} = 40(-\operatorname{cosec}^2\theta)\dfrac{d\theta}{dt}$

$\Rightarrow \quad 2 = -40\operatorname{cosec}^2\theta\dfrac{d\theta}{dt}$

$\Rightarrow \quad \dfrac{d\theta}{dt} = \dfrac{-1}{20\operatorname{cosec}^2\theta}$ ...(ii) [1]

Now, when $x = 30$ m, then $\tan\theta = \dfrac{4}{3}$ [using Eq. (i)]

$\Rightarrow \quad \cot\theta = \dfrac{3}{4} \Rightarrow \operatorname{cosec}\theta = \sqrt{1+\cot^2\theta} = \sqrt{1+\dfrac{9}{16}} = \dfrac{5}{4}$

$\therefore$ From Eq. (ii), we get $\dfrac{d\theta}{dt} = \dfrac{-1}{20\cdot\dfrac{25}{16}} = \dfrac{-4}{125}$ rad/s [1]

13. Given that L represents the number of litres of water in the pool, t seconds after the pool has been plugged off to drain, then

$$L = 200(10-t)^2$$

$\therefore$ Rate at which the water is running out,

$$\frac{dL}{dt} = -200\cdot 2(10-t)\cdot(-1) = 400(10-t)$$ [1]

[here, we take negative sign, because the water is decreasing]

Rate at which the water is running out at the end of 5 s

$= 400(10-5) = 2000$ L/s = Final rate [1]

Initial rate (at $t=0$) $= \left(\dfrac{dL}{dt}\right)_{t=0} = 4000$ L/s [1]

$\therefore$ Average rate during 5 s $= \dfrac{\text{Initial rate} + \text{Final rate}}{2}$

$= \dfrac{4000+2000}{2} = 3000$ L/s

Hence, the water flows out during the first 5 s with average rate of 3000 L/s. [1]

14. Let r be the radius, h be the height and V be the volume of the sand cone.

Also given that, $\dfrac{dV}{dt} = 12\ \text{cm}^3/\text{s},\ h = \dfrac{1}{6}r$

$\Rightarrow \quad r = 6h$ and $h = 4$ cm [1]

Volume of sand cone,

$$V = \frac{1}{3}\pi r^2 h$$ [1]

$\Rightarrow \quad V = \dfrac{1}{3}\pi(6h)^2 h$ [$\because r = 6h$]

$\Rightarrow \quad V = \dfrac{1}{3}\pi\times 36h^2\times h = 12\pi h^3$ [1]

On differentiating both sides w.r.t. t, we get

$$\frac{dV}{dt} = 12\pi\times 3h^2\frac{dh}{dt} = 36\pi h^2\frac{dh}{dt}$$ [1]

$\Rightarrow \quad 12 = 36\pi(4)^2\dfrac{dh}{dt}$

$\Rightarrow \quad \dfrac{dh}{dt} = \dfrac{12}{36\pi\times 16} = \dfrac{1}{48\pi}$ cm/s [1]

Hence, the height of the sand cone is increasing at the rate of $\dfrac{1}{48\pi}$ cm/s, when the height is 4 cm. [1]

15. **Hint** $\because \dfrac{dV}{dt} = 0.1\ \text{cm}^3/\text{s}$

(i) To find $\dfrac{dh}{dt}$, where $h = 6$ cm

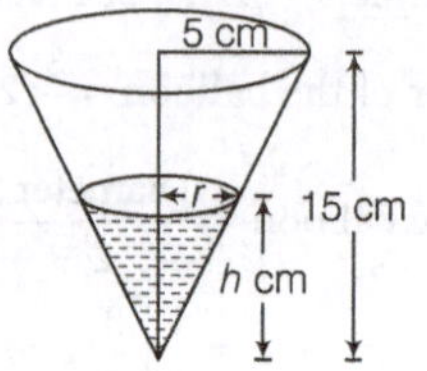

$\left[\textbf{Ans. } \dfrac{1}{40\pi}\text{ cm/s}\right]$

(ii) Water surface area (A) at any time $t = \pi r^2$

$= \pi\dfrac{h^2}{9}$ $\left[\text{from part (i)}, \dfrac{5}{r} = \dfrac{15}{h} \Rightarrow r = \dfrac{h}{3}\right]$

$\Rightarrow \quad \dfrac{dA}{dt} = \dfrac{2\pi}{9}h\dfrac{dh}{dt}$

Now, $\left(\dfrac{dA}{dt}\right)_{h=6} = \dfrac{2\pi}{9}\times 6\times\dfrac{1}{40\pi}$

$\left[\because \dfrac{dh}{dt} = \dfrac{1}{40\pi}, \text{ from part (i)}\right]$

$\left[\textbf{Ans. } \dfrac{1+\sqrt{10}}{30}\ \text{cm}^2/\text{s}\right]$

(iii) Wetted surface area (S) of the vessel at any time $t = \pi r l$

$= \pi\dfrac{h}{3}\sqrt{r^2+h^2} = \pi\dfrac{h}{3}\sqrt{\dfrac{h^2}{9}+h^2}$

$= \pi\cdot\dfrac{h}{3}\cdot\dfrac{\sqrt{10}h}{3} = \dfrac{\pi}{9}\sqrt{10}h^2$

Now, $\dfrac{dS}{dt} = \dfrac{2\pi\sqrt{10}}{9}h\dfrac{dh}{dt}$

$\Rightarrow \quad \left(\dfrac{dS}{dt}\right)_{\text{at } h=6} = \dfrac{2\pi\sqrt{10}}{9}\times 6\times\dfrac{1}{40\pi}$ $\left[\textbf{Ans. } \dfrac{\sqrt{10}}{30}\ \text{cm}^2/\text{s}\right]$

16. **Hint** $r = l\sin\dfrac{\pi}{6} = \dfrac{l}{2}$ and $h = l\cos\dfrac{\pi}{6} = \dfrac{l\sqrt{3}}{2}$.

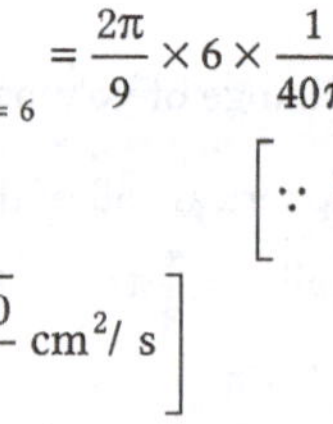

$$V = \frac{\sqrt{3}}{24}\pi l^3$$

$\Rightarrow \quad \dfrac{dV}{dt} = \dfrac{\sqrt{3}}{8}\pi l^2\dfrac{dl}{dt}$ $\left[\textbf{Ans. } \dfrac{1}{2\sqrt{3}\pi}\text{ cm/s}\right]$

17. Let CD be the height of kite and AB be the height of boy, then height of kite $CD = h = 151.5$ m.

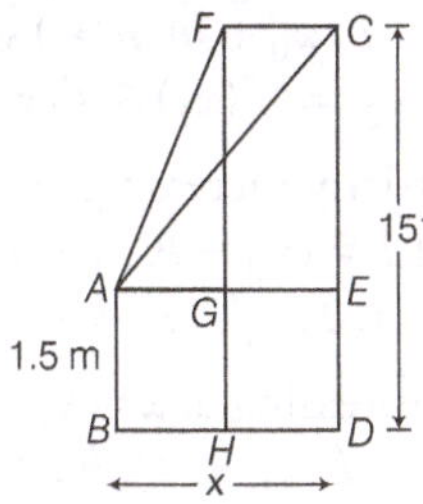

[2]

Let $DB = x$ m $= EA$

Since, the kite is 250 m away from the boy.

So, $AC = y = 250$ m

Speed of the kite,

$$v = \frac{dx}{dt} = 10 \text{ m/s}$$ [1/2]

From the figure, we get

$$EC = 151.5 - 1.5 = 150 \text{ m}$$ [1]

In right angled ΔCEA, we get

$$AE^2 + EC^2 = AC^2 \quad \text{[by Pythagoras theorem]}$$

$$\Rightarrow x^2 + (150)^2 = y^2 \quad \text{...(i)}$$

$$\Rightarrow x^2 + (150)^2 = (250)^2$$

$$\Rightarrow x^2 = (250)^2 - (150)^2$$

$$\Rightarrow x^2 = (250+150)(250-150) = 400 \times 100$$

$$\Rightarrow x = 20 \times 10 = 200$$ [1]

On differentiating both sides of Eq. (i) w.r.t. t, we get

$$2x \cdot \frac{dx}{dt} + 0 = 2y \frac{dy}{dt}$$

$$\Rightarrow 2y \cdot \frac{dy}{dt} = 2x \frac{dx}{dt}$$

$$\Rightarrow \frac{dy}{dt} = \frac{x}{y} \cdot \frac{dx}{dt} = \frac{200}{250} \times 10 = 8 \text{ m/s}$$

$$\left[\because \frac{dx}{dt} = 10 \text{ m/s}\right]$$ [1]

Hence, the required rate at which the string is being let out is 8 m/s. [1/2]

TOPIC 03 Increasing and Decreasing Functions

Let I be an open interval contained in the domain of a real valued function f, then we can define increasing or decreasing functions as given below

Increasing Function

A function f is called a increasing function in I, if $x_1 < x_2 \Rightarrow f(x_1) \le f(x_2)$ for all $x_1, x_2 \in I$. The graphical representation of such function is given below

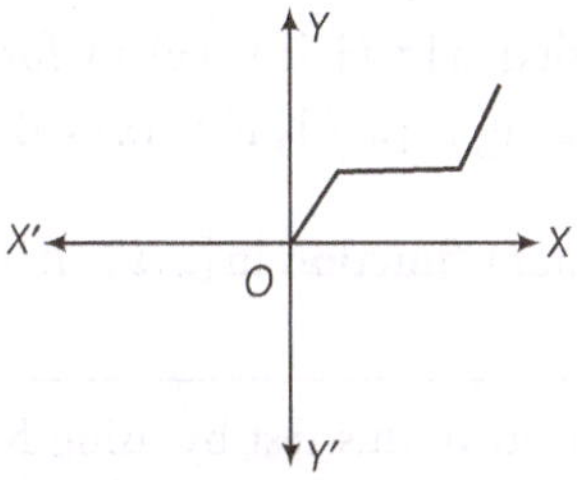

Strictly Increasing Function

A function f is called a strictly increasing function in I, if $x_1 < x_2 \Rightarrow f(x_1) < f(x_2)$ for all $x_1, x_2 \in I$.

The graphical representation of such function is given below

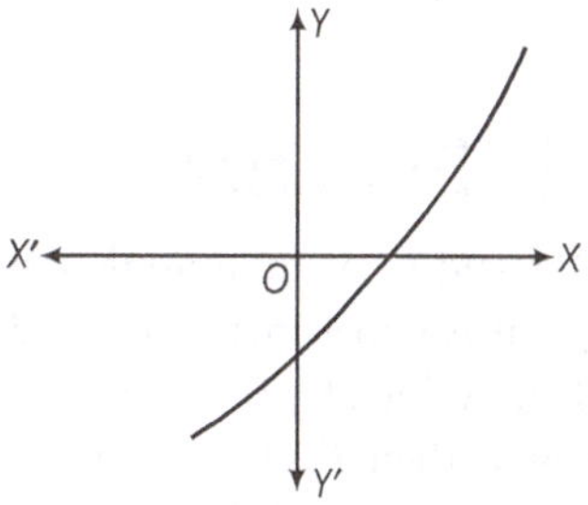

Example 1 Show that $f(x) = 3x + 5$ is a strictly increasing function on R.

Sol. We have, $f(x) = 3x + 5$

Let $x_1, x_2 \in R$, such that $x_1 < x_2$.

Then, $x_1 < x_2$

$$\Rightarrow 3x_1 < 3x_2 \quad \text{[multiplying both sides by 3]}$$

$$\Rightarrow 3x_1 + 5 < 3x_2 + 5 \quad \text{[adding 5 on both sides]}$$

$$\Rightarrow f(x_1) < f(x_2)$$

Thus, $x_1 < x_2$

$$\Rightarrow f(x_1) < f(x_2), \forall x_1, x_2 \in R$$

Hence, $f(x)$ is strictly increasing on R.

Decreasing Function

A function f is called a decreasing function in I, if

$$x_1 < x_2$$

$\Rightarrow f(x_1) \geq f(x_2)$ for all $x_1, x_2 \in I$.

The graphical representation of such function is given below

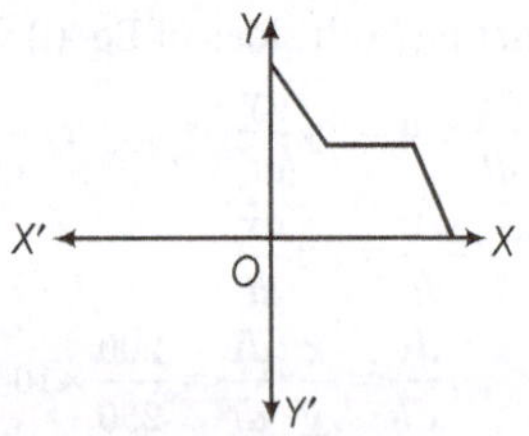

Strictly Decreasing Function

A function f is called a strictly decreasing function in I, if $x_1 < x_2 \Rightarrow f(x_1) > f(x_2)$ for all $x_1, x_2 \in I$. The graphical representation of such function is given below

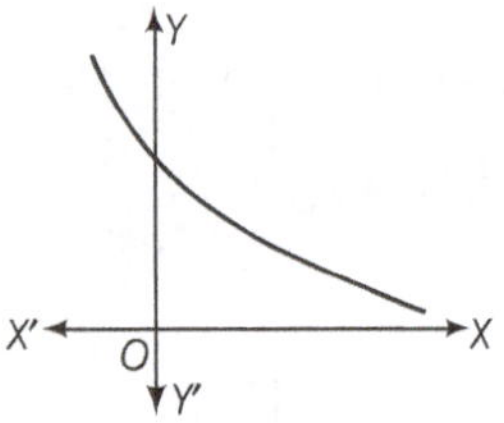

Monotonic Function

A function $f(x)$ is said to be **monotonic** (or monotone) in an interval I, if it is either increasing or decreasing in the interval I. If the value of $f(x)$ increases with the increasing value of x, then $f(x)$ is called **monotonically increasing** function and if $f(x)$ decreases with the increasing value of x, then $f(x)$ is called **monotonically decreasing** e.g. e^x, $\log_e x$, $5x+4$ etc are monotonically increasing function and $-x$, e^{-x}, $\cot^{-1} x$ etc are monotonically decreasing function.

Increasing and Decreasing Functions at a Point

Let x_0 be a point in the domain of definition of a real valued function f. Then, f is said to be **increasing or strictly increasing, decreasing or strictly decreasing** at x_0, if there exists an open interval I containing x_0, such that f is increasing or strictly increasing, decreasing or strictly decreasing respectively, in I.

In other words,

(i) f is said to be increasing at $x = x_0$, if there exists an interval $I = (x_0 - h, x_0 + h)$, $h > 0$ such that for all $x_1, x_2 \in I$; $x_1 < x_2 \Rightarrow f(x_1) \leq f(x_2)$.

(ii) f is said to be strictly increasing at $x = x_0$, if there exists an interval $I = (x_0 - h, x_0 + h)$, $h > 0$ such that for all $x_1, x_2 \in I$; $x_1 < x_2 \Rightarrow f(x_1) < f(x_2)$.

(iii) f is said to be decreasing at $x = x_0$, if there exists an interval $I = (x_0 - h, x_0 + h)$, $h > 0$ such that for all $x_1, x_2 \in I$; $x_1 < x_2 \Rightarrow f(x_1) \geq f(x_2)$.

(iv) f is said to be strictly decreasing at $x = x_0$, if there exists an interval $I = (x_0 - h, x_0 + h)$, $h > 0$ such that for all $x_1, x_2 \in I$; $x_1 < x_2 \Rightarrow f(x_1) > f(x_2)$.

Note The interval I may be finite or infinite.

Example 2 If a is a real number such that $0 < a < 1$. Show that the function $f(x) = a^x$ is strictly decreasing on R.

Sol. We have, $f(x) = a^x$, $0 < a < 1$

Let $x_1, x_2 \in R$ such that $x_1 < x_2$.

Then, $x_1 < x_2 \Rightarrow a^{x_1} > a^{x_2}$

[$\because 0 < a < 1$, when $x_1 < x_2$, then $a^{x_1} > a^{x_2}$]

$\Rightarrow f(x_1) > f(x_2)$, $\forall x_1, x_2 \in R$

Hence, $f(x)$ is strictly decreasing on R.

First Derivative Test for Monotonic Functions

To check or find that given function is increasing or decreasing, we use first derivative test as a theorem which is given below

> **Theorem** Let f be continuous on $[a, b]$ and differentiable on the open interval (a, b). Then,
>
> (i) f is **increasing** in $[a, b]$, if $f'(x) > 0$ for each $x \in (a, b)$.
>
> (ii) f is **decreasing** in $[a, b]$, if $f'(x) < 0$ for each $x \in (a, b)$.
>
> (iii) f is a **constant function** in $[a, b]$, if $f'(x) = 0$ for each $x \in (a, b)$.

Proof (i) We can prove this test by using Mean Value theorem.

Let $x_1, x_2 \in [a, b]$ be such that $x_1 < x_2$. Then, f is continuous and differentiable and $f'(x) > 0$, so by Mean Value theorem, there exists a point c between x_1 and x_2 such that

$$f'(c) = \frac{f(x_2) - f(x_1)}{x_2 - x_1}$$

$$\Rightarrow \quad f(x_2) - f(x_1) = f'(c)(x_2 - x_1)$$

$\Rightarrow \quad f(x_2) - f(x_1) > 0$ [as $f'(c) > 0$]

$\Rightarrow \quad f(x_2) > f(x_1)$

Thus, $x_1 < x_2$

$\Rightarrow \quad f(x_1) < f(x_2), \forall x_1, x_2 \in [a, b]$

Hence, f is an increasing function in $[a, b]$.
Similarly, we can prove other parts.

Note

(i) f is strictly increasing in (a, b), if $f'(x) > 0$ for each $x \in (a, b)$.
(ii) f is strictly decreasing in (a, b), if $f'(x) < 0$ for each $x \in (a, b)$.
(iii) A function will be increasing (decreasing) in R, if it is so as every interval of R.
(iv) If for a given interval $I \subseteq R$, function f increases for some values in I and decreases for the other values in I, then we say function is neither increasing nor decreasing.

Example 3 Prove that the function $f(x) = x^3 - 6x^2 + 12x + 5$ is increasing on R. **[ISC 2019]**

Sol. We have, $f(x) = x^3 - 6x^2 + 12x + 5$

On differentiating both sides w.r.t. x, we get

$$f'(x) = 3x^2 - 12x + 12 = 3(x^2 - 4x + 4) = 3(x-2)^2 \geq 0$$

$\therefore \quad f'(x) \geq 0, \forall x \in R$

Hence, $f(x)$ is an increasing function.

Example 4 Show that the function $f(x) = \cos\left(2x + \frac{\pi}{4}\right)$ is increasing on $\left(\frac{3\pi}{8}, \frac{7\pi}{8}\right)$.

Sol. Given, $f(x) = \cos\left(2x + \frac{\pi}{4}\right)$

On differentiating both sides w.r.t. x, we get

$$f'(x) = -\sin\left(2x + \frac{\pi}{4}\right)\frac{d}{dx}\left(2x + \frac{\pi}{4}\right)$$

$$\Rightarrow \quad f'(x) = -2\sin\left(2x + \frac{\pi}{4}\right)$$

Since, $\frac{3\pi}{8} < x < \frac{7\pi}{8} \Rightarrow \frac{3\pi}{4} < 2x < \frac{7\pi}{4}$

$$\Rightarrow \quad \frac{3\pi}{4} + \frac{\pi}{4} < 2x + \frac{\pi}{4} < \frac{7\pi}{4} + \frac{\pi}{4}$$

$$\Rightarrow \quad \pi < 2x + \frac{\pi}{4} < 2\pi \Rightarrow \sin\left(2x + \frac{\pi}{4}\right) < 0$$

[$\because$ sine function is negative in third and fourth quadrants]

$$\Rightarrow \quad -\sin\left(2x + \frac{\pi}{4}\right) > 0 \Rightarrow -2\sin\left(2x + \frac{\pi}{4}\right) > 0$$

$$\Rightarrow \quad f'(x) > 0$$

$\Rightarrow f(x)$ is increasing on $\left(\frac{3\pi}{8}, \frac{7\pi}{8}\right)$.

Example 5 Show that the function $f(x) = \cos^2 x$ is strictly decreasing on $\left(0, \frac{\pi}{2}\right)$.

Sol. We have, $f(x) = \cos^2 x$

On differentiating both sides w.r.t. x, we get

$$f'(x) = -2\cos x \sin x = -\sin 2x < 0 \text{ in } \left(0, \frac{\pi}{2}\right)$$

$\left[\because \sin 2x > 0 \text{ in } \left(0, \frac{\pi}{2}\right)\right]$

$$\Rightarrow \quad f'(x) < 0 \, \forall x \in \left(0, \frac{\pi}{2}\right)$$

Hence, $f(x) = \cos^2 x$ is strictly decreasing function on $\left(0, \frac{\pi}{2}\right)$.

Example 6 Show that $f(x) = \log \sin x$ is

(i) strictly increasing on $\left(0, \frac{\pi}{2}\right)$.

(ii) strictly decreasing on $\left(\frac{\pi}{2}, \pi\right)$. **[NCERT]**

Sol. We have, $f(x) = \log \sin x$

On differentiating both sides w.r.t. x, we get

$$f'(x) = \frac{1}{\sin x} \cdot \cos x \Rightarrow f'(x) = \cot x$$

(i) We know that, for each $x \in \left(0, \frac{\pi}{2}\right)$, $\cot x > 0$

$$\Rightarrow \quad f'(x) > 0$$

So, $f(x)$ is strictly increasing in $(0, \pi/2)$.

(ii) We know that, for each $x \in \left(\frac{\pi}{2}, \pi\right)$,

$$\cot x < 0 \Rightarrow f'(x) < 0$$

So, $f(x)$ is strictly decreasing in $\left(\frac{\pi}{2}, \pi\right)$.

Working Rule to Find the Interval in which Function is Increasing or Decreasing

Suppose a function $f(x)$, where $x \in R$ or ($x \in$ an interval) is given to us and we have to find the interval in which it is increasing or decreasing. Then, we use the following steps

I. First, write the given function $f(x)$, where $x \in R$ or an interval and then find $f'(x)$.

II. Put $f'(x) = 0$ and find the value (or values) of x in R or given interval.

III. Divide the number line (R) or given interval in which x lies into disjoint sub intervals with the help of values of x obtained in step II.

IV. In each sub interval, check that $f'(x) > 0$ or $f'(x) < 0$.

(i) If $f'(x) > 0$, then $f(x)$ is strictly increasing in that interval.

(ii) If $f'(x) < 0$, then $f(x)$ is strictly decreasing in that interval.

V. From step IV, we get those intervals in which function $f(x)$ is increasing or decreasing. If $f(x)$ is increasing in some sub interval and decreasing in some other sub interval, then in whole interval or number line, function $f(x)$ is neither increasing nor decreasing.

Note A strictly increasing function is an increasing function but an increasing function may or may not be strictly increasing (same is true for decreasing function).

Example 7 Find the intervals in which the function f given by $f(x) = 4x^3 - 6x^2 - 72x + 30$ is strictly increasing and strictly decreasing. Also, check on whole real line. [NCERT]

Sol. Given, $f(x) = 4x^3 - 6x^2 - 72x + 30, \forall x \in R$

On differentiating both sides w.r.t. x, we get

$$f'(x) = 12x^2 - 12x - 72$$

On putting $f'(x) = 0$, we get

$$12x^2 - 12x - 72 = 0$$

$\Rightarrow \quad 12(x^2 - x - 6) = 0$

$\Rightarrow \quad 12(x-3)(x+2) = 0$

$\Rightarrow \quad x = 3, -2$

We have, $x = -2$ and $x = 3$, which divides the number line into three disjoint sub intervals.

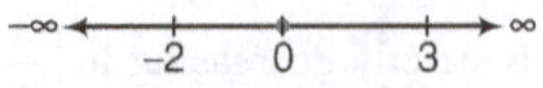

Thus, we have sub intervals $(-\infty, -2)$, $(-2, 3)$ and $(3, \infty)$.

Now, check that $f'(x) > 0$ or $f'(x) < 0$.

In the interval $(-\infty, -2)$, $f'(x) > 0$

$\left[\begin{array}{l}\text{as at } x = -4 \in (-\infty, -2), (x-3) < 0, \\ (x+2) < 0, \text{ so } (x-3)(x+2) > 0\end{array}\right]$

$\Rightarrow \quad f(x)$ is strictly increasing in $(-\infty, -2)$.

In the interval $(-2, 3)$, $f'(x) < 0$

[as at $x = 1 \in (-2, 3)$, $(x-3) < 0$, $(x+2) > 0$ so, $(x-3)(x+2) < 0$]

$\Rightarrow \quad f(x)$ is strictly decreasing in $(-2, 3)$.

In the interval $(3, \infty)$, $f'(x) > 0$

[as at $x = 4 \in (3, \infty)$, $(x-3) > 0$, $(x+2) > 0$ so, $(x-3)(x+2) > 0$]

$\Rightarrow \quad f(x)$ is strictly increasing in $(3, \infty)$.

Since, the function $f(x)$ is strictly increasing in $(-\infty, -2)$ and $(3, \infty)$ and strictly decreasing in $(-2, 3)$, so f is neither increasing nor decreasing in R.

Example 8 Find interval(s) in which the function $f(x) = \sin x + \cos x$, $x \in \left(0, \frac{\pi}{2}\right)$ is strictly increasing or decreasing.

Sol. Given function is $f(x) = \sin x + \cos x$

On differentiating both sides w.r.t. x, we get

$$f'(x) = \cos x - \sin x$$

Put $f'(x) = 0$

$\Rightarrow \quad \cos x - \sin x = 0$

$\Rightarrow \quad \tan x = 1$

$\Rightarrow \quad x = \frac{\pi}{4} \in \left(0, \frac{\pi}{2}\right)$

Now, $\frac{\pi}{4}$ divides the interval $\left(0, \frac{\pi}{2}\right)$ into two sub intervals $\left(0, \frac{\pi}{4}\right)$ and $\left(\frac{\pi}{4}, \frac{\pi}{2}\right)$.

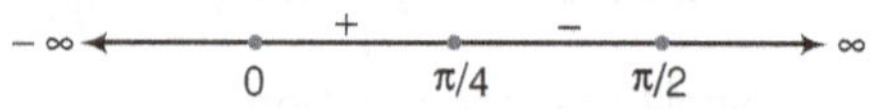

In interval $\left(0, \frac{\pi}{4}\right)$, $\cos x > \sin x$

$\therefore \quad \cos x - \sin x > 0$

$\Rightarrow \quad f'(x) > 0$

So, $f(x)$ is strictly increasing function in $\left(0, \frac{\pi}{4}\right)$.

In interval $\left(\frac{\pi}{4}, \frac{\pi}{2}\right)$, $\cos x < \sin x$

$\therefore \quad \cos x - \sin x < 0$

$\Rightarrow \quad f'(x) < 0$

So, $f(x)$ is strictly decreasing function in $\left(\frac{\pi}{4}, \frac{\pi}{2}\right)$.

Example 9 Find the intervals on which the function $f(x) = 5 + 36x + 3x^2 - 2x^3$ is

(i) increasing. (ii) decreasing.

Sol. We have, $f(x) = 5 + 36x + 3x^2 - 2x^3$

On differentiating both sides w.r.t. x, we get

$$f'(x) = 36 + 6x - 6x^2$$
$$= -6(x^2 - x - 6)$$
$$= -6(x+2)(x-3)$$

(i) For $f(x)$ to be increasing, $f'(x) \geq 0$

$\Rightarrow \quad -6(x+2)(x-3) \geq 0$

$\Rightarrow \quad (x+2)(x-3) \leq 0$

$\Rightarrow \quad -2 \leq x \leq 3$

Hence, $f(x)$ is increasing in $[-2, 3]$.

(ii) For $f(x)$ to be decreasing, $f'(x) \leq 0$

$\Rightarrow \quad -6(x+2)(x-3) \leq 0$

$\Rightarrow \quad (x+2)(x-3) \geq 0$

$\Rightarrow \quad x \leq -2$ or $x \geq 3$

Hence, $f(x)$ is decreasing on $(-\infty, -2] \cup [3, \infty)$.

Example 10 Find the interval in which $f(x) = x^x, x > 0$ is increasing or decreasing.

Sol. We have, $f(x) = x^x$, $x > 0$

$\therefore$ dom $(f) = (0, \infty)$

Now, $\quad f(x) = e^{\log x^x} = e^{x \log x}$ ...(i)

On differentiating Eq. (i) both sides w.r.t. x, we get

$$f'(x) = e^{\log x^x} \frac{d}{dx}(x \log x)$$

$$\Rightarrow \quad f'(x) = x^x\left(x \frac{1}{x} + \log x \cdot 1\right)$$

$$\Rightarrow \quad f'(x) = x^x(1 + \log x)$$

For $f(x)$ to be increasing, $f'(x) > 0$

$\Rightarrow \quad x^x(1 + \log x) > 0$

$\Rightarrow \quad 1 + \log x > 0 \quad [\because x^x > 0, x > 0]$

$\Rightarrow \quad \log x > -1$

$\Rightarrow \quad x > e^{-1}$

$\Rightarrow \quad x \in \left(\frac{1}{e}, \infty\right)$

Thus, $f(x)$ is increasing in $\left(\frac{1}{e}, \infty\right)$.

For $f(x)$ to be decreasing, $f'(x) < 0$

$x^x(1 + \log x) < 0$

$\Rightarrow \quad 1 + \log x < 0 \quad [\because x^x > 0, x > 0]$

$\Rightarrow \quad \log x < -1 \Rightarrow x < e^{-1}$

$\Rightarrow \quad x \in \left(0, \frac{1}{e}\right)$

Thus, $f(x)$ is decreasing in $\left(0, \frac{1}{e}\right)$.

Hence, $f(x)$ is increasing in $\left(\frac{1}{e}, \infty\right)$ and decreasing in $\left(0, \frac{1}{e}\right)$.

Topic Practice 3

Very Short Answer Type Questions

(2 Marks)

1 (i) Show that the function given by $f(x) = 7x - 3$ is strictly increasing on R. **[NCERT]**

(ii) Prove that $f(x) = ax + b$, where a and b are constants and $a > 0$ is strictly increasing function for all real values of x without using the derivative.

2 (i) Show that $f(x) = x^2$ is strictly decreasing in $(-\infty, 0)$.

(ii) Prove that $f(x) = \frac{3}{x} + 7$ is strictly decreasing for $x \in R, (x \neq 0)$.

3 Show that the function f given by $f(x) = x^3 - 3x^2 + 4x, x \in R$ is strictly increasing on R. **[NCERT]**

4 Let I be an interval disjoint from $(-1, 1)$. Prove that function $f(x) = \left(x + \frac{1}{x}\right)$ is strictly increasing on I.

5 Show that the function $f(x) = \tan x - x$ is always increasing in $x \in R$. **[NCERT Exemplar]**

6 Show that the function f given by $f(x) = \tan^{-1}(\sin x + \cos x), x > 0$ is always an strictly increasing function in $\left(0, \frac{\pi}{4}\right)$. **[NCERT]**

7 Show that $f(x) = \frac{x}{\sin x}$ is increasing on $\left(0, \frac{\pi}{2}\right)$.

Short Answer Type Questions

(4 Marks)

8 Which of the following functions are strictly decreasing on $\left(0, \frac{\pi}{2}\right)$. (Each part carries 4 Marks) **[NCERT]**

(i) $\cos x$ (ii) $\cos 2x$
(iii) $\cos 3x$ (iv) $\tan x$

9 Show that $f(x) = 2x + \cot^{-1} x + \log(\sqrt{1 + x^2} - x)$ is increasing in R. **[NCERT Exemplar]**

10 Find the least value of a, such that the function f given by $f(x)=x^2+ax+1$ is strictly increasing on (1, 2). **[NCERT]**

11 Find the value(s) of x for which $y=[x(x-2)]^2$ is an increasing function. **[NCERT]**

12 Find the intervals in which the following functions is strictly increasing or strictly decreasing. (Each part carries 4 Marks)

(i) $f(x)=-2x^3-9x^2-12x+1$ **[NCERT]**

(ii) $f(x)=\frac{3}{10}x^4-\frac{4}{5}x^3-3x^2+\frac{36x}{5}+11$

(iii) $f(x)=\sin^4 x+\cos^4 x, 0\le x\le\frac{\pi}{2}$

13 Find the intervals in which the following functions is increasing or decreasing. (Each part carries 4 Marks)

(i) $f(x)=\frac{4\sin x-2x-x\cos x}{2+\cos x}$ **[NCERT]**

(ii) $f(x)=x^4-\frac{4x^3}{3}$

(iii) $f(x)=2x^3+9x^2+12x+20$

(iv) $f(x)=\frac{x}{\log x}$

14 Prove that the function f defined by $f(x)=x^2-x+1$ is neither increasing nor decreasing in (–1, 1). Hence find the interval in which $f(x)$, is

(i) strictly increasing.

(ii) strictly decreasing.

Long Answer Type Questions

6 Marks

15 Find the intervals in which the function f given by $f(x)=\sin x+\cos x, 0\le x\le 2\pi$ is strictly increasing or strictly decreasing. **[NCERT]**

16 Find the intervals in which $f(x)=\sin 3x-\cos 3x$, $0<x<\pi$, is strictly increasing or strictly decreasing.

17 Prove that $y=\frac{4\sin\theta}{2+\cos\theta}-\theta$ is an increasing function of θ on $\left[0,\frac{\pi}{2}\right]$.

Hints & Solutions

1. (i) Here, $f'(x)=7>0, \forall x\in R$

$\therefore$ f is strictly increasing on R. [1]

(ii) Let $x_1, x_2 \in R$.

Now, consider $x_1<x_2$

$\Rightarrow \quad ax_1<ax_2$

[multiplying both sides by a as $a>0$, given]

$\Rightarrow \quad ax_1+b<ax_2+b$ [adding b on both sides]

$\Rightarrow \quad f(x_1)<f(x_2)$ [$\because f(x)=ax+b$]

Thus, $x_1<x_2 \Rightarrow f(x_1)<f(x_2)$

Hence, f is strictly increasing on R. [1]

2. (i) Here, $f'(x)=2x<0, \forall x\in(-\infty,0)$

$\therefore f$ is strictly decreasing function in $(-\infty, 0)$. [1]

(ii) Given function is $f(x)=\frac{3}{x}+7,\ x\ne 0$

$\Rightarrow \quad f(x)=3x^{-1}+7$

On differentiating both sides w.r.t. x, we get

$$f'(x)=3(-1)x^{-2}+0$$

$$=\frac{-3}{x^2}<0, \forall x\in R-\{0\}$$

$\therefore f(x)$ is strictly decreasing for $x\in R, (x\ne 0)$.

Hence proved. [1]

3. **Hint** $f'(x)=3x^2-6x+4=3(x^2-2x+1)+1$

$$=3(x-1)^2+1>0, \forall x\in R$$

4. We have, $f(x)=x+\frac{1}{x}$ and $I=R-(-1,1)$

$$=(-\infty,-1]\cup[1,\infty).$$

Clearly, $f'(x)=1-\frac{1}{x^2}$ [1/2]

$$=\frac{x^2-1}{x^2}>0,\ \forall\ x\in I$$

[$\because x^2>1, \forall\ x\in I$ and $x^2-1>0, \forall\ x\in I$] [1]

Hence, $f(x)$ is strictly increasing on I. [1/2]

5. Given function is $f(x)=\tan x-x$.

On differentiating both sides w.r.t. x, we get

$f'(x)=\sec^2 x-1$ [1/2]

Since, range of $\sec^2 x$ is $[1,\infty)$.

$\therefore \quad f'(x)\ge 0, \forall\ x\in R$ [1]

Hence, $f(x)$ is always increasing function. [1/2]

6. Here, $f'(x)=\frac{1}{1+(\sin x+\cos x)^2}\times(\cos x-\sin x)$

$=\frac{(\cos x-\sin x)}{1+(\sin x+\cos x)^2}$ [1/2]

In the interval $\left(0, \frac{\pi}{4}\right)$, $\cos x > \sin x > 0$

$\therefore \quad \cos x - \sin x > 0$ [1/2]

or $\quad \dfrac{\cos x - \sin x}{1 + (\sin x + \cos x)^2} > 0$

$\Rightarrow \quad f'(x) > 0, \forall\ x \in \left(0, \frac{\pi}{4}\right)$

Hence, $f(x)$ is strictly increasing in $\left(0, \frac{\pi}{4}\right)$. [1]

7. We have, $f(x) = \dfrac{x}{\sin x}$

$\Rightarrow \quad f'(x) = \dfrac{\sin x \cdot 1 - x \cdot \cos x}{\sin^2 x}$

$= \dfrac{\sin x - x \cos x}{\sin^2 x}$ [1/2]

Clearly, $\quad \sin^2 x > 0, \forall x \in \left(0, \frac{\pi}{2}\right)$.

and $\sin x - x \cos x > 0$

$\Rightarrow \quad \sin x > x \cos x$

$\Rightarrow \tan x > x$, which is true, $\forall x \in \left(0, \frac{\pi}{2}\right)$.

Thus, $f'(x) > 0, \forall\ x \in \left(0, \frac{\pi}{2}\right)$. [1]

So, $f(x)$ is increasing on $\left(0, \frac{\pi}{2}\right)$. [1/2]

8. **Hint** Find $\dfrac{dy}{dx}$ and see which is smaller than 0 in $\left(0, \frac{\pi}{2}\right)$.

[**Ans.** (i) and (ii) are strictly decreasing]

9. **Hint** $f'(x) = \dfrac{1 + 2x^2}{1 + x^2} - \dfrac{1}{\sqrt{1 + x^2}}$

$= \dfrac{1 + 2x^2 - \sqrt{1 + x^2}}{1 + x^2}$

For increasing function, $f'(x) \geq 0$

$\Rightarrow \quad \dfrac{1 + 2x^2 - \sqrt{1 + x^2}}{1 + x^2} \geq 0$

$\Rightarrow \quad 1 + 2x^2 \geq \sqrt{1 + x^2}$

$\Rightarrow \quad 1 + 4x^4 + 4x^2 \geq 1 + x^2$

$\Rightarrow \quad 4x^4 + 3x^2 \geq 0$, which is true for all $x \in R$.

So, $f'(x) \geq 0, \forall\ x \in R$.

10. Given, $f(x) = x^2 + ax + 1$

On differentiating both sides w.r.t. x, we get

$f'(x) = 2x + a$

For the interval (1, 2), i.e. $1 < x < 2$ [1]

$\Rightarrow \quad 2 < 2x < 4$

$\Rightarrow \quad 2 + a < 2x + a < 4 + a$

$\Rightarrow \quad 2 + a < f'(x) < 4 + a$

Since, $f(x)$ is strictly increasing.

$\therefore \quad f'(x) > 0$ [1]

$\Rightarrow \quad 2 + a > 0 \Rightarrow a > -2$

Hence, the least value of a is -2. [2]

11. Given, $y = [x(x-2)]^2 = [x^2 - 2x]^2$

On differentiating both sides w.r.t. x, we get

$\dfrac{dy}{dx} = 2(x^2 - 2x) \cdot \dfrac{d}{dx}(x^2 - 2x)$

$= 2(x^2 - 2x)(2x - 2)$

$= 2[2x^3 - 6x^2 + 4x]$

$= 4x[x^2 - 3x + 2]$

$= 4x(x - 2)(x - 1)$ [1]

On putting $\dfrac{dy}{dx} = 0$, we get

$4x(x - 2)(x - 1) = 0$

$\Rightarrow \quad x = 0$, 1 and 2

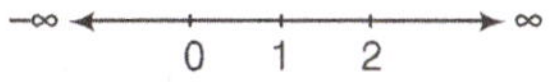

[1]

These values divide the real line into four disjoint intervals $(-\infty, 0)$, (0, 1), (1, 2) and $(2, \infty)$. [1]

In each interval, nature of $y(x)$ is given below

Interval	Sign of $f(x)$	Nature of $y(x)$
$(-\infty, 0)$	$(-)(-)(-) = -$ve	Strictly decreasing
(0, 1)	$(+)(-)(-) = +$ ve	Strictly increasing
(1, 2)	$(+)(-)(+) = -$ ve	Strictly decreasing
$(2, \infty)$	$(+)(+)(+) = +$ ve	Strictly increasing

Therefore, $y(x)$ is increasing in (0, 1) and $(2, \infty)$.

$\Rightarrow \ 0 < x < 1$ and $x > 2$. [1]

12. (i) Given, $f(x) = -2x^3 - 9x^2 - 12x + 1$

On differentiating both sides w.r.t. x, we get

$f'(x) = -6x^2 - 18x - 12$ [1]

$\Rightarrow \quad f'(x) = -6(x^2 + 3x + 2)$

$\Rightarrow \quad f'(x) = -6(x^2 + 2x + x + 2)$

$= -6[x(x + 2) + 1(x + 2)]$

$= -6(x + 2)(x + 1)$

Now, put $f'(x) = 0$ [1]

$\Rightarrow \ -6(x + 2)(x + 1) = 0$

$\Rightarrow \quad x = -2, -1$

The points, $x = -2$ and $x = -1$ divide the real line into their disjoint intervals $(-\infty, -2)$, $(-2, -1)$ and $(-1, \infty)$.

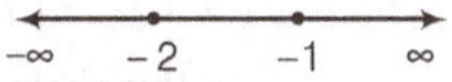

The nature of function in these intervals are given below

Interval	Sign of $f'(x)$ $f'(x) = -6(x+2)(x+1)$	Nature of function
$(-\infty, -2)$	$(-)(-)(-) = (-) < 0$	Strictly decreasing
$(-2, -1)$	$(-)(+)(-) = (+) > 0$	Strictly increasing
$(-1, \infty)$	$(-)(+)(+) = (-) < 0$	Strictly decreasing

[1]

Hence, $f(x)$ is strictly increasing in the interval $(-2, -1)$ and $f(x)$ is strictly decreasing in the interval
$(-\infty, -2) \cup (-1, \infty)$. [1]

(ii) Given, $f(x) = \frac{3}{10}x^4 - \frac{4}{5}x^3 - 3x^2 + \frac{36x}{5} + 11$

On differentiating both sides w.r.t. x, we get

$$f'(x) = \frac{12x^3}{10} - \frac{12x^2}{5} - 6x + \frac{36}{5} + 0 \quad [1]$$

Put $f'(x) = 0$

$$\Rightarrow \frac{12x^3}{10} - \frac{12x^2}{5} - 6x + \frac{36}{5} = 0$$

$$\Rightarrow \frac{6x^3 - 12x^2 - 30x + 36}{5} = 0$$

$$\Rightarrow x^3 - 2x^2 - 5x + 6 = 0 \quad \left[\text{divide by } \frac{6}{5}\right]$$

$$\Rightarrow (x-1)(x^2 - x - 6) = 0$$

$$\Rightarrow (x-1)(x+2)(x-3) = 0$$

$$\Rightarrow x - 1 = 0$$

or $x + 2 = 0$

or $x - 3 = 0$

$\therefore \quad x = -2, 1, 3$ [1]

Now, we find the intervals in which $f(x)$ is strictly increasing or strictly decreasing.

Interval	Sign of $f'(x)$ $f'(x) = (x-1)(x+2)(x-3)$	Nature of function
$(-\infty, -2)$	$(-)(-)(-) = (-) < 0$	Strictly decreasing
$(-2, 1)$	$(-)(+)(-) = (+) > 0$	Strictly increasing
$(1, 3)$	$(+)(+)(-) = (-) < 0$	Strictly decreasing
$(3, \infty)$	$(+)(+)(+) = (+) > 0$	Strictly increasing

[1]

(a) $f(x)$ is strictly increasing in the interval $(-2, 1) \cup (3, \infty)$.

(b) $f(x)$ is strictly decreasing in the interval $(-\infty, -2) \cup (1, 3)$. [1]

(iii) Given, $f(x) = \sin^4 x + \cos^4 x$, $x \in \left[0, \frac{\pi}{2}\right]$.

On differentiating both sides w.r.t. x, we get
$f'(x) = 4\sin^3 x \cos x + 4\cos^3 x(-\sin x)$

[by chain rule of derivative]

$$= 4\sin^3 x \cos x - 4\cos^3 x \sin x$$

$$= -4\sin x \cos x(\cos^2 x - \sin^2 x)$$

$$= -2\sin 2x \cos 2x$$

$[\because \cos 2x = \cos^2 x - \sin^2 x \text{ and } \sin 2x = 2\sin x \cos x]$

$$= -\sin 4x \quad [1]$$

Now, put $f'(x) = 0 \Rightarrow -\sin 4x = 0$

$$\Rightarrow \sin 4x = 0$$

$$\Rightarrow 4x = 0, \pi, 2\pi, \ldots \quad \left[\because x \in \left[0, \frac{\pi}{2}\right] \Rightarrow 4x \in [0, 2\pi]\right]$$

$$\Rightarrow x = \frac{\pi}{4} \text{ as } \frac{\pi}{4} \in \left[0, \frac{\pi}{2}\right] \quad [1]$$

The point $x = \pi/4$ divides the interval $\left[0, \frac{\pi}{2}\right]$ into two disjoint intervals $\left[0, \frac{\pi}{4}\right)$ and $\left(\frac{\pi}{4}, \frac{\pi}{2}\right]$.

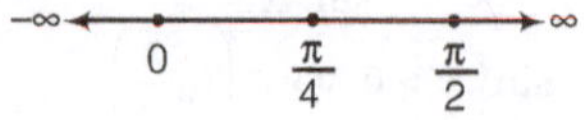

[1/2]

The nature of function in these intervals are given below

Interval	Test value	Sign of $f'(x)$, $f'(x) = -\sin 4x$	Nature of function
$\left[0, \frac{\pi}{4}\right)$	$x = \frac{\pi}{6}$	$f'\left(\frac{\pi}{6}\right) = -\sin\frac{4\pi}{6}$ $= -\sin\frac{2\pi}{3} = -\frac{\sqrt{3}}{2} < 0$	Strictly decreasing
$\left(\frac{\pi}{4}, \frac{\pi}{2}\right]$	$x = \frac{\pi}{3}$	$f'\left(\frac{\pi}{3}\right) = -\sin\frac{4\pi}{3}$ $= -\left(-\frac{\sqrt{3}}{2}\right) = \frac{\sqrt{3}}{2} > 0$	Strictly increasing

[1]

So, $f(x)$ is strictly increasing in the interval $\left(\frac{\pi}{4}, \frac{\pi}{2}\right]$ and $f(x)$ is strictly decreasing in the interval $\left[0, \frac{\pi}{4}\right)$. [1/2]

13. (i) Given, $f(x) = \frac{4\sin x - 2x - x\cos x}{2 + \cos x}$

$$= \frac{4\sin x - x(2 + \cos x)}{2 + \cos x}$$

$$= \frac{4\sin x}{2 + \cos x} - \frac{x(2 + \cos x)}{2 + \cos x}$$

$$= \frac{4\sin x}{2 + \cos x} - x \quad [1]$$

On differentiating both sides w.r.t. x, we get

$$f'(x) = 4\left\{\frac{(2 + \cos x)\cos x - \sin x(0 - \sin x)}{(2 + \cos x)^2}\right\} - 1$$

$$= 4\left\{\frac{2\cos x + \cos^2 x + \sin^2 x}{(2+\cos x)^2}\right\} - 1$$

$[\because \cos^2 x + \sin^2 x = 1]$

$$= \frac{8\cos x + 4}{(2+\cos x)^2} - 1 = \frac{8\cos x + 4 - (2+\cos x)^2}{(2+\cos x)^2}$$

$$= \frac{8\cos x + 4 - 4 - \cos^2 x - 4\cos x}{(2+\cos x)^2}$$

$$= \frac{4\cos x - \cos^2 x}{(2+\cos x)^2}$$

$$= \frac{\cos x(4-\cos x)}{(2+\cos x)^2}$$ [1]

We know that, $-1 \le \cos x \le 1$

$\Rightarrow 4 - \cos x > 0$ and $(2+\cos x)^2 > 0$

(a) For $f(x)$ to be increasing,

$f'(x) \ge 0$, when $\cos x \ge 0$

$[\because \cos x$ is positive in I and IV quadrants$]$

Thus, $f(x)$ is increasing in the interval

$\left(0, \frac{\pi}{2}\right] \cup \left[\frac{3\pi}{2}, 2\pi\right)$. [1]

(b) For $f(x)$ to be decreasing,

$f'(x) \le 0$, when $\cos x \le 0$

$[\because \cos x$ is negative in II and III quadrants$]$

Hence, $f(x)$ is decreasing in the interval $\left[\frac{\pi}{2}, \frac{3\pi}{2}\right]$. [1]

(ii) Similar as Example 9.

[**Ans.** Increasing in $[1, \infty)$, decreasing in $(-\infty, 1]$]

(iii) Similar as Example 9.

[**Ans.** Increasing in $(-\infty, -2] \cup [-1, \infty)$, decreasing in $[-2, -1]$]

(iv) **Hint** $f(x) = \frac{x}{\log x}$

$\therefore \quad f'(x) = \frac{\log x - 1}{(\log x)^2}, x \ne 1$

Now, $f'(x) \ge 0$, $x \ge e$ and $f'(x) \le 0$, $x \in (0, e] - \{1\}$

[**Ans.** $f(x)$ is increasing in $[e, \infty)$, $f(x)$ is decreasing in $(0, e] - \{1\}$]

14. **Hint** $f'(x) = 2x - 1$, which is both positive and negative in $(-1, 1)$.

Hence, $f(x)$ is neither increasing nor decreasing, further proceed as Example 7.

[**Ans.** (i) $\left(\frac{1}{2}, 1\right)$ (ii) $\left(-1, \frac{1}{2}\right)$]

15. Similar as Example 8.

[**Ans.** f is strictly increasing in the intervals $\left[0, \frac{\pi}{4}\right)$ and $\left(\frac{5\pi}{4}, 2\pi\right]$, and f is strictly decreasing in the interval $\left(\frac{\pi}{4}, \frac{5\pi}{4}\right)$]

16. Given, $f(x) = \sin 3x - \cos 3x, 0 < x < \pi$

On differentiating both sides w.r.t. x, we get

$$f'(x) = 3\cos 3x + 3\sin 3x$$ [1]

On putting $f'(x) = 0$

$\Rightarrow \quad \sin 3x = -\cos 3x$

$\Rightarrow \quad \tan 3x = -1$

$\Rightarrow \quad 3x = \frac{3\pi}{4}, \frac{7\pi}{4}, \frac{11\pi}{4}$

$[\because \tan\theta$ is negative in II and IV quadrants$]$

$\Rightarrow \quad x = \frac{\pi}{4}, \frac{7\pi}{12}, \frac{11\pi}{12}$ [1]

Now, we find intervals and check in which interval $f(x)$ is strictly increasing or strictly decreasing.

Interval	Test value	$f'(x) = 3(\cos 3x + \sin 3x)$	Sign of $f'(x)$
$0 < x < \frac{\pi}{4}$	At $x = \frac{\pi}{6}$	$3\left(\cos\frac{\pi}{2} + \sin\frac{\pi}{2}\right)$ $= 3(0+1) = 3$	+ ve
$\frac{\pi}{4} < x < \frac{7\pi}{12}$	At $x = \frac{\pi}{3}$	$3(\cos\pi + \sin\pi)$ $= 3(-1+0) = -3$	− ve
$\frac{7\pi}{12} < x < \frac{11\pi}{12}$	At $x = \frac{3\pi}{4}$	$3\left(\cos\frac{9\pi}{4} + \sin\frac{9\pi}{4}\right)$ $= 3\left(\frac{1}{\sqrt{2}} + \frac{1}{\sqrt{2}}\right) = 3\sqrt{2}$	+ ve
$\frac{11\pi}{12} < x < \pi$	At $x = \frac{23\pi}{24}$	$3\left(\cos\frac{23\pi}{8} + \sin\frac{23}{8}\pi\right)$ < 0	− ve

[2]

Here, we see that $f'(x) > 0$, for $0 < x < \frac{\pi}{4}$ and $\frac{7\pi}{12} < x < \frac{11\pi}{12}$, so $f(x)$ is strictly increasing in the intervals $\left(0, \frac{\pi}{4}\right)$ and $\left(\frac{7\pi}{12}, \frac{11\pi}{12}\right)$. [1]

While $f'(x) < 0$ in $\frac{\pi}{4} < x < \frac{7\pi}{12}$ and $\frac{11\pi}{12} < x < \pi$.

So, $f(x)$ is strictly decreasing in the intervals $\left(\frac{\pi}{4}, \frac{7\pi}{12}\right)$ and $\left(\frac{11\pi}{12}, \pi\right)$. [1]

17. Let $y = f(\theta) = \dfrac{4\sin\theta}{2+\cos\theta} - \theta$

On differentiating both sides w.r.t. θ, we get

$$f'(\theta) = \frac{(2+\cos\theta)(4\cos\theta) - 4\sin\theta\,(0-\sin\theta)}{(2+\cos\theta)^2} - 1 \quad [1]$$

[by quotient rule of derivative]

$$= \frac{8\cos\theta + 4\cos^2\theta + 4\sin^2\theta}{(2+\cos\theta)^2} - 1$$

$$= \frac{8\cos\theta + 4}{(2+\cos\theta)^2} - 1 \quad [\because \sin^2\theta + \cos^2\theta = 1] \; [1]$$

$$= \frac{8\cos\theta + 4 - 4 - \cos^2\theta - 4\cos\theta}{(2+\cos\theta)^2}$$

$$= \frac{4\cos\theta - \cos^2\theta}{(2+\cos\theta)^2} = \frac{\cos\theta\,(4-\cos\theta)}{(2+\cos\theta)^2} \quad [1]$$

For all $x \in \left(0, \dfrac{\pi}{2}\right)$, $\dfrac{\cos\theta\,(4-\cos\theta)}{(2+\cos\theta)^2} > 0$ [1]

$\Rightarrow \quad f'(\theta) > 0, \forall\, \theta \in \left(0, \dfrac{\pi}{2}\right)$ [1]

Therefore, $f(\theta)$ is strictly increasing in $\left(0, \dfrac{\pi}{2}\right)$.

Also, the given function is continuous at $\theta = 0$ and $\theta = \dfrac{\pi}{2}$.

Hence, $f(\theta)$ is increasing in $\left[0, \dfrac{\pi}{2}\right]$. **Hence proved.** [1]

TOPIC 04 Maxima and Minima

Here, we will use the concept of derivatives to calculate the maximum or minimum values of various functions. We will find the turning points of the graph of a function and then find points at which the graph reaches its highest (or lowest) locally. Also, find the absolute maximum and absolute minimum of a function.

Maximum and Minimum Values in an Interval

Let f be a function defined on an interval I (i.e. I is the domain of f).

(i) **Maximum Value of a Function** A function $f(x)$ is said to have a maximum value in I, if there exists a point c in interval I, such that $f(c) > f(x)$ for all $x \in I$. Here, the number $f(c)$ is called the (absolute) **maximum value of f** in I and point c is called a **point of maximum value of f** in I.

(ii) **Minimum Value of a Function** A function $f(x)$ is said to have a minimum value in I, if there exists a point c in interval I, such that $f(c) < f(x)$ for all values of x in I. Here, the number $f(c)$ is called the (absolute) **minimum value of f** in I and the point c is called a **point of minimum value of f** in I.

(iii) **Extreme Value of a Function** A function $f(x)$ is said to have an extreme value in I, if there exists a point c in interval I, such that $f(c)$ is either a maximum value or minimum value in the interval. Then, $f(c)$ is called the **extreme value of f** in that interval and c is the extreme point.

Note Graphs of certain particular functions help us to find maximum value and minimum value at a point. Also, from graph, we can find maximum/minimum value of a function at a point in which it is not even differentiable.

Example 1 Find the maximum and minimum values of f, if any of the function given by $f(x) = |x|$, $x \in R$. Also, find the maximum value in $[-2, 1]$.

Sol. We have, $f(x) = |x|$

Its graph is given below

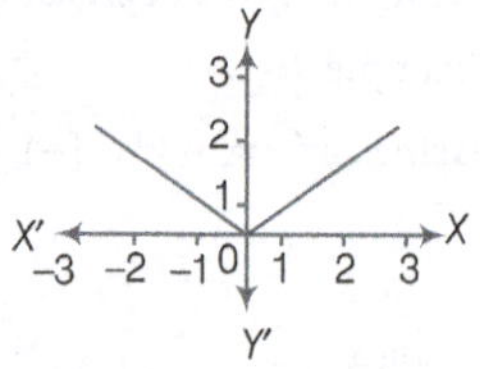

Here, $f(x) \geq 0$, $\forall x \in R$ and $f(x) = 0$, if $x = 0$.

$\therefore$ Minimum value of $f(x) = 0$ at point $x = 0$.

Also, f has no maximum value in R, so no point of maximum value in R. Now, if domain of $f = [-2, 1]$, then maximum value of f is $|-2| = 2$ and minimum value is 0.

Note Here, function $f(x)$ is not differentiable at $x = 0$, but minimum value exist.

Some Important Results

(i) Every monotonic function, i.e. either increasing or decreasing function assumes its maximum/minimum value at the end points of the domain of the function.

(ii) Every continuous function on a closed interval has a maximum and a minimum value.

e.g. Let $f(x)=x, x \in (0, 1)$. In (0, 1), $f(x)$ has neither the maximum value nor the minimum value. If we include the points 0 and 1 in the domain, i.e. if domain is $[0,1]$, then $f(x)=x$ has minimum value 0 at $x=0$ and maximum value 1 at $x=1$.

Note If a function f defined on an interval I, then following possibilities are arises

(i) It may attain the maximum value at a point in I but not the minimum value at any point in I.
(ii) It may attain the minimum value at a point in I but not the maximum value at any point in I.
(iii) It may attain both the maximum and minimum values at some point in I.
(iv) It may not attain both the maximum and minimum values at any point in I.

Local Maxima and Local Minima

Consider points P, Q, R and S on the graph, at which the function changes its nature from decreasing to increasing or *vice-versa*. These points may be called **turning points** or **stationary points** of the given function. At turning points, the graph has either a little hill or a little valley.

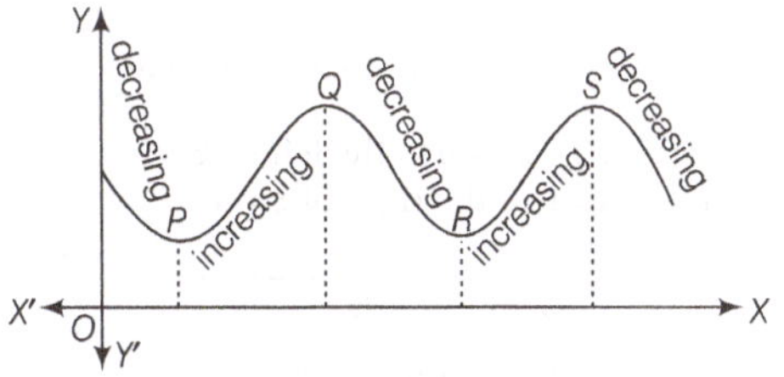

Here, points P and R may be regarded as points of local minimum value or relative minimum value and points Q and S may be regarded as points of local maximum value or relative maximum value for the function.

The local maximum value and local minimum value of the function are referred to as local maxima and local minima, respectively of the function.

Definition Let f be a real valued function and c be an interior point in the domain of f, then

(i) c is called a point of local maxima, if there is an $h>0$ such that $f(c)>f(x)$ for all x in $(c-h, c+h)$. Here, value $f(c)$ is called the **local maximum value (or relative maximum value)** of f.

(ii) c is called a point of local minima, if there is an $h>0$ such that $f(c)<f(x)$ for all x in $(c-h, c+h)$. Here, value $f(c)$ is called the **local minimum value (or relative minimum value)** of f.

Geometrical Interpretation

(i) Suppose $x=c$ is a point of local maxima of f, then the graph of f around c will be as shown in Fig. (i).

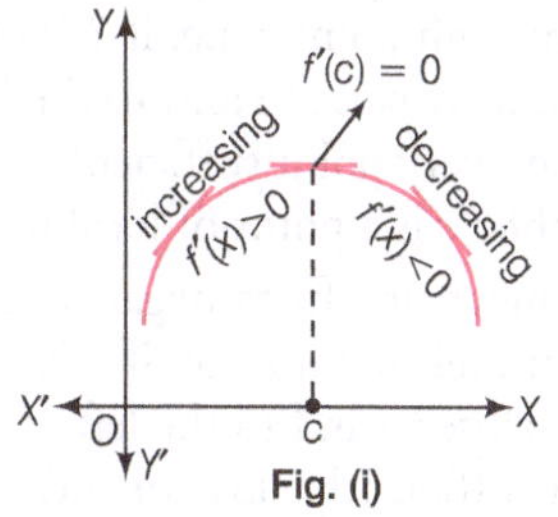

Fig. (i)

(ii) Similarly, if c is a point of local minima of f, then the graph of f around c will be as shown in the Fig. (ii).

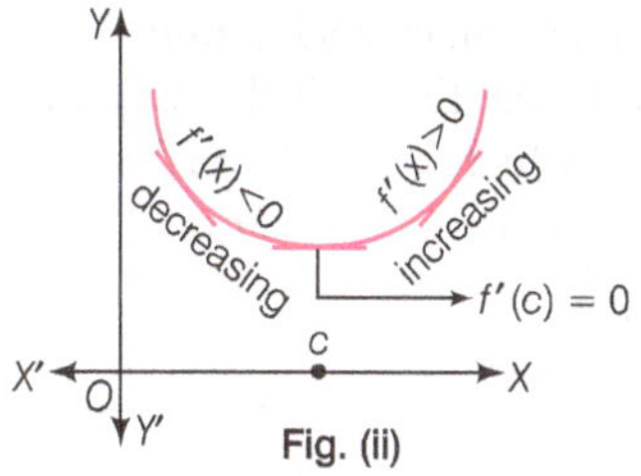

Fig. (ii)

Thus, the nature of f in intervals is given below

Interval	f in Fig. (i)	f in Fig. (ii)
$(c-h, c)$	increasing [i.e. $f'(x)>0$]	decreasing [i.e. $f'(x)<0$]
$(c, c+h)$	decreasing [i.e. $f'(x)<0$]	increasing [i.e. $f'(x)>0$]

Thus, this suggest that $f'(c)$ must be zero.

Some Important Theorems

Theorem 1. Let f be a function defined on an open interval I. Suppose $c \in I$ be any point. If f has a local maxima or a local minima at $x=c$, then either $f'(c)=0$ or f is not differentiable at c.

Note The converse of above theorem need not be true that is a point at which the derivative vanishes need not be a point of local maxima or local minima. e.g. If $f(x)=x^3$, then $f'(x)=3x^2$ and so $f'(0)=0$. But 0 is neither a point of local maxima nor a point of local minima.

Critical Point A point c in the domain of a function f at which either $f'(c)=0$ or f is not differentiable, is called a **critical point** of f. If f is continuous at point c and $f'(c)=0$, then there exists a $h>0$ such that f is differentiable in the interval $(c-h, c+h)$.

Theorem 2. (First Derivative Test) Let f be a function defined on an open interval I and f be continuous at a critical point c in I.

(i) If $f'(x)$ changes sign from positive to negative as x increases through point c, i.e. if $f'(x) > 0$ at every point sufficiently close to and to the left of c and $f'(x) < 0$ at every point sufficiently close to and to the right of c, then c is a point of local maxima.

(ii) If $f'(x)$ changes sign from negative to positive as x increases through point c, i.e. if $f'(x) < 0$ at every point sufficiently close to and to the left of c and $f'(x) > 0$ at every point sufficiently close to and to the right of c, then c is a point of local minima.

(iii) If $f'(x)$ does not change sign as x increases through c, then c is neither a point of local maxima nor a point of local minima. Infact, such a point is called **point of inflexion.** In the figure, if the tangent to the curve (i.e. at point B) which is parallel to X-axis crosses the curve, is said to be **point of inflexion.**

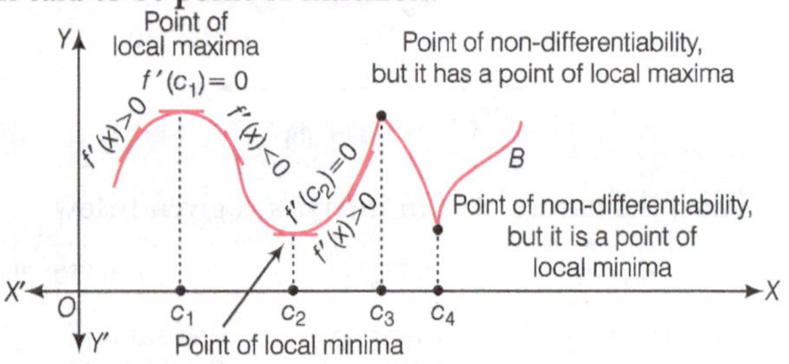

Note If c is a point of local maxima of f, then f(c) is a local maximum value of f. Similarly, if c is a point of local minima of f, then f(c) is a local minimum value of f.

Working Rule to Find the Local Maxima /Minima by First Derivative Test

Suppose $f(x)$ be the given function, then to find local maxima and local minima of $f(x)$ by first derivative test, we use the following steps

I. Firstly, write the given function $f(x)$ and differentiate it w.r.t. x, i.e. find $f'(x)$.

II. Put $f'(x) = 0$ and solve it to find critical points (say a and b) which could possibly be the points of local maxima or local minima of f.

III. Take these points one-by-one and check that it is a point of local maxima/minima, i.e. check the following.

	Values of x	Sign of $f'(x)$	Nature of point
Close to a	to the right of a and to the left of a	> 0 < 0	Local minima
Close to b	to the right of b and to the left of b	< 0 > 0	Local maxima

IV. Now, find the local maximum or minimum value of function by putting corresponding point in given function in place of x.

Note If we get two or more than two critical points, then for making above Step III easier, we can divide the real number line into intervals and then check the nature of function in each interval.

Example 2 Find the points of local maxima and local minima of the function $f(x) = (x-1)^3 (x+1)^2$.

Sol. We have, $f(x) = (x-1)^3 (x+1)^2$

$$\therefore \; f'(x) = 3(x-1)^2 (x+1)^2 + (x-1)^3 \, 2(x+1)$$

$$= (x-1)^2 (x+1)[3(x+1) + 2(x-1)]$$

$$= (x-1)^2 (x+1)(5x+1)$$

For local maxima or local minima, put $f'(x) = 0$,

$$\Rightarrow (x-1)^2 (x+1)(5x+1) = 0 \Rightarrow x = -\frac{1}{5}, -1, 1$$

For $x = -1$, $f'(x) > 0$ to the left of $x = -1$ and $f'(x) < 0$ to the right of $x = -1$.

$\therefore$ $x = -1$ is a point of local maxima.

For $x = -\frac{1}{5}$, $f'(x) < 0$ to the left of $x = -\frac{1}{5}$ and $f'(x) > 0$ to the right of $x = -\frac{1}{5}$.

$\therefore$ $x = -\frac{1}{5}$ is a point of local minima.

For $x = 1$, $f'(x) > 0$ to the left of $x = 1$ and $f'(x) > 0$ to the right of $x = 1$.

$$\underset{-\infty \quad\quad -1 \quad\quad -1/5 \quad\quad 1 \quad\quad \infty}{+ \quad\quad - \quad\quad + \quad\quad +}$$

Thus, we have the following table

	Value of x	Sign of $f'(x)$	Nature of point
Close to -1	to the right of -1 and to the left of -1	< 0 > 0	Local maxima
Close to $\frac{-1}{5}$	to the right of $\frac{-1}{5}$ and to the left of $\frac{-1}{5}$	> 0 < 0	Local minima

At $x = \frac{-1}{5}$,

$$f\left(-\frac{1}{5}\right) = \left(-\frac{1}{5} - 1\right)^3 \left(-\frac{1}{5} + 1\right)^2 = \left(\frac{-6}{5}\right)^3 \left(\frac{4}{5}\right)^2 = -\frac{3456}{3125}$$

At $x = -1$, $f(-1) = (-1-1)^3 (-1+1)^2 = 0$

Hence, the point of local maxima is -1 and the local maximum value $= 0$ and the point of local minima is $-\frac{1}{5}$ and the local minimum value $= \frac{-3456}{3125}$.

Example 3 Find all the points of local maxima and minima of the function $f(x) = x^3 - 6x^2 + 9x - 8$.

Sol. We have, $f(x) = x^3 - 6x^2 + 9x - 8$

On differentiating both sides w.r.t. x, we get

$$f'(x) = 3x^2 - 12x + 9$$

Put $f'(x) = 0$

$\Rightarrow \quad 3x^2 - 12x + 9 = 0$

$\Rightarrow \quad 3(x^2 - 4x + 3) = 0$

$\Rightarrow \quad 3(x-1)(x-3) = 0 \quad$ ...(i)

$\Rightarrow \quad x = 1, 3$

These are the critical points.

Now, for values close to 1 and to the right of 1, $f'(x) < 0$ and for values close to 1 and to the left of 1, $f'(x) > 0$.

$\therefore$ $x = 1$ is a point of local maxima.

For values close to 3 and to the right of 3, $f'(x) > 0$ and for values close to 3 and to the left of 3, $f'(x) < 0$.

$\therefore \quad x = 3$ is a point of local minima.

Hence, $x = 1$ is a point of local maxima and $x = 3$ is a point of local minima for given function.

Example 4 Find the local maxima or local minima value, if any of the function $f(x) = \dfrac{1}{x^2 + 2}$.

Sol. We have, $f(x) = \dfrac{1}{x^2+2} \Rightarrow f'(x) = \dfrac{-2x}{(x^2+2)^2}$

For a local maxima or local minima, put $f'(x) = 0$

$$\Rightarrow -\frac{2x}{(x^2+2)^2} = 0 \Rightarrow x = 0$$

Now, when x is slightly less than 0, i.e. when x is negative, then $f'(x) = -\dfrac{2x}{(x^2+2)^2}$ is positive.

When x is slightly greater than 0, then

$f'(x) = -\dfrac{2x}{(x^2+2)^2}$ is negative.

Thus, $f'(x)$ changes sign from positive to negative.

So, $x = 0$ is a point of local maxima and local maximum value is $f(0) = \dfrac{1}{0+2} = \dfrac{1}{2}$.

Theorem 3 **(Second Derivative Test)** Let f be a function defined on an interval I and $c \in I$ and f be twice differentiable at c. Then,

(i) $x = c$ is a point of local maxima, if

$$f'(c) = 0 \quad \text{and} \quad f''(c) < 0$$

The value $f(c)$ is local maximum value of f.

(ii) $x = c$ is a point of local minima, if $f'(c) = 0$ and $f''(c) > 0$.

The value $f(c)$ is local minimum value of f.

(iii) The test fails, if $f'(c) = 0$ and $f''(c) = 0$.

In this case, we go back to the first derivative test and find whether c is a point of local maxima or local minima.

Note As f is twice differentiable at c, we mean second order derivative of f exists at c.

Working Rule to Find the Local Maxima/ Minima by Second Derivative Test

Suppose $f(x)$ be the given function. Then, to find local maxima and local minima by second derivative test, we use the following steps

I. First, write the given function and differentiate it w.r.t. x, i.e. find first derivative.

II. Put first derivative, i.e. $f'(x) = 0$ and find the critical points which could be possibly the points of local maxima or local minima.

III. Find second derivative of $f(x)$, i.e. again differentiate $f'(x)$ w.r.t. x to get $f''(x)$.

IV. Check the sign of $f''(x)$ at each critical point obtained in step II to get local maxima/minima, i.e. Suppose $x = a$ is a critical point, then if at $x = a$,

(i) $f''(a) < 0$, then a is point of local maxima.

(ii) $f''(a) > 0$, then a is point of local minima.

(iii) $f''(a) = 0$, then test fails.

V. Now, find the local maximum or minimum value of function by putting corresponding point in the given function in place of x.

Example 5 Find the local maxima and local minima and the corresponding local maximum and local minimum values of the following functions.

(i) $f(x) = x\sqrt{1-x}$, where $x \le 1$ **[NCERT]**

(ii) $f(x) = \dfrac{x}{(x-1)(x-4)}$, where $1 < x < 4$.

Sol. (i) Given, $f(x) = x\sqrt{1-x}$

On differentiating twice w.r.t. x, we get

$$f'(x) = \frac{-x}{2\sqrt{1-x}} + \sqrt{1-x} = \frac{(2-3x)}{2\sqrt{1-x}}$$

$$\text{and } f''(x) = \frac{1}{2}\left[\frac{\sqrt{1-x}\,(0-3) - (2-3x) \times \dfrac{-1}{2\sqrt{1-x}}}{(\sqrt{1-x})^2}\right]$$

$$= \frac{(3x-4)}{4(1-x)^{3/2}}$$

For local maxima and local minima, put $f'(x) = 0$

$$\Rightarrow \quad (2-3x) = 0 \Rightarrow x = \frac{2}{3}$$

and $f''\left(\frac{2}{3}\right) = \dfrac{\left(3\times\frac{2}{3} - 4\right)}{4\left(1-\frac{2}{3}\right)^{3/2}} = \dfrac{-3^{3/2}}{2} < 0$

$\therefore \quad x = \frac{2}{3}$ is a point of local maxima.

Hence, local maximum value $= f\left(\frac{2}{3}\right) = \frac{2}{3\sqrt{3}}$.

(ii) Given, $f(x) = \dfrac{x}{(x-1)(x-4)} = \dfrac{x}{(x^2-5x+4)}$

On differentiating twice w.r.t. x, we get

$$f'(x) = \frac{(x^2-5x+4)1 - x(2x-5)}{(x^2-5x+4)^2} = \frac{4-x^2}{(x^2-5x+4)^2}$$

and $f''(x) = \dfrac{\left[\begin{array}{r}(x^2-5x+4)^2(-2x)-(4-x^2)2\\ (x^2-5x+4)(2x-5)\end{array}\right]}{(x^2-5x+4)^4}$

$$\Rightarrow f''(x) = \frac{2[(x^2-5x+4)(-x)-(4-x^2)(2x-5)]}{(x^2-5x+4)^3}$$

$$= \frac{2[-x^3+5x^2-4x-(8x-20-2x^3+5x^2)]}{(x^2-5x+4)^3}$$

$$= \frac{2[x^3-12x+20]}{(x^2-5x+4)^3}$$

For local maxima and local minima, put $f'(x) = 0$

$$\Rightarrow \quad (4-x^2) = 0 \Rightarrow x = \pm 2$$

But $1 < x < 4 \Rightarrow x = 2$ $\qquad [\because x = -2 \notin (1, 4)]$

Now, $f''(2) = \dfrac{2[2^3-(12\times 2)+20]}{(2^2-(5\times 2)+4)^3} = \dfrac{2(4)}{(-2)^3} = -1 < 0.$

$\therefore$ $x = 2$ is a point of local maxima.

Thus, local maximum value $= f(2)$

$$= \frac{2}{(2-1)(2-4)} = \frac{2}{-2} = -1$$

Example 6 Find all the points of local maxima and local minima of $f(x) = -x + 2\sin x$ on $[0, 2\pi]$. Also, find local maximum and minimum values.

Sol. We have, $f(x) = -x + 2\sin x$

On differentiating both sides w.r.t. x, we get

$$f'(x) = -1 + 2\cos x \qquad \text{...(i)}$$

For local maxima and local minima, put $f'(x) = 0$

$$\Rightarrow \quad -1 + 2\cos x = 0 \Rightarrow \cos x = \frac{1}{2}$$

$$\Rightarrow \quad x = 2n\pi \pm \frac{\pi}{3}$$

$$\Rightarrow \quad x = \frac{\pi}{3}, \frac{5\pi}{3} \in [0, 2\pi]$$

On differentiating both sides of Eq. (i) w.r.t. x, we get

$$f''(x) = -2\sin x$$

At $x = \pi/3$, $f''\left(\frac{\pi}{3}\right) = -2\sin\frac{\pi}{3} = -\sqrt{3} < 0$

$\therefore \quad x = \frac{\pi}{3}$ is a point of local maxima.

At $x = \frac{5\pi}{3}$, $f''\left(\frac{5\pi}{3}\right) = -2\sin\frac{5\pi}{3} = \sqrt{3} > 0$

$\therefore \quad x = \frac{5\pi}{3}$ is a point of local minima.

Hence, the points of local maxima is $\frac{\pi}{3}$ and local minima is $\frac{5\pi}{3}$.

On putting $x = \frac{\pi}{3}$ in $f(x)$, we get

$$f\left(\frac{\pi}{3}\right) = -\frac{\pi}{3} + 2\sin\frac{\pi}{3} = -\frac{\pi}{3} + 2\times\frac{\sqrt{3}}{2} = \frac{-\pi}{3} + \sqrt{3}$$

which is the required local maximum value.

On putting $x = \frac{5\pi}{3}$ in $f(x)$, we get

$$f\left(\frac{5\pi}{3}\right) = -\frac{5\pi}{3} + 2\sin\frac{5\pi}{3}$$

$$= \frac{-5\pi}{3} + 2\times\left(\frac{-\sqrt{3}}{2}\right) = \frac{-5\pi}{3} - \sqrt{3}$$

which is the required local minimum value.

Example 7 Prove that the area of right angled triangle of given hypotenuse is maximum when the triangle is isosceles. **[ISC 2020]**

Sol. Let ΔABC be right angled triangle, right angle at B.

Let $AB = x$, $BC = y$, $AC = h$

Length of hypotenuse of ΔABC is fixed.

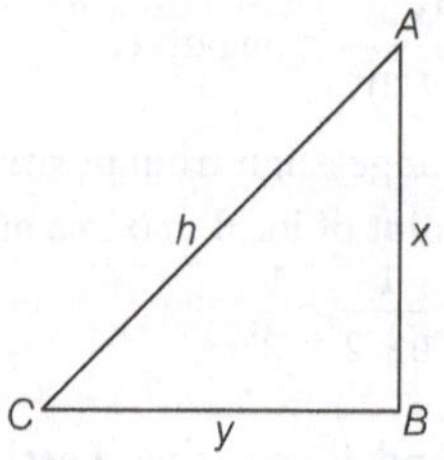

$$\therefore \quad h^2 = x^2 + y^2 \qquad \text{...(i)}$$

$$\Rightarrow \quad y^2 = h^2 - x^2$$

Let A be the area of ΔABC.

$$\therefore \quad A = \frac{1}{2}xy$$

$$\Rightarrow \quad A^2 = \frac{1}{4}x^2y^2$$

$$\Rightarrow \quad Z = \frac{1}{4}x^2y^2 \quad [\text{ say } A^2 = Z]$$

$$\Rightarrow \quad Z = \frac{1}{4}x^2(h^2 - x^2)$$

$$\Rightarrow \quad Z = \frac{1}{4}(h^2x^2 - x^4)$$

$$\Rightarrow \quad \frac{dZ}{dx} = \frac{1}{4}(2h^2x - 4x^3)$$

For maxima or minima $\frac{dZ}{dx} = 0$

$$\therefore \frac{1}{4}(2h^2x - 4x^3) = 0 \Rightarrow h^2 = 2x^2 \quad [\because x \neq 0]$$

$$\frac{d^2Z}{dx^2} = \frac{1}{4}[2h^2 - 12x^2]$$

$$= \frac{1}{4}(2h^2 - 6h^2) = -h^2 < 0$$

$\therefore$ Area of triangle is maximum when $h^2 = 2x^2$

Now, putting the value of h^2 in Eq. (i), we get

$$2x^2 = x^2 + y^2 \Rightarrow x = y$$

$$\therefore \quad AB = BC$$

$\therefore$ Area of right angle triangle of given hypotenuse is maximum when the triangle is isosceles.

Example 8 Show that the surface area of a closed cuboid with square base and given volume is minimum, when it is a cube. **[ISC 2017]**

Sol. Let V be the fixed volume of a closed cuboid with length x, breadth x and height y.

Let S be its surface area, then

$$V = x \times x \times y$$

$$\Rightarrow \quad y = \frac{V}{x^2} \quad \text{...(i)}$$

Now, $$S = 2(x^2 + xy + xy)$$

$$\Rightarrow \quad S = 2(x^2 + 2xy) = 2\left(x^2 + \frac{2V}{x}\right) \quad [\text{using Eq. (i)}]$$

$$\Rightarrow \quad S = 2\left(x^2 + \frac{2V}{x}\right)$$

On differentiating w.r.t. x, we get

$$\frac{dS}{dx} = 2\left(2x - \frac{2V}{x^2}\right) \text{ and } \frac{d^2S}{dx^2} = \left(4 + \frac{8V}{x^3}\right)$$

Now, put $\frac{dS}{dx} = 0 \Rightarrow 2\left(2x - \frac{2V}{x^2}\right) = 0$

$$\Rightarrow \quad 2x = \frac{2V}{x^2} \Rightarrow x^3 = V \Rightarrow V = x^3$$

$$\Rightarrow \quad x \times x \times y = x^3 \Rightarrow y = x$$

Now, when $y = x$, then we have $V = x^3$

$$\therefore \quad \left(\frac{d^2S}{dx^2}\right)_{y=x} = 4 + \frac{8x^3}{x^3} = 12 > 0$$

So, S is minimum when length = x, breadth = x and height = x, i.e. when it is cube.

Example 9 A closed right circular cylinder has volume $\frac{539}{2}$ cu units. Find the radius and the height of the cylinder so that the total surface area is minimum. **[ISC 2010]**

Sol. Let h be the height and r be the radius of cylinder.

Given, volume of cylinder, $V = \pi r^2 h = \frac{539}{2}$

$$\Rightarrow \quad h = \frac{539}{2\pi r^2} \quad \text{...(i)}$$

Total surface area of cylinder $S = 2\pi rh + 2\pi r^2$

$$= 2\pi r\left(\frac{539}{2\pi r^2}\right) + 2\pi r^2 \quad [\text{from Eq. (i)}]$$

$$= \frac{539}{r} + 2\pi r^2 \quad \text{...(ii)}$$

For maxima and minima, $\frac{dS}{dr} = 0$

$$\Rightarrow \quad 539\left(\frac{-1}{r^2}\right) + 4\pi r = 0 \Rightarrow 4\pi r^3 = 539$$

[differentiating Eq. (ii) w.r.t. r]

$$\Rightarrow \quad r^3 = \frac{539}{4\pi} = \frac{539 \times 7}{4 \times 22} = \frac{49 \times 7}{4 \times 2}$$

$$\Rightarrow \quad r^3 = \frac{7^3}{2^3} \Rightarrow r = \frac{7}{2} \text{ units} \quad [\text{taking cube root}]$$

Example 10 Show that the radius of a closed right circular cylinder of given surface area and maximum volume is equal to half of its height. **[ISC 2020]**

Sol. Let r be the radius of the circular base and h be the height of the cylinder.

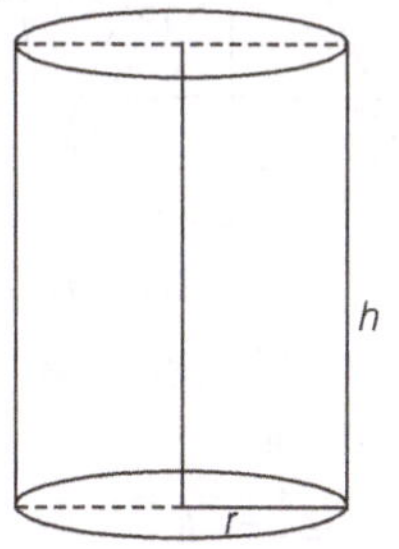

Let S (given) and V denotes its surface area and volume of cylinder. Then,

$$S = 2\pi r^2 + 2\pi rh$$

$$\Rightarrow \quad h = \frac{S - 2\pi r^2}{2\pi r} \quad \text{... (i)}$$

$\therefore \quad V = \pi r^2 h = \pi r^2 \left(\frac{S - 2\pi r^2}{2\pi r} \right)$

$\Rightarrow \quad V = \frac{1}{2}(Sr - 2\pi r^3)$

On differentiating it w.r.t. r, we get

$$\frac{dV}{dr} = \frac{1}{2}(S - 6\pi r^2) \text{ and } \frac{d^2V}{dr^2} = -6\pi r$$

Now, $\frac{dV}{dr} = 0 \Rightarrow S - 6\pi r^2 = 0 \Rightarrow r^2 = \frac{S}{6\pi}$

$\Rightarrow \quad r = \sqrt{\frac{S}{6\pi}}$

For, $\quad r = \sqrt{\frac{S}{6\pi}}, \frac{d^2V}{dr^2} = -3\pi\sqrt{\frac{S}{6\pi}} < 0$

$\Rightarrow V$ is maximum at $r = \sqrt{\frac{S}{6\pi}}$

Now, putting the value of $S = 6\pi r^2$ in Eq. (i), we get

$$h = \frac{6\pi r^2 - 2\pi r^2}{2\pi r} = \frac{4\pi r^2}{2\pi r} = 2r$$

$\Rightarrow \quad r = \frac{h}{2}$

Hence, volume is maximum when $r = \frac{h}{2}$

Example 11 A cone is inscribed in a sphere of radius 12 cm. If the volume of the cone is maximum, find its height. **[ISC 2018]**

Sol. Let r be the radius and h be the height of cone, which inscribed in a sphere of radius 12 cm.

$\therefore \quad OD = h - 12 \quad [\because AD = h]$

$\Rightarrow \quad x = h - 12$

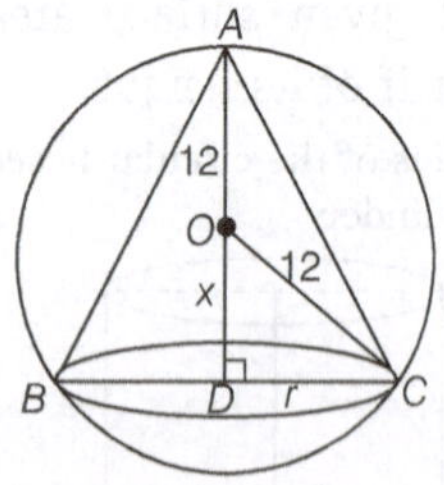

In $\Delta OCD, 12^2 = x^2 + r^2 \Rightarrow 144 = (h-12)^2 + r^2$

$\Rightarrow \quad r^2 = 144 - h^2 + 24h - 144$

$\Rightarrow \quad r^2 = 24h - h^2$

Volume of cone, $V = \frac{1}{3}\pi r^2 h$

$\Rightarrow \quad V = \frac{\pi}{3}(24h - h^2)h = \frac{\pi}{3}(24h^2 - h^3)$

On differentiating both sides w.r.t. h, we get

$$\frac{dV}{dh} = \frac{1}{3}(48h - 3h^2)$$

For maxima or minima, put $\frac{dV}{dx} = 0$

$\Rightarrow \quad 48h - 3h^2 = 0 \Rightarrow h = 16$

Again differentiating w.r.t. h, we get

$$\frac{d^2V}{dh^2} = (16 - 2h)$$

$\Rightarrow \quad \left(\frac{d^2V}{dh^2}\right)_{h=16} = (16 - 32) < 0$

Here, the volume is maximum when $h = 16$ cm.

Example 12 The sum of surface areas of a sphere and a cuboid with sides $\frac{x}{3}$, x and $2x$ is constant. Show that the sum of their volumes is minimum, if x is equal to three times the radius of the sphere.

Sol. Let r be the radius of the sphere and dimensions of cuboid are $\frac{x}{3}$, x, $2x$, respectively.

$\Rightarrow \quad 4\pi r^2 + 2\left[\frac{x}{3} \times x + x \times 2x + 2x \times \frac{x}{3}\right] = k$ (constant) [given]

$\Rightarrow \quad 4\pi r^2 + 6x^2 = k \Rightarrow r^2 = \frac{k - 6x^2}{4\pi}$

$\Rightarrow \quad r = \sqrt{\frac{k - 6x^2}{4\pi}}$ ...(i)

Sum of the volumes, $V = \frac{4}{3}\pi r^3 + \frac{x}{3} \times x \times 2x$

$\Rightarrow \quad V = \frac{4}{3}\pi\left(\frac{k - 6x^2}{4\pi}\right)^{3/2} + \frac{2}{3}x^3$

On differentiating both sides w.r.t. x, we get

$$\frac{dV}{dx} = \frac{4}{3}\pi \times \frac{3}{2}\left(\frac{k - 6x^2}{4\pi}\right)^{1/2}\left(\frac{-12x}{4\pi}\right) + \frac{2}{3} \times 3x^2$$

$$= 2\pi\sqrt{\frac{k - 6x^2}{4\pi}}\left(\frac{-3x}{\pi}\right) + 2x^2$$

$$= (-6x)\sqrt{\frac{k - 6x^2}{4\pi}} + 2x^2$$

For maximum or minimum value, put $\frac{dV}{dx} = 0$

$\Rightarrow \quad (-6x)\sqrt{\frac{k - 6x^2}{4\pi}} + 2x^2 = 0$

$\Rightarrow \quad 2x^2 = 6x\sqrt{\frac{k - 6x^2}{4\pi}} \Rightarrow x = 3\sqrt{\frac{k - 6x^2}{4\pi}}$

$\Rightarrow \quad x = 3r$ [using Eq. (i)]

Again, differentiating $\frac{dV}{dx}$ w.r.t. x, we get

$$\frac{d^2V}{dx^2} = \frac{-6}{2\sqrt{\pi}}\frac{d}{dx}(x\sqrt{k - 6x^2}) + 4x$$

$$= \frac{-3}{\sqrt{\pi}}\left(\sqrt{k-6x^2} + x \cdot \frac{1}{2} \cdot \frac{1}{\sqrt{k-6x^2}}(-12x)\right) + 4x$$

$$= \frac{-3}{\sqrt{\pi}}\left(\frac{k-6x^2-6x^2}{\sqrt{k-6x^2}}\right) + 4x = \frac{3(12x^2-k)}{\sqrt{\pi}\sqrt{k-6x^2}} + 4x$$

$$\left[\frac{d^2V}{dx^2}\right]_{x=\frac{3}{2\sqrt{\pi}}\sqrt{k-6x^2}} = \frac{3\left(12x^2 - \frac{4\pi x^2}{9} - 6x^2\right)}{\sqrt{\pi}\sqrt{\frac{4\pi x^2}{9} + 6x^2 - 6x^2}} + 4x$$

$$= \frac{3\left(6x^2 - \frac{4\pi x^2}{9}\right)}{\sqrt{\pi}\left(\frac{2\sqrt{\pi}x}{3}\right)} + 4x = \frac{3\left(\frac{54x^2 - 4\pi x^2}{9}\right)}{\frac{2\pi x}{3}} + 4x$$

$$= \frac{54x^2 - 4\pi x^2}{2\pi x} + 4x = \frac{2x^2(27-2\pi)}{2\pi x} + 4x$$

$$= \frac{x(27-2\pi)}{\pi} + 4x > 0$$

$\therefore V$ is minimum, when $x = 3\sqrt{\dfrac{k-6x^2}{4\pi}}$.

But $r = \sqrt{\dfrac{k-6x^2}{4\pi}} \Rightarrow x = 3r$

Hence, V is minimum when x is equal to three times the radius of the sphere.

Example 13 A wire of length 50 m is cut into two pieces. One piece of the wire is bent in the shape of a square and the other in the shape of a circle. What should be the length of each piece so that the combined area of the two is minimum? **[ISC 2014]**

Sol. Let x be the radius of circle and y be the side of square.

Circumference of circle $= 2\pi x$

Perimeter of square $= 4y$

Also, given, $2\pi x + 4y = 50$ ...(i)

Let A be the sum of the area of circle and square.

Then, $A = \pi x^2 + y^2$

$$= \pi x^2 + \left(\frac{50 - 2\pi x}{4}\right)^2 \quad \text{[from Eq. (i)]}$$

On differentiating both sides w.r.t. x, we get

$$\frac{dA}{dx} = 2\pi x + 2\frac{(50-2\pi x)}{4}\frac{d}{dx}\left(\frac{50-2\pi x}{4}\right)$$

$$= 2\pi x + \frac{2(50-2\pi x)}{4} \times \left(\frac{-2\pi}{4}\right)$$

$$= 2\pi x - \frac{(50-2\pi x)\pi}{4} = 2\pi x - \frac{50\pi}{4} + \frac{\pi^2 x}{2}$$

For maxima or minima, put $\dfrac{dA}{dx} = 0$

$$\Rightarrow \quad 2\pi x - \frac{50\pi}{4} + \frac{\pi^2 x}{2} = 0$$

$$\Rightarrow \quad 8\pi x - 50\pi + 2\pi^2 x = 0$$

$$\Rightarrow \quad 8x - 50 + 2\pi x = 0$$

$$\Rightarrow \quad \pi x + 4x = 25$$

$$\therefore \quad x = \frac{25}{4+\pi}$$

Now, $\dfrac{d^2A}{dx^2} = 2\pi + \dfrac{\pi^2}{2}$ which is always positive.

So, A is minimum when $x = \dfrac{25}{4+\pi}$.

Then, $4y = 50 - \dfrac{2\pi \times 25}{4+\pi}$ [from Eq. (i)]

$$\Rightarrow \quad 4y = \frac{200 + 50\pi - 50\pi}{4+\pi}$$

$$\therefore \quad y = \frac{50}{4+\pi}$$

Hence, A is minimum when $y = 2x$, i.e. side of square = Diameter of circle.

Example 14 A running track of 440 m is to be laid out enclosing a football field. The football field is in the shape of a rectangle with a semi-circle at each end. If the area of the rectangular portion is to be maximum, then find the length of its sides. Also, calculate the area of the football field. **[ISC 2023]**

Sol. Let $ABCD$ be a rectangle and let the semi-circle be described on side AB and CD as diameter respectively.

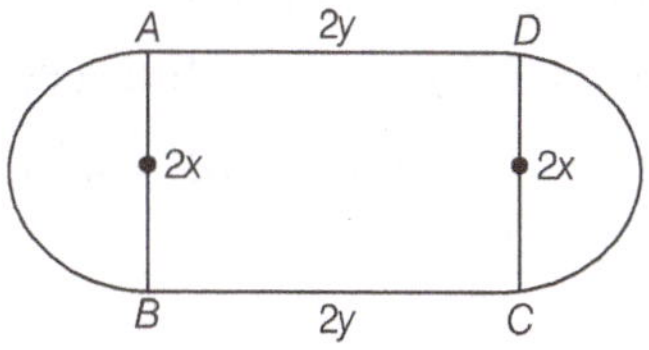

Let $AB = 2x$ and $AD = 2y$

Given, perimeter of ground = 440 m

Then, $440 = 4y + 2\pi x$ ...(i)

A = Area of rectangular field

$\therefore \quad A = 2x \cdot 2y = 4xy$

$\Rightarrow \quad A = x4y = x(440 - 2\pi x)$ [from Eq. (i)]

$\Rightarrow \quad A = 440x - 2\pi x^2$

$$\Rightarrow \quad \frac{dA}{dx} = 440 - 4\pi x \Rightarrow \frac{d^2A}{dx^2} = -4\pi < 0$$

$\therefore$ Area of rectangular field is maximum.

$\therefore$ For maxima or minimum, put $\dfrac{dA}{dx} = 0$

$$\Rightarrow \quad 440 - 4\pi x = 0 \Rightarrow x = \frac{440}{4\pi} = \frac{110}{\pi}$$

$\Rightarrow \quad x = \dfrac{110 \times 7}{22} = 35$

On substitute $x = 5$ in Eq. (i), we get

$440 = 4y + 2 \times \pi \times 35$

or $\quad 4y = 440 - 2 \times \dfrac{22}{7} \times 35 \quad$ [from Eq. (i)]

$\Rightarrow \quad 4y = 440 - 220 = 220 \Rightarrow y = \dfrac{220}{4} = 55$

Length of sides = 55 m and 35 m

Area of football field $= 4xy + \pi x^2$

$= 4 \times 35 \times 55 + \dfrac{22}{7} \times 35 \times 35$

$= 7700 + 3850 = 11550 \text{ m}^2$

Example 15 Show that the height of the cylinder of maximum volume that can be inscribed in a sphere of radius R is $\dfrac{2R}{\sqrt{3}}$. Find the volume of the largest cylinder inscribed in a sphere of radius R. **[NCERT]**

Sol. Let we have a sphere of radius R and a cylinder is inscribed in it. $EB = r$ be the radius of the cylinder and $BC = h$ be the height of cylinder.

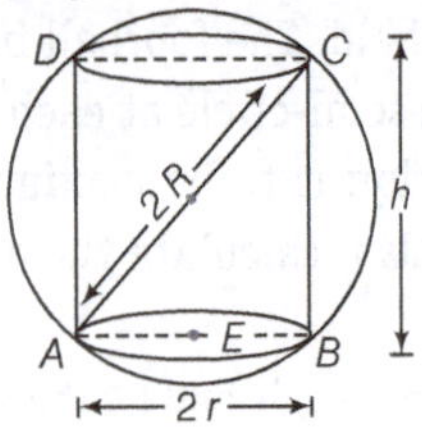

In right angled ΔABC, we have

$(AC)^2 = (AB)^2 + (BC)^2 \quad$ [using Pythagoras theorem]

$\Rightarrow (2R)^2 = (2r)^2 + h^2 \Rightarrow 4R^2 = 4r^2 + h^2$

$\Rightarrow \quad r^2 = \dfrac{1}{4}(4R^2 - h^2) \quad$ ...(i)

Volume of cylinder, $V = \pi r^2 h$

$\Rightarrow \quad V = \pi \left[\dfrac{1}{4}(4R^2 - h^2)\right] h \quad$ [from Eq. (i)]

$\Rightarrow \quad V = \dfrac{\pi}{4}(4R^2 h - h^3) \quad$ ...(ii)

On differentiating V w.r.t. h, we get

$\dfrac{dV}{dh} = \dfrac{\pi}{4}(4R^2 - 3h^2) \quad$ ...(iii)

For maxima or minima, put $\dfrac{dV}{dh} = 0$

$\Rightarrow \dfrac{\pi}{4}(4R^2 - 3h^2) = 0 \Rightarrow 4R^2 = 3h^2$

$\Rightarrow \quad h = \dfrac{2R}{\sqrt{3}} \quad$ [$\because$ height cannot be negative]

On differentiating both sides of Eq. (iii) w.r.t. h, we get

$\dfrac{d^2V}{dh^2} = -\dfrac{3}{2}\pi h$

At $h = \dfrac{2R}{\sqrt{3}}, \dfrac{d^2V}{dh^2} = -\dfrac{3}{2}\pi \times \dfrac{2R}{\sqrt{3}} = -\sqrt{3}\,\pi R < 0 \quad [\because R > 0]$

$\therefore$ Volume of cylinder is maximum at $h = \dfrac{2R}{\sqrt{3}}$.

From Eq. (i), we get $r^2 = \dfrac{1}{4}\left(4R^2 - \dfrac{4R^2}{3}\right) = \dfrac{2R^2}{3}$

$\therefore$ Volume of largest cylinder inscribed in a sphere,

$V = \pi\left(\dfrac{2R^2}{3}\right) \times \dfrac{2R}{\sqrt{3}} = \dfrac{1}{\sqrt{3}} \times \left(\dfrac{4}{3}\pi R^3\right)$

$= \dfrac{1}{\sqrt{3}} \times$ Volume of sphere

Hence, height of the cylinder of maximum volume is $\dfrac{2R}{\sqrt{3}}$ and volume of largest cylinder inscribed in sphere is $\dfrac{1}{\sqrt{3}}$ times volume of sphere.

Note For maximum volume, the diagonal of cylinder passes through the centre of the sphere i.e. diagonal is a diameter of sphere.

Example 16 Prove that the semi-vertical angle of the right circular cone of given volume and least curved area is $\cot^{-1}\sqrt{2}$. **[ISC 2023]**

Sol. Let r be the radius and h be the height of given cone.

Then, volume $(V) = \dfrac{1}{3}\pi r^2 h \Rightarrow h = \dfrac{3V}{\pi r^2}$

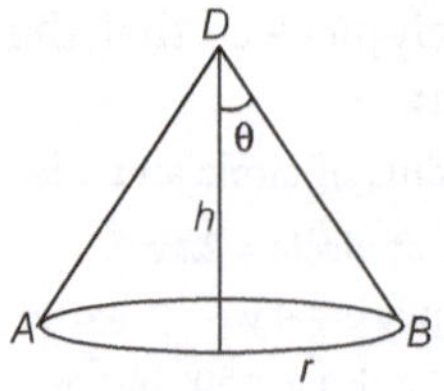

Let C be the curved surface area of the cone.

Then, $\quad C = \pi r l$

$\Rightarrow \quad C^2 = \pi^2 r^2 l^2 = \pi^2 r^2 (r^2 + h^2) \quad [\because l^2 = r^2 + h^2]$

Let $\quad C^2 = S$

$\therefore \quad S = \pi^2 (r^4 + r^2 h^2)$

$\Rightarrow \quad S = \pi^2\left[r^4 + r^2\left(\dfrac{9V^2}{\pi^2 r^4}\right)\right] \quad \left[\because h = \dfrac{3V}{\pi r^2}\right]$

$\Rightarrow \quad S = \pi^2\left(r^4 + \dfrac{9V^2}{\pi^2 r^2}\right)$

C is maximum or minimum according to S is maximum or minimum.

$$\therefore \quad \frac{dS}{dr} = \pi^2\left(4r^3 - \frac{18V^2}{\pi^2 r^3}\right)$$

For maximum or minimum, we must have

$$\frac{dS}{dr} = 0 \Rightarrow \pi^2\left(4r^3 - \frac{18V^2}{\pi^2 r^3}\right) = 0 \Rightarrow V^2 = \frac{2}{9}\pi^2 r^6$$

Again, differentiating w.r.t. r, we get

$$\frac{d^2S}{dr^2} = \pi^2\left(12r^2 + \frac{54V^2}{\pi^2 r^4}\right) > 0$$

[by second derivative test]

So, S is minimum when

$$V^2 = \frac{2}{9}\pi^2 r^6$$

$$\Rightarrow \quad \frac{2}{9}\pi^2 r^6 = \frac{1}{9}\pi^2 r^4 h^2 \qquad \left[\because V = \frac{1}{3}\pi r^2 h\right]$$

$$\Rightarrow \quad 2r^2 = h^2 \Rightarrow h = \sqrt{2}r$$

$$\Rightarrow \quad \frac{h}{r} = \sqrt{2} \Rightarrow \cot\theta = \sqrt{2} \Rightarrow \theta = \cot^{-1}\sqrt{2}$$

Hence, curve surface area is minimum when $\theta = \cot^{-1}\sqrt{2}$.

Example 17 Mrs. Roy designs a window in her son's study room, so that the room gets maximum sunlight. She designs the window in the shape of a rectangle surmounted by an equilateral triangle. If the perimeter of the window is 12 m, find the dimensions of the window that will admit maximum sunlight into the room.

[ISC 2024]

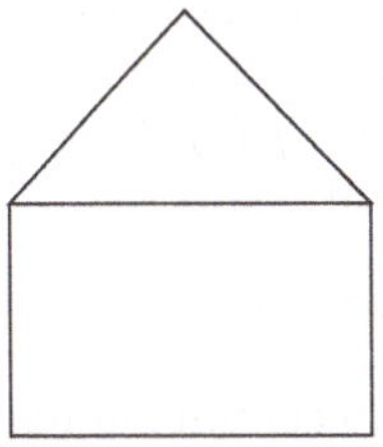

Sol. Let x be the length and y be the width of the rectangular portion of the window as shown in the figure.

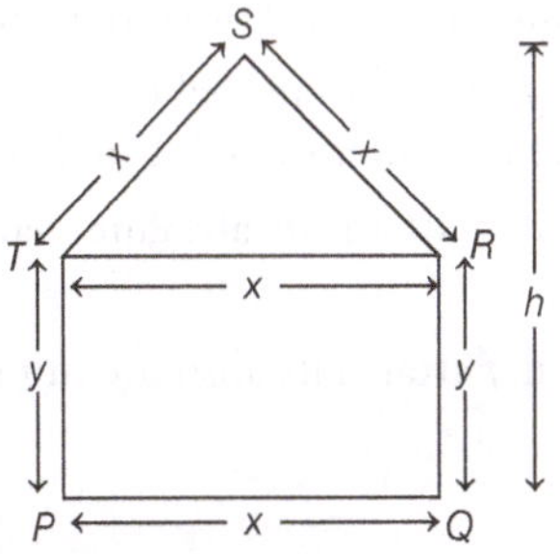

An equilateral triangle with side x placed on the rectangular shape.

$\because$ Perimeter of window $= PQ + QR + RS + ST + TP$

$$12 = x + y + x + x + y$$

$$12 = 3x + 2y \qquad \text{...(i)}$$

Now, the area of the window

$$A = \text{Area of rectangle} + \text{Area of equilateral triangle}$$

$$= xy + \frac{\sqrt{3}}{4}x^2$$

$$= x\left[\frac{12-3x}{2}\right] + \frac{\sqrt{3}}{4}x^2 \qquad [\because \text{using Eq. (i)}]$$

$$= 6x - \frac{3}{2}x^2 + \frac{\sqrt{3}}{4}x^2$$

$$= x^2\left(\frac{\sqrt{3}}{4} - \frac{3}{2}\right) + 6x$$

For maximum sunlight, area of window should be maximum.

$$\text{Now, } \frac{dA}{dx} = 2x\left(\frac{\sqrt{3}}{4} - \frac{3}{2}\right) + 6$$

$$= x\left(\frac{\sqrt{3}}{2} - 3\right) + 6$$

$$\text{For maximum, } \frac{dA}{dx} = 0$$

$$\Rightarrow \quad x\left(\frac{\sqrt{3}}{2} - 3\right) + 6 = 0$$

$$\Rightarrow \quad x = \frac{6}{\left(3 - \frac{\sqrt{3}}{2}\right)}$$

$$= \left(\frac{12}{6-\sqrt{3}}\right) \times \frac{6+\sqrt{3}}{6+\sqrt{3}}$$

$$= \frac{4}{11}(6+\sqrt{3})\text{ m}$$

$$\text{Also, } \frac{d^2A}{dx^2} = \left(\frac{\sqrt{3}}{2} - 3\right) < 0$$

Hence, the area is maximum at $x = \frac{4}{11}(6+\sqrt{3})$.

$$\text{So, from Eq. (i), } y = \frac{12-3x}{2}$$

$$= 6 - \frac{3}{2} \times \frac{4}{11}(6+\sqrt{3})$$

$$= 6 - \frac{6}{11}(6+\sqrt{3})$$

$$= \frac{66 - 36 - 6\sqrt{3}}{11} = \frac{30 - 6\sqrt{3}}{11}$$

$$= \frac{6}{11}(5-\sqrt{3})$$

Hence, the length of window (rectangular portion) is $\frac{4}{11}(6+\sqrt{3})$ m and the width of (rectangular portion) is $\frac{6}{11}(5-\sqrt{3})$ m

and the height of the window

$$h = y + \text{Height of triangle}$$
$$= \frac{6}{11}(5-\sqrt{3}) + \frac{\sqrt{3}}{2} \times \frac{4}{11}(6+\sqrt{3})$$
$$= \frac{30}{11} - \frac{6\sqrt{3}}{11} + \frac{12\sqrt{3}}{11} + \frac{6}{11}$$
$$= \frac{36}{11} + \frac{6\sqrt{3}}{11} = \frac{6}{11}(6+\sqrt{3}) \text{ m}$$

Example 18 The volume of a closed rectangular metal box with a square base is 4096 cm^3. The cost of polishing the outer surface of the box is ₹ 4 per cm^2. Find the dimensions of the box for the minimum cost of polishing it. **[ISC 2019]**

Sol. Let the length of side of the square base of closed rectangular metal box be x cm with and its height be y cm.

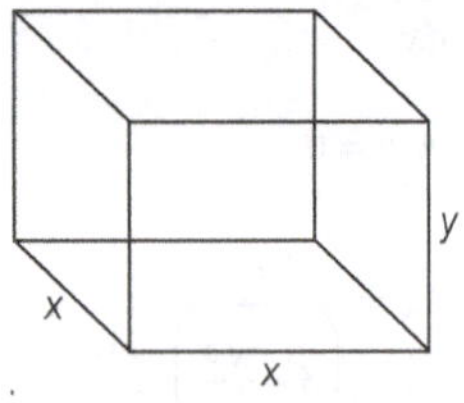

Then, Volume of rectangular box $= x \times x \times y = x^2y$

$$\Rightarrow \quad 4096 = x^2y \Rightarrow y = \frac{4096}{x^2}$$

Let c denotes the cost of the box

$$c = 4 \times 2x^2 + 4 \times 4xy$$
$$= 8x^2 + 16x \cdot \frac{4096}{x^2}$$
$$= 8x^2 + \frac{65536}{x} \quad \text{...(i)}$$

On differentiating both sides w.r.t. x, we get

$$\frac{dc}{dx} = 16x - \frac{65536}{x^2} \quad \text{...(ii)}$$

Now, $\frac{dc}{dx} = 0$

$$\Rightarrow \quad 16x - \frac{65536}{x^2} = 0 \Rightarrow 16x^3 = 65536$$
$$\Rightarrow \quad x^3 = 4096 = 16^3$$
$$\Rightarrow \quad x = 16$$

Again differentiating Eq. (ii) w.r.t. x, we get

$$\frac{d^2c}{dx^2} = 16 - 65536(-2)\cdot\frac{1}{x^3} = 16 + \frac{131072}{x^3} > 0$$

So for $x = 16$, cost in minimum

$$\therefore \quad y = \frac{4096}{x^2} = \frac{4096}{16^2} = 16$$

Hence, dimension of the box for the minimum cost of polishing is 16 cm, 16 cm and 16 cm.

Maximum and Minimum Values of a Function in Closed Interval

A function may have a number of local maxima or local minima in a given interval. A local maximum value may not be the greatest and a local minimum value may not be the least value of the function in any given interval.

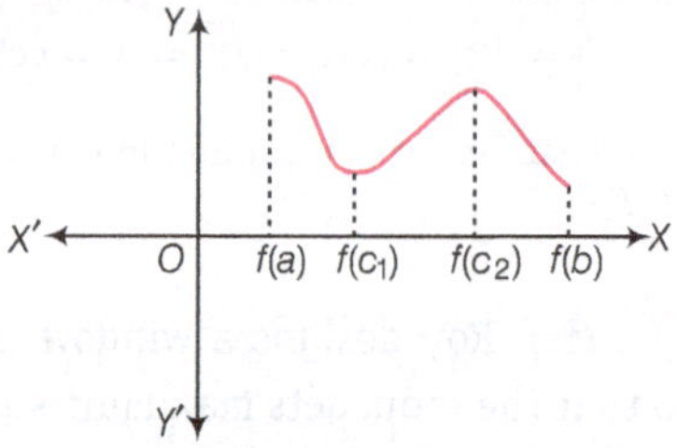

If a function $f(x)$ is continuous on a closed interval, say $[a, b]$, then it attains the **absolute** maximum value or **global** maximum (absolute minimum value or global minimum) at critical points or at the end points of the interval $[a, b]$. Thus, to find the absolute maximum (absolute minimum) value of the function, we choose the largest and smallest amongst the numbers $f(a), f(c_1), f(c_2), f(b)$, where c_1 and c_2 are the critical points.

Important Theorems

Theorem 1. Let f be a continuous function on an interval $I = [a, b]$. Then, f has the absolute maximum value and f attains it atleast once in I. Also, f has the absolute minimum value and attains it atleast once in I.

Theorem 2. Let f be a differentiable function on a closed interval I and c be any interior point of I. Then,

(i) $f'(c) = 0$, if f attains its absolute maximum value at c.

(ii) $f'(c) = 0$, if f attains its absolute minimum value at c.

Method to Find Absolute Maximum /Minimum Values in an Interval $[a, b]$

Suppose $f(x)$ be the given function. Then, to find absolute maximum and absolute minimum values in the given interval, we use the following steps

I. Find all critical points of f in the interval, i.e. find points at which either $f'(x) = 0$ or f is not differentiable.

II. Take the end points of the interval.

III. At all these points listed in steps I and II, calculate the values of f.

IV. Identify the maximum and minimum values of f out of the values calculated in step III. This maximum value will be the absolute maximum (greatest) value of f and the minimum value will be the absolute minimum (least) value of f.

Example 19 Find absolute maximum and minimum values of a function f given by

$$f(x) = 12x^{4/3} - 6x^{1/3},\ x \in [-1, 1].$$ **[NCERT]**

Sol. We have, $f(x) = 12x^{4/3} - 6x^{1/3}$

On differentiating both sides w.r.t. x, we get

$$f'(x) = 12 \times \frac{4}{3}x^{1/3} - 6 \times \frac{1}{3}x^{-2/3}$$

$$= 16x^{1/3} - \frac{2}{x^{2/3}} = \frac{2(8x-1)}{x^{2/3}}$$

For critical points, put $f'(x) = 0$

$$\Rightarrow \quad \frac{2(8x-1)}{x^{2/3}} = 0 \Rightarrow 8x - 1 = 0 \Rightarrow x = \frac{1}{8}$$

Also, $f'(x)$ is not defined at $x = 0$, so critical points are $x = 0$ and $x = \frac{1}{8}$ and end points of interval are -1 and 1.

Now, $f(-1) = 12(-1)^{4/3} - 6(-1)^{1/3} = 12 + 6 = 18$

$$f(0) = 12(0) - 6(0) = 0$$

$$f\left(\frac{1}{8}\right) = 12\left(\frac{1}{8}\right)^{4/3} - 6\left(\frac{1}{8}\right)^{1/3} = 12\left(\frac{1}{16}\right) - 6\left(\frac{1}{2}\right) = \frac{-9}{4}$$

and $f(1) = 12(1)^{4/3} - 6(1)^{1/3} = 6$

Hence, absolute maximum value of function f is 18 at $x = -1$ and absolute minimum value of function f is $\frac{-9}{4}$ at $x = \frac{1}{8}$.

Example 20 Find the maximum and minimum values of $(x + \sin 2x)$ on $[0, \pi]$.

Sol. Let $f(x) = x + \sin 2x$

On differentiating both sides w.r.t. x, we get

$$f'(x) = (1 + 2\cos 2x)$$

For critical points, put $f'(x) = 0$

$$\Rightarrow \cos 2x = \frac{-1}{2},\ \text{where } x \in [0, \pi]$$

$$\Rightarrow \quad 2x = \frac{2\pi}{3}, \frac{4\pi}{3} \Rightarrow x = \frac{\pi}{3}, \frac{2\pi}{3}$$

Now, $f\left(\frac{\pi}{3}\right) = \frac{\pi}{3} + \sin\frac{2\pi}{3} = \frac{\pi}{3} + \frac{\sqrt{3}}{2} = \frac{2\pi + 3\sqrt{3}}{6}$,

$$f\left(\frac{2\pi}{3}\right) = \frac{2\pi}{3} + \sin\frac{4\pi}{3} = \frac{2\pi}{3} - \sin\frac{\pi}{3} = \frac{4\pi - 3\sqrt{3}}{6},$$

$$f(0) = 0 \text{ and } f(\pi) = \pi + \sin 2\pi = \pi$$

Hence, the minimum value of $f(x)$ is 0 at $x = 0$ and the maximum value of $f(x)$ is π at $x = \pi$.

Topic Practice 4

Short Answer Type Questions

(4 Marks)

1 Find the points at which the function f given by $f(x) = (x-4)^4 (x+1)^3$ has
(i) local maxima.
(ii) local minima.

2 Find all the points of local maxima and local minima of the function
$$f(x) = -\frac{3}{4}x^4 - 8x^3 - \frac{45}{2}x^2 + 105.$$ **[NCERT Exemplar]**

3 It is given that at $x = 1$, the function $x^4 - 62x^2 + ax + 9$ attains maximum value on the interval $[0, 2]$. Find the value of a. **[NCERT]**

4 Find the least value of $f(x) = e^x + e^{-x}$.

5 Find the maximum and minimum values, if any of the following functions. (Each part carries 4 Marks)
(i) $f(x) = |x + 2| - 1$
(ii) $g(x) = -|x + 1| + 3$
(iii) $f(x) = |\sin 4x + 3|$

6 Find the local maximum and local minimum values of $\frac{(x-1)(x-6)}{x-10}$, $x \neq 10$.

7 Find the local maximum and local minimum value of the following functions.
(i) $f(x) = (\sin x - \cos x)$, where $0 < x < \frac{\pi}{2}$ **[NCERT]**
(ii) $f(x) = (2\cos x + x)$, where $0 < x < 2\pi$

8 Show that $\sin^p\theta\cos^q\theta$ attains a maximum value, when $\theta = \tan^{-1}\sqrt{\frac{p}{q}}$.

9 Prove that the maximum value of $\left(\frac{1}{x}\right)^x$ is $e^{1/e}$.

10 Prove that the largest rectangle with a given perimeter is a square.

11 Let AP and BQ be two vertical poles at points A and B, respectively. If $AP = 16$ m, $BQ = 22$ m and $AB = 20$ m, then find the distance of a point R on AB from the point A such that $RP^2 + RQ^2$ is minimum.

12 Find the points of absolute maximum and minimum of $f(x) = (x-1)^{1/3}(x-2);\ 1 \le x \le 9$.

13 Find the absolute maximum and absolute minimum values of the function f given by $f(x) = \cos^2 x + \sin x,\ x \in [0, \pi]$.

Long Answer Type Questions

6 Marks

14 Show that the height of a closed right circular cylinder of given surface and maximum volume is equal to diameter of base. **[NCERT]**

15 A page is to have a total area of 80 sq cm with a margin of 1 cm at the top and on each side and a margin of 1.5 cm at the bottom. What should be the dimensions of the page, so that the printed area will be maximum? **[ISC 2012]**

16 An Apache helicopter of enemy is flying along the curve given by $y = x^2 + 7$. A soldier placed at (3, 7) wants to shoot down the helicopter, when it is nearest to him. Find the nearest distance. **[NCERT Exemplar]**

17 If an open box with square base is to be made of a given quantity of card board of area c^2, then show that the maximum volume of the box is $\frac{c^3}{6\sqrt{3}}$ cu units. **[ISC 2008]**

18 A square piece of tin of side 18 cm is to made into a box without top, by cutting a square from each corner and folding up the flaps to form the box. What should be the side of the square to cut off, so that the volume of the box is the maximum possible? Find maximum volume. **[NCERT]**

19 A metal box with a square base and vertical sides is to contain 1024 cm^3. If the material for the top and bottom costs ₹ 5 per cm^2 and the material for the sides costs ₹ 2.50 per cm^2. Then, find the least cost of the box. **[NCERT Exemplar]**

20 The sum of the perimeter of a circle and square is k, where k is some constant. Prove that the sum of their areas is least, when the side of square is double the radius of the circle. **[NCERT]**

Hints & Solutions

1. Similar as Example 2.
[**Ans.** (i) Local maxima at $x = 8/7$.
(ii) Local minima at $x = 4$.

2. Similar as Example 3.
[**Ans.** Local maxima $= 0, -5$; Local minima $= -3$]

3. **Hint** $f'(x) = 4x^3 - 124x + a$, put $f'(1) = 0$ [**Ans.** $a = 120$]

4. **Hint** $\frac{dy}{dx} = e^x - e^{-x} = 0 \Rightarrow e^{2x} = 1 \Rightarrow x = 0$ [**Ans.** 2]

5. Similar as Example 5.
[**Ans.** (i) Minimum value $= -1$, no maximum value
(ii) Maximum value $= 3$, no minimum value
(iii) Minimum value $= 2$, maximum value $= 4$]

6. Let $y = \frac{(x-1)(x-6)}{x-10} = \frac{x^2 - 7x + 6}{x-10}$

On differentiating both sides w.r.t. x, we get

$$\frac{dy}{dx} = \frac{(x-10)(2x-7) - (x^2 - 7x + 6)\cdot 1}{(x-10)^2}$$

[using quotient rule of derivative]

$$= \frac{2x^2 - 7x - 20x + 70 - x^2 + 7x - 6}{(x-10)^2}$$

$$= \frac{x^2 - 20x + 64}{(x-10)^2} = \frac{(x-4)(x-16)}{(x-10)^2}$$

For local maxima and local minima, put $dy/dx = 0$

$$\Rightarrow \frac{(x-4)(x-16)}{(x-10)^2} = 0 \Rightarrow (x-4)(x-16) = 0$$

$\therefore$ $x = 4, 16$ [1]

For $x = 4$,

When x is slightly < 4, then $\frac{dy}{dx} = \frac{(-)(-)}{(+)} =$ Positive

When x is slightly > 4, then $\frac{dy}{dx} = \frac{(+)(-)}{(+)} =$ Negative

Thus, $\frac{dy}{dx}$ changes sign from positive to negative.

So, y is local maxima at $x = 4$.

$\therefore$ Local maximum value at $x = 4$ is

$$y = \frac{(4-1)(4-6)}{4-10} = \frac{3\times(-2)}{-6} = 1$$ [1]

For $x = 16$,

When x is slightly < 16, then $\frac{dy}{dx} = \frac{(+)(-)}{(+)}$ = Negative

When x is slightly > 16, then $\frac{dy}{dx} = \frac{(+)(+)}{(+)}$ = Positive

Thus, $\frac{dy}{dx}$ changes sign from negative to positive. [1]

So, y is local minima at $x = 16$.

$\therefore$ Local minimum value at $x = 16$ is

$$y = \frac{(16-1)(16-6)}{16-10} = \frac{15\times 10}{6} = 25$$ [1]

7. Similar as Example 6.

[**Ans.** (i) Local maximum value $= \sqrt{2}$ and no local minimum value exist (ii) Local maximum value $= \left(\sqrt{3} + \frac{\pi}{6}\right)$ and local minimum value $= \left(\frac{5\pi}{6} - \sqrt{3}\right)$]

8. **Hint** $\frac{dy}{d\theta} = \sin^p\theta \cdot q\cos^{q-1}\theta \times (-\sin\theta)$

$$+ \cos^q\theta \cdot p\sin^{p-1}\theta \times (\cos\theta) = 0$$

$\Rightarrow \sin^{p-1}\theta\cos^{q-1}\theta(-q\sin^2\theta + p\cos^2\theta) = 0$

$\Rightarrow \tan\theta = \pm\sqrt{p/q}$

9. **Hint** Let $y = x^{-x} \Rightarrow \frac{dy}{dx} = -x^{-x}(1 + \log x)$

$\Rightarrow \frac{dy}{dx} = 0 \Rightarrow x = \frac{1}{e}$

10. **Hint** Let x be length and y be breadth of rectangle.

Given, $2(x + y) = p$, then $A = xy = x\left(\frac{p}{2} - x\right)$

$\because \frac{dA}{dx} = 0$, we get $x = y$.

11. **Hint** Let $AR = x$, then $BR = (20 - x)$

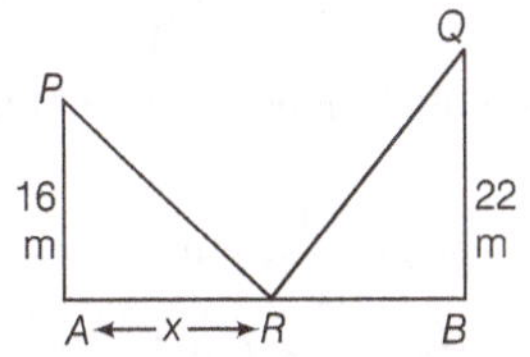

$\because RP^2 + RQ^2 = x^2 + (20-x)^2 + 740$ [**Ans.** 10 m]

12. We have, $f(x) = (x-1)^{1/3}(x-2)$

On differentiating both sides w.r.t. x, we get

$f'(x) = (x-1)^{1/3}\cdot 1 + (x-2)\cdot\frac{1}{3}(x-1)^{-2/3}$

[by product rule of derivative]

$$= (x-1)^{-2/3}\left[x - 1 + \frac{1}{3}(x-2)\right]$$ [1]

$$= (x-1)^{-2/3}\left[\frac{3x-3+x-2}{3}\right]$$

$$= (x-1)^{-2/3}\left(\frac{4x-5}{3}\right)$$

Put $f'(x) = 0$

$\Rightarrow \frac{1}{3}(x-1)^{-2/3}(4x-5) = 0 \Rightarrow x = \frac{5}{4}$ [1]

Now, $f(1) = (1-1)^{1/3}(1-2) = 0$

$$f\left(\frac{5}{4}\right) = \left(\frac{5}{4} - 1\right)^{1/3}\left(\frac{5}{4} - 2\right) = \left(\frac{1}{4}\right)^{1/3}\left(\frac{-3}{4}\right) = \frac{-3}{4\cdot\sqrt[3]{4}}$$

and $f(9) = (9-1)^{1/3}(9-2) = (8)^{1/3}\cdot 7 = 2\times 7 = 14$ [1]

Hence, $f(x)$ is absolute maximum at $x = 9$ and absolute minimum at $x = \frac{5}{4}$. [1]

13. We have, $f(x) = \cos^2 x + \sin x,\ x \in [0, \pi]$

On differentiating both sides w.r.t. x, we get

$f'(x) = -2\cos x\cdot\sin x + \cos x$

For critical points, put $f'(x) = 0$

$\Rightarrow -2\cos x\sin x + \cos x = 0$

$\Rightarrow \cos x(1 - 2\sin x) = 0$

$\Rightarrow \cos x = 0$ or $1 - 2\sin x = 0$

$\Rightarrow x = (2n+1)\frac{\pi}{2}$ or $\sin x = \frac{1}{2}$

$\Rightarrow x = (2n+1)\frac{\pi}{2}$ or $\sin x = \sin\frac{\pi}{6}$

$\Rightarrow x = (2n+1)\frac{\pi}{2}$ or $x = n\pi + (-1)^n\cdot\frac{\pi}{6}$,

where $n = 0, \pm 1, \pm 2, \ldots$

$\Rightarrow x = \frac{\pi}{2}, \frac{\pi}{6}, \frac{5\pi}{6}$ [1]

Then, we evaluate the value of f at critical points $x = \frac{\pi}{6}, \frac{\pi}{2}, \frac{5\pi}{6}$ and at the end points of the interval $[0, \pi]$.

At $x = 0$, $f(0) = \cos^2 0 + \sin 0 = 1$

At $x = \frac{\pi}{6}$, $f\left(\frac{\pi}{6}\right) = \cos^2\frac{\pi}{6} + \sin\frac{\pi}{6}$

$$= \left(\frac{\sqrt{3}}{2}\right)^2 + \frac{1}{2} = \frac{3}{4} + \frac{1}{2} = \frac{5}{4}$$ [1]

At $x = \frac{\pi}{2}$, $f\left(\frac{\pi}{2}\right) = \cos^2\frac{\pi}{2} + \sin\frac{\pi}{2} = 0 + 1 = 1$

At $x = \frac{5\pi}{6}$, $f\left(\frac{5\pi}{6}\right) = \cos^2\frac{5\pi}{6} + \sin\frac{5\pi}{6}$

$$= \cos^2\left(\pi - \frac{\pi}{6}\right) + \sin\left(\pi - \frac{\pi}{6}\right)$$ [1]

$$= \cos^2\left(\frac{\pi}{6}\right) + \sin\left(\frac{\pi}{6}\right) = \left(\frac{\sqrt{3}}{2}\right)^2 + \frac{1}{2} = \frac{3+2}{4} = \frac{5}{4}$$

At $x = \pi$, $f(\pi) = \cos^2 \pi + \sin \pi = 1$

Hence, the absolute maximum value is 5/4 and absolute minimum value is 1. [1]

14. Hint Let r be the radius and h be the height of cylinder.

Given, $S = 2\pi r^2 + 2\pi rh$

$$\Rightarrow \quad h = \frac{S - 2\pi r^2}{2\pi r}$$

$$\because \quad V = \pi r^2 h = \pi r^2 \left(\frac{S - 2\pi r^2}{2\pi r} \right) = \frac{rS - 2\pi r^3}{2}$$

Now, $\frac{dV}{dr} = 0$, we get $h = 2r$

15. Let the length of page be x cm and breadth be y cm.

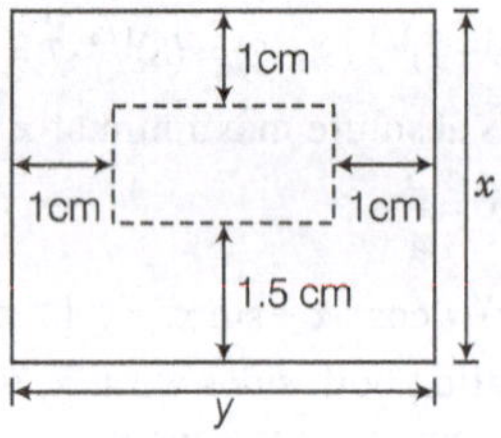

According to the question,

Area of a page = 80

$$\therefore \quad xy = 80 \text{ cm}^2 \quad \text{...(i) [1]}$$

Length of printed material = $(x - 2.5)$ cm

and breadth of printed material = $(y - 2)$ cm

$\therefore$ Area of the printed area,

$$A = (x - 2.5)(y - 2)$$

$$= xy - 2x - 2.5y + 5 \quad [1]$$

$$= 80 - 2x - 2.5 \times \frac{80}{x} + 5 \quad \text{[from Eq. (i)]}$$

$$A = 85 - 2x - \frac{200}{x} \quad [1]$$

On differentiating both sides w.r.t. x, we get

$$\frac{dA}{dx} = -2 + \frac{200}{x^2} \quad [1/2]$$

For maxima and minima,

Put $\frac{dA}{dx} = 0 \Rightarrow -2 + \frac{200}{x^2} = 0$ [1/2]

$$\Rightarrow \quad \frac{200}{x^2} = 2 \Rightarrow x^2 = 100$$

$\therefore \quad x = 10$ cm [taking positive square root]

Now, $\frac{d^2A}{dx^2} = \frac{-2 \times 200}{x^3} = \frac{-400}{x^3}$ [1]

$$\therefore \quad \left(\frac{d^2A}{dx^2} \right)_{x = 10} = \frac{-400}{(10)^3} = \frac{-4}{10} < 0$$

So, A will be maximum when $x = 10$ cm.

$$\because \quad xy = 80$$

$$\therefore \quad y = \frac{80}{10} = 8 \text{ cm} \quad [\text{put } x = 10]$$

Hence, dimensions are length of page = 10 cm and breadth of page = 8 cm [1]

16. Hint Let $A(h, k)$ be any point on the curve $y = x^2 + 7$ and $B(3, 7)$ be the given point.

$\therefore$ Distance between A and B is

$$AB = \sqrt{(h-3)^2 + (k-7)^2}$$

Since, the point $A(h, k)$ lies on the curve.

$$\therefore \quad k = h^2 + 7$$

$$\Rightarrow \quad AB = \sqrt{(h-3)^2 + (h^2 + 7 - 7)^2}$$

$$\text{or} \quad AB^2 = (h-3)^2 + (h^2)^2$$

Let $AB^2 = f(h)$, then AB is maximum or minimum accordingly as $f(h)$ is maximum or minimum.

$$\therefore \quad f(h) = (h+1)^2 + h^4 \quad [\textbf{Ans. } \sqrt{5}]$$

17. Let the length of side of the square base of open box be x units and its height be y units.

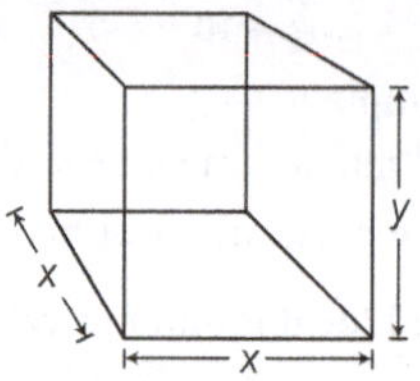

$\therefore$ Area of the cardboard used $= x^2 + 4xy$ [1]

$$\Rightarrow \quad c^2 = x^2 + 4xy \quad \text{[given]}$$

$$\Rightarrow \quad y = \frac{c^2 - x^2}{4x} \quad \text{...(i) [1]}$$

Now, volume of the box, $V = x^2 y$

$$\Rightarrow \quad V = x^2 \cdot \left(\frac{c^2 - x^2}{4x} \right) \quad \text{[from Eq. (i)]}$$

$$\Rightarrow \quad V = \frac{1}{4} x (c^2 - x^2) = \frac{1}{4}(c^2 x - x^3) \quad [1]$$

On differentiating both sides w.r.t. x, we get

$$\frac{dV}{dx} = \frac{1}{4}(c^2 - 3x^2) \quad \text{...(ii)}$$

For maximum volume, put $\frac{dV}{dx} = 0$

$$\Rightarrow \quad c^2 = 3x^2$$

$$\Rightarrow \quad x^2 = \frac{c^2}{3} \Rightarrow x = \frac{c}{\sqrt{3}} \quad \text{[using positive sign] [1]}$$

Again, differentiating both sides of Eq. (ii) w.r.t. x, we get

$$\frac{d^2V}{dx^2} = \frac{1}{4}(-6x) = \frac{-3}{2} x < 0$$

At $x = \frac{c}{\sqrt{3}}$, $\frac{d^2V}{dx^2} = -\frac{3}{2} \cdot \left(\frac{c}{\sqrt{3}} \right) < 0$

So, the volume (V) is maximum at $x = \frac{c}{\sqrt{3}}$. [1]

Hence, maximum volume of the box,

$$(V)_{x=\frac{c}{\sqrt{3}}} = \frac{1}{4}\left(c^2 \cdot \frac{c}{\sqrt{3}} - \frac{c^3}{3\sqrt{3}}\right)$$

$$= \frac{1}{4} \cdot \frac{(3c^3 - c^3)}{3\sqrt{3}} = \frac{1}{4} \cdot \frac{2c^3}{3\sqrt{3}}$$

$$= \frac{c^3}{6\sqrt{3}} \text{ cu units}$$ [1]

18. Let the side of square piece to be cut x cm.

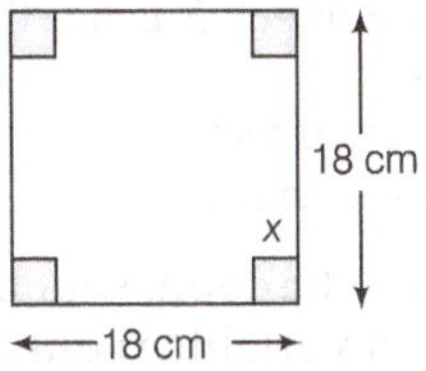

$\therefore$ Length of box, $l = 18 - 2x$

Breadth of box, $b = 18 - 2x$

Height of box, $h = x$

We know that,

Volume of box, $V = lbh$

$\therefore \quad V = (18 - 2x) \cdot (18 - 2x) \cdot x$

$= 2(9 - x) \cdot 2(9 - x) \cdot x$

$= 4(9 - x)^2 \cdot x$ ...(i)

$= 4(81 - 18x + x^2) \cdot x$

$\Rightarrow \quad V = 4(x^3 - 18x^2 + 81x)$ [1]

On differentiating V w.r.t. x, we get

$$\frac{dV}{dx} = 4(3x^2 - 36x + 81)$$

$$= 4 \cdot 3(x^2 - 12x + 27)$$

$$= 12(x^2 - 12x + 27)$$ ...(ii) [1]

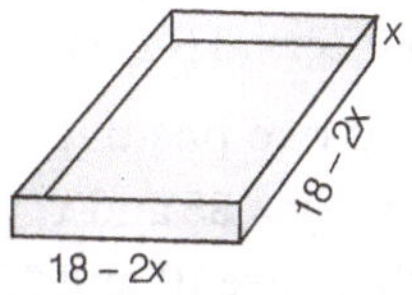

For maximum or minimum volume V, put $\frac{dV}{dx} = 0$

$\Rightarrow \quad 12(x^2 - 12x + 27) = 0$

$\Rightarrow \quad x^2 - 12x + 27 = 0 \Rightarrow x(x - 9) - 3(x - 9) = 0$

$\Rightarrow \quad (x - 9)(x - 3) = 0 \Rightarrow x - 9 = 0$ and $x - 3 = 0$

$\Rightarrow \quad x = 9$ and $x = 3$ [1]

But $x = 9$ is not possible, as whole tin piece will be cut off into two equal parts.

$\therefore \quad x = 3$

Again, differentiating both sides of Eq. (ii) w.r.t. x, we get

$$\frac{d^2V}{dx^2} = 12(2x - 12) = 12 \cdot 2(x - 6) = 24(x - 6)$$ [1]

At $x = 3$, $\left[\frac{d^2V}{dx^2}\right]_{x=3} = 24(3 - 6) = 24(-3) = -72 < 0$ [1]

So, volume is maximum at $x = 3$ cm.

Maximum volume $= 4(9 - 3)^2 \cdot 3$ [from Eq. (i)]

$= 4 \cdot 36 \cdot 3 = 432 \text{ cm}^3$ [1]

19. **Hint** Side of a square base is x and height is y.

$V = x^2 y$ and cost $= 2x^2 \times 5 + 4xy \times 2.50$ [**Ans.** ₹ 1920]

20. Let x be the side of square and r be the radius of circle.

Then, perimeter of a circle $= 2\pi r$

and perimeter of a square $= 4x$

Given, sum of perimeter of circle and square $= k$

$\Rightarrow \quad 2\pi r + 4x = k$

$\Rightarrow \quad x = \frac{k - 2\pi r}{4}$ ...(i) [1]

Now, sum of areas of a circle and a square is

$$A = x^2 + \pi r^2 = \left[\frac{k - 2\pi r}{4}\right]^2 + \pi r^2$$

$$\Rightarrow \quad A = \left(\frac{1}{16}\right)(k^2 - 4k\pi r + 4\pi^2 r^2) + \pi r^2$$

On differentiating twice w.r.t. r, we get

$$\frac{dA}{dr} = \left(\frac{1}{16}\right)(-4k\pi + 8\pi^2 r) + 2\pi r$$ [1]

and $\frac{d^2A}{dr^2} = \frac{1}{16}[0 + 8\pi^2] + 2\pi = 2\pi + \frac{\pi^2}{2} > 0$ [1]

For maximum or minimum value, put $\frac{dA}{dr} = 0$

$$\Rightarrow \quad 2\pi r - \frac{4k\pi}{16} + \frac{8\pi^2 r}{16} = 0 \Rightarrow r\left(2\pi + \frac{\pi^2}{2}\right) = \frac{k\pi}{4}$$

$$\Rightarrow \quad r = \frac{\left(\frac{k\pi}{4}\right)}{2\pi + \frac{\pi^2}{2}} = \frac{k}{8 + 2\pi}$$ ...(ii) [1]

Now, $\left(\frac{d^2A}{dr^2}\right)_{r=\frac{k}{8+2\pi}} = +\text{ve}$ [1]

$\therefore A$ is least, when $r = \frac{k}{8 + 2\pi}$ and put this value in Eq. (i), we get

$$x = \frac{1}{4}\left(k - 2\pi \times \frac{k}{8 + 2\pi}\right) = \frac{1}{4}\left[\frac{8k + 2\pi k - 2\pi k}{8 + 2\pi}\right]$$

$\Rightarrow \quad x = \frac{2k}{8 + 2\pi} = 2\left(\frac{k}{8 + 2\pi}\right) = 2r$ [using Eq. (ii)]

Hence, A (i.e. sum of their areas) is least, when side of the square is double the radius of the circle. [1]

Chapter Practice

Multiple Choice Type Questions

1 Mark

1 For the curve $y^2 = 2x^3 - 7$, the slope of the normal at (2, 3) is [ISC 2023]

(a) 4 (b) $\frac{1}{4}$ (c) – 4 (d) $\frac{-1}{4}$

2 An edge of a variable cube is increasing at the rate of 10 cm/s. How fast will the volume of the cube increase if the edge is 5 cm long? [ISC 2023]

(a) 75 cm^3/s (b) 750 cm^3/s
(c) 7500 cm^3/s (d) 1250 cm^3/s

3 The radius of a circle is increasing uniformly at the rate of 3 cm/s. If radius is 10 cm, the area of the circle is increasing at the rate of

(a) $\frac{4}{3}cm^2/s$ (b) $60\pi cm^2/s$
(c) $6\pi cm^2/s$ (d) None of these

4 If $f(x) = a(x - \cos x)$ is strictly decreasing in R, then a belongs to

(a) {0} (b) $(0, \infty)$
(c) $(-\infty, 0)$ (d) $(-\infty, \infty)$

5 In which one of the following intervals is the function $f(x) = x^3 - 12x$ increasing? [ISC 2024]

(a) $(-2, 2)$ (b) $(-\infty, -2) \cup (2, \infty)$
(c) $(-2, \infty)$ (d) $(-\infty, 2)$

6 The interval in which the function $f(x) = 5 + 36x - 3x^2$ increases will be [ISC 2023]

(a) $(-\infty, 6)$ (b) $(6, \infty)$ (c) $(-6, 6)$ (d) $(0, -6)$

7 The smallest value of polynomial $x^3 - 18x^2 + 96x$ in [0, 9] is

(a) 126 (b) 0 (c) 135 (d) 160

Assertion-Reason Type Questions

1 Mark

Directions (Q. Nos. 8-11) *In the questions given below are two statements labelled as Assertion (A) and Reason (R). In the context of the two statements, which one of the following is correct?*

(a) Both A and R are correct; R is the correct explanation of A
(b) Both A and R are correct; R is not the correct explanation of A
(c) A is correct; R is incorrect
(d) R is correct; A is incorrect

8 **Assertion (A)** A balloon, which always remains spherical, has a variable radius. The rate, at which its volume is increasing with the radius when the radius is 10 cm, is 400 π cm^3/cm.

Reason (R) Rate of change of volume (v) of balloon with respect to radius (r) is

$$\frac{dv}{dr} = \left(\frac{2}{3}\pi\right) \cdot 3r^2$$

9 **Assertion (A)** The function $f(x) = x^2 - 4x + 6$ is strictly increasing in the interval $(2, \infty)$.

Reason (R) The function $f(x) = x^2 - 4x + 6$ is strictly decreasing in the interval $(-\infty, 2)$.

10 Consider the information given below

The function f is given by

$$f(x) = 2x^3 - 3x^2 - 36x + 7.$$

Assertion (A) The given function f is strictly increasing in intervals $(-\infty, +2)$ and $(-3, \infty)$.

Reason (R) The given function f is strictly decreasing in interval $(-2, 3)$.

11 **Assertion (A)** If two positive numbers x and y are such that $x + y = 35$ and x^2y^5 is maximum, then the numbers are 10 and 25.

Reason (R) If f be a function defined on an interval I and $c \in I$ and also, if f be twice differentiable at c, then $x = c$ is a point of local maxima if $f'(c) = 0$ and $f''(c) < 0$ and the value $f(c)$ is local maximum value of f.

Very Short Answer Type Questions

2 Marks

12 (i) Find the slope of tangent to the curve $y = x^2 + x + 1$ at $x = 1$.

(ii) Find the slope of normal to the curve $y = \sin^2 x$ at $x = \pi/4$.

13 Find the equation of normal to the curve $y = x^3 + 5x^2 + 2$ at $(1, -1)$.

14 Find a point on the curve $y = x^2 - 4x$ at which tangent to the curve is parallel to the X-axis.

15 If the slope of the curve $y = \frac{ax}{b - x}$ at the point $(1, 1)$ is 2. Then, find the value of a and b.

16 (i) The side of a square is increasing at the rate of 0.2 cm/s. Find the rate of increase of the perimeter of the square.

(ii) The radius of a circle is increasing at the rate of 0.9 cm/s. What is the rate of increase of its circumference?

17 A stone is dropped into a quiet lake and waves moves in circles at a speed of 5 cm/s. At the instant when the radius of the circular wave is 8 cm, how fast is the enclosed area increasing? **[NCERT]**

18 An edge of a variable cube is increasing at the rate of 3 cm/s. How fast is the volume of the cube increasing, when the edge is 10 cm long?

19 The volume of a sphere is increasing at the rate of 8 cm^3/s. Find the rate at which its surface area is increasing when the radius of the sphere is 12 cm.

20 The surface area of a spherical bubble is increasing at the rate of 2 cm^2 /s. Find the rate at which the volume of the bubbles is increasing at the instant, when its radius is 6 cm.

21 At what points of the ellipse $16x^2 + 9y^2 = 400$ does the ordinate decrease at the same rate at which the abscissa increase?

22 (i) Show that $f(x) = \left(x - \frac{1}{x}\right)$ is increasing for all $x \in R, x \neq 0$.

(ii) Show that the function given by $f(x) = e^{2x}$ is strictly increasing on R. **[NCERT]**

23 Show that the function $f(x) = x^3 - 3x^2 + 6x - 100$ is increasing on R.

24 Find the values of k for which $f(x) = kx^3 - 9kx^2 + 9x + 3$ is increasing on R.

Short Answer Type Questions

4 Marks

25 Find the points on the curve $y = 4x^3 - 3x + 5$ at which the equation of the tangent is parallel to the X-axis. **[ISC 2018]**

26 Find the equation of tangent and normal to the ellipse $\frac{x^2}{a^2} + \frac{y^2}{b^2} = 1$ at (x_1, y_1).

27 Find the equations of tangent and normal to curve $x = 1 - \cos\theta$ and $y = \theta - \sin\theta$ at $\theta = \pi/4$.

28 For the curve $y = 4x^3 - 2x^5$, find all the points at which the tangent passes through the origin. **[NCERT]**

29 Find the equation of the normal lines to the curve $3x^2 - y^2 = 8$, which are parallel to the line $x + 3y = 4$. **[NCERT Exemplar]**

30 Find the points on the curve $y = x^3 - 3x^2 + 2x$ at which the tangent to the curve is parallel to the line $y - 2x + 3 = 0$.

31 Find a point on the parabola $f(x) = (x - 3)^2$, where the tangent is parallel to the chord joining the points (3, 0) and (4, 1).

32 Find the equations of all lines having slope −1, that are tangent to the curve $y = \frac{1}{x - 1}, x \neq 1$. **[NCERT]**

33 The side of an equilateral triangle is increasing at the rate of 2 cm/s. At what rate is its area increasing, when the side of the triangle is 20 cm?

34 If x and y are the sides of two squares such that $y = x - x^2$, then find the rate of change of the area of second square with respect to the area of first quadrant. **[NCERT Exemplar]**

35 Find the intervals in which the function given by $f(x) = \sin 3x, x \in \left[0, \frac{\pi}{2}\right]$ is

(i) increasing (ii) decreasing.

36 Find the intervals of the function $f(x) = 4\sin^3 x - 6\sin^2 x + 12\sin x + 100$ is strictly decreasing. **[NCERT Exemplar]**

37 Determine the interval in which the function $f(x) = 2x^3 - 15x^2 + 36x + 1$ is strictly increasing and strictly decreasing.

Directions (Q. Nos. 38-41) *Find the interval(s) in which the following functions are*

(i) *increasing.* (ii) *decreasing.*

38 $f(x) = \log(1+x) - \frac{x}{1+x}, x \neq -1$

39 $f(x) = (x+2)e^{-x}$

40 Find the maximum profit that a company can make, if the profit function is given by $P(x) = 41 + 24x - 18x^2$. **[NCERT]**

41 The sum of two numbers is 24. Find the numbers, so that their product is maximum. **[NCERT]**

Long Answer Type Questions

6 Marks

42 Find the equations of tangents to curve $3x^2 - y^2 = 8$, which passes through point $\left(\frac{4}{3}, 0\right)$.

43 Find the point on the curve $y = \frac{x}{1+x^2}$, where the tangent to the curve has the greatest slope.

44 Find the point on the curve $y^2 = 2x$, which is at a minimum distance from point (1, 4).

45 Show that of all the rectangles inscribed in a given fixed circle, the square has the maximum area.

46 Show that the rectangle of maximum perimeter which can be inscribed in a circle of radius 10 cm is a square of side $10\sqrt{2}$ cm. **[ISC 2015]**

47 Find the maximum volume of the cylinder which can be inscribed in a sphere of radius $3\sqrt{3}$ cm. **[ISC 2013]**

48 A wire of length 20 m is available to fence off a flower bed in the form of a sector of a circle. What must be the radius of the circle, if we wish to have a flower bed with the greatest possible area? **[ISC 2009]**

49 A rectangle is inscribed in a semi-circle of radius r with one of its sides on the diameter of the semi-circle. Find the dimensions of the rectangle to get maximum area. Also, find the maximum area. **[ISC 2016]**

Case-Based Type Questions

6 Marks

50 In order to set up a rainwater harvesting system, a tank to collect rainwater is to be dug. The tank should have a square base and a capacity of 250 m^3. The cost of land is ₹ 5000 per square metre and cost of digging increases with depth and for the whole tank, it is ₹ 40000 h^2, where h is the depth of the tank in metres x is the side of the square base of the tank in metres.

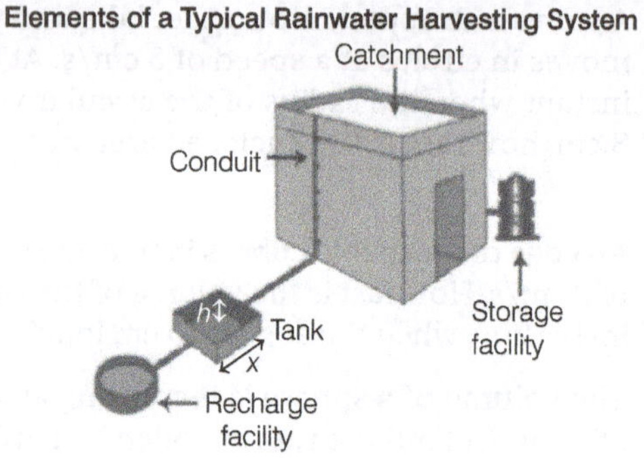

Based on the above information, answer the following questions.

(i) Find the total cost C of digging the tank in terms of x.

(ii) Find $\frac{dC}{dx}$.

(iii) (a) Find the value of x for which cost C is minimum.

(b) Check whether the cost function $C(x)$ expressed in terms of x is increasing or not, where $x > 0$.

51 Sumit has bought a closed cylindrical dustbin. The radius of the dustbin is r cm and height is h cm. It has a volume of 20π cm^3. **[ISC 2024]**

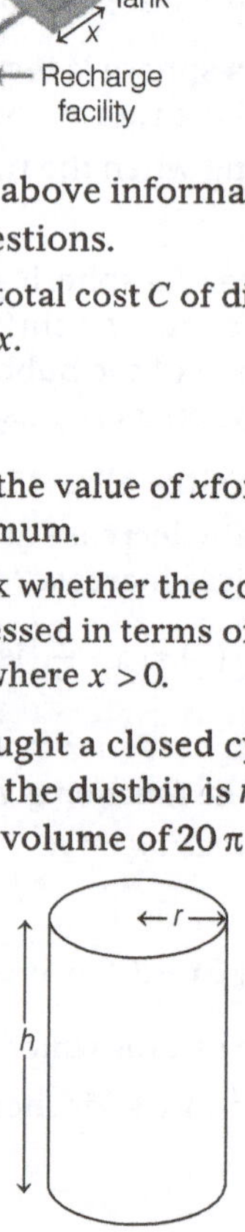

(i) Express h in terms of r, using the given volume.

(ii) Prove that the total surface area of the dustbin is $2\pi r^2 + \frac{40\pi}{r}$.

(iii) Sumit wants to paint the dustbin. The cost of painting the base and top of the dustbin is ₹ 2 per cm^2 and the cost of painting the curved side is ₹ 25 per cm^2. Find the total cost in terms of r, for painting the outer surface of the dustbin including the base and top.

(iv) Calculate the minimum cost for painting the dustbin.

Answers

1. (d) 2. (b) 3. (b) 4. (c) 5. (b) 6. (a)
7. (b) 8. (c) 9. (b) 10. (d) 11. (a) 12. (i) 3 (ii) −1
13. $x + 13y + 12 = 0$ 14. $(2, -4)$ 15. $a = 1, b = 2$ 16. (i) 0.8 cm/s (ii) 1.8 π cm/s
17. $80\pi \text{ cm}^2/\text{s}$ 18. $900 \text{ cm}^3/\text{s}$ 19. $\frac{4}{3} \text{ cm}^2/\text{s}$ 20. $6 \text{ cm}^3/\text{s}$ 21. $\left(3, \frac{16}{3}\right)$ and $\left(-3, \frac{-16}{3}\right)$
24. $k \in \left(0, \frac{1}{3}\right)$ 25. $\left(\frac{1}{2}, 4\right)$ and $\left(-\frac{1}{2}, 6\right)$ 26. $\frac{xx_1}{a^2} + \frac{yy_1}{b^2} = 1, \frac{a^2x}{x_1} - \frac{b^2y}{y_1} = a^2 - b^2$
27. $y - (\sqrt{2} - 1)x = \frac{\pi}{4} - \frac{4}{\sqrt{2}} + 2,\ y + (\sqrt{2} + 1)x = \frac{\pi}{4}$ 28. (0, 0), (1, 2) and (−1, −2)
29. $x + 3y = \pm 8$ 30. (2, 0) and (0, 0) 31. $\left(\frac{7}{2}, \frac{1}{4}\right)$ 32. $x + y = 3$ and $x + y - 1 = 0$
33. $20\sqrt{3} \text{ cm}^2/\text{s}$ 34. $2x^2 - 3x + 1$ 35. (i) $\left[0, \frac{\pi}{6}\right]$ (ii) $\left[\frac{\pi}{6}, \frac{\pi}{2}\right]$ 36. $\left(\frac{\pi}{2}, \pi\right)$
37. Strictly increasing in $(-\infty, 2) \cup (3, \infty)$ and strictly decreasing in $(2, 3)$.
38. Increasing in $[0, \infty)$ and decreasing in $(-\infty, -1) \cup (-1, 0)$. 39. Increasing in $(-\infty, -1]$ and decreasing in $[-1, \infty)$.
40. ₹ 49 41. 12, 12 42. $y = -3x + 4$ and $y = 3x - 4$ 43. (0, 0) 44. (2, 2)
47. $108\pi \text{ cm}^3$ 48. 5 cm 49. r^2
50. (i) $C = 5000x^2 + \frac{40000 \times (250)^2}{x^4}$

(ii) $\frac{dC}{dx} = 10000x - \frac{160000 \times (250)^2}{x^5}$

(iii) (a) $x = 10$

(b) $C(x)$ is increasing in $[10, \infty)$.

51. (i) $h = \frac{20}{\pi^2}$ (iii) ₹ $\left(4\pi r^2 + \frac{100\pi}{r}\right)$ (iv) ₹ 942.85

CHAPTER

08

Indefinite Integrals

We know how to find the derivative of a given function. But the question arises, can we find a function whose derivative is known to us. The functions that could have possibly given function as a derivative are called **anti-derivatives** of the function. The formula that gives all these anti-derivatives is called the **indefinite integral** of the function and such process of finding anti-derivatives is called the **integration** or **anti-differentiation**.

- Integration as an Inverse Process of Differentiation
- Methods of Integration
- Some Special Integrals

TOPIC 01 Integration as an Inverse Process of Differentiation

Let $F(x)$ and $f(x)$ be two functions connected together such that $\frac{d}{dx}F(x)=f(x)$, then $F(x)$ is called **integral** or **anti-derivative** or **primitive** of $f(x)$.

Note that, if $\frac{d}{dx}F(x)=f(x)$, then for any arbitrary constant C, $\frac{d}{dx}[F(x)+C]=f(x)$. Thus, $F(x)+C$ is also an anti-derivative of $f(x)$. Since, the integral of a function is not unique, therefore it is called **indefinite integral.**

We represent it by $\int f(x)\,dx$, i.e. $\int f(x)\,dx=F(x)+C$, where C is an arbitrary constant (also called **constant of integration**) and symbol '$\int$' stands for the sign of integration. Some symbols/terms/phrases, related to integration, with their meaning are given in following table.

Symbols/Terms/Phrases	Meaning
$\int f(x)\,dx$	Integral of f with respect to x
$f(x)$ in $\int f(x)\,dx$	Integrand
x in $\int f(x)\,dx$	Variable of integration
Integrate	Find the integral
An integral of f	A function F such that $F'(x)=f(x)$
Integration	The process of finding the integral
Constant of integration	Any real number C, considered as constant function

Anti-derivatives of Some Standard Functions

	Derivatives	Indefinite integrals (Anti-derivatives)
1.	$\frac{d}{dx}(x)=1$	$\int dx = x + C$
2.	$\frac{d}{dx}\left(\frac{x^{n+1}}{n+1}\right)=x^n, n \neq -1$	$\int x^n dx = \frac{x^{n+1}}{n+1}+C, n\neq -1$
3.	$\frac{d}{dx}\left(\frac{(ax+b)^{n+1}}{a\cdot(n+1)}\right)=(ax+b)^n$, $a\neq 0$ and $n \neq -1$	$\int (ax+b)^n dx = \frac{(ax+b)^{n+1}}{a\cdot(n+1)}+C$, $a\neq 0$ and $n\neq -1$
4.	$\frac{d}{dx}(\sin x)=\cos x$	$\int \cos x\, dx = \sin x + C$
5.	$\frac{d}{dx}(-\cos x)=\sin x$	$\int \sin x\, dx = -\cos x + C$
6.	$\frac{d}{dx}(\tan x)=\sec^2 x$	$\int \sec^2 x\, dx = \tan x + C$
7.	$\frac{d}{dx}(-\cot x)=\text{cosec}^2 x$	$\int \text{cosec}^2 x\, dx = -\cot x + C$
8.	$\frac{d}{dx}(\sec x)=\sec x\cdot\tan x$	$\int \sec x\cdot \tan x\, dx = \sec x + C$
9.	$\frac{d}{dx}(-\text{cosec}\, x)=\text{cosec}\, x\cdot\cot x$	$\int \text{cosec}\, x\cdot\cot x\, dx = -\text{cosec}\, x + C$
10.	$\frac{d}{dx}(\sin^{-1}x)=\frac{1}{\sqrt{1-x^2}}$	$\int \frac{dx}{\sqrt{1-x^2}}=\sin^{-1}x+C$
11.	$\frac{d}{dx}(-\cos^{-1}x)=\frac{1}{\sqrt{1-x^2}}$	$\int \frac{dx}{\sqrt{1-x^2}}=-\cos^{-1}x+C$
12.	$\frac{d}{dx}(\tan^{-1}x)=\frac{1}{1+x^2}$	$\int \frac{dx}{1+x^2}=\tan^{-1}x+C$
13.	$\frac{d}{dx}(-\cot^{-1}x)=\frac{1}{1+x^2}$	$\int \frac{dx}{1+x^2}=-\cot^{-1}x+C$
14.	$\frac{d}{dx}(\sec^{-1}x)=\frac{1}{x\sqrt{x^2-1}}$	$\int \frac{dx}{x\sqrt{x^2-1}}=\sec^{-1}x+C$
15.	$\frac{d}{dx}(-\text{cosec}^{-1}x)=\frac{1}{x\sqrt{x^2-1}}$	$\int \frac{dx}{x\sqrt{x^2-1}}=-\text{cosec}^{-1}x+C$
16.	$\frac{d}{dx}(e^x)=e^x$	$\int e^x dx = e^x + C$
17.	$\frac{d}{dx}(\log\lvert x\rvert)=\frac{1}{x}$	$\int \frac{1}{x}dx=\log\lvert x\rvert + C$
18.	$\frac{d}{dx}\left(\frac{a^x}{\log a}\right)=a^x, a>0, a\neq 1$	$\int a^x dx = \frac{a^x}{\log a}+C, a>0, a\neq 1$

Note

(i) The derivative of function is unique but integral of a function is not unique.

(ii) Integrals of a function differ by a constant.

Example 1 Evaluate the following integrals.

(i) $\int x^6 dx$ (ii) $\int \frac{1}{x^{3/4}}dx$ (iii) $\int (3x-2)^7 dx$

(iv) $\int 5^x dx$ (v) $\int a^{3\log_a x} dx$

Sol. (i) Let $I=\int x^6 dx$

$$=\frac{x^{6+1}}{6+1}+C \quad \left[\because \int x^n dx = \frac{x^{n+1}}{n+1}+C, \text{ if } n\neq -1\right]$$

$$=\frac{x^7}{7}+C$$

(ii) Let $I=\int\left[\frac{1}{x^{3/4}}\right]dx=\int x^{-3/4}dx$

$$=\frac{x^{-\frac{3}{4}+1}}{-\frac{3}{4}+1}+C \quad \left[\because \int x^n dx=\frac{x^{n+1}}{n+1}+C\right]$$

$$=\frac{x^{1/4}}{1/4}+C=4x^{1/4}+C$$

(iii) Let $I=\int(3x-2)^7 dx$

$$=\frac{(3x-2)^{7+1}}{(7+1)\cdot 3}+C$$

$$\left[\because \int (ax+b)^n dx=\frac{(ax+b)^{n+1}}{(n+1)\cdot a}+C, a\neq 0 \text{ and } n\neq -1\right]$$

$$=\frac{(3x-2)^8}{24}+C$$

(iv) Let $I=\int 5^x dx=\frac{5^x}{\log 5}+C \quad \left[\because \int a^x dx=\frac{a^x}{\log a}+C\right]$

(v) Let $I=\int a^{3\log_a x}dx=\int a^{\log_a x^3}dx \quad [\because m\log n=\log n^m]$

$$=\int x^3 dx \quad [\because a^{\log_a f(x)}=f(x)]$$

$$=\frac{x^4}{4}+C \quad \left[\because \int x^n dx=\frac{x^{n+1}}{n+1}+C, \text{ if } n\neq -1\right]$$

Note

(i) While solving an integral, constant of integration should be written, otherwise answer would be wrong.

(ii) If more than one constant of integration is used while solving the integral, then at the end of the solution write only one constant of integration.

Properties of Indefinite Integrals

(i) $\frac{d}{dx}\int f(x)dx=f(x)$ and $\int f'(x)dx=f(x)+C$

where, C is any arbitrary constant.

(ii) $\int \{f(x)\pm g(x)\}\,dx=\int f(x)\,dx\pm\int g(x)\,dx$

(iii) $\int k\cdot f(x)\,dx=k\cdot\int f(x)\,dx$ where, k is any non-zero real number.

(iv) Properties (ii) and (iii) can be generalised to a finite number of function, i.e. if $f_1, f_2, \ldots, f_n$ are functions and $k_1, k_2, \ldots, k_n$ are non-zero real numbers, then

$$\int [k_1 f_1(x) + k_2 f_2(x) + \ldots + k_n f_n(x)]\, dx$$
$$= k_1 \int f_1(x) dx + k_2 \int f_2(x)\, dx + \ldots + k_n \int f_n(x) dx$$

Thus, the integral of the sum of a number of functions is equal to the sum of the integrals of the functions.

Example 2 Evaluate $\int \frac{(1+x)^2}{\sqrt{x}} dx.$

Firstly, expand numerator by using $(a+b)^2 = a^2 + b^2 + 2ab$ and then integrate it.

Sol. Let $I = \int \frac{(1+x)^2}{\sqrt{x}} dx = \int \frac{(1+x^2+2x)}{\sqrt{x}} dx$

$$= \int \frac{1}{\sqrt{x}} dx + \int \frac{x^2}{\sqrt{x}} dx + 2\int \frac{x}{\sqrt{x}} dx \text{ [by property (iv)]}$$

$$= \int x^{-\frac{1}{2}} dx + \int x^{2-\frac{1}{2}} dx + 2\int x^{1-\frac{1}{2}} dx$$

$$= \int x^{-1/2} dx + \int x^{3/2} dx + 2\int x^{1/2} dx$$

$$= \frac{x^{-\frac{1}{2}+1}}{-\frac{1}{2}+1} + C_1 + \frac{x^{\frac{3}{2}+1}}{\frac{3}{2}+1} + C_2 + \frac{2x^{\frac{1}{2}+1}}{\frac{1}{2}+1} + C_3$$

$$\left[\because \int x^n dx = \frac{x^{n+1}}{n+1} + C\right]$$

$$= \frac{x^{1/2}}{1/2} + \frac{x^{5/2}}{5/2} + \frac{2x^{3/2}}{3/2} + C, \text{ where } C = C_1 + C_2 + C_3$$

$$= 2x^{1/2} + \frac{2}{5}x^{5/2} + \frac{4}{3}x^{3/2} + C$$

$$= 2\sqrt{x} + \frac{2}{5}x^{5/2} + \frac{4}{3}x^{3/2} + C$$

Example 3 Evaluate the following integrals.

(i) $\int \sqrt{ax+b}\, dx$ (ii) $\int \frac{dx}{\sqrt{x+a}+\sqrt{x+b}}$ [NCERT]

Sol. (i) Let $I = \int \sqrt{ax+b}\, dx = \int (ax+b)^{1/2} dx$

$$= \frac{(ax+b)^{(1/2)+1}}{((1/2)+1)\cdot a} + C = \frac{2}{3}\frac{(ax+b)^{3/2}}{a} + C$$

$$= \frac{2}{3a}(ax+b)^{3/2} + C$$

(ii) Let $I = \int \frac{dx}{\sqrt{x+a}+\sqrt{x+b}}$

$$= \int \frac{(\sqrt{x+a}-\sqrt{x+b})}{(\sqrt{x+a}+\sqrt{x+b})(\sqrt{x+a}-\sqrt{x+b})} dx$$

[rationalising denominator]

$$= \int \frac{\sqrt{x+a}-\sqrt{x+b}}{(\sqrt{x+a})^2-(\sqrt{x+b})^2} dx = \int \frac{(\sqrt{x+a}-\sqrt{x+b})}{(x+a)-(x+b)} dx$$

$$= \frac{1}{a-b}\int [(x+a)^{1/2} - (x+b)^{1/2}] dx$$

$$= \frac{1}{a-b}\left[\frac{2}{3}(x+a)^{3/2} - \frac{2}{3}(x+b)^{3/2}\right] + C$$

$$= \frac{2}{3(a-b)}[(x+a)^{3/2} - (x+b)^{3/2}] + C$$

Example 4 Find the anti-derivative F of f defined by $f(x) = 4x^5 - 6x$, where $F(0) = 2$.

Firstly, find the integral of $f(x)$, say $F(x)$. Further, use the condition $F(0) = 2$ to get the value of C. Finally, put the value of C in $F(x)$ and get the required result.

Sol. Given, $f(x) = 4x^5 - 6x$

On integrating both sides, we get

$$\int f(x)\, dx = \int (4x^5 - 6x)\, dx$$

$$\Rightarrow \quad F(x) = \frac{4x^{5+1}}{5+1} - \frac{6x^2}{2} + C \quad \left[\because \int x^n\, dx = \frac{x^{n+1}}{n+1} + C\right]$$

$$\Rightarrow \quad F(x) = \frac{4}{6}x^6 - \frac{6}{2}x^2 + C$$

$$\Rightarrow \quad F(x) = \frac{2}{3}x^6 - 3x^2 + C \quad \ldots(i)$$

Also, given $F(0) = 2$, therefore putting $x = 0$ in Eq. (i), we get

$$F(0) = \frac{2}{3}(0) - 3(0) + C$$

$$\Rightarrow \quad 2 = 0 - 0 + C \Rightarrow C = 2$$

Now, putting $C = 2$ in Eq. (i), we get

$$F(x) = \frac{2x^6}{3} - 3x^2 + 2$$

Example 5 Evaluate the following integrals.

(i) $\int (\sin x + \cos x)\, dx$ (ii) $\int \sin x \left(\cot x + \frac{1}{\sin^3 x}\right) dx$

Sol. (i) Let $I = \int (\sin x + \cos x) dx$

$$= \int \sin x\, dx + \int \cos x\, dx$$

$$= -\cos x + \sin x + C$$

(ii) Let $I = \int \sin x \left(\cot x + \frac{1}{\sin^3 x}\right) dx$

$$= \int \left(\sin x \times \cot x + \frac{\sin x}{\sin^3 x}\right) dx$$

$$= \int \left(\sin x \times \frac{\cos x}{\sin x}\right) dx + \int \frac{1}{\sin^2 x} dx$$

$$= \int \cos x\, dx + \int \text{cosec}^2 x\, dx$$

$$= \sin x - \cot x + C$$

Topic Practice 1

Very Short Answer Type Questions

2 Marks

1 Evaluate the following integrals. (Each part carries 2 Marks)

(i) $\int (2\sin x + x)dx$ (ii) $\int (x^2+1)^2 dx$

(iii) $\int \frac{x^4+x^2}{x} dx$ (iv) $\int (\sec^2 x + x^2)dx$

(v) $\int b^{4\log_b x} dx$

2 Verify the following, using the concept of integration as an anti-derivative.

$$\int \frac{x^3}{x+1} dx = x - \frac{x^2}{2} + \frac{x^3}{3} - \log|x+1| + C$$

[NCERT Exemplar]

3 Integrate $\left(\frac{2a}{\sqrt{x}} - \frac{b}{x^2} + 3c\sqrt[3]{x^2}\right)$ w.r.t. x.. [NCERT Exemplar]

4 Write the anti-derivative of $\left(3\sqrt{x} + \frac{1}{\sqrt{x}}\right)$.

Directions (Q. Nos. 5-8) *Evaluate the following integrals.*

5 $\int \frac{x^3+5x^2+4x+1}{x^2} dx$ [ISC 2018]

6 $\int \frac{x^3-x^2+x-1}{x-1} dx$ 7 $\int \frac{(x^3+8)(x-1)}{x^2-2x+4} dx$

8 If $\frac{d}{dx} f(x) = 4x^3 - \frac{3}{x^4}$ such that $f(2)=0$. Then, find $f(x)$. [NCERT]

Directions (Q. Nos. 9-13) *Evaluate the following integrals.*

9 Evaluate $\int \frac{\sec^2 x}{\text{cosec}^2 x} dx$ [ISC 2019]

10 $\int \frac{\sin^2 x - \cos^2 x}{\sin^2 x \cos^2 x} dx$ 11 $\int \frac{2+3\cos x}{\sin^2 x} dx$

12 Evaluate $\int \frac{1+\cos x}{\sin^2 x} dx$ [ISC 2023]

13 $\int \frac{e^{6\log x} - e^{5\log x}}{e^{4\log x} - e^{3\log x}} dx$ [NCERT Exemplar]

Short Answer Type Questions

4 Marks

14 Evaluate $\int \frac{x^4}{x^2+1} dx$.

15 Evaluate $\int \frac{(a^x+b^x)^2}{a^x b^x} dx$.

Hints & Solutions

1. (i) $\int (2\sin x + x)dx = \int (2\sin x)dx + \int x\,dx = -2\cos x + C$ [2]

(ii) $\int (x^2+1)^2 dx = \int (x^4+2x^2+1)dx$ [1]

$$= \frac{x^5}{5} + \frac{2x^3}{3} + x + C$$ [1]

(iii) $\int \left(\frac{x^4+x^2}{x}\right) dx = \int (x^3+x)dx = \frac{x^4}{4} + \frac{x^2}{2} + C$ [2]

(iv) $\int (\sec^2 x + x^2)dx = \tan x + \frac{x^3}{3} + C$ [2]

(v) Similar as Example 1(v) $\left[\textbf{Ans. } \frac{x^5}{5} + C\right]$

2. Consider, $\frac{d}{dx}\left(x - \frac{x^2}{2} + \frac{x^3}{3} - \log|x+1| + C\right)$

$$= 1 - \frac{2x}{2} + \frac{3x^2}{3} - \frac{1}{x+1}$$

$$= 1 - x + x^2 - \frac{1}{x+1}$$ [1]

$$= \frac{(x+1)(x^2-x+1)-1}{x+1}$$

$$= \frac{(x^3+1)-1}{x+1} = \frac{x^3}{x+1}$$

$[\because a^3+b^3 = (a+b)(a^2-ab+b^2)]$

Hence, $x - \frac{x^2}{2} + \frac{x^3}{3} - \log|x+1| + C = \int \frac{x^3}{x+1} dx$ [1]

3. Let $I = \int \left(\frac{2a}{\sqrt{x}} - \frac{b}{x^2} + 3c\sqrt[3]{x^2}\right) dx$

$$= \int \frac{2a}{\sqrt{x}} dx - \int \frac{b}{x^2} dx + \int 3c\sqrt[3]{x^2}\, dx$$

$$= 2a\int x^{-1/2} dx - b\int x^{-2} dx + 3c\int x^{2/3} dx$$ [1]

$$= 2a\left[\frac{x^{(-1/2)+1}}{(-1/2)+1}\right] - b\left[\frac{x^{-2+1}}{-2+1}\right] + 3c\left[\frac{x^{(2/3)+1}}{(2/3)+1}\right] + C$$

$\left[\because \int x^n dx = \frac{x^{n+1}}{n+1}\right]$

$$= 2a\left[\frac{x^{1/2}}{1/2}\right] - b\left[\frac{x^{-1}}{(-1)}\right] + 3c\left[\frac{x^{5/3}}{5/3}\right] + C$$

$$= 4a\sqrt{x} + \frac{b}{x} + \frac{9c}{5} x^{5/3} + C$$ [1]

4. **Hint** $3\int \sqrt{x}dx+\int \frac{1}{\sqrt{x}}dx = 3\int x^{1/2}dx+\int x^{-1/2}dx.$

[Ans. $2(x^{3/2}+x^{1/2})+C$]

5. Let $I=\int \frac{x^3+5x^2+4x+1}{x^2}dx$

$\Rightarrow \quad I=\int\left(x+5+\frac{4}{x}+\frac{1}{x^2}\right)dx$ [1]

$\Rightarrow \quad I=\frac{x^2}{2}+5x+4\log|x|-\frac{1}{x}+C$ [1]

6. **Hint** Write $x^3-x^2+x-1=x^2(x-1)+1(x-1)$

$=(x^2+1)(x-1)$

$\left[\textbf{Ans. } \frac{x^3}{3}+x+C\right]$

7. Let $I=\int \frac{(x^3+8)(x-1)}{x^2-2x+4}dx$

$=\int \frac{(x+2)(x^2+2^2-2x)(x-1)}{(x^2-2x+4)}dx$

$=\int (x+2)(x-1)\,dx=\int (x^2+x-2)\,dx$ [1]

$=\frac{x^3}{3}+\frac{x^2}{2}-2x+C$ [1]

8. **Hint** Firstly integrate, further to find C, put $x=2$ and use the condition $f(2)=0$.

$\left[\textbf{Ans. } x^4+\frac{1}{x^3}-\frac{129}{8}\right]$

9. Let $I=\int \frac{\sec^2 x}{\text{cosec}^2 x}dx$

$=\int \frac{1}{\cos^2 x}\times\frac{\sin^2 x}{1}dx=\int \tan^2 x$

$=\int(\sec^2 x-1)\,dx$

$=\tan x-x+C$

10. Let $I=\int \frac{\sin^2 x-\cos^2 x}{\sin^2 x\cos^2 x}dx$

$=\int\left(\frac{\sin^2 x}{\sin^2 x\cos^2 x}-\frac{\cos^2 x}{\sin^2 x\cos^2 x}\right)dx$ [1]

$=\int(\sec^2 x-\text{cosec}^2 x)dx=\int \sec^2 x\,dx-\int \text{cosec}^2 x\,dx$

$=\tan x-(-\cot x)+C$

$=\tan x+\cot x+C$ [1]

11. Let $I=\int \frac{2+3\cos x}{\sin^2 x}dx=\int\left(\frac{2}{\sin^2 x}+\frac{3\cos x}{\sin^2 x}\right)dx$

$=2\int \frac{1}{\sin^2 x}dx+3\int \frac{\cos x}{\sin^2 x}dx$

$=2\int \text{cosec}^2 x\,dx+3\int\left(\frac{\cos x}{\sin x}\right)\cdot\frac{1}{\sin x}dx$ [1]

$=2\int \text{cosec}^2 x\,dx+3\int \cot x\cdot\text{cosec}\,x\,dx$

$=2(-\cot x)+3(-\text{cosec}\,x)+C$

$=-2\cot x-3\,\text{cosec}\,x+C$ [1]

12. Let $I=\int \frac{1+\cos x}{\sin^2 x}dx$

$I=\int(\text{cosec}^2 x+\text{cosec}x\cot x)\,dx$

$I=-\cot x-\text{cosec}\,x+C$

13. Let $I=\int \frac{e^{6\log x}-e^{5\log x}}{e^{4\log x}-e^{3\log x}}dx=\int \frac{e^{\log x^6}-e^{\log x^5}}{e^{\log x^4}-e^{\log x^3}}dx$

$=\int \frac{x^6-x^5}{x^4-x^3}dx \qquad [\because e^{\log f(x)}=f(x)]$ [1]

$=\int \frac{x^5(x-1)}{x^3(x-1)}dx=\int x^2dx=\frac{x^3}{3}+C$ [1]

14. Let $I=\int \frac{x^4}{x^2+1}dx=\int \frac{x^4-1+1}{x^2+1}dx$

$=\int \frac{x^4-1}{x^2+1}dx+\int \frac{1}{x^2+1}dx$ [1]

$=\int\left(\frac{(x^2-1)(x^2+1)}{x^2+1}+\frac{1}{x^2+1}\right)dx$ [1]

$[\because a^4-b^4=(a^2-b^2)(a^2+b^2)]$

$=\int(x^2-1)dx+\int \frac{1}{x^2+1}dx$

$=\int x^2dx-\int dx+\int \frac{dx}{x^2+1}$ [1]

$=\frac{x^3}{3}-x+\tan^{-1}x+C \quad \left[\because \int \frac{dx}{x^2+1}=\tan^{-1}x+C\right]$ [1]

15. Let $I=\int \frac{(a^x+b^x)^2}{a^x\cdot b^x}dx=\int\left(\frac{a^{2x}+b^{2x}+2a^x\cdot b^x}{a^x\cdot b^x}\right)dx$ [1]

$[\because (a+b)^2=a^2+b^2+2ab]$

$=\int\left(\frac{a^{2x}}{a^x\cdot b^x}+\frac{b^{2x}}{a^x\cdot b^x}+\frac{2a^x\cdot b^x}{a^x\cdot b^x}\right)dx$

$=\int\left(\frac{a^x}{b^x}+\frac{b^x}{a^x}+2\right)dx$ [1]

$=\int\left(\frac{a}{b}\right)^x dx+\int\left(\frac{b}{a}\right)^x dx+2\int dx$ [1]

$=\frac{\left(\frac{a}{b}\right)^x}{\log\left(\frac{a}{b}\right)}+\frac{\left(\frac{b}{a}\right)^x}{\log\left(\frac{b}{a}\right)}+2x+C, \text{ if } a\neq b$

$\left[\because \int a^x dx=\frac{a^x}{\log a}+C, a>0,\ a\neq 1\right]$ [1]

TOPIC 02 Method of Integration

In previous topic, we discussed the integrals of those functions which are in standard forms. But there exist some functions which cannot be integrated directly. For such integrals we have the following method to solve

(i) Integration by substitution
(ii) Integration by parts
(iii) Integration by partial fractions

Method of Substitution

The method of reducing a given integral into one of the standard integrals by a proper substitution is called **method of substitution.**

To evaluate an integral of the type $\int f'(x)[f(x)]^n\,dx$ or $\int \frac{f'(x)}{f(x)}\,dx$, we substitute $f(x)=t$, which reduces the above integrals to $\int t^n\,dt$ or $\int \frac{1}{t}\,dt$ respectively.

$$\left[\because f(x)=t \Rightarrow f'(x)=\frac{dt}{dx} \Rightarrow f'(x)\,dx=dt\right]$$

Thus, $\int f'(x)[f(x)]^n\,dx=\int t^n\,dt=\frac{t^{n+1}}{n+1}+C$

$$=\frac{(f(x))^{n+1}}{n+1}+C,\ n\neq -1$$

or $\int \frac{f'(x)}{f(x)}\,dx=\int \frac{1}{t}\,dt=\log|t|+C=\log|f(x)|+C.$

Note It is often important to guess what will be the useful substitution. Usually, we make a substitution for a function whose derivative also occurs in the integrand.

Example 1 Evaluate $\int \frac{e^{\tan^{-1}x}}{1+x^2}\,dx.$

Sol. Let $I=\int \frac{e^{\tan^{-1}x}}{1+x^2}\,dx$

Here, integrand has differentiation of $\tan^{-1}x$, so we substitute for $\tan^{-1}x$.

Now, put $\tan^{-1}x=t$

$\Rightarrow \frac{1}{1+x^2}\,dx=dt$ [differentiating both sides w.r.t. x]

Now, $I=\int e^t\,dt$

Thus, $I=\int e^t\,dt=e^t+C$

On putting $t=\tan^{-1}x$, we get

$$I=e^{\tan^{-1}x}+C$$

Example 2 Evaluate $\int \cos 6x\sqrt{1+\sin 6x}\,dx.$ [NCERT]

Sol. Let $I=\int \cos 6x\sqrt{1+\sin 6x}\,dx$

Now, put $1+\sin 6x=t$

$\Rightarrow \cos 6x\cdot 6\,dx=dt \Rightarrow \cos 6x\,dx=\frac{dt}{6}$

$\therefore\quad I=\frac{1}{6}\int \sqrt{t}\,dt=\frac{1}{6}\frac{t^{1/2+1}}{\frac{1}{2}+1}+C$

$=\frac{1}{6}\cdot\frac{t^{3/2}}{\frac{3}{2}}+C=\frac{1}{6}\times\frac{2}{3}t^{3/2}+C$

$=\frac{1}{9}(1+\sin 6x)^{3/2}+C$ $[\because t=1+\sin 6x]$

Example 3 Integrate the following function w.r.t. x.

$$\frac{\tan^4\sqrt{x}\sec^2\sqrt{x}}{\sqrt{x}}$$ [NCERT]

Sol. Let $I=\int \frac{\tan^4\sqrt{x}\sec^2\sqrt{x}}{\sqrt{x}}\,dx$

Now, put $\tan\sqrt{x}=t$

$\Rightarrow \sec^2\sqrt{x}\cdot\frac{1}{2\sqrt{x}}\,dx=dt \Rightarrow \frac{\sec^2\sqrt{x}}{\sqrt{x}}\,dx=2dt$

$\therefore\quad I=\int t^4(2\,dt)=2\int t^4\,dt$

$=2\cdot\frac{t^5}{5}+C=\frac{2}{5}\tan^5\sqrt{x}+C$ [put $t=\tan\sqrt{x}$]

Example 4 Evaluate $\int \frac{dx}{1+\tan x}.$

Given integrand is not in standard form, so firstly convert in $\sin x$ and $\cos x$ form. Further, adjust them and use suitable substitution to integrate easily.

Sol. Let $I=\int \frac{dx}{1+\tan x}=\int \frac{dx}{1+\frac{\sin x}{\cos x}}$

$=\int \frac{\cos x}{\cos x+\sin x}\,dx=\int \frac{2\cos x\,dx}{2(\cos x+\sin x)}$

$=\frac{1}{2}\int \frac{(\cos x+\sin x)+(\cos x-\sin x)}{\cos x+\sin x}\,dx$

[adding and subtracting $(\sin x)$ in numerator]

$$= \frac{1}{2}\int 1\,dx + \frac{1}{2}\int \frac{\cos x - \sin x}{\cos x + \sin x}\,dx$$

Now, put $\cos x + \sin x = t \Rightarrow (-\sin x + \cos x)\,dx = dt$

Then, we get

$$I = \frac{1}{2}\int 1\,dx + \frac{1}{2}\int \frac{dt}{t} = \frac{x}{2} + \frac{1}{2}\log|t| + C$$

$$= \frac{x}{2} + \frac{1}{2}\log|\cos x + \sin x| + C \quad [\because t = \cos x + \sin x]$$

Some Standard Formulae

Some standard formulae involving trigonometric functions are given below. These formulae are obtained by using substitution technique.

(i) $\int \tan x\,dx = -\log|\cos x| + C = \log|\sec x| + C$

(ii) $\int \cot x\,dx = \log|\sin x| + C$

(iii) $\int \sec x\,dx = \log|\sec x + \tan x| + C$

$$= \log\left|\tan\left(\frac{\pi}{4} + \frac{x}{2}\right)\right| + C$$

(iv) $\int \operatorname{cosec} x\,dx = \log|\operatorname{cosec} x - \cot x| + C$

$$= \log\left|\tan\frac{x}{2}\right| + C$$

Proof

(i) Let $I = \int \tan x\,dx = \int \frac{\sin x}{\cos x}\,dx$

Now, put $\cos x = t \Rightarrow -\sin x\,dx = dt$

$\Rightarrow \quad \sin x\,dx = -dt$

$$\therefore \quad I = -\int \frac{1}{t}\,dt = -\log|t| + C$$

$$= -\log|\cos x| + C \quad [\because t = \cos x]$$

$$= \log|(\cos x)^{-1}| + C$$

$$= \log|\sec x| + C \quad \left[\because \frac{1}{\cos x} = \sec x\right]$$

(ii) Put $\sin x = t$ and then solve same as above.

(iii) Let $I = \int \sec x\,dx$

On multiplying numerator and denominator by $(\sec x + \tan x)$, we get

$$I = \int \frac{\sec x(\sec x + \tan x)}{\sec x + \tan x}\,dx$$

$$I = \int \frac{(\sec^2 x + \sec x \tan x)}{(\sec x + \tan x)}\,dx$$

Put $\sec x + \tan x = t$

$\Rightarrow \quad (\sec x \tan x + \sec^2 x)\,dx = dt$

$$\therefore \quad I = \int \frac{1}{t}\,dt = \log|t| + C$$

$$\Rightarrow I = \log|\sec x + \tan x| + C \quad [\because t = \sec x + \tan x]$$

(iv) Firstly, multiplying numerator and denominator by $(\operatorname{cosec} x - \cot x)$. Further, put $\operatorname{cosec} x - \cot x = t$ and then solve as part (iii).

Some Important Deductions

(i) $\int \sin(ax+b)\,dx = \frac{-\cos(ax+b)}{a} + C$

(ii) $\int \cos(ax+b)\,dx = \frac{\sin(ax+b)}{a} + C$

(iii) $\int \tan(ax+b)dx = -\frac{1}{a}\log|\cos(ax+b)| + C$

$= \frac{1}{a}\log|\sec(ax+b)| + C$

(iv) $\int \cot(ax+b)\,dx = \frac{1}{a}\log|\sin(ax+b)| + C$

(v) $\int \sec(ax+b)\,dx = \frac{1}{a}\log|\sec(ax+b) + \tan(ax+b)| + C$

(vi) $\int \operatorname{cosec}(ax+b)\,dx = \frac{1}{a}\log|\operatorname{cosec}(ax+b) - \cot(ax+b)| + C$

(vii) $\int \sec(ax+b)\tan(ax+b)\,dx = \frac{1}{a}\sec(ax+b) + C$

(viii) $\int \operatorname{cosec}(ax+b)\cot(ax+b)\,dx = -\frac{1}{a}\operatorname{cosec}(ax+b) + C$

(ix) $\int \sec^2(ax+b)\,dx = \frac{1}{a}\tan(ax+b) + C$

(x) $\int \operatorname{cosec}^2(ax+b)\,dx = -\frac{1}{a}\cot(ax+b) + C$

(xi) $\int e^{(ax+b)}\,dx = \frac{e^{(ax+b)}}{a} + C$ (xii) $\int \frac{1}{ax+b}\,dx = \frac{1}{a}\log|ax+b| + C$

Note Above integrals can be derived by substituting $(ax+b) = t$ and $dx = \frac{1}{a}\,dt$.

Example 5 Evaluate the following integrals.

(i) $\int \frac{\tan(\log x)}{x}\,dx$ (ii) $\int \sec^2(7-4x)\,dx$ **[NCERT]**

Sol. (i) Let $I = \int \frac{\tan(\log x)}{x}\,dx$

Putting $\log x = t$, we get $\frac{1}{x}\,dx = dt$

and hence $I = \int \tan t\,dt = \log|\sec t| + C$

$$= \log|\sec(\log x)| + C$$

(ii) Let $I = \int \sec^2(7-4x)dx = \frac{1}{(-4)}\tan(7-4x) + C$

$$\left[\because \int \sec^2(ax+b)dx = \frac{1}{a}\tan(ax+b) + C\right]$$

$$= -\frac{1}{4}\tan(7-4x) + C$$

Integration using Trigonometric Identities

When the integrand involves trigonometric functions, then some known trigonometric identities help us to evaluate integral easily.

Important Trigonometric Identities

Some useful trigonometric identities are given below

1. $\sin 2x = 2\sin x \cos x = \dfrac{2\tan x}{1+\tan^2 x}$
2. $\cos 2x = \cos^2 x - \sin^2 x = 2\cos^2 x - 1$
   $= 1 - 2\sin^2 x = \dfrac{1-\tan^2 x}{1+\tan^2 x}$
3. $\tan 2x = \dfrac{2\tan x}{1-\tan^2 x}$
4. $\sin 3x = -\sin^3 x + 3\cos^2 x \sin x = -4\sin^3 x + 3\sin x$
5. $\cos 3x = \cos^3 x - 3\sin^2 x \cos x = 4\cos^3 x - 3\cos x$
6. $\tan 3x = \dfrac{3\tan x - \tan^3 x}{1 - 3\tan^2 x}$
7. $\sin x = 2\sin \dfrac{x}{2} \cos \dfrac{x}{2}$
8. $1 - \cos x = 2\sin^2 \dfrac{x}{2}$
9. $1 + \cos x = 2\cos^2 \dfrac{x}{2}$
10. $\tan \dfrac{x}{2} = \operatorname{cosec} x - \cot x = \sqrt{\dfrac{1-\cos x}{1+\cos x}}$
    $= \dfrac{\sin x}{1+\cos x} = \dfrac{1-\cos x}{\sin x}$
11. $1 \pm \sin 2x = (\cos x \pm \sin x)^2$
12. $\sin (x \pm y) = \sin x \cos y \pm \cos x \sin y$
13. $\cos (x+y) = \cos x \cos y - \sin x \sin y$
14. $\cos (x-y) = \cos x \cos y + \sin x \sin y$
15. $\tan (x+y) = \dfrac{\tan x + \tan y}{1 - \tan x \tan y}$
16. $\tan (x-y) = \dfrac{\tan x - \tan y}{1 + \tan x \tan y}$
17. $2\sin A \cos B = \sin (A+B) + \sin (A-B)$
18. $2\cos A \sin B = \sin (A+B) - \sin (A-B)$
19. $2\cos A \cos B = \cos (A+B) + \cos (A-B)$
20. $2\sin A \sin B = \cos (A-B) - \cos (A+B)$
21. $\sin A + \sin B = 2\sin \left(\dfrac{A+B}{2}\right) \cdot \cos \left(\dfrac{A-B}{2}\right)$
22. $\sin A - \sin B = 2\cos \left(\dfrac{A+B}{2}\right) \cdot \sin \left(\dfrac{A-B}{2}\right)$
23. $\cos A + \cos B = 2\cos \left(\dfrac{A+B}{2}\right) \cdot \cos \left(\dfrac{A-B}{2}\right)$
24. $\cos A - \cos B = -2\sin \left(\dfrac{A+B}{2}\right) \cdot \sin \left(\dfrac{A-B}{2}\right)$
    $= 2\sin \left(\dfrac{A+B}{2}\right) \cdot \sin \left(\dfrac{B-A}{2}\right)$
25. **Inverse Trigonometric Functions**
    (i) $\sin^{-1}(\sin x) = x$ (ii) $\cos^{-1}(\cos x) = x$
    (iii) $\tan^{-1}(\tan x) = x$ (iv) $\operatorname{cosec}^{-1}(\operatorname{cosec} x) = x$
    (v) $\sec^{-1}(\sec x) = x$ (vi) $\cot^{-1}(\cot x) = x$

Example 6 Evaluate the integral $\int \dfrac{\sin x}{\sin (x+a)} dx.$

Sol. Let $I = \int \dfrac{\sin x}{\sin (x+a)} dx$

Now, put $x + a = t \Rightarrow dx = dt$

$\therefore \quad I = \int \dfrac{\sin (t-a)}{\sin t} dt = \int \dfrac{\sin t \cos a - \cos t \sin a}{\sin t} dt$

[$\because \sin (A-B) = \sin A \cos B - \cos A \sin B$]

$= \cos a \int dt - \sin a \int \cot t \, dt$

$= (\cos a)\, t - \sin a \log |\sin t| + C_1$

$= (x+a) \cos a - \sin a \log |\sin (x+a)| + C_1$

[$\because t = x + a$]

$= x \cos a - \sin a \log |\sin (x+a)| + C_1 + a \cos a$

$= x \cos a - \sin a \log |\sin (x+a) + C,$

where, $C = C_1 + a \cos a$

Example 7 Evaluate $\int \dfrac{1}{\cos (x-\alpha) \cos (x-\beta)} dx.$

Sol. Let $I = \int \dfrac{1}{\cos (x-\alpha) \cos (x-\beta)} dx$

$= \int \dfrac{1}{\cos (x-\alpha) \cos (x-\beta)} \times \dfrac{\sin (\beta-\alpha)}{\sin (\beta-\alpha)} dx$

[multiply numerator and denominator by $\sin (\beta-\alpha)$]

$= \dfrac{1}{\sin (\beta-\alpha)} \int \dfrac{\sin [(x-\alpha)-(x-\beta)]}{\cos (x-\alpha) \cos (x-\beta)} dx$

[adding and subtracting x in $(\beta-\alpha)$ of numerator]

$= \dfrac{1}{\sin (\beta-\alpha)}$

$\int \dfrac{\sin (x-\alpha) \cdot \cos (x-\beta) - \cos (x-\alpha) \cdot \sin (x-\beta)}{\cos (x-\alpha) \cos (x-\beta)} dx$

[$\because \sin (A-B) = \sin A \cos B - \cos A \sin B$]

$$= \frac{1}{\sin(\beta-\alpha)} \int \left[\frac{\sin(x-\alpha)\cos(x-\beta)}{\cos(x-\alpha)\cos(x-\beta)} - \frac{\cos(x-\alpha)\sin(x-\beta)}{\cos(x-\alpha)\cos(x-\beta)}\right]dx$$

$$= \frac{1}{\sin(\beta-\alpha)} \int [\tan(x-\alpha) - \tan(x-\beta)]\,dx$$

$$= \frac{1}{\sin(\beta-\alpha)} [-\log|\cos(x-\alpha)| + \log|\cos(x-\beta)|] + C$$

$$\left[\because \int \tan x\,dx = -\log|\cos x|\right]$$

$$= \frac{1}{\sin(\beta-\alpha)} \log\left|\frac{\cos(x-\beta)}{\cos(x-\alpha)}\right| + C$$

$$\left[\because \log m - \log n = \log\frac{m}{n}\right]$$

Example 8 Evaluate $\int \frac{1}{\sqrt{\sin^3 x \sin(x+\alpha)}}\,dx.$ **[NCERT]**

Sol. Let $I = \int \frac{1}{\sqrt{\sin^3 x \sin(x+\alpha)}}\,dx$

$$= \int \frac{1}{\sqrt{\sin^3 x (\sin x \cos\alpha + \cos x \sin\alpha)}}\,dx$$

$$[\because \sin(A+B) = \sin A \cos B + \cos A \sin B]$$

$$= \int \frac{1}{\sqrt{\sin^4 x (\cos\alpha + \cot x \sin\alpha)}}\,dx$$

$$= \int \frac{1}{\sin^2 x \sqrt{\cos\alpha + \cot x \sin\alpha}}\,dx$$

$$= \int \frac{\operatorname{cosec}^2 x}{\sqrt{\cos\alpha + \cot x \sin\alpha}}\,dx$$

Now, putting $\cos\alpha + \cot x \sin\alpha = t$

$\Rightarrow -\operatorname{cosec}^2 x \sin\alpha\,dx = dt \Rightarrow \operatorname{cosec}^2 x\,dx = \frac{-dt}{\sin\alpha}$

$$\therefore \quad I = \frac{-1}{\sin\alpha} \int \frac{dt}{\sqrt{t}} = \frac{-1}{\sin\alpha}[2\sqrt{t}] + C$$

$$= \frac{-1}{\sin\alpha}[2\sqrt{\cos\alpha + \cot x \sin\alpha}] + C$$

$$= \frac{-2}{\sin\alpha}\sqrt{\cos\alpha + \frac{\cos x \sin\alpha}{\sin x}} + C$$

$$= \frac{-2}{\sin\alpha}\sqrt{\frac{\sin x \cos\alpha + \cos x \sin\alpha}{\sin x}} + C$$

$$= -\frac{2}{\sin\alpha}\sqrt{\frac{\sin(x+\alpha)}{\sin x}} + C$$

$$[\because \sin(A+B) = \sin A \cos B + \cos A \sin B]$$

Example 9 Evaluate $\int \tan^{-1}\left(\frac{\cos x - \sin x}{\cos x + \sin x}\right)dx.$

Sol. Let $I = \int \tan^{-1}\left(\frac{\cos x - \sin x}{\cos x + \sin x}\right)dx$

$$= \int \tan^{-1}\left(\frac{\frac{\cos x}{\cos x} - \frac{\sin x}{\cos x}}{\frac{\cos x}{\cos x} + \frac{\sin x}{\cos x}}\right)dx$$

[dividing numerator and denominator by cos x]

$$= \int \tan^{-1}\left(\frac{1-\tan x}{1+\tan x}\right)dx$$

$$= \int \tan^{-1}\left(\frac{\tan\frac{\pi}{4} - \tan x}{1 + \tan\frac{\pi}{4}\tan x}\right)dx \quad \left[\because \tan\frac{\pi}{4} = 1\right]$$

$$= \int \tan^{-1}\left[\tan\left(\frac{\pi}{4} - x\right)\right]dx$$

$$\left[\because \tan(x-y) = \frac{\tan x - \tan y}{1 + \tan x \tan y}\right]$$

$$= \int \left(\frac{\pi}{4} - x\right)dx \quad [\because \tan^{-1}(\tan\theta) = \theta]$$

$$= \int \frac{\pi}{4}dx - \int x\,dx = \frac{\pi}{4}x - \frac{x^2}{2} + C$$

Some Standard Integrals and Methods to Evaluate it

Integral	Methods
$\int \sin^p x\,dx$ or $\int \cos^p x\,dx$ where, $p \in N$ and $p \le 4$	To evaluate, we express $\sin^p x$ (or $\cos^p x$) in terms of sines and cosines of multiples of x. For which we use the following trigonometrical identities. (i) $\sin^2 x = \frac{1-\cos 2x}{2}$ (ii) $\cos^2 x = \frac{1+\cos 2x}{2}$ (iii) $\sin^3 x = \frac{3\sin x - \sin 3x}{4}$ (iv) $\cos^3 x = \frac{\cos 3x + 3\cos x}{4}$
$\int \sin^p x \cos^q x\,dx$ where, $p, q \in N$	To evaluate it, use the following If p is odd, then put $\cos x = t$ If q is odd, then put $\sin x = t$ If p and q both are odd, then put either $\sin x = t$ or $\cos x = t$. If p and q both are even, then express $\sin^p x \cos^q x$ in terms of sines and cosines of multiples of x by using trigonometric results.
$\int \sin^p x \cos^q x$ where, $p, q \in Q$ and $p+q$ is a negative even integer.	To evaluate it, change the integrand $\sin^p x \cos^q x$ in terms of $\tan x$ and $\sec^2 x$ by dividing numerator and denominator by $\cos^k x$, where $k = -(p+q)$ and then substitute $\tan x = t$.

Integral	Methods
$\int \sin px \cos qx\, dx$, $\int \sin px \sin qx\, dx$, $\int \cos px \cos qx\, dx$	To evaluate these type of integral, firstly multiply and divide by 2 and then use the following trigonometrical identities $2\sin A\cos B = \sin(A+B)+\sin(A-B)$ $2\cos A\sin B = \sin(A+B)-\sin(A-B)$ $2\cos A\cos B = \cos(A+B)+\cos(A-B)$ $2\sin A\sin B = \cos(A-B)-\cos(A+B)$
$\int \tan^p x \sec^{2q} x\, dx$ or $\int \cot^p x \,\text{cosec}^{2q} x\, dx$ where, p and $q \in N$	To evaluate these type of integral, firstly write the given integral as $\int \tan^p x(\sec^2 x)^{q-1}\cdot\sec^2 x\, dx$ or $\int \cot^p x(\text{cosec}^2 x)^{q-1}\cdot\text{cosec}^2 x\, dx$ and then put $\tan x = t$ (or $\cot x = t$)
$\int \tan^{2p+1} x \sec^{2q+1} x dx$ or $\int \cot^{2p+1} x \text{cosec}^{2q+1} x dx$, where p and q are non-negative integers.	To evaluate these type of integral, firstly write the given integral as $\int (\tan^2 x)^p (\sec^2 x)^q \sec x \tan x\, dx$ or $\int (\cot^2 x)^p (\text{cosec}^2 x)^q \cot x \,\text{cosec}\, x\, dx$ and then put $\sec x = t$ (or $\text{cosec}\, x = t$)

Example 10 Evaluate $\int \cos^2 x\, dx$.

Sol. Let $I = \int \cos^2 x\, dx$

$$= \int \frac{1+\cos 2x}{2} dx \qquad \left[\because \cos^2 x = \frac{1+\cos 2x}{2}\right]$$

$$= \frac{1}{2}\int (1+\cos 2x) dx = \frac{1}{2}\left(x + \frac{\sin 2x}{2}\right) + C$$

$$\left[\int \cos(ax+b)dx = \frac{\sin(ax+b)}{a} + C\right]$$

$$= \frac{x}{2} + \frac{\sin 2x}{4} + C$$

Example 11 Evaluate $\int \frac{1}{x^2}\sin^2\left(\frac{1}{x}\right) dx$. **[ISC 2017]**

Sol. Let $I = \int \frac{1}{x^2}\sin^2\left(\frac{1}{x}\right) dx$

Put $\frac{1}{x} = t$

On differentiating both sides w.r.t. x, we get

$$\frac{-1}{x^2} dx = dt \Rightarrow \frac{1}{x^2} dx = -dt$$

$$\therefore \quad I = \int \sin^2 t(-dt) = -\int \sin^2 t\, dt = -\int \frac{1-\cos 2t}{2} dt$$

$$= -\left[\int \frac{1}{2} dt - \frac{1}{2}\int \cos 2t\, dt\right]$$

$$= -\left[\frac{1}{2}t - \frac{1}{2}\frac{\sin 2t}{2}\right] + C = \frac{1}{4}\sin 2t - \frac{1}{2}t + C$$

Now, by putting value of t, we get

$$I = \frac{1}{4}\sin\left(\frac{2}{x}\right) - \left(\frac{1}{2x}\right) + C$$

Example 12 Evaluate $\int \cos^4 x\, dx$.

Sol. Let $I = \int \cos^4 x\, dx = \int (\cos^2 x)^2 dx$

$$= \int \left(\frac{1+\cos 2x}{2}\right)^2 dx \qquad \left[\because \cos^2 x = \frac{1+\cos 2x}{2}\right]$$

$$= \frac{1}{4}\int (1 + 2\cos 2x + \cos^2 2x) dx$$

$$= \frac{1}{4}\int \left(1 + 2\cos 2x + \frac{1+\cos 2(2x)}{2}\right) dx$$

$$= \frac{1}{4}\int \left(1 + 2\cos 2x + \frac{1+\cos 4x}{2}\right) dx$$

$$= \frac{1}{4}\int \left(\frac{2 + 4\cos 2x + 1 + \cos 4x}{2}\right) dx$$

$$= \frac{1}{8}\int (3 + 4\cos 2x + \cos 4x) dx$$

$$= \frac{1}{8}\left(3x + 4\cdot\frac{\sin 2x}{2} + \frac{\sin 4x}{4}\right) + C$$

$$= \frac{3}{8}x + \frac{\sin 2x}{4} + \frac{\sin 4x}{32} + C$$

Example 13 Evaluate $\int \sin^3 x \cos^4 x\, dx$ **[ISC 2020]**

Sol. Let $I = \int \sin^3 x \cos^4 x\, dx$

$$\Rightarrow I = \int \sin^2 x \cos^4 x \sin x\, dx$$

$$\Rightarrow I = \int (1-\cos^2 x)\cos^4 x \sin x\, dx$$

Put $\cos x = t$

$\Rightarrow \sin x\, dx = dt$

$$\therefore \quad I = -\int (1-t^2)t^4 dt$$

$$I = \int (t^6 - t^4)\, dt$$

$$I = \frac{t^7}{7} - \frac{t^5}{5} + C$$

$$I = \frac{\cos^7 x}{7} - \frac{\cos^5 x}{5} + C \qquad [\because t = \cos x]$$

Example 14 Evaluate $\int \cos 2x \cos 4x \cos 6x\, dx$. **[NCERT]**

There is no standard integral formula for given integral. So, we simplify the integral by using the formula $2\cos A\cos B = [\cos(A+B) + \cos(A-B)]$ and then integrate it.

Sol. Let $I = \int \cos 2x \cdot \cos 4x \cdot \cos 6x \, dx$

$$= \frac{1}{2}\int (2\cos 4x \cdot \cos 2x) \cdot \cos 6x \, dx$$

$$= \frac{1}{2}\int [\cos(4x + 2x) + \cos(4x - 2x)] \cdot \cos 6x \, dx$$

$[\because 2\cos A \cdot \cos B = \cos(A + B) + \cos(A - B)]$

$$= \frac{1}{2}\int (\cos 6x + \cos 2x) \cdot \cos 6x \, dx$$

$$= \frac{1}{2}\int (\cos^2 6x + \cos 6x \cdot \cos 2x) dx$$

$$= \frac{1}{4}\int (2\cos^2 6x + 2\cos 6x \cdot \cos 2x) dx$$

$$= \frac{1}{4}\int (1 + \cos 12x + \cos 8x + \cos 4x) dx$$

$\left[\because \cos^2\theta = \frac{1 + \cos 2\theta}{2} \text{ and } 2\cos x \cos y = \cos(x + y) + \cos(x - y)\right]$

$$= \frac{1}{4}\left(x + \frac{\sin 12x}{12} + \frac{\sin 8x}{8} + \frac{\sin 4x}{4}\right) + C$$

$\left[\because \int \cos ax \, dx = \frac{1}{a}\sin ax\right]$

$$= \frac{x}{4} + \frac{1}{48}\sin 12x + \frac{1}{32}\sin 8x + \frac{1}{16}\sin 4x + C$$

Example 15 Evaluate $\int \tan^2 x \sec^4 x \, dx$.

[NCERT Exemplar]

Firstly, write $\sec^4 x$ as $\sec^2 x \cdot \sec^2 x$ and use the formula $\sec^2 x = 1 + \tan^2 x$, further put $\tan x = t$ and then integrate it.

Sol. Let $I = \int \tan^2 x \sec^4 x \, dx = \int \tan^2 x \sec^2 x \sec^2 x \, dx$

$$= \int \tan^2 x (1 + \tan^2 x) \sec^2 x \, dx \quad [\because \sec^2 x = 1 + \tan^2 x]$$

Now, put $\tan x = t \Rightarrow \sec^2 x \, dx = dt$

$$\therefore \quad I = \int t^2(1 + t^2) \, dt = \int (t^2 + t^4) dt = \frac{t^3}{3} + \frac{t^5}{5} + C$$

$$= \frac{\tan^5 x}{5} + \frac{\tan^3 x}{3} + C \quad [\because t = \tan x]$$

Integration by Parts

Let u and v be two differentiable functions of a single variable x, then the integral of the product of these two functions

= Ist function × Integral of the IInd function

− Integral of [Derivatives of Ist function × Integral of the IInd function]

i.e. $$\int \underset{\text{I}}{u} \cdot \underset{\text{II}}{v} \, dx = u \int v \, dx - \int \left(\frac{d}{dx}(u) \int v \, dx\right) dx$$

If in the product, two functions are of different types, then take that function as first function (i.e. u) which comes first in word **ILATE**, where

- I : Inverse trigonometric function. e.g. $\sin^{-1} x$
- L : Logarithmic function. e.g. $\log x$
- A : Algebraic function. e.g. $1, x, x^2$
- T : Trigonometric function. e.g. $\sin x, \cos x$
- E : Exponential function. e.g. e^x

Note

(i) If the integrand contains a logarithmic or an inverse trigonometric function and the second function is not given, we take second function as 1. e.g. In the integral of $\int \sin^{-1} x \, dx$, we take second function as unity (i.e. 1).

(ii) Integration by parts is not applicable in all cases. For instance, the method does not work for $\int \sqrt{x} \sin x \, dx$. The reason is that there does not exist any function whose derivative is $\sqrt{x} \sin x$.

Working Rule to Evaluate Integration by Parts

Let the given integration is of the form $I = \int u \cdot v \, dx$, where u and v are the functions of x. Then, to evaluate such integrals, we use the following steps

I. Firstly, choose the Ist and IInd functions with the help of ILATE, i.e. take that function as I function which comes first in ILATE and take other function as IInd function.

II. Now, integrate by using integration by parts, i.e.

$$\int \underset{\text{I II}}{u.v} \, dx = u \underbrace{\int v \, dx}_{\text{I Integral}} - \underbrace{\int \left(\frac{d}{dx}(u) \int v \, dx\right) dx}_{\text{II Integral}}$$

III. From Step II, we get one of the three possible cases

(i) If IInd integral is in simple form, then integrate it by using appropriate method.

(ii) If IInd integral is the product of two functions, then again use Steps I and II.

(iii) If IInd integral is same as the given integral, then put I in place of II integral. Finally, simplify it and get the required result.

Example 16 Evaluate $\int x \cos x \, dx$.

Sol. Let $I = \int x \cos x \, dx$

Here, we see that integrand is the product of algebraic and trigonometric functions and algebraic function comes first in the word ILATE, so we consider it as Ist function and trigonometric function as IInd function.

$\therefore \quad I = \int \underset{\text{I}}{x} \cos \underset{\text{II}}{x}\, dx$

$= x \int \cos x\, dx - \int \left(\frac{d}{dx}(x) \int \cos x\, dx \right) dx$

$\left[\because \int \underset{\text{I}}{u} \cdot \underset{\text{II}}{v}\, dx = u \int v\, dx - \int \left(\frac{d}{dx}(u) \int v\, dx \right) dx \right]$

$= x \sin x - \int 1 \cdot \sin x\, dx$

$= x \sin x - \int \sin x\, dx$

$= x \sin x + \cos x + C$

Note Suppose $I = \int x \cos x\, dx = x(\sin x + k) - \int (\sin x + k)\, dx$

$= x(\sin x + k) - \int \sin x\, dx - \int k\, dx$

$= x(\sin x + k) + \cos x - kx + C$

$= x \sin x + \cos x + C$

which shows that adding a constant to the integral of the IInd function is unnecessary. So, we write the constant of integration at the last part of the integral while integrating.

Example 17 Evaluate $\int e^x \cos x\, dx$.

Firstly, apply integration by parts to integrate it. Now, if we again get IInd integral as product of two functions, then again apply integration by parts.

Sol. Let $I = \int e^x \cos x\, dx$ ... (i)

By using the order of functions in ILATE, take $\cos x$ as Ist function and e^x as IInd function.

$\therefore \quad I = \int \underset{\text{I}}{\cos x}\, \underset{\text{II}}{e^x}\, dx$

$\Rightarrow \quad I = \cos x \int e^x\, dx - \int \left[\frac{d}{dx}(\cos x) \int e^x\, dx \right] dx$

$\left[\because \int \underset{\text{I}}{u} \cdot \underset{\text{II}}{v}\, dx = u \int v\, dx - \int \left(\frac{d}{dx}(u) \int v\, dx \right) dx \right]$

$\Rightarrow \quad I = \cos x\, e^x - \int (-\sin x)\, e^x\, dx$

$\Rightarrow \quad I = e^x \cos x + \int \underset{\text{I}}{\sin x}\, \underset{\text{II}}{e^x}\, dx$

[$\because$ integrand is the product of two functions, so we again choose Ist and IInd functions by using ILATE]

$\Rightarrow I = e^x \cos x + \sin x \int e^x dx$

$- \int \left(\frac{d}{dx}(\sin x) \int e^x\, dx \right) dx$

$\left[\because \int u \cdot v\, dx = u \int v\, dx - \int \left(\frac{d}{dx}(u) \int v\, dx \right) dx \right]$

$\Rightarrow I = e^x \cos x + \sin x\, e^x - \int \cos x\, e^x\, dx$

$\Rightarrow I = e^x \cos x + e^x \sin x - I + C_1$ [from Eq. (i)]

$\Rightarrow 2I = e^x (\cos x + \sin x) + C_1$

$\Rightarrow \quad I = \frac{e^x}{2}(\cos x + \sin x) + C$, where $C = \frac{C_1}{2}$

Note Above integral can also be solved by taking e^x as Ist function and $\cos x$ as IInd function.

Example 18 Evaluate $\int \log|1 + x^2|\, dx$.

Here, we are unable to guess a function, whose derivative is $\log(1 + x^2)$. So, take $\log(1 + x^2)$ as the Ist function and the constant function 1 as the IInd function, then integrate it by parts.

Sol. Let $I = \int \log|1 + x^2|\, dx = \int \underset{\text{I}}{\log|1 + x^2|} \cdot \underset{\text{II}}{1}\, dx$

$= \log|1 + x^2| \int 1\, dx - \int \left[\frac{d}{dx} \log|1 + x^2| \int 1\, dx \right] dx$

[using integration by parts]

$= \log|1 + x^2| \cdot x - \int \frac{1}{1 + x^2}(2x) \cdot x\, dx$

$= x \log|1 + x^2| - 2\int \frac{x^2}{1 + x^2} dx$

$= x \log|1 + x^2| - 2\int \frac{1 + x^2 - 1}{1 + x^2} dx$

$= x \log|1 + x^2| - 2\int \left(1 - \frac{1}{1 + x^2} \right) dx$

$= x \log|1 + x^2| - 2\int dx + 2\int \frac{dx}{1 + x^2} + C$

$= x \log|1 + x^2| - 2x + 2\tan^{-1} x + C$

Integral of the Type $\int e^x [f(x) + f'(x)]\, dx$

In this type of integral, integrand is the product of two functions. One is in exponential form and second function is the sum of two functions in which one is derivative of other function. Then, to evaluate such integrals, we directly use the following formula

$$\int e^x [f(x) + f'(x)]\, dx = e^x f(x) + C$$

Proof It can be proved by using integration by parts as given below

Let $I = \int e^x [f(x) + f'(x)]\, dx$

$= \int e^x f(x) dx + \int \underset{\text{I}}{e^x} \underset{\text{II}}{f'(x)} dx$

$= \int e^x f(x)\, dx + e^x \int f'(x) dx - \int \left[\frac{d}{dx}(e^x) \int f'(x) \right] dx$

[using integration by parts]

$= \int e^x f(x)\, dx + e^x f(x) - \int e^x f(x)\, dx + C$

$= e^x f(x) + C$

Note Sometimes, it may be possible that the IInd function is not in standard form i.e. not in the form $f(x) + f'(x)$. In that case, we try to make it in standard form, if it is possible, otherwise we use some another ways to integrate it.

Example 19 Evaluate $\int e^x (\sin x + \cos x)\, dx$.

Sol. Let $I = \int e^x (\sin x + \cos x)\, dx$

and $f(x) = \sin x$, then $f'(x) = \cos x$

So, the given integral is of the form

$$I = \int e^x [f(x) + f'(x)]\, dx$$

We know that

$$\int e^x [f(x) + f'(x)]\, dx = e^x f(x) + C$$

$$\therefore \quad I = e^x \sin x + C$$

Example 20 Evaluate $\int \frac{x-3}{(x-1)^3} e^x\, dx$.

Here, the integrand $e^x \frac{x-3}{(x-1)^3}$ is not in the form of $e^x [f(x) + f'(x)]$, so we firstly convert it in the form of $e^x [f(x) + f'(x)]$ and then simplify it.

Sol. Let $I = \int \frac{x-3}{(x-1)^3} e^x\, dx = \int \frac{x-1-2}{(x-1)^3} e^x\, dx$

$$= \int e^x \left(\frac{x-1}{(x-1)^3} - \frac{2}{(x-1)^3} \right) dx$$

$$= \int e^x \left(\frac{1}{(x-1)^2} - \frac{2}{(x-1)^3} \right) dx \quad \text{...(i)}$$

Now, let $f(x) = \frac{1}{(x-1)^2}$

$$\Rightarrow \quad f'(x) = \frac{-2}{(x-1)^3}$$

Then, Eq. (i) becomes of the form

$$I = \int e^x [f(x) + f'(x)]\, dx$$

Also, we know that,

$$\int e^x [f(x) + f'(x)]\, dx = e^x f(x) + C$$

Hence, $I = \frac{e^x}{(x-1)^2} + C$.

Integration by Partial Fractions

To evaluate an integral of the form $\int \frac{P(x)}{Q(x)} dx$, where $P(x)$ and $Q(x)$ are polynomials in x, $Q(x) \neq 0$ and $Q(x)$ has only linear and quadratic factors, we use this method.

By this method, it is always possible to write $\frac{P(x)}{Q(x)}$ as a sum of simple rational functions. Each such fraction is called **a partial fraction**.

Working Rule

I. Check whether the rational function $\frac{P(x)}{Q(x)}$ is proper or improper. [If degree of $P(x) <$ degree of $Q(x)$, then the rational function is called **proper**, otherwise it is called **improper**].

II. If $\frac{P(x)}{Q(x)}$ is a proper fraction, then we go to next step directly. If $\frac{P(x)}{Q(x)}$ is an improper fraction, then we divide $P(x)$ by $Q(x)$, so that $\frac{P(x)}{Q(x)}$ is expressed in the form of $T(x) + \frac{P_1(x)}{Q(x)}$, where $T(x)$ is a polynomial in x and $\frac{P_1(x)}{Q(x)}$ is a proper rational function.

III. Now, the decomposition of proper fraction $\frac{P(x)}{Q(x)}$ or $\frac{P_1(x)}{Q(x)}$ into the partial fractions depends mainly upon the nature of the factors of $Q(x)$.

According to nature of factors of $Q(x)$, corresponding form of the partial fraction is given below

S.No.	Form of the rational function	Form of the partial fraction
1.	$\frac{px \pm q}{(x \pm a)(x \pm b)}, a \neq b$	$\frac{A}{x \pm a} + \frac{B}{x \pm b}$
2.	$\frac{px \pm q}{(x \pm a)^2}$	$\frac{A}{(x \pm a)} + \frac{B}{(x \pm a)^2}$
3.	$\frac{px^2 \pm qx \pm r}{(x \pm a)(x \pm b)(x \pm c)}$	$\frac{A}{(x \pm a)} + \frac{B}{(x \pm b)} + \frac{C}{(x \pm c)}$
4.	$\frac{px^2 \pm qx \pm r}{(x \pm a)(x \pm b)^2}$	$\frac{A}{(x \pm a)} + \frac{B}{(x \pm b)} + \frac{C}{(x \pm b)^2}$
5.	$\frac{px^2 \pm qx \pm r}{(x \pm a)^3}$	$\frac{A}{(x \pm a)} + \frac{B}{(x \pm a)^2} + \frac{C}{(x \pm a)^3}$
6.	$\frac{px^2 \pm qx \pm r}{(x \pm a)(x^2 \pm bx \pm c)}$	$\frac{A}{(x \pm a)} + \frac{Bx + C}{x^2 \pm bx \pm c}$ where, $x^2 \pm bx \pm c$ cannot be factorised further.

Using the form of rational function, write $\frac{P(x)}{Q(x)}$ or $\frac{P_1(x)}{Q(x)}$ in suitable form of partial fraction and assume it Eq. (i).

IV. Multiply both sides of Eq. (i) by $Q(x)$ and assume this as Eq. (ii), then for finding the values of constants A, B, C, etc., we use the following two methods

Method 1 Contains factor of the form $(x \pm a)$, $(x \pm b)$, $(x \pm c)$, then put $(x \pm a)$, $(x \pm b)$, $(x \pm c)$ equal to zero for finding values of x and then put these values of x in Eq. (ii) to get the required values of A, B, C, etc.

Method 2 Simplify RHS of Eq. (ii) to convert it into a polynomial in x and then equate coefficients of x^3, x^2, x and constant terms from both sides to get equations in $A, B, C, \ldots$ etc. On solving these equations, we get values of A, B and C.

V. Put the values of $A, B, C, \ldots$ etc., in Eq. (i) and get the required partial fraction form.

VI. Integrate each fraction by suitable method and get the required answer.

Example 21 Resolve $\frac{x^3 - 6x^2 + 10x - 2}{x^2 - 5x + 6}$ into partial fractions.

Sol. Here, degree of numerator > degree of denominator.

So, it is an improper fraction.

Now, divide numerator by denominator, we get

$$\frac{x^3 - 6x^2 + 10x - 2}{x^2 - 5x + 6} = (x - 1) + \frac{(-x + 4)}{x^2 - 5x + 6} \quad \text{...(i)}$$

Now, $$\frac{-x + 4}{x^2 - 5x + 6} = \frac{-x + 4}{(x - 2)(x - 3)}$$

$[\because x^2 - 5x + 6 = x^2 - 2x - 3x + 6 = (x - 2)(x - 3)]$

So, let $$\frac{-x + 4}{x^2 - 5x + 6} = \frac{A}{x - 2} + \frac{B}{x - 3} \quad \text{...(ii)}$$

[from fraction table, it is of the form 1]

$$\Rightarrow -x + 4 = A(x - 3) + B(x - 2) \quad \text{...(iii)}$$

[multiply both sides by $x^2 - 5x + 6$]

On putting $x - 3 = 0$, i.e. $x = 3$ in Eq. (iii), we get

$$-3 + 4 = A(0) + B(3 - 2) \Rightarrow B = 1$$

Again, putting $x - 2 = 0$, i.e. $x = 2$ in Eq. (iii), we get

$$-2 + 4 = A(2 - 3) + B(0) \Rightarrow A = -2$$

Now, putting the values of A and B in Eq. (ii), we get

$$\frac{-x + 4}{x^2 - 5x + 6} = \frac{-2}{x - 2} + \frac{1}{x - 3}$$

Hence, $$\frac{x^3 - 6x^2 + 10x - 2}{x^2 - 5x + 6} = x - 1 - \frac{2}{x - 2} + \frac{1}{x - 3}$$

[from Eq. (i)]

Example 22 Evaluate $\int \frac{x}{(x - 1)^2 (x + 2)} dx.$ [NCERT]

Firstly, write the given integrand into partial fraction form and then integrate.

Sol. Let $I = \int \frac{x}{(x - 1)^2 (x + 2)} dx$

Here, integrand is a proper rational function.

So, by using the form of partial fraction, we write

$$\frac{x}{(x-1)^2(x+2)} = \frac{A}{(x-1)} + \frac{B}{(x-1)^2} + \frac{C}{(x+2)} \quad \text{...(i)}$$

$$\Rightarrow \frac{x}{(x-1)^2(x+2)} = \frac{A(x-1)(x+2) + B(x+2) + C(x-1)^2}{(x-1)^2(x+2)}$$

$$\Rightarrow x = A(x-1)(x+2) + B(x+2) + C(x-1)^2 \quad \text{...(ii)}$$

On putting $x = 1$ in Eq. (ii), we get

$$1 = A(1-1)(1+2) + B(1+2) + C(1-1)^2$$

$$\Rightarrow \quad 1 = 3B \Rightarrow B = 1/3$$

On putting $x = -2$ in Eq. (ii), we get

$$-2 = A(-2-1)(-2+2) + B(-2+2) + C(-2-1)^2$$

$$\Rightarrow \quad -2 = 0 + 0 + 9C \Rightarrow C = \frac{-2}{9}$$

On putting $x = 0$ in Eq. (ii), we get

$$0 = A(0-1)(0+2) + B(0+2) + C(0-1)^2$$

$$\Rightarrow \quad 0 = -2A + 2B + C$$

$$\Rightarrow \quad 0 = -2A + 2\cdot\frac{1}{3} - \frac{2}{9} \quad \left[\because B = \frac{1}{3}, C = -\frac{2}{9}\right]$$

$$\Rightarrow \quad 0 = -2A + \frac{2}{3} - \frac{2}{9}$$

$$\Rightarrow \quad 0 = -2A + \frac{6-2}{9}$$

$$\Rightarrow \quad 2A = 4/9 \Rightarrow A = 2/9$$

Now, putting the values of A, B and C in Eq. (i), we get

$$\frac{x}{(x-1)^2(x+2)} = \frac{2/9}{(x-1)} + \frac{1/3}{(x-1)^2} + \frac{-2/9}{(x+2)}$$

$$\therefore I = \int \frac{x}{(x-1)^2(x+2)} dx$$

$$= \frac{2}{9}\int \frac{dx}{x-1} + \frac{1}{3}\int \frac{dx}{(x-1)^2} - \frac{2}{9}\int \frac{dx}{x+2}$$

$$= \frac{2}{9}\log|x-1| + \frac{1}{3}\int (x-1)^{-2} dx - \frac{2}{9}\log|x+2| + C$$

$$= \frac{2}{9}\log|x-1| + \frac{1}{3}\cdot\frac{(x-1)^{-1}}{(-1)} - \frac{2}{9}\log|x+2| + C$$

$$= \frac{2}{9}\log|x-1| - \frac{1}{3(x-1)} - \frac{2}{9}\log|x+2| + C$$

$$= \frac{2}{9}\left(\log\left|\frac{x-1}{x+2}\right|\right) - \frac{1}{3(x-1)} + C$$

$$\left[\because \log m - \log n = \log\frac{m}{n}\right]$$

Example 23 Evaluate $\int \frac{x}{(x^2+1)(x-1)}\,dx.$ **[NCERT]**

Sol. Let $I = \int \frac{x}{(x^2+1)(x-1)}\,dx$

Here, integrand $= \frac{x}{(x^2+1)(x-1)} = \frac{P(x)}{Q(x)}$ (say)

where, degree of $P(x)$ is less than degree of $Q(x)$, so it is a proper fraction.

Now, let $\frac{x}{(x^2+1)(x-1)} = \frac{A}{(x-1)} + \frac{Bx+C}{x^2+1}$ ...(i)

On multiplying both sides of Eq. (i) by $(x^2+1)(x-1)$, we get

$$x = A(x^2+1) + (Bx+C)(x-1) \quad ...(ii)$$

On putting $x = 1$ in Eq. (ii), we get

$$1 = A(1+1) + (B+C)(0)$$

$$\Rightarrow \quad 1 = 2A \Rightarrow A = \frac{1}{2}$$

On equating the coefficients of x^2 and x from both sides of Eq. (ii), we get

$$0 = A + B \text{ and } 1 = -B + C$$

$$\Rightarrow \quad 0 = \frac{1}{2} + B \Rightarrow B = -\frac{1}{2} \quad \left[\because A = \frac{1}{2}\right]$$

and $\quad 1 = -\left(-\frac{1}{2}\right) + C$

$$\Rightarrow \quad C = 1 - \frac{1}{2} = \frac{1}{2}$$

From Eq. (i), we get

$$\frac{x}{(x^2+1)(x-1)} = \frac{1}{2(x-1)} + \frac{-\frac{1}{2}x + \frac{1}{2}}{x^2+1} \quad ...(iii)$$

Now, putting partial fraction form of integrand from Eq. (iii) in given integral, we get

$$I = \int \frac{1}{2(x-1)}\,dx + \frac{1}{2}\int \frac{(-x+1)}{x^2+1}\,dx$$

$$= \frac{1}{2}\log|x-1| + \frac{1}{2}\left[-\int \frac{x}{x^2+1} \times \frac{2}{2}\,dx + \int \frac{1}{x^2+1}\,dx\right]$$

$$= \frac{1}{2}\log|x-1| - \frac{1}{4}\int \frac{2x}{x^2+1}\,dx + \frac{1}{2}\int \frac{1}{x^2+1}\,dx$$

$$= \frac{1}{2}\log|x-1| - \frac{1}{4}\log|x^2+1| + \frac{1}{2}\tan^{-1} x + C$$

$\left[\text{for evaluating } \int \frac{2x}{x^2+1}\,dx, \text{ put } x^2+1 = t \Rightarrow 2x\,dx = dt, \text{ then } \int \frac{2x}{x^2+1}\,dx = \int \frac{1}{t}\,dt = \log|t| = \log|x^2+1|\right]$

Example 24 $\int \frac{\log x}{(x+1)^2}\,dx.$

Sol. Let $I = \int \frac{\log x}{(x+1)^2}\,dx = \int \log x \cdot \frac{1}{(x+1)^2}\,dx$

On applying integration by parts, we get

$$I = \log x \cdot \int \frac{dx}{(x+1)^2} - \int \left(\frac{d}{dx}(\log x) \cdot \int \frac{dx}{(x+1)^2}\right) dx$$

$$\left[\because \int u \cdot v\,dx = u\int v\,dx - \int\left(\frac{d}{dx}(u)\int v\,dx\right) dx\right]$$

$$= \log x \cdot \frac{(-1)}{x+1} + \int \frac{1}{x(x+1)}\,dx$$

$$\left[\because \int \frac{1}{(x+1)^2}\,dx = -\frac{1}{(x+1)}\right]$$

$$= \frac{-\log x}{x+1} + I_1, \text{ where } I_1 = \int \frac{dx}{x(x+1)} \text{ (say)} \quad ...(i)$$

Now, using partial fraction method, consider

$$\frac{1}{x(x+1)} = \frac{A}{x} + \frac{B}{x+1}$$

$$\Rightarrow \quad 1 = A(x+1) + Bx$$

On putting $x = 0$, we get $A = 1$

Again, putting $x = -1$, we get $B = -1$

$$\therefore \quad I_1 = \int\left(\frac{1}{x} - \frac{1}{x+1}\right) dx = \int \frac{1}{x}\,dx - \int \frac{dx}{x+1}$$

$$= \log|x| - \log|x+1| + C \quad ...(ii)$$

Now, from Eqs. (i) and (ii), we get

$$I = \frac{-\log x}{x+1} + \log|x| - \log|x+1| + C$$

$$= \frac{-\log x}{x+1} + \log\left|\frac{x}{x+1}\right| + C \quad \left[\because \log m - \log n = \log \frac{m}{n}\right]$$

Topic Practice 2

Very Short Answer Type Questions

2 Marks

Directions (Q. Nos. 1-22) *Evaluate the following integrals.*

1 $\int \frac{3ax}{b^2 + c^2x^2}\,dx$ **[NCERT Exemplar]**

2 $\int \frac{(\log x)^2}{x}\,dx$ **[NCERT]**

3 $\int \frac{1}{x\cos^2(1+\log x)}\,dx$ **[ISC 2007]**

4 $\int x^2(e^{x^3})\cos(2e^{x^3})\,dx$ **[ISC 2006]**

5 $\int \sin(ax+b)\cos(ax+b)\,dx$ [NCERT]

6 $\int \frac{1}{x+\sqrt{x}}dx$ [ISC 2013]

7 $\int \frac{x}{(x+1)^2}dx$ [ISC 2010]

8 $\int \frac{\sqrt{1+x^2}}{x^4}dx$ [NCERT Exemplar]

9 $\int \frac{\operatorname{cosec} x}{\log\tan\left(\frac{x}{2}\right)}dx$ [ISC 2011]

10 $\int \frac{(x+1)(x+\log x)^2}{x}dx$ [NCERT]

11 $\int \frac{x^3\sin(\tan^{-1}x^4)}{1+x^8}dx$ [NCERT]

12 $\int \cos^3 x\, e^{\log\sin x}\,dx$ [NCERT]

13 $\int \frac{2\cos x-3\sin x}{6\cos x+4\sin x}dx$ [NCERT]

14 $\int \frac{e^{2x}}{2+e^x}dx$ [ISC 2008]

15 $\int \cos^{-1}(\sin x)\,dx$

16 $\int \frac{\sin 4x}{\cos 2x}dx$

17 $\int \frac{\cos 2x}{(\sin x+\cos x)^2}dx$ [NCERT]

18 $\int \frac{\sin x+\cos x}{\sqrt{1+\sin 2x}}dx$

19 $\int \frac{\cos 2x+2\sin^2 x}{\cos^2 x}dx$

20 $\int x\cdot e^x\,dx$ [NCERT]

21 $\int x\log x\,dx$ [NCERT]

22 $\int e^x(\tan x+\log\sec x)\,dx$ [ISC 2012]

Short Answer Type Questions

4 Marks

Directions (Q. Nos. 23-59) *Evaluate the following integrals.*

23 $\int \frac{(x^4-x)^{1/4}}{x^5}dx$ [NCERT]

24 $\int \frac{1}{x^2(x^4+1)^{3/4}}dx$ [NCERT]

25 $\int \frac{x^2-x+2}{x^2+1}dx$

26 $\int \sqrt{\frac{1+x}{1-x}}\,dx,\ x\neq 1$ [NCERT Exemplar]

27 $\int \frac{\cos x}{\sin x+\sqrt{\sin x}}dx$ [ISC 2005]

28 $\int \frac{\sin x-x\cos x}{x(x+\sin x)}dx$

29 $\int \frac{\sqrt{\tan x}}{\sin x\cdot\cos x}dx$ [NCERT]

30 $\int \frac{\cos x-\cos 2x}{1-\cos x}dx$

31 $\int \tan^{-1}\sqrt{\frac{1+\cos x}{1-\cos x}}\,dx$

32 $\int \frac{\sin^8 x-\cos^8 x}{1-2\sin^2 x\cos^2 x}dx$ [NCERT]

33 $\int \frac{\sin^6 x+\cos^6 x}{\sin^2 x\cdot\cos^2 x}dx$ [NCERT Exemplar]

34 $\int \sin x\sin 2x\sin 3x\,dx$ [NCERT]

35 $\int \tan^3 x\,dx$ [ISC 2016]

36 $\int e^{2x}\sin x\,dx$

37 $\int \tan^{-1}x\,dx$ [NCERT]

38 $\int \tan^{-1}\sqrt{x}\,dx$ [ISC 2018]

39 $\int \sin^{-1}\left(\frac{2x}{1+x^2}\right)dx$

40 $\int \frac{x\sin^{-1}x}{\sqrt{1-x^2}}dx$

41 $\int \frac{\cos^{-1}x}{x^2}dx$ [ISC 2013]

42 $\int \frac{\sqrt{x^2+1}\,[\log(x^2+1)-2\log(x)]}{x^4}dx$ [NCERT]

43 $\int \left[\log(\log x)+\frac{1}{(\log x)^2}\right]dx$ [NCERT]

44 $\int \frac{(x^2+1)\,e^x}{(x+1)^2}dx$

45 $\int \frac{(2x-5)\,e^{2x}}{(2x-3)^3}dx$

46 $\int \frac{e^x(2+\sin 2x)}{\cos^2 x} dx$ [ISC 2014]

47 $\int e^{2x}\left(\frac{1-\sin 2x}{1-\cos 2x}\right) dx$

48 $\int \frac{\sin x}{(1-\cos x)(2-\cos x)} dx$

49 $\int \frac{e^x}{(1+e^x)(2+e^x)} dx$ [NCERT]

50 $\int \frac{2x}{(x^2+1)(x^2+3)} dx$ [NCERT]

51 $\int \frac{(3\sin\phi-2)\cos\phi}{5-\cos^2\phi-4\sin\phi} d\phi$ [NCERT]

52 $\int \frac{\sin 2x}{(1+\sin x)(2+\sin x)} dx$ [ISC 2017]

53 $\int \frac{(2x-1)}{(x-1)(x+2)(x-3)} dx$ [NCERT Exemplar]

54 $\int \frac{e^x}{(e^x-1)^2(e^x+2)} dx$

55 $\int \frac{2x}{(x^2+1)(x^2+2)^2} dx$

56 $\int \frac{dx}{x(x^3+1)}$

57 $\int \frac{1}{(x^4-1)} dx$

58 $\int \frac{x^2+x+1}{(x^2+1)(x+2)} dx$

59 $\int \frac{x^4}{(x-1)(x^2+1)} dx$ [NCERT]

Long Answer Type Questions

6 Marks

Directions (Q. Nos. 60-66) *Evaluate the following integrals.*

60 $\int \sqrt{\frac{1-\sqrt{x}}{1+\sqrt{x}}} dx$ [NCERT]

61 $\int \frac{(\cos 5x+\cos 4x)}{1-2\cos 3x} dx$ [NCERT Exemplar]

62 $\int \frac{x^2}{(x\sin x+\cos x)^2} dx$

63 $\int \frac{x+\sin x}{1+\cos x} dx$ [ISC 2014]

64 $\int e^{-3x}\cos^3 x\, dx$ [NCERT Exemplar]

65 $\int e^{\tan^{-1}x}\left(\frac{1+x+x^2}{1+x^2}\right) dx$ [NCERT Exemplar]

66 $\int \frac{\sec x}{1+\operatorname{cosec} x} dx$ [ISC 2015]

Hints & Solutions

1. Let $I = \int \frac{3ax}{b^2+c^2x^2} dx$

Now, put $b^2+c^2x^2 = t \Rightarrow 2c^2x\,dx = dt$

$\Rightarrow x\,dx = \frac{dt}{2c^2}$

$\therefore \quad I = \frac{3a}{2c^2}\int \frac{dt}{t} = \frac{3a}{2c^2}\log|t| + C$ [1]

$= \frac{3a}{2c^2}\log|b^2+c^2x^2| + C$

$= \frac{3a}{2c^2}\log(b^2+c^2x^2) + C$ $[\because b^2+c^2x^2>0]$ [1]

2. Let $I = \int \frac{(\log x)^2}{x} dx$

Now, put $\log x = t \Rightarrow \frac{1}{x}dx = dt$ [1]

$\therefore \quad I = \int t^2 dt = \frac{t^3}{3} + C = \frac{(\log x)^3}{3} + C$ $[\because t = \log x]$ [1]

3. Let $I = \int \frac{1}{x\cos^2(1+\log x)} dx$

Put $1+\log x = t \Rightarrow \frac{1}{x}dx = dt$ [1/2]

$\therefore \quad I = \int \frac{dt}{\cos^2 t} = \int \sec^2 t\, dt$ [1/2]

$= \tan t + C = \tan(1+\log x) + C$

[put $t = 1+\log|x|$] [1]

4. Let $I = \int x^2(e^{x^3})\cos(2e^{x^3})\,dx$

Put $2e^{x^3} = t \Rightarrow 2e^{x^3}\cdot 3x^2\,dx = dt$

$\Rightarrow e^{x^3}\cdot x^2\,dx = \frac{1}{6}dt$ [1]

$\therefore \quad I = \frac{1}{6}\int \cos t\, dt = \frac{1}{6}\sin t + C$

$= \frac{1}{6}\sin(2e^{x^3}) + C$ [put $t = 2e^{x^3}$] [1]

5. Hint Put $\sin(ax+b) = t$

[**Ans.** $\frac{1}{2a}\cdot\sin^2(ax+b) + C$]

6. Let $I = \int \frac{1}{x + \sqrt{x}} dx$

Put $x = t^2 \Rightarrow dx = 2t\, dt$

$$I = \int \frac{2t\, dt}{t^2 + t} = 2\int \frac{1}{1+t} dt \quad [1]$$

$$= 2 \log|1+t| + C$$

$$= 2 \log|1+\sqrt{x}| + C \left[\because \int \frac{1}{x} dx = \log|x| + C\right] [1]$$

7. Let $I = \int \frac{x}{(x+1)^2} dx$

Put $(1+x) = t \Rightarrow dx = dt$

$$\therefore \quad I = \int \frac{(t-1)\, dt}{t^2} = \int \frac{t}{t^2} dt - \int \frac{1}{t^2} dt \quad [1]$$

$$= \int \frac{1}{t} dt - \int t^{-2} dt$$

$$= \log|t| - \frac{t^{-2+1}}{-2+1} + C$$

$$= \log|t| + \frac{1}{t} + C$$

$$= \log|1+x| + \frac{1}{1+x} + C \quad [\text{put } t = (1+x)] \; [1]$$

8. Let $I = \int \frac{\sqrt{1+x^2}}{x^4} dx = \int \frac{\sqrt{1+x^2}}{x} \cdot \frac{1}{x^3} dx$

$$= \int \sqrt{\frac{1+x^2}{x^2}} \cdot \frac{1}{x^3} dx = \int \sqrt{\frac{1}{x^2} + 1} \cdot \frac{1}{x^3} dx \quad [1]$$

Now, putting $1 + \frac{1}{x^2} = t^2$

$$\Rightarrow \frac{-2}{x^3} dx = 2t\, dt \Rightarrow -\frac{1}{x^3} dx = t\, dt$$

$$\therefore \quad I = \int -t^2 dt = -\frac{t^3}{3} + C$$

$$= -\frac{1}{3}\left(1 + \frac{1}{x^2}\right)^{3/2} + C \quad [1]$$

9. **Hint** Put $\log\left(\tan\frac{x}{2}\right) = t$. Then, $I = \int \frac{1}{t} dt$

$\left[\textbf{Ans. } \log\left|\log\tan\left(\frac{x}{2}\right)\right| + C\right]$

10. **Hint** Put $x + \log x = t \Rightarrow \left(1 + \frac{1}{x}\right) dx = dt$

$\left[\textbf{Ans. } \frac{1}{3}(x + \log x)^3 + C\right]$

11. **Hint** Put $\tan^{-1} x^4 = t \Rightarrow \frac{1}{1+x^8} \cdot 4x^3 dx = dt$

$\left[\textbf{Ans. } -\frac{1}{4}\cos(\tan^{-1} x^4) + C\right]$

12. **Hint** $e^{\log f(x)} = f(x)$ therefore $e^{\log \sin x} = \sin x$ and then Put $\cos x = t$. $\left[\textbf{Ans. } -\frac{1}{4}\cos^4 x + C\right]$

13. **Hint** Firstly, write the given integral as

$$\frac{1}{2}\int \frac{2\cos x - 3\sin x}{3\cos x + 2\sin x} dx$$

and then put $3\cos x + 2\sin x = t$.

$\left[\textbf{Ans. } \frac{1}{2}\log|2\sin x + 3\cos x| + C\right]$

14. Let $I = \int \frac{e^{2x}}{2+e^x} dx = \int \frac{e^x \cdot e^x}{e^x + 2} dx$

Put $e^x = t \Rightarrow e^x\, dx = dt$ [1/2]

$$\therefore \quad I = \int \frac{t\, dt}{t+2} = \int \frac{t+2-2}{t+2} dt$$

$$= \int \frac{t+2}{t+2} dt - 2\int \frac{1}{t+2} dt \quad [1/2]$$

$$= \int 1 dt - 2\int \frac{dt}{t+2} = t - 2\log|t+2| + C$$

$$= e^x - 2\log|e^x + 2| + C \quad [\text{put } t = e^x] \; [1]$$

15. Let $I = \int \cos^{-1}(\sin x) dx$

$$\Rightarrow I = \int \cos^{-1}\left[\cos\left(\frac{\pi}{2} - x\right)\right] dx \left[\because \cos\left(\frac{\pi}{2} - \theta\right) = \sin\theta\right]$$

[1]

$$= \int \left(\frac{\pi}{2} - x\right) dx \quad [\because \cos^{-1}(\cos\theta) = \theta]$$

$$= \frac{\pi}{2}\int dx - \int x\, dx = \frac{\pi}{2}x - \frac{x^2}{2} + C \quad [1]$$

16. Let $I = \int \frac{\sin 4x}{\cos 2x} dx = \int \frac{\sin[2\cdot(2x)]}{\cos 2x} dx$

$$= \int \frac{2\sin 2x \cdot \cos 2x}{\cos 2x} dx \; [\because \sin 2x = 2\sin x \cdot \cos x] \; [1]$$

$$= 2\int \sin 2x\, dx = -\frac{2\cos 2x}{2} + C = -\cos 2x + C \quad [1]$$

17. **Hint** First, write

$\cos 2x = \cos^2 x - \sin^2 x = (\cos x + \sin x)(\cos x - \sin x)$

and then put $\sin x + \cos x = t$

[**Ans.** $\log|\sin x + \cos x| + C$]

18. **Hint** Use the formula, $1 + \sin 2x = (\cos x + \sin x)^2$

[**Ans.** $x + C$]

19. Let $I = \int \frac{\cos 2x + 2\sin^2 x}{\cos^2 x} dx$

$$= \int \frac{1 - 2\sin^2 x + 2\sin^2 x}{\cos^2 x} dx \quad [\because \cos 2x = 1 - 2\sin^2 x]$$

[1]

$$= \int \frac{1}{\cos^2 x} dx = \int \sec^2 x\, dx = \tan x + C \quad [1]$$

20. Let $I = \int \underset{\text{I}}{x} \cdot \underset{\text{II}}{e^x} dx = x\int e^x dx - \int \left[\frac{d}{dx}x(\int e^x dx)\right]dx$ [1]

[using integration by parts]

$= x \cdot e^x - \int 1 \cdot e^x dx = x \cdot e^x - e^x + C$ [1]

21. Let $I = \int x \log x \, dx = \int \underset{\text{I}}{(\log x)} \cdot \underset{\text{II}}{x} \, dx$

$= \log x \int x \, dx - \int \left[\frac{d}{dx}(\log x)(\int x \, dx)\right]dx$ [1]

[using integration by parts]

$= \frac{x^2}{2} \cdot \log x - \int \frac{1}{x} \cdot \frac{x^2}{2} dx = \frac{x^2}{2}\log x - \frac{1}{2}\int x \, dx$

$= \frac{x^2}{2}\log x - \frac{1}{2} \cdot \frac{x^2}{2} + C = \frac{x^2}{2}\log x - \frac{x^2}{4} + C$ [1]

22. Hint $\frac{d}{dx}(\log \sec x) = \tan x$. **[Ans.** $e^x \log(\sec x) + C$]

23. Let $I = \int \frac{(x^4 - x)^{1/4}}{x^5} dx = \int \frac{\left[x^4\left(1 - \frac{1}{x^3}\right)\right]^{1/4}}{x^5} dx$

[taking x^4 common from numerator] [1]

$= \int \frac{(x^4)^{1/4}\left(1 - \frac{1}{x^3}\right)^{1/4}}{x^5} dx = \int \frac{x\left(1 - \frac{1}{x^3}\right)^{1/4}}{x^5} dx$ [1]

$= \int \frac{\left(1 - \frac{1}{x^3}\right)^{1/4}}{x^4} dx$

Now, put $1 - \frac{1}{x^3} = t \Rightarrow \frac{3}{x^4} dx = dt$ [1]

$\Rightarrow \frac{dx}{x^4} = \frac{1}{3} dt \Rightarrow I = \frac{1}{3}\int t^{1/4} dt$

$= \frac{1}{3} \frac{t^{5/4}}{5/4} + C = \frac{4}{15} t^{5/4} + C$

$= \frac{4}{15}\left(1 - \frac{1}{x^3}\right)^{5/4} + C$ $\left[\because t = 1 - \frac{1}{x^3}\right]$ [1]

24. Let $I = \int \frac{1}{x^2 (x^4 + 1)^{3/4}} dx = \int \frac{1}{x^2\left\{x^4\left(1 + \frac{1}{x^4}\right)\right\}^{3/4}} dx$ [1]

$= \int \frac{1}{x^2 \cdot x^3 \left(1 + \frac{1}{x^4}\right)^{3/4}} dx = \int \frac{1}{x^5\left(1 + \frac{1}{x^4}\right)^{3/4}} dx$ [1]

Now, put $1 + \frac{1}{x^4} = t \Rightarrow -\frac{4}{x^5} dx = dt$

$\Rightarrow \frac{1}{x^5} dx = -\frac{dt}{4}$ [1]

$\therefore I = \frac{1}{-4}\int \frac{1}{t^{3/4}} dt = -\frac{1}{4}\left[\frac{t^{1/4}}{1/4}\right] + C$

$= -(1 + x^{-4})^{1/4} + C$ $[\because t = 1 + x^{-4}]$ [1]

25. Hint Write the given integral as

$$\int \left(1 - \frac{x}{x^2 + 1} + \frac{1}{x^2 + 1}\right) dx$$

$\left[\textbf{Ans. } x - \frac{1}{2}\log|x^2 + 1| + \tan^{-1} x + C\right]$

26. Hint $I = \int \sqrt{\frac{1 + x}{1 - x}} dx = \int \sqrt{\frac{(1 + x)(1 + x)}{(1 - x)(1 + x)}} dx$

$= \int \frac{1 + x}{\sqrt{1 - x^2}} dx = \int \frac{dx}{\sqrt{1 - x^2}} + \int \frac{x}{\sqrt{1 - x^2}} dx$

Put $1 - x^2 = t$ in second integral

[**Ans.** $\sin^{-1}(x) - \sqrt{1 - x^2} + C$]

27. Let $I = \int \frac{\cos x}{\sin x + \sqrt{\sin x}} dx$

$I = \int \frac{\cos x}{\sqrt{\sin x}\,(1 + \sqrt{\sin x})} dx$ [1]

Put $\sqrt{\sin x} = t \Rightarrow \frac{1}{2\sqrt{\sin x}} \cdot \cos x \, dx = dt$ [1]

$\left[\because \frac{d}{dx}\sqrt{x} = \frac{1}{2\sqrt{x}} dx\right]$

$\therefore$ $I = 2\int \frac{dt}{(1 + t)} = 2 \log|1 + t| + C$ [1]

$= 2 \log|1 + \sqrt{\sin x}| + C$ [put $t = \sqrt{\sin x}$] [1]

28. Let $I = \int \frac{\sin x - x \cos x}{x(x + \sin x)} dx$

$= \int \frac{(\sin x + x) - (x \cos x + x)}{x(x + \sin x)} dx$ [1]

$= \int \frac{dx}{x} - \int \frac{1 + \cos x}{x + \sin x} dx$ [1]

$= \log|x| - \int \frac{1 + \cos x}{x + \sin x} dx$

Put $x + \sin x = t \Rightarrow (1 + \cos x)\, dx = dt$ [1]

$\therefore$ $I = \log|x| - \int \frac{dt}{t} = \log|x| - \log|t| + C$

$= \log\left|\frac{x}{t}\right| + C = \log\left|\frac{x}{x + \sin x}\right| + C$ [1]

29. Let $I = \int \frac{\sqrt{\tan x}}{\sin x \cdot \cos x} dx$

On multiplying numerator and denominator by $\sqrt{\tan x}$, we get

$I = \int \frac{\sqrt{\tan x}}{\sin x \cdot \cos x} \times \frac{\sqrt{\tan x}}{\sqrt{\tan x}} dx$ [1]

$= \int \frac{\tan x}{\sin x \cdot \cos x \sqrt{\tan x}} dx$

$= \int \frac{\sin x / \cos x}{\sin x \cdot \cos x \sqrt{\tan x}} dx = \int \frac{\sec^2 x}{\sqrt{\tan x}} dx$ [1]

Now, put $\tan x = t \Rightarrow \sec^2 x\,dx = dt$

$$\therefore\ I = \int \frac{dt}{\sqrt{t}} = \int t^{-1/2} dt = \frac{t^{-\frac{1}{2}+1}}{-\frac{1}{2}+1} + C = \frac{t^{1/2}}{1/2} + C$$

$= 2t^{1/2} + C = 2\sqrt{\tan x} + C$ [$\because t = \tan x$] [2]

30. **Hint** By using the formula, $\cos 2x = 2\cos^2 x - 1$, given integral reduces to

$$\int \frac{-(2\cos^2 x - \cos x - 1)dx}{1-\cos x} = \int \frac{(2\cos x + 1)(1-\cos x)}{(1-\cos x)} dx$$

[**Ans.** $2\sin x + x + C$]

31. Let $I = \int \tan^{-1}\sqrt{\frac{1+\cos x}{1-\cos x}}\,dx = \int \tan^{-1}\sqrt{\frac{2\cos^2\frac{x}{2}}{2\sin^2\frac{x}{2}}}\,dx$

$\left[\because \cos^2\frac{x}{2} = \frac{1+\cos x}{2} \text{ and } \sin^2\frac{x}{2} = \frac{1-\cos x}{2}\right]$ [1]

$= \int \tan^{-1}\sqrt{\cot^2\frac{x}{2}}\,dx = \int \tan^{-1}\cdot\cot\frac{x}{2}dx$ [1]

$= \int \tan^{-1}\left[\tan\left(\frac{\pi}{2}-\frac{x}{2}\right)\right]dx$ $\left[\because \tan\left(\frac{\pi}{2}-\theta\right) = \cot\theta\right]$

$= \int\left(\frac{\pi}{2}-\frac{x}{2}\right)dx$ [1]

$= \frac{\pi}{2}x - \frac{x^2}{2\cdot 2} + C = \frac{\pi}{2}x - \frac{x^2}{4} + C$

[$\because \tan^{-1}(\tan\theta) = \theta$] [1]

32. $\int \frac{\sin^8 x - \cos^8 x}{1-2\sin^2 x\cos^2 x}dx = \int \frac{\{(\sin^4 x)^2 - (\cos^4 x)^2\}}{1-2\sin^2 x\cos^2 x}dx$ [1]

$= \int \frac{(\sin^4 x - \cos^4 x)(\sin^4 x + \cos^4 x)}{1-2\sin^2 x\cos^2 x}dx$

[$\because a^2 - b^2 = (a-b)(a+b)$]

$= \int \frac{\left[(\sin^2 x - \cos^2 x)(\sin^2 x + \cos^2 x)\{(\sin^2 x)^2 + (\cos^2 x)^2\}\right]}{1-2\sin^2 x\cos^2 x}dx$ [1]

$= \int \frac{\left[(\sin^2 x - \cos^2 x)1\{(\sin^2 x + \cos^2 x)^2 - 2\sin^2 x\cdot\cos^2 x\}\right]}{1-2\sin^2 x\cos^2 x}dx$

[$\because a^2 + b^2 = (a+b)^2 - 2ab$] [1]

$= \int \frac{-\cos 2x\,[1-2\sin^2 x\cdot\cos^2 x]}{1-2\sin^2 x\cos^2 x}dx$

[$\because \sin^2 x + \cos^2 x = 1$ and $\cos 2x = \cos^2 x - \sin^2 x$]

$= -\int \cos 2x\,dx = -\frac{\sin 2x}{2} + C$ [1]

33. Let $I = \int \frac{\sin^6 x + \cos^6 x}{\sin^2 x\cos^2 x}dx$

$\Rightarrow I = \int \frac{(\sin^2 x)^3 + (\cos^2 x)^3}{\sin^2 x\cos^2 x}dx$

$= \int \frac{(\sin^2 x + \cos^2 x)^3 - 3\sin^2 x\cos^2 x(\sin^2 x + \cos^2 x)}{\sin^2 x\cos^2 x}dx$ [1]

[$\because a^3 + b^3 = (a+b)^3 - 3ab(a+b)$]

$= \int \frac{(1)^3 - 3\sin^2 x\cos^2 x}{\sin^2 x\cos^2 x}dx$ [$\because \sin^2 x + \cos^2 x = 1$]

$= \int \frac{1}{\sin^2 x\cos^2 x}dx - 3\int \frac{\sin^2 x\cos^2 x}{\sin^2 x\cos^2 x}dx$

$= \int \frac{\sin^2 x + \cos^2 x}{\sin^2 x\cos^2 x}dx - 3\int 1\,dx$ [$\because 1 = \sin^2 x + \cos^2 x$] [1]

$= \int\left[\frac{\sin^2 x}{\sin^2 x\cos^2 x} + \frac{\cos^2 x}{\sin^2 x\cos^2 x}\right]dx - 3\int 1dx$ [1]

$= \int(\sec^2 x + \text{cosec}^2 x)\,dx - 3\int 1dx$

$= \int \sec^2 x\,dx + \int \text{cosec}^2 x\,dx - 3\int 1\,dx$

$= \tan x - \cot x - 3x + C$ [1]

34. Similar as Example 14.

$\left[\textbf{Ans.} -\frac{\cos 4x}{16} + \frac{\cos 6x}{24} - \frac{\cos 2x}{8} + C\right]$

35. Let $I = \int \tan^3 x\,dx$

$\Rightarrow I = \int \tan^2 x\tan x\,dx$ [1/2]

$\Rightarrow I = \int(\sec^2 x - 1)\tan x\,dx$ [1/2]

$\Rightarrow I = \int(\tan x\sec^2 x - \tan x)\,dx$

$\Rightarrow I = \int \tan x\sec^2 x\,dx - \int \tan x\,dx$ [1/2]

On putting $\tan x = t$ and $\sec^2 x\,dx = dt$ in first integral, we get

$I = \int t\,dt - \int \tan x\,dx$ [1/2]

$\Rightarrow I = \frac{t^2}{2} + \log|\cos x| + C$ [1]

$\therefore \int \tan^3 x\,dx = \frac{1}{2}\tan^2 x + \log|\cos x| + C$ [1]

36. Similar as Example 17. $\left[\textbf{Ans.} \frac{1}{5}e^{2x}(2\sin x - \cos x) + C\right]$

37. Let $I = \int \tan^{-1} x\,dx = \int \underset{\text{II}}{1}\cdot\underset{\text{I}}{\tan^{-1}} x\,dx$

Using integration by parts, taking $\tan^{-1} x$ as Ist function and 1 as IInd function, we get

$I = \tan^{-1} x\cdot\int 1dx - \int\left[\frac{d}{dx}(\tan^{-1} x)\cdot\int 1\,dx\right]dx$ [1]

$= (\tan^{-1} x)\cdot x - \int \frac{1}{1+x^2}\cdot x\,dx$

$= x\tan^{-1} x - \frac{1}{2}\int \frac{2x}{1+x^2}dx$

$= x\tan^{-1} x - I_1$, where $I_1 = \frac{1}{2}\int \frac{2x}{1+x^2}dx$ ...(i) [1]

Now, put $1 + x^2 = t \Rightarrow 2x\,dx = dt$

$\therefore \quad I_1 = \frac{1}{2}\int \frac{dt}{t} = \frac{1}{2}\log|t| + C_1$

$= \frac{1}{2}\log|1+x^2| + C_1 \qquad [\because t = 1+x^2]$ [1]

Now, from Eq. (i), we get

$I = x\tan^{-1}x - \frac{1}{2}\log|1+x^2| - C_1$

$= x\tan^{-1}x - \frac{1}{2}\log|1+x^2| + C$, where $C = -C_1$ [1]

38. We have, $I = \int \tan^{-1}\sqrt{x}\,dx$

Put $x = t^2 \Rightarrow dx = 2t\,dt$

$\therefore \quad I = \int \underset{\text{I}}{2t}\,\underset{\text{II}}{\tan^{-1}t}\,dt$ [1]

Using integration by part

$I = 2\left[\tan^{-1}t\int t\,dt - \int\left(\frac{d}{dt}(\tan^{-1}t)\int t\,dt\right)\cdot dt\right] + C$

$I = 2\left[\tan^{-1}t\cdot\frac{t^2}{2} - \int\frac{1}{1+t^2}\times\frac{t^2}{2}\,dt\right] + C$ [1]

$I = t^2\tan^{-1}t - \int\frac{t^2+1}{t^2+1}\,dt + \int\frac{1}{1+t^2}\,dt + C$

$I = t^2\tan^{-1}t - \int dt + \int\frac{1}{1+t^2}\,dt + C$ [1]

$I = t^2\tan^{-1}t - t + \tan^{-1}t + C$

$I = (t^2+1)\tan^{-1}t - t + C$

$I = (x+1)\tan^{-1}\sqrt{x} - \sqrt{x} + C \qquad [\because t^2 = x]$ [1]

39. Hint

(i) On substituting $x = \tan\theta$ and $dx = \sec^2\theta\,d\theta$, given integral reduces to $\int 2\theta\cdot\sec^2\theta\,d\theta$

(ii) After integrating by parts and then substitute $\theta = \tan^{-1}x$

[**Ans.** $2[x\tan^{-1}x - \log(1+x^2)] + C$]

40. Let $I = \int\frac{x\sin^{-1}x}{\sqrt{1-x^2}}\,dx$

Now, put $\quad x = \sin t \Rightarrow \sin^{-1}x = t$

$\Rightarrow \frac{1}{\sqrt{1-x^2}}\,dx = dt$

$\therefore \quad I = \int t\sin t\,dt$ [1]

Using integration by parts, taking t as the Ist function and $\sin t$ as the IInd function, we get

$I = t\int\sin t\,dt - \int\left[\frac{d}{dt}(t)\cdot\int\sin t\,dt\right]dt$ [1]

$\Rightarrow \quad I = -t\cos t - \int 1\times(-\cos t)\,dt$

$= -t\cos t + \int\cos t\,dt$

$\Rightarrow \quad I = -t\cos t + \sin t + C$ [1]

$\Rightarrow \quad I = -t\sqrt{1-\sin^2 t} + \sin t + C$

$[\because \cos^2 t = 1-\sin^2 t \Rightarrow \cos t = \sqrt{1-\sin^2 t}]$

$\therefore \quad I = -(\sin^{-1}x)\sqrt{1-x^2} + x + C$

$[\because t = \sin^{-1}x$ and $x = \sin t]$ [1]

41. Let $I = \int\frac{\cos^{-1}x}{x^2}\,dx$

Put $x = \cos\theta \Rightarrow dx = -\sin\theta\,d\theta$ and $\theta = \cos^{-1}x$

$\therefore \quad I = \int -\left(\theta\cdot\frac{\sin\theta}{\cos\theta}\cdot\frac{1}{\cos\theta}\right)d\theta$

$\Rightarrow \quad I = -\int \underset{\text{I}}{\theta}\cdot\underset{\text{II}}{(\tan\theta\cdot\sec\theta)}\,d\theta$ [1]

Using integration by parts, we get

$I = -[\theta\cdot\sec\theta - \int 1\cdot\sec\theta\,d\theta]$

$\left[\because \int \underset{\text{I}}{f(x)}.\underset{\text{II}}{g(x)}dx = f(x)\int g(x) - \int\left(\frac{d}{dx}f(x)\int g(x)dx\right)dx\right]$

$= -\theta\sec\theta + \int\sec\theta\,d\theta$ [1]

$= -\theta\sec\theta + \log|\sec\theta + \tan\theta| + C$

$= (-\cos^{-1}x)\cdot\frac{1}{x} + \log\left|\left(\frac{1}{x} + \sqrt{\sec^2\theta - 1}\right)\right| + C$

$\left[\text{put } \cos\theta = x \Rightarrow \sec\theta = \frac{1}{x}\right]$ [1]

$= \frac{-\cos^{-1}x}{x} + \log\left|\frac{1}{x} + \sqrt{\frac{1}{x^2} - 1}\right| + C$

$= \frac{-\cos^{-1}x}{x} + \log\left|\frac{1}{x} + \frac{\sqrt{1-x^2}}{x}\right| + C$ [1]

42. Let $I = \int\frac{\sqrt{x^2+1}\,[\log(x^2+1) - 2\log(x)]}{x^4}\,dx$

$= \int\frac{\sqrt{x^2+1}\log\left(\frac{x^2+1}{x^2}\right)}{x^4}\,dx$

$\left[\because n\log m = \log m^n \text{ and } \log m - \log n = \log\frac{m}{n}\right]$

$= \int\frac{x\sqrt{1+\frac{1}{x^2}}\log\left(1+\frac{1}{x^2}\right)}{x^4}\,dx$

$= \int\frac{\sqrt{1+\frac{1}{x^2}}\log\left(1+\frac{1}{x^2}\right)}{x^3}\,dx$ [1]

Now, put $1 + \frac{1}{x^2} = t \Rightarrow \frac{-2}{x^3}\,dx = dt \Rightarrow \frac{dx}{x^3} = -\frac{dt}{2}$

$\therefore \quad I = -\frac{1}{2}\int\sqrt{t}\log t\,dt$

[1]

$$= -\frac{1}{2}\left[\log t \times \frac{t^{3/2}}{3/2} - \int \frac{t^{3/2}}{3/2} \times \frac{1}{t}\, dt\right]$$

[using integration by parts]

$$= -\frac{1}{3}[t^{3/2} \log t - \int \sqrt{t}\, dt]$$ [1]

$$= -\frac{1}{3}\left[t^{3/2} \log t - \frac{t^{3/2}}{3/2}\right] + C$$

$$= -\frac{1}{3} t^{3/2}\left[\log t - \frac{2}{3}\right] + C$$

$$= -\frac{1}{3}\left(1 + \frac{1}{x^2}\right)^{3/2}\left[\log\left(1 + \frac{1}{x^2}\right) - \frac{2}{3}\right] + C$$

$\left[\because t = 1 + \frac{1}{x^2}\right]$ [1]

43. Let $I = \int\left[\log(\log x) + \frac{1}{(\log x)^2}\right] dx$

$$= \int \log(\log x)\, dx + \int \frac{dx}{(\log x)^2} = I_1 + I_2$$ ...(i) [1]

where, $I_1 = \int \log(\log x)\, dx$ and $I_2 = \int \frac{dx}{(\log x)^2}$

Consider, $I_1 = \int \log(\log x)\, dx$

Let us take 1 as the IInd function, thus

$$I_1 = \int \log(\log x) \cdot 1\, dx$$

$$= \log(\log x) \cdot x - \int \frac{1}{(\log x)} \cdot \frac{1}{x} \cdot x\, dx$$

[using integration by parts] [1]

$$= x \cdot \log(\log x) - \int (\log x)^{-1} \cdot 1\, dx$$

Again, consider 1 as the IInd function and applying integration by parts, we get

$$I_1 = x \cdot \log(\log x) - \left\{(\log x)^{-1} \cdot x - \int (-1)(\log x)^{-2} \cdot \frac{1}{x} \cdot x\, dx\right\}$$ [1]

$$= x \cdot \log(\log x) - \frac{x}{(\log x)} - \int \frac{dx}{(\log x)^2}$$

$$= x \cdot \log(\log x) - \frac{x}{(\log x)} - I_2 + C$$

Now, substituting the value of I_1 in Eq. (i), we get

$$I = x \cdot \log(\log x) - \frac{x}{(\log x)} - I_2 + C + I_2$$

$$= x \cdot \log(\log x) - \frac{x}{\log x} + C$$ [1]

44. Let $I = \int e^x \frac{x^2 + 1}{(x+1)^2}\, dx$

$$\Rightarrow I = \int e^x\left(1 - \frac{2x}{(x+1)^2}\right) dx$$ [1]

$$= \int e^x\, dx - 2\int e^x \frac{x}{(x+1)^2}\, dx$$

$$\Rightarrow I = e^x - 2\int e^x \frac{x+1-1}{(x+1)^2}\, dx$$ [1]

$$\Rightarrow I = e^x - 2\int e^x\left\{\frac{1}{x+1} + \frac{-1}{(x+1)^2}\right\} dx$$

$$\Rightarrow I = e^x - 2\left\{\int e^x \cdot \frac{1}{x+1}\, dx - \int e^x \frac{1}{(x+1)^2}\, dx\right\}$$

$$I = e^x - 2\left\{\frac{1}{x+1} e^x - \int -\frac{1}{(x+1)^2} e^x dx - \int e^x \frac{1}{(x+1)^2} dx\right\}$$

[using integration by part] [1]

$$\Rightarrow I = e^x - 2\left\{\begin{array}{l}\frac{1}{x+1} e^x + \int e^x \cdot \frac{1\, dx}{(x+1)^2} \\ -\int e^x \cdot \frac{1}{(x+1)^2} dx\end{array}\right\} + C$$

$$\Rightarrow I = e^x - 2\frac{e^x}{x+1} + C$$ [1]

45. Let $I = \int \frac{(2x-5)e^{2x}}{(2x-3)^3}\, dx = \int \frac{(2x-3-2)e^{2x}}{(2x-3)^3}\, dx$

$$= \int \frac{e^{2x}}{(2x-3)^2}\, dx - 2\int \frac{e^{2x}}{(2x-3)^3}\, dx$$

$$= \int \underset{\text{II}}{e^{2x}} \underset{\text{I}}{(2x-3)^{-2}}\, dx - 2\int e^{2x}(2x-3)^{-3}\, dx$$ [1]

$$= \left[(2x-3)^{-2} \int e^{2x} dx - \int\left\{\frac{d}{dx}(2x-3)^{-2} \int e^{2x}\, dx\right\} dx\right] - 2\int e^{2x}(2x-3)^{-3}\, dx$$

[using integration by parts] [1]

$$= (2x-3)^{-2} \frac{e^{2x}}{2} - \int -2(2x-3)^{-3} \times 2 \times \frac{e^{2x}}{2}\, dx - 2\int e^{2x}(2x-3)^{-3}\, dx$$ [1]

$$= \frac{e^{2x}(2x-3)^{-2}}{2} + 2\int e^{2x}(2x-3)^{-3}\, dx - 2\int e^{2x}(2x-3)^{-3}\, dx$$

$$= \frac{e^{2x}(2x-3)^{-2}}{2} + C$$ [1]

46. Given that, $\int e^x \frac{(2 + \sin 2x)}{\cos^2 x}\, dx$

$$= \int e^x \frac{(2 + 2\sin x \cos x)}{\cos^2 x}\, dx$$

$[\because \sin 2x = 2 \sin x \cos x]$ [1]

$$= 2\int e^x\left[\frac{1}{\cos^2 x} + \frac{\sin x \cos x}{\cos^2 x}\right] dx$$ [1]

$= 2\int e^x (\sec^2 x + \tan x)\,dx$

$= 2\int e^x(\tan x + \sec^2 x)dx$ [1]

$= 2e^x \tan x + C$

$[\because \int e^x [f(x) + f'(x)]\,dx = e^x f(x) + C]$ [1]

47. Let $I = \int e^{2x}\left(\dfrac{1-\sin 2x}{1-\cos 2x}\right)dx$

$= \int e^{2x}\left(\dfrac{1-2\sin x\cos x}{2\sin^2 x}\right)dx$ [1]

$[\because 1-\cos 2x = 2\sin^2 x$ and $\sin 2x = 2\sin x\cos x]$

$= \dfrac{1}{2}\int e^{2x}(\text{cosec}^2 x - 2\cot x)\,dx$ [1]

$= \dfrac{1}{2}\int e^{2x}\,\text{cosec}^2 x\,dx - \int e^{2x}\cot x\,dx$

$= \dfrac{1}{2}[-e^{2x}\cot x + \int 2e^{2x}\cot x\,dx] - \int e^{2x}\cot x\,dx$ [1]

$= -\dfrac{e^{2x}}{2}\cot x + \int e^{2x}\cot x\,dx - \int e^{2x}\cot x\,dx + C$

$= -\dfrac{e^{2x}}{2}\cot x + C$ [1]

48. Let $I = \int \dfrac{\sin x}{(1-\cos x)(2-\cos x)}dx$

Now, put $-\cos x = t \Rightarrow \sin x\,dx = dt$

$\therefore \quad I = \int \dfrac{dt}{(1+t)(2+t)}$ [1]

Now, decompose the rational function into partial fraction.

Let $\dfrac{1}{(1+t)(2+t)} = \dfrac{A}{(1+t)} + \dfrac{B}{(2+t)}$

$\Rightarrow \dfrac{1}{(1+t)(2+t)} = \dfrac{A(2+t)+B(1+t)}{(1+t)(2+t)}$

$\Rightarrow \quad 1 = A(2+t) + B(1+t)$ ...(i)

On putting $t = -1$ in Eq. (i), we get

$1 = A(2-1) + 0 \Rightarrow A = 1$

On putting $t = -2$ in Eq. (i), we get

$1 = 0 + B(1-2)$

$\Rightarrow \quad B = -1$

$\therefore \quad \dfrac{1}{(1+t)(2+t)} = \dfrac{1}{(1+t)} + \dfrac{-1}{(2+t)}$ [1]

Now, $I = \int \dfrac{dt}{(1+t)(2+t)}$

$= \int \left[\dfrac{1}{(1+t)} - \dfrac{1}{(2+t)}\right]dt$ [1]

$= \int \dfrac{dt}{1+t} - \int \dfrac{dt}{2+t}$

$= \log|1+t| - \log|2+t| + C = \log\left|\dfrac{1+t}{2+t}\right| + C$

$\left[\because \log m - \log n = \log\dfrac{m}{n}\right]$

$= \log\left|\dfrac{1-\cos x}{2-\cos x}\right| + C \quad [\because t = -\cos x]$ [1]

49. **Hint** Substitute $e^x = t$ and $e^x\,dx = dt$, then given integral reduces to $\int \dfrac{dt}{(1+t)(2+t)}$. Further, use partial fractions and then integrate.

$\left[\textbf{Ans. } \log\left|\dfrac{1+e^x}{2+e^x}\right| + C\right]$

50. **Hint** Firstly, put $x^2 = t \Rightarrow 2x\,dx = dt$ and then

$I = \int \dfrac{dt}{(t+1)(t+3)}$.

$\left[\textbf{Ans. } \dfrac{1}{2}\log\left|\dfrac{x^2+1}{x^2+3}\right| + C\right]$

51. **Hint** (i) Write the given integral as $\int \dfrac{(3\sin\phi - 2)\cos\phi}{\sin^2\phi - 4\sin\phi + 4}d\phi$

(ii) On substituting $\sin\phi = t$ and $\cos\phi\,d\phi = dt$, then above integral reduces to $\int \dfrac{(3t-2)}{(t-2)^2}dt$.

(iii) Now, use partial fraction and then integrate.

$\left[\textbf{Ans. } 3\log|2-\sin\phi| + \dfrac{4}{2-\sin\phi} + C\right]$

52. Let $I = \int \dfrac{\sin 2x}{(1+\sin x)(2+\sin x)}dx$

$= \int \dfrac{2\sin x \cdot \cos x}{(1+\sin x)(2+\sin x)}dx$

Put $\sin x = t$ [1]

On differentiating both sides w.r.t. x, we get

$\cos x\,dx = dt$

$\therefore \quad I = 2\int \dfrac{t\,dt}{(1+t)(2+t)}$ ...(i)

Let $\dfrac{t}{(1+t)(2+t)} = \dfrac{A}{(1+t)} + \dfrac{B}{(2+t)}$

$\Rightarrow \quad t \equiv A(2+t) + B(1+t)$ [1]

Putting $t = -1$, we get

$A = -1$

and putting $t = -2$, we get

$B = 2$

$\therefore \quad \dfrac{t}{(1+t)(2+t)} = \dfrac{-1}{(1+t)} + \dfrac{2}{(2+t)}$ [1]

$\therefore$ From Eq. (i), we get

$$I = 2\int\left(\frac{-1}{1+t} + \frac{2}{2+t}\right)dt$$
$$= 2\int\frac{-1}{1+t}\,dt + 4\int\frac{1}{2+t}\,dt$$
$$= -2\log|1+t| + 4\log|2+t| + C$$
$$= -2\log|1+\sin x| + 4\log|2+\sin x| + C$$

$[\because t = \sin x]$ [1]

53. **Hint** $\frac{2x-1}{(x-1)(x+2)(x-3)} = \frac{A}{x-1} + \frac{B}{x+2} + \frac{C}{x-3}$

$\left[\textbf{Ans. } \log\left|\frac{\sqrt{x-3}}{(x-1)^{1/6}(x+2)^{1/3}}\right| + C\right]$

54. Let $I = \int\frac{e^x dx}{(e^x-1)^2(e^x+2)}$

Put $e^x = t \Rightarrow e^x dx = dt$

$\therefore \quad I = \int\frac{dt}{(t-1)^2(t+2)}$

Now, let $\frac{1}{(t-1)^2(t+2)} = \frac{A}{(t-1)} + \frac{B}{(t-1)^2} + \frac{C}{(t+2)}$

$\Rightarrow \quad 1 = A(t-1)(t+2) + B(t+2) + C(t-1)^2$

$\Rightarrow \quad 1 = A(t^2+t-2) + B(t+2) + C(t^2-2t+1)$

$\Rightarrow \quad 1 = t^2(A+C) + t(A+B-2C) - 2A + 2B + C$ [1]

On comparing the coefficient of t^2, t and the constant term from the both sides, we get

$A + C = 0$, $A + B - 2C = 0$ and $-2A + 2B + C = 1$

$\Rightarrow \quad A = -C,$ ...(i)

$A + B = 2C$ ...(ii)

and $\quad -2A + 2B + C = 1$ ...(iii)

On substituting $A = -C$ in Eqs. (ii) and (iii), we get

$-C + B = 2C \Rightarrow B = 3C$ ...(iv)

and $\quad 2C + 2B + C = 1$

$\Rightarrow \quad 2C + 2(3C) + C = 1$ [from Eq. (iv)]

$\Rightarrow \quad 9C = 1 \Rightarrow C = \frac{1}{9}$ [1]

Now, from Eqs. (i) and (iv), we get

$A = \frac{-1}{9}, B = \frac{1}{3}$

Now, $I = \int\left[-\frac{1}{9}\frac{1}{(t-1)} + \frac{1}{3}\frac{1}{(t-1)^2} + \frac{1}{9}\frac{1}{(t+2)}\right]dt$ [1]

$$= -\frac{1}{9}\int\frac{dt}{t-1} + \frac{1}{3}\int\frac{dt}{(t-1)^2} + \frac{1}{9}\int\frac{dt}{t+2}$$
$$= -\frac{1}{9}\log|t-1| + \frac{1}{3}\cdot\frac{(t-1)^{-2+1}}{(-2+1)} + \frac{1}{9}\log|t+2| + C$$
$$= \frac{1}{9}\log\left|\frac{t+2}{t-1}\right| - \frac{1}{3}\cdot\frac{1}{(t-1)} + C$$
$$= \frac{1}{9}\log\left|\frac{e^x+2}{e^x-1}\right| - \frac{1}{3}\frac{1}{(e^x-1)} + C$$

[putting $t = e^x$] [1]

55. Solve as Question 54.

$\left[\textbf{Ans. } \log|x^2+1| - \log|x^2+2| + \frac{1}{x^2+2} + C\right]$

56. Let $I = \int\frac{dx}{x(x^3+1)}$, $I = \int\frac{dx}{x(x+1)(x^2-x+1)}$

$[\because a^3 + b^3 = (a+b)(a^2+b^2-ab)]$

Decompose the rational function into partial fraction.

Again, let

$$\frac{1}{x(x+1)(x^2-x+1)} = \frac{A}{x} + \frac{B}{x+1} + \frac{Cx+D}{x^2-x+1}$$

$\Rightarrow \quad 1 = A(x+1)(x^2-x+1) + Bx(x^2-x+1) + (Cx+D)x(x+1)$

$\Rightarrow \quad 1 = A(x^3-x^2+x+x^2-x+1) + B(x^3-x^2+x) + (Cx+D)(x^2+x)$

$\Rightarrow \quad 1 = A(x^3+1) + B(x^3-x^2+x) + (Cx^3+Dx^2+Cx^2+Dx)$

$\Rightarrow 1 = (A+B+C)x^3 + (-B+D+C)x^2 + (B+D)x + A$ [1]

On comparing the coefficients of different powers of x from both sides, we get

$A + B + C = 0$ ...(i)

$-B + D + C = 0$ ...(ii)

$B + D = 0$ ...(iii)

and $\quad A = 1$ ...(iv)

From Eqs. (ii) and (iii), we get

$C - 2B = 0$ ...(v)

From Eqs. (i) and (iv), we get

$B + C = -1$ ...(vi)

From Eqs. (v) and (vi), we get

$B = -\frac{1}{3}$ and $C = -\frac{2}{3} \Rightarrow D = \frac{1}{3}$

[using Eq. (iii)] [1]

Now, $I = \int\frac{dx}{x(x^3+1)} = \int\left[\frac{1}{x} - \frac{1}{3(x+1)} + \frac{-\frac{2x}{3}+\frac{1}{3}}{x^2-x+1}\right]dx$

$\Rightarrow \quad I = \int\frac{dx}{x} - \frac{1}{3}\int\frac{dx}{x+1} + \frac{1}{3}\int\frac{1-2x}{x^2-x+1}\,dx$

$\Rightarrow \quad I = \log|x| - \frac{1}{3}\log|x+1| - \frac{1}{3}\int\frac{2x-1}{x^2-x+1}\,dx$ [1]

Now, put $t = x^2 - x + 1 \Rightarrow dt = (2x-1)dx$

$\therefore \quad I = \log|x| - \frac{1}{3}\log|x+1| - \frac{1}{3}\int\frac{dt}{t}$

$$= \log|x| - \frac{1}{3}\log|x+1| - \frac{1}{3}\log|t| + C$$
$$= \log|x| - \frac{1}{3}\log|x+1| - \frac{1}{3}\log|x^2-x+1| + C$$

[put $t = x^2 - x + 1$]

$$= \log|x| - \frac{1}{3}\log|(x+1)(x^2-x+1)| + C$$

$[\because \log m + \log n = \log mn]$

$$= \log|x| - \frac{1}{3}\log|x^3+1| + C$$

$$= \log|x| - \log|x^3+1|^{1/3} + C$$

$$= \log\frac{|x|}{|x^3+1|^{1/3}} + C$$

$\left[\because \log m - \log n = \log\frac{m}{n}\right]$ [1]

57. **Hint** (i) Firstly, write the given integral as $\int\frac{dx}{(x-1)(x+1)(x^2+1)}$.

(ii) Let $\frac{1}{(x-1)(x+1)(x^2+1)} = \frac{A}{x-1} + \frac{B}{x+1} + \frac{Cx+D}{x^2+1}$

$\left[\textbf{Ans. } \frac{1}{4}\log\left|\frac{x-1}{x+1}\right| - \frac{1}{2}\tan^{-1}x + C\right]$

58. Let $I = \int\frac{x^2+x+1}{(x^2+1)(x+2)}dx$

Using partial fraction method, we get

$$\frac{x^2+x+1}{(x^2+1)(x+2)} = \frac{A}{x+2} + \frac{Bx+C}{x^2+1} \quad ...(i)$$

$\Rightarrow \quad x^2+x+1 = A(x^2+1) + (Bx+C)(x+2)$

$\Rightarrow \quad x^2+x+1 = x^2(A+B) + x(2B+C) + (A+2C)$

On comparing the coefficients of x^2, x and constant terms from both sides, we get

$A + B = 1 \quad ...(ii)$

$2B + C = 1 \quad ...(iii)$

and $\quad A + 2C = 1 \quad ...(iv)$ [1]

On substituting the value of B from Eq. (ii) in Eq. (iii), we get

$2(1-A) + C = 1 \Rightarrow 2 - 2A + C = 1$

$\Rightarrow \quad 2A - C = 1 \quad ...(v)$

Now, solving Eqs. (iv) and (v), we get

$C = \frac{1}{5}$ and $A = \frac{3}{5}$

On putting the value of A in Eq. (ii), we get

$B = 1 - \frac{3}{5} = \frac{2}{5}$ [1]

Thus, from Eq. (i), we get

$$\frac{x^2+x+1}{(x^2+1)(x+2)} = \frac{3}{5}\cdot\frac{1}{(x+2)} + \frac{1}{5}\cdot\frac{(2x+1)}{x^2+1}$$

$$\Rightarrow I = \frac{3}{5}\int\frac{dx}{x+2} + \frac{1}{5}\int\frac{(2x+1)}{x^2+1}dx \quad [1]$$

$$= \frac{3}{5}\int\frac{dx}{x+2} + \frac{1}{5}\int\frac{2x}{x^2+1}dx + \frac{1}{5}\int\frac{dx}{x^2+1}$$

$$= \frac{3}{5}\log|x+2| + \frac{1}{5}\log|x^2+1| + \frac{1}{5}\tan^{-1}x + C$$

$\left[\because \int\frac{dx}{x^2+a^2} = \frac{1}{a}\tan^{-1}\left(\frac{x}{a}\right) + C \text{ and } \int\frac{f'(x)}{f(x)}dx = \log|f(x)| + C\right]$ [1]

59. **Hint** Firstly, write the given integral as

$$\int\left[(x+1) + \left(\frac{1}{x^3-x^2+x-1}\right)\right]dx$$

$$= \int(x+1)dx + \int\frac{dx}{(x-1)(x^2+1)}$$

$\left[\textbf{Ans. } \frac{x^2}{2} + x + \frac{1}{2}\log|x-1| - \frac{1}{4}\log|x^2+1| - \frac{1}{2}\tan^{-1}x + C\right]$

60. Let $I = \int\sqrt{\frac{1-\sqrt{x}}{1+\sqrt{x}}}\,dx.$

Now, putting $\sqrt{x} = \cos t \Rightarrow x = \cos^2 t$

$\Rightarrow dx = 2\cos t(-\sin t)\,dt$

$$\therefore \quad I = \int\sqrt{\frac{1-\cos t}{1+\cos t}}(-2\sin t\cos t)\,dt \quad [1]$$

$$\Rightarrow I = -2\int\sqrt{\frac{2\sin^2\frac{t}{2}}{2\cos^2\frac{t}{2}}}\cdot 2\sin\frac{t}{2}\cos\frac{t}{2}\cdot\cos t\,dt$$

$\left[\because 1-\cos x = 2\sin^2\frac{x}{2}, 1+\cos x = 2\cos^2\frac{x}{2} \text{ and } \sin 2t = 2\sin t\cos t\right]$

$$= -4\int\sin^2\frac{t}{2}\cdot\cos t\,dt \quad [1]$$

$$= -4\int\frac{1-\cos t}{2}\cdot\cos t\,dt \quad \left[\because \sin^2\frac{\theta}{2} = \frac{1-\cos\theta}{2}\right]$$

$$= -2\int(\cos t - \cos^2 t)\,dt \quad [1]$$

$$= -2\int\left(\cos t - \frac{1+\cos 2t}{2}\right)dt \quad [1]$$

$$= -2\sin t + t + \frac{1}{2}\sin 2t + C$$

$$= -2\sin t + t + \frac{1}{2}\times 2\sin t\cdot\cos t + C \quad [1]$$

$$= -2\sqrt{1-\cos^2 t} + t + \frac{1}{2}[2\sqrt{1-\cos^2 t}\cdot\cos t] + C$$

$$= -2\sqrt{1-x} + \cos^{-1}\sqrt{x} + \sqrt{x}\sqrt{1-x} + C$$

$[\because \cos^2 t = x]$

$$= -2\sqrt{1-x} + \cos^{-1}\sqrt{x} + \sqrt{x-x^2} + C \quad [1]$$

61. Let $I=\int \frac{\cos 5x+\cos 4x}{1-2\cos 3x}dx=\int \frac{2\cos\frac{9x}{2}\cdot\cos\frac{x}{2}}{1-2\left(2\cos^2\frac{3x}{2}-1\right)}dx$ [1]

$\left[\because \cos C+\cos D=2\cos\frac{C+D}{2}\cdot\cos\frac{C-D}{2}\right.$
$\left.\text{and } \cos x=2\cos^2\left(\frac{x}{2}\right)-1\right]$

$\Rightarrow \quad I=\int \frac{2\cos\frac{9x}{2}.\cos\frac{x}{2}}{3-4\cos^2\frac{3x}{2}}dx$

$=-\int \frac{2\cos\frac{9x}{2}\cdot\cos\frac{x}{2}}{4\cos^2\frac{3x}{2}-3}dx$ [1]

$=-\int \frac{2\cos\frac{9x}{2}\cdot\cos\frac{x}{2}\cdot\cos\frac{3x}{2}}{4\cos^3\frac{3x}{2}-3\cos\frac{3x}{2}}dx$

$\left[\text{multiply and divide by } \cos\frac{3x}{2}\right]$ [1]

$=-\int \frac{2\cos\frac{9x}{2}\cdot\cos\frac{x}{2}\cdot\cos\frac{3x}{2}}{\cos 3\cdot\left(\frac{3x}{2}\right)}dx$

$[\because \cos 3\theta=4\cos^3\theta-3\cos\theta]$

$=-\int 2\cos\frac{3x}{2}\cdot\cos\frac{x}{2}dx$

$=-\int\left\{\cos\left(\frac{3x}{2}+\frac{x}{2}\right)+\cos\left(\frac{3x}{2}-\frac{x}{2}\right)\right\}dx$ [1]

$[\because 2\cos A\cos B=\cos(A+B)+\cos(A-B)]$

$=-\int(\cos 2x+\cos x)\,dx$ [1]

$=-\left[\frac{\sin 2x}{2}+\sin x\right]+C$

$=-\frac{1}{2}\sin 2x-\sin x+C$ [1]

62. Let $I=\int \frac{x^2}{(x\sin x+\cos x)^2}dx$

$=\int \frac{x\cos x}{(x\sin x+\cos x)^2}\,x\sec x\,dx$ ...(i) [1]

[multiplying numerator by $\cos x$ and $\sec x$]

$I=\int \underbrace{\frac{x\cos x}{(x\sin x+\cos x)^2}}_{\text{II}}\times\underbrace{x\sec x}_{\text{I}}\,dx$ [1]

$=x\sec x\frac{(-1)}{x\sin x+\cos x}$
$-\int(1\cdot\sec x+x\sec x\tan x)\frac{-dx}{x\sin x+\cos x}$ [1]

$\left[\therefore I_1=\int\frac{x\cos x}{(x\sin x+\cos x)^2}dx\right.$
Let $x\sin x+\cos x=t$
$\Rightarrow (x\cos x+\sin x-\sin x)dx=dt$
or $x\cos x\,dx=dt$
$\left.\therefore I_1=\int\frac{dt}{t^2}=-\frac{1}{t}=\frac{-1}{x\sin x+\cos x}\right]$

$=\frac{-x\sec x}{x\sin x+\cos x}+\int\sec x\left(1+\frac{x\sin x}{\cos x}\right)\frac{dx}{x\sin x+\cos x}$ [1]

$=\frac{-x\sec x}{x\sin x+\cos x}+\int\sec^2 x\,dx$ [1]

$=\frac{-\sec x}{x\sin x+\cos x}+\tan x+C$ [1]

63. Let $I=\int\frac{x+\sin x}{1+\cos x}dx$

Then, $I=\int\frac{x}{1+\cos x}dx+\int\frac{\sin x}{1+\cos x}dx$

$\Rightarrow \quad I=I_1+I_2$ (say) ...(i) [1]

Now, $I_1=\int\frac{x}{1+\cos x}dx$

$=\int\frac{x}{2\cos^2 x/2}dx=\frac{1}{2}\int \underset{\text{I}}{x}\,\underset{\text{II}}{\sec^2}\frac{x}{2}dx$

$\left[\because \cos x=2\cos^2\frac{x}{2}-1\right]$ [1]

Using integration by parts, we get

$I_1=\frac{1}{2}\left[x\cdot\tan\frac{x}{2}\cdot 2-\int 1\cdot\tan\frac{x}{2}\cdot 2dx\right]$ [1]

$=\frac{1}{2}\left[2x\tan\frac{x}{2}-2\int\tan\frac{x}{2}dx\right]$

$=x\tan\frac{x}{2}-\int\tan\frac{x}{2}dx$ [1/2]

and $I_2=\int\frac{\sin x}{1+\cos x}dx$

$=\int\frac{2\sin x/2\cdot\cos x/2}{2\cos^2 x/2}dx$

$=\int\tan x/2\,dx$ [1]

$\left[\because \sin x=2\sin\frac{x}{2}\cos\frac{x}{2} \text{ and } \cos x=2\cos^2\frac{x}{2}-1\right]$

From Eq. (i),

$$I = I_1 + I_2$$

$$I = x\tan\frac{x}{2} - \int \tan\frac{x}{2}\,dx + \int \tan\frac{x}{2}\,dx \quad [1]$$

$$I = x\tan\frac{x}{2} + C \quad [1/2]$$

64. **Hint** $I = \int e^{-3x}\cos^3 x\,dx$

$$I = \int e^{-3x}\left[\frac{\cos 3x + 3\cos x}{4}\right]dx$$

$$= \frac{1}{4}\left[\int e^{-3x}\cos 3x\,dx + 3\int e^{-3x}\cos x\,dx\right]$$

Further, similar as Example 17.

$$\left[\textbf{Ans. } I = \frac{e^{-3x}}{24}[\sin 3x - \cos 3x] - \frac{9}{40}e^{-3x}\cos x + \frac{3}{40}e^{-3x}\sin x + C\right]$$

65. Let $I = \int e^{\tan^{-1}x}\left(\frac{1+x+x^2}{1+x^2}\right)dx$

$$= \int e^{\tan^{-1}x}\left(\frac{1+x^2}{1+x^2} + \frac{x}{1+x^2}\right)dx \quad [1]$$

$$= \int e^{\tan^{-1}x}dx + \int \frac{x\,e^{\tan^{-1}x}}{1+x^2}dx$$

$\Rightarrow \quad I = I_1 + I_2$ (say) [1]

Now, consider $I_2 = \int \frac{x\,e^{\tan^{-1}x}}{1+x^2}dx$

Now, put $\tan^{-1}x = t \Rightarrow x = \tan t$

and $\frac{1}{1+x^2}dx = dt$

$$\therefore \quad I_2 = \int \underset{\text{I}}{\tan t}\cdot \underset{\text{II}}{e^t}\,dt \quad [1]$$

$$= \tan t\int e^t\,dt - \int\left[\frac{d}{dt}(\tan t)\int e^t\,dt\right]dt$$

$$= \tan t\cdot e^t - \int \sec^2 t\cdot e^t\,dt + C \quad [1]$$

$$= \tan t\cdot e^t - \int (1+\tan^2 t)\,e^t\,dt + C$$

$$[\because \sec^2\theta = 1 + \tan^2\theta]$$

$$\Rightarrow \quad I_2 = \tan t\cdot e^t - \int (1+x^2)\frac{e^{\tan^{-1}x}}{1+x^2}dx + C \quad [1]$$

$$\Rightarrow \quad I_2 = x\,e^{\tan^{-1}x} - \int e^{\tan^{-1}x}dx + C \quad [\text{put } t = \tan^{-1}x]$$

$$\therefore \quad I = \int e^{\tan^{-1}x}dx + x\,e^{\tan^{-1}x} - \int e^{\tan^{-1}x}dx + C$$

$$= x\,e^{\tan^{-1}x} + C \quad [1]$$

66. Let $I = \int \frac{\sec x}{1+\operatorname{cosec} x}dx = \int \frac{\sin x}{\cos x(1+\sin x)}dx$

$$= \int \frac{\sin x}{\cos x(1+\sin x)} \times \frac{\cos x}{\cos x}dx \quad [1]$$

$$= \int \frac{\sin x\cos x}{\cos^2 x(1+\sin x)}dx$$

$$= \int \frac{\sin x\cos x}{(1-\sin^2 x)(1+\sin x)}dx$$

$$= \int \frac{\sin x\cos x}{(1+\sin x)^2(1-\sin x)}dx$$

Put $\sin x = t \Rightarrow \cos x\,dx = dt$

$$\therefore \quad I = \int \frac{t}{(1+t)^2(1-t)}dt \quad [1]$$

By using partial fraction, consider

$$\frac{t}{(1+t)^2(1-t)} = \frac{A}{(1+t)} + \frac{B}{(1+t)^2} + \frac{C}{(1-t)}$$

$$\Rightarrow \quad t = A(1+t)(1-t) + B(1-t) + C(1+t)^2$$

$$\Rightarrow \quad t = A(1-t^2) + B(1-t) + C(1+t^2+2t) \quad [1]$$

On equating the coefficient of t^2, t and constant, we get $0 = -A + C, 1 = -B + 2C$ and $0 = A + B + C$

On solving, we get

$$A = \frac{1}{4}, B = -\frac{1}{2} \text{ and } C = \frac{1}{4}$$

$$\therefore \quad \frac{t}{(1+t)^2(1-t)} = \frac{1}{4(1+t)} - \frac{1}{2(1+t)^2} + \frac{1}{4(1-t)} \quad [1]$$

$$\therefore \quad I = \int\left[\frac{1}{4(1+t)} - \frac{1}{2(1+t)^2} + \frac{1}{4(1-t)}\right]dt$$

$$= \frac{1}{4}\log|1+t| - \frac{1}{2}\frac{(1+t)^{-2+1}}{(-2+1)} - \frac{1}{4}\log|1-t| + C$$

$$= \frac{1}{4}\log|1+t| + \frac{1}{2(1+t)} - \frac{1}{4}\log|1-t| + C \quad [1]$$

$$= \frac{1}{4}\log\left|\frac{1+t}{1-t}\right| + \frac{1}{2(1+t)} + C$$

$$\left[\because \log m - \log n = \log\left(\frac{m}{n}\right)\right]$$

$$= \frac{1}{4}\log\left|\frac{1+\sin x}{1-\sin x}\right| + \frac{1}{2(1+\sin x)} + C$$

[put $t = \sin x$] [1]

TOPIC 03 Some Special Integrals

In this topic, we will discuss some important formulae and apply them to evaluate many integrals.

Integrals of the Type $\int \frac{dx}{x^2 \pm a^2}$, $\int \frac{dx}{a^2 - x^2}$, $\int \frac{dx}{\sqrt{x^2 \pm a^2}}$, $\int \frac{dx}{\sqrt{a^2 - x^2}}$

For any constant $a > 0$, we have the following results

(i) $\int \frac{dx}{x^2 - a^2} = \frac{1}{2a} \log \left| \frac{x-a}{x+a} \right| + C$

(ii) $\int \frac{dx}{a^2 - x^2} = \frac{1}{2a} \log \left| \frac{a+x}{a-x} \right| + C$

(iii) $\int \frac{dx}{x^2 + a^2} = \frac{1}{a} \tan^{-1} \frac{x}{a} + C$

(iv) $\int \frac{dx}{\sqrt{x^2 - a^2}} = \log |x + \sqrt{x^2 - a^2}| + C, |x| > a$

(v) $\int \frac{dx}{\sqrt{a^2 - x^2}} = \sin^{-1} \frac{x}{a} + C, |x| < a$

(vi) $\int \frac{dx}{\sqrt{x^2 + a^2}} = \log |x + \sqrt{x^2 + a^2}| + C$

Proof

(i) Let $I = \int \frac{dx}{x^2 - a^2}$

$$= \int \frac{1}{(x-a)(x+a)} \times \frac{2a}{2a} dx$$

[multiplying numerator and denominator by $2a$]

$$= \frac{1}{2a} \int \frac{(x+a)-(x-a)}{(x-a)(x+a)} dx$$

$$= \frac{1}{2a} \int \left[\frac{1}{(x-a)} - \frac{1}{(x+a)} \right] dx$$

$$= \frac{1}{2a} \left[\int \frac{1}{(x-a)} dx - \int \frac{1}{(x+a)} dx \right]$$

$$= \frac{1}{2a} [\log |x-a| - \log |x+a|] + C$$

$$= \frac{1}{2a} \log \left| \frac{x-a}{x+a} \right| + C$$

(ii) Similarly, we can prove second formula.

(iii) Now, put $x = a \tan \theta$ and $dx = a \sec^2 \theta \, d\theta$ in $\int \frac{dx}{x^2 + a^2}$, we get

$$\int \frac{dx}{x^2 + a^2} = \int \frac{a \sec^2 \theta}{a^2 \tan^2 \theta + a^2} d\theta$$

$$= \int \frac{a \sec^2 \theta}{a^2 (\sec^2 \theta)} d\theta \quad [\because \sec^2 \theta = \tan^2 \theta + 1]$$

$$= \frac{1}{a} \int d\theta = \frac{1}{a} \theta + C$$

$$\Rightarrow \quad \int \frac{dx}{x^2 + a^2} = \frac{1}{a} \tan^{-1} \frac{x}{a} + C$$

$$\left[\because x = a \tan \theta \Rightarrow \tan \theta = \frac{x}{a} \Rightarrow \theta = \tan^{-1} \frac{x}{a} \right]$$

Similarly, we can prove other formulae by using following substitutions

(iv) Put $x = a \sec \theta$

(v) Put $x = a \sin \theta$

(vi) Put $x = a \tan \theta$

Note (i) Before using the above formulae, make the coefficient of x^2 unity.

(ii) If we have integral of the form $\int \frac{dx}{(x \pm c)^2 \pm d^2}$ or $\int \frac{dx}{d^2 - (x \pm c)^2}$ or $\int \frac{dx}{\sqrt{(x \pm c)^2 \pm d^2}}$ or $\int \frac{dx}{\sqrt{d^2 - (x \pm c)^2}}$, then to evaluate it we can directly replace x by $x \pm c$ in the corresponding standard formulae.

e.g. $\int \frac{dx}{\sqrt{3^2 - (x+2)^2}} = \sin^{-1}\left(\frac{x+2}{3}\right) + C$

$$\left[\because \int \frac{dx}{\sqrt{a^2 - x^2}} = \sin^{-1}\left(\frac{x}{a}\right) + C \right]$$

Some Standard Substitutions which are Useful in Evaluating Integrals

Expression	Substitution
1. $a^2 - x^2$ or $\sqrt{a^2 - x^2}$	$x = a\sin\theta$ or $a\cos\theta$
2. $a^2 + x^2$ or $\sqrt{a^2 + x^2}$	$x = a\tan\theta$ or $a\cot\theta$
3. $x^2 - a^2$ or $\sqrt{x^2 - a^2}$	$x = a\sec\theta$ or $a\,\text{cosec}\,\theta$
4. $\sqrt{\frac{a+x}{a-x}}$ or $\sqrt{\frac{a-x}{a+x}}$	$x = a\cos 2\theta$
5. $\sqrt{\frac{x-\alpha}{\beta - x}}$ or $\sqrt{(x-\alpha)(\beta - x)}$	$x = \alpha\cos^2\theta + \beta\sin^2\theta$
6. $\sqrt{\frac{x-\alpha}{x-\beta}}$ or $\sqrt{(x-\alpha)(x-\beta)}$	$x = \alpha\sec^2\theta - \beta\tan^2\theta$ or $\alpha\,\text{cosec}^2\theta - \beta\cot^2\theta$
7. $\sqrt{\frac{x}{a-x}}$ or $\sqrt{\frac{a-x}{x}}$	$x = a\sin^2\theta$ or $x = a\cos^2\theta$
8. $\sqrt{\frac{x}{a+x}}$ or $\sqrt{\frac{a+x}{x}}$	$x = a\tan^2\theta$ or $x = a\cot^2\theta$

Example 1 Find the following integrals.

(i) $\int \frac{dx}{x^2 - 16}$ (ii) $\int \frac{dx}{\sqrt{9 - 25x^2}}$

Sol. (i) Let $I = \int \frac{dx}{x^2 - 16} = \int \frac{dx}{x^2 - 4^2}$

$$= \frac{1}{2(4)} \log\left|\frac{x-4}{x+4}\right| + C = \frac{1}{8}\log\left|\frac{x-4}{x+4}\right| + C$$

(ii) Let $I = \int \frac{dx}{\sqrt{9 - 25x^2}} = \int \frac{dx}{\sqrt{25\left(\frac{9}{25} - x^2\right)}}$

$$= \frac{1}{5}\int \frac{dx}{\sqrt{\left(\frac{3}{5}\right)^2 - x^2}} = \frac{1}{5}\sin^{-1}\left(\frac{x}{(3/5)}\right) + C$$

$$= \frac{1}{5}\sin^{-1}\left(\frac{5x}{3}\right) + C$$

Integral of the Type $\int \frac{dx}{ax^2 + bx + c}$

To evaluate this type of integrals, we proceed as follows

I. Firstly, take a common from denominator to make coefficient of x^2 unity, i.e. $I = \int \frac{dx}{a\left(x^2 + \frac{b}{a}x + \frac{c}{a}\right)}$

II. Add and subtract $(b/2a)^2$ in denominator and try to write denominator in the form $X^2 \pm k^2$ or $k^2 - X^2$

where, $X^2 = \left(x \pm \frac{b}{2a}\right)^2$ and $k^2 = \left(\frac{c}{a} \mp \frac{b^2}{4a^2}\right)$.

III. Substitute $x \pm \frac{b}{2a} = t$ and reduce the integral obtained in step II into one of the form $\frac{1}{a}\int \frac{dt}{t^2 \pm k^2}$ or $\frac{1}{a}\int \frac{dt}{k^2 - t^2}$.

Example 2 Evaluate $\int \frac{1}{9x^2 + 6x + 5}\,dx$.

Sol. Let $I = \int \frac{1}{9x^2 + 6x + 5}\,dx = \frac{1}{9}\int \frac{1}{x^2 + \frac{2}{3}x + \frac{5}{9}}\,dx$

[take 9 common from denominator]

$$= \frac{1}{9}\int \frac{1}{x^2 + 2\cdot\frac{1}{3}\cdot x + \left(\frac{1}{3}\right)^2 + \frac{5}{9} - \left(\frac{1}{3}\right)^2}\,dx$$

[here $a = 9$ and $b = 6$, adding and subtracting $\left(\frac{b}{2a}\right)^2 = \left(\frac{6}{2\times 9}\right)^2 = \left(\frac{1}{3}\right)^2$ from denominator]

$$= \frac{1}{9}\int \frac{1}{x^2 + \frac{2}{3}x + \left(\frac{1}{3}\right)^2 + \frac{5}{9} - \frac{1}{9}}\,dx$$

$$= \frac{1}{9}\int \frac{1}{\left(x + \frac{1}{3}\right)^2 + \left(\frac{2}{3}\right)^2}\,dx$$

$$= \frac{1}{9}\left(\frac{1}{2/3}\right)\tan^{-1}\left(\frac{x + 1/3}{2/3}\right) + C$$

$\left[\because \int \frac{dx}{a^2 + x^2} = \frac{1}{a}\tan^{-1}\left(\frac{x}{a}\right)\right]$

$$= \frac{1}{6}\tan^{-1}\left(\frac{3x+1}{2}\right) + C$$

Integral of the Type $\int \frac{dx}{\sqrt{ax^2 + bx + c}}$

To evaluate such integrals, we do same steps as previous integral. The only difference is that, here reduced integral (obtained after step II) will be of the form $\frac{1}{a}\int \frac{dt}{\sqrt{t^2 \pm k^2}}$ or $\frac{1}{a}\int \frac{dt}{\sqrt{k^2 - t^2}}$, which can be integrated by using suitable formulae.

Example 3 Evaluate $\int \frac{dx}{\sqrt{3-x+x^2}}$.

Sol. Let $I = \int \frac{dx}{\sqrt{3-x+x^2}} = \int \frac{dx}{\sqrt{x^2-x+3}}$

$$= \int \frac{dx}{\sqrt{x^2 - 2\times x \times \frac{1}{2} + \left(\frac{1}{2}\right)^2 - \left(\frac{1}{2}\right)^2 + 3}}$$

$\left[\text{here } a=1, b=-1, \text{ adding and subtracting } \left(\frac{b}{2a}\right)^2 = \left(\frac{-1}{2}\right)^2 = \left(\frac{1}{2}\right)^2 \text{ from denominator}\right]$

$$= \int \frac{dx}{\sqrt{\left(x-\frac{1}{2}\right)^2 + 3 - \frac{1}{4}}}$$

$$= \int \frac{dx}{\sqrt{\left(x-\frac{1}{2}\right)^2 + \frac{11}{4}}}$$

Now, put $x - \frac{1}{2} = t \Rightarrow dx = dt$

$$\therefore\ I = \int \frac{dt}{\sqrt{t^2 + \left(\frac{\sqrt{11}}{2}\right)^2}} = \log\left|t + \sqrt{t^2 + \left(\frac{\sqrt{11}}{2}\right)^2}\right| + C$$

$\left[\because \int \frac{dx}{\sqrt{x^2+a^2}} = \log|x + \sqrt{x^2+a^2}|\right]$

$$= \log\left|\left(x-\frac{1}{2}\right) + \sqrt{\left(x-\frac{1}{2}\right)^2 + \left(\frac{\sqrt{11}}{2}\right)^2}\right| + C \quad \left[\because t = x - \frac{1}{2}\right]$$

Hence, $I = \log\left|\left(x-\frac{1}{2}\right) + \sqrt{3-x+x^2}\right| + C.$

Example 4 Evaluate $\int \frac{e^x}{\sqrt{5-4e^x-e^{2x}}}\,dx.$

Sol. Let $I = \int \frac{e^x}{\sqrt{5-4e^x-e^{2x}}}\,dx$

Now, put $e^x = t \Rightarrow e^x dx = dt$

$$\therefore\ I = \int \frac{dt}{\sqrt{5-4t-t^2}} = \int \frac{dt}{\sqrt{-(t^2+4t-5)}}$$

$$= \int \frac{dt}{\sqrt{-[(t+2)^2-5-4]}}$$

$\left[\text{adding and subtracting } \left(\frac{b}{2a}\right)^2 = \left(\frac{4}{2\times 1}\right)^2 = (2)^2 \text{ from denominator}\right]$

$$= \int \frac{dt}{\sqrt{9-(t+2)^2}} = \int \frac{dt}{\sqrt{(3)^2-(t+2)^2}}$$

$$= \sin^{-1}\left(\frac{t+2}{3}\right) + C \qquad \left[\because \int \frac{dx}{\sqrt{a^2-x^2}} = \sin^{-1}\frac{x}{a}\right]$$

$$= \sin^{-1}\left(\frac{e^x+2}{3}\right) + C \qquad [\because t = e^x]$$

Integrals of the Type $\int \frac{px+q}{ax^2+bx+c}\,dx$ and $\int \frac{px+q}{\sqrt{ax^2+bx+c}}\,dx$

To evaluate such integrals, we firstly write the numerator as

$$px + q = A\left\{\frac{d}{dx}(ax^2+bx+c)\right\} + B = A(2ax+b) + B$$

Then, find A and B by comparing the coefficients of like powers of x from both sides. Now, put the resultant value of $(px+q)$ in given integral and then given integral is reduced to one of the known forms which can be integrate easily.

Example 5 Evaluate $\int \frac{x+7}{x^2+4x+7}\,dx.$ **[ISC 2024]**

Sol. Let $I = \int \frac{x+7}{x^2+4x+7}\,dx$

Let us assume that

$$x + 7 = A\frac{d}{dx}(x^2+4x+7) + B = A(2x+4) + B$$

On comparing the coefficients of x and constant terms both sides, we get

$$2A = 1 \Rightarrow A = \frac{1}{2}$$

and $4A + B = 7$

$\Rightarrow \quad B = 5$

So, $x + 7 = \frac{1}{2}(2x+4) + 5$

$$\therefore\ I = \int \frac{\frac{1}{2}(2x+4)+5}{x^2+4x+7}\,dx$$

$$= \frac{1}{2}\int \frac{2x+4}{x^2+4x+7}\,dx + 5\int \frac{1}{x^2+4x+7}\,dx$$

$$= \frac{1}{2}\ln|x^2+4x+7| + 5\int \frac{1}{(x+2)^2+3}\,dx$$

$$= \frac{1}{2}\ln|x^2+4x+7| + \frac{5}{\sqrt{3}}\tan^{-1}\left(\frac{x+2}{\sqrt{3}}\right) + C$$

Hence, $\int \frac{x+7}{x^2+4x+7}dx$

$= \frac{1}{2}\ln|x^2+4x+7| + \frac{5}{\sqrt{3}}\tan^{-1}\left(\frac{x+2}{\sqrt{3}}\right) + C$

where, C is an integrating constant.

Example 6 Evaluate $\int \frac{x+3}{\sqrt{5-4x-2x^2}}dx$.

Sol. Let $x+3 = A\frac{d}{dx}(5-4x-2x^2) + B$

$\Rightarrow \quad x+3 = A(-4-4x) + B$ ...(i)

$\Rightarrow \quad x+3 = -4A - 4Ax + B$

$\Rightarrow \quad x+3 = -4Ax + (B-4A)$

On equating the coefficient of x and constant term from both sides, we get $1 = -4A$ and $3 = B - 4A$

$\Rightarrow \quad A = -\frac{1}{4}$ and $B = 3 + 4\times\left(-\frac{1}{4}\right)$

$\Rightarrow \quad A = -\frac{1}{4}$ and $B = 2$

$\therefore$ From Eq. (i), we get $(x+3) = -\frac{1}{4}(-4-4x) + 2$

Now, the given integral can be written as

$$I = \int \frac{x+3}{\sqrt{5-4x-2x^2}}dx = \int \frac{-\frac{1}{4}(-4-4x)+2}{\sqrt{5-4x-2x^2}}dx$$

$$= -\frac{1}{4}\int \frac{(-4-4x)}{\sqrt{5-4x-2x^2}}dx + 2\int \frac{dx}{\sqrt{5-4x-2x^2}}$$

$$= -\frac{1}{4}I_1 + 2I_2 \text{ (say)} \quad \text{...(ii)}$$

where, $I_1 = \int \frac{(-4-4x)}{\sqrt{5-4x-2x^2}}dx$, $I_2 = \int \frac{dx}{\sqrt{5-4x-2x^2}}$

Consider $I_1 = \int \frac{(-4-4x)}{\sqrt{5-4x-2x^2}}dx$

Now, put $5-4x-2x^2 = t \Rightarrow (-4-4x)\,dx = dt$

$$\therefore \quad I_1 = \int \frac{dt}{\sqrt{t}} = \int t^{-\frac{1}{2}}dt = 2\sqrt{t} + C_1$$

$$= 2\sqrt{5-4x-2x^2} + C_1 \quad [\because t = 5-4x-2x^2]$$

and $I_2 = \int \frac{dx}{\sqrt{5-4x-2x^2}}$

$$= \int \frac{dx}{\sqrt{(-2)\left(x^2+2x-\frac{5}{2}\right)}}$$

$$= \frac{1}{\sqrt{2}}\int \frac{dx}{\sqrt{-\left(x^2+2\cdot x\cdot 1+1^2-1^2-\frac{5}{2}\right)}}$$

[adding and subtracting $(1)^2$ from denominator]

$$= \frac{1}{\sqrt{2}}\int \frac{dx}{\sqrt{-\left[(x+1)^2-\left(\sqrt{\frac{7}{2}}\right)^2\right]}}$$

$$= \frac{1}{\sqrt{2}}\int \frac{dx}{\sqrt{\left(\sqrt{\frac{7}{2}}\right)^2-(x+1)^2}}$$

$$= \frac{1}{\sqrt{2}}\sin^{-1}\left(\frac{x+1}{\sqrt{7/2}}\right) + C_2 \quad \left[\because \int \frac{dx}{\sqrt{a^2-x^2}} = \sin^{-1}\left(\frac{x}{a}\right)\right]$$

$$= \frac{1}{\sqrt{2}}\sin^{-1}\left[\frac{\sqrt{2}(x+1)}{\sqrt{7}}\right] + C_2$$

Now, putting the values of I_1 and I_2 in Eq. (ii), we get

$$I = -\frac{1}{4}\times 2\sqrt{5-4x-2x^2} - \frac{1}{4}C_1 + 2\cdot\frac{1}{\sqrt{2}}\sin^{-1}\left[\frac{\sqrt{2}(x+1)}{\sqrt{7}}\right] + 2C_2$$

$$= -\frac{1}{2}\sqrt{5-4x-2x^2} + \sqrt{2}\sin^{-1}\left[\frac{\sqrt{2}(x+1)}{\sqrt{7}}\right] + C$$

where, $C = -\frac{1}{4}C_1 + 2C_2$

Integrals of the Type $\int\sqrt{a^2 \pm x^2}\,dx$ and $\int\sqrt{x^2-a^2}\,dx$

For any constant $a > 0$, we have the following results

(i) $\int\sqrt{x^2-a^2}\,dx = \frac{x}{2}\sqrt{x^2-a^2} - \frac{a^2}{2}\log|x+\sqrt{x^2-a^2}| + C$

(ii) $\int\sqrt{x^2+a^2}\,dx = \frac{x}{2}\sqrt{x^2+a^2} + \frac{a^2}{2}\log|x+\sqrt{x^2+a^2}| + C$

(iii) $\int\sqrt{a^2-x^2}\,dx = \frac{x}{2}\sqrt{a^2-x^2} + \frac{a^2}{2}\sin^{-1}\frac{x}{a} + C$

Proof

(i) Let $I = \int \underset{\text{I}}{\sqrt{x^2-a^2}} \times \underset{\text{II}}{1}\,dx$ ...(i)

$$= \sqrt{x^2-a^2}\int 1dx - \int\left[\frac{d}{dx}(\sqrt{x^2-a^2})\int 1\,dx\right]dx$$

$$\left[\because \int \underset{\text{I}}{u}\cdot\underset{\text{II}}{v}\,dx = u\int v dx - \int\left(\frac{d}{dx}(u)\int v dx\right)dx\right]$$

$$= \sqrt{x^2 - a^2} \times x - \int \left[\frac{1}{2\sqrt{x^2 - a^2}} \times 2x \right] x\, dx$$

$$= x\sqrt{x^2 - a^2} - \int \frac{x^2}{\sqrt{x^2 - a^2}}\, dx$$

$$= x\sqrt{x^2 - a^2} - \int \frac{x^2 - a^2 + a^2}{\sqrt{x^2 - a^2}}\, dx$$

[adding and subtracting a^2]

$$= x\sqrt{x^2 - a^2} - \int \sqrt{x^2 - a^2}\, dx - \int \frac{a^2\, dx}{\sqrt{x^2 - a^2}}$$

$$\Rightarrow \quad I = x\sqrt{x^2 - a^2} - I - a^2 \int \frac{1\, dx}{\sqrt{x^2 - a^2}}$$

$$\Rightarrow 2I = x\sqrt{x^2 - a^2} - a^2 [\log |x + \sqrt{x^2 - a^2}|]$$

$$\left[\because \int \frac{1}{\sqrt{x^2 - a^2}}\, dx = \log |x + \sqrt{x^2 - a^2}| \right]$$

$$\Rightarrow \quad I = \frac{x}{2}\sqrt{x^2 - a^2} - \frac{a^2}{2} [\log |x + \sqrt{x^2 - a^2}|] + C$$

Similarly, we can prove other formulae given (ii) and (iii).

Note Given formulae also hold good when x is replaced by $x + c$, where c is a constant.

Example 7 Integrate the following functions.

(i) $\sqrt{1 - 4x^2}$ (ii) $\sqrt{1 + \frac{x^2}{9}}$

Sol. (i) Let $I = \int \sqrt{1 - 4x^2}\, dx = \int \sqrt{4\left(\frac{1}{4} - x^2\right)}\, dx$

$$= \int 2\sqrt{\left(\frac{1}{2}\right)^2 - x^2}\, dx = 2\int \sqrt{\left(\frac{1}{2}\right)^2 - x^2}\, dx$$

$$= 2\left[\frac{x}{2}\sqrt{\left(\frac{1}{2}\right)^2 - x^2} + \frac{\left(\frac{1}{2}\right)^2}{2} \sin^{-1}\left(\frac{x}{\left(\frac{1}{2}\right)}\right) \right] + C$$

$$\left[\because \int \sqrt{a^2 - x^2} = \frac{x}{2}\sqrt{a^2 - x^2} + \frac{a^2}{2}\sin^{-1}\left(\frac{x}{a}\right) + C \right]$$

$$= x\sqrt{\frac{1}{4} - x^2} + \frac{1}{4}\sin^{-1}(2x) + C$$

$$= \frac{x}{2}\sqrt{1 - 4x^2} + \frac{1}{4}\sin^{-1}(2x) + C$$

(ii) Let $I = \int \sqrt{1 + \frac{x^2}{9}}\, dx = \int \frac{\sqrt{9 + x^2}}{3}\, dx$

$$= \frac{1}{3}\int \sqrt{3^2 + x^2}\, dx$$

$$= \frac{1}{3}\left[\frac{x}{2}\sqrt{3^2 + x^2} + \frac{3^2}{2}\log |x + \sqrt{3^2 + x^2}| \right] + C$$

$$\left[\because \int \sqrt{a^2 + x^2} = \frac{x}{2}\sqrt{a^2 + x^2} + \frac{a^2}{2}\log |x + \sqrt{x^2 + a^2}| + C \right]$$

$$= \frac{x}{6}\sqrt{9 + x^2} + \frac{3}{2}\log |x + \sqrt{9 + x^2}| + C$$

Integral of the Type $\int \sqrt{ax^2 + bx + c}\, dx$

To evaluate this type of integral we proceed as follows

I. Firstly, take a common from integrand to make coefficient of x^2 unity,

i.e. $I = \int \sqrt{a\left(x^2 + \frac{b}{a}x + \frac{c}{a}\right)}\, dx$

II. Add and subtract $\left(\frac{b}{2a}\right)^2$ from integrand inside the square root and convert it in the form $\sqrt{X^2 \pm k^2}$ or $\sqrt{k^2 - X^2}$, where $X^2 = \left(x \pm \frac{b}{2a}\right)^2$ and $k^2 = \left(\frac{c}{a} \mp \frac{b^2}{4a^2}\right)$.

III. Substitute $x \pm \frac{b}{2a} = t$ and reduce the integral obtained from Step II into one of the form

$$\int \sqrt{t^2 \pm k^2}\, dt$$

or $$\int \sqrt{k^2 - t^2}\, dt$$

Then, apply suitable formula to integrate.

Example 8 Evaluate $\int \sqrt{x^2 - 8x + 7}\, dx$.

Sol. Let $I = \int \sqrt{x^2 - 8x + 7}\, dx$

Here, the coefficient of x^2 is unity.

$\therefore \quad I = \int \sqrt{x^2 - 8x + 7}\, dx$

$$= \int \sqrt{x^2 - 8x + 7 + 4^2 - (4)^2}\, dx$$

[here $a = 1$ and $b = -8$, adding and subtracting $\left(\frac{b}{2a}\right)^2 = \left(\frac{-8}{2}\right)^2 = (4)^2$, under the square root]

$$= \int \sqrt{(x-4)^2 + 7 - 16}\, dx$$
$$= \int \sqrt{(x-4)^2 - (3)^2}\, dx$$

Now, put $x - 4 = t \Rightarrow dx = dt$

$$\therefore \quad I = \int \sqrt{t^2 - 3^2}\, dt$$
$$= \frac{t}{2}\sqrt{t^2 - 3^2} - \frac{(3)^2}{2} \log\left|t + \sqrt{t^2 - 3^2}\right| + C$$
$$\left[\because \int \sqrt{x^2 - a^2}\, dx = \frac{x}{2}\sqrt{x^2 - a^2} - \frac{a^2}{2}\log|x + \sqrt{x^2 - a^2}|\right]$$
$$= \frac{(x-4)}{2}\sqrt{(x-4)^2 - (3)^2} - \frac{(3)^2}{2}\log|x - 4 + \sqrt{(x-4)^2 - (3)^2}| + C$$
$$= \frac{x-4}{2}\sqrt{x^2 - 8x + 7} - \frac{9}{2}\log|(x-4) + \sqrt{x^2 - 8x + 7}| + C$$

Example 9 Evaluate $\int \sqrt{x^2 + 4x + 6}\, dx$.

Sol. Let $I = \int \sqrt{x^2 + 4x + 6}\, dx$

$$= \int \sqrt{x^2 + 4x + 2^2 + 6 - 4}\, dx$$
$$= \int \sqrt{(x+2)^2 + (\sqrt{2})^2}\, dx$$
$$= \frac{(x+2)}{2}\sqrt{x^2 + 4x + 6} + \frac{2}{2}\log|(x+2) + \sqrt{x^2 + 4x + 6}| + C$$
$$\left[\because \int \sqrt{x^2 + a^2}\, dx = \frac{x}{2}\sqrt{x^2 + a^2} + \frac{a^2}{2}\log|x + \sqrt{x^2 + a^2}|\right]$$
$$\Rightarrow I = \frac{x+2}{2}\sqrt{x^2 + 4x + 6} + \log|(x+2) + \sqrt{x^2 + 4x + 6}| + C$$

Example 10 Evaluate $\int \sqrt{1 + 3x - x^2}\, dx$. **[NCERT]**

Sol. Let $I = \int \sqrt{1 + 3x - x^2}\, dx = \int \sqrt{-(x^2 - 3x - 1)}\, dx$

$$= \int \sqrt{-\left(x^2 - 3x + \left(\frac{3}{2}\right)^2 - \left(\frac{3}{2}\right)^2 - 1\right)}\, dx$$
$$\left[\text{adding and subtracting } \left(\frac{b}{2a}\right)^2 = \left(\frac{3}{2}\right)^2\right]$$
$$= \int \sqrt{-\left\{\left(x - \frac{3}{2}\right)^2 - \frac{9}{4} - 1\right\}}\, dx$$
$$= \int \sqrt{-\left\{\left(x - \frac{3}{2}\right)^2 - \left(\frac{9+4}{4}\right)\right\}}\, dx$$
$$= \int \sqrt{-\left\{\left(x - \frac{3}{2}\right)^2 - \frac{13}{4}\right\}}\, dx$$
$$= \int \sqrt{\left(\frac{\sqrt{13}}{2}\right)^2 - \left(x - \frac{3}{2}\right)^2}\, dx$$
$$= \frac{\left(x - \frac{3}{2}\right)}{2}\sqrt{1 + 3x - x^2} + \frac{13}{4 \times 2}\sin^{-1}\left\{\frac{\left(x - \frac{3}{2}\right)}{\frac{\sqrt{13}}{2}}\right\} + C$$
$$\left[\because \int \sqrt{a^2 - x^2}\, dx = \frac{x}{2}\sqrt{a^2 - x^2} + \frac{a^2}{2}\sin^{-1}\frac{x}{a} + C\right]$$
$$= \frac{2x - 3}{4}\sqrt{1 + 3x - x^2} + \frac{13}{8}\sin^{-1}\left(\frac{2x - 3}{\sqrt{13}}\right) + C$$

Integral of the Type $\int (px + q)\sqrt{ax^2 + bx + c}\, dx$

To evaluate such integrals, we firstly write $(px + q)$ as

$$px + q = A\frac{d}{dx}(ax^2 + bx + c) + B = A(2ax + b) + B.$$

Then, find A and B by comparing the coefficient of like powers of x from both sides. Now, put this value of $(px + q)$ in the given integral and then given integral is reduce to one of the known forms which can be integrate easily.

Example 11 Evaluate $\int (x - 3)\sqrt{x^2 + 3x - 18}\, dx$.

Sol. Let $I = \int (x - 3)\sqrt{x^2 + 3x - 18}\, dx$

Now, let $x - 3 = A\frac{d}{dx}(x^2 + 3x - 18) + B$

$$\Rightarrow \quad x - 3 = A(2x + 3) + B$$

On equating the coefficients of x and constant term from both sides, we get

$$2A = 1 \text{ and } 3A + B = -3 \Rightarrow A = \frac{1}{2}$$

and $3 \times \frac{1}{2} + B = -3 \Rightarrow B = -\frac{9}{2}$

Thus, the given integral reduces in the following form

$$I = \int \left\{\frac{1}{2}(2x + 3) - \frac{9}{2}\right\}\sqrt{x^2 + 3x - 18}\, dx$$
$$\Rightarrow \quad I = \frac{1}{2}\int (2x + 3)\sqrt{x^2 + 3x - 18}\, dx - \frac{9}{2}\int \sqrt{x^2 + 3x - 18}\, dx$$
$$= \frac{1}{2}I_1 - \frac{9}{2}I_2 \text{ (say)} \quad \text{...(i)}$$

where, $I_1 = \int (2x + 3)\sqrt{x^2 + 3x - 18}\, dx$

Now, put $x^2+3x-18=t$

$\Rightarrow \quad (2x+3)\,dx = dt$

$$\therefore \quad I_1 = \int t^{1/2}\,dt = \frac{2}{3}t^{3/2} + C_1$$

$$= \frac{2}{3}(x^2+3x-18)^{3/2} + C_1 \quad [\because t = x^2+3x-18]$$

and $I_2 = \int \sqrt{x^2+3x-18}\,dx$

$$= \int \sqrt{\left(x+\frac{3}{2}\right)^2 - \frac{81}{4}}\,dx$$

$$= \int \sqrt{\left(x+\frac{3}{2}\right)^2 - \left(\frac{9}{2}\right)^2}\,dx$$

$$= \frac{\left(x+\frac{3}{2}\right)}{2}\sqrt{x^2+3x-18} - \frac{81}{8}\log\left|\left(x+\frac{3}{2}\right)+\sqrt{x^2+3x-18}\right| + C_2$$

$$\left[\because \int \sqrt{x^2-a^2}\,dx = \frac{x}{2}\sqrt{x^2-a^2} - \frac{a^2}{2}\log|x+\sqrt{x^2-a^2}|\right]$$

$$= \frac{2x+3}{4}\sqrt{x^2+3x-18} - \frac{81}{8}\log\left|\frac{2x+3}{2}+\sqrt{x^2+3x-18}\right| + C_2$$

On putting the values of I_1 and I_2 in Eq. (i), we get

$$I = \frac{1}{2}\left[\frac{2}{3}(x^2+3x-18)^{3/2} + C_1\right] - \frac{9}{2}\left[\frac{2x+3}{4}\sqrt{x^2+3x-18} - \frac{81}{8}\log\left|\frac{2x+3}{2}+\sqrt{x^2+3x-18}\right| + C_2\right]$$

$$\Rightarrow I = \frac{1}{3}(x^2+3x-18)^{3/2} - \frac{9}{8}(2x+3)\sqrt{x^2+3x-18} + \frac{729}{16}\log\left|\frac{2x+3}{2}+\sqrt{x^2+3x-18}\right| + C,$$

where, $C = \dfrac{C_1}{2} - \dfrac{9C_2}{2}$

Example 12 Evaluate $\int (3-2x)\sqrt{2+x-x^2}\,dx$.

Sol. Let $I = \int (3-2x)\cdot\sqrt{2+x-x^2}\,dx$ ...(i)

Put $(3-2x) = A\dfrac{d}{dx}(2+x-x^2) + B$

$\Rightarrow \quad 3-2x = A(1-2x) + B$ ...(ii)

$\Rightarrow \quad 3-2x = (A+B) - 2Ax$

On comparing the coefficient of x and constant term, we get

$$-2A = -2$$

$\Rightarrow \quad A = 1$

and $\quad A+B = 3$

$\Rightarrow \quad B = 3-1 = 2$

Now, Eq. (ii) becomes $(3-2x) = (1-2x)+2$

On putting $3-2x = (1-2x)+2$ in Eq. (i), we get

$$I = \int (1-2x)\sqrt{2+x-x^2}\,dx + 2\int\sqrt{2+x-x^2}\,dx$$

$$= I_1 + I_2 \text{ (say)} \quad ...(iii)$$

Now, consider $I_1 = \int (1-2x)\sqrt{2+x-x^2}\,dx$

Put $2+x-x^2 = t \Rightarrow (1-2x)dx = dt$

$$\therefore\ I_1 = \int\sqrt{t}\,dt = \frac{2}{3}(t)^{3/2} + C_1 = \frac{2}{3}(2+x-x^2)^{3/2} + C_1 \quad ...(iv)$$

and $I_2 = 2\int\sqrt{2+x-x^2}\,dx$

$$= 2\int\sqrt{-(x^2-x-2)}\,dx$$

$$= 2\int\sqrt{-\left[x^2 - 2\cdot\frac{1}{2}x + \left(\frac{1}{2}\right)^2 - \left(\frac{1}{2}\right)^2 - 2\right]}\,dx$$

$$= 2\int\sqrt{-\left[\left(x-\frac{1}{2}\right)^2 - \frac{9}{4}\right]}\,dx$$

$$= 2\int\sqrt{\left(\frac{3}{2}\right)^2 - \left(x-\frac{1}{2}\right)^2}\,dx$$

$$= 2\times\frac{1}{2}\left[\left(x-\frac{1}{2}\right)\sqrt{\left(\frac{3}{2}\right)^2 - \left(x-\frac{1}{2}\right)^2} + \left(\frac{3}{2}\right)^2\sin^{-1}\left(\frac{x-\frac{1}{2}}{3/2}\right)\right] + C_2$$

$$\left[\because \int\sqrt{a^2-x^2}\,dx = \frac{1}{2}\left[x\sqrt{a^2-x^2} + a^2\sin^{-1}\left(\frac{x}{a}\right)\right] + C\right]$$

$$\Rightarrow I_2 = \frac{(2x-1)}{2}\sqrt{2+x-x^2} + \frac{9}{4}\sin^{-1}\left(\frac{2x-1}{3}\right) + C_2 \quad ...(v)$$

From Eqs. (iii), (iv) and (v), we get

$$I = \frac{2}{3}(2+x-x^2)^{3/2} + \frac{(2x-1)}{2}\sqrt{2+x-x^2} + \frac{9}{4}\sin^{-1}\left(\frac{2x-1}{3}\right) + C$$

where, $C = C_1 + C_2$

Integral of the Types $\int \frac{dx}{a\sin x + b\cos x}$, $\int \frac{dx}{a + b\sin x}$, $\int \frac{dx}{a + b\cos x}$ and $\int \frac{dx}{a\sin x + b\cos x + c}$

To evaluate these type of integrals we proceed as follows

Step I Put $\sin x = \frac{2\tan\frac{x}{2}}{1+\tan^2\frac{x}{2}}$ and $\cos x = \frac{1-\tan^2\frac{x}{2}}{1+\tan^2\frac{x}{2}}$ and simplify.

Step II Replace $1+\tan^2\frac{x}{2}$ in the numerator by $\sec^2\frac{x}{2}$.

Step III Put $\tan\frac{x}{2} = t$, so that $\frac{1}{2}\sec^2\frac{x}{2}dx = dt$.

Step IV Evaluate the integral obtained in step III by using methods discussed earlier.

Note To evaluate the integral $\int \frac{dx}{a\sin x + b\cos x}$, we may also proceed as follows

Step I Put $a = r\cos\theta$ and $b = r\sin\theta$, where $r = \sqrt{a^2+b^2}$ and $\theta = \tan^{-1}\left(\frac{b}{a}\right)$. This will reduce the given integral to $\frac{1}{r}\int \frac{dx}{\sin(x+\theta)}$.

Step II Evaluate the integral and then substitute the value of r and θ.

Example 13 Evaluate $\int \frac{dx}{1-3\sin x}$.

Use the substitution $\sin x = \frac{2\tan\frac{x}{2}}{1+\tan^2\frac{x}{2}}$, further put $\tan\frac{x}{2} = t$ and then integrate it.

Sol. Let $I = \int \frac{dx}{1-3\sin x}$

$$= \int \frac{dx}{1-3\left(\frac{2\tan\frac{x}{2}}{1+\tan^2\frac{x}{2}}\right)} \qquad \left[\because \sin x = \frac{2\tan\frac{x}{2}}{1+\tan^2\frac{x}{2}}\right]$$

$$= \int \frac{\left(1+\tan^2\frac{x}{2}\right)}{\left(\tan^2\frac{x}{2} - 6\tan\frac{x}{2} + 1\right)}dx$$

$$= \int \frac{\sec^2\frac{x}{2}}{\tan^2\frac{x}{2} - 6\tan\frac{x}{2} + 1}dx$$

$$\left[\because \sec^2\frac{x}{2} - \tan^2\frac{x}{2} = 1 \Rightarrow \sec^2\frac{x}{2} = 1 + \tan^2\frac{x}{2}\right]$$

Now, put $\tan\frac{x}{2} = t$

$$\Rightarrow \sec^2\frac{x}{2}\cdot\frac{1}{2}dx = dt \Rightarrow \sec^2\frac{x}{2}dx = 2dt$$

$$\therefore \quad I = \int \frac{2dt}{t^2 - 6t + 1} = 2\int \frac{dt}{t^2 - 6t + 9 + 1 - 9}$$

$$\left[\text{adding and subtracting } \left(\frac{b}{2a}\right)^2 = \left(\frac{-6}{2}\right)^2 = 9 \text{ in denominator}\right]$$

$$= 2\int \frac{dt}{(t-3)^2 - 8} = 2\int \frac{dt}{(t-3)^2 - (2\sqrt{2})^2}$$

$$= \frac{2\times 1}{2\times 2\sqrt{2}}\log\left|\frac{t-3-2\sqrt{2}}{t-3+2\sqrt{2}}\right| + C$$

$$\left[\because \int \frac{dx}{x^2-a^2} = \frac{1}{2a}\log\left|\frac{x-a}{x+a}\right|\right]$$

$$= \frac{1}{2\sqrt{2}}\log\left|\frac{\tan\frac{x}{2} - 3 - 2\sqrt{2}}{\tan\frac{x}{2} - 3 + 2\sqrt{2}}\right| + C \qquad \left[\because \tan\frac{x}{2} = t\right]$$

Example 14 Evaluate $\int \frac{dx}{\sqrt{3}\sin x + \cos x}$.

Sol. Let $I = \int \frac{dx}{\sqrt{3}\sin x + \cos x}$

Now, put $\sqrt{3} = r\cos\theta$ and $1 = r\sin\theta$.

Then, $r = \sqrt{(\sqrt{3})^2 + 1^2} = \sqrt{3+1} = 2$

and $\theta = \tan^{-1}\left(\frac{1}{\sqrt{3}}\right) = \frac{\pi}{6}$

$\left[\because \text{integral of type } \int \frac{dx}{a\sin x + b\cos x}\text{, put } a = r\cos\theta \text{ and } b = r\sin\theta\text{, where } r = \sqrt{a^2+b^2} \text{ and } \theta = \tan^{-1}\left(\frac{b}{a}\right)\right]$

$$\therefore \quad I = \int \frac{dx}{r\cos\theta\sin x + r\sin\theta\cos x}$$

$$= \frac{1}{r}\int \frac{dx}{\sin(x+\theta)} = \frac{1}{2}\int \operatorname{cosec}(x+\theta)\,dx \qquad [\because r = 2]$$

$$= \frac{1}{2}\log\left|\operatorname{cosec}(x+\theta) - \cot(x+\theta)\right| + C$$

$$= \frac{1}{2}\log\left|\frac{1-\cos(x+\theta)}{\sin(x+\theta)}\right| + C$$

$$= \frac{1}{2}\log\left|\frac{2\sin^2\left(\frac{x+\theta}{2}\right)}{2\sin\left(\frac{x+\theta}{2}\right)\cos\left(\frac{x+\theta}{2}\right)}\right| + C$$

$$\left[\because 1-\cos\theta = 2\sin^2\frac{\theta}{2} \text{ and } \sin\theta = 2\sin\frac{\theta}{2}\cos\frac{\theta}{2}\right]$$

$$= \frac{1}{2}\log\left|\tan\left(\frac{x+\theta}{2}\right)\right| + C$$

$$= \frac{1}{2}\log\left|\tan\left(\frac{x}{2}+\frac{\pi}{12}\right)\right| + C \qquad \left[\because \theta = \frac{\pi}{6}\right]$$

Integrals of the Type

$$\int\frac{dx}{a\sin^2 x + b\cos^2 x}, \int\frac{dx}{a+b\sin^2 x}, \int\frac{dx}{a+b\cos^2 x}, \int\frac{dx}{(a\sin x + b\cos x)^2}, \int\frac{dx}{a\cos^2 x + b\sin^2 x + c}$$

To evaluate these type of integrals, we proceed as follows

***Step* I** Divide numerator and denominator by $\cos^2 x$.

***Step* II** Replace $\sec^2 x$, if any in denominator by $1+\tan^2 x$.

***Step* III** Put $\tan x = t$ so that $\sec^2 x\, dx = dt$.

***Step* IV** Evaluate the integral obtained in Step III by using the methods discussed earlier.

Example 15 Evaluate $\int\frac{dx}{3+2\cos^2 x}$.

Sol. Let $I = \int\frac{dx}{3+2\cos^2 x}$

On dividing numerator and denominator by $\cos^2 x$,

we get $= \int\frac{\sec^2 x\,dx}{3\sec^2 x + 2}$

$$= \int\frac{\sec^2 x}{3(1+\tan^2 x)+2}dx$$

[replacing $\sec^2 x$ by $1+\tan^2 x$]

$$= \int\frac{\sec^2 x}{3\tan^2 x + 5}dx$$

Now, put $\tan x = t \Rightarrow \sec^2 x\,dx = dt$

$$\therefore \quad I = \int\frac{dt}{3t^2+5} = \frac{1}{3}\int\frac{dt}{t^2+\left(\sqrt{\frac{5}{3}}\right)^2}$$

$$= \frac{1}{3}\cdot\frac{1}{\frac{\sqrt{5}}{\sqrt{3}}}\cdot\tan^{-1}\left(\frac{t}{\sqrt{5/3}}\right)+C$$

$$\left[\because \int\frac{dx}{x^2+a^2} = \frac{1}{a}\tan^{-1}\left(\frac{x}{a}\right)+C\right]$$

$$= \frac{1}{\sqrt{15}}\tan^{-1}\left(\frac{\sqrt{3}\tan x}{\sqrt{5}}\right)+C \qquad [\because t = \tan x]$$

Example 16 Evaluate $\int\frac{1}{4\sin^2 x + 5\cos^2 x}dx$.

Sol. Let $I = \int\frac{1}{4\sin^2 x + 5\cos^2 x}dx$

On dividing numerator and denominator by $\cos^2 x$, we get

$$I = \int\frac{\sec^2 x\,dx}{4\tan^2 x + 5}$$

Now, put $\tan x = t \Rightarrow \sec^2 x\,dx = dt$

$$\therefore \quad I = \int\frac{dt}{4t^2+5} = \frac{1}{4}\int\frac{dt}{t^2+\left(\frac{\sqrt{5}}{2}\right)^2}$$

$$= \frac{1}{4}\cdot\frac{1}{(\sqrt{5}/2)}\cdot\tan^{-1}\left(\frac{t}{\sqrt{5}/2}\right)+C$$

$$\left[\because \int\frac{dx}{x^2+a^2} = \frac{1}{a}\tan^{-1}\left(\frac{x}{a}\right)+C\right]$$

$$= \frac{1}{2\sqrt{5}}\tan^{-1}\left(\frac{2\tan x}{\sqrt{5}}\right)+C \qquad [\because t = \tan x]$$

Example 17 Evaluate $\int\frac{dx}{(2\sin x + 3\cos x)^2}$.

Sol. Let $I = \int\frac{dx}{(2\sin x + 3\cos x)^2}$

On dividing numerator and denominator by $\cos^2 x$, we get

$$I = \int\frac{\sec^2 x\,dx}{(2\tan x + 3)^2}$$

Now, put $\tan x = t \Rightarrow \sec^2 x\,dx = dt$

$$\therefore \quad I = \int\frac{dt}{(2t+3)^2} = \int(2t+3)^{-2}dt = \frac{(2t+3)^{-1}}{(-1)\cdot(2)}+C$$

$$\left[\because \int(ax+b)^n dx = \frac{(ax+b)^{n+1}}{(n+1)\cdot a}+C\right]$$

$$= \frac{-1}{2(2\tan x+3)}+C \qquad [\because t = \tan x]$$

Integral of the Type $\int \frac{a\sin x + b\cos x}{c\sin x + d\cos x}dx$

To evaluate this type of integral, we proceed as follows

Step I Write $a\sin x + b\cos x = A\frac{d}{dx}(c\sin x + d\cos x)$ $+B(c\sin x + d\cos x)$.

Step II Obtain the values of A and B by equating the coefficients of $\sin x$ and $\cos x$ on both sides.

Step III Put the value of $a\sin x + b\cos x$ in the given integral and integrate it by appropriate method.

Example 18 Evaluate $\int \frac{4\sin x + 5\cos x}{5\sin x + 4\cos x}dx$.

It is an integration of the form $\int \frac{a\sin x + b\cos x}{c\sin x + d\cos x}dx$. So, write $4\sin x + 5\cos x = A\frac{d}{dx}(5\sin x + 4\cos x)$ $+B(5\sin x + 4\cos x)$

Sol. Let $I = \int \frac{4\sin x + 5\cos x}{5\sin x + 4\cos x}dx$

Now, let $4\sin x + 5\cos x = A\frac{d}{dx}(5\sin x + 4\cos x)$ $+B(5\sin x + 4\cos x)$

$$= A(5\cos x - 4\sin x) + B(5\sin x + 4\cos x)$$

$\Rightarrow 4\sin x + 5\cos x = (5A + 4B)\cos x + (5B - 4A)\sin x$

On comparing the coefficients of $\sin x$ and $\cos x$, we get

$$5A + 4B = 5 \text{ and } 5B - 4A = 4$$

On solving these two equations, we get

$$A = \frac{9}{41} \text{ and } B = \frac{40}{41}$$

$$\therefore \quad I = \int \frac{\left(\frac{9}{41}(5\cos x - 4\sin x) + \frac{40}{41}(5\sin x + 4\cos x)\right)}{(5\sin x + 4\cos x)}dx$$

$$= \frac{9}{41}\int \frac{5\cos x - 4\sin x}{5\sin x + 4\cos x}dx + \frac{40}{41}\int dx$$

Now, put $5\sin x + 4\cos x = t$

$\Rightarrow \quad (5\cos x - 4\sin x)\,dx = dt$

$$\therefore \; I = \frac{9}{41}\int \frac{dt}{t} + \frac{40}{41}x = \frac{9}{41}\log|t| + \frac{40}{41}x + C$$

$$= \frac{40}{41}x + \frac{9}{41}\log|5\sin x + 4\cos x| + C$$

$[\because t = 5\sin x + 4\cos x]$

Integral of the Type $\int \frac{a\sin x + b\cos x + c}{p\sin x + q\cos x + r}dx$

To evaluate this integral, we proceed as follows

Step I Write $\frac{a\sin x + b\cos x + c}{p\sin x + q\cos x + r}$

$$= A\frac{d}{dx}(p\sin x + q\cos x + r) + B(p\sin x + q\cos x + r) + C$$

Step II Obtain the values of A, B and C by equating the coefficients of $\sin x$, $\cos x$ and constant terms.

Step III Put the value of $a\sin x + b\cos x + c$ in the given integral and integrate it by using appropriate method.

Example 19 Evaluate $\int \frac{5\cos x + 6}{2\cos x + \sin x + 3}dx$.

Sol. Let $I = \int \frac{5\cos x + 6}{2\cos x + \sin x + 3}dx$

Now, let us write $5\cos x + 6 = A\frac{d}{dx}(2\cos x + \sin x + 3)$ $+B(2\cos x + \sin x + 3) + C$

$\Rightarrow \quad 5\cos x + 6 = A(-2\sin x + \cos x)$ $+B(2\cos x + \sin x + 3) + C$

$\Rightarrow 5\cos x + 6 = \sin x(-2A + B) + \cos x(A + 2B) + 3B + C$

On equating the coefficients of $\cos x$, $\sin x$ and the constant terms, we get

$$-2A + B = 0 \quad \text{...(i)}$$

$$A + 2B = 5 \quad \text{...(ii)}$$

and $$3B + C = 6 \quad \text{...(iii)}$$

On multiplying Eq. (ii) by 2 and then adding it to Eq. (i), we get

$$(2A + 4B) + (-2A + B) = 10 + 0$$

$\Rightarrow \quad 5B = 10$

$\Rightarrow \quad B = 2$

$\Rightarrow \quad A = 1$ [from Eq. (i)]

and $\quad C = 0$ [from Eq. (iii)]

Thus, $5\cos x + 6 = 1(-2\sin x + \cos x)$ $+2(2\cos x + \sin x + 3)$

Now, $$I = \int \frac{(-2\sin x + \cos x)}{2\cos x + \sin x + 3}dx + 2\int dx$$

$$= \log|2\cos x + \sin x + 3| + 2x + C$$

$$\left[\because \int \frac{f'(x)}{f(x)}dx = \log|f(x)| + C\right]$$

Integral of the Type

$$\int \frac{x^2 \pm 1}{x^4 + kx^2 + 1} dx, \text{ where } k \in R$$

To evaluate these type of integrals, we proceed as follows

Step I Divide numerator and denominator by x^2.

Step II Make perfect square of the form $\left(x \mp \frac{1}{x}\right)^2$ in the denominator.

Step III Substitute $x + \frac{1}{x} = t$ or $x - \frac{1}{x} = t$ by which integration is possible.

Step IV Evaluate the integral using appropriate formula.

Note (i) If we put $k = 0$ in the integral $\int \frac{x^2 \pm 1}{x^2 + kx^2 + 1} dx$, then we get the integral of the type $\int \frac{x^2 \pm 1}{x^4 + 1} dx$.

(ii) If the given integral is of the form $\int \frac{dx}{x^4 + kx^2 + 1} dx$, $k \in R$, then first write the given integral as

$$\int \frac{dx}{x^4 + kx^2 + 1} = \frac{1}{2}\int \frac{2dx}{x^4 + kx^2 + 1} = \frac{1}{2}\int \frac{(x^2+1)-(x^2-1)}{x^4 + kx^2 + 1} dx$$

$$= \frac{1}{2}\left\{\int \frac{(x^2+1)}{x^4 + kx^2 + 1} dx - \int \frac{x^2 - 1}{x^4 + kx^2 + 1} dx\right\}$$

further integrate easily.

(iii) Evaluation of integral of type $\int \frac{1}{x^4 + 1} dx$ can be understood with the example given below

Example 20 Evaluate $\int \frac{1}{x^4 + 1} dx$.

Sol. Let $I = \int \frac{1}{x^4+1} dx = \frac{1}{2}\int \frac{2}{x^4+1} dx$

$$= \frac{1}{2}\int \frac{(x^2+1)-(x^2-1)}{x^4+1} dx$$

$$= \frac{1}{2}\int \frac{x^2+1}{x^4+1} dx - \frac{1}{2}\int \frac{x^2-1}{x^4+1} dx$$

$$= \frac{1}{2} I_1 - \frac{1}{2} I_2 \text{ (say)} \quad \text{...(i)}$$

where, $I_1 = \int \frac{x^2+1}{x^4+1} dx$ and $I_2 = \int \frac{x^2-1}{x^4+1} dx$.

Consider, $I_1 = \int \frac{x^2+1}{x^4+1} dx$

On dividing numerator and denominator by x^2, we get

$$= \int \frac{1 + \frac{1}{x^2}}{x^2 + \frac{1}{x^2}} dx = \int \frac{1 + \frac{1}{x^2}}{x^2 + \frac{1}{x^2} + 2 - 2} dx = \int \frac{1 + \frac{1}{x^2}}{\left(x - \frac{1}{x}\right)^2 + 2} dx$$

Now, put $x - \frac{1}{x} = t \Rightarrow \left(1 + \frac{1}{x^2}\right) dx = dt$

$$\therefore \quad I_1 = \int \frac{dt}{t^2 + (\sqrt{2})^2} = \frac{1}{\sqrt{2}} \tan^{-1}\left(\frac{t}{\sqrt{2}}\right) + C_1$$

$$= \frac{1}{\sqrt{2}} \tan^{-1}\left(\frac{x^2-1}{\sqrt{2}x}\right) + C_1 \quad \left[\because t = \frac{x^2-1}{x}\right] \quad \text{...(ii)}$$

Now, consider $I_2 = \int \frac{x^2-1}{x^4+1} dx$

On dividing numerator and denominator by x^2, we get

$$I_2 = \int \frac{1 - \frac{1}{x^2}}{x^2 + \frac{1}{x^2}} dx = \int \frac{1 - \frac{1}{x^2}}{x^2 + \frac{1}{x^2} + 2 - 2} dx$$

$$= \int \frac{1 - \frac{1}{x^2}}{\left(x + \frac{1}{x}\right)^2 - 2} dx$$

Now, put $x + \frac{1}{x} = t \Rightarrow \left(1 - \frac{1}{x^2}\right) dx = dt$

$$\therefore \quad I_2 = \int \frac{dt}{t^2 - (\sqrt{2})^2} = \frac{1}{2\sqrt{2}} \log\left|\frac{t - \sqrt{2}}{t + \sqrt{2}}\right| + C_2$$

$$\left[\because \int \frac{dx}{x^2 - a^2} = \frac{1}{2a} \log\left|\frac{x-a}{x+a}\right| + C\right]$$

$$= \frac{1}{2\sqrt{2}} \log\left|\frac{x^2 + 1 - \sqrt{2}x}{x^2 + 1 + \sqrt{2}x}\right| + C_2 \quad \left[\because t = \frac{x^2+1}{x}\right] \quad \text{...(iii)}$$

Now, using Eqs. (i), (ii) and (iii), we get

$$I = \frac{1}{2\sqrt{2}} \tan^{-1}\left(\frac{x^2-1}{\sqrt{2}x}\right) - \frac{1}{4\sqrt{2}} \log\left|\frac{x^2+1-\sqrt{2}x}{x^2+1+\sqrt{2}x}\right| + C,$$

where $C = \frac{1}{2}C_1 + \frac{1}{2}C_2$.

Example 21 Evaluate $\int \frac{x^2 - 1}{x^4 + x^2 + 1} dx$.

Sol. Let $I = \int \frac{x^2 - 1}{x^4 + x^2 + 1} dx$

$$\Rightarrow \quad I = \int \frac{1 - \frac{1}{x^2}}{x^2 + 1 + \frac{1}{x^2}} dx$$

[dividing numerator and denominator by x^2]

$$= \int \frac{\left(1-\frac{1}{x^2}\right)}{\left(x^2+\frac{1}{x^2}\right)+1}\,dx = \int \frac{\left(1-\frac{1}{x^2}\right)dx}{\left(x^2+\frac{1}{x^2}+2\right)+1-2}$$

[adding and subtracting 2 from denominator]

$$= \int \frac{\left(1-\frac{1}{x^2}\right)dx}{\left(x+\frac{1}{x}\right)^2-1}$$

Now, put $x+\frac{1}{x}=t \Rightarrow \left(1-\frac{1}{x^2}\right)dx = dt$

$$\therefore \quad I = \int \frac{dt}{t^2-1^2} = \frac{1}{2}\log\left|\frac{t-1}{t+1}\right| + C$$

$$\left[\because \int \frac{dx}{x^2-a^2} = \frac{1}{2a}\log\left|\frac{x-a}{x+a}\right| + C\right]$$

$$\Rightarrow \quad I = \frac{1}{2}\log\left|\frac{x+\frac{1}{x}-1}{x+\frac{1}{x}+1}\right| + C$$

$$= \frac{1}{2}\log\left|\frac{x^2+1-x}{x^2+1+x}\right| + C \qquad \left[\because t = x+\frac{1}{x}\right]$$

Integrals of the Types $\int \sqrt{\tan x}\,dx$ and $\int \sqrt{\cot x}\,dx$

Let us discuss these one-by-one

(i) $\int \sqrt{\tan x}\,dx$

Let $I = \int \sqrt{\tan x}\,dx$

Now, put $\sqrt{\tan x} = t \Rightarrow \tan x = t^2$

$$\Rightarrow \quad \sec^2 x\,dx = 2t\,dt$$

$$\Rightarrow \quad dx = \frac{2t\,dt}{\sec^2 x} = \frac{2t\,dt}{1+\tan^2 x} = \frac{2t\,dt}{1+t^4} \quad [\because \tan x = t^2]$$

$$\therefore \quad I = \int \sqrt{t^2}\cdot\frac{2t}{1+t^4}\,dt$$

$$= \int t\cdot\frac{2t\,dt}{1+t^4} = \int \frac{2t^2}{1+t^4}\,dt$$

$$= \int \frac{(t^2-1)+(t^2+1)}{1+t^4}\,dt$$

$$= \int \frac{t^2-1}{t^4+1}\,dt + \int \frac{t^2+1}{t^4+1}\,dt$$

$$= \int \frac{1-\frac{1}{t^2}}{t^2+\frac{1}{t^2}}\,dt + \int \frac{1+\frac{1}{t^2}}{t^2+\frac{1}{t^2}}\,dt$$

$$= \int \frac{1-\frac{1}{t^2}}{\left(t^2+\frac{1}{t^2}+2\right)-2}\,dt + \int \frac{1+\frac{1}{t^2}}{\left(t^2+\frac{1}{t^2}-2\right)+2}\,dt$$

$$= \int \frac{1-\frac{1}{t^2}}{\left(t+\frac{1}{t}\right)^2-2}\,dt + \int \frac{1+\frac{1}{t^2}}{\left(t-\frac{1}{t}\right)^2+2}\,dt$$

Put $t+\frac{1}{t}=u$ and $t-\frac{1}{t}=v$, so that $\left(1-\frac{1}{t^2}\right)dt = du$ and $\left(1+\frac{1}{t^2}\right)dt = dv$

$$\therefore \quad I = \int \frac{du}{u^2-2} + \int \frac{dv}{v^2+2}$$

$$= \int \frac{du}{u^2-(\sqrt{2})^2} + \int \frac{dv}{v^2+(\sqrt{2})^2}$$

$$= \frac{1}{2\sqrt{2}}\log\left|\frac{u-\sqrt{2}}{u+\sqrt{2}}\right| + \frac{1}{\sqrt{2}}\tan^{-1}\frac{v}{\sqrt{2}} + C$$

$$= \frac{1}{2\sqrt{2}}\log\left|\frac{t+\frac{1}{t}-\sqrt{2}}{t+\frac{1}{t}+\sqrt{2}}\right| + \frac{1}{\sqrt{2}}\tan^{-1}\frac{t-\frac{1}{t}}{\sqrt{2}} + C$$

$$\left[\because u = t+\frac{1}{t} \text{ and } v = t-\frac{1}{t}\right]$$

$$= \frac{1}{2\sqrt{2}}\log\left|\frac{t^2-t\sqrt{2}+1}{t^2+t\sqrt{2}+1}\right| + \frac{1}{\sqrt{2}}\tan^{-1}\frac{t^2-1}{t\sqrt{2}} + C$$

$$= \frac{1}{2\sqrt{2}}\log\left|\frac{\tan x-\sqrt{2\tan x}+1}{\tan x+\sqrt{2\tan x}+1}\right|$$

$$+ \frac{1}{\sqrt{2}}\tan^{-1}\frac{\tan x-1}{\sqrt{2\tan x}} + C \quad [\because t = \sqrt{\tan x}]$$

(ii) Similarly, by putting $\sqrt{\cot x} = t$, we can see

$$\int \sqrt{\cot x}\,dx = -\frac{1}{\sqrt{2}}\tan^{-1}\left(\frac{\cot x-1}{\sqrt{2\cot x}}\right)$$

$$-\frac{1}{2\sqrt{2}}\log\left|\frac{\cot x-\sqrt{2\cot x}+1}{\cot x+\sqrt{2\cot x}+1}\right| + C$$

Topic Practice 3

Very Short Answer Type Questions

(2 Marks)

Directions (Q. Nos. 1-13) *Evaluate the following integrals.*

1 $\int \frac{x^2}{x^2-4} dx$ [ISC 2008]

2 $\int \frac{2y^2}{y^2+4} dy$ [ISC 2017]

3 $\int \frac{x^3}{\sqrt{1-x^8}} dx$ [NCERT]

4 $\int \frac{e^x}{\sqrt{9-e^{2x}}} dx$

5 $\int \frac{\sin 2x \cos 2x}{\sqrt{9-\cos^4 (2x)}} dx$ [NCERT]

6 $\int \frac{dx}{x^2+4x+8}$

7 $\int \frac{dx}{5-8x-x^2}$

8 $\int \frac{1}{\sqrt{x^2-4x}} dx$

9 $\int x^2\sqrt{a^6-x^6}\, dx$

10 $\int \sqrt{x^2-2x}\, dx$

11 $\int \sqrt{2x-x^2}\, dx$

12 $\int \frac{dx}{4+5\cos x}$

13 $\int \frac{dx}{1+3\sin^2 x}$ [NCERT]

Short Answer Type Questions

(4 Marks)

Directions (Q. Nos. 14-26) *Evaluate the following integrals.*

14 $\int \frac{dx}{x(x^3+8)}$

15 $\int \frac{x^3}{x^4+3x^2+2} dx$ [NCERT Exemplar]

16 $\int \frac{x+2}{\sqrt{x^2+5x+6}} dx$

17 $\int \frac{x+3}{\sqrt{5-4x+x^2}} dx$

18 $\int \frac{6x+7}{\sqrt{(x-5)(x-4)}} dx$

19 $\int \frac{x+2}{\sqrt{4x-x^2}} dx$

20 $\int \frac{x^2-3x+1}{\sqrt{1-x^2}} dx$

21 $\int \sqrt{5-2x+x^2}\, dx$ [NCERT Exemplar]

22 $\int (3x-2)(\sqrt{x^2+x+1})\, dx$

23 $\int (x+3)\sqrt{3-4x-x^2}\, dx$

24 $\int (x-3)\sqrt{3-2x-x^2}\, dx$

25 $\int (3x+5)\sqrt{4+3x-2x^2}\, dx$

26 $\int \frac{dx}{2\sin^2 x+5\cos^2 x}$ [NCERT Exemplar]

Long Answer Type Questions

(6 Marks)

Directions (Q. Nos. 27-37) *Evaluate the following integrals.*

27 $\int \frac{\cos\theta}{(4+\sin^2\theta)(5-4\cos^2\theta)} d\theta$

28 $\int \frac{x^2}{(x^2+4)(x^2+9)} dx$

29 $\int \frac{(x^2+1)(x^2+2)}{(x^2+3)(x^2+4)} dx$

30 $\int \frac{\sin x+\cos x}{\sqrt{9+16\sin 2x}} dx$ [ISC 2016]

31 $\int \frac{dx}{x\{6(\log x)^2+7\log x+2\}}$ [ISC 2012]

32 $\int \frac{2\sin 2\theta-\cos\theta}{6-\cos^2\theta-4\sin\theta} d\theta$ [ISC 2010]

33 $\int \frac{x-1}{\sqrt{x^2-x}} dx$ [ISC 2018]

34 $\int \frac{x^2-5x-1}{x^4+x^2+1} dx$ [ISC 2011]

35 $\int \frac{1}{\cos^4 x+\sin^4 x} dx$

36 $\int \frac{1}{\sin^4 x+\sin^2 x\cos^2 x+\cos^4 x} dx$

37 $\int [\sqrt{\cot x}+\sqrt{\tan x}]\, dx$

Hints & Solutions

1. Let $I=\int \frac{x^2}{x^2-4}dx=\int \frac{x^2-4+4}{x^2-4}dx$

$=\int \frac{x^2-4}{x^2-4}dx+\int \frac{4}{x^2-4}dx$ [1]

$=\int dx+4\int \frac{1}{(x)^2-(2)^2}dx$ [1/2]

$=x+4\times\frac{1}{2\times 2}\log\left|\frac{x-2}{x+2}\right|+C$

$\left[\because \int \frac{1}{x^2-a^2}dx=\frac{1}{2a}\log\left|\frac{x-a}{x+a}\right|+C\right]$

$=x+\log\left|\frac{x-2}{x+2}\right|+C$ [1/2]

2. **Hint** $\int \frac{2y^2}{y^2+4}dy=2\left[\int \frac{y^2+4-4}{y^2+4}dy\right]$

$=2\left[\int dy-4\int \frac{dy}{y^2+4}\right]$

$\left[\textbf{Ans. } 2y-4\tan^{-1}\left(\frac{y}{2}\right)+C\right]$

3. **Hint** (i) Write the given integral as $\int \frac{x^3}{\sqrt{1-(x^4)^2}}dx$

(ii) Put $x^4=t$ and then use the formula

$\int \frac{dx}{\sqrt{a^2-x^2}}=\sin^{-1}\left(\frac{x}{a}\right)+C$

$\left[\textbf{Ans. } \frac{1}{4}\sin^{-1}(x^4)+C\right]$

4. Let $I=\int \frac{e^x}{\sqrt{9-e^{2x}}}dx=\int \frac{e^x}{\sqrt{(3)^2-(e^x)^2}}dx$

Now, put $e^x=t\Rightarrow e^x\,dx=dt$ [1]

$\therefore\ I=\int \frac{dt}{\sqrt{(3)^2-t^2}}=\sin^{-1}\frac{t}{3}+C=\sin^{-1}\left(\frac{e^x}{3}\right)+C$ [1]

$\left[\because \int \frac{dx}{\sqrt{a^2-x^2}}=\sin^{-1}\left(\frac{x}{a}\right)\text{and } t=e^x\right]$

5. Let $I=\int \frac{\sin 2x\cos 2x}{\sqrt{9-\cos^4(2x)}}dx=\int \frac{\sin 2x\cos 2x}{\sqrt{3^2-[\cos^2(2x)]^2}}dx$

Now, put $\cos^2(2x)=t$

$\Rightarrow\ 2\cos(2x)[-\sin(2x)]\cdot 2\,dx=dt$

$\Rightarrow\ \sin 2x\cdot\cos 2x\,dx=-\frac{dt}{4}$ [1]

$\therefore\ I=-\frac{1}{4}\int \frac{dt}{\sqrt{3^2-t^2}}=-\frac{1}{4}\sin^{-1}\left(\frac{t}{3}\right)+C$

$=-\frac{1}{4}\sin^{-1}\left(\frac{\cos^2 2x}{3}\right)+C$ [1]

6. Similar as Example 2. $\left[\textbf{Ans. } \frac{1}{2}\tan^{-1}\left(\frac{x+2}{2}\right)+C\right]$

7. Let $I=\int \frac{dx}{5-8x-x^2}=\int \frac{dx}{5-2\cdot4\cdot x-x^2-(4)^2+(4)^2}$

$=\int \frac{dx}{5+16-[x^2+(4)^2+2\cdot4\cdot x]}$

$=\int \frac{dx}{21-(x+4)^2}$ [1]

$=\int \frac{dx}{(\sqrt{21})^2-(x+4)^2}$

$=\frac{1}{2\sqrt{21}}\log\left|\frac{\sqrt{21}+x+4}{\sqrt{21}-x-4}\right|+C$ [1]

$\left[\because \int \frac{dx}{a^2-x^2}=\frac{1}{2a}\log\left|\frac{a+x}{a-x}\right|+C\right]$

8. Let $I=\int \frac{dx}{\sqrt{x^2-4x}}=\int \frac{dx}{\sqrt{x^2-2\cdot2\cdot x+2^2-2^2}}$ [1]

$=\int \frac{dx}{\sqrt{(x-2)^2-2^2}}$

$=\log|(x-2)+\sqrt{(x-2)^2-2^2}|+C$

$=\log|(x-2)+\sqrt{x^2-4x}|+C$ [1]

9. **Hint** (i) $\int x^2\sqrt{a^6-x^6}dx=\int x^2\sqrt{(a^3)^2-(x^3)^2}\,dx$

(ii) Put $x^3=t$

$\left[\textbf{Ans. } \frac{1}{6}\left(x^3\sqrt{a^6-x^6}+a^6\sin^{-1}\left(\frac{x^3}{a^3}\right)\right)+C\right]$

10. Let $I=\int\sqrt{x^2-2x}\,dx$

$=\int\sqrt{(x^2-2x+1)-1}\,dx$

$=\int\sqrt{(x-1)^2-1^2}\,dx$ [1]

$=\frac{(x-1)}{2}\sqrt{x^2-2x}-\frac{1}{2}\log|(x-1)+\sqrt{x^2-2x}|+C$ [1]

11. Let $I=\int\sqrt{2x-x^2}\,dx$

$=\int\sqrt{-(x^2-2x)}\,dx$

$=\int\sqrt{-(x^2-2x+1-1)}\,dx$

$=\int\sqrt{-((x-1)^2-1)}\,dx$ [1]

$=\int\sqrt{1^2-(x-1)^2}\,dx$

$=\frac{(x-1)}{2}\sqrt{2x-x^2}+\frac{1}{2}\sin^{-1}(x-1)+C$ [1]

12. Similar as Example 13. $\left[\textbf{Ans. } \frac{1}{3}\log\left|\frac{3+\tan\frac{x}{2}}{3-\tan\frac{x}{2}}\right|+C\right]$

13. **Hint** $\int \frac{dx}{1+3\sin^2 x} = \int \frac{\sec^2 x\,dx}{\sec^2 x+3\tan^2 x} = \int \frac{\sec^2 x\,dx}{4\tan^2 x+1}$

$\left[\textbf{Ans. } \frac{1}{2}\tan^{-1}(2\tan x)+C\right]$

14. Let $I = \int \frac{dx}{x(x^3+8)} = \int \frac{x^2}{x^3(x^3+8)}dx$

[multiply numerator and denominator by x^2]

Now, put $x^3+8=t$

$\Rightarrow 3x^2\,dx = dt \Rightarrow x^2\,dx = \frac{dt}{3}$ [1]

$\therefore \quad I = \frac{1}{3}\int \frac{dt}{(t-8)t} = \frac{1}{3}\int \frac{dt}{t^2-8t}$

$= \frac{1}{3}\int \frac{dt}{t^2-8t+(4)^2-(4)^2}$ [1]

[adding and subtracting by $(4)^2$ from denominator]

$= \frac{1}{3}\int \frac{dt}{(t-4)^2-(4)^2}$ [1]

$= \frac{1}{3}\times\frac{1}{2\times 4}\log\left|\frac{t-4-4}{t-4+4}\right|+C$

$= \frac{1}{24}\log\left|\frac{t-8}{t}\right|+C$

$= \frac{1}{24}\log\left|\frac{x^3}{x^3+8}\right|+C \quad [\because t = x^3+8]$ [1]

15. **Hint** (i) Write the given integral as

$\int \frac{x^2\cdot x}{(x^2)^2+3x^2+2}dx$

(ii) Put $x^2=t$, then above integral reduces to

$\frac{1}{2}\int \frac{t}{t^2+3t+2}dt$

(iii) Similar as Example 5. $\left[\textbf{Ans. } \log\left|\frac{x^2+2}{\sqrt{x^2+1}}\right|+C\right]$

16. Similar as Example 6.

$\left[\textbf{Ans. } \sqrt{x^2+5x+6}-\frac{1}{2}\log\left|\left(x+\frac{5}{2}\right)+\sqrt{x^2+5x+6}\right|+C\right]$

17. Similar as Example 6.

$[\textbf{Ans. } \sqrt{5-4x+x^2}+5\log|(x-2)+\sqrt{5-4x+x^2}|+C]$

18. **Hint** Firstly, write the given integral as

$\int \frac{6x+7}{\sqrt{x^2-9x+20}}dx$ and then similar as Example 6.

$\left[\textbf{Ans. } 6\sqrt{x^2-9x+20}+34\log\left|\left(x-\frac{9}{2}\right)+\sqrt{\left(x-\frac{9}{2}\right)^2-\frac{1}{4}}\right|+C\right]$

19. **Hint** Firstly, put $x+2 = A\frac{d}{dx}(4x-x^2)+B$ and then similar as Example 6.

$\left[\textbf{Ans. } -\sqrt{4x-x^2}+4\sin^{-1}\left(\frac{x-2}{2}\right)+C\right]$

20. Let $I = \int \frac{x^2-3x+1}{\sqrt{1-x^2}}dx = (-1)\int \frac{-x^2+3x-1}{\sqrt{1-x^2}}dx$

$= (-1)\int \frac{1-x^2+3x-2}{\sqrt{1-x^2}}dx$

[adding and subtracting 1 from numerator]

$= (-1)\int\left[\frac{1-x^2}{\sqrt{1-x^2}}+\frac{3x-2}{\sqrt{1-x^2}}\right]dx$ [1/2]

$= (-1)\int\left[\sqrt{1-x^2}+\frac{3x-2}{\sqrt{1-x^2}}\right]dx$

$= (-1)\left[\int\sqrt{1-x^2}\,dx+\int\frac{3x-2}{\sqrt{1-x^2}}dx\right]$

$= (-1)[I_1+I_2]$ (say) ...(i) [1/2]

Now, $I_1 = \int\sqrt{1-x^2}dx = \frac{1}{2}[x\sqrt{1-x^2}+\sin^{-1}(x)]+C_1$ ...(ii) [1]

and $I_2 = \int\frac{3x-2}{\sqrt{1-x^2}}dx = \int\frac{3x}{\sqrt{1-x^2}}dx-2\int\frac{dx}{\sqrt{1-x^2}}$

$= -\frac{3}{2}\int\frac{-2x}{\sqrt{1-x^2}}dx-2\int\frac{dx}{\sqrt{1-x^2}}$

$= -\frac{3}{2}\times 2\sqrt{1-x^2}-2\sin^{-1}(x)+C_2$

$\left[\because \int\frac{f'(x)}{\sqrt{f(x)}}dx = 2\sqrt{f(x)}+C\right]$

$= -3\sqrt{1-x^2}-2\sin^{-1}(x)+C_2$ ...(iii) [1]

From Eqs. (i), (ii) and (iii), we have

$I = (-1)\left[\frac{x}{2}\sqrt{1-x^2}+\frac{1}{2}\sin^{-1}(x)-2\sin^{-1}(x)-3\sqrt{1-x^2}+C_3\right]$

[where, $C_3 = C_1+C_2$]

$= \frac{3}{2}\sin^{-1}(x)-\frac{x}{2}\sqrt{1-x^2}+3\sqrt{1-x^2}+C$ [1]

where, $C = -C_3$

21. Similar as Example 8.

$\left[\textbf{Ans. } \frac{(x-1)}{2}\sqrt{5-2x+x^2}+2\log|(x-1)+\sqrt{5-2x+x^2}|+C\right]$

22. Similar as Example 11.

$\left[\textbf{Ans. } (x^2+x+1)^{3/2}-\frac{7}{4}\left(x+\frac{1}{2}\right)\sqrt{x^2+x+1}-\frac{21}{16}\log\left|\left(x+\frac{1}{2}\right)+\sqrt{x^2+x+1}\right|+C\right]$

23. Similar as Example 12.

$$\left[\textbf{Ans. } -\frac{1}{3}(3-4x-x^2)^{3/2}+\frac{1}{2}(x+2)\sqrt{3-4x-x^2}+\frac{7}{2}\sin^{-1}\left(\frac{x+2}{\sqrt{7}}\right)+C\right]$$

24. Similar as Example 12.

$$\left[\textbf{Ans. } -\frac{1}{3}(3-2x-x^2)^{3/2}-4\left[\frac{(x+1)}{2}\sqrt{3-2x-x^2}+2\sin^{-1}\left(\frac{x+1}{2}\right)\right]+C\right]$$

25. Let $I=\int(3x+5)\sqrt{4+3x-2x^2}\,dx$

Put $3x+5=A\frac{d}{dx}(4+3x-2x^2)+B$

$\Rightarrow \quad 3x+5=A(3-4x)+B$

$\Rightarrow \quad 3x+5=-4Ax+(3A+B)$ [1/2]

On comparing the coefficients of x and constant terms, we get

$-4A=3$ and $3A+B=5$

$\Rightarrow \quad A=\frac{-3}{4}$ and $B=5-3A=5+\frac{9}{4}=\frac{29}{4}$

Now, $(3x+5)=\frac{-3}{4}(3-4x)+\frac{29}{4}$

$\therefore \quad I=-\frac{3}{4}\int(3-4x)\sqrt{4+3x-2x^2}\,dx+\frac{29}{4}\int\sqrt{4+3x-2x^2}\,dx$

$=\frac{-3}{4}I_1+\frac{29}{4}I_2$ (say) [1]

Here, $I_1=\int(3-4x)\sqrt{4+3x-2x^2}\,dx$

Put $4+3x-2x^2=t \Rightarrow (3-4x)\,dx=dt$

$\therefore \quad I_1=\int\sqrt{t}\,dt=\frac{2}{3}t^{3/2}+C_1=\frac{2}{3}(3-4x)^{3/2}+C_1$ [1]

and $I_2=\int\sqrt{4+3x-2x^2}\,dx$

$$=\sqrt{2}\int\sqrt{2+\frac{3}{2}x-x^2}\,dx$$

$$=\sqrt{2}\int\sqrt{-\left(x^2-\frac{3}{2}x-2\right)}\,dx$$

$$=\sqrt{2}\int\sqrt{-\left(x^2-2\cdot\frac{3}{2}\cdot x+\left(\frac{3}{4}\right)^2-2-\frac{9}{16}\right)}\,dx$$

$$=\sqrt{2}\int\sqrt{-\left[\left(x-\frac{3}{4}\right)^2-\frac{41}{16}\right]}\,dx$$

$$=\sqrt{2}\int\sqrt{\left(\frac{\sqrt{41}}{4}\right)^2-\left(x-\frac{3}{4}\right)^2}\,dx$$

$$=\frac{\sqrt{2}}{2}\left[\left(x-\frac{3}{4}\right)\sqrt{\left(\frac{\sqrt{41}}{4}\right)^2-\left(x-\frac{3}{4}\right)^2}+\frac{41}{16}\sin^{-1}\left(\frac{4x-3}{\sqrt{41}}\right)\right]+C_2 \quad [1]$$

$$\therefore \quad I=-\frac{1}{2}(3-4x)^{3/2}+\frac{29}{4\sqrt{2}}\left[\left(x-\frac{3}{4}\right)\sqrt{4+3x-2x^2}+\frac{41\sqrt{2}}{16}\sin^{-1}\left(\frac{4x-3}{\sqrt{41}}\right)\right]+C$$

$\left[\text{where, } C=-\frac{3}{4}C_1+\frac{29}{4}C_2\right]$ [1/2]

26. Similar as Example 16.

$$\left[\textbf{Ans. } \frac{1}{\sqrt{10}}\tan^{-1}\left(\frac{\sqrt{2}\tan x}{\sqrt{5}}\right)+C\right]$$

27. Let $I=\int\frac{\cos\theta}{(4+\sin^2\theta)(5-4\cos^2\theta)}\,d\theta$

$$=\int\frac{\cos\theta}{(4+\sin^2\theta)[5-4(1-\sin^2\theta)]}\,d\theta$$

$$=\int\frac{\cos\theta}{(4+\sin^2\theta)(5-4+4\sin^2\theta)}\,d\theta$$

$$=\int\frac{\cos\theta}{(4+\sin^2\theta)(1+4\sin^2\theta)}\,d\theta \quad [1]$$

Put $\sin\theta=t \Rightarrow \cos\theta\,d\theta=dt$

Then, $I=\int\frac{dt}{(4+t^2)(1+4t^2)}$ ...(i)

Again, let $\frac{1}{(4+t^2)(1+4t^2)}=\frac{A}{4+t^2}+\frac{B}{1+4t^2}$ ...(ii)

[by partial fractions]

At $t=0$, $\frac{A}{4}+\frac{B}{1}=\frac{1}{4\times1}$ [1]

$\Rightarrow \quad A+4B=1$ ...(iii)

At $t=1$, $\frac{A}{5}+\frac{B}{5}=\frac{1}{5\times5}$

$\Rightarrow \quad 5A+5B=1$ ...(iv) [1]

On solving Eqs. (iii) and (iv), we get

$A=-\frac{1}{15}$ and $B=\frac{4}{15}$

On putting $A=-\frac{1}{15}$ and $B=\frac{4}{15}$ in Eq. (ii), we get

$$\frac{1}{(4+t^2)(1+4t^2)}=\frac{-\frac{1}{15}}{4+t^2}+\frac{\frac{4}{15}}{1+4t^2} \quad [1]$$

$$\Rightarrow \quad \frac{1}{(4+t^2)(1+4t^2)}=\frac{-1}{15(4+t^2)}+\frac{4}{15(1+4t^2)}$$

On integrating both sides w.r.t. t, we get

$$\int\frac{1}{(4+t^2)(1+4t^2)}\,dt=\frac{-1}{15}\int\frac{1}{4+t^2}\,dt+\frac{4}{15}\int\frac{1}{1+4t^2}\,dt$$

$$= \frac{-1}{15}\int \frac{1}{2^2+t^2} + \frac{4}{15\times 4}\int \frac{1}{\left(\frac{1}{2}\right)^2 + t^2} dt \quad [1]$$

$$= \frac{-1}{15}\cdot\frac{1}{2}\tan^{-1}\frac{t}{2} + \frac{1}{15}\cdot\frac{1}{1/2}\tan^{-1}\frac{t}{1/2} + C$$

$$\left[\because \int \frac{dx}{x^2+a^2} = \frac{1}{a}\tan^{-1}\frac{x}{a} + C\right]$$

$$= \frac{-1}{30}\tan^{-1}\left(\frac{\sin\theta}{2}\right) + \frac{2}{15}\tan^{-1}(2\sin\theta) + C$$

$[\because t = \sin\theta]$ [1]

28. Let $I = \int \frac{x^2}{(x^2+4)(x^2+9)} dx = \frac{1}{2}\int \frac{2x^2+4+9-4-9}{(x^2+4)(x^2+9)} dx$

[adding and subtracting 4 and 9 from numerator]

$$= \frac{1}{2}\int \frac{x^2+4}{(x^2+4)(x^2+9)} dx + \frac{1}{2}\int \frac{x^2+9}{(x^2+4)(x^2+9)} dx - \frac{1}{2}\int \frac{13}{(x^2+4)(x^2+9)} dx \quad [1]$$

$$= \frac{1}{2}\int \frac{dx}{x^2+9} + \frac{1}{2}\int \frac{dx}{x^2+4} - \frac{1}{2}\int \frac{13\,dx}{(x^2+4)(x^2+9)} \quad [1]$$

$$= \frac{1}{2}\cdot\frac{1}{3}\tan^{-1}\left(\frac{x}{3}\right) + \frac{1}{2}\cdot\frac{1}{2}\tan^{-1}\left(\frac{x}{2}\right) - \frac{1}{2}\cdot\frac{13}{5}\int\left(\frac{1}{(x^2+4)} - \frac{1}{(x^2+9)}\right)dx$$

$$\left[\because \int \frac{dx}{x^2+a^2} = \frac{1}{a}\tan^{-1}\frac{x}{a}\right] \quad [1]$$

$$= \frac{1}{6}\tan^{-1}\left(\frac{x}{3}\right) + \frac{1}{4}\tan^{-1}\left(\frac{x}{2}\right) - \frac{13}{10}\cdot\frac{1}{2}\tan^{-1}\left(\frac{x}{2}\right) + \frac{13}{10}\cdot\frac{1}{3}\tan^{-1}\left(\frac{x}{3}\right) + C \quad [1]$$

$$= \frac{1}{6}\tan^{-1}\left(\frac{x}{3}\right) + \frac{1}{4}\tan^{-1}\left(\frac{x}{2}\right) - \frac{13}{20}\tan^{-1}\left(\frac{x}{2}\right) + \frac{13}{30}\tan^{-1}\left(\frac{x}{3}\right) + C \quad [1]$$

$$= \tan^{-1}\left(\frac{x}{3}\right)\left(\frac{1}{6}+\frac{13}{30}\right) + \tan^{-1}\left(\frac{x}{2}\right)\left(\frac{1}{4}-\frac{13}{20}\right) + C$$

$$= \tan^{-1}\left(\frac{x}{3}\right)\left(\frac{5+13}{30}\right) + \tan^{-1}\left(\frac{x}{2}\right)\left(\frac{5-13}{20}\right) + C$$

$$= \frac{18}{30}\tan^{-1}\left(\frac{x}{3}\right) - \frac{8}{20}\tan^{-1}\left(\frac{x}{2}\right) + C$$

$$= \frac{3}{5}\tan^{-1}\left(\frac{x}{3}\right) - \frac{2}{5}\tan^{-1}\left(\frac{x}{2}\right) + C \quad [1]$$

29. Firstly, convert it into simple form by putting $x^2 = t$,

i.e. write $\frac{(x^2+1)(x^2+2)}{(x^2+3)(x^2+4)} = \frac{(t+1)(t+2)}{(t+3)(t+4)}$

$$= \frac{t^2+3t+2}{t^2+7t+12}$$

Now, degree of numerator and denominator is same, so it can be written as $1 - \frac{4t+10}{t^2+7t+12}$. [1]

[divide numerator by denominator]

Thus, $\frac{(x^2+1)(x^2+2)}{(x^2+3)(x^2+4)} = 1 - \frac{(4t+10)}{t^2+7t+12}$ $[\because x^2 = t]$

$$= 1 - \frac{4t+10}{(t+3)(t+4)} \quad \text{...(i)}$$

$[\because t^2+7t+12 = t^2+4t+3t+12 = (t+3)(t+4)]$ [1/2]

Now, consider $\frac{4t+10}{(t+4)(t+3)} = \frac{A}{(t+4)} + \frac{B}{(t+3)}$ [1]

$$\Rightarrow \frac{4t+10}{(t+3)(t+4)} = \frac{A(t+3)+B(t+4)}{(t+4)(t+3)}$$

$$\Rightarrow 4t+10 = At + 3A + Bt + 4B$$

$$\Rightarrow 4t+10 = t(A+B) + (3A+4B) \quad [1/2]$$

On comparing the coefficients of t and constant term from both sides, we get

$$A + B = 4$$

$\Rightarrow 3A + 3B = 12$ [multiply both sides by 3] ...(ii)

and $3A + 4B = 10$ ...(iii)

On subtracting Eq. (iii) from Eq. (ii), we get

$$-B = 2 \Rightarrow B = -2$$

Then, from Eq. (iii), we get

$$3A + 4(-2) = 10$$

$$\Rightarrow 3A = 18 \Rightarrow A = 6$$

$$\therefore \frac{4t+10}{(t+4)(t+3)} = \frac{6}{t+4} - \frac{2}{t+3} \quad [1]$$

On putting this value in Eq. (i), we get

$$\frac{(x^2+1)(x^2+2)}{(x^2+3)(x^2+4)} = 1 - \left[\frac{6}{t+4} - \frac{2}{t+3}\right]$$

$$= 1 - \left(\frac{6}{(x^2+4)} - \frac{2}{(x^2+3)}\right) \quad [\because t = x^2] \quad [1]$$

Now, given integral,

$$I = \int 1dx - \int\left(\frac{6}{x^2+2^2} - \frac{2}{x^2+(\sqrt{3})^2}\right)dx$$

$$= x - 6\left(\frac{1}{2}\tan^{-1}\frac{x}{2}\right) + 2\left(\frac{1}{\sqrt{3}}\tan^{-1}\frac{x}{\sqrt{3}}\right) + C$$

$$\left[\because \int \frac{1}{a^2+x^2}dx = \frac{1}{a}\tan^{-1}\frac{x}{a}\right]$$

$$= x - 3\tan^{-1}\frac{x}{2} + \frac{2}{\sqrt{3}}\tan^{-1}\frac{x}{\sqrt{3}} + C \quad [1]$$

Note The substitution $x^2 = t$ was made only for the partial fraction part and not for the integration part.

30. Let $I = \int \frac{\sin x + \cos x}{\sqrt{9 + 16 \sin 2x}} dx$

Put $\sin x - \cos x = t$ [1]

$\Rightarrow (\cos x + \sin x)\, dx = dt$

Again, $(\sin x - \cos x)^2 = t^2$

$\Rightarrow \sin^2 x + \cos^2 x - 2 \sin x \cos x = t^2$

$\Rightarrow 1 - 2 \sin x \cos x = t^2$

$\Rightarrow 1 - \sin 2x = t^2$

$\Rightarrow \sin 2x = 1 - t^2$ [1]

$\therefore I = \int \frac{dt}{\sqrt{9 + 16(1 - t^2)}}$ [1]

$= \int \frac{dt}{\sqrt{9 + 16 - 16t^2}} = \int \frac{dt}{\sqrt{25 - 16t^2}}$ [1/2]

$= \int \frac{dt}{4\sqrt{\left(\frac{5}{4}\right)^2 - (t)^2}}$

$= \frac{1}{4} \int \frac{dt}{\sqrt{(5/4)^2 - t^2}}$ [1]

$= \frac{1}{4} \sin^{-1} \frac{4t}{5} + C$ [1]

$\left[\because \int \frac{dx}{\sqrt{a^2 - x^2}} = \sin^{-1} \frac{x}{a} + C\right]$

$= \frac{1}{4} \sin^{-1} \left\{\frac{4}{5}(\sin x - \cos x)\right\} + C$ [1/2]

31. Let $I = \int \frac{dx}{x\{6(\log x)^2 + 7 \log x + 2\}}$

Put $\log x = t \Rightarrow \frac{1}{x} dx = dt$

$\therefore I = \int \frac{dt}{6t^2 + 7t + 2}$ [1]

$= \frac{1}{6} \int \frac{dt}{t^2 + \frac{7}{6}t + \frac{1}{3}}$

$= \frac{1}{6} \int \frac{dt}{t^2 + 2 \cdot \frac{7}{12} t + \left(\frac{7}{12}\right)^2 + \frac{1}{3} - \left(\frac{7}{12}\right)^2}$ [1]

$= \frac{1}{6} \int \frac{dt}{\left(t + \frac{7}{12}\right)^2 - \left(\frac{1}{12}\right)^2}$ [1]

$= \frac{1}{6} \cdot \frac{1}{2 \cdot \frac{1}{12}} \log \left|\frac{\left(t + \frac{7}{12}\right) - \frac{1}{12}}{\left(t + \frac{7}{12}\right) + \frac{1}{12}}\right| + C$ [1]

$= \log \left|\frac{12t + 7 - 1}{12t + 7 + 1}\right| + C$ [1]

$= \log \left|\frac{12t + 6}{12t + 8}\right| + C = \log \left|\frac{6t + 3}{6t + 4}\right| + C$

$= \log \left|\frac{6 \log x + 3}{6 \log x + 4}\right| + C$ $[\because t = \log x]$ [1]

32. Let $I = \int \frac{2 \sin 2\theta - \cos \theta}{6 - \cos^2 \theta - 4 \sin \theta} d\theta$

$= \int \frac{2 \cdot 2 \sin \theta \cdot \cos \theta - \cos \theta}{6 - (1 - \sin^2 \theta) - 4 \sin \theta} d\theta$ [1]

$[\because \sin 2\theta = 2 \sin \theta \cdot \cos \theta, \cos^2 \theta = 1 - \sin^2 \theta]$

$= \int \frac{\cos \theta\, (4 \sin \theta - 1)}{6 - 1 + \sin^2 \theta - 4 \sin \theta} d\theta$

$= \int \frac{\cos \theta\, (4 \sin \theta - 1)}{\sin^2 \theta - 4 \sin \theta + 5} d\theta$ [1]

Put $\sin \theta = t \Rightarrow \cos\, d\theta = dt$

$\therefore I = \int \frac{(4t - 1)}{t^2 - 4t + 5} dt = \int \frac{2(2t - 4) + 7}{t^2 - 4t + 5} dt$

$I = 2\int \frac{2t - 4}{t^2 - 4t + 5} dt + \int \frac{7}{t^2 - 4t + 5} dt$

$\Rightarrow I = I_1 + I_2$ ...(i) [1]

Now, $I_1 = 2\int \frac{2t - 4}{t^2 - 4t + 5} dt = 2\int \frac{1}{z} dz$

$[\text{put } t^2 - 4t + 5 = z \Rightarrow (2t - 4)dt = dz]$

$= 2 \log|z| + C_1$

$\Rightarrow I_1 = 2 \log |(t^2 - 4t + 5)| + C_1$

$[\text{put } z = t^2 - 4t + 5]$ [1]

$= 2 \log |(\sin^2 \theta - 4 \sin \theta + 5)| + C_1$

$[\text{put } t = \sin\theta]$

Now, $I_2 = \int \frac{7}{t^2 - 4t + 5} dt = \int \frac{7}{(t - 2)^2 + (1)^2} dt$

$= 7 \tan^{-1}(t - 2) + C_2$ [1]

$= 7 \tan^{-1}(\sin\theta - 2) + C_2$ $[\text{put } t = \sin\theta]$

$\therefore$ From Eq (i),

$I = 2 \log |\sin^2 \theta - 4 \sin\theta + 5|$

$+ 7 \tan^{-1} (\sin \theta - 2) + C$

$[\text{put } C_1 + C_2 = C]$ [1]

33. We have, $I = \int \frac{x - 1}{\sqrt{x^2 - x}} dx$

$\Rightarrow I = \frac{1}{2} \int \frac{2x - 2}{\sqrt{x^2 - x}} dx$ [1]

$= \frac{1}{2}\left[\int \frac{2x - 1}{\sqrt{x^2 - x}} dx - \int \frac{1}{\sqrt{x^2 - x}} dx\right]$ [1]

$$\Rightarrow \quad I=\frac{1}{2}\left[\int \frac{2x-1}{\sqrt{x^2-x}}dx-\int \frac{dx}{\sqrt{x^2-x+\frac{1}{4}-\frac{1}{4}}}\right] \quad [1]$$

$$\Rightarrow \quad I=\frac{1}{2}\left[\int \frac{dt}{\sqrt{t}}-\int \frac{dx}{\sqrt{\left(x-\frac{1}{2}\right)^2-\left(\frac{1}{2}\right)^2}}\right] \quad [1]$$

[$\because$ put $x^2-x=t \Rightarrow (2x-1)dx=dt$]

$$\Rightarrow \quad I=\frac{1}{2}\left[2\sqrt{t}-\log\left|\left(x-\frac{1}{2}\right)+\sqrt{x^2-x}\right|\right]+C \quad [1]$$

$$\Rightarrow \quad I=\sqrt{x^2-x}-\frac{1}{2}\log\left|\left(x-\frac{1}{2}\right)+\sqrt{x^2-x}\right|+C \quad [1]$$

34. Let $I=\int \frac{x^2-5x-1}{x^4+x^2+1}dx$

$$\Rightarrow \quad I=\int \frac{x^2-1}{x^4+x^2+1}dx-5\int \frac{x}{x^4+x^2+1}dx$$

$$\Rightarrow \quad I=I_1-5I_2 \text{ (say)} \quad \text{...(i) [1/2]}$$

Now, $I_1=\int \frac{x^2-1}{x^4+x^2+1}dx$

$$=\int \frac{x^2\left(1-\frac{1}{x^2}\right)}{x^2\left(x^2+1+\frac{1}{x^2}\right)}dx$$

$$=\int \frac{(1-1/x^2)}{\left(x^2+\frac{1}{x^2}+1\right)}dx=\int \frac{\left(1-\frac{1}{x^2}\right)}{\left(x+\frac{1}{x}\right)^2-1}dx \ [1]$$

Put $x+\frac{1}{x}=t$

$$\Rightarrow \left(1-\frac{1}{x^2}\right)dx=dt$$

$$\therefore \quad I_1=\int \frac{dt}{t^2-1}=\frac{1}{2}\log\frac{|t-1|}{|t+1|}+C_1$$

$$\left[\because \int \frac{dx}{x^2-a^2}=\frac{1}{2a}\log\left|\frac{x-a}{x+a}\right|\right] \ [1]$$

$$I_1=\frac{1}{2}\log\left|\frac{x+\frac{1}{x}-1}{x+\frac{1}{x}+1}\right|+C_1 \quad \left[\text{put } t=x+\frac{1}{x}\right]$$

$$=\frac{1}{2}\log\left|\frac{x^2-x+1}{x^2+x+1}\right|+C_1 \quad [1]$$

Now, $I_2=\int \frac{x}{x^4+x^2+1}dx$

Put $x^2=t \Rightarrow 2x\,dx=dt$

$$\therefore \quad I_2=\frac{1}{2}\int \frac{dt}{t^2+t+1}=\frac{1}{2}\int \frac{dt}{\left(t+\frac{1}{2}\right)^2+\left(\frac{\sqrt{3}}{2}\right)^2} \ [1/2]$$

$$=\frac{1}{2}\times\frac{2}{\sqrt{3}}\tan^{-1}\left(\frac{\left(t+\frac{1}{2}\right)\times 2}{\sqrt{3}}\right)+C_2$$

$$\left[\because \int \frac{1}{x^2+a^2}dx=\frac{1}{a}\tan^{-1}\left(\frac{x}{a}\right)+C\right] \ [1]$$

$$=\frac{1}{\sqrt{3}}\tan^{-1}\left(\frac{2t+1}{\sqrt{3}}\right)+C_2$$

$$=\frac{1}{\sqrt{3}}\tan^{-1}\left(\frac{2x^2+1}{\sqrt{3}}\right)+C_2 \quad [\text{put } t=x^2]$$

$$\therefore \quad I=\frac{1}{2}\log\left|\frac{x^2-x+1}{x^2+x+1}\right|-\frac{5}{\sqrt{3}}\tan^{-1}\left(\frac{2x^2+1}{\sqrt{3}}\right)+C$$

[put $C_1-5C_2=C$] [1]

35. Let $I=\int \frac{1}{\cos^4 x+\sin^4 x}dx$

On dividing numerator and denominator by $\cos^4 x$, we get

$$I=\int \frac{\sec^4 x}{1+\tan^4 x}dx$$

$$\Rightarrow \quad I=\int \frac{(\sec^2 x)(\sec^2 x)}{1+\tan^4 x}dx \quad [1]$$

$$\Rightarrow \quad I=\int \frac{\sec^2 x(1+\tan^2 x)}{1+\tan^4 x}dx$$

[$\because 1+\tan^2 x=\sec^2 x$]

Now, put $\tan x=t \Rightarrow \sec^2 x\,dx=dt$

$$\therefore \quad I=\int \frac{1+t^2}{1+t^4}dt \quad [1]$$

Again, dividing numerator and denominator by t^2, we get

$$I=\int \frac{1+\frac{1}{t^2}}{t^2+\frac{1}{t^2}+2-2}dt=\int \frac{1+\frac{1}{t^2}}{\left(t-\frac{1}{t}\right)^2+2}dt$$

[adding and subtracting 2 from denominator] [1]

Again, putting $t-\frac{1}{t}=u$

$$\Rightarrow \quad \left(1+\frac{1}{t^2}\right)dt=du, \text{ we get}$$

$$I = \int \frac{du}{u^2 + (\sqrt{2})^2} \Rightarrow I = \frac{1}{\sqrt{2}} \tan^{-1}\left(\frac{u}{\sqrt{2}}\right) + C$$

$$\left[\because \int \frac{dx}{a^2 + x^2} = \frac{1}{a}\tan^{-1}\left(\frac{x}{a}\right)\right] \text{[1]}$$

$$\Rightarrow I = \frac{1}{\sqrt{2}} \tan^{-1}\left(\frac{t - \frac{1}{t}}{\sqrt{2}}\right) + C \qquad \left[\because u = t - \frac{1}{t}\right]$$

$$\Rightarrow I = \frac{1}{\sqrt{2}} \tan^{-1}\left(\frac{t^2 - 1}{\sqrt{2}t}\right) + C \qquad \text{[1]}$$

$$\Rightarrow I = \frac{1}{\sqrt{2}} \tan^{-1}\left(\frac{\tan^2 x - 1}{\sqrt{2}\tan x}\right) + C \qquad [\because t = \tan x] \text{ [1]}$$

36. Hint Let $I = \int \frac{1}{\sin^4 x + \sin^2 x \cos^2 x + \cos^4 x} dx$

On dividing numerator and denominator by $\cos^4 x$, we get

$$I = \int \frac{\sec^4 x}{\tan^4 x + \tan^2 x + 1} dx$$

$$= \int \frac{(\sec^2 x)(\sec^2 x)}{\tan^4 x + \tan^2 x + 1} dx$$

Now, put $\tan x = t \Rightarrow \sec^2 x\, dx = dt$

$$[\because \sec^2 x = 1 + \tan^2 x = 1 + t^2]$$

$$\therefore \quad I = \int \frac{1 + t^2}{t^4 + t^2 + 1} dt \qquad [\because t = \tan x]$$

Further, solve as Example 21.

$$\left[\textbf{Ans. } I = \frac{1}{\sqrt{3}} \tan^{-1}\left(\frac{\tan^2 x - 1}{\sqrt{3}\tan x}\right) + C\right]$$

37. Hint $I = \int [\sqrt{\cot x} + \sqrt{\tan x}] dx = \int \sqrt{\tan x}\,(1 + \cot x)\, dx$

Now, put $\tan x = t^2$

$$\Rightarrow \quad \sec^2 x\, dx = 2t\, dt$$

$$\Rightarrow \quad dx = \frac{2t\, dt}{1 + t^4}$$

$$\Rightarrow \quad I = \int t\left[1 + \frac{1}{t^2}\right]\frac{2t}{(1 + t^4)} dt$$

$$\Rightarrow \quad I = 2\int \frac{t^2 + 1}{t^4 + 1} dt$$

Further, solve as I_1, of Example 20.

$$\left[\textbf{Ans. } I = \sqrt{2} \tan^{-1}\left(\frac{\tan x - 1}{\sqrt{2\tan x}}\right) + C\right]$$

Chapter Practice

Multiple Choice Type Questions

1 Mark

1 Evaluate $\int \frac{x}{x^2+1}dx.$ **[ISC 2023]**

(a) $2\log(x^2+1)+C$ (b) $\frac{1}{2}\log(x^2+1)+C$

(c) $e^{x^2+1}+C$ (d) $\log x+\frac{x^2}{2}+C$

2 If $\int(\cot x-\text{cosec}^2 x)e^x dx = e^x f(x)+C$, then $f(x)$ will be **[ISC 2024]**

(a) $\cot x + \text{cosec}\, x$ (b) $\cot^2 x$

(c) $\cot x$ (d) $\text{cosec}\, x$

3 $\int e^x\left(\frac{1-x}{1+x^2}\right)^2 dx$ is equal to

(a) $\frac{e^x}{1+x^2}+C$ (b) $\frac{-e^x}{1+x^2}+C$

(c) $\frac{e^x}{(1+x^2)^2}+C$ (d) $\frac{-e^x}{(1+x^2)^2}+C$

4 If $\int\frac{1}{(x+2)(x^2+1)}dx = a\log|1+x^2|+b\tan^{-1}x + \frac{1}{5}\log|x+2|+C$, then

(a) $a=\frac{-1}{10}, b=\frac{-2}{5}$ (b) $a=\frac{1}{10}, b=\frac{-2}{5}$

(c) $a=\frac{-1}{10}, b=\frac{2}{5}$ (d) $a=\frac{1}{10}, b=\frac{2}{5}$

5 $\int\frac{1}{\sqrt{9x-4x^2}}dx$ is equal to

(a) $\frac{1}{9}\sin^{-1}\left(\frac{9x-8}{8}\right)+C$ (b) $\frac{1}{2}\sin^{-1}\left(\frac{8x-9}{9}\right)+C$

(c) $\frac{1}{3}\sin^{-1}\left(\frac{9x-8}{8}\right)+C$ (d) $\frac{1}{2}\sin^{-1}\left(\frac{9x-8}{9}\right)+C$

Assertion-Reason Type Questions

1 Mark

Directions (Q. Nos. 6-9) *In the questions given below are two statements labelled as Assertion (A) and Reason (R). In the context of the two statements, which one of the following is correct?*

(a) Both A and R are correct; R is the correct explanation of A

(b) Both A and R are correct; R is not the correct explanation of A

(c) A is correct; R is incorrect

(d) R is correct; A is incorrect

6 **Assertion** (A) $\int\frac{1}{9+4x^2}dx=\frac{1}{6}\tan^{-1}\frac{2x}{3}+C$

Reason (R) $\int\frac{1}{x^2+a^2}dx=\frac{1}{a}\tan^{-1}\frac{x}{a}+C$

7 **Assertion (A)** $\int\cos^{-1}(\sin x)dx=\frac{\pi}{2}x+\frac{x^2}{2}+C$

Reason (R) $\cos\left(\frac{\pi}{2}-x\right)=\sin x$

8 **Assertion (A)** $\int 2^{3x+2}dx=\frac{2^{3x+2}}{\log 8}+C$

Reason (R) If $\int f(x)dx=F(x)+C$, then

$$f(ax+b)\,dx=\frac{F(ax+b)}{a}+C$$

9 **Assertion (A)** $\int x^2\log x\,dx=\frac{x^3}{3}\left(\log x+\frac{1}{3}\right)+C$

Reason (R) $\int uv\,dx = u\int v\,dx-\int\left(\frac{d}{dx}(u)\int v\,dx\right)dx$

Very Short Answer Type Questions

2 Marks

10 Evaluate $\int\frac{\sec^2|\log x|}{x}dx.$

11 Evaluate $\int\frac{\log|\sin x|}{\tan x}dx.$

12 Evaluate $\int\frac{x+\cos 6x}{3x^2+\sin 6x}dx.$

[**Hint** Put $3x^2+\sin 6x=t$]

13 Evaluate $\int\sec x^\circ\tan x^\circ dx.$ $\left[\textbf{Hint} \text{ Write } x^\circ=\frac{\pi x}{180}\right]$

14 Evaluate $\int e^{3\log x}(x^4+1)^{-1}dx.$

$\left[\textbf{Hint } I=\int\frac{x^3}{(x^4+1)}dx\right]$

15 Evaluate $\int \frac{\sin^6 x}{\cos^8 x} dx$.

16 Evaluate $\int \frac{\sec^2 x}{\operatorname{cosec}^2 x} dx$.

17 Evaluate $\int \frac{2}{1+\cos 2x} dx$.

18 Evaluate $\int \sqrt{1+\sin x}\, dx$.

$\left[\textbf{Hint } 1+\sin x = \left(\cos\frac{x}{2} + \sin\frac{x}{2}\right)^2\right]$ **[NCERT Exemplar]**

19 Evaluate $\int \sqrt{\tan x}(1+\tan^2 x) dx$.

20 Evaluate $\int \frac{\sin^6 x + \cos^6 x}{\sin^2 x \cos^2 x} dx$.

21 Evaluate $\int (\operatorname{cosec}^2 x - \cot x) e^x dx$.

22 Given, $\int e^x (\tan x + 1) \sec x \, dx = e^x f(x) + C$. Write $f(x)$ satisfying above.

23 Evaluate $\int \frac{x}{x^4 - 1} dx$.

$\left[\textbf{Hint } \int \frac{x}{x^4-1} dx = \int \frac{x}{(x^2)^2 - 1} dx, \text{ put } x^2 = t\right]$

[NCERT Exemplar]

24 Evaluate $\int x\sqrt{x^4 - 1}\, dx$.

Short Answer Type Questions

4 Marks

25 Evaluate $\int \frac{\sqrt{x}}{x+1} dx$.

$\left[\textbf{Hint } \int \frac{\sqrt{x}}{x+1} dx = \int \frac{x\, dx}{\sqrt{x}(x+1)}\right]$

26 Evaluate $\int \frac{\sin(x-a)}{\sin(x+a)} dx$. [**Hint** Put $x + a = t$]

27 Evaluate $\int \frac{\sin 2x}{(a+b\cos x)^2} dx$.

[**Hint** $\sin 2x = 2\sin x \cos x$ and put $a + b\cos x = t$]

28 Evaluate $\int \frac{\cos x}{\left(\cos\frac{x}{2} + \sin\frac{x}{2}\right)^3} dx$.

$\left[\textbf{Hint } \text{Use } \cos x = \cos^2\frac{x}{2} - \sin^2\frac{x}{2} \text{ and simplify it, then put } \cos\frac{x}{2} + \sin\frac{x}{2} = t\right]$

29 Evaluate $\int \sin^4 x\, dx$.

$\left[\textbf{Hint } \sin^4 x = \left(\frac{1-\cos 2x}{2}\right)^2 \text{ and } \cos^2 2x = \frac{1+\cos 4x}{2}\right]$

30 Evaluate $\int \sin 4x \cdot \cos 3x\, dx$.

31 Evaluate $\int \tan^8 x \sec^4 x\, dx$. **[NCERT Exemplar]**

32 Evaluate $\int x \sin^{-1} x\, dx$.

33 Evaluate $\int \sec^3 x\, dx$.

[**Hint** $\int \sec^3 x\, dx = \int \underset{\text{II}}{\sec^2 x} \cdot \underset{\text{I}}{\sec x}\, dx$]

34 Evaluate $\int \sin(\log x)\, dx$.

[**Hint** Put $\log x = t \Rightarrow x = e^t \Rightarrow dx = e^t\, dt$

$\therefore I = \int e^t \sin t\, dt$, apply integration by parts]

35 Evaluate $\int \left(\frac{1+\sin x}{1+\cos x}\right) e^x dx$.

$\left[\textbf{Hint } 1+\sin x = 1 + 2\sin\frac{x}{2}\cos\frac{x}{2} \text{ and } 1+\cos x = 2\cos^2\frac{x}{2}\right]$

36 Evaluate $\int \frac{xe^{2x}}{(1+2x)^2} dx$.

37 Evaluate $\int \frac{(3x+1)}{(x+1)^2 (x+3)} dx$.

38 Evaluate $\int \frac{dx}{x(x^5+3)}$.

[**Hint** Multiply numerator and denominator by x^4]

39 Evaluate $\int \frac{5x}{(x+1)(x^2+9)} dx$. **[NCERT]**

40 Evaluate $\int \frac{x^2}{(x^2+a^2)(x^2+b^2)} dx$. **[NCERT Exemplar]**

41 Evaluate $\int \frac{x^2+1}{(x^2+4)(x^2+25)} dx$.

42 Evaluate $\int \frac{2x^2+1}{x^2(x^2+4)} dx$.

[**Hint** Put $x^2 = t$ and then use partial fractions]

43 Evaluate $\int \frac{x}{x^4+x^2+1} dx$. [**Hint** Put $x^2 = t$]

44 Evaluate $\int \frac{5x-2}{1+2x+3x^2} dx$.

$\left[\textbf{Hint } \text{Let } 5x - 2 = A\frac{d}{dx}(1+2x+3x^2) + B\right]$

45 Evaluate $\int \frac{x+2}{\sqrt{x^2+2x+3}}dx.$

[**Hint** Write given integral as

$$\int \frac{(x+1)}{\sqrt{x^2+2x+3}}dx + \int \frac{1}{\sqrt{x^2+2x+3}}dx]$$

46 Evaluate $\int \frac{x+2}{\sqrt{4x-x^2}}dx.$

[**Hint** Let $x+2 = A\frac{d}{dx}(4x-x^2)+B$] **[NCERT]**

47 Evaluate $\int \frac{dx}{\sin x+\sqrt{3}\cos x}dx.$

48 Evaluate $\int \frac{x^2}{x^4-x^2+12}dx.$

[**Hint** $\int \frac{x^2}{x^4-x^2+12}dx = \int \frac{x^2}{(x^2-4)(x^2-3)}dx$]

[NCERT Exemplar]

Long Answer Type Questions

6 Marks

49 Evaluate $\int x(\log x)^2 dx.$

[**Hint** Take $(\log x)^2$ as Ist function and x as IInd function] **[NCERT]**

50 Evaluate $\int \frac{3x+5}{x^3-x^2-x+1}dx.$

[**Hint** Use the partial fractions] **[NCERT]**

51 Evaluate $\int \frac{x^2+x+1}{(x+1)^2(x+2)}dx.$

52 Evaluate $\int \frac{\tan\theta+\tan^3\theta}{1+\tan^3\theta}d\theta.$

Case-Based Type Question

6 Marks

53 Let $f(x)$ be a function and $f'(x)$ be its derivative. Now, teacher ask Raju, can you answer my question. Raju says, "What is your question?"

Teacher wrote question on blackboard.

After reading the question, Raju gave the answer as $e^x f(x)+C$.

On the basis of above information, answer the following questions.

(i) If $\int e^x\left(\frac{1}{x^2}-\frac{2}{x^3}\right)dx = e^x f(x)+C$, then Find the value of $f(x)$.

(ii) Find the value of $\int e^x \sec x(1+\tan x)dx$.

(iii) Find the value of $\int \frac{e^x}{x}\{x(\log x)^2+2\log x\}dx$.

(iv) Find the value of $\int [\tan(\log x)+\sec^2(\log x)]dx$.

Answers

1. (b) 2. (c) 3. (c) 4. (c) 5. (b) 6. (a)
7. (d) 8. (a) 9. (d)

10. $\tan(\log|x|) + C$

11. $\dfrac{(\log|\sin x|)^2}{2} + C$

12. $\dfrac{1}{6}\log\left|3x^2 + \sin 6x\right| + C$

13. $\dfrac{180}{\pi}\sec x° + C$

14. $\dfrac{1}{4}\log(x^4 + 1) + C$

15. $\dfrac{\tan^7 x}{7} + C$

16. $\tan x - x + C$

17. $\tan x + C$

18. $-2\cos\dfrac{x}{2} + 2\sin\dfrac{x}{2} + C$

19. $\dfrac{2}{3}(\tan x)^{3/2} + C$

20. $\tan x - \cot x - 3x + C$

21. $-e^x \cot x + C$

22. $f(x) = \sec x$

23. $\dfrac{1}{4}\log\left|\dfrac{x^2-1}{x^2+1}\right| + C$

24. $\dfrac{1}{2}\left[\dfrac{x^2\sqrt{x^4-1}}{2} - \dfrac{1}{2}\log\left|x^2 + \sqrt{x^4-1}\right|\right] + C$

25. $2[\sqrt{x} - \tan^{-1}\sqrt{x}] + C$

26. $(x + a)\cos 2a - \sin 2a \log|\sin(x + a)| + C$

27. $-\dfrac{2}{b^2}\left[\log|a + b\cos x| + \dfrac{a}{a + b\cos x}\right] + C$

28. $-\dfrac{2}{\cos\dfrac{x}{2} + \sin\dfrac{x}{2}} + C$

29. $\dfrac{3}{8}x - \dfrac{\sin 2x}{4} + \dfrac{\sin 4x}{32} + C$

30. $-\dfrac{\cos 7x}{14} - \dfrac{\cos x}{2} + C$

31. $\dfrac{\tan^{11} x}{11} + \dfrac{\tan^9 x}{9} + C$

32. $\dfrac{\sin^{-1} x}{4}(2x^2 - 1) + \dfrac{x}{4}\sqrt{1 - x^2} + C$

33. $\dfrac{1}{2}[\sec x \tan x + \log|\sec x + \tan x|] + C$

34. $\dfrac{x}{2}[\sin(\log x) - \cos(\log x)] + C$

35. $e^x \tan\dfrac{x}{2} + C$

36. $\dfrac{1}{4}\cdot\dfrac{e^{2x}}{1 + 2x} + C$

37. $2\log\left|\dfrac{x+1}{x+3}\right| + \dfrac{1}{(x+1)} + C$

38. $\dfrac{1}{15}\log\left|\dfrac{x^5}{x^5 + 3}\right| + C$

39. $-\dfrac{1}{2}\log|x + 1| + \dfrac{1}{4}\log(x^2 + 9) + \dfrac{3}{2}\tan^{-1}\dfrac{x}{3} + C$

40. $\dfrac{1}{a^2 - b^2}\left[a\tan^{-1}\dfrac{x}{a} - b\tan^{-1}\dfrac{x}{b}\right] + C$

41. $-\dfrac{1}{14}\tan^{-1}\left(\dfrac{x}{2}\right) + \dfrac{8}{35}\tan^{-1}\left(\dfrac{x}{5}\right) + C$

42. $-\dfrac{1}{4x} + \dfrac{7}{8}\tan^{-1}\left(\dfrac{x}{2}\right) + C$

43. $\dfrac{1}{\sqrt{3}}\tan^{-1}\left(\dfrac{2x^2 + 1}{\sqrt{3}}\right) + C$

44. $\dfrac{5}{6}\log\left|1 + 2x + 3x^2\right| - \dfrac{11}{3\sqrt{2}}\tan^{-1}\left(\dfrac{3x + 1}{\sqrt{2}}\right) + C$

45. $\sqrt{x^2 + 2x + 3} + \log\left|(x + 1) + \sqrt{x^2 + 2x + 3}\right| + C$

46. $-\sqrt{4x - x^2} + 4\sin^{-1}\left(\dfrac{x-2}{2}\right) + C$

47. $\dfrac{1}{2}\log\left|\tan\left(\dfrac{x}{2} + \dfrac{\pi}{6}\right)\right| + C$

48. $\dfrac{1}{7}\log\left|\dfrac{x-2}{x+2}\right| + \dfrac{\sqrt{3}}{7}\tan^{-1}\dfrac{x}{\sqrt{3}} + C$

49. $\dfrac{x^2}{2}(\log|x|)^2 - \dfrac{x^2}{2}\log|x| + \dfrac{x^2}{4} + C$

50. $\dfrac{1}{2}\log\left|\dfrac{x+1}{x-1}\right| - \dfrac{4}{(x-1)} + C$

51. $-2\log|x + 1| - \dfrac{1}{(x+1)} + 3\log|x + 2| + C$

52. $-\dfrac{1}{3}\log|1 + \tan\theta| + \dfrac{1}{6}\log|\tan^2\theta - \tan\theta + 1| + \dfrac{1}{\sqrt{3}}\tan^{-1}\left(\dfrac{2\tan\theta - 1}{\sqrt{3}}\right) + C$

53. (i) $\dfrac{1}{x^2}$ (ii) $e^x \sec x + C$ (iii) $e^x(\log x)^2$ (iv) $x\tan(\log x) + C$

CHAPTER

09

Definite Integrals

An integral of the form of $\int_a^b f(x)\,dx$ is known as **definite integral**, where a and b are called the **lower** and **upper limits** of a definite integral. The value of definite integral is given by either as the limit of a sum or if it has an anti-derivative F, then its value is the difference between the values of F at the end points, i.e. $F(b) - F(a)$. Here, $\int_a^b f(x)dx$ is read as 'the integral of $f(x)$ from a to b'.

- Fundamental Theorem of Integral Calculus
- Properties of Definite Integrals

TOPIC 01 Fundamental Theorem of Integral Calculus

Fundamental theorem of integral calculus is a connection between indefinite integral and definite integral and it makes the definite integral as a practical tool for Science and Engineering.

Area Function

The space occupied by the curve $y = f(x)$ with the axis and the given coordinates $x = a$ and $x = b$ is called **area of bounded region.**

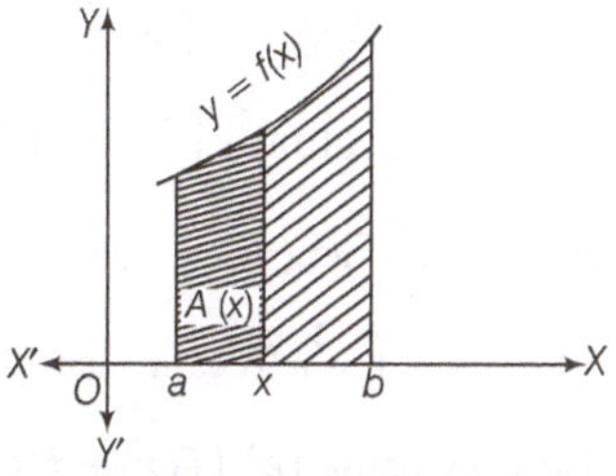

Let x be any point in $[a, b]$, then, $\int_a^x f(x)dx$ represents the area of the shaded region $A(x)$. The area of shaded region depends upon the value of x or we can say area of this shaded region is a function of x and denoted by $A(x)$.

Then, function $A(x)$ is known as **area function** and is given by $A(x) = \int_a^x f(x)dx$.

First Fundamental Theorem of Integral Calculus

Let f be a continuous function defined on the closed interval $[a, b]$ and $A(x)$ be the area of function, i.e. $A(x) = \int_a^x f(x)dx$. Then, $A'(x) = f(x)$, for all $x \in [a, b]$.

Second Fundamental Theorem of Integral Calculus

Let f be a continuous function defined on the closed interval $[a, b]$ and F be an anti-derivative of f.

Then, $\int_a^b f(x)\,dx = [F(x)]_a^b = F(b) - F(a)$

In other words, $\int_a^b f(x)\,dx$ = (Value of the anti-derivative F at the upper limit b) − (Value of the same anti-derivative at the lower limit a).

Note (i) In $\int_a^b f(x)\,dx$, the function f needs to be well-defined and continuous in $[a, b]$.

(iii) Using fundamental theorem of integral calculus, we can verify the answer of limit of a sum.

Steps for Calculating the Definite Integrals

Suppose given integral is $\int_a^b f(x)\,dx$, then to calculate, we use the following steps

I. Find the indefinite integral $\int f(x)\,dx$ by using suitable method. Let it be, $F(x)$, i.e. $\int f(x)\,dx = F(x)$.

II. Evaluate $[F(x)]_a^b = F(b) - F(a)$, which gives the required value.

Thus, $\int_a^b f(x)\,dx = [F(x)]_a^b = F(b) - F(a)$.

Note There is no need to keep integration constant C because if we consider $F(x)+C$ instead of $F(x)$, we get

$\int_a^b f(x)\,dx = [F(x)+C]_a^b = [F(b)+C]-[F(a)+C] = F(b)-F(a)$

Thus, the arbitrary constant disappears in evaluating the value of the definite integral.

Example 1 Evaluate $\int_1^2 (4x^3 - 5x^2 + 6x + 9)\,dx$. **[NCERT]**

Sol. Let $I = \int_1^2 (4x^3 - 5x^2 + 6x + 9)\,dx$ and

$$f(x) = 4x^3 - 5x^2 + 6x + 9$$

Then, $\int f(x)dx = \int (4x^3 - 5x^2 + 6x + 9)dx$

$$= \frac{4x^4}{4} - \frac{5x^3}{3} + \frac{6x^2}{2} + 9x$$

$$= x^4 - \frac{5}{3}x^3 + 3x^2 + 9x = F(x) \text{ (say)}$$

Now, by the fundamental theorem of integral calculus, we get

$I = [F(x)]_1^2 = F(2) - F(1)$

$$= \left[(2)^4 - \frac{5}{3}(2)^3 + 3(2)^2 + 9(2)\right] - \left[(1)^4 - \frac{5}{3}(1)^3 + 3(1)^2 + 9(1)\right]$$

$$= \left[16 - \frac{40}{3} + 12 + 18\right] - \left[1 - \frac{5}{3} + 3 + 9\right]$$

$$= \left[46 - \frac{40}{3}\right] - \left[13 - \frac{5}{3}\right] = \left[\frac{138-40}{3}\right] - \left[\frac{39-5}{3}\right]$$

$$= \frac{98}{3} - \frac{34}{3} = \frac{64}{3}$$

Example 2 Evaluate $\int_0^{\pi/2} \cos^2 x\,dx$.

Sol. Let $I = \int_0^{\pi/2} \cos^2 x\,dx$

Here, $\int \cos^2 dx = \int \left(\frac{\cos 2x + 1}{2}\right)dx$ $[\because \cos 2x = 2\cos^2 x - 1]$

$$= \frac{1}{2}\int \cos 2x\,dx + \frac{1}{2}\int 1\,dx$$

$$= \frac{1}{2}\left[\frac{\sin 2x}{2}\right] + \frac{1}{2}x = \frac{1}{4}\sin 2x + \frac{1}{2}x = F(x) \text{ (say)}$$

Now, by the fundamental theorem of integral calculus, we get

$$I = [F(x)]_0^{\pi/2} = F(\pi/2) - F(0)$$

$$= \left[\frac{1}{4}\sin 2\left(\frac{\pi}{2}\right) + \frac{1}{2}\left(\frac{\pi}{2}\right)\right] - \left[\frac{1}{4}\sin(0) + \frac{1}{2}(0)\right]$$

$$= \left[\frac{1}{4}(0) + \frac{\pi}{4}\right] - [0+0] = \frac{\pi}{4}$$

Example 3 Evaluate $\int_0^{\pi/2} e^x (\sin x - \cos x)\,dx$.

Sol. Let $I = \int_0^{\pi/2} e^x (\sin x - \cos x)\,dx$

$$\Rightarrow I = -\int_0^{\pi/2} e^x (\cos x - \sin x)\,dx$$

Now, by using $\int e^x [f(x) + f'(x)]\,dx = e^x f(x)$, we get

$I = -[e^x \cos x]_0^{\pi/2}$ [here, $f(x) = \cos x$]

$$= -e^{\pi/2}\cos\frac{\pi}{2} + e^0 \cos(0) = 0 + 1(1) = 1$$

Example 4 Evaluate $\int_0^1 |2x+1|\, dx$. **[ISC 2023]**

Sol. Let $I = \int_0^1 |2x+1|\, dx$

$= \int_0^1 (2x+1)\, dx \qquad [\because 2x+1>0;\ x \in (0,1)]$

$= [x^2 + x]_0^1 = (1+1) - 0 = 2$

Evaluation of Definite Integral by Substitution

To evaluate $\int_a^b f(x)\,dx$ by substitution, we follow the following steps

I. First, make suitable substitution, so that given integral reduces to a known form.

II. Change the upper and lower limits corresponding to the new variable.

III. Integrate the new integral with respect to the new variable.

Example 5 Evaluate $\int_1^3 \frac{1}{x(1+\log x)}\, dx$.

Sol. Let $I = \int_1^3 \frac{dx}{x(1+\log x)}$

Now, putting $\log x = t \Rightarrow \frac{1}{x}dx = dt$

Lower limit When $x = 1$, then $t = \log 1 \Rightarrow t = 0$

Upper limit When $x = 3$, then $t = \log 3$

Now, $I = \int_0^{\log 3} \frac{dt}{(1+t)} = [\log|1+t|]_0^{\log 3}$

$= \log|1+\log 3| - \log|1+0|$

$= \log|1+\log 3| - \log 1$

$= \log|1+\log 3| - 0 \qquad [\because \log 1 = 0]$

$= \log|1+\log 3|$

Example 6 Evaluate $\int_0^{\pi/2} \sqrt{\sin\phi}\, \cos^5 \phi\, d\phi$.

Sol. Let $I = \int_0^{\pi/2} \sqrt{\sin\phi}\, \cos^5\phi\, d\phi$

$= \int_0^{\pi/2} \sqrt{\sin\phi}\, \cos^4\phi \cos\phi\, d\phi$

$= \int_0^{\pi/2} \sqrt{\sin\phi}\,(1-\sin^2\phi)^2 \cos\phi\, d\phi$

Now, put $\sin\phi = t \Rightarrow \cos\phi\, d\phi = dt$

Lower limit When $\phi = 0$, then $t = 0$

Upper limit When $\phi = \frac{\pi}{2}$, then $t = 1$

Now, $I = \int_0^1 \sqrt{t}(1-t^2)^2\, dt = \int_0^1 \sqrt{t}(1+t^4-2t^2)\, dt$

$= \int_0^1 (t^{1/2} + t^{9/2} - 2t^{5/2})\, dt$

$= \left[\frac{t^{3/2}}{3/2} + \frac{t^{11/2}}{11/2} - \frac{2t^{7/2}}{7/2}\right]_0^1$

$= \left[\frac{2}{3}t^{3/2} + \frac{2}{11}t^{11/2} - \frac{4}{7}t^{7/2}\right]_0^1$

$= \frac{2}{3} + \frac{2}{11} - \frac{4}{7}$

$= \frac{154+42-132}{11\times 3\times 7} = \frac{64}{231}$

Example 7 Evaluate $\int_{\pi/6}^{\pi/3} \frac{\sin x + \cos x}{\sqrt{\sin 2x}}\, dx$.

Sol. Let $I = \int_{\pi/6}^{\pi/3} \frac{\sin x + \cos x}{\sqrt{\sin 2x}}\, dx$

We know that,

$(\sin x - \cos x)^2 = \sin^2 x + \cos^2 x - 2\sin x \cos x$

$\Rightarrow (\sin x - \cos x)^2 = 1 - \sin 2x$

$[\because \sin^2 x + \cos^2 x = 1 \text{ and } 2\sin x\cos x = \sin 2x]$

$\Rightarrow \sin 2x = 1 - (\sin x - \cos x)^2$

Now, putting $\sin x - \cos x = t$ ...(i)

$\Rightarrow (\cos x + \sin x)\, dx = dt$

Also, when $x = \frac{\pi}{6}$, then

$\Rightarrow t = \sin\frac{\pi}{6} - \cos\frac{\pi}{6} = \frac{1}{2} - \frac{\sqrt{3}}{2} = \frac{1-\sqrt{3}}{2}$

When $x = \frac{\pi}{3}$, then

$t = \sin\frac{\pi}{3} - \cos\frac{\pi}{3} = \frac{\sqrt{3}}{2} - \frac{1}{2} = \frac{\sqrt{3}-1}{2}$

$\therefore I = \int_{\frac{1-\sqrt{3}}{2}}^{\frac{\sqrt{3}-1}{2}} \frac{1}{\sqrt{1-t^2}}\, dt$

$= \int_{\frac{1-\sqrt{3}}{2}}^{\frac{\sqrt{3}-1}{2}} \frac{1}{\sqrt{1-t^2}}\, dt = [\sin^{-1} t]_{\frac{1-\sqrt{3}}{2}}^{\frac{\sqrt{3}-1}{2}}$

$= \left[\sin^{-1}\left(\frac{\sqrt{3}-1}{2}\right) - \sin^{-1}\left\{-\left(\frac{\sqrt{3}-1}{2}\right)\right\}\right]$

$= \left[\sin^{-1}\left(\frac{\sqrt{3}-1}{2}\right) + \sin^{-1}\left(\frac{\sqrt{3}-1}{2}\right)\right]$

$[\because \sin^{-1}(-\theta) = -\sin^{-1}\theta]$

$= 2\sin^{-1}\left(\frac{\sqrt{3}-1}{2}\right)$

Topic Practice 1

Very Short Answer Type Questions

2 Marks

Directions (Q. Nos. 1-11) *Evaluate the following integrals.*

1 $\int_0^{\pi/4} \tan x\, dx$

2 $\int_{\pi/6}^{\pi/4} \operatorname{cosec} x\, dx$ **[NCERT]**

3 $\int_2^3 [x] dx$, where $[x]$ is the greatest integer function.

4 $\int_0^{\pi/4} \sqrt{1+\sin 2x}\, dx$ **[NCERT Exemplar]**

5 $\int_0^1 \frac{dx}{\sqrt{1+x}-\sqrt{x}}$

6 $\int_0^1 \frac{dx}{e^x + e^{-x}}$ **[NCERT Exemplar]**

7 $\int_e^{e^2} \frac{dx}{x \log x}$

8 $\int_2^4 \frac{x}{x^2+1} dx$

9 $\int_0^1 x\, e^{x^2} dx$

10 $\int_0^1 \frac{x}{\sqrt{1+x^2}} dx$ **[NCERT Exemplar]**

11 $\int_0^{\pi/2} \cos x\, e^{\sin x} dx$ **[NCERT Exemplar]**

12 If $\int_0^a \frac{1}{4+x^2} dx = \frac{\pi}{8}$, then find the value of a.

Short Answer Type Questions

4 Marks

Directions (Q. Nos. 13-19) *Evaluate the following integrals.*

13 Evaluate $\int_0^1 \frac{xe^x}{(1+x)^2} dx$ **[ISC 2011]**

14 Prove that $\int_1^3 \frac{1}{x^2(x+1)} dx = \frac{2}{3} + \log \frac{2}{3}$. **[NCERT]**

15 Evaluate $\int_1^2 \frac{dx}{\sqrt{(x-1)(2-x)}}$.

16 Evaluate $\int_0^1 x(\tan^{-1} x)\, dx$.

17 If $f(x) = \int_0^x t \sin t\, dt$, then write the value of $f'(x)$.

18 Evaluate $\int_0^1 x \cdot \sqrt{\frac{1-x^2}{1+x^2}}\, dx$.

19 Prove that $\int_0^{\pi/4} 2\tan^3 x\, dx = 1 - \log 2$.

Directions (Q. Nos. 20-25) *Evaluate the following integrals.*

20 $\int_0^{\pi/4} \frac{1}{\cos^2 x + 4\sin^2 x} dx$

21 $\int_0^{1/\sqrt{2}} \frac{\sin^{-1} x}{(1-x^2)^{3/2}} dx$

22 $\int_0^1 x(\tan^{-1} x)^2\, dx$ **[NCERT Exemplar]**

23 $\int_{\pi/3}^{\pi/2} \frac{\sqrt{1+\cos x}}{(1-\cos x)^{5/2}} dx$ **[NCERT Exemplar]**

24 $\int_0^{\pi/4} \frac{dx}{\cos^3 x \sqrt{2\sin 2x}}$

25 $\int_0^{\pi/4} \frac{\sin x + \cos x}{9 + 16\sin 2x} dx$ **[NCERT]**

Long Answer Type Questions

6 Marks

26 Evaluate $\int_0^{\pi} e^{2x} \cdot \sin\left(\frac{\pi}{4} + x\right) dx$.

27 Evaluate $\int_0^{\pi/2} \sin 2x \tan^{-1}(\sin x)\, dx$. **[NCERT]**

28 Evaluate $\int_0^{\pi/2} \frac{\sin x \cos x}{\cos^2 x + 3\cos x + 2} dx$.

Hints & Solutions

1. Let $I = \int_0^{\pi/4} \tan x\, dx = [\log|\sec x|]_0^{\pi/4}$ [1]

$= \log\left|\sec\frac{\pi}{4}\right| - \log|\sec 0|$

$= \log\sqrt{2} - \log 1 = \log\sqrt{2} - 0 = \log\sqrt{2}$ [1]

2. Let $I = \int_{\pi/6}^{\pi/4} \operatorname{cosec} x\, dx = [\log|\operatorname{cosec} x - \cot x|]_{\pi/6}^{\pi/4}$ [1]

$= \log\left|\operatorname{cosec}\frac{\pi}{4} - \cot\frac{\pi}{4}\right| - \log\left|\operatorname{cosec}\frac{\pi}{6} - \cot\frac{\pi}{6}\right|$

$= \log|\sqrt{2}-1| - \log|2-\sqrt{3}|$

$= \log\left|\frac{\sqrt{2}-1}{2-\sqrt{3}}\right|$ [1]

3. **Hint** $\int_2^3 [x]\,dx = \int_2^3 2\,dx$ [$\because$ if $2 < x < 3$, then $[x] = 2$]
[**Ans.** 2]

4. **Hint** Use the formula, $1 + \sin 2x = (\cos x + \sin x)^2$.
[**Ans.** 1]

5. **Hint** Rationalise the denominator, i.e. multiply numerator and denominator by $\sqrt{1+x} + \sqrt{x}$.
$\left[\textbf{Ans. } \frac{4\sqrt{2}}{3}\right]$

6. Let $I = \int_0^1 \frac{dx}{e^x + e^{-x}} = \int_0^1 \frac{e^x}{e^{2x}+1}\,dx$

Now, put $e^x = t \Rightarrow e^x dx = dt$

Upper limit When $x = 1$, then $t = e^1 = e$

Lower limit When $x = 0$, then $t = e^0 = 1$ [1]

$$\therefore \quad I = \int_1^e \frac{dt}{t^2+1} = [\tan^{-1} t]_1^e$$
$$= \tan^{-1} e - \tan^{-1} 1$$
$$= \tan^{-1} e - \frac{\pi}{4} \quad [1]$$

7. Let $I = \int_e^{e^2} \frac{dx}{x \log x}$

Now, put $\log x = t \Rightarrow \frac{1}{x}dx = dt$

Lower limit When $x = e$, then $t = \log e = 1$

Upper limit When $x = e^2$, then $t = \log e^2 = 2 \log e = 2$ [1]

Now, $I = \int_1^2 \frac{dt}{t} = [\log t]_1^2$
$= \log 2 - \log 1 = \log 2$ [$\because \log 1 = 0$] [1]

8. **Hint** On putting $1 + x^2 = t$, given integral reduces to
$\frac{1}{2}\int_5^{17} \frac{dt}{t}$. $\left[\textbf{Ans. } \frac{1}{2}\log\left(\frac{17}{5}\right)\right]$

9. Let $I = \int_0^1 x e^{x^2}\,dx$

Now, put $x^2 = t \Rightarrow 2x\,dx = dt$

Upper limit when $x = 1$, then $t = 1^2 = 1$

Lower limit When $x = 0$, then $t = 0$ [1]

$$\therefore \quad I = \int_0^1 e^t \frac{dt}{2} = \frac{1}{2}[e^t]_0^1 = \frac{1}{2}[e^1 - e^0] = \frac{1}{2}(e-1) \quad [1]$$

10. **Hint** On putting $1 + x^2 = t$, given integral reduces to
$\frac{1}{2}\int_1^2 \frac{dt}{\sqrt{t}}$. [**Ans.** $\sqrt{2} - 1$]

11. **Hint** On putting $\sin x = t$, given integral reduces to $\int_0^1 e^t dt$. [**Ans.** $e - 1$]

12. **Hint** $\frac{1}{2}\tan^{-1}\left(\frac{a}{2}\right) = \frac{\pi}{8}$

$$\Rightarrow \quad \tan^{-1}\left(\frac{a}{2}\right) = \frac{\pi}{4}$$
$$\Rightarrow \quad \frac{a}{2} = \tan\left(\frac{\pi}{4}\right) \quad [\textbf{Ans. } a = 2]$$

13. Let $I = \int_0^1 \frac{xe^x}{(1+x)^2}\,dx$

$$= \int_0^1 \frac{[(1+x)-1]\,e^x}{(1+x)^2}\,dx$$

[adding and subtracting 1 in numerator] [1]

$$= \int_0^1 \left(\frac{e^x}{(1+x)} - \frac{e^x}{(1+x)^2}\right)dx \quad [1]$$
$$= \int_0^1 e^x\left(\frac{1}{(1+x)} - \frac{1}{(1+x)^2}\right)dx$$
$$\therefore \quad I = \left[\frac{e^x}{(1+x)}\right]_0^1 = \left(\frac{e^1}{2} - \frac{e^0}{1+0}\right)$$

[using $\int e^x \{f(x) + f'(x)\}\,dx = e^x f(x) + C$]

$$\Rightarrow \quad I = \left(\frac{e}{2} - 1\right) \quad [2]$$

14. To prove, $\int_1^3 \frac{1}{x^2(x+1)}\,dx = \frac{2}{3} + \log\frac{2}{3}$

Let $\frac{1}{x^2(x+1)} = \frac{A}{x} + \frac{B}{x^2} + \frac{C}{x+1}$ ...(i)

[by partial fraction]

$\Rightarrow \; 1 = Ax(x+1) + B(x+1) + Cx^2$ ...(ii)

On putting $x = 0, -1$ respectively in Eq. (ii), we get
$1 = B(0+1)$ and $1 = C(-1)^2 \Rightarrow B = 1$ and $C = 1$ [1]

On equating the coefficient of x^2 from both sides of Eq. (ii), we get
$0 = A + C \Rightarrow A = -C \Rightarrow A = -1$

$$\therefore \int_1^3 \frac{1}{x^2(x+1)}\,dx = \int_1^3 \left(-\frac{1}{x} + \frac{1}{x^2} + \frac{1}{x+1}\right)dx \quad [1]$$
$$= \left[-\log|x| - \frac{1}{x} + \log|x+1|\right]_1^3$$
$$= \left[\log\left|\frac{x+1}{x}\right| - \frac{1}{x}\right]_1^3$$

$\left[\because \log\left(\frac{m}{n}\right) = \log m - \log n\right]$

$$= \left(\log\left|\frac{4}{3}\right| - \frac{1}{3}\right) - \left(\log\left|\frac{2}{1}\right| - \frac{1}{1}\right) \quad [1]$$
$$= \left[\log\frac{4}{3} - \log 2\right] + \left[1 - \frac{1}{3}\right]$$
$$= \log\left(\frac{4}{3} \times \frac{1}{2}\right) + \frac{2}{3}$$
$$= \log\frac{2}{3} + \frac{2}{3} \quad [1]$$

15. **Hint** $\int \frac{dx}{\sqrt{(x-1)(2-x)}} = \int \frac{dx}{\sqrt{\left(\frac{1}{2}\right)^2 - \left(x-\frac{3}{2}\right)^2}}$ and

use $\sin^{-1}(-x) = -\sin^{-1}x, \forall x \in [-1, 1]$. [**Ans.** π]

16. Let $I = \int_0^1 \underset{\text{II}}{x} \underset{\text{I}}{\tan^{-1} x}\, dx = \left[\tan^{-1} x \cdot \frac{x^2}{2} - \int \frac{1}{1+x^2} \cdot \frac{x^2}{2} dx\right]_0^1$

[using integration by parts] [1]

$= \left[\frac{x^2}{2} \cdot \tan^{-1} x - \frac{1}{2}\int \frac{x^2+1-1}{1+x^2} dx\right]_0^1$ [1]

$= \left[\frac{x^2}{2}\tan^{-1} x\right]_0^1 - \frac{1}{2}\int_0^1 dx + \frac{1}{2}\int_0^1 \frac{dx}{1+x^2}$

$= \left[\frac{1}{2}\tan^{-1}(1) - 0\right] - \frac{1}{2}(1-0) + \frac{1}{2}[\tan^{-1} x]_0^1$ [1]

$= \frac{1}{2}\cdot\frac{\pi}{4} - \frac{1}{2} + \frac{1}{2}[\tan^{-1}(1) - \tan^{-1}(0)]$

$= \frac{\pi}{8} - \frac{1}{2} + \frac{\pi}{8} = \frac{\pi}{4} - \frac{1}{2}$ [1]

17. We have, $f(x) = \int_0^x \underset{\text{I}}{t}\, \underset{\text{II}}{\sin t}\, dt$

$= \left[t\int \sin t\, dt - \int\left[\frac{d}{dt}(t)\int \sin t\, dt\right]dt\right]_0^x$

[using integration by parts] [1]

$= [t(-\cos t)]_0^x - \int_0^x (-\cos t)dt = [-t\cos t]_0^x + [\sin t]_0^x$ [1]

$= -x\cos x + 0 + \sin x - 0 = \sin x - x\cos x$ [1]

Thus, $f(x) = \sin x - x\cos x$

On differentiating both sides w.r.t. x, we get

$f'(x) = \cos x - \left[x\frac{d}{dx}(\cos x) + \cos x\frac{d}{dx}(x)\right]$

[by product rule of derivative]

$= \cos x - [x(-\sin x) + \cos x]$

$= \cos x + x\sin x - \cos x = x\sin x$ [1]

18. **Hint** On putting $x^2 = t$, then the given integral reduces to $\frac{1}{2}\int_0^1 \sqrt{\frac{1-t}{1+t}}\, dt = \frac{1}{2}\int_0^1 \frac{1-t}{\sqrt{1-t^2}} dt$

$= \frac{1}{2}\left\{\int_0^1 \frac{dt}{\sqrt{1-t^2}} - \int_0^1 \frac{t}{\sqrt{1-t^2}} dt\right\}$ $\left[\textbf{Ans. } \frac{\pi}{4} + \frac{1}{2}\right]$

19. **Hint** Write $\tan^3 x = \tan^2 x \cdot \tan x = (\sec^2 x - 1)\tan x$ $= \sec^2 x \tan x - \tan x$, then the given integral reduces to $2\int_0^{\pi/4} \sec^2 x \cdot \tan x\, dx - 2\int_0^{\pi/4} \tan x\, dx$.

20. Let $I = \int_0^{\pi/4} \frac{dx}{\cos^2 x + 4\sin^2 x} = \int_0^{\pi/4} \frac{\sec^2 x}{1 + 4\tan^2 x} dx$

[dividing numerator and denominator by $\cos^2 x$] [1]

Now, put $\tan x = t \Rightarrow \sec^2 x\, dx = dt$

Lower limit When $x = 0$, then $t = 0$.

Upper limit When $x = \frac{\pi}{4}$, then $t = 1$. [1]

$\therefore \quad I = \int_0^1 \frac{dt}{1+4t^2} = \int_0^1 \frac{dt}{1^2 + (2t)^2}$

$= \left[\frac{\tan^{-1}(2t)}{2}\right]_0^1$ [1]

$= \frac{1}{2}[\tan^{-1} 2 - \tan^{-1} 0] = \frac{1}{2}\tan^{-1} 2$ [1]

21. Let $I = \int_0^{1/\sqrt{2}} \frac{\sin^{-1} x}{(1-x^2)^{3/2}} dx$

Now, put $x = \sin\theta \Rightarrow dx = \cos\theta\, d\theta$.

Lower limit When $x = 0$, then $\theta = 0$.

Upper limit When $x = \frac{1}{\sqrt{2}}$, then $\theta = \frac{\pi}{4}$. [1]

Now, $I = \int_0^{\pi/4} \frac{\theta\cos\theta}{(1-\sin^2\theta)^{3/2}} d\theta = \int_0^{\pi/4} \frac{\theta\cos\theta}{(\cos^2\theta)^{3/2}} d\theta$

$= \int_0^{\pi/4} \frac{\theta\cos\theta}{\cos^3\theta} d\theta$ $I = \int_0^{\pi/4} \underset{\text{I}}{\theta} \sec^2\theta\, d\theta$ [1]

Using integrating by parts, we have

$I = [\theta\tan\theta]_0^{\pi/4} - \int_0^{\pi/4} \tan\theta\, d\theta$ [1]

$= \frac{\pi}{4}\cdot\tan\frac{\pi}{4} - 0 + [\log|\cos\theta|]_0^{\pi/4}$

$= \frac{\pi}{4}\cdot 1 + \log\left(\cos\frac{\pi}{4}\right) - \log(\cos 0)$

$= \frac{\pi}{4} + \log\frac{1}{\sqrt{2}} - \log 1$

$= \frac{\pi}{4} - \frac{1}{2}\log 2$ [1]

22. Let $I = \int_0^1 x(\tan^{-1} x)^2 dx$ ...(i)

Now, put $x = \tan\theta \Rightarrow dx = \sec^2\theta\, d\theta$

Upper limit When $x = 1$, $\tan\theta = 1 \Rightarrow \theta = \tan^{-1}(1) = \frac{\pi}{4}$

Lower limit When $x = 0$, $\tan\theta = 0 \Rightarrow \theta = \tan^{-1}(0) = 0$

Now, from Eq. (i), we have

$I = \int_0^{\pi/4} \tan\theta \cdot \theta^2 \cdot \sec^2\theta\, d\theta = \int_0^{\pi/4} \underset{\text{I}}{\theta^2} \underset{\text{II}}{(\tan\theta \cdot \sec^2\theta)} d\theta$ [1]

$= \left[\theta^2 \cdot \frac{\tan^2\theta}{2}\right]_0^{\pi/4} - \int_0^{\pi/4} 2\theta \cdot \frac{\tan^2\theta}{2} d\theta$

$\left[\because \int \tan x \sec^2 x\, dx = \frac{\tan^2 x}{2}\right]$ [1]

$$= \frac{1}{2}\left[\frac{\pi^2}{16}\left(\tan\frac{\pi}{4}\right)^2 - 0\right] - \int_0^{\pi/4} \underset{\text{I}}{\theta}\cdot\underset{\text{II}}{(\sec^2\theta - 1)}d\theta$$

$[\because \sec^2\theta - \tan^2\theta = 1]$

$$= \frac{\pi^2}{32} - \left[\theta\cdot(\tan\theta - \theta) - \int 1\cdot(\tan\theta - \theta)d\theta\right]_0^{\pi/4}$$ [1]

$$= \frac{\pi^2}{32} - [\theta\cdot\tan\theta - \theta^2]_0^{\pi/4} + \int_0^{\pi/4}(\tan\theta - \theta)d\theta$$

$$= \frac{\pi^2}{32} - \left[\frac{\pi}{4}\tan\frac{\pi}{4} - \frac{\pi^2}{16} - 0\right] + \left[\log|\sec\theta| - \frac{\theta^2}{2}\right]_0^{\pi/4}$$

$$= \frac{\pi^2}{32} - \frac{\pi}{4} + \frac{\pi^2}{16} + \log\sqrt{2} - \frac{\pi^2}{32} - 0$$

$$= \frac{\pi^2 - 4\pi}{16} + \log\sqrt{2}$$ [1]

23. Hint (i) Let

$$I = \int_{\pi/3}^{\pi/2} \frac{\sqrt{1+\cos x}\,dx}{(1-\cos x)^{5/2}} = \int_{\pi/3}^{\pi/2} \frac{\sqrt{1-\cos^2 x}}{(1-\cos x)^{\frac{5}{2}+\frac{1}{2}}}dx$$

[multiplying numerator and denominator by $\sqrt{1-\cos x}$]

$$= \int_{\pi/3}^{\pi/2} \frac{\sin x}{(1-\cos x)^3}dx$$

(ii) Put $1 - \cos x = t$ and simplify it. $\left[\textbf{Ans. } \frac{3}{2}\right]$

24. Let $I = \int_0^{\pi/4} \frac{dx}{\cos^3 x\sqrt{2\sin 2x}}$

$$= \int_0^{\pi/4} \frac{dx}{\cos^3 x\sqrt{2(2\sin x\cos x)}}$$ [1/2]

$[\because \sin 2x = 2\sin x \cos x]$

$$= \frac{1}{2}\int_0^{\pi/4} \frac{dx}{\cos^3 x\cos^{1/2} x\sin^{1/2} x}$$

$$= \frac{1}{2}\int_0^{\pi/4} \frac{dx}{\cos^{7/2} x\sin^{1/2} x}$$ [1]

$$= \frac{1}{2}\int_0^{\pi/4} \frac{\sec^4 x}{\cos^{7/2-4} x\sin^{1/2} x}dx$$

[dividing numerator and denominator by $\cos^4 x$]

$$= \frac{1}{2}\int_0^{\pi/4} \frac{\sec^4 x}{\cos^{-1/2} x\sin^{1/2} x}dx$$

$$= \frac{1}{2}\int_0^{\pi/4} \frac{\sec^2 x(1+\tan^2 x)}{\tan^{1/2} x}dx \quad [\because \sec^2 x - \tan^2 x = 1]$$ [1]

Now, put $\tan x = t \Rightarrow \sec^2 x\,dx = dt$

Lower limit When $x = 0$, then $t = \tan 0 = 0$

Upper limit When $x = \frac{\pi}{4}$, then $t = \tan\frac{\pi}{4} = 1$

$$\therefore I = \frac{1}{2}\int_0^1\left(\frac{1+t^2}{t^{1/2}}\right)dt = \frac{1}{2}\int_0^1 (t^{-1/2} + t^{3/2})\,dt$$ [1/2]

$$= \frac{1}{2}\left[2t^{1/2} + \frac{2}{5}t^{5/2}\right]_0^1 = (1)^{1/2} + \frac{1}{5}(1)^{5/2} - 0 = 1 + \frac{1}{5} = \frac{6}{5}$$ [1]

25. Let $I = \int_0^{\pi/4} \frac{\sin x + \cos x}{9 + 16\sin 2x}dx$

We know that,

$$(\sin x - \cos x)^2 = \sin^2 x + \cos^2 x - 2\sin x\cos x$$

$$\Rightarrow (\sin x - \cos x)^2 = 1 - \sin 2x$$

$[\because \sin^2 x + \cos^2 x = 1 \text{ and } 2\sin x\cos x = \sin 2x]$

$$\Rightarrow \quad \sin 2x = 1 - (\sin x - \cos x)^2$$

$$\therefore \quad I = \int_0^{\pi/4} \frac{\sin x + \cos x}{9 + 16(1 - (\sin x - \cos x)^2)}dx$$

Now, put $(\sin x - \cos x) = t$

$$\Rightarrow \quad \cos x + \sin x = \frac{dt}{dx}$$ ...(i) [1]

$$\Rightarrow \quad (\cos x + \sin x)dx = dt$$

Lower limit When $x = 0$, then $t = 0 - \cos 0 = -1$

Upper limit when $x = \frac{\pi}{4}$, then $t = \sin\frac{\pi}{4} - \cos\frac{\pi}{4} = 0$

$$\therefore \; I = \int_{-1}^0 \frac{1}{9 + 16(1-t^2)}dt$$

$$= \int_{-1}^0 \frac{1}{9 + 16 - 16t^2}dt = \int_{-1}^0 \frac{1}{25 - 16t^2}dt$$

$$= \frac{1}{16}\int_{-1}^0 \frac{1}{\left(\frac{5}{4}\right)^2 - t^2}dt$$ [1]

$$= \frac{1}{16}\cdot\frac{1}{2\cdot\frac{5}{4}}\left[\log\left|\frac{\frac{5}{4}+t}{\frac{5}{4}-t}\right|\right]_{-1}^0$$

$$\left[\because \int \frac{1}{a^2 - x^2}dx = \frac{1}{2a}\log\left|\frac{a+x}{a-x}\right|\right]$$ [1]

$$= \frac{1}{40}\left[\log\left|\frac{5+4t}{5-4t}\right|\right]_{-1}^0 = \frac{1}{40}\left[\log 1 - \log\frac{1}{9}\right]$$

$$\left[\because \log\left(\frac{m}{n}\right) = \log m - \log n\right]$$

$$= \frac{1}{40}[\log 1 - (\log 1 - \log 9)] = \frac{1}{40}\log 9$$ [1]

26. Let $I = \int_0^{\pi} e^{2x}\sin\left(\frac{\pi}{4} + x\right)dx$

Again, let $I_1 = \int \underset{\text{II}}{e^{2x}}\,\underset{\text{I}}{\sin}\left(\frac{\pi}{4} + x\right)dx$ ... (i)

$$= \sin\left(\frac{\pi}{4} + x\right)\int e^{2x}dx - \int\left\{\frac{d}{dx}\sin\left(\frac{\pi}{4} + x\right)\int e^{2x}dx\right\}dx$$ [1]

[using integration by parts]

$$= \sin\left(\frac{\pi}{4}+x\right)\frac{e^{2x}}{2} - \int \cos\left(\frac{\pi}{4}+x\right)\frac{e^{2x}}{2}\,dx$$

$$= \frac{e^{2x}}{2}\sin\left(\frac{\pi}{4}+x\right) - \frac{1}{2}\int \underset{\text{II}}{e^{2x}} \underset{\text{I}}{\cos}\left(\frac{\pi}{4}+x\right)dx \quad [1]$$

$$= \frac{e^{2x}}{2}\sin\left(\frac{\pi}{4}+x\right)$$

$$-\frac{1}{2}\left[\cos\left(\frac{\pi}{4}+x\right)\frac{e^{2x}}{2} - \int -\sin\left(\frac{\pi}{4}+x\right)\frac{e^{2x}}{2}\,dx\right]$$

[using integration by parts]

$$= \frac{e^{2x}}{2}\sin\left(\frac{\pi}{4}+x\right) - \frac{e^{2x}}{4}\cos\left(\frac{\pi}{4}+x\right)$$

$$-\frac{1}{4}\int e^{2x}\sin\left(\frac{\pi}{4}+x\right)dx \quad [1]$$

$$\Rightarrow \quad I_1 = \frac{e^{2x}}{4}\left\{2\sin\left(\frac{\pi}{4}+x\right) - \cos\left(\frac{\pi}{4}+x\right)\right\} - \frac{1}{4}I_1$$

[from Eq. (i)]

$$\Rightarrow I_1 + \frac{1}{4}I_1 = \frac{e^{2x}}{4}\left\{2\sin\left(\frac{\pi}{4}+x\right) - \cos\left(\frac{\pi}{4}+x\right)\right\}$$

$$\Rightarrow \quad \frac{5}{4}I_1 = \frac{e^{2x}}{4}\left\{2\sin\left(\frac{\pi}{4}+x\right) - \cos\left(\frac{\pi}{4}+x\right)\right\}$$

$$\Rightarrow \quad I_1 = \frac{e^{2x}}{5}\left\{2\sin\left(\frac{\pi}{4}+x\right) - \cos\left(\frac{\pi}{4}+x\right)\right\} \quad [1]$$

$$\therefore\ I = [I_1]_0^{\pi} = \left[\frac{e^{2x}}{5}\left\{2\sin\left(\frac{\pi}{4}+x\right) - \cos\left(\frac{\pi}{4}+x\right)\right\}\right]_0^{\pi}$$

$$= \frac{1}{5}\left[e^{2\pi}\left\{2\sin\left(\frac{\pi}{4}+\pi\right) - \cos\left(\frac{\pi}{4}+\pi\right)\right\}\right.$$

$$\left. - e^0\left\{2\sin\left(\frac{\pi}{4}+0\right) - \cos\left(\frac{\pi}{4}+0\right)\right\}\right] \quad [1]$$

$$= \frac{1}{5}\left[e^{2\pi}\left\{-2\sin\frac{\pi}{4} + \cos\frac{\pi}{4}\right\} - e^0\left\{2\sin\frac{\pi}{4} - \cos\frac{\pi}{4}\right\}\right]$$

$$= \frac{1}{5}\left[e^{2\pi}\left\{-2\times\frac{1}{\sqrt{2}} + \frac{1}{\sqrt{2}}\right\} - 1\left\{2\times\frac{1}{\sqrt{2}} - \frac{1}{\sqrt{2}}\right\}\right]$$

$$= \frac{1}{5}\left[e^{2\pi}\left\{-\frac{1}{\sqrt{2}}\right\} - \frac{1}{\sqrt{2}}\right]$$

$$= -\frac{1}{5\sqrt{2}}[e^{2\pi}+1] \quad [1]$$

27. Let $I = \int_0^{\pi/2} \sin 2x \tan^{-1}(\sin x)\,dx$

$$= \int_0^{\pi/2} 2\sin x \cos x \tan^{-1}(\sin x)\,dx$$

[$\because \sin 2x = 2\sin x\cos x$] [1]

Now, put $\sin x = t \Rightarrow \cos x\,dx = dt$

Lower limit When $x = 0$, then $t = 0$

Upper limit When $x = \frac{\pi}{2}$, then $t = \sin\frac{\pi}{2} = 1$

Now, $I = \int_0^1 2t\tan^{-1} t\,dt = 2\int_0^1 t\cdot\tan^{-1} t\,dt$

$$= 2\left(\left[(\tan^{-1} t)\frac{t^2}{2}\right]_0^1 - \int_0^1 \frac{1}{1+t^2}\cdot\frac{t^2}{2}\,dt\right) \quad [1½]$$

[using integration by parts]

$$= 2\left[\frac{\tan^{-1}1}{2} - 0\right] - \int_0^1 \frac{t^2}{1+t^2}\,dt$$

$$= 2\left(\frac{\pi}{8}\right) - \int_0^1 \frac{(1+t^2)-1}{1+t^2}\,dt$$

[adding and subtracting 1in numerator] [1½]

$$= \frac{\pi}{4} - \int_0^1\left(1 - \frac{1}{1+t^2}\right)dt = \frac{\pi}{4} - [t - \tan^{-1} t]_0^1$$

$$= \frac{\pi}{4} - [1 - \tan^{-1}1 - (0-0)]$$

$$= \frac{\pi}{4} - 1 + \frac{\pi}{4} = \frac{\pi}{2} - 1 \quad [2]$$

28. **Hint** (i) Put $\cos x = t$.

(ii) Use the integral of the form $\int \frac{(px+q)}{ax^2+bx+c}\,dx$

$\left[\textbf{Ans. } \log\left(\frac{9}{8}\right)\right]$

TOPIC 02 Properties of Definite Integrals

Some important properties which will be useful in evaluating the definite integrals are given below

(i) $\int_a^b f(x)\,dx = \int_a^b f(t)\,dt$

This property shows that, the value of a definite integral does not change if the variable is changed.

(ii) $\int_a^b f(x)\,dx = -\int_b^a f(x)\,dx$

This property shows that, when we interchange the limits, then it changes by negative sign.

Special case $\int_a^a f(x)\,dx = 0.$

(iii) $\int_a^b f(x)\,dx = \int_a^c f(x)\,dx + \int_c^b f(x)\,dx$, where $a < c < b$.

Special case If $a < c_1 < c_2 < \ldots < c_n < b$, then

$$\int_a^b f(x)\,dx = \int_a^{c_1} f(x)\,dx + \int_{c_1}^{c_2} f(x)\,dx + \int_{c_2}^{c_3} f(x)\,dx + \ldots + \int_{c_n}^{b} f(x)\,dx.$$

(iv) $\int_a^b f(x)\,dx = \int_a^b f(a+b-x)\,dx$

(v) $\int_0^a f(x)\,dx = \int_0^a f(a-x)\,dx$

[it is a particular case of property (iv)]

(vi) $\int_0^{2a} f(x)\,dx = \int_0^a f(x)\,dx + \int_0^a f(2a-x)\,dx$

(vii) $\int_0^{2a} f(x)\,dx = \begin{cases} 2\int_0^a f(x)\,dx, & \text{if } f(2a-x) = f(x) \\ 0, & \text{if } f(2a-x) = -f(x) \end{cases}$

Special case

$$\int_0^a f(x)\,dx = \begin{cases} 2\int_0^{a/2} f(x)\,dx, & \text{if } f(a-x) = f(x) \\ 0, & \text{if } f(a-x) = -f(x) \end{cases}$$

(viii) $\int_{-a}^a f(x)\,dx$

$$= \begin{cases} 2\int_0^a f(x)\,dx, & \text{if } f \text{ is an even function, i.e. } f(-x) = f(x) \\ 0 & \text{if } f \text{ is an odd function, i.e. } f(-x) = -f(x) \end{cases}$$

Example 1 Evaluate the integral $\int_0^4 g(x)\,dx$, where

$$g(x) = \begin{cases} \sin 2x, & 0 \le x \le \pi \\ 3, & \pi < x < 4 \end{cases}.$$

Sol. Let $I = \int_0^4 g(x)dx = \int_0^\pi (\sin 2x)dx + \int_\pi^4 (3)dx$

$$= \left[-\frac{\cos 2x}{2}\right]_0^\pi + 3[x]_\pi^4$$

$$= -\frac{1}{2}[\cos 2\pi - \cos 2\times 0] + 3[4-\pi]$$

$$= -\frac{1}{2}[(1)-(1)] + 3(4-\pi)$$

$$= 3(4-\pi)$$

Example 2 Evaluate $\int_{-3}^3 |x+2|\,dx$. **[ISC 2010]**

Sol. Let $I = \int_{-3}^3 |x+2|\,dx$

Now, $|x+2| = \begin{cases} x+2, & x \ge -2 \\ -(x+2), & x < -2 \end{cases}$

$\therefore \quad I = \int_{-3}^{-2} -(x+2)\,dx + \int_{-2}^{3} (x+2)\,dx$

$$= -\left[\frac{x^2}{2} + 2x\right]_{-3}^{-2} + \left[\frac{x^2}{2} + 2x\right]_{-2}^{3}$$

$$= -\left[\frac{4}{2} - 4 - \frac{9}{2} + 6\right] + \left[\frac{9}{2} + 6 - \frac{4}{2} + 4\right]$$

$$= -2 - 2 + \frac{9}{2} + \frac{9}{2} + 8 = 4 + 9 = 13$$

Example 3 Evaluate

$$\int_2^5 [|x-2| + |x-3| + |x-5|]\,dx.$$

Sol. Let $I = \int_2^5 [|x-2| + |x-3| + |x-5|]\,dx$

Now, let us first define the given absolute functions.

Clearly, $|x-2| = \begin{cases} (x-2), & \text{if } x \ge 2 \\ -(x-2), & \text{if } x < 2 \end{cases}$,

$|x-3| = \begin{cases} (x-3), & \text{if } x \ge 3 \\ -(x-3), & \text{if } x < 3 \end{cases}$

and $|x-5| = \begin{cases} (x-5), & \text{if } x \ge 5 \\ -(x-5), & \text{if } x < 5 \end{cases}$

Now, divide the given limit at $x = 3$, i.e. write I as

$$I = \int_2^3 [|x-2| + |x-3| + |x-5|]\, dx + \int_3^5 [|x-2| + |x-3| + |x-5|]\, dx$$

[using property (iii)]

$$= \int_2^3 [(x-2) + (-(x-3)) + (-(x-5))]\, dx + \int_3^5 [(x-2) + (x-3) + (-(x-5))]\, dx$$

$$= \int_2^3 [x - 2 - x + 3 - x + 5]\, dx + \int_3^5 [x - 2 + x - 3 - x + 5]\, dx$$

$$= \int_2^3 (6-x)\, dx + \int_3^5 x\, dx$$

$$= \left[6x - \frac{x^2}{2}\right]_2^3 + \left[\frac{x^2}{2}\right]_3^5$$

$$= \left\{\left(18 - \frac{9}{2}\right) - \left(12 - \frac{4}{2}\right)\right\} + \left[\frac{25}{2} - \frac{9}{2}\right]$$

$$= \frac{27}{2} - \frac{20}{2} + \frac{25}{2} - \frac{9}{2} = \frac{7}{2} + \frac{16}{2} = \frac{23}{2}$$

Example 4 Using properties of definite integrals, evaluate $\int_0^{\pi/2} \frac{\sqrt{\sin x}}{\sqrt{\sin x} + \sqrt{\cos x}}\, dx.$ **[ISC 2014]**

Sol. Let $I = \int_0^{\pi/2} \frac{\sqrt{\sin x}}{\sqrt{\sin x} + \sqrt{\cos x}}\, dx$ ...(i)

$$\therefore \quad I = \int_0^{\pi/2} \frac{\sqrt{\sin\left(\frac{\pi}{2} - x\right)}}{\sqrt{\sin\left(\frac{\pi}{2} - x\right)} + \sqrt{\cos\left(\frac{\pi}{2} - x\right)}}\, dx$$

$$\left[\because \int_0^a f(x)\, dx = \int_0^a f(a-x)dx\right]$$

$$\Rightarrow \quad I = \int_0^{\pi/2} \frac{\sqrt{\cos x}}{\sqrt{\cos 2x} + \sqrt{\sin x}} dx \quad \text{...(ii)}$$

On adding Eqs. (i) and (ii), we get

$$2I = \int_0^{\pi/2} \frac{\sqrt{\sin x} + \sqrt{\cos x}}{\sqrt{\cos x} + \sqrt{\sin x}} dx$$

$$\Rightarrow \quad 2I = \int_0^{\pi/2} 1 dx = [x]_0^{\pi/2} = \frac{\pi}{2} - 0 \Rightarrow I = \frac{\pi}{4}$$

Example 5 Evaluate $\int_0^1 \log\left(\frac{1}{x} - 1\right) dx.$ **[ISC 2013]**

Sol. Let $I = \int_0^1 \log\left(\frac{1}{x} - 1\right) dx$

$$\Rightarrow \quad I = \int_0^1 \log\left(\frac{1-x}{x}\right) dx \quad \text{...(i)}$$

Using $\int_0^a f(x)\, dx = \int_0^a f(a-x)\, dx$, we get

$$I = \int_0^1 \log\left(\frac{1-(1-x)}{(1-x)}\right) dx$$

$$I = \int_0^1 \log\left(\frac{x}{1-x}\right) dx \quad \text{...(ii)}$$

On adding Eqs. (i) and (ii), we get

$$2I = \int_0^1 \log\left(\frac{1-x}{x}\right) dx + \int_0^1 \log\left(\frac{x}{1-x}\right) dx$$

$$= \int_0^1 \log\left(\left(\frac{1-x}{x}\right)\left(\frac{x}{1-x}\right)\right) dx$$

[using product rule of logarithm, i.e. $\log m + \log n = \log mn$]

$$= \int_0^1 \log 1\, dx = 0 \quad [\because \log 1 = 0]$$

$$\Rightarrow \quad 2I = 0 \Rightarrow I = 0$$

Example 6 Evaluate $\int_0^{\pi/4} \log(1 + \tan\theta)\, d\theta.$ **[ISC 2017, 2007; NCERT]**

Sol. Let $I = \int_0^{\pi/4} \log(1 + \tan\theta)\, dx$ ...(i)

$$\Rightarrow \quad I = \int_0^{\pi/4} \log\left[1 + \tan\left(\frac{\pi}{4} - \theta\right)\right] d\theta$$

$$\left[\because \int_0^a f(x)\, dx = \int_0^a f(a-x)\, dx\right]$$

$$= \int_0^{\pi/4} \log\left(1 + \frac{1 - \tan\theta}{1 + \tan\theta}\right) d\theta$$

$$\left[\because \tan(A-B) = \frac{\tan A - \tan B}{1 + \tan A \tan B}\right]$$

$$= \int_0^{\pi/4} \log\left(\frac{2}{1 + \tan\theta}\right) d\theta$$

$$= \int_0^{\pi/4} \{\log 2 - \log(1 + \tan\theta)\}\, d\theta \quad \text{...(ii)}$$

$$\left[\because \log\left(\frac{m}{n}\right) = \log m - \log n\right]$$

On adding Eqs. (i) and (ii), we get

$$2I = \int_0^{\pi/4} \log 2\, d\theta$$

$$= \log 2 \int_0^{\pi/4} 1\, d\theta = \log 2\, [\theta]_0^{\pi/4}$$

$$= \log 2\left(\frac{\pi}{4} - 0\right)$$

$$\Rightarrow \quad 2I = \frac{\pi}{4} \log 2$$

$$\Rightarrow \quad I = \frac{\pi}{8} \log 2$$

Example 7 Evaluate $\int_0^{\pi/2} \frac{\cos^2 x}{1+\sin x \cos x} dx.$ **[ISC 2018]**

Sol. Let $I = \int_0^{\pi/2} \frac{\cos^2 x}{1+\sin x \cos x} dx$ ...(i)

$$I = \int_0^{\pi/2} \frac{\cos^2\left(\frac{\pi}{2}-x\right)}{1+\sin\left(\frac{\pi}{2}-x\right)\cos\left(\frac{\pi}{2}-x\right)} dx$$

$$\left[\because \int_0^a f(x)dx = \int_0^a f(a-x)\,dx\right]$$

$$I = \int_0^{\pi/2} \frac{\sin^2 x}{1+\cos x \sin x} dx \quad \text{...(ii)}$$

On adding Eqs. (i) and (ii), we get

$$2I = \int_0^{\pi/2} \frac{(\cos^2 x + \sin^2 x)\,dx}{1+\sin x \cos x}$$

$$\Rightarrow I = \frac{1}{2}\int_0^{\pi/2} \frac{dx}{1+\sin x \cos x} \quad [\because \sin^2\theta + \cos^2\theta = 1]$$

$$I = \int_0^{\pi/2} \frac{\sec^2 x}{\sec^2 x + \tan x} dx$$

[dividing numerator and denominator by $\cos^2 x$]

$$= \int_0^{\pi/2} \frac{\sec^2 x}{\tan^2 x + \tan x + 1} dx$$

Put $\tan x = t \Rightarrow \sec^2 x\,dx = dt$

When $x = 0$, then $t = 0$ and when $x = \frac{\pi}{2}$ then $t = \infty$

$$\therefore I = \int_0^{\infty} \frac{dt}{t^2+t+1} = \int_0^{\infty} \frac{dt}{t^2+t+\frac{1}{4}+1-\frac{1}{4}}$$

$$\Rightarrow I = \int_0^{\infty} \frac{dt}{\left(t+\frac{1}{2}\right)^2 + \left(\frac{\sqrt{3}}{2}\right)^2}$$

$$= \frac{2}{\sqrt{3}}\left[\tan^{-1}\frac{2t+1}{\sqrt{3}}\right]_0^{\infty}$$

$$\Rightarrow I = \frac{2}{\sqrt{3}}\left(\tan^{-1}\infty - \tan^{-1}\frac{1}{\sqrt{3}}\right)$$

$$= \frac{2}{\sqrt{3}}\left(\frac{\pi}{2}-\frac{\pi}{6}\right) = \frac{2\pi}{3\sqrt{3}}$$

Example 8 Evaluate $\int_0^{\pi} \frac{x \tan x}{\sec x + \tan x} dx.$

Sol. Let $I = \int_0^{\pi} \frac{x \tan x}{\sec x + \tan x} dx$ ...(i)

$$\therefore I = \int_0^{\pi} \frac{(\pi - x)\tan(\pi - x)}{\sec(\pi - x) + \tan(\pi - x)} dx$$

$$\left[\because \int_0^a f(x)\,dx = \int_0^a f(a-x)\,dx\right]$$

$$= \int_0^{\pi} \frac{-(\pi - x)\tan x}{-\sec x - \tan x} dx$$

$$\Rightarrow I = \int_0^{\pi} \frac{(\pi - x)\tan x}{\sec x + \tan x} dx \quad \text{...(ii)}$$

On adding Eqs. (i) and (ii), we get

$$2I = \pi \int_0^{\pi} \frac{\tan x}{\sec x + \tan x} dx$$

$$= \pi \int_0^{\pi} \frac{\tan x(\sec x - \tan x)}{(\sec x + \tan x)(\sec x - \tan x)} dx$$

$$= \pi \int_0^{\pi} \frac{\tan x \cdot \sec x - \tan^2 x}{\sec^2 x - \tan^2 x} dx$$

$$= \pi\left[\int_0^{\pi} \sec x \cdot \tan x\,dx - \int_0^{\pi} \tan^2 x\,dx\right]$$

$$= \pi\left\{[\sec x]_0^{\pi} - \int_0^{\pi}(\sec^2 x - 1)\,dx\right\}$$

$$= \pi\{[\sec\pi - \sec 0] - [\tan x - x]_0^{\pi}\}$$

$$= \pi\{[-1-1] - [(\tan\pi - \pi) - (\tan 0 - 0)]\}$$

$$= \pi\{-2 - [(-\pi) - 0]\} = \pi(\pi - 2)$$

$$\Rightarrow I = \frac{\pi}{2}(\pi - 2)$$

Example 9 Evaluate the integral $\int_0^{2\pi} \frac{1}{1+e^{\sin x}} dx.$ **[ISC 2024]**

Sol. Let $I = \int_0^{2\pi} \frac{1}{1+e^{\sin x}} dx$

$$\therefore I = \int_0^{\pi}\left[\frac{1}{1+e^{\sin x}} + \frac{1}{1+e^{\sin(2\pi - x)}}\right] dx$$

$$\left[\because \int_0^{2a} f(x)\,dx = \int_0^a \{f(x) + f(2a-x)\}\,dx\right]$$

$$= \int_0^{\pi}\left[\frac{1}{1+e^{\sin x}} + \frac{1}{1+e^{-\sin x}}\right] dx$$

$$[\because \sin(2\pi - x) = -\sin x]$$

$$= \int_0^{\pi}\left[\frac{1}{1+e^{\sin x}} + \frac{e^{\sin x}}{e^{\sin x}+1}\right] dx$$

$$= \int_0^{\pi} \frac{1+e^{\sin x}}{1+e^{\sin x}} dx = \int_0^{\pi} 1\,dx = [x]_0^{\pi} = \pi$$

Example 10 Evaluate $\int_0^{2\pi} \cos^5 x\,dx.$

Sol. Let $I = \int_0^{2\pi} \cos^5 x\,dx = 2\int_0^{\pi} \cos^5 x\,dx$

$$\left[\because \int_0^{2a} f(x)dx = 2\int_0^a f(x)\,dx, \text{ if } f(2a-x) = f(x), \text{ here } \cos^5(2\pi - x) = \cos^5 x\right]$$

$$= 2 \times 0 = 0 \quad \left[\because \int_0^{2a} f(x) = 0, \text{ if } f(2a-x) = -f(x), \text{ here } \cos^5(\pi - x) = -\cos^5 x\right]$$

Example 11 Evaluate the integral $\int_{-\pi/2}^{\pi/2} \sin^2 x\, dx$.

Sol. Let $I = \int_{-\pi/2}^{\pi/2} \sin^2 x\, dx$

Here, $f(x) = \sin^2 x$

Now, $f(-x) = \sin^2(-x) = [\sin(-x)]^2$

$= (-\sin x)^2 = \sin^2 x = f(x)$

$[\because \sin(-\theta) = -\sin\theta]$

So, $f(x)$ is an even function.

$\therefore \quad I = \int_{-\pi/2}^{\pi/2} \sin^2 x\, dx$

$= 2\int_0^{\pi/2} \sin^2 x\, dx$

$\left[\because \int_{-a}^{a} f(x)\,dx = 2\int_0^a f(x)\,dx, \text{ if } f(x) \text{ is an even function, here } \sin^2 x \text{ is an even function.}\right]$

$= 2\int_0^{\pi/2}\left[\frac{1-\cos 2x}{2}\right] dx \quad [\because \cos 2x = 1 - 2\sin^2 x]$

$= \int_0^{\pi/2} (1-\cos 2x)\, dx$

$= \left[x - \frac{\sin 2x}{2}\right]_0^{\pi/2}$

$= \left[\frac{\pi}{2} - \frac{\sin \pi}{2}\right] - [0 - 0]$

$= \frac{\pi}{2} - 0 = \frac{\pi}{2}$

Topic Practice 2

Very Short Answer Type Questions

(2 Marks)

1 Evaluate $\int_0^3 f(x)dx$, where

$$f(x) = \begin{cases} \cos 2x, & 0 \le x \le \frac{\pi}{2} \\ 3, & \frac{\pi}{2} < x \le 3 \end{cases}.$$ **[ISC 2015]**

2 If $g(x) = \int_0^x \cos 4t\, dt$, then prove that $g(x) = g(x + \pi)$.

Directions (Q. Nos. 3-7) *Evaluate the following integrals.*

3 $\int_1^2 \frac{\sqrt{x}}{\sqrt{3-x} + \sqrt{x}} dx$ **[ISC 2012; NCERT]**

4 $\int_0^{\pi/2} \frac{\tan^7 x}{\cot^7 x + \tan^7 x} dx.$

5 $\int_0^{\pi/2} \frac{\sin x - \cos x}{1 + \sin x \cos x} dx.$ **[ISC 2016]**

6 $\int_0^{\pi/2} \log(\tan x)\, dx.$ **[ISC 2009]**

7 $\int_{-\pi/3}^{\pi/3} \sin^3 x\, dx$

8 Prove that $\int_0^{\pi/2} \frac{3\sin\theta + 4\cos\theta}{\sin\theta + \cos\theta} d\theta = \frac{7\pi}{4}.$ **[ISC 2005]**

9 Show that $\int_0^a f(x)\, g(x)\, dx = 2\int_0^a f(x)\, dx$, if f and g are defined as

$f(x) = f(a-x)$ and $g(x) + g(a-x) = 4.$

10 Prove that $\int_{-1}^{1} \log\left(\frac{2-x}{2+x}\right) dx = 0$

11 Evaluate $\int_0^9 f(x)\, dx$, where $f(x)$ is defined by

$$f(x) = \begin{cases} \sin x, \text{ if } 0 \le x \le \pi/2 \\ 1, \text{ if } \frac{\pi}{2} < x \le 5 \\ e^{x-5}, \text{ if } 5 < x \le 9 \end{cases}.$$ **[ISC 2008)]**

12 Evaluate $\int_0^2 (x - [x])\, dx$, where $[x]$ is the greatest integer of x.

Directions (Q. Nos. 13-17) *Evaluate the following integrals.*

13 $\int_{-2}^{2} \frac{x^2}{1+5^x} dx$

14 $\int_0^{\pi/2} \frac{dx}{1+\sqrt{\tan x}}$

15 $\int_{\pi/6}^{\pi/3} \frac{dx}{1+\sqrt{\cot x}}$

16 $\int_0^1 x(1-x)^n\, dx$ **[NCERT]**

17 $\int_0^{\pi/2} \log\left(\frac{4+3\sin x}{4+3\cos x}\right) dx$ **[NCERT]**

18 Prove that $\int_0^{2\pi} \frac{x\cos x}{1+\cos x} dx = 2\pi^2.$ **[ISC 2006]**

19 Evaluate $\int_0^1 \tan^{-1}\left(\frac{2x-1}{1+x-x^2}\right) dx.$ **[NCERT]**

Long Answer Type Questions

6 Marks

Directions (Q. Nos. 20-27) *Evaluate the following integrals.*

20 $\int_0^{3/2} |x \cos \pi x| \, dx.$

21 $\int_0^1 \cot^{-1}\{1 - x + x^2\} \, dx.$

22 $\int_0^{\pi/2} \frac{x \sin x \cos x}{\sin^4 x + \cos^4 x} dx$

23 $\int_0^1 \frac{\log(1+x)}{1+x^2} dx$

24 $\int_0^{\pi/2} [2 \log (\sin x) - \log (\sin 2x)] \, dx$ **[NCERT]**

25 $\int_{-1}^1 \frac{x^3 + |x| + 1}{x^2 + 2|x| + 1} dx$

26 $\int_{-\pi}^{\pi} (\cos ax - \sin bx)^2 \, dx$

27 $\int_0^{\pi} x \log |\sin x| \, dx$

Hints & Solutions

1. Given, $f(x) = \begin{cases} \cos 2x, & 0 \le x \le \frac{\pi}{2} \\ 3, & \frac{\pi}{2} < x \le 3 \end{cases}$

Let $I = \int_0^3 f(x) dx$

$= \int_0^{\pi/2} f(x) dx + \int_{\pi/2}^3 f(x) \, dx$

$= \int_0^{\pi/2} \cos 2x dx + \int_{\pi/2}^3 3 \, dx$

$= \left[\frac{\sin 2x}{2}\right]_0^{\frac{\pi}{2}} + [3x]_{\frac{\pi}{2}}^3$ [1]

$= \frac{1}{2}\left[\sin 2 \times \frac{\pi}{2} - \sin 0\right] + 3\left[3 - \frac{\pi}{2}\right]$

$= \frac{1}{2}[\sin \pi - 0] + \frac{3}{2}(6 - \pi)$

$= \frac{1}{2}[0] + \frac{3}{2}(6 - \pi)$

$= \frac{3}{2}(6 - \pi)$ [1]

2. Given, $g(x) = \int_0^x \cos 4t \, dt$

Now, $g(x + \pi) = \int_0^{x+\pi} \cos 4t \, dt$

$= \int_0^x \cos 4t \, dt + \int_x^{x+\pi} \cos 4t \, dt$

$= g(x) + I_1$ (say) ...(i) [1]

Now, $I_1 = \int_x^{x+\pi} \cos 4t \, dt = \left[\frac{\sin 4t}{4}\right]_x^{x+\pi}$

$= \frac{\sin 4(x+\pi)}{4} - \frac{\sin 4x}{4}$

$= \frac{\sin(4\pi + 4x)}{4} - \frac{\sin 4x}{4}$

$= \frac{\sin 4x}{4} - \frac{\sin 4x}{4} = 0$

Then, Eq. (i) becomes $g(x + \pi) = g(x)$.

Hence proved. [1]

3. Let $I = \int_1^2 \frac{\sqrt{x}}{\sqrt{3-x} + \sqrt{x}} dx$ ...(i)

$\Rightarrow I = \int_1^2 \frac{\sqrt{3-x}}{\sqrt{3-x} + \sqrt{x}} dx$ ...(ii)

$\left[\because \int_a^b f(x) \, dx = \int_a^b f(a + b - x) \, dx\right]$ [1]

On adding Eqs. (i) and (ii), we get

$2I = \int_1^2 \frac{\sqrt{x} + \sqrt{3-x}}{\sqrt{3-x} + \sqrt{x}} dx$

$\Rightarrow 2I = \int_1^2 1 \, dx = [x]_1^2 \Rightarrow I = \frac{1}{2}[2-1] = \frac{1}{2}$ [1]

4. Let $I = \int_0^{\pi/2} \frac{\tan^7 x}{\cot^7 x + \tan^7 x} dx$ ...(i)

$\Rightarrow I = \int_0^{\pi/2} \frac{\tan^7\left(\frac{\pi}{2} - x\right)}{\cot^7\left(\frac{\pi}{2} - x\right) + \tan^7\left(\frac{\pi}{2} - x\right)} dx$

$\left[\because \int_0^a f(x) \, dx = \int_0^a f(a - x) \, dx\right]$

$\Rightarrow I = \int_0^{\pi/2} \frac{\cot^7 x}{\tan^7 x + \cot^7 x} dx$ ...(ii) [1]

$\left[\because \tan\left(\frac{\pi}{2} - x\right) = \cot x \text{ and } \cot\left(\frac{\pi}{2} - x\right) = \tan x\right]$

On adding Eqs. (i) and (ii), we get

$2I = \int_0^{\pi/2} \frac{\tan^7 x + \cot^7 x}{\tan^7 x + \cot^7 x} dx$

$= \int_0^{\pi/2} 1 \, dx = [x]_0^{\pi/2} = \frac{\pi}{2} - 0 = \frac{\pi}{2} \Rightarrow I = \frac{\pi}{4}$ [1]

5. Let $I = \int_0^{\pi/2} \frac{\sin x - \cos x}{1 + \sin x \cos x} dx$

$\Rightarrow I = \int_0^{\pi/2} \frac{\sin(\pi/2 - x) - \cos(\pi/2 - x)}{1 + \sin(\pi/2 - x) \cos(\pi/2 - x)} dx$

$[\because \int_0^a f(x) \, dx = \int_0^a f(a - x) \, dx]$

$\Rightarrow I = \int_0^{\pi/2} \frac{\cos x - \sin x}{1 + \cos x \sin x} dx$ [1]

$$\Rightarrow I = -\int_0^{\pi/2} \frac{\sin x - \cos x}{1 + \sin x \cos x}\, dx = -I$$

$\Rightarrow \quad 2I = 0$

$\Rightarrow \quad I = 0$ [1]

6. Let $I = \int_0^{\pi/2} \log(\tan x)\, dx$ ...(i)

Using $\int_0^a f(x)\, dx = \int_0^a f(a-x)\, dx$, we get

$$I = \int_0^{\pi/2} \log\left[\tan\left(\frac{\pi}{2} - x\right)\right] dx$$

$$= \int_0^{\pi/2} \log(\cot x)\, dx \quad \text{...(ii) [1/2]}$$

On adding Eqs. (i) and (ii),we get

$$2I = \int_0^{\pi/2} \log(\tan x)\, dx + \int_0^{\pi/2} \log(\cot x)\, dx$$

$$\Rightarrow \quad 2I = \int_0^{\pi/2} \log(\tan x \cdot \cot x)\, dx \quad \text{[1]}$$

$$\Rightarrow \quad 2I = \int_0^{\pi/2} \log 1\, dx$$

$\Rightarrow \quad 2I = 0$

$\Rightarrow \quad I = 0$ $[\because \log 1 = 0]$ [1/2]

7. Let $I = \int_{-\pi/3}^{\pi/3} \sin^3 x\, dx$

Here, $f(x) = \sin^3 x$

$\therefore \quad f(-x) = \sin^3(-x) = -\sin x^3 = -f(x)$

Thus, $f(x)$ is an odd function. [1]

$\therefore \quad I = 0 \quad \left[\because \int_{-a}^{a} f(x)dx = 0, \text{ if } f(-x) = -f(x)\right]$ [1]

8. Let $I = \int_0^{\pi/2} \frac{3\sin\theta + 4\cos\theta}{\sin\theta + \cos\theta}\, d\theta$ ...(i)

Using $\int_0^a f(x)\, dx = \int_0^a f(a-x)\, dx$, we get

$$I = \int_0^{\pi/2} \frac{3\sin\left(\frac{\pi}{2} - \theta\right) + 4\cos\left(\frac{\pi}{2} - \theta\right)}{\sin\left(\frac{\pi}{2} - \theta\right) + \cos\left(\frac{\pi}{2} - \theta\right)}\, d\theta$$

$$\Rightarrow \quad I = \int_0^{\pi/2} \frac{3\cos\theta + 4\sin\theta}{\cos\theta + \sin\theta}\, d\theta$$

$\left[\because \sin\left(\frac{\pi}{2} - \theta\right) = \cos\theta\right]$ ...(ii)

On adding Eqs. (i) and (ii),we get

$$2I = \int_0^{\pi/2} \frac{\begin{bmatrix} 3\sin\theta + 4\cos\theta \\ + 3\cos\theta + 4\sin\theta \end{bmatrix}}{\sin\theta + \cos\theta}\, d\theta \quad \text{[1]}$$

$$\Rightarrow \quad 2I = \int_0^{\pi/2} \frac{7(\sin\theta + \cos\theta)}{\sin\theta + \cos\theta}\, d\theta$$

$$\Rightarrow \quad 2I = \int_0^{\pi/2} 7\, d\theta = 7\,[\theta]_0^{\pi/2} = 7\,[\pi/2 - 0]$$

$$\Rightarrow \quad 2I = \frac{7\pi}{2} \Rightarrow I = \frac{7}{4}\pi \quad \text{[1]}$$

9. Let $I = \int_0^a f(x) g(x)\, dx$ ...(i)

$\Rightarrow I = \int_0^a f(a-x)\, g(a-x)\, dx$

$\left[\because \int_0^a f(x)\, dx = \int_0^a f(a-x)\, dx\right]$

$\Rightarrow \quad I = \int_0^a f(x)\{4 - g(x)\}\, dx$ ...(ii) [1]

$[\because f(x) = f(a-x) \text{ and } g(x) + g(a-x) = 4, \text{ given}]$

On adding Eqs. (i) and (ii), we get

$2I = \int_0^a 4 f(x)\, dx$

$\Rightarrow \quad I = 2\int_0^a f(x)\, dx$ [1]

10. **Hint** Let $f(x) = \log\left(\frac{2-x}{2+x}\right)$, then

$$f(-x) = \log\left(\frac{2+x}{2-x}\right) = \log\left(\frac{2-x}{2+x}\right)^{-1} = (-1)\log\left(\frac{2-x}{2+x}\right)$$

$= -f(x)$

Thus, $f(x)$ is an odd function.

11. Given function is

$$f(x) = \begin{cases} \sin x, & \text{if } 0 \le x \le \pi/2 \\ 1, & \text{if } \pi/2 < x \le 5 \\ e^{x-5}, & \text{if } 5 < x \le 9 \end{cases}$$

Now, $\int_0^9 f(x) = \int_0^{\pi/2} \sin x\, dx + \int_{\pi/2}^5 1\, dx + \int_5^9 e^{x-5}\, dx$ [1]

$$= -[\cos x]_0^{\pi/2} + [x]_{\pi/2}^5 + [e^{x-5}]_5^9$$

$$= -\left(\cos\frac{\pi}{2} - \cos 0\right) + \left(5 - \frac{\pi}{2}\right) + (e^4 - e^0) \quad \text{[1]}$$

$$= 0 + 1 + 5 - \frac{\pi}{2} + e^4 - 1 = 5 - \frac{\pi}{2} + e^4 \quad \text{[1]}$$

12. Let $I = \int_0^2 (x - [x])\, dx = \int_0^2 x\, dx - \int_0^2 [x]\, dx$

$$= \int_0^2 x\, dx - \left[\int_0^1 0\, dx + \int_1^2 1\, dx\right] \quad \text{[2]}$$

$$\left[\because [x] = \begin{cases} 0, \text{ if } 0 \le x < 1 \\ 1, \text{ if } 1 \le x < 2 \end{cases}\right]$$

$$= \left[\frac{x^2}{2}\right]_0^2 - 0 + [x]_1^2 = \frac{2^2}{2} - 0 - [2 - 1] = 2 - 1 = 1 \quad \text{[2]}$$

13. Let $I = \int_{-2}^{2} \frac{x^2}{1 + 5^x}\, dx$ ...(i)

$$= \int_{-2}^{2} \frac{(2 - 2 - x)^2}{1 + 5^{2-2-x}}\, dx$$

$\left[\because \int_a^b f(x)\, dx = \int_a^b f(a + b - x)\, dx\right]$

$$= \int_{-2}^{2} \frac{x^2}{1 + 5^{-x}}\, dx \quad \text{[1]}$$

$\Rightarrow I = \int_{-2}^{2} \frac{5^x}{5^x + 1} x^2\, dx$ ... (ii) [1/2]

On adding Eqs. (i) and (ii), we get

$$2I = \int_{-2}^{2} \left(\frac{1 + 5^x}{5^x + 1}\right) x^2\, dx = \int_{-2}^{2} x^2\, dx \quad \text{[1]}$$

$\Rightarrow 2I = 2\int_0^2 x^2\, dx$

$[\because x^2 \text{ is even, so } \int_{-2}^{2} x^2\, dx = 2\int_0^2 x^2\, dx]$ [1/2]

$\Rightarrow \quad I = \left[\frac{x^3}{3}\right]_0^2 = \frac{1}{3}(2^3 - 0) = \frac{8}{3}$ [1]

14. Let $I = \int_0^{\pi/2} \frac{dx}{1+\sqrt{\tan x}}$

$\Rightarrow \quad I = \int_0^{\pi/2} \frac{\sqrt{\cos x}}{\sqrt{\cos x} + \sqrt{\sin x}}\, dx$ ...(i) [1]

$\Rightarrow \quad I = \int_0^{\pi/2} \frac{\sqrt{\cos\left(\frac{\pi}{2} - x\right)}}{\sqrt{\cos\left(\frac{\pi}{2} - x\right)} + \sqrt{\sin\left(\frac{\pi}{2} - x\right)}}\, dx$

$[\because \int_0^a f(x)dx = \int_0^a f(a-x)dx]$ [1]

$\Rightarrow \quad I = \int_0^{\pi/2} \frac{\sqrt{\sin x}}{\sqrt{\sin x} + \sqrt{\cos x}}\, dx$ ...(ii)

On adding Eqs. (i) and (ii), we get

$2I = \int_0^{\pi/2} \frac{\sqrt{\cos x} + \sqrt{\sin x}}{\sqrt{\cos x} + \sqrt{\sin x}}\, dx$ [1]

$\Rightarrow 2I = \int_0^{\pi/2} 1\, dx = [x]_0^{\pi/2} = \frac{\pi}{2} \Rightarrow I = \frac{\pi}{4}$ [1]

15. **Hint** Use the property, $\int_a^b f(x)\, dx = \int_a^b f(a+b-x)\, dx$

Here, $a + b = \frac{\pi}{6} + \frac{\pi}{3} = \frac{\pi}{2}$

Now, solve as Question 14. $\left[\textbf{Ans. } \frac{\pi}{12}\right]$

16. Let $I = \int_0^1 x(1-x)^n\, dx \Rightarrow I = \int_0^1 (1-x)\{1-(1-x)\}^n\, dx$

$\left[\because \int_0^a f(x)\, dx = \int_0^a f(a-x)\, dx\right]$ [1]

$= \int_0^1 (1-x)\, x^n\, dx = \int_0^1 (x^n - x^{n+1})\, dx$ [1]

$= \left[\frac{x^{n+1}}{n+1} - \frac{x^{n+2}}{n+2}\right]_0^1 = \left[\frac{1}{n+1} - \frac{1}{n+2}\right] - 0$ [1]

$= \frac{(n+2)-(n+1)}{(n+1)(n+2)} = \frac{1}{(n+1)(n+2)}$ [1]

17. Let $I = \int_0^{\pi/2} \log\left(\frac{4+3\sin x}{4+3\cos x}\right) dx$

$= \int_0^{\pi/2} \log(4 + 3\sin x)dx - \int_0^{\pi/2} \log(4+3\cos x)dx$

$\left[\because \log\frac{m}{n} = \log m - \log n\right]$ [1]

$= \int_0^{\pi/2} \log\left[4 + 3\sin\left(\frac{\pi}{2} - x\right)\right] dx$

$- \int_0^{\pi/2} \log(4+3\cos x)dx$ [1½]

$\left[\because \int_0^a f(x)dx = \int_0^a f(a-x)dx\right]$

$= \int_0^{\pi/2} \log(4+3\cos x)dx - \int_0^{\pi/2} \log(4+3\cos x)dx$

$\therefore \quad I = 0$ [1½]

18. Let $I = \int_0^{2\pi} \frac{x\cos x}{1+\cos x}\, dx$ ...(i)

Using $\int_0^a f(x)\, dx = \int_0^a f(a-x)\, dx$, we get

$I = \int_0^{2\pi} \frac{(2\pi - x)\cos(2\pi - x)}{1 + \cos(2\pi - x)}\, dx$

$\Rightarrow \quad I = \int_0^{2\pi} \frac{(2\pi - x)\cos x}{1+\cos x}$ ...(ii) [1]

On adding Eqs. (i) and (ii),we get

$2I = \int_0^{2\pi} \frac{(x + 2\pi - x)\cos x}{1+\cos x}\, dx$

$\Rightarrow \quad 2I = 2\pi \int_0^{2\pi} \frac{\cos x + 1 - 1}{1+\cos x}\, dx$

[adding and subtracting 1 in numerator]

$= 2\pi \int_0^{2\pi} \frac{1+\cos x}{1+\cos x} dx - 2\pi \int_0^{2\pi} \frac{1}{1+\cos x}\, dx$ [1]

$= 2\pi \int_0^{2\pi} 1\, dx - 2\pi \int_0^{2\pi} \frac{1}{1+\cos x} dx$

$= 2\pi\,[x]_0^{2\pi} - 2\pi \int_0^{2\pi} \frac{1}{2\cos^2\frac{x}{2}}\, dx$ [1]

$= 2\pi\,[2\pi - 0] - \pi \int_0^{2\pi} \sec^2 \frac{x}{2}\, dx$

$= 4\pi^2 - \pi\left[2\tan\frac{x}{2}\right]_0^{2\pi}$

$\Rightarrow \quad 2I = 4\pi^2 - 2\pi[\tan\pi - 0]$

$\Rightarrow \quad 2I = 4\pi^2 - 2\pi[0]$

$\Rightarrow \quad I = 2\pi^2$ [1]

19. Let $I = \int_0^1 \tan^{-1}\left(\frac{2x-1}{1+x-x^2}\right) dx$

$= \int_0^1 \tan^{-1}\left(\frac{x + (x-1)}{1 - x(x-1)}\right) dx$ [1]

$= \int_0^1 \{\tan^{-1} x + \tan^{-1}(x-1)\}\, dx$

$\left[\because \tan^{-1} A + \tan^{-1} B = \tan^{-1}\left(\frac{A+B}{1-AB}\right)\right]$ [1]

$\Rightarrow \quad I = \int_0^1 \{\tan^{-1} x - \tan^{-1}(1-x)\}\, dx$ ...(i)

Also, $I = \int_0^1 [\tan^{-1}(1-x) - \tan^{-1}\{1-(1-x)\}]\, dx$

$$\left[\because \int_0^a f(x)dx = \int_0^a f(a-x)\,dx\right] \text{[1]}$$

$\Rightarrow \quad I = \int_0^1 [\tan^{-1}(1-x) - \tan^{-1}(x)]\, dx \qquad$ ...(ii)

On adding Eqs. (i) and (ii), we get

$$2I = 0 \Rightarrow I = 0 \qquad \text{[1]}$$

20. Let $I = \int_0^{3/2} |x \cos \pi x|\, dx$

Here, $x \cos \pi x = 0 \Rightarrow x = 0$ or $\cos \pi x = 0$

$\Rightarrow \quad x = 0$ or $\cos \pi x = \cos \dfrac{\pi}{2} = \cos \dfrac{3\pi}{2}$

$\Rightarrow \quad x = 0$ or $\pi x = \dfrac{\pi}{2}$ or $\pi x = \dfrac{3\pi}{2}$

$\Rightarrow \quad x = 0$ or $x = \dfrac{1}{2}$ or $\pi x = \dfrac{3}{2}$

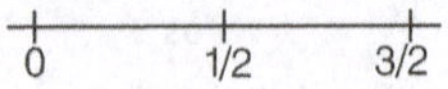

[1]

For $0 < x < \dfrac{1}{2}$; $x > 0$ and $\cos \pi x > 0$, then

$\therefore x \cos \pi x > 0$

For $\dfrac{1}{2} < x < \dfrac{3}{2}$; $x > 0$ and $\cos \pi x < 0$, then [1/2]

$\therefore x \cos \pi x < 0$

$$\therefore |x \cos \pi x| = \begin{cases} x \cos \pi x, & \text{for } 0 < x \le \dfrac{1}{2} \\ -x \cos \pi x, & \text{for } \dfrac{1}{2} \le x \le \dfrac{3}{2} \end{cases} \qquad \text{[1/2] [1]}$$

Now, $\int_0^{3/2} |x \cos \pi x|\, dx = \int_0^{1/2} x \cos \pi x\, dx + \int_{1/2}^{3/2} -(x \cos \pi x)\, dx$ [1]

$$= \left[x \frac{\sin \pi x}{\pi} - \int \frac{\sin \pi x}{\pi}\, dx\right]_0^{1/2} - \left[x \frac{\sin \pi x}{\pi} - \int \frac{\sin \pi x}{\pi}\, dx\right]_{1/2}^{3/2}$$

[using integration by parts] [1]

$$= \left[\frac{x}{\pi}\sin \pi x + \frac{1}{\pi^2}\cos \pi x\right]_0^{1/2} - \left[\frac{x}{\pi}\sin \pi x + \frac{1}{\pi^2}\cos \pi x\right]_{1/2}^{3/2}$$

$$= \left[\left(\frac{1}{2\pi}\sin\frac{\pi}{2} + \frac{1}{\pi^2}\cos\frac{\pi}{2}\right) - \left(0 + \frac{1}{\pi^2}\cos 0\right)\right]$$

$$- \left[\left(\frac{3}{2\pi}\sin\frac{3\pi}{2} + \frac{1}{\pi^2}\cos\frac{3\pi}{2}\right) - \left(\frac{1}{2\pi}\sin\frac{\pi}{2} + \frac{1}{\pi^2}\cos\frac{\pi}{2}\right)\right]$$

$$= \left[\frac{1}{2\pi} - \frac{1}{\pi^2} - \frac{3}{2\pi}(-1) + \frac{1}{2\pi}\right]$$

$$= \frac{1}{\pi} - \frac{1}{\pi^2} + \frac{3}{2\pi}$$

$$= \frac{5}{2\pi} - \frac{1}{\pi^2} \qquad \text{[1]}$$

21. Let $I = \int_0^1 \cot^{-1}\{1 - x + x^2\}\, dx = \int_0^1 \tan^{-1}\left\{\dfrac{1}{1 - x + x^2}\right\} dx$

$$= \int_0^1 \tan^{-1}\left\{\frac{x + (1-x)}{1 - x + x^2}\right\} dx$$

[adding and subtracting x in numerator] [1]

$$= \int_0^1 \tan^{-1}\left(\frac{x + (1-x)}{1 - x(1-x)}\right) dx$$

$$= \int_0^1 (\tan^{-1} x + \tan^{-1}(1-x))\, dx$$

$$\left[\because \tan^{-1} A + \tan^{-1} B = \tan^{-1}\left(\frac{A+B}{1-AB}\right)\right] \text{[1]}$$

$$= \int_0^1 \tan^{-1} x\, dx + \int_0^1 \tan^{-1}(1-x)\, dx$$

$$= \int_0^1 \tan^{-1} x\, dx + \int_0^1 \tan^{-1}(1-(1-x))\, dx$$

$$\left[\because \int_0^a f(x)\, dx = \int_0^a f(a-x)\, dx\right] \text{[1]}$$

$$= \int_0^1 \tan^{-1} x + \int_0^1 \tan^{-1} x\, dx$$

$$= 2\int_0^1 \tan^{-1} x = 2\int_0^1 (\underset{\text{I}}{\tan^{-1} x})\underset{\text{II}}{1}\, dx \qquad \text{[1]}$$

$$= 2\left\{[\tan^{-1} x \cdot x]_0^1 - \int_0^1 \frac{1}{1+x^2} \cdot x\, dx\right\}$$

[using integration by parts]

$$= 2\,[\tan^{-1}(1) - 0] - \int_0^1 \frac{2x}{1+x^2} dx \qquad \text{[1]}$$

$$= 2 \cdot \frac{\pi}{4} - [\log(1+x^2)]_0^1$$

$$= \frac{\pi}{2} - [\log 2 - \log 1] = \frac{\pi}{2} - \log 2 \qquad [\because \log 1 = 0] \text{ [1]}$$

22. Let $I = \int_0^{\pi/2} \dfrac{x \sin x \cos x}{\sin^4 x + \cos^4 x} dx \qquad$ ...(i)

Using $\int_0^a f(x)\, dx = \int_0^a f(a-x) dx$, we get

$$I = \int_0^{\pi/2} \frac{\left(\frac{\pi}{2} - x\right) \sin\left(\frac{\pi}{2} - x\right) \cos\left(\frac{\pi}{2} - x\right)}{\sin^4\left(\frac{\pi}{2} - x\right) + \cos^4\left(\frac{\pi}{2} - x\right)} dx$$

$$\Rightarrow \quad I = \int_0^{\pi/2} \frac{\left(\frac{\pi}{2} - x\right) \cos x \sin x}{\cos^4 x + \sin^4 x} dx \qquad \text{...(ii)}$$

$$\left[\because \cos\left(\frac{\pi}{2} - \theta\right) = \sin \theta \text{ and } \sin\left(\frac{\pi}{2} - \theta\right) = \cos \theta\right] \text{[1]}$$

On adding Eqs. (i) and (ii), we get

$$2I = \frac{\pi}{2} \int_0^{\pi/2} \frac{\cos x \sin x}{\sin^4 x + \cos^4 x} dx$$

$$\Rightarrow \quad I = \frac{\pi}{4} \int_0^{\pi/2} \frac{\sin x \cos x}{(\sin^2 x)^2 + (1 - \sin^2 x)^2} dx$$

$$[\because \cos^2 \theta = 1 - \sin^2 \theta]$$

Now, put $\sin^2 x = t \Rightarrow 2\sin x\cos x\, dx = dt$

$\Rightarrow \quad \sin x\cos x\, dx = \frac{dt}{2}$

Lower limit When $x = 0$, then $t = \sin^2 0 = 0$ [1]

Upper limit When $x = \frac{\pi}{2}$, then $t = \sin^2\frac{\pi}{2} = 1$

Now, $I = \frac{\pi}{4}\int_0^1 \frac{1}{t^2 + (1-t)^2}\frac{dt}{2}$

$\Rightarrow \quad I = \frac{\pi}{8}\int_0^1 \frac{1}{t^2 + (1 + t^2 - 2t)}dt$ [1]

$\Rightarrow \quad I = \frac{\pi}{8}\int_0^1 \frac{1}{2t^2 - 2t + 1}dt$

$\Rightarrow \quad I = \frac{\pi}{16}\int_0^1 \frac{1}{t^2 - t + \frac{1}{2}}dt$

$\Rightarrow \quad I = \frac{\pi}{16}\int_0^1 \frac{1}{t^2 - t + \left(\frac{1}{2}\right)^2 - \left(\frac{1}{2}\right)^2 + \frac{1}{2}}dt$ [1]

$\left[\text{adding and subtracting by } \left(\frac{1}{2}\right)^2 \text{ from denominator}\right]$

$\Rightarrow \quad I = \frac{\pi}{16}\int_0^1 \frac{1}{\left(t - \frac{1}{2}\right)^2 + \left(\frac{1}{2}\right)^2}dt$

$\Rightarrow \quad I = \frac{\pi}{16}\cdot\frac{1}{(1/2)}\left[\tan^{-1}\left(\frac{t - \frac{1}{2}}{\frac{1}{2}}\right)\right]_0^1 = \frac{\pi}{8}\left[\tan^{-1} 2\left(t - \frac{1}{2}\right)\right]_0^1$

$\left[\because \int \frac{1}{x^2 + a^2}dx = \frac{1}{a}\tan^{-1}\frac{x}{a}\right]$

$\Rightarrow \quad I = \frac{\pi}{8}\left[\tan^{-1} 2\left(1 - \frac{1}{2}\right) - \tan^{-1} 2\left(0 - \frac{1}{2}\right)\right]$ [1]

$\Rightarrow \quad I = \frac{\pi}{8}[\tan^{-1}(1) - \tan^{-1}(-1)]$

$\left[\because \tan^{-1}(-1) = -\tan^{-1}(1) = -\frac{\pi}{4}\right]$

$\Rightarrow \quad I = \frac{\pi}{8}\left[\frac{\pi}{4} + \frac{\pi}{4}\right] = \frac{\pi^2}{16}$ [1]

23. **Hint** Let $I = \int_0^1 \frac{\log(1+x)}{1+x^2}dx$ ...(i)

Now, put $x = \tan\theta \Rightarrow dx = \sec^2\theta\, d\theta$

Lower limit When $x = 0$, then $\tan\theta = 0 \Rightarrow \theta = 0$

Upper limit When $x = 1$, then $\tan\theta = 1 \Rightarrow \theta = \frac{\pi}{4}$

Now, $I = \int_0^{\pi/4} \frac{\log|1 + \tan\theta|}{(1 + \tan^2\theta)}\sec^2\theta\, d\theta$

$= \int_0^{\pi/4} \frac{\log|1 + \tan\theta|}{\sec^2\theta}\sec^2\theta\, d\theta$

$[\because \sec^2\theta = 1 + \tan^2\theta]$

$\Rightarrow \quad I = \int_0^{\pi/4} \log(1 + \tan\theta)\, d\theta$ ...(ii)

$\left[\textbf{Ans. } \frac{\pi}{8}\log 2\right]$

24. Let $I = \int_0^{\pi/2} (2\log(\sin x) - \log(\sin 2x))dx$

$= \int_0^{\pi/2} [\log(\sin^2 x) - \log(\sin 2x)]dx$

$[\because m\log n = \log n^m]$

$= \int_0^{\pi/2} \log\left(\frac{\sin^2 x}{\sin 2x}\right)dx \quad \left[\because \log m - \log n = \log\frac{m}{n}\right]$

[1/2]

$= \int_0^{\pi/2} \log\left(\frac{\sin^2 x}{2\sin x\cos x}\right)dx \quad [\because \sin 2x = 2\sin x\cos x]$

$= \int_0^{\pi/2} \log\left(\frac{\tan x}{2}\right)dx$

$= \int_0^{\pi/2} [\log(\tan x) - \log 2]\, dx$ [1]

$= \int_0^{\pi/2} \log(\tan x)\, dx - \int_0^{\pi/2} \log 2\, dx$

$= \int_0^{\pi/2} \log(\tan x)dx - \log 2\int_0^{\pi/2} 1\, dx$

$\Rightarrow I = I_1 - (\log 2)[x]_0^{\pi/2} = I_1 - \left(\frac{\pi}{2} - 0\right)\log 2$ ...(i) [1]

where, $I_1 = \int_0^{\pi/2} \log(\tan x)\, dx$ ...(ii)

Now, $I_1 = \int_0^{\pi/2} \log\left[\tan\left(\frac{\pi}{2} - x\right)\right]dx$

$\left[\because \int_0^a f(x)\, dx = \int_0^a f(a - x)\, dx\right]$

$\Rightarrow \quad I_1 = \int_0^{\pi/2} \log(\cot x)\, dx$ ...(iii) [1]

On adding Eqs. (ii) and (iii), we get

$2I_1 = \int_0^{\pi/2} [\log(\tan x) + \log(\cot x)]dx$

$= \int_0^{\pi/2} \log(\tan x\cot x)\, dx$

$[\because \log m + \log n = \log(mn)]$

$= \int_0^{\pi/2} \log 1\, dx = 0 \quad \left[\because \tan x = \frac{1}{\cot x}\right]$ [1]

$\Rightarrow \quad I_1 = 0$

From Eq. (i), we get $I = 0 - \frac{\pi}{2}\log 2$

$\Rightarrow \quad I = -\frac{\pi}{2}\log 2$ [1½]

25. **Hint** Let $I = \int_{-1}^1 \frac{x^3 + |x| + 1}{x^2 + 2|x| + 1}dx$

$= \int_{-1}^1 \frac{x^3}{x^2 + 2|x| + 1}dx + \int_{-1}^1 \frac{|x| + 1}{x^2 + 2|x| + 1}dx$

$$= 0 + 2\int_0^1 \frac{|x|+1}{x^2 + 2|x| + 1}dx$$

$$\left[\because \int_{-1}^{1} f(x)dx = \begin{cases} 2\int_0^1 f(x)dx, \text{ if } f(x) \text{ is even function} \\ 0, \quad \text{if } f(x) \text{ is odd function} \end{cases}\right]$$

$$= 2\int_0^1 \frac{(x+1)}{x^2 + 2x + 1}dx \qquad [\because |x| = x, \text{ if } x \ge 0]$$

$$= 2\int_0^1 \frac{(x+1)}{(x+1)^2}dx \quad [\textbf{Ans. } 2\log 2]$$

26. Let $I = \int_{-\pi}^{\pi} (\cos ax - \sin bx)^2\, dx$

$$= 2\int_0^{\pi} (\cos ax - \sin bx)^2\, dx$$

$$\left[\because \int_{-a}^{a} f(x)\,dx = \begin{cases} 2\int_0^a f(x)dx, \text{ if } f(x) \text{ is even} \\ 0, \quad \text{if } f(x) \text{ is odd} \end{cases} \text{ and the given integrand is an even function}\right] \text{[1]}$$

$$= 2\int_0^{\pi} [\cos^2 ax + \sin^2 bx - 2\sin bx \cos ax]dx$$

$$= 2\int_0^{\pi} [\cos^2 ax + \sin^2 bx - \{\sin(bx + ax) + \sin(bx - ax)\}]dx$$

$$[\because 2\sin A \cos B = \sin(A+B) + \sin(A-B)] \quad \text{[1]}$$

$$= 2\left[\int_0^{\pi} \cos^2 ax\, dx + \int_0^{\pi} \sin^2 bx\, dx - \int_0^{\pi} \sin(b+a)x\, dx - \int_0^{\pi} \sin(b-a)x\, dx\right]$$

$$= 2\left[\int_0^{\pi} \left(\frac{1+\cos 2ax}{2}\right)dx + \int_0^{\pi}\left(\frac{1-\cos 2bx}{2}\right)dx - \int_0^{\pi} \sin(b+a)x\, dx - \int_0^{\pi} \sin(b-a)x\, dx\right] \text{[1]}$$

$$= 2\left[\int_0^{\pi}\left(\frac{1}{2} + \frac{\cos 2ax}{2}\right)dx + \int_0^{\pi}\left(\frac{1}{2} - \frac{\cos 2bx}{2}\right)dx - \int_0^{\pi}\sin(b+a)x\, dx - \int_0^{\pi}\sin(b-a)x\, dx\right]$$

$$= 2\left[\int_0^{\pi}\left(\frac{1}{2} + \frac{1}{2}\right)dx + \frac{1}{2}\int_0^{\pi}\cos 2ax\, dx - \frac{1}{2}\int_0^{\pi}\cos 2bx\, dx - \int_0^{\pi}\sin(b+a)x\, dx - \int_0^{\pi}\sin(b-a)x\, dx\right] \text{[1]}$$

$$= 2\left[[x]_0^{\pi} + \frac{1}{2}\left[\frac{\sin 2ax}{2a}\right]_0^{\pi} - \frac{1}{2}\left[\frac{\sin 2bx}{2b}\right]_0^{\pi} + \left[\frac{\cos(b+a)x}{(b+a)}\right]_0^{\pi} + \left[\frac{\cos(b-a)x}{(b-a)}\right]_0^{\pi}\right] \text{[1]}$$

$$= 2\left[\pi + \frac{1}{4a}[\sin 2a\pi] - \frac{1}{4b}[\sin 2b\pi] + \frac{1}{b+a}\cdot[\cos(b+a)\pi - 1] + \frac{1}{(b-a)}[\cos(b-a)\pi - 1]\right]$$

$$[\because \cos 0 = 1]$$

$$= 2\left[\pi + \frac{1}{4a}\sin 2a\pi - \frac{1}{4b}\sin 2b\pi + \frac{1}{b+a}\cos(b+a)\pi - \frac{1}{b+a} + \frac{1}{b-a}\cos(b-a)\pi - \frac{1}{b-a}\right] \text{[1]}$$

27. Let $I = \int_0^{\pi} x \log|\sin x|\, dx$ ...(i)

$$\Rightarrow I = \int_0^{\pi} (\pi - x)\log|\sin(\pi - x)|dx$$

$$= \int_0^{\pi} (\pi - x)\log|\sin x|\, dx \quad \text{...(ii)}$$

On adding Eqs. (i) and (ii), we get

$$2I = \pi\int_0^{\pi} \log|\sin x|\, dx \quad \text{...(iii) [1]}$$

$$\Rightarrow 2I = 2\pi\int_0^{\pi/2} \log|\sin x|\, dx$$

$$\left[\because \int_0^{2a} f(x)dx = 2\int_0^a f(x)dx, \text{ if } f(2a - x) = f(x)\right]$$

$$\Rightarrow I = \pi\int_0^{\pi/2} \log|\sin x|\, dx \quad \text{...(iv)}$$

$$\Rightarrow I = \pi\int_0^{\pi/2} \log|\sin(\pi/2 - x)|dx$$

$$\left[\because \int_0^a f(x)\,dx = \int_0^a f(a-x)\,dx\right]$$

$$= \pi\int_0^{\pi/2} \log|\cos x|\, dx \quad \text{...(v) [1]}$$

On adding Eqs. (iv) and (v), we get

$$2I = \pi\int_0^{\pi/2} (\log|\sin x| + \log|\cos x|)dx$$

$$\Rightarrow 2I = \pi\int_0^{\pi/2} \log|\sin x \cos x|\, dx$$

$$\Rightarrow 2I = \pi\int_0^{\pi/2} \log\left|\frac{2\sin x\cos x}{2}\right|dx$$

[multiply by 2 from numerator and denominator]

$$\Rightarrow 2I = \pi\int_0^{\pi/2} (\log|\sin 2x| - \log 2)dx \quad \text{[1]}$$

$$2I = \pi\int_0^{\pi/2} \log|\sin 2x|\, dx - \pi\int_0^{\pi/2} \log 2\, dx$$

$$\Rightarrow 2I = \pi\int_0^{\pi/2} \log|\sin 2x|\, dx - \pi\log 2[x]_0^{\pi/2} \quad \text{[1]}$$

Now, put $2x = t \Rightarrow dx = \frac{1}{2}dt$

Lower limit When $x = 0$, then $t = 0$

Upper limit When $x = \frac{\pi}{2}$, then $t = \pi$

$$\therefore \quad 2I = \frac{\pi}{2}\int_0^{\pi} \log|\sin t|dt - \frac{\pi^2}{2}\log 2$$

$$\Rightarrow 2I = \frac{\pi}{2}\int_0^{\pi} \log|\sin x|\, dx - \frac{\pi^2}{2}\log 2 \quad \text{[1]}$$

$$\Rightarrow 2I = I - \frac{\pi^2}{2}\log 2 \quad \text{[from Eq. (iii)]}$$

$$\therefore \quad I = -\frac{\pi^2}{2}\log 2 = \frac{\pi^2}{2}\log\left(\frac{1}{2}\right) \quad \text{[1]}$$

Chapter Practice

Multiple Choice Type Questions

(1 Mark)

1 If $\int_0^a 3x^2 dx = 8$, then the value of a is

(a) 2 (b) 4 (c) 8 (d) 10

2 Evaluate $\int_{-1}^{1} x^{17} \cos^4 x\, dx$. [ISC 2023]

(a) ∞ (b) 1 (c) -1 (d) 0

3 $\int_0^{\pi/2} \sqrt{1-\sin 2x}\, dx$ is equal to

(a) $2\sqrt{2}$ (b) $2(\sqrt{2}+1)$ (c) 2 (d) $2(\sqrt{2}-1)$

4 $\int_{-\pi/2}^{\pi/2} (x^3 + x\cos x + \tan^5 x + 1)dx$ is equal to

(a) 0 (b) 2 (c) π (d) 1

5 $\int_{-1}^{1} x\,|x|\,dx$ is equal to

(a) 0 (b) 1
(c) 2 (d) None of these

Assertion-Reason Type Questions

(1 Mark)

Directions (Q. Nos. 6-9) *In the questions given below are two statements labelled as Assertion (A) and Reason (R). In the context of the two statements, which one of the following is correct?*

(a) Both A and R are correct; R is the correct explanation of A
(b) Both A and R are correct; R is not the correct explanation of A
(c) A is correct; R is incorrect
(d) R is correct; A is incorrect

6 **Assertion (A)** $\int_{-\pi}^{\pi} x\tan^2 x\, dx = 0$

Reason (R) If $f(x)$ is an even function, then $\int_{-a}^{a} f(x)dx = 2\int_0^a f(x)dx$.

7 **Assertion (A)** $\int_1^e \frac{e^x}{x}(1+\log x)dx = e^e$

Reason (R) $\int e^x\, f(x) + f'(x)dx = e^x f(x) + C$

8 **Assertion (A)** $\int_{-3}^{3} |x+2|\, dx = 13$

Reason (R)

$$\int_{-a}^{a} f(x)\, dx = \begin{cases} 2\int_0^a f(x), \text{ if } f \text{ is an even function} \\ \quad \text{i.e. } f(-x) = f(x) \\ 0, \text{ if } f \text{ is an odd function,} \\ \quad \text{i.e. } f(x) = -f(x) \end{cases}$$

9 **Assertion (A)** $\int_0^{\pi} \cos^2 x\, dx = \frac{\pi}{2}$

Reason (R) $\int_a^b f(x)\, dx = \int_a^b f(a+b-x)\, dx$

Very Short Answer Type Questions

(2 Marks)

10 Evaluate $\int_0^2 \sqrt{4-x^2}\, dx$

11 Evaluate $\int_0^1 \frac{dx}{4-x^2}$

12 Evaluate $\int_0^{\pi} \left(\sin^2\frac{x}{2} - \cos^2\frac{x}{2}\right) dx$. [NCERT]

13 Evaluate $\int_4^5 |x-5|dx$. [ISC 2020]

14 Evaluate $\int_0^2 x\sqrt{x+2}\, dx$. [NCERT]

15 Evaluate $\int_{-1}^{1} \sin^5 x \cos^4 x\, dx$. [NCERT]

16 Evaluate $\int_1^2 \left(\frac{1}{x} - \frac{1}{2x^2}\right) e^{2x} dx$. [NCERT]

17 Evaluate $\int_0^1 \frac{x^4+1}{x^2+1} dx$.

18 Evaluate $\int_1^2 \frac{5x^2}{x^2+4x+3} dx$. [NCERT]

19 Evaluate $\int_2^4 \frac{(x^2+x)}{\sqrt{2x+1}} dx$.

[**Hint** Integrate by parts by taking (x^2+x) as I function and $\frac{1}{\sqrt{2x+1}}$ as II function]

20 Evaluate $\int_{1/3}^{1} \frac{(x-x^3)^{1/3}}{x^4} dx$. [NCERT]

21 Evaluate $\int_0^4 (|x|+|x-2|+|x-4|)\, dx$.

22 Evaluate $\int_0^{\pi/2} |\cos x - \sin x| dx$.

23 Evaluate $\int_{\pi/5}^{3\pi/10} \frac{\sin x}{(\sin x + \cos x)} dx$.

24 Evaluate $\int_0^{\pi/2} \frac{x}{(\sin x + \cos x)} dx$.

Short Answer Type Questions

4 Marks

25 Evaluate $\int_0^{\pi} x \sin x \cos^2 x \, dx$.

[**Hint** Use $\int_0^{\pi} x \sin x \cos^2 x \, dx = (\pi - x) \sin (\pi - x) \cos (\pi - x) \, dx$]

26 Evaluate $\int_0^{\pi} \frac{x \sin x}{1 + \cos^2 x} dx$.

[**Hint** $\int_0^a f(x) dx = \int_0^a f(a - x) \, dx$]

27 Evaluate $\int_0^{\pi/2} \frac{x + \sin x}{1 + \cos x} dx$.

28 Evaluate $\int_0^{\pi} \frac{x}{a^2 \cos^2 x + b^2 \sin^2 x} dx$.

29 Evaluate $\int_0^{\pi/2} \log \sin x \, dx$. [NCERT]

Long Answer Type Questions

6 Marks

30 Evaluate $\int_0^{3/2} |x \sin \pi x| \, dx$.

31 Evaluate $\int_0^2 (x^2 + 2x + 1) dx$, as limit of sum.

32 Evaluate $\int_0^3 (2x^2 + e^x) dx$, as limit of sum.

33 Evaluate $\int_{-\pi/4}^{\pi/4} \log (\cos x + \sin x) dx$.

[**Hint** Use $\int_a^b f(x) \, dx = \int_a^b f(a + b - x) \, dx$]

[NCERT Exemplar]

34 Prove that $\int_0^{\pi} \frac{x}{1 + \cos\alpha \sin x} dx = \frac{\pi\alpha}{\sin\alpha}$.

Case-Based Type Question

6 Marks

35 In a school, Madam Sharma explains the additive property of definite integration which is as follows:

$$\int_a^b f(x) dx = \int_a^{c_1} f(x) dx + \int_{c_1}^{c_2} f(x) dx + \ldots + \int_{c_n}^b f(x) dx$$

where, $a < c_1 < c_2 \ldots < c_n < b$

After explaining it, she asks some questions to her class which are as follows. Now, answer these questions.

(i) Find the value of $\int_1^4 f(x) dx$,

where $f(x) = \begin{cases} 7x + 3, & 1 \le x \le 3 \\ 8x, & 3 \le x \le 4 \end{cases}$

(ii) Find the value of $\int_0^{2\pi} |\sin x| dx$.

(iii) Find the value of $\int_0^2 2x[x] dx$.

(iv) Find the value of $\int_0^4 |x - 1| dx$.

Answers

1. (a)	2. (d)	3. (d)	4. (c)
5. (a)	6. (b)	7. (a)	8. (a)
9. (b)	10. π	11. $\frac{1}{4} \log 3$	12. 0
13. $\frac{1}{2}$	14. $\frac{16\sqrt{2}}{15} (\sqrt{2} + 1)$	15. 0	16. $\frac{e^2 (e^2 - 2)}{4}$
17. $\frac{3\pi - 4}{6}$	18. $5 - \frac{45}{2} \log \frac{5}{4} + \frac{5}{2} \log \frac{3}{2}$	19. $\sqrt{\frac{57 - 5\sqrt{5}}{5}}$	20. 6
21. 20	22. $2 (\sqrt{2} - 1)$	23. $\frac{\pi}{20}$	24. $\frac{\pi}{4\sqrt{2}} \log \left\lvert \frac{\sqrt{2} + 1}{\sqrt{2} - 1} \right\rvert$
25. $\frac{\pi}{3}$	26. $\frac{\pi^2}{4}$	27. $\frac{\pi}{2}$	28. $\frac{\pi^2}{2ab}$
29. $-\frac{\pi}{2} \log 2$	30. $\frac{2}{\pi} + \frac{1}{\pi^2}$	31. $\frac{26}{3}$	32. $17 + e^3$
33. $\frac{\pi}{8} \log \left(\frac{1}{2}\right)$	35. (i) 64 (ii) 4	(iii) 3	(iv) 5

CHAPTER

10

Differential Equations

In this chapter, we will study some basic concepts related to differential equation, general and particular solutions of a differential equation, and some methods to solve differential equations.

- Order, Degree and Solution of Differential Equation
- Solution of Differential Equation of First Order and First Degree
- Linear Differential Equations

TOPIC 01 Order, Degree and Solution of Differential Equation

Differential Equation

An equation involving independent variable (variables), dependent variable and derivative or derivatives of dependent variable with respect to independent variable (variables) is called a **differential equation. e.g.**

$2x\frac{dy}{dx}-3y=5$ and $4\frac{d^2y}{dx^2}+\left(\frac{dy}{dx}\right)^3=0$ are differential equations, but

$2x-3y=0$ is not a differential equation as derivatives of dependent variable (y) with respect to independent variable (x) is not present.

Ordinary Differential Equation

A differential equation involving derivative or derivatives of the dependent variable with respect to only one independent variable is called **an ordinary differential equation. e.g.** $2\frac{d^2y}{dx^2}+5\left(\frac{dy}{dx}\right)^3=0$ is an ordinary differential equation, because here dependent variable y have derivatives with respect to only one independent variable, i.e. x.

There are differential equation involving derivatives with respect to more than one independent variables, such equation is called the **partial differential equation**. But here, we will only deal with ordinary differential equation.

Note The derivatives are denoted by the symbols

$\frac{dy}{dx}, \frac{d^2y}{dx^2}, \ldots, \frac{d^ny}{dx^n}$ or $y', y'', \ldots, y^{(n)}$ or $y_1, y_2, \ldots, y_n$.

If the derivative is of higher order say n, then it is convenient to use y_n to represent nth order derivative.

Order of a Differential Equation

The order of the highest order derivative occurring in a differential equation, is called the **order of differential equation.**

e.g. (i) $\frac{dy}{dx} - \sin x = 0$ (ii) $\frac{d^3y}{dx^3} + x^2\left(\frac{d^2y}{dx^2}\right) = 0$

Here, in e.g. (i), equation has the highest derivative of first order and in e.g. (ii), equation has the highest derivative of third order. So, orders of the differential equations in e.g. (i) and (ii) are 1 and 3, respectively.

Degree of a Differential Equation

The highest power (positive integral index) of the highest order derivative involved in a differential equation, when it is written as a polynomial in derivatives, is called the **degree of differential equation.**

e.g. $\left(\frac{d^3y}{dx^3}\right)^2 + x\left(\frac{d^2y}{dx^2}\right) + 3y\left(\frac{dy}{dx}\right) = 0$

In this differential equation, highest order derivative is $\left(\frac{d^3y}{dx^3}\right)$, whose highest power is 2. So, degree of differential equation is 2.

Note

(i) The order and degree (if defined) of a differential equation are always positive integers.

(ii) If the given differential equation is not a polynomial equation in its derivatives, then its degree is not defined.

e.g. $\frac{d^2y}{dx^2} + \sin\left(\frac{dy}{dx}\right) = 0$ is not a polynomial equation in derivatives, because by using expansion of sin x, the differential equation becomes $\frac{d^2y}{dx^2} + \left\{\frac{dy}{dx} - \frac{\left(\frac{dy}{dx}\right)^3}{3!} + \frac{\left(\frac{dy}{dx}\right)^5}{5!} - \ldots\right\} = 0$, which is not a polynomial in derivatives, as it is not finite, so its degree is not defined.

(iii) If the differential equation have radicals (like $\sqrt{\ }$, $\sqrt[3]{\ }$, etc.) and fractions $\left(\text{like } \frac{1}{\left(\frac{dy}{dx}\right)}, \frac{1}{\sqrt{1+\frac{d^2y}{dx^2}}}, \text{etc.}\right)$, then to find degree, first made it free from radicals and fractions by simplifying it.

Example 1 Find the order and degree (if defined) of each of the following differential equation.

(i) $\frac{dy}{dx} - \sec x = 0$ (ii) $y''' + y^2 + e^{y'} = 0$

(iii) $y = x\frac{dy}{dx} + \sqrt{1 + \left(\frac{dy}{dx}\right)^2}$

Sol. (i) Given differential equation is $\frac{dy}{dx} - \sec x = 0$.

The highest order derivative occurring in the differential equation is $\frac{dy}{dx}$, so its order is 1. It is a polynomial in $\frac{dy}{dx}$ and highest power raised to $\frac{dy}{dx}$ is 1.

So, its degree is 1.

(ii) Given differential equation is $y''' + y^2 + e^{y'} = 0$

The highest order derivative occurring in the differential equation is y''', so its order is 3.

The given differential equation is not a polynomial equation in derivatives of y, so its degree is not defined.

(iii) Given differential equation is $y = x\frac{dy}{dx} + \sqrt{1 + \left(\frac{dy}{dx}\right)^2}$.

It has radical sign in power, i.e. not have positive integer powers, so we first convert it into differential equation having positive integer powers.

We can rewrite the given differential equations as

$$y - x\frac{dy}{dx} = \sqrt{1 + \left(\frac{dy}{dx}\right)^2}$$

$$\Rightarrow y^2 + x^2\left(\frac{dy}{dx}\right)^2 - 2xy\frac{dy}{dx} = 1 + \left(\frac{dy}{dx}\right)^2$$

[squaring both sides]

$$\Rightarrow (x^2 - 1)\left(\frac{dy}{dx}\right)^2 - 2xy\frac{dy}{dx} + y^2 - 1 = 0$$

which represents a quadratic polynomial in $\frac{dy}{dx}$.

Since, highest order derivative is $\frac{dy}{dx}$.

So, the order of differential equation is 1 and the degree of differential equation is 2.

Example 2 Find the order and degree of differential equation $y = px + \sqrt{a^2p^2 + b^2}$, where $p = dy/dx$.

Sol. Given differential equation is $y = px + \sqrt{a^2p^2 + b^2}$

where, $p = \frac{dy}{dx}$.

$$\Rightarrow y - px = \sqrt{a^2p^2 + b^2}$$

$$\Rightarrow (y - px)^2 = a^2p^2 + b^2$$

$$\Rightarrow \quad y^2 + p^2x^2 - 2xpy = a^2p^2 + b^2$$
$$\Rightarrow \quad (x^2 - a^2)p^2 - 2xyp + (y^2 - b^2) = 0$$
$$\Rightarrow \quad (x^2 - a^2)\left(\frac{dy}{dx}\right)^2 - 2xy\left(\frac{dy}{dx}\right) + (y^2 - b^2) = 0$$

Clearly, order = 1 and degree = 2.

Example 3 Write the sum of the order and degree of the differential equation $\frac{d}{dx}\left\{\left(\frac{dy}{dx}\right)^3\right\} = 0.$

Sol. Given equation is $\frac{d}{dx}\left\{\left(\frac{dy}{dx}\right)^3\right\} = 0$

$$\Rightarrow \quad 3\left(\frac{dy}{dx}\right)^2 \frac{d^2y}{dx^2} = 0$$

Clearly, the highest order derivative occurring in the differential equation is d^2y/dx^2.

So, its order is 2. Also, it is a polynomial equation in derivatives and highest power raised to d^2y/dx^2 is 1, so its degree is 1.

Hence, the sum of the order and degree of the above differential equation is $2 + 1 = 3$.

Solution of a Differential Equation

A solution of differential equation will be a function of independent variable, which will satisfy the given differential equation.

In other words, suppose a differential equation is given to us, in which y is dependent variable and x is independent variable. Then, the function $\phi(x)$ will be its solution, if it satisfy the given differential equation, i.e. when the function ϕ is substituted for the unknown y (dependent variable) in the given differential equation, LHS becomes equal to RHS. The solution of a differential equation is of two types, which are given below

(i) General solution (ii) Particular solution

General Solution of a Differential Equation

If the solution of a differential equation of order n, contains n arbitrary constants, then it is called the **general solution.**

e.g. The general solution of $\frac{d^2y}{dx^2} + y = 0$ is $y = A\cos x + B\sin x$.

But $y = A\cos x + \sin x$ and $y = \cos x + B\sin x$ is not the general solution of given differential equation, as it contains only one arbitrary constant.

Method to Verify that Given Function is a Solution of Differential Equation

Suppose, a differential equation is given to us in which y is dependent variable and x is independent variable. Then, to verify whether the function $y = \phi(x)$ is a solution of given differential equation or not, we differentiate $y = \phi(x)$ with respect to x as many times as the order of given differential equation. Then, put $y = \phi(x)$ and values of its derivatives into LHS of given differential equation and check that LHS = RHS or not. If LHS = RHS, then function $y = \phi(x)$ is a solution of given differential equation, otherwise not.

Note

(i) If it is possible to obtain the given differential equation by using given function $y = \phi(x)$ and its derivatives, then the given function $y = \phi(x)$ is a solution of given differential equation.

(ii) Sometimes, a relation between dependent variable (y) and independent variable (x) is given to us, where y is not directly expressed as function of x (e.g. $y - \cos y = x$) and we have to check whether the given relation is a solution of given differential equation or not. In such case, we differentiate the given relation as many times as the order of differential equation to get the given differential equation. If we obtained the given differential equation. Then, the given relation is a solution, otherwise not.

Example 4 Show that the function $y = \frac{b}{x+b}$ is a solution of the differential equation $x\frac{dy}{dx} + y = y^2$.

Sol. Given equation can be rewritten as $(x + b)y = b$ ...(i)

On differentiating both sides w.r.t. x, we get

$$(1+0)y + (x+b)\frac{dy}{dx} = 0$$

$$\Rightarrow \quad x + b = -\frac{y}{dy/dx} \Rightarrow b = -x - \frac{y}{dy/dy}$$

On putting the values of b and $x + b$ in Eq. (i), we get

$$\left(-\frac{y}{dy/dx}\right)y = -x - \frac{y}{dy/dx}$$

$$-y^2 = -x\frac{dy}{dx} - y \Rightarrow y^2 = x\frac{dy}{dx} + y$$

Example 5 Verify that the function $y = e^{-3x}$ is a solution of the differential equation $\frac{d^2y}{dx^2} + \frac{dy}{dx} - 6y = 0.$

Sol. Given differential equation is

$$\frac{d^2y}{dx^2} + \frac{dy}{dx} - 6y = 0 \quad \text{...(i)}$$

and given function is $y = e^{-3x}$. ...(ii)

Here, order of the given differential equation is 2.

So, we differentiate Eq. (ii) two times.

On differentiating Eq. (ii), w.r.t. x two times, we get

$$\frac{dy}{dx} = -3e^{-3x} \text{ and } \frac{d^2y}{dx^2} = 9e^{-3x}$$

On putting the values of y, $\frac{dy}{dx}$ and $\frac{d^2y}{dx^2}$ in LHS of Eq. (i), we get

$$\text{LHS} = 9e^{-3x} + (-3e^{-3x}) - 6e^{-3x}$$
$$= 9e^{-3x} - 3e^{-3x} - 6e^{-3x} = 0 = \text{RHS}$$

Hence, the given function is a solution of given differential equation.

Example 6 Verify that $y = A\cos x - B\sin x$ is a solution of the differential equation $\frac{d^2y}{dx^2} + y = 0$.

Sol. Given, $y = A\cos x - B\sin x$ ...(i)

Here, order of the given differential equation is 2. So, we differentiate the Eq. (i) two times.

On differentiating both sides of Eq. (i) w.r.t. x two times, we get

$$\frac{dy}{dx} = -A\sin x - B\cos x$$
$$\Rightarrow \frac{d^2y}{dx^2} = -A\cos x + B\sin x$$
$$\Rightarrow \frac{d^2y}{dx^2} = -(A\cos x - B\sin x)$$
$$\Rightarrow \frac{d^2y}{dx^2} = -y \quad \text{[from Eq. (i)]}$$
$$\Rightarrow \frac{d^2y}{dx^2} + y = 0,$$

which is the given differential equation.

Hence, $y = A\cos x - B\sin x$ is a solution of given equation.

Particular Solution of a Differential Equation

The solution of a differential equation obtained by giving particular values to the arbitrary constants in the general solution, is called the **particular solution**. In other words, the solution free from arbitrary constant is called the **particular solution.**

e.g. The general solution of $\frac{d^2y}{dx^2} + y = 0$ is

$$y = A\cos x + B\sin x.$$

If $A = B = 1$, then $y = \cos x + \sin x$ is a particular solution of the given differential equation.

Initial Value Problems

An initial value problem is a differential equation together with specified value of the unknown function and its derivatives at a point of the domain of definition of independent variable.

These specified values are called initial conditions and given for specify a particular solution of the differential equation. Often, initial conditions are of the form $y(x_0) = y_0$ and / or $y'(x_0) = y_{01}$, $y''(x_0) = y_{02}$ and so on.

e.g.

(i) $x\frac{dy}{dx} = 1$, $y(1) = 0$

(ii) $\frac{d^2y}{dx^2} - 3\frac{dy}{dx} + 2y = 0$, $y(0) = 2$, $y'(0) = 3$ are initial value problems.

(i) If the differential equation in the initial value problem is of order 1, then initial value problem involves only specified value of the unknown function, i.e. $y(x_0) = y_0$.

(ii) A function is said to be a solution of initial value problem, if it satisfy the given differential equation and its initial conditions.

Example 7 Show that $y = x^2 + 2x + 1$ is the solution of the initial value problem

$$\frac{d^3y}{dx^3} = 0,\ y(0) = 1,\ y'(0) = 2,\ y''(0) = 2.$$

Sol. Given function is

$$y = x^2 + 2x + 1 \quad \text{...(i)}$$

Here, order of the given differential equation is 3. So, we differentiate Eq. (i) three times.

On differentiating Eq. (i) w.r.t. x three times, we get

$$\frac{dy}{dx} = 2x + 2 \quad \text{...(ii)}$$
$$\frac{d^2y}{dx^2} = 2 \quad \text{...(iii)}$$

$\frac{d^3y}{dx^3} = 0$, which is the given differential equation.

So, $y = x^2 + 2x + 1$ is the solution of given differential equation.

Now, $y(0) = (0)^2 + 2(0) + 1 = 1$ [using Eq. (i)]

$$y'(0) = \left(\frac{dy}{dx}\right)_{\text{at } x=0} = 2(0) + 2 = 2 \quad \text{[using Eq. (ii)]}$$

and $$\left(\frac{d^2y}{dx^2}\right)_{\text{at } x=0} = 2 \quad \text{[using Eq. (iii)]}$$

Hence, $y = x^2 + 2x + 1$ is the solution of initial value problem.

Topic Practice 1

Very Short Answer Type Questions

(2 Marks)

Directions (Q. Nos. 1-5) *Find the order and degree, of each of the following differential equations, if defined.*

1 $y+\frac{dy}{dx}=\frac{1}{4}\int y\,dx$

2 $\left(\frac{d^2y}{dx^2}\right)^3+\left(\frac{dy}{dx}\right)^2+\sin\left(\frac{dy}{dx}\right)+1=0$ **[NCERT]**

3 $\left[1+\left(\frac{dy}{dx}\right)^2\right]^{3/2}=\frac{d^2y}{dx^2}$.

4 $x-\sin\left(\frac{dy}{dx}\right)=0$.

5 $\log_e\left(1+\frac{d^2y}{dx^2}\right)=x$

Short Answer Type Questions

(4 Marks)

6 Show that $y=Ae^{mx}+Be^{nx}$ is a solution of the differential equation $\frac{d^2y}{dx^2}-(m+n)\frac{dy}{dx}+mny=0$.

7 Verify that $y=e^{m\sin^{-1}x}$ is a solution of the differential equation $(1-x^2)\frac{d^2y}{dx^2}-x\frac{dy}{dx}-m^2y=0$. **[ISC 2020]**

8 Prove that $(x^2-y^2)=c(x^2+y^2)^2$ is the general solution of the differential equation $(x^3-3xy^2)\,dx=(y^3-3x^2y)\,dy$, where c is a parameter. **[NCERT]**

Hints & Solutions

1. Given differential equation is

$$y+\frac{dy}{dx}=\frac{1}{4}\int y\,dx \quad \text{...(i)}$$

Let us first remove the integral sign by differentiating it w.r.t. x.

On differentiating Eq. (i) w.r.t. x, we get

$$\frac{dy}{dx}+\frac{d^2y}{dx^2}=\frac{1}{4}y \quad [1]$$

Since, the highest order derivative is $\frac{d^2y}{dx^2}$. So, its order is 2.

Also, it is a polynomial equation in $\frac{d^2y}{dx^2}$ and $\frac{dy}{dx}$, where highest power of $\frac{d^2y}{dx^2}$ is 1. So, its degree is 1. [1]

2. Given differential equation is

$$\left(\frac{d^2y}{dx^2}\right)^3+\left(\frac{dy}{dx}\right)^2+\sin\left(\frac{dy}{dx}\right)+1=0$$

Since, the highest order derivative is $\frac{d^2y}{dx^2}$. So, its order is 2. [1]

Degree is not defined as it is not a polynomial in derivatives. [1]

3. Given differential equation is $\left[1+\left(\frac{dy}{dx}\right)^2\right]^{3/2}=\frac{d^2y}{dx^2}$.

On squaring both sides, we get

$$\left[1+\left(\frac{dy}{dx}\right)^2\right]^3=\left(\frac{d^2y}{dx^2}\right)^2 \quad [1]$$

Here, highest order derivative is $\frac{d^2y}{dx^2}$, whose highest power is 2.

So, order of differential equation is 2 and degree is also 2. [1]

4. Given differential equation is $x-\sin\left(\frac{dy}{dx}\right)=0$.

Since, the highest order derivative is $\frac{dy}{dx}$. So, its order is 1. [1/2]

Now, if possible, then convert the given differential equation into polynomial equation of derivatives.

Consider, $x-\sin\left(\frac{dy}{dx}\right)=0$

$$\Rightarrow \quad \sin\left(\frac{dy}{dx}\right)=x \quad [1]$$

$\Rightarrow \frac{dy}{dx}=\sin^{-1}x$, which is a polynomial in $\frac{dy}{dx}$.

Also, highest power of $\frac{dy}{dx}$ is 1. So, its degree is 1. [1/2]

5. Given differential equation is

$\log_e\left(1+\frac{d^2y}{dx^2}\right)=x$, which can be rewritten as $1+\frac{d^2y}{dx^2}=e^x$

Clearly, the order of differential equation is 2 and its degree is 1. [2]

6. Given, $y=Ae^{mx}+Be^{nx}$ ...(i)

On differentiating both sides of Eq. (i) w.r.t. x, we get

$$\frac{dy}{dx}=A\cdot e^{mx}\cdot m+Be^{nx}\cdot n \quad \text{...(ii) [1]}$$

Again, on differentiating both sides of Eq. (ii) w.r.t. x, we get

$$\frac{d^2y}{dx^2} = m\cdot Ae^{mx}\cdot m + n\cdot Be^{nx}\cdot n$$

$$\Rightarrow \quad \frac{d^2y}{dx^2} = m^2Ae^{mx} + n^2Be^{nx}$$ [1]

Now, consider LHS $= \dfrac{d^2y}{dx^2} - (m+n)\dfrac{dy}{dx} + mny$

$= m^2Ae^{mx} + n^2Be^{nx} - (m+n)(mAe^{mx} + nBe^{nx}) + mn(Ae^{mx} + Be^{nx})$ [1]

$= m^2Ae^{mx} + n^2Be^{nx} - m^2Ae^{mx} - mnBe^{nx} - nmAe^{mx} - n^2Be^{nx} + mnAe^{mx} + mnBe^{nx}$

$= 0 =$ RHS

Thus, LHS = RHS

Hence, $y = Ae^{mx} + Be^{nx}$ is a solution of given equation.

Hence proved. [1]

7. **Hint** $\dfrac{dy}{dx} = \dfrac{my}{\sqrt{1-x^2}} \Rightarrow (1-x^2)\left(\dfrac{dy}{dx}\right)^2 = m^2y^2$

$$\Rightarrow (1-x^2)2\left(\frac{dy}{dx}\right)\frac{d^2y}{dx^2} + \left(\frac{dy}{dx}\right)^2(-2x) = m^2 2y\frac{dy}{dx}$$

On dividing both sides by $2\left(\dfrac{dy}{dx}\right)$ to verify required result.

8. The given differential equation is

$$(x^3 - 3xy^2)\,dx = (y^3 - 3x^2y)\,dy \quad \text{...(i)}$$

and the given function is

$$(x^2 - y^2) = c(x^2 + y^2)^2 \quad \text{...(ii)}$$

On differentiating Eq. (ii) w.r.t. x, we get

$$2x - 2y\frac{dy}{dx} = 2c(x^2+y^2)\left(2x + 2y\frac{dy}{dx}\right)$$

$$\Rightarrow \left(x - y\frac{dy}{dx}\right) = 2c(x^2+y^2)\left(x + y\frac{dy}{dx}\right) \quad \text{...(iii)}$$ [1]

$$\Rightarrow \left(x - y\frac{dy}{dx}\right) = \frac{2(x^2-y^2)}{(x^2+y^2)^2}(x^2+y^2)\left(x + y\frac{dy}{dx}\right)$$

[using Eq. (ii)]

$$\Rightarrow (x^2+y^2)\left(x - y\frac{dy}{dx}\right) = 2(x^2-y^2)\left(x + y\frac{dy}{dx}\right)$$ [1]

$$\Rightarrow (x^2+y^2)\,x - (x^2+y^2)\,y\frac{dy}{dx} = 2(x^2-y^2)\,x + 2(x^2-y^2)\,y\frac{dy}{dx}$$

$$\Rightarrow \{x(x^2+y^2) - 2x(x^2-y^2)\} = \{2y(x^2-y^2) + y(x^2+y^2)\}\frac{dy}{dx}$$ [1]

$$\Rightarrow \quad (3xy^2 - x^3) = (3x^2y - y^3)\frac{dy}{dx}$$

$$\Rightarrow \quad (x^3 - 3xy^2)\,dx = (y^3 - 3x^2y)\,dy$$

which is the given differential equation.

Hence, the given function is the solution of the given differential equation. [1]

TOPIC 02 Solution of Differential Equation of First Order and First Degree

A first order and first degree differential equation is of the form $\dfrac{dy}{dx} = F(x, y)$, where $F(x, y)$ is a function of x and y. We can solve such equations easily, if it will belong to any one of the following forms

(i) Variable separable form

(ii) Homogeneous form

(iii) Linear form

Differential Equation with Variable Separable

A first order and first degree differential equation $\dfrac{dy}{dx} = F(x, y)$ is in the form of **variable separable**, if the function F can be expressed as the product of the functions of x and the functions of y. Suppose a first order and first degree differential equation is given to us, i.e.

$$\frac{dy}{dx} = F(x, y) \quad \text{...(i)}$$

Now, expressed it as $\dfrac{dy}{dx} = h(y)\cdot g(x)$ ...(ii)

If $h(y) \neq 0$, then separate the variables, i.e. write Eq. (ii) as $\dfrac{1}{h(y)}dy = g(x)dx$

On integrating both sides, we get

$$\int \frac{1}{h(y)}dy = \int g(x)dx \text{ or } H(y) = G(x) + C$$

which is the required solution of given differential equation, where $H(y)$, $G(x)$ are the anti-derivatives of $\dfrac{1}{h(y)}$, $g(x)$ respectively and C is the arbitrary constant.

Example 1 Solve the differential equation

$$\frac{dy}{dx} = (1 + x^2)(1 + y^2).$$ [NCERT]

Sol. Given differential equation is $\frac{dy}{dx} = (1 + x^2)(1 + y^2)$

On separating the variables, we get

$$\left(\frac{1}{1+y^2}\right)dy = (1+x^2)dx$$

On integrating both sides, we get

$$\int \frac{1}{1+y^2}\,dy = \int (1 + x^2)\,dx$$

$$\Rightarrow \quad \tan^{-1} y = x + \frac{x^3}{3} + C$$

where, C is a constant of integration.

Note Here, is no need to introduce arbitrary constants of integration on both sides because both constant may be combined together and give just one arbitrary constant.

Example 2 Find the general solution of the differential equation $(x + 2)\frac{dy}{dx} = x^2 + 5x - 3,\ x \neq -2.$

Sol. Given differential equation is $(x + 2)\frac{dy}{dx} = x^2 + 5x - 3$

$$\Rightarrow \quad dy = \frac{x^2 + 5x - 3}{(x + 2)}\,dx \qquad \text{[separating the variables]}$$

On integrating both sides, we get

$$\int dy = \int \frac{x^2 + 5x - 3}{(x + 2)}\,dx$$

$$\Rightarrow \quad y = \int \left\{(x + 3) - \frac{9}{(x + 2)}\right\} dx$$

[dividing $(x^2 + 5x - 3)$ by $(x + 2)$]

$$\Rightarrow \quad y = \frac{x^2}{2} + 3x - 9\log|x + 2| + C$$

which is the required general solution.

Example 3 Solve the differential equation

$$\frac{dy}{dx} = e^{x+y} + x^2 e^y.$$ [ISC 2011]

Sol. Given differential equation is

$$\frac{dy}{dx} = e^{x+y} + x^2 e^y$$

$$\Rightarrow \quad \frac{dy}{dx} = e^y(e^x + x^2)$$

$$\Rightarrow \quad \frac{1}{e^y}dy = (e^x + x^2)\,dx$$

$$\Rightarrow \quad e^{-y}dy = (e^x + x^2)dx \qquad \text{[separating the variables]}$$

On integrating both sides, we get

$$\int e^{-y}dy = \int (e^x + x^2)\,dx$$

$$\Rightarrow \quad e^{-y} = e^x + \frac{x^3}{3} + C_1$$

$$\Rightarrow e^{-y} = e^x + \frac{x^3}{3} + C, \text{ where } C = C_1$$

which is the required solution.

Example 4 Find the particular solution of differential equation $\frac{dy}{dx} = -4xy^2$, given that $y = 1$, when $x = 0$.

Sol. Given differential equation is

$$\frac{dy}{dx} = -4xy^2 \qquad \text{...(i)}$$

$$\Rightarrow \quad \frac{dy}{y^2} = -4x\,dx \qquad \text{[separating the variables]}$$

On integrating both sides, we get

$$\int \frac{dy}{y^2} = -\int 4x\,dx \Rightarrow -\frac{1}{y} = -2x^2 + C$$

$$\Rightarrow \quad y = \frac{1}{2x^2 - C} \qquad \text{...(ii)}$$

which is a general solution of the given differential equation.

Also, given $y = 1$, when $x = 0$

On putting $x = 0$ and $y = 1$ in Eq. (ii), we get

$$1 = \frac{1}{2(0)^2 - C} \Rightarrow C = -1$$

On putting the value of C in Eq. (ii), we get

$$y = \frac{1}{2x^2 - (-1)}$$

$$\Rightarrow \quad y = \frac{1}{2x^2 + 1}$$

which is a particular solution of given differential equation.

Differential Equation Reducible to Variable Separable Form

If the given differential equation is of the form $\frac{dy}{dx} = f(ax + by + c)$, then it can be reduced to variable separable form by substituting $ax + by + c = z$.

To convert it into variable separable form, we use the following steps

I. Write the given differential equation, i.e.

$$\frac{dy}{dx} = f(ax + by + c)$$

II. Consider, $ax + by + c = z$ and differentiate it w.r.t. x, i.e. $a + b\frac{dy}{dx} = \frac{dz}{dx} \Rightarrow \frac{dy}{dx} = \frac{1}{b}\left(\frac{dz}{dx} - a\right)$

III. Substitute the value of $ax + by + c$ and $\frac{dy}{dx}$ from Step II to Step I, i.e. $\frac{1}{b}\left(\frac{dz}{dx} - a\right) = f(z)$

$\Rightarrow \frac{dz}{dx} = a + b\,f(z)$, which is the required differential equation.

Example 5 Solve the differential equation

$$\frac{dy}{dx} = \frac{x + y + 2}{2(x + y) - 1}$$ [ISC 2019]

Sol. We have, $\frac{dy}{dx} = \frac{x + y + 2}{2(x + y) - 1}$ ...(i)

Put $x + y = u$

$$\Rightarrow 1 + \frac{dy}{dx} = \frac{du}{dx} \Rightarrow \frac{dy}{dx} = \frac{du}{dx} - 1$$

$\therefore$ From Eq. (i), we get

$$\frac{du}{dx} - 1 = \frac{u + 2}{2(u) - 1} \Rightarrow \frac{du}{dx} = \frac{u + 2}{2u - 1} + 1$$

$$\Rightarrow \frac{du}{dx} = \frac{3u + 1}{2u - 1} \Rightarrow \left(\frac{2u - 1}{3u + 1}\right) du = dx$$

$$\Rightarrow \left(\frac{2}{3} - \frac{5/3}{3u + 1}\right) du = dx$$

$$\Rightarrow \frac{2}{3}\left(1 - \frac{5/2}{3u + 1}\right) du = dx$$

On, integration both sides, we get

$$\Rightarrow \frac{2}{3}\int\left[1 - \frac{5}{2(3u + 1)}\right] du = dx$$

$$\Rightarrow \frac{2}{3}\left[x - \frac{5}{2}\frac{\log|3u + 1|}{3}\right] = x + C$$

$$= \frac{2}{3}\left[x - \frac{5}{6}\log|3x + 3y + 1|\right] = x + C \quad [\because u = x + y]$$

$$\Rightarrow x - \frac{2}{3}x + \frac{5}{9}\log|3x + 3y + 1| + C = 0$$

$$\Rightarrow \frac{x}{3} + \frac{5}{9}\log|3x + 3y + 1| + C = 0$$

Homogeneous Differential Equations

A function $F(x, y)$ is said to be **homogeneous function** of degree n, if $F(x, y) = x^n g\left(\frac{y}{x}\right)$ or $y^n h\left(\frac{x}{y}\right)$

e.g. $F(x, y) = \frac{x + 2y}{x - y}$ is a homogeneous function of degree 0, as $F(x, y) = x^0\left[\frac{1 + 2\left(\frac{y}{x}\right)}{1 - \frac{y}{x}}\right]$

A differential equation of the form $\frac{dy}{dx} = F(x, y)$ is called a **homogeneous differential equation,** if $F(x, y)$ is a homogeneous function of degree zero.

Thus, if $F(x, y) = g\left(\frac{y}{x}\right)$ or $h\left(\frac{x}{y}\right)$, then the differential equation is homogeneous.

e.g. $\frac{dy}{dx} = \frac{x + 2y}{x - y}$ is a homogeneous differential equation.

Method to Check Whether Given Differential Equation is Homogeneous or Not

Suppose, a differential equation is given to us, then to check whether it is homogeneous or not, we use the following steps

I. First, write the given differential equation as
$$\frac{dy}{dx} = F(x, y) \text{ or } \frac{dx}{dy} = F(x, y)$$

II. Replace y by λy and x by λx in $F(x, y)$.

III. If it is possible to write $F(\lambda x, \lambda y) = \lambda^0\, F(x, y)$, then the given differential equation is homogeneous, otherwise the given differential equation is not homogeneous.

Note Generally, we use this method, only when we have to show that the differential equation is homogeneous.

Example 6 Show that the differential equation $x\cos\left(\frac{y}{x}\right)\frac{dy}{dx} = y\cos\left(\frac{y}{x}\right) + x$ is homogeneous.

Sol. Given differential equation is,

$$x\cos\left(\frac{y}{x}\right)\frac{dy}{dx} = y\cos\left(\frac{y}{x}\right) + x$$

$$\Rightarrow \frac{dy}{dx} = \frac{y\cos(y/x) + x}{x\cos(y/x)}$$

Let $$F(x, y) = \frac{y\cos(y/x) + x}{x\cos(y/x)} \quad \text{...(i)}$$

On replacing y by λy and x by λx in Eq. (i), we get

$$F(\lambda x, \lambda y) = \frac{\lambda y \cos\left(\frac{\lambda y}{\lambda x}\right) + \lambda x}{\lambda x \cos\left(\frac{\lambda y}{\lambda x}\right)}$$
$$= \frac{\lambda[y \cos(y/x) + x]}{\lambda x \cos(y/x)}$$
$$= \lambda^0 F(x, y) \quad \text{[from Eq. (i)]}$$

Since, power of λ is 0 (zero), so $F(x, y)$ is a homogeneous function of degree 0. Hence, given differential equation is a homogeneous differential equation.

Note In short, to check whether the given differential equation is homogeneous or not, we check degree of each term of numerator and denominator of $F(x, y)$. If degree is same, then differential equation is homogeneous, otherwise not.

Solution of Homogeneous Differential Equation

Suppose given differential equation is of the form $f(x, y)dy = g(x, y)dx$, then to find its solution, we use the following steps

I. Write the given differential equation in the form

$$\frac{dy}{dx} = F(x, y), \text{ where } F(x, y) = \frac{g(x, y)}{f(x, y)} \quad \ldots\text{(i)}$$

or

$$\frac{dx}{dy} = F(x, y), \text{ where } F(x, y) = \frac{f(x, y)}{g(x, y)} \quad \ldots\text{(i)}$$

and check whether it is homogeneous or not. If Eq. (i) is homogeneous differential equation, then go to next step.

II. *Case* I If $F(x, y) = h\left(\frac{y}{x}\right)$, then put $y = vx$ and $\frac{dy}{dx} = v + x\frac{dv}{dx}$ in Eq. (i).

Case II If $F(x, y) = h\left(\frac{x}{y}\right)$, then put $x = vy$ and $\frac{dx}{dy} = v + y\frac{dv}{dy}$ in Eq. (i).

III. Write the equation obtained in step II in variable separable form and then integrate.

IV. If case I occurred, then replace v by $\frac{y}{x}$ otherwise for case II, replace v by $\frac{x}{y}$ in the equation obtained in step III, to get the required solution.

Example 7 Solve the following differential equation for a particular solution $y - x\frac{dy}{dx} = x + y\frac{dy}{dx}$, when $y = 0$ and $x = 1$. **[ISC 2011]**

Sol. Given, $y - x\frac{dy}{dx} = x + y\frac{dy}{dx}$

$$\Rightarrow \quad y - x = (y + x)\frac{dy}{dx} \Rightarrow \frac{dy}{dx} = \frac{y - x}{y + x}$$

It is a homogeneous differential equation because degree of numerator and denominator is same.

Put $y = vx$, then $\frac{dy}{dx} = v + x\frac{dv}{dx}$

Now, $v + x\frac{dv}{dx} = \frac{vx - x}{vx + x} \Rightarrow v + x\frac{dv}{dx} = \frac{x(v-1)}{x(v+1)}$

$$\Rightarrow \quad v + x\frac{dv}{dx} = \frac{v-1}{v+1} \Rightarrow x\frac{dv}{dx} = \frac{v-1}{v+1} - v$$

$$\Rightarrow \quad x\frac{dv}{dx} = \frac{v - 1 - v(v+1)}{v+1}$$

$$\Rightarrow \quad x\frac{dv}{dx} = \frac{v - 1 - v^2 - v}{v+1} \Rightarrow x\frac{dv}{dx} = \frac{-(1+v^2)}{v+1}$$

$$\Rightarrow \quad \frac{-(v+1)dv}{1+v^2} = \frac{dx}{x}$$

On integrating both sides, we get

$$\frac{1}{2}\int \frac{2v}{1+v^2}dv + \int \frac{dv}{1+v^2} = \int -\frac{dx}{x}$$

$$\Rightarrow \quad \frac{1}{2}\log|1+v^2| + \tan^{-1} v = -\log|x| + C$$

$$\Rightarrow \quad \frac{1}{2}\log\left|1 + \frac{y^2}{x^2}\right| + \tan^{-1}\left(\frac{y}{x}\right) = -\log|x| + C \quad \ldots\text{(i)}$$

$$\left[\text{put } v = \frac{y}{x}\right]$$

Also given, $y = 0$ when $x = 1$ [given]

$$\therefore \quad \frac{1}{2}\log|1| + \tan^{-1}(0) = -\log|1| + C$$

$$\Rightarrow \quad 0 + 0 = 0 + C \quad [\because \log 1 = 0]$$

$$\Rightarrow \quad C = 0$$

On putting $C = 0$ in Eq. (i), we get

$$\frac{1}{2}\log\left|1 + \frac{y^2}{x^2}\right| + \tan^{-1}\left(\frac{y}{x}\right) + \log|x| = 0$$

$$\Rightarrow \quad \log\left(\frac{\sqrt{x^2+y^2}}{x}\right) + \tan^{-1}\left(\frac{y}{x}\right) + \log|x| = 0$$

$$\Rightarrow \log\sqrt{x^2+y^2} - \log|x| + \tan^{-1}\left(\frac{y}{x}\right) + \log|x| = 0$$

$$\Rightarrow \quad \log\sqrt{x^2+y^2} + \tan^{-1}\left(\frac{y}{x}\right) = 0$$

Example 8 Solve the differential equation

$$(x^2 - y^2)dx + 2xydy = 0 \quad \text{[ISC 2023]}$$

Sol. Given, $(x^2 - y^2)\,dx + 2xy\,dy = 0$

$$\Rightarrow \quad 2xy\,dy = (y^2 - x^2)\,dx$$

$$\Rightarrow \quad \frac{dy}{dx} = \frac{y^2 - x^2}{2xy}$$

which is a homogeneous differential equation.

Put $y = vx \Rightarrow \frac{dy}{dx} = v + x\frac{dv}{dx}$

$$\therefore \quad v + \frac{xdv}{dx} = \frac{v^2x^2 - x^2}{2x(vx)} = \frac{x^2(v^2 - 1)}{2x^2v} = \frac{v^2 - 1}{2v}$$

$$\Rightarrow \quad x\frac{dv}{dx} = \frac{v^2 - 1}{2v} - v$$

$$\Rightarrow \quad x\frac{dv}{dx} = \frac{v^2 - 1 - 2v^2}{2v} = \frac{-(1 + v^2)}{2v}$$

$$\Rightarrow \quad \frac{2v}{v^2 + 1}\,dv = -\frac{dx}{x}$$

On integrating both sides,

$$\int \frac{2v}{v^2 + 1}\,dv = -\int \frac{dx}{x}$$

$$\Rightarrow \quad \log|v^2 + 1| = -\log x + \log C$$

$$\Rightarrow \log|v^2 + 1| + \log x = \log C$$

$$\Rightarrow \quad \log[(v^2 + 1)\,x] = \log C \Rightarrow (v^2 + 1)\,x = C$$

$$\Rightarrow \quad \left(\frac{y^2}{x^2} + 1\right)x = C \qquad \left[\because v = \frac{y}{x}\right]$$

$$\Rightarrow \quad (y^2 + x^2) = Cx \Rightarrow x^2 + y^2 - Cx = 0,$$

where C is an arbitrary constant.

Example 9 Find the general solution of

$$y^2dx + (x^2 - xy + y^2)\,dy = 0. \quad \text{[NCERT Exemplar]}$$

Sol. Given differential equation is

$$y^2dx + (x^2 - xy + y^2)dy = 0$$

$$\Rightarrow \quad y^2dx = -(x^2 - xy + y^2)dy$$

$$\Rightarrow \quad y^2\frac{dx}{dy} = -(x^2 - xy + y^2)$$

$$\Rightarrow \quad \frac{dx}{dy} = -\left(\frac{x^2}{y^2} - \frac{x}{y} + 1\right) \qquad \text{...(i)}$$

which is a homogeneous differential equation as

$$\frac{dx}{dy} = F\left(\frac{x}{y}\right)$$

$\therefore$ Put $\frac{x}{y} = v$ or $x = vy$

$$\Rightarrow \quad \frac{dx}{dy} = v + y\frac{dv}{dy}$$

On substituting these values in Eq. (i), we get

$$v + y\frac{dv}{dy} = -(v^2 - v + 1)$$

$$\Rightarrow \quad y\frac{dv}{dy} = -v^2 + v - 1 - v$$

$$\Rightarrow \quad y\frac{dv}{dy} = -v^2 - 1$$

$$\Rightarrow \quad \frac{dv}{v^2 + 1} = -\frac{dy}{y}$$

On integrating both sides, we get

$$\int \frac{dv}{v^2 + 1} = \int -\frac{dy}{y}$$

$$\Rightarrow \quad \tan^{-1}(v) = -\log|y| + C$$

$$\Rightarrow \tan^{-1}\left(\frac{x}{y}\right) + \log|y| = C \qquad \left[\text{put } v = \frac{x}{y}\right]$$

which is the required general solution.

Topic Practice 2

Very Short Answer Type Questions

(2 Marks)

Directions (Q. Nos. 1-14) *Solve the following differential equations.*

1 $\frac{dy}{dx} = \sqrt{4 - y^2}\ (-2 < y < 2)$ **[NCERT]**

2 $\frac{dy}{dx} + \sqrt{\frac{1 - y^2}{1 - x^2}} = 0$ **[NCERT]**

3 $(x + 1)\,dy - 2xydx = 0$ **[ISC 2014]**

4 $\frac{dy}{dx} = \sin^{-1}x$ **[NCERT]**

5 $xy\frac{dy}{dx} = (x + 2)(y + 2)$

6 $\frac{dy}{dx} = 1 - xy + y - x$ **[ISC 2017]**

7 $\text{cosec}^3 x\,dy - \text{cosec}\,y\,dx = 0$ **[ISC 2010]**

8 $\tan y\,dx + \sec^2 y \tan x\,dy = 0$ **[ISC 2017]**

9 $\cos x\,(1 + \cos y)\,dx - \sin y\,(1 + \sin x)\,dy = 0$

10 $x\sqrt{1 - y^2}\,dx + y\sqrt{1 - x^2}\,dy = 0$

11 $y \log y\, dx - x\, dy = 0$ [NCERT]

12 $(1 + y^2) \tan^{-1} x\, dx + 2y(1 + x^2)\, dy = 0$ [NCERT Exemplar]

13 $(x \cos y) dx = e^x (x \log x + 1) dx$ [ISC 2009]

14 $\log\left(\frac{dy}{dx}\right) = 2x - 3y$ [ISC 2013]

15 Solve $\frac{dy}{dx} = y \tan x$, when $x = 0$ and $y = 1$. [NCERT]

16 Given that $\frac{dy}{dx} = e^{-2y}$ and $y = 0$, when $x = 5$. Find the value of x, when $y = 3$. [NCERT Exemplar]

Short Answer Type Questions

4 Marks

17 Solve $(x - 1)\frac{dy}{dx} = 2x^3 y$.

18 Solve the following differential equation.

$$e^x \tan y\, dx + (1 - e^x) \sec^2 y\, dy = 0$$

19 Solve the differential equation

$$(xy^2 + x)dx + (x^2 y + y)dy = 0$$ [ISC 2012]

20 Solve the differential equation

$$x(x^2 - x^2y^2)dy + y(y^2 + x^2y^2)dx = 0$$ [ISC 2006]

21 Solve the differential equation

$$\frac{dy}{dx} - e^{y+x} = e^{x-y}$$ [ISC 2005]

22 Find the particular solution of the differential equation $\frac{dy}{dx} = 1 + x + y + xy$, given that $y = 0$, when $x = 1$.

23 If $y(x)$ is a solution of $\left(\frac{2 + \sin x}{1 + y}\right)\frac{dy}{dx} = -\cos x$ and $y(0) = 1$, then find the value of $y\left(\frac{\pi}{2}\right)$. [NCERT Exemplar]

24 Solve the differential equation.

$$\sin^{-1}\left(\frac{dy}{dx}\right) = x + y$$ [ISC 2015]

25 Solve the differential equation.

$$x\frac{dy}{dx} - y = \sqrt{x^2 + y^2}$$ [ISC 2007, 2002]

26 Find the particular solution of the differential equation $\frac{dy}{dx} - \frac{y}{x} + \operatorname{cosec}\left(\frac{y}{x}\right) = 0$, $y = 0$ when $x = 1$.

27 Find the general solution of the following differential equation.

$$x \cos\left(\frac{y}{x}\right)\frac{dy}{dx} = y \cos\left(\frac{y}{x}\right) + x, x \neq 0$$

28 Solve the differential equation

$$x^2\frac{dy}{dx} = x^2 - 2y^2 + xy.$$

29 Find the solution of the differential equation $(x\, dy - y\, dx)\, y \sin\left(\frac{y}{x}\right) = (y\, dx + x\, dy)\, x \cos\left(\frac{y}{x}\right)$. [NCERT]

30 Solve the differential equation

$$e^{x/y}\left(1 - \frac{x}{y}\right) + (1 + e^{x/y})\frac{dx}{dy} = 0, \text{ when } x = 0, y = 1.$$ [ISC 2015]

Long Answer Type Questions

6 Marks

31 Solve the following differential equation.

$$x(x^2 - 1)\frac{dy}{dx} = 1, y = 0, \text{ when } x = 2$$ [NCERT]

32 Show that the differential equation $(x - y)\frac{dy}{dx} = x + 2y$ is a homogeneous and solve it. [NCERT]

33 Solve the differential equation $\left[x \sin^2\left(\frac{y}{x}\right) - y\right] dx + x\, dy = 0$, given $y = \frac{\pi}{4}$, when $x = 1$.

34 Solve the differential equation $x^2 dy + (xy + y^2)\, dx = 0$, when $x = 1$ and $y = 1$. [ISC 2016]

35 Show that the differential equation $\frac{dy}{dx} = \frac{y^2}{xy - x^2}$ is homogeneous and also solve it.

36 Find the general solution of differential equation $(x^3 - 3xy^2)\, dx = (y^3 - 3x^2 y)\, dy$.

37 Solve the following differential equation.

$$(3xy + y^2)dx + (x^2 + xy)\, dy = 0$$ [ISC 2014]

Hints & Solutions

1. Given differential equation is $\frac{dy}{dx}=\sqrt{4-y^2}$

On separating the variables, we get $\frac{dy}{\sqrt{4-y^2}}=dx$ [1]

On integrating both sides, we get

$$\int \frac{dy}{\sqrt{4-y^2}}=\int dx \Rightarrow \sin^{-1}\left(\frac{y}{2}\right)=x+C$$

$$\Rightarrow \frac{y}{2}=\sin(x+C) \quad \left[\because \int \frac{dy}{\sqrt{a^2-y^2}}=\sin^{-1}\left(\frac{y}{a}\right)\right]$$

$$\Rightarrow y=2\sin(x+C),$$

which is the required solution. [1]

2. Given differential equation is

$$\frac{dy}{dx}+\sqrt{\frac{1-y^2}{1-x^2}}=0 \Rightarrow \frac{dy}{dx}=-\frac{\sqrt{1-y^2}}{\sqrt{1-x^2}}$$

On separating the variables, we get

$$\frac{1}{\sqrt{1-y^2}}dy=-\frac{1}{\sqrt{1-x^2}}dx$$ [1]

On integrating both sides, we get

$$\int \frac{1}{\sqrt{1-y^2}}dy=-\int \frac{1}{\sqrt{1-x^2}}dx$$

$$\Rightarrow \sin^{-1}y=-\sin^{-1}x+C$$

$$\Rightarrow \sin^{-1}x+\sin^{-1}y=C,$$

which is the required general solution. [1]

3. Given differential equation can be written as

$$(x+1)\frac{dy}{dx}=2xy$$

On separating the variables, we get

$$\frac{dy}{y}=\frac{2x}{x+1}dx$$

On integrating both sides, we get

$$\int \frac{dy}{y}=2\int \frac{x}{x+1}dx$$

$$\Rightarrow \int \frac{dy}{y}=2\int \frac{(x+1)-1}{(x+1)}dx$$ [1]

$$\Rightarrow \int \frac{dy}{y}=2\left[\int dx-\int \frac{1}{(x+1)}dx\right]$$

$$\Rightarrow \log|y|=2\int dx-2\int \frac{1}{x+1}dx$$

$$\Rightarrow \log|y|=2x-2\log|x+1|+C$$

$$\Rightarrow \log|y|=2(x-\log|x+1|)+C,$$

which is the required solution. [1]

4. **Hint** Evaluate $\int \sin^{-1}x\,dx$ by using integration by parts.

[**Ans.** $y=x(\sin^{-1}x)+\sqrt{1-x^2}+C$]

5. Given differential equation is

$$xy\frac{dy}{dx}=(x+2)(y+2) \quad ...(i)$$

On separating the variables, we get

$$\frac{y}{y+2}dy=\frac{x+2}{x}dx$$ [1/2]

On integrating both sides, we get

$$\int \frac{y}{y+2}dy=\int \frac{x+2}{2}dx$$

$$\Rightarrow \int\left(\frac{y+2-2}{y+2}\right)dy=\int \frac{x+2}{x}dx$$

$$\Rightarrow \int \frac{y+2}{y+2}dy-\int \frac{2}{y+2}dy=\int \frac{x}{x}dx+\int \frac{2}{x}dx$$ [1]

$$\Rightarrow \int dy-2\int \frac{1}{y+2}dy=\int dx+2\int \frac{1}{x}dx$$

$$\Rightarrow y-2\log|y+2|=x+2\log|x|+C$$ [1/2]

6. **Hint** Write the given equation as $\frac{dy}{dx}=(1-x)(1+y)$ and solve it. $\left[\textbf{Ans. } \log|1+y|=x-\frac{x^2}{2}+C\right]$

7. Given, $\operatorname{cosec}^3 x\,dy-\operatorname{cosec} y\,dx=0$

$$\Rightarrow \frac{dy}{\operatorname{cosec} y}-\frac{dx}{\operatorname{cosec}^3 x}=0$$

$$\Rightarrow \sin y\,dy-\sin^3 x\,dx=0$$

$$\Rightarrow \sin y\,dy=\sin^3 x\,dx$$ [1]

On integrating both sides, we get

$$\int \sin y\,dy=\int\left(\frac{3\sin x-\sin 3x}{4}\right)dx$$

$$[\because \sin 3x=3\sin x-4\sin^3 x]$$

$$\Rightarrow -\cos y=\frac{-3}{4}\cos x+\frac{\cos 3x}{12}+C$$

$$\Rightarrow \frac{3}{4}\cos x-\cos y-\frac{\cos 3x}{12}=C$$ [1]

8. Given, $\tan y\,dx+\sec^2 y\tan x\,dy=0$

$$\tan y\,dx=-\sec^2 y\tan x\,dy$$

$$\Rightarrow \frac{1}{\tan x}dx=\frac{-\sec^2 y}{\tan y}dy$$

[dividing both sides by $\tan x\tan y$] [1]

On integrating both sides, we get

$$\Rightarrow -\int \cot x\,dx=\int \frac{\sec^2 y}{\tan y}dy$$

$$\Rightarrow -\log|\sin x|=\log|\tan y|+\log|C_1|$$

$$\Rightarrow \log|\sin x|+\log|\tan y|+\log C_1=0$$

$$\Rightarrow \log|\sin x\cdot\tan y\cdot C_1|=0 \quad [\because \log_a b=c\Rightarrow b=a^c]$$

$\Rightarrow \quad \sin x \cdot \tan y \cdot C_1 = 1 \Rightarrow \sin x \cdot \tan y = \dfrac{1}{C_1}$

$\Rightarrow \quad \sin x \cdot \tan y = C$, where $\dfrac{1}{C_1} = C$ [1]

9. Hint

(i) Write the given equation as $\dfrac{\cos x}{1+\sin x}dx = \dfrac{\sin y}{1+\cos y}dy$

(ii) Put $1+\sin x = u$ in LHS and $1+\cos y = v$ in RHS to solve it.

[**Ans.** $(1+\sin x)(1+\cos y) = C$]

10. Hint Write the given equation as $\dfrac{x}{\sqrt{1-x^2}}dx = \dfrac{-y}{\sqrt{1-y^2}}dy$ and solve it. [**Ans.** $\sqrt{1-x^2} + \sqrt{1-y^2} = C$]

11. Hint Write the given equation as $\dfrac{dy}{y\log y} = \dfrac{1}{x}dx$ and solve it. [**Ans.** $y = e^{cx}$]

12. Hint Write the given equation as $\dfrac{\tan^{-1}x}{1+x^2}dx = \dfrac{-2y}{1+y^2}dy$ and solve it. $\left[\textbf{Ans. } \dfrac{1}{2}(\tan^{-1}x)^2 + \log|1+y^2| = C\right]$

13. Given, $(x\cos y)dy = e^x(x\log x + 1)dx$

$\Rightarrow \quad \cos y\, dy = e^x\left(\dfrac{x\log x + 1}{x}\right)dx$

$\Rightarrow \quad \cos y\, dy = e^x\left(\log x + \dfrac{1}{x}\right)dx$ [1]

On integrating both sides, we get

$$\int \cos y\, dy = \int e^x\left(\log x + \frac{1}{x}\right)dx$$

$\Rightarrow \quad \sin y = e^x \log x + C$

$[\because \int e^x[f(x)+f'(x)]dx = e^x f(x) + C]$ [1]

14. Given differential equation is $\log\left(\dfrac{dy}{dx}\right) = 2x - 3y$

$\Rightarrow \quad \dfrac{dy}{dx} = e^{2x-3y} \Rightarrow \dfrac{dy}{dx} = e^{2x}e^{-3y}$

On separating the variables, we get [1]

$$\frac{1}{e^{-3y}}dy = e^{2x}dx$$ [1/2]

On integrating both sides, we get

$$\int e^{3y}dy = \int e^{2x}dx \Rightarrow \frac{e^{3y}}{3} = \frac{e^{2x}}{2} + C$$

which is the required general solution of given differential equation. [1/2]

15. Given differential equation is $\dfrac{dy}{dx} = y\tan x$.

On separating the variables, we get

$$\frac{1}{y}dy = \tan x\, dx$$

On integrating both sides, we get

$$\int \frac{1}{y}dy = \int \tan x\, dx$$

$\Rightarrow \quad \log|y| = \log|\sec x| + \log|C|$

$\Rightarrow \quad \log|y| = \log|(C\sec x)|$

$[\because \log m + \log n = \log mn]$

$\Rightarrow \quad y = C\sec x$ ...(i) [1]

$[\because \log m = \log n \Rightarrow m = n]$

Also, given $x = 0$ and $y = 1$

$\therefore \quad 1 = C\sec 0$

$\Rightarrow \quad 1 = C \times 1 \Rightarrow C = 1$

On putting $C = 1$ in Eq. (i), we get

$$y = \sec x$$

which is the required solution. [1]

16. Hint (i) $\int e^{2y}dy = \int 1dx$

(ii) Put $y = 3$, to get the required value of x. $\left[\textbf{Ans. } \dfrac{e^6+9}{2}\right]$

17. Given differential equation is $(x-1)\dfrac{dy}{dx} = 2x^3y$.

On separating the variables, we get

$$\frac{dy}{y} = \frac{2x^3}{(x-1)}dx$$ [1]

$\Rightarrow \quad \dfrac{dy}{y} = 2\left(\dfrac{x^3}{x-1}\right)dx \Rightarrow \dfrac{dy}{y} = 2\left[\dfrac{(x^3-1)+1}{x-1}\right]dx$

$$= 2\left[\frac{(x-1)(x^2+x+1)}{(x-1)} + \frac{1}{(x-1)}\right]dx$$

$[\because a^3 - b^3 = (a-b)(a^2+ab+b^2)]$

$\Rightarrow \quad \dfrac{dy}{y} = 2\left(x^2+x+1+\dfrac{1}{x-1}\right)dx$ [1]

On integrating both sides, we get

$$\int\frac{dy}{y} = 2\int\left(x^2+x+1+\frac{1}{x-1}\right)dx$$ [1]

$\Rightarrow \quad \log|y| = 2\left(\dfrac{x^3}{3} + \dfrac{x^2}{2} + x + \log|x-1|\right) + C,$

which is the required solution. [1]

18. Hint Differential equation reduces to

$\int \dfrac{e^x}{(e^x-1)}dx = \int \dfrac{\sec^2 y}{\tan y}dy$ and for simplifying this put $e^x - 1 = t$ and $\tan y = z$. $\left[\textbf{Ans. } y = \tan^{-1}\left(\dfrac{e^x-1}{C}\right)\right]$

19. Given, $(xy^2 + x)dx + (x^2y + y)dy = 0$

$\Rightarrow \quad x(y^2+1)dx + y(x^2+1)dy = 0$

$\Rightarrow \quad \dfrac{x}{x^2+1}dx + \dfrac{y}{y^2+1}dy = 0$ [1]

On integrating both sides, we get

$$\frac{1}{2}\int \frac{2x}{x^2+1}dx + \frac{1}{2}\int \frac{2y}{y^2+1}dy = 0$$

[multiplying numerator and denominator by 2]

$$\Rightarrow \quad \frac{1}{2}\log|x^2+1| + \frac{1}{2}\log|y^2+1| = C \quad [1]$$

$$\left[\because \int \frac{2x}{x^2+1}dx = \int \frac{d(x^2+1)}{x^2+1} = \log|x^2+1|\right]$$

$$\log\sqrt{x^2+1} + \log\sqrt{y^2+1} = C$$

$$\Rightarrow \quad \log(\sqrt{x^2+1}\sqrt{y^2+1}) = C$$

$$\Rightarrow \quad \sqrt{x^2+1}\sqrt{y^2+1} = e^C \quad [1]$$

$$[\because \log_a b = c \Rightarrow b = a^c]$$

On squaring both sides, we get

$$(x^2+1)(y^2+1) = e^{2C} \Rightarrow (x^2+1)(y^2+1) = C'$$

where, $e^{2C} = C' = \text{Constant}$ [1]

20. Given, $x(x^2 - x^2y^2)dy + y(y^2 + x^2y^2)dx = 0$

$$\Rightarrow \quad x^3(1-y^2)dy + y^3(1+x^2)dx = 0$$

$$\Rightarrow \quad \frac{(1-y^2)}{y^3}dy + \frac{(1+x^2)}{x^3}dx = 0 \quad [1]$$

$$\Rightarrow \quad \left(\frac{1}{y^3} - \frac{1}{y}\right)dy + \left(\frac{1}{x^3} + \frac{1}{x}\right)dx = 0 \quad [1]$$

On integrating both sides, we get

$$\int\left(\frac{1}{y^3} - \frac{1}{y}\right)dy + \int\left(\frac{1}{x^3} + \frac{1}{x}\right)dx = 0$$

$$\Rightarrow \quad \frac{-1}{2y^2} - \log|y| - \frac{1}{2x^2} + \log|x| = C \quad [1]$$

$$\Rightarrow \quad \log|y| - \log|x| + C = -\left(\frac{1}{2x^2} + \frac{1}{2y^2}\right)$$

$$\Rightarrow \quad \log\left|\frac{y}{x}\right| + C = -\left(\frac{1}{2x^2} + \frac{1}{2y^2}\right)$$

$$\left[\because \log m - \log n = \log\frac{m}{n}\right] \quad [1]$$

21. Given, $\frac{dy}{dx} - e^{x+y} = e^{x-y}$

$$\Rightarrow \quad \frac{dy}{dx} - e^x \cdot e^y = e^x \cdot e^{-y}$$

$$\Rightarrow \quad \frac{dy}{dx} = e^x \cdot e^y + e^x \cdot e^{-y}$$

$$\Rightarrow \quad \frac{dy}{dx} = e^x(e^y + e^{-y}) \quad [1]$$

$$\Rightarrow \quad \frac{dy}{e^y + e^{-y}} = e^x dx$$

$$\Rightarrow \quad \frac{e^y dy}{1 + e^{2y}} = e^x dx \quad [1]$$

On integrating both sides, we get

$$\int \frac{e^y}{1+e^{2y}}dy = \int e^x dx$$

$$\Rightarrow \quad \int \frac{dt}{1+t^2} = e^x + C$$

$$[\text{put } e^y = t \Rightarrow e^y dy = dt] \quad [1]$$

$$\Rightarrow \quad \tan^{-1} t = e^x + C$$

$$\Rightarrow \quad \tan^{-1}(e^y) = e^x + C \quad [\text{put } t = e^y]$$

$$\therefore \quad e^y = \tan(e^x + C) \quad [1]$$

22. Given, $\frac{dy}{dx} = 1 + x + y + xy$

$$\Rightarrow \quad \frac{dy}{dx} = 1(1+x) + y(1+x)$$

$$\Rightarrow \quad \frac{dy}{dx} = (1+x)(1+y) \quad \text{...(i) [1/2]}$$

On separating the variables, we get

$$\frac{1}{(1+y)}dy = (1+x)dx \quad \text{...(ii) [1]}$$

On integrating both sides of Eq. (ii), we get

$$\int \frac{1}{1+y}dy = \int(1+x)dx$$

$$\Rightarrow \quad \log|1+y| = x + \frac{x^2}{2} + C \quad \text{...(iii) [1]}$$

On substituting $x = 1$, $y = 0$ in Eq. (iii), we get

$$\log|1+0| = 1 + \frac{1}{2} + C$$

$$\Rightarrow \quad C = -\frac{3}{2} \quad [\because \log 1 = 0] \quad [1]$$

Now, substituting the value of C in Eq. (iii), we get

$$\log|1+y| = x + \frac{x^2}{2} - \frac{3}{2}$$

which is the required particular solution of differential equation. [1/2]

23. Given that, $\left(\frac{2+\sin x}{1+y}\right)\frac{dy}{dx} = -\cos x$

$$\Rightarrow \quad \frac{dy}{1+y} = -\frac{\cos x}{2+\sin x}dx$$

On integrating both sides, we get

$$\int \frac{1}{1+y}dy = -\int \frac{\cos x}{2+\sin x}dx$$

$$\Rightarrow \quad \log|1+y| = -\log|2+\sin x| + \log|C| \quad [1]$$

$$\Rightarrow \log|1+y| + \log|2+\sin x| = \log|C|$$

$$\Rightarrow \quad \log|(1+y)(2+\sin x)| = \log|C|$$

$$\Rightarrow \quad (1+y)(2+\sin x) = C$$

$$\Rightarrow \quad 1 + y = \frac{C}{2+\sin x} \Rightarrow y = \frac{C}{2+\sin x} - 1 \quad \text{...(i) [1]}$$

It is given that, when $x = 0$, then $y = 1$.

$$\therefore \quad 1 = \frac{C}{2} - 1 \Rightarrow C = 4$$

On putting $C = 4$ in Eq. (i), we get [1]

$$y = \frac{4}{2+\sin x} - 1$$

Now, $$y\left(\frac{\pi}{2}\right) = \frac{4}{2+\sin\frac{\pi}{2}} - 1$$

$$= \frac{4}{2+1} - 1 = \frac{4}{3} - 1 = \frac{1}{3}$$ [1]

24. Given differential equation can be rewritten as

$$\left(\frac{dy}{dx}\right) = \sin(x+y) \quad \text{...(i)}$$

Put $x + y = v \Rightarrow 1 + \frac{dy}{dx} = \frac{dv}{dx}$

$$\Rightarrow \quad \frac{dy}{dx} = \frac{dv}{dx} - 1$$

$\therefore$ Eq. (i) becomes

$$\frac{dv}{dx} - 1 = \sin v \Rightarrow \frac{dv}{dx} = 1 + \sin v$$ [1]

$$\Rightarrow \quad \frac{dv}{1+\sin v} = dx$$ [1/2]

On integrating both sides, we get

$$\int \frac{1}{1+\sin v} \times \frac{1-\sin v}{1-\sin v} dv = \int dx$$

$$\Rightarrow \quad \int \frac{1-\sin v}{1-\sin^2 v} dv = \int dx$$ [1]

$$\Rightarrow \quad \int \frac{1-\sin v}{\cos^2 v} dv = \int dx$$

$$\Rightarrow \quad \int (\sec^2 v - \tan v \sec v) dv = dx$$ [1/2]

$$\Rightarrow \quad [\tan v - \sec v] = x + C$$

$\Rightarrow \quad \tan(x+y) - \sec(x+y) = x + C$ [put $v = x + y$] [1]

25. Given, $$x\frac{dy}{dx} - y = \sqrt{x^2 + y^2}$$

$$\Rightarrow \quad x\frac{dy}{dx} = y + \sqrt{x^2 + y^2}$$

$$\Rightarrow \quad \frac{dy}{dx} = \frac{y}{x} + \sqrt{1 + \frac{y^2}{x^2}}$$ [1]

Put $\quad y = vx$

Then, $$\frac{dy}{dx} = v + x\frac{dv}{dx}$$

$$\therefore \quad v + x\frac{dv}{dx} = v + \sqrt{1+v^2}$$

$$\Rightarrow \quad x\frac{dv}{dx} = \sqrt{1+v^2}$$

$$\Rightarrow \quad \frac{dv}{\sqrt{1+v^2}} = \frac{dx}{x}$$ [1]

On integrating both sides, we get

$$\int \frac{dv}{\sqrt{1+v^2}} = \int \frac{dx}{x}$$

$$\Rightarrow \quad \log|v + \sqrt{1+v^2}| = \log|x| + \log|C|$$ [1]

$$\Rightarrow \quad \log\left|\frac{y}{x} + \sqrt{1 + \frac{y^2}{x^2}}\right| = \log|Cx| \quad \left[\text{put } v = \frac{y}{x}\right]$$

$$\Rightarrow \quad \log\left|\frac{y + \sqrt{x^2+y^2}}{x}\right| = \log|Cx|$$

$$\Rightarrow \quad \frac{y+\sqrt{x^2+y^2}}{x} = Cx$$

$$\Rightarrow \quad y + \sqrt{x^2+y^2} = Cx^2$$ [1]

26. Given differential equation is

$$\frac{dy}{dx} - \frac{y}{x} + \operatorname{cosec}\left(\frac{y}{x}\right) = 0 \Rightarrow \frac{dy}{dx} = \frac{y}{x} - \operatorname{cosec}\left(\frac{y}{x}\right) \quad \text{...(i)}$$ [1/2]

which is a homogeneous differential equation as $\frac{dy}{dx} = f\left(\frac{y}{x}\right)$. [1/2]

On putting $y = vx$ and $\frac{dy}{dx} = v + x\frac{dv}{dx}$ in Eq. (i), we get

$$v + x\frac{dv}{dx} = v - \operatorname{cosec} v$$

$$\Rightarrow \quad x\frac{dv}{dx} = -\operatorname{cosec} v$$

$$\Rightarrow \quad \sin v \, dv = -\frac{dx}{x}$$ [1]

On integrating both sides, we get

$$\int \sin v \, dv = -\int \frac{dx}{x} \Rightarrow -\cos v = -\log|x| + C$$

$$\Rightarrow \quad \cos v = \log|x| - C$$

$$\Rightarrow \quad \cos\left(\frac{y}{x}\right) = \log|x| - C \quad \left[\text{put } v = \frac{y}{x}\right] \quad \text{...(ii)}$$ [1]

Also, given $y = 0$, when $x = 1$.

Then, $\cos 0 = \log 1 - C \Rightarrow 1 = 0 - C \Rightarrow C = -1$

So, Eq. (ii) becomes $\cos\left(\frac{y}{x}\right) = \log|x| + 1$

which is the required equation. [1]

27. Hint

(i) Write the given equation as $\frac{dy}{dx} = \frac{\left(\frac{y}{x}\right)\cos\left(\frac{y}{x}\right) + 1}{\cos\left(\frac{y}{x}\right)}$.

(ii) Substitute $y = vx$ to solve it. $\left[\textbf{Ans. } \sin\left(\frac{y}{x}\right) = \log|Cx|\right]$

28. Hint

(i) Write the given equation as $\frac{dy}{dx} = 1 - 2\left(\frac{y}{x}\right)^2 + \left(\frac{y}{x}\right)$.

(ii) Substitute $y = vx$ and $\frac{dy}{dx} = v + x\frac{dv}{dx}$ to solve it.

$$\left[\textbf{Ans. } \frac{x+\sqrt{2}y}{x-\sqrt{2}y} = (Cx)^{2\sqrt{2}}\right]$$

29. Given differential equation can be rewritten as

$$xy \sin\left(\frac{y}{x}\right) dy - y^2 \sin\left(\frac{y}{x}\right) dx = xy \cos\left(\frac{y}{x}\right) dx + x^2 \cos\left(\frac{y}{x}\right) dy$$

$$\Rightarrow \left[xy \sin\left(\frac{y}{x}\right) - x^2 \cos\left(\frac{y}{x}\right)\right] dy = \left[xy \cos\left(\frac{y}{x}\right) + y^2 \sin\left(\frac{y}{x}\right)\right] dx$$

$$\Rightarrow \frac{dy}{dx} = \frac{xy \cos\left(\frac{y}{x}\right) + y^2 \sin\left(\frac{y}{x}\right)}{xy \sin\left(\frac{y}{x}\right) - x^2 \cos\left(\frac{y}{x}\right)}$$

$$\Rightarrow \frac{dy}{dx} = \frac{\frac{y}{x} \cos\left(\frac{y}{x}\right) + \left(\frac{y}{x}\right)^2 \sin\left(\frac{y}{x}\right)}{\frac{y}{x} \sin\left(\frac{y}{x}\right) - \cos\left(\frac{y}{x}\right)} \quad \text{...(i) [1]}$$

[dividing numerator and denominator by x^2]

Clearly, the given differential equation is homogeneous as $\frac{dy}{dx} = f\left(\frac{y}{x}\right)$.

Now, put $y = vx \Rightarrow \frac{dy}{dx} = v + x\frac{dv}{dx}$ ...(ii) [1/2]

From Eqs. (i) and (ii), we get

$$v + x\frac{dv}{dx} = \frac{v \cos v + v^2 \sin v}{v \sin v - \cos v} \quad \left[\because v = \frac{y}{x}\right]$$

$$\Rightarrow x\frac{dv}{dx} = \frac{v \cos v + v^2 \sin v - v^2 \sin v + v \cos v}{v \sin v - \cos v}$$

$$\Rightarrow x\frac{dv}{dx} = \frac{2v \cos v}{v \sin v - \cos v} \quad \text{[1/2]}$$

On separating the variables, we get

$$\frac{v \sin v - \cos v}{v \cos v} dv = 2\frac{dx}{x}$$

On integrating both sides, we get

$$\int \left(\tan v - \frac{1}{v}\right) dv = 2\int \frac{dx}{x}$$

$$\Rightarrow \log|\sec v| - \log|v| = 2\log|x| + \log|C_1| \quad \text{[1]}$$

$$\Rightarrow \log\left|\frac{\sec v}{v}\right| - \log|x|^2 = \log|C_1|$$

$$\Rightarrow \log\left|\frac{\sec v}{vx^2}\right| = \log|C_1|$$

$$\Rightarrow \frac{\sec v}{vx^2} = C_1 \Rightarrow \frac{\sec\left(\frac{y}{x}\right)}{\frac{y}{x}(x^2)} = C_1 \quad \left[\because v = \frac{y}{x}\right]$$

$$\Rightarrow \frac{\sec\left(\frac{y}{x}\right)}{xy} = C_1 \Rightarrow \sec\left(\frac{y}{x}\right) = C_1(xy)$$

which is the required solution. [1]

30. Given differential equation is

$$(1 + e^{\frac{x}{y}})\frac{dx}{dy} + e^{\frac{x}{y}}\left(1 - \frac{x}{y}\right) = 0$$

$$\Rightarrow \frac{dx}{dy} = \frac{-e^{\frac{x}{y}}\left(1 - \frac{x}{y}\right)}{(1 + e^{\frac{x}{y}})} \quad \text{...(i) [1]}$$

Put $\frac{x}{y} = v \Rightarrow x = vy$, then

$$\frac{dx}{dy} = v + y\frac{dv}{dy} \quad \text{...(ii)}$$

From Eqs. (i) and (ii), we get

$$v + y\frac{dv}{dy} = -e^v\frac{(1-v)}{(1+e^v)} \Rightarrow y\frac{dv}{dy} = \frac{-e^v(1-v)}{(1+e^v)} - v$$

$$\Rightarrow y\frac{dv}{dy} = \frac{-e^v(1-v) - v(1+e^v)}{(1+e^v)}$$

$$\Rightarrow y\frac{dv}{dy} = \frac{-e^v + ve^v - v - ve^v}{1+e^v}$$

$$\Rightarrow y\frac{dv}{dy} = -\frac{(v+e^v)}{(1+e^v)} \quad \text{[1]}$$

On separating the variables, we get

$$\frac{(1+e^v)}{(v+e^v)}dv = -\frac{1}{y}dy$$

On integrating both sides, we get

$$\int \frac{(1+e^v)}{(v+e^v)}dv = -\int \frac{dy}{y}$$

$$\Rightarrow \log|v+e^v| = -\log|y| + \log|C|$$

$$\left[\because \text{put } v + e^v = t \Rightarrow (1+e^v)dv = dt \quad \therefore \int \frac{1+e^v}{v+e^v}dv = \int \frac{1}{t}dt = \log|t| = \log|v+e^v|\right]$$

$$\Rightarrow \log\left|\frac{x}{y} + e^{\frac{x}{y}}\right| + \log|y| = \log|C| \quad \left[\text{put } v = \frac{x}{y}\right]$$

$$\Rightarrow \log\left|y\left(\frac{x}{y} + e^{\frac{x}{y}}\right)\right| = \log|C| \quad \text{[1]}$$

$$\Rightarrow x + y.e^{x/y} = C \quad \text{...(iii)}$$

Also, given, $x = 0$, $y = 1$

Then, from Eq. (iii), we get

$$0+1e^0 = C \Rightarrow C = 1$$

$\therefore$ Required equation is $x + ye^{x/y} = 1$. [1]

31. Given differential equation is

$$x(x^2-1)\frac{dy}{dx} = 1 \Rightarrow \frac{dy}{dx} = \frac{1}{x(x^2-1)}$$

$$\Rightarrow \frac{dy}{dx} = \frac{1}{x(x-1)(x+1)} \quad [\because a^2-b^2=(a-b)(a+b)]$$

$$\Rightarrow dy = \frac{dx}{x(x-1)(x+1)}$$

On integrating both sides, we get

$$\int dy = \int \frac{dx}{x(x-1)(x+1)} + C$$

$$\Rightarrow y = I + C \quad \text{...(i) [1]}$$

where, $I = \int \frac{dx}{x(x-1)(x+1)}$

Let $\frac{1}{x(x-1)(x+1)} = \frac{A}{x} + \frac{B}{x-1} + \frac{C}{x+1}$

$$\Rightarrow 1 = A(x-1)(x+1) + Bx(x+1) + Cx(x-1) \quad [1]$$

On comparing coefficients of x^2, x and constant terms from both sides, we get

$$A+B+C=0 \quad \text{...(ii)}$$

$$B-C=0 \quad \text{...(iii)}$$

and $-A = 1 \Rightarrow A = -1$

On putting $A=-1$ in Eq. (ii), we get

$$B+C=1 \quad \text{...(iv)}$$

Now, adding Eqs. (iii) and (iv), we get

$$2B = 1 \Rightarrow B = \frac{1}{2}$$

On putting $B = \frac{1}{2}$ in Eq. (iii), we get

$$\frac{1}{2} - C = 0 \Rightarrow C = \frac{1}{2}$$

$$\therefore \quad A=-1,\ B=\frac{1}{2} \text{ and } C=\frac{1}{2} \quad [1]$$

Thus, $\frac{1}{x(x-1)(x+1)} = \frac{-1}{x} + \frac{1/2}{x-1} + \frac{1/2}{x+1}$

On integrating both sides w.r.t. x, we get

$$I = \int \frac{1}{x(x-1)(x+1)}dx = \int \frac{-1}{x}dx + \frac{1}{2}\int\frac{dx}{x-1} + \frac{1}{2}\int\frac{dx}{x+1}$$

$$\Rightarrow I = -\log|x| + \frac{1}{2}\log|x-1| + \frac{1}{2}\log|x+1|$$

On putting the value of I in Eq. (i), we get

$$y = -\log|x| + \frac{1}{2}\log|x-1| + \frac{1}{2}\log|x+1| + C \quad \text{...(v) [1]}$$

Also, given that $y=0$, when $x=2$

On putting $y=0$ and $x=2$ in Eq. (v), we get

$$0 = -\log 2 + \frac{1}{2}\log 1 + \frac{1}{2}\log 3 + C$$

$$\Rightarrow C = \log 2 - \frac{1}{2}\log 1 - \frac{1}{2}\log 3$$

$$\Rightarrow C = \log 2 - \log\sqrt{3} \quad [\because \log 1 = 0]$$

$$\Rightarrow C = \log\frac{2}{\sqrt{3}} \quad [1]$$

On putting the value of C in Eq. (v), we get

$$y = -\log|x| + \frac{1}{2}\log|x-1| + \frac{1}{2}\log|x+1| + \log\frac{2}{\sqrt{3}}$$

which is the required solution. [1]

32. Given differential equation is

$$(x-y)\frac{dy}{dx} = x+2y \Rightarrow \frac{dy}{dx} = \frac{x+2y}{x-y} \quad \text{...(i)}$$

Let $F(x,y) = \frac{x+2y}{x-y}$, then

$$F(\lambda x, \lambda y) = \frac{\lambda x + 2\lambda y}{\lambda x - \lambda y} = \frac{\lambda(x+2y)}{\lambda(x-y)} = \frac{\lambda^0(x+2y)}{x-y} = \lambda^0 F(x,y)$$

So, $F(x,y)$ is a homogeneous function of degree zero. Therefore, given differential equation is a homogeneous differential equation. [1]

Also, the given differential equation can be written as

$$\frac{dy}{dx} = \frac{1+2(y/x)}{1-(x/y)} = f\left(\frac{y}{x}\right) \quad \text{...(ii)}$$

On putting $y = vx$ and $\frac{dy}{dx} = v + x\frac{dv}{dx}$ in Eq. (i), we get

$$v + x\frac{dv}{dx} = \frac{x+2vx}{x-vx} \Rightarrow v + x\frac{dv}{dx} = \frac{1+2v}{1-v}$$

$$\Rightarrow x\frac{dv}{dx} = \frac{1+2v}{1-v} - v \Rightarrow x\frac{dv}{dx} = \frac{1+2v-v+v^2}{1-v}$$

$$\Rightarrow x\frac{dv}{dx} = \frac{1+v+v^2}{-(v-1)}$$

On separating the variables, we get

$$\frac{(v-1)}{v^2+v+1}dv = -\frac{dx}{x} \quad [1]$$

On integrating both sides, we get

$$\int \frac{v-1}{v^2+v+1}dv = -\int\frac{dx}{x}$$

$$\Rightarrow \frac{1}{2}\int\frac{2(v-1)}{v^2+v+1}dv = -\int\frac{dx}{x}$$

$$\Rightarrow \frac{1}{2}\int\frac{2v-2}{v^2+v+1}dv = -\int\frac{dx}{x}$$

$$\Rightarrow \frac{1}{2}\int\frac{(2v+1)-3}{v^2+v+1}dv = -\int\frac{dx}{x}$$

$$\Rightarrow \frac{1}{2}\int\left(\frac{2v+1}{v^2+v+1}\right)dv - \frac{3}{2}\int\frac{dv}{v^2+v+1} = -\int\frac{dx}{x} \quad [1]$$

$$\therefore \frac{1}{2}\log|v^2+v+1|-\frac{3}{2}\int \frac{dv}{\left(v+\frac{1}{2}\right)^2+1-\frac{1}{4}} = -\log|x|+C_1$$

$$\left[\begin{array}{l}\because \text{put } v^2+v+1=t \Rightarrow (2v+1)\,dv = dt \\ \therefore \int \frac{(2v+1)}{v^2+v+1}\,dv = \int \frac{dt}{t} = \log|t| = \log|v^2+v+1|\end{array}\right]$$

$$\Rightarrow \frac{1}{2}\log|v^2+v+1|-\frac{3}{2}\int \frac{dv}{\left(v+\frac{1}{2}\right)^2+\left(\frac{\sqrt{3}}{2}\right)^2}$$

$$= -\log|x|+C_1 \quad [1]$$

$$\Rightarrow \frac{1}{2}\log|v^2+v+1|-\frac{3}{2}\frac{1}{\left(\frac{\sqrt{3}}{2}\right)}\tan^{-1}\left[\frac{\left(v+\frac{1}{2}\right)}{\frac{\sqrt{3}}{2}}\right]$$

$$= -\log|x|+C_1 \quad \left[\because \int \frac{dx}{x^2+a^2} = \frac{1}{a}\tan^{-1}\left(\frac{x}{a}\right)\right]$$

$$\Rightarrow \frac{1}{2}\log|v^2+v+1|-\frac{3}{2}\cdot\frac{2}{\sqrt{3}}\tan^{-1}\left(\frac{2v+1}{\sqrt{3}}\right)$$

$$= -\log|x|+C_1$$

$$\Rightarrow \frac{1}{2}\log\left|\frac{y^2}{x^2}+\frac{y}{x}+1\right|-\frac{3}{2}\cdot\frac{2}{\sqrt{3}}\tan^{-1}\left(\frac{\frac{2y}{x}+1}{\sqrt{3}}\right)$$

$$= -\log|x|+C_1 \quad \left[\text{put } v = \frac{y}{x}\right]$$

$$\Rightarrow \frac{1}{2}\log\left|\frac{y^2+xy+x^2}{x^2}\right|-\sqrt{3}\tan^{-1}\left(\frac{2y+x}{\sqrt{3}x}\right)$$

$$= -\log|x|+C_1$$

$$\Rightarrow \frac{1}{2}\log|y^2+xy+x^2|-\frac{1}{2}\log|x^2|$$

$$-\sqrt{3}\tan^{-1}\left(\frac{2y+x}{\sqrt{3}x}\right) = -\log|x|+C_1$$

$$\left[\because \log\frac{m}{n} = \log m - \log n\right] \quad [1]$$

$$\Rightarrow \frac{1}{2}\log|y^2+xy+x^2|-\log|x|-\sqrt{3}\tan^{-1}\left(\frac{2y+x}{\sqrt{3}x}\right)$$

$$= -\log|x|+C_1$$

$$\Rightarrow \frac{1}{2}\log|y^2+xy+x^2| = \sqrt{3}\tan^{-1}\left(\frac{2y+x}{\sqrt{3}x}\right)+C_1$$

$$\Rightarrow \log|y^2+xy+x^2| = 2\sqrt{3}\tan^{-1}\left(\frac{2y+x}{\sqrt{3}x}\right)+2C_1$$

$$\Rightarrow \log|y^2+xy+x^2| = 2\sqrt{3}\tan^{-1}\left(\frac{2y+x}{\sqrt{3}x}\right)+C \quad \text{...(iii)}$$

[put $C = 2C_1$]

which is the required general solution. [1]

33. Given differential equation is

$$\left[x\sin^2\left(\frac{y}{x}\right)-y\right]dx + x\,dy = 0$$

$$\Rightarrow \frac{dy}{dx} = \frac{y-x\sin^2\left(\frac{y}{x}\right)}{x} \quad \text{...(i)} \ [1/2]$$

Let $F(x, y) = \dfrac{y-x\sin^2\left(\frac{y}{x}\right)}{x}$

Then, $F(\lambda x, \lambda y) = \dfrac{\lambda y-\lambda x\sin^2\left(\frac{\lambda y}{\lambda x}\right)}{\lambda x}$

$$= \frac{\lambda\left[y-x\sin^2\left(\frac{y}{x}\right)\right]}{\lambda x} = \lambda^0 F(x, y)$$

So, $\dfrac{dy}{dx} = F(x, y)$ is a homogeneous differential equation. [1/2]

Put $y = vx$ and $\dfrac{dy}{dx} = v + x\dfrac{dv}{dx}$ in Eq. (i), we get [1/2]

$$v + x\frac{dv}{dx} = \frac{vx - x\sin^2\left(\frac{vx}{x}\right)}{x}$$

$$\Rightarrow v + x\frac{dv}{dx} = v - \sin^2(v)$$

$$\Rightarrow x\frac{dv}{dx} = -\sin^2(v) \quad [1]$$

$$\Rightarrow \operatorname{cosec}^2 v\,dv = -\frac{dx}{x}$$

On integrating both sides, we get

$$\int \operatorname{cosec}^2 v\,dv + \int \frac{dx}{x} = 0 \quad [1]$$

$$\Rightarrow -\cot v + \log|x| = C$$

$$\Rightarrow -\cot\left(\frac{y}{x}\right) + \log|x| = C \quad \left[\text{put } v = \frac{y}{x}\right] \text{...(ii)} \ [1]$$

Also, given that $y = \dfrac{\pi}{4}$, when $x = 1$.

$$\therefore -\cot\frac{\pi}{4} + \log|1| = C$$

$$\Rightarrow C = -1+0$$

$$\Rightarrow C = -1 \quad [1/2]$$

So, the required particular solution is

$$-\cot\left(\frac{y}{x}\right) + \log|x| = -1$$

$$\Rightarrow 1 + \log|x| - \cot\left(\frac{y}{x}\right) = 0 \quad [1]$$

34. Given differential equation is

$x^2dy + (xy + y^2)\,dx = 0$

$\Rightarrow \quad x^2dy = -(xy + y^2)\,dx$

$\Rightarrow \quad \frac{dy}{dx} = -\left(\frac{yx + y^2}{x^2}\right)$

$\Rightarrow \quad \frac{dy}{dx} = -\left(\frac{y}{x}\right) - \left(\frac{y}{x}\right)^2$ ...(i)

which is a homogeneous, as $\frac{dy}{dx} = f\left(\frac{y}{x}\right)$. [1]

On putting $y = vx$ and $\frac{dy}{dx} = v + x\frac{dv}{dx}$ in Eq. (i), we get

$v + x\frac{dv}{dx} = -v - v^2 \Rightarrow x\frac{dv}{dx} = -2v - v^2$ [1]

$\Rightarrow \quad \frac{1}{2v + v^2}\,dv = -\frac{1}{x}\,dx$

$\Rightarrow \quad \frac{1}{v(2 + v)}\,dv = -\frac{1}{x}\,dx$

$\Rightarrow \quad \frac{2}{2v(2 + v)}\,dv = -\frac{1}{x}\,dx$

$\Rightarrow \quad \frac{1}{2}\left(\frac{1}{v} - \frac{1}{v + 2}\right)dv = -\frac{1}{x}\,dx$ [1]

$\Rightarrow \quad \frac{1}{2}\int\frac{1}{v}\,dv - \frac{1}{2}\int\frac{1}{v + 2}\,dv = -\int\frac{1}{x}\,dx + \log C$

$\Rightarrow \quad \frac{1}{2}\log|v| - \frac{1}{2}\log|v + 2| = -\log|x| + \log C$

$\Rightarrow \quad \frac{1}{2}\log\left|\frac{v}{v + 2}\right| = \log\left|\frac{C}{x}\right|$

$\Rightarrow \quad \log\left|\frac{v}{v + 2}\right| = 2\log\left|\frac{C}{x}\right|$

$\Rightarrow \quad \frac{v}{v + 2} = \left(\frac{C}{x}\right)^2$ [1]

$\Rightarrow \quad \frac{\frac{y}{x}}{\frac{y}{x} + 2} = \left(\frac{C}{x}\right)^2$ $\left[\text{put } v = \frac{y}{x}\right]$

$\Rightarrow \quad \frac{y}{y + 2x} = \left(\frac{C}{x}\right)^2$

It is given that $y = 1$, when $x = 1$.

$\therefore \quad \frac{1}{1 + 2} = \left(\frac{C}{1}\right)^2 \Rightarrow \frac{1}{3} = C^2$ [1]

Hence, the particular solution of given differential equation is

$$\frac{y}{y + 2x} = \frac{1/3}{x^2} \Rightarrow \frac{y}{y + 2x} = \frac{1}{3x^2}$$

$\Rightarrow 3x^2y = y + 2x$, which is the required solution. [1]

35. Hint (i) Show that the given differential equation is homogeneous.

(ii) Write the given equation as $\frac{dy}{dx} = \frac{\left(\frac{y}{x}\right)^2}{\left(\frac{y}{x}\right) - 1}$.

(iii) Substitute $y = vx$ to solve it. $\left[\textbf{Ans. } \frac{y}{x} - \log|y| = C\right]$

36. Given differential equation can be rewritten as

$$\frac{dy}{dx} = \frac{x^3 - 3xy^2}{y^3 - 3x^2y} = \frac{1 - 3\left(\frac{y}{x}\right)^2}{\left(\frac{y}{x}\right)^3 - 3\left(\frac{y}{x}\right)} \quad \text{...(i)}$$

which is a homogeneous differential equation, as

$\frac{dy}{dx} = f\left(\frac{y}{x}\right)$ [1/2]

On putting $y = vx$ and $\frac{dy}{dx} = v + x\frac{dv}{dx}$ in Eq. (i), we get

$\Rightarrow \quad v + x\frac{dv}{dx} = \frac{1 - 3v^2}{v^3 - 3v}$

$\Rightarrow \quad x\frac{dv}{dx} = \frac{1 - 3v^2}{v^3 - 3v} - v$

$\Rightarrow \quad x\frac{dv}{dx} = \frac{1 - 3v^2 - v^4 + 3v^2}{v^3 - 3v}$

$\Rightarrow \quad x\frac{dv}{dx} = \frac{1 - v^4}{v^3 - 3v}$

$\Rightarrow \quad \left(\frac{v^3 - 3v}{1 - v^4}\right)dv = \frac{dx}{x}$ [1]

On integrating both sides, we get

$$\int\left(\frac{v^3 - 3v}{1 - v^4}\right)dv = \int\frac{dx}{x}$$

$\Rightarrow \quad \int\left(\frac{v^3 - 3v}{1 - v^4}\right)dv = \log|x| + \log|C_1|$ ...(ii)

$\Rightarrow \quad \int\frac{v^3}{1 - v^4}\,dv - 3\int\frac{v}{1 - v^4}\,dv = \log|C_1x|$

$\Rightarrow \quad I_1 - 3I_2 = \log|C_1x|$ ...(iii)

where, $I_1 = \int\frac{v^3}{1 - v^4}\,dv$ and $I_2 = \int\frac{v}{1 - v^4}\,dv$ [1]

Put $1 - v^4 = t$, then $-4v^3dv = dt \Rightarrow v^3\,dv = -\frac{dt}{4}$

$\therefore \quad I_1 = \int\frac{-dt}{4t} = -\frac{1}{4}\log|t| = -\frac{1}{4}\log|1 - v^4|$

[put $t = 1 - v^4$]

and $I_2 = \int\frac{v\,dv}{1 - v^4} = \int\frac{v\,dv}{1 - (v^2)^2}$ [1]

Put $v^2 = z$, then $v\,dv = \frac{dz}{2}$

$$\therefore \quad I_2 = \frac{1}{2}\int \frac{dz}{1-z^2} = \frac{1}{2\times 2}\log\left|\frac{1+z}{1-z}\right|$$

$$\left[\because \int \frac{dx}{a^2-x^2} = \frac{1}{2a}\log\left|\frac{a+x}{a-x}\right|\right]$$

$$= \frac{1}{4}\log\left|\frac{1+v^2}{1-v^2}\right| \quad [\text{put } z = v^2]$$

On substituting the values of I_1 and I_2 in Eq. (iii), we get

$$-\frac{1}{4}\log|1-v^4| - \frac{3}{4}\log\left|\frac{1+v^2}{1-v^2}\right| = \log|C_1x| \quad [1]$$

$$\Rightarrow \quad -\frac{1}{4}\log\left|(1-v^4)\left(\frac{1+v^2}{1-v^2}\right)^3\right| = \log|C_1x|$$

$$\Rightarrow \quad -\frac{1}{4}\log\left|(1-v^2)(1+v^2)\times\frac{(1+v^2)^3}{(1-v^2)^3}\right| = \log|C_1x|$$

$$\Rightarrow \quad \log\left|\frac{(1+v^2)^4}{(1-v^2)^2}\right|^{-1/4} = \log|C_1x| \quad [1/2]$$

$$\Rightarrow \quad \left[\frac{(1+v^2)^4}{(1-v^2)^2}\right]^{-1/4} = C_1x$$

$$\Rightarrow \quad \frac{(1+v^2)^4}{(1-v^2)^2} = (C_1x)^{-4}$$

[raising power (– 4) on both sides]

$$\Rightarrow \quad \frac{\left(1+\frac{y^2}{x^2}\right)^4}{\left(1-\frac{y^2}{x^2}\right)^2} = \frac{1}{C_1^4x^4} \quad \left[\text{put } v = \frac{y}{x}\right]$$

$$\Rightarrow \quad \frac{(x^2+y^2)^4}{x^4(x^2-y^2)^2} = \frac{1}{C_1^4x^4}$$

$$\Rightarrow \quad (x^2-y^2)^2 = C_1^4(x^2+y^2)^4$$

$$\Rightarrow \quad (x^2-y^2) = C_1^2(x^2+y^2)^2 \quad [\text{taking square root}]$$

$$\Rightarrow \quad x^2-y^2 = C(x^2+y^2)^2 \quad [\text{put } C_1^2 = C] \; [1]$$

which is the required general solution.

37. Hint (i) Write the given differential equation as

$$\frac{dy}{dx} = -\frac{\left[3\left(\frac{y}{x}\right)+\left(\frac{y}{x}\right)^2\right]}{1+\left(\frac{y}{x}\right)}.$$

(ii) Substitute $y = vx$ to solve it.

$$\left[\textbf{Ans. } y(y+2x) = \frac{c}{x^2}\right]$$

TOPIC 03 Linear Differential Equations

A differential equation of the form

$$A_0\frac{d^ny}{dx^n} + A_1\frac{d^{n-1}y}{dx^{n-1}} + A_2\frac{d^{n-2}y}{dx^{n-2}} + \ldots + A_{n-1}\frac{dy}{dx} + A_ny = Q$$

where, $A_0, A_1, A_2, \ldots, A_{n-1}, A_n$ are either constants or functions of independent variable x, is called the **linear differential equation.**

e.g. $\frac{d^3y}{dx^2} + x^2\frac{d^2y}{dx^2} + 2xy = x^2$ is a linear differential equation, but $xy\frac{d^2y}{dx^2} + 2\left(\frac{dy}{dx}\right)^2 + ay = x$ is a non-linear differential equation.

Note Linear differential equation is always of 1 degree.

Linear Differential Equation of First Order

A first order differential equation in which the degree of dependent variable and its derivative is one and they do not get multiplied together, is called the **linear differential equation** of first order.

Here, we will study two types of linear differential equation of first order, as given below

Type I A differential equation of the form $\frac{dy}{dx} + Py = Q$, where P and Q are constants or functions of x only.

e.g. $\frac{dy}{dx} + 2y = \sin x$. Here, $P = 2$ and $Q = \sin x$.

Type II A differential equation of the form $\frac{dx}{dy} + Px = Q$, where P and Q are constants or functions of y only.

e.g. $\frac{dx}{dy} - \frac{x}{y} = y^2$.

Here, $P = -\frac{1}{y}$ and $Q = y^2$.

In type II, x is the dependent variable and y is the independent variable.

Integrating Factor (IF)

Linear differential equations are solved when they are multiplied by a factor, which is called the integrating factor, because by multiplying such factor the left hand side of the differential equation become exact differential of same function.

For type I Differential equation, IF is $e^{\int P dx}$.

For type II Differential equation, IF is $e^{\int P dy}$.

Example 1 What will be the integrating factor of given differential equation $y\,dx + (x - y^2)\,dy = 0$?

Sol. Given differential equation is

$$y\,dx + (x - y^2)\,dy = 0$$

$$\Rightarrow \quad y\frac{dx}{dy} + (x - y^2) = 0$$

$$\Rightarrow \quad y\frac{dx}{dy} + x = y^2$$

$$\Rightarrow \quad \frac{dx}{dy} + \frac{1}{y}x = y \text{ [dividing both sides by } y]$$

which is of the form $\frac{dx}{dy} + Px = Q$.

Here, $P = \frac{1}{y}$ and $Q = y$

$\therefore$ Integrating Factor, $\text{IF} = e^{\int P dy} = e^{\int \frac{1}{y} dy}$

$= e^{\log y} = y \quad [\because e^{\log f(x)} = f(x)]$

Method to Solve First Order Linear Differential Equation

To solve a first order linear differential equation, we use the following steps

I. Express the given differential either in the form

$$\frac{dy}{dx} + Py = Q \quad \text{or} \quad \frac{dx}{dy} + Px = Q.$$

II. If the given differential equation is of the form $\frac{dy}{dx} + Py = Q$, then identify P and Q, which are constants or functions of x only.

III. Find the integrating factor IF by using the formula $e^{\int P dx}$.

IV. Now, the solution of the given differential equation is given by

$$y \cdot \text{IF} = \int (Q \times \text{IF})\,dx + C$$

In case, the first order linear differential equation is of the form $\frac{dx}{dy} + Px = Q$, where P and Q are constants or functions of y only.

Then, $\text{IF} = e^{\int P dy}$ and the solution of the differential equation is given by

$$x \cdot \text{IF} = \int (Q \times \text{IF})\,dy + C$$

Example 2 Solve the differential equation

$$\tan x \frac{dy}{dx} + 2y = \sec x.$$

[ISC 2005]

Sol. Given, $\frac{dy}{dx} + \frac{2y}{\tan x} = \frac{\sec x}{\tan x}$

On comparing above equation with the linear differential equation $\frac{dy}{dx} + Py = Q$,

we get

$$P = \frac{2}{\tan x} \text{ and } Q = \frac{\sec x}{\tan x} = \operatorname{cosec} x$$

$$\therefore \quad \text{IF} = e^{\int P dx} = e^{\int \frac{2}{\tan x} dx} = e^{2\log|\sin x|}$$

$$= e^{\log \sin^2 x} = \sin^2 x$$

The solution is $y \times \text{IF} = \int (Q \times \text{IF})\,dx + C$

$$\Rightarrow \quad y\sin^2 x = \int \operatorname{cosec} x \times \sin^2 x\,dx + C$$

$$\Rightarrow \quad y\sin^2 x = \int \sin x\,dx + C$$

$$\Rightarrow \quad y\sin^2 x = -\cos x + C$$

$$\Rightarrow \quad y = -\operatorname{cosec} x \cot x + C\operatorname{cosec}^2 x$$

Example 3 Find the general solution of the differential equation $e^{2x}\frac{dy}{dx} + 3e^{2x}y = 1$.

Sol. Given differential equation is $e^{2x}\frac{dy}{dx} + 3e^{2x}y = 1$

$$\Rightarrow \quad e^{2x}\left(\frac{dy}{dx} + 3y\right) = 1$$

$$\Rightarrow \quad \frac{dy}{dx} + 3y = e^{-2x}$$

This is the form of $\frac{dy}{dx} + Py = Q$.

Here, $\quad P = 3$ and $Q = e^{-2x}$

Now, Integrating Factor, $\text{IF} = e^{\int 3dx} = e^{3x}$

and the solution of differential equation is given by

$$y \times \text{IF} = \int (Q \times \text{IF})\,dx + C$$

$$\Rightarrow \quad y \times e^{3x} = \int (e^{-2x} \times e^{3x})\,dx + C = \int e^x dx + C$$

$$\Rightarrow \quad ye^{3x} = e^x + C$$

which is the required solution.

Example 4 Solve the differential equation

$$y\,dx - (x + 2y^2)\,dy = 0.$$

[ISC 2006]

Sol. Given, $y\,dx - (x + 2y^2)dy = 0$

$$\Rightarrow \quad y\,dx = (x + 2y^2)dy$$

$$\Rightarrow \quad \frac{dx}{dy} = \frac{x + 2y^2}{y} \Rightarrow \frac{dx}{dy} - \frac{x}{y} = 2y$$

On comparing above equation with linear differential equation $\frac{dx}{dy} + Px = Q$, we get

$$P = -\frac{1}{y} \text{ and } Q = 2y$$

$$\therefore \quad \text{IF} = e^{\int P\,dy} = e^{-\int \frac{1}{y} dy}$$

$$= e^{-\log|y|} = e^{\log\frac{1}{|y|}} = \frac{1}{y}$$

The solution is $x \times \text{IF} = \int (Q \times \text{IF})\,dy + C$

$$\Rightarrow \quad \frac{x}{y} = \int \frac{2y}{y}\,dy + C$$

$$\Rightarrow \quad \frac{x}{y} = 2\int dy + C \Rightarrow \frac{x}{y} = 2y + C$$

$$\Rightarrow \quad x = 2y^2 + yC$$

Example 5 Solve the differential equation

$$(x^2 - 1)\frac{dy}{dx} + 2xy = \frac{2}{x^2 - 1}.$$

Sol. Given differential equation is $(x^2 - 1)\frac{dy}{dx} + 2xy = \frac{2}{x^2 - 1}$

On dividing both sides by $(x^2 - 1)$, we get

$$\frac{dy}{dx} + \frac{2x}{x^2 - 1} \cdot y = \frac{2}{(x^2 - 1)^2} \quad \text{...(i)}$$

which is a linear differential equation of the form

$$\frac{dy}{dx} + Py = Q$$

Here, $P = \frac{2x}{x^2 - 1}$ and $Q = \frac{2}{(x^2 - 1)^2}$

Now, $\text{IF} = e^{\int P\,dx} = e^{\int \frac{2x}{x^2 - 1} dx}$

$$= e^{\log(x^2 - 1)} = x^2 - 1$$

$$\left[\begin{array}{l} \because \text{put } x^2 - 1 = t \Rightarrow 2x\,dx = dt \\ \therefore \int \frac{2x}{x^2 - 1}\,dx = \int \frac{1}{t}\,dt = \log|t| = \log|x^2 - 1| \end{array}\right]$$

and the solution of differential equation is given by

$$y \times \text{IF} = \int (Q \times \text{IF})\,dx + C$$

$$\Rightarrow \quad y(x^2 - 1) = \int \frac{2}{(x^2 - 1)^2} \cdot (x^2 - 1)\,dx + C$$

$$\Rightarrow \quad y(x^2 - 1) = \int \frac{2}{(x^2 - 1)}\,dx + C$$

$$\Rightarrow \quad y(x^2 - 1) = \frac{2}{2 \times 1} \log\left|\frac{x - 1}{x + 1}\right| + C$$

$$\left[\because \int \frac{1}{x^2 - a^2}\,dx = \frac{1}{2a} \log\left|\frac{x - a}{x + a}\right| + C\right]$$

which is the required solution.

Topic Practice 3

Very Short Answer Type Questions

2 Marks

1 Find the integrating factor of the following differential equation. (Each part carries 2 Marks)

(i) $\frac{dy}{dx} + \frac{y}{2x} = 6x^2$ (ii) $\frac{dy}{dx} + x^2 y = 5x$

(iii) $\frac{dx}{dy} + \cot y x = y^3$

2 Find the integrating factor of the differential equation $\left(\frac{e^{-2\sqrt{x}}}{\sqrt{x}} - \frac{y}{\sqrt{x}}\right)\frac{dx}{dy} = 1.$

3 Write the integrating factor of the differential equation $(1 + y^2) + (2xy - \cot y)\frac{dy}{dx} = 0.$

4 Find the general solution of the differential equation $\frac{dy}{dx} + \frac{2y}{x} = x.$

5 Solve $\frac{dy}{dx} + y = \cos x - \sin x.$

6 Solve $\frac{dy}{dx} - 2y = \cos 3x.$

Short Answer Type Questions

4 Marks

7 Solve the differential equation $(y + \log x)dx - x\,dy = 0$, given that $y = 0$, when $x = 1$ **[ISC 2010]**

8 Solve $\sin x \frac{dy}{dx} - y = \sin x \tan\frac{x}{2}$ **[ISC 2018]**

9 Solve $\cos^2 x \frac{dy}{dx} + y = \tan x.$ **[NCERT]**

10 Solve the differential equation

$$(1 + y^2)dx = (\tan^{-1} y - x)\,dy$$ **[ISC 2023]**

11 Solve the differential equation
$$(x+1)\frac{dy}{dx}-y=e^{3x}(x+1)^2$$
[ISC 2008]

12 Find the general solution of the differential equation $(1+y^2)+(x-e^{\tan^{-1}y})\frac{dy}{dx}=0$.
[NCERT Exemplar]

13 Solve $(x^2+1)\frac{dy}{dx}-2xy=(x^2+2)(x^2+1)$.

14 Solve the differential equation
$$(1+x^2)dy+2xy\,dx=\sec^2 x\,dx.$$

15 Find the general solution of the differential equation $(x\log x)\frac{dy}{dx}+y=\frac{2}{x}\log x$.

16 Solve the differential equation $(y+3x^2)\frac{dx}{dy}=x$.

17 Solve the following differential equation for a particular solution $dy=(5x-4y)dx$; when $y=0$ and $x=0$. **[ISC 2009]**

18 Find the general solution of $(x+y)\frac{dy}{dx}=1$. **[NCERT]**

19 If $y(t)$ is a solution of $(1+t)\frac{dy}{dt}-ty=1$ and $y(0)=-1$, then show that $y(1)=\frac{-1}{2}$.
[NCERT Exemplar]

Long Answer Type Questions

6 Marks

20 Solve the differential equation
$\frac{dy}{dx}-3y\cot x=\sin 2x$, given $y=2$, when $x=\frac{\pi}{2}$.
[NCERT; ISC 2012]

21 Solve the differential equation
$(x^2+1)\frac{dy}{dx}+2xy=\sqrt{x^2+4}$.

22 Solve the following differential equation.
$ye^y dx=(y^3+2xe^y)dy$, given that $x=0, y=1$
[ISC 2013]

Hints & Solutions

1. (i) Given differential equation is
$$\frac{dy}{dx}+\frac{y}{2x}=6x^2$$
On comparing with $\frac{dy}{dx}+Py=Q$, we get $P=\frac{1}{2x}$ [1]

$\therefore$ Integrating factor, $\text{IF}=e^{\int P dx}=e^{\int \frac{1}{2x}dx}$
$$=e^{\frac{1}{2}\log x}=e^{\log\sqrt{x}}=\sqrt{x}$$ [1]

(ii) Similar as part (i). $\left[\textbf{Ans. } e^{\frac{x^3}{3}}\right]$

(iii) Given differential equation is $\frac{dx}{dy}+\cot y x=y^3$

On comparing with $\frac{dx}{dy}+Px=Q$, we get
$$P=\cot y$$ [1]
$\therefore\quad \text{IF}=e^{\int P dy}=e^{\int \cot y\,dy}=e^{\log \sin y}=\sin y$ [1]

2. The given differential equation can be rewritten as
$$\frac{dy}{dx}=\frac{e^{-2\sqrt{x}}}{\sqrt{x}}-\frac{y}{\sqrt{x}}$$
$$\Rightarrow\quad \frac{dy}{dx}+\frac{y}{\sqrt{x}}=\frac{e^{-2\sqrt{x}}}{\sqrt{x}}$$
which is a linear differential equation of the form
$$\frac{dy}{dx}+Py=Q$$
Here, $P=\frac{1}{\sqrt{x}}$ and $Q=\frac{e^{-2\sqrt{x}}}{\sqrt{x}}$. [1]

Now, Integrating Factor,
$$\text{IF}=e^{\int P dx}=e^{\int \frac{1}{\sqrt{x}}dx}=e^{\int \frac{1}{\sqrt{x}}dx}=e^{2\sqrt{x}}$$ [1]

3. Given equation can be rewritten as
$$(\cot y-2xy)\frac{dy}{dx}=1+y^2$$
$$\Rightarrow\quad \frac{\cot y-2xy}{(1+y^2)}=\frac{dx}{dy}$$
$$\Rightarrow\quad \frac{dx}{dy}=\frac{\cot y}{1+y^2}-\frac{2xy}{1+y^2}$$
$$\Rightarrow\quad \frac{dx}{dy}+\frac{2y}{1+y^2}\cdot x=\frac{\cot y}{1+y^2}$$
which is a linear differential equation of the form

$$\frac{dx}{dy} + Px = Q$$

Here, $P = \dfrac{2y}{1+y^2}$ and $Q = \dfrac{\cot y}{1+y^2}$. [1]

Now, Integrating Factor, $IF = e^{\int P dy} = e^{\int \frac{2y}{1+y^2} dy}$

Put $1 + y^2 = t \Rightarrow 2y\,dy = dt$

$\therefore \quad IF = e^{\int \frac{dt}{t}} = e^{\log(t)} = t = 1 + y^2$ [1]

4. Hint (i) $IF = e^{\int \frac{2}{x}dx} = e^{2\log x} = e^{\log x^2} = x^2$

(ii) Solution is given by $y \cdot x^2 = \int x \cdot x^2 dx + C$

$$\left[\textbf{Ans. } y = \frac{x^2}{4} + Cx^{-2}\right]$$

5. Hint

(i) $IF = e^x$

(ii) Use the formula, $\int e^x[f(x) + f'(x)]dx = e^x f(x) + C$ to simplify the solution.

[**Ans.** $ye^x = e^x \cos x + C$]

6. Hint (i) $IF = e^{\int -2dx} = e^{-2x}$

(ii) For simplifying the solution.

Let $I = \int \underset{I}{e^{-2x}} \underset{II}{\cos 3x}\, dx$

$$= e^{-2x} \cdot \frac{\sin 3x}{3} - \int e^{-2x}(-2)\frac{\sin 3x}{3}dx$$

$$= \frac{e^{-2x}\sin 3x}{3} + \frac{2}{3}\int \underset{I}{e^{-2x}} \underset{II}{\sin 3x}\, dx$$

$$= \frac{e^{-2x}\sin 3x}{3} + \frac{2}{3}\left[\int e^{-2x}\left(\frac{-\cos 3x}{3}\right) - \int e^{-2x}(-2)\left(\frac{-\cos 3x}{3}\right)dx\right]$$

$$= \frac{e^{-2x}\sin 3x}{3} - \frac{2}{9}e^{-2x}\cos 3x - \frac{4}{9}I$$

$$\left[\textbf{Ans. } y = \frac{1}{13}(3\sin 3x - 2\cos 3x) + Ce^{2x}\right]$$

7. Given differential equation can be rewritten as

$$\frac{dy}{dx} - \frac{y}{x} = \frac{\log x}{x}$$

which is a linear differential equation of the form

$$\frac{dy}{dx} + Py = Q$$

Here, $\quad P = -\dfrac{1}{x}$ and $Q = \dfrac{\log x}{x}$.

Now, Integrating Factor, $IF = e^{\int \frac{-1}{x}dx} = e^{-\log x} = x^{-1}$ [1]

and the solution of differential equation is given by

$$y \cdot x^{-1} = \int \left(\frac{\log x}{x} \cdot x^{-1}\right)dx + C$$

$\Rightarrow \quad \dfrac{y}{x} = \int \dfrac{\log x}{x^2}dx + C$ ...(i) [1]

Now, put $\log x = t$

$\Rightarrow \quad \dfrac{1}{x}dx = dt$

$\Rightarrow \quad x = e^t$

$\therefore$ From Eq. (i), we get

$$\frac{y}{x} = \int \frac{t}{e^t}dt + C$$

$\Rightarrow \quad \dfrac{y}{x} = \int (\underset{I}{t} \cdot \underset{II}{e^{-t}})dt + C$ [1]

$\Rightarrow \quad \dfrac{y}{x} = t \cdot \dfrac{e^{-t}}{(-1)} - \int 1 \cdot \dfrac{e^{-t}}{(-1)}dt + C$

[using integrating by parts]

$\Rightarrow \quad \dfrac{y}{x} = -t\,e^{-t} + \int e^{-t}dt + C$

$\Rightarrow \quad \dfrac{y}{x} = -t\,e^{-t} - e^{-t} + C$

$\Rightarrow \quad \dfrac{y}{x} = -\log x\left(\dfrac{1}{x}\right) - \dfrac{1}{x} + C$

$[\because e^{-t} = e^{-\log x} = e^{\log x^{-1}} = x^{-1}]$

$\Rightarrow \quad y = -\log x - 1 + Cx$

$\Rightarrow \quad y = Cx - (\log x + 1)$ ...(i)

$\because y = 0$ when $x = 1$

$\therefore \quad 0 = C - (\log 1 + 1)$

$\Rightarrow \quad C = 1$ $[\because \log 1 = 0]$

On putting $C = 1$ in Eq. (i), we get

$y = x - (\log x + 1)$ [1]

8. We have, $\sin x \dfrac{dy}{dx} - y = \sin x \tan \dfrac{x}{2}$

$\Rightarrow \quad \dfrac{dy}{dx} - y \operatorname{cosec} x = \tan \dfrac{x}{2}$

This is the form of $\dfrac{dy}{dx} + Py = Q$

where, $P = -\operatorname{cosec} x$ and $Q = \tan \dfrac{x}{2}$ [1]

Now, $\quad IF = e^{\int P dx} = e^{\int - \quad dx} = e^{-\log \tan \frac{x}{2}}$

$= \dfrac{1}{\tan x/2}$ [1]

and the solution of the given differential equation is

$$y \cdot IF = \int Q \cdot IF\, dx + C$$

$\dfrac{y}{\tan \frac{x}{2}} = \int \tan \dfrac{x}{2} \cdot \dfrac{1}{\tan \frac{x}{2}}dx + C$ [1]

$$\Rightarrow \quad \frac{y}{\tan\frac{x}{2}} = \int dx + C = x + C$$

$$\Rightarrow \quad y = x\tan\frac{x}{2} + C\tan\frac{x}{2}$$ [1]

9. Hint

(i) Given differential equation can be rewritten as $\frac{dy}{dx} + \sec^2 x\, y = \sec^2 x \tan x$

Here, $P = \sec^2 x$ and $Q = \sec^2 x \cdot \tan x$.

(ii) $\text{IF} = e^{\tan x}$

[**Ans.** $y \cdot e^{\tan x} = e^{\tan x}(\tan x - 1) + C$]

10. We have, $(1 + y^2)\, dx = (\tan^{-1} y - x)\, dy$

$$\frac{dx}{dy} = \frac{\tan^{-1} y}{1+y^2} - \frac{x}{1+y^2} \Rightarrow \frac{dx}{dy} + \frac{x}{1+y^2} = \frac{\tan^{-1} y}{1+y^2}$$

This is a linear differential equation in form $\frac{dx}{dy} + Px = Q$,

where $P = \frac{1}{1+y^2}$ and $Q = \frac{\tan^{-1} y}{1+y^2}$

$$\text{IF} = e^{\int P dy} = e^{\int \frac{1}{1+y^2} dy} = e^{\tan^{-1} y}$$

Solution of the given differential equation is

$$x \cdot \text{IF} = \int Q \cdot \text{IF}\, dy \Rightarrow xe^{\tan^{-1} y} = \int \frac{\tan^{-1} y}{1+y^2} e^{\tan^{-1} y}\, dy$$

Put $\tan^{-1} y = t \Rightarrow \frac{1}{1+y^2} dy = dt$

$$\therefore \quad xe^{\tan^{-1} y} = \int te^t dt$$

Integrating by parts in RHS, we have

$$xe^{\tan^{-1} y} = t\int e^t dt - \int\left[\frac{d}{dt}(t)\cdot\int e^t \cdot dt\right]dt$$

$$\Rightarrow xe^{\tan^{-1} y} = te^t - \int e^t dt + C$$

$$\Rightarrow xe^{\tan^{-1} y} = te^t - e^t + C$$

$$\Rightarrow xe^{\tan^{-1} y} = e^{\tan^{-1} y}[(\tan^{-1} y) - 1] + C \qquad [\because t = \tan^{-1} y]$$

$$\Rightarrow \quad x = \tan^{-1} y - 1 + Ce^{-\tan^{-1} y}$$

11. Given, $(x+1)\frac{dy}{dx} - y = e^{3x}(x+1)^2$

$$\Rightarrow \quad \frac{dy}{dx} - \frac{y}{x+1} = e^{3x}(x+1) \qquad \text{...(i)}$$

On comparing, above equation with the linear differential equation $\frac{dy}{dx} + Py = Q$, we get,

$$P = \frac{-1}{x+1} \text{ and } Q = e^{3x}(x+1)$$ [1]

$$\therefore \quad \text{IF} = e^{\int P dx} = e^{-\int \frac{1}{x+1} dx} = e^{-\log|x+1|}$$

$$= e^{\log\left(\frac{1}{x+1}\right)} = \frac{1}{x+1} \qquad [\because e^{\log x} = x]$$ [1]

$\therefore$ The solution is $y \times \text{IF} = \int Q \times \text{IF}\, dx + C$

$$\Rightarrow \quad y \times \frac{1}{x+1} = \int \frac{e^{3x}(x+1)dx}{x+1} + C$$ [1]

$$\Rightarrow \quad \frac{y}{x+1} = \frac{e^{3x}}{3} + C$$

$$\Rightarrow \quad y = \frac{e^{3x}}{3}(1+x) + C(1+x)$$ [1]

12. Given differential equation is $(1+y^2) + (x - e^{\tan^{-1} y})\frac{dy}{dx} = 0$

$$\Rightarrow \quad (1+y^2) = -(x - e^{\tan^{-1} y})\frac{dy}{dx}$$

$$\Rightarrow \quad (1+y^2)\frac{dx}{dy} = -x + e^{\tan^{-1} y}$$

$$\Rightarrow \quad (1+y^2)\frac{dx}{dy} + x = e^{\tan^{-1} y}$$ [1]

$$\Rightarrow \quad \frac{dx}{dy} + \frac{x}{1+y^2} = \frac{e^{\tan^{-1} y}}{1+y^2}$$

[dividing both sides by $(1+y^2)$]

which is a linear differential equation of the form.

$$\frac{dx}{dy} + Px = Q$$

Here, $P = \frac{1}{1+y^2}$ and $Q = \frac{e^{\tan^{-1} y}}{1+y^2}$.

Now, $\text{IF} = e^{\int P dy} = e^{\int \frac{1}{1+y^2} dy} = e^{\tan^{-1} y}$

and the required solution is given by [1]

$$x \cdot \text{IF} = \int Q \cdot \text{IF}\, dy + C_1$$

$$\Rightarrow \quad x \cdot e^{\tan^{-1} y} = \int \frac{e^{\tan^{-1} y}}{1+y^2} \cdot e^{\tan^{-1} y} dy + C_1$$

$$\Rightarrow \quad x \cdot e^{\tan^{-1} y} = \int \frac{(e^{\tan^{-1} y})^2}{1+y^2} dy + C_1$$ [1]

Put $\tan^{-1} y = t$, then $\frac{1}{1+y^2} dy = dt$

$$\therefore \quad x \cdot e^{\tan^{-1} y} = \int e^{2t} dt + C_1$$

$$\Rightarrow \quad x \cdot e^{\tan^{-1} y} = \frac{1}{2} e^{2\tan^{-1} y} + C_1$$

$$\Rightarrow \quad 2x e^{\tan^{-1} y} = e^{2\tan^{-1} y} + 2C_1$$

$$\Rightarrow \quad 2x e^{\tan^{-1} y} = e^{2\tan^{-1} y} + C \qquad [\because C = 2C_1]$$ [1]

13. Hint (i) Here, $P = \frac{-2x}{x^2+1}$ and $Q = x^2 + 2$

(ii) $\text{IF} = \dfrac{1}{x^2+1}$

(iii) The required solution is given by

$$\frac{y}{x^2+1} = \int \left(1+\frac{1}{x^2+1}\right)dx + C$$

$[\textbf{Ans. } y = (1+x^2)(x+\tan^{-1}x + C)]$

14. Hint (i) Given differential equation can be rewritten as

$$\frac{dy}{dx} + \frac{2x}{1+x^2}y = \frac{\sec^2 x}{1+x^2}$$

Here, $P = \dfrac{2x}{1+x^2}$ and $Q = \dfrac{\sec^2 x}{1+x^2}$.

(ii) $\text{IF} = 1 + x^2$

(iii) The required solution is given by

$$y\cdot(1+x^2) = \int \sec^2 x\, dx + C$$

$$\left[\textbf{Ans. } y = \frac{\tan x}{1+x^2} + \frac{C}{1+x^2}\right]$$

15. Hint Given differential equation can be rewritten as

$$\frac{dy}{dx} + \frac{y}{x\log x} = \frac{2}{x^2}$$

$$\text{IF} = e^{\int \frac{1}{x\log x}dx} = e^{\log\log x} = \log x$$

So, required solution is

$$y\log x = \int \underset{\text{II}}{\frac{2}{x^2}} \underset{\text{I}}{\log x}\, dx + C$$

$$= \log x \times 2\left(-\frac{1}{x}\right) - \int \frac{2}{x}\left(-\frac{1}{x}\right)dx + C$$

$$\left[\textbf{Ans. } y\log x = -\frac{2}{x}\log x - \frac{2}{x} + C\right]$$

16. Hint Write given equation as $\dfrac{dy}{dx} - \dfrac{y}{x} = 3x$ and solve it.

$[\textbf{Ans. } y = 3x^2 + Cx]$

17. Given, $dy = (5x - 4y)dx$

$$\Rightarrow \frac{dy}{dx} = 5x - 4y \Rightarrow \frac{dy}{dx} + 4y = 5x$$

On comparing above equation with linear differential equation $\dfrac{dy}{dx} + Py = Q$, we get

$P = 4, Q = 5x$ [1]

$\therefore \quad \text{IF} = e^{\int P\,dx} = e^{\int 4\,dx} = e^{4x}$ [1/2]

$\therefore$ The solution is $y \times \text{IF} = \int Q \times \text{IF}\, dx + C$

$\Rightarrow \quad ye^{4x} = \int 5xe^{4x}dx + C = 5\int \underset{\text{I}}{x}\underset{\text{II}}{e^{4x}}\, dx + C$ [1/2]

$$= \frac{5xe^{4x}}{4} - 5\int \frac{e^{4x}}{4}dx + C$$

[using integration by parts]

$$\Rightarrow \quad y\cdot e^{4x} = \frac{5}{4}xe^{4x} - \frac{5e^{4x}}{16} + C$$

$\Rightarrow \quad y = \dfrac{5}{4}x - \dfrac{5}{16} + Ce^{-4x}$ ...(i) [1]

Also, given $x = 0$ when $y = 0$

So, $0 = 0 - \dfrac{5}{16} + C \Rightarrow C = \dfrac{5}{16}$

On putting the value of C in Eq. (i), we get

$$y = \frac{5x}{4} - \frac{5}{16} + \frac{5e^{-4x}}{16}$$

$$\Rightarrow \quad 16y = 20x - 5 + 5e^{-4x}$$

$\Rightarrow \quad 16y = 20x + 5[e^{-4x} - 1]$ [1]

18. Hint Write the given equation as $\dfrac{dx}{dy} - x = y$ and solve it.

$[\textbf{Ans. } x + y + 1 = Ce^y]$

19. Given differential equation is $(1+t)\dfrac{dy}{dx} - ty = 1$

and it can be rewritten as $\dfrac{dy}{dt} - \dfrac{t}{(1+t)}y = \dfrac{1}{1+t}$

Here, $P = \dfrac{-t}{1+t}$ and $Q = \dfrac{1}{1+t}$

Now, $\text{IF} = e^{\int \frac{-t}{1+t}dt} = e^{-\int\left(1-\frac{1}{1+t}\right)dt} = e^{-[t-\log(1+t)]}$

$= e^{-t}\cdot e^{\log(1+t)} = (1+t)e^{-t}$ [1]

and the solution of differential equation is given by

$$y(1+t)e^{-t} = \int (1+t)\cdot e^{-t}\cdot\frac{1}{(1+t)}dt + C$$

$$\Rightarrow y\cdot(1+t)e^{-t} = \int e^{-t}dt + C$$

$\Rightarrow y\cdot(1+t)e^{-t} = -e^{-t} + C$ ...(i) [1]

Also, it is given that $y = -1$, when $t = 0$.

$\therefore$ From Eq. (i), we get

$$(-1)(1+0)e^{-0} = -e^{-0} + C$$

$\Rightarrow \quad -1 = -1 + C \Rightarrow C = 0$ [1]

Now, from Eq. (i), we get $y = \dfrac{-1}{(1+t)}$

$\therefore \quad y(1) = \dfrac{-1}{(1+1)} = \dfrac{-1}{2}$ **Hence proved.** [1]

20. Given, $\dfrac{dy}{dx} - (3\cot x)y = \sin 2x$

which is a linear differential equation of the form

$$\frac{dy}{dx} + Py = Q$$

Here, $P = -3\cot x$ and $Q = \sin 2x$. [1]

Now, $\text{IF} = e^{\int P\,dx} = e^{-3\int \cot x\,dx}$

$= e^{-3\log(\sin x)} = e^{\log(\sin x)^{-3}} = \dfrac{1}{\sin^3 x}$ [1]

and the required solution is given by

$$y \times \text{IF} = \int (Q \times \text{IF})\,dx + C$$

$$\Rightarrow \quad y \times \frac{1}{\sin^3 x} = \int \frac{1}{\sin^3 x} \sin 2x\,dx + C$$

$$\Rightarrow \quad y \times \frac{1}{\sin^3 x} = 2\int \frac{\sin x \cos x}{\sin^3 x}\,dx + C$$ [1]

[$\because \sin 2x = 2\sin x \cos x$]

$$\Rightarrow \quad \frac{1}{\sin^3 x} \times y = 2\int \frac{\cos x}{\sin^2 x}\,dx + C$$

$$\Rightarrow \quad \frac{y}{\sin^3 x} = 2\int \cot x \operatorname{cosec} x\,dx + C$$ [1/2]

$$\Rightarrow \quad \frac{y}{\sin^3 x} = -2\operatorname{cosec} x + C$$

$$\Rightarrow \quad y = -2\left(\frac{1}{\sin x} \times \sin^3 x\right) + C\sin^3 x$$

$$\Rightarrow \quad y = -2\sin^2 x + C\sin^3 x \quad \text{...(i)}$$ [1]

Also, given $y = 2$ and $x = \frac{\pi}{2}$, therefore from Eq. (i), we get

$$2 = -2\sin^2\left(\frac{\pi}{2}\right) + C\sin^3\left(\frac{\pi}{2}\right)$$

$$\Rightarrow \quad 2 = -2 + C$$

$$\Rightarrow \quad C = 4$$ [1]

On putting the value of C in Eq. (i), we get

$$y = -2\sin^2 x + 4\sin^3 x$$

$$\Rightarrow \quad y = 4\sin^3 x - 2\sin^2 x$$

which is the required solution. [1/2]

21. Given differential equation is

$$(x^2 + 1)\frac{dy}{dx} + 2xy = \sqrt{x^2 + 4}$$

$$\Rightarrow \quad \frac{dy}{dx} + \frac{2xy}{(1 + x^2)} = \frac{\sqrt{x^2 + 4}}{(1 + x^2)}$$ [1]

which is a linear differential equation of the form

$$\frac{dy}{dx} + Py = Q$$

Here, $P = \frac{2x}{1 + x^2}$ and $Q = \frac{\sqrt{x^2+4}}{(1 + x^2)}$. [1]

Now, Integrating Factor, $\text{IF} = e^{\int P dx} = e^{\int \frac{2x}{(1+x^2)}dx}$

$$= e^{\log|1 + x^2|} = (1 + x^2)$$ [1]

and the required solution is given by

$$y \cdot \text{IF} = \int (Q \cdot \text{IF})\,dx + C$$

$$\Rightarrow \quad y \cdot (1 + x^2) = \int \frac{\sqrt{x^2 + 4}}{(1 + x^2)} \cdot (1 + x^2)\,dx + C$$ [1]

$$\Rightarrow \quad y \cdot (1 + x^2) = \int \sqrt{x^2 + (2)^2}\,dx + C$$

$$\Rightarrow \quad y \cdot (1 + x^2) = \frac{x}{2}\sqrt{x^2+4} + \frac{4}{2}\log\left|x + \sqrt{x^2+4}\right| + C$$ [1]

$$\left[\because \int \sqrt{x^2 + a^2}\,dx = \frac{x}{2}\sqrt{x^2 + a^2} + \frac{a^2}{2}\log|x + \sqrt{x^2 + a^2}|\right]$$

$$\therefore \quad y(1 + x^2) = \frac{x}{2}\sqrt{x^2 + 4} + 2\log|x + \sqrt{x^2 + 4}| + C$$

which is the required solution. [1]

22. **Hint** Write the given differential equation as

$$\frac{dx}{dy} = y^2 e^{-y} + \frac{2x}{y}$$

$$\Rightarrow \quad \frac{dx}{dy} - \frac{2}{y}x = y^2 e^{-y}$$

[**Ans.** $x = y^2(e^{-1} - e^{-y})$]

Chapter Practice

Multiple Choice Type Questions

1 Mark

1 The order and the degree of differential equation $1+\left(\frac{dy}{dx}\right)^2=\frac{d^2y}{dx^2}$ are [ISC 2024]

(a) 2 and $\frac{3}{2}$ (b) 2 and 3 (c) 3 and 4 (d) 2 and 1

2 If $y=e^{-x}(A\cos x+B\sin x)$, then y is a solution of

(a) $\frac{d^2y}{dx^2}+2\frac{dy}{dx}=0$ (b) $\frac{d^2y}{dx^2}-2\frac{dy}{dx}+2y=0$

(c) $\frac{d^2y}{dx^2}+2\frac{dy}{dx}+2y=0$ (d) $\frac{d^2y}{dx^2}+2y=0$

3 The solution of $\frac{dy}{dx}+y=e^{-x}$, $y(0)=0$ is

(a) $y=e^x(x-1)$ (b) $y=xe^{-x}$

(c) $y=xe^{-x}+1$ (d) $y=(x+1)e^{-x}$

4 The general solution of the differential equation $x\,dy-(1+x^2)dx=dx$ is

(a) $y=2x+\frac{x^3}{3}+C$ (b) $y=2\log x+\frac{x^3}{3}+C$

(c) $y=\frac{x^2}{2}+C$ (d) $y=2\log x+\frac{x^2}{2}+C$

5 The integrating factor of differential equation $\frac{dy}{dx}+y=\frac{1+y}{x}$ is

(a) $\frac{x}{e^x}$ (b) $\frac{e^x}{x}$ (c) xe^x (d) e^x

Assertion-Reason Type Questions

1 Mark

Directions (Q. Nos. 6-9) *In the questions given below are two statements labelled as Assertion (A) and Reason (R). In the context of the two statements, which one of the following is correct?*

(a) Both A and R are correct; R is the correct explanation of A
(b) Both A and R are correct; R is not the correct explanation of A
(c) A is correct; R is incorrect
(d) R is correct; A is incorrect

6 **Assertion (A)** The general solution of the differential equation $x\frac{dy}{dx}+2y=x^2 (x\neq 0)$ is $y=\frac{x^2}{4}+kx^{-2}$.

Reason (R) The number of arbitrary constant in the general solution is equal to the order of the differential equation.

7 **Assertion (A)** The order of the differential equation whose solution is $y=c_1e^{2x+c_2}+c_3e^{2x+c_4}$ is 4.

Reason (R) Order of the differential equation is the order of the highest order derivative occurring in the differential equation.

8 **Assertion (A)** Integrating factor of $\frac{dy}{dx}+\frac{y}{2x}=3x^2$ is $x^{1/2}$.

Reason (R) Integrating factor of $\frac{dy}{dx}+Py=Q$ is $e^{\int P\,dx}$.

9 **Assertion (A)** Order of differential equation $\frac{dy}{dx}+\sin\left(\frac{dy}{dx}\right)=0$ is 1.

Reason (R) The highest order derivative involved in a differential equation, is called order of differential equation.

Very Short Answer Type Questions

2 Marks

Directions (Q. Nos. 10-12) *Find the order and degree of the following differential equations.*

10 $\frac{d^4y}{dx^4}+\sin\left(\frac{d^3y}{dx^3}\right)=0$ [NCERT]

11 $\frac{d^2y}{dx^2}=\sqrt{1+\left(\frac{dy}{dx}\right)^2}$

12 $x\frac{dy}{dx}+\frac{2}{(dy/dx)}=y^2$

13 State whether $y = e^{-x}(x+a)$ is a solution of differential equation $\frac{dy}{dx} + y = e^{-x}$.

14 Show that the function $y = (A+Bx)\,e^{3x}$ is a solution of the equation $\frac{d^2y}{dx^2} - 6\frac{dy}{dx} + 9y = 0$.

15 Show that the function ϕ, defined by $\phi(x) = \cos x$, $(x \in R)$, satisfies the initial value problem $\frac{d^2y}{dx^2} + y = 0$, $y(0) = 1$, $y'(0) = 0$.

16 Solve $\frac{dy}{dx} = 2^{y-x}$. **[NCERT Exemplar]**

17 Solve $\sqrt{a+x}\frac{dy}{dx} + x = 0$.

18 Write the solution of differential equation $(e^x + e^{-x})\,dy = (e^x - e^{-x})\,dx$.

19 If $\frac{dy}{dx} = ye^x$ and $x = 0$, $y = e$, then find the value of y, when $x = 1$. **[NCERT Exemplar]**

20 Solve $2(y+3) - xy\frac{dy}{dx} = 0$, given that $y(1) = -2$. **[NCERT Exemplar]**

Short Answer Type Questions

4 Marks

Directions (Q. Nos. 21-24) *Solve each of the following differential equations.*

21 $(1+y^2)(1+\log x)\,dx + x\,dy = 0$

22 $\frac{dy}{dx} + \frac{1+\cos 2y}{1-\cos 2x} = 0$

23 $(1+e^{2x})\,dy + (1+y^2)\,e^x\,dx = 0$, given $y = 1$, when $x = 0$. **[NCERT]**

24 $(x+1)\frac{dy}{dx} = 2e^{-y} - 1$, $y = 0$, when $x = 0$

25 Solve $(1+x^2)\frac{dy}{dx} + 2xy - 4x^2 = 0$ subject to the initial condition $y(0) = 0$.

Long Answer Type Questions

6 Marks

26 Solve the differential equation

$$\frac{dy}{dx} = \frac{e^x(\sin^2 x + \sin 2x)}{y(2\log y + 1)}.$$

27 Solve the differential equation $\frac{dy}{dx} = 1 + x + y^2 + xy^2$, when $y = 0$, $x = 0$. **[NCERT Exemplar]**

28 Solve $x^2\frac{dy}{dx} = x^2 + xy + y^2$. **[NCERT Exemplar]**

29 Solve $x^2\frac{dy}{dx} - xy = 1 + \cos\left(\frac{y}{x}\right)$, $x \neq 0$ and $x = 1$, $y = \frac{\pi}{2}$. **[NCERT Exemplar]**

30 Solve the following differential equation

$$2ye^{\frac{x}{y}}dx + \left(y - 2xe^{\frac{x}{y}}\right)dy = 0, \text{ given } x = 0 \text{ and } y = 1.$$

[ISC 2024]

31 Find the particular solution of the differential equation $(1+x^2)\frac{dy}{dx} = e^{m\tan^{-1}x} - y$, given that $y = 1$, when $x = 0$.

32 Find the general solution of $(1+\tan y)(dx - dy) + 2x\,dy = 0$. **[NCERT Exemplar]**

Case-Based Type Questions

6 Marks

33 Reshma a Mathematics teacher of Class XII, writes a differential equation $\frac{dy}{dx} + (\sec x)\,y = \tan x$ on the blackboard and asks some questions which are based on above differential equation to check the preparation of the topic, then answer the following questions.

(i) What is the form of given equation?

(ii) Write the value of $(P^2 - Q^2)$.

(iii) Find the integration factor of equation $\frac{dy}{dx} + y\sec x = \tan x$.

(iv) What is the solution of $\frac{dy}{dx} + Py = Q$?

34 The electromotive force (e) or emf is the energy provided by a cell or battery per Columb of charge passing through it. To give the knowledge about emf, Mathematics teacher of Class XII writes the equation of electromotive forces for an electric circuit. Containing resistance and self inductance is $E = Ri + L\frac{di}{dt}$, where E is the electromotive force given to the

circuit, R the resistance and L is the coefficient of induction.

Then, answer the following questions which are based on above information.

(i) What is the form of the equation $E = Ri + L\frac{di}{dt}$?

(ii) Find the integrating factor of equation $E = Ri + L\frac{di}{dt}$.

(iii) What is the solution of the eqution $E = Ri + L\frac{di}{dt}$?

(iv) Find the current i at time t when $E = 0$.

Answers

1. (d)
2. (c)
3. (b)
4. (d)
5. (b)
6. (b)
7. (d)
8. (a)
9. (d)
10. Order = 4, degree = not defined
11. Order = 2, degree = 2
12. Order = 1, degree = 2
13. Yes
16. $2^{-x} - 2^{-y} = k$
17. $y = -\frac{2}{3}(a + x)^{3/2} + 2a\sqrt{a + x} + C$
18. $y = \log|e^x + e^{-x}| + C$
19. $y = e^e$
20. $x^2(y + 3)^3 = e^{y+2}$
21. $\tan^{-1} y + \log|x| + \frac{(\log|x|)^2}{2} = C$
22. $\tan y = \cot x + C$
23. $\tan^{-1} y + \tan^{-1} e^x = \frac{\pi}{2}$
24. $(x + 1)(2 - e^y) = 1$
25. $y = \frac{4x^3}{3(1 + x^2)}$
26. $y^2(\log y) = e^x \sin^2 x + C$
27. $y = \tan\left(x + \frac{x^2}{2}\right)$
28. $\tan^{-1}\left(\frac{y}{x}\right) = \log|x| + C$
29. $\tan\left(\frac{y}{2x}\right) = \frac{-1}{2x^2} + \frac{3}{2}$
30. $y = \ln\left|\frac{2}{x}\sqrt{\left(\frac{x^2 - 1}{3}\right)}\right|$
31. $y\,(m + 1)\,e^{\tan^{-1} x} = e^{(m+1)\tan^{-1} x} + m$
32. $x(\sin y + \cos y) = \sin y + Ce^{-y}$
33. (i) Linear form (ii) 1 (iii) $\sec x + \tan x$ (iv) $y\,(\text{IF}) = \int Q(\text{IF})\,dx + C$
34. (i) Linear form (ii) $e^{(R/L)t}$ (iii) $\frac{E}{R} + Ce^{(-R/L)T}$ (iv) $Ce^{-\frac{Rt}{L}}$

CHAPTER

11

Probability

In this chapter, we will discuss the concept of conditional probability of an event given that another event has occurred, which will be helpful in understanding the Baye's theorem, multiplication rule of probability, independence and dependence of events. We will also study random variable, its probability distribution; mean and variance of probability distribution and Binomial distribution.

- Conditional Probability
- Multiplication Theorem on Probability, Independent & Dependent Events
- Theorem of Total Probability and Baye's Theorem
- Random Variable and Its Probability Distribution

TOPIC 01 Conditional Probability

Quick Review of Probability

- An operation which can produce some well-defined outcomes is called an **experiment.**
- An experiment is called **random experiment**, if it satisfies the following two conditions
  (i) It has more than one possible outcomes.
  (ii) It is not possible to predict the outcome in advance.
- A possible result of a random experiment is called its **outcome.**
- The set of all possible outcomes of a random experiment is called its **sample space.** It is usually denoted by S. Each element of a sample space is called a sample point or an event point.
- When a random experiment is repeated under identical conditions and it does not give the same result each time but may result in anyone of the several possible outcomes, then each such action is called a **trial** and the outcomes are called **cases.** The number of times the experiment is repeated, is called the **number of trials.**
- A subset of the sample space associated with a random experiment is called an **event.**
- The empty set ϕ and the sample space S describe events (as S and ϕ are also subset of S). The empty set ϕ is called an **impossible event** and whole sample space S is called the **sure event.**

- If an event has only one sample point of a sample space, then it is called a **simple** or **elementary event.**
- If an event has more than one sample point, then it is called a **compound event.**
- The given events are said to be **equally likely**, if none of them is expected to occur in preference to the other.
- Two or more events are said to be **mutually exclusive**, if the happening of one excludes the happening of the other i.e. if no two of them can occur together. If A and B are mutually exclusive events, then $(A \cap B) = \phi$.
- A set of events are said to be **exhaustive**, if one of them necessarily occurs whenever the experiment is performed.

  Let $E_1, E_2, \ldots, E_n$ be subsets of sample space S. Then, events $E_1, E_2, \ldots, E_n$ are exhaustive events, if $E_1 \cup E_2 \cup \ldots \cup E_n = S$.
- Let A be an event in a sample space S, then **complement of** A is the set of all sample points, which are not in A and it is denoted by A' or $\bar{A}$.

  i.e. $A' = \{n : n \in S, n \notin A\}$

Probability of an Event

If there are n elementary equally likely events associated with a random experiment and m of them are favourable to an event A, then the **probability of happening or occurrence of** A is denoted by $P(A)$ and defined as

$$P(A) = \frac{m}{n} = \frac{\left[\text{Number of elementary events favourable to event } A\right]}{\left[\text{Total number of elementary events to the experiment}\right]}$$

Note

(i) $0 \le P(A) \le 1$ (ii) $P(A \cup A') = 1$

(iii) $P(A \cap A') = 0$ (iv) $P(A')' = P(A)$

(v) Probability of impossible event is zero.

(vi) Probability of sure event is 1.

(vii) Sometimes, we have to select r objects from n distinct objects, then we use the formula, ${}^nC_r = \frac{n!}{r!(n-r)!}$, $0 \le r \le n$.

Important Laws on Probability

1. **Addition Theorem of Probability**

   (i) For two events A and B,

   $$P(A \cup B) = P(A) + P(B) - P(A \cap B)$$
   $$= P(A - B) + P(B - A) + P(A \cap B)$$
   $$= P(A) + P(B - A)$$
   $$= P(B) + P(A - B)$$

   If A and B are mutually exclusive events, then $P(A \cup B) = P(A) + P(B)$

   [for mutually exclusive events, $P(A \cap B) = 0$]

   (ii) For three events A, B and C,

   $$P(A \cup B \cup C) = P(A) + P(B) + P(C) - P(A \cap B) - P(B \cap C) - P(A \cap C) + P(A \cap B \cap C)$$

   If A, B and C are mutually exclusive events, then

   $$P(A \cup B \cup C) = P(A) + P(B) + P(C)$$

   [$\because$ for mutually exclusive events, $P(A \cap B) = P(B \cap C) = P(C \cap A) = P(A \cap B \cap C) = 0$]

Note If $A_1, A_2, A_3, \ldots, A_n$ are mutually exclusive events associated with a random experiment, then $P(A_1 \cup A_2 \cup A_3 \cup \ldots \cup A_n) = P(A_1) + P(A_2) + P(A_3) + \ldots + P(A_n)$.

2. If A and B are two events associated with a random experiment, then

   (i) $P(\bar{A} \cap B) = P(B) - P(A \cap B)$

   (ii) $P(A \cap \bar{B}) = P(A) - P(A \cap B)$

   (iii) $P[(A \cap \bar{B}) \cup (\bar{A} \cap B)] = P(A) + P(B) - 2P(A \cap B)$

   (iv) $P(\bar{A} \cap \bar{B}) = 1 - P(A \cup B)$

   (v) $P(\bar{A} \cup \bar{B}) = 1 - P(A \cap B)$

   (vi) $P(A) = P(A \cap B) + P(A \cap \bar{B})$
   $= P(A - B) + P(A \cap B)$

   (vii) $P(B) = P(A \cap B) + P(B \cap \bar{A})$
   $= P(B - A) + P(A \cap B)$

   (viii) P(exactly one of A, B occurs)
   $= P(A) + P(B) - 2P(A \cap B)$
   $= P(A \cup B) - P(A \cap B)$

3. If A, B and C are three events, then

   P(exactly one of A, B, C occurs)
   $$= P(A) + P(B) + P(C) - 2P(A \cap B) - 2P(B \cap C) - 2P(A \cap C) + 3P(A \cap B \cap C)$$

4. $P(\bar{A}) = 1 - P(A)$

Note If $A \subseteq B$, then

(i) $P(A) \le P(B)$

(ii) $P(B - A) = P(B) - P(A)$

Conditional Event

If A and B are events of a sample space S that associated with a random experiment and A occurs after the occurrence of B, then occurrence of event A under the condition that B has already occurred is called conditional event. It is denoted by A/B. Similarly, we define B/A.

Conditional Probability

If A and B are two events associated with the same sample space of a random experiment, then **conditional probability** of the event A given that B has occurred, i.e. $P(A/B)$ is given by

$$P\left(\frac{A}{B}\right)=\frac{P(A\cap B)}{P(B)}, \text{ provided } P(B)\neq 0$$

Probability of occurrence of event B, when A has already occurred i.e. $P(B/A)$ is given by

$$P\left(\frac{B}{A}\right)=\frac{P(B\cap A)}{P(A)}, \text{ provided } P(A)\neq 0$$

Properties of Conditional Probability

Let A and B be the events of a sample space S of an experiment, then

(i) The conditional probability of an event A given that B has occurred lies between 0 and 1, i.e. $0\leq P(A/B)\leq 1$.

(ii) $P(S/A)=P(A/A)=1$

(iii) If A and B are any two events of a sample space S and C is an event of S, such that $P(C)\neq 0$, then
$P\{(A\cup B)/C\}=P(A/C)+P(B/C)-P\{(A\cap B)/C\}$
In particular, if A and B are disjoint events, then

$$P\left(\frac{A\cup B}{C}\right)=P\left(\frac{A}{C}\right)+P\left(\frac{B}{C}\right)$$

(iv) The conditional property of an event A given that B has occurred lies between 0 and 1.

(v) $P(A'/B)=1-P(A/B)$, where A' is complement of A.

Note (i) $P(S/A)=P(A/A)=1$

(ii) If A and B are mutually exclusive events, then $P(A/B)=0=P(B/A)$

Method to Solve Problem Based on Conditional Probability

To solve problems based on conditional probability, we use the following steps

I. First, write the sample space for given experiment and then assume the given events as A, B, which are associated with sample space.

II. Find the probability of that event A or B, which is already occurred and find $P(A\cap B)$.

III. Find the required conditional probability by using suitable formula

$$P\left(\frac{A}{B}\right)=\frac{P(A\cap B)}{P(B)} \text{ or } P\left(\frac{B}{A}\right)=\frac{P(A\cap B)}{P(A)}.$$

Note If elementary events of the sample space are not equally likely, then probabilities $P(A\cap B)$ and $P(A)$ or $P(B)$ being calculated accordingly.

Example 1 If $P(A)=\frac{6}{11}$, $P(B)=\frac{5}{11}$ and $P(A\cup B)=\frac{7}{11}$, then find

(i) $P(A\cap B)$ (ii) $P(A/B)$ (iii) $P(B/A)$. **[NCERT]**

Sol. Given, $P(A)=\frac{6}{11}$, $P(B)=\frac{5}{11}$ and $P(A\cup B)=\frac{7}{11}$

(i) $P(A\cup B)=P(A)+P(B)-P(A\cap B)$

$$\Rightarrow \frac{7}{11}=\frac{6}{11}+\frac{5}{11}-P(A\cap B)$$

$$\therefore P(A\cap B)=\frac{6}{11}+\frac{5}{11}-\frac{7}{11}=\frac{4}{11}$$

(ii) $P\left(\frac{A}{B}\right)=\frac{P(A\cap B)}{P(B)}=\frac{4/11}{5/11}=\frac{4}{5}$ $\left[\because P(A\cap B)=\frac{4}{11}\right]$

(iii) $P\left(\frac{B}{A}\right)=\frac{P(A\cap B)}{P(A)}=\frac{4/11}{6/11}=\frac{4}{6}=\frac{2}{3}$

Example 2 Evaluate $P(A\cup B)$, if $2P(A)=P(B)=\frac{5}{13}$ and $P\left(\frac{A}{B}\right)=\frac{2}{3}$. **[ISC 2024]**

Sol. Given, $2P(A)=P(B)=\frac{5}{13}$

and $P\left(\frac{A}{B}\right)=\frac{2}{5}$

We know that

$$P\left(\frac{A}{B}\right)=\frac{P(A\cap B)}{P(B)}$$

$$\Rightarrow \frac{2}{5}=\frac{P(A\cap B)}{5/13}$$

$$\Rightarrow P(A\cap B)=\frac{2}{13}$$

$$\therefore P(A\cup B)=P(A)+P(B)-P(A\cap B)$$
$$=P(A)+2P(A)-P(A\cap B)$$
$$=3P(A)-P(A\cap B)$$
$$=\frac{15}{26}-\frac{2}{13}=\frac{11}{26}$$

Hence, $P(A\cup B)=\frac{11}{26}$

Example 3 In a college, 70% students pass in Physics, 75% pass in Mathematics and 10% students fail in both. One student is chosen at random. What is the probability that

(i) he passes in Physics and Mathematics?

(ii) he passes Mathematics given that he passes in Physics?

(iii) he passes in Physics given that he passes in Mathematics? **[ISC 2014]**

Sol. Given, $P(A)$ = Probability of students passed in Physics

$$= \frac{70}{100}$$

$P(B)$ = Probability of students passed in Mathematics

$$= \frac{75}{100}$$

$P(A' \cap B')$ = Probability of students fail in both = 10/100

$\because P(A' \cap B') = P(A \cup B)' = 1 - P(A \cup B)$

$$\Rightarrow P(A \cup B) = 1 - P(A' \cap B') = 1 - \frac{10}{100} = \frac{90}{100}$$

(i) Probability of passing in Physics and Mathematics

$$= P(A \cap B) = P(A) + P(B) - P(A \cup B)$$

$$= \frac{70}{100} + \frac{75}{100} - \frac{90}{100} = \frac{55}{100} = \frac{11}{20}$$

(ii) P (he passes in Mathematics given that he passes in Physics), $P\left(\frac{B}{A}\right) = \frac{P(A \cap B)}{P(A)}$

$$= \frac{55/100}{70/100} = \frac{55}{70} = \frac{11}{14}$$

(iii) P (he passes in Physics given that he passes in Mathematics) $P\left(\frac{A}{B}\right) = \frac{P(A \cap B)}{P(B)}$

$$= \frac{55/100}{75/100} = \frac{55}{75} = \frac{11}{15}$$

Example 4 Given that, the two numbers appearing on throwing two dice are different. Find the probability of the events

(i) the sum of numbers on the dice is 4.

(ii) the sum of numbers on the dice is not 4. **[NCERT]**

Sol. Here, two dice are thrown, so number of outcomes in the sample space, $S = 6 \times 6 = 36$ (equally likely sample events) i.e. $n(S) = 36$.

Let E be the event of getting sum of the numbers on the dice is 4 and F be the event that numbers appearing on the two dice are different.

Then, $E = \{(1, 3), (2, 2), (3, 1)\} \Rightarrow n(E) = 3$

$$\text{and } F = \left\{\begin{matrix} (1, 2), (1, 3), (1, 4), (1, 5), (1, 6), \\ (2, 1), (2, 3), (2, 4), (2, 5), (2, 6), \\ (3, 1), (3, 2), (3, 4), (3, 5), (3, 6), \\ (4, 1), (4, 2), (4, 3), (4, 5), (4, 6), \\ (5, 1), (5, 2), (5, 3), (5, 4), (5, 6), \\ (6, 1), (6, 2), (6, 3), (6, 4), (6, 5) \end{matrix}\right\}$$

$\Rightarrow n(F) = 30$

Here, $E \cap F = \{(1, 3), (3, 1)\} = 2$

$$\therefore \quad P(F) = \frac{\text{Number of favourable outcomes}}{\text{Total number of outcomes}}$$

$$= \frac{30}{36} = \frac{5}{6}$$

$$\text{and } P(E \cap F) = \frac{2}{36} = \frac{1}{18}$$

(i) The probability that the sum of numbers on the dice showing different number is 4,

$$P\left(\frac{E}{F}\right) = \frac{P(E \cap F)}{P(F)} = \frac{1/18}{5/6} = \frac{1}{15}$$

(ii) The probability that the sum of numbers on the dice showing different numbers is not 4,

$$P\left(\frac{E'}{F}\right) = 1 - P\left(\frac{E}{F}\right) = 1 - \frac{1}{15} = \frac{14}{15}$$

Example 5 Consider the experiment of tossing a coin. If the coin shows head, toss it again but if it shows tail, then throw a die. Find the conditional probability of the event that 'the die shows a number greater than 4' given that there is atleast one tail. **[NCERT]**

Sol. The outcomes of the experiment can be represented in the following tree diagram.

The sample space S of the experiment is given as

$$S = \{(H, H), (H, T), (T, 1), (T, 2), (T, 3), (T, 4), (T, 5), (T, 6)\}$$

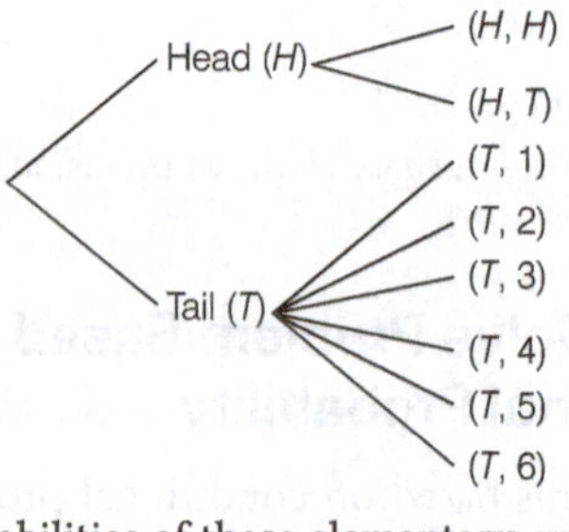

The probabilities of these elementary events are

$$P\{(H, H)\} = \frac{1}{2} \times \frac{1}{2} = \frac{1}{4}, \; P\{(H, T)\} = \frac{1}{2} \times \frac{1}{2} = \frac{1}{4},$$

$$P\{(T, 1)\} = \frac{1}{2} \times \frac{1}{6} = \frac{1}{12}, \; P\{(T, 2)\} = \frac{1}{2} \times \frac{1}{6} = \frac{1}{12},$$

$P\{(T,3)\} = \frac{1}{2} \times \frac{1}{6} = \frac{1}{12}$, $P\{(T,4)\} = \frac{1}{2} \times \frac{1}{6} = \frac{1}{12}$,

$P\{(T,5)\} = \frac{1}{2} \times \frac{1}{6} = \frac{1}{12}$ and $P\{(T,6)\} = \frac{1}{2} \times \frac{1}{6} = \frac{1}{12}$

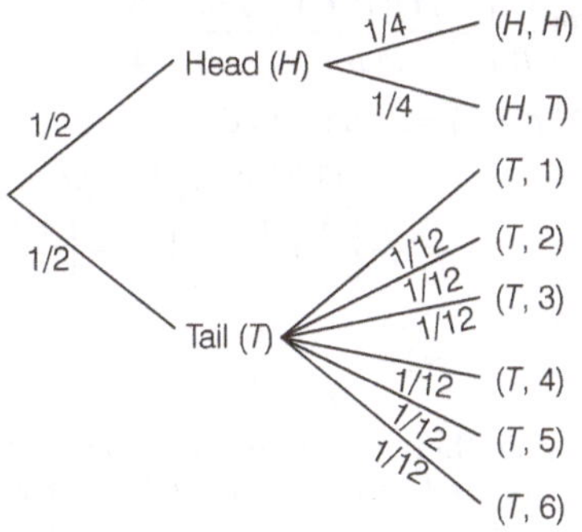

Consider the following events

A = the die shows a number greater than 4

and B = there is atleast one tail.

We have, $A = \{(T,5), (T,6)\}$,

$B = \{(H,T), (T,1), (T,2), (T,3), (T,4), (T,5), (T,6)\}$

and $A \cap B = \{(T,5), (T,6)\}$

$\therefore \quad P(B) = P\{(H,T)\} + P\{(T,1)\} + P\{(T,2)\} + P\{(T,3)\} + P\{(T,4)\} + P\{(T,5)\} + P\{(T,6)\}$

$\Rightarrow \quad P(B) = \frac{1}{4} + \frac{1}{12} + \frac{1}{12} + \frac{1}{12} + \frac{1}{12} + \frac{1}{12} + \frac{1}{12} = \frac{3}{4}$

and $P(A \cap B) = P\{(T,5)\} + P\{(T,6)\} = \frac{1}{12} + \frac{1}{12} = \frac{1}{6}$

$\therefore$ Required probability, $P\left(\frac{A}{B}\right) = \frac{P(A \cap B)}{P(B)} = \frac{1/6}{3/4} = \frac{4}{18} = \frac{2}{9}$

Note Here, the elementary events are not equally likely. So, we cannot say that $P(B) = \frac{7}{8}$, $P(A \cap B) = \frac{2}{8}$.

Topic Practice 1

Very Short Answer Type Questions

2 Marks

1 The probability that atleast one of the two events A and B occurs is 0.6. If A and B occur simultaneously with probability 0.3, then evaluate $P(\overline{A}) + P(\overline{B})$. **[NCERT Exemplar]**

2 If A and B are events such that $P(A) = \frac{1}{2}$, $P(B) = \frac{1}{3}$ and $P(A \cap B) = \frac{1}{4}$, then find

(i) $P\left(\frac{A}{B}\right)$ (ii) $P\left(\frac{B}{A}\right)$. **[ISC 2018]**

3 Three events A, B and C have probabilities $\frac{2}{5}, \frac{1}{3}$ and $\frac{1}{2}$, respectively. If $P(A \cap C) = \frac{1}{5}$ and $P(B \cap C) = \frac{1}{4}$, then find the values of $P(C/B)$ and $P(A' \cap C')$. **[NCERT Exemplar]**

Short Answer Type Questions

4 Marks

4 If a leap year is selected at random, then what is the chance that it will contain 53 Tuesday? **[NCERT]**

5 If $P(A) = 0.8$, $P(B) = 0.5$ and $P\left(\frac{B}{A}\right) = 0.4$, then find the value of $P(A \cup B)$. **[NCERT]**

6 If $P(B) = \frac{3}{5}$, $P(A/B) = \frac{1}{2}$ and $P(A \cup B) = \frac{4}{5}$, then find $P(A \cup B)' + P(A' \cup B)$. **[NCERT Exemplar]**

7 If $P(A) = \frac{2}{5}$, $P(B) = \frac{3}{10}$ and $P(A \cap B) = \frac{1}{5}$, then find $P(A'/B') \cdot P(B'/A')$. **[NCERT Exemplar]**

8 A and B are two events such that $P(A) \neq 0$.

Find $P\left(\frac{B}{A}\right)$, if (i) A is a subset of B. (ii) $A \cap B = \phi$. **[NCERT]**

9 A fair die is rolled. Consider the following events

$A = \{2,4,6\}, B = \{4,5\}$ and $C = \{3,4,5,6\}$

Find (i) $P(A \cup B / C)$ (ii) $P(A \cap B / C)$

10 Two coins are tossed once, if E: tail appears on one coin and F: one coin shows head, then find $P\left(\frac{E}{F}\right)$. **[NCERT]**

11 A die is thrown three times. Events A and B are defined as below

A : 4 on the third throw

B : 6 on the first and 5 on the second throw.

Find the probability of A, given that B has already occurred. **[NCERT]**

12 A die is thrown twice and the sum of the numbers appearing is observed to be 8. What is the conditional probability that the number 5 has appeared atleast once? **[NCERT]**

13 A black and a red die are rolled. Find the conditional probability of obtaining a sum greater than 9, given that the black die resulted in a 5. **[NCERT]**

14 An instructor has a question bank consisting of 300 easy true/false questions, 200 difficult true/false questions, 500 easy multiple choice questions and 400 difficult multiple choice questions. If a question is selected at random from the question bank, then what is the probability that it will be an easy question, given that it is a multiple choice questions? **[NCERT]**

15 In a hostel, 60% of the students read Hindi newspaper, 40% read English newspaper and 20% read both Hindi and English newspapers. A student is selected at random,

(i) find the probability that he/she reads neither Hindi nor English newspaper.

(ii) if he/she reads Hindi newspaper, then find the probability that she reads English newspaper.

(iii) if he/she reads English newspaper, then find the probability he/she reads Hindi newspaper. **[NCERT]**

Hints & Solutions

1. We know that, $A \cup B$ denotes the occurrence of atleast one of A and B and $A \cap B$ denotes the occurrence of both A and B, simultaneously.

Then, $P(A \cup B) = 0.6$ and $P(A \cap B) = 0.3$

$\because P(A \cup B) = P(A) + P(B) - P(A \cap B)$

$\therefore \quad 0.6 = P(A) + P(B) - 0.3 \Rightarrow P(A) + P(B) = 0.9$ [1]

$\Rightarrow \{[1 - P(\bar{A})] + [1 - P(\bar{B})]\} = 0.9$

$[\because P(A) = 1 - P(\bar{A})$ and $P(B) = 1 - P(\bar{B})]$

$\Rightarrow P(\bar{A}) + P(\bar{B}) = 2 - 0.9 = 1.1$ [1]

2. Given, $P(A) = \frac{1}{2}$, $P(B) = \frac{1}{3}$ and $P(A \cap B) = \frac{1}{4}$

(i) $P\left(\frac{A}{B}\right) = \frac{P(A \cap B)}{P(B)} = \frac{1/4}{1/3} = \frac{3}{4}$ [1]

(ii) $P\left(\frac{B}{A}\right) = \frac{P(A \cap B)}{P(A)} = \frac{1/4}{1/2} = \frac{2}{4} = \frac{1}{2}$ [1]

Thus, the required value of $P(A/B)$ and $P(B/A)$ are $\frac{3}{4}$ and $\frac{1}{2}$, respectively.

3. Given, $P(A) = \frac{2}{5}$, $P(B) = \frac{1}{3}$, $P(C) = \frac{1}{2}$, $P(A \cap C) = \frac{1}{5}$ and $P(B \cap C) = \frac{1}{4}$

$\therefore \quad P\left(\frac{C}{B}\right) = \frac{P(B \cap C)}{P(B)} = \frac{1/4}{1/3} = \frac{3}{4}$ [1]

and $P(A' \cap C') = 1 - P(A \cup C)$

$= 1 - [P(A) + P(C) - P(A \cap C)]$

$= 1 - \left(\frac{2}{5} + \frac{1}{2} - \frac{1}{5}\right) = 1 - \left(\frac{4+5-2}{10}\right)$

$= 1 - \frac{7}{10} = \frac{3}{10}$ [1]

4. In a leap year, there are 366 days, i.e. 52 weeks and 2 days extra. There are 52 tuesday and 2 days extra.

For the remaining two days, there are following 7 cases

(i) Sunday and Monday
(ii) Monday and Tuesday
(iii) Tuesday and Wednesday
(iv) Wednesday and Thursday
(v) Thursday and Friday
(vi) Friday and Saturday
(vii) Saturday and Sunday

Out of these seven possibilities, only two are favourable to the events "53 tuesday". [2]

$\therefore$ Total number of cases = 7 and favourable cases = 2

Hence, required probability is 2/7. [2]

5. **Hint** $P(A \cap B) = P(A) \times P(B/A)$

and $P(A \cup B) = P(A) + P(B) - P(A \cap B)$ **[Ans.** 0.98]

6. Here, $P(B) = \frac{3}{5}$, $P(A/B) = \frac{1}{2}$ and $P(A \cup B) = \frac{4}{5}$

Since, $\quad P(A/B) = \frac{P(A \cap B)}{P(B)}$

$\Rightarrow \quad P(A \cap B) = P(A/B) \cdot P(B)$

$= \frac{1}{2} \times \frac{3}{5} = \frac{3}{10}$ [1]

Also, $P(A \cup B) = P(A) + P(B) - P(A \cap B)$

$\Rightarrow \quad P(A) = \frac{4}{5} - \frac{3}{5} + \frac{3}{10} = \frac{1}{2}$

$\therefore \quad P(A \cup B)' = 1 - P(A \cup B) = 1 - \frac{4}{5} = \frac{1}{5}$ [1]

and $P(A' \cup B) = P(A') + P(B) - P(A' \cap B)$ [1]

$= P(A') + P(B) - P(B) + P(A \cap B)$

$= P(A') + P(A \cap B) = \frac{1}{2} + \frac{3}{10} = \frac{4}{5}$

$\Rightarrow \quad P(A \cup B)' + P(A' \cup B) = \frac{1}{5} + \frac{4}{5} = \frac{5}{5} = 1$ [1]

7. **Hint** $P\left(\frac{A'}{B'}\right)\times P\left(\frac{B'}{A'}\right)=\frac{[1-P(A\cup B)]^2}{[1-P(B)][1-P(A)]}$ $\left[\textbf{Ans. } \frac{25}{42}\right]$

8. **Hint** $P(A\cap B)=P(A)$ [**Ans.** (i) 1 (ii) 0]

9. Given events are $A=\{2,4,6\}$, $B=\{4,5\}$ and $C=\{3,4,5,6\}$

Sample space, $S=\{1,2,3,4,5,6\}$

Now, $A\cup B=\{2,4,5,6\}$, $A\cap B=\{4\}$

$(A\cup B)\cap C=\{2,4,5,6\}\cap\{3,4,5,6\}=\{4,5,6\}$

and $A\cap B\cap C=\{4\}\cap\{3,4,5,6\}=\{4\}$ [1]

$\therefore$ $n(S)=6$, $n[((A\cup B)\cap C)]=3$, $n(A\cap B\cap C)=1$

and $n(C)=4$

(i) $P\left(\frac{A\cup B}{C}\right)=\frac{P((A\cup B)\cap C)}{P(C)}=\frac{n((A\cup B)\cap C)/n(S)}{n(C)/n(S)}$

$=\frac{3/6}{4/6}=\frac{3}{4}$ [1½]

(ii) $P\left(\frac{A\cap B}{C}\right)=\frac{P(A\cap B\cap C)}{P(C)}$

$=\frac{n(A\cap B\cap C)/n(S)}{n(C)/n(S)}$

$=\frac{1/6}{4/6}=\frac{1}{4}$ [1½]

10. **Hint** $P(E)=\frac{2}{4}$, $P(F)=\frac{2}{4}$, $P(E\cap F)=\frac{2}{4}$

Now, $P\left(\frac{E}{F}\right)=\frac{P(E\cap F)}{P(F)}$ [**Ans.** 1]

11. **Hint** $P(B)=\frac{6}{216}$, $P(A\cap B)=\frac{1}{216}$

Now, $P\left(\frac{A}{B}\right)=\frac{P(A\cap B)}{P(B)}$ $\left[\textbf{Ans. } \frac{1}{6}\right]$

12. **Hint** Let E : sum of numbers is 8

and F : number 5 appear at least once

Then, $P(E)=\frac{5}{36}$, $P(F)=\frac{11}{36}$ and $P(E\cap F)=\frac{2}{36}$

Required probability $=P\left(\frac{F}{E}\right)$ $\left[\textbf{Ans. } \frac{2}{5}\right]$

13. **Hint** A = sum greater than 9

and B = black die resulted 5

$\therefore$ $P(A)=\frac{6}{36}$, $P(B)=\frac{6}{36}$, $P(A\cap B)=\frac{2}{36}$,

Now, $P\left(\frac{A}{B}\right)=\frac{P(A\cap B)}{P(B)}$ $\left[\textbf{Ans. } \frac{1}{3}\right]$

14. Total number of questions,

$n(S)=300+200+500+400=1400$

Let E be the event that question is easy and F be the event that question is a multiple choice.

Then, $n(E)=500+300=800$ [1]

$\therefore$ $P(E)=\frac{\text{Number of easy questions}}{\text{Total number of questions}}$

$=\frac{n(E)}{n(S)}=\frac{800}{1400}=\frac{4}{7}$ [1]

Also, $n(F)=500+400=900$

$\therefore$ $P(F)=\frac{\text{Number of multiple choice questions}}{\text{Total number of questions}}$

$=\frac{n(F)}{n(S)}=\frac{900}{1400}=\frac{9}{14}$ [1/2]

and $P(E\cap F)$

$=\frac{\text{Total number of easy multiple choice questions}}{\text{Total number of questions}}$

$=\frac{500}{1400}=\frac{5}{14}$ [1/2]

$\therefore$ $P\left(\frac{E}{F}\right)=\frac{P(E\cap F)}{P(F)}$

$=\frac{5/14}{9/14}=\frac{5}{9}$ [1]

15. Let H = student reading Hindi newspaper

and E = student reading English newspaper

Let $n(S)=100$, then $n(H)=60$,

$n(E)=40$ and $n(H\cap E)=20$

$\therefore P(H)=\frac{n(H)}{n(S)}=\frac{60}{100}=\frac{3}{5}$

$P(E)=\frac{n(E)}{n(S)}=\frac{40}{100}=\frac{2}{5}$

and $P(H\cap E)=\frac{n(H\cap E)}{n(S)}=\frac{20}{100}=\frac{1}{5}$ [1]

(i) Required probability = P(student reads neither Hindi nor English newspaper)

$=P(H'\cap E')=P(H\cup E)'=1-P(H\cup E)$

$=1-[P(H)+P(E)-P(H\cap E)]$

$=1-\left[\frac{3}{5}+\frac{2}{5}-\frac{1}{5}\right]=1-\frac{4}{5}=\frac{1}{5}$ [1]

(ii) Required probability = P(student reads English newspaper, if he/she reads Hindi newspaper)

$\therefore$ $P\left(\frac{E}{H}\right)=\frac{P(E\cap H)}{P(H)}=\frac{1/5}{3/5}=\frac{1}{3}$ [1]

(iii) Required probability = P(student reads Hindi newspaper when it is given that he/she reads English newspaper)

$\therefore$ $P\left(\frac{H}{E}\right)=\frac{P(H\cap E)}{P(E)}=\frac{1/5}{2/5}=\frac{1}{2}$ [1]

TOPIC 02 | Multiplication Theorem on Probability and Independent & Dependent Events

Multiplication Theorem

Let A and B be two events associated with a random experiment, then

$$P(A \cap B) = \begin{cases} P(A) \cdot P(B/A), \text{ where } P(A) \neq 0 \\ P(B) \cdot P(A/B), \text{ where } P(B) \neq 0 \end{cases}$$

Here, $A \cap B$ denotes the simultaneous occurrence of the events A and B. The event $A \cap B$ is also written as AB.

The above result is known as the **multiplication rule of probability.**

Example 1 Find the probability of drawing a diamond card in each of the two consecutive draws from a well-shuffled pack of cards, if the card drawn is not replaced after the first draw.

Sol. Let A be the event of drawing a diamond card in the first draw and B be the event of drawing a diamond card in the second draw. Then, $P(A) = \frac{13}{52} = \frac{1}{4}$

After drawing a diamond card in first draw, 51 cards are left out of which 12 cards are diamond cards.

$\therefore$ $P(B/A)$ = Probability of drawing a diamond card in second draw when a diamond card has already been drawn in first draw

$$\Rightarrow \quad P\left(\frac{B}{A}\right) = \frac{12}{51} = \frac{4}{17}$$

Now, required probability,

$$P(A \cap B) = P(A) \cdot P\left(\frac{B}{A}\right) = \frac{1}{4} \times \frac{4}{17} = \frac{1}{17}$$

Example 2 A bag contains 19 tickets, numbered from 1 to 19. A ticket is drawn and then another ticket is drawn without replacement. Find the probability that both tickets will show even numbers.

Sol. Let A be the event of drawing an even numbered ticket in first draw and B be the event of drawing an even numbered ticket in the second draw. Then,

Required probability $= P(A \cap B) = P(A) \cdot P(B/A)$ ...(i)

Since, there are 19 tickets numbered 1 to 19 in the bag, out of which 9 are even numbered *viz.* 2, 4, 6, 8, 10, 12, 14, 16 and 18.

Therefore, $P(A) = \frac{9}{19}$

Since, the ticket drawn in the first draw is not replaced, therefore second ticket drawn is from the remaining 18 tickets, out of which 8 are even numbered.

$$\therefore \quad P\left(\frac{B}{A}\right) = \frac{8}{18} = \frac{4}{9}$$

Hence, required probability $= P(A \cap B)$

$= P(A) \cdot P(B/A)$ [from Eq. (i)]

$= \frac{9}{19} \times \frac{4}{9} = \frac{4}{19}$

Extension of Multiplication Theorem

(i) If A, B and C are three events associated with a random experiment, then

$$P(A \cap B \cap C) = P(A) \cdot P\left(\frac{B}{A}\right) \cdot P\left(\frac{C}{A \cap B}\right)$$

(ii) If $A_1, A_2, \ldots, A_n$ are n events associated with a random experiment, then

$$P(A_1 \cap A_2 \cap \ldots \cap A_n) = P(A_1) P\left(\frac{A_2}{A_1}\right) \ldots P\left(\frac{A_n}{A_1 \cap A_2 \cap \ldots \cap A_{n-1}}\right)$$

Example 3 Three cards are drawn successively without replacement from a pack of 52 well-shuffled cards. What is the probability that first two cards are king and the third card drawn is an ace?

Sol. There are 52 cards in a pack.

$\therefore \quad n(S) = 52$

Let A = event that the card drawn is king and B = event that the card drawn is an ace. Now, $P(A) = 4/52$

$P\left(\frac{A}{A}\right)$ = Probability of drawing second king when one king has already been drawn $= 3/51$

[$\because$ remaining cards are $(52-1) = 51$]

$P(B/AA)$ = Probability of drawing third card to be an ace when two kings have already been drawn $= \frac{4}{50}$

Now, probability of getting first two cards are king and third card is an ace $= P(A \cap A \cap B)$

$= P(A) \cdot P\left(\frac{A}{A}\right) \cdot P\left(\frac{B}{AA}\right)$

[by multiplication theorem]

$= \frac{4}{52} \times \frac{3}{51} \times \frac{4}{50}$

$= \frac{2}{5525}$

Example 4 A bag contains 5 white, 7 red and 8 black balls. If four balls are drawn one by one without replacement, then find the probability of getting all white balls.

Sol. Let A, B, C and D denote events of getting a white ball in first, second, third and fourth draw, respectively.

Then, required probability $= P(A \cap B \cap C \cap D)$

$= P(A)\,P(B/A)\,P(C/A \cap B)\,P(D/A \cap B \cap C)$ ...(i)

Now, $P(A)$ = Probability of drawing a white ball in first draw

$= \frac{5}{20} = \frac{1}{4}$

When a white ball is drawn in the first draw, there are 19 balls left in the bag, out of which 4 are white.

$\therefore \quad P(B/A) = \frac{4}{19}$

Since, the ball drawn is not replaced, therefore after drawing a white ball in second draw, there are 18 balls left in the bag, out of which 3 are white.

$\therefore \quad P(C/A \cap B) = \frac{3}{18} = \frac{1}{6}$

After drawing a white ball in third draw, there are 17 balls left in the bag, out of which 2 are white.

$\therefore \quad P(D/A \cap B \cap C) = \frac{2}{17}$

Hence, required probability

$= P(A \cap B \cap C \cap D)$

$= P(A) \cdot P(B/A)\,P(C/A \cap B)\,P(D/A \cap B \cap C)$

$= \frac{1}{4} \times \frac{4}{19} \times \frac{1}{6} \times \frac{2}{17} = \frac{1}{969}$

Example 5 Two balls are drawn from an urn containing 3 white, 5 red and 2 black balls, one by one without replacement. What is the probability that atleast one ball is red? **[ISC 2019]**

Sol. Let A be the event of not getting a red ball in first draw and B be the event of not getting a red ball in secod draw. Then,

Required probability = Probability that at least one ball is red.

$= 1 -$ Probability of none is red

$= 1 - P(A \text{ and } B) = 1 - P(A \cap B)$

$= 1 - P(A)P(B/A)$ ...(i)

Now, $P(A)$ = Probability of not getting a red ball in first draw

$\Rightarrow P(A)$ = Probability of getting an other colour (white or black) ball in first draw

$\Rightarrow P(A) = \frac{5}{10} = \frac{1}{2}$

When another colour ball is drawn in first draw there are 4 other colour (white or black) balls and 5 red balls, out of which one other colour ball can be drawn in ${}^4C_1$ ways.

$\therefore \quad P\left(\frac{B}{A}\right) = \frac{4}{9}$

Substituting these values in Eq. (i), we get

Required probability $= 1 - P(A) \cdot P\left(\frac{B}{A}\right)$

$= 1 - \frac{1}{2} \times \frac{4}{9} = 1 - \frac{2}{9} = \frac{7}{9}$

Independent Events

Two events A and B are said to be independent, if the occurrence or non-occurrence of one event does not affect the occurrence or non-occurrence of another event. Two events E and F are said to be **independent**, if

$$P\left(\frac{F}{E}\right) = P(F), \text{ provided } P(E) \neq 0$$

and $$P\left(\frac{E}{F}\right) = P(E), \text{ provided } P(F) \neq 0.$$

In other words, let E and F be two events associated with the same random experiment, then E and F are said to be **independent**, if $P(E \cap F) = P(E) \cdot P(F)$.

Some Important Results

1. Two events E and F are said to be dependent, if they are not independent,

   i.e. $\quad P(E \cap F) \neq P(E) \cdot P(F)$

2. Two experiments are said to be independent, if for every pair of events E and F, where E is associated with the first experiment and F with the second experiment, the probability of the simultaneous occurrence of the events E and F is the product of $P(E)$ and $P(F)$ calculated separately on the basis of two experiments,

   i.e. $\quad P(E \cap F) = P(E) \cdot P(F)$

3. **Difference between independent events and mutually exclusive events**

   (i) Term independent is defined in terms of probability of events whereas mutually exclusive is defined in terms of subset of sample space.

   (ii) Mutually exclusive events never have an outcome common, but independent events may have common outcome. In other words, two independent events having non-zero probabilities of occurrence cannot be mutually exclusive and conversely i.e. two mutually exclusive events having non-zero probabilities of occurrence cannot be independent.

4. Three events A, B and C are said to be mutually independent, if

$$P(A \cap B) = P(A) \cdot P(B)$$
$$P(A \cap C) = P(A) \cdot P(C)$$
$$P(B \cap C) = P(B) \cdot P(C)$$
and $$P(A \cap B \cap C) = P(A) \cdot P(B) \cdot P(C)$$

If atleast one of the above is not true for three given events, then events are not independent.
i.e. dependent.

Properties of Independent Events

If A and B are independent events, then

(i) A and B' are also independent events.
(ii) A' and B are also independent events.
(iii) A' and B' are also independent events.

Example 6 Let A and B be two events such that

$$P(A) = \frac{1}{2}, P(B) = p \text{ and } P(A \cup B) = \frac{3}{5}$$

Find 'p' if A and B are independent events. **[ISC 2020]**

Sol. Given, $P(A) = \frac{1}{2}$, $P(B) = p$ and $P(A \cup B) = \frac{3}{5}$

A and B are independent events.

$\therefore \quad P(A \cap B) = P(A) \times P(B) = \frac{1}{2} \times p = \frac{p}{2}$

We know that,

$$P(A \cup B) = P(A) + P(B) - P(A \cap B)$$
$$\Rightarrow \quad \frac{3}{5} = \frac{1}{2} + p - \frac{p}{2}$$
$$\Rightarrow \quad \frac{p}{2} = \frac{3}{5} - \frac{1}{2}$$
$$\Rightarrow \quad \frac{p}{2} = \frac{1}{10}$$
$$\Rightarrow \quad p = \frac{1}{5}$$

Example 7 The probability of the event A occurring is $\frac{1}{3}$ and of the event B occurring is $\frac{1}{2}$. If A and B are independent events, then find the probability of neither A nor B occurring. **[ISC 2023]**

Sol. Given, $P(A) = \frac{1}{3}$ and $P(B) = \frac{1}{2}$

where A and B are independent events.

$\therefore P(A \cap B) = P(A) \cdot P(B) = \frac{1}{3} \times \frac{1}{2} = \frac{1}{6}$

$\therefore P(A \cup B)' = 1 - P(A \cup B)$

$$= 1 - (P(A) + P(B) - P(A \cap B))$$
$$= 1 - \frac{1}{3} - \frac{1}{2} + \frac{1}{6} = \frac{6 - 2 - 3 + 1}{6} = \frac{2}{6} = \frac{1}{3}$$

Example 8 A problem in Mathematics is given to three students A, B and C. Their chances of solving the problem are $\frac{1}{2}, \frac{1}{3}$ and $\frac{1}{4}$ respectively. Find the probability that

(a) exactly two students will solve the problem.
(b) atleast two of them will solve the problem. **[ISC 2023]**

Sol. Consider the events

A = Problem solved by A
B = Problem solved by B
C = Problem solved by C

Given, $P(A) = \frac{1}{2}$, $P(B) = \frac{1}{3}$, $P(C) = \frac{1}{4}$

and $P(\bar{A}) = \frac{1}{2}$, $P(\bar{B}) = \frac{2}{3}$, $P(\bar{C}) = \frac{3}{4}$

(a) P(exactly two students will solve the problem)

$$= P(AB\bar{C}) + P(A\bar{B}C) + P(\bar{A}BC)$$
$$= P(A) \times P(B) \times P(\bar{C}) + P(A) \times P(\bar{B}) \times P(C) + P(\bar{A}) \times P(B) \times P(C)$$
$$= \frac{1}{2} \times \frac{1}{3} \times \frac{3}{4} + \frac{1}{2} \times \frac{2}{3} \times \frac{1}{4} + \frac{1}{2} \times \frac{1}{3} \times \frac{1}{4}$$
$$= \frac{3 + 2 + 1}{24} = \frac{6}{24} = \frac{1}{4}$$

(b) P (atleast two of them will solve the problem)

$$= P(AB\bar{C}) + P(A\bar{B}C) + P(\bar{A}BC) + P(ABC)$$
$$= P(A) \times P(B) \times P(\bar{C}) + P(A) \times P(\bar{B}) \times P(C) + P(\bar{A}) \times P(B) \times P(C) + P(A) \times P(B) \times P(C)$$
$$= \frac{1}{2} \times \frac{1}{3} \times \frac{3}{4} + \frac{1}{2} \times \frac{2}{3} \times \frac{1}{4} + \frac{1}{2} \times \frac{1}{3} \times \frac{1}{4} + \frac{1}{2} \times \frac{1}{3} \times \frac{1}{4}$$
$$= \frac{3 + 2 + 1 + 1}{24} = \frac{7}{24}$$

Example 9 Teena is practising for an upcoming Rifle Shooting tournament. The probability of her shooting the target in the 1st, 2nd, 3rd and 4th shots are 0.4, 0.3, 0.2 and 0.1 respectively. Find the probability of atleast one shot of Teena hitting the target. **[ISC 2024]**

Sol. Given, probability of her shooting the target in

$$P(\text{1st shot}) = 0.4$$
$$P(\text{2nd shot}) = 0.3$$
$$P(\text{3rd shot}) = 0.2$$
and $$P(\text{4th shot}) = 0.1$$

∴ The probability of atleast one shot of Teena hit the target

$= 1 -$ Probability of none of the shot hitting the target

$= 1 - [(1-0.4)(1-0.3)(1-0.2)(1-0.1)]$

$= 1 - (0.6 \times 0.7 \times 0.8 \times 0.9) = 1 - 0.3024 = 0.6976$

Example 10 Three persons *A*, *B* and *C* shoot to hit a target. Their probabilities of hitting the target $\frac{5}{6}, \frac{4}{5}$ and $\frac{3}{4}$, respectively. Find the probability that

(i) Exactly two persons hit the target.

(ii) At least one person hits the target. **[ISC 2020]**

Sol. Given, $P(A) = \frac{5}{6}$

$P(B) = 4/5$

$P(C) = 3/4$

$P(\overline{A}) = 1 - P(A) = 1 - \frac{5}{6} = \frac{1}{6}$

$P(\overline{B}) = 1 - P(B) = 1 - \frac{4}{5} = \frac{1}{5}$

$P(\overline{C}) = 1 - P(C) = 1 - \frac{3}{4} = \frac{1}{4}$

(i) Probability of exactly two persons hitting the target

$= P(AB\overline{C}) + P(A\overline{B}C) + P(\overline{A}BC)$

$= P(A) \times P(B) \times P(\overline{C}) + P(A) \times P(\overline{B}) \times P(C) + P(\overline{A}) \times P(B) \times P(C)$

$= \frac{5}{6} \times \frac{4}{5} \times \frac{1}{4} + \frac{5}{6} \times \frac{1}{5} \times \frac{3}{4} + \frac{1}{6} \times \frac{4}{5} \times \frac{3}{4}$

$= \frac{20 + 15 + 12}{120} = \frac{47}{120}$

(ii) Probability of atleast one person hit the target

$= 1 -$ Probability of none hit the target

$= 1 - P(\overline{A}\overline{B}\overline{C})$

$= 1 - P(\overline{A}) \times P(\overline{B}) \times P(\overline{C})$

$= 1 - \frac{1}{6} \times \frac{1}{5} \times \frac{1}{4}$

$= 1 - \frac{1}{120} = \frac{119}{120}$

Example 11 Two horses are considered for a race. The probability of selection of the first horse is 1/4 and that of the second is 1/3. What is the probability that

(i) both of them will be selected?

(ii) only one of them will be selected?

(iii) none of them will be selected? **[ISC 2009]**

Sol. Let *A* : Selection of I Horse

B : Selection of II Horse [given]

$\therefore \quad P(A) = P(\text{I Horse selection}) = \frac{1}{4}$

and $P(B) = P(\text{II Horse selection}) = \frac{1}{3}$

(i) *P* (both of them will be selected)

$= P(AB) = P(A)\,P(B)$

[since, *A* and *B* are independent events]

$= \frac{1}{4} \times \frac{1}{3} = \frac{1}{12}$

(ii) *P* (only one of them will be selected)

$= P(A\overline{B}) + P(\overline{A}B)$

$= P(A)\,P(\overline{B}) + P(\overline{A})\,P(B)$

[If *A* and *B* independent, then *A* and $\overline{B}$, $\overline{A}$ and *B* are independent]

$= \frac{1}{4} \times \left(1 - \frac{1}{3}\right) + \left(1 - \frac{1}{4}\right) \times \frac{1}{3}$

$= \frac{1}{4} \times \frac{2}{3} + \frac{3}{4} \times \frac{1}{3} = \frac{1}{6} + \frac{1}{4} = \frac{2+3}{12} = \frac{5}{12}$

(iii) *P* (None of them will be selected)

$= P(\overline{AB}) = P(\overline{A})\,P(\overline{B})$

$= \left(1 - \frac{1}{4}\right)\left(1 - \frac{1}{3}\right) = \frac{3}{4} \times \frac{2}{3} = \frac{1}{2}$

Example 12 There are two bags. One bag contains six green and three red balls. The second bag contains five green and four red balls. One ball is transferred from the first bag to the second bag. Then, one ball is drawn from the second bag. Find the probability that it is a red ball. **[ISC 2010]**

Sol. **Bag I** 6 green and 3 red balls

Bag II 5 green and 4 red balls

***Case* I** When one green ball is transferred from bag I to bag II,

Then, its probability, $P_1 = \frac{6}{6+3} = \frac{6}{9} = \frac{2}{3}$

Now, bag II contains 6 green and 4 red balls.

Probability that a red ball drawn from bag II,

Then its probability, $P_2 = \frac{4}{6+4} = \frac{4}{10} = \frac{2}{5}$

Probability of both the events occurring together

$$= P_1 P_2 = \frac{2}{3} \times \frac{2}{5} = \frac{4}{15} \quad \text{...(i)}$$

[multiplication theorem for independent events]

***Case* II** When one red ball is transferred from bag I to bag II $P_3 = \frac{3}{6+3} = \frac{3}{9} = \frac{1}{3}$

Now, bag II contains 5 green and 5 red balls.

Probability that a red ball is drawn from bag II,

$$P_4 = \frac{5}{5+5} = \frac{5}{10} = \frac{1}{2}$$

Probability of both the events occurring together

$$= P_3P_4 = \frac{1}{3} \times \frac{1}{2} = \frac{1}{6} \quad \text{...(ii)}$$

On adding Eqs. (i) and (ii), we get the required probability

$$P_1P_2 + P_3P_4 = \frac{4}{15} + \frac{1}{6} = \frac{8+5}{30} = \frac{13}{30}$$

Dependent Events

Two events are said to be **dependent**, if the occurrence or non-occurrence of the one event in any trial affects the probability of the other subsequent trials. If the occurrence of one event affects the happening of the other events, then they are said to be **dependent events**.

Example 13 A committee of 4 persons has to be chosen from 8 boys and 6 girls, consisting of atleast one girl. Find the probability that the committee consists of more girls than boys. **[ISC 2016]**

Sol. Given, number of boys = 8

and number of girls = 6

We have to make a committee of 4 persons.

If the committee consists of more girls than boys, then

Number of ways this can be done

$$= {}^8C_0 \times {}^6C_4 + {}^8C_1 \times {}^6C_3$$

$$= 1 \times \frac{6!}{4!\,2!} + 8 \times \frac{6!}{3!\,3!}$$

$$= \frac{6 \times 5}{2} + \frac{8 \times 6 \times 5 \times 4}{3 \times 2}$$

$$= 15 + 160 = 175$$

$\therefore$ Total number of ways

$$= {}^8C_0 \times {}^6C_4 + {}^8C_1 \times {}^6C_3 + {}^8C_2 \times {}^6C_2 + {}^8C_3 \times {}^6C_1$$

$$= 15 + 8 \times 20 + 28 \times 15 + 56 \times 6$$

$$= 15 + 160 + 420 + 336 = 931$$

Hence, required probability

$$= \frac{175}{931} = 0.187$$

Example 14 Bag A contains three red and four white balls; bag B contains two red and three white balls. If one ball is drawn from bag A and two balls from bag B, find the probability that

(i) one ball is red and two balls are white.

(ii) all the three balls are of the same colour. **[ISC 2013]**

Sol. **Bag** A : Three red balls and four white balls

Bag B : Two red balls and three white balls

(i) P (one red ball and two white balls)

$= P$ (1 white ball from bag A and 1 white and 1 red ball from bag B) $+ P$ (1 red ball from bag A and 2 white balls from Bag B)

$$= \frac{{}^4C_1}{{}^7C_1} \times \frac{{}^2C_1 \times {}^3C_1}{{}^5C_2} + \frac{{}^3C_1}{{}^7C_1} \times \frac{{}^3C_2}{{}^5C_2}$$

$$= \frac{4}{7} \times \frac{2 \times 3 \times 2}{5 \times 4} + \frac{3}{7} \times \frac{3 \times 2}{5 \times 4}$$

$$= \frac{12}{35} + \frac{9}{70} = \frac{24+9}{70} = \frac{33}{70}$$

(ii) P (all balls are of same colour)

$= P$ (all white balls) $+ P$ (all red balls)

$= P$ (1 white ball from bag A and 2 white balls from bag B) $+ P$ (1 red ball from bag A and 2 red balls from bag B).

$$= \frac{{}^4C_1}{{}^7C_1} \times \frac{{}^3C_2}{{}^5C_2} + \frac{{}^3C_1}{{}^7C_1} \times \frac{{}^2C_2}{{}^5C_2}$$

$$= \frac{4}{7} \times \frac{3}{5 \times 2} + \frac{3}{7} \times \frac{1 \times 2}{5 \times 4} = \frac{6}{35} + \frac{3}{70}$$

$$= \frac{12+3}{70} = \frac{15}{70} = \frac{3}{14}$$

Topic Practice 2

Very Short Answer Type Questions

2 Marks

1 Two cards are drawn at random and without replacement from a pack of 52 playing cards. Find the probability that both the cards are black. **[NCERT]**

2 An urn contains 10 black and 5 white balls. Two balls are drawn from the urn one after the other without replacement. What is the probability that both drawn balls are black?

3 A fair coin and an unbiased die are tossed. Let A be the event 'head appears on the coin' and B be the event '3 on the die'. Check whether A and B are independent events or not. **[NCERT]**

4 Prove that if E and F are independent events, then the events E and F' are also independent.

5 A die marked 1, 2, 3 in red and 4, 5, 6 in green is tossed. Let A be the event, 'number is odd' and B be the event, 'number is green'. Are A and B independent? **[NCERT]**

6 In a race, the probabilities of A and B winning the race are $\frac{1}{3}$ and $\frac{1}{6}$ respectively. Find the probability of neither of them winning the race. **[ISC 2018]**

7 Kamal and Monica appear for an interview for two vacancies. The probability of Kamal's selection is $1/3$ and that of Monica's selection is $1/5$. Find the probability that only one of them will be selected. **[ISC 2007]**

8 The probability of A, B and C solving a problem are $\frac{1}{3}, \frac{2}{7}$ and $\frac{3}{8}$, respectively. If all try and solve the problem simultaneously, find the probability that only one of them will solve it. **[ISC 2006]**

9 Akhil and Vijay appear for an interview for two vacancies. The probability of Akhil's selection is $\frac{1}{4}$ and Vijay's selection is $\frac{2}{3}$. Find the probability that only one of them will be selected. **[ISC 2010]**

10 There are 3 urns A, B and C. Urn A contains 4 red balls and 3 black balls. Urn B contains 5 red balls and 4 black balls. Urn C contains 4 red balls and 4 black balls. One ball is drawn from each of these urns. What is the probability that the 3 balls drawn consist of 2 red balls and 1 black ball? **[ISC 2008]**

11 A candidate is selected for interview of management trainees in 3 companies. For the first company, there are 12 candidates for the second there are 15 candidates and for the third, there are 10 candidates. Find the probability that he is selected by atleast one of the companies. **[ISC 2005]**

Short Answer Type Questions

4 Marks

12 If A and B are independent events, then prove that

(i) $P(A) = P(A \cap B) + P(A \cap \bar{B})$.

(ii) $P(A \cup B) = P(A \cap B) + P(A \cap \bar{B}) + P(\bar{A} \cap B)$.

[NCERT Exemplar]

13 Given two independent events A and B such that $P(A) = 0.3$ and $P(B) = 0.6$. Find

(i) $P(A \text{ and not } B)$ (ii) $P(A \text{ or } B)$.

14 If A and B are two independent events, then prove that the probability of occurrence of atleast one of A and B is given by $1 - P(A') \cdot P(B')$.

15 If A and B are two events such that $P(A) = \frac{1}{4}$, $P(B) = \frac{1}{2}$ and $P(A \cap B) = \frac{1}{8}$, then find P (not A and not B). **[NCERT]**

16 Two balls are drawn at random with replacement from a box containing 10 black and 8 red balls. Find the probability that

(i) both balls are red.

(ii) first ball is black and second ball is red.

[NCERT]

17 Probability of solving specific problem independently by A and B are $1/2$ and $1/3$, respectively. If both try to solve the problem independently, then find the probability that

(i) the problem is solved.

(ii) exactly one of them solves the problem.

[NCERT]

18 Bag A contains 5 white and 4 black balls, any bag B contains 7 white and 6 black balls. One ball is drawn from the bag A and without noticing its colour, is put in the bag B. If the ball is drawn from bag B, then find the probability that it is black in colour. **[ISC 2009]**

19 A word consists of 9 different alphabets, in which there are 4 consonants and 5 vowels. Three alphabets are chosen at random. What is the probability that more than one vowel will be selected? **[ISC 2011]**

Long Answer Type Questions

6 Marks

20 Two dice are thrown together and the total score is noted. The events E, F and G are 'a total of 4', 'a total of 9 or more' and 'a total divisible by 5', respectively. Calculate $P(E)$, $P(F)$ and $P(G)$ and decide which pairs of events, if any are independent? **[NCERT Exemplar]**

21 If A and B are two independent events such that $P(\overline{A}\cap B)=\frac{2}{15}$ and $P(A\cap\overline{B})=\frac{1}{6}$, then find $P(A)$ and $P(B)$.

22 A bag contains 5 white and 4 black balls and another bag contains 7 white and 9 black balls. A ball is drawn from the first bag and two balls drawn from the second bag. What is the probability of drawing one white and two black balls? **[ISC 2014]**

Hints & Solutions

1. There are 26 black cards in a pack of 52 cards.

Required probability $= P(E \text{ and } F) = P(E)\cdot P\left(\frac{F}{E}\right)$

where, E : First card drawn is black and F : Second card drawn is black.

$$P(E)=\frac{\text{Number of favourable outcomes}}{\text{Total number of outcomes}}=\frac{26}{52}=\frac{1}{2}$$

$P\left(\frac{F}{E}\right)=\frac{25}{51}$ [after drawing 1 black card, there will be 25 black cards left] [1]

$\therefore$ Required probability,

$$P(E\cap F)=P(E)\cdot P\left(\frac{F}{E}\right)=\frac{1}{2}\times\frac{25}{51}=\frac{25}{102}$$ [1]

2. **Hint** $P(BB)=\frac{10}{15}\times\frac{9}{14}$ $\left[\textbf{Ans. } \frac{3}{7}\right]$

3. If a fair coin and an unbiased die are tossed, then the sample space S is given by

$$S=\begin{Bmatrix}(H,1),(H,2),(H,3),(H,4),(H,5),(H,6),\\(T,1),(T,2),(T,3),(T,4),(T,5),(T,6)\end{Bmatrix}$$

$\Rightarrow n(S)=12$

Also, A : Head appears on the coin and B : 3 appears on die.

$\Rightarrow$ $A=$ Event having head on coin

$=\{(H,1),(H,2),(H,3),(H,4),(H,5),(H,6)\}$

$B=$ Event having 3 on die

$=\{(H,3),(T,3)\}$; $A\cap B=\{(H,3)\}$

$\therefore n(A)=6, n(B)=2, n(A\cap B)=1$ [1]

Hence, $P(A)=\frac{n(A)}{n(S)}=\frac{6}{12}=\frac{1}{2}$, $P(B)=\frac{n(B)}{n(S)}=\frac{2}{12}=\frac{1}{6}$

and $P(A\cap B)=\frac{n(A\cap B)}{n(S)}=\frac{1}{12}$

Now, $P(A)\times P(B)=\frac{1}{2}\times\frac{1}{6}=\frac{1}{12}$

$=P(A\cap B)$

Hence, A and B are independent events. [1]

4. Given, E and F are independent events, therefore

$\Rightarrow$ $P(E\cap F)=P(E)\,P(F)$ ...(i)

Now, we have

$P(E\cap F')+P(E\cap F)=P(E)$

$\Rightarrow P(E\cap F')=P(E)-P(E\cap F)$ [1]

$\Rightarrow P(E\cap F')=P(E)-P(E)P(F)$ [using Eq. (i)]

$\Rightarrow$ $P(E\cap F')=P(E)[1-P(F)]$

$\Rightarrow$ $P(E\cap F')=P(E)P(F')$

$\therefore$ E and F' are also independent events.

Hence proved. [1]

5. When a die is thrown, then sample space,

$S=\{1,2,3,4,5,6\}\Rightarrow n(S)=6$

Also, A : Number is odd and B : Number is green

$\therefore$ $A=\{1,3,5\}$, $B=\{4,5,6\}$ and $A\cap B=\{5\}$

$\Rightarrow n(A)=3, n(B)=3, n(A\cap B)=1$

Now, $P(A)=\frac{n(A)}{n(S)}=\frac{3}{6}=\frac{1}{2}$, $P(B)=\frac{n(B)}{n(S)}=\frac{3}{6}=\frac{1}{2}$,

$P(A\cap B)=\frac{n(A\cap B)}{n(S)}=\frac{1}{6}$ [1]

and $P(A)\times P(B)=\frac{1}{2}\times\frac{1}{2}=\frac{1}{4}\neq\frac{1}{6}=P(A\cap B)$

$\therefore$ $P(A\cap B)\neq P(A)\times P(B)$

Thus, A and B are not independent events. [1]

6. Given, $P(A)=\frac{1}{3}$, $P(B)=\frac{1}{6}$

$\therefore$ $P(A')=1-\frac{1}{3}=\frac{2}{3}$ and $P(B')=1-\frac{1}{6}=\frac{5}{6}$ [1]

Thus, required probability $=P(A')\times P(B')$

$=\frac{2}{3}\times\frac{5}{6}=\frac{5}{9}$ [1]

7. Let $E_1=$ Kamal's selection after appearing for an interview and $E_2=$ Monica's selection after appearing for an interview

Then, $P(E_1)=\frac{1}{3}$ and $P(E_2)=\frac{1}{5}$ [given] [1/2]

P (either Kamal's or Monica's selection)

$=P(E_1\,\overline{E}_2)+P(\overline{E}_1\,E_2)$

$=P(E_1)\,P(\overline{E}_2)+P(\overline{E}_1)\,P(E_2)$ [1/2]

[since, E_1 and E_2 are independent events]

$=\frac{1}{3}\times\left(1-\frac{1}{5}\right)+\left(1-\frac{1}{3}\right)\times\frac{1}{5}$

$=\frac{1}{3}\times\frac{4}{5}+\frac{2}{3}\times\frac{1}{5}=\frac{4}{15}+\frac{2}{15}=\frac{6}{15}=\frac{2}{5}$ [1]

8. Let A : Problem is solved by A

B : Problem is solved by B

C : Problem is solved by C

Given, $P(A)=\frac{1}{3}$, $P(B)=\frac{2}{7}$ and $P(C)=\frac{3}{8}$

P (only one of A, B and C solve the problem)

$=P(\overline{A}\overline{B}C)+P(\overline{A}B\overline{C})+P(A\overline{B}\overline{C})$

$=P(\overline{A})P(\overline{B})P(C)+P(\overline{A})P(B)P(\overline{C})$

$$+P(A)P(\bar{B})P(\bar{C})$$ [1]

[since, A, B and C are independent events]

$$=\left(1-\frac{1}{3}\right)\left(1-\frac{2}{7}\right)\times\frac{3}{8}+\left(1-\frac{1}{3}\right)\times\frac{2}{7}$$

$$\times\left(1-\frac{3}{8}\right)+\frac{1}{3}\times\left(1-\frac{2}{7}\right)\left(1-\frac{3}{8}\right)$$

$$=\frac{2}{3}\times\frac{5}{7}\times\frac{3}{8}+\frac{2}{3}\times\frac{2}{7}\times\frac{5}{8}+\frac{1}{3}\times\frac{5}{7}\times\frac{5}{8}$$

$$=\frac{1}{3\times7\times8}(30+20+25)$$

$$=\frac{75}{3\times7\times8}=\frac{25}{56}$$ [1]

9. Given, probability of Akhil's selection; $P(A)=\frac{1}{4}$

Probability of Vijay's selection; $P(B)=\frac{2}{3}$ [1/2]

Probability that only one of them will be selected for an interview = P (A selected and B is not selected for an interview) + P(B selected and A is not selected for an interview)

$$=P(A)\times P(\bar{B})+P(B)\times P(\bar{A})$$

$$=\frac{1}{4}\times\left(1-\frac{2}{3}\right)+\frac{2}{3}\times\left(1-\frac{1}{4}\right)$$

$$=\frac{1}{4}\times\frac{1}{3}+\frac{2}{3}\times\frac{3}{4}=\frac{1}{12}+\frac{6}{12}=\frac{7}{12}$$ [1½]

10. Urn A : 4 red balls and 3 black balls

Urn B : 5 red balls and 4 black balls

Urn C : 4 red balls and 4 black balls

Three balls are drawn in such a way that 2 are red balls and 1 is black ball. [1]

∴ Required probability

$$=P(R_AR_BB_C)+P(R_AB_BR_C)+P(B_AR_BR_C)$$

$$=\frac{4}{7}\times\frac{5}{9}\times\frac{4}{8}+\frac{4}{7}\times\frac{4}{9}\times\frac{4}{8}+\frac{3}{7}\times\frac{5}{9}\times\frac{4}{8}$$

$$=\frac{4}{8}\left(\frac{20}{63}+\frac{16}{63}+\frac{15}{63}\right)$$

$$=\frac{1}{2}\times\frac{51}{63}=\frac{17}{42}$$ [1]

11. Let C_1, C_2 and C_3 be the companies,

$P(C_1)$ = Probability of selection in $C_1=\frac{1}{12}$

$P(C_2)$ = Probability of selection in $C_2=\frac{1}{15}$

$P(C_3)$ = Probability of selection in $C_3=\frac{1}{10}$ [1/2]

Probability of no selection in all,

$$P(\overline{C_1C_2C_3})=P(\bar{C}_1)\,P(\bar{C}_2)\,P(\bar{C}_3)$$

[C_1, C_2 and C_3 are in dependents]

$$=\left(1-\frac{1}{12}\right)\times\left(1-\frac{1}{15}\right)\times\left(1-\frac{1}{10}\right)$$ [1/2]

$$=\frac{11}{12}\times\frac{14}{15}\times\frac{9}{10}=\frac{231}{300}$$

Probability of selection in atleast one of the companies

= 1 – Probability of no selection in all

$$=1-\frac{231}{300}=1-0.77=0.23$$ [1]

12. (i) **Hint** RHS $=P(A\cap B)+P(A\cap\bar{B})$

$$=P(A)\cdot P(B)+P(A)\cdot P(\bar{B})=P(A)[P(B)+P(\bar{B})]$$

$$=P(A)[P(B)+1-P(B)]=P(A)=\text{LHS}$$

(ii) Similar as part (i).

13. **Hint** (i) P(A and not B) $=P(A)-P(A\cap B)$

$$=0.3-(0.3)(0.6)$$

[∵ A and B are independent events]

(ii) P(A or B) $=P(A)+P(B)-P(A\cap B)$

$$=0.3+0.6-0.18$$

[**Ans.** (i) 0.12 (ii) 0.72]

14. Required probability $=P(A\cup B)$

$$=P(A)+P(B)-P(A)\cdot P(B)$$

$$=P(A)\,[1-P(B)]+1-P(B')$$ [2]

$$=P(A)P(B')-P(B')+1$$

$$=1-P(B')[1-P(A)]$$

$$=1-P(A')P(B')$$ **Hence proved.** [2]

15. **Hint** P(not A and not B) $=P(A')\times P(B')$

[∵ A and B are independent events]

$$=[1-P(A)]\,[1-P(B)]$$

$$=\left(1-\frac{1}{4}\right)\left(1-\frac{1}{2}\right)$$ $\left[\textbf{Ans. } \frac{3}{8}\right]$

16. **Hint** (i) $P(RR)=\frac{8}{18}\times\frac{8}{18}$

(ii) $P(BR)=\frac{10}{18}\times\frac{8}{18}$ $\left[\textbf{Ans. } \text{(i)}\frac{16}{81}\ \text{(ii)}\frac{20}{81}\right]$

17. We have, $P(A)=\frac{1}{2}$ and $P(B)=\frac{1}{3}$

∴ $P(\bar{A})=1-P(A)=1-\frac{1}{2}=\frac{1}{2}$

and $P(\bar{B})=1-P(B)=1-\frac{1}{3}=\frac{2}{3}$ [1]

(i) P(problem is solved)

= P(atleast one of them will solve the problem)

= 1 – P(none of them solve the problem)

$$=1-P(\bar{A})\cdot P(\bar{B})$$

[∵ A and B are independent events, then $\bar{A}$ and $\bar{B}$ are also independent events]

$$=1-\frac{1}{2}\times\frac{2}{3}=1-\frac{1}{3}=\frac{2}{3}$$ [1]

(ii) P (exactly one of them solves the problem)

$$= P(A \cap \bar{B}) + P(\bar{A} \cap B)$$

$$= P(A) \cdot P(\bar{B}) + P(\bar{A}) \cdot P(B)$$ [1]

[$\because$ A and B are independent events, then A, $\bar{B}$ and $\bar{A}$, B are also independent events]

$$= \frac{1}{2} \times \frac{2}{3} + \frac{1}{2} \times \frac{1}{3} = \frac{3}{6} = \frac{1}{2}$$ [1]

18. Given, Bag A : 5 white and 4 black balls

Bag B : 7 white and 6 black balls

***Case* I** When 1 white ball is transferred from bag A to bag B.

Then, its probability,

$$P_1 = \frac{5}{5+4} = \frac{5}{9}$$ [1]

Now, bag B contains 8 white and 6 black balls. Then, the probability of drawing a ball from bag B black in colour,

$$P_2 = \frac{6}{8+6} = \frac{6}{14} = \frac{3}{7}$$

Thus, the probability of both occurring together $= P_1 P_2$

$$= \frac{5}{9} \times \frac{3}{7} = \frac{15}{63} \quad ...(i)$$

[multiplication theorem for independent events]

***Case* II** When 1 black ball is transferred from bag A to bag B. [1]

Then, its probability,

$$(P_3) = \frac{4}{5+4} = \frac{4}{9}$$

Now, the bag B contains 7 white and 7 black balls. Then, the probability of drawing a ball from bag B black in colour, P_4

$$= \frac{7}{7+7} = \frac{7}{14} = \frac{1}{2}$$ [1]

Thus, the probability of both occuring together

$$= P_3 P_4 = \frac{4}{9} \times \frac{1}{2} = \frac{2}{9} \quad ...(i)$$

On adding Eqs. (i) and (ii) we get the required probability

$$= \frac{15}{63} + \frac{2}{9} = \frac{15+14}{63} = \frac{29}{63}$$ [1]

19. In a given word consists of 9 different alphabets, there are 4 constants and 5 vowels. Three alphabets are chosen at random.

$\therefore$ Probability that more than one vowel will be selected

$= P$ (two vowels and one constant) $+ P$ (three vowels)

$$= \frac{{}^5C_2 \times {}^4C_1}{{}^9C_3} + \frac{{}^5C_3}{{}^9C_3}$$ [2]

$$= \frac{1}{{}^9C_3}\left(\frac{5 \times 4 \times 4}{2 \times 1} + \frac{5 \times 4 \times 3}{3 \times 2 \times 1}\right)$$

$$= \frac{3 \times 2 \times 1}{9 \times 8 \times 7}(40+10) = \frac{1}{84} \times 50 = \frac{25}{42}$$ [2]

20. Two dice are thrown together, so number of outcomes in the sample space is 36

$\Rightarrow \quad n(S) = 36$

E = Total of 4 $= \{(2, 2), (3, 1), (1, 3)\}$

$\Rightarrow \quad n(E) = 3$ [1]

F = Total of 9 or more

$$= \begin{Bmatrix} (3, 6), (6, 3), (4, 5), (5, 4), (4, 6), \\ (6, 4), (5, 5), (5, 6), (6, 5), (6, 6) \end{Bmatrix}$$

$\Rightarrow \quad n(F) = 10$ [1]

and $\quad G$ = Total divisible by 5

$= \{(1, 4), (4, 1), (2, 3), (3, 2), (4, 6), (6, 4), (5, 5)\}$

$\Rightarrow \quad n(G) = 7$ [1]

Here, $(E \cap F) = \phi$ and $(E \cap G) = \phi$

Also, $(F \cap G) = \{(4, 6), (6, 4), (5, 5)\}$

$\Rightarrow \quad n(F \cap G) = 3$ and $(E \cap F \cap G) = \phi$ [1]

$$\therefore \quad P(E) = \frac{n(E)}{n(S)} = \frac{3}{36} = \frac{1}{12}$$

$$P(F) = \frac{n(F)}{n(S)} = \frac{10}{36} = \frac{5}{18},$$ [1]

$$\text{and} \quad P(G) = \frac{n(G)}{n(S)} = \frac{7}{36}$$

$$P(F \cap G) = \frac{3}{36} = \frac{1}{12}$$

$$\text{and} \quad P(F) \cdot P(G) = \frac{5}{18} \times \frac{7}{36} = \frac{35}{648}$$

Here, we see that $P(F \cap G) \neq P(F) \cdot P(G)$

[since only F and G have common events, so only F and G are used here]

Hence, there is no pair which is independent. [1]

21. Given, A and B are two independent events with

$$P(\bar{A} \cap B) = \frac{2}{15} \text{ and } P(A \cap \bar{B}) = \frac{1}{6}.$$

We know that if A and B are independent events, then $\bar{A}$, B and A, $\bar{B}$ are independent events. [1]

$$\text{Now,} \quad P(\bar{A} \cap B) = \frac{2}{15} \Rightarrow P(B) \cdot P(\bar{A}) = \frac{2}{15}$$

$$\Rightarrow \quad P(B) \cdot [1 - P(A)] = \frac{2}{15}$$

$$\Rightarrow \quad P(B) - P(A) \cdot P(B) = \frac{2}{15} \quad ...(i)$$ [1]

$$\text{and } P(A \cap \bar{B}) = \frac{1}{6} \Rightarrow P(A) \cdot P(\bar{B}) = \frac{1}{6}$$

$$\Rightarrow \quad P(A) \cdot [1 - P(B)] = \frac{1}{6}$$

$$\Rightarrow \quad P(A) - P(A)P(B) = \frac{1}{6} \quad ...(ii)$$

On subtracting Eq. (i) from Eq. (ii), we get

$$P(A)-P(B)=\frac{1}{6}-\frac{2}{15}=\frac{5-4}{30}=\frac{1}{30}$$

$$\Rightarrow \quad P(A)=\frac{1}{30}+P(B) \quad \text{...(iii)}$$

[1]

Now, substituting the value of $P(A)$ in Eq. (i), we get

$$P(B)-\left[\frac{1}{30}+P(B)\right]\cdot P(B)=\frac{2}{15}$$

Let $P(B)=x$, then

$$x-\left(\frac{1}{30}+x\right)x=\frac{2}{15}$$

[1]

$$\Rightarrow \quad 30x-(1+30x)x=4$$

$$\Rightarrow \quad 30x-x-30x^2=4 \Rightarrow 30x^2-29x+4=0$$

$$\Rightarrow \quad (6x-1)(5x-4)=0 \Rightarrow x=\frac{1}{6} \text{ or } \frac{4}{5}$$

$$\Rightarrow \quad P(B)=\frac{1}{6} \text{ or } \frac{4}{5} \quad [\because x=P(B)]$$

[1]

Now, if $P(B)=\frac{1}{6}$, then $P(A)=\frac{1}{5}$ [from Eq. (iii)]

and if $P(B)=\frac{4}{5}$, then $P(A)=\frac{5}{6}$ [1]

22. Given, Bag I : 5 white and 4 black balls

Bag II : 7 white and 9 black balls

***Case* I** 1 black ball from 1st bag, 1 black and 1 white balls from 2nd bag.

$$P(A)=\frac{{}^4C_1}{{}^9C_1}\times\left(\frac{{}^7C_1\times{}^9C_1}{{}^{16}C_2}\right)=\frac{7}{15\times 2}=\frac{7}{30} \quad [3]$$

***Case* II** 1 white ball from 1st bag, 2 black balls from 2nd bag.

$$P(B)=\frac{{}^5C_1}{{}^9C_1}\times\left(\frac{{}^9C_2}{{}^{16}C_2}\right)=\frac{5\times 9\times 8\times 2}{2\times 9\times 16\times 15}=\frac{1}{6}$$

$\therefore$ Required probability $=P(A)+P(B)$

$$=\frac{7}{30}+\frac{1}{6}=\frac{12}{30}=\frac{2}{5} \quad [3]$$

TOPIC 03 Theorem of Total Probability and Baye's Theorem

Partition of a Sample Space

A set of mutually exclusive and exhaustive events $E_1, E_2, \ldots, E_n$ is said to represent a partition of the sample space S, if it satisfies the following conditions

(i) $E_i \cap E_j = \phi, i \neq j; i, j = 1, 2, \ldots, n$

(ii) $E_1 \cup E_2 \cup \ldots \cup E_n = S$

(iii) $P(E_i) > 0, \forall\, i = 1, 2, \ldots, n$.

In other words, the events $E_1, E_2, \ldots, E_n$ represent a partition of the sample space S, if they are pairwise disjoint, exhaustive and have non-zero probabilities.

Note The partition of a sample space is not unique. There can be several partitions of the same sample space.

Theorem of Total Probability

Let $\{E_1, E_2, \ldots, E_n\}$ be a partition of the sample space S and suppose that each of the events $E_1, E_2, \ldots, E_n$ has non-zero probability of occurrence.

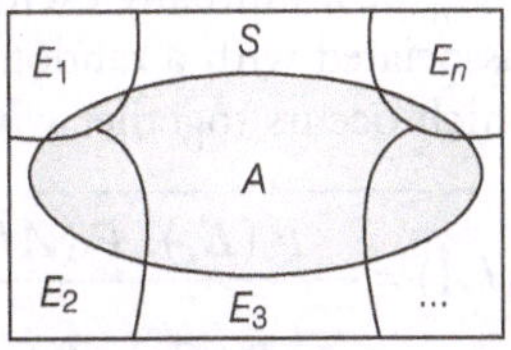

Let A be any event associated with S, then

$$P(A)=P(E_1)\cdot P(A/E_1)+P(E_2)\cdot P(A/E_2)+\ldots+P(E_n)\cdot P(A/E_n)$$

$$=\sum_{j=1}^{n} P(E_j)\cdot P(A/E_j)$$

Example 1 Bag A contains 1 white, 2 blue and 3 red balls. Bag B contains 3 white, 3 blue and 2 red balls. Bag C contains 2 white, 3 blue and 4 red balls. One bag is selected at random and then two balls are drawn from the selected bag. Find the probability that the balls drawn are white and red. **[ISC 2017]**

Sol. Let E_1 is event of selecting bag A.

E_2 is event of selecting bag B.

E_3 is event of selecting bag C.

E is event of drawing two balls which one of the three bags is selected randomly.

$$\therefore P(E_1)=\frac{1}{3}, P(E_2)=\frac{1}{3} \text{ and } P(E_3)=\frac{1}{3}$$

Now, $P(E/E_1)$ = Probability of drawing two balls, which are white and red, from bag A.

$$=\frac{1\times{}^3C_1}{{}^6C_2}$$

[$\because$ bag A contains 1 white 2 blue and 3 red balls]

$$= \frac{1 \times 3}{15} = \frac{1}{5}$$

$P(E/E_2)$ = Probability of drawing two balls, which are white and red, from bag B

$$= \frac{^3C_1 \times {^2C_1}}{^8C_2}$$

[$\because$ bag B contains 3 white, 3 blue and 2 red balls]

$$= \frac{3 \times 2}{28} = \frac{3}{14}$$

$P(E/E_3)$ = Probability of drawing two balls, which are white and red, from bag C

$$= \frac{^2C_1 \times {^4C_1}}{^9C_2}$$

[$\because$ bag C contains 2 white, 3 blue and 4 red balls]

$$= \frac{2 \times 4}{36} = \frac{2}{9}$$

Now, by using the law of total probability, we get

$$P(E) = P(E_1)P(E/E_2) + P(E_2)P(E/E_2) + P(E_3)P(E/E_3)$$

$$= \frac{1}{3} \times \frac{1}{5} + \frac{1}{3} \times \frac{3}{14} + \frac{1}{3} \times \frac{2}{9}$$

$$= \frac{1}{15} + \frac{1}{14} + \frac{2}{27} = \frac{401}{1890}$$

Example 2 An urn contains 10 white and 3 black balls while another urn contains 3 white and 5 black balls. Two balls are drawn from the first urn and put into the second urn and then a ball is drawn from the second urn. Find the probability that the ball drawn from the second urn is a white ball. **[ISC 2016]**

Sol. Here, there are three cases:

***Case* I** When the balls transferred from Urn I to Urn II are white.

Here, the probability of transferring two white balls from Urn I

$$= \frac{^{10}C_2}{^{13}C_2} = \frac{\frac{10 \times 9}{2 \times 1}}{\frac{13 \times 12}{2 \times 1}} = \frac{15}{26}$$

In Urn II, white balls = 3 + 2 = 5

$\therefore$ Probability of drawing a white ball from Urn II

$$= \frac{^5C_1}{^{10}C_1} = \frac{5}{10} = \frac{1}{2}$$

$\therefore$ Probability of these events occurring together

$$= \frac{15}{26} \times \frac{1}{2} = \frac{15}{52}.$$

***Case* II** When one white and one black is transferred from Urn I to Urn II.

$\therefore$ The probability of transferring a white ball and a black ball from Urn I into Urn II

$$= \frac{^{10}C_1 \times {^3C_1}}{^{13}C_2} = \frac{10 \times 3}{\frac{13 \times 12}{2 \times 1}} = \frac{30}{13 \times 6} = \frac{5}{13}$$

Now, in Urn II, white balls = 4 and black balls = 6

$\therefore$ P (getting a white ball from Urn II)

$$= \frac{^4C_1}{^{10}C_1} = \frac{4}{10} = \frac{2}{5}$$

$\therefore$ Probability of these events occurring together

$$= \frac{5}{13} \times \frac{2}{5} = \frac{2}{13}$$

***Case* III** When two black balls are transferred from Urn I to Urn II.

$\therefore$ P (transferring 2 black balls from Urn I to Urn II)

$$= \frac{^3C_1}{^{13}C_2} = \frac{3}{\frac{13 \times 12}{2 \times 1}} = \frac{3}{13 \times 6} = \frac{1}{26}$$

Now, in Urn II, white balls = 3 and balls = 5 + 2 = 7.

$\therefore$ P (getting a white ball) $= \frac{^3C_1}{^{10}C_1} = \frac{3}{10}$

Now, probability of these events occurring together

$$= \frac{1}{26} \times \frac{3}{10} = \frac{3}{260}$$

Since, all the three cases are mutually exclusive. Thus, only one of them can happen at a time.

Hence, the required probability of drawing a white ball

$$= \frac{15}{52} + \frac{2}{13} + \frac{3}{260} = \frac{118}{260} = \frac{59}{130}$$

Baye's Theorem

If $E_1, E_2, \ldots, E_n$ are non-empty events, which constitute a partition of sample space S, i.e. $E_1, E_2, \ldots, E_n$ are pairwise disjoint,

$E_1 \cup E_2 \cup \ldots \cup E_n = S$ and $P(E_i) > 0, \forall i = 1, 2, 3, \ldots, n$.

Also, let A be any event of non-zero probability, then

$$P(E_i/A) = \frac{P(E_i) \cdot P(A/E_i)}{\sum_{j=1}^{n} P(E_j) \cdot P(A/E_j)}, \text{ for any } i = 1, 2, 3, \ldots, n$$

Or

Let $E_1, E_2, E_3, \ldots, E_n$ be n mutually exclusive and exhaustive events associated with a random experiment. If A is an event, which occurs together with E_i's. Then,

$$P(E_i/A) = \frac{P(E_i) \cdot P(A/E_i)}{\sum_{j=1}^{n} P(E_j) \cdot P(A/E_j)}$$

Here, events $E_1, E_2, \ldots, E_n$ are called **hypothesis**. The probability $P(E_i)$ is called the **priori probability** of the hypothesis E_i and the conditional probability $P(E_i/A)$ is called a posteriori probability of the hypothesis E_i. Baye's theorem is also called the formula for the probability of causes.

Method to Solve the Problems Based on Baye's Theorem

To solve problems based on Baye's theorem, we use the following steps

I. Identify the events, which constitute a partition of sample space S and name them E_1, E_2, E_3 and so on.

II. Assume the other event of non-zero probability as A.

III. Find the probabilities of $E_1, E_2, E_3, \ldots$.

IV. Find the conditional probabilities of A with $E_1, E_2, E_3, \ldots$.

V. Use Baye's theorem to find required probability, i.e. $P(E_i / A)$.

Example 3 In an automobile factory, certain parts are to be fixed into the chassis in a section before it moves into another section. On a given day, one of the three persons A, B and C carries out this task. A has 45% chance, B has 35% chance and C has 20% chance of doing the task. The probability that A, B and C will take more than the allotted time is $\frac{1}{6}, \frac{1}{10}$ and $\frac{1}{20}$, respectively. If it is found that the time taken is more than the allotted time, then what is the probability that A has done the task? **[ISC 2016]**

Sol. Let E_1, E_2, E_3 and A be the events defined as follows

$E_1 = A$ has done the task

$E_2 = B$ has done the task

$E_3 = C$ has done the task and

A = Person takes more than the allotted time.

$$\therefore \quad P(E_1) = \frac{45}{100} = \frac{9}{20}, \; P(E_2) = \frac{35}{100} = \frac{7}{20}$$

$$P(E_3) = \frac{20}{100} = \frac{4}{20}, \; P(A/E_1) = \frac{1}{6}$$

$$P(A/E_2) = \frac{1}{10} \text{ and } P(A/E_3) = \frac{1}{20}$$

By Baye's theorem, we have

$$P\left(\frac{E_1}{A}\right) = \frac{P(E_1)\,P(A/E_1)}{\left[\begin{array}{r} P(E_1)\,P(A/E_1) + P(E_2)\,P(A/E_2) \\ + P(E_3)\,P(A/E_3) \end{array}\right]}$$

$$= \frac{\frac{9}{20} \times \frac{1}{6}}{\frac{9}{20} \times \frac{1}{6} + \frac{7}{20} \times \frac{1}{10} + \frac{4}{20} \times \frac{1}{20}}$$

$$= \frac{0.075}{0.075 + 0.035 + 0.01} = 0.625$$

Example 4 A fair die is rolled. If face 1 turns up, a ball is drawn from Bag A. If face 2 or 3 turns up, a ball is drawn from Bag B. If face 4 or 5 or 6 turns up, a ball is drawn from Bag C. Bag A contains 3 red and 2 white balls, Bag B contains 3 red and 4 white balls and Bag C contains 4 red and 5 white balls. The die is rolled, a Bag is picked up and a ball is drawn. If the drawn ball is red, what is the probability that it is drawn from Bag B? **[ISC 2017]**

Sol. Let us define the following events.

E_1 : Bag A is chosen.

E_2 : Bag B is chosen.

E_3 : Bag C is chosen.

Then, $P(E_1) = \frac{1}{6}$

$$P(E_2) = \frac{2}{6} = \frac{1}{3}; \; P(E_3) = \frac{3}{6} = \frac{1}{2}$$

Also, let event E : The drawn ball is red.

Then, $P(E/E_1) = \frac{3}{5}$

$$P(E/E_2) = \frac{3}{7}; \; P(E/E_3) = \frac{4}{9}$$

Now, required probability $= P(E_2/E)$

$$= \frac{P(E/E_2)P(E_2)}{\begin{array}{r} P(E/E_2)P(E_2) + P(E/E_1)P(E_1) \\ + P(E/E_3)P(E_3) \end{array}}$$

$$P(E_2/E) = \frac{\frac{3}{7} \times \frac{1}{3}}{\frac{3}{7} \times \frac{1}{3} + \frac{3}{5} \times \frac{1}{6} + \frac{4}{9} \times \frac{1}{2}} = \frac{\frac{1}{7}}{\frac{1}{7} + \frac{1}{10} + \frac{2}{9}}$$

$$= \frac{\frac{1}{7}}{\frac{90 + 63 + 2 \times 70}{630}} = \frac{1}{7} \times \frac{630}{293} = \frac{90}{293}$$

Example 5 Box I contains two white and three black balls. Box II contains four white and one black balls and box III contains three white and four black balls. A die having three red, two yellow and one green face, is thrown to select the box, if red face turns up, we pick up box I, if a yellow face turns up we pick up box II, otherwise, we pick up box III. Then, we draw a ball from the selected box. If the ball drawn is white, what is the probability that the dice had turned up with a red face? **[ISC 2015]**

Sol. Let B and W denote for black and white balls.

Given, Bag I = $\{2W, 3B\}$

Bag II = $\{4W, 1B\}$

and Bag III = $\{3W, 4B\}$

Let E_1 = A die have a red face,

E_2 = A die have a yellow face

and E_3 = A die have green face.

Total number of face is a die is six.

Then, $P(E_1) = \frac{3}{6} = \frac{1}{2}, P(E_2) = \frac{2}{6} = \frac{1}{3}$

and $P(E_3) = \frac{1}{6}$

Let E = Event of drawing a white ball

Now, $P\left(\frac{E}{E_1}\right) = \frac{1}{2} \times \frac{2}{5} = \frac{1}{5}; P\left(\frac{E}{E_2}\right) = \frac{1}{3} \times \frac{4}{5} = \frac{4}{15}$

and $P(E_3) = \frac{1}{6} \times \frac{3}{7} = \frac{1}{14}$

∴ The probability that the white ball is selected when a die turn up red face.

$$P\left(\frac{E_1}{E}\right) = \frac{P(E_1)P\left(\frac{E}{E_1}\right)}{P(E_1)P\left(\frac{E}{E_1}\right) + P(E_2)P\left(\frac{E}{E_2}\right) + P(E_3)P\left(\frac{E}{E_3}\right)}$$

[by using Baye's theorem]

$$= \frac{\frac{1}{2} \times \frac{1}{5}}{\frac{1}{2} \times \frac{1}{5} + \frac{1}{3} \times \frac{4}{15} + \frac{1}{6} \times \frac{1}{14}} = \frac{\frac{1}{10}}{\frac{1}{10} + \frac{4}{45} + \frac{1}{84}}$$

$$= \frac{\frac{1}{10}}{\frac{378 + 336 + 45}{3780}} = \frac{3780}{10 \times 759} = \frac{378}{759}$$

Example 6 In a company, 15% of the employees are graduates and 85% of the employees are non-graduates. As per the annual report of the company, 80% of the graduate employees and 10% of the non-graduate employees are in the administrative positions. Find the probability that an employee selected at random from those working in administrative positions will be a graduate. **[ISC 2023]**

Sol. Consider the event

E_1 = Employees are graduate

E_2 = Employees are non-graduates

A = Employees are in the administrative position

Given, $P(E_1) = 15\% = \frac{15}{100}, P(E_2) = 85\% = \frac{85}{100},$

$P(A/E_1) = 80\% = \frac{80}{100}$

and $P(A/E_2) = 10\% = \frac{10}{100}$

∴ Required probability = $P(E_1/A)$

By Baye's theorem,

$$P(E_1/A) = \frac{P(E_1) \times P(A/E_1)}{P(E_1) \times P(A/E_1) + P(E_2) \times P(A/E_2)}$$

$$= \frac{\frac{15}{100} \times \frac{80}{100}}{\frac{15}{100} \times \frac{80}{100} + \frac{85}{100} \times \frac{10}{100}}$$

$$= \frac{1200}{1200 + 850} = \frac{1200}{2050} = \frac{120}{205} = \frac{24}{41}$$

Example 7 Given three identical Boxes A, B and C, Box A contains 2 gold and 1 silver coin, Box B contains 1 gold and 2 silver coins and Box C contains 3 silver coins. A person chooses a Box at random and takes out a coin. If the coin drawn is of silver, find the probability that it has been drawn from the box which has the remaining two coins also of silver. **[ISC 2019]**

Sol. Given boxes A, B and C are identical, so each has equal probability of selecting boxes.

∴ $P(A) = \frac{1}{3}, P(B) = \frac{1}{3}$ and $P(C) = \frac{1}{3}$

Here, we see that only box C has all three silver coins.

Let E = Event of getting one silver coin.

Now, $P\left(\frac{E}{A}\right) = \frac{1}{{}^3C_1} = \frac{1}{3}$

$P\left(\frac{E}{B}\right) = \frac{{}^2C_1}{{}^3C_1} = \frac{2}{3}$

and $P\left(\frac{E}{C}\right) = \frac{{}^3C_1}{{}^3C_1} = \frac{3}{3}$

By using Baye's theorem

$$P\left(\frac{C}{E}\right) = \frac{P(C)\, P\left(\frac{E}{C}\right)}{\left[P(A)\, P\left(\frac{E}{A}\right) + P(B)P\left(\frac{E}{B}\right) + P(C)\, P\left(\frac{E}{C}\right)\right]}$$

$$= \frac{\frac{1}{3} \times \frac{3}{3}}{\frac{1}{3} \times \frac{1}{3} + \frac{1}{3} \times \frac{2}{3} + \frac{1}{3} \times \frac{3}{3}} = \frac{\frac{1}{3}}{\frac{1}{3}\left[\frac{1}{3} + \frac{2}{3} + \frac{3}{3}\right]}$$

$$= \frac{1}{\frac{6}{3}} = \frac{3}{6} = \frac{1}{2}$$

Topic Practice 3

Short Answer Type Questions

4 Marks

1 Bag I contains 3 black and 2 white balls, bag II contains 2 black and 4 white balls. A bag and a ball is selected at random. Determine the probability of selecting a black ball. [NCERT Exemplar]

2 The bag A contains 3 white and 2 black balls while the bag B contains 2 white and 5 black balls. One of the bags is chosen at random and a ball is drawn from it. What is the probability that the ball is white? [ISC 2007]

3 An urn contains 2 white and 2 black balls. A ball is drawn at random. If it is white, it is not replaced into the urn. Otherwise, it is replaced with another ball of the same colour. The process is repeated. Find the probability that the third ball drawn is black. [ISC 2015]

4 A bag contains 4 white and 5 black balls. Another bag contains 9 white and 7 black balls. A ball is transferred from the first bag to the second bag and then a ball is drawn at random from the second bag. Find the probability that the ball drawn is white. [NCERT Exemplar]

5 For A, B and C the chances of being selected as the manager of a firm are $4:1:2$, respectively. The probabilities for them to introduce a radical change in the marketing strategy are 0.3, 0.8 and 0.5, respectively. If a change takes place, then find the probability that it is due to the appointment of B. [ISC 2013]

Long Answer Type Questions

6 Marks

6 Bag I contains 3 red and 4 black balls and bag II contains 4 red and 5 black balls. One ball is transferred from bag I to bag II and then ball is drawn from bag II. The ball so drawn is found to be red in colour. Find the probability that the transferred ball is black. [NCERT]

7 Bag A contains 2 white, 1 black and 3 red balls, bag B contains 3 white, 2 black and 4 red balls and bag C contains 4 white, 3 black and 2 red balls. One bag is chosen at random and 2 balls are drawn at random from that bag. If the randomly drawn balls happen to be red and black, then what is the probability that both balls come from bag B? [ISC 2011]

8 A shopkeeper sells three types of flower seeds A_1, A_2 and A_3. They are sold as a mixture, where the proportions are $4:4:2$, respectively. The germination rates of the three types of seeds are 45%, 60% and 35%. Calculate the probability

(i) of a randomly chosen seed to germinate.

(ii) that it will not germinate given that the seed is of type A_3.

(iii) that it is of the type A_2 given that a randomly chosen seed does not germinate.

[NCERT Exemplar]

9 In a class of 75 students, 15 are above average, 45 are average and the rest below average achievers. The probability that an above average achieving student fail is 0.005, that an average achieving student fails is 0.05 and the probability of a below average achieving student failing is 0.15. If a student is known to have passed, then what is the probability that he is a below average achiever? [ISC 2012]

10 A laboratory blood test is 99% effective in detecting a certain disease,when it is infact present. However, the test also yields a false positive result for 0.5% of the healthy person tested (i.e. if a healthy person is tested, then with probability 0.005, the test will imply he has the disease). If 0.1% of the population actually has the disease, then what is the probability that a person has disease, given that his test result is positive? [NCERT]

11 By examining the chest X-ray, the probability that TB is detected when a person is actually suffering is 0.99. The probability of an healthy person diagnosed to have TB is 0.001. In a certain city, 1 in 1000 people suffers from TB. A person is selected at random and is diagnosed to have TB. What is the probability that he actually has TB? [NCERT Exemplar]

12 Two groups are competing for the position on the board of directors of a corporation. The probability that the first and the second groups will win are 0.6 and 0.4, respectively. Further, if the first group wins the probability of introducing a new product is 0.7 and the corresponding probability is 0.3, if the second group wins. Find the probability that the new product introduce was by second group. **[NCERT]**

13 An item is manufactured by three machines A, B and C. Out of the total number of items manufactured during a specified period, 50% are manufactured on A, 30% on B and 20% on C. 2% of the items produced on A and 2% of items produced on B are defective and 3% of these produced on C are defective. All the items are stored at one godown. One item is drawn at random and is found to be defective. What is the probability that it was manufactured on machine A? **[NCERT Exemplar]**

14 Suppose a girl throws a die. If she gets a 5 or 6, she tosses a coin three times and notes the number of heads. If she gets 1, 2, 3 or 4, she tosses a coin once and notes whether a head or tail is obtained. If she obtained exactly one head, then what is the probability that she threw 1, 2, 3 or 4 with the die? **[NCERT]**

15 A factory has three machines A, B and C producing 1500, 2500 and 3000 bulbs per day, respectively. Machine A produces 1.5% defective bulbs, machine B produces 2% defective bulbs and machine C produces 2.5% defective bulbs. At the end of the day, a bulb is drawn at random and is found to be defective. What is the probability that the defective bulb has been produced by machine B? **[ISC 2010]**

16 A card from a pack of 52 cards is lost. From the remaining cards of the pack, two cards are drawn and are found to be diamonds. Find the probability of the lost card being a diamond. **[NCERT]**

17 An insurance company insured 4000 doctors, 8000 teachers and 12000 engineers. The probability of a doctor, a teacher and an engineer dying before the age of 58 yr are 0.01, 0.03 and 0.05, respectively. If one of the insured persons dies before the age of 58 yr, then find the probability that he is a doctor. **[ISC 2009]**

18 A manufacturing firm produces steel pipes in three plants A, B and C with daily production of 500, 1000 and 2000 units, respectively. The fractions of defective steel pipes output produced by the plants A, B and C are respectively 0.005, 0.008 and 0.010. If a pipe is selected from a day's total production and found to be defective, then find out the probability that it came from the first plant. **[ISC 2005]**

Hints & Solutions

1. **Hint** Let E_1 = Bag I is selected; E_2 = Bag II is selected and A = Black ball is drawn

Then, $P(E_1) = P(E_2) = \frac{1}{2}, P\left(\frac{A}{E_1}\right) = \frac{3}{5}, P\left(\frac{A}{E_2}\right) = \frac{2}{6}$

$\therefore$ Required probability,

$$P(A) = P(E_1) \times P\left(\frac{A}{E_1}\right) + P(E_2) \times P\left(\frac{A}{E_2}\right)$$

$\left[\textbf{Ans. } \frac{7}{15}\right]$

2. Similar as Quesiton 1. $\left[\textbf{Ans. } \frac{31}{70}\right]$

3. Let E_{pq} denote the event that the first ball drawn has colour P and second ball drawn has colour q.

Let B denote the event that the third ball drawn is black. [1]

Now, $P(E_{ww}) = \frac{2}{4} \times \frac{1}{3} = \frac{1}{6}$, $P(E_{wb}) = \frac{2}{4} \times \frac{2}{3} = \frac{1}{3}$

$P(E_{bw}) = \frac{2}{4} \times \frac{2}{5} = \frac{1}{5}$, $P(E_{bb}) = \frac{2}{4} \times \frac{3}{5} = \frac{3}{10}$

Also, $P(B/E_{ww}) = \frac{2}{2} = 1$, $P(B/E_{wb}) = \frac{3}{4}$

$P(B/E_{bw}) = \frac{3}{4}$, $P(B/E_{bb}) = \frac{4}{6} = \frac{2}{3}$ [1½]

Now, by total probability,

$$P(B) = P(E_{ww})P(B/E_{ww}) + P(E_{wb}) P(B/E_{wb}) + P(E_{bw}) P P(B/E_{bw}) + P(E_{bb}) P P(B/E_{bb})$$

$$= \frac{1}{6} \times 1 + \frac{1}{3} \times \frac{3}{4} + \frac{1}{5} \times \frac{3}{4} + \frac{3}{10} \times \frac{2}{3}$$

$$= \frac{1}{6} + \frac{1}{4} + \frac{3}{20} + \frac{1}{5} = \frac{23}{30}$$ [1½]

4. Given first bag contains

W_1 = {4 white balls}, B_1 = {5 black balls},

and second bag contains

W_2 = {9 white balls} and B_2 = {7 black balls}

Let E_1 be the event that ball transferred from the first bag is white and E_2 be the event that the ball transferred from the first bag is black. Also, E is the event that the ball drawn from the second bag is white.

$$\therefore \quad P\left(\frac{E}{E_1}\right)=\frac{10}{17} \text{ and } P\left(\frac{E}{E_2}\right)=\frac{9}{17}$$ [1]

[if we transferred one white ball from bag I to bag II, then the second bag contains (9 + 1), i.e. 10 white balls. Similarly, if we transferred one black ball from bag I to bag II, then the second bag contains (7 +1), i.e. 8 black balls]

$$P(E_1)=\frac{4}{9} \text{ and } P(E_2)=\frac{5}{9}$$ [1]

∴ Required probability,

$$P(E)=P(E_1)\cdot P\left(\frac{E}{E_1}\right)+P(E_2)\cdot P\left(\frac{E}{E_2}\right)$$ [1]

$$=\frac{4}{9}\times\frac{10}{17}+\frac{5}{9}\times\frac{9}{17}=\frac{40+45}{153}=\frac{85}{153}=\frac{5}{9}$$ [1]

5. Let E_1, E_2 and E_3 be the events of chances of A, B and C being selecting as the managers, respectively and S be the event for selected person as the manager of a firm. Since, the ratio of chances between A, B and C is $4:1:2$.

So, the total chances = 7

Therefore, $P(E_1)=\frac{4}{7}$, $P(E_2)=\frac{1}{7}$ and $P(E_3)=\frac{2}{7}$ [1]

Also given, the probability for them introduce a radical change in market strategy,

$$P\left(\frac{S}{E_1}\right)=0.3,\ P\left(\frac{S}{E_2}\right)=0.8,\ P\left(\frac{S}{E_3}\right)=0.5$$ [1]

By using Baye's theorem,

$$P\left(\frac{E_2}{S}\right)=\frac{P(E_2)\cdot P\left(\frac{S}{E_2}\right)}{P(E_1)\cdot P\left(\frac{S}{E_1}\right)+P(E_2)\cdot P\left(\frac{S}{E_2}\right)+P(E_3)\cdot P\left(\frac{S}{E_3}\right)}$$

$$=\frac{\frac{1}{7}\times 0.8}{\frac{4}{7}\times 0.3+\frac{1}{7}\times 0.8+\frac{2}{7}\times 0.5}$$ [1]

$$=\frac{\frac{0.8}{7}}{\frac{1.2}{7}+\frac{0.8}{7}+\frac{1}{7}}=\frac{\frac{8}{70}}{\frac{12}{70}+\frac{8}{70}+\frac{1}{7}}$$

$$=\frac{\frac{8}{70}}{\frac{12+8+10}{70}}=\frac{8}{70}\times\frac{70}{30}=\frac{8}{30}=\frac{4}{15}$$ [1]

6. Let E_1 = Red ball is transferred from bag I to bag II and E_2 = Black ball is transferred from bag I to bag II

So, E_1 and E_2 are mutually exclusive and exhaustive events.

$$\therefore \quad P(E_1)=\frac{3}{3+4}=\frac{3}{7} \text{ and } P(E_2)=\frac{4}{3+4}=\frac{4}{7}$$ [2]

Let E be the event that the ball drawn is red.

Then, $$P\left(\frac{E}{E_1}\right)=\frac{4+1}{(4+1)+5}=\frac{5}{10}=\frac{1}{2}$$ [1]

and $$P\left(\frac{E}{E_2}\right)=\frac{4}{4+(5+1)}=\frac{4}{10}=\frac{2}{5}$$

∴ Required probability,

$$P\left(\frac{E_2}{E}\right)=\frac{P\left(\frac{E}{E_2}\right)\cdot P(E_2)}{P\left(\frac{E}{E_1}\right)\cdot P(E_1)+P\left(\frac{E}{E_2}\right)\cdot P(E_2)}$$ [1]

$$=\frac{\frac{2}{5}\times\frac{4}{7}}{\frac{1}{2}\times\frac{3}{7}+\frac{2}{5}\times\frac{4}{7}}$$ [by using Baye's theorem] [1]

$$=\frac{\frac{8}{35}}{\frac{3}{14}+\frac{8}{35}}=\frac{\frac{8}{35}}{\frac{105+112}{14\times 35}}$$

$$=\frac{8\times 14}{217}=\frac{16}{31}$$

Hence, the probability that the transferred ball is black, is $\frac{16}{31}$. [1]

7. Let E_1, E_2 and E_3 be the events for chosen bags A, B and C, respectively. So, $P(E_1)=P(E_2)=P(E_3)=\frac{1}{3}$ [1]

Bag A contains 2 white, 1 black and 3 red balls.
Bag B contains 3 white, 2 black and 4 red balls.
Bag C contains 4 white, 3 black and 2 red balls. [1]

If A be the event of choosing two balls, i.e. one red and one black

$$\therefore \quad P\left(\frac{A}{E_1}\right)=\frac{{}^3C_1\,{}^1C_1}{{}^6C_2}=\frac{3\times 1}{\frac{6\times 5}{2\times 1}}=\frac{1}{5}$$

$$P\left(\frac{A}{E_2}\right)=\frac{{}^4C_1\times{}^2C_1}{{}^9C_2}=\frac{4\times 2}{\frac{9\times 8}{2\times 1}}=\frac{2}{9}$$

$$P\left(\frac{A}{E_3}\right)=\frac{{}^2C_1\times{}^3C_1}{{}^9C_2}=\frac{2\times 3}{\frac{9\times 8}{2\times 1}}=\frac{1}{6}$$ [1½]

Probability that both balls drawn from the bag B, having red and black balls

$$P\left(\frac{E_2}{A}\right)=\frac{P(E_2)P\left(\frac{A}{E_2}\right)}{P(E_1)P\left(\frac{A}{E_1}\right)+P(E_2)P\left(\frac{A}{E_2}\right)+P(E_3)P\left(\frac{A}{E_3}\right)}$$

$$= \frac{\frac{1}{3}\times\frac{2}{9}}{\frac{1}{3}\times\frac{1}{5}+\frac{1}{3}\times\frac{2}{9}+\frac{1}{3}\times\frac{1}{6}}$$

$$= \frac{\frac{1}{3}\times\frac{2}{9}}{\frac{1}{3}\left(\frac{1}{5}+\frac{2}{9}+\frac{1}{6}\right)} = \frac{2/9}{\frac{1}{5}+\frac{2}{9}+\frac{1}{6}}$$ [1½]

$$= \frac{2/9}{\frac{18+20+15}{90}} = \frac{2/9}{53/90} = \frac{2}{9}\times\frac{90}{53} = \frac{2}{53}\times 10 = \frac{20}{53}$$ [1]

8. We have, $A_1 : A_2 : A_3 = 4:4:2$

$\therefore \quad P(A_1) = \frac{4}{10}, P(A_2) = \frac{4}{10}$

and $P(A_3) = \frac{2}{10}$ [1]

where A_1, A_2 and A_3 denote the event of choosing flower seeds A_1, A_2 and A_3 respectively. Let E be the event that a seed germinates and $\bar{E}$ be the event that a seed does not germinate.

Then, $P\left(\frac{E}{A_1}\right) = \frac{45}{100}, P\left(\frac{E}{A_2}\right) = \frac{60}{100}, P\left(\frac{E}{A_3}\right) = \frac{35}{100}$

and $P\left(\frac{\bar{E}}{A_1}\right) = \frac{55}{100}, P\left(\frac{\bar{E}}{A_2}\right) = \frac{40}{100}, P\left(\frac{\bar{E}}{A_3}\right) = \frac{65}{100}$ [1]

(i) Probability that a randomly chosen seed to germinate,

$$P(E) = P(A_1)\cdot\left(\frac{E}{A_1}\right) + P(A_2)\cdot P\left(\frac{E}{A_2}\right) + P(A_3)\cdot P\left(\frac{E}{A_3}\right)$$

$$= \frac{4}{10}\times\frac{45}{100} + \frac{4}{10}\times\frac{60}{100} + \frac{2}{10}\times\frac{35}{100}$$

$$= \frac{180}{1000} + \frac{240}{1000} + \frac{70}{1000} = \frac{490}{1000} = 0.49$$ [1]

(ii) $P\left(\frac{\bar{E}}{A_3}\right) = 1 - P\left(\frac{E}{A_3}\right) = 1 - \frac{35}{100} = \frac{65}{100}$ [1]

(iii) $P\left(\frac{A_2}{\bar{E}}\right)$

$$= \frac{P(A_2)\cdot P\left(\frac{\bar{E}}{A_2}\right)}{P(A_1)\cdot P\left(\frac{\bar{E}}{A_1}\right) + P(A_2)\cdot P\left(\frac{\bar{E}}{A_2}\right) + P(A_3)\cdot P\left(\frac{\bar{E}}{A_3}\right)}$$ [1]

$$= \frac{\frac{4}{10}\times\frac{40}{100}}{\frac{4}{10}\times\frac{55}{100}+\frac{4}{10}\times\frac{40}{100}+\frac{2}{10}\times\frac{65}{100}}$$

$$= \frac{\frac{160}{1000}}{\frac{220}{1000}+\frac{160}{1000}+\frac{130}{1000}} = \frac{\frac{160}{1000}}{\frac{510}{1000}} = \frac{16}{51}$$

$= 0.313725 = 0.314$ [1]

9. Let E_1, E_2 and E_3 be the events of achievers for above average, average and below average respectively.

The total number of students = 75 [1]

Let A be the event of passed student.

So, $\quad P(E_1) = \frac{15}{75} = \frac{1}{5}$ and $P(E_2) = \frac{45}{75} = \frac{3}{5}$

$P(E_3) = \frac{75-(15+45)}{75} = \frac{15}{75} = \frac{1}{5}$ [1]

Also, $P\left(\frac{A}{E_1}\right) = 1 - 0.005 = 1 - \frac{5}{1000} = \frac{995}{1000} = \frac{199}{200}$ [1]

$P\left(\frac{A}{E_2}\right) = 1 - 0.05 = 1 - \frac{5}{100} = \frac{95}{100} = \frac{19}{20}$

$P\left(\frac{A}{E_3}\right) = 1 - 0.15 = 1 - \frac{15}{100} = \frac{85}{100} = \frac{17}{20}$ [1]

The probability of below average achievers students who have passed

$$P\left(\frac{E_3}{A}\right) = \frac{P(E_3)\cdot P(A/E_3)}{P(E_1)\cdot P(A/E_1) + P(E_2)\cdot P(A/E_2) + P(E_3)\cdot P(A/E_3)}$$

$$= \frac{\frac{1}{5}\times\frac{17}{20}}{\frac{1}{5}\times\frac{199}{200}+\frac{3}{5}\times\frac{19}{20}+\frac{1}{5}\times\frac{17}{20}}$$ [1]

[by using Baye's theorem]

$$= \frac{\frac{17}{100}}{\frac{199}{1000}+\frac{57}{100}+\frac{17}{100}} = \frac{17/100}{\frac{199+570+170}{1000}}$$

$$= \frac{17}{100}\times\frac{1000}{939} = \frac{170}{939}$$ [1]

10. Let E_1 = Event that the person has disease and E_2 = Event that the person is healthy.

Then, E_1 and E_2 are mutually exclusive and exhaustive events. [1]

$\therefore \quad P(E_1) = 0.1\% = \frac{0.1}{100} = 0.001$

and $\quad P(E_2) = 1 - 0.001 = 0.999$

Let E : Event that test is positive. [1]

$P\left(\frac{E}{E_1}\right) = P$ (result is positive, given that person has disease)

$= 99\% = \frac{99}{100} = 0.99$ [1]

$P\left(\frac{E}{E_2}\right) = P$ (result is positive, given that person does not have disease)

$= 0.5\% = \frac{0.5}{100} = 0.005$ [1]

Probability that a person has disease, given that test result is positive, is given by

$$P\left(\frac{E_1}{E}\right)=\frac{P(E_1)\cdot P\left(\frac{E}{E_1}\right)}{P(E_1)\cdot P\left(\frac{E}{E_1}\right)+P(E_2)\cdot P\left(\frac{E}{E_2}\right)}$$

[by Baye's theorem]

$$=\frac{0.001\times 0.99}{0.001\times 0.99+0.999\times 0.005}=\frac{0.00099}{0.00099+0.004995}$$

$$=\frac{0.00099}{0.005985}=\frac{990}{5985}=\frac{110}{665}=\frac{22}{133}$$ [1]

Hence, the required probability is $\frac{22}{133}$. [1]

11. Let E_1 be the event that person is suffering from TB and E_2 be the event that person is not suffering from TB. Let E be the event that the doctor diagnoses that person has TB. Then,

$$P(E_1)=\frac{1}{1000}$$ [1]

$$P(E_2)=1-\frac{1}{1000}=\frac{999}{1000}$$ [1]

$P\left(\frac{E}{E_1}\right)=P$ (TB is detected when a person is actually Suffering) $=0.99=\frac{990}{1000}$ [1]

and $P\left(\frac{E}{E_2}\right)=P$ (TB is detected when a person is not actually suffering) $=0.001=\frac{1}{1000}$ [1]

P (A selected person has actually TB), is given by

$$P\left(\frac{E_1}{E}\right)=\frac{P(E_1)\cdot P\left(\frac{E}{E_1}\right)}{\left[P(E_1)\cdot P\left(\frac{E}{E_1}\right)+P(E_2)\cdot P\left(\frac{E}{E_2}\right)\right]}$$ [1]

[by Baye's theorem]

$$=\frac{\left(\frac{1}{1000}\right)\left(\frac{990}{1000}\right)}{\left(\frac{1}{1000}\right)\left(\frac{990}{1000}\right)+\left(\frac{999}{1000}\right)\left(\frac{1}{1000}\right)}=\frac{\frac{990}{1000000}}{\left(\frac{990+999}{1000000}\right)}$$

$$=\frac{990}{1989}=\frac{110}{221}$$

Hence, the probability that a selected person has actually TB is $\frac{110}{221}$. [1]

12. **Hint** E_1 and E_2 be the events of first group and second group wins and E be the new product is introduced.

Then, $P(E_1)=0.6$, $P(E_2)=0.4$, $P\left(\frac{E}{E_1}\right)=0.7$

and $P\left(\frac{E}{E_2}\right)=0.3$

Determine $P\left(\frac{E_2}{E}\right)$ by using Baye's theorem.

$\left[\textbf{Ans. } \frac{2}{9}\right]$

13. **Hint** $P(A)=50\%$, $P(B)=30\%$, $P(C)=20\%$,

$$P\left(\frac{D}{A}\right)=2\%,\ P\left(\frac{D}{B}\right)=2\%,\ P\left(\frac{D}{C}\right)=3\%$$

Required probability,

$$P\left(\frac{A}{D}\right)=\frac{50\%\times 2\%}{50\%\times 2\%+30\%\times 2\%+20\%\times 3\%}$$

$\left[\textbf{Ans. } \frac{5}{11}\right]$

14. Let E_1 = Event that 5 or 6 is shown on die
and E_2 = Event that 1, 2, 3 or 4 is shown on die.
Here, $n(E_1)=2$ and $n(E_2)=4$
Also, $n(S)=6$ [1]

$\therefore\quad P(E_1)=\frac{2}{6}=\frac{1}{3}$ and $P(E_2)=\frac{4}{6}=\frac{2}{3}$ [1]

Let E = The event that exactly one head show up.

$\therefore\ P\left(\frac{E}{E_1}\right)=P$ (exactly one head show up when coin is tossed thrice) [1]

$$=P\{HTT, THT, TTH\}=\frac{3}{8}$$

[$\because$ total number of outcomes $=2^3=8$]

$P\left(\frac{E}{E_2}\right)=P$ (head shows up when coin is tossed once) $=\frac{1}{2}$ [1]

The probability that the girl threw 1, 2, 3 or 4 with the die, if she obtained exactly one head, is given by

$$P\left(\frac{E_2}{E}\right)=\frac{P(E_2)\cdot P\left(\frac{E}{E_2}\right)}{P(E_1)\cdot P\left(\frac{E}{E_1}\right)+P(E_2)\cdot P\left(\frac{E}{E_2}\right)}$$

[by Baye's theorem] [1]

$$=\frac{\frac{2}{3}\times\frac{1}{2}}{\frac{1}{3}\times\frac{3}{8}+\frac{2}{3}\times\frac{1}{2}}=\frac{\frac{1}{3}}{\frac{1}{8}+\frac{1}{3}}=\frac{8}{8+3}=\frac{8}{11}$$ [1]

15. Given, factory A production per day $=1500$
The factory B production per day $=2500$
The factory C production per day $=3000$
The total production of factores A, B and C

$$=1500+2500+3000=7000$$ [1]

Let E_1 = Event of selecting a bulb produced by A,
E_2 = Event of selecting a bulb produced by B,

E_3 = Event of selecting a bulb produced by C.

Let S be the event of selecting a defective bulb. [1]

$$P(S/E_1) = 1.5\% = \frac{1.5}{100},$$

$$P(S/E_2) = 2\% = \frac{2}{100} \text{ and } P(S/E_3) = 2.5\% = \frac{2.5}{100}$$

Also, $P(E_1) = \frac{1500}{7000} = \frac{3}{14}$,

$$P(E_2) = \frac{2500}{7000} = \frac{5}{14} \text{ and } P(E_3) = \frac{3000}{7000} = \frac{3}{7}$$ [1]

∴ The probability that the selecting bulb produced by B is defective,

$$P(E_2/S) = \frac{P(E_2)\cdot P(S/E_2)}{P(E_1)\cdot P(S/E_1) + P(E_2)\cdot P(S/E_2) + P(E_3)\cdot P(S/E_3)}$$

[by using Baye's theorem] [1]

$$= \frac{\frac{5}{14}\times\frac{2}{100}}{\frac{3}{14}\times\frac{1.5}{100} + \frac{5}{14}\times\frac{2}{100} + \frac{3}{7}\times\frac{2.5}{100}}$$

$$= \frac{\frac{5}{14}\times\frac{2}{100}}{\frac{1}{100}\left(\frac{3}{14}\times 1.5 + \frac{5}{14}\times 2 + \frac{3}{7}\times 2.5\right)}$$ [1]

$$= \frac{\frac{5}{14}\times 2}{\frac{3}{14}\times 1.5 + \frac{5}{14}\times 2 + \frac{3}{7}\times 2.5}$$

$$= \frac{\frac{10}{14}}{\frac{4.5}{14} + \frac{10}{14} + \frac{7.5}{7}} = \frac{\frac{10}{14}}{\frac{4.5 + 10 + 15}{14}}$$

$$= \frac{\frac{10}{14}}{\frac{29.5}{14}} = \frac{10}{14}\times\frac{14}{29.5} = \frac{10}{29.5} = \frac{100}{295} = \frac{20}{59}$$ [1]

16. **Hint** E_1 = Missing card is diamond

E_2 = Missing card is not diamond

and A = Drawing two diamond cards from the remaining cards

$$\therefore P(E_1) = \frac{1}{4}, P(E_2) = \frac{3}{4},$$

$$P\left(\frac{A}{E_1}\right) = \frac{12}{51}\times\frac{11}{50}, P\left(\frac{A}{E_2}\right) = \frac{13}{51}\times\frac{12}{50}$$

$$P\left(\frac{E_1}{A}\right) = \frac{P(E_1)\times P\left(\frac{A}{E_1}\right)}{P(E_1)\times P\left(\frac{A}{E_1}\right) + P(E_2)\times P\left(\frac{A}{E_2}\right)}\left[\textbf{Ans. } \frac{11}{50}\right]$$

17. **Hint** E_1 = There are two white and two other colour balls in the bag

E_2 = There are three white and one other colour balls in the bag

E_3 = There are all white balls in the bag

and A = Drawing two white balls from the bag

$$\therefore \quad P(E_1) = P(E_2) = P(E_3) = \frac{1}{3},$$

$$P\left(\frac{A}{E_1}\right) = \frac{^2C_2}{^4C_2} = \frac{1}{6}, P\left(\frac{A}{E_2}\right) = \frac{^3C_2}{^4C_2} = \frac{1}{2}$$

and $P\left(\frac{A}{E_3}\right) = \frac{^4C_2}{^4C_2} = 1$

Now, find $P\left(\frac{E_3}{A}\right)$. $\left[\textbf{Ans. } \frac{3}{5}\right]$

18. Given, per day production from plant A = 500 units, per day production from plant B = 1000 units and per day production from plant C = 2000 units

Let the events be

E_1 = Selecting the pipe from (plant) A

E_2 = Selecting the pipe from (plant) B

E_3 = Selecting the pipe from (plant) C.

Let D be the event of selecting defective pipe. [1]

Now, $P(E_1) = \frac{500}{500 + 1000 + 2000} = \frac{500}{3500} = \frac{1}{7}$

$$P(E_2) = \frac{1000}{3500} = \frac{2}{7}$$

and $$P(E_3) = \frac{2000}{3500} = \frac{4}{7}$$

Now, the probability that defective pipe produce from plant A, $P(D/E_1) = 0.005$

The probability that defective pipe produce from plant B, $P(D/E_2) = 0.008$

The probability that the defective pipe produce from plant C, $P(D/E_3) = 0.010$ [2]

∴ The probability that the selecting pipe produce from plant A is defective is

$$P(E_1/D) = \frac{P(E_1)\cdot P(D/E_1)}{P(E_1)\cdot P(D/E_1) + P(E_2)\cdot P(D/E_2) + P(E_3)\cdot P(D/E_3)}$$ [1]

[by using Baye's theorem]

$$= \frac{\frac{1}{7}\times 0.005}{\frac{1}{7}\times 0.005 + \frac{2}{7}\times 0.008 + \frac{4}{7}\times 0.010}$$

$$= \frac{\frac{1}{7}\times 0.005}{\frac{1}{7}(0.005 + 2\times 0.008 + 4\times 0.010)}$$

$$= \frac{0.005}{0.005 + 0.016 + 0.04} = \frac{0.005}{0.061} = \frac{5}{61}$$ [2]

TOPIC 04 Random Variable and Its Probability Distribution

Random Variable

A random variable is a real valued function, whose domain is the sample space of a random experiment. Generally, it is denoted by capital letter X. Also, more than one random variables can be defined on the same sample space.

e.g. Let a coin be tossed twice.

Then, sample space, $S = \{HT, TH, HH, TT\}$

If X denotes the number of heads in two tosses, then X is a random variable and for each outcome, its value is

$$X(TT) = 0,\ X(HT) = 1,\ X(TH) = 1 \text{ and } X(HH) = 2$$

Clearly, values of X are 0, 1and 2.

Let Y denotes the number of heads minus the number of tails for each outcome of the above sample space S and for each outcome, its value is

$$Y(HH) = 2-0 = 2,\ Y(HT) = 1-1 = 0,$$
$$Y(TH) = 1-1 = 0 \text{ and } Y(TT) = 0-2 = -2$$

Thus, X and Y are two different random variables defined on the same sample space S.

Example 1 A bag contains 2 black and 1 green balls. One ball is drawn at random and then put back in the box after noting its colour. The process repeated again. Let X denotes the number of green balls recorded in the two draws, describe X.

Sol. Given a bag contains 2 black and 1 green balls. Black balls are denoted by b_1, b_2 and green ball is denoted by g_1, then the sample space for two draws is

$S = \{b_1b_1, b_1b_2, b_2b_1, b_2b_2, b_1g_1, b_2g_1, g_1b_1, g_1b_2, g_1g_1\}$

Now, X denotes the number of green balls. Then,

$$X(b_1b_1) = X(b_1b_2) = X(b_2b_1) = X(b_2b_2) = 0,$$
$$X(b_1g_1) = X(b_2g_1) = X(g_1b_1) = X(g_1b_2) = 1$$

and $X(g_1g_1) = 2$

Hence, X is a random variable whose range is {0, 1, 2}.

Probability Distribution of a Random Variable

The system in which the values of a random variable are given along with their corresponding probability, is called probability distribution.

If X is a random variable and takes the values of $x_1, x_2, x_3, \ldots, x_n$ with respective probabilities $p_1, p_2, p_3, \ldots, p_n$.

Then, the probability distribution of X is represented by

X	x_1	x_2	x_3	...	x_n
$P(X)$	p_1	p_2	p_3	...	p_n

where $p_i > 0$ and $\sum_{i=1}^{n} p_i = 1; i = 1, 2, 3, \ldots, n.$

Note If x_i is one of the possible values of a random variable X, then statement $X = x_i$ is true only at some point(s) of the sample space. Hence, the probability that X takes value x_i is always non-zero, i.e. $P(X = x_i) \neq 0$.

Example 2 Two cards are drawn successively with replacement from a well-shuffled deck of 52 cards. Find the probability distribution of the number of aces. **[NCERT]**

Sol. Let the number of aces is a random variable denoted by X. Here, two cards are drawn. Let A denotes an ace card and B denotes a non-ace card, then sample space for two cards is $S = \{AB, BA, AA, BB\}$.

Then, $X(AB) = 1$, $X(BA) = 1$, $X(AA) = 2$ and $X(BB) = 0$.

So, X takes the values 0, 1 or 2. Since, the draws are done with replacement, two draws form independent experiments.

$$\therefore\ P(X = 0) = P(BB) = P(B) \times P(B) = \frac{48}{52} \times \frac{48}{52} = \frac{144}{169}$$

[$\because$ in 52 cards, 4 aces and remaining 48 are non-ace cards]

$$P(X = 1) = P(AB \text{ or } BA) = P(AB) + P(BA)$$
$$= P(A) \cdot P(B) + P(B) \cdot P(A)$$
$$= \frac{4}{52} \times \frac{48}{52} + \frac{48}{52} \times \frac{4}{52} = \frac{12}{169} + \frac{12}{169} = \frac{24}{169}$$

and $P(X = 2) = P(AA) = P(A) \cdot P(A) = \frac{4}{52} \times \frac{4}{52} = \frac{1}{169}$

Hence, the required probability distribution is

X	0	1	2
$P(X)$	$\frac{144}{169}$	$\frac{24}{169}$	$\frac{1}{169}$

Verification Sum of probabilities,

$$\sum_{i=1}^{n} p_i = \frac{144}{169} + \frac{24}{169} + \frac{1}{169} = \frac{144 + 24 + 1}{169} = \frac{169}{169} = 1$$

Example 3 From a lot of 15 bulbs which include 5 defectives, a sample of 2 bulbs is drawn at random (without replacement). Find the probability distribution of the number of defective bulbs.

Sol. Total number of bulbs = 15

Number of defective bulbs = 5

∴ Good bulbs = 15 − 5 = 10

Let X be the random variable of number of defective bulbs.

∴ $X = 0, 1, 2,$

$P(X=0)=\frac{10}{15}\times\frac{9}{14}=\frac{9}{21}; P(X=1)=\frac{10}{15}\times\frac{5}{14}+\frac{5}{15}\times\frac{10}{14}=\frac{10}{21}$

$P(X=2)=\frac{5}{15}\times\frac{4}{14}=\frac{2}{21}$

∴ Required probability distribution table is

X	0	1	2
P(X)	$\frac{9}{21}$	$\frac{10}{21}$	$\frac{2}{21}$

Mean of a Random Variable

Let X be a random variable taking values $x_1, x_2, x_3, \ldots, x_n$ with probabilities $p_1, p_2, p_3, \ldots, p_n$, respectively. Then, mean of X denoted by μ is the number $\sum_{i=1}^{n} x_i p_i$, i.e. the mean of X is the weighted average of the possible values of X, each value being weighted by its probability with which it occurs. It is also called the expectation of X, denoted by $E(X)$.

Then, $$E(X)=\mu=\sum_{i=1}^{n} x_i p_i = x_1p_1+x_2p_2+\ldots+x_np_n$$

Thus, in other words we can say that the mean or expectation of a random variable X is the sum of the products of all possible values of X by their respective probabilities.

Note (i) If we replace probabilities by relative frequencies, we can write $\bar{x}=\sum_{i=1}^{n} x_i \cdot f(x_i)$

(ii) For continuous distribution, we have $\bar{x}=\int_{l_1}^{l_2} x\, f(x)\, dx$

(iii) The mean of the discrete random variable x is also called the expected value $E(x)$ provided the series $\Sigma p_i \cdot x_i$ is convergent.

(iv) Mean is a measure of location or central tendency in the sense that it roughly locates a middle or average value of the random variable.

(v) Random variables with different probability distributions can have equal means.

Method of Finding the Mean of a Random Variable

Suppose a random experiment is given to us, then to find mean of a random variable associated with random experiment, we use the following steps

I. First, identify the random variable (say X) associated with given random experiment and then find all possible values $x_1, x_2, x_3, \ldots$, which X can take.

II. For each value of X obtained in step I, find the probability.

III. Write the probability distribution table for random variable X.

IV. Calculate mean by using the formula, mean $\bar{X}=\sum_{i=1}^{n} x_i\, p(x_i)$, i.e. multiply each value of x_i by the corresponding probability and then find their sum to get required mean.

Example 4 Five bad eggs are mixed with 10 good ones. If 3 eggs are drawn one by one with replacement, then find the probability distribution of the number of good eggs drawn. **[ISC 2010]**

Sol. Let the random variable be X.

Since, number of drawing eggs = 3

So, the value of X can be 0, 1, 2 and 3.

For $P(X=0)=P(0 \text{ good ege})$

$=\frac{5}{15}\times\frac{5}{15}\times\frac{5}{15}=\frac{1}{3}\times\frac{1}{3}\times\frac{1}{3}=\frac{1}{27}$

For $P(X=1)=P(1 \text{good ege})$

$=\frac{10}{15}\times\frac{5}{15}\times\frac{5}{15}+\frac{5}{15}\times\frac{10}{15}\times\frac{5}{15}+\frac{5}{15}\times\frac{5}{15}\times\frac{10}{15}$

$=\frac{2}{3}\times\frac{1}{3}\times\frac{1}{3}+\frac{1}{3}\times\frac{2}{3}\times\frac{1}{3}+\frac{1}{3}\times\frac{1}{3}\times\frac{2}{3}$

$=\frac{2}{27}+\frac{2}{27}+\frac{2}{27}=\frac{6}{27}$

For $P(X=2)=P(2 \text{ good eges})$

$=\frac{10}{15}\times\frac{10}{15}\times\frac{5}{15}+\frac{10}{15}\times\frac{5}{15}\times\frac{10}{15}+\frac{5}{15}\times\frac{10}{15}\times\frac{10}{15}$

$=\frac{2}{3}\times\frac{2}{3}\times\frac{1}{3}+\frac{2}{3}\times\frac{1}{3}\times\frac{2}{3}+\frac{1}{3}\times\frac{2}{3}\times\frac{2}{3}$

$=\frac{4}{27}+\frac{4}{27}+\frac{4}{27}=\frac{4+4+4}{27}=\frac{12}{27}$

For $P(X=3)=P(3 \text{ good eges})$

$=\frac{10}{15}\times\frac{10}{15}\times\frac{10}{15}=\frac{2}{3}\times\frac{2}{3}\times\frac{2}{3}=\frac{8}{27}$

∴ Required probability distribution is

X	P(X)
0	1/27
1	6/27
2	12/27
3	8/27

Example 5 A box contains 4 red and 5 black marbles. Find the probability distribution of the red marbles in a random draw of three marbles. Also, find the mean. **[ISC 2011]**

Sol Let X be the number of red marbles drawn from the box.

The total number of red marbles = 4

The total number of black marbles = 5

Since, 3 red marbles are drawn. So, the value of X may be 0, 1, 2, and 3.

$\therefore P(X=0) = P($ no red marbles)

$= P$ (all black marbles)

$$= \frac{{}^5C_3 \times {}^4C_0}{{}^9C_3} = \frac{{}^5C_3}{{}^9C_3} = \frac{\frac{5!}{(5-3)!3!}}{\frac{9!}{(9-3)!3!}}$$

$$= \frac{\frac{5!}{2!3!}}{\frac{9!}{6!3!}} = \frac{\frac{4\times 5}{2}}{\frac{9\times 8\times 7}{3\times 2}} = \frac{\frac{20}{2}}{\frac{504}{6}} = \frac{20}{2}\times\frac{6}{504}$$

$$= \frac{60}{504} = \frac{10}{84} = \frac{5}{42}$$

$P(X=1) = P$ (1 red ball and 2 black balls)

$$= \frac{{}^4C_1 \times {}^5C_2}{{}^9C_3} = \frac{\frac{4!}{(4-1)!}\times\frac{5!}{(5-2)!2!}}{\frac{9!}{(9-3)!3!}}$$

$$= \frac{\frac{4!}{3!}\times\frac{5!}{3!2!}}{\frac{9!}{6!3!}} = \frac{4\times\frac{5\times 4}{2}}{\frac{9\times 8\times 7}{3\times 2}} = \frac{40}{84} = \frac{20}{42}$$

$P(X=2) = P$ (2 red balls and 1 black ball)

$$= \frac{{}^4C_2 \times {}^5C_1}{{}^9C_3} = \frac{\frac{4!}{2!2!}\times\frac{5!}{4!}}{\frac{9!}{6!3!}}$$

$$= \frac{\frac{4\times 3}{2}\times\frac{5}{1}}{84} = \frac{30}{84} = \frac{15}{42}$$

$P(X=3) = P$ (3 red balls or 0 black ball)

$$= \frac{{}^4C_3 \times {}^5C_0}{{}^9C_3} = \frac{\frac{4!}{3!}\times 1}{\frac{9!}{6!3!}} = \frac{4}{84} = \frac{2}{42}$$

So, the following table distribution of X is given below

X	0	1	2	3
P(X)	5/42	20/42	15/42	2/42

Table for making mean and variance,

$X = x_i$	p_i	$p_i x_i$	$p_i x_i^2$
0	5/42	0	0
1	20/42	20/42	20/42
2	15/42	30/42	60/42
3	2/42	6/42	18/42
Total		$\sum p_i x_i = \frac{56}{42}$	$\sum p_i x_i^2 = \frac{98}{42} = 2.333$

We know that,

$$\text{Mean }(\bar{x}) = \sum p_i \bar{x}_i = \frac{56}{42} = 1.333$$

Example 6 **Two numbers are selected at random (without replacement) from positive integers 2, 3, 4, 5, 6 and 7. Let X denotes the larger of the two numbers obtained. Find the mean of the probability distribution of X.**

Sol. The total number of pairs will be formed by taking two numbers at a time $= {}^6C_1 \times {}^5C_1 = 30$.

Let X denotes larger of the two numbers be obtained.

Obviously X may have values 3, 4, 5, 6 and 7.

Now, $P(X=3) = P$

[getting (2,3), (3,2) out of 30 pairs]

$$= \frac{2}{30} = \frac{1}{15}$$

$P(X=4) = P$

[getting (2,4), (3,4), (4,2), (4,3) out of 30 pairs]

$$= \frac{4}{30} = \frac{2}{15}$$

$P(X=5) = P$

[getting (2,5), (5,2), (3,5), (5,3), (4,5),(5,4) out of 30 pairs]

$$= \frac{6}{30} = \frac{3}{15}$$

$P(X=6) = P$

[getting (2,6), (6,2), (3,6), (6,3), (4,6),(6,4), (5,6), (6,5) out of 30 pairs]

$$= \frac{8}{30} = \frac{4}{15}$$

$P(X=7) = P$

[getting (2,7), (7,2), (3,7), (7,3), (4,7), (7,4), (5,7), (7,5), (6,7), (7,6) out of 30 pairs]

$$= \frac{10}{30} = \frac{5}{15}$$

Therefore, required probability distribution is

X	3	4	5	6	7
P(X)	1/15	2/15	3/15	4/15	5/15

$\therefore$ Required mean $= \mu = \Sigma x_i p_i$

$$= 3\times\frac{1}{15} + 4\times\frac{2}{15} + 5\times\frac{3}{15} + 6\times\frac{4}{15} + 7\times\frac{5}{15}$$

$$= \frac{3}{15} + \frac{8}{15} + \frac{15}{15} + \frac{24}{15} + \frac{35}{15} = \frac{85}{15} = \frac{17}{3}$$

Example 7 **An urn contains 4 white and 3 red balls. Let X be the number of red balls in a random draw of 3 balls. Find the mean of X.**

Sol. When 3 balls are drawn at random, there may be no red ball, 1 red ball, 2 red balls or 3 red balls.

Let X denotes the random variable showing the number of red balls in a draw of 3 balls.

Then, X can take the values 0, 1, 2 or 3.

$P(X=0) = P$ (getting no red ball)

$= P$ (getting 3 white balls)

$$= \frac{^4C_3}{^7C_3} = \left(\frac{4\times3\times2}{3\times2\times1}\times\frac{3\times2\times1}{7\times6\times5}\right) = \frac{4}{35}$$

$P(X=1) = P$ (getting 1 red and 2 white balls)

$$= \frac{^3C_1 \times {^4C_2}}{^7C_3} = \left(\frac{3\times4\times3}{2}\times\frac{3\times2\times1}{7\times6\times5}\right) = \frac{18}{35}$$

$P(X=2) = P$ (getting 2 red and 1 white balls)

$$= \frac{^3C_2 \times {^4C_1}}{^7C_3} = \left(\frac{3\times2}{2\times1}\times4\times\frac{3\times2\times1}{7\times6\times5}\right) = \frac{12}{35}$$

$P(X=3) = P$ (getting 3 red balls)

$$= \frac{^3C_3}{^7C_3} = \frac{3\times2\times1}{7\times6\times5} = \frac{1}{35}$$

Thus, the probability distribution of X is given below

$X = x_i$	0	1	2	3
p_i	$\frac{4}{35}$	$\frac{18}{35}$	$\frac{12}{35}$	$\frac{1}{35}$

$\therefore$ Mean, $\mu = \Sigma x_i p_i$

$$= 0\times\frac{4}{35} + 1\times\frac{18}{35} + 2\times\frac{12}{35} + 3\times\frac{1}{35} = \frac{45}{35} = \frac{9}{7}$$

Topic Practice 4

Very Short Answer Type Questions

(2 Marks)

1 State whether the following distribution is a probability distribution of a random variable or not.

X	3	2	1	0	−1
P(X)	0.3	0.2	0.4	0.1	0.05

[NCERT]

2 The probability distribution of a discrete random variable X is given below

X	2	3	4	5
P(X)	$5/k$	$7/k$	$9/k$	$11/k$

Find the value of k. **[NCERT Exemplar]**

3 The random variable X has a probability distribution $P(X)$ of the following form, where λ is some number.

$$P(X) = \begin{cases} \lambda, & X = 0 \\ 3\lambda, & X = 1 \\ 4\lambda, & X = 2 \\ 5\lambda, & X = 3 \\ 0, & \text{otherwise} \end{cases}$$

Find the value of λ.

4 If the probability distribution of a random variable X is given below.

X	0	1	2	3	4
P(X)	$\frac{1}{15}$	$\frac{3}{15}$	$\frac{4}{15}$	$\frac{5}{15}$	$\frac{2}{15}$

Find the probability that the random variable has atleast 2 value.

Short Answer Type Questions

(4 Marks)

5 A coin is biased so that the head is 3 times as likely to occur as tail. If the coin is tossed twice, then find the probability distribution of number of tails. **[NCERT]**

6 3 defective bulbs are mixed up with 7 good ones. 3 bulbs are drawn at random. Find the probability distribution of defective bulbs.

7 Three cards are drawn successively with replacement from a well-shuffled pack of 52 cards. Find the probability distribution of the number of spades. Also, find the mean of the distribution.

8 From a lot of 30 bulbs which includes 6 defectives, a sample of 4 bulbs is drawn at random one-by-one with replacement. Find the probability distribution of the number of defective bulbs. Hence, find the mean of the distributions.

9 A coin is biased so that the head is 2 times as likely to occur as tail. If the coin is tossed twice, find the probability distribution of number of tails. Hence, find the mean of the distribution.

10 In a meeting, 70% of the members favour a certain proposal, 30% being opposite. A member is selected at random and let $X = 0$, if he opposed and $X = 1$, if he is in favour. Find $E(X)$. **[NCERT]**

11 Suppose 10000 tickets are sold in a lottery each for ₹ 1. First prize is of ₹ 3000 and the second prize is of ₹ 2000. There are three third prizes of ₹ 500 each. If you buy one ticket, then what is your expectation? **[NCERT Exemplar]**

Long Answer Type Questions

(6 Marks)

12 The probability distribution of a random variable X is given as under

$$P(X=x)=\begin{cases} kx^2, & x=1,2,3 \\ 2kx, & x=4,5,6 \\ 0, & \text{otherwise} \end{cases}$$

where, k is a constant. Calculate

(i) $E(X)$ (ii) $E(X^2)$

(iii) $P(X \geq 4)$ **[NCERT Exemplar]**

13 From a lot of 6 items containing 2 defective items, a sample of 4 items are drawn at random. Let the random variable X denote the number of defective items in the sample. If the sample is drawn without replacement, find

(i) The probability distribution of X

(ii) Mean of X **[ISC 2018]**

14 An urn contains 3 white and 6 red balls. Four balls are drawn one-by-one with replacement from the urn. Find the probability distribution of the number of red balls drawn. Also, find mean of the distribution.

15 Three numbers are selected at random (without replacement) from first six positive integers. Let X denotes the largest of the three numbers obtained. Find the probability distribution of X. Also, find the mean of the distribution.

Hints & Solutions

1. **Hint** $\sum_{i=1}^{n} p_i = 1.05$ [**Ans.** No]

2. **Hint** $\Sigma P(X)=1 \Rightarrow \frac{32}{k}=1$ [**Ans.** $k=32$]

3. **Hint** Use $\sum_{i=1}^{n} p_i = 1$ $\left[\textbf{Ans. } \lambda = \frac{1}{13}\right]$

4. P (random variable has atleast 2 value)

$$= P(X=2)+P(X=3)+P(X=4)$$

$$= \frac{4}{15}+\frac{5}{15}+\frac{2}{15}=\frac{11}{15}$$ [2]

5. Let X be the random variable which denotes the number of tails when a biased coin is tossed twice.

So, X may have values 0, 1 or 2.

Since, the coin is biased in which head is 3 times as likely to occur as a tail.

$\therefore \quad P(H)=\frac{3}{4}$ and $P(T)=\frac{1}{4}$ [1]

$$P(X=0)=P(HH)=P(H)\cdot P(H)=\left(\frac{3}{4}\right)^2=\frac{9}{16}$$

$P(X=1)=P$ (one tail and one head)

$$= P(HT, TH) = P(HT)+P(TH)$$

$$= P(H)\cdot P(T)+P(T)\cdot P(H)$$

$$= \frac{3}{4}\times\frac{1}{4}+\frac{1}{4}\times\frac{3}{4}$$

$$= \frac{3}{16}+\frac{3}{16}=\frac{6}{16}=\frac{3}{8}$$

$P(X=2)=P(\text{two tails})=P(TT)=P(T)\cdot P(T)$

$$= \left(\frac{1}{4}\right)^2=\frac{1}{16}$$ [2]

Therefore, the required probability distribution is as follows

X	0	1	2
$P(X)$	9/16	3/8	1/16

[1]

6. Given, defective bulbs = 3 and good bulbs = 7

Here, total number of bulbs = 3 + 7 = 10

Let X denotes the number of defective bulbs.

Then, X takes the values 0, 1, 2 and 3.

Now, $P(X=0)=P$ (getting 0 defective bulb)

$$= \frac{({}^3C_0 \times {}^7C_3)}{{}^{10}C_3} = \frac{\left(1\times\frac{7\times6\times5}{3\times2\times1}\right)}{\left(\frac{10\times9\times8}{3\times2\times1}\right)}$$

$$= \frac{7\times6\times5}{10\times9\times8}=\frac{7}{24}$$ [1/2]

$P(X=1)=P$ (getting 1 defective bulb)

$$= \frac{({}^3C_1 \times {}^7C_2)}{{}^{10}C_3} = \frac{\left(3\times\frac{7\times6}{2\times1}\right)}{\left(\frac{10\times9\times8}{3\times2\times1}\right)}$$

$$= \frac{3\times7\times6\times3}{10\times9\times8}=\frac{21}{40}$$ [1/2]

$P(X=2)=P$ (getting 2 defective bulbs)

$$= \frac{({}^3C_2 \times {}^7C_1)}{{}^{10}C_3} = \frac{\left(\frac{3\times2}{2\times1}\times7\right)}{\left(\frac{10\times9\times8}{3\times2\times1}\right)}$$

$$= \frac{3\times2\times7\times3}{10\times9\times8}=\frac{7}{40}$$ [1]

$P(X=3)=P$ (getting 3 defective bulbs)

$$= \frac{({}^3C_3 \times {}^7C_0)}{{}^{10}C_3} = \frac{1\times1}{\left(\frac{10\times9\times8}{3\times2\times1}\right)}$$

$$= \frac{3 \times 2 \times 1}{10 \times 9 \times 8} = \frac{1}{120}$$ [1]

∴ Required probability distribution as follows

X	0	1	2	3
P (X)	7/24	21/40	7/40	1/120

[1]

7. Let X be a random variable that denotes the number of spades in a draw of three cards. So, X can takes values 0, 1, 2 and 3.

Now, $P(X = 0) = P$ (no spade)

$$= \frac{39}{52} \times \frac{39}{52} \times \frac{39}{52} = \frac{3}{4} \times \frac{3}{4} \times \frac{3}{4} = \frac{27}{64}$$

[∵ cards are drawn with replacement]

$P(X = 1) = P$ (one spade and two non-spade)

$= P$ (I card is spade, II and III cards are non-spade) $+ P$ (I card is non-spade, II card is spade and III is non-spade) $+ P$ (I and II cards are non-spade and III card is spade)

$$= \frac{13}{52} \times \frac{39}{52} \times \frac{39}{52} + \frac{39}{52} \times \frac{13}{52} \times \frac{39}{52} + \frac{39}{52} \times \frac{39}{52} \times \frac{13}{52}$$

$$= 3\left(\frac{1}{4} \times \frac{3}{4} \times \frac{3}{4}\right) = \frac{27}{64}$$ [1]

$P(X = 2) = P$ (two spade and one non-spade)

$$= \frac{13}{52} \times \frac{13}{52} \times \frac{39}{52} + \frac{13}{52} \times \frac{39}{52} \times \frac{13}{52} + \frac{39}{52} \times \frac{13}{52} \times \frac{13}{52}$$

$$= 3\left(\frac{1}{4} \times \frac{1}{4} \times \frac{3}{4}\right) = \frac{9}{64}$$

∴ $P(X = 3) = P$ (all are spade cards)

$$= \frac{13}{52} \times \frac{13}{52} \times \frac{13}{52}$$

$$= \frac{1}{4} \times \frac{1}{4} \times \frac{1}{4} = \frac{1}{64}$$ [1]

Thus, the required probability distribution is as follows

X	0	1	2	3
P(X)	27/64	27/64	9/64	1/64

[1]

Now, mean of above distribution is given by

$$E(X) = \sum_{x=0}^{3} X \cdot P(X = x)$$

$$= 0 \cdot P(X = 0) + 1 \cdot P(X = 1) + 2 \cdot P(X = 2) + 3 \cdot P(X = 3)$$

$$= 0 \cdot \frac{27}{64} + 1 \cdot \frac{27}{64} + 2 \cdot \frac{9}{64} + 3 \cdot \frac{1}{64}$$

$$= \frac{27 + 18 + 3}{64} = \frac{48}{64} = \frac{3}{4}$$ [1]

8. Let X = Number of defective bulbs out of 4 bulbs drawn with replacement $X = 0, 1, 2, 3, 4$

p = Probability of defective bulb $= \frac{6}{30} = \frac{1}{5}$ [1]

q = Probability of good bulb = 4/5 [1]

$X = x_i$	0	1	2	3	4
$P(X) = p_i$	$\left(\frac{4}{5}\right)^4 = \frac{256}{625}$	$4 \cdot \frac{1}{5} \cdot \frac{64}{125} = \frac{256}{625}$	$6 \cdot \frac{1}{25} \cdot \frac{16}{25} = \frac{96}{625}$	$4 \cdot \frac{1}{125} \cdot \frac{4}{5} = \frac{16}{625}$	$\left(\frac{1}{5}\right)^4 = \frac{1}{625}$

[1]

Mean $(\mu) = \Sigma p_i x_i$

$$= 0 \times \frac{256}{625} + 1 \times \frac{256}{625} + 2 \times \frac{96}{625} + 3 \times \frac{16}{625} + 4 \times \frac{1}{625}$$

$$= \frac{4}{5}$$ [1]

9. Here, $P(\text{head}) = \frac{2}{3}$, $P(\text{tail}) = \frac{1}{3}$

Let X be the number of tails in two tosses.

Then, $X = 0, 1, 2$ [1]

X	0	1	2
P(X)	$\frac{2}{3} \times \frac{2}{3} = \frac{4}{9}$	$\frac{2}{3} \times \frac{1}{3} + \frac{1}{3} \times \frac{2}{3} = \frac{4}{9}$	$\frac{1}{3} \times \frac{1}{3} = \frac{1}{9}$
XP(X)	0	4/9	2/9

[2]

∴ Mean $= \Sigma XP(X) = \frac{6}{9} = \frac{2}{3}$ [2]

10. Hint

X	0	1
P(X)	3/10	7/10

$\left[\textbf{Ans. } E(X) = \frac{7}{10}\right]$

11. Hint

X	0	500	2000	3000
P (X)	$\frac{9995}{10000}$	$\frac{3}{10000}$	$\frac{1}{10000}$	$\frac{1}{10000}$
XP(X)	0	$\frac{1500}{10000}$	$\frac{2000}{10000}$	$\frac{3000}{10000}$

∵ $E(X) = \Sigma XP(X)$ [**Ans.** 0.65]

12. The probability distribution table for given function is

X	1	2	3	4	5	6	otherwise
P(X)	k	$4k$	$9k$	$8k$	$10k$	$12k$	0

[1]

We know that, $\Sigma P_i = 1$

∴ $k + 4k + 9k + 8k + 10k + 12k + 0 = 1$

$\Rightarrow 44k = 1 \Rightarrow k = \frac{1}{44}$ [1]

(i) $E(X) = \Sigma X \cdot P(X)$

$= 1 \times k + 2 \times 4k + 3 \times 9k + 4 \times 8k + 5 \times 10k + 6 \times 12k + 0$

$= k + 8k + 27k + 32k + 50k + 72k$

$= 190k = 190 \times \frac{1}{44} = \frac{95}{22}$ $\left[\because k = \frac{1}{44}\right]$ [1]

(ii) $E(X^2) = \Sigma X^2 P(X)$

$= (1) \times k + (2)^2 \times 4k + (3)^2 \times 9k + (4)^2 \times 8k + (5)^2 \times 10k + (6)^2 \times 12k$

$= k + 16k + 81k + 128k + 250k + 432k$

$= 908k = 908 \times \frac{1}{44} = 20.64$ (approx.) [1]

(iii) $P(X \geq 4) = P(X = 4) + P(X = 5) + P(X = 6)$

$= 30k = 30 \times \frac{1}{44} = 0.68$ [2]

13. Given, total number of items = 6

Defective items = 2,

Non-defective items $= 6 - 2 = 4$

(i) Let X denotes the number of defective items.

Then, X takes the values, $X = 0, 1, 2$

Now, $P(X = 0) = P$(getting non-defective item)

$= \frac{^4C_4 \times {^2C_0}}{^6C_4} = \frac{1}{15}$ [1]

$P(X = 1) = P$(getting one defective item)

$= \frac{^4C_3 \times {^2C_1}}{^6C_4} = \frac{4 \times 2}{15} = \frac{8}{15}$ [1]

$P(X = 2) = P$(getting two defective items)

$= \frac{^4C_2 \times {^2C_2}}{^6C_4} = \frac{6}{15}$ [1]

$\therefore$ Required probability distribution

X	0	1	2
P(X)	$\frac{1}{15}$	$\frac{8}{15}$	$\frac{6}{15}$

[1]

(ii) Mean of $X = \Sigma (X_i) P_i(X)$

$= 0 \times \frac{1}{15} + 1 \times \frac{8}{15} + 2 \times \frac{6}{15}$

$= \frac{0 + 8 + 12}{15} = \frac{20}{15} = \frac{4}{3}$

14. Consider p = probability of getting a red ball $= \frac{6}{9} = \frac{2}{3}$

and q = probability of getting a white ball $= \frac{3}{9} = \frac{1}{3}$

Let X denotes the number of red balls in four draws.

Then, X can take values 0, 1, 2, 3 and 4. [1/2]

Now, $P(X = 0) = P$ (no red balls) $= P$ (all black balls)

$= \frac{1}{3} \times \frac{1}{3} \times \frac{1}{3} \times \frac{1}{3} = \frac{1}{81}$

$P(X = 1) = P$ (one red and three blacks balls)

$= \frac{2}{3} \times \frac{1}{3} \times \frac{1}{3} \times \frac{1}{3} + \frac{1}{3} \times \frac{2}{3} \times \frac{1}{3} \times \frac{1}{3} + \frac{1}{3} \times \frac{1}{3} \times \frac{2}{3} \times \frac{1}{3}$

$+ \frac{1}{3} \times \frac{1}{3} \times \frac{1}{3} \times \frac{2}{3} = 4 \times \frac{2}{81} = \frac{8}{81}$

$P(X = 2) = P$ (two red and two black balls)

$= 6 \times \frac{4}{81} = \frac{24}{81}$

$P(X = 3) = P$ (three red and one black ball)

$= 4 \times \frac{8}{81} = \frac{32}{81}$

$P(X = 4) = P$ (all red balls)

$= 1 \times \frac{16}{81} = \frac{16}{81}$ [2½]

Hence, the probability distribution is shown below

X	0	1	2	3	4
P(X)	$\frac{1}{81}$	$\frac{8}{81}$	$\frac{24}{81}$	$\frac{32}{81}$	$\frac{16}{81}$

Now, mean of distribution, $E(X) = \Sigma X \cdot P(X)$ [1]

$= 0 \cdot \frac{1}{81} + 1 \cdot \frac{8}{81} + 2 \cdot \frac{24}{81} + 3 \cdot \frac{32}{81} + 4 \cdot \frac{16}{81}$

$= \frac{1}{81}[0 + 8 + 48 + 96 + 64] = \frac{216}{81} = \frac{8}{3}$ [1]

15. Given, X denotes the largest of the three positive integers.

So, the random variable X may have values 3, 4, 5 or 6.

$P(X = 3) = P$ (getting 3 and two numbers less than 3)

$= \frac{^1C_1 \times {^2C_2}}{^6C_3} = \frac{1}{20}$ [1]

$P(X = 4) = P$ (getting 4 and two numbers less than 4)

$= \frac{^1C_1 \times {^3C_2}}{^6C_3} = \frac{3}{20}$ [1]

$P(X = 5) = P$ (getting 5 and two numbers less than 5)

$= \frac{^1C_1 \times {^4C_2}}{^6C_3} = \frac{6}{20}$ [1]

$P(X = 6) = P$ (getting 6 and two numbers less than 6)

$= \frac{^1C_1 \times {^5C_2}}{^6C_3} = \frac{10}{20}$ [1]

$\therefore$ Probability distribution is shown below

X	3	4	5	6
P(X)	$\frac{1}{20}$	$\frac{3}{20}$	$\frac{6}{20}$	$\frac{10}{20}$

Now, mean of distribution, $E(X) = \Sigma X \cdot P(X)$

$= 3 \times \frac{1}{20} + 4 \times \frac{3}{20} + 5 \times \frac{6}{20} + 6 \times \frac{10}{20}$

$= \frac{3 + 12 + 30 + 60}{20}$

$= \frac{105}{20} = \frac{21}{4}$ [1]

Chapter Practice

Multiple Choice Type Questions

(1 Mark)

1 Three dice are thrown simultaneously. The probability of obtaining a total score of 5 is

(a) $\frac{5}{216}$ (b) $\frac{1}{6}$ (c) $\frac{1}{36}$ (d) $\frac{1}{49}$

2 A die is thrown once. Let A be the event that the number obtained is greater than 3. Let B be the event that the number obtained is less than 5. Then, $P(A \cup B)$ is

(a) $\frac{2}{5}$ (b) $\frac{3}{5}$ (c) 0 (d) 1

3 If A and B are two events such that $P(B) = \frac{3}{5}$, $P(A/B) = \frac{1}{2}$ and $P(A \cup B) = \frac{4}{5}$, then $P(A)$ is equal to

(a) $\frac{3}{10}$ (b) $\frac{1}{5}$ (c) $\frac{1}{2}$ (d) $\frac{3}{5}$

4 If $P\left(\frac{A}{B}\right) = 0.3$, $P(A) = 0.4$ and $P(B) = 0.8$, then $P\left(\frac{B}{A}\right)$ is equal to

(a) 0.6 (b) 0.3 (c) 0.06 (d) 0.4

5 A bag contains 3 white, 4 black and 2 red balls. If 2 balls are drawn at random (without replacement), then the probability that both the balls are white, is

(a) $\frac{1}{18}$ (b) $\frac{1}{36}$ (c) $\frac{1}{12}$ (d) $\frac{1}{24}$

6 The events E and F are independent. If $P(E) = 0.3$ and $P(E \cup F) = 0.5$, then $P\left(\frac{E}{F}\right) - P\left(\frac{F}{E}\right)$ is equal to

(a) $\frac{1}{7}$ (b) $\frac{2}{7}$ (c) $\frac{3}{35}$ (d) $\frac{1}{70}$

7 X and Y are independent events such that $P(X \cap \bar{Y}) = \frac{2}{5}$ and $P(X) = \frac{3}{5}$. Then, $P(Y)$ is equal to

(a) $\frac{2}{3}$ (b) $\frac{2}{5}$ (c) $\frac{1}{3}$ (d) $\frac{1}{5}$

Assertion-Reason Type Questions

(1 Mark)

Directions (Q. Nos. 8-11) *In the questions given below are two statements labelled as Assertion (A) and Reason (R). In the context of the two statements, which one of the following is correct?*

(a) Both A and R are correct; R is the correct explanation of A
(b) Both A and R are correct; R is not the correct explanation of A
(c) A is correct; R is incorrect
(d) R is correct; A is incorrect

8 Two coins are tossed once.

Assertion (A) If E : tail appears on one coin and F : one coin shows head, then $P(E/F)$ is 1.

Reason (R) If E : no tail appears and F : no head appears, then $P(E/F)$ is 0.

9 **Assertion (A)** Consider the experiment of drawing a card from a deck of 52 playing cards, in which the elementary events are assumed to be equally likely. If E and F denote the events the card drawn is a spade and the card drawn is an ace respectively, then

$P(E/F) = \frac{1}{4}$ and $P(F/E) = \frac{1}{13}$.

Reason (R) E and F are two events such that the probability of occurrence of one of them is not affected by occurrence of the other. Such events are called independent events.

10 **Assertion (A)** Two coins are tossed simultaneously. The probability getting two heads, if it is known that atleast one head comes up, is $\frac{1}{3}$.

Reason (R) Let E and F be two events with a random experiment,

$$P\left(\frac{F}{E}\right) = \frac{P(E \cap F)}{P(E)}.$$

11 **Assertion (A)** If $P(A) = \frac{3}{5}$ and $P(B) = \frac{1}{5}$, then $P(A \cap B)$, if A and B are independent events, is $\frac{3}{25}$.

Reason (R) Two cards are drawn at random and without replacement from a pack of 52 playing cards. Then, the probability that both the cards are black, is $\frac{25}{102}$.

Very Short Answer Type Questions

(2 Marks)

12 In class XII of a school, 40% of students study Mathematics, 30% of students study Biology and 10% of class study both Mathematics and Biology. If a student is selected at random from the class, then find the probability that he will studying Mathematics or Biology.

13 A die has two faces each with number 1, three faces each with number 2 and one face with number 3. If die is rolled once, then determine probability of not getting 3.

14 If $P(A) = \frac{7}{13}$, $P(B) = \frac{9}{13}$ and $P(A \cap B) = \frac{4}{13}$, then find $P\left(\frac{A'}{B}\right)$. **[NCERT Exemplar]**

15 If $P(A) = 0.4$, $P(B) = 0.8$ and $P\left(\frac{B}{A}\right) = 0.6$, then find $P(A \cup B)$. **[NCERT Exemplar]**

16 A coin is tossed 4 times. Find the mean of the probability distribution of the number of tails.

Short Answer Type Questions

(4 Marks)

17 If A and B are two events such that $P(B) = \frac{3}{5}$, $P\left(\frac{A}{B}\right) = \frac{1}{2}$ and $P(A \cup B) = \frac{4}{5}$, then find $P(A)$. **[NCERT Exemplar]**

18 If A and B are two events such that $P(A) = \frac{1}{2}$, $P(B) = \frac{1}{3}$ and $P\left(\frac{A}{B}\right) = \frac{1}{4}$, then find $P(A' \cap B')$. **[NCERT Exemplar]**

19 If A and B are two events such that $P(A) = \frac{3}{8}$, $P(B) = \frac{5}{8}$ and $P(A \cup B) = \frac{3}{4}$, then find $P\left(\frac{A}{B}\right) \cdot P\left(\frac{A'}{B}\right)$. **[NCERT Exemplar]**

20 If a mother, father and son line up at random for a family picture as E (son on one end) and F (father is on middle), then find $P(E/F)$. **[NCERT]**

21 A bag contains 8 red and 5 white balls. Two successive draws of 3 balls are made at random from the bag without replacements. Find the probability that the first draw yields 3 white balls and the second draw 3 red balls. **[ISC 2012]**

22 A purse contains 4 silver and 5 copper coins. A second purse contains 3 silver and 7 copper coins. If a coin is taken out at random from one of the purses, then what is the probability that it is a copper coin? **[ISC 2011]**

23 An article manufactured by a company consists of two parts A and B. In the process of manufacture of part A, 9 out of 104 parts may be defective. Similarly, 5 out of 100 are likely to be defective in the manufacture of part B. Calculate the probability that the article manufactured will not be defective. **[ISC 2009]**

24 12 cards, numbered 1 to 12 are placed in a box, mixed up thoroughly and then a card is drawn at random from the box. If it is known that the number on the drawn card is more than 3, then find the probability that it is an even number.

25 In a college, 30% students fail in Physics, 25% fail in Mathematics and 10% fail in both. One student is chosen at random. Find the probability that she fails in Physics, if she failed in Mathematics. **[NCERT Exemplar]**

26 A bag contains 5 red, 7 green and 4 white balls. 3 balls are drawn one after another without replacement. Find the probability that

(i) the balls are white, green and green, respectively.

(ii) out of 3 balls, one is white and 2 is green.

27 A bag contains 4 red and 5 black balls. Another bag contains 3 red and 6 black balls. One ball is drawn from bag I and two balls are drawn from bag II. Find the probability that out of three, two are black and one is red.

28 A class consists of 50 students out of which there are 10 girls. In the class 2 girls and 5 boys are rank holders in an examination. If a student is selected at random from the class and is found to be a rank holder, then what is the probability that the student selected is a girl? **[ISC 2008]**

29 A box contains 3 orange balls, 3 green balls and 2 blue balls. Three balls are drawn at random from the box without replacement. Find the probability of drawing 2 green balls and one blue ball. **[NCERT Exemplar]**

30 Two events E and F are independent. If $P(E) = 0.3$ and $P(E \cup F) = 0.5$, then find $P\left(\frac{E}{F}\right) - P\left(\frac{F}{E}\right)$. **[NCERT Exemplar]**

31 In a group of students, there are 3 boys and 3 girls. 4 students are to be selected at random from the group. Find the probability that either 3 boys and 1 girl or 3 girls and 1 boy are selected.

32 Three persons A, B and C fire at a target in turn, starting with A. Their probability of hitting the target are 0.4, 0.3 and 0.2, respectively. Find the probability that exactly two of them hit the target. **[NCERT Exemplar]**

33 Three bags contains a number of red and white balls as follows. Bag I : 3 red balls, Bag II : 2 red balls and 1 white ball and Bag III : 3 white balls. The probability that bag i will be chosen and a ball is selected from it is $\frac{i}{6}$, where $i = 1, 2, 3$. What is the probability that

(i) a red ball will be selected?

(ii) a white ball will be selected? **[NCERT Exemplar]**

34 A box contains 2 gold and 3 silver coins. Another box contains 3 gold and 3 silver coins. A box is chosen at random and coin is drawn from it. If the selected coin is a gold coin, then find the probability that it was drawn from second box.

35 The random variable X has a probability distribution $P(X)$ of the following form, where k is some number $P(X) = \begin{cases} k, & \text{if } X = 0 \\ 2k, & \text{if } X = 1 \\ 3k, & \text{if } X = 2 \\ 0, & \text{otherwise} \end{cases}$

(i) Determine the value of k.

(ii) Find $P(X < 2)$, $P(X \leq 2)$ and $P(X \geq 2)$. **[NCERT]**

36 The random variable X can take only the values 0, 1, 2. If $P(X = 0) = P(X = 1) = p$ and $E(X^2) = E(X)$, then find the value of p. **[NCERT Exemplar]**

37 Find the probability distribution of number of doublets in three tosses of a pair of dice.

38 Two cards are drawn simultaneously (without replacement) from a well-shuffled deck of 52 cards. Find the mean of number of red cards.

39 In a die game, a player pays a stake of ₹ 1 for each throw of a die. She receives ₹ 5, if the die shows a 3; ₹ 2, if the die shows a 1 or 6 and nothing otherwise. What is the player's expected profit per throw over a long series of throws? **[NCERT Exemplar]**

40 A and B throw two dice each. If A gets a sum of 9 on his two dice, then find the probability of B getting a higher sum. **[ISC 2006]**

Long Answer Type Questions

6 Marks

41 Three persons, Aman, Bipin and Mohan attempt a Mathematics problem independently. The odds favour of Aman and Mohan solving the problem are 3 : 2 and 4 : 1, respectively and the odds against Bipin solving the problem are 2 : 1. Find

(i) the probability that all the three persons will solve the problem.

(ii) the probability that problem will be solved. **[ISC 2013]**

42 Aman and Bhuwan throw a pair of dice alternatively. In order to win, they have to get a sum of 8. Find their respective probabilities of winning, if Aman starts the game. **[ISC 2011]**

43 An insurence company insured 1500 scooter drivers, 2500 car derivers and 4500 truck drivers. The probability of a scooter, a car and a truck meeting with an accident is 0.01, 0.02 and 0.04 respectively. If one of the insured persons meets with an accident, then find the probability that he is a scooter driver. **[ISC 2007]**

44 A man is known to speak truth 3 out of 4 times. He throws a die and reports that it is a six. Find the probability that it is actually a six.

45 If a machine is correctly setup, it produces 90% acceptable items. If it is incorrectly setup, it produces only 40% acceptable items. Past experience shows that 80% of the setups are correctly done. If after a certain setup, the machine produces 2 acceptable items, then find the probability that machine is correctly setup. [NCERT]

46 A company has two plants which manufacture scooters. Plant I manufactures 80% of the scooters while plant II manufactures 20% of the scooters. At plant I, 85 out of 100 scooters are rated as being of standard quality, while at plant II only 65 out of 100 scooters are rated as being of standard quality. If a scooter is of standard quality, what is the probability that it came from plant I? [ISC 2006]

47 Suppose 5% of men and 0.25% of women have grey hair. A grey haired person is selected at random. What is the probability of this person being male? (Assume that these are equal number of males and females) [NCERT]

Case-Based Type Questions

6 Marks

48 Suppose we have four boxes A, B, C, D containing coloured marbles as given below

Boxes	Marble colour		
	Red	White	Black
A	1	6	3
B	6	2	2
C	8	1	1
D	0	6	4

One of the boxes has been selected at random and a single marble drawn from it. If the marble is red, then what is the probability that it was drawn from

(i) box A? (ii) box B?

(iii) box C? [NCERT]

49 A building contractor undertakes a job to construct 4 flats on a plot along with parking area. Due to strike the probability of many construction workers not being present for the job is 0.65. The probability that many are not present and still the work gets completed on time is 0.35. The probability that work will be completed on time when all workers are present is 0.80.

Let E_1 : represent the event when many workers were not present for the job;

E_2 : represent the event when all workers were present; and

E : represent completing the construction work on time.

Based on the above information, answer the following questions.

(i) What is the probability that all the workers are present for the job ?

(ii) What is the probability that construction will be completed on time ?

(iii)(a) What is the probability that many workers are not present given that the construction work is completed on time?

Or

(b) What is the probability that all workers were present given that the construction job was completed on time ?

50 A primary school teacher wants to teach the concept of 'larger number' to the students of Class II.

To teach this concept, he conducts an activity in his class. He asks the children to select two numbers from a set of numbers given as 2, 3, 4, 5 one after the other without replacement.

All the outcomes of this activity are tabulated in the form of ordered pairs given below.

	2	3	4	5
2	(2, 2)	(2, 3)	(2, 4)	
3	(3, 2)	(3, 3)		(3, 5)
4	(4, 2)		(4, 4)	(4, 5)
5		(5, 3)	(5, 4)	(5, 5)

(i) Complete the table given above.

(ii) Find the total number of ordered pairs having one larger number.

(iii) Let the random variable X denote the larger of two numbers in the ordered pair.

Now, complete the probability distribution table for X given below

X	3	4	5
$P(X = x)$			

(iv) Find the value of $P(X < 5)$.

(v) Calculate the expected value of the probability distribution. [ISC 2024]

Answers

1. (c) **2.** (d) **3.** (c) **4.** (a) **5.** (c) **6.** (d) **7.** (c) **8.** (b) **9.** (a) **10.** (b)

11. (b) **12.** 0.6 **13.** $\frac{5}{6}$ **14.** $\frac{5}{9}$ **15.** 0.96 **16.** Mean = 2 **17.** $\frac{1}{2}$ **18.** $\frac{1}{4}$ **19.** $\frac{6}{25}$

20. 1 **21.** $\frac{7}{429}$ **22.** $\frac{113}{180}$ **23.** 0.8677 **24.** $\frac{5}{9}$ **25.** $\frac{2}{5}$ **26.** (i) 0.05 (ii) 0.15 **27.** $\frac{25}{54}$ **28.** $\frac{1}{11}$

29. $\frac{3}{28}$ **30.** $\frac{1}{70}$ **31.** $\frac{2}{5}$ **32.** 0.188 **33.** (i) $\frac{7}{18}$ (ii) $\frac{11}{18}$ **34.** $\frac{5}{9}$ **35.** (i) $k = \frac{1}{6}$ (ii) $\frac{1}{2}$, 1, $\frac{1}{2}$ **36.** $p = \frac{1}{2}$

37.

X	0	1	2	3
$P(X)$	$\frac{125}{216}$	$\frac{75}{216}$	$\frac{15}{216}$	$\frac{1}{216}$

38. Mean = 1 **39.** 0.50 **40.** $\frac{1}{54}$ **41.** (i) $\frac{4}{25}$ (ii) $\frac{31}{75}$ **42.** $\frac{31}{67}$ **43.** $\frac{3}{49}$ **44.** $\frac{3}{8}$ **45.** 0.953

46. 0.84 **47.** $\frac{20}{21}$ **48.** (i) $\frac{1}{15}$ (ii) $\frac{2}{5}$ (iii) $\frac{8}{15}$

49. (i) $P(E_2) = 0.35$ (ii) $P(E) = 0.5075$ (iii) $P\left(\frac{E_1}{E}\right) = 0.448$ (iv) $P\left(\frac{E_2}{E}\right) = 0.552$

50. (i) All outcomes of this cutting are tabulated in the form of ordered pairs given below

	2	3	4	5
2	(2, 2)	(2, 3)	(2, 4)	(2, 5)
3	(3, 2)	(3, 3)	(3, 4)	(3, 5)
4	(4, 2)	(4, 3)	(4, 4)	(4, 5)
5	(5, 2)	(5, 3)	(5, 4)	(5, 5)

(ii) 12

(iii)

X	3	4	5
$P(X = x)$	$\frac{1}{6}$	$\frac{1}{3}$	$\frac{1}{2}$

(iv) $\frac{1}{2}$ (v) $\frac{13}{3}$

CHAPTER

12

Vectors

In this chapter, we will study some of the basic concepts about vectors, various operations on vectors, and their algebraic and geometric properties.

- Basic Concepts of Vectors and Section Formulae
- Scalar (or Dot) Product of Two Vectors
- Vector (or Cross) Product of Two Vectors

TOPIC 01 Basic Concepts of Vectors and Section Formulae

Scalar Quantities or Scalars

Those quantities which have magnitude but no direction, are called scalar quantities or scalars. **e.g.** The height of Ram may be 1.6 m. Here, height involves only one value (magnitude), which is a real number. Some scalar quantities are length, mass, time, distance, speed, area, volume, temperature, work, density, voltage, resistance, etc. A scalar quantity is represented by a real number alongwith a suitable unit.

Vector Quantities or Vectors

Those quantities which have magnitude as well as direction are called vector quantities or vectors. **e.g.** A football player hit the ball to give a pass to another player of his team. Hence, he apply a quantity (called force) which involves muscular strength (magnitude) and direction in which another player is positioned. Some vector quantities are force, displacement, velocity, acceleration, weight, momentum, electric field intensity, etc.

Example 1 Classify the following measures as scalars and vectors.

(i) 40 watt (ii) 20 m/s^2

(iii) 100 m^2 (iv) 2 m North-West

Sol. (i) 40 watt represents power, which is a scalar.

(ii) 20 m/s^2 represents acceleration, which is a vector.

(iii) 100 m^2 represents an area, which is a scalar.

(iv) 2 m North-West has magnitude as well as direction, so it is a vector.

Representation of a Vector as a Directed Line Segment (or Notation for a Vector)

Any straight line 'l' in plane or three dimensional space can be given two directions by means of arrowheads. A line with one of these directions prescribed is called a **directed line** and if we restrict the line l to the line segment AB, then a magnitude is prescribed on the line l with one of the two directions, so we obtain a **directed line segment**.

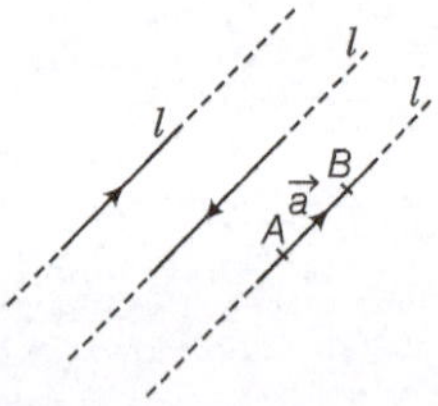

Thus, a directed line segment has magnitude as well as direction, so it is called **vector** denoted as $\overrightarrow{AB}$ (or simply as $\vec{a}$) and read as vector 'AB' (or vector 'a').

Here, the point A from where the vector $\overrightarrow{AB}$ starts is called its **initial point** and the point B where it ends is called its **terminal point**. Since, the initial and terminal points of $\overrightarrow{AB}$ are not interchangeable so the vectors $\overrightarrow{AB}$ and $\overrightarrow{BA}$ must be different. Generally, **vectors are denoted by** $\vec{a}, \vec{b}, \vec{c}$ etc.

Note The arrow indicates the direction of the vector.

Magnitude (or Length or Modulus) of a Vector

The length of the vector $\overrightarrow{AB}$ or $\vec{a}$ is called the **magnitude** (or modulus) of $\overrightarrow{AB}$ or $\vec{a}$ and it is represented by $|\overrightarrow{AB}|$ or $|\vec{a}|$ or a. Since, the length is never negative, the notation $|\overrightarrow{AB}| < 0$ has no meaning.

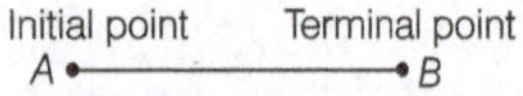

In other words, the distance between **initial point** or **origin** and **terminal point** or **end point** of a vector is called its length or magnitude.

Types of Vectors

There are various types of vectors as given below

(i) **Like Vectors** Two vectors $\vec{a}$ and $\vec{b}$ are said to be **like vectors**, if they have the same directions and they said to be **unlike vectors**, if they have opposite directions.

(ii) **Zero or Null Vector** A vector whose magnitude is zero, i.e. whose initial and terminal points coincide, is called a null vector or zero vector. It is denoted by $\vec{0}$ and it cannot be assigned a definite direction, as its magnitude is zero. Otherwise, it may be regarded as having any direction. Thus, $\overrightarrow{AA}, \overrightarrow{BB}$ represent the zero vectors.

(iii) **Unit Vector** A vector whose magnitude is one unit (i.e. unity) is called a unit vector. The unit vector in the direction of $\vec{a}$ is denoted by $\hat{a}$ and read as 'a cap'.

(iv) **Proper Vector** If vector, which is not a zero vector, is called proper vector. i.e. If $|\vec{a}| \neq 0$, where $\vec{a}$ be any vector, the $\vec{a}$ is called proper vector.

(v) **Coinitial Vectors** Two or more vectors having the same initial point are called coinitial vectors.

Note Two equal coinitial vectors must coincide.

(vi) **Collinear or Parallel Vectors** Two or more vectors are said to be collinear, if they are parallel to same line, irrespective of their magnitudes and directions.

(vii) **Non-collinear Vectors** These vectors whose directions are neither parallel nor coincident, are called non-collinear vectors.

(viii) **Equal Vectors** Two vectors are said to be **equal,** if they have same magnitude and direction regardless of the positions of their initial points. Symbolically if $\vec{a}$ and $\vec{b}$ are equal, then it is written as $\vec{a} = \vec{b}$.

(ix) **Negative of a Vector** A vector whose magnitude is same as that of a given vector but the direction is opposite to that of it, is called negative of the given vector. **e.g.** Let $\overrightarrow{AB}$ be a vector, then $-\overrightarrow{AB}$ or $\overrightarrow{BA}$ is its negative vector.

(x) **Coplanar Vectors** Three or more vectors, which either lie in the same plane or are parallel to the same plane, are called coplanar vectors.

(xi) **Non-coplanar Vectors** Three or more vectors, which do not lie in the same plane nor parallel to the same plane are called non-coplanar vectors.

(xii) **Localised Vectors** These vectors which are restricted to pass through a given point (origin) are called localised vectors.

(xiii) **Reciprocal Vectors** Two vectors are said to be reciprocal vectors, if they have the same direction but whose magnitude (or modulus or length) are reciprocal of each other. Thus, if $\hat{a}$ denotes the unit vector in the direction of a vector $\vec{a}$, then

$$\vec{a} = |\vec{a}|\,\hat{a} \text{ and } \frac{1}{\vec{a}} = \frac{\hat{a}}{|\vec{a}|}.$$

Note

(i) Two vectors are always coplanar.

(ii) If the value of a vector depends only on its magnitude and direction and is independent of its position in the space, it is called **free or non-localised vector.** Throughout this chapter, we will be dealing with free vectors only.

Example 2 In the given parallelogram *ABCD*, identify the vectors are

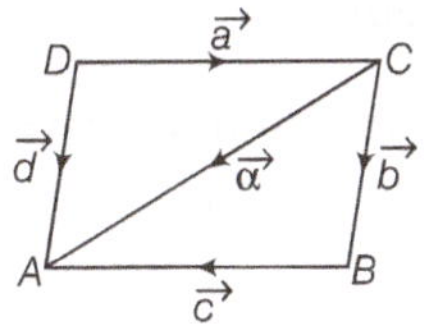

(i) equal.
(ii) collinear but not equal.
(iii) coinitial vector.

Sol. (i) $\vec{b}$ and $\vec{d}$ are equal vectors.

(ii) $\vec{a}$ and $\vec{c}$ are collinear vectors but not equal.
[here, $\vec{a}$ and $\vec{c}$ have opposite directions]

(iii) $\vec{\alpha}$ and $\vec{b}$; $\vec{d}$ and $\vec{a}$ are coinitial vectors.

Position Vector of a Point

Let $O\ (0, 0, 0)$ be the origin and P be a point in space having coordinates (x, y, z) with respect to the origin O.

Then, the vector $\overrightarrow{OP}$ or $\vec{r}$ is called the **position vector** of the point P with respect to O. Here, O is its initial point and P is its terminal point.

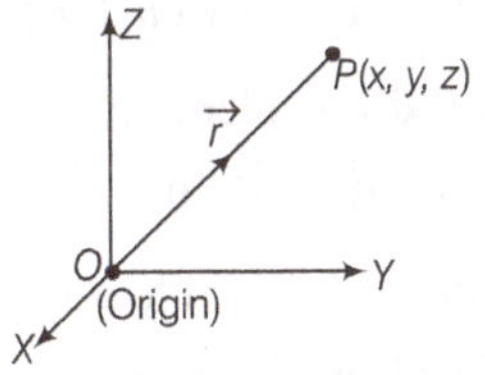

By using the distance formula, the magnitude of $\overrightarrow{OP}$ or $\vec{r}$ is given by

$$|\overrightarrow{OP}| = |\vec{r}| = \sqrt{x^2 + y^2 + z^2}$$

Generally, we denote the position vector of points A, B, C, etc., with respect to the origin O by $\vec{a}, \vec{b}, \vec{c}$, etc., respectively.

Addition of Vectors (Combination of Two Directed Line Segments)

There are two laws of vector addition, which are given below

1. Triangle Law of Vector Addition

Suppose two vectors $\vec{a}$ and $\vec{b}$ are represented by the two adjacent sides of a triangle such that the initial point of one coincides with the terminal point of the other (say $\overrightarrow{AB}$ and $\overrightarrow{BC}$), then their sum (or resultant) $\vec{c}$ is represented by the third side $\overrightarrow{AC}$ of ΔABC.

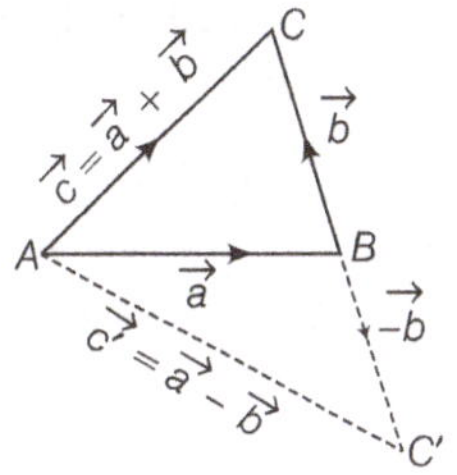

Thus, $\vec{a} + \vec{b} = \vec{c}$ or $\overrightarrow{AB} + \overrightarrow{BC} = \overrightarrow{AC}$

This is known as the **triangle law** of vector addition.

Difference of Two Vectors

Suppose a vector $\overrightarrow{BC'}$ or $\vec{b}'$ is constructed, such that its magnitude is same as the vector $\overrightarrow{BC}$ and direction opposite to $\overrightarrow{BC}$,

i.e. $\overrightarrow{BC'} = -\overrightarrow{BC}$ or $\vec{b}' = -\vec{b}$.

Then, by triangle law, we have

$$\overrightarrow{AC'} = \overrightarrow{AB} + \overrightarrow{BC'} = \overrightarrow{AB} + (-\overrightarrow{BC})$$
$$= \overrightarrow{AB} - \overrightarrow{BC} \quad \text{or} \quad \vec{c}' = \vec{a} - \vec{b}$$

Here, the vector $\overrightarrow{AC'}$ or $\vec{c}'$ is said to be represent the **difference** of $\vec{a}$ and $\vec{b}$.

Example 3 If *A*, *B* and *C* are the vertices of a ΔABC, then what is the value of $\overrightarrow{AB} + \overrightarrow{BC} + \overrightarrow{CA}$?

Sol. By triangle law of vector addition, we get

$$\overrightarrow{AB} + \overrightarrow{BC} = \overrightarrow{AC}$$

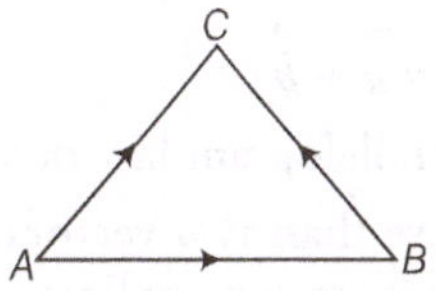

$$\Rightarrow \quad \overrightarrow{AB} + \overrightarrow{BC} + \overrightarrow{CA} = \overrightarrow{CA} + \overrightarrow{AC}$$

$\Rightarrow \overrightarrow{AB} + \overrightarrow{BC} + \overrightarrow{CA} = \overrightarrow{CA} - \overrightarrow{CA}$ $\quad [\because \overrightarrow{AC} = -\overrightarrow{CA}]$

$\therefore \quad \overrightarrow{AB} + \overrightarrow{BC} + \overrightarrow{CA} = \vec{0}$

Note When the sides of a triangle are taken in order, it leads to zero resultant as the initial and terminal points get coincided.

Example 4 Vectors drawn from the origin O to the points A, B and C are respectively $\vec{a}$, $\vec{b}$ and $4\vec{a}-3\vec{b}$. Find $\overrightarrow{AC}$ and $\overrightarrow{BC}$.

Sol. We have, $\overrightarrow{OA} = \vec{a}$, $\overrightarrow{OB} = \vec{b}$ and $\overrightarrow{OC} = 4\vec{a} - 3\vec{b}$.

Clearly, from ΔOAC, we get $\overrightarrow{OA} + \overrightarrow{AC} = \overrightarrow{OC}$

[using triangle law of addition]

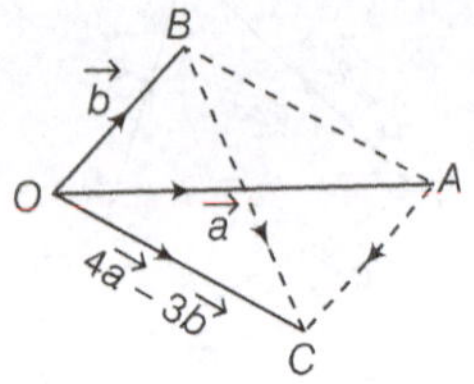

$\Rightarrow \quad \overrightarrow{AC} = \overrightarrow{OC} - \overrightarrow{OA} = 4\vec{a} - 3\vec{b} - \vec{a}$

$= 3\vec{a} - 3\vec{b} = 3(\vec{a} - \vec{b})$

and from ΔOBC, we get

$\overrightarrow{OB} + \overrightarrow{BC} = \overrightarrow{OC}$ [using triangle law of addition]

$\Rightarrow \quad \overrightarrow{BC} = \overrightarrow{OC} - \overrightarrow{OB}$

$= 4\vec{a} - 3\vec{b} - \vec{b}$

$= 4\vec{a} - 4\vec{b} = 4(\vec{a} - \vec{b})$

2. Parallelogram Law of Vector Addition

Suppose two vectors $\vec{a}$ and $\vec{b}$ are represented by the two adjacent sides of a parallelogram, then their sum $\vec{c}$ is represented by the diagonal of the parallelogram, which is coinitial with the given vectors.

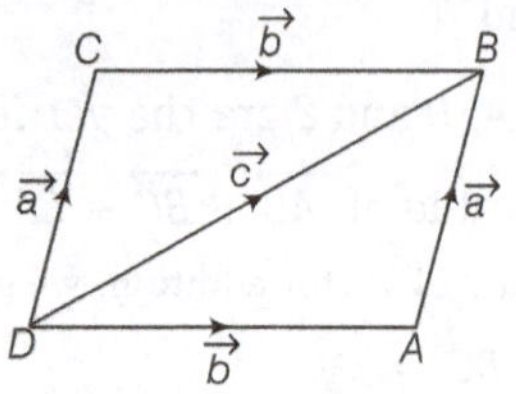

Mathematically, $\vec{c} = \vec{a} + \vec{b}$

This is known as **parallelogram law** of vector addition.

The **addition of more than two vectors** (vector polygon) can also be found by repeated application of the triangle laws.

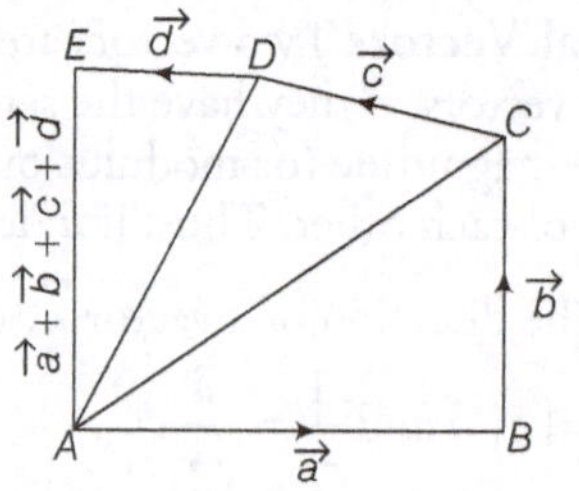

Thus, in the figure,

$\vec{a} + \vec{b} + \vec{c} + \vec{d} = \overrightarrow{AB} + \overrightarrow{BC} + \overrightarrow{CD} + \overrightarrow{DE}$

$= \overrightarrow{AC} + \overrightarrow{CD} + \overrightarrow{DE}$ $\quad [\because \overrightarrow{AB} + \overrightarrow{BC} = \overrightarrow{AC}]$

$= \overrightarrow{AD} + \overrightarrow{DE}$ $\quad [\because \overrightarrow{AC} + \overrightarrow{CD} = \overrightarrow{AD}]$

$= \overrightarrow{AE}$

$\therefore$ The vector $\overrightarrow{AE}$ is the sum of the given vectors and the polygon $ABCDEA$ is a vector polygon.

Note

(i) For applying parallelogram law, vectors should have same initial point.

(ii) From the above figure, using the triangle law of vector addition, we have

$\overrightarrow{DA} + \overrightarrow{AB} = \overrightarrow{DB}$ or $\overrightarrow{DA} + \overrightarrow{DC} = \overrightarrow{DB}$ $\quad [\because \overrightarrow{AB} = \overrightarrow{DC}]$

which is parallelogram law. Thus, we may say that the two laws of vector addition are equivalent to each other.

Properties of Vector Addition

Suppose $\vec{a}$, $\vec{b}$ and $\vec{c}$ are any three vectors, then

(i) Vector addition is **commutative,**

i.e. $\quad \vec{a} + \vec{b} = \vec{b} + \vec{a}$

(ii) Vector addition is **associative,**

i.e. $\quad (\vec{a} + \vec{b}) + \vec{c} = \vec{a} + (\vec{b} + \vec{c})$

(iii) **Existence of additive identity**

$\vec{a} + \vec{0} = \vec{a} = \vec{0} + \vec{a}$

where $\vec{0}$ is called additive identity.

(iv) **Existence of additive inverse**

$(\vec{a}) + (-\vec{a}) = \vec{0} = (-\vec{a}) + (\vec{a})$

where, vector $-\vec{a}$ is called the negative (or additive inverse) of $\vec{a}$.

Note The associative property of vector addition enables us to write the sum of three vectors $\vec{a}$, $\vec{b}$ and $\vec{c}$ as $\vec{a} + \vec{b} + \vec{c}$ without using brackets.

Example 5 If $\vec{a}$ and $\vec{b}$ are two non-collinear vectors having the same initial point. What are the vectors represented by $\vec{a}+\vec{b}$ and $\vec{a}-\vec{b}$?

Sol. According to the given condition, we have the following figure

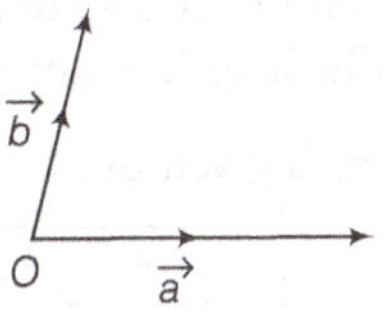

Let us make the following parallelogram.

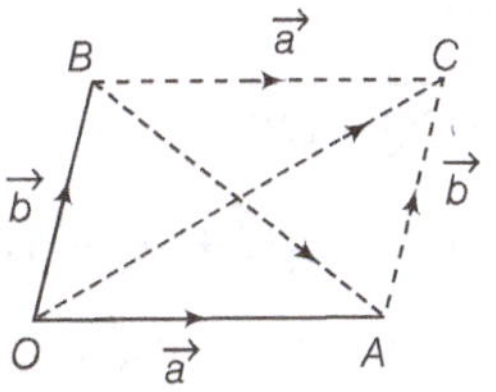

Clearly, by parallelogram law, we have

$$\overrightarrow{OC} = \overrightarrow{OA} + \overrightarrow{AC} = \vec{a} + \vec{b}$$

and $$\overrightarrow{BA} = \overrightarrow{BC} + \overrightarrow{CA} = \vec{a} + (-\vec{b}) = \vec{a} - \vec{b}$$

Thus, $\vec{a}+\vec{b}$ and $\vec{a}-\vec{b}$ represent the diagonals of the parallelogram.

Representation of a Vector in Terms of Position Vectors of Its End Points

Let $\vec{p}$ and $\vec{q}$ be the position vectors of points P and Q, respectively.

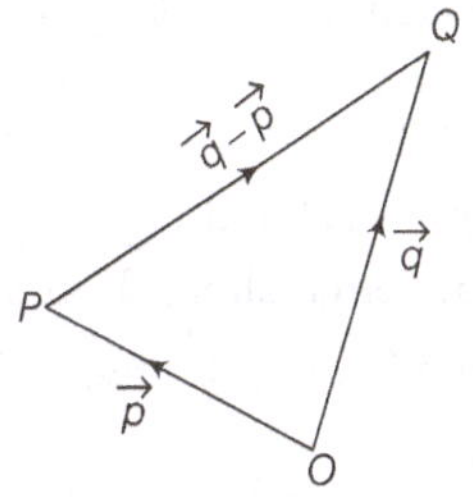

In ΔOPQ,

$$\overrightarrow{OP} + \overrightarrow{PQ} = \overrightarrow{OQ}$$

[by using triangle law of vector addition]

$\Rightarrow$ $$\overrightarrow{PQ} = \overrightarrow{OQ} - \overrightarrow{OP}$$

$\Rightarrow \overrightarrow{PQ}$ = Position vector of Q – Position vector of P

$$= \vec{q} - \vec{p}.$$

Multiplication of a Vector by a Scalar

Let λ be a scalar and $\vec{a}$ be a vector, then $\lambda\vec{a}$ is defined as a vector whose magnitude is $|\lambda|$ times the magnitude of $\vec{a}$, i.e. $|\lambda\vec{a}| = |\lambda||\vec{a}|$ and the direction is same or opposite of $\vec{a}$, according as λ is positive or negative.

e.g. When $\lambda = -2$, then $\lambda\vec{a} = -2\vec{a}$, which is a vector having magnitude double to the magnitude of $\vec{a}$ and direction opposite to that of the direction of $\vec{a}$.

Note

(i) $1\vec{a} = \vec{a}$ (ii) $(-1)\vec{a} = -\vec{a}$ (iii) $0\vec{a} = \vec{0}$

(iv) For any value of λ, the vector $\lambda\vec{a}$ is always collinear to the vector $\vec{a}$.

(v) If $\lambda = \frac{1}{\vec{a}}$, provided $\vec{a} \neq \vec{0}$ (i.e. $\vec{a}$ is not a null vector).

Then, $|\lambda\vec{a}$ λ $\vec{a}$ $\frac{1}{\vec{a}}\cdot|\vec{a}|$ 1

So, $\lambda\vec{a}$ represents the unit vector in the direction of $\vec{a}$ and we write it as $\hat{a} = \frac{1}{|\vec{a}|}\cdot\vec{a}$.

(vi) For any scalar k, $k\cdot\vec{0}$ $\vec{0}$.

Properties of Multiplication of a Vector by a Scalar

The addition of vectors and the multiplication of a vector by a scalar, together constitute the following distribution law

Let $\vec{a}$ and $\vec{b}$ be any two vectors and k and m be any two scalars, then

(i) $k\vec{a} + m\vec{a} = (k+m)\vec{a}$ (ii) $k(\vec{a}+\vec{b}) = k\vec{a} + k\vec{b}$

(iii) $k(m\vec{a}) = km(\vec{a})$

Components of a Vector

Two Dimensions

(i) Let a point P lie in a plane, say XY-plane and has coordinates (x, y). Then, $\overrightarrow{OP} = x\hat{i} + y\hat{j}$, where $\hat{i}$ and $\hat{j}$ are unit vectors along OX and OY-axes, respectively. Also, $|\overrightarrow{OP}| = \sqrt{x^2 + y^2}$.

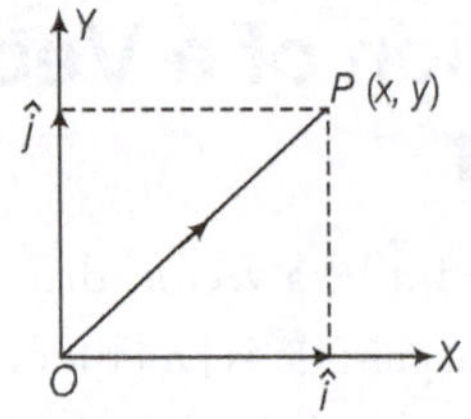

(ii) If $P(x_1, y_1)$ and $Q(x_2, y_2)$ are two points in any plane, then

$\overrightarrow{PQ} = \overrightarrow{OQ} - \overrightarrow{OP} = (x_2 - x_1)\hat{i} + (y_2 - y_1)\hat{i}$ and distance between P and Q is

$$|\overrightarrow{PQ}| = \sqrt{(x_2 - x_1)^2 + (y_2 - y_1)^2}$$

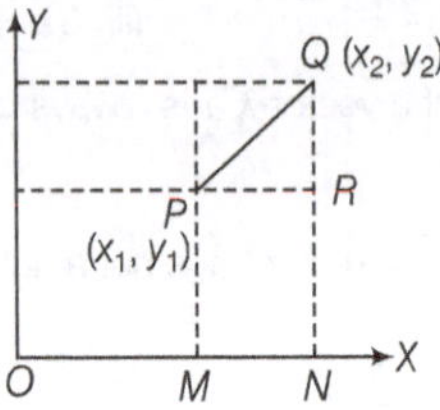

$\therefore$ Component of $\overrightarrow{PQ}$ along X-axis is $(x_2 - x_1)$ and the **vector component** along X-axis is $(x_2 - x_1)\hat{i}$.

Similarly, the component of $\overrightarrow{PQ}$ along Y-axis is $(y_2 - y_1)$ and the **vector component** along Y-axis is $(y_2 - y_1)\hat{j}$.

Three Dimensions

(i) Let a point P in a space has coordinates (x, y, z) and $\hat{i}$, $\hat{j}$ and $\hat{k}$ are unit vectors along OX, OY and OZ-axes, respectively. Then, the position vector of P with respect to O is given by

$\overrightarrow{OP}$ (or $\vec{r}$) $= x\hat{i} + y\hat{j} + z\hat{k}$, where $\hat{i}$, $\hat{j}$ and $\hat{k}$ are called the **unit vectors.**

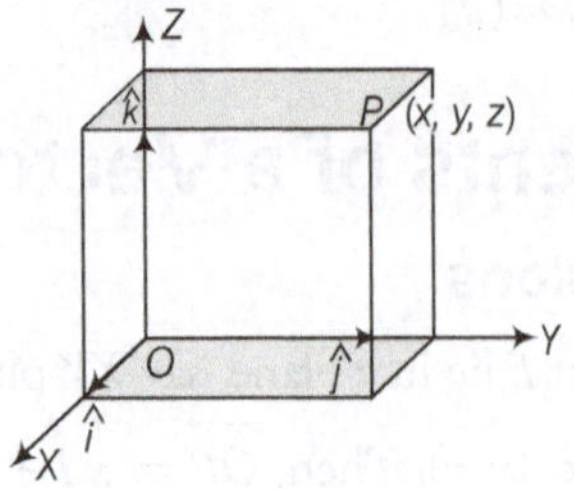

This form of vector $\overrightarrow{OP}$ is called **component form.** Here, x, y and z are called the **scalar components** and $x\hat{i}$, $y\hat{j}$ and $z\hat{k}$ are called the **vector components** of $\overrightarrow{OP}$ (or $\vec{r}$) along the respective axes.

Sometimes x, y and z are also termed as **rectangular components.** The length of any vector $\vec{r} = x\hat{i} + y\hat{j} + z\hat{k}$ is given by

$$|\vec{r}| = |x\hat{i} + y\hat{j} + z\hat{k}| = \sqrt{x^2 + y^2 + z^2}.$$

(ii) If $P(x_1, y_1, z_1)$ and $Q(x_2, y_2, z_2)$ are two points in any plane, then

$$\overrightarrow{PQ} = \overrightarrow{OQ} - \overrightarrow{OP}$$
$$= (x_2 - x_1)\hat{i} + (y_2 - y_1)\hat{j} + (z_2 - z_1)\hat{k}$$

and distance between P and Q is given by

$$|\overrightarrow{PQ}| = \sqrt{(x_2 - x_1)^2 + (y_2 - y_1)^2 + (z_2 - z_1)^2}$$

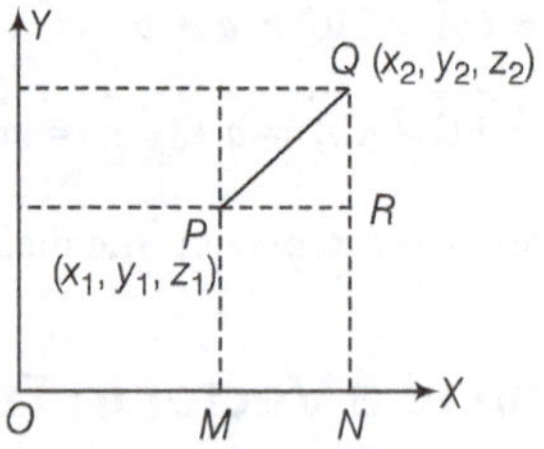

$\therefore$ **Component** of $\overrightarrow{PQ}$ along X-axis is $x_2 - x_1$ and **vector component** of $\overrightarrow{PQ}$ along X-axis is $(x_2 - x_1)\hat{i}$.

Similarly, components of $\overrightarrow{PQ}$ along Y-axis and Z-axis are $(y_2 - y_1)$ and $(z_2 - z_1)$ respectively and **vector components** along Y-axis and Z-axis are $(y_2 - y_1)\hat{j}$ and $(z_2 - z_1)\hat{k}$, respectively.

Example 6 If $\vec{a} = 2\hat{i} + 3\hat{j} + 4\hat{k}$, then find its scalar and vector components.

Sol. We have, $\vec{a} = 2\hat{i} + 3\hat{j} + 4\hat{k}$.

Clearly, the scalar components are 2, 3, 4 and the vector components are $2\hat{i}$, $3\hat{j}$, $4\hat{k}$.

Example 7 Find a vector in the direction of vector $\vec{a} = \hat{i} - 2\hat{j}$ that has magnitude 7 units. **[NCERT Exemplar]**

Sol. We have, $\vec{a} = \hat{i} - 2\hat{j}$, then

$$|\vec{a}| = \sqrt{(1)^2 + (-2)^2} = \sqrt{1+4} = \sqrt{5}$$

The unit vector in the direction of the given vector $\vec{a}$ is

$$\hat{a} = \frac{1}{|\vec{a}|} \cdot \vec{a} = \frac{1}{\sqrt{5}}(\hat{i} - 2\hat{j}) = \frac{1}{\sqrt{5}}\hat{i} - \frac{2}{\sqrt{5}}\hat{j}$$

Now, the vector having magnitude 7 units and in the direction of $\vec{a} = 7\hat{a}$

$$= 7\left(\frac{1}{\sqrt{5}}\hat{i} - \frac{2}{\sqrt{5}}\hat{j}\right)$$

$$= \frac{7}{\sqrt{5}}\hat{i} - \frac{14}{\sqrt{5}}\hat{j}$$

Important Results in Component Form

If $\vec{a}$ and $\vec{b}$ are any two vectors given in the component form such that $\vec{a} = a_1\hat{i} + a_2\hat{j} + a_3\hat{k}$ and $\vec{b} = b_1\hat{i} + b_2\hat{j} + b_3\hat{k}$. Then,

(i) the sum (or resultant) of the vectors $\vec{a}$ and $\vec{b}$ is given by $\vec{a} + \vec{b} = (a_1 + b_1)\hat{i} + (a_2 + b_2)\hat{j} + (a_3 + b_3)\hat{k}$.

(ii) the difference of the vectors $\vec{a}$ and $\vec{b}$ is given by $\vec{a} - \vec{b} = (a_1 - b_1)\hat{i} + (a_2 - b_2)\hat{j} + (a_3 - b_3)\hat{k}$.

(iii) the vectors $\vec{a}$ and $\vec{b}$ are equal, if and only if $a_1 = b_1$, $a_2 = b_2$ and $a_3 = b_3$.

(iv) the multiplication of vector $\vec{a}$ by any scalar λ is given by $\lambda\vec{a} = (\lambda a_1)\hat{i} + (\lambda a_2)\hat{j} + (\lambda a_3)\hat{k}$.

(v) The vectors $\vec{a}$ and $\vec{b}$ are collinear (or parallel) if and only if there exists a non-zero scalar λ such that $\vec{b} = \lambda\vec{a}$.

$$\Rightarrow (b_1\hat{i} + b_2\hat{j} + b_3\hat{k}) = \lambda(a_1\hat{i} + a_2\hat{j} + a_3\hat{k})$$

$$\Rightarrow \quad b_1 = a_1\lambda,\ b_2 = a_2\lambda$$

and $$b_3 = a_3\lambda$$

$$\Rightarrow \quad \frac{b_1}{a_1} = \frac{b_2}{a_2} = \frac{b_3}{a_3} = \lambda$$

Thus, the vectors $\vec{a}$ and $\vec{b}$ are collinear (or parallel) iff

$$\frac{b_1}{a_1} = \frac{b_2}{a_2} = \frac{b_3}{a_3} = \lambda \quad \text{[non-zero constant]}$$

Example 8 If $\vec{a} = 3\hat{i} - 2\hat{j} + \hat{k}$ and $\vec{b} = 2\hat{i} - 4\hat{j} - 3\hat{k}$, then find $|\vec{a} - 2\vec{b}|$.

Sol. We have, $\vec{a} = 3\hat{i} - 2\hat{j} + \hat{k}$ ...(i)

and $\vec{b} = 2\hat{i} - 4\hat{j} - 3\hat{k}$

$\Rightarrow$ $2\vec{b} = 2(2\hat{i} - 4\hat{j} - 3\hat{k})$

[multiplying by 2 on both sides]

$\Rightarrow$ $2\vec{b} = 4\hat{i} - 8\hat{j} - 6\hat{k}$ ...(ii)

On subtracting Eq. (ii) from Eq. (i), we get

$$\vec{a} - 2\vec{b} = (3\hat{i} - 2\hat{j} + \hat{k}) - (4\hat{i} - 8\hat{j} - 6\hat{k})$$

$$= (3-4)\hat{i} + (-2+8)\hat{j} + (1+6)\hat{k}$$

[subtracting corresponding terms]

$$= -\hat{i} + 6\hat{j} + 7\hat{k}$$

Now, $|\vec{a} - 2\vec{b}| = |-\hat{i} + 6\hat{j} + 7\hat{k}| = \sqrt{(-1)^2 + (6)^2 + (7)^2}$

$$= \sqrt{1+36+49} = \sqrt{86}$$

Example 9 For what values of a, the vectors $2\hat{i} - 3\hat{j} + 4\hat{k}$ and $a\hat{i} + 6\hat{j} - 8\hat{k}$ are collinear?

Sol. Let given vectors are $\vec{a} = 2\hat{i} - 3\hat{j} + 4\hat{k}$ and $\vec{b} = a\hat{i} + 6\hat{j} - 8\hat{k}$.

We know that vectors $\vec{a} = a_1\hat{i} + a_2\hat{j} + a_3\hat{k}$ and $\vec{b} = b_1\hat{i} + b_2\hat{j} + b_3\hat{k}$ are collinear, iff $\frac{b_1}{a_1} = \frac{b_2}{a_2} = \frac{b_3}{a_3}$.

$$\therefore \quad \frac{a}{2} = \frac{6}{-3} = \frac{-8}{4} \Rightarrow \frac{a}{2} = -2 \Rightarrow a = -4$$

Direction Cosines and Direction Ratios of a Vector

Suppose $\overrightarrow{OP}$ (or $\vec{r}$) is the position vector of a point $P(x, y, z)$ shown in the figure.

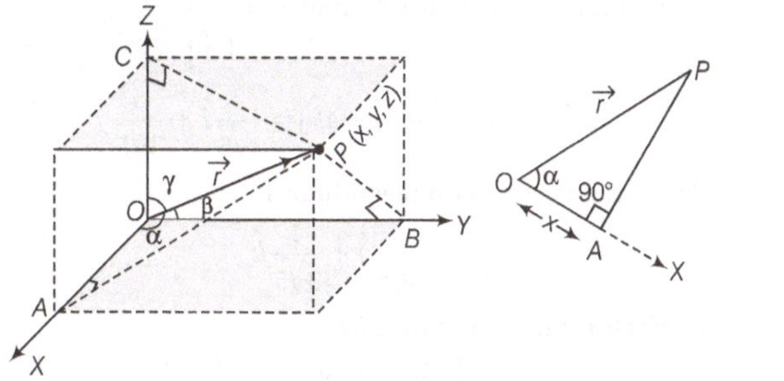

Here, the angles α, β and γ made by the vector $\overrightarrow{OP}$ with positive directions of coordinates axes OX, OY and OZ respectively, are called **direction angles**. The cosine values of these angles, i.e. $\cos\alpha, \cos\beta$ and $\cos\gamma$ are known as the **direction cosines** of $\overrightarrow{OP}$ (or $\vec{r}$).

Generally, they are denoted by l, m and n respectively, i.e. $l = \cos\alpha$, $m = \cos\beta$ and $n = \cos\gamma$.

In the figure, the ΔOAP is a right angled triangle, so we have, $\cos\alpha = \frac{x}{r}$, where $r = |\vec{r}|$.

Similarly, from right angled ΔOBP and ΔOCP, we have $\cos\beta = \frac{y}{r}$ and $\cos\gamma = \frac{z}{r}$. Thus, the coordinates of the point P may also be expressed as $(r\cos\alpha, r\cos\beta, r\cos\gamma)$ or (lr, mr, nr).

In point $P(lr, mr, nr)$, the numbers lr, mr and nr are proportional to the direction cosines, so these numbers are called the **direction ratios** of vector $\vec{r}$ and denoted as x, y and z, respectively.

Suppose a position vector is $\vec{a} = a_1\hat{i} + a_2\hat{j} + a_3\hat{k}$, then a_1, a_2 and a_3 are called the **direction ratios** of $\vec{a}$.

Note

(i) In general, it may be noted that $l^2 + m^2 + n^2 = 1$ but $x^2 + y^2 + z^2 \neq 1$.

(ii) If it is given that l, m and n are direction cosines of a vector, then $l\hat{i} + m\hat{j} + n\hat{k} = (\cos\alpha)\hat{i} + (\cos\beta)\hat{j} + (\cos\gamma)\hat{k}$ is the unit vector in the direction of that vector, where α, β and γ are the angles which the vector makes with X, Y and Z-axes, respectively.

Example 10 Find a vector of magnitude 20 units parallel to the vector $2\hat{i} + 5\hat{j} + 4\hat{k}$. **[ISC 2024]**

Sol. We have, $\vec{a} = 2\hat{i} + 5\hat{j} + 4\hat{k}$

$\therefore \quad |\vec{a}| = \sqrt{2^2 + 5^2 + 4^2} = \sqrt{4 + 25 + 16} = \sqrt{45} = 3\sqrt{5}$

Now, unit vector in direction of $\vec{a} = \dfrac{\vec{a}}{|\vec{a}|}$

$$\hat{a} = \frac{1}{3\sqrt{5}}[2\hat{i} + 5\hat{j} + 4\hat{k}] = \frac{2}{3\sqrt{5}}\hat{i} + \frac{5}{3\sqrt{5}}\hat{j} + \frac{4}{3\sqrt{5}}\hat{k}$$

Thus, the vector with magnitude 1

$$= \frac{2}{3\sqrt{5}}\hat{i} + \frac{5}{3\sqrt{5}}\hat{j} + \frac{4}{3\sqrt{5}}\hat{k}$$

$\therefore$ Vector with magnitude 20

$$= 20 \times \left[\frac{2}{3\sqrt{5}}\hat{i} + \frac{5}{3\sqrt{5}}\hat{j} + \frac{4}{3\sqrt{5}}\hat{k}\right]$$

$$= \frac{40}{3\sqrt{5}}\hat{i} + \frac{100}{3\sqrt{5}}\hat{j} + \frac{80}{3\sqrt{5}}\hat{k}$$

$$= \frac{8\sqrt{5}}{3}\hat{i} + \frac{20\sqrt{5}}{3}\hat{j} + \frac{16\sqrt{5}}{3}\hat{k}$$

Example 11 Find a vector $\vec{a}$ of magnitude $5\sqrt{2}$, making an angle of $\frac{\pi}{4}$ with X-axis, $\frac{\pi}{2}$ with Y-axis and an acute angle θ with Z-axis.

Sol. Given, vector $\vec{a}$ makes an angle $\frac{\pi}{4}$ with X-axis and $\frac{\pi}{2}$ with Y-axis.

So, $\quad l = \cos\frac{\pi}{4}$ and $m = \cos\frac{\pi}{2}$

$\Rightarrow \quad l = \frac{1}{\sqrt{2}}$ and $m = 0$

We know that, $l^2 + m^2 + n^2 = 1$

$\therefore \quad \left(\frac{1}{\sqrt{2}}\right)^2 + (0)^2 + n^2 = 1 \Rightarrow \frac{1}{2} + n^2 = 1$

$\Rightarrow \quad n^2 = 1 - \frac{1}{2} \Rightarrow n = \pm\frac{1}{\sqrt{2}}$

$\Rightarrow \quad n = \frac{1}{\sqrt{2}}$ [$\because \vec{a}$ makes acute angle with Z-axis, so we take a positive sign]

$\therefore \quad \cos\theta = \frac{1}{\sqrt{2}}$ [$\because \theta$ is an acute angle with Z-axis]

Thus, the direction cosines of $\vec{a}$ are $\frac{1}{\sqrt{2}}, 0, \frac{1}{\sqrt{2}}$.

Now, vector $\vec{a} = |\vec{a}|\left(\cos\frac{\pi}{4}\hat{i} + \cos\frac{\pi}{2}\hat{j} + \cos\theta\hat{k}\right)$

$$= 5\sqrt{2}\left(\frac{1}{\sqrt{2}}\hat{i} + (0)\hat{j} + \frac{1}{\sqrt{2}}\hat{k}\right) = 5\hat{i} + 5\hat{k}$$

Example 12 Write the direction ratios of the vector $\vec{a} = \hat{i} + \hat{j} - 2\hat{k}$ and hence calculate its direction cosines. **[NCERT]**

Sol. We have, vector $\vec{a} = \hat{i} + \hat{j} - 2\hat{k}$

We know that, direction ratios of a vector $\vec{r} = x\hat{i} + y\hat{j} + z\hat{k}$ are the scalar components x, y and z of the vector.

So, direction ratios are 1, 1 and -2.

Now, $|\vec{a}| = |\hat{i} + \hat{j} - 2\hat{k}| = \sqrt{(1)^2 + (1)^2 + (-2)^2}$

$= \sqrt{1 + 1 + 4} = \sqrt{6}$

Suppose l, m and n are the direction cosines of given vector $\vec{a}$.

Then, $\quad l = \frac{x}{|\vec{a}|}$, $m = \frac{y}{|\vec{a}|}$ and $n = \frac{z}{|\vec{a}|}$

$\Rightarrow \quad l = \frac{1}{\sqrt{6}}$, $m = \frac{1}{\sqrt{6}}$ and $n = \frac{-2}{\sqrt{6}}$

Hence, the required direction cosines are $\left(\frac{1}{\sqrt{6}}, \frac{1}{\sqrt{6}}, \frac{-2}{\sqrt{6}}\right)$.

Section Formulae

Let A and B be two points represented by position vectors $\overrightarrow{OA}$ and $\overrightarrow{OB}$ respectively, with respect to the origin. Then, the line segment joining the points A and B may be divided by a third point C (say) in two ways which are given below.

Internal Division

Let a point C divide the line joining A, B internally in the ratio of $m:n$. Then, the position vector of point C is given by

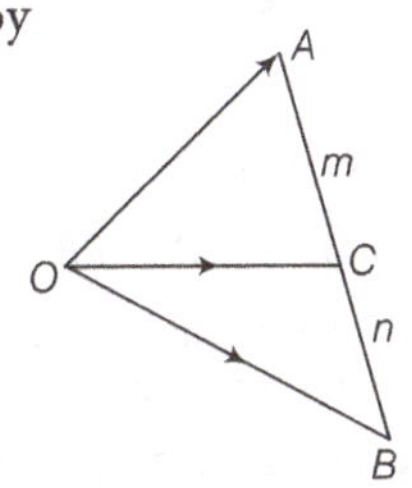

$$\overrightarrow{OC} = \frac{m\,\overrightarrow{OB} + n\,\overrightarrow{OA}}{m+n}$$

where, m and n are positive scalars.

External Division

Let a point C divide the line joining AB externally in the ratio of $m:n$. Then, the position vector of point C is given by

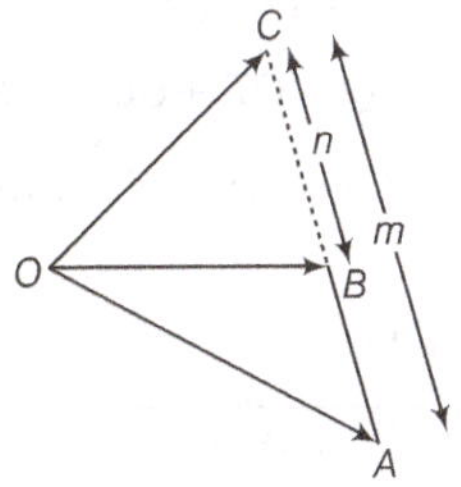

$$\overrightarrow{OC} = \frac{m\,\overrightarrow{OB} - n\,\overrightarrow{OA}}{m-n}$$

where, m and n are positive scalars.

Note If C is a mid-point, then the position vector of point C is given by $\overrightarrow{OC} = \frac{\overrightarrow{OB} + \overrightarrow{OA}}{2}$.

Example 13 Find the position vectors of the points which divide the line joining the two points $3\vec{a} - 2\vec{b}$ and $2\vec{a} - 5\vec{b}$ internally and externally in the ratio 3 : 2.

Sol. Let A and B be the given points whose position vectors are $3\vec{a} - 2\vec{b}$ and $2\vec{a} - 5\vec{b}$ respectively, with respect to the origin O, i.e. $\overrightarrow{OA} = 3\vec{a} - 2\vec{b}$ and $\overrightarrow{OB} = 2\vec{a} - 5\vec{b}$.

Let P and Q be the points, which divides the line joining A and B internally and externally respectively, in the ratio 3 : 2.

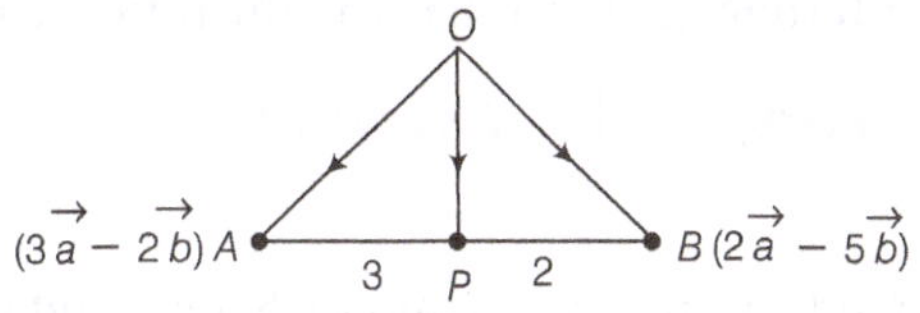

Then, by using section formula of internal division, we get

$$\overrightarrow{OP} = \frac{3\,\overrightarrow{OB} + 2\overrightarrow{OA}}{3+2}$$

$$= \frac{3(2\vec{a} - 5\vec{b}) + 2(3\vec{a} - 2\vec{b})}{5}$$

$$= \frac{6\vec{a} - 15\vec{b} + 6\vec{a} - 4\vec{b}}{5}$$

$$= \frac{12\vec{a} - 19\vec{b}}{5} = \frac{12}{5}\vec{a} - \frac{19}{5}\vec{b}$$

Now, by using section formula of external division, we get

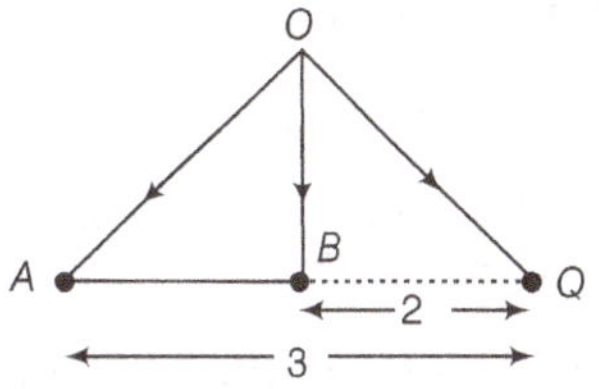

$$\overrightarrow{OQ} = \frac{3\,\overrightarrow{OB} - 2\,\overrightarrow{OA}}{3-2} = \frac{3(2\vec{a} - 5\vec{b}) - 2(3\vec{a} - 2\vec{b})}{1}$$

$$= \frac{6\vec{a} - 15\vec{b} - 6\vec{a} + 4\vec{b}}{1} = -11\vec{b}$$

Topic Practice 1

Very Short Answer Type Questions

(2 Marks)

1. If A, B, P, Q and R be the five points in a plane, then show that the sum of the vectors $\overrightarrow{AP}, \overrightarrow{AQ}, \overrightarrow{AR}, \overrightarrow{PB}, \overrightarrow{QB}$ and $\overrightarrow{RB}$ is $3\,\overrightarrow{AB}$.

2. If O be the centre of a regular hexagon $PQRSTU$, then prove that
$$\overrightarrow{OP} + \overrightarrow{OQ} + \overrightarrow{OR} + \overrightarrow{OS} + \overrightarrow{OT} + \overrightarrow{OU} = \vec{0}.$$

3. Find a unit vector in the direction $3\hat{i} - 8\hat{j} + 2\hat{k}$.

4 If the position vectors of two points A and B are $2\hat{i}+3\hat{j}+8\hat{k}$ and $3\hat{i}+4\hat{j}+5\hat{k}$ respectively, then find the direction cosines of the vectors $\overrightarrow{AB}$.

5 Find the position vectors of the points which divide the join of the points $2\vec{a}-5\vec{b}$ and $3\vec{a}-\vec{b}$ internaly and externally in the ratio 3 : 4.

Short Answer Type Questions

4 Marks

6 Find a vector of magnitude 5 units and parallel to the resultant of $\vec{a}=2\hat{i}+3\hat{j}-3\hat{k}$ and $\vec{b}=\hat{i}-2\hat{j}+3\hat{k}$. **[NCERT]**

7 Let $\vec{a}=\hat{i}+\hat{j}+\hat{k}$, $\vec{b}=4\hat{i}-2\hat{j}+3\hat{k}$ and $\vec{c}=\hat{i}-2\hat{j}+\hat{k}$ and find a vector of magnitude 6 units which is parallel to the vector $2\vec{a}-\vec{b}+3\vec{c}$.

8 Show that the vector $\hat{i}+\hat{j}+\hat{k}$ is equally inclined to the axes OX, OY and OZ.

9 A vector $\vec{r}$ is inclined at equal angles to the three axes. If the magnitude of $\vec{r}$ is $2\sqrt{3}$ units, then find the value of $\vec{r}$.

10 Show that the vectors $\vec{a}=3\hat{i}-2\hat{j}+\hat{k}$, $\vec{b}=\hat{i}-3\hat{j}+5\hat{k}$ and $\vec{c}=2\hat{i}+\hat{j}-4\hat{k}$ form a right angled triangle.

11 If a vector $\vec{r}$ has magnitude 14 and direction ratios 2, 3 and – 6. Then, find the direction cosines and components of $\vec{r}$, given that $\vec{r}$ makes an acute angle with X-axis. **[NCERT Exemplar]**

12 If a unit vector $\vec{a}$ makes angle $\frac{\pi}{4}$ with $\hat{i}$, $\frac{\pi}{3}$ with $\hat{j}$ and an acute angle θ with $\hat{k}$, then find the components of $\vec{a}$ and the angle θ.

13 Find the position vector of a point C which divides the line segment joining A and B, whose position vectors are $2\vec{a}+\vec{b}$ and $\vec{a}-3\vec{b}$, externally in the ratio 1 : 2. Also, show that A is the mid-point of the line segment BC.

14 Points L, M and N divide the side BC, CA and AB of ΔABC in the ratio 1 : 4, 3 : 2 and 3 : 7, respectively. Prove that $\overrightarrow{AL}+\overrightarrow{BM}+\overrightarrow{CN}$ is a vector parallel to $\overrightarrow{CK}$, where K divides AB in the ratio 1 : 3.

Hints & Solutions

1. Applying triangle law of addition of vectors in triangles APB, AQB and ARB, we get

$$\overrightarrow{AP}+\overrightarrow{PB}=\overrightarrow{AB},\ \overrightarrow{AQ}+\overrightarrow{QB}=\overrightarrow{AB}$$

and $\overrightarrow{AR}+\overrightarrow{RB}=\overrightarrow{AB}$ **[1]**

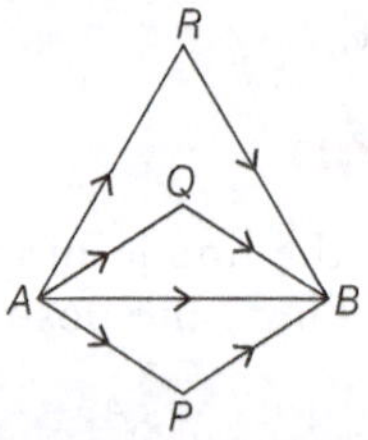

On adding all these, we get

$$\overrightarrow{AP}+\overrightarrow{PB}+\overrightarrow{AQ}+\overrightarrow{QB}+\overrightarrow{AR}+\overrightarrow{RB}=3\overrightarrow{AB}$$ **[1]**

2. We know that the centre of a regular hexagon bisects all the diagonals passing through it.

$\therefore\ \overrightarrow{OP}=-\overrightarrow{OS},\ \overrightarrow{OQ}=-\overrightarrow{OT}$ and $\overrightarrow{OU}=-\overrightarrow{OR}$

$\Rightarrow \overrightarrow{OP}+\overrightarrow{OS}=\vec{0},\ \overrightarrow{OQ}+\overrightarrow{OT}=\vec{0}$ and $\overrightarrow{OU}+\overrightarrow{OR}=\vec{0}$ **[1]**

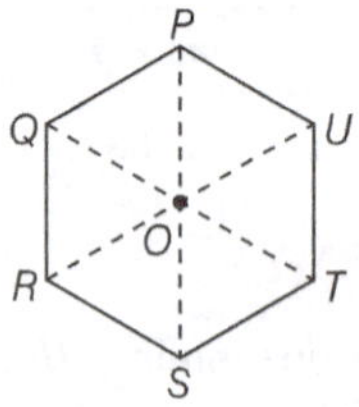

On adding all of them, we get

$$\overrightarrow{OP}+\overrightarrow{OS}+\overrightarrow{OQ}+\overrightarrow{OT}+\overrightarrow{OU}+\overrightarrow{OR}=\vec{0}$$

$$\Rightarrow \overrightarrow{OP}+\overrightarrow{OQ}+\overrightarrow{OR}+\overrightarrow{OS}+\overrightarrow{OT}+\overrightarrow{OU}=\vec{0}$$

Hence proved. [1]

3. Let $\vec{r}=3\hat{i}-8\hat{j}+2\hat{k}$

Then, $|\vec{r}|=\sqrt{(3)^2+(-8)^2+(2)^2}$

$=\sqrt{9+64+4}=\sqrt{77}$ **[1]**

$\therefore$ Unit vector in the direction of the given vector

$$=\frac{\vec{r}}{|\vec{r}|}=\frac{3\hat{i}-8\hat{j}+2\hat{k}}{\sqrt{77}}$$

$$=\frac{3\hat{i}}{\sqrt{77}}-\frac{8\hat{j}}{\sqrt{77}}+\frac{2\hat{k}}{\sqrt{77}}$$ **[1]**

4. $\because\ \overrightarrow{AB}=$ Position vector of $\vec{B}$ – Position vector of $\vec{A}$

$=(3\hat{i}+4\hat{j}+5\hat{k})-(2\hat{i}+3\hat{j}+8\hat{k})$

$=\hat{i}-\hat{j}-3\hat{k}$ **[1]**

Now, $|\overrightarrow{AB}|=\sqrt{(1)^2+(-1)^2+(-3)^2}$

$$= \sqrt{1+1+9} = \sqrt{11}$$ [1/2]

Now, unit vector along $|\overrightarrow{AB}| = \dfrac{\overrightarrow{AB}}{|\overrightarrow{AB}|}$

$$= \frac{\hat{i}-\hat{j}-3\hat{k}}{\sqrt{11}} = \frac{1}{\sqrt{11}}\hat{i} - \frac{1}{\sqrt{11}}\hat{j} - \frac{3}{\sqrt{11}}\hat{k}$$ [1/2]

Therefore, the direction cosines of $\overrightarrow{AB}$ are

$$\frac{1}{\sqrt{11}}, \frac{-1}{\sqrt{11}} \text{ and } \frac{-3}{\sqrt{11}}$$

5. Similar as Example 13. $\left[\textbf{Ans. } \dfrac{17\vec{a}-23\vec{b}}{7},\ \vec{a}+17\vec{b}\right]$

6. **Hint** Required vector $= \dfrac{5(\vec{a}+\vec{b})}{|\vec{a}+\vec{b}|}$. $\left[\textbf{Ans. } \dfrac{15}{\sqrt{10}}\hat{i} + \dfrac{5}{\sqrt{10}}\hat{j}\right]$

7. Given, $\vec{a} = \hat{i}+\hat{j}+\hat{k}$, $\vec{b} = 4\hat{i}-2\hat{j}+3\hat{k}$

and $\vec{c} = \hat{i}-2\hat{j}+\hat{k}$

Now, $2\vec{a} - \vec{b} + 3\vec{c}$

$$= 2(\hat{i}+\hat{j}+\hat{k}) - (4\hat{i}-2\hat{j}+3\hat{k}) + 3(\hat{i}-2\hat{j}+\hat{k})$$

$$= 2\hat{i}+2\hat{j}+2\hat{k}-4\hat{i}+2\hat{j}-3\hat{k}+3\hat{i}-6\hat{j}+3\hat{k}$$

$$= \hat{i}-2\hat{j}+2\hat{k}$$ [1]

Now, we find a unit vector in the direction of vector $2\vec{a}-\vec{b}+3\vec{c}$, which is equal to

$$\frac{2\vec{a}-\vec{b}+3\vec{c}}{|2\vec{a}-\vec{b}+3\vec{c}|} = \frac{\hat{i}-2\hat{j}+2\hat{k}}{\sqrt{(1)^2+(-2)^2+(2)^2}}$$ [1]

$$= \frac{\hat{i}-2\hat{j}+2\hat{k}}{\sqrt{1+4+4}} = \frac{\hat{i}-2\hat{j}+2\hat{k}}{\sqrt{9}}$$

$$= \frac{\hat{i}-2\hat{j}+2\hat{k}}{3} = \frac{1}{3}\hat{i} - \frac{2}{3}\hat{j} + \frac{2}{3}\hat{k}$$ [1]

So, vector of magnitude 6 units parallel to the vector

$$2\vec{a}-\vec{b}+3\vec{c} = 6\left(\frac{1}{3}\hat{i} - \frac{2}{3}\hat{j} + \frac{2}{3}\hat{k}\right) = 2\hat{i}-4\hat{j}+4\hat{k}$$ [1]

8. The direction ratios of $\hat{i}+\hat{j}+\hat{k}$ are (1, 1, 1). [1]

So, its direction cosines are $\dfrac{1}{\sqrt{1+1+1}}, \dfrac{1}{\sqrt{1+1+1}}, \dfrac{1}{\sqrt{1+1+1}}$

i.e. $\dfrac{1}{\sqrt{3}}, \dfrac{1}{\sqrt{3}}, \dfrac{1}{\sqrt{3}}$ [1]

Suppose vector $\hat{i}+\hat{j}+\hat{k}$ makes angles α, β, γ with the coordinates axes.

Then, $\cos\alpha = \cos\beta = \cos\gamma = \dfrac{1}{\sqrt{3}}$ [1]

Hence, the vector $\hat{i}+\hat{j}+\hat{k}$ is equally inclined to the axes *OX*, *OY* and *OZ*, respectively. [1]

9. We have, $|\vec{r}| = 2\sqrt{3}$

Since, $\vec{r}$ is equally inclined to the three axes. So, the direction cosines of $\vec{r}$ will be same, i.e. $l = m = n$. [1]

We know that, $l^2 + m^2 + n^2 = 1$

$$\Rightarrow \quad l^2 + l^2 + l^2 = 1$$ [1/2]

$$\Rightarrow \quad l^2 = \frac{1}{3} \Rightarrow l = \pm\left(\frac{1}{\sqrt{3}}\right)$$ [1/2]

So, $\hat{r} = \pm\left(\dfrac{1}{\sqrt{3}}\hat{i} + \dfrac{1}{\sqrt{3}}\hat{j} + \dfrac{1}{\sqrt{3}}\hat{k}\right)$ [1]

Now, $\vec{r} = \hat{r}\cdot|\vec{r}|$ $\left[\because \hat{r} = \dfrac{\vec{r}}{|\vec{r}|}\right]$

$$= \pm\left[\frac{1}{\sqrt{3}}\hat{i} + \frac{1}{\sqrt{3}}\hat{j} + \frac{1}{\sqrt{3}}\hat{k}\right] 2\sqrt{3} \quad [\because |\vec{r}| = 2\sqrt{3}]$$

$$= \pm(2\hat{i}+2\hat{j}+2\hat{k}) = \pm 2(\hat{i}+\hat{j}+\hat{k})$$ [1]

10. Given, $\vec{a} = 3\hat{i}-2\hat{j}+\hat{k}$, $\vec{b} = \hat{i}-3\hat{j}+5\hat{k}$

and $\vec{c} = 2\hat{i}+\hat{j}-4\hat{k}$

Now, $|\vec{a}| = \sqrt{(3)^2+(-2)^2+(1)^2} = \sqrt{9+4+1} = \sqrt{14}$, [1]

$|\vec{b}| = \sqrt{(1)^2+(-3)^2+(5)^2} = \sqrt{1+9+25} = \sqrt{35}$ [1]

and $|\vec{c}| = \sqrt{(2)^2+(1)^2+(-4)^2} = \sqrt{4+1+16} = \sqrt{21}$ [1]

$\because \ |\vec{a}|^2 + |\vec{c}|^2 = 14 + 21 = 35$

$\therefore \quad |\vec{a}|^2 + |\vec{c}|^2 = |\vec{b}|^2$

Hence, the vectors form a right angled triangle. [1]

11. Given, $|\vec{r}| = 14$ and if $\vec{r} = a\hat{i}+b\hat{j}+c\hat{k}$, then $a = 2\lambda, b = 3\lambda$ and $c = -6\lambda$ for some $\lambda \neq 0$.

$\therefore$ Direction cosines l, m and n are $l = \dfrac{a}{\vec{r}} = \dfrac{2\lambda}{14} = \dfrac{\lambda}{7}$,

$$m = \frac{b}{\vec{r}} = \frac{3\lambda}{14} \text{ and } n = \frac{c}{\vec{r}} = \frac{-6\lambda}{14} = \frac{-3\lambda}{7}$$ [1]

Also, we know that $l^2 + m^2 + n^2 = 1$

$$\therefore \quad \frac{\lambda^2}{49} + \frac{9\lambda^2}{196} + \frac{9\lambda^2}{49} = 1$$ [1]

$$\Rightarrow \frac{4\lambda^2 + 9\lambda^2 + 36\lambda^2}{196} = 1 \Rightarrow 49\lambda^2 = 196 \Rightarrow \lambda^2 = \frac{196}{49}$$

$$\lambda^2 = 4 \Rightarrow \lambda = \pm 2$$ [1]

So, the direction cosines l, m and n are $\dfrac{2}{7}, \dfrac{3}{7}$ and $\dfrac{-6}{7}$.

[$\because \vec{r}$ makes an acute angle with *X*-axis, so we will take positive value of λ]

$$\because \quad \vec{r} = \hat{r}.|\vec{r}|$$

$$\therefore \quad \vec{r} = (l\hat{i}+m\hat{j}+n\hat{k})\cdot|\vec{r}| = \left(\frac{2}{7}\hat{i} + \frac{3}{7}\hat{j} - \frac{6}{7}\hat{k}\right)\cdot 14$$

$$= 4\hat{i}+6\hat{j}-12\hat{k}$$

Thus, the components of $\vec{r}$ are $4\hat{i}, 6\hat{j}$ and $-12\hat{k}$. [1]

12. We know that, if a vector $\vec{a}$ makes angles α, β and γ with $\hat{i}, \hat{j}$ and $\hat{k}$ respectively, then

$$\cos^2\alpha + \cos^2\beta + \cos^2\gamma = 1$$

It is given that, $\alpha = \frac{\pi}{4}$, $\beta = \frac{\pi}{3}$ and $\gamma = \theta$ an acute angle. [1]

$$\therefore \quad \cos^2\alpha + \cos^2\beta + \cos^2\gamma = 1$$

$$\Rightarrow \quad \cos^2\frac{\pi}{4} + \cos^2\frac{\pi}{3} + \cos^2\theta = 1$$

$$\Rightarrow \quad \frac{1}{2} + \frac{1}{4} + \cos^2\theta = 1 \Rightarrow \cos^2\theta = \frac{1}{4}$$

$$\Rightarrow \quad \cos\theta = \frac{1}{2} \quad [\because \theta \text{ is an acute angle, } \cos\theta > 0]$$

$$\Rightarrow \quad \theta = \frac{\pi}{3} \Rightarrow \gamma = \frac{\pi}{3}$$ [1]

Now, $$\vec{a} = |\vec{a}|\{(\cos\alpha)\hat{i} + (\cos\beta)\hat{j} + (\cos\gamma)\hat{k}\}$$

$$\Rightarrow \quad \vec{a} = \left(\cos\frac{\pi}{4}\right)\hat{i} + \left(\cos\frac{\pi}{3}\right)\hat{j} + \left(\cos\frac{\pi}{3}\right)\hat{k}$$ [1]

$$\left[\because |\vec{a}| = 1,\ \alpha = \frac{\pi}{4},\ \beta = \frac{\pi}{3} \text{ and } \gamma = \frac{\pi}{3}\right]$$

$$\Rightarrow \quad \vec{a} = \frac{1}{\sqrt{2}}\hat{i} + \frac{1}{2}\hat{j} + \frac{1}{2}\hat{k}$$

Thus, the components of $\vec{a}$ are $\left(\frac{1}{\sqrt{2}}\hat{i}, \frac{1}{2}\hat{j}, \frac{1}{2}\hat{k}\right)$. [1]

13. Given, $\overrightarrow{OA} = 2\vec{a} + \vec{b}$ and $\overrightarrow{OB} = \vec{a} - 3\vec{b}$ ...(i)

Also, it is given that C is the point which divides the line joining A and B externally in the ratio 1:2. Then, by using section formula of external division, we get

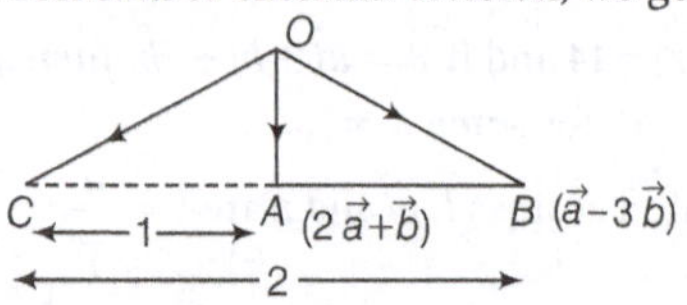

$$\overrightarrow{OC} = \frac{2\overrightarrow{OA} - \overrightarrow{OB}}{2-1}$$ [1]

$$\Rightarrow \quad \overrightarrow{OC} = \frac{2(2\vec{a} + \vec{b}) - 1(\vec{a} - 3\vec{b})}{1}$$ [from Eq. (i)]

$$= 4\vec{a} + 2\vec{b} - \vec{a} + 3\vec{b} = 3\vec{a} + 5\vec{b}$$ ...(ii) [1]

Now, we have to show that A is the mid-point of BC

i.e. to show $\overrightarrow{OA} = \dfrac{\overrightarrow{OB} + \overrightarrow{OC}}{2}$ [1]

Consider, $$\frac{\overrightarrow{OB} + \overrightarrow{OC}}{2} = \frac{\vec{a} - 3\vec{b} + 3\vec{a} + 5\vec{b}}{2}$$

[from Eqs. (i) and (ii)]

$$= \frac{4\vec{a} + 2\vec{b}}{2}$$

$$= 2\vec{a} + \vec{b} = \overrightarrow{OA}$$ [from Eq. (i)]

Thus, $$\frac{\overrightarrow{OB} + \overrightarrow{OC}}{2} = \overrightarrow{OA}$$

Hence, A is mid-point of line segment BC. [1]

14. Let $\vec{a}$, $\vec{b}$ and $\vec{c}$ be the position vectors of the vertices A, B and C of ΔABC, then the position vectors of L, M and N are $\dfrac{4\vec{b} + \vec{c}}{5}$, $\dfrac{3\vec{a} + 2\vec{c}}{5}$ and $\dfrac{7\vec{a} + 3\vec{b}}{10}$, respectively.

Also, K divides AB in the ratio 1:3. Therefore, the position vector of K is $\dfrac{\vec{b} + 3\vec{a}}{4}$. [2]

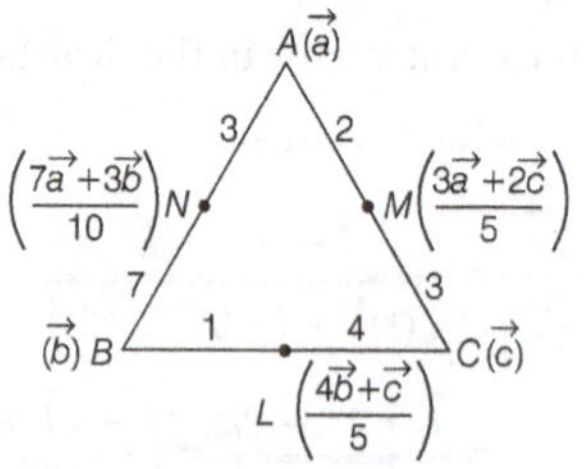

Now, $\overrightarrow{AL} + \overrightarrow{BM} + \overrightarrow{CN}$

$$= \frac{4\vec{b} + \vec{c}}{5} - \vec{a} + \frac{3\vec{a} + 2\vec{c}}{5} - \vec{b} + \frac{7\vec{a} + 3\vec{b}}{10} - \vec{c}$$

$$= \frac{3\vec{a} + \vec{b} - 4\vec{c}}{10} = \frac{4}{10}\overrightarrow{CK}$$ [1]

Hence, $\overrightarrow{AL} + \overrightarrow{BM} + \overrightarrow{CN}$ is parallel to $\overrightarrow{CK}$. [1]

TOPIC 02 Scalar (or Dot) Product of Two Vectors

Let $\vec{a}$ and $\vec{b}$ be two non-zero vectors inclined at an angle θ. Then, the scalar product or dot product of $\vec{a}$ and $\vec{b}$ is denoted by $\vec{a}\cdot\vec{b}$ and defined as

$$\vec{a}\cdot\vec{b} = |\vec{a}||\vec{b}|\cos\theta,\ 0 \le \theta \le \pi$$

or $$\vec{a}\cdot\vec{b} = ab\cos\theta, 0 \le \theta \le \pi$$

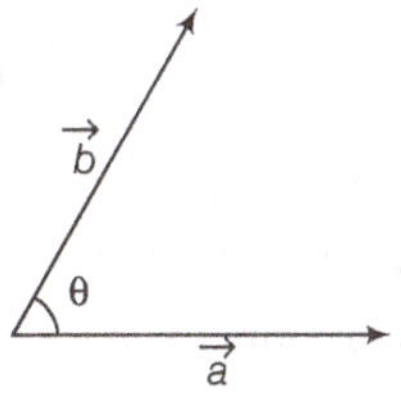

where $a = |\vec{a}|$, $b = |\vec{b}|$ and θ is the angle between $\vec{a}$ and $\vec{b}$.

Note If either $\vec{a} = \vec{0}$ or $\vec{b} = \vec{0}$, then θ is not defined and in this case we define, $\vec{a}\cdot\vec{b} = 0$.

Important Results on Scalar Product of Two Vectors

(i) The scalar product of two vectors (i.e. $\vec{a}\cdot\vec{b}$) is a real number.

(ii) Let $\vec{a}$ and $\vec{b}$ be two non-zero vectors, then $\vec{a}\cdot\vec{b} = 0$ if and only if $\vec{a}$ and $\vec{b}$ are perpendicular to each other, i.e. $\vec{a}\cdot\vec{b} = 0 \Leftrightarrow \vec{a} \perp \vec{b}$ i.e. $a_1b_1 + a_2b_2 + a_3b_3 = 0$.

(iii) Two vectors $\vec{a}$ and $\vec{b}$ are parallel, if there exists a scalar λ such that $\vec{a} = \lambda\vec{b}$, i.e. $\dfrac{a_1}{b_1} = \dfrac{a_2}{b_2} = \dfrac{a_3}{b_3} = \lambda$.

In other words, two vectors are parallel, if their corresponding components are proportional.

(iv) If $\theta = 0$, then $\vec{a}\cdot\vec{b} = |\vec{a}||\vec{b}|$. Also, $\vec{a}\cdot\vec{a} = |\vec{a}|^2$.

(v) If $\theta = \pi$, then $\vec{a}\cdot\vec{b} = -|\vec{a}||\vec{b}|$.

Also, $\vec{a}\cdot(-\vec{a}) = -|\vec{a}|^2$.

(vi) For mutually perpendicular unit vectors $\hat{i}, \hat{j}$ and $\hat{k}$, $\hat{i}\cdot\hat{i} = \hat{j}\cdot\hat{j} = \hat{k}\cdot\hat{k} = 1$ and $\hat{i}\cdot\hat{j} = \hat{j}\cdot\hat{k} = \hat{k}\cdot\hat{i} = 0$.

(vii) The angle between two non-zero vectors $\vec{a}$ and $\vec{b}$ is given by $\cos\theta = \dfrac{\vec{a}\cdot\vec{b}}{|\vec{a}||\vec{b}|}$ or $\theta = \cos^{-1}\left(\dfrac{\vec{a}\cdot\vec{b}}{|\vec{a}||\vec{b}|}\right)$.

Example 1 Find the angle between two vectors $\vec{a}$ and $\vec{b}$ with magnitude 2 and 1 respectively, such that $\vec{a}\cdot\vec{b} = \sqrt{3}$.

Sol. Given, $|\vec{a}| = 2, |\vec{b}| = 1$ and $\vec{a}\cdot\vec{b} = \sqrt{3}$.

Let θ be the angle between $\vec{a}$ and $\vec{b}$.

Then, $$\cos\theta = \frac{\vec{a}\cdot\vec{b}}{|\vec{a}||\vec{b}|} \Rightarrow \cos\theta = \frac{\sqrt{3}}{2\times 1} \quad \text{[given]}$$

$$\Rightarrow \cos\theta = \frac{\sqrt{3}}{2} \Rightarrow \cos\theta = \cos\frac{\pi}{6} \quad \left[\because \cos\frac{\pi}{6} = \frac{\sqrt{3}}{2}\right]$$

$$\Rightarrow \theta = \frac{\pi}{6}$$

Hence, the angle between $\vec{a}$ and $\vec{b}$ is $\frac{\pi}{6}$.

Example 2 If the two vectors $3\hat{i} + \alpha\hat{j} + \hat{k}$ and $2\hat{i} - \hat{j} + 8\hat{k}$ are perpendicular to each other, then find the value of α. **[ISC 2023]**

Sol. Given, vectors $3\hat{i} + \alpha\hat{j} + \hat{k}$ and $2\hat{i} - \hat{j} + 8\hat{k}$ are perpendicular to each other.

$$\therefore 3\cdot 2 + \alpha\cdot(-1) + 1\cdot(8) = 0 \quad [\because \vec{a}\cdot\vec{b} = 0]$$

$$\Rightarrow 6 - \alpha + 8 = 0$$

$$\Rightarrow \alpha = 14$$

Geometrical Interpretation of Scalar Product

Let $\overrightarrow{OA}$ and $\overrightarrow{OB}$ represent the vectors $\vec{a}$ and $\vec{b}$ respectively, then $a = |\vec{a}| = |\overrightarrow{OA}| = |OA|$ and $b = |\vec{b}| = |\overrightarrow{OB}| = OB$.

Let θ be the angle between $\vec{a}$ and $\vec{b}$ and M, N be the feet of perpendicular from B, A on OA and OB respectively.

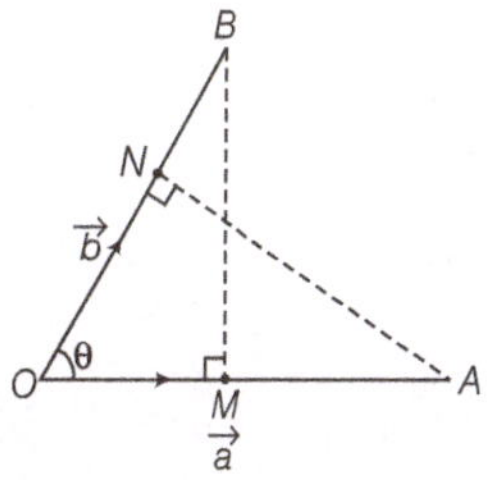

In ΔOBM and ΔOAN,

$$OM = OB\cos\theta \text{ and } ON = OA\cos\theta = a\cos\theta = b\cos\theta$$

Here, OM and ON are known as **projection of $\vec{b}$ on $\vec{a}$ and $\vec{a}$ on $\vec{b}$**, respectively.

Now, $\vec{a}\cdot\vec{b} = |a||b|\cos\theta = |\vec{a}|(|\vec{b}|\cos\theta) = |\vec{a}|\cdot OM$

$= |\vec{a}|$ (projection of $\vec{b}$ on $\vec{a}$)

Similarly, $\vec{a}\cdot\vec{b} = |\vec{a}||\vec{b}|\cos\theta = |\vec{b}|(|\vec{a}|\cos\theta) = |\vec{b}|\cdot ON$

$= |\vec{b}|\cdot$ (projection of $\vec{a}$ on $\vec{b}$)

Thus, the scalar product of two vector is the product of modulus of either vectors and the projection of the other in its direction.

Some Results Related to Projection of a Vector

(i) **Projection of vector $\vec{a}$ on $\vec{b}$** is given by $\vec{a}\cdot\hat{b}$ or $\dfrac{\vec{a}\cdot\vec{b}}{|\vec{b}|}$

and **projection of vector $\vec{b}$ on $\vec{a}$** is given by $\vec{b}\cdot\hat{a}$ or $\dfrac{\vec{a}\cdot\vec{b}}{|\vec{a}|}$

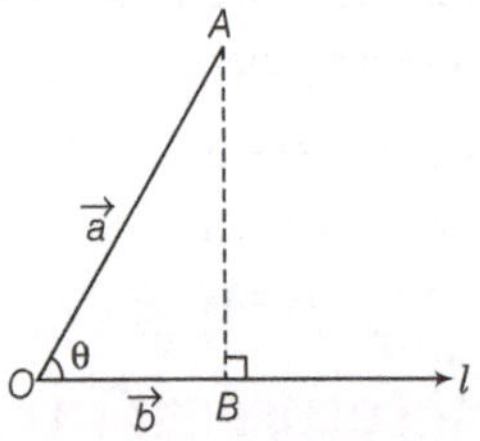

(ii) If $\theta = 0$, then the projection vector of $\overrightarrow{AB}$ will be $\overrightarrow{AB}$ itself and if $\theta = \pi$, then the projection vector of $\overrightarrow{AB}$ will be $\overrightarrow{BA}$.

(iii) If $\theta = \dfrac{\pi}{2}$ or $\theta = \dfrac{3\pi}{2}$, then the projection vector of $\overrightarrow{AB}$ will be zero vector.

(iv) Let α, β and γ be the direction angles of vector $\vec{a} = a_1\hat{i} + a_2\hat{j} + a_3\hat{k}$, then its direction cosines may be given as

$$\cos\alpha = \frac{\vec{a}\cdot\hat{i}}{|\vec{a}||\hat{i}|} = \frac{a_1}{|\vec{a}|},\ \cos\beta = \frac{\vec{a}\cdot\hat{j}}{|\vec{a}||\hat{j}|} = \frac{a_2}{|\vec{a}|}$$

$$\text{and } \cos\gamma = \frac{\vec{a}\cdot\hat{k}}{|\vec{a}||\hat{k}|} = \frac{a_3}{|\vec{a}|}.$$

Here, $|\vec{a}|\cos\alpha$, $|\vec{a}|\cos\beta$ and $|\vec{a}|\cos\gamma$ are respectively, the projection of $\vec{a}$ along OX, OY and OZ, i.e. the scalar components a_1, a_2 and a_3 of the vector $\vec{a}$ are precisely the projections of $\vec{a}$ along X, Y and Z-axes, respectively.

Note (i) If $\hat{a}$ is a unit vector, then it may be expressed as
$$\hat{a} = \cos\alpha\hat{i} + \cos\beta\hat{j} + \cos\gamma\hat{k}.$$
(ii) Square of a vector is always equal to square of its modulus.

Example 3 If $\vec{a} = 2\hat{i} + \hat{j} + 2\hat{k}$ and $\vec{b} = 5\hat{i} - 3\hat{j} + \hat{k}$, find the projection of $\vec{b}$ on $\vec{a}$. **[ISC 2024]**

Sol. We have,

$$\vec{a} = 2\hat{i} + \hat{j} + 2\hat{k}$$

and $$\vec{b} = 5\hat{i} - 3\hat{j} + \hat{k}$$

The projection of $\vec{b}$ on $\vec{a}$ is given by

$$= \frac{\vec{b}\cdot\vec{a}}{|\vec{a}|}$$

$$= \frac{(5\hat{i} - 3\hat{j} + \hat{k})\cdot(2\hat{i} + \hat{j} + 2\hat{k})}{\sqrt{2^2 + 1^2 + 2^2}}$$

$$= \frac{10 - 3 + 2}{\sqrt{4 + 1 + 4}}$$

$$= \frac{9}{\sqrt{9}} = \frac{9}{3} = 3$$

$\therefore$ The projection of $\vec{b}$ on $\vec{a}$ is 3.

Properties of Scalar Product of Two Vectors

(i) Scalar product of two vectors is **commutative**, i.e. for vectors $\vec{a}$ and $\vec{b}$, we have $\vec{a}\cdot\vec{b}=\vec{b}\cdot\vec{a}$.

(ii) Scalar product of vectors is **distributive over addition**, i.e. for vectors $\vec{a}$, $\vec{b}$ and $\vec{c}$, we have

$$\vec{a}\cdot(\vec{b}+\vec{c})=\vec{a}\cdot\vec{b}+\vec{a}\cdot\vec{c}.$$

(iii) If m is any scalar and $\vec{a}$ and $\vec{b}$ be two non-zero vectors.

Then, $(m\vec{a})\cdot(\vec{b})=m(\vec{a}\cdot\vec{b})=(\vec{a})\cdot(m\vec{b})$

Note For any two vectors $\vec{a}$ and $\vec{b}$,

(i) $\vec{a}\cdot(-\vec{b})=-(\vec{a}\cdot\vec{b})=(-\vec{a})\cdot(\vec{b})$

(ii) $(-\vec{a})\cdot(-\vec{b})=\vec{a}\cdot\vec{b}$

(iv) **Scalar product of two vectors in component form.** Suppose two vectors $\vec{a}$ and $\vec{b}$ are given in component form, say $\vec{a}=a_1\hat{i}+a_2\hat{j}+a_3\hat{k}$

and $\vec{b}=b_1\hat{i}+b_2\hat{j}+b_3\hat{k}$.

Then, their scalar product is given by

$$\vec{a}\cdot\vec{b}=(a_1\hat{i}+a_2\hat{j}+a_3\hat{k})\cdot(b_1\hat{i}+b_2\hat{j}+b_3\hat{k})$$
$$=a_1b_1+a_2b_2+a_3b_3$$

Example 4 Find $(\vec{a}+2\vec{b})\cdot(3\vec{a}-\vec{b})$, if $\vec{a}=\hat{i}+\hat{j}+2\hat{k}$ and $\vec{b}=3\hat{i}+2\hat{j}-\hat{k}$.

Sol. We have, $\vec{a}=\hat{i}+\hat{j}+2\hat{k}$ and $\vec{b}=3\hat{i}+2\hat{j}-\hat{k}$

Clearly, $\vec{a}+2\vec{b}=(\hat{i}+\hat{j}+2\hat{k})+2(3\hat{i}+2\hat{j}-\hat{k})$

$=\hat{i}+\hat{j}+2\hat{k}+6\hat{i}+4\hat{j}-2\hat{k}=7\hat{i}+5\hat{j}+0\hat{k}$

and $3\vec{a}-\vec{b}=3(\hat{i}+\hat{j}+2\hat{k})-(3\hat{i}+2\hat{j}-\hat{k})$

$=(3\hat{i}+3\hat{j}+6\hat{k})-(3\hat{i}+2\hat{j}-\hat{k})$

$=0\hat{i}+\hat{j}+7\hat{k}$

Now, $(\vec{a}+2\vec{b})\cdot(3\vec{a}-\vec{b})=(7\hat{i}+5\hat{j}+0\hat{k})\cdot(0\hat{i}+\hat{j}+7\hat{k})$

$=7(0)+5(1)+0(7)=0+5+0=5$

Example 5 If $\vec{a}$, $\vec{b}$, $\vec{c}$ are three mutually perpendicular vectors of equal magnitude, prove that $(\vec{a}+\vec{b}+\vec{c})$ is equally inclined with vectors $\vec{a}$, $\vec{b}$ and $\vec{c}$. **[ISC 2017]**

Sol. Given, $|\vec{a}|=|\vec{b}|=|\vec{c}|=a$ (say) ...(i)

$\because$ $\vec{a}$, $\vec{b}$ and $\vec{c}$ are mutually perpendicular vectors, then

$$\vec{a}\cdot\vec{b}=\vec{b}\cdot\vec{c}=\vec{c}\cdot\vec{a}=0 \quad ...(ii)$$

Now, consider $|\vec{a}+\vec{b}+\vec{c}|^2=(\vec{a}+\vec{b}+\vec{a})\cdot(\vec{a}+\vec{b}+\vec{c})$

$=\vec{a}\cdot\vec{a}+\vec{b}\cdot\vec{b}+\vec{c}\cdot\vec{c}+2(\vec{a}\cdot\vec{b}+\vec{b}\cdot\vec{c}+\vec{c}\cdot\vec{a})$

$=|\vec{a}|^2+|\vec{b}|^2+|\vec{c}|^2$ [by using Eq. (ii)]

$=3a^2$ [by Eq. (i)]

Let $(\vec{a}+\vec{b}+\vec{c})$ make angle α, β and γ with vector $\vec{a}$, $\vec{b}$ and $\vec{c}$, respectively

Then, $(\vec{a}+\vec{b}+\vec{c})\cdot\vec{a}=|\vec{a}+\vec{b}+\vec{c}\ \ \vec{a}\ \cos\alpha$

$=(\sqrt{3}a\cdot a\cdot\cos\alpha)=\sqrt{3}a^2\cos\alpha$

$\Rightarrow(\vec{a}\cdot\vec{a}+\vec{b}\cdot\vec{a}+\vec{c}\cdot\vec{a})=\sqrt{3}a^2\cos\alpha$

$\Rightarrow\quad |\vec{a}|^2=\sqrt{3}a^2\cos\alpha \Rightarrow a^2=\sqrt{3}a^2\cos\alpha$

$\Rightarrow\quad \cos\alpha=\dfrac{1}{\sqrt{3}}\Rightarrow \alpha=\cos^{-1}\left(\dfrac{1}{\sqrt{3}}\right)$

Similarly, $\beta=\cos^{-1}\left(\dfrac{1}{\sqrt{3}}\right)$ and $\gamma=\cos^{-1}\left(\dfrac{1}{\sqrt{3}}\right)$

$\therefore\quad \alpha=\beta=\gamma=\cos^{-1}\left(\dfrac{1}{\sqrt{3}}\right)$

Thus, $(\vec{a}+\vec{b}+\vec{c})$ is equally inclined to $\vec{a}$, $\vec{b}$ and $\vec{c}$ and the required angle is $\cos^{-1}\left(\dfrac{1}{\sqrt{3}}\right)$.

Topic Practice 2

Very Short Answer Type Questions

2 Marks

1 If $\vec{a}=3\hat{i}+2\hat{j}-3\hat{k}$ and $\vec{b}=2\hat{i}+5\hat{j}+3\hat{k}$, then find $\vec{a}\cdot\vec{b}$ and $\vec{b}\cdot\vec{a}$.

2 If $\vec{a}=(\hat{i}+3\hat{j}-2\hat{k})$, $\vec{b}=2\hat{i}+3\hat{j}+\hat{k}$ and $\vec{c}=3\hat{i}+2\hat{j}-4\hat{k}$, then find the value of $(\vec{a}+\vec{b})\cdot\vec{c}$.

3 If $\vec{a}$ and $\vec{b}$ are two unit vectors such that $\vec{a}+\vec{b}$ is also a unit vector, then find the angle between $\vec{a}$ and $\vec{b}$.

4 If $\hat{a}$ is a unit vector and $(\vec{x}-\hat{a})\cdot(\vec{x}+\hat{a})=8$, then find $|\vec{x}|$. **[NCERT Exemplar]**

5 Using vectors, prove that angle in a semi-circle is a right angle. **[ISC 2015]**

6 In a ΔABC, using vectors prove that $c^2 = a^2 + b^2 - 2ab\cos C$. **[ISC 2014]**

7 If $\hat{a}, \hat{b}$ and $\hat{c}$ are mutually perpendicular unit vectors, then find the value of $|2\hat{a} + \hat{b} + \hat{c}|$.

8 In any ΔABC, prove by vector method
$$\cos B = \frac{c^2 + a^2 - b^2}{2ca}$$ **[ISC 2010]**

9 If $\vec{a}$ and $\vec{b}$ are unit vectors such that $2\vec{a} - 4\vec{b}$ and $10\vec{a} + 8\vec{b}$ are perpendicular to each other. Then, find the angle between the vectors $\vec{a}$ and $\vec{b}$. **[ISC 2005]**

10 Find $|\vec{a} - \vec{b}|$, if two vectors $\vec{a}$ and $\vec{b}$ are such that $|\vec{a}| = 2$, $|\vec{b}| = 3$ and $\vec{a} \cdot \vec{b} = 4$.

11 If $\vec{a} = 2\hat{i} + 2\hat{j} + 3\hat{k}$, $\vec{b} = -\hat{i} + 2\hat{j} + \hat{k}$ and $\vec{c} = 3\hat{i} + \hat{j}$ are such that $\vec{a} + \lambda\vec{b}$ is perpendicular to $\vec{c}$, then find the value of λ.

Short Answer Type Questions

4 Marks

12 If the dot products of a vector with vectors $3\hat{i} - 5\hat{k}, 2\hat{i} + 7\hat{j}$ and $\hat{i} + \hat{j} + \hat{k}$ are respectively -1, 6 and 5, then find the vector.

13 Vectors $\vec{a}$ $\vec{b}$ and $\vec{c}$ are such that $\vec{a} + \vec{b} + \vec{c} =$ and $|\vec{a}| = 3$, $|\vec{b}| = 5$ and $|\vec{c}| = 7$. Then, find the angle between $\vec{a}$ and $\vec{b}$.

14 If $\vec{a}, \vec{b}, \vec{c}$ are unit vectors such that $\vec{a} + \vec{b} + \vec{c} = \vec{0}$, then find the value of $\vec{a} \cdot \vec{b} + \vec{b} \cdot \vec{c} + \vec{c} \cdot \vec{a}$.

15 The scalar product of the vector $\vec{a} = \hat{i} + \hat{j} + \hat{k}$ with a unit vector along the sum of vectors $\vec{b} = 2\hat{i} + 4\hat{j} - 5\hat{k}$ and $\vec{c} = \lambda\hat{i} + 2\hat{j} + 3\hat{k}$ is equal to one. Find the value of λ and hence find the unit vector along $\vec{b} + \vec{c}$.

16 If $\hat{a}$ and $\hat{b}$ are unit vectors inclined at an angle θ, then prove that $\sin\frac{\theta}{2} = \frac{1}{2}|\hat{a} - \hat{b}|$.

17 Find the values of x for which the angle between the vectors $\vec{a} = 2x^2\hat{i} + 4x\hat{j} + \hat{k}$ and $\vec{b} = 7\hat{i} - 2\hat{j} + x\hat{k}$ is obtuse.

18 Find the values of a for which the vectors $\vec{r} = (a^2 - 4)\hat{i} + 2\hat{j} - (a^2 - 9)\hat{k}$ makes an acute angles with the coordinate axes.

19 Prove that for any two vectors $\vec{a}$ and $\vec{b}$, $|\vec{a} + \vec{b}| \le |\vec{a}| + |\vec{b}|$.

20 Find the value of p for which the vectors $\vec{a} = 3\hat{i} + 2\hat{j} + 9\hat{k}$ and $\vec{b} = \hat{i} + p\hat{j} + 3\hat{k}$ are
(i) perpendicular. (ii) parallel.

21 If $\vec{a}$, $\vec{b}$ and $\vec{c}$ are three mutually perpendicular vectors of equal magnitude, then find the angle between $\vec{a}$ and $(\vec{a} + \vec{b} + \vec{c})$.

22 Let $\vec{a}, \vec{b}$ and $\vec{c}$ be three vectors of magnitudes 3, 4 and 5, respectively. If each one is perpendicular to the sum of the other two vectors, then prove that $|\vec{a} + \vec{b} + \vec{c}| = 5\sqrt{2}$. **[NCERT]**

23 If with reference to a right handed system of mutually perpendicular unit vectors $\hat{i}, \hat{j}$ and $\hat{k}$, we have $\vec{\alpha} = 3\hat{i} - \hat{j}$ and $\vec{\beta} = 2\hat{i} + \hat{j} - 3\hat{k}$. Express $\vec{\beta}$ in the form of $\vec{\beta} = \vec{\beta}_1 + \vec{\beta}_2$, where $\vec{\beta}_1$ is parallel to $\vec{\alpha}$ and $\vec{\beta}_2$ is perpendicular to $\vec{\alpha}$. **[NCERT]**

Hints & Solutions

1. We have, $\vec{a} = 3\hat{i} + 2\hat{j} - 3\hat{k}$, $\vec{b} = 2\hat{i} + 5\hat{j} + 3\hat{k}$

$\therefore \quad \vec{a} \cdot \vec{b} = (3\hat{i} + 2\hat{j} - 3\hat{k}) \cdot (2\hat{i} + 5\hat{j} + 3\hat{k})$
$= 6 + 10 - 9 = 7$

and $\quad \vec{b} \cdot \vec{a} = (2\hat{i} + 5\hat{j} + 3\hat{k}) \cdot (3\hat{i} + 2\hat{j} - 3\hat{k})$
$= 6 + 10 - 9 = 7$

2. Hint First, add the vectors $\vec{a}$ and $\vec{b}$ and then their sum will be multiplied by vector $\vec{c}$. **[Ans.** 25]

3. Given, $|a| = 1$, $|b| = 1$ and $\vec{a} + \vec{b} = 1$

Now, consider $|\vec{a} + \vec{b}|^2 = (\vec{a} + \vec{b}) \cdot (\vec{a} + \vec{b})$

$= \vec{a} \cdot \vec{a} + \vec{b} \cdot \vec{a} + \vec{a} \cdot \vec{b} + \vec{b} \cdot \vec{b}$

$= |\vec{a}|^2 + 2\,\vec{a} \cdot \vec{b} + |\vec{b}|^2$

[$\because \vec{a} \cdot \vec{b} \quad \vec{b} \cdot \vec{a}$ and $\vec{x} \cdot \vec{x} = |\vec{x}|^2$]

$\Rightarrow \; 1 = 1 + 2\,\vec{a} \cdot \vec{b} + 1 \;$ [$\because |\vec{a} + \vec{b}| = |\vec{a}| = |\vec{b}| = 1$, given] [1]

$\Rightarrow \; 2\,\vec{a} \cdot \vec{b} = -1 \Rightarrow |\vec{a}||\vec{b}| \cos\theta = -\frac{1}{2}$

[$\because \vec{a} \cdot \vec{b} = |\vec{a}|\,|\vec{b}| \cos\theta$]

$\Rightarrow \quad \cos\theta = -\frac{1}{2}$ $\quad [\because |\vec{a}| = |\vec{b}| = 1]$

$\Rightarrow \quad \cos\theta = \cos\frac{2\pi}{3} \Rightarrow \theta = \frac{2\pi}{3}$

Hence, the angle between $\vec{a}$ and $\vec{b}$ is $\frac{2\pi}{3}$. **[1]**

4. Given, $\hat{a}$ is a unit vector.

$\therefore \quad |\hat{a}| = 1$

Now, consider $(\vec{x} - \hat{a})\cdot(\vec{x} + \hat{a}) = \vec{x}\cdot\vec{x} + \vec{x}\cdot\hat{a} - \hat{a}\cdot\vec{x} - \hat{a}\cdot\hat{a}$

$= |\vec{x}|^2 + \vec{x}\cdot\hat{a} - \vec{x}\cdot\hat{a} - |\hat{a}|^2 \quad [\because \vec{x}\cdot\hat{a} = \hat{a}\cdot\vec{x}]$ **[1]**

$\Rightarrow \quad (\vec{x} - \hat{a})\cdot(\vec{x} + \hat{a}) = |\vec{x}|^2 - |\hat{a}|^2$

$\Rightarrow \quad 8 = |\vec{x}|^2 - (1)^2 \quad$ [given, $(\vec{x} - \hat{a})\cdot(\vec{x} + \hat{a}) = 8$]

$\Rightarrow 8 + 1 = |\vec{x}|^2 \Rightarrow 9 = |\vec{x}|^2$

$\therefore \quad |\vec{x}| = 3$ [magnitude is always positive] **[1]**

5. Let O be the centre of a semi-circle and AB be a diameter of a semi-circle. Let C be a point on the circumference, then prove that $\angle ACB = 90°$.

Take O as origin and let $\overrightarrow{OB} = \vec{a}$ and $\overrightarrow{OC} = \vec{b}$,

then $\overrightarrow{OA} = -\overrightarrow{OB} = \vec{a}$

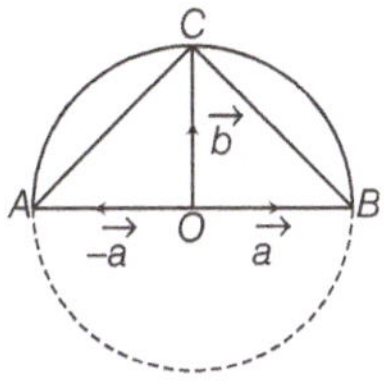

[1]

Now, $\overrightarrow{AC} = \overrightarrow{OC} - \overrightarrow{OA} = \vec{b} + \vec{a}$

$\overrightarrow{BC} = \overrightarrow{OC} - \overrightarrow{OB} = \vec{b} - \vec{a}$

$\therefore \quad \overrightarrow{AC}\cdot\overrightarrow{BC} = (\vec{b} + \vec{a})\cdot(\vec{b} - \vec{a})$

$= \vec{b}\cdot\vec{b} - \vec{b}\cdot\vec{a} + \vec{a}\cdot\vec{b} - \vec{a}\cdot\vec{a}$

$= \vec{b}\cdot\vec{b} - \vec{a}\cdot\vec{a} = r^2 - r^2$

[where, r radius of a semi-circle]

$= 0$

$\Rightarrow \quad \overrightarrow{AC} \perp \overrightarrow{BC}$

$\therefore \quad \angle ACB = 90°$

Hence, the angle in a semi-circle is a right angle. **[1]**

6. In ΔABC, let $\overrightarrow{BC} = \vec{a}, \overrightarrow{CA} = \vec{b}$ and $\overrightarrow{AC} = \vec{c}$

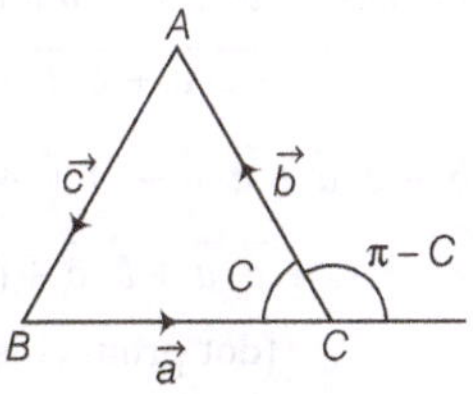

$\therefore \quad |\overrightarrow{BC}| = a, |\overrightarrow{CA}| = b$ and $|\overrightarrow{AB}| = c$

By triangle law of addition,

$\overrightarrow{BA} = \overrightarrow{BC} + \overrightarrow{CA} \Rightarrow -\vec{c} = \vec{a} + \vec{b}$

Now, $(-\vec{c})\cdot(-\vec{c}) = (\vec{a} + \vec{b})\cdot(\vec{a} + \vec{b})$

$\Rightarrow \quad c^2 = \vec{a}\cdot(\vec{a} + \vec{b}) + \vec{b}\cdot(\vec{a} + \vec{b})$ **[1]**

$\Rightarrow \quad c^2 = \vec{a}\cdot\vec{a} + \vec{a}\cdot\vec{b} + \vec{b}\cdot\vec{a} + \vec{b}\cdot\vec{b}$

$\Rightarrow \quad c^2 = a^2 + b^2 + 2\vec{a}\cdot\vec{b}$

$\Rightarrow \quad c^2 = a^2 + b^2 + 2|\vec{a}||\vec{b}|\cos(\pi - C)$

$[\because a^2 \cdot b^2 = |\vec{a}||\vec{b}|\cos(\pi - C)]$

$\Rightarrow \quad c^2 = a^2 + b^2 - 2ab\cos C$ **Hence proved. [1]**

7. We have, $\hat{a}$, $\hat{b}$ and $\hat{c}$ are mutually perpendicular unit vectors, i.e. $\hat{a}\cdot\hat{b} = \hat{b}\cdot\hat{c} = \hat{c}\cdot\hat{a} = 0$ ...(i)

and $\quad |\hat{a}| = |\hat{b}| = |\hat{c}| = 1$ ...(ii)

Now, $|2\hat{a} + \hat{b} + \hat{c}|^2 = (2\hat{a} + \hat{b} + \hat{c})\cdot(2\hat{a} + \hat{b} + \hat{c})$ **[1]**

$= 4(\hat{a}\cdot\hat{a}) + 2(\hat{a}\cdot\hat{b}) + 2(\hat{a}\cdot\hat{c}) + 2(\hat{b}\cdot\hat{a})$

$+ (\hat{b}\cdot\hat{b}) + (\hat{b}\cdot\hat{c}) + 2(\hat{c}\cdot\hat{a}) + (\hat{c}\cdot\hat{b}) + (\hat{c}\cdot\hat{c})$

[dot product is distributive over addition] **[1/2]**

$= 4(|\hat{a}|^2) + 2(0) + 2(0) + 2(0) + |\hat{b}|^2 + (0) + 2(0) + (0) + |\hat{c}|^2$

[from Eq. (i) and $\hat{a}\cdot\hat{a} = |\hat{a}|^2$]

$= 4(1) + 1 + 1 = 4 + 1 + 1 = 6$

$\Rightarrow |2\hat{a} + \hat{b} + \hat{c}| = \sqrt{6}$ [length cannot be negative] **[1/2]**

8. Let ABC be a triangle with $\overrightarrow{BC} = \vec{a}$, $\overrightarrow{CA} = \vec{b}$ and $\overrightarrow{AB} = \vec{c}$.

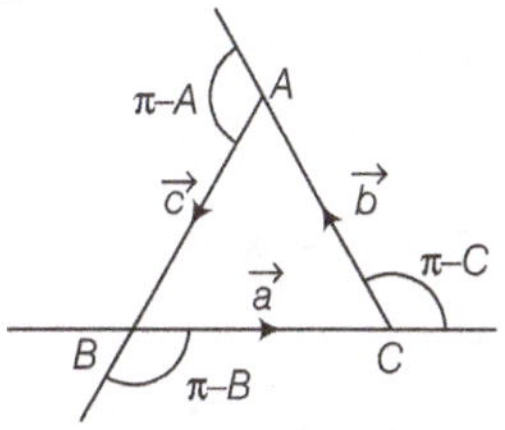

$\therefore \quad |\overrightarrow{BC}| = a, |\overrightarrow{CA}| = b$ and $|\overrightarrow{AB}| = c$

By triangle law of addition, $\overrightarrow{BC} + \overrightarrow{CA} = \overrightarrow{BA}$

$\Rightarrow \quad \overrightarrow{BC} + \overrightarrow{CA} + \overrightarrow{AB} = \vec{0}$

$\Rightarrow \quad \vec{a} + \vec{b} + \vec{c} = \vec{0}$

$\Rightarrow \quad \vec{a} + \vec{c} = -\vec{b}$

$\Rightarrow \quad (\vec{a} + \vec{c})\cdot(\vec{a} + \vec{c}) = (-\vec{b})\cdot(-\vec{b})$ **[1]**

[multiply by same product]

$\Rightarrow \quad |\vec{a}|^2 + |\vec{c}|^2 + 2\vec{a}\cdot\vec{c} = |\vec{b}|^2$

$\Rightarrow \quad a^2 + c^2 + 2|\vec{a}||\vec{c}|\cos c = b^2$

$\Rightarrow \quad 2|\vec{a}||\vec{c}|\cos(\pi - B) = b^2 - c^2 - a^2$

$\Rightarrow \quad -2ac\cos B = b^2 - c^2 - a^2$

$\Rightarrow \quad 2ac\cos B = a^2 + c^2 - b^2$

$\therefore \quad \cos B = \dfrac{a^2 + c^2 - b^2}{2ac}$ **Hence proved.** [1]

9. Given, $2\vec{a} - 4\vec{b}$ and $10\vec{a} + 8\vec{b}$ are perpendicular to each other.

$\therefore \quad (2\vec{a} - 4\vec{b})\cdot(10\vec{a} + 8\vec{b}) = 0 \quad [\because \vec{a} \perp \vec{b} \text{ then } \vec{a}\cdot\vec{b} = 0]$

$\Rightarrow 20(\vec{a}\cdot\vec{a}) + 16(\vec{a}\cdot\vec{b}) - 40(\vec{b}\cdot\vec{a}) - 32(\vec{b}\cdot\vec{b}) = 0$

$\Rightarrow \quad 20|\vec{a}|^2 - 24(\vec{a}\cdot\vec{b}) - 32|\vec{b}|^2 = 0$ [1]

$\Rightarrow \quad 20 - 24(\vec{a}\cdot\vec{b}) - 32 = 0 \quad [\because |\vec{a}| = |\vec{b}| = 1]$

$\Rightarrow \quad -24\vec{a}\cdot\vec{b} - 12 = 0 \Rightarrow 24|\vec{a}||\vec{b}|\cos\theta = -12$

$\Rightarrow \quad 24\cos\theta = -12 \quad [\because |\vec{a}| = |\vec{b}| = 1]$

$\Rightarrow \quad \cos\theta = \dfrac{-12}{24} = \dfrac{-1}{2} \Rightarrow \theta = \pi - \dfrac{\pi}{3} = \dfrac{2\pi}{3}$ [1]

10. Given, $|\vec{a}| = 2$, $|\vec{b}| = 3$ and $\vec{a}\cdot\vec{b} = 4$

Now, consider $|\vec{a} - \vec{b}|^2 = (\vec{a} - \vec{b})^2 = (\vec{a} - \vec{b})\cdot(\vec{a} - \vec{b})$

$= \vec{a}\cdot\vec{a} - \vec{a}\cdot\vec{b} - \vec{b}\cdot\vec{a} + \vec{b}\cdot\vec{b}$

$= |\vec{a}|^2 - \vec{a}\cdot\vec{b} - \vec{a}\cdot\vec{b} + |\vec{b}|^2$

$= |\vec{a}|^2 - 2\vec{a}\cdot\vec{b} + |\vec{b}|^2 \quad [\because \vec{a}\cdot\vec{b} = \vec{b}\cdot\vec{a}]$ [1]

$\therefore |\vec{a} - \vec{b}|^2 = (2)^2 - 2(4) + (3)^2 = 4 - 8 + 9 = 5$

$\therefore \quad |\vec{a} - \vec{b}| = \sqrt{5}$ [taking square root on both sides] [1]

11. We have, $\vec{a} = 2\hat{i} + 2\hat{j} + 3\hat{k}$, $\vec{b} = -\hat{i} + 2\hat{j} + \hat{k}$

and $\quad \vec{c} = 3\hat{i} + \hat{j}$

Now, $\vec{a} + \lambda\vec{b} = (2\hat{i} + 2\hat{j} + 3\hat{k}) + \lambda(-\hat{i} + 2\hat{j} + \hat{k})$

$= 2\hat{i} + 2\hat{j} + 3\hat{k} - \lambda\hat{i} + 2\lambda\hat{j} + \lambda\hat{k}$

$= (2 - \lambda)\hat{i} + (2 + 2\lambda)\hat{j} + (3 + \lambda)\hat{k}$ [1]

Since, $\vec{a} + \lambda\vec{b}$ is perpendicular to $\vec{c}$.

$\therefore \quad (\vec{a} + \lambda\vec{b})\cdot\vec{c} = 0$

$\Rightarrow \quad [(2 - \lambda)\hat{i} + (2 + 2\lambda)\hat{j} + (3 + \lambda)\hat{k}]\cdot(3\hat{i} + \hat{j}) = 0$

$\Rightarrow \quad (2 - \lambda)(3) + (2 + 2\lambda)(1) + (3 + \lambda)(0) = 0$

$\Rightarrow \quad 6 - 3\lambda + 2 + 2\lambda = 0$

$\Rightarrow \quad -\lambda + 8 = 0$ [1]

$\therefore \quad \lambda = 8$

12. Let $\vec{a} = 3\hat{i} - 5\hat{k}$, $\vec{b} = 2\hat{i} + 7\hat{j}$ and $\vec{c} = \hat{i} + \hat{j} + \hat{k}$ be three given vectors. Let $\vec{r} = x\hat{i} + y\hat{j} + z\hat{k}$ be a vector such that its dot products with $\vec{a}, \vec{b}$ and $\vec{c}$ are -1, 6 and 5 respectively, we have

$\vec{r}\cdot\vec{a} = (x\hat{i} + y\hat{j} + z\hat{k})\cdot(3\hat{i} - 5\hat{k}) \Rightarrow -1 = 3x - 5z$ ...(i) [1]

$\vec{r}\cdot\vec{b} = (x\hat{i} + y\hat{j} + z\hat{k})\cdot(2\hat{i} + 7\hat{j}) \Rightarrow 6 = 2x + 7y$ ...(ii)

and $\vec{r}\cdot\vec{c} = (x\hat{i} + y\hat{j} + z\hat{k})\cdot(\hat{i} + \hat{j} + \hat{k}) \Rightarrow 5 = x + y + z$ ...(iii) [1½]

On solving Eqs. (i), (ii) and (iii), we get

$x = 3, y = 0$ and $z = 2$ [1]

Hence, the required vector is $\vec{r} = 3\hat{i} + 2\hat{k}$. [1/2]

13. Given, $\quad \vec{a} + \vec{b} + \vec{c} = \vec{0} \Rightarrow \vec{a} + \vec{b} = -\vec{c}$

$\Rightarrow \quad (\vec{a} + \vec{b})^2 = (-\vec{c})^2$ [squaring on both sides]

$\Rightarrow (\vec{a} + \vec{b})\cdot(\vec{a} + \vec{b}) = (-\vec{c})\cdot(-\vec{c})$ [1]

$\Rightarrow \quad \vec{a}\cdot\vec{a} + \vec{a}\cdot\vec{b} + \vec{b}\cdot\vec{a} + \vec{b}\cdot\vec{b} = \vec{c}\cdot\vec{c}$

$\Rightarrow \quad |\vec{a}|^2 + \vec{a}\cdot\vec{b} + \vec{a}\cdot\vec{b} + |\vec{b}|^2 = |\vec{c}|^2 \quad [\because \vec{a}\cdot\vec{b} = \vec{b}\cdot\vec{a}]$

$\Rightarrow \quad |\vec{a}|^2 + 2\vec{a}\cdot\vec{b} + |\vec{b}|^2 = |\vec{c}|^2$ [1]

$\Rightarrow \quad |\vec{a}|^2 + 2|\vec{a}||\vec{b}|\cos\theta + |\vec{b}|^2 = |\vec{c}|^2$ ...(i)

$[\because \vec{a}\cdot\vec{b} = |\vec{a}||\vec{b}|\cos\theta]$

On putting the values of $|\vec{a}| = 3$, $|\vec{b}| = 5$ and $|\vec{c}| = 7$ in Eq. (i), we get

$(3)^2 + 2 \times 3 \times 5 \times \cos\theta + (5)^2 = (7)^2$

$\Rightarrow \quad 9 + 30\cos\theta + 25 = 49$ [1]

$\Rightarrow \quad 30\cos\theta = 49 - 34$

$\Rightarrow \quad \cos\theta = \dfrac{15}{30} = \dfrac{1}{2} \Rightarrow \cos\theta = \cos\dfrac{\pi}{3}$

$\therefore \quad \theta = \dfrac{\pi}{3}$

Hence, the angle between $\vec{a}$ and $\vec{b}$ is $\dfrac{\pi}{3}$. [1]

14. Given, $|\vec{a}| = |\vec{b}| = |\vec{c}| = 1$ and $\vec{a} + \vec{b} + \vec{c} = \vec{0}$ ...(i)

Now, consider $(\vec{a} + \vec{b} + \vec{c})\cdot(\vec{a} + \vec{b} + \vec{c}) = \vec{0}\cdot\vec{0} = 0$

$\Rightarrow \vec{a}\cdot(\vec{a} + \vec{b} + \vec{c}) + \vec{b}\cdot(\vec{a} + \vec{b} + \vec{c}) + \vec{c}\cdot(\vec{a} + \vec{b} + \vec{c}) = 0$

$\Rightarrow \vec{a}\cdot\vec{a} + \vec{a}\cdot\vec{b} + \vec{a}\cdot\vec{c} + \vec{b}\cdot\vec{a} + \vec{b}\cdot\vec{b} + \vec{b}\cdot\vec{c}$

$+ \vec{c}\cdot\vec{a} + \vec{c}\cdot\vec{b} + \vec{c}\cdot\vec{c} = 0$ [1]

$\Rightarrow |\vec{a}|^2 + \vec{a}\cdot\vec{b} + \vec{c}\cdot\vec{a} + \vec{a}\cdot\vec{b} + |\vec{b}|^2 + \vec{b}\cdot\vec{c}$

$+ \vec{c}\cdot\vec{a} + \vec{b}\cdot\vec{c} + |\vec{c}|^2 = 0$

[dot product is commutative] [1]

$$\Rightarrow |\vec{a}|^2 + |\vec{b}|^2 + |\vec{c}|^2 + 2\vec{a}\cdot\vec{b} + 2\vec{b}\cdot\vec{c} + 2\vec{c}\cdot\vec{a} = 0$$

$$\Rightarrow 1+1+1+2(\vec{a}\cdot\vec{b} + \vec{b}\cdot\vec{c} + \vec{c}\cdot\vec{a}) = 0 \quad \text{[from Eq. (i)]} \text{ [1]}$$

$$\Rightarrow 2(\vec{a}\cdot\vec{b} + \vec{b}\cdot\vec{c} + \vec{c}\cdot\vec{a}) = -3$$

$$\Rightarrow (\vec{a}\cdot\vec{b} + \vec{b}\cdot\vec{c} + \vec{c}\cdot\vec{a}) = -\frac{3}{2} \quad \text{[1]}$$

15. Given, $\vec{a} = \hat{i} + \hat{j} + \hat{k}$, $\vec{b} = 2\hat{i} + 4\hat{j} - 5\hat{k}$

and $\vec{c} = \lambda\hat{i} + 2\hat{j} + 3\hat{k}$

Now, $\vec{b} + \vec{c} = 2\hat{i} + 4\hat{j} - 5\hat{k} + \lambda\hat{i} + 2\hat{j} + 3\hat{k}$

$$= (2+\lambda)\hat{i} + 6\hat{j} - 2\hat{k}$$

$$\therefore \quad |\vec{b} + \vec{c}| = \sqrt{(2+\lambda)^2 + (6)^2 + (-2)^2}$$

$$= \sqrt{4 + \lambda^2 + 4\lambda + 36 + 4}$$

$$= \sqrt{\lambda^2 + 4\lambda + 44} \quad \text{[1]}$$

The unit vector along $\vec{b} + \vec{c}$ is given by

$$\frac{\vec{b} + \vec{c}}{|\vec{b} + \vec{c}|} = \frac{(2+\lambda)\hat{i} + 6\hat{j} - 2\hat{k}}{\sqrt{\lambda^2 + 4\lambda + 44}} \quad \text{...(i) [1/2]}$$

Given, scalar product of $(\hat{i} + \hat{j} + \hat{k})$ with above unit vector is 1,

i.e. $$(\hat{i} + \hat{j} + \hat{k})\cdot\frac{\vec{b} + \vec{c}}{|\vec{b} + \vec{c}|} = 1 \quad \text{[1/2]}$$

$$\Rightarrow (\hat{i} + \hat{j} + \hat{k})\cdot\frac{(2+\lambda)\hat{i} + 6\hat{j} - 2\hat{k}}{\sqrt{\lambda^2 + 4\lambda + 44}} = 1$$

$$\Rightarrow \frac{1(2+\lambda) + 1(6) + 1(-2)}{\sqrt{\lambda^2 + 4\lambda + 44}} = 1 \quad \text{[1/2]}$$

$$\Rightarrow \frac{2 + \lambda + 6 - 2}{\sqrt{\lambda^2 + 4\lambda + 44}} = 1$$

$$\Rightarrow \lambda + 6 = \sqrt{\lambda^2 + 4\lambda + 44}$$

$$\Rightarrow (\lambda + 6)^2 = \lambda^2 + 4\lambda + 44 \quad \text{[squaring on both sides]}$$

$$\Rightarrow \lambda^2 + 36 + 12\lambda = \lambda^2 + 4\lambda + 44$$

$$\Rightarrow 8\lambda = 8 \Rightarrow \lambda = 1 \quad \text{[1]}$$

Hence, the value of λ is 1.

On putting the value of λ in Eq. (i), we get

Unit vector along $\vec{b} + \vec{c} = \dfrac{(2+1)\hat{i} + 6\hat{j} - 2\hat{k}}{\sqrt{(1)^2 + 4(1) + 44}}$

$$= \frac{3\hat{i} + 6\hat{j} - 2\hat{k}}{\sqrt{1 + 4 + 44}} = \frac{3\hat{i} + 6\hat{j} - 2\hat{k}}{\sqrt{49}}$$

$$= \frac{3}{7}\hat{i} + \frac{6}{7}\hat{j} - \frac{2}{7}\hat{k} \quad \text{[1/2]}$$

16. We know that, $|\vec{x}\cdot\vec{x}| = |\vec{x}|^2$ [1/2]

$$\Rightarrow |\hat{a} - \hat{b}|^2 = (\hat{a} - \hat{b})\cdot(\hat{a} - \hat{b}) \quad \text{[1/2]}$$

$$\Rightarrow |\hat{a} - \hat{b}|^2 = \hat{a}\cdot\hat{a} - \hat{a}\cdot\hat{b} - \hat{b}\cdot\hat{a} + \hat{b}\cdot\hat{b}$$

$$\Rightarrow |\hat{a} - \hat{b}|^2 = |\hat{a}|^2 - 2\hat{a}\cdot\hat{b} + |\hat{b}|^2 \quad [\because \hat{a}\cdot\hat{b} = \hat{b}\cdot\hat{a}] \text{ [1]}$$

$$\Rightarrow |\hat{a} - \hat{b}|^2 = |\hat{a}|^2 - 2|\hat{a}||\hat{b}|\cos\theta + |\hat{b}|^2$$

$$[\because \hat{a}\cdot\hat{b} = |\hat{a}||\hat{b}|\cos\theta]$$

$$\Rightarrow |\hat{a} - \hat{b}|^2 = 1 - 2\cdot1\cdot1\cos\theta + 1 \quad [\text{given } |\hat{a}| = |\hat{b}| = 1]$$

$$\Rightarrow |\hat{a} - \hat{b}|^2 = 2 - 2\cos\theta \quad \text{[1]}$$

$$\Rightarrow |\hat{a} - \hat{b}|^2 = 2(1 - \cos\theta) = 2\left[2\sin^2\left(\frac{\theta}{2}\right)\right] = 4\sin^2\frac{\theta}{2}$$

$$\Rightarrow \sin^2\frac{\theta}{2} = \frac{1}{4}|\hat{a} - \hat{b}|^2 \Rightarrow \sin\frac{\theta}{2} = \frac{1}{2}|\hat{a} - \hat{b}| \quad \text{[1]}$$

17. Let θ be the angle between vectors $\vec{a}$ and $\vec{b}$.

Then, $\cos\theta = \dfrac{\vec{a}\cdot\vec{b}}{|\vec{a}||\vec{b}|}$ [1]

For the angle θ to be obtuse, we must have $\cos\theta < 0$

$$\Rightarrow \frac{\vec{a}\cdot\vec{b}}{|\vec{a}||\vec{b}|} < 0 \quad \text{[1]}$$

$$\Rightarrow \vec{a}\cdot\vec{b} < 0 \quad [\because |\vec{a}|, |\vec{b}| > 0]$$

$$\Rightarrow (2x^2\hat{i} + 4x\hat{j} + \hat{k})\cdot(7\hat{i} - 2\hat{j} + x\hat{k}) < 0$$

$$\Rightarrow 14x^2 - 8x + x < 0 \Rightarrow 7x(2x - 1) < 0 \quad \text{[1]}$$

$$\Rightarrow x(2x - 1) < 0 \Rightarrow 0 < x < \frac{1}{2}$$

Hence, the angle between the given vectors is obtuse, if $x \in (0, 1/2)$. [1]

18. For vector $\vec{r}$ to be inclined acute angles with the coordinate axes, we must have

$$\vec{r}\cdot\hat{i} > 0, \vec{r}\cdot\hat{j} > 0 \text{ and } \vec{r}\cdot\hat{k} > 0 \quad \text{[1]}$$

Consider, $\vec{r}\cdot\hat{i} > 0$ and $\vec{r}\cdot\hat{k} > 0$ $\quad [\because \vec{r}\cdot\vec{j} = 2 > 0]$

$$\Rightarrow (a^2 - 4) > 0 \text{ and} -(a^2 - 9) > 0$$

$$[\because \vec{r}\cdot\hat{i} = a^2 - 4 \text{ and } \vec{r}\cdot\hat{k} = -(a^2 - 9)] \text{ [1]}$$

$$\Rightarrow (a - 2)(a + 2) > 0 \text{ and} (a + 3)(a - 3) < 0$$

$$\Rightarrow a < -2 \text{ or } a > 2 \text{ and } -3 < a < 3 \quad \text{[1]}$$

$$\Rightarrow a \in (-3, -2) \cup (2, 3). \quad \text{[1]}$$

19. When either $\vec{a} = \vec{0}$ or $\vec{b} = \vec{0}$, then $|\vec{a} + \vec{b}| = |\vec{a}| + |\vec{b}|$.

Thus, the inequality holds trivially in this case. [1]

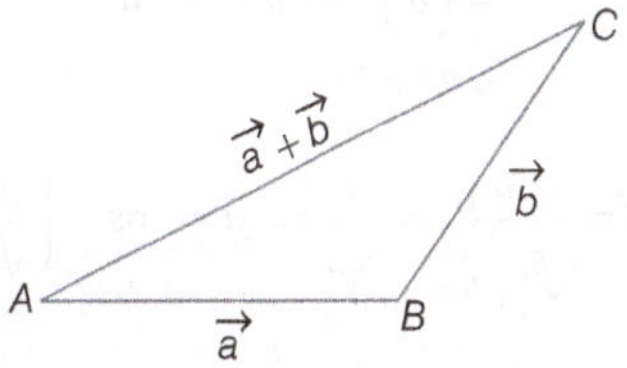

When $|\vec{a}| \neq 0 \neq |\vec{b}|$.

Then, $|\vec{a}+\vec{b}|^2 = (\vec{a}+\vec{b})^2 = (\vec{a}+\vec{b})\cdot(\vec{a}+\vec{b})$

$= \vec{a}\cdot\vec{a} + \vec{a}\cdot\vec{b} + \vec{b}\cdot\vec{a} + \vec{b}\cdot\vec{b}$ [1]

$= |\vec{a}|^2 + |\vec{b}|^2 + 2\vec{a}\cdot\vec{b}$

$\Rightarrow |\vec{a}+\vec{b}|^2 \leq |\vec{a}|^2 + |\vec{b}|^2 + 2|\vec{a}\cdot\vec{b}|$ $[\because x \leq |x|, \forall x \in R]$

$\Rightarrow |\vec{a}+\vec{b}|^2 \leq |\vec{a}|^2 + |\vec{b}|^2 + 2|\vec{a}||\vec{b}|$ $[\because |\vec{a}\cdot\vec{b}| \leq |\vec{a}||\vec{b}|]$ [1]

$\Rightarrow |\vec{a}+\vec{b}|^2 \leq (|\vec{a}|+|\vec{b}|)^2 \Rightarrow |\vec{a}+\vec{b}| \leq |\vec{a}|+|\vec{b}|$ [1]

20. (i) If vectors $\vec{a}$ and $\vec{b}$ are perpendicular, then $\vec{a}\cdot\vec{b} = 0$ [1]

$\Rightarrow (3\hat{i} + 2\hat{j} + 9\hat{k}).(\hat{i} + p\hat{j} + 3\hat{k}) = 0$

$\Rightarrow 3 + 2p + 27 = 0 \Rightarrow p = -15$ [1]

(ii) We know that, the vectors $\vec{a} = a_1\hat{i} + a_2\hat{j} + a_3\hat{k}$ and $\vec{b} = b_1\hat{i} + b_2\hat{j} + b_3\hat{k}$ are parallel iff

$\Rightarrow \frac{a_1}{b_1} = \frac{a_2}{b_2} = \frac{a_3}{b_3} = l$

So, the given vectors $\vec{a} = 3\hat{i} + 2\hat{j} + 9\hat{k}$

and $\vec{b} = \hat{i} + p\hat{j} + 3\hat{k}$ will be parallel iff

$\frac{3}{1} = \frac{2}{p} = \frac{9}{3} \Rightarrow 3 = \frac{2}{p} \Rightarrow p = \frac{2}{3}$ [2]

21. Given $\vec{a}$, $\vec{b}$ and $\vec{c}$ are mutually perpendicular vectors with equal magnitude.

$\therefore$ We have, $\vec{a}\cdot\vec{b} = \vec{b}\cdot\vec{c} = \vec{c}\cdot\vec{a} = 0$

and $|\vec{a}| = |\vec{b}| = |\vec{c}|$ ...(i) [1]

Let θ be the angle between $\vec{a}$ and $(\vec{a}+\vec{b}+\vec{c})$.

Then, $\cos\theta = \frac{\vec{a}\cdot(\vec{a}+\vec{b}+\vec{c})}{|\vec{a}||\vec{a}+\vec{b}+\vec{c}|} = \frac{\vec{a}\cdot\vec{a}+\vec{a}\cdot\vec{b}+\vec{a}\cdot\vec{c}}{|\vec{a}||\vec{a}+\vec{b}+\vec{c}|}$

$= \frac{|\vec{a}|^2+0+0}{|\vec{a}||\vec{a}+\vec{b}+\vec{c}|} = \frac{|\vec{a}|}{|\vec{a}+\vec{b}+\vec{c}|}$ [from Eq. (i)] [1]

Now, $|\vec{a}+\vec{b}+\vec{c}|^2 = (\vec{a}+\vec{b}+\vec{c})\cdot(\vec{a}+\vec{b}+\vec{c})$

$= \vec{a}^2 + \vec{b}^2 + \vec{c}^2 + 2\vec{a}\cdot\vec{b} + 2\vec{b}\cdot\vec{c} + 2\vec{c}\cdot\vec{a}$

$\therefore |\vec{a}+\vec{b}+\vec{c}|^2 = |\vec{a}|^2 + |\vec{b}|^2 + |\vec{c}|^2 + 0 + 0 + 0$ [1/2]

$= |\vec{a}|^2 + |\vec{a}|^2 + |\vec{a}|^2$ [from Eq. (i)]

$= 3|\vec{a}|^2$ [1/2]

$\therefore \cos\theta = \frac{|\vec{a}|}{\sqrt{3}|\vec{a}|} = \frac{1}{\sqrt{3}} \Rightarrow \theta = \cos^{-1}\left(\frac{1}{\sqrt{3}}\right)$ [1]

22. We have, $|\vec{a}| = 3$, $|\vec{b}| = 4$ and $|\vec{c}| = 5$

It is given that,

$\vec{a} \perp (\vec{b}+\vec{c})$, $\vec{b} \perp (\vec{c}+\vec{a})$ and $\vec{c} \perp (\vec{a}+\vec{b})$ [1/2]

$\Rightarrow \vec{a}\cdot(\vec{b}+\vec{c}) = 0$, $\vec{b}\cdot(\vec{c}+\vec{a}) = 0$ and $\vec{c}\cdot(\vec{a}+\vec{b}) = 0$ [1]

$\Rightarrow \vec{a}\cdot\vec{b} + \vec{a}\cdot\vec{c} = 0$, $\vec{b}\cdot\vec{c} + \vec{b}\cdot\vec{a} = 0$

and $\vec{c}\cdot\vec{a} + \vec{c}\cdot\vec{b} = 0$

Adding all these, we get

$2(\vec{a}\cdot\vec{b} + \vec{b}\cdot\vec{c} + \vec{c}\cdot\vec{a}) = 0$

$\Rightarrow \vec{a}\cdot\vec{b} + \vec{b}\cdot\vec{c} + \vec{c}\cdot\vec{a} = 0$ ...(i) [1/2]

Now, consider

$|\vec{a}+\vec{b}+\vec{c}|^2 = |\vec{a}|^2 + |\vec{b}|^2 + |\vec{c}|^2 + 2(\vec{a}.\vec{b} + \vec{b}.\vec{c} + \vec{c}.\vec{a})$ [1]

$\Rightarrow |\vec{a}+\vec{b}+\vec{c}|^2 = 3^2 + 4^2 + 5^2 + 0$ [using Eq. (i)]

$\Rightarrow |\vec{a}+\vec{b}+\vec{c}| = \sqrt{50} = 5\sqrt{2}$ [1]

23. Since, $\vec{\beta}_1$ is parallel to $\vec{\alpha}$.

Therefore, $\vec{\beta}_1 = \lambda\vec{\alpha}$ for some scalar λ. ...(i) [1]

It is given that, $\vec{\beta} = \vec{\beta}_1 + \vec{\beta}_2$

$\Rightarrow \vec{\beta}_2 = \vec{\beta} - \vec{\beta}_1 = \vec{\beta} - \lambda\vec{\alpha}$ ...(ii) [1/2]

Also, it is given that, $\vec{\beta}_2$ is perpendicular to $\vec{\alpha}$, therefore

$\Rightarrow \vec{\beta}_2\cdot\vec{\alpha} = 0 \Rightarrow (\vec{\beta} - \lambda\vec{\alpha})\cdot\vec{\alpha} = 0$ [1/2]

$\Rightarrow \vec{\beta}\cdot\vec{\alpha} - \lambda(\vec{\alpha}\cdot\vec{\alpha}) = 0$ [using Eq. (ii)]

$\Rightarrow \lambda = \frac{\vec{\beta}\cdot\vec{\alpha}}{\vec{\alpha}\cdot\vec{\alpha}}$ [1/2]

Also, given $\vec{\alpha} = 3\hat{i} - \hat{j}$ and $\vec{\beta} = 2\hat{i} + \hat{j} - 3\hat{k}$

Now, $\vec{\beta}\cdot\vec{\alpha} = (2\hat{i} + \hat{j} - 3\hat{k})\cdot(3\hat{i} - \hat{j}) = 6 - 1 + 0 = 5$

and $\vec{\alpha}\cdot\vec{\alpha} = (3\hat{i} - \hat{j})\cdot(3\hat{i} - \hat{j}) = 9 + 1 = 10$

$\therefore \lambda = \frac{\vec{\beta}\cdot\vec{\alpha}}{\vec{\alpha}\cdot\vec{\alpha}} = \frac{5}{10} = \frac{1}{2}$ [1/2]

From Eq. (i), we get

$\vec{\beta}_1 = \lambda\vec{\alpha} \Rightarrow \vec{\beta}_1 = \frac{1}{2}(3\hat{i} - \hat{j}) = \frac{3}{2}\hat{i} - \frac{1}{2}\hat{j}$

and $\vec{\beta}_2 = \vec{\beta} - \vec{\beta}_1$

$\Rightarrow \vec{\beta}_2 = (2\hat{i} + \hat{j} - 3\hat{k}) - \left(\frac{3}{2}\hat{i} - \frac{1}{2}\hat{j}\right)$

$= \frac{1}{2}\hat{i} + \frac{3}{2}\hat{j} - 3\hat{k}$

Hence, $\vec{\beta}_1 = \frac{3}{2}\hat{i} - \frac{1}{2}\hat{j}$ and $\vec{\beta}_2 = \frac{1}{2}\hat{i} + \frac{3}{2}\hat{j} - 3\hat{k}$ [1]

TOPIC 03 Vector (or Cross) Product of Two Vectors

Let $\vec{a}$ and $\vec{b}$ be two non-zero vectors inclined at an angle θ. Then, the vector (or cross) product of $\vec{a}$ and $\vec{b}$ is denoted by $\vec{a} \times \vec{b}$, read as $\vec{a}$ cross $\vec{b}$ and defined as

$$\vec{a} \times \vec{b} = |\vec{a}||\vec{b}| \sin\theta\, \hat{n}$$

where, $\hat{n}$ is a unit vector perpendicular to both vectors $\vec{a}$ and $\vec{b}$, such that $\vec{a}, \vec{b}$ and $\hat{n}$ form a right handed system.

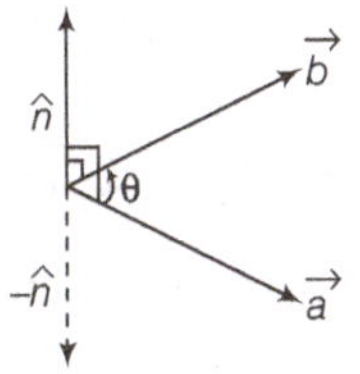

Also, $|\vec{a} \times \vec{b}| = |\vec{a}||\vec{b}| \sin\theta |\hat{n}|$

$$= ab \sin\theta \qquad [\because |\vec{a}| = a, |\vec{b}| = b \text{ and } |\hat{n}| = 1]$$

Note

(i) Either $\vec{a} = \vec{0}$ or $\vec{b} = \vec{0}$, then θ is not defined as $\vec{0}$ has no direction and in this case $\vec{a} \times \vec{b} = \vec{0}$.

(ii) Unit vector perpendicular of two vectors $\vec{a}$ and $\vec{b}$ is given by $\hat{n} = \dfrac{\vec{a} \times \vec{b}}{|\vec{a} \times \vec{b}|}$

(iii) **Lagrange's Identity** If $\vec{a}$ and $\vec{b}$ are two vectors, then $(\vec{a} \times \vec{b})^2 = |\vec{a}|^2 |\vec{b}|^2 - (\vec{a} \cdot \vec{b})^2$ which are known as relation between dot and cross product.

(iv) **Geometrically interpreted** The cross product is a vector perpendicular to both vectors whose magnitude is equal to the area of the parallelogram whose adjacent sides are the vectors $\vec{a}$ and $\vec{b}$.

Example 1 If vectors $\vec{a}$ and $\vec{b}$ are such that $\vec{a} = 3, |\vec{b}| = \dfrac{2}{3}$ and $\vec{a} \times \vec{b}$ is a unit vector, then find the angle between $\vec{a}$ and $\vec{b}$.

Sol. Given, $|\vec{a}| = 3, |\vec{b}| = \dfrac{2}{3}$.

Let θ be the angle between $\vec{a}$ and $\vec{b}$.

Since, $\quad \vec{a} \times \vec{b} = 1$

$\therefore \quad |\vec{a} \quad \vec{b} \sin\theta = 1 \Rightarrow 3 \times \dfrac{2}{3} \sin\theta = 1 \Rightarrow 2\sin\theta = 1$

$\Rightarrow \qquad \sin\theta = \dfrac{1}{2} \Rightarrow \theta = \dfrac{\pi}{6}$

Important Results on Vector Product of Two Vectors

(i) The vector product of two vectors $(\vec{a} \times \vec{b})$ is a vector.

(ii) Let $\vec{a}$ and $\vec{b}$ be two non-zero vectors. Then, $\vec{a} \times \vec{b} = \vec{0}$ if and only if $\vec{a}$ and $\vec{b}$ are parallel (or **collinear**) to each other, i.e. $\vec{a} \times \vec{b} = \vec{0} \Leftrightarrow \vec{a} \parallel \vec{b}$.

(iii) $\vec{a} \times \vec{a} = \vec{0}$, as $\theta = 0°$ and $\vec{a} \times (-\vec{a}) = \vec{0}$, as $\theta = \pi$.

(iv) If $\theta = \dfrac{\pi}{2}$, then $\vec{a} \times \vec{b} = |\vec{a}||\vec{b}|$.

(v) For mutually perpendicular unit vectors $\hat{i}, \hat{j}$ and $\hat{k}$,

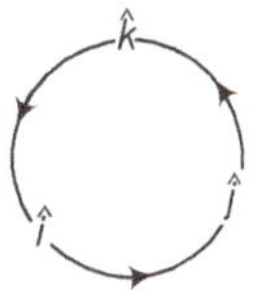

$$\hat{i} \times \hat{i} = \hat{j} \times \hat{j} = \hat{k} \times \hat{k} = \vec{0}$$

and $\quad \hat{i} \times \hat{j} = \hat{k}, \hat{j} \times \hat{k} = \hat{i}, \hat{k} \times \hat{i} = \hat{j};$

$\quad \hat{j} \times \hat{i} = -\hat{k}, \hat{k} \times \hat{j} = -\hat{i}$ and $\hat{i} \times \hat{k} = -\hat{j}$.

(vi) The **angle between two non-zero vectors $\vec{a}$ and $\vec{b}$** in terms of vector products is given by $\sin\theta = \dfrac{|\vec{a} \times \vec{b}|}{|\vec{a}||\vec{b}|}$.

(vii) Vectors of magnitude λ normal to the plane of $\vec{a}$ and $\vec{b}$ are given as $\dfrac{\pm\lambda(\vec{a} \times \vec{b})}{|\vec{a} \times \vec{b}|}$.

Properties of Vector Product of Two Vectors

(i) The vector product is not **commutative**, for vectors $\vec{a}$ and $\vec{b}$, we have $(\vec{a} \times \vec{b}) = -(\vec{b} \times \vec{a})$

(ii) The vector product is distributive over addition, i.e. for vectors $\vec{a}, \vec{b}$ and $\vec{c}$, we have

$$\vec{a} \times (\vec{b} + \vec{c}) = \vec{a} \times \vec{b} + \vec{a} \times \vec{c}$$

(iii) If m is any scalar and $\vec{a}$ and $\vec{b}$ be the two non-zero vectors, then $(m\vec{a}) \times \vec{b} = m(\vec{a} \times \vec{b}) = \vec{a} \times (m\vec{b})$

Example 2 For any three vectors $\vec{a}$, $\vec{b}$ and $\vec{c}$, prove that $\vec{a}\times(\vec{b}-\vec{c})=(\vec{a}\times\vec{b})-(\vec{a}\times\vec{c})$.

Sol. We have, LHS $=\vec{a}\times(\vec{b}-\vec{c})=\vec{a}\times[\vec{b}+(-\vec{c})]$

$=(\vec{a}\times\vec{b})+\vec{a}\times(-\vec{c})$ [by distributive law]

$=(\vec{a}\times\vec{b})+[-(\vec{a}\times\vec{c})]$ $[\because \vec{a}\times(m\vec{c})=m(\vec{a}\times\vec{c})]$

$=(\vec{a}\times\vec{b}\ -(\vec{a}\times\vec{c})=$ RHS

Note We can use this result as standard result.

Example 3 If $\vec{a}\times\vec{b}=\vec{a}\times\vec{c}$ where $\vec{a}$, $\vec{b}$ and $\vec{c}$ are non-zero vectors, then prove that either $\vec{b}=\vec{c}$ or $\vec{a}$ and $(\vec{b}\cdot\vec{c})$ are parallel. **[ISC 2024]**

Sol. Given, $\vec{a}\times\vec{b}=\vec{a}\times\vec{c}$, where $\vec{a}$, $\vec{b}$ and $\vec{c}$ are non-zero vectors.

Since, $\vec{a}\times\vec{b}=\vec{a}\times\vec{c}$

$\Rightarrow \vec{a}\times\vec{b}-\vec{a}\times\vec{c}=0$

$\Rightarrow \vec{a}\times(\vec{b}-\vec{c})=0$

$\Rightarrow \vec{a}\,||\,(\vec{b}-\vec{c})$ or $\vec{b}-\vec{c}=0$ $[\because \vec{a}\neq 0]$

$\Rightarrow \vec{a}\,||\,(\vec{b}-\vec{c})$ or $\vec{b}=\vec{c}$

Vector Product of Two Vectors in Component Form

Suppose two vectors $\vec{a}$ and $\vec{b}$ are given in component form, say $\vec{a}=a_1\hat{i}+a_2\hat{j}+a_3\hat{k}$ and $\vec{b}=b_1\hat{i}+b_2\hat{j}+b_3\hat{k}$, then their vector product is given by

$$\vec{a}\times\vec{b}=\begin{vmatrix}\hat{i}&\hat{j}&\hat{k}\\a_1&a_2&a_3\\b_1&b_2&b_3\end{vmatrix}$$

Example 4 Find a vector of magnitude 3, which is perpendicular to both the vectors $3\hat{i}+\hat{j}-4\hat{k}$ and $6\hat{i}+5\hat{j}-2\hat{k}$.

Sol. Let two given vectors be $\vec{a}=3\hat{i}+\hat{j}-4\hat{k}$ and $\vec{b}=6\hat{i}+5\hat{j}-2\hat{k}$.

Using vector product of two vectors, we get

$$\vec{a}\times\vec{b}=\begin{vmatrix}\hat{i}&\hat{j}&\hat{k}\\3&1&-4\\6&5&-2\end{vmatrix}$$

$=\hat{i}\,\{1(-2)-5(-4)\}-\hat{j}\,\{3(-2)-6(-4)\}+\hat{k}\,\{3(5)-6(1)\}$

[expanding the determinant along R_1]

$=\hat{i}(-2+20)-j(-6+24)+\hat{k}(15-6)$

$=18\hat{i}-18\hat{j}+9\hat{k}$

and $|\vec{a}\times\vec{b}|=\sqrt{18^2+(-18)^2+9^2}=\sqrt{729}=27$

Hence, required vector $=\dfrac{\lambda(\vec{a}\times\vec{b})}{|\vec{a}\times\vec{b}|}$

$=\dfrac{3(18\hat{i}-18\hat{j}+9\hat{k})}{27}$ [given $\lambda=3$]

$=\dfrac{18}{9}\hat{i}-\dfrac{18}{9}\hat{j}+\dfrac{9}{9}\hat{k}=2\hat{i}-2\hat{j}+\hat{k}$

Example 5 If $\vec{a}=\hat{i}-2\hat{j}+3\hat{k}$, $\vec{b}=2\hat{i}+3\hat{j}-5\hat{k}$, prove that $\vec{a}$ and $\vec{a}\times\vec{b}$ are perpendicular. **[ISC 2019]**

Sol. Given vectors are

$\vec{a}=\hat{i}-2\hat{j}+3\hat{k}$ and $\vec{b}=2\hat{i}+3\hat{j}-5\hat{k}$.

Now, $\vec{a}\times\vec{b}=\begin{vmatrix}\hat{i}&\hat{j}&\hat{k}\\1&-2&3\\2&3&-5\end{vmatrix}$

$=\hat{i}(10-9)-\hat{j}(-5-6)+\hat{k}(3+4)$

$=\hat{i}+11\hat{j}+7\hat{k}$

Now, $\vec{a}\cdot(\vec{a}\times\vec{b})=(\hat{i}-2\hat{j}+3\hat{k})\cdot(\hat{i}+11\hat{j}+7\hat{k})$

$=1-22+21=22-22=0$

Hence, $\vec{a}$ is perpendicular to $\vec{a}\times\vec{b}$.

Example 6 Find a unit vector perpendicular to each of the vectors $\vec{a}+\vec{b}$ and $\vec{a}-\vec{b}$, where $\vec{a}=3\hat{i}+2\hat{j}+2\hat{k}$ and $\vec{b}=\hat{i}+2\hat{j}-2\hat{k}$. **[ISC 2016]**

Sol. Given, $\vec{a}=3\hat{i}+2\hat{j}+2\hat{k}$ and $\vec{b}=\hat{i}+2\hat{j}-2\hat{k}$

Now, $\vec{a}+\vec{b}=4\hat{i}+4\hat{j}=\vec{c}$ (say)

and $\vec{a}-\vec{b}=2\hat{i}+4\hat{k}=\vec{d}$ (say)

Now, $\vec{c}\times\vec{d}=\begin{vmatrix}\hat{i}&\hat{j}&\hat{k}\\4&4&0\\2&0&4\end{vmatrix}$

$=\hat{i}\,(16-0)-\hat{j}\,(16-0)+\hat{k}\,(0-8)$

$=16\hat{i}-16\hat{j}-8\hat{k}$

$$\therefore \text{ Required unit vector} = \frac{16\hat{i} - 16\hat{j} - 8\hat{k}}{|16\hat{i} - 16\hat{j} - 8\hat{k}|}$$

$$= \pm \frac{16\hat{i} - 16\hat{j} - 8\hat{k}}{\sqrt{(16)^2 + (-16)^2 + (-8)^2}}$$

$$= \pm \frac{16\hat{i} - 16\hat{j} - 8\hat{k}}{24} = \pm \left(\frac{2}{3}\hat{i} - \frac{2}{3}\hat{j} - \frac{1}{3}\hat{k}\right)$$

Example 7 If A, B, C are three non-collinear points with position vectors $\vec{a}$, $\vec{b}$, $\vec{c}$ respectively, then show that the length of the perpendicular from C on AB is $\dfrac{|(\vec{a} \times \vec{b}) + (\vec{b} \times \vec{c}) + (\vec{c} \times \vec{a})|}{|\vec{b} - \vec{a}|}$. **[ISC 2018]**

Sol. We have, A, B, C are three non-collinear points with position vectors $\vec{a}, \vec{b}, \vec{c}$ respectively.

Let position vector of $\overrightarrow{CD}$ be d.

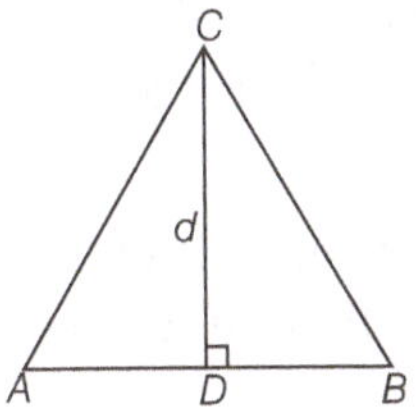

$$\overrightarrow{AB} = \vec{b} - \vec{a}$$
$$\overrightarrow{AC} = \vec{c} - \vec{a}$$
$$\overrightarrow{BC} = \vec{c} - \vec{b}$$

Now, area of ΔABC

$$= \frac{1}{2}|\overrightarrow{AB} \times \overrightarrow{AC}| = \frac{1}{2}|(\vec{b} - \vec{a}) \times (\vec{c} - \vec{a})|$$

$$= \frac{1}{2}|(\vec{b} \times \vec{c}) - (\vec{a} \times \vec{c}) - (\vec{b} \times \vec{a}) + (\vec{a} \times \vec{a})|$$

$$= \frac{1}{2}|\vec{b} \times \vec{c} + \vec{c} \times \vec{a} + \vec{a} \times \vec{b}|$$

$[\because \vec{a} \times \vec{c} = -\vec{c} \times \vec{a} \text{ and } \vec{a} \times \vec{a} = 0]$ ...(i)

Also, area of $\Delta ABC = \frac{1}{2}|\overrightarrow{AB}||\overrightarrow{CD}| = \frac{1}{2}|\vec{b} - \vec{a}|\, d$ ...(ii)

From Eqs. (i) and (ii), we get

$$\frac{1}{2}|\vec{b} - \vec{a}|\, d = \frac{1}{2}|(\vec{a} \times \vec{b}) + (\vec{b} \times \vec{c}) + (\vec{c} \times \vec{a})|$$

$$\Rightarrow \quad d = \frac{|(\vec{a} \times \vec{b}) + (\vec{b} \times \vec{c}) + (\vec{c} \times \vec{a})|}{|\vec{b} - \vec{a}|}$$

Hence, length of perpendicular from C on AB is

$$\frac{|(\vec{a} \times \vec{b}) + (\vec{b} \times \vec{c}) + (\vec{c} \times \vec{a})|}{|\vec{b} - \vec{a}|}$$

Applications of Vector Product of Two Vectors

Vector product of two vectors can be used to find the area of some geometrical figures which are given below

1. **Area of a triangle** The area of triangle having adjacent sides $\vec{a}$ and $\vec{b}$ is given by

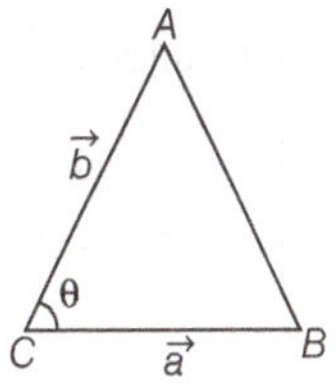

$$\text{Area} = \frac{1}{2}|\vec{a} \times \vec{b}|$$

2. **Area of a triangle** The area of ΔABC is

$$\frac{1}{2}|\overrightarrow{AB} \times \overrightarrow{AC}| \text{ or } \frac{1}{2}|\overrightarrow{BC} \times \overrightarrow{BA}| \text{ or } \frac{1}{2}|\overrightarrow{CB} \times \overrightarrow{CA}|.$$

3. **Area of a parallelogram** The area of a parallelogram having adjacent sides $\vec{a}$ and $\vec{b}$ is given by

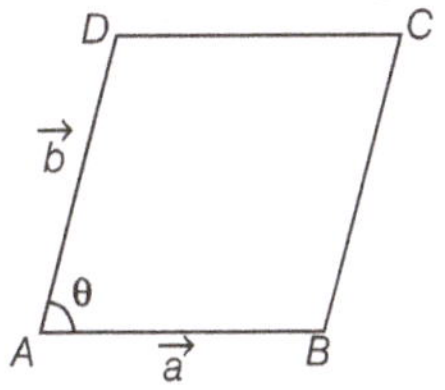

$$\textbf{Area} = |\vec{a} \times \vec{b}|$$

4. **Area of a parallelogram** The area of a parallelogram having diagonals $\vec{d_1}$ and $\vec{d_2}$ is given by

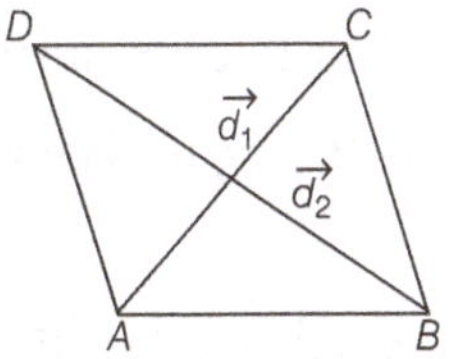

$$\text{Area} = \frac{1}{2}|\vec{d_1} \times \vec{d_2}|$$

where, $\overrightarrow{AC} = \vec{d_1}$ and $\overrightarrow{BD} = \vec{d_2}$ are diagonals.

Example 8 Using vectors, find the area of the triangle whose vertices are

$A(3, -1, 2)$, $B(1, -1, -3)$ and $C(4, -3, 1)$. **[ISC 2020]**

Sol. We have,

$$\vec{A} = 3\hat{i} - \hat{j} + 2\hat{k},\ \vec{B} = \hat{i} - \hat{j} - 3\hat{k} \text{ and } \vec{C} = 4\hat{i} - 3\hat{j} + \hat{k}$$

$$\overrightarrow{AB} = -2\hat{i} - 5\hat{k} \text{ and } \overrightarrow{AC} = i - 2\hat{j} - \hat{k}$$

The area of the given triangle is $\frac{1}{2}|\overrightarrow{AB} \times \overrightarrow{AC}|$

$$\text{Now}, \overrightarrow{AB} \times \overrightarrow{AC} = \begin{vmatrix} \hat{i} & \hat{j} & \hat{k} \\ -2 & 0 & -5 \\ 1 & -2 & -1 \end{vmatrix} = 10\hat{i} - 7\hat{j} + 4\hat{k}$$

$$\text{Therefore}, |\overrightarrow{AB} \times \overrightarrow{AC}| = \sqrt{100 + 49 + 16} = \sqrt{165}$$

Thus, the required area is $\frac{\sqrt{165}}{2}$.

Example 9 Find the area of the parallelogram whose diagonals are $\hat{i} - 3\hat{j} + \hat{k}$ and $\hat{i} + \hat{j} + \hat{k}$. **[ISC 2023]**

Sol. Area of parallelogram whose diagonals are $\vec{d_1}$ and $\vec{d_2}$ is $\frac{1}{2}|\vec{d_1} \times \vec{d_2}|$.

$\therefore$ Here, $\vec{d_1} = \hat{i} - 3\hat{j} + \hat{k}$ and $\vec{d_2} = \hat{i} + \hat{j} + \hat{k}$

$$\vec{d_1} \times \vec{d_2} = \begin{vmatrix} \hat{i} & \hat{j} & \hat{k} \\ 1 & -3 & 1 \\ 1 & 1 & 1 \end{vmatrix}$$

$$= (-3 - 1)\hat{i} - (1 - 1)\hat{j} + (1 + 3)\hat{k}$$

$$= -4\hat{i} + 4\hat{k}$$

$$\Rightarrow |\vec{d_1} \times \vec{d_2}| = \sqrt{(-4)^2 + 4^2} = \sqrt{16 + 16} = 4\sqrt{2}$$

$$\therefore \text{Area of parallelogram} = \frac{1}{2} \times 4\sqrt{2} = 2\sqrt{2} \text{ sq units}$$

Example 10 A ΔOAB is determined by the vectors $\vec{a}$ and $\vec{b}$ as shown in the figure below. Show that the triangle has

the area, is given by $\Delta = \frac{1}{2}\sqrt{|\vec{a}|^2|\vec{b}|^2 - (\vec{a} \cdot \vec{b})^2}$.

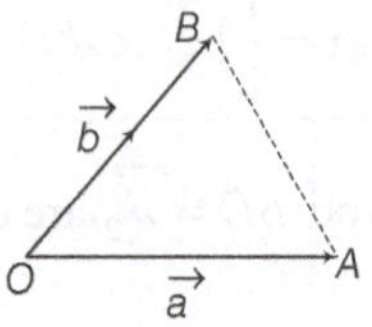

Sol. We know that, area of triangle, $\Delta = \frac{1}{2}|\overrightarrow{OA} \times \overrightarrow{OB}|$

$$\Rightarrow \quad \Delta^2 = \frac{1}{4}|\vec{a} \times \vec{b}|^2 \quad \text{...(i)}$$

$$\text{Now}, |\vec{a} \times \vec{b}|^2 + (\vec{a} \cdot \vec{b})^2 = |\vec{a}|^2|\vec{b}|^2 \sin^2\theta + |\vec{a}|^2|\vec{b}|^2 \cos^2\theta$$

$$= |\vec{a}|^2|\vec{b}|^2(\sin^2\theta + \cos^2\theta) = |\vec{a}|^2|\vec{b}|^2 \times 1 = |\vec{a}|^2|\vec{b}|^2$$

$$\Rightarrow |\vec{a} \times \vec{b}|^2 = |\vec{a}|^2|\vec{b}|^2 - (\vec{a} \cdot \vec{b})^2$$

$\therefore$ From Eq. (i), we get

$$\Delta^2 = \frac{1}{4}\left[|\vec{a}|^2|\vec{b}|^2 - (\vec{a} \cdot \vec{b})^2\right] \Rightarrow \Delta = \frac{1}{2}\sqrt{|\vec{a}|^2|\vec{b}|^2 - (\vec{a} \cdot \vec{b})^2}$$

Topic Practice 3

Very Short Answer Type Questions

2 Marks

1 Find the magnitude of $\vec{a}$ given by $\vec{a} = (\hat{i} + 3\hat{j} - 2\hat{k}) \times (-\hat{i} + 3\hat{k})$.

2 Find λ and μ, if $(2\hat{i} + 6\hat{j} + 27\hat{k}) \times (\hat{i} + \lambda\hat{j} + \mu\hat{k}) = \vec{0}$. **[NCERT]**

3 Find a vector of magnitude 9, which is perpendicular to both the vectors $4\hat{i} - \hat{j} + 3\hat{k}$ and $-2\hat{i} + \hat{j} - 2\hat{k}$.

4 If $\vec{a}$ $2\hat{i}$ $\hat{j} + 3\hat{k}$ and $\vec{b} = 3\hat{i} + 5\hat{j} - 2\hat{k}$, then find $|\vec{a} \times \vec{b}|$.

5 Given $|\vec{a}| = 10$, $|\vec{b}| = 2$ and $\vec{a} \cdot \vec{b} = 12$, find $|\vec{a} \times \vec{b}|$.

6 If $\vec{a}$ and $\vec{b}$ are unit vector and θ is the angle between them, then show that $|\vec{a} - \vec{b}| = 2\sin\frac{\theta}{2}$. **[ISC 2013]**

7 Find $\vec{a} \cdot \vec{b}$, if $|\vec{a}| = 2$, $|\vec{b}| = 5$ and $|\vec{a} \times \vec{b}| = 8$. **[ISC 2008]**

8 Find a unit vector perpendicular to the vectors $4\hat{i} + 3\hat{j} + \hat{k}$ and $2\hat{i} - \hat{j} + 2\hat{k}$. Determine the sine of the angle between these two vectors. **[ISC 2007]**

9 The vectors $-2\hat{i} + 4\hat{j} + 4\hat{k}$ and $-4\hat{i} - 2\hat{k}$ represent the diagonals BD and AC of a parallelogram $ABCD$. Then, find the area of the parallelogram. **[ISC 2006]**

10 Find the area of a parallelogram whose diagonals are determined by the vectors $\vec{a} = 3\hat{i} + \hat{j} - 2\hat{k}$ and $\vec{b} = \hat{i} - 3\hat{j} + 4\hat{k}$. **[ISC 2009]**

Short Answer Type Questions

(4 Marks)

11 Find a unit vector perpendicular to each of the vectors $\vec{a}+\vec{b}$ and $\vec{a}-\vec{b}$, where $\vec{a}=\hat{i}+\hat{j}+\hat{k}$ and $\vec{b}=\hat{i}+2\hat{j}+3\hat{k}$. **[NCERT]**

12 If the three vectors $\vec{a}$, $\vec{b}$ and $\vec{c}$ are given as $a_1\hat{i}+a_2\hat{j}+a_3\hat{k}, b_1\hat{i}+b_2\hat{j}+b_3\hat{k}$ and $c_1\hat{i}+c_2\hat{j}+c_3\hat{k}$. Then, show that $\vec{a}\times(\vec{b}+\vec{c})=(\vec{a}\times\vec{b})+(\vec{a}\times\vec{c})$. **[NCERT Exemplar]**

13 For any three vectors $\vec{a}$, $\vec{b}$ and $\vec{c}$, evaluate $\vec{a}\times(\vec{b}+\vec{c})+\vec{b}\times(\vec{c}+\vec{a})+\vec{c}\times(\vec{a}+\vec{b})$.

14 If $\vec{a}\times\vec{b}=\vec{c}\times\vec{d}$ and $\vec{a}\times\vec{c}=\vec{b}\times\vec{d}$, then show that $\vec{a}-\vec{d}$ is parallel to $\vec{b}-\vec{c}$.

15 In any ΔABC, prove by vector method
$$\frac{a}{\sin A}=\frac{b}{\sin B}=\frac{c}{\sin C}.$$
[ISC 2012]

16 (i) Prove by vector method that the diameter of a circle will subtend a right angle at a point on its circumference.

(ii) If $\vec{a}$, $\vec{b}$ and $\vec{c}$ represent the position vectors of the points with coordinates (2, –10, 2), (3, 1, 2) and (2, 1, 3) respectively, find the value of $\vec{a}\times(\vec{b}\times\vec{c})$. **[ISC 2009]**

17 If $\vec{a},\vec{b}$ and $\vec{c}$ are three vectors such that $\vec{a}+\vec{b}+\vec{c}=\vec{0}$, then prove that $\vec{a}\times\vec{b}=\vec{b}\times\vec{c}=\vec{c}\times\vec{a}$.

18 If $\vec{r}=x\hat{i}+y\hat{j}+z\hat{k}$, then find $(\vec{r}\times\hat{i})\cdot(\vec{r}\times\hat{j})+xy$.

19 If $\vec{a}=\hat{i}+\hat{j}+\hat{k}$ and $\vec{b}=\hat{j}-\hat{k}$, then find a vector $\vec{c}$ such that $\vec{a}\times\vec{c}=\vec{b}$ and $\vec{a}\cdot\vec{c}=3$.

20 If D, E and F are the mid-points of the sides of a ΔABC, then prove by vector method that area of $\Delta DEF=\frac{1}{4}$(area of ΔABC). **[ISC 2011, 2001]**

Hints & Solutions

1. We have, $\vec{a}=(\hat{i}+3\hat{j}-2\hat{k})\times(-\hat{i}+0\hat{j}+3\hat{k})$

$$\Rightarrow \vec{a}=\begin{vmatrix}\hat{i}&\hat{j}&\hat{k}\\1&3&-2\\-1&0&3\end{vmatrix}=(9+0)\hat{i}-(3-2)\hat{j}+(0+3)\hat{k}$$
$$=9\hat{i}-\hat{j}+3\hat{k}$$ [1]

$$\therefore \quad |\vec{a}|=\sqrt{9^2+(-1)^2+3^2}=\sqrt{81+1+9}=\sqrt{91}$$ [1]

2. We have, $(2\hat{i}+6\hat{j}+27\hat{k})\times(\hat{i}+\lambda\hat{j}+\mu\hat{k})=\vec{0}$

$$\Rightarrow \begin{vmatrix}\hat{i}&\hat{j}&\hat{k}\\2&6&27\\1&\lambda&\mu\end{vmatrix}=\vec{0}$$

$$\Rightarrow (6\mu-27\lambda)\hat{i}-(2\mu-27)\hat{j}+(2\lambda-6)\hat{k}=0\hat{i}+0\hat{j}+0\hat{k}$$ [1]

On equating the coefficients of $\hat{i}$, $\hat{j}$ and $\hat{k}$ both sides, we get
$$6\mu-27\lambda=0,\ 2\mu-27=0 \text{ and } 2\lambda-6=0$$
$$\Rightarrow \quad \lambda=3 \text{ and } \mu=\frac{27}{2}$$ [1]

3. Let $\vec{a}=4\hat{i}-\hat{j}+3\hat{k}$ and $\vec{b}=-2\hat{i}+\hat{j}-2\hat{k}$. Then,

$$\vec{a}\times\vec{b}=\begin{vmatrix}\hat{i}&\hat{j}&\hat{k}\\4&-1&3\\-2&1&-2\end{vmatrix}=(2-3)\hat{i}-(-8+6)\hat{j}+(4-2)\hat{k}$$
$$=-\hat{i}+2\hat{j}+2\hat{k}$$

and $|\vec{a}\times\vec{b}|=\sqrt{(-1)^2+2^2+2^2}=\sqrt{1+4+4}=\sqrt{9}=3$ [1]

$$\therefore \text{ Required vector}=9\left\{\frac{\vec{a}\times\vec{b}}{|\vec{a}\times\vec{b}|}\right\}=\frac{9}{3}(-\hat{i}+2\hat{j}+2\hat{k})$$
$$=-3\hat{i}+6\hat{j}+6\hat{k}$$ [1]

4. We have, $\vec{a}=2\hat{i}+\hat{j}+3\hat{k}$ and $\vec{b}=3\hat{i}+5\hat{j}-2\hat{k}$

Now, $$\vec{a}\times\vec{b}=\begin{vmatrix}\hat{i}&\hat{j}&\hat{k}\\2&1&3\\3&5&-2\end{vmatrix}$$ [1/2]

$$=\hat{i}(-2-15)-\hat{j}(-4-9)+\hat{k}(10-3)$$
$$=\hat{i}(-17)-\hat{j}(-13)+\hat{k}(7)$$
$$=-17\hat{i}+13\hat{j}+7\hat{k}$$ [1/2]

$$\therefore \quad |\vec{a}\times\vec{b}|=\sqrt{(-17)^2+(13)^2+(7)^2}$$
$$=\sqrt{289+169+49}=\sqrt{507}=13\sqrt{3}$$ [1]

5. Given, $|\vec{a}|=10$, $|\vec{b}|=2$ and $\vec{a}\cdot\vec{b}=12$

We know that, $(\vec{a}\cdot\vec{b})^2+|\vec{a}\times\vec{b}|^2=|\vec{a}|^2|\vec{b}|^2$

$$\therefore \quad 12^2+|\vec{a}\times\vec{b}|^2=(10)^2\times(2)^2$$ [1]

$$\Rightarrow \quad |\vec{a}\times\vec{b}|^2=400-144 \Rightarrow |\vec{a}\times\vec{b}|^2=256$$

$$\Rightarrow \quad |\vec{a}\times\vec{b}|=16$$ [taking positive square root] [1]

6. Given, $|\vec{a}|=1$ and $|\vec{b}|=1$ and θ is the angle between $\vec{a}$ and $\vec{b}$. Now, $|\vec{a}-\vec{b}|^2=(\vec{a}-\vec{b})^2=a^2+b^2-2\vec{a}\cdot\vec{b}$

$$=a^2+b^2-2|\vec{a}||\vec{b}|\cos\theta$$

[$\because \vec{a}\cdot\vec{b}=|\vec{a}||\vec{b}|\cos\theta$]

$= 1 + 1 - 2\cos\theta$ [1]

$= 2 - 2\cos\theta = 2(1 - \cos\theta) = 2 \times 2\sin^2\frac{\theta}{2} = 4\sin^2\frac{\theta}{2}$

$\therefore \quad |\vec{a} - \vec{b}|^2 = 4\sin^2\frac{\theta}{2} \Rightarrow |\vec{a} - \vec{b}| = 2\sin\frac{\theta}{2}$

[taking positive square root]

Hence proved. [1]

7. Given, $|\vec{a} \times \vec{b}| = 8$, $|\vec{a}| = 2$, $|\vec{b}| = 5$

$\because \quad \vec{a} \times \vec{b} = |\vec{a}||\vec{b}|\sin\theta \cdot \hat{n} \Rightarrow |\vec{a} \times \vec{b}| = |\vec{a}||\vec{b}|\sin\theta$

$\Rightarrow \quad \sin\theta = \frac{|\vec{a} \times \vec{b}|}{|\vec{a}||\vec{b}|} \Rightarrow \sin\theta = \frac{8}{2 \times 5} = \frac{4}{5}$ [1]

$\therefore \quad \cos\theta = \sqrt{1 - \sin^2\theta} = \sqrt{1 - \left(\frac{4}{5}\right)^2} = \frac{3}{5}$

Now, $\quad \vec{a} \cdot \vec{b} = |\vec{a}||\vec{b}|\cos\theta = 2 \times 5 \times \frac{3}{5} = 6$ [1]

8. Let $\vec{a} = 4\hat{i} + 3\hat{j} + \hat{k}$ and $\vec{b} = 2\hat{i} - \hat{j} + 2\hat{k}$

Now, $\vec{a} \times \vec{b} = \begin{vmatrix} \hat{i} & \hat{j} & \hat{k} \\ 4 & 3 & 1 \\ 2 & -1 & 2 \end{vmatrix} = (6+1)\hat{i} - (8-2)\hat{j} + (-4-6)\hat{k}$

$= 7\hat{i} - 6\hat{j} - 10\hat{k}$ [1]

Now, unit vector perpendicular to $\vec{a}$ and $\vec{b}$,

$\hat{n} = \frac{\vec{a} \times \vec{b}}{|\vec{a} \times \vec{b}|} = \frac{7\hat{i} - 6\hat{j} - 10\hat{k}}{\sqrt{7^2 + (-6)^2 + (-10)^2}}$

$= \frac{7\hat{i} - 6\hat{j} - 10\hat{k}}{\sqrt{49 + 36 + 100}} = \frac{7\hat{i} - 6\hat{j} - 10\hat{k}}{\sqrt{185}}$

Now, $|\vec{a} \times \vec{b}| = |\vec{a}||\vec{b}|\sin\theta$

$\therefore \quad \sqrt{185} = \sqrt{16 + 9 + 1}\sqrt{4 + 1 + 4}\sin\theta$

$\Rightarrow \quad \sin\theta = \frac{\sqrt{185}}{\sqrt{26}\sqrt{9}} = \frac{\sqrt{185}}{3\sqrt{26}}$ [1]

9. Given diagonals of parallelogram are

$\overrightarrow{BD} = -2\hat{i} + 4\hat{j} + 4\hat{k}$ and $\overrightarrow{AC} = -4\hat{i} - 2\hat{k}$

Now, area of parallelogram $= \frac{1}{2}|\overrightarrow{BD} \times \overrightarrow{AC}|$

$\therefore \quad \overrightarrow{BD} \times \overrightarrow{AC} = \begin{vmatrix} \hat{i} & \hat{j} & \hat{k} \\ -2 & 4 & 4 \\ -4 & 0 & -2 \end{vmatrix}$

$= \hat{i}(-8-0) - \hat{j}(4+16) + \hat{k}(0+16)$

$= -8\hat{i} - 20\hat{j} + 16\hat{k}$ [1]

$\Rightarrow \quad |\overrightarrow{BD} \times \overrightarrow{AC}| = \sqrt{(-8)^2 + (-20)^2 + (16)^2} = \sqrt{720}$

$\therefore$ Area of parallelogram $= \frac{1}{2}|\overrightarrow{BD} \times \overrightarrow{AC}| = \frac{1}{2} \times \sqrt{720}$

$= \frac{1}{2} \times 12\sqrt{5} = 6\sqrt{5}$ sq units [1]

10. Given, diagonals of a parallelogram are

$\vec{a} = 3\hat{i} + \hat{j} - 2\hat{k}$ and $\vec{b} = \hat{i} - 3\hat{j} + 4\hat{k}$

Now, $\vec{a} \times \vec{b} = \begin{vmatrix} \hat{i} & \hat{j} & \hat{k} \\ 3 & 1 & -2 \\ 1 & -3 & 4 \end{vmatrix}$

$= [(4-6)\hat{i} - (12+2)\hat{j} + (-9-1)\hat{k}]$

$= [-2\hat{i} - 14\hat{j} - 10\hat{k}]$

$\therefore$ Area of parallelogram $= \frac{1}{2}|\vec{a} \times \vec{b}|$

$= \frac{1}{2}|-2\hat{i} - 14\hat{j} - 10\hat{k}|$ [1]

$= \frac{1}{2} \times \sqrt{(-2)^2 + (-14)^2 + (-10)^2}$

$= \frac{1}{2} \times \sqrt{4 + 196 + 100}$

$= \frac{1}{2} \times \sqrt{300} = \frac{10\sqrt{3}}{2} = 5\sqrt{3}$ sq units [1]

11. We have, $\vec{a} = \hat{i} + \hat{j} + \hat{k}$ and $\vec{b} = \hat{i} + 2\hat{j} + 3\hat{k}$

Now, $\vec{a} + \vec{b} = (\hat{i} + \hat{j} + \hat{k}) + (\hat{i} + 2\hat{j} + 3\hat{k}) = 2\hat{i} + 3\hat{j} + 4\hat{k}$

and $\vec{a} - \vec{b} = (\hat{i} + \hat{j} + \hat{k}) - (\hat{i} + 2\hat{j} + 3\hat{k}) = 0\hat{i} - \hat{j} - 2\hat{k}$ [1]

A vector $\vec{c}$ perpendicular to both $\vec{a} + \vec{b}$ and $\vec{a} - \vec{b}$ is given by

$\vec{c} = (\vec{a} + \vec{b}) \times (\vec{a} - \vec{b}) = (2\hat{i} + 3\hat{j} + 4\hat{k}) \times (0\hat{i} - \hat{j} - 2\hat{k})$ [1]

$\Rightarrow \quad \vec{c} = \begin{vmatrix} \hat{i} & \hat{j} & \hat{k} \\ 2 & 3 & 4 \\ 0 & -1 & -2 \end{vmatrix} = (-6+4)\hat{i} - (-4-0)\hat{j} + (-2-0)\hat{k}$

$= -2\hat{i} + 4\hat{j} - 2\hat{k}$ [1]

and $|\vec{c}| = \sqrt{(-2)^2 + (4)^2 + (-2)^2}$

$= \sqrt{4 + 16 + 4} = \sqrt{24} = 2\sqrt{6}$

$\therefore$ Required unit vector $= \frac{1}{|\vec{c}|}\vec{c} = \frac{1}{2\sqrt{6}}(-2\hat{i} + 4\hat{j} - 2\hat{k})$

$= -\frac{1}{\sqrt{6}}\hat{i} + \frac{2}{\sqrt{6}}\hat{j} - \frac{1}{\sqrt{6}}\hat{k}$ [1]

12. Clearly, $\vec{b} + \vec{c} = (b_1\hat{i} + b_2\hat{j} + b_3\hat{k}) + (c_1\hat{i} + c_2\hat{j} + c_3\hat{k})$

$= (b_1 + c_1)\hat{i} + (b_2 + c_2)\hat{j} + (b_3 + c_3)\hat{k}$ [1]

$\therefore \vec{a} \times (\vec{b} + \vec{c}) = \begin{vmatrix} \hat{i} & \hat{j} & \hat{k} \\ a_1 & a_2 & a_3 \\ b_1 + c_1 & b_2 + c_2 & b_3 + c_3 \end{vmatrix}$ [1]

$= \begin{vmatrix} \hat{i} & \hat{j} & \hat{k} \\ a_1 & a_2 & a_3 \\ b_1 & b_2 & b_3 \end{vmatrix} + \begin{vmatrix} \hat{i} & \hat{j} & \hat{k} \\ a_1 & a_2 & a_3 \\ c_1 & c_2 & c_3 \end{vmatrix}$

[by property of determinant] [1]

$$= (\vec{a} \times \vec{b}) + (\vec{a} \times \vec{c})$$

Hence, $\vec{a} \times (\vec{b} + \vec{c}) = (\vec{a} \times \vec{b}) + (\vec{a} \times \vec{c})$. [1]

13. Clearly, $\vec{a} \times (\vec{b} + \vec{c}) + \vec{b} \times (\vec{c} + \vec{a}) + \vec{c} \times (\vec{a} + \vec{b})$

$$= (\vec{a} \times \vec{b}) + (\vec{a} \times \vec{c}) + (\vec{b} \times \vec{c}) + (\vec{b} \times \vec{a}) + (\vec{c} \times \vec{a}) + (\vec{c} \times \vec{b})$$ [1½]

$$= (\vec{a} \times \vec{b}) - (\vec{c} \times \vec{a}) + (\vec{b} \times \vec{c}) - (\vec{a} \times \vec{b}) + (\vec{c} \times \vec{a}) - (\vec{b} \times \vec{c})$$ [1½]

$= 0$ $\quad [\because \vec{b} \times \vec{a} = -(\vec{a} \times \vec{b}), \vec{a} \times \vec{c} = -(\vec{c} \times \vec{a})$ and $\vec{c} \times \vec{b} = -(\vec{b} \times \vec{c})]$ [1]

14. Given, $\vec{a} \times \vec{b} = \vec{c} \times \vec{d}$ ...(i)

and $\vec{a} \times \vec{c} = \vec{b} \times \vec{d}$ ...(ii)

On subtracting Eq. (ii) from Eq. (i), we get

$$\vec{a} \times \vec{b} - \vec{a} \times \vec{c} = \vec{c} \times \vec{d} - \vec{b} \times \vec{d}$$

$\Rightarrow \vec{a} \times (\vec{b} - \vec{c}) = (\vec{c} - \vec{b}) \times \vec{d}$ [1½]

$\Rightarrow \vec{a} \times (\vec{b} - \vec{c}) = -(\vec{b} - \vec{c}) \times \vec{d}$

$\Rightarrow \vec{a} \times (\vec{b} - \vec{c}) = \vec{d} \times (\vec{b} - \vec{c})$ $\quad [\because \vec{a} \times \vec{b} = -(\vec{b} \times \vec{a})]$

$\Rightarrow \vec{a} \times (\vec{b} - \vec{c}) - \vec{d} \times (\vec{b} - \vec{c}) = 0$ [1½]

$\Rightarrow (\vec{a} - \vec{d}) \times (\vec{b} - \vec{c}) = 0$

Hence, $(\vec{a} - \vec{d})$ is parallel to $(\vec{b} - \vec{c})$. [1]

15. In ΔABC, let $\overrightarrow{BC} = \vec{a}$, $\overrightarrow{CA} = \vec{b}$ and $\overrightarrow{AB} = \vec{c}$

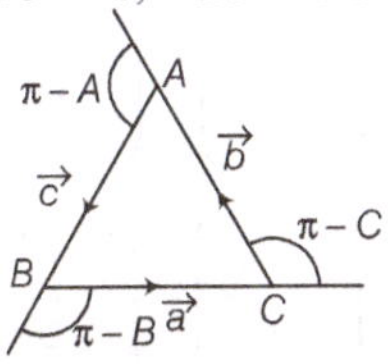

$\therefore \quad |\overrightarrow{BC}| = a$, $|\overrightarrow{CA}| = b$ and $|\overrightarrow{AB}| = c$

$$\overrightarrow{BC} + \overrightarrow{CA} = \overrightarrow{BA}$$

By triangle law of addition,

$\Rightarrow \overrightarrow{BC} + \overrightarrow{CA} + \overrightarrow{AB} = \vec{0}$ $\quad [\because \overrightarrow{BA} = -\overrightarrow{AB}]$

$\Rightarrow \vec{a} + \vec{b} + \vec{c} = \vec{0}$ [1]

$\Rightarrow \vec{a} \times (\vec{a} + \vec{b} + \vec{c}) = \vec{a} \times \vec{0}$

$\Rightarrow (\vec{a} \times \vec{a} + \vec{a} \times \vec{b} + \vec{a} \times \vec{c}) = \vec{0}$

$\Rightarrow \vec{a} \times \vec{b} = -(\vec{a} \times \vec{c})$ $\quad [\because \vec{a} \times \vec{a} = \vec{0}]$

$\Rightarrow \vec{a} \times \vec{b} = \vec{c} \times \vec{a}$ $\quad [\because (\vec{a} \times \vec{b}) = -(\vec{b} \times \vec{a})]$ ...(i)

Similarly, $\vec{c} \times \vec{a} = \vec{b} \times \vec{c}$ ...(ii)

From Eqs. (i) and (ii), we get

$$\vec{a} \times \vec{b} = \vec{b} \times \vec{c} = \vec{c} \times \vec{a}$$ [1]

$\Rightarrow |\vec{a} \times \vec{b}| = |\vec{b} \times \vec{c}| = |\vec{c} \times \vec{a}|$

$\Rightarrow ab\sin(\pi - C) = bc\sin(\pi - A) = ca\sin(\pi - B)$ [1]

$\Rightarrow ab\sin C = bc\sin A = ca\sin B$

$\Rightarrow \dfrac{\sin C}{c} = \dfrac{\sin A}{a} = \dfrac{\sin B}{b}$ $\quad$ [dividing by abc]

$\Rightarrow \dfrac{a}{\sin A} = \dfrac{b}{\sin B} = \dfrac{c}{\sin C}$ $\quad$ [taking reciprocal]

Hence proved. [1]

16. (i) Given, AB is the diameter of the circle.

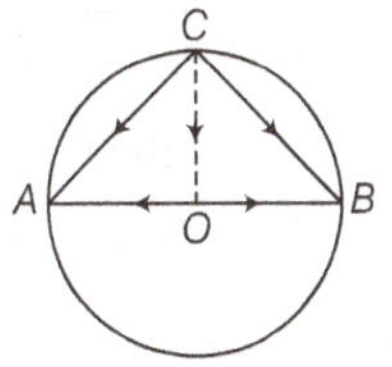

[1]

In ΔAOC, $\overrightarrow{CA} = \overrightarrow{CO} + \overrightarrow{OA}$ ...(i)

[triangle law of addition]

and in ΔBOC, $\overrightarrow{CB} = \overrightarrow{CO} + \overrightarrow{OB}$ ...(ii)

[triangle law of addition]

Now, $\overrightarrow{CA} \cdot \overrightarrow{CB} = (\overrightarrow{CO} + \overrightarrow{OA}) \cdot (\overrightarrow{CO} + \overrightarrow{OB})$ [1]

[from Eqs. (i) and (ii)]

$$= \overrightarrow{CO} \cdot \overrightarrow{CO} + \overrightarrow{CO} \cdot \overrightarrow{OB} + \overrightarrow{OA} \cdot \overrightarrow{CO} + \overrightarrow{OA} \cdot \overrightarrow{OB}$$

$$= CO^2 + \overrightarrow{CO} \cdot \overrightarrow{OB} - \overrightarrow{OB} \cdot \overrightarrow{CO} - \overrightarrow{OA} \cdot \overrightarrow{OA}$$

$[\because \overrightarrow{OB} = -\overrightarrow{OA}]$

$= CO^2 - OA^2 = 0$ $\quad [\because CO = OA = \text{radius}]$

$\therefore \quad \overrightarrow{CA} \perp \overrightarrow{CB} \Rightarrow \angle ACB = 90°$

Hence diameter of a circle will subtend a right angle at a point on its circumference.

(ii) Given, $\vec{a} = 2\hat{i} - 10\hat{j} + 2\hat{k}$, $\vec{b} = 3\hat{i} + \hat{j} + 2\hat{k}$

and $\vec{c} = 2\hat{i} + \hat{j} + 3\hat{k}$

Now, $\vec{b} \times \vec{c} = \begin{vmatrix} \hat{i} & \hat{j} & \hat{k} \\ 3 & 1 & 2 \\ 2 & 1 & 3 \end{vmatrix}$ [1]

$$= (3-2)\hat{i} - (9-4)\hat{j} + (3-2)\hat{k} = \hat{i} - 5\hat{j} + \hat{k}$$

$\therefore \vec{a} \times (\vec{b} \times \vec{c}) = \begin{vmatrix} \hat{i} & \hat{j} & \hat{k} \\ 2 & -10 & 2 \\ 1 & -5 & 1 \end{vmatrix}$

$$= (-10+10)\hat{i} - (2-2)\hat{j} + (-10+10)\hat{k}$$

$= 0\hat{i} + 0\hat{j} + 0\hat{k} = \vec{0}$ [1]

17. To prove, $\vec{a} \times \vec{b} = \vec{b} \times \vec{c} = \vec{c} \times \vec{a}$

We have, $\vec{a} + \vec{b} + \vec{c} = \vec{0} \Rightarrow \vec{a} \times (\vec{a} + \vec{b} + \vec{c}) = \vec{a} \times \vec{0}$

[taking cross product with $\vec{a}$]

$\Rightarrow (\vec{a} \times \vec{a}) + (\vec{a} \times \vec{b}) + (\vec{a} \times \vec{c}) = \vec{0}$

[using distributive law] [1]

$\Rightarrow (\vec{a} \times \vec{b}) - (\vec{c} \times \vec{a}) = \vec{0}$

[$\because \vec{a} \times \vec{a} = 0$ and $\vec{a} \times \vec{c} = -\vec{c} \times \vec{a}$]

$\Rightarrow \vec{a} \times \vec{b} = \vec{c} \times \vec{a}$ ...(i) [1]

Again, $\vec{a} + \vec{b} + \vec{c} = \vec{0} \Rightarrow \vec{b} \times (\vec{a} + \vec{b} + \vec{c}) = \vec{b} \times \vec{0}$

[taking cross product with $\vec{b}$]

$\Rightarrow (\vec{b} \times \vec{a}) + (\vec{b} \times \vec{b}) + (\vec{b} \times \vec{c}) = \vec{0}$ [1]

$\Rightarrow -(\vec{a} \times \vec{b}) + (\vec{b} \times \vec{c}) = \vec{0}$

[$\because \vec{b} \times \vec{b} = 0$, $\vec{b} \times \vec{a} = -\vec{a} \times \vec{b}$]

$\Rightarrow \vec{a} \times \vec{b} = \vec{b} \times \vec{c}$ ...(ii)

From Eqs. (i) and (ii), we get

$\vec{a} \times \vec{b} = \vec{b} \times \vec{c} = \vec{c} \times \vec{a}$ **Hence proved.** [1]

18. We have, $\vec{r} = x\hat{i} + y\hat{j} + z\hat{k}$

Now, $\vec{r} \times \hat{i} = (x\hat{i} + y\hat{j} + z\hat{k}) \times \hat{i}$

$= x(\hat{i} \times \hat{i}) + y(\hat{j} \times \hat{i}) + z(\hat{k} \times \hat{i})$

$= x \cdot 0 + y(-\hat{k}) + z(\hat{j}) = -y\hat{k} + z\hat{j}$ [1]

[$\because \hat{i} \times \hat{i} = \vec{0}$, $\hat{j} \times \hat{i} = -\hat{k}$ and $\hat{k} \times \hat{i} = \hat{j}$]

and $\vec{r} \times \hat{j} = (x\hat{i} + y\hat{j} + z\hat{k}) \times \hat{j}$

$= x(\hat{i} \times \hat{j}) + y(\hat{j} \times \hat{j}) + z(\hat{k} \times \hat{j})$

$= x\hat{k} + y \cdot 0 + z(-\hat{i})$ [1]

$= x\hat{k} - z\hat{i}$ [1]

Now, $(\vec{r} \times \hat{i}) \cdot (\vec{r} \times \hat{j}) = (-y\hat{k} + z\hat{j}) \cdot (x\hat{k} - z\hat{i})$

$= -yx + 0 + 0 - 0 = -xy$

$\therefore (\vec{r} \times \hat{i}) \cdot (\vec{r} \times \hat{j}) + xy = -xy + xy = 0$ [1]

19. Given, $\vec{a} = \hat{i} + \hat{j} + \hat{k}$ and $\vec{b} = \hat{j} - \hat{k}$ and $\vec{c} = x\hat{i} + y\hat{j} + z\hat{k}$

$$\therefore \vec{a} \times \vec{c} = \begin{vmatrix} \hat{i} & \hat{j} & \hat{k} \\ 1 & 1 & 1 \\ x & y & z \end{vmatrix} = \hat{i}(z - y) - \hat{j}(z - x) + \hat{k}(y - x)$$

[1]

Now, $\vec{a} \times \vec{c} = \vec{b}$ [given]

$\Rightarrow \hat{i}(z - y) + \hat{j}(x - z) + \hat{k}(y - x) = 0\hat{i} + 1\hat{j} + (-1)\hat{k}$

[$\because \vec{b} = \hat{j} - \hat{k}$]

On comparing the coefficients from both sides, we get

$z - y = 0$, $x - z = 1$ and $y - x = -1$

$\Rightarrow y = z$ and $x - y = 1$ ...(i)

Also, given $\vec{a} \cdot \vec{c} = 3$

$\Rightarrow (\hat{i} + \hat{j} + \hat{k}) \cdot (x\hat{i} + y\hat{j} + z\hat{k}) = 3$

$\Rightarrow x + y + z = 3$ [1]

$\Rightarrow x + 2y = 3$ [$\because z = y$] ...(ii)

On solving Eqs. (i) and (ii), we get

$3y = 2 \Rightarrow y = \frac{2}{3} = z$ [$\because y = z$]

From Eq. (i), we get $x = 1 + y = 1 + \frac{2}{3} = \frac{5}{3}$ [1]

Hence, $\vec{c} = \frac{5}{3}\hat{i} + \frac{2}{3}\hat{j} + \frac{2}{3}\hat{k}$. [1]

20. Let the position vectors of A, B and C be $\vec{a}$, $\vec{b}$ and $\vec{c}$, respectively.

Given, D, E and F are the mid-points of the sides of the ΔABC.

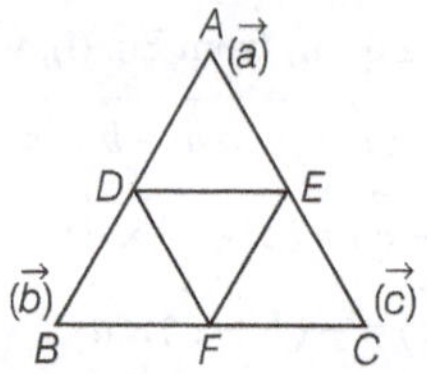

$\therefore$ Position vectors of D, E and F are $\frac{\vec{a} + \vec{b}}{2}$, $\frac{\vec{a} + \vec{c}}{2}$ and $\frac{\vec{b} + \vec{c}}{2}$, respectively.

Now, $\overrightarrow{AB} = \vec{b} - \vec{a}$ and $\overrightarrow{AC} = \vec{c} - \vec{a}$ [1]

Then, $\overrightarrow{EF} = \left(\frac{\vec{b} + \vec{c}}{2}\right) - \left(\frac{\vec{a} + \vec{c}}{2}\right) = \frac{1}{2}(\vec{b} - \vec{a})$

and $\overrightarrow{DF} = \left(\frac{\vec{b} + \vec{c}}{2}\right) - \left(\frac{\vec{a} + \vec{b}}{2}\right) = \frac{1}{2}(\vec{c} - \vec{a})$ [1]

Now, Area of $\Delta ABC = \frac{1}{2}|\overrightarrow{AB} \times \overrightarrow{AC}|$

$= \frac{1}{2}|(\vec{b} - \vec{a}) \times (\vec{c} - \vec{a})|$ ...(i)

$\therefore$ Area of $\Delta DEF = \frac{1}{2}|\overrightarrow{EF} \times \overrightarrow{DF}|$ [1]

$= \frac{1}{2}\left|\frac{1}{2}(\vec{b} - \vec{a}) \times \frac{1}{2}(\vec{c} - \vec{a})\right|$

$= \frac{1}{4} \times \frac{1}{2}|(\vec{b} - \vec{a}) \times (\vec{c} - \vec{a})|$

$= \frac{1}{4} \times$ Area of ΔABC [from Eq. (i)]

Hence proved. [1]

Chapter Practice

Multiple Choice Type Questions

(1 Mark)

1 If $\vec{a}+\vec{b}=\hat{i}$ and $\vec{a}=2\hat{i}-2\hat{j}+2\hat{k}$, then $|\vec{b}|$ equals

(a) $\sqrt{14}$ (b) 3 (c) $\sqrt{12}$ (d) $\sqrt{17}$

2 If $\vec{a}=3\hat{i}-2\hat{j}+\hat{k}$ and $\vec{b}=2\hat{i}-4\hat{j}-3\hat{k}$, then the value of $|\vec{a}-2\vec{b}|$ will be **[ISC 2024]**

(a) $\sqrt{85}$ (b) $\sqrt{86}$ (c) $\sqrt{87}$ (d) $\sqrt{88}$

3 The vectors $\vec{a}=a_1\hat{i}+a_2\hat{j}+a_3\hat{k}$ and $\vec{b}=b_1\hat{i}+b_2\hat{j}+b_3\hat{k}$ are collinear, if

(a) $a_1b_1+a_2b_2+a_3b_3=0$

(b) $\frac{a_1}{b_1}=\frac{a_2}{b_2}=\frac{a_3}{b_3}$

(c) $a_1=b_1, a_2=b_2, a_3=b_3$

(d) $a_1+a_2+a_3=b_1+b_2+b_3$

4 If $\vec{a}\cdot\vec{b}=\frac{1}{2}|\vec{a}||\vec{b}|$, then the angle between $\vec{a}$ and $\vec{b}$ is

(a) 0° (b) 30° (c) 60° (d) 90°

5 If $|\vec{a}|=3, |\vec{b}|=\frac{\sqrt{2}}{3}$ and $\vec{a}\times\vec{b}$ is a unit vector, then the angle between $\vec{a}$ and $\vec{b}$ **[ISC 2023]**

(a) $\frac{\pi}{6}$ (b) $\frac{\pi}{4}$ (c) $\frac{\pi}{3}$ (d) $\frac{\pi}{2}$

Assertion-Reason Type Questions

(1 Mark)

Directions (Q. Nos. 6-9) *In the questions given below are two statements labelled as Assertion (A) and Reason (R). In the context of the two statements, which one of the following is correct?*

(a) Both A and R are correct; R is the correct explanation of A

(b) Both A and R are correct; R is not the correct explanation of A

(c) A is correct; R is incorrect

(d) R is correct; A is incorrect

6 **Assertion (A)** The points A, B and C with position vectors, $\vec{a}=3\hat{i}-4\hat{j}-4\hat{k}$, $\vec{b}=2\hat{i}-\hat{j}+\hat{k}$ and $\vec{c}=\hat{i}-3\hat{j}-5\hat{k}$ respectively, form the vertices of a right angled triangle.

Reason (R) Three points A, B, C form a right angled triangle, then sum of squares of magnitudes of any two vectors (corresponding to sides) equals square of magnitude of third vector (corresponding to the third side).

7 **Assertion (A)** The projection of the vector $\vec{a}=2\hat{i}+3\hat{j}+2\hat{k}$ on the vector $\vec{b}=\hat{i}+2\hat{j}+\hat{k}$ is $\frac{5}{3}\sqrt{6}$.

Reason (R) The projection of vector $\vec{a}$ on vector $\vec{b}$ is $\frac{1}{|\vec{a}|}(\vec{a}\cdot\vec{b})$.

8 **Assertion (A)** For any two vectors $\vec{a}$ and $\vec{b}$, we always have $|\vec{a}+\vec{b}|\le|\vec{a}|+|\vec{b}|$. (triangle inequality)

Reason (R) The inequality holds trivially in case either $\vec{a}=0$ or $\vec{b}=0$.

9 **Assertion (A)** The angle between vectors $\vec{a}$ and $\vec{b}$ having the same length $\sqrt{2}$ and scalar product -1 is $\frac{2\pi}{3}$.

Reason (R) The angle between two vectors $\vec{a}$ and $\vec{b}$ is $\theta=\cos^{-1}\left(\frac{\vec{a}\cdot\vec{b}}{|\vec{a}||\vec{b}|}\right)$.

Very Short Answer Type Questions

2 Marks

10 Write the direction ratio's of the vector $3\vec{a} + 2\vec{b}$, where $\vec{a} = \hat{i} + \hat{j} - 2\hat{k}$ and $\vec{b} = 2\hat{i} - 4\hat{j} + 5\hat{k}$.

11 Find $\vec{a} \cdot \vec{b}$, if $\vec{a} = -\hat{i} + \hat{j} - 2\hat{k}$ and $\vec{b} = 2\hat{i} + 3\hat{j} - \hat{k}$.

12 For what value of λ, the vectors $\hat{i} + 2\lambda\hat{j} + \hat{k}$ and $2\hat{i} + \hat{j} - 3\hat{k}$ are perpendicular?

13 If $|\vec{a}| = \sqrt{3}, |\vec{b}| = 2$ and the angle between $\vec{a}$ and $\vec{b}$ is 60°, then find $\vec{a} \cdot \vec{b}$.

14 Find λ, when projection of $\vec{a} = \lambda\hat{i} + \hat{j} + 4\hat{k}$ on $\vec{b} = 2\hat{i} + 6\hat{j} + 3\hat{k}$ is 4 units.

15 Write the value of $(\hat{k} \times \hat{j}) \cdot \hat{i} + \hat{j} \cdot \hat{k}$.

16 If $\vec{a} \cdot \vec{a} = 0$ and $\vec{a} \cdot \vec{b} = 0$, then what can be concluded about $\vec{b}$?

17 P and Q are two points with position vectors $3\vec{a} - 2\vec{b}$ and $\vec{a} + \vec{b}$, respectively. Write the position vector of a point R which divides the line segment PQ in the ratio 2 : 1 externally.

18 Find $|\vec{x}|$, if for a unit vector $\hat{a}$, $(\vec{x} - \hat{a}) \cdot (\vec{x} + \hat{a}) = 15$.

19 Find the vector product of the vectors $3\hat{i} - \hat{k}$ and $-\hat{i} - \hat{j} + 5\hat{k}$.

20 Find the area of parallelogram determined by the vectors $\hat{i} + 2\hat{j} + 3\hat{k}$ and $3\hat{i} - 2\hat{j} + \hat{k}$.

21 If $\vec{a}$ and $\vec{b}$ are two non-zero vectors such that $|\vec{a} \times \vec{b}| = \vec{a} \cdot \vec{b}$, find the angle between $\vec{a}$ and $\vec{b}$. **[ISC 2024]**

22 Write the angle between the vectors $\vec{a} \times \vec{b}$ and $\vec{b} \times \vec{a}$.

23 If $(\vec{a} \times \vec{b})^2 + (\vec{a} \cdot \vec{b})^2 = 225$ and $|\vec{a}| = 5$, then write the value of $|\vec{b}|$.

24 The two vectors $\hat{j} + \hat{k}$ and $3\hat{i} - \hat{j} + 4\hat{k}$ represent the two sides AB and AC respectively of triangle ABC. Find the length of the median through A.

25 If $\vec{a}$ and $\vec{b}$ are two vectors such that $|\vec{a} + \vec{b}| = |\vec{a}|$, then prove that vector $2\vec{a} + \vec{b}$ is perpendicular to vector $\vec{b}$.

26 Find λ, if $(2\hat{i} + 6\hat{j} + 14\hat{k}) \times (\hat{i} - \lambda\hat{j} + 7\hat{k}) = \vec{0}$.

27 Find the projection of the vector $\vec{a} = 2\hat{i} + 3\hat{j} + 2\hat{k}$ on the vector $\vec{b} = 2\hat{i} + 2\hat{j} + \hat{k}$.

28 If $\vec{a}$ and $\vec{b}$ are unit vectors, then what is the angle between $\vec{a}$ and $\vec{b}$, so that $\sqrt{2}\vec{a} - \vec{b}$ is a unit vector?

29 Write the number of vectors of unit length perpendicular to both the vectors $\vec{a} = 2\hat{i} + \hat{j} + 2\hat{k}$ and $\vec{b} = \hat{j} + \hat{k}$.

30 If the points with position vectors $10\hat{i} + 3\hat{j}$, $12\hat{i} - 5\hat{j}$ and $\lambda\hat{i} + 11\hat{j}$ are collinear, find the value of λ.

31 If $\vec{a} = \hat{i} + 2\hat{j} - \hat{k}$ and $\vec{b} = 3\hat{i} + \hat{j} - 5\hat{k}$, then find a unit vector in the direction of $\vec{a} - \vec{b}$.

32 Find the projection of $\vec{b} + \vec{c}$ on $\vec{a}$, where $\vec{a} = 2\hat{i} - 2\hat{j} + \hat{k}$, $\vec{b} = \hat{i} + 2\hat{j} - 2\hat{k}$ and $\vec{c} = 2\hat{i} - \hat{j} + 4\hat{k}$.

33 Find $|\vec{a} - \vec{b}|$, if two vectors $\vec{a}$ and $\vec{b}$ are such that $|\vec{a}| = 2, |\vec{b}| = 3$ and $\vec{a} \cdot \vec{b} = 5$.

34 Find the unit vector perpendicular to $3\hat{i} + \hat{j} + 2\hat{k}$ and $2\hat{i} - 2\hat{j} + 4\hat{k}$.

35 Given $\vec{a} = \hat{i} - 2\hat{j} + \hat{k}, \vec{b} = 2\hat{i} + \hat{j} + \hat{k}$ and $\vec{c} = \hat{i} + 2\hat{j} - \hat{k}$. Then, find $\vec{a} \times (\vec{b} \times \vec{c})$. **[ISC 2008, 2002]**

Short Answer Type Questions

4 Marks

36 Find the position vector of a point R which divides the line joining two points P and Q whose position vectors are $\hat{i} + 2\hat{j} - \hat{k}$ and $-\hat{i} + \hat{j} + \hat{k}$ respectively, in the ratio 2 : 1

(i) internally. (ii) externally.

37 If $\hat{a}, \hat{b}$ are two unit vectors and θ is angle between them, then what is the value of $\left|\frac{\hat{a}-\hat{b}}{2}\right|$?

38 Find a unit vector perpendicular to both of the vectors $3\vec{a}+2\vec{b}$ and $3\vec{a}-2\vec{b}$, where $\vec{a}=\hat{i}+\hat{j}+\hat{k}$ and $\vec{b}=\hat{i}+2\hat{j}+3\hat{k}$.

39 Show that the points A, B and C with position vectors $2\hat{i}-\hat{j}+\hat{k}, \hat{i}-3\hat{j}-5\hat{k}$ and $3\hat{i}-4\hat{j}-4\hat{k}$ respectively, are the vertices of a right-angled triangle. Hence, find the area of triangle.

40 If $\vec{a}, \vec{b}$ and $\vec{c}$ are mutually perpendicular vectors of equal magnitudes, find the angles which the vector $2\vec{a}+\vec{b}+2\vec{c}$ makes with the vectors $\vec{a}, \vec{b}$ and $\vec{c}$.

41 If $\vec{a}, \vec{b}$ and $\vec{c}$ are three mutually perpendicular vectors of equal magnitude x, then show that $\vec{a}+\vec{b}+\vec{c}$ is equally inclined to $\vec{a}, \vec{b}$ and $\vec{c}$. Also, find the angle.

42 Find the unit vector perpendicular to the plane ABC, where the position vectors of A, B and C are $2\hat{i}-\hat{j}+\hat{k}, \hat{i}+\hat{j}+2\hat{k}$ and $2\hat{i}+3\hat{k}$, respectively.

43 If $\vec{b}\times\vec{c}=\vec{c}\times\vec{a}\neq\vec{0}$, then prove that $\vec{a}+\vec{b}=\lambda\vec{c}$, where λ is a scalar.

44 If $\vec{a}, \vec{b}$ and $\vec{c}$ are three vectors such that $|\vec{a}|=5$, $|\vec{b}|=12$, $|\vec{c}|=13$ and $\vec{a}+\vec{b}+\vec{c}=\vec{0}$, then find the value of $\vec{a}\cdot\vec{b}+\vec{b}\cdot\vec{c}+\vec{c}\cdot\vec{a}$.

45 If $\vec{a}+\vec{b}+\vec{c}=\vec{0}$, $|\vec{a}|=\sqrt{37}$, $|\vec{b}|=3$ and $|\vec{c}|=4$, then what will be the angle between $\vec{b}$ and $\vec{c}$?

46 Prove that in any ΔABC, $\cos C=\frac{a^2+b^2-c^2}{2ab}$, where a, b and c are the magnitudes of the sides opposite to the vertices A, B and C, respectively. [NCERT Exemplar]

Case-Based Type Questions

(6 Marks)

47 A person is standing at point $P(0, 0, 0)$ on a ground at some distance from a building. The three corner points of a building are $A(0, 1, 2)$, $B(2, -1, 3)$ and $C(1, -3, 1)$. And the height of the building is equal to the magnitude of the perpendicular vector at point B.

The angle of elevation made by the person to the top of the building is θ.

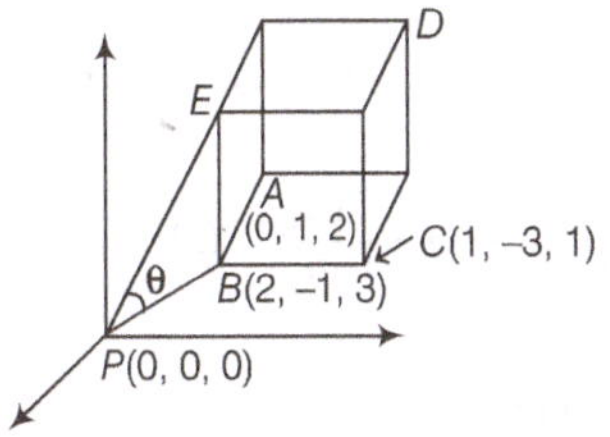

On the basis of the given information, answer the following questions.

(i) Find the angle between the vectors $\overrightarrow{AB}$ and $\overrightarrow{BC}$.

(ii) Find a vector, which is perpendicular to $\overrightarrow{BA}$ and $\overrightarrow{BC}$.

(iii) Find the angle θ.

(iv) Find the area of base region covered by the building.

48 In unlock period, the students are sitting in the classroom with some spaces, as per the guidelines of central board of education.

The position of three special students Sumit, Harish and Anil in the class are respectively, $A(2, 1, -1)$, $B(1, 0, -3)$ and $C(-1, 2, 1)$.

Based on the given information, answer the following questions.

(i) Find the distance between Sumit and Harish.

(ii) If we want to insert one student between Sumit and Harish such that student is 2 units distance from Sumit and 1 unit distance from Harish and all three are in a line. Then, find the position of inserted student.

(iii) Find the area of the region covered by these three persons.

(iv) Find a unit vector, which is perpendicular to the vectors A, B and C.

Answers

1. (b) 2. (b) 3. (b) 4. (c) 5. (b) 6. (a)

7. (c) 8. (b) 9. (a)

10. 7, −5, 4 11. 3 12. $\lambda = \frac{1}{2}$ 13. $\sqrt{3}$ 14. $\lambda = 5$ 15. −1

16. $\vec{b}$ can be any vector 17. $-\vec{a} + 4\vec{b}$ 18. 4 19. $-\hat{i} - 14\hat{j} - 3\hat{k}$ 20. $8\sqrt{3}$ sq units 21. $\frac{\pi}{4}$

22. π 23. 3 24. $\frac{\sqrt{34}}{2}$ 26. $\lambda = -3$ 27. 4 units 28. $\theta = \frac{\pi}{4}$

29. 2 30. $\lambda = 8$ 31. $\frac{-2}{\sqrt{21}}\hat{i} + \frac{1}{\sqrt{21}}\hat{j} + \frac{4}{\sqrt{21}}\hat{k}$ 32. 2 33. $\sqrt{3}$

34. $\frac{\hat{i}}{\sqrt{3}} - \frac{\hat{j}}{\sqrt{3}} - \frac{\hat{k}}{\sqrt{3}}$ 35. $-9\hat{i} - 6\hat{j} - 3\hat{k}$

36. (i) $\left(-\frac{1}{3}\right)\hat{i} + \left(\frac{4}{3}\right)\hat{j} + \left(\frac{1}{3}\right)\hat{k}$ (ii) $-3\hat{i} + 3\hat{k}$ 37. $\sin\frac{\theta}{2}$ 38. $-12\hat{i} + 24\hat{j} - 12\hat{k}$

39. $\frac{\sqrt{210}}{2}$ sq units 40. $\cos^{-1}\frac{2}{3}, \cos^{-1}\frac{1}{3}, \cos^{-1}\frac{2}{3}$ 41. $\cos^{-1}\left(\frac{x}{(\vec{a} + \vec{b} + \vec{c})}\right)$

42. $\frac{3}{\sqrt{14}}\hat{i} + \frac{2}{\sqrt{14}}\hat{j} - \frac{1}{\sqrt{14}}\hat{k}$ 44. −169 45. $\theta = 60°$

47. (i) 90° (ii) $-6\hat{i} - 3\hat{j} + 6\hat{k}$ (iii) $\tan^{-1}\left(\frac{9}{\sqrt{14}}\right)$ (iv) 9

48. (i) $\sqrt{6}$ (ii) $\left(\frac{4}{3}, \frac{1}{3}, -\frac{7}{3}\right)$ (iii) $\frac{1}{2}\sqrt{80}$ (iv) $\frac{8\hat{j} - 4\hat{k}}{4\sqrt{5}}$

CHAPTER

13

Three Dimensional Geometry I : Lines

In this chapter, we will study the direction cosines, direction ratios of a line and discuss about the different forms of equations of the lines in space under different conditions.

- Direction Cosines and Direction Ratios of a Line
- Lines in Space

TOPIC 01 Direction Cosines and Direction Ratios of a Line

We know that the position of a point in a plane can be determined, if the coordinates (x, y) of the point with reference to two mutually perpendicular lines, called *X* **and** *Y***-axes**, are known. But in order to locate a point in space, two coordinate axes is insufficient. So, we need three coordinate axes called *X*, *Y* **and** *Z***-axes**.

Coordinate Axes and Coordinate Planes in Three-Dimensional Geometry

Let $X'OX, Y'OY$ and $Z'OZ$ be three mutually perpendicular lines intersecting at O. The point O is called the **origin** and the lines $X'OX, Y'OY$ and $Z'OZ$ are called **X-axis, Y-axis** and **Z-axis**, respectively. These three lines are also called the **rectangular coordinate axes**. These lines constitute the rectangular coordinate system.

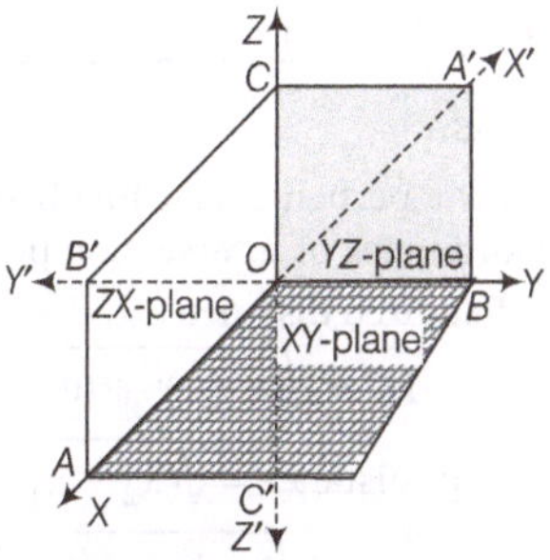

The axes X, Y and Z, when taken in pairs, determine three mutually perpendicular planes XOY, YOZ and ZOX or simply XY-plane, YZ-plane and ZX-plane, called **rectangular coordinate planes** which divide the space into eight parts called **octants.**

Note Equation of YZ-plane is $x = 0$, equation of ZX-plane is $y = 0$ and equation of XY-plane is $z = 0$.

Coordinates of a Point in Space

The coordinates of a point are the distances from the origin to the feet of the perpendiculars, drawn from the point on the respective coordinate axes.

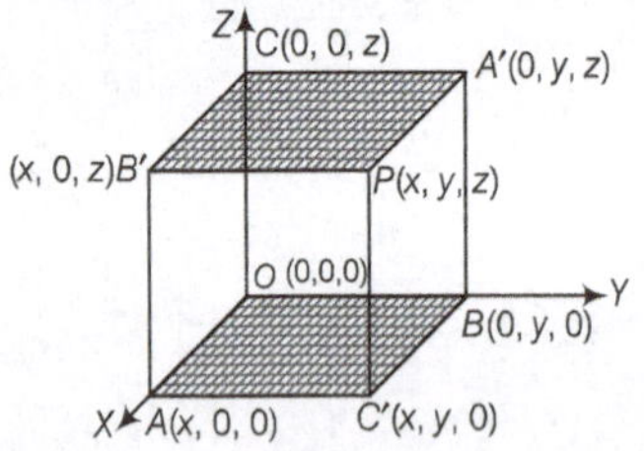

The coordinates of any point on the X-axis, Y-axis and Z-axis will be as $A(x, 0, 0)$, $B(0, y, 0)$ and $C(0, 0, z)$, respectively.

The coordinates of any point on XY, YZ and ZX-planes may be taken as $(x, y, 0)$, $(0, y, z)$ and $(x, 0, z)$, respectively.

Note Fact about coordinates of point $P(x, y, z)$

x = Perpendicular distance of P from YZ-plane

y = Perpendicular distance of P from XZ-plane

z = Perpendicular distance of P from XY-plane

Equation of Planes Parallel to Coordinate Planes

Let $P(x, y, z)$ be any point on the given plane, then

(i) the equation of a plane parallel to XY-plane is $z = c$.

(ii) the equation of a plane parallel to YZ-plane is $x = a$.

(iii) the equation of a plane parallel to ZX-plane is $y = b$. where a, b and c are constants.

Equation of Coordinate Axes

(i) The equation of the X-axis is given by $y = 0$ and $z = 0$.

(ii) The equation of the Y-axis is given by $z = 0$ and $x = 0$.

(iii) The equation of the Z-axis is given by $x = 0$ and $y = 0$.

Equation of Lines Parallel to Coordinate Axes

(i) The equation of a line parallel to X-axis is given by $y = b$ and $z = c$.

(ii) The equation of a line parallel to Y-axis is given by $z = c$ and $x = a$.

(iii) The equation of a line parallel to Z-axis is given by $x = a$ and $y = b$, where a, b and c are constants.

Some Important Formulae

(i) **Distance between two points** Let $P(x_1, y_1, z_1)$ and $Q(x_2, y_2, z_2)$ be two points referred to a system of rectangular axes, then

$$PQ = \sqrt{(x_2 - x_1)^2 + (y_2 - y_1)^2 + (z_2 - z_1)^2}.$$

Note The distance of any point $P(x_1, y_1, z_1)$ from the origin is given by $OP = \sqrt{x_1^2 + y_1^2 + z_1^2}$.

(ii) **Section formula** Let the two given points be $P(x_1, y_1, z_1)$ and $Q(x_2, y_2, z_2)$ and the point $R(x, y, z)$ divides PQ in the ratio $m : n$ internally, then

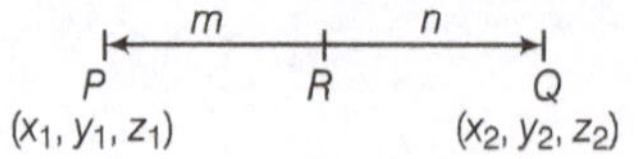

$$R = \left(\frac{mx_2 + nx_1}{m + n}, \frac{my_2 + ny_1}{m + n}, \frac{mz_2 + nz_1}{m + n}\right)$$

If the point R divides PQ externally in the ratio $m : n$, then

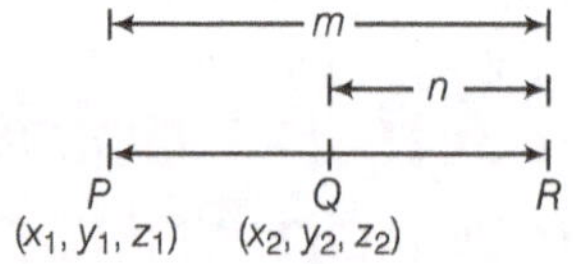

$$R = \left(\frac{mx_2 - nx_1}{m - n}, \frac{my_2 - ny_1}{m - n}, \frac{mz_2 - nz_1}{m - n}\right)$$

(iii) **Mid-point of a line** The mid-point of the line joining points $A(x_1, y_1, z_1)$ and $B(x_2, y_2, z_2)$ is $\left(\frac{x_1 + x_2}{2}, \frac{y_1 + y_2}{2}, \frac{z_1 + z_2}{2}\right)$.

(iv) **Centroid of a triangle** The centroid of ΔABC with vertices $A(x_1, y_1, z_1)$, $B(x_2, y_2, z_2)$ and $C(x_3, y_3, z_3)$ is

$$= \left(\frac{x_1 + x_2 + x_3}{3}, \frac{y_1 + y_2 + y_3}{3}, \frac{z_1 + z_2 + z_3}{3}\right)$$

Example 1 Find the distance of a point $P(a, b, c)$ from X-axis.

Sol. Draw a perpendicular line from P to the X-axis, then coordinates of intersection point is $Q(a, 0, 0)$.

$\therefore$ Required distance,

$$PQ = \sqrt{(a - a)^2 + (0 - b)^2 + (0 - c)^2}$$

$$[\because \text{distance} = \sqrt{(x_2 - x_1)^2 + (y_2 - y_1)^2 + (z_2 - z_1)^2}]$$

$$= \sqrt{0 + b^2 + c^2} = \sqrt{b^2 + c^2}$$

Direction Cosines of a Line

As we know that if a directed line (say L) passing through the origin makes angles α, β and γ with the positive directions of X, Y and Z-axes respectively, called **direction angles**, then cosine values of these angles, i.e. $\cos\alpha$, $\cos\beta$ and $\cos\gamma$ are known as the **direction cosines** of the **directed line** L (or $\overrightarrow{OA}$).

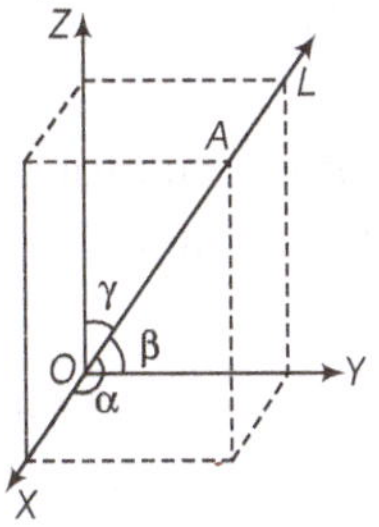

The direction cosines are represented by l, m and n. Thus, $l = \cos\alpha$, $m = \cos\beta$ and $n = \cos\gamma$.

If the direction of directed line is reversed (i.e. opposite), then the direction angles are replaced by their supplements, i.e. $\pi - \alpha$, $\pi - \beta$ and $\pi - \gamma$. Also, the signs of direction cosines are reversed, i.e. $(-l, -m, -n)$.

Thus, the direction cosines of a line are either $< l, m, n >$ or $< -l, -m, -n >$, where $l = \cos\alpha$, $m = \cos\beta$ and $n = \cos\gamma$.

Note

(i) A line in space can be extended in two opposite directions and so it has two sets of direction cosines. To have a unique set of direction cosines for a given line in space, we must take the given line as a directed line.

(ii) If the given line in space does not pass through the origin, then in order to find its direction cosines, we draw a line through the origin and parallel to the given line. Now, take one of the directed lines from the origin and find its direction cosines and then use the result that two parallel lines have same set of direction cosines.

(iii) (a) DC's of the X-axis are 1, 0, 0.
(b) DC's of the Y-axis are 0, 1, 0.
(c) DC's of the Z-axis are 0, 0, 1.

Example 2 If a line makes angles $90°$, $135°$, $45°$ with the positive direction of X, Y and Z-axes, respectively. Find its direction cosines. **[NCERT]**

Sol. Let direction cosines of the line be l, m and n.

Given, $\alpha = 90°, \beta = 135°$ and $\gamma = 45°$

Then, $l = \cos\alpha = \cos 90° = 0$,

$$m = \cos\beta = \cos 135° = \frac{-1}{\sqrt{2}}$$

and $$n = \cos\gamma = \cos 45° = \frac{1}{\sqrt{2}}$$

Hence, the direction cosines of a line are $0, \frac{-1}{\sqrt{2}}$ and $\frac{1}{\sqrt{2}}$.

Relation between Direction Cosines of a Line

Let direction cosines of a line RS be l, m and n. Now, draw a line passing through origin and parallel to the given line. Take a point $P(x, y, z)$ on this line and draw a perpendicular PA from P on X-axis.

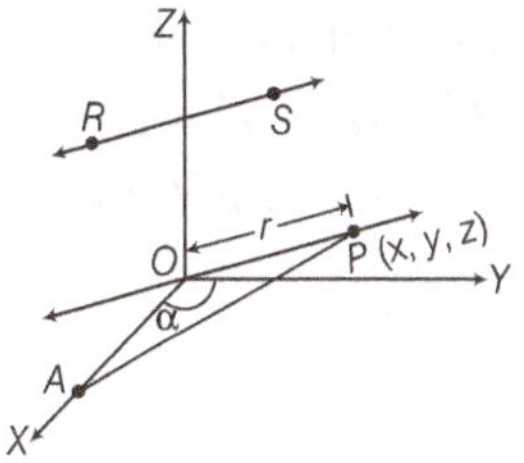

Let $OP = r$. Then, in right angled ΔOAP,

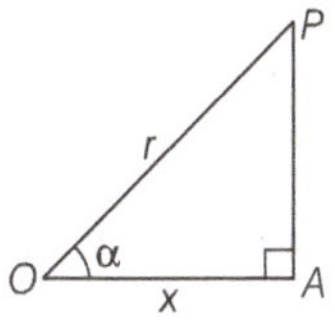

$$\cos\alpha = \frac{OA}{OP} = \frac{x}{r} \Rightarrow x = lr$$

Similarly, $y = mr$ and $z = nr$

Now, $x^2 + y^2 + z^2 = r^2(l^2 + m^2 + n^2)$

$\Rightarrow \quad r^2 = r^2(l^2 + m^2 + n^2)$

$[\because$ distance $OP = r \Rightarrow x^2 + y^2 + z^2 = r^2]$

$$\Rightarrow \quad \boxed{l^2 + m^2 + n^2 = 1}$$

which is the required relation between direction cosines of a line.

Note The coordinates of the point $P(x, y, z)$ can be written as (lr, mr, nr).

Example 3 Find the direction cosines of a line which makes equal angles with coordinate axes. **[NCERT]**

Sol. Let the line makes an angle α with each of the three coordinate axes, then its direction cosines are $l = \cos\alpha$, $m = \cos\alpha$ and $n = \cos\alpha$.

We know that, $l^2 + m^2 + n^2 = 1$

$\Rightarrow \cos^2\alpha + \cos^2\alpha + \cos^2\alpha = 1 \Rightarrow 3\cos^2\alpha = 1$

$\Rightarrow \cos^2\alpha = \frac{1}{3} \Rightarrow \cos\alpha = \pm\frac{1}{\sqrt{3}}$

Hence, the direction cosines of a line are $\frac{1}{\sqrt{3}}, \frac{1}{\sqrt{3}}, \frac{1}{\sqrt{3}}$ or $\frac{-1}{\sqrt{3}}, \frac{-1}{\sqrt{3}}, \frac{-1}{\sqrt{3}}$.

Direction Cosines of a Line Passing through Two Points

The direction cosines of a line passing through the points $A(x_1, y_1, z_1)$ and $B(x_2, y_2, z_2)$ are given by

$$\frac{x_2 - x_1}{AB}, \frac{y_2 - y_1}{AB} \text{ and } \frac{z_2 - z_1}{AB}$$

where, $AB = \sqrt{(x_2 - x_1)^2 + (y_2 - y_1)^2 + (z_2 - z_1)^2}$.

Direction Ratios of a Line

Any three numbers a, b and c proportional to the direction cosines l, m and n respectively, are called the direction ratios or direction numbers of the line.

Suppose, $\frac{l}{a} = \frac{m}{b} = \frac{n}{c} = k$ (say), k being a constant.

Then, $l = ak$, $m = bk$ and $n = ck$

But we know that, $l^2 + m^2 + n^2 = 1$

$\therefore (ak)^2 + (bk)^2 + (ck)^2 = 1 \Rightarrow k^2(a^2 + b^2 + c^2) = 1$

$$\Rightarrow \quad k = \pm \frac{1}{\sqrt{a^2 + b^2 + c^2}}$$

$$\therefore \quad l = \pm \frac{a}{\sqrt{a^2 + b^2 + c^2}}, \; m = \pm \frac{b}{\sqrt{a^2 + b^2 + c^2}}$$

$$\text{and} \quad n = \pm \frac{c}{\sqrt{a^2 + b^2 + c^2}}$$

Thus, if a, b and c are direction ratios, then direction cosines are

$$\left(\frac{\pm a}{\sqrt{a^2+b^2+c^2}}, \frac{\pm b}{\sqrt{a^2+b^2+c^2}}, \frac{\pm c}{\sqrt{a^2+b^2+c^2}} \right),$$

where signs should be taken all positive or all negative.

For any line, if a, b and c are direction ratios of a line, then ka, kb, kc; $k \neq 0$ is also a set of direction ratios. So, any two sets of direction ratios of a line are also proportional.

Hence, for a line, there are infinitely many sets of direction ratios.

Direction Ratios of a Line Passing through Two Points

The direction ratios of a line passing through two points $P(x_1, y_1, z_1)$ and $Q(x_2, y_2, z_2)$ are given by $x_2 - x_1$, $y_2 - y_1$ and $z_2 - z_1$.

Note Direction ratios of two parallel lines are proportional, as two parallel lines have same set of direction cosines.

Direction Ratios and Direction Cosines of a Vector

Let $\vec{r} = a\hat{i} + b\hat{j} + c\hat{k}$ be a vector then coefficients of $\hat{i}, \hat{j}, \hat{k}$ i.e. a, b, c are called direction ratios of $\vec{r}$ and the direction cosines of $\vec{r}$ are given by

$$\frac{a}{\sqrt{a^2 + b^2 + c^2}}, \frac{b}{\sqrt{a^2 + b^2 + c^2}}, \frac{c}{\sqrt{a^2 + b^2 + c^2}}$$

Example 4 If a line has direction ratios 2, –1, 2, then determine its direction cosines. **[NCERT]**

Sol. Given direction ratios are (2, –1, 2), i.e. $a = 2$, $b = -1$ and $c = 2$.

$$\therefore \sqrt{a^2 + b^2 + c^2} = \sqrt{(2)^2 + (-1)^2 + (2)^2} = \sqrt{9} = 3$$

Now, direction cosines are

$$l = \frac{a}{\sqrt{a^2 + b^2 + c^2}} = \frac{2}{3}, \; m = \frac{b}{\sqrt{a^2 + b^2 + c^2}} = \frac{-1}{3}$$

$$\text{and} \quad n = \frac{c}{\sqrt{a^2 + b^2 + c^2}} = \frac{2}{3}$$

Example 5 Find the direction ratios and direction cosines of the line passing through two points (2, –4, 5) and (0, 1, –1).

Sol. Let $A(x_1, y_1, z_1) = (2, -4, 5)$ and $B(x_2, y_2, z_2) = (0, 1, -1)$.

Then, DR's of line AB are $(0 - 2, 1 + 4, -1 - 5)$, i.e. $(-2, 5, -6)$

Now, DC's of AB are

$$\left(\frac{-2}{\sqrt{(-2)^2 + 5^2 + (-6)^2}}, \frac{5}{\sqrt{(-2)^2 + 5^2 + (-6)^2}}, \frac{-6}{\sqrt{(-2)^2 + 5^2 + (-6)^2}} \right)$$

Hence, DC's of line AB are $\left(\frac{-2}{\sqrt{65}}, \frac{5}{\sqrt{65}}, \frac{-6}{\sqrt{65}} \right)$.

Example 6 Find the direction cosines of the sides of the triangle whose vertices are (3, 5, –4), (–1, 1, 2) and (–5, –5, –2). **[NCERT]**

Sol. Let the vertices of ΔABC be $A(3, 5, -4)$, $B(-1, 1, 2)$ and $C(-5, -5, -2)$. Then, the direction ratios of side AB are

$$[(-1-3), (1-5), 2-(-4)], \text{ i.e. } (-4, -4, 6).$$

[$\because$ if the given points are $A(x_1, y_1, z_1)$ and $B(x_2, y_2, z_2)$, then DR's of $AB = (x_2 - x_1, y_2 - y_1, z_2 - z_1)$]

and the direction cosines of AB are

$$\left(\frac{-4}{2\sqrt{17}}, \frac{-4}{2\sqrt{17}}, \frac{6}{2\sqrt{17}} \right) \text{ or } \left(\frac{-2}{\sqrt{17}}, \frac{-2}{\sqrt{17}}, \frac{3}{\sqrt{17}} \right)$$

$\left[\because \text{ if } a, b \text{ and } c \text{ are direction ratios, then direction cosines are } \left(\frac{a}{\sqrt{a^2 + b^2 + c^2}}, \frac{b}{\sqrt{a^2 + b^2 + c^2}}, \frac{c}{\sqrt{a^2 + b^2 + c^2}} \right) \right]$

Similarly, the direction ratios of side BC are $[\{-5-(-1)\}, (-5-1), (-2-2)]$, i.e. $(-4, -6, -4)$ and the direction cosines of BC are

$$\left(\frac{-4}{2\sqrt{17}}, \frac{-6}{2\sqrt{17}}, \frac{-4}{2\sqrt{17}} \right) \text{ or } \left(\frac{-2}{\sqrt{17}}, \frac{-3}{\sqrt{17}}, \frac{-2}{\sqrt{17}} \right).$$

The direction ratios of side AC are $[(-5-3), (-5-5), \{(-2-(-4)\}]$, i.e. $(-8, -10, 2)$ and the direction cosines of AC are $\left(\frac{-8}{2\sqrt{42}}, \frac{-10}{2\sqrt{42}}, \frac{2}{2\sqrt{42}} \right)$ or $\left(\frac{-4}{\sqrt{42}}, \frac{-5}{\sqrt{42}}, \frac{1}{\sqrt{42}} \right)$.

Angle Between Two Lines in Terms of Direction Cosines/Direction Ratios

We know that there are always two angles θ and $\pi - \theta$ between two intersecting lines, as shown in the figure.

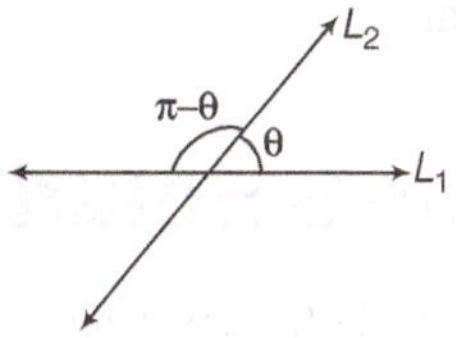

Now, we will define the formula to find the angle between two lines whose direction cosines/ratios are given.

Angle between Two Lines whose Direction Cosines are Given

Let L_1 and L_2 be two lines with direciton cosines $< l_1, m_1, n_1 >$ and $< l_2, m_2, n_2 >$, respectively and let θ be the acute angle between L_1 and L_2. Then, θ is given by

$$\cos\theta = | l_1l_2 + m_1m_2 + n_1n_2 |$$

or

$$\sin\theta = \sqrt{(l_1m_2 - l_2m_1)^2 + (m_1n_2 - m_2n_1)^2 + (n_1l_2 - n_2l_1)^2}$$
$$= \sqrt{\Sigma(l_1m_2 - l_2m_1)^2}$$

Condition of Perpendicularity and Parallelism

(i) Two lines are perpendicular iff

$$l_1l_2 + m_1m_2 + n_1n_2 = 0$$

(ii) Two lines are parallel iff $l_1 = l_2, m_1 = m_2 = n_1 = n_2$

Angle between Two Lines whose Direction Ratios are Given

Let L_1 and L_2 be two lines with direction ratios $< a_1, b_1, c_1 >$ and $< a_2, b_2, c_2 >$, respectively and let θ be the acute angle between L_1 and L_2, then θ is given by

$$\cos\theta = \frac{|a_1a_2 + b_1b_2 + c_1c_2|}{\sqrt{a_1^2 + b_1^2 + c_1^2}\sqrt{a_2^2 + b_2^2 + c_2^2}}$$

or

$$\sin\theta = \frac{\sqrt{\Sigma(a_1b_2 - a_2b_1)^2}}{\sqrt{a_1^2 + b_1^2 + c_1^2}\sqrt{a_2^2 + b_2^2 + c_2^2}}$$

Condition of Perpendicularity and Parallelism

(i) Two lines are perpendicular iff

$$a_1a_2 + b_1b_2 + c_1c_2 = 0.$$

(ii) Two lines are parallel iff $\frac{a_1}{a_2} = \frac{b_1}{b_2} = \frac{c_1}{c_2}$.

Example 7 Find the angle between the lines with direction ratios proportional to 4, – 3, 5 and 3, 4, 5, respectively.

Sol. Let θ be the acute angle between the given lines.

Here, $a_1 = 4, b_1 = -3, c_1 = 5$ and $a_2 = 3, b_2 = 4, c_2 = 5$

$$\because \cos\theta = \frac{|a_1a_2 + b_1b_2 + c_1c_2|}{\sqrt{a_1^2 + b_1^2 + c_1^2}\sqrt{a_2^2 + b_2^2 + c_2^2}}$$

$$\therefore \cos\theta = \frac{|4 \times 3 + (-3) \times 4 + 5 \times 5|}{\sqrt{4^2 + (-3)^2 + 5^2}\sqrt{3^2 + 4^2 + 5^2}}$$

$$= \frac{|12 - 12 + 25|}{\sqrt{16 + 9 + 25}\sqrt{9 + 16 + 25}} = \frac{25}{\sqrt{50}\sqrt{50}} = \frac{25}{50} = \frac{1}{2}$$

$$\Rightarrow \cos\theta = \cos\left(\frac{\pi}{3}\right) \Rightarrow \theta = \frac{\pi}{3}$$

Example 8 Find the angle between the lines whose direction cosines are given by the equations $3l + m + 5n = 0$, $6mn - 2nl + 5lm = 0$. **[NCERT Exemplar]**

Sol. The given equations are $3l + m + 5n = 0$ ...(i)

and $6mn - 2nl + 5lm = 0$ ...(ii)

Now, from Eq. (i), we get $m = -3l - 5n$ ...(iii)

On substituting $m = -3l - 5n$ in Eq. (ii), we get

$$6(-3l - 5n)n - 2nl + 5l(-3l - 5n) = 0$$

$\Rightarrow$ $30n^2 + 45ln + 15l^2 = 0 \Rightarrow 2n^2 + 3ln + l^2 = 0$

$\Rightarrow$ $2n^2 + 2nl + nl + l^2 = 0 \Rightarrow 2n(n + l) + l(n + l) = 0$

$\Rightarrow$ $(n + l)(2n + l) = 0$

$\Rightarrow$ Either $l = -n$ or $l = -2n$

If $l = -n$, then $m = -2n$ [using Eq. (iii)]

and if $l = -2n$, then $m = n$. [using Eq. (iii)]

Thus, the direction ratios of two lines are proportional to $(-n, -2n, n)$ and $(-2n, n, n)$ i.e. $(-1, -2, 1)$ and $(-2, 1, 1)$, respectively.

Now, let θ be the acute angle between the lines, then

$$\cos\theta = \frac{|a_1a_2 + b_1b_2 + c_1c_2|}{\sqrt{a_1^2 + b_1^2 + c_1^2}\sqrt{a_2^2 + b_2^2 + c_2^2}}$$

$$= \frac{|2 - 2 + 1|}{\sqrt{1 + 4 + 1}\sqrt{4 + 1 + 1}} = \frac{1}{6} \Rightarrow \theta = \cos^{-1}\left(\frac{1}{6}\right)$$

Condition for Collinearity of Three Points

Suppose $A(x_1, y_1, z_1)$, $B(x_2, y_2, z_2)$ and $C(x_3, y_3, z_3)$ are three points in a space. Then, direction ratios of line joining A and B, B and C are $(x_2 - x_1, y_2 - y_1, z_2 - z_1)$ and $(x_3 - x_2, y_3 - y_2, z_3 - z_2)$, respectively. If direction ratios of AB and BC are proportional, then these points are collinear, otherwise not.

Example 9 Show that the points $A(2, 3, -4)$, $B(1, -2, 3)$ and $C(3, 8, -11)$ are collinear. **[NCERT]**

Sol. Given points are $A(2, 3, -4)$, $B(1, -2, 3)$ and $C(3, 8, -11)$.

Direction ratios of line joining A and B are

$[1-2, -2-3, 3-(-4)]$, i.e. $(-1, -5, 7)$.

Direction ratios of line joining B and C are

$(3-1, 8+2, -11-3)$, i.e. $(2, 10, -14)$.

Now, ratios of DR's of AB and BC are

$$\frac{-1}{2}, \frac{-5}{10}, \frac{7}{-14}, \text{ i.e. } -\frac{1}{2}, -\frac{1}{2}, -\frac{1}{2}.$$

Thus, the direction ratios of AB and BC are proportional. So, AB is parallel to BC. But B is common to both AB and BC.

Hence, A, B and C are collinear points.

Topic Practice 1

Very Short Answer Type Questions

2 Marks

1 Find the distance of a point (2, 3, 4) from X-axis.

2 Write the direction cosines of a line parallel to Z-axis.

3 If a line makes angles 90°, 60° and 30° with the positive direction of X, Y and Z-axes respectively, then find its direction cosines.

4 If a line makes angles 90°, 60° and θ with X, Y and Z-axes respectively, where θ is acute, then find θ.

5 If a line makes angles 90° and 60° respectively with the positive directions of X and Y-axes, find the angle which it makes with the positive direction of Z-axis.

6 Find the direction cosines of a line whose direction ratios are 2, –6, 3.

7 If $P = (1, 5, 4)$ and $Q = (4, 1, -2)$, then find the direction ratios of PQ.

8 Find the direction cosines of the line segment joining the points $A(7, -5, 9)$ and $B(5, -3, 8)$.

9 Find the direction ratios of a line whose direction cosines are $\frac{1}{2}, \frac{1}{\sqrt{2}}, \frac{1}{2}$.

Short Answer Type Questions

4 Marks

10 If a line makes angles α, β and γ with the positive direction of coordinate axes, then write the value of $\sin^2\alpha + \sin^2\beta + \sin^2\gamma$. [ISC 2024]

11 Show that the line through the points $(1, -1, 2)$, $(3, 4, -2)$ is perpendicular to the line through the points $(0, 3, 2)$ and $(3, 5, 6)$. [NCERT]

12 Show that the points $(2, 3, 4)$, $(-1, -2, 1)$ and $(5, 8, 7)$ are collinear. [NCERT]

Hints & Solutions

1. Similar as Example 1. [**Ans.** 5 units]

2. As we know that two parallel lines have same set of direction cosines. Therefore, required direction cosines are the direction cosines of Z-axis, i.e. 0, 0, 1. [2]

3. Similar as Example 2. $\left[\textbf{Ans. } 0, \frac{1}{2}, \frac{\sqrt{3}}{2}\right]$

4. Given, $\alpha = 90°$, $\beta = 60°$ and $\gamma = \theta$.

Then, $\cos^2 90° + \cos^2 60° + \cos^2\theta = 1$

$[\because \cos^2\alpha + \cos^2\beta + \cos^2\gamma = 1]$

$$\Rightarrow 0 + \frac{1}{4} + \cos^2\theta = 1 \Rightarrow \cos^2\theta = \frac{3}{4} \Rightarrow \cos\theta = \pm\frac{\sqrt{3}}{2}$$

$$\Rightarrow \cos\theta = \frac{\sqrt{3}}{2} \Rightarrow \theta = 30° \quad [\because \theta \text{ is an acute angle}]$$ [2]

5. Solve as Question 4. [**Ans.** 30°, 150°]

6. Similar as Example 4. $\left[\textbf{Ans. } \frac{2}{7}, \frac{-6}{7}, \frac{3}{7}\right]$

7. Similar as Example 5. [**Ans.** 3, – 4, – 6]

8. Similar as Example 5. $\left[\textbf{Ans. } -\frac{2}{3}, \frac{2}{3}, \frac{-1}{3}\right]$

9. As we know that any three numbers proportional to the direction cosines are called the direction ratios.

So, infinite sets of direction ratios can be found, one of them is $1, \sqrt{2}, 1$. [multiplying direction cosines by 2] [2]

10. Since, the line makes angles α, β and γ with positive direction of coordinate axes, therefore $\cos\alpha$, $\cos\beta$ and $\cos\gamma$ are the direction cosines of the line.

So, we have $\cos^2\alpha + \cos^2\beta + \cos^2\gamma = 1$ [2]

$$\Rightarrow 1 - \sin^2\alpha + 1 - \sin^2\beta + 1 - \sin^2\gamma = 1$$

$[\because \sin^2 x + \cos^2 x = 1]$

$$\Rightarrow 3 - 1 = \sin^2\alpha + \sin^2\beta + \sin^2\gamma$$

Hence, $\sin^2\alpha + \sin^2\beta + \sin^2\gamma = 2$ [2]

11. **Hint** If a_1, b_1, c_1 and a_2, b_2, c_2 are the direction ratios of the lines, then the lines are perpendicular, if $a_1a_2 + b_1b_2 + c_1c_2 = 0$.

12. Similar as Example 9.

TOPIC 02 Lines in Space

A line (or straight line) is a curve such that all the points on the line segment joining any two points of it lies on it. A line in space can be determined uniquely, if

(i) its direction and the coordinates of a point on it are known.

(ii) it passes through two given points.

Now, we will find the vector and cartesian equations of a line in space.

Equation of a Line through a Given Point and Parallel to a Given Vector

Vector Equation

The vector equation of a line l passing through a point A with position vector $\vec{a}$ and parallel to a given vector $\vec{b}$ is $\vec{r} = \vec{a} + \lambda \vec{b}$, where $\vec{r}$ is the position vector of an arbitrary point P on the line and λ is a real number. The vector equation of a straight line passing through the origin and parallel to given vector $\vec{b}$ is

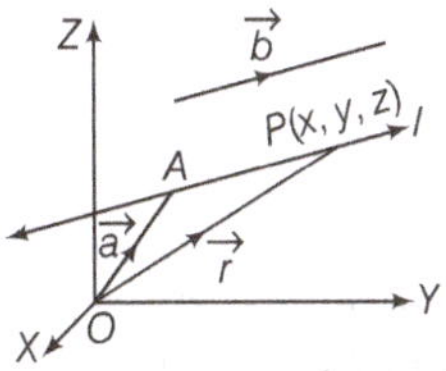

$$\boxed{\vec{r} = \lambda \vec{b}}$$

Note (i) If $\vec{b} = a'\hat{i} + b'\hat{j} + c'\hat{k}$, then a', b' and c' are direction ratios of the line and conversely, if a', b' and c' are direction ratios of a line, then $\vec{b} = a'\hat{i} + b'\hat{j} + c'\hat{k}$ will be parallel to the line.

(ii) If $\vec{r} = (a_1\hat{i} + a_2\hat{j} + a_3\hat{k}) + \lambda(b_1\hat{i} + b_2\hat{j} + b_3\hat{k})$, then coordinates of any point on the line are given by considering $\vec{r} = x\hat{i} + y\hat{j} + z\hat{k}$ and comparing the coefficient of $\hat{i}$, $\hat{j}$ and $\hat{k}$, i.e. first write

$$x\hat{i} + y\hat{j} + z\hat{k} = (a_1\hat{i} + a_2\hat{j} + a_3\hat{k}) + \lambda(b_1\hat{i} + b_2\hat{j} + b_3\hat{k})$$
$$= (a_1 + \lambda b_1)\hat{i} + (a_2 + \lambda b_2)\hat{j} + (a_3 + \lambda b_3)\hat{k}$$
$$\Rightarrow \quad x = a_1 + \lambda b_1;\ y_2 = a_2 + \lambda b_2 \text{ and } z = a_3 + \lambda b_3$$

Cartesian Equation

The cartesian equation of a line passing through a point $A(x_1, y_1, z_1)$ and having direction ratios a, b and c is

$$\boxed{\frac{x - x_1}{a} = \frac{y - y_1}{b} = \frac{z - z_1}{c}}$$

[Symmetrical form]

where, (x, y, z) are coordinates of any point on the line.

If l, m and n are the direction cosines of the line, then equation of the line is

$$\boxed{\frac{x - x_1}{l} = \frac{y - y_1}{m} = \frac{z - z_1}{n}}$$

The cartesian equation of a line passing through origin and having direction ratios (a, b, c) is $\frac{x}{a} = \frac{y}{b} = \frac{z}{c}$.

Note To find the coordinates of any point on the line, consider $\frac{x - x_1}{a} = \frac{y - y_1}{b} = \frac{z - z_1}{c} = \lambda$, where λ is some real number

$\Rightarrow x = a\lambda + x_1$, $y = b\lambda + y_1$ and $z = c\lambda + z_1$. Then, $(x = x_1 + a\lambda, y = y_1 + b\lambda, z = z_1 + c\lambda)$ represent the coordinates of any point on the line.

Method to Convert Vector Equation of Line in Cartesian Form Suppose vector equation of line $\vec{r} = \vec{a} + \lambda \vec{b}$ is given, then to convert it into cartesian form. First, put the values of $\vec{a}$, $\vec{b}$ and $\vec{r} = x\hat{i} + y\hat{j} + z\hat{k}$. Then, compare the coefficients of $\hat{i}$, $\hat{j}$ and $\hat{k}$ from both sides, to get required equation in cartesian form.

Method to Convert Cartesian Equation of a Line in Vector Form First, compare the given equation with $\frac{x - x_1}{a} = \frac{y - y_1}{b} = \frac{z - z_1}{c}$ to get (x_1, y_1, z_1) and a, b, c, then put these values in $\vec{r} = (x_1\hat{i} + y_1\hat{j} + z_1\hat{k}) + \lambda(a\hat{i} + b\hat{j} + c\hat{k})$ and get the required vector equation.

Example 1 Find the vector and the cartesian equations of the line passing through the point (5, 2, – 4) and which is parallel to the vector $5\hat{i} + \hat{j} - 7\hat{k}$.

Sol. Given point is (5, 2, – 4), whose position vector will be $\vec{a} = 5\hat{i} + 2\hat{j} - 4\hat{k}$ and parallel vector is $\vec{b} = 5\hat{i} + \hat{j} - 7\hat{k}$

The required vector equation of line is

$$\vec{r} = 5\hat{i} + 2\hat{j} - 4\hat{k} + \lambda(5\hat{i} + \hat{j} - 7\hat{k})$$

For cartesian equation, write

$$\vec{r} = (5 + 5\lambda)\hat{i} + (2 + \lambda)\hat{j} - (4 + 7\lambda)\hat{k}$$
$$\Rightarrow (x\hat{i} + y\hat{j} + z\hat{k}) = (5 + 5\lambda)\hat{i} + (2 + \lambda)\hat{j} - (4 + 7\lambda)\hat{k}$$

On comparing the coefficients of $\hat{i}$, $\hat{j}$ and $\hat{k}$, we get

$$x = 5 + 5\lambda,\ y = 2 + \lambda \text{ and } z = -(4 + 7\lambda)$$

$$\Rightarrow \quad \frac{x-5}{5}=\lambda, \frac{y-2}{1}=\lambda \text{ and } \frac{z+4}{-7}=\lambda$$

$$\therefore \quad \frac{x-5}{5}=\frac{y-2}{1}=\frac{z+4}{-7}=\lambda$$

Thus, the required cartesian equation of the given line is

$$\frac{x-5}{5}=\frac{y-2}{1}=\frac{z+4}{-7}.$$

Alternate Method

As the given line is parallel to the vector $5\hat{i}+\hat{j}-7\hat{k}$, therefore direction ratios of the given line are 5, 1, – 7.

Now, the equation of line passing through the point $(5, 2, -4)$ and having direction ratios 5, 1, – 7 is

$$\frac{x-5}{5}=\frac{y-2}{1}=\frac{z+4}{-7}.$$

Note In rectangular coordinate system as X, Y and Z-axes passes through the origin, therefore

Equation of X-axis is $\frac{x-0}{1}=\frac{y-0}{0}=\frac{z-0}{0}$

[$\because$ direction cosines of X-axis are (1, 0, 0)]

$\Rightarrow \quad y=0$ and $z=0$

Equation of Y-axis is $\frac{x-0}{0}=\frac{y-0}{1}=\frac{z-0}{0} \Rightarrow x=0$ and $z=0$

and equation of Z-axis is $\frac{x-0}{0}=\frac{y-0}{0}=\frac{z-0}{1} \Rightarrow x=0$ and $y=0$.

Example 2 Find the equation of the lines passing through the point (2, 1, 3) and perpendicular to the lines $\frac{x-1}{1}=\frac{y-2}{2}=\frac{z-3}{3}$ and $\frac{x}{-3}=\frac{y}{2}=\frac{z}{5}$. **[ISC 2019]**

Sol. Given equation of lines are

$$\frac{x-1}{1}=\frac{y-2}{2}=\frac{z-3}{3}, \frac{x}{-3}=\frac{y}{2}=\frac{z}{5}$$

and whose direction ratios

are $< a_1, b_1, c_1 > = < 1, 2, 3 >$

and $< a_2, b_2, c_2 > = < -3, 2, 5 >$.

Now, equation of line passing through (2, 1, 3) and having direction ratios $< a, b, c >$ is

$$\frac{x-2}{a}=\frac{y-1}{b}=\frac{z-3}{c} \quad \text{...(i)}$$

Since, the line (i) is perpendicular to the given lines.

$\therefore \quad aa_1+bb_1+cc_1=0$ and $aa_2+bb_2+cc_2=0$

$\Rightarrow \quad a\times 1+b\times 2+c\times 3=0$

and $\quad a\times(-3)+b\times 2+c\times 5=0$

$\Rightarrow \quad a+2b+3c=0$ and $-3a+2b+5c=0$

Using cross-multiplication, we get

$$\frac{a}{2\times 5-3\times 2}=\frac{-b}{1\times 5-(-3)\times 3}=\frac{c}{1\times 2-(-3)\times 2}$$

$$\Rightarrow \quad \frac{a}{10-6}=-\frac{b}{5+9}=\frac{c}{2+6}=\frac{a}{4}=\frac{b}{-14}=\frac{c}{8}$$

Put the values of a, b and c in Eq. (i), we get

$$\frac{x-2}{4}=\frac{y-1}{-14}=\frac{z-3}{8}$$

or $$\frac{x-2}{2}=\frac{y-1}{-7}=\frac{z-3}{4}$$

Equation of a Line Passing through Two Given Points

Vector Equation

The vector equation of a line passing through two points A and B with position vectors $\vec{a}$ and $\vec{b}$ is given by

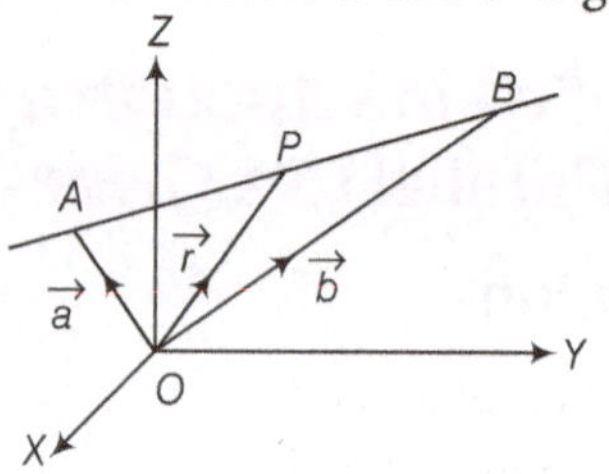

$$\vec{r}=\vec{a}+\lambda(\vec{b}-\vec{a})$$

where, $\vec{r}$ is the position vector of any point P on the line and λ is a real number.

Cartesian Equation

The equation of a line passing through two points $A(x_1, y_1, z_1)$ and $B(x_2, y_2, z_2)$ is given by

$$\frac{x-x_1}{x_2-x_1}=\frac{y-y_1}{y_2-y_1}=\frac{z-z_1}{z_2-z_1}$$

[symmetrical form]

where, (x, y, z) are coordinates of any point on the line.

Example 3 Find the equation of a line passing through the points $P(-1, 3, 2)$ and $Q(-4, 2, -2)$. Also, if the point $R(5, 5, \lambda)$ is collinear with the points P and Q, then find the value of λ. **[ISC 2014]**

Sol. The equation of the line passing through $P(-1, 3, 2)$ and $Q(-4, 2, -2)$ will be $\frac{x+1}{-4+1}=\frac{y-3}{2-3}=\frac{z-2}{-2-2}$

$$\left[\because \frac{x-x_1}{x_2-x_1}=\frac{y-y_1}{y_2-y_1}=\frac{z-z_1}{z_2-z_1}\right]$$

$$\Rightarrow \quad \frac{x+1}{-3}=\frac{y-3}{-1}=\frac{z-2}{-4}$$

$$\Rightarrow \quad \frac{x+1}{3}=\frac{y-3}{1}=\frac{z-2}{4}=r \text{ (say)} \quad \text{[multiplying by } -1]$$

$\therefore$ Any point on the above line PQ is

$(3r-1, r+3, 4r+2)$

Given, the point $R(5, 5, \lambda)$ lies on the line PQ.

$\therefore$ $(3r-1, r+3, 4r+2) = (5, 5, \lambda)$, for some $r \in R$

$\Rightarrow$ $3r - 1 = 5 \Rightarrow 3r = 6 \Rightarrow r = 2$ and $4r + 2 = \lambda$

$\Rightarrow 4 \times 2 + 2 = \lambda \Rightarrow 10 = \lambda$

Hence, the value of λ is 10.

Example 4 Find the cartesian and vector equation for the line passing through the points $A(-1, 1, 2)$ and $B(2, 4, 5)$.

Sol. Given points are $A(x_1, y_1, z_1) = A(-1, 1, 2)$

and $B(x_2, y_2, z_2) = B(2, 4, 5)$

We know that the cartesian equation of a line passing through two points is

$$\frac{x-x_1}{x_2-x_1} = \frac{y-y_1}{y_2-y_1} = \frac{z-z_1}{z_2-z_1}$$

$$\therefore \quad \frac{x-(-1)}{2-(-1)} = \frac{y-1}{4-1} = \frac{z-2}{5-2} \Rightarrow \frac{x+1}{3} = \frac{y-1}{3} = \frac{z-2}{3}$$

or $$\frac{x+1}{1} = \frac{y-1}{1} = \frac{z-2}{1} \qquad \text{...(i)}$$

which is the required cartesian equation of the given line.

To find the vector equation of line, compare Eq. (i) with $\frac{x-x_1}{a} = \frac{y-y_1}{b} = \frac{z-z_1}{c}$, we get

$$x_1 = -1, y_1 = 1, z_1 = 2 \text{ and } a = 1, b = 1, c = 1$$

Now, the required vector equation is given by

$$\vec{r} = (x_1\hat{i} + y_1\hat{j} + z_1\hat{k}) + \lambda(a\hat{i} + b\hat{j} + c\hat{k})$$

$$\therefore \quad \vec{r} = -\hat{i} + \hat{j} + 2\hat{k} + \lambda(\hat{i} + \hat{j} + \hat{k})$$

Angle between Two Lines

Let L_1 and L_2 be two lines and θ be the acute angle between them.

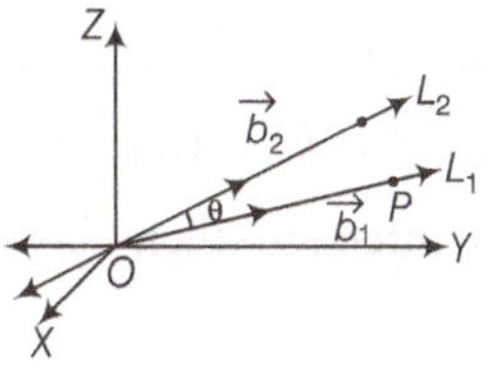

Vector Form

Let the vector equations of lines L_1 and L_2 be $\vec{r} = \vec{a}_1 + \lambda\vec{b}_1$ and $\vec{r} = \vec{a}_2 + \mu\vec{b}_2$, then angle between these two lines is given by

$$\cos\theta = \left|\frac{\vec{b}_1 \cdot \vec{b}_2}{|\vec{b}_1||\vec{b}_2|}\right|$$

where, λ and μ are scalars.

If two lines are perpendicular, then $\vec{b}_1 \cdot \vec{b}_2 = 0$ and if two lines are parallel, then $\vec{b}_1 = \lambda\vec{b}_2$.

Cartesian Form

Let the cartesian equations of lines L_1 and L_2 be

$$\frac{x-x_1}{a_1} = \frac{y-y_1}{b_1} = \frac{z-z_1}{c_1}$$

and $$\frac{x-x_2}{a_2} = \frac{y-y_2}{b_2} = \frac{z-z_2}{c_2}.$$

Then, angle between the lines L_1 and L_2 is given by

$$\cos\theta = \frac{|a_1a_2 + b_1b_2 + c_1c_2|}{\sqrt{a_1^2 + b_1^2 + c_1^2}\sqrt{a_2^2 + b_2^2 + c_2^2}}$$

The angle between the lines in terms of $\sin\theta$ is given by

$$\sin\theta = \frac{\sqrt{(a_1b_2 - a_2b_1)^2 + (b_1c_2 - b_2c_1)^2 + (c_1a_2 - c_2a_1)^2}}{\sqrt{a_1^2 + b_1^2 + c_1^2}\sqrt{a_2^2 + b_2^2 + c_2^2}}$$

where, a_1, b_1, c_1 and a_2, b_2, c_2 are direction ratios of lines L_1 and L_2, respectively.

If two lines are **perpendicular**, then $a_1a_2 + b_1b_2 + c_1c_2 = 0$ and if two lines are **parallel**, then $\frac{a_1}{a_2} = \frac{b_1}{b_2} = \frac{c_1}{c_2}$.

If l_1, m_1, n_1 and l_2, m_2, n_2 are direction cosines of lines L_1 and L_2, then angle between the lines is given by

$$\cos\theta = |l_1l_2 + m_1m_2 + n_1n_2| = |\Sigma l_1l_2|$$

$$[\because l_1^2 + m_1^2 + n_1^2 = 1 = l_2^2 + m_2^2 + n_2^2]$$

and $$\sin\theta = \sqrt{(l_1m_2 - l_2m_1)^2 + (m_1n_2 - m_2n_1)^2 + (n_1l_2 - n_2l_1)^2}$$

$$= \sqrt{\Sigma(l_1m_2 - l_2m_1)^2} \qquad \text{[Lagrange's identity]}$$

Example 5 Find the angle between the lines

(i) $\vec{r} = 2\hat{i} - 5\hat{j} + \hat{k} + \lambda(3\hat{i} + 2\hat{j} + 6\hat{k})$ and $\vec{r} = 7\hat{i} - 6\hat{k} + \mu(\hat{i} + 2\hat{j} + 2\hat{k})$.

(ii) $\frac{x}{2} = \frac{y}{2} = \frac{z}{1}$ and $\frac{x-5}{4} = \frac{y-2}{1} = \frac{z-3}{8}$.

Sol. (i) Given lines are $\vec{r} = 2\hat{i} - 5\hat{j} + \hat{k} + \lambda(3\hat{i} + 2\hat{j} + 6\hat{k})$

and $\vec{r} = 7\hat{i} - 6\hat{k} + \mu(\hat{i} + 2\hat{j} + 2\hat{k})$

On comparing with $\vec{r} = \vec{a_1} + \lambda\vec{b_1}$ and $\vec{r} = \vec{a_2} + \mu\,\vec{b_2}$,
we get $\vec{b_1} = 3\hat{i} + 2\hat{j} + 6\hat{k}$ and $\vec{b_2} = \hat{i} + 2\hat{j} + 2\hat{k}$

∴ The angle between the lines is given by

$$\cos\theta = \left|\frac{\vec{b_1}\cdot\vec{b_2}}{|\vec{b_1}||\vec{b_2}|}\right| = \left|\frac{(3\hat{i}+2\hat{j}+6\hat{k})\cdot(\hat{i}+2\hat{j}+2\hat{k})}{\sqrt{3^2+2^2+6^2}\sqrt{1^2+2^2+2^2}}\right|$$

$$= \left|\frac{3+4+12}{\sqrt{9+4+36}\sqrt{1+4+4}}\right| = \frac{19}{\sqrt{49}\sqrt{9}}$$

$$= \frac{19}{7\times 3} = \frac{19}{21} \Rightarrow \theta = \cos^{-1}\left(\frac{19}{21}\right)$$

(ii) Given equations of lines are $\frac{x}{2} = \frac{y}{2} = \frac{z}{1}$

and $\frac{x-5}{4} = \frac{y-2}{1} = \frac{z-3}{8}$

Here, direction ratios of two lines are (2, 2, 1) and (4, 1, 8).

Let θ be the acute angle between the given lines, then

$$\cos\theta = \frac{|a_1a_2 + b_1b_2 + c_1c_2|}{\sqrt{a_1^2+b_1^2+c_1^2}\sqrt{a_2^2+b_2^2+c_2^2}}$$

$$\Rightarrow \cos\theta = \frac{|2\times 4 + 2\times 1 + 1\times 8|}{\sqrt{2^2+2^2+1^2}\sqrt{4^2+1^2+8^2}}$$

$$= \frac{|8+2+8|}{\sqrt{4+4+1}\sqrt{16+1+64}}$$

$$= \frac{18}{\sqrt{9}\sqrt{81}} = \frac{18}{3\times 9} = \frac{2}{3} \Rightarrow \theta = \cos^{-1}\left(\frac{2}{3}\right)$$

Example 6 Find the equations of the two lines passing through the origin which intersect the line $\frac{x-3}{2} = \frac{y-3}{1} = \frac{z}{1}$ at angles of $\frac{\pi}{3}$ each. **[NCERT Exemplar]**

Sol. Given equation of the line is $\frac{x-3}{2} = \frac{y-3}{1} = \frac{z}{1} = \lambda$ (say)

$$\Rightarrow \quad x = 2\lambda + 3,\ y = \lambda + 3 \text{ and } z = \lambda \quad \text{...(i)}$$

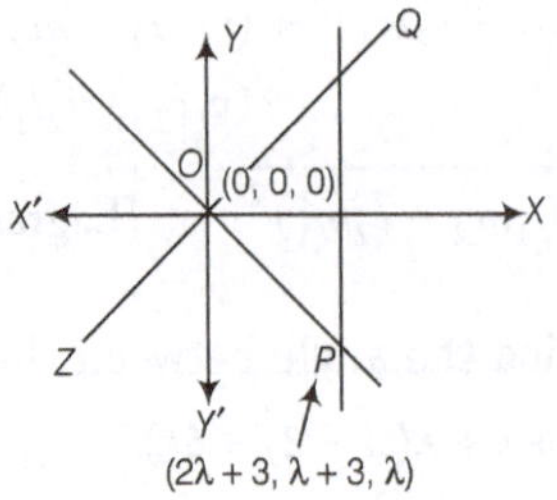

Since, direction ratios of the given line are (2, 1, 1) and the required lines make angle $\frac{\pi}{3}$ with the given line.

$$\therefore \quad \cos\frac{\pi}{3} = \frac{a_1a_2 + b_1b_2 + c_1c_2}{\sqrt{a_1^2+b_1^2+c_1^2}\sqrt{a_2^2+b_2^2+c_2^2}}$$

$$\therefore \quad \cos\frac{\pi}{3} = \frac{2(2\lambda+3) + 1\cdot(\lambda+3) + 1\cdot\lambda}{\sqrt{2^2+1^2+1^2}\sqrt{(2\lambda+3)^2+(\lambda+3)^2+\lambda^2}}$$

[∵ direction ratios of OP are $(2\lambda+3)$, $(\lambda+3)$ and λ]

$$\Rightarrow \quad \frac{1}{2} = \frac{6\lambda+9}{\sqrt{6}\sqrt{4\lambda^2+9+12\lambda+\lambda^2+9+6\lambda+\lambda^2}}$$

$$\Rightarrow \quad \frac{\sqrt{6}}{2} = \frac{6\lambda+9}{\sqrt{6\lambda^2+18\lambda+18}}$$

$$\Rightarrow \quad 6\sqrt{(\lambda^2+3\lambda+3)} = 2(6\lambda+9)$$

$$\Rightarrow \quad 6\sqrt{(\lambda^2+3\lambda+3)} = 6(2\lambda+3)$$

$$\Rightarrow \quad (\lambda^2+3\lambda+3) = (4\lambda^2+9+12\lambda)$$

[squaring on both sides]

$$\Rightarrow \quad 3\lambda^2 + 9\lambda + 6 = 0 \Rightarrow \lambda^2 + 3\lambda + 2 = 0$$

$$\Rightarrow \quad (\lambda+1)(\lambda+2) = 0,\ \lambda = -1, -2$$

So, the direction ratios of required lines are (1, 2, −1) and (−1, 1, −2). [put $\lambda = -1, -2$ in DR's of OP]

Since, the required lines passes through origin.

∴ The equations of required lines are $\frac{x}{1} = \frac{y}{2} = \frac{z}{-1}$

and $\frac{x}{-1} = \frac{y}{1} = \frac{z}{-2}$.

Point of Intersection of Lines

To check whether the two given lines intersect or not and to find point of intersection (if intersect) we follow the following procedure

Vector Form

Let the two lines be

$$\vec{r} = (a_1\hat{i} + a_2\hat{j} + a_3\hat{k}) + \lambda(b_1\hat{i} + b_2\hat{j} + b_3\hat{k}) \quad \text{...(i)}$$

and $$\vec{r} = (a_1'\hat{i} + a_2'\hat{j} + a_3'\hat{k}) + \mu(b_1'\hat{i} + b_2'\hat{j} + b_3'\hat{k}) \quad \text{...(ii)}$$

If Eqs. (i) and (ii) intersect, then they have a common point.

So, we have $(a_1\hat{i} + a_2\hat{j} + a_3\hat{k}) + \lambda(b_1\hat{i} + b_2\hat{j} + b_3\hat{k})$

$$= (a_1'\hat{i} + a_2'\hat{j} + a_3'\hat{k}) + \mu(b_1'\hat{i} + b_2'\hat{j} + b_3'\hat{k})$$

$$\Rightarrow \quad (a_1 + \lambda b_1)\hat{i} + (a_2 + \lambda b_2)\hat{j} + (a_3 + \lambda b_3)\hat{k}$$

$$= (a_1' + \mu b_1')\hat{i} + (a_2' + \mu b_2')\hat{j} + (a_3' + \mu b_3')\hat{k}$$

$$\therefore \quad a_1 + \lambda b_1 = a_1' + \mu b_1',\ a_2 + \lambda b_2 = a_2' + \mu b_2'$$

and $a_3 + \lambda b_3 = a_3' + \mu b_3'$

Now, find the value of λ and μ by solving any two of above equations. If the values of λ and μ satisfy the third equation, then the two lines intersect, otherwise not. If intersect, then the point of intersection can be obtain by substituting the value of λ (or μ) in Eq. (i) [or Eq. (ii)].

Example 7 Show that lines $\vec{r} = (\hat{i} + \hat{j} - \hat{k}) + \lambda(3\hat{i} - \hat{j})$ and $\vec{r} = (4\hat{i} - \hat{k}) + \mu(2\hat{i} + 3\hat{k})$ intersect each other. Find their point of intersection.

Sol. Given lines are $\vec{r} = (\hat{i} + \hat{j} - \hat{k}) + \lambda(3\hat{i} - \hat{j})$ ...(i)

and $\vec{r} = (4\hat{i} - \hat{k}) + \mu(2\hat{i} + 3\hat{k})$ ...(ii)

Clearly, these lines will intersect, if $(\hat{i} + \hat{j} - \hat{k}) + \lambda(3\hat{i} - \hat{j}) = (4\hat{i} - \hat{k}) + \mu(2\hat{i} + 3\hat{k})$, for some particular values of λ and μ.

Collecting the like terms, we get

$$(1 + 3\lambda)\hat{i} + (1 - \lambda)\hat{j} - \hat{k} = (4 + 2\mu)\hat{i} + (-1 + 3\mu)\hat{k}$$

On equating the coefficients of $\hat{i}$, we get

$$1 + 3\lambda = 4 + 2\mu \Rightarrow 3\lambda - 2\mu = 3$$

On equating the coefficients of $\hat{j}$, we get

$$1 - \lambda = 0 \Rightarrow \lambda = 1$$

On equating the coefficients of $\hat{k}$, we get

$$-1 = -1 + 3\mu \Rightarrow \mu = 0$$

$\therefore$ $\mu = 0$ and $\lambda = 1$

Also, these values satisfy $3\lambda - 2\mu = 3$, therefore the given lines intersect.

On putting $\lambda = 1$ in Eq. (i), we get

$$\vec{r} = (\hat{i} + \hat{j} - \hat{k}) + 1(3\hat{i} - \hat{j})$$
$$= 4\hat{i} + 0\hat{j} - \hat{k}$$

Hence, the point of intersection of given lines is $(4, 0, -1)$.

Cartesian Form

Let two lines be $L_1 : \dfrac{x - x_1}{a_1} = \dfrac{y - y_1}{b_1} = \dfrac{z - z_1}{c_1} = \lambda$ (say)

and $L_2 : \dfrac{x - x_2}{a_2} = \dfrac{y - y_2}{b_2} = \dfrac{z - z_2}{c_2} = \mu$ (say)

Consider the coordinates of general points on L_1 and L_2, i.e. $(x_1 + a_1\lambda, y_1 + b_1\lambda, z_1 + c_1\lambda)$ ...(i)

and $(x_2 + a_2\mu, y_2 + b_2\mu, z_2 + c_2\mu)$ ...(ii)

where, λ and μ are some real constants. If the lines L_1 and L_2 intersect, then they have a common point.

$\therefore$ $(x_1 + a_1\lambda, y_1 + b_1\lambda, z_1 + c_1\lambda) = (x_2 + a_2\mu, y_2 + b_2\mu, z_2 + c_2\mu)$

for some constants λ and μ.

$\Rightarrow$ $x_1 + a_1\lambda = x_2 + a_2\mu$,

$y_1 + b_1\lambda = y_2 + b_2\mu$

and $z_1 + c_1\lambda = z_2 + c_2\mu$

Now, find the value of λ and μ by solving any two of above equations. If the values of λ and μ satisfy the third equation, then the two lines intersect, otherwise not. If intersect, then the point of intersection can be obtain by substituting the value of λ(or μ) in Eq. (i) [or Eq. (ii)].

Example 8 Show that the lines $\dfrac{x+1}{3} = \dfrac{y+3}{5} = \dfrac{z+5}{7}$ and $\dfrac{x-2}{1} = \dfrac{y-4}{3} = \dfrac{z-6}{5}$ intersect. Also, find their point of intersection.

Sol. The given lines are

$$\frac{x+1}{3} = \frac{y+3}{5} = \frac{z+5}{7} = \lambda \text{ (let)} \quad ...(i)$$

and $$\frac{x-2}{1} = \frac{y-4}{3} = \frac{z-6}{5} = \mu \text{ (let)} \quad ...(ii)$$

Then, any point on line (i) is

$$P(3\lambda - 1, 5\lambda - 3, 7\lambda - 5) \quad ...(iii)$$

and any point on line (ii) is

$$Q(\mu + 2, 3\mu + 4, 5\mu + 6) \quad ...(iv)$$

Clearly, the lines (i) and (ii) will intersect, if

$$(3\lambda - 1, 5\lambda - 3, 7\lambda - 5) = (\mu + 2, 3\mu + 4, 5\mu + 6),$$

for some particular value of λ and μ.

$\Rightarrow$ $3\lambda - 1 = \mu + 2, 5\lambda - 3 = 3\mu + 4$

and $7\lambda - 5 = 5\mu + 6$

$\Rightarrow$ $3\lambda - \mu = 3,$ ...(v)

$5\lambda - 3\mu = 7$ ...(vi)

and $7\lambda - 5\mu = 11$ ...(vii)

On multiplying Eq. (v) by 3 and then subtracting Eq. (vi) from it, we get

$$9\lambda - 3\mu - 5\lambda + 3\mu = 9 - 7$$

$\Rightarrow$ $4\lambda = 2 \Rightarrow \lambda = \dfrac{1}{2}$

On putting the value of λ in Eq. (v), we get

$$3 \times \frac{1}{2} - \mu = 3$$

$\Rightarrow$ $\dfrac{3}{2} - \mu = 3 \Rightarrow \mu = -\dfrac{3}{2}$

On putting the values of λ and μ in Eq. (vii), we get

$$7 \times \frac{1}{2} - 5\left(-\frac{3}{2}\right) = 11$$

$\Rightarrow$ $\dfrac{7}{2} + \dfrac{15}{2} = 11 \Rightarrow \dfrac{22}{2} = 11$

$\Rightarrow$ $11 = 11$, which is true.

Hence, lines (i) and (ii) intersect and their point of intersection is

$$P\left(3 \times \frac{1}{2} - 1, 5 \times \frac{1}{2} - 3, 7 \times \frac{1}{2} - 5\right) \quad \left[\text{put } \lambda = \frac{1}{2} \text{ in Eq. (iii)}\right]$$

i.e. $P\left(\dfrac{1}{2}, -\dfrac{1}{2}, -\dfrac{3}{2}\right)$.

Shortest Distance between Two Lines

Two lines in space will be one of the following forms

(i) Intersecting (ii) Parallel

(iii) Neither parallel nor intersecting

If two lines in space intersect at a point, then the shortest distance between them is zero. If two lines in space are parallel, then the shortest distance between them will be the perpendicular distance, i.e. the length of the perpendicular drawn from a point on one line onto the other line.

Coplanar and Skew-Lines

Two lines lying in the same plane are called **coplanar lines** and these lines are either parallel or intersecting. If two lines are neither intersecting nor parallel, then such pair of lines are **non-coplanar** and are called **skew-lines.**

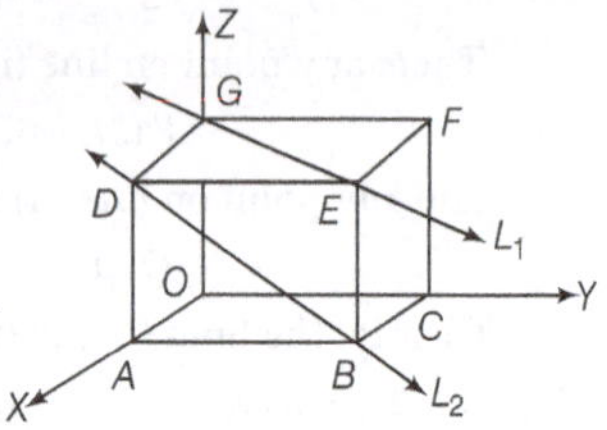

In the given figure, line GE (lie in ceiling $DEFG$) and BD (lie in wall $ABED$) are skew-lines, since they are not parallel and also never meet.

Shortest Distance between Two Skew-Lines

For skew-lines, **the line of shortest distance** will be perpendicular to both the lines and it is unique also.

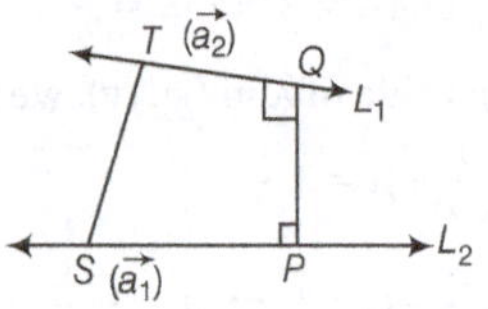

In the figure, the shortest distance between two skew-lines L_1 and L_2 is the length of the line segment PQ .

Vector Form

Let the equations of L_1 and L_2 be $\vec{r} = \vec{a_1} + \lambda \vec{b_1}$ and $\vec{r} = \vec{a_2} + \mu \vec{b_2}$. Then, shortest distance PQ between these two skew-lines is

$$SD = \frac{\left|(\vec{a_2} - \vec{a_1}) \cdot (\vec{b_1} \times \vec{b_2})\right|}{|\vec{b_1} \times \vec{b_2}|}$$

Condition for Two Given Lines to be Intersect The given lines $\vec{r} = \vec{a_1} + \lambda \vec{b_1}$ and $\vec{r} = \vec{a_2} + \mu \vec{b_2}$ will intersect, if the shortest distance between them is zero.

i.e. $$\frac{\left|(\vec{a_2} - \vec{a_1}) \cdot (\vec{b_1} \times \vec{b_2})\right|}{|\vec{b_1} \times \vec{b_2}|} = 0$$

$$\Rightarrow \quad (\vec{a_2} - \vec{a_1}) \cdot (\vec{b_1} \times \vec{b_2}) = 0$$

Method to Find the Shortest Distance

Let two lines be $\vec{r} = \vec{a_1} + \vec{b_1}\lambda$ and $\vec{r} = \vec{a_2} + \vec{b_2}\mu$, which are the standard equations of lines.

Then, for finding the shortest distance between the two lines, we use the following steps

I. First, check whether the given equations are in standard form or not. If they are not in standard form, then write them in standard form.

II. Find $\vec{a_1}, \vec{a_2}, \vec{b_1}$ and $\vec{b_2}$ by comparing with standard form, say

$$\vec{a_1} = a_1'\hat{i} + a_2'\hat{j} + a_3'\hat{k},\ \vec{b_1} = b_1'\hat{i} + b_2'\hat{j} + b_3'\hat{k}$$

and $$\vec{a_2} = a_1''\hat{i} + a_2''\hat{j} + a_3''\hat{k}, \vec{b_2} = b_1''\hat{i} + b_2''\hat{j} + b_3''\hat{k}.$$

III. Compute the value of $\vec{b_1} \times \vec{b_2}$ by using the formula

$$\vec{b_1} \times \vec{b_2} = \begin{vmatrix} \hat{i} & \hat{j} & \hat{k} \\ b_1' & b_2' & b_3' \\ b_1'' & b_2'' & b_3'' \end{vmatrix}$$

$$= \hat{i}(b_2'b_3'' - b_3'b_2'') - \hat{j}(b_1'b_3'' - b_3'b_1'') + \hat{k}(b_1'b_2'' - b_2'b_1'')$$

IV. Determine the value of $\vec{a_2} - \vec{a_1}$ and $|\vec{b_1} \times \vec{b_2}|$.

V. Now, put the values obtained in steps III and IV in shortest distance formula

i.e. $$SD = \frac{\left|(\vec{a_2} - \vec{a_1}) \cdot (\vec{b_1} \times \vec{b_2})\right|}{|\vec{b_1} \times \vec{b_2}|}$$

and simplify it to get the required shortest distance.

Example 9 Find the shortest distance between the lines $\vec{r} = (t+1)\hat{i} + (2-t)\hat{j} + (1+t)3\hat{k}$ and $\vec{r} = (2s+2)\hat{i} - (1-s)\hat{j} + (2s-1)3\hat{k}$.

Sol. Given lines are $\vec{r} = (t+1)\hat{i} + (2-t)\hat{j} + (1+t)3\hat{k}$

and $\vec{r} = (2s+2)\hat{i} - (1-s)\hat{j} + (2s-1)3\hat{k}$

Clearly, the given equations are not in standard form. Let us write these equations in standard form, i.e.

$$\vec{r} = (\hat{i} + 2\hat{j} + 3\hat{k}) + t(\hat{i} - \hat{j} + 3\hat{k}) \quad \text{...(i)}$$

$$\vec{r} = (2\hat{i} - \hat{j} - 3\hat{k}) + s(2\hat{i} + \hat{j} + 6\hat{k}) \quad \text{...(ii)}$$

On comparing Eqs. (i) and (ii) with $\vec{r} = \vec{a}_1 + \lambda \vec{b}_1$ and $\vec{r} = \vec{a}_2 + \mu \vec{b}_2$, we get

Let $\vec{a}_1 = \hat{i} + 2\hat{j} + 3\hat{k}$, $\vec{b}_1 = \hat{i} - \hat{j} + 3\hat{k}$,

$\vec{a}_2 = 2\hat{i} - \hat{j} - 3\hat{k}$ and $\vec{b}_2 = 2\hat{i} + \hat{j} + 6\hat{k}$.

Then, $\vec{a}_2 - \vec{a}_1 = \hat{i} - 3\hat{j} - 6\hat{k}$

We know that $\vec{b}_1 \times \vec{b}_2 = \begin{vmatrix} \hat{i} & \hat{j} & \hat{k} \\ 1 & -1 & 3 \\ 2 & 1 & 6 \end{vmatrix} = -9\hat{i} + 3\hat{k}$

$$\therefore \text{Shortest distance} = \left| \frac{(\vec{b}_1 \times \vec{b}_2)\cdot(\vec{a}_2 - \vec{a}_1)}{|\vec{b}_1 \times \vec{b}_2|} \right|$$

$$= \left| \frac{-9-18}{\sqrt{81+9}} \right| = \frac{27}{3\sqrt{10}} = \frac{9\sqrt{10}}{10}$$

Example 10 Find the shortest distance between the lines $\vec{r} = (1+\lambda)\hat{i} + (2-3\lambda)\hat{j} + (3+2\lambda)\hat{k}$ and $\vec{r} = (4\hat{i} + 5\hat{j} + 6\hat{k}) + \mu(2\hat{i} + 3\hat{j} + \hat{k})$. **[NCERT]**

Sol. Given lines are $\vec{r} = (1+\lambda)\hat{i} + (2-3\lambda)\hat{j} + (3+2\lambda)\hat{k}$ ...(i)

and $\vec{r} = (4\hat{i} + 5\hat{j} + 6\hat{k}) + \mu(2\hat{i} + 3\hat{j} + \hat{k})$. ...(ii)

Clearly, first equation is not in standard form. Let us write first equation of line in standard form, i.e.

$$\vec{r} = (\hat{i} + 2\hat{j} + 3\hat{k}) + \lambda(\hat{i} - 3\hat{j} + 2\hat{k}) \quad \text{...(iii)}$$

On comparing Eqs. (iii) and (ii) with $\vec{r} = a_1 + \lambda b_1$ and $\vec{r} = a_2 + \mu b_2$ respectively, we get

$$\vec{a}_1 = \hat{i} + 2\hat{j} + 3\hat{k},\ \vec{b}_1 = \hat{i} - 3\hat{j} + 2\hat{k}$$

and $\vec{a}_2 = 4\hat{i} + 5\hat{j} + 6\hat{k},\ \vec{b}_2 = 2\hat{i} + 3\hat{j} + \hat{k}$

Clearly, $\vec{b}_1 \times \vec{b}_2 = \begin{vmatrix} \hat{i} & \hat{j} & \hat{k} \\ 1 & -3 & 2 \\ 2 & 3 & 1 \end{vmatrix}$

$$= \hat{i}(-3-6) - \hat{j}(1-4) + \hat{k}(3+6)$$

$$= -9\hat{i} + 3\hat{j} + 9\hat{k}$$

$\Rightarrow$ $|\vec{b}_1 \times \vec{b}_2| = |-9\hat{i} + 3\hat{j} + 9\hat{k}| = \sqrt{(-9)^2 + (3)^2 + (9)^2}$

$$= \sqrt{81+9+81} = \sqrt{171} = 3\sqrt{19}$$

Now, $\vec{a}_2 - \vec{a}_1 = (4\hat{i} + 5\hat{j} + 6\hat{k}) - (\hat{i} + 2\hat{j} + 3\hat{k})$

$$= 3\hat{i} + 3\hat{j} + 3\hat{k}$$

$$\text{Required SD} = \frac{|(\vec{a}_2 - \vec{a}_1)\cdot(\vec{b}_1 \times \vec{b}_2)|}{|\vec{b}_1 \times \vec{b}_2|}$$

$$= \frac{|(3\hat{i} + 3\hat{j} + 3\hat{k})\cdot(-9\hat{i} + 3\hat{j} + 9\hat{k})|}{3\sqrt{19}}$$

$$= \frac{|-27+9+27|}{3\sqrt{19}} = \frac{9}{3\sqrt{19}} = \frac{3}{\sqrt{19}} \text{ units}$$

which is the required shortest distance.

Cartesian Form

Let L_1 and L_2 be two skew-lines with equations

$$L_1: \frac{x - x_1}{a_1} = \frac{y - y_1}{b_1} = \frac{z - z_1}{c_1}$$

and $$L_2: \frac{x - x_2}{a_2} = \frac{y - y_2}{b_2} = \frac{z - z_2}{c_2}$$

Then, the shortest distance between these lines is

$$\left| \frac{\begin{vmatrix} x_2 - x_1 & y_2 - y_1 & z_2 - z_1 \\ a_1 & b_1 & c_1 \\ a_2 & b_2 & c_2 \end{vmatrix}}{\sqrt{(b_1c_2 - b_2c_1)^2 + (c_1a_2 - c_2a_1)^2 + (a_1b_2 - a_2b_1)^2}} \right|$$

Condition for Two Given Lines to be Intersect Let the two lines be

$$L_1: \frac{x - x_1}{a_1} = \frac{y - y_1}{b_1} = \frac{z - z_1}{c_1}$$

and $$L_2: \frac{x - x_2}{a_2} = \frac{y - y_2}{b_2} = \frac{z - z_2}{c_2}.$$

The lines L_1 and L_2 will intersect, if the shortest distance between them is zero.

i.e. $$\begin{vmatrix} x_2 - x_1 & y_2 - y_1 & z_2 - z_1 \\ a_1 & b_1 & c_1 \\ a_2 & b_2 & c_2 \end{vmatrix} = 0$$

Method to Find the Shortest Distance

Suppose two lines $\frac{x - x_1}{a_1} = \frac{y - y_1}{b_1} = \frac{z - z_1}{c_1}$ and $\frac{x - x_2}{a_2} = \frac{y - y_2}{b_2} = \frac{z - z_2}{c_2}$ are given to us, then for finding the shortest distance between these lines, we use the following steps

I. First, check whether the given equations are in standard form or not. If they are not in standard form, then write them in standard form.

II. Find $x_1, y_1, z_1; x_2, y_2, z_2; a_1, b_1, c_1$ and a_2, b_2, c_2 by comparing the given equations with standard equation of lines.

III. Compute the value of the determinant
$$\begin{vmatrix} x_2-x_1 & y_2-y_1 & z_2-z_1 \\ a_1 & b_1 & c_1 \\ a_2 & b_2 & c_2 \end{vmatrix}$$
by expanding along R_1 or C_1.

IV. Compute the value of
$$\sqrt{(b_1c_2-b_2c_1)^2+(c_1a_2-c_2a_1)^2+(a_1b_2-a_2b_1)^2}.$$

V. Put the values obtained in steps III and IV in shortest distance formula, i.e.
$$SD = \left| \frac{\begin{vmatrix} x_2-x_1 & y_2-y_1 & z_2-z_1 \\ a_1 & b_1 & c_1 \\ a_2 & b_2 & c_2 \end{vmatrix}}{\sqrt{(b_1c_2-b_2c_1)^2+(c_1a_2-c_2a_1)^2+(a_1b_2-a_2b_1)^2}} \right|$$
and simplify it to get required shortest distance.

Note If direction cosines of the lines are given, i.e. (l_1, m_1, n_1) and (l_2, m_2, n_2), then replace (a_1, b_1, c_1) by (l_1, m_1, n_1) and (a_2, b_2, c_2) by (l_2, m_2, n_2) in the above formula to find shortest distance.

Example 11 Find the shortest distance between the lines $\frac{1-x}{-2} = \frac{2-y}{-3} = \frac{z-3}{4}$ and $\frac{x-2}{3} = \frac{y-4}{4} = \frac{z-5}{5}$.

Sol. Given lines are $\frac{1-x}{-2} = \frac{2-y}{-3} = \frac{z-3}{4}$

and $\frac{x-2}{3} = \frac{y-4}{4} = \frac{z-5}{5}$ which are not in standard form.

Given equations of lines can be written in standard form as
$$\frac{x-1}{2} = \frac{y-2}{3} = \frac{z-3}{4} \text{ and } \frac{x-2}{3} = \frac{y-4}{4} = \frac{z-5}{5}$$

On comparing the given equations of lines with
$$\frac{x-x_1}{a_1} = \frac{y-y_1}{b_1} = \frac{z-z_1}{c_1} \text{ and } \frac{x-x_2}{a_2} = \frac{y-y_2}{b_2} = \frac{z-z_2}{c_2},$$

we get $x_1 = 1, y_1 = 2, z_1 = 3; a_1 = 2, b_1 = 3, c_1 = 4$

and $x_2 = 2, y_2 = 4, z_2 = 5; a_2 = 3, b_2 = 4, c_2 = 5$

On putting these values in $\begin{vmatrix} x_2-x_1 & y_2-y_1 & z_2-z_1 \\ a_1 & b_1 & c_1 \\ a_2 & b_2 & c_2 \end{vmatrix}$,

we get $\begin{vmatrix} 2-1 & 4-2 & 5-3 \\ 2 & 3 & 4 \\ 3 & 4 & 5 \end{vmatrix} = \begin{vmatrix} 1 & 2 & 2 \\ 2 & 3 & 4 \\ 3 & 4 & 5 \end{vmatrix}$

$= 1(15-16) - 2(10-12) + 2(8-9) = -1 + 4 - 2 = 1$

Now, $\sqrt{(b_1c_2-b_2c_1)^2+(c_1a_2-c_2a_1)^2+(a_1b_2-a_2b_1)^2}$

$= \sqrt{(3\times5-4\times4)^2+(4\times3-5\times2)^2+(2\times4-3\times3)^2}$

$= \sqrt{(15-16)^2+(12-10)^2+(8-9)^2}$

$= \sqrt{(-1)^2+(2)^2+(-1)^2} = \sqrt{1+4+1} = \sqrt{6}$

$$\therefore \quad SD = \left| \frac{\begin{vmatrix} x_2-x_1 & y_2-y_1 & z_2-z_1 \\ a_1 & b_1 & c_1 \\ a_2 & b_2 & c_2 \end{vmatrix}}{\sqrt{(b_1c_2-b_2c_1)^2+(c_1a_2-c_2a_1)^2+(a_1b_2-a_2b_1)^2}} \right|,$$

$= \frac{1}{\sqrt{6}}$ units, which is the required shortest distance.

Example 12 Prove that the lines
$$\frac{x-2}{1} = \frac{y-4}{4} = \frac{z-6}{7} \text{ and } \frac{x+1}{3} = \frac{y+3}{5} = \frac{z+5}{7}$$
are coplanar.

Sol. Given lines are
$$\frac{x-2}{1} = \frac{y-4}{4} = \frac{z-6}{7} \text{ and } \frac{x+1}{3} = \frac{y+3}{5} = \frac{z+5}{7}$$

On comparing these with $\frac{x-x_1}{a_1} = \frac{y-y_1}{b_1} = \frac{z-z_1}{c_1}$ and $\frac{x-x_2}{a_2} = \frac{y-y_2}{b_2} = \frac{z-z_2}{c_2}$, we get

$x_1 = 2, y_1 = 4, z_1 = 6,$
$a_1 = 1, b_1 = 4, c_1 = 7$

and $x_2 = -1, y_2 = -3, z_2 = -5,$
$a_2 = 3, b_2 = 5, c_2 = 7$

Since, DR's of given lines are not proportional so they cannot be parallel to each other.

Now, these lines are coplanar, if
$$\begin{vmatrix} x_2-x_1 & y_2-y_1 & z_2-z_1 \\ a_1 & b_1 & c_1 \\ a_2 & b_2 & c_2 \end{vmatrix} = 0$$

Consider, $\begin{vmatrix} -1-2 & -3-4 & -5-6 \\ 1 & 4 & 7 \\ 3 & 5 & 7 \end{vmatrix} = \begin{vmatrix} -3 & -7 & -11 \\ 1 & 4 & 7 \\ 3 & 5 & 7 \end{vmatrix}$

$= \begin{vmatrix} 3 & 7 & 11 \\ 3 & 5 & 7 \\ 1 & 4 & 7 \end{vmatrix}$

[taking negative sign common from R_1 and interchanging R_2 and R_3]

$= 3(35-28) - 7(21-7) + 11(12-5)$ [expanding along R_1]

$= 21 - 98 + 77 = 0$

Hence, the given lines are coplanar.

Distance between Parallel Lines

If two lines L_1 and L_2 are parallel, then they are coplanar.

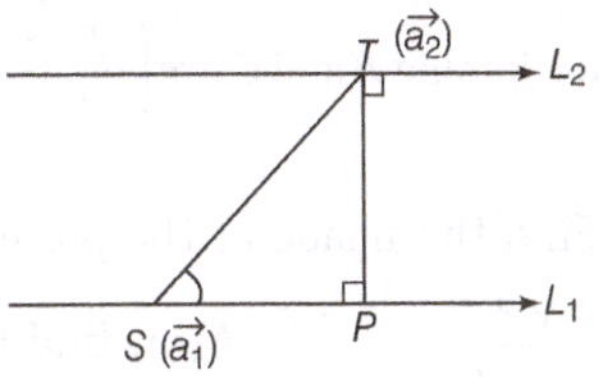

Then, shortest distance TP between parallel lines

$L_1: \vec{r} = \vec{a_1} + \lambda \vec{b}$ and $L_2: \vec{r} = \vec{a_2} + \mu \vec{b}$ is

$$d = |\overrightarrow{PT}| = \left|\frac{\vec{b} \times (\vec{a_2} - \vec{a_1})}{|\vec{b}|}\right|$$

Note To find the distance between two lines, first check whether they are parallel or not.

Example 13 Find the vector equation of the line passing through the point (−1, 2, 1) and parallel to the line $\vec{r} = 2\hat{i} + 3\hat{j} - \hat{k} + \lambda(\hat{i} - 2\hat{j} + \hat{k})$. Also, find the distance between these lines. **[ISC 2011]**

Sol. Given line is $\vec{r} = (2\hat{i} + 3\hat{j} - \hat{k}) + \lambda(\hat{i} - 2\hat{j} + \hat{k})$ ...(i)

Equation of line parallel to line (i) and passing through $(-1, 2, 1)$ is $\vec{r} = (-\hat{i} + 2\hat{j} + \hat{k}) + \mu(\hat{i} - 2\hat{j} + \hat{k})$ ...(ii)

On comparing Eqs. (i) and (ii) with

$$\vec{r} = \vec{a_1} + \lambda\vec{b} \text{ and } \vec{r} = \vec{a_2} + \mu\vec{b},$$

we get $\vec{a_1} = 2\hat{i} + 3\hat{j} - \hat{k}$, $\vec{a_2} = -\hat{i} + 2\hat{j} + \hat{k}$

and $\vec{b} = \hat{i} - 2\hat{j} + \hat{k}$

Now, $\vec{a_2} - \vec{a_1} = (-\hat{i} + 2\hat{j} + \hat{k}) - (2\hat{i} + 3\hat{j} - \hat{k}) = -3\hat{i} - \hat{j} + 2\hat{k}$

Now, $(\vec{a_2} - \vec{a_1}) \times \vec{b} = (-3\hat{i} - \hat{j} + 2\hat{k}) \times (\hat{i} - 2\hat{j} + \hat{k})$

$$= \begin{vmatrix} \hat{i} & \hat{j} & \hat{k} \\ -3 & -1 & 2 \\ 1 & -2 & 1 \end{vmatrix}$$

$$= (-1 + 4)\hat{i} - (-3 - 2)\hat{j} + (6 + 1)\hat{k}$$

$$= 3\hat{i} + 5\hat{j} + 7\hat{k}$$

∴ Shortest distance between the lines (i) and (ii)

$$= \frac{|(\vec{a_2} - \vec{a_1}) \times \vec{b}|}{|\vec{b}|} = \frac{|3\hat{i} + 5\hat{j} + 7\hat{k}|}{|\hat{i} - 2\hat{j} + \hat{k}|}$$

$$= \frac{\sqrt{9 + 25 + 49}}{\sqrt{1 + 4 + 1}} = \frac{\sqrt{83}}{\sqrt{6}} \text{ units}$$

Distance of a Point From a Line

Vector Form

To determine the perpendicular distance from a given point $P(\vec{\alpha})$ to a given line $\vec{r} = \vec{a} + \lambda\vec{b}$ we follow the following procedure

Let L be the foot of perpendicular drawn from the point $P(\vec{\alpha})$ on the given line and then the position vector of L will be $\vec{a} + \lambda\vec{b}$, for same $\lambda \in R$.

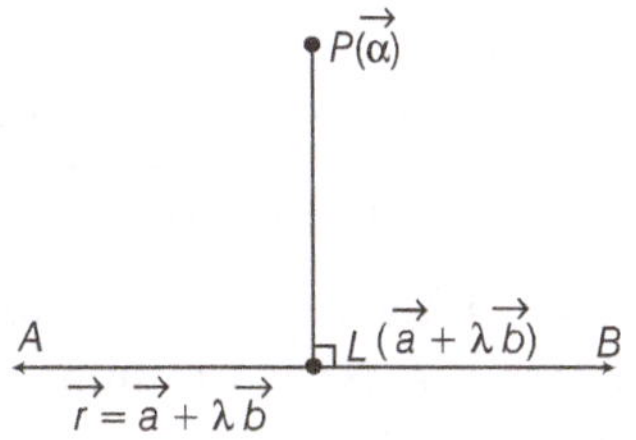

Now, $\overrightarrow{PL} = \vec{a} + \lambda\vec{b} - \vec{\alpha} = \vec{a} - \vec{\alpha} + \lambda\vec{b}$.

Since, $\overrightarrow{PL}$ is perpendicular to the line which is parallel to $\vec{b}$.

Therefore, $\overrightarrow{PL} \cdot \vec{b} = 0$

$$\Rightarrow \quad (\vec{a} - \vec{\alpha} + \lambda\vec{b}) \cdot \vec{b} = 0$$

$$\Rightarrow \quad (\vec{a} - \vec{\alpha}) \cdot \vec{b} + \lambda(\vec{b} \cdot \vec{b}) = 0$$

$$\Rightarrow \quad \lambda = -\frac{(\vec{a} - \vec{\alpha}) \cdot \vec{b}}{|\vec{b}|^2}$$

On substituting the value of λ in $\vec{a} + \lambda\vec{b}$ and $\overrightarrow{PL} = \vec{a} - \vec{\alpha} + \lambda\vec{b}$, we obtain the position vector of L and vector $\overrightarrow{PL}$. The magnitude of $\overrightarrow{PL}$ gives the length of perpendicular.

Cartesian Form

To determine the perpendicular distance from a given point $P(\alpha, \beta, \gamma)$ to a given line

$$\frac{x - x_1}{a} = \frac{y - y_1}{b} = \frac{z - z_1}{c} = \lambda \text{ (say)}$$

we follow the following procedure

Let L be the foot of the perpendicular drawn from $P(\alpha, \beta, \gamma)$ on the given line and then the coordinate of L will be $(x_1 + a\lambda, y_1 + b\lambda, z_1 + c\lambda)$, for some $\lambda \in R$.

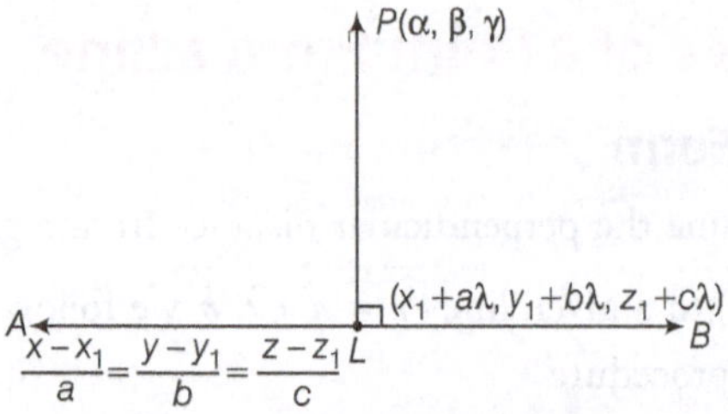

Clearly, direction ratios of AB are a, b, c and direction ratios of PL are $(x_1 + a\lambda - \alpha,\ y_1 + b\lambda - \beta,\ z_1 + c\lambda - \gamma)$. Since, PL is perpendicular to AB, therefore

$(x_1 + a\lambda - \alpha)a + (y_1 + b\lambda - \beta)b + (z_1 + c\lambda - \gamma)c = 0.$

After simplifying, we get

$$\lambda = \frac{[a(\alpha - x_1) + b(\beta - y_1) + c(\gamma - z_1)]}{a^2 + b^2 + c^2}$$

On putting the value of λ in $(x_1 + a\lambda, y_1 + b\lambda, z_1 + c\lambda)$, we obtain coordinates of L. Now, we can find the length of PL using distance formula.

Example 14 Find the coordinates of the foot of perpendicular drawn from a point $A(1, 8, 4)$ to the line joining the points $B(0, -1, 3)$ and $C(2, -3, -1)$.

Sol. Let D be the foot of perpendicular drawn from A to the line BC.

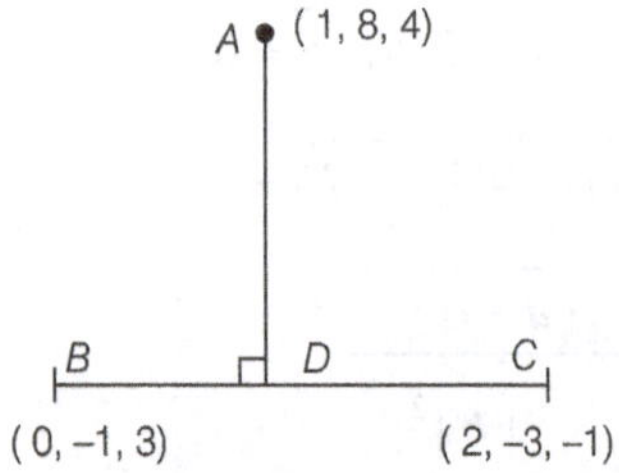

Now, equation of line passing through B and C is

$$\frac{x}{2} = \frac{y+1}{-2} = \frac{z-3}{-4} \text{ or } \frac{x}{1} = \frac{y+1}{-1} = \frac{z-3}{-2}$$

$$\left[\because \frac{x - x_1}{x_2 - x_1} = \frac{y - y_1}{y_2 - y_1} = \frac{z - z_1}{z_2 - z_1}\right]$$

Now, let $\frac{x}{1} = \frac{y+1}{-1} = \frac{z-3}{-2} = \lambda$

$\Rightarrow \quad x = \lambda,\ y = -\lambda - 1$ and $z = -2\lambda + 3$

So, coordinates of D are $(\lambda, -\lambda - 1, -2\lambda + 3)$ for some value of λ.

Now, direction ratios of line AD are

$$< \lambda - 1, -\lambda - 9, -2\lambda - 1 >$$

As, $AD \perp BC$

$\therefore \quad 1(\lambda - 1) - 1(-\lambda - 9) - 2(-2\lambda - 1) = 0 \Rightarrow \lambda = -\frac{5}{3}$

Now, the coordinates of D are $\left(-\frac{5}{3}, \frac{2}{3}, \frac{19}{3}\right)$.

Hence, the coordinates of foot of perpendicular drawn from A to line joining B and C are $\left(-\frac{5}{3}, \frac{2}{3}, \frac{19}{3}\right)$.

Example 15 Find the image of the point $(2, -1, 5)$ in the line $\frac{x-11}{10} = \frac{y+2}{-4} = \frac{z+8}{-11}$. Also, find the length of the perpendicular from the point $(2, -1, 5)$ to the line. **[ISC 2016]**

Sol. Given line is $\frac{x-11}{10} = \frac{y+2}{-4} = \frac{z+8}{-11} = \lambda$ (say) ...(i)

Any point on line (i) is $(10\lambda + 11, -4\lambda - 2, -11\lambda - 8)$.

Let N be the foot of perpendicular drawn from the point $P(2, -1, 5)$ to the line (i).

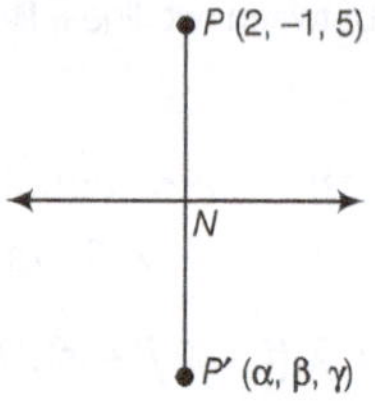

Then, the coordinates of N be $(10\lambda + 11, -4\lambda - 2, -11\lambda - 8)$ for some λ.

Now, we need to find a suitable value of λ so that this point becomes N.

Clearly, direction number of NP are

$< 10\lambda + 11 - 2, -4\lambda - 2 + 1, -11\lambda - 8 - 5 >$

i.e. $\quad < 10\lambda + 9, -4\lambda - 1, -11\lambda - 13 >$

and direction number of the line (i) are $< 10, -4, -11 >$.

$\because NP$ is perpendicular to the given line.

$\therefore \quad 10(10\lambda + 9) - 4(-4\lambda - 1) - 11(-11\lambda - 13) = 0$

$\Rightarrow \quad 100\lambda + 90 + 16\lambda + 4 + 121\lambda + 143 = 0$

$\Rightarrow \quad 237\lambda + 237 = 0 \Rightarrow \lambda = -1$

On substituting the value of λ in the coordinate of point N, we get $(1, 2, 3)$.

Let image of point $P(2, -1, 5)$ in the line (i) be $P'(\alpha, \beta, \gamma)$.

Then, point N be the mid-point of PP'.

$\therefore \quad 1 = \frac{2+\alpha}{2},\ 2 = \frac{-1+\beta}{2},\ 3 = \frac{5+\gamma}{2}$

$\Rightarrow \alpha = 0, \beta = 5, \gamma = 1$

Hence, image of point $P(2, -1, 5)$ is $P'(0, 5, 1)$.

Now, the required length of perpendicular of

$$NP = \sqrt{(1-2)^2 + (2+1)^2 + (3-5)^2}$$
$$= \sqrt{1^2 + 3^2 + 2^2} = \sqrt{14}$$

Topic Practice 2

Very Short Answer Type Questions

(2 Marks)

1 Find the direction cosines of the line
$$\frac{4-x}{2}=\frac{y}{6}=\frac{1-z}{3}.$$

2 The equation of a line is $5x-3=15y+7=3-10z$. Write the direction cosines of the line.

3 If the equation of line AB is $\frac{3-x}{1}=\frac{y+2}{-2}=\frac{z-5}{4}$, then write the direction ratios of line parallel to above line AB.

4 Find the cartesian equation of the line which passes through the point $(-2,4,-5)$ and is parallel to the line $\frac{x+3}{3}=\frac{4-y}{5}=\frac{z+8}{6}$.

5 If the cartesian equation of a line is $\frac{3-x}{5}=\frac{y+4}{7}=\frac{2z-6}{4}$, then write the vector equation for the line.

6 A line passes through the point with position vector $2\hat{i}-3\hat{j}+4\hat{k}$ and makes angles 60°, 120° and 45° with X, Y and Z-axes, respectively. Find the equation of the line in the cartesian form.

7 The cartesian equation of a line is $2x-3=3y+1=5-6z$. Find the vector equation of a line passing through $(7,-5,0)$ and parallel to the given line. **[ISC 2018]**

8 Find the vector equation of the line passing through the point $A(1,2,-1)$ and parallel to the line $5x-25=14-7y=35z$.

9 Find the vector equation of the line which is parallel to the vector $3\hat{i}-2\hat{j}+6\hat{k}$ and which passes through the point $(1,-2,3)$. **[NCERT Exemplar]**

10 The x-coordinate of a point on the line joining the points $P(2,2,1)$ and $Q(5,1,-2)$ is 4. Find its z-coordinate.

11 Find the cartesian equation of line that passing through the points $(1,-1,3)$ and $(3,4,-2)$.

12 Find the vector equation of line passing through the points $(1,-1,2)$ and $(3,2,1)$.

13 Prove that the lines $x=py+q$, $z=ry+s$ and $x=p'y+q'$, $z=r'y+s'$ are perpendicular, if $pp'+rr'+1=0$. **[NCERT Exemplar]**

Short Answer Type Questions

(4 Marks)

14 Find the points on the line $\frac{x+2}{3}=\frac{y+1}{2}=\frac{z-3}{2}$ at a distance of 5 units from the point $P(1,3,3)$.

15 The cartesian equations of a line is $6x-2=3y+1=2z-2$. Find the direction cosines of the line. Write down the cartesian and vector equations of a line passing through the point $(2,-1,-1)$ which are parallel to the given line.

16 Find the direction cosines of the line $\frac{x+2}{2}=\frac{2y-7}{6}=\frac{5-z}{6}$. Also, find the vector equation of the line through the point $A(-1,2,3)$ and parallel to the given line.

17 A line passes through the point $(2,-1,3)$ and is perpendicular to the lines $\vec{r}=(\hat{i}+\hat{j}-\hat{k})+\lambda(2\hat{i}-2\hat{j}+\hat{k})$ and $\vec{r}=(2\hat{i}-\hat{j}-3\hat{k})+\mu(\hat{i}+2\hat{j}+2\hat{k})$. Obtain its equation in vector forms. **[ISC 2023]**

18 Find the angle between the pair of lines given by $\vec{r}=3\hat{i}+2\hat{j}-4\hat{k}+\lambda(\hat{i}+2\hat{j}+2\hat{k})$ and $\vec{r}=5\hat{i}-2\hat{j}+\mu(3\hat{i}+2\hat{j}+6\hat{k})$.

19 Find the angle between the pair of lines $\frac{-x+2}{-2}=\frac{y-1}{7}=\frac{z+3}{-3}$ and $\frac{x+2}{-1}=\frac{2y-8}{4}=\frac{z-5}{4}$ and check whether the lines are parallel or perpendicular.

20 Find the angle between the lines $2x=3y=-z$ and $6x=-y=-4z$.

21 Find the value of p so that the lines $\frac{1-x}{3}=\frac{7y-14}{2p}=\frac{z-3}{1}$ and $\frac{7-7x}{3p}=\frac{5-y}{1}=\frac{11-z}{7}$ are at right angles.

22 By computing shortest distance, determine whether the following pair of lines intersect or not $\vec{r}=(4\hat{i}+5\hat{j})+\lambda(\hat{i}+2\hat{j}-3\hat{k})$ and
$$\vec{r}=(\hat{i}-\hat{j}+2\hat{k})+\mu(2\hat{i}+4\hat{j}-5\hat{k}).$$

23 Find the shortest distance between the lines $\frac{x-3}{1}=\frac{y-5}{-2}=\frac{z-7}{1}$ and $\frac{x+1}{7}=\frac{y+1}{-6}=\frac{z+1}{1}$.

24 Show that the lines $\frac{x-1}{3}=\frac{y+1}{2}=\frac{z-1}{5}$ and $\frac{x+2}{4}=\frac{y-1}{3}=\frac{z+1}{-2}$ do not intersect each other.

25 Show that the lines $\frac{5-x}{-4}=\frac{y-7}{4}=\frac{z+3}{-5}$ and $\frac{x-8}{7}=\frac{2y-8}{2}=\frac{z-5}{3}$ are coplanar.

26 Find the shortest distance between the lines $\vec{r_1}=\hat{i}+2\hat{j}+3\hat{k}+\lambda(2\hat{i}+3\hat{j}+4\hat{k})$ and $\vec{r_2}=2\hat{i}+4\hat{j}+5\hat{k}+\mu(4\hat{i}+6\hat{j}+8\hat{k})$. **[ISC 2015]**

27 Find the foot of perpendicular from $P(1, 2, -3)$ to the line $\frac{x+1}{2}=\frac{y-3}{-2}=\frac{z}{-1}$. Also, find the image of P in the given line.

Long Answer Type Questions

6 Marks

28 Determine the equation of the line passing through the point $(-1, -3, -2)$ and perpendicular to the lines $\frac{x}{1}=\frac{y}{2}=\frac{z}{3}$ and $\frac{x+2}{-3}=\frac{y-1}{2}=\frac{z+1}{5}$. **[ISC 2020]**

29 Show that the lines $\frac{x-4}{1}=\frac{y+3}{-4}=\frac{z+1}{7}$ and $\frac{x-1}{2}=\frac{y+1}{-3}=\frac{z+10}{8}$ intersect. Find the coordinates of their point of intersection. **[ISC 2017]**

30 Find the shortest distance between the lines $\frac{x-8}{3}=\frac{y+9}{-16}=\frac{z-10}{7}$ and $\frac{x-15}{3}=\frac{y-29}{8}=\frac{5-z}{5}$. Also, find the equations of the shortest distance. **[ISC 2012]**

31 Find the perpendicular distance of point (1, 0, 0) from the line $\frac{x-1}{2}=\frac{y+1}{-3}=\frac{z+10}{8}$. Also, find the coordinate of foot of perpendicular and equation of perpendicular.

Hints & Solutions

1. Given equation of line is $\frac{4-x}{2}=\frac{y}{6}=\frac{1-z}{3}$.

It can be rewritten in standard form as $\frac{x-4}{-2}=\frac{y}{6}=\frac{z-1}{-3}$.

Here, DR's of line are $-2, 6, -3$. [1]

Now, $\sqrt{(-2)^2+6^2+(-3)^2}=\sqrt{4+36+9}=\sqrt{49}=7$

So, DC's of line are $-\frac{2}{7}, \frac{6}{7}, -\frac{3}{7}$. [1]

2. Given equation of a line is

$$5x-3=15y+7=3-10z \quad \text{...(i)}$$

To convert the equation in standard form

$$\frac{x-x_1}{a}=\frac{y-y_1}{b}=\frac{z-z_1}{c} \quad \text{...(ii)}$$

Let us divide Eq. (i) by LCM (coefficient of x, y and z).
i.e. LCM (5, 15, 10) = 30

Now, Eq. (i) becomes $\frac{5x-3}{30}=\frac{15y+7}{30}=\frac{3-10z}{30}$

$$\Rightarrow \frac{5\left(x-\frac{3}{5}\right)}{30}=\frac{15\left(y+\frac{7}{15}\right)}{30}=\frac{-10\left(z-\frac{3}{10}\right)}{30}$$

$$\Rightarrow \frac{x-\frac{3}{5}}{6}=\frac{y+\frac{7}{15}}{2}=\frac{z-\frac{3}{10}}{-3}$$ [1]

On comparing the above equation with Eq. (ii), we get $6, 2, -3$ are the direction ratios of the given line.
Now, the direction cosines of given line are

$$\frac{6}{\sqrt{6^2+2^2+(-3)^2}}, \frac{2}{\sqrt{6^2+2^2+(-3)^2}}, \frac{-3}{\sqrt{6^2+2^2+(-3)^2}}$$

i.e. $\frac{6}{7}, \frac{2}{7}, \frac{-3}{7}$ $[\because \sqrt{36+4+9}=\sqrt{49}=7]$ [1]

3. Hint Given equation can be rewritten in standard form as

$$\frac{x-3}{-1}=\frac{y+2}{-2}=\frac{z-5}{4}$$

(i) Direction ratios of two parallel lines are proportional
(ii) Direction ratios of given line are $-1, -2, 4$.
[Ans. $-1, -2, 4$**]**

4. Since, the required line is parallel to the line

$$\frac{x+3}{3}=\frac{4-y}{5}=\frac{z+8}{6} \text{ or } \frac{x+3}{3}=\frac{y-4}{-5}=\frac{z+8}{6}$$

$\therefore$ DR's of required line are $(3, -5, 6)$. [1]

Now, the required cartesian equation of the line passing through the point $(-2, 4, -5)$ having DR's $(3, -5, 6)$ is

$$\frac{x+2}{3}=\frac{y-4}{-5}=\frac{z+5}{6}.$$ [1]

5. Given cartesian equation of a line is $\frac{3-x}{5}=\frac{y+4}{7}=\frac{2z-6}{4}$

On rewriting the given equation in standard form, we get

$$\frac{x-3}{-5}=\frac{y+4}{7}=\frac{z-3}{2}=\lambda \text{ (say)}$$

$\Rightarrow \quad x = -5\lambda + 3,\ y = 7\lambda - 4$ and $z = 2\lambda + 3$ [1/2]

Now, $x\hat{i} + y\hat{j} + z\hat{k} = (-5\lambda + 3)\hat{i} + (7\lambda - 4)\hat{j} + (2\lambda + 3)\hat{k}$

$\Rightarrow \quad \vec{r} = (3\hat{i} - 4\hat{j} + 3\hat{k}) + \lambda(-5\hat{i} + 7\hat{j} + 2\hat{k})$ [1]

which is the required equation of a line in vector form. [1/2]

6. Hint DC's of required line are cos 60°, cos 120° and cos 45°; i.e. $\frac{1}{2}, \frac{-1}{2}, \frac{1}{\sqrt{2}}$ and a point on the line is (2, –3, 4).

[**Ans.** $\frac{x-2}{1/2} = \frac{y+3}{-1/2} = \frac{z-4}{1/\sqrt{2}}$

or $2x - 4 = -2y - 6 = \sqrt{2}(z-4)$]

7. Given cartesian equation of line is

$$2x - 3 = 3y + 1 = 5 - 6z$$

$$\Rightarrow \frac{x - \frac{3}{2}}{\frac{1}{2}} = \frac{y + \frac{1}{3}}{\frac{1}{3}} = \frac{z - \frac{5}{6}}{-\frac{1}{6}} \Rightarrow \frac{x - \frac{3}{2}}{3} = \frac{y + \frac{1}{3}}{2} = \frac{z - \frac{5}{6}}{-1}$$ [1]

$\Rightarrow$ Direction ratios of line are (3, 2, – 1).

Now, the direction ratios of a line parallel to given line are 3, 2, –1.

$\therefore$ Vector equation of line passing through (7 – 5, 0) and parallel to given line is

$$\vec{r} = (7\hat{i} - 5\hat{j}) + \lambda(3\hat{i} + 2\hat{j} - \hat{k}).$$ [1]

8. Similar as Question 7.

[**Ans.** $\vec{r} = (\hat{i} + 2\hat{j} - \hat{k}) + \lambda(7\hat{i} - 5\hat{j} + \hat{k})$]

9. Similar as Example 1.

[**Ans.** $\vec{r} = \hat{i} - 2\hat{j} + 3\hat{k} + \lambda(3\hat{i} - 2\hat{j} + 6\hat{k})$]

10. Similar as Example 3. [**Ans.** $z = -1$]

11. Similar as Example 4. $\left[\textbf{Ans. } \frac{x-1}{2} = \frac{y+1}{5} = \frac{z-3}{-5}\right]$

12. Hint Let $\vec{a}$ and $\vec{b}$ are the position vectors of (1, – 1, 2) and (3, 2, 1), respectively.

Then, $\vec{a} = \hat{i} - \hat{j} + 2\hat{k}$ and $\vec{b} = 3\hat{i} + 2\hat{j} + \hat{k}$.

Now, the required equation of line is given by $\vec{r} = \vec{a} + \lambda(\vec{b} - \vec{a})$. [**Ans.** $\vec{r} = (\hat{i} - \hat{j} + 2\hat{k}) + \lambda(2\hat{i} + 3\hat{j} - \hat{k})$]

13. We have, $x = py + q$, $z = ry + s$ and $x = p'y + q'$, $z = r'y + s'$

$$\therefore \quad \frac{x-q}{p} = \frac{y}{1} = \frac{z-s}{r} \text{ and } \frac{x-q'}{p'} = \frac{y}{1} = \frac{z-s'}{r'}$$

Direction ratios of above lines are

$$a_1 = p, b_1 = 1, c_1 = r \text{ and } a_2 = p', b_2 = 1, c_2 = r'$$ [1]

We know that two lines are perpendicular if

$$a_1a_2 + b_1b_2 + c_1c_2 = 0$$

$\Rightarrow \quad p \times p' + 1 \times 1 + r \times r' = 0$

$\Rightarrow \quad pp' + 1 + rr' = 0$ **Hence proved.** [1]

14. Given equation of line is $\frac{x+2}{3} = \frac{y+1}{2} = \frac{z-3}{2}$

We find any random point on the line as follows

$$\frac{x+2}{3} = \frac{y+1}{2} = \frac{z-3}{2} = \lambda \text{ (say)}$$

$$\Rightarrow \quad \frac{x+2}{3} = \lambda, \frac{y+1}{2} = \lambda, \frac{z-3}{2} = \lambda$$

$\Rightarrow \quad x = 3\lambda - 2,\ y = 2\lambda - 1,\ z = 2\lambda + 3$

So, the required point will be of the form,

$$Q(3\lambda - 2, 2\lambda - 1, 2\lambda + 3)$$ ...(i) [1]

Now, given that distance between two points $P(1, 3, 3)$ and $Q(3\lambda - 2, 2\lambda - 1, 2\lambda + 3)$ is 5 units,

i.e. $PQ = 5$

$\Rightarrow \sqrt{[(3\lambda - 2 - 1)^2 + (2\lambda - 1 - 3)^2 + (2\lambda + 3 - 3)^2]} = 5$

$\left[\because \text{distance} = \sqrt{(x_2 - x_1)^2 + (y_2 - y_1)^2 + (z_2 - z_1)^2}\right]$

$\Rightarrow \quad \sqrt{(3\lambda - 3)^2 + (2\lambda - 4)^2 + (2\lambda)^2} = 5$ [1]

On squaring both sides, we get

$$(3\lambda - 3)^2 + (2\lambda - 4)^2 + (2\lambda)^2 = 25$$

$\Rightarrow \quad 9\lambda^2 + 9 - 18\lambda + 4\lambda^2 + 16 - 16\lambda + 4\lambda^2 = 25$

$\Rightarrow \quad 17\lambda^2 - 34\lambda = 0 \Rightarrow 17\lambda(\lambda - 2) = 0$ [1]

$\Rightarrow$ Either $17\lambda = 0$ or $\lambda - 2 = 0$

$\Rightarrow \quad \lambda = 0$ or 2

On putting $\lambda = 0$ and $\lambda = 2$ in Eq .(i), we get the required points as $Q(-2, -1, 3)$ or $Q(4, 3, 7)$. [1]

15. Given equation of line is

$$6x - 2 = 3y + 1 = 2z - 2$$

or $$\frac{6x-2}{6} = \frac{3y+1}{6} = \frac{2z-2}{6}$$

or $$\frac{6\left(x - \frac{2}{6}\right)}{6} = \frac{3\left(y + \frac{1}{3}\right)}{6} = \frac{2\left(z - \frac{2}{2}\right)}{6}$$

or $$\frac{x - \frac{1}{3}}{1} = \frac{y + \frac{1}{3}}{2} = \frac{z-1}{3}$$

Clearly, DR's of given line are 1, 2, 3.

$\therefore$ DC's of given line are $\frac{1}{\sqrt{14}}, \frac{2}{\sqrt{14}}, \frac{3}{\sqrt{14}}$

$\left[\because \sqrt{1^2 + 2^2 + 3^2} = \sqrt{1 + 4 + 9} = \sqrt{14}\right]$ [1]

Now, equation of a line passing through the point (2, – 1, – 1) and parallel to the given line is

$$\frac{x-2}{1} = \frac{y+1}{2} = \frac{z+1}{3}$$ [1]

To find the vector form, consider

$$\frac{x-2}{1} = \frac{y+1}{2} = \frac{z+1}{3} = \lambda \text{ (say)}$$ [1/2]

$\Rightarrow \quad x = \lambda + 2,\ y = 2\lambda - 1,\ z = 3\lambda - 1$ [1/2]

$\therefore \quad x\hat{i} + y\hat{j} + z\hat{k} = (\lambda + 2)\hat{i} + (2\lambda - 1)\hat{j} + (3\lambda - 1)\hat{k}$

$= (2\hat{i} - \hat{j} - \hat{k}) + \lambda(\hat{i} + 2\hat{j} + 3\hat{k})$

$\Rightarrow \quad \vec{r} = (2\hat{i} - \hat{j} - \hat{k}) + \lambda(\hat{i} + 2\hat{j} + 3\hat{k}),$ [1]

which is the required equation of line in vector form.

16. Solve as Question 15.

$$\left[\textbf{Ans.} \left(\frac{2}{7}, \frac{3}{7}, \frac{-6}{7}\right); \vec{r} = -\hat{i} + 2\hat{j} + 3\hat{k} + \lambda(2\hat{i} + 3\hat{j} - 6\hat{k})\right]$$

17. Similar as Example 2.

$$\left[\textbf{Ans.}\ \vec{r} = (2\hat{i} - \hat{j} + 3\hat{k}) + \lambda(-6\hat{i} - 3\hat{j} + 6\hat{k}) \text{ and } \frac{2-x}{6} = \frac{-y-1}{3} = \frac{z-3}{6}\right]$$

18. Similar as Example 5 (i). $\left[\textbf{Ans.}\ \theta = \cos^{-1}\left(\frac{19}{21}\right)\right]$

19. Similar as Example 5 (ii). $\left[\textbf{Ans.}\ \frac{\pi}{2}\right.$; given pair of lines are perpendicular to each other]

20. **Hint** (i) The given equations of lines can be rewritten as

$$\frac{x-0}{3} = \frac{y-0}{2} = \frac{z-0}{-6} \text{ and } \frac{x-0}{2} = \frac{y-0}{-12} = \frac{z-0}{-3}.$$

(ii) Similar as Example 5 (ii). $\left[\textbf{Ans.}\ \theta = \frac{\pi}{2}\right]$

21. **Hint** Given equations of lines can be written as

$$\frac{x-1}{-3} = \frac{y-2}{2p/7} = \frac{z-3}{1} \quad \text{...(i)}$$

and $$\frac{x-1}{-3p/7} = \frac{y-5}{-1} = \frac{z-11}{-7} \quad \text{...(ii)}$$

Since, Eqs. (i) and (ii) are perpendicular.

$$\therefore -3\left(\frac{-3p}{7}\right) + \frac{2p}{7}(-1) + 1(-7) = 0 \quad [\textbf{Ans.}\ p = 7]$$

22. Given equations of lines are

$$\vec{r} = (4\hat{i} + 5\hat{j}) + \lambda(\hat{i} + 2\hat{j} - 3\hat{k})$$

and $\vec{r} = (\hat{i} - \hat{j} + 2\hat{k}) + \mu(2\hat{i} + 4\hat{j} - 5\hat{k})$

On comparing with $\vec{r} = a_1 + \lambda b_1$ and $\vec{r} = \vec{a_2} + \mu\vec{b_2}$,

we get $\quad \vec{a_1} = 4\hat{i} + 5\hat{j}, \vec{b_1} = \hat{i} + 2\hat{j} - 3\hat{k}$

and $\quad \vec{a_2} = \hat{i} - \hat{j} + 2\hat{k}, \vec{b_2} = 2\hat{i} + 4\hat{j} - 5\hat{k}$ [1]

Now, $\vec{a_2} - \vec{a_1} = \hat{i} - \hat{j} + 2\hat{k} - 4\hat{i} - 5\hat{j} = -3\hat{i} - 6\hat{j} + 2\hat{k}$

and $\vec{b_1} \times \vec{b_2} = \begin{vmatrix} \hat{i} & \hat{j} & \hat{k} \\ 1 & 2 & -3 \\ 2 & 4 & -5 \end{vmatrix}$

$$= \hat{i}(-10 + 12) - \hat{j}(-5 + 6) + \hat{k}(4 - 4)$$

$$= 2\hat{i} - \hat{j} + 0\hat{k}$$ [1]

$$\therefore |\vec{b_1} \times \vec{b_2}| = \sqrt{(2)^2 + (-1)^2 + (0)^2} = \sqrt{4+1} = \sqrt{5}$$

$\because$ Shortest distance between two lines is

$$\text{SD} = \left|\frac{(\vec{b_1} \times \vec{b_2}) \cdot (\vec{a_2} - \vec{a_1})}{|\vec{b_1} \times \vec{b_2}|}\right|$$ [1]

$$\therefore \quad \text{SD} = \left|\frac{(2\hat{i} - \hat{j} + 0\hat{k}) \cdot (-3\hat{i} - 6\hat{j} + 2\hat{k})}{\sqrt{5}}\right|$$

$$= \left|\frac{-6 + 6 + 0}{\sqrt{5}}\right| = 0$$

Hence, the two lines intersect each other. [1]

23. Similar as Example 11. [**Ans.** $2\sqrt{29}$ units]

24. Given equations of lines are

$$\frac{x-1}{3} = \frac{y+1}{2} = \frac{z-1}{5} \text{ and } \frac{x+2}{4} = \frac{y-1}{3} = \frac{z+1}{-2}$$

On comparing above equations with

$$\frac{x-x_1}{a_1} = \frac{y-y_1}{b_1} = \frac{z-z_1}{c_1}$$

and $$\frac{x-x_2}{a_2} = \frac{y-y_2}{b_2} = \frac{z-z_2}{c_2}, \text{ we get}$$

$$x_1 = 1, y_1 = -1, z_1 = 1, a_1 = 3, b_1 = 2, c_1 = 5$$

and $x_2 = -2, y_2 = 1, z_2 = -1, a_2 = 4, b_2 = 3, c_2 = -2$ [1]

Now, consider $\begin{vmatrix} x_2 - x_1 & y_2 - y_1 & z_2 - z_1 \\ a_1 & b_1 & c_1 \\ a_2 & b_2 & c_2 \end{vmatrix} = \begin{vmatrix} -3 & 2 & -2 \\ 3 & 2 & 5 \\ 4 & 3 & -2 \end{vmatrix}$ [1]

$$= -3(-4 - 15) - 2(-6 - 20) - 2(9 - 8)$$

$$= -3(-19) - 2(-26) - 2(1)$$

$$= 57 + 52 - 2 = 107 \neq 0$$ [1]

$\Rightarrow$ Shortest distance will not be zero.

Hence, the given lines do not intersect each other. [1]

25. Similar as Example 12.

26. Given equations of lines are

$$\vec{r} = \hat{i} + 2\hat{j} + 3\hat{k} + \lambda(2\hat{i} + 3\hat{j} + 4\hat{k}) \text{ and}$$

$$\vec{r} = 2\hat{i} + 4\hat{j} + 5\hat{k} + \mu(4\hat{i} + 6\hat{j} + 8\hat{k})$$

On comparing with $\vec{r} = \vec{a_1} + \lambda\vec{b_1}$ and $\vec{r} = \vec{a_2} + \lambda\vec{b_2}$,

we get

$$\vec{a_1} = \hat{i} + 2\hat{j} + 3\hat{k}, \vec{b_1} = 2\hat{i} + 3\hat{j} + 4\hat{k}$$

and $\quad \vec{a_2} = 2\hat{i} + 4\hat{j} + 5\hat{k}, \vec{b_2} = 4\hat{i} + 6\hat{j} + 8\hat{k}$ [1]

Now, $(\vec{a_2} - \vec{a_1}) = (2\hat{i} + 4\hat{j} + 5\hat{k}) - (\hat{i} + 2\hat{j} + 3\hat{k})$

$$= \hat{i} + 2\hat{j} + 2\hat{k}$$

and $(\vec{b_1} \times \vec{b_2}) = \begin{vmatrix} \hat{i} & \hat{j} & \hat{k} \\ 2 & 3 & 4 \\ 4 & 6 & 8 \end{vmatrix}$

$$= \hat{i}(24 - 24) - \hat{j}(16 - 16) + \hat{k}(12 - 12)$$

$$= 0i - 0j + 0k$$

It means given lines are parallel. [1]

$\therefore$ The shortest distance between two parallel lines is

$$= \frac{|\vec{b} \times (\vec{a_2} - \vec{a_1})|}{|\vec{b}|} = \frac{|(2\hat{i} + 3\hat{j} + 4\hat{k}) \times (\hat{i} + 2\hat{j} + 2\hat{k})|}{|2\hat{i} + 3\hat{j} + 4\hat{k}|}$$

$[\because \vec{b} = \vec{b_1} = \vec{b_2}]$ [1]

$$= \frac{\left\| \begin{vmatrix} \hat{i} & \hat{j} & \hat{k} \\ 2 & 3 & 4 \\ 1 & 2 & 2 \end{vmatrix} \right\|}{\sqrt{2^2+3^2+4^2}} = \frac{|\hat{i}(6-8)-\hat{j}(4-4)+\hat{k}(4-3)|}{\sqrt{4+9+16}}$$

$$= \frac{|-2\hat{i}-0\hat{j}+\hat{k}|}{\sqrt{29}} = \frac{\sqrt{(-2)^2+0+(1)^2}}{\sqrt{29}} = \frac{\sqrt{4+1}}{\sqrt{29}} = \sqrt{\frac{5}{29}}$$ [1]

27. Similar as Example 15. [**Ans.** Foot of perpendicular $= (1, 1, -1)$ and image of $P(1,0,1)$]

28. Let the equation of line passing through the point $(-1, -3, -2)$ is

$$\frac{x+1}{a} = \frac{y+3}{b} = \frac{z+2}{c}$$

Since, the above line is perpendicular to the line

$$\frac{x}{1} = \frac{y}{2} = \frac{z}{3}$$

and $\dfrac{x+2}{-3} = \dfrac{y-1}{2} = \dfrac{z+1}{5}$

$\therefore \quad a + 2b + 3c = 0$ ... (i)

and $-3a + 2b + 5c = 0$ ... (ii)

By cross-multiplication, we have

$$\frac{a}{10-6} = \frac{-b}{5+9} = \frac{c}{2+6}$$

$$\frac{a}{4} = \frac{b}{-14} = \frac{c}{8}$$

$$\frac{a}{2} = \frac{b}{-7} = \frac{c}{4} = \lambda$$

$\Rightarrow a = 2\lambda,\ b = -7\lambda,\ c = 4\lambda$

$\therefore$ Equation of line is

$$\frac{x+1}{2} = \frac{y+3}{-7} = \frac{z+2}{4}$$

29. Similar as Example 8. [**Ans.** $(5, -7, 6)$]

30. Given equation of lines are

$$\frac{x-8}{3} = \frac{y+9}{-16} = \frac{z-10}{7} = \lambda \text{ (say)} \quad \text{...(i)}$$

and $$\frac{x-15}{3} = \frac{y-29}{8} = \frac{z-5}{-5} = \mu \text{ (say)} \quad \text{...(ii)}$$

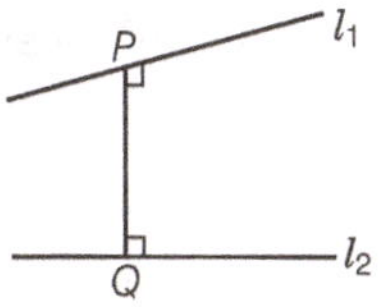

Any point P on line (i) is

$P(3\lambda + 8, -16\lambda - 9, 7\lambda + 10)$ ...(iii)

and any point Q on line (ii) is

$Q(3\mu + 15, 8\mu + 29, -5\mu + 5)$ ...(iv)

Now, direction ratios of PQ are

$(3\mu + 15 - 3\lambda - 8,\ 8\mu + 29 + 16\lambda + 9, -5\mu + 5 - 7\lambda - 10)$

i.e. $(3\mu - 3\lambda + 7,\ 8\mu + 16\lambda + 38, -5\mu - 7\lambda - 5)$ [1]

Now, $|PQ|$ will be the shortest distance between lines (i) and (ii) if PQ is perpendicular to both lines (i) and (ii).

$\therefore 3(3\mu - 3\lambda + 7) - 16(8\mu + 16\lambda + 38) + 7(-5\mu - 7\lambda - 5) = 0$

$[\because a_1a_2 + b_1b_2 + c_1c_2 = 0]$

$\Rightarrow 9\mu - 9\lambda + 21 - 128\mu - 256\lambda - 608 - 35\mu - 49\lambda - 35 = 0$

$\Rightarrow -154\mu - 314\lambda - 622 = 0$

$\Rightarrow 77\mu + 157\lambda + 311 = 0$ [dividing by (-2)] ...(v) [1]

and $3(3\mu - 3\lambda + 7) + 8(8\mu + 16\lambda + 38) - 5(-5\mu - 7\lambda - 5) = 0$

$[\because a_1a_2 + b_1b_2 + c_1c_2 = 0]$

$\Rightarrow 9\mu - 9\lambda + 21 + 64\mu + 128\lambda + 304 + 25\mu + 35\lambda + 25 = 0$

$\Rightarrow 98\mu + 154\lambda + 350 = 0$

$\Rightarrow 7\mu + 11\lambda + 25 = 0$ [dividing by 14] ...(vi)

On multiplying Eq. (vi) by 11 and then subtracting from Eq. (v), we get

$(77\mu + 157\lambda + 311) - (77\mu + 121\lambda + 275) = 0$ [1]

$\Rightarrow 36\lambda + 36 = 0 \Rightarrow \lambda = -1$

On putting the value of λ in Eq. (v), we get

$77\mu + 157(-1) + 311 = 0$

$\Rightarrow 77\mu - 157 + 311 = 0$

$\Rightarrow 77\mu + 154 = 0$

$\Rightarrow \mu = -2$ [1]

On putting the values of λ and μ in Eqs. (iii) and (iv), we get

Coordinates of $P = (-3 + 8, 16 - 9, -7 + 10) = (5, 7, 3)$

and coordinates of $Q = (-6 + 15, -16 + 29, 10 + 5)$
$= (9, 13, 15)$

$\therefore$ Shortest distance between two lines,

$$PQ = \sqrt{(9-5)^2 + (13-7)^2 + (15-3)^2}$$

$[\because \text{distance} = (\sqrt{(x_2 - x_1)^2 + (y_2 - y_1)^2 + (z_2 - z_1)^2})]$

$= \sqrt{16 + 36 + 144} = \sqrt{196} = 14$ units [1]

Equation of line PQ of shortest distance is

$$\frac{x-5}{9-5} = \frac{y-7}{13-7} = \frac{z-3}{15-3}$$

$$\left[\because \frac{x-x_1}{x_2-x_1} = \frac{y-y_1}{y_2-y_1} = \frac{z-z_1}{z_2-z_1}\right]$$

$$\therefore \quad \frac{x-5}{4} = \frac{y-7}{6} = \frac{z-3}{12}$$

Hence, $\dfrac{x-5}{2} = \dfrac{y-7}{3} = \dfrac{z-3}{6}$ is the required equation of the line which gives shortest distance. [1]

31. Similar as Example 15.

[**Ans.** Length of perpendicular is $\sqrt{24}$, coordinate of foot of perpendicular is $(3, -4, -2)$ and equation of perpendicular is $\dfrac{x-1}{1} = \dfrac{y}{-2} = \dfrac{z}{-1}$]

Chapter Practice

Multiple Choice Type Questions

1 Mark

1 Direction cosines of the line $\frac{x-1}{2}=\frac{1-y}{3}-\frac{2z-1}{12}$ are

(a) $\frac{2}{7},\frac{3}{7},\frac{6}{7}$ (b) $\frac{2}{\sqrt{157}},-\frac{3}{\sqrt{157}},\frac{12}{\sqrt{157}}$

(c) $\frac{2}{7},-\frac{3}{7},-\frac{6}{7}$ (d) $\frac{2}{7},-\frac{3}{7},\frac{6}{7}$

2 The angle between the lines $2x=3y=-z$ and $6x=-y=-4z$ is

(a) $0°$ (b) $30°$

(c) $45°$ (d) $90°$

3 The coordinates of a point on the line $\frac{x+2}{3}=\frac{y+1}{2}=\frac{z-3}{2}$ at a distance of $\frac{6}{\sqrt{2}}$ from the point (1, 2, 3) is

(a) (56, 43, 111) (b) $\left(\frac{56}{17},\frac{43}{17},\frac{111}{17}\right)$

(c) (2, 1, 3) (d) (−2, −1, −3)

4 The two lines $x=ay+b$, $z=cy+d$ and $x=a'y+b'$, $z=c'y+d'$ are perpendicular to each other, if

(a) $\frac{a}{a'}+\frac{c}{c'}=1$ (b) $\frac{a}{a'}+\frac{c}{c'}=-1$

(c) $aa'+cc'=1$ (d) $aa'+cc'=-1$

5 The lines $\frac{x-2}{1}=\frac{y-3}{1}=\frac{4-z}{k}$ and $\frac{x-1}{k}=\frac{y-4}{2}=\frac{z-5}{-2}$ are mutually perpendicular if the value of k is

(a) $-\frac{2}{3}$ (b) $\frac{2}{3}$ (c) -2 (d) 2

Assertion-Reason Type Questions

1 Mark

Directions (Q. Nos. 6-9) *In the questions given below are two statements labelled as Assertion (A) and Reason (R). In the context of the two statements, which one of the following is correct?*

(a) Both A and R are correct; R is the correct explanation of A

(b) Both A and R are correct but R is not the correct explanation of A

(c) A is correct but R is incorrect

(d) R is correct but A is incorrect

6 **Assertion (A)** The points (1, 2, 3), (−2, 3, 4) and (7, 0, 1) are collinear.

Reason (R) If a line makes angles $\frac{\pi}{2},\frac{3\pi}{4}$ and $\frac{\pi}{4}$ with X, Y and Z-axes respectively, then its direction cosines are $0, \frac{-1}{\sqrt{2}}$ and $\frac{1}{\sqrt{2}}$.

7 **Assertion (A)** The cartesian equation of the line which passes through the point (−2, 4 −5) and parallel to the line given by $\frac{x+3}{3}=\frac{y-4}{5}=\frac{z+8}{6}$ is $\frac{x+3}{-2}=\frac{y-4}{4}=\frac{z+8}{-5}$.

Reason (R) If the cartesian equation of a line is $\frac{x-5}{3}=\frac{y+4}{7}=\frac{z-6}{2}$, then its vector form is $\vec{r}=5\hat{i}-4\hat{j}+6\hat{k}+\lambda(3\hat{i}+7\hat{j}+2\hat{k})$.

8 **Assertion** (A) The lines $\vec{r}=\vec{a}_1+\lambda\vec{b}_1$ and $\vec{r}=\vec{a}_2+\mu\vec{b}_2$ are perpendicular when $\vec{b}_1\cdot\vec{b}_2=0$.

Reason (R) The angle θ between the lines $\vec{r}=\vec{a}_1+\lambda\vec{b}_1$ and $\vec{r}=\vec{a}_2+\mu\vec{b}_2$ is given by

$$\cos\theta=\frac{\vec{b}_1\cdot\vec{b}_2}{|\vec{b}_1||\vec{b}_2|}.$$

9 **Assertion (A)** The image of a point (0, 2, 3) about the line $\frac{x+3}{5}=\frac{y-1}{2}=\frac{z+4}{3}$ is (4, 4, − 5).

Reason (R) Mid-point of line segment joining (x_1, y_1, z_1) and (x_2, y_2, z_2) is

$$\left(\frac{x_1+x_2}{2},\frac{y_1+y_2}{2},\frac{z_1+z_2}{2}\right).$$

Very Short Answer Type Questions

(2 Marks)

10 Find the direction cosines of the line passing through two points (–2, 4, – 5) and (1, 2, 3).

11 If a line has direction ratio (2, –1, – 2), then what are its direction cosines?

12 Show that the line joining the origin to the point (2,1,1) is perpendicular to the line determined by the points (3, 5, – 1) and (4, 3, – 1). **[NCERT Exemplar]**

13 Equation of a line is

$$\frac{4-x}{2}=\frac{y+3}{2}=\frac{z+2}{1}.$$

Find the direction cosines of a line parallel to the above line.

14 Cartesian equation of line

AB is $\frac{2x-1}{2}=\frac{4-y}{7}=\frac{z+1}{2}$. Write the direction ratios of a line parallel to AB.

15 What is the cartesian equation of the line $\vec{r}=(3\hat{i}-\hat{j}+4\hat{k})+\lambda(\hat{i}+2\hat{j}+3\hat{k})$? **[NCERT Exemplar]**

16 Write the vector equation of the line $\frac{x-5}{3}=\frac{y+4}{7}=\frac{6-z}{2}$.

17 Find the equation of line passing through the point (2, 1, 3) having the direction ratios 1, 1, – 2.

18 Find the equation of a line parallel to Y-axis and passing through the origin.

19 Write the condition for the lines $\vec{r}=\vec{a_1}+\lambda\vec{b_1}$ and $\vec{r}=\vec{a_2}+\lambda\vec{b_2}$ to be intersecting.

20 Show that the lines $\frac{x-5}{7}=\frac{y+2}{-5}=\frac{z}{1}$ and $\frac{x}{1}=\frac{y}{2}=\frac{z}{3}$ are perpendicular to each other.

21 Find the coordinates of the point, where the line passing through (5, 1, 6) and (3, 4, 1) cross YZ-plane.

Short Answer Type Questions

(4 Marks)

22 Find the equation of a line passing through the point (–1, 3, – 2) and perpendicular to the lines $\frac{x}{1}=\frac{y}{2}=\frac{z}{3}$ and $\frac{x+2}{-3}=\frac{y-1}{2}=\frac{z+1}{5}$. **[ISC 2013]**

23 Show that the lines $\vec{r}=3\hat{i}+2\hat{j}-4\hat{k}+\lambda(\hat{i}+2\hat{j}+2\hat{k})$ and $\vec{r}=5\hat{i}-2\hat{j}+\mu(3\hat{i}+2\hat{j}+6\hat{k})$ are intersecting. Also, find their point of intersecting.

24 Find the shortest distance between the lines $\vec{r}=(\hat{i}+2\hat{j}+\hat{k})+\lambda(\hat{i}-\hat{j}+\hat{k})$ and $\vec{r}=(2\hat{i}-\hat{j}-\hat{k})+\mu(2\hat{i}+\hat{j}+2\hat{k})$.

25 Find the shortest distance between the lines whose vector equations are $\vec{r}=4\hat{i}-\hat{j}+2\hat{k}+\lambda(\hat{i}+2\hat{j}-3\hat{k})$ and $\vec{r}=2\hat{i}+\hat{j}-\hat{k}+\mu(3\hat{i}+2\hat{j}-4\hat{k})$. **[ISC 2010]**

26 Find the shortest distance between the lines

$$\vec{r}=(1-t)\,\hat{i}+(t-2)\,\hat{j}+(3-2t)\,\hat{k}$$

and $\vec{r}=(s+1)\,\hat{i}+(2s-1)\,\hat{j}-(2s+1)\,\hat{k}$.

27 Find the shortest distance between the pair of lines $\frac{x}{5}=\frac{y-2}{2}=\frac{z-3}{3}$ and $\frac{x+3}{5}=\frac{y-1}{2}=\frac{z+4}{3}$.

28 Find the shortest distance between the lines $x+1=2y=-12z$ and $x=y+2=6z-6$.

29 Find the foot of the perpendicular drawn from the point $A(1, 0, 3)$ to the join of the points $B(4, 7, 1)$ and $C(3, 5, 3)$.

30 Find the image of the point (2, – 1, 5) in the line $\vec{r}=(11\hat{i}-2\hat{j}-8\hat{k})+\lambda(10\hat{i}-4\hat{j}-11\hat{k})$.

31 A line passing through the point A with position vector $\vec{a}=4\hat{i}+2\hat{j}+2\hat{k}$ is parallel to the vector $\vec{b}=2\hat{i}+3\hat{j}+6\hat{k}$. Find the length of the perpendicular drawn on this line from a point P with position vector $\vec{r}=\hat{i}+2\hat{j}+3\hat{k}$.

Long Answer Type Questions

6 Marks

32 If a variable line in two adjacent positions has direction cosines l, m, n and $l + \delta l, m + \delta m, n + \delta n$, then show that the small angle $\delta\theta$ between the two positions is given by $\delta\theta^2 = \delta l^2 + \delta m^2 + \delta n^2$. **[NCERT Exemplar]**

33 If l_1, m_1, n_1 and l_2, m_2, n_2 are the direction cosines of two mutually perpendicular lines, then show that direction cosines of the line perpendicular to both of these are $m_1n_2 - m_2n_1, n_1l_2 - n_2l_1$ and $l_1m_2 - l_2m_1$. **[NCERT]**

34 Find the vector and cartesian equations of line passing through the point (1, 2, – 4) and perpendicular to two lines

$$\frac{x-8}{3} = \frac{y+19}{-16} = \frac{z-10}{7}$$

and $\dfrac{x-15}{3} = \dfrac{y-29}{8} = \dfrac{z-5}{-5}$.

35 Show that the two lines are coplanar

$\dfrac{x-a+d}{\alpha-\delta} = \dfrac{y-a}{\alpha} = \dfrac{z-a-d}{\alpha+\delta}$ and

$\dfrac{x-b+c}{\beta-\gamma} = \dfrac{y-b}{\beta} = \dfrac{z-b-c}{\beta+\gamma}$. **[NCERT]**

Answers

1. (d)	**2.** (d)	**3.** (b)
4. (d)	**5.** (a)	**6.** (b)
7. (d)	**8.** (a)	**9.** (a)
10. $\left(\frac{3}{\sqrt{77}}, \frac{-2}{\sqrt{77}}, \frac{8}{\sqrt{77}}\right)$	**11.** $\left(\frac{2}{3}, \frac{-1}{3}, \frac{-2}{3}\right)$	**13.** $\left(\frac{-2}{3}, \frac{2}{3}, \frac{1}{3}\right)$
14. (1, −7, 2)	**15.** $\frac{x-3}{1} = \frac{y+1}{2} = \frac{z-4}{3}$	**16.** $\vec{r} = (5\hat{i} - 4\hat{j} + 6\hat{k}) + \lambda(3\hat{i} + 7\hat{j} - 2\hat{k})$
17. $\frac{x-2}{1} = \frac{y-1}{1} = \frac{z-3}{-2}$	**18.** $\frac{x}{0} = \frac{y}{1} = \frac{z}{0}$	
19. $(\vec{b_1} \times \vec{b_2}) \cdot (\vec{a_2} - \vec{a_1}) = 0$	**21.** $\left(0, \frac{17}{2}, \frac{-13}{2}\right)$	**22.** $\frac{x+1}{2} = \frac{y-3}{-7} = \frac{z+2}{4}$
23. (−1, −6, −12)	**24.** $\frac{3\sqrt{2}}{2}$ units	**25.** $\frac{2}{\sqrt{5}}$ units
26. $\frac{8}{\sqrt{29}}$ units	**27.** $\sqrt{21}$	**28.** 2 units
29. $\left(\frac{5}{3}, \frac{7}{3}, \frac{17}{3}\right)$	**30.** (0, 5, 1)	
31. $\sqrt{10}$ units	**34.** $\frac{x-1}{2} = \frac{y-2}{3} = \frac{z+4}{6}$; $\vec{r} = (\hat{i} + 2\hat{j} - 4\hat{k}) + \lambda(2\hat{i} + 3\hat{j} + 6\hat{k})$	

CHAPTER

14

Three Dimensional Geometry II : The Plane

- Equation of Plane in Different Forms
- Angle between Two Planes
- Distance of a Point from a Plane
- Distance between Parallel Planes
- Angle between a Line and a Plane

A plane is a **surface** such that a line segment joining any two points on it, lies wholly on it. A straight line, which is perpendicular to every line lying on a plane is called a **normal** to the plane. Every normal to a plane is parallel to each other.

Equation of Plane in Different Forms

A plane is determined uniquely, if any one of the following is known

(i) The normal to the plane and its distance from the origin is given, i.e. equation of a plane in normal form.

(ii) It passes through a point and is perpendicular to a given direction.

(iii) It passes through three given non-collinear points.

Equation of a Plane in Normal Form

Suppose ABC is a plane and ON is a normal line to given plane.

Vector Equation

The equation of plane, which is at a distance of d from the origin and having unit vector $\hat{n}$ along ON is

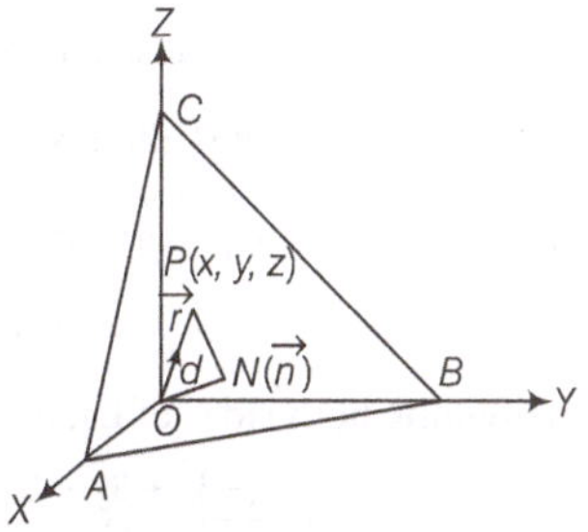

$$\boxed{\vec{r}\cdot\hat{n}=d} \quad \ldots(\text{i})$$

where, $\vec{r}$ is the position vector of any point P on the plane and $\hat{n}=\dfrac{\vec{n}}{|\vec{n}|}$.

Note (i) Eq. (i) of the given plane can be written as $\vec{r}\cdot\frac{\vec{n}}{|\vec{n}|}=d$

or $\vec{r}\cdot\vec{n}=p$, where $p=|\vec{n}|d$.

(ii) The equation $\vec{r}\cdot\vec{n}=p$ is called the **standard form** of the vector equation of a plane.

Cartesian Equation (General Equation of a Plane)

Let $P(x, y, z)$ be any point on the plane.

Then, $\quad \overrightarrow{OP}=\vec{r}=x\hat{i}+y\hat{j}+z\hat{k}$.

Again, let l, m and n be the direction cosines of unit normal $\hat{n}$. Then, $\hat{n}=l\hat{i}+m\hat{j}+n\hat{k}$.

Now, from Eq. (i), we get

$$(x\hat{i}+y\hat{j}+z\hat{k})\cdot(l\hat{i}+m\hat{j}+n\hat{k})=d$$

i.e. $$\boxed{lx+my+nz=d} \quad \dots\text{(ii)}$$

which is the required equation of plane in **normal form.** If the direction cosines of a normal to the plane are converted into a direction ratios, then the transformed equation is said to be **general form** of equation of plane.

Thus, general equation of plane be $ax+by+cz+d=0$.

Note (i) Vector and cartesian equation of plane can also be written as $\vec{r}\cdot\vec{n}=d$ (or $\vec{r}\cdot(a\hat{i}+b\hat{j}+c\hat{k})=d$) and $ax+by+cz=d$, respectively, where a, b, c are DR's of normal to the plane. But, in this case d will not represent the perpendicular distance of the plane from the origin.

(ii) If $\vec{r}\cdot(a\hat{i}+b\hat{j}+c\hat{k})=d$ represent the vector equation of plane, then its corresponding cartesian equation is $ax+by+cz=d$.

(iii) In the equation $\vec{r}\cdot\vec{n}=d$, if $\vec{n}$ is not a unit vector, then to convert $\vec{r}\cdot\vec{n}=d$ into normal form, divide both sides by $|\vec{n}|$.

(iv) In the equation $ax+by+cz=d$, if a, b, c are direction ratios of normal to the plane, then to convert $ax+by+cz=d$ into normal form, divide both sides by $\sqrt{a^2+b^2+c^2}$.

Example 1 Find the vector equation of the plane which is at a distance of $4/\sqrt{5}$ from the origin and its normal vector from the origin is $3\hat{i}-4\hat{j}+5\hat{k}$. Also, find the cartesian equation of the plane.

Sol. Given distance of plane from the origin, $d=4/\sqrt{5}$ and normal vector, $\vec{n}=3\hat{i}-4\hat{j}+5\hat{k}$.

Now, unit normal vector,

$$\hat{n}=\frac{\vec{n}}{|\vec{n}|}=\frac{3\hat{i}-4\hat{j}+5\hat{k}}{\sqrt{3^2+(-4)^2+(5)^2}}=\frac{3\hat{i}-4\hat{j}+5\hat{k}}{\sqrt{9+16+25}}$$

Clearly, the required vector equation of plane is $\vec{r}\cdot\hat{n}=d$

$$\Rightarrow \quad \vec{r}\cdot\left(\frac{3\hat{i}-4\hat{j}+5\hat{k}}{\sqrt{9+16+25}}\right)=\frac{4}{\sqrt{5}}$$

$$\Rightarrow \quad \vec{r}\cdot\left(\frac{3\hat{i}-4\hat{j}+5\hat{k}}{\sqrt{50}}\right)=\frac{4}{\sqrt{5}}$$

$$\Rightarrow \quad \vec{r}\cdot\left(\frac{3\hat{i}-4\hat{j}+5\hat{k}}{5\sqrt{2}}\right)=\frac{4}{\sqrt{5}}$$

$$\Rightarrow \quad \vec{r}\cdot(3\hat{i}-4\hat{j}+5\hat{k})=4\sqrt{10} \quad \dots\text{(i)}$$

which is the required vector equation of the plane.

Now, putting $\vec{r}=x\hat{i}+y\hat{j}+z\hat{k}$ in Eq. (i), we get

$$(x\hat{i}+y\hat{j}+z\hat{k})\cdot(3\hat{i}-4\hat{j}+5\hat{k})=4\sqrt{10}$$

$$\Rightarrow \quad 3x-4y+5z=4\sqrt{10}$$

which is the required cartesian equation of the plane.

Example 2 Find the cartesian equation of a plane which is at a distance of 6 units from the origin and which has a normal with direction ratios $(2, -1, -2)$.

Sol. Given direction ratios of normal to the plane are $(2, -1, -2)$.

So, direction cosines of the normal are

$$\left(\frac{2}{\sqrt{(2)^2+(-1)^2+(-2)^2}}, \frac{-1}{\sqrt{(2)^2+(-1)^2+(-2)^2}}, \frac{-2}{\sqrt{(2)^2+(-1)^2+(-2)^2}}\right)$$

i.e. $\left(\frac{2}{3}, \frac{-1}{3}, \frac{-2}{3}\right)$

Also, it is given that distance from origin to the plane, is $d=6$.

Now, the required equation of plane is given by

$$lx+my+nz=d$$

$$\Rightarrow \quad \frac{2}{3}x-\frac{1}{3}y-\frac{2}{3}z=6$$

$$\Rightarrow \quad 2x-y-2z=18$$

Example 3 Find the direction cosines of the unit vector, perpendicular to the given plane $\vec{r}\cdot(3\hat{i}-5\hat{j}+3\hat{k})+3=0$ passing through the origin.

Sol. Given equation of plane can be written as

$$\vec{r}\cdot(-3\hat{i}+5\hat{j}-3\hat{k})=3 \quad [\because d>0]\dots\text{(i)}$$

Now, $|-3\hat{i}+5\hat{j}-3\hat{k}|=\sqrt{(-3)^2+(5)^2+(-3)^2}$

$$=\sqrt{9+25+9}=\sqrt{43}$$

On dividing both sides of Eq. (i) by $\sqrt{43}$, we get

$$\vec{r}\cdot\frac{(-3\hat{i}+5\hat{j}-3\hat{k})}{\sqrt{43}}=\frac{3}{\sqrt{43}}$$

$$\Rightarrow \quad \vec{r}\cdot\left(\frac{-3}{\sqrt{43}}\hat{i}+\frac{5}{\sqrt{43}}\hat{j}-\frac{3}{\sqrt{43}}\hat{k}\right)=\frac{3}{\sqrt{43}}$$

which is in the form of $\vec{r}\cdot\hat{n}=d$, where $\hat{n}$ is a unit vector perpendicular to the plane through the origin.

$\therefore \quad \hat{n} = \left(-\frac{3}{\sqrt{43}}\hat{i} + \frac{5}{\sqrt{43}}\hat{j} - \frac{3}{\sqrt{43}}\hat{k}\right)$

Hence, direction cosines of $\hat{n}$ are $\left(-\frac{3}{\sqrt{43}}, \frac{5}{\sqrt{43}}, -\frac{3}{\sqrt{43}}\right)$.

Example 4 Find the distance of the plane $2x - 3y + 4z - 6 = 0$ from the origin and the coordinates of the foot of the perpendicular drawn from origin to the given plane. **[NCERT]**

Sol. Given equation of the plane can be written as

$$2x - 3y + 4z = 6 \quad \text{...(i)}$$

Now, dividing both sides of Eq. (i) by

$\sqrt{2^2 + (-3)^2 + 4^2} = \sqrt{29}$, we get

$$\frac{2}{\sqrt{29}}x - \frac{3}{\sqrt{29}}y + \frac{4}{\sqrt{29}}z = \frac{6}{\sqrt{29}} \quad \text{...(ii)}$$

This is of the form $lx + my + nz = d$, where d is the distance of the plane from the origin. So, the distance of the plane from the origin is $\frac{6}{\sqrt{29}}$.

Also, direction cosines of normal to the plane are

$$\left(\frac{2}{\sqrt{29}}, \frac{-3}{\sqrt{29}}, \frac{4}{\sqrt{29}}\right)$$

Now, let the coordinates of the foot of the perpendicular drawn from origin to the plane is $P(x_1, y_1, z_1)$.

Then, the direction ratios of the line OP are (x_1, y_1, z_1).

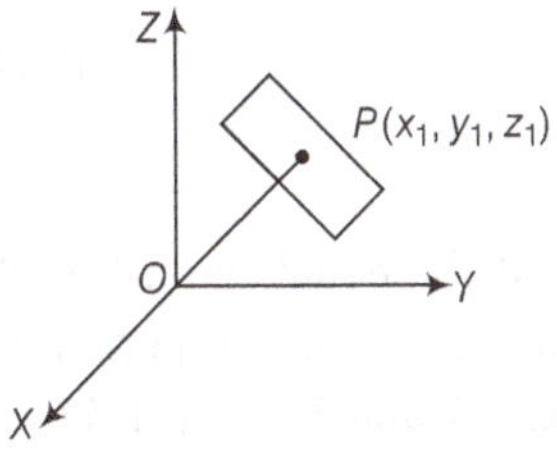

We know that direction cosines and direction ratios of a line are proportional.

$$\therefore \quad \frac{x_1}{\frac{2}{\sqrt{29}}} = \frac{y_1}{\frac{-3}{\sqrt{29}}} = \frac{z_1}{\frac{4}{\sqrt{29}}} = k \text{ (say)}$$

$$\Rightarrow \quad x_1 = \frac{2k}{\sqrt{29}}, y_1 = \frac{-3k}{\sqrt{29}} \text{ and } z_1 = \frac{4k}{\sqrt{29}}$$

As the point $P(x_1, y_1, z_1)$ lies on the plane.

So, $P(x_1, y_1, z_1)$ will satisfy the Eq. (ii).

$$\therefore \quad \frac{2}{\sqrt{29}}x_1 - \frac{3}{\sqrt{29}}y_1 + \frac{4}{\sqrt{29}}z_1 = \frac{6}{\sqrt{29}} \quad \text{...(iii)}$$

Now, putting the values of x_1, y_1 and z_1 in Eq. (iii), we get

$$\frac{2}{\sqrt{29}}\left(\frac{2k}{\sqrt{29}}\right) - \frac{3}{\sqrt{29}}\left(\frac{-3k}{\sqrt{29}}\right) + \frac{4}{\sqrt{29}}\left(\frac{4k}{\sqrt{29}}\right) = \frac{6}{\sqrt{29}}$$

$$\Rightarrow \quad \frac{4k}{29} + \frac{9k}{29} + \frac{16k}{29} = \frac{6}{\sqrt{29}}$$

$$\Rightarrow \quad \frac{29k}{29} = \frac{6}{\sqrt{29}} \Rightarrow k = \frac{6}{\sqrt{29}}$$

Thus, $x_1 = \frac{2}{\sqrt{29}} \times \frac{6}{\sqrt{29}} = \frac{12}{29}$

$y_1 = \frac{-3}{\sqrt{29}} \times \frac{6}{\sqrt{29}} = \frac{-18}{29}$

and $z_1 = \frac{4}{\sqrt{29}} \times \frac{6}{\sqrt{29}} = \frac{24}{29}$

Hence, the coordinates of the foot of the perpendicular are $\left(\frac{12}{29}, \frac{-18}{29}, \frac{24}{29}\right)$.

Note If d is the distance from the origin and , m and n are the direction cosines of the normal to the plane through the origin, then the foot of the perpendicular is (d, md, nd).

Equation of a Plane Passing through a Given Point and Perpendicular to a Given Vector (One Point Form)

In the space, there can be many planes that are perpendicular to the given vector, but through a given point $A(x_1, y_1, z_1)$ only one such plane exist.

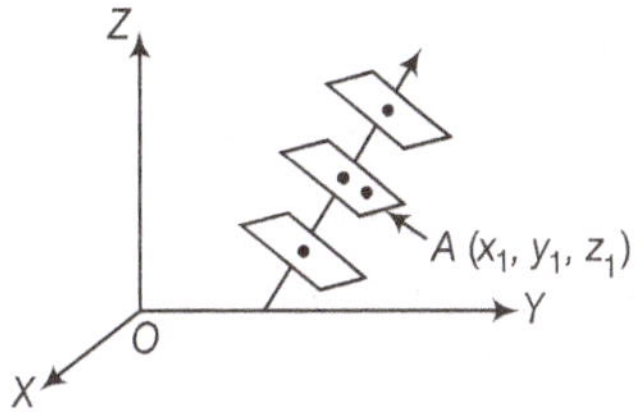

Vector Equation

The vector equation of a plane passing through a given point A with position vector $\vec{a}$ and perpendicular to a given vector $\vec{n}$ is

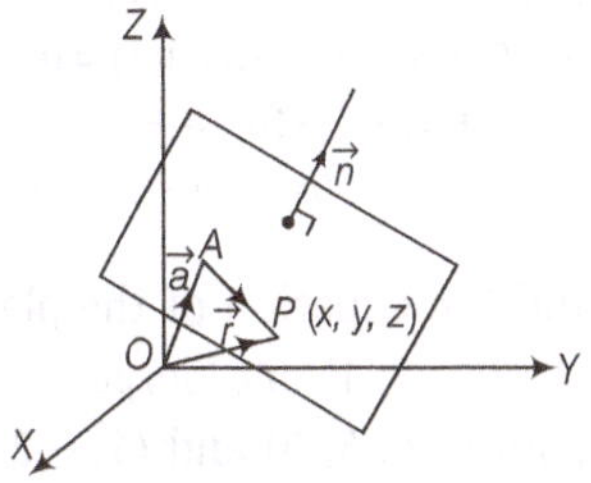

$$(\vec{r} - \vec{a}) \cdot \vec{n} = 0$$

where, $\vec{r}$ is the position vector of any point $P(x, y, z)$ on the plane.

Note Equation of a plane passing through the origin and perpendicular to given vector $\vec{n}$ is $\vec{r} \cdot \vec{n} = 0$.

Cartesian Equation

The cartesian equation of a plane passing through a given point $A(x_1, y_1, z_1)$ and perpendicular to a line having direction ratios (a, b, c) is

$$a(x - x_1) + b(y - y_1) + c(z - z_1) = 0$$

We call this as **one point form** of equation of plane.

Example 5 Find the vector and cartesian equation of the plane, which passes through the point (5, 2, –4) and perpendicular to the line with direction ratios (2, 3, –1). **[NCERT]**

Sol. Given point is (5, 2, –4), its position vector is

$\vec{a} = 5\hat{i} + 2\hat{j} - 4\hat{k}$, and direction ratios of normal to the plane are 2, 3, –1.

$\therefore$ Normal vector, $\vec{n}$ to the plane is $\vec{n} = 2\hat{i} + 3\hat{j} - \hat{k}$

Now, vector equation of the plane passing through one point is given by $(\vec{r} - \vec{a}).\vec{n} = 0$

$\therefore \quad [\vec{r} - (5\hat{i} + 2\hat{j} - 4\hat{k})]\cdot(2\hat{i} + 3\hat{j} - \hat{k}) = 0$

$\Rightarrow \vec{r}\cdot(2\hat{i} + 3\hat{j} - \hat{k}) = (5\hat{i} + 2\hat{j} - 4\hat{k})\cdot(2\hat{i} + 3\hat{j} - \hat{k})$

$\Rightarrow \vec{r}\cdot(2\hat{i} + 3\hat{j} - \hat{k}) = 10 + 6 + 4$

$\Rightarrow \vec{r}\cdot(2\hat{i} + 3\hat{j} - \hat{k}) = 20,$

which is the required vector equation.

On putting $\vec{r} = x\hat{i} + y\hat{j} + z\hat{k}$, we get

$(x\hat{i} + y\hat{j} + z\hat{k})\cdot(2\hat{i} + 3\hat{j} - \hat{k}) = 20$

$\Rightarrow \quad 2x + 3y - z = 20$

which is the required equation of plane in cartesian form.

Alternate Method

Here, point $A(x_1, y_1, z_1) = (5, 2, -4)$ and direction ratios of normal to the plane a, b, c are 2, 3, –1, respectively. Since, the cartesian equation of plane passing through one point is given by

$$a(x - x_1) + b(y - y_1) + c(z - z_1) = 0$$

$\therefore \quad 2(x - 5) + 3(y - 2) - 1(z + 4) = 0$

$\Rightarrow \quad 2x + 3y - z - 10 - 6 - 4 = 0$

$\Rightarrow \quad 2x + 3y - z = 20$

Example 6 Find the equation of the plane passing through the point (2, – 3, 1) and perpendicular to the line joining the points (4, 5, 0) and (1, – 2, 4). **[ISC 2020]**

Sol. Equation of the plane passing through the point (2, – 3, 1) and perpendicular to the line joining the points (4, 5, 0) and (1, – 2, 4).

Here, direction ratios of normal to the line joining the points (4, 5, 0) and (1, – 2, 4) are (1 –4, – 2 – 5, 4 – 0) = (– 3, – 7, 4).

Equation of plane is

$$-3(x - 2) - 7(y + 3) + 4(z - 1) = 0$$

$\Rightarrow \quad -3x + 6 - 7y - 21 + 4z - 4 = 0$

$\Rightarrow \quad 3x + 7y - 4z + 19 = 0$

Example 7 Find the vector equation of the plane passing through the point $5\hat{i} + 2\hat{j} - 3\hat{k}$ and perpendicular to each of the planes $\vec{r}\cdot(2\hat{i} - \hat{j} + 2\hat{k}) = 0$ and $\hat{r}\cdot(\hat{i} + 3\hat{j} - 5\hat{k}) + 3 = 0.$

Sol. Let $\vec{n}$ be a vector normal to the required plane.

Given, $\vec{n_1} = 2\hat{i} - \hat{j} + 2\hat{k}$

and $\quad \vec{n_2} = \hat{i} + 3\hat{j} - 5\hat{k}$

Since, the required plane is to be perpendicular to each of the two given planes.

$\therefore \quad \vec{n} = \vec{n_1} \times \vec{n_2} = (2\hat{i} - \hat{j} + 2\hat{k}) \times (\hat{i} + 3\hat{j} - 5\hat{k})$

$$= \begin{vmatrix} \hat{i} & \hat{j} & \hat{k} \\ 2 & -1 & 2 \\ 1 & 3 & -5 \end{vmatrix} = -\hat{i} + 12\hat{j} + 7\hat{k}$$

Hence, the required plane is that which passes through the point $(5\hat{i} + 2\hat{j} - 3\hat{k})$ and is perpendicular to the vector $-\hat{i} + 12\hat{j} + 7\hat{k}$

$\therefore \quad [\vec{r} - (5\hat{i} + 2\hat{j} - 3\hat{k})]\cdot(-\hat{i} + 12\hat{j} + 7\hat{k}) = 0$

$\Rightarrow \vec{r}\cdot(-\hat{i} + 12\hat{j} + 7\hat{k}) = (5\hat{i} + 2\hat{j} - 3\hat{k})\cdot(-\hat{i} + 12\hat{j} + 7\hat{k})$

$[\because (\vec{r} - \vec{a})\cdot\vec{n_1} \times \vec{n_2} = 0]$

$\Rightarrow \quad \vec{r}(\hat{i} - 12\hat{j} - 7\hat{k}) = 2$

Example 8 Find the equation of the plane passing through the point (1, 1, – 1) and perpendicular to the planes $x + 2y + 3z = 7$ and $2x - 3y + 4z = 0.$ **[ISC 2023]**

Sol. Let the equation of plane passing through (1, 1, – 1) is

$$a(x - 1) + b(y - 1) + c(z + 1) = 0 \quad \text{...(i)}$$

Since, this plane is perpendicular to plane

$x + 2y + 3z = 7$ and $2x - 3y + 4z = 0$

$\therefore \quad a + 2b + 3c = 7 \quad$ ...(ii)

$2a - 3b + 4c = 0 \quad$ ...(iii)

Solving Eqs. (ii) and (iii) by cross-multiplication method,

$$\frac{a}{8 + 9} = \frac{b}{6 - 4} = \frac{c}{-3 - 4}$$

$\Rightarrow \quad \frac{a}{17} = \frac{b}{2} = \frac{c}{-7} = \lambda$

$\Rightarrow \quad a = 17\lambda, b = 2\lambda, c = -7\lambda$

Putting the values of a, b, c in Eq. (i), we get

$17(x - 1) + 2(y - 1) - 7(z + 1) = 0$

$\Rightarrow \quad 17x - 17 + 2y - 2 - 7z - 7 = 0$

$\Rightarrow \quad 17x + 2y - 7z = 26$

which is equation of required plane.

Equation of Plane Passing through Three Non-collinear Points

Vector Equation

The equation of plane passing through three non-collinear points R, S and T with position vectors $\vec{a}$, $\vec{b}$ and $\vec{c}$ is

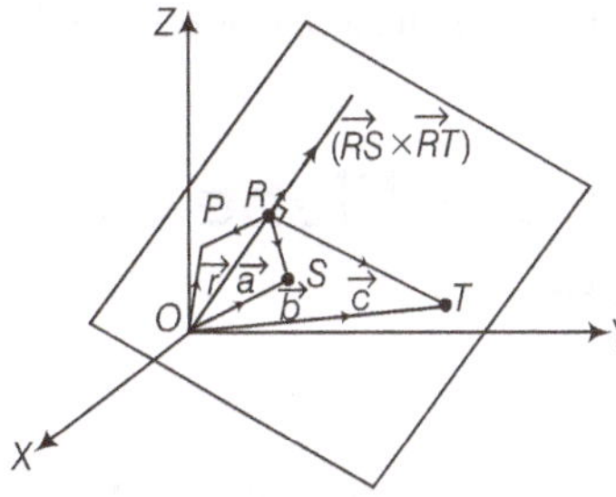

$$(\vec{r}-\vec{a})\cdot[(\vec{b}-\vec{a})\times(\vec{c}-\vec{a})]=0$$

where, $\vec{r}$ is the position vector of any point P on the plane.

Cartesian Equation

The cartesian equation of a plane passing through three non-collinear points $R(x_1, y_1, z_1), S(x_2, y_2, z_2)$ and $T(x_3, y_3, z_3)$ is

$$\begin{vmatrix} x-x_1 & y-y_1 & z-z_1 \\ x_2-x_1 & y_2-y_1 & z_2-z_1 \\ x_3-x_1 & y_3-y_1 & z_3-z_1 \end{vmatrix}=0$$

where, $P(x, y, z)$ be any point on the plane.

Note

(i) The given three points must be non-collinear. If the three points were on the same line, then there will be many planes that will contain them.

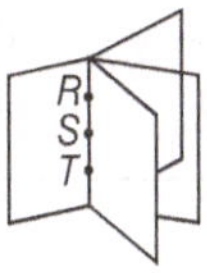

(ii) The points $A(x_1, y_1, z_1)$, $B(x_2, y_2, z_2)$ and $C(x_3, y_3, z_3)$ are non-collinear, if DR's of AB and BC are not proportional.

(iii) To show four points are coplanar, find the equation of plane passing through three points and then satisfy the fourth point.

Example 9 Find the vector equation of the plane passing through the points $R(2, 5, -3)$, $S(-2, -3, 5)$ and $T(5, 3, -3)$. **[NCERT]**

Sol. First, check the condition of non-collinear points.

Here, DR's of RS are $-4, -8, 8$

and DR's of ST are $7, 6, -8$.

$\because$ DR's of RS and ST are not proportional.

$\therefore$ The points are non-collinear.

Let the position vectors of given points $R(2, 5, -3)$, $S(-2,-3,5)$ and $T(5,3,-3)$ be $\vec{a}, \vec{b}$ and $\vec{c}$, respectively.

Then, $\vec{a}=2\hat{i}+5\hat{j}-3\hat{k}$, $\vec{b}=-2\hat{i}-3\hat{j}+5\hat{k}$

and $\vec{c}=5\hat{i}+3\hat{j}-3\hat{k}$.

The vector equation of a plane passing through three non-collinear points is $(\vec{r}-\vec{a})\cdot[(\vec{b}-\vec{a})\times(\vec{c}-\vec{a})]=0$

$$\therefore\ [\vec{r}-(2\hat{i}+5\hat{j}-3\hat{k})]\cdot[\{(-2\hat{i}-3\hat{j}+5\hat{k})-(2\hat{i}+5\hat{j}-3\hat{k})\}\times\{(5\hat{i}+3\hat{j}-3\hat{k})-(2\hat{i}+5\hat{j}-3\hat{k})\}]=0$$

$$\Rightarrow [\vec{r}-(2\hat{i}+5\hat{j}-3\hat{k})]\cdot[(-4\hat{i}-8\hat{j}+8\hat{k})\times(3\hat{i}-2\hat{j})]=0 \quad \text{...(i)}$$

Now, $(-4\hat{i}-8\hat{j}+8\hat{k})\times(3\hat{i}-2\hat{j})=\begin{vmatrix} \hat{i} & \hat{j} & \hat{k} \\ -4 & -8 & 8 \\ 3 & -2 & 0 \end{vmatrix}$

$$=\hat{i}(0+16)-\hat{j}(0-24)+\hat{k}(8+24)=16\hat{i}+24\hat{j}+32\hat{k}$$

From Eq. (i), we get

$$[\vec{r}-(2\hat{i}+5\hat{j}-3\hat{k})]\cdot(16\hat{i}+24\hat{j}+32\hat{k})=0$$

$$\Rightarrow \vec{r}\cdot(16\hat{i}+24\hat{j}+32\hat{k})=(2\hat{i}+5\hat{j}-3\hat{k})\cdot(16\hat{i}+24\hat{j}+32\hat{k})$$

$$\Rightarrow \vec{r}\cdot(16\hat{i}+24\hat{j}+32\hat{k})=32+120-96$$

$$\Rightarrow \vec{r}\cdot(16\hat{i}+24\hat{j}+32\hat{k})=56$$

which is the required equation of the plane in vector form.

Example 10 Find the cartesian equation of the plane passing through the points $A(2, 2, -1)$, $B(3, 4, 2)$ and $C(7, 0, 6)$.

Sol. Here, DR's of AB are $1, 2, 3$ and DR's of BC are $4, -4, 4$.

$\because$ DR's of AB and BC are not proportional.

$\therefore$ The points are non-collinear.

Since, the cartesian equation of plane passing through three points $A(x_1, y_1, z_1)$, $B(x_2, y_2, z_2)$ and $C(x_3, y_3, z_3)$ is given by

$$\begin{vmatrix} x-x_1 & y-y_1 & z-z_1 \\ x_2-x_1 & y_2-y_1 & z_2-z_1 \\ x_3-x_1 & y_3-y_1 & z_3-z_1 \end{vmatrix}=0$$

$$\therefore \begin{vmatrix} x-2 & y-2 & z+1 \\ 3-2 & 4-2 & 2+1 \\ 7-2 & 0-2 & 6+1 \end{vmatrix}=0$$

$$\Rightarrow \begin{vmatrix} x-2 & y-2 & z+1 \\ 1 & 2 & 3 \\ 5 & -2 & 7 \end{vmatrix}=0$$

Expanding along R_1, we get

$$(x-2)(14+6)-(y-2)(7-15)+(z+1)(-2-10)=0$$

$$\Rightarrow 20(x-2)+8(y-2)-12(z+1)=0$$

$\Rightarrow \quad 5(x-2)+2(y-2)-3(z+1)=0$ [dividing by 4]

$\Rightarrow \quad 5x+2y-3z=17$

which is the required equation of the plane in cartesian form.

Equation of a Plane in Intercept Form

The equation of a plane having intercepts of length a, b and c with coordinate axes X, Y and Z respectively is

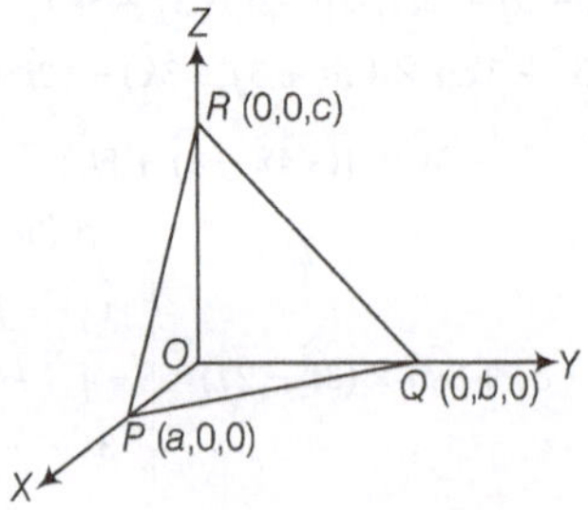

$$\boxed{\frac{x}{a}+\frac{y}{b}+\frac{z}{c}=1}$$

which is known as **intercept form.**

Example 11 Find the equation of the plane with intercept 2, 3 and 4 on the X, Y and Z-axes, respectively.

Sol. Here, $a=2$, $b=3$ and $c=4$

$\therefore$ Equation of plane is $\frac{x}{2}+\frac{y}{3}+\frac{z}{4}=1$

$\Rightarrow \quad \frac{6x+4y+3z}{12}=1$

$\Rightarrow \quad 6x+4y+3z=12$

which is the required equation of plane.

Example 12 Write the equation of the plane passing through the point (2, 4, 6) and making equal intercepts on the coordinate axes. [ISC 2023]

Sol. Equation of plane in intercept form is $\frac{x}{a}+\frac{y}{b}+\frac{z}{c}=1$

Here, $a=b=c$

$\therefore x+y+z=a$

Since, this plane is passing through (2, 4, 6).

$\therefore 2+4+6=a \Rightarrow a=12$

$\therefore$ Required equation of plane is

$x+y+z=12$

Example 13 Reduce the equation of the plane $4x+3y-6z-12=0$ into intercept form and find its intercepts on the coordinate axes.

Sol. Given equation of plane is $4x+3y-6z=12$

On dividing both sides by 12, we get

$\frac{4x}{12}+\frac{3y}{12}-\frac{6z}{12}=1 \Rightarrow \frac{x}{3}+\frac{y}{4}-\frac{z}{2}=1$

$\Rightarrow \quad \frac{x}{3}+\frac{y}{4}+\frac{z}{(-2)}=1$

which is the intercept form of equation of plane.

On comparing with $\frac{x}{a}+\frac{y}{b}+\frac{z}{c}=1$, we get

$a=3$, $b=4$ and $c=-2$

So, intercept on X, Y and Z-axes are 3, 4 and -2 units, respectively.

Equation of a Plane containing Two Lines

Vector Form

If two lines $\vec{r}=\vec{a_1}+\lambda\vec{b_1}$ and $\vec{r}=\vec{a_2}+\mu\vec{b_2}$ are coplanar, then the vector $(\vec{b_1}\times\vec{b_2})$ is perpendicular to their common plane and this plane passes through to the each points $\vec{a_1}$ and $\vec{a_2}$, then vector equation of the required plane is

$$(\vec{r}-\vec{a_1})\cdot(\vec{b_1}\times\vec{b_2})=0 \text{ or } (\vec{r}-\vec{a_2})\cdot(\vec{b_1}\times\vec{b_2})=0$$

Cartesian Form

The cartesian equation of the required plane is

$$\begin{vmatrix} x-x_1 & y-y_1 & z-z_1 \\ a_1 & b_1 & c_1 \\ a_2 & b_2 & c_2 \end{vmatrix}=0$$

or

$$\begin{vmatrix} x-x_2 & y-y_2 & z-z_2 \\ a_1 & b_1 & c_1 \\ a_2 & b_2 & c_2 \end{vmatrix}=0$$

Example 14 Find the equation of the plane which contains the lines $\frac{x-2}{1}=\frac{y-4}{4}=\frac{z-6}{7}$ and $\frac{x+1}{3}=\frac{y+3}{5}=\frac{z+5}{7}$

Sol. Given lines are

$$\frac{x-2}{1}=\frac{y-4}{4}=\frac{z-6}{7}$$

and $$\frac{x+1}{3}=\frac{y+3}{5}=\frac{z+5}{7}.$$

Here, the points and direction ratios of given lines are

$x_1 = 2,\ y_1 = 4,\ z_1 = 6,$

$a_1 = 1,\ b_1 = 4,\ c_1 = 7$

and $x_2 = -1,\ y_2 = -3,\ z_2 = -5,$

$a_2 = 3,\ b_2 = 5,\ c_2 = 7$

Now, equation of the plane containing these lines is

$$\begin{vmatrix} x - x_1 & y - y_1 & z - z_1 \\ a_1 & b_1 & c_1 \\ a_2 & b_2 & c_2 \end{vmatrix} = 0$$

$$\Rightarrow \begin{vmatrix} x - 2 & y - 4 & z - 6 \\ 1 & 4 & 7 \\ 3 & 5 & 7 \end{vmatrix} = 0$$

Expanding along R_1, we get

$$(x - 2)(28 - 35) - (y - 4)(7 - 21) + (z - 6)(5 - 12) = 0$$

$$\Rightarrow -7(x - 2) + 14(y - 4) - 7(z - 6) = 0$$

$$\Rightarrow -7x + 14 + 14y - 56 - 7z + 42 = 0$$

$$\Rightarrow -7x + 14y - 7z = 0$$

$$\Rightarrow x - 2y + z = 0 \quad \text{[dividing by } (-7)]$$

which is the required equation of plane containing given lines. **Hence proved.**

Angle between Two Planes

The angle between two planes is defined as the angle between their normals, if θ is an angle between the two planes, then other angle will be $180° - \theta$. We will take the acute angle as the angle between two planes.

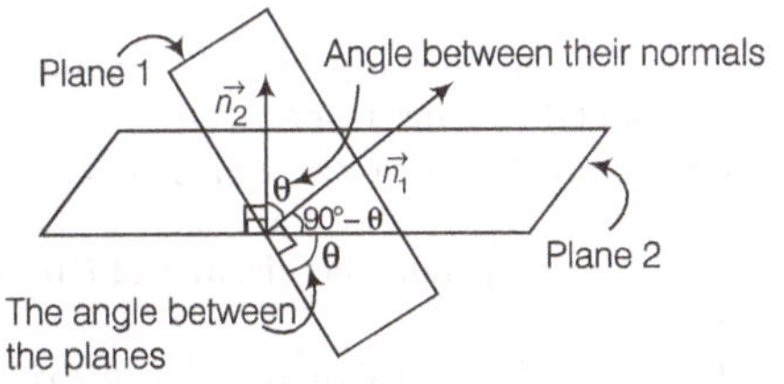

Vector Form

If $\vec{n}_1$ and $\vec{n}_2$ are normals to the planes and θ is the angle between the planes $\vec{r} \cdot \vec{n}_1 = d_1$ and $\vec{r} \cdot \vec{n}_2 = d_2$.

Then, $$\boxed{\cos\theta = \left| \frac{\vec{n}_1 \cdot \vec{n}_2}{|\vec{n}_1|\,|\vec{n}_2|} \right|}$$

Two planes are perpendicular to each other, if their normals are perpendicular, i.e. $\vec{n}_1 \cdot \vec{n}_2 = 0$ and two planes are parallel to each other, if their normals are parallel, i.e. $\vec{n_1} = \lambda \vec{n_2}$ for some scalar λ.

Cartesian Form

If θ is the angle between two planes

$$a_1 x + b_1 y + c_1 z + d_1 = 0$$

and $$a_2 x + b_2 y + c_2 z + d_2 = 0.$$

Then, $$\boxed{\cos\theta = \left| \frac{a_1 a_2 + b_1 b_2 + c_1 c_2}{\sqrt{a_1^2 + b_1^2 + c_1^2}\sqrt{a_2^2 + b_2^2 + c_2^2}} \right|}$$

Two planes are **perpendicular** to each other, if $a_1 a_2 + b_1 b_2 + c_1 c_2 = 0$ and **parallel**, if $\frac{a_1}{a_2} = \frac{b_1}{b_2} = \frac{c_1}{c_2}$.

Example 15 Find the angle between the planes whose vector equations are $\vec{r} \cdot (2\hat{i} + 2\hat{j} - 3\hat{k}) = 5$ and $\vec{r} \cdot (3\hat{i} - 3\hat{j} + 5\hat{k}) = 3$.

Sol. Given planes are

$$\vec{r} \cdot (2\hat{i} + 2\hat{j} - 3\hat{k}) = 5 \text{ and } \vec{r} \cdot (3\hat{i} - 3\hat{j} + 5\hat{k}) = 3$$

Here, $\vec{n_1} = 2\hat{i} + 2\hat{j} - 3\hat{k}$ and $\vec{n_2} = 3\hat{i} - 3\hat{j} + 5\hat{k}$

$$\therefore \vec{n_1} \cdot \vec{n_2} = (2\hat{i} + 2\hat{j} - 3\hat{k}) \cdot (3\hat{i} - 3\hat{j} + 5\hat{k})$$

$$= 2 \cdot 3 + 2 \cdot (-3) + (-3) \cdot 5$$

$$= 6 - 6 - 15 = -15$$

$$|\vec{n_1}| = \sqrt{(2)^2 + (2)^2 + (-3)^2} = \sqrt{4 + 4 + 9} = \sqrt{17}$$

and $$|\vec{n_2}| = \sqrt{(3)^2 + (-3)^2 + (5)^2}$$

$$= \sqrt{9 + 9 + 25} = \sqrt{43}$$

We know that angle between two planes is given by

$$\cos\theta = \left| \frac{\vec{n_1} \cdot \vec{n_2}}{|\vec{n_1}||\vec{n_2}|} \right| \quad \text{...(i)}$$

On putting the values of $\vec{n_1} \cdot \vec{n_2}$, $|\vec{n_1}|$ and $|\vec{n_2}|$ in Eq. (i), we get

$$\cos\theta = \left| \frac{-15}{\sqrt{17}\sqrt{43}} \right| \Rightarrow \cos\theta = \frac{15}{\sqrt{731}}$$

$$\Rightarrow \theta = \cos^{-1}\left(\frac{15}{\sqrt{731}}\right) \text{ which is the required angle.}$$

Example 16 Find the angle between the two planes $3x - 6y + 2z - 7 = 0$ and $2x + 2y - 2z - 5 = 0$.

Sol. Given equations of planes are

$$3x - 6y + 2z - 7 = 0 \text{ and } 2x + 2y - 2z - 5 = 0$$

On comparing with $a_1 x + b_1 y + c_1 z + d_1 = 0$

and $a_2 x + b_2 y + c_2 z + d_2 = 0$, we get

$$a_1 = 3, b_1 = -6, c_1 = 2 \text{ and } a_2 = 2, b_2 = 2, c_2 = -2$$

Now, the angle between two planes is given by

$$\theta = \cos^{-1}\left|\frac{a_1a_2 + b_1b_2 + c_1c_2}{\sqrt{a_1^2 + b_1^2 + c_1^2}\sqrt{a_2^2 + b_2^2 + c_2^2}}\right|$$

$$= \cos^{-1}\left|\frac{3\times 2 + (-6)\times 2 + 2\times(-2)}{\sqrt{3^2 + (-6)^2 + (2)^2}\sqrt{2^2 + 2^2 + (-2)^2}}\right|$$

$$= \cos^{-1}\left|\frac{6-12-4}{\sqrt{9+36+4}\sqrt{4+4+4}}\right|$$

$$= \cos^{-1}\left|\frac{-10}{\sqrt{49}\sqrt{12}}\right|$$

$$= \cos^{-1}\left(\frac{10}{7\times 2\sqrt{3}}\right) = \cos^{-1}\left(\frac{5\sqrt{3}}{21}\right)$$

Example 17 Find the equation of the plane parallel to the plane $3x - 2y + z + 5 = 0$ and passing through the point (1, 1, 2).

Sol. Equation of plane passing through the point (1, 1, 2) is of the form $a(x-1) + b(y-1) + c(z-2) = 0$ ...(i)

where a, b, c and DR's of normal to the plane.

Since, plane (i) is parallel to the given plane, therefore DR's of their normals will be proportional.

Thus, we get $\frac{a}{3} = \frac{b}{-2} = \frac{c}{1} = \lambda$ (say)

[∵ DR's of normal to given plane are 3, − 2, 1]

$\Rightarrow \quad a = 3\lambda, b = -2\lambda$ and $c = \lambda$

On putting the values of a, b, c in Eq (i), we get

$$3(x-1) - 2(y-1) + (z-2) = 0$$

[∵ $\lambda \neq 0$, dividing both side by λ]

$\Rightarrow \quad 3x - 2y + z - 3 = 0,$

which is the required equation of plane.

Distance of a Point from a Plane

Vector Form

Let a point P with position vector $\vec{a}$ and the plane π_1, whose equation is $\vec{r}\cdot\vec{n} = d$.

Then, perpendicular distance $= \frac{|\vec{a}\cdot\vec{n} - d|}{|\vec{n}|}$

Note (i) The length of perpendicular drawn from the origin O to the plane $\vec{r}\cdot\vec{n} = d$ is $\frac{|d|}{|\vec{n}|}$.

(ii) The position vector of the foot of perpendicular drawn from the point $P(\vec{a})$ to plane $\vec{r}\cdot\vec{n} = d$ is $\vec{a} + \lambda\vec{n}$, where $\lambda = -\frac{\vec{a}\cdot\vec{n} - d}{|\vec{n}|^2}$.

Cartesian Form

Let $P(x_1, y_1, z_1)$ be the given point and $ax + by + cz = d$ be the cartesian equation of the given plane.

Then, perpendicular distance $= \left|\frac{ax_1 + by_1 + cz_1 - d}{\sqrt{a^2 + b^2 + c^2}}\right|$

Note The length of the perpendicular from the origin to the plane $ax + by + cz + d = 0$ is $\frac{|d|}{\sqrt{a^2 + b^2 + c^2}}$.

Example 18 In the figure given below, if the coordinates of the point P are (a, b, c), then what are the perpendicular distances of P from XY, YZ and ZX planes respectively? **[ISC 2024]**

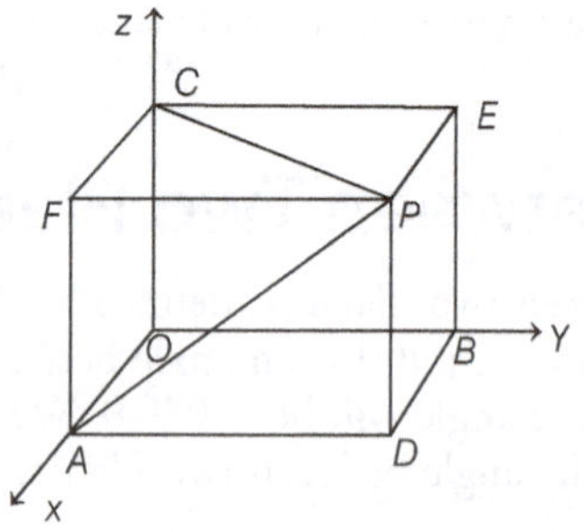

Sol. Let PD, PE and PF are the perpendicular distance of P from XY, YZ and ZX-planes respectively.

Now, for any point $P(a, b, c)$, a is perpendicular distance of P from YZ-plane, b is perpendicular distance of P from XZ-plane and c is perpendicular distance of P from XY-plane.

Hence, the perpendicular distances of $P(a, b, c)$ from XY, YZ and ZX-planes are c, a and b, respectively.

Example 19 Find the length of the perpendicular from origin to the plane $\vec{r}\cdot(3\hat{i} - 4\hat{j} - 12\hat{k}) + 39 = 0$. **[ISC 2019]**

Sol. We know that the equation of plane, which is at a distance of d from the origin and having unit vector $\hat{n}$ is

$$\vec{r}\cdot\hat{n} = d \quad ...(i)$$

Given equation of plane can be written as

$$\vec{r}\cdot(3\hat{i} - 4\hat{j} - 12\hat{k}) = -39$$

or $$\vec{r}\cdot(-3\hat{i} + 4\hat{j} + 12\hat{k}) = 39 \quad ...(ii)$$

Now, $\sqrt{(-3)^2+(4)^2+(12)^2}=\sqrt{9+16+144}$
$=\sqrt{169}=13$

On dividing both sides of Eq. (ii) by 13, we get

$$\frac{\vec{r}\cdot(-3\hat{i}+4\hat{j}+12\hat{k})}{13}=\frac{39}{13}$$

$$\Rightarrow \quad \vec{r}\left(\frac{-3}{13}\hat{i}+\frac{4}{13}\hat{j}+\frac{12}{13}\hat{k}\right)=3 \quad \text{...(iii)}$$

On comparing Eqs. (i) and (iii), we get

$$d=3$$

Example 20 Find the distance of a point (2, 2, −1) from the plane

(i) $\vec{r}\cdot(3\hat{i}-3\hat{j}+5\hat{k})=7$ (ii) $3x-3y+5z=7$

Sol. (i) Let the position vector of given point is

$$\vec{a}=2\hat{i}+2\hat{j}-\hat{k}.$$

Here, $\vec{n}=3\hat{i}-3\hat{j}+5\hat{k}$ and $d=7$

$$\therefore \text{ Required distance }=\frac{|\vec{a}\cdot\vec{n}-d|}{|\vec{n}|}$$

$$=\frac{|(2\hat{i}+2\hat{j}-\hat{k})\cdot(3\hat{i}-3\hat{j}+5\hat{k})-7|}{\sqrt{(3)^2+(-3)^2+(5)^2}}$$

$$=\frac{|(6-6-5)-7|}{\sqrt{9+9+25}}$$

$$=\frac{|-12|}{\sqrt{43}}=\frac{12}{\sqrt{43}}$$

(ii) Given point is $(x_1, y_1, z_1)=(2, 2, -1)$ and equation of plane is $3x-3y+5z=7$

$$\therefore \text{ Required distance }=\left|\frac{ax_1+by_1+cz_1-d}{\sqrt{a^2+b^2+c^2}}\right|$$

$$=\left|\frac{3\times2-3\times2+5\times(-1)-7}{\sqrt{3^2+(-3)^2+5^2}}\right|$$

$$=\left|\frac{6-6-5-7}{\sqrt{9+9+25}}\right|=\frac{|-12|}{\sqrt{43}}=\frac{12}{\sqrt{43}}$$

Example 21 Find the equation of the planes parallel to the plane $2x-4y+4z=7$ and which are at a distance of five units from the point (3, −1, 2). **[ISC 2013]**

Sol. The equation of the plane parallel to the plane $2x-4y+4z=7$ is given by

$$2x-4y+4z+k=0 \quad \text{...(i)}$$

Since, the required plane (*i*) is at a distance of 5 units from the point (3, −1, 2).

$$\therefore \quad \left|\frac{2(3)-4(-1)+4(2)+k}{\sqrt{4+16+16}}\right|=5$$

[∵ perpendicular distance from (x_1, y_1, z_1) to the plane $ax+by+cz\ d=0$ is $\left|\frac{ax_1+by_1+cz_1}{\sqrt{a^2+b^2+c^2}}\right|$]

$$\Rightarrow \quad \left|\frac{6+4+8+k}{\sqrt{36}}\right|=5 \Rightarrow \frac{18+k}{6}=\pm5$$

$$\Rightarrow \quad k=\pm30-18 \Rightarrow k=12 \text{ or } k=-30-18$$

$$\therefore \quad k=-48$$

Hence, the possible equations of required plane are $2x-4y+4z+12=0$ and $2x-4y+4z-48=0$.

[put $k=12$ and $k=-48$ in Eq. (i)]

Example 22 A variable plane which remains at a constant distance $3p$ from the origin cuts the coordinate axes at A, B, C. Show that the locus of the centroid of ΔABC is $\frac{1}{x^2}+\frac{1}{y^2}+\frac{1}{z^2}=\frac{1}{p^2}$.

Sol. Let the equation of variable plane is $\frac{x}{a}+\frac{y}{b}+\frac{z}{c}=1$ ...(i)

Clearly, above plane (i) meets the X-axis, Y-axis and Z-axis at the point $A(a, 0, 0)$, $B(0, b, 0)$ and $C(0, 0, c)$, respectively.

Now, let (α, β, γ) be the coordinates of the centroid of ΔABC.

Then, $\alpha=\frac{a+0+0}{3}$, $\beta=\frac{0+b+0}{3}$ and $\gamma=\frac{0+0+c}{3}$

$$\Rightarrow \quad \alpha=\frac{a}{3}, \beta=\frac{b}{3} \text{ and } \gamma=\frac{c}{3}$$

$$\Rightarrow \quad a=3\alpha, b=3\beta \text{ and } c=3\gamma \quad \text{...(ii)}$$

∵ $3p$ = length of the perpendicular from (0, 0, 0) to the plane (i)

$$\Rightarrow \quad 3p=\frac{\left|\frac{0}{a}+\frac{0}{b}+\frac{0}{c}-1\right|}{\sqrt{\frac{1}{a^2}+\frac{1}{b^2}+\frac{1}{c^2}}}$$

$$\Rightarrow \quad 3p=\frac{1}{\sqrt{\frac{1}{a^2}+\frac{1}{b^2}+\frac{1}{c^2}}}$$

$$\Rightarrow \quad \frac{1}{a^2}+\frac{1}{b^2}+\frac{1}{c^2}=\frac{1}{9p^2}$$

$$\Rightarrow \quad \frac{1}{9\alpha^2}+\frac{1}{9\beta^2}+\frac{1}{9\gamma^2}=\frac{1}{9p^2} \quad \text{[using Eq. (ii)]}$$

$$\Rightarrow \quad \frac{1}{\alpha^2}+\frac{1}{\beta^2}+\frac{1}{\gamma^2}=\frac{1}{p^2}$$

Hence, the locus of centroid is $\frac{1}{x^2}+\frac{1}{y^2}+\frac{1}{z^2}=\frac{1}{p^2}$.

Hence proved.

Example 23 Find the image of a point having position vector $(3\hat{i} - 2\hat{j} + \hat{k})$ in the plane $\vec{r} \cdot (3\hat{i} - \hat{j} + 4\hat{k}) = 2$. **[ISC 2018]**

Or

Find the image of the point (3, – 2, 1) in the plane $3x - y + 4z = 2$. **[ISC 2020]**

Sol. Let point $Q(\alpha, \beta, \gamma)$ are image of point $P(3, -2, 1)$ in the plane $\vec{r} \cdot (3\hat{i} - \hat{j} + 4\hat{k}) = 2$

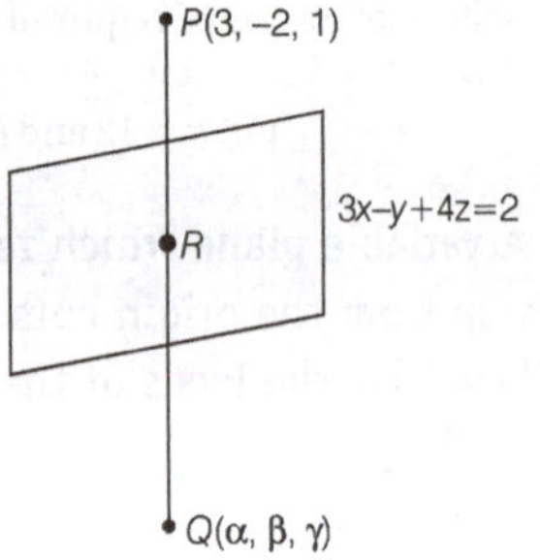

Direction ratio of normal to the plane is (3, –1, 4) and direction ratio of line $PQ(\alpha - 3, \beta + 2, \gamma - 1)$.

Line PQ is parallel to the normal of plane.

$$\therefore \quad \frac{\alpha - 3}{3} = \frac{\beta + 2}{-1} = \frac{\gamma - 1}{4} = \lambda$$

$$\Rightarrow \quad \alpha = 3\lambda + 3, \ \beta = -\lambda - 2, \ \gamma = 4\lambda + 1$$

$\because$ R is mid-point PQ.

$$\therefore \quad R\left(\frac{3\lambda + 6}{2}, \frac{-\lambda - 4}{2}, \frac{4\lambda + 2}{2}\right)$$

Since, R lies on plane $3x - y + 4z = 2$.

$$\therefore \quad 3\left(\frac{3\lambda + 6}{2}\right) - \left(\frac{-\lambda - 4}{2}\right) + 4\left(\frac{4\lambda + 2}{2}\right) = 2$$

$$\Rightarrow 9\lambda + 18 + \lambda + 4 + 16\lambda + 8 = 4$$

$$\Rightarrow \quad \lambda = -1$$

$$\therefore \quad Q(-3 + 3, 1 - 2, -4 + 1) = Q(0, -1, -3)$$

Hence, image of point $P(3, -2, 1)$ in the plane is $(0, -1, -3)$.

Distance between Parallel Planes

Let $a_1x + b_1y + c_1z + d_1 = 0$ and $a_1x + b_1y + c_1z + d$ be two parallel planes. Then, for the distance between them, we take a point $P(x_1, y_1, z_1)$ on any one of given planes and find the perpendicular distance from $P(x_1, y_1, z_1)$ to the other plane.

Example 24 Find the distance between the parallel planes $2x - y + 2z + 3 = 0$ and $4x - 2y + 4z + 5 = 0$.

Sol. Given equations of planes are

$$2x - y + 2z + 3 = 0 \quad \text{...(i)}$$

and

$$4x - 2y + 4z + 5 = 0 \quad \text{...(ii)}$$

The given planes are parallel, as DR's of normals are proportional.

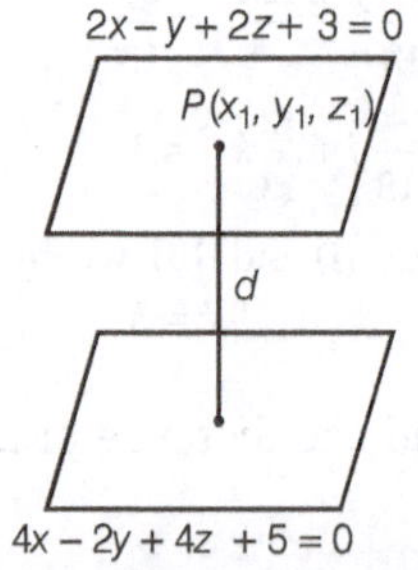

Let $P(x_1, y_1, z_1)$ be any point lies on the plane (i).

Then, $$2x_1 - y_1 + 2z_1 + 3 = 0$$

$$\Rightarrow \quad 2x_1 - y_1 + 2z_1 = -3 \quad \text{...(iii)}$$

Now, perpendicular distance d from the point $P(x_1, y_1, z_1)$ to plane (ii) is

$$d = \left|\frac{4x_1 - 2y_1 + 4z_1 + 5}{\sqrt{(4)^2 + (-2)^2 + (4)^2}}\right| = \left|\frac{2(2x_1 - y_1 + 2z_1) + 5}{\sqrt{16 + 4 + 16}}\right|$$

$$= \left|\frac{2(-3) + 5}{\sqrt{36}}\right| = \left|\frac{-6 + 5}{6}\right| = \frac{|-1|}{6} = \frac{1}{6} \quad \text{[from Eq. (iii)]}$$

Intersection of a Line and a Plane

Let P be the point of intersection of the line

$$\frac{x - x_1}{a} = \frac{y - y_1}{b} = \frac{z - z_1}{c} \quad \text{...(i)}$$

and plane $Ax + By + Cz + D = 0$ ...(ii)

Since, P lies on the line (i), therefore its coordinates will be $(x_1 + ar, y_1 + br, z_1 + cr)$.

Since, P lies on the plane (ii), therefore

$$A(x_1 + ar) + B(y_1 + br) + C(z_1 + cr) + D = 0$$

$$\Rightarrow \quad \boxed{r = -\frac{Ax_1 + By_1 + Cz_1 + D}{aA + bB + cC}}$$

Example 25 Find the point of intersection of the line $\frac{x-1}{2} = \frac{y-2}{-3} = \frac{z+3}{4}$ and the plane $2x + 4y - z + 1 = 0$.

Sol. Let the point of intersection of the given line and plane is P. Since P lies on the given line.

$\therefore$ its coordinates are $(2r + 1, -3r + 2, 4r - 3)$.

Since, P also, lies on the given plane, therefore

$$2(2r + 1) + 4(-3r + 2) - 1(4r - 3) + 1 = 0$$

$$\Rightarrow \quad r = \frac{7}{6} \Rightarrow P \equiv \left(\frac{10}{3}, \frac{-3}{2}, \frac{5}{3}\right)$$

Angle between a Line and a Plane

The angle between a line and a plane is the complement of the angle between the line and normal to the plane.

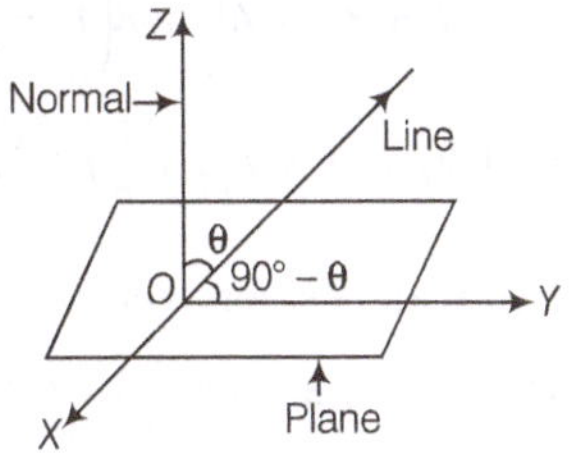

Vector Form

If the equation of the line is $\vec{r} = \vec{a} + \lambda \vec{b}$ and the equation of the plane is $\vec{r} \cdot \vec{n} = d$, then the angle θ between the line and the normal to the plane is given by

$$\cos \theta = \left| \frac{\vec{b} \cdot \vec{n}}{|\vec{b}||\vec{n}|} \right|$$

Let ϕ be the angle between line and plane, then it is equal to the $(90° - \theta)$.

Now, $\sin \phi = \sin (90° - \theta) = \cos\theta \Rightarrow \sin \phi = \cos\theta$

$$\Rightarrow \quad \sin \phi = \left| \frac{\vec{b} \cdot \vec{n}}{|\vec{b}||\vec{n}|} \right| \text{ or } \phi = \sin^{-1} \left| \frac{\vec{b} \cdot \vec{n}}{|\vec{b}||\vec{n}|} \right|$$

which is the required angle between a line and a plane.

Deduction

(i) If the line $\vec{r} = \vec{a} + \lambda \vec{b}$ is parallel to the plane $\vec{r} \cdot \vec{n} = d$, (i.e. normal line is perpendicular to the line) then $\vec{n} \cdot \vec{b} = 0$. $[\because \theta = 0°]$

(ii) If the line $\vec{r} = \vec{a} + \lambda \vec{b}$ is perpendicular to the plane $\vec{r} \cdot \vec{n} = d$, i.e. normal line is parallel to the line, then $\vec{n} = \mu \vec{b}$. $[\because \theta = 90°]$

Cartesian Form

If the equation of a line is $\frac{x - x_1}{a_1} = \frac{y - y_1}{b_1} = \frac{z - z_1}{c_1}$ and equation of a plane is $a_2 x + b_2 y + c_2 z = d_2$, then the angle between line and plane is given by

$$\sin \phi = \left| \frac{a_1 a_2 + b_1 b_2 + c_1 c_2}{\sqrt{a_1^2 + b_1^2 + c_1^2}\sqrt{a_2^2 + b_2^2 + c_2^2}} \right|$$

Deduction

(i) If line is perpendicular to plane, then $\frac{a_1}{a_2} = \frac{b_1}{b_2} = \frac{c_1}{c_2}$.

(ii) If the line is parallel to the plane, then $a_1 a_2 + b_1 b_2 + c_1 c_2 = 0$.

Example 26 Find the angle between the line $\vec{r} = (-\hat{i} + 3\hat{k}) + \lambda (2\hat{i} + 3\hat{j} + 6\hat{k})$ and plane $\vec{r} \cdot (10\hat{i} + 2\hat{j} - 11\hat{k}) = 3$. **[NCERT]**

Sol. Given equation of line is

$$\vec{r} = (-\hat{i} + 3\hat{k}) + \lambda (2\hat{i} + 3\hat{j} + 6\hat{k})$$

and equation of plane is $\vec{r} \cdot (10\hat{i} + 2\hat{j} - 11\hat{k}) = 3$.

On comparing with $\vec{r} = \vec{a} + \lambda \vec{b}$ and $\vec{r} \cdot \vec{n} = d$, we get

$$\vec{b} = (2\hat{i} + 3\hat{j} + 6\hat{k}) \text{ and } \vec{n} = 10\hat{i} + 2\hat{j} - 11\hat{k}$$

The angle ϕ between the line and the plane is

$$\sin \phi = \left| \frac{\vec{b} \cdot \vec{n}}{|\vec{b}||\vec{n}|} \right|$$

$$= \left| \frac{(2\hat{i} + 3\hat{j} + 6\hat{k}) \cdot (10\hat{i} + 2\hat{j} - 11\hat{k})}{\sqrt{(2)^2 + (3)^2 + (6)^2}\sqrt{(10)^2 + (2)^2 + (-11)^2}} \right|$$

$$= \left| \frac{(2)(10) + (3)(2) + (6)(-11)}{\sqrt{4 + 9 + 36}\sqrt{100 + 4 + 121}} \right|$$

$$= \left| \frac{20 + 6 - 66}{\sqrt{49}\sqrt{225}} \right|$$

$$= \left| \frac{-40}{7 \times 15} \right| = \frac{8}{21}$$

$$\therefore \quad \phi = \sin^{-1}\left(\frac{8}{21}\right)$$

Example 27 Find the distance between the line $\vec{r} = 3\hat{i} + 5\hat{j} - 2\hat{k} + \lambda(3\hat{i} + \hat{j} + 3\hat{k})$ and the plane determined by the points $A(1, 1, 0)$, $B(1, 2, 1)$ and $C(-2, 2, -1)$.

Sol. Given line is $\vec{r} = 3\hat{i} + 5\hat{j} - 2\hat{k} + \lambda(3\hat{i} + \hat{j} + 3\hat{k})$.

Now, equation of the plane passing through points $A(1, 1, 0)$, $B(1, 2, 1)$ and $C(-2, 2, -1)$ is

$$\begin{vmatrix} x-1 & y-1 & z \\ 0 & 1 & 1 \\ -3 & 1 & -1 \end{vmatrix} = 0$$

$$\Rightarrow \quad \{(x-1)(-1-1) - (y-1)(0+3) + z(0+3)\} = 0$$

$$\Rightarrow \quad (x-1)(-2) - (y-1)(3) + 3z = 0$$

$$\Rightarrow -2x + 2 - 3y + 3 + 3z = 0 \text{ or } 2x + 3y - 3z - 5 = 0$$

Since, $2(3)+3(1)-3(3)=0$, so the line is parallel to the plane.

$\therefore$ Distance between the line and the plane

= Distance of plane from any point on the line

$$= \left|\frac{2(3)+3(5)+(-3)(-2)-5}{\sqrt{(2)^2+(3)^2+(-3)^2}}\right| = \sqrt{22}$$

[$\because$ (3, 5, – 2) lies on the given line]

Condition for a Line to lie in a Plane

Vector Form

If the line $\vec{r} = \vec{a} + \lambda \vec{b}$ lies in the plane $\vec{r} \cdot \vec{n} = \vec{d}$, then

(i) $\vec{b} \cdot \vec{n} = 0$ (ii) $\vec{a} \cdot \vec{n} = d$.

Cartesian Form

If the line $\dfrac{x - x_1}{l} = \dfrac{y - y_1}{m} = \dfrac{z - z_1}{n}$

lies in the plane $ax + by + cz + d = 0$, then

(i) $ax_1 + by_1 + cz_1 + d = 0$

(ii) $al + bm + cn = 0$

Example 28 Show that the plane

$\vec{r}(-5\hat{i} + 2\hat{j} + 12\hat{k}) = 47$ contains the line

$$\vec{r} = \hat{i} + 2\hat{j} + 4\hat{k} + \lambda\left(\hat{i} + \frac{1}{2}\hat{j} + \frac{1}{3}\hat{k}\right).$$

Sol. Since, line $\vec{r} = \hat{i} + 2\hat{j} + 4\hat{k} + \lambda\left(\hat{i} + \frac{1}{2}\hat{j} + \frac{1}{3}\hat{k}\right)$ passes through the point with position vector $\vec{a} = \hat{i} + 2\hat{j} + 4\hat{k}$ and parallel to the vector $\vec{b} = \hat{i} + \frac{1}{2} + \frac{1}{3}\hat{k}$, the plane $\vec{r}(-5\hat{i} + 2\hat{j} + 12\hat{k}) = 47$ contains the given line, if

(i) it is passes through $\hat{i} + 2\hat{j} + 4\hat{k}$

(ii) it is parallel to the line. Here, we have

$(\hat{i} + 2\hat{j} + 4\hat{k})(-5\hat{i} + 2\hat{j} + 12\hat{k}) = -5 + 4 + 48 = 47$ so, the plane passes through the point $\hat{i} + 2\hat{j} + 4\hat{k}$ and

$\left(\hat{i} + \frac{1}{2}\hat{j} + \frac{1}{3}\hat{k}\right)(-5\hat{i} + 2\hat{j} + 12\hat{k}) = -5 + 1 + 4 = 0.$

Therefore, the plane is parallel to the line. Hence, the plane contains the given line.

Chapter Practice

Multiple Choice Type Questions

1 Mark

1 The reflection of the point (α, β, γ) in the XY-plane is **[NCERT Exemplar]**

(a) $(\alpha, \beta, 0)$ (b) $(0, 0, \gamma)$
(c) $(-\alpha, -\beta, \gamma)$ (d) $(\alpha, \beta, -\gamma)$

2 The distance of the point $2\hat{i} + \hat{j} - \hat{k}$ from the plane $\vec{r} \cdot (\hat{i} - 2\hat{j} + 4\hat{k}) = 9$ will be **[ISC 2023]**

(a) 13 (b) $\frac{13}{\sqrt{21}}$ (c) 21 (d) $\frac{21}{\sqrt{13}}$

3 Find the equation of plane passing through the points $P(1, 1, 1)$, $Q(3, -1, 2)$, $R(-3, 5, -4)$.

(a) $x + 2y = 0$ (b) $x - y - 2 = 0$
(c) $-x + 2y - 2 = 0$ (d) $x + y - 2 = 0$

4 Perpendicular distance between the planes $2x - y + 2z = 1$ and $4x - 2y + 4z = 1$ is

(a) $\frac{1}{3}$ (b) 3 (c) $\frac{1}{6}$ (d) 6

Assertion-Reason Type Questions

1 Mark

Directions (Q. Nos. 5-8) *In the questions given below are two statements labelled as Assertion (A) and Reason (R). In the context of the two statements, which one of the following is correct?*

(a) Both A and R are correct; R is the correct explanation of A
(b) Both A and R are correct; R is not the correct explanation of A
(c) A is correct; R is incorrect
(d) R is correct; A is incorrect

5 **Assertion (A)** One point form of equation of plane is $a(x - x_1) + b(y - y_1) + c(z - z_1) = 0$, where (x_1, y_1, z_1) is the given point and (a, b, c) is the direction ratios of the line perpendicular to the plane.

Reason (R) The equation of a plane having intercepts of length a, b and c with coordinate axes X, Y and Z respectively is $\frac{x}{a} + \frac{y}{b} + \frac{z}{c} = 1$.

6 **Assertion (A)** The angle between the two planes $2x + 4y - 2z = 5$ and $6x - 8y - 2z = 14$ is $\cos^{-1}\left(\frac{2\sqrt{39}}{39}\right)$.

Reason (R) The angle between the line $\vec{r} = \vec{a} + \lambda\vec{b}$ and the plane $\vec{r} \cdot \vec{n} = d$ is given by $\sin^{-1}\left|\frac{\vec{b} \cdot \vec{n}}{|\vec{b}||\vec{n}|}\right|$.

7 **Assertion (A)** The distance of the origin from the plane $2x + 6y - 3z + 7 = 0$ is 1.

Reason (R) The perpendicular distance of the point $P(x_1, y_1, z_1)$ from the plane $ax + by + cz = d$ is given by $\left|\frac{ax_1 + by_1 + cz_1 - d}{\sqrt{a^2 + b^2 + c^2}}\right|$.

8 **Assertion (A)** The distance between two parallel planes $3x - 2y + 2z + 8 = 0$ and $9x - 6y + 6z + 1 = 0$ is $\frac{23\sqrt{7}}{51}$ units.

Reason (R) The angle between the line $\vec{r} = \vec{a} + \lambda\vec{b}$ and the plane $\vec{r}\vec{n} = d$ is given by $\cos^{-1}\left|\frac{\vec{b} \cdot \vec{n}}{|\vec{b}||\vec{n}|}\right|$.

Very Short Answer Type Questions

2 Marks

9 Find the vector equation of a plane which is at a distance of 5 units from the origin and its normal vector is $2\hat{i} - 3\hat{j} + 6\hat{k}$.

10 Find the vector equation of a plane which is at a distance of 7 units from the origin and normal to the vector $3\hat{i} + 5\hat{j} - 6\hat{k}$. **[NCERT]**

11 Determine the direction cosines of the normal to the plane $x + y + z = 1$ and the distance from the origin. **[NCERT Exemplar]**

12 Find the vector and cartesian equation of the planes that passes through the point (1, 0, −2) and the normal to the plane is $\hat{i}+\hat{j}-\hat{k}$. [NCERT]

13 Write the vector equation of the plane passing through the point (a, b, c) and parallel to the plane $\vec{r}\cdot(\hat{i}+\hat{j}+\hat{k})=2$.

14 If the line drawn from the point (−2, −1, −3) meets a plane at right angle at the point (1, −3, 3), then find the equation of the plane. [NCERT Exemplar]

15 Write the sum of intercepts cut off by the plane $\vec{r}\cdot(2\hat{i}+\hat{j}-\hat{k})-5=0$ on the three axes.

16 Find the equation of the plane with intercept 3 on the Y-axis and parallel to ZOX-plane.

17 Check whether the given planes are parallel or perpendicular

(i) $2x+y+3z-2=0$ and $x-2y+5=0$.

(ii) $2x-2y+4z+5=0$ and $3x-3y+6z-1=0$.

[NCERT]

18 Find the distance of the plane $3x-4y+12z=3$ from the origin.

19 Find the distance between the planes $2x-y+2z=5$ and $5x-2.5y+5z=20$.

20 Write the vector equation of the line passing through the point (1, 2, 3) and perpendicular to the plane $\vec{r}\cdot(\hat{i}+2\hat{j}-5\hat{k})+9=0$.

21 Find the value of λ, such that the line $\frac{x-2}{6}=\frac{y-1}{\lambda}=\frac{z+5}{-4}$ is perpendicular to the plane $3x-y-2z=7$.

22 Find the value of λ for which the line $\frac{x-1}{2}=\frac{y-1}{3}=\frac{z-1}{\lambda}$ is parallel to the plane $\vec{r}\cdot(2\hat{i}+3\hat{j}+4\hat{k})=4$.

Short Answer Type Questions

4 Marks

23 Find the coordinates of the foot of the perpendicular drawn from the origin to the plane $2x+3y+4z-12=0$. [NCERT]

24 Find the equation of a plane which bisects perpendicularly the line joining the points $A(2, 3, 4)$ and $B(4, 5, 8)$ at right angles. [NCERT Exemplar]

25 Find the equation of the plane passing through the points $A(2, 1, -3)$, $B(-3, -2, 1)$ and $C(2, 4, -1)$. [ISC 2011]

26 A plane makes intercepts − 6, 3, 4 respectively, on the coordinate axes. Find the length of the perpendicular from the origin on it.

27 A plane meets the coordinates axes at A, B and C such that the centroid of the ΔABC is the point (α, β, γ). Show that the equation of the plane is $\frac{x}{\alpha}+\frac{y}{\beta}+\frac{z}{\gamma}=3$.

28 Find the equation of the plane through the point $P(1, 4, -2)$ and it is parallel to the plane $-2x+y-3z=0$.

29 Find the equation of the plane passing through the points (2, −3, 1) and (−1, 1, −7) and perpendicular to the plane $x-2y+5z+1=0$. [ISC 2014]

30 Find the equation of the plane through the point (1, 2, 3) and perpendicular to the planes $x+y+2z=3$ and $3x+2y+z=4$. [ISC 2007]

31 A plane passes through the point (4, 2, 4) and is perpendicular to the planes $2x+5y+4z+1=0$ and $4x+7y+6z+2=0$. Then, find the equation of plane. [ISC 2005]

32 Find the length and the foot of the perpendicular from the point (7, 14, 5) to the plane $2x+4y-z=2$.

33 Find the distance between the parallel planes $\vec{r}\cdot(2\hat{i}-\hat{j}-2\hat{k})=6$ and $\vec{r}\cdot(6\hat{i}-3\hat{j}-6\hat{k})=27$.

34 Find the image of the point (1,3,4) in the plane $x-y+z=5$.

35 Find the intersection point of the line $\frac{x+1}{2}=\frac{y+2}{3}=\frac{z+3}{4}$ and the plane $x+y+4z=6$.

36 Find the coordinates of the point, where the line $\frac{x-2}{3}=\frac{y+1}{4}=\frac{z-2}{2}$ intersects the plane $x-y+z-5=0$. Also, find the angle between the line and the plane.

37 Find the distance between the point $(-1, -5, -10)$ and the point of intersection of the line $\frac{x-2}{3}=\frac{y+1}{4}=\frac{z-2}{12}$ and plane $x-y+z=5$.

38 Find the equation of the plane passing through the points $(-1, 2, 0)$, $(2, 2, -1)$ and parallel to the line $\frac{x-1}{1}=\frac{2y+1}{2}=\frac{z+1}{-1}$.

39 Find the equation of plane passing through the point $A(1, 2, 1)$ and perpendicular to the line joining points $P(1, 4, 2)$ and $Q(2, 3, 5)$. Also, find the distance of this plane from the line $\frac{x+3}{2}=\frac{y-5}{-1}=\frac{z-7}{-1}$.

40 Find the equation of the line passing through the point $(3, 0, 1)$ and parallel to the planes $x+2y=0$ and $3y-z=0$. **[NCERT Exemplar]**

Long Answer Type Questions

6 Marks

41 Show that the four points $A(4, 5, 1)$, $B(0, -1, -1)$, $C(3, 9, 4)$ and $D(-4, 4, 4)$ are coplanar. Find the equation of the plane containing them.

42 If from a point $P(a, b, c)$ perpendiculars PA and PB are drawn to YZ and ZX-planes, then find the vector equation of the plane OAB.

43 Find the equation of the two planes passing through the points $(0, 4, -3)$ and $(6, -4, 3)$, if the sum of their intercepts on the three axes is zero. **[ISC 2006]**

44 Find the vector and cartesian equations of the plane passing through the point $(-1, 3, 2)$ and perpendicular to each of the planes $x+2y+3z=5$ and $3x+3y+z=0$.

45 Find the direction ratios of the normal to the plane, which passes through the point $(1, 0, 0)$ and $(0, 1, 0)$ and makes angle $\frac{\pi}{4}$ with the plane $x+y=3$. Also, find the equation of the plane.

46 Find the equation of the plane, which intersect X and Y-axes at the points $A(4, 0, 0)$ and $B(0, 6, 0)$ and the intercept on Z-axis is two more than the arithmetic mean of z-coordinates of A and B. Also, find the perpendicular distance from origin to the plane.

47 Find the equation of the plane that contains the point $(1, -1, 2)$ and is perpendicular to both the planes $2x+3y-2z=5$ and $x+2y-3z=8$. Hence, find the distance of point $P(-2, 5, 5)$ from the plane obtained above.

48 Find the coordinates of the point where the line through the points $(3, -4, -5)$ and $(2, -3, 1)$, crosses the plane determined by the points $(1, 2, 3)$, $(4, 2, -3)$ and $(0, 4, 3)$.

49 Find the vector equation of the plane passing through the three points with position vectors $\hat{i}+\hat{j}-2\hat{k}$, $2\hat{i}-\hat{j}+\hat{k}$ and $\hat{i}+2\hat{j}+\hat{k}$. Also, find the coordinates of the point of intersection of this plane and the line $\vec{r}=3\hat{i}-\hat{j}-\hat{k}+\lambda(2\hat{i}-2\hat{j}+\hat{k})$.

50 Find the coordinates of the point, where the line joining the points $(1, -2, 3)$ and $(2, -1, 5)$ cuts the plane $x-2y+3z=19$. Hence, find the distance of this point from the point $(5, 4, 1)$. **[ISC 2008]**

51 Find the coordinates of the point P where the line through $A(3, -4, -5)$ and $B(2, -3, 1)$ crosses the plane passing through three points $L(2, 2, 1)$, $M(3, 0, 1)$ and $N(4, -1, 0)$. Also, find the ratio in which P divides the line segment AB.

52 Find the distance between the line $\frac{x-5}{3}=\frac{y-4}{3}=\frac{z-8}{1}$ and the plane determined by the points $A(2, -2, 1)$, $B(4, 1, 3)$ and $C(-2, -2, 5)$.

53 Show that the equation $by+cz+d=0$ represents a plane parallel to the X-axis. Find the equation of a plane which is parallel to the X-axis and passes through the points $A(2, 3, 1)$ and $B(4, -5, 3)$.

54 Find the distance between the point $(7, 2, 4)$ and the plane determined by the points $A(2, 5, -3)$, $B(-2, -3, 5)$ and $C(5, 3, -3)$.

55 Find the distance of the point $(-1, -5, -10)$ from the point of intersection of the line $\vec{r}=2\hat{i}-\hat{j}+2\hat{k}+\lambda(3\hat{i}+4\hat{j}+12\hat{k})$ and the plane $\vec{r}\cdot(\hat{i}-\hat{j}+\hat{k})=5$

56 Find the distance of the point $P(3, 4, 4)$ from the point, where the line joining the points $A(3, -4, -5)$ and $B(2, -3, 1)$ intersects the plane $2x+y+z=7$.

57 Find the distance of the point $(2, 3, 4)$ from the plane $3x+2y+2z+5=0$ measured parallel to the line $\frac{x+3}{3}=\frac{y-2}{6}=\frac{z}{2}$.

58 Find the equation of plane containing the lines $\frac{x-8}{3}=\frac{y+19}{-16}=\frac{z-10}{7}$ and $\frac{x-38}{3}=\frac{y+29}{8}=\frac{z-5}{-5}$.

59 If lines $\frac{x-1}{2}=\frac{y+1}{3}=\frac{z-1}{4}$ and $\frac{x-3}{1}=\frac{y-k}{2}=\frac{z}{1}$ intersect, then find the value of k and also find the equation of plane containing these lines.

60 Find the vector and cartesian equation of a plane containing the two lines

$\vec{r}=(2\hat{i}+\hat{j}-3\hat{k})+\lambda(\hat{i}+2\hat{j}+5\hat{k})$ and

$\vec{r}=(3\hat{i}+3\hat{j}+2\hat{k})+\mu(3\hat{i}-2\hat{j}+5\hat{k})$.

Also, show that the line

$\vec{r}=(2\hat{i}+5\hat{j}+2\hat{k})+\alpha(3\hat{i}-2\hat{j}+5\hat{k}$ lies in the plane.

61 A line with positive direction cosines passes through the point $P(2,-1,2)$ and makes equal angles with the coordinate axes. The line meets the plane $2x+y+z=9$ at point Q. Find the length of the line segment PQ.

62 If the plane $ax+by=0$ is rotated about its line of intersection with the plane $z=0$ through an angle α, then prove that the equation of the plane in its new position is

$ax+by\pm(\sqrt{a^2+b^2}\tan\alpha)z=0$. **[NCERT Exemplar]**

Case-Based Type Question

(6 Marks)

63 A mobile tower is situated at the top of a hill. Consider the surface on which the tower stands as a plane having points $A(1,0,2)$, $B(3,-1,1)$ and $C(1,2,1)$ on it. The mobile tower is tied with three cables from the points A, B and C such that it stands vertically on the ground. The top of the tower is at point $P(2,3,1)$ as shown in the figure below. The foot of the perpendicular from the point P on the plane is at the point $Q\left(\frac{43}{29},\frac{77}{29},\frac{9}{29}\right)$. **[ISC 2024]**

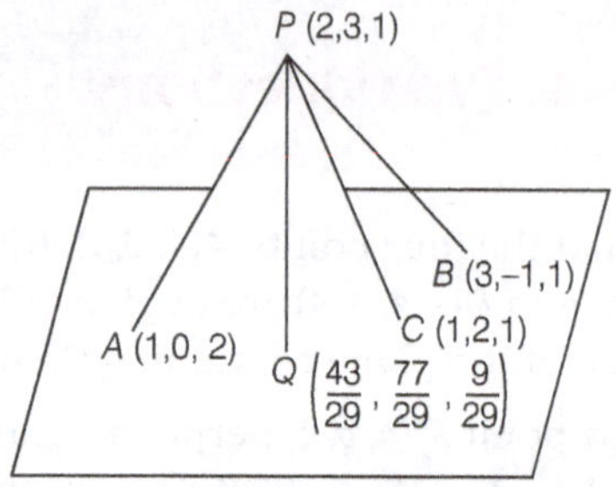

Answer the following questions.

(i) Find the equation of the plane containing the points A, B and C.

(ii) Find the equation of the line PQ.

(iii) Calculate the height of the tower.

Answers

1. (d)
2. (b)
3. (d)
4. (c)
5. (b)
6. (b)
9. (a)
7. (a)
8. (c)

1. $\vec{r}\cdot(2\hat{i}-3\hat{j}+6\hat{k})=35$
10. $\vec{r}\cdot\left(\frac{3}{\sqrt{70}}\hat{i}+\frac{5}{\sqrt{70}}\hat{j}-\frac{6}{\sqrt{70}}\hat{k}\right)=7$
11. $\frac{1}{\sqrt{3}},\frac{1}{\sqrt{3}},\frac{1}{\sqrt{3}}$, $d=\frac{1}{\sqrt{3}}$ units
12. $\vec{r}\cdot(\hat{i}+\hat{j}-\hat{k})=3$ and $x+y-z=3$
13. $\vec{r}\cdot(\hat{i}+\hat{j}+\hat{k})=a+b+c$
14. $3x-2y+6z-27=0$
15. $\frac{5}{2}$
16. $y=3$
17. (i) Perpendicular (ii) Parallel
18. $\frac{3}{13}$
19. 1 unit
20. $\vec{r}=\hat{i}+2\hat{j}+3\hat{k}+\lambda(\hat{i}+2\hat{j}-5\hat{k})$
21. $\lambda=-2$
22. $\lambda=\frac{-13}{4}$
23. $\frac{24}{29},\frac{36}{29},\frac{48}{29}$
24. $x+y+2z=19$
25. $18x-10y+15z+19=0$
26. $\frac{12}{\sqrt{29}}$ units
28. $2x-y+3z+8=0$
29. $4x+7y+2z+11=0$
30. $3x-5y+z+4=0$
31. $x+2y-3z+4=0$
32. $3\sqrt{21}$; (1, 2, 8)
33. 1 unit
34. (3, 1, 6)
35. (1,1,1)
36. $(2,-1,2)$ and $\theta=\sin^{-1}\frac{1}{\sqrt{87}}$
37. 13 units
38. $x+2y+3z=3$
39. $x-y+3z-2=0$, $\sqrt{11}$
40. $\frac{x-3}{-2}=\frac{y}{1}=\frac{z-1}{3}$
41. $5x-7y+11z+4=0$
42. $\vec{r}\cdot(bc\hat{i}+ac\hat{j}-ab\hat{k})=0$
43. $2x-3y-6z-6=0$
44. $\vec{r}\cdot(7\hat{i}-8\hat{j}+3\hat{k})+25=0$ and $7x-8y+3z+25=0$
45. $x+y\pm\sqrt{2}z=1$
46. $\frac{12}{7}$
47. $5x-4y-z-7=0$, $\sqrt{42}$ units
48. $(1,-2,7)$
49. $\vec{r}=\hat{i}+\hat{j}-2\hat{k}$ and $(1,1,-2)$
50. $(2,-1,5)$; $5\sqrt{2}$ units
51. $(1,-2,7)$ and P divides the line joining points A and B externally in the ratio 2 : 1
52. $\frac{6}{\sqrt{34}}$ units
53. $y+4z-7=0$
54. $\sqrt{29}$ units
55. 13 units
56. 7 units
57. 7 units
58. $2x+3y+6z=19$
59. $k=\frac{9}{2}$, $5x-2y-z-6=0$
60. $\vec{r}(10\hat{i}+5\hat{j}-4\hat{k})=37$ and $10x+5y-4z=37$
61. $\sqrt{3}$ units
63. (i) $3x+2y+4z=1$ (ii) $\frac{x-2}{3}=\frac{y-3}{2}=\frac{z-1}{4}$ (iii) $\frac{5}{\sqrt{29}}$ unit

CHAPTER 15

Application of Integrals

In this chapter, we will study a specific application of integral to find the areas of bounded regions, area between lines and arcs of circles, parabolas and ellipses in their standard form only, we will also deal with finding the area between two curves.

- Area under Simple Curves (Single Curve and Lines)
- Area between Two Curves

TOPIC 01 Area under Simple Curves (Single Curve and Lines)

Curve Sketching

For curve sketching of the function $y = f(x)$, we follow the following steps

1. Symmetry

(i) **Symmetry about the Y-axis** If the given equation remains same when x is replaced by $(-x)$, then the given curve is symmetrical about Y-axis.

(ii) **Symmetry about the X-axis** If the given equation remains same when y is replaced by $(-y)$, then the given curve is symmetrical about X-axis.

(iii) **Symmetry about the origin** If the given equation remains same when both x and y are replaced by $-x$ and $-y$ respectively, then the given curve is symmetrical about origin.

(iv) **Symmetry about the line $y = x$** If the given equation remains same when x and y are interchanged with each other, then the given curve is symmetrical about the line $y = x$.

(v) **Symmetry about the line $y = -x$** If the given equation remains same, when x and y are replaced with $-y$ and $-x$, then the given curve is symmetrical about the line $y = -x$.

2. Points of Intersection with the Axes

For finding the intersecting points with X-axis and Y-axis, put $y = 0$ and $x = 0$, respectively.

3. Origin

If the curve satisfies $(0, 0)$, then it will pass through origin.

4. Turning Points

Put $f'(x) = 0$ for obtaining the turning point. Turning points gives the position of maxima or minima point and nature of curve.

5. Increasing or Decreasing

Intervals in which for the given curve $f'(x) > 0$, then $f(x)$ is increasing and in which $f'(x) < 0$, then $f(x)$ is decreasing.

Sketches of Some Standard Curves

	Equation of curve	Sketch
1. (a)	**Straight lines** $x = a$ and $x = -a$, where $a > 0$	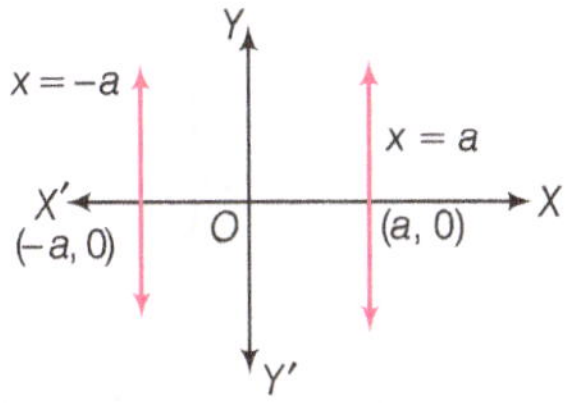
(b)	**Straight lines** $y = b$ and $y = -b$, where $b > 0$	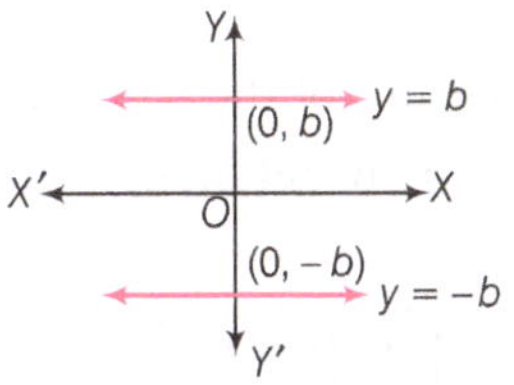
2.	**Straight lines** $y = x$ and $y = -x$	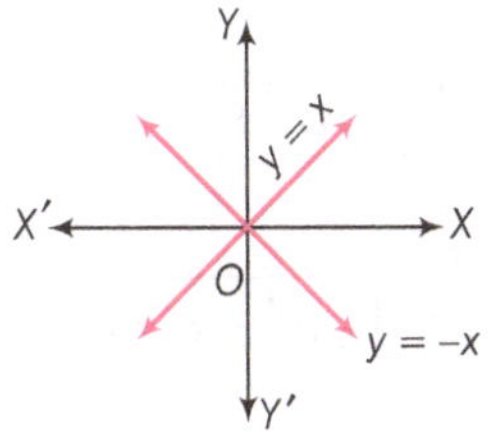
3.	**Straight lines** $\frac{x}{a} + \frac{y}{b} = 1, a \neq b$ $x + y = a, a = b$	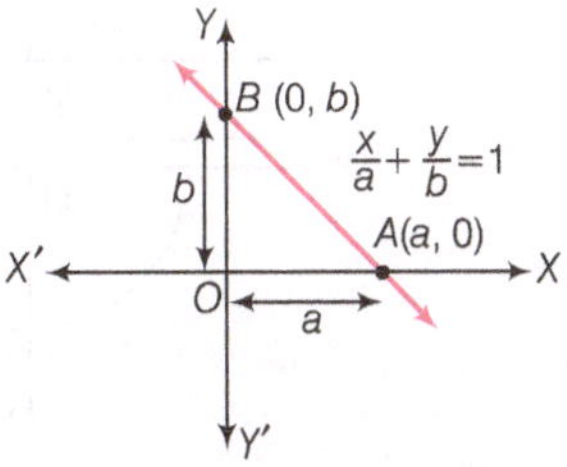
4.	**Modulus function** $y = \lvert x \rvert$ $y = \begin{cases} x, \text{ for } x \geq 0 \\ -x, \text{ for } x < 0 \end{cases}$	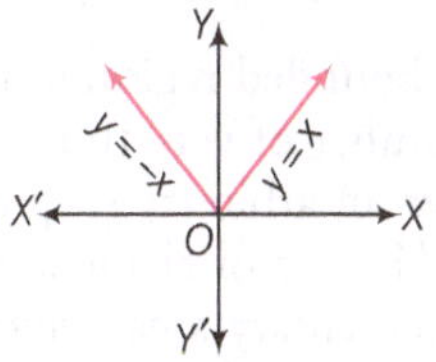
5.	**Circle** $x^2 + y^2 = a^2$ **Centre** $= (0, 0)$ **Radius** $= a$	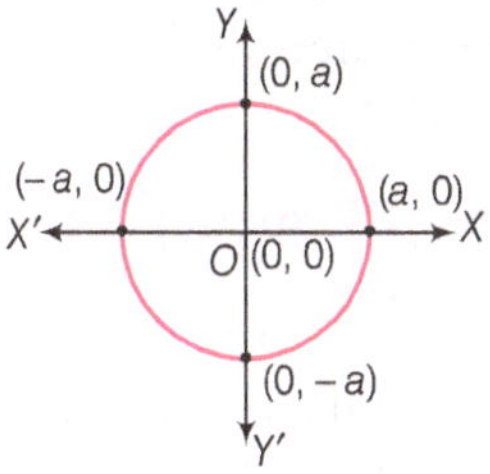
6. (a)	**Parabola** $y^2 = 4ax$ (or $y^2 = -4ax$) **Vertex,** $O = (0, 0)$, **Focus,** $S = (a, 0)$ or $(-a, 0)$. **Length of latusrectum** $= 4a$	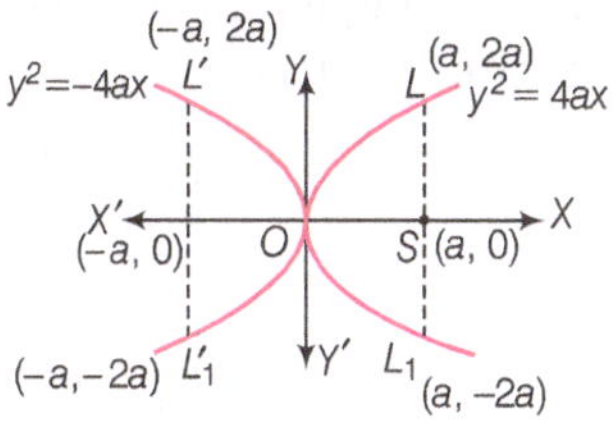
(b)	**Parabola** $x^2 = 4ay$ (or $x^2 = -4ay$) **Vertex,** $O = (0, 0)$, **Focus,** $S = (0, a)$ or $(0, -a)$. **Length of latusrectum** $= 4a$	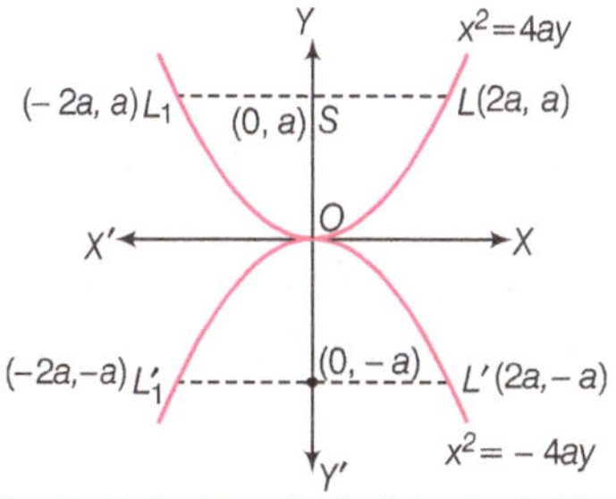
7. (a)	**Ellipse** $\frac{x^2}{a^2} + \frac{y^2}{b^2} = 1$, when $a > b$ **Vertices** $= (\pm a, 0)$, **Centre,** $O = (0, 0)$	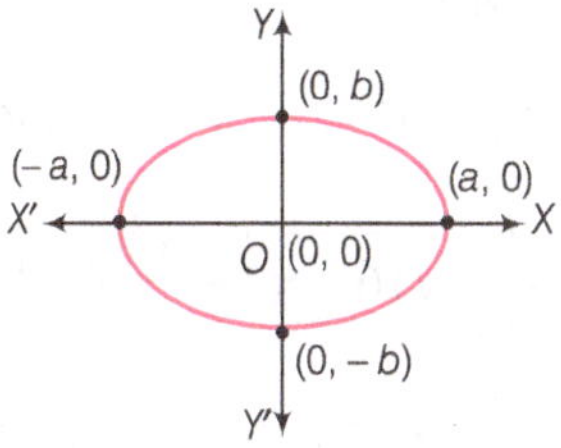
(b)	**Ellipse** $\frac{x^2}{a^2} + \frac{y^2}{b^2} = 1$, when $a < b$ **Vertices** $= (0, \pm b)$ **Centre,** $O = (0, 0)$	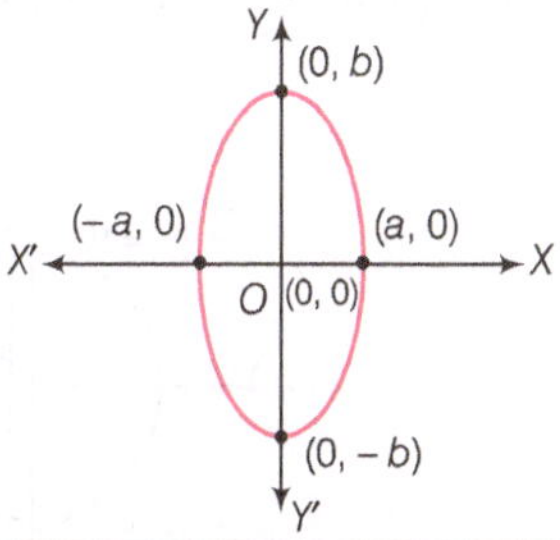

Area of Bounded Region

Area of bounded region can be assumed as composed of large number of very thin vertical (or horizontal) strips. Consider an arbitrary strip of height y and width dx. Then, dA (area of elementary strip) = $y\,dx$. This area is called elementary area, which is located at an arbitrary position within the region, so by adding up the elementary areas of thin strips across the region, we get the required area.

Area of Region Bounded by X-axis, Lines $x = a$, $x = b$ and Curve $y = f(x)$

The area of the region $PQRSP$ bounded by the curve $y = f(x)$, the X-axis and lines $x = a$ and $x = b$, will be the result of adding up the elementary areas of thin vertical strips across the region $PQRSP$.

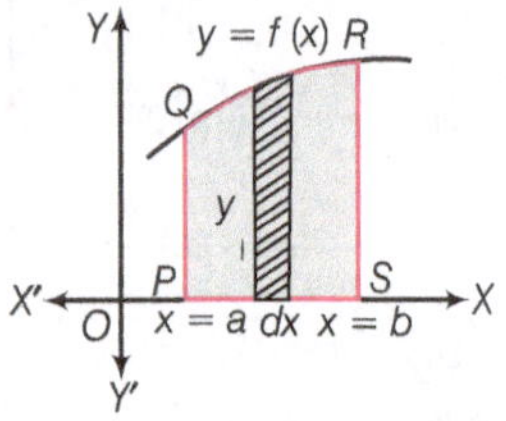

Thus, $$\text{Area} = \int_a^b dA = \int_a^b y\,dx = \int_a^b f(x)\,dx$$

e.g. The area of the region bounded by the curve $x^2 + y^2 = 16$ and lines $x = 1$ and $x = 2$ in I quadrant is given by

$$\text{Area} = \int_1^2 y\,dx$$

$$= \int_1^2 \sqrt{4^2 - x^2}\,dx \quad \text{[here, we take a vertical strip]}$$

$$= \left[\frac{x}{2}\sqrt{16 - x^2} + \frac{4^2}{2}\sin^{-1}\frac{x}{4}\right]_1^2$$

$$\left[\because \int \sqrt{a^2 - x^2}\,dx = \frac{x}{2}\sqrt{a^2 - x^2} + \frac{a^2}{2}\sin^{-1}\left(\frac{x}{a}\right) + C\right]$$

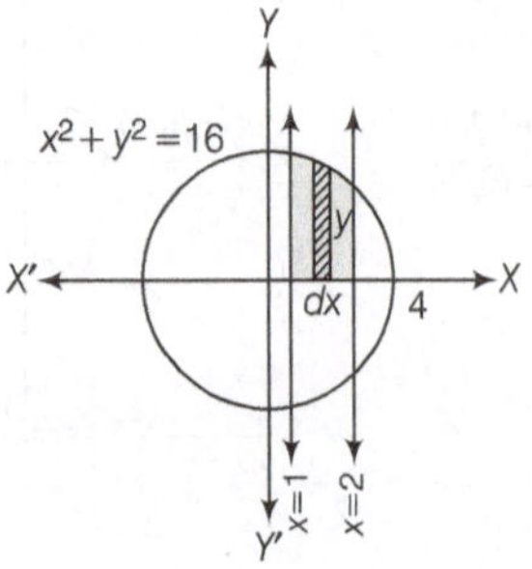

$$= \left[\frac{2}{2}\sqrt{16-4} + 8\sin^{-1}\frac{2}{4} - \left(\frac{1}{2}\sqrt{16-1} + 8\sin^{-1}\frac{1}{4}\right)\right]$$

$$= \left[2\sqrt{3} + 8 \times \frac{\pi}{6} - \left(\frac{1}{2}\sqrt{15} + 8\sin^{-1}\frac{1}{4}\right)\right]$$

$$= \left[2\sqrt{3} + \frac{4\pi}{3} - \left(\frac{\sqrt{15}}{2} + 8\sin^{-1}\frac{1}{4}\right)\right] \text{ sq units}$$

Area of Region Bounded by Y-axis, Lines $y = c$, $y = d$ and the Curve $x = f(y)$

The area of region $PQRSP$ bounded by the curve $x = f(y)$, the Y-axis and lines $y = c$ and $y = d$ is given by

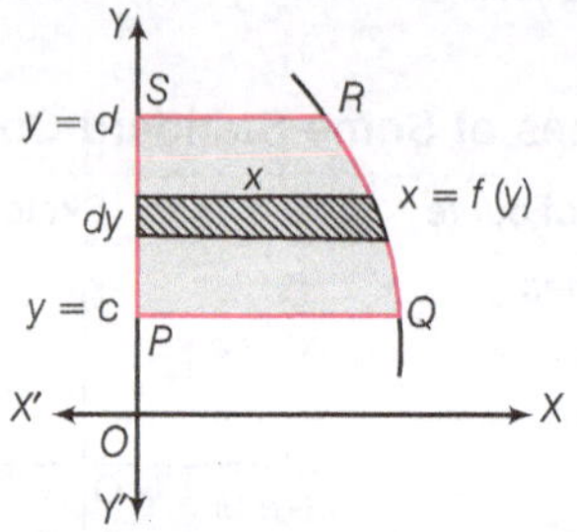

$$\text{Area} = \int_c^d dA = \int_c^d x\,dy = \int_c^d f(y)\,dy$$

e.g. The area of the region bounded by the curve $x^2 + y^2 = 16$ and lines $y = 1$ and $y = 2$ in I quadrant is given by

$$A = \int_1^2 x\,dy = \int_1^2 \sqrt{4^2 - y^2}\,dy$$

[here, we take a horizontal strip]

$$= \left[\frac{y}{2}\sqrt{16 - y^2} + \frac{4^2}{2}\sin^{-1}\frac{y}{4}\right]_1^2$$

$$\left[\because \int \sqrt{a^2 - x^2}\,dx = \frac{x}{2}\sqrt{a^2 - x^2} + \frac{a^2}{2}\sin^{-1}\left(\frac{x}{a}\right) + C\right]$$

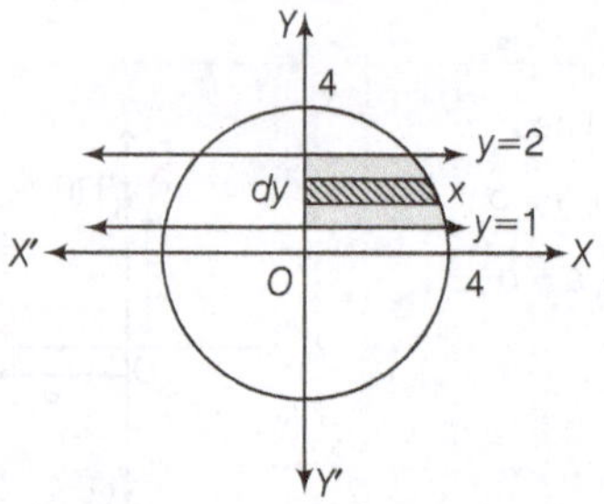

$$= \left[\frac{2}{2}\sqrt{16-4} + 8\sin^{-1}\frac{2}{4} - \left(\frac{1}{2}\sqrt{16-1} + 8\sin^{-1}\frac{1}{4}\right)\right]$$

$$= \left[2\sqrt{3} + 8 \times \frac{\pi}{6} - \left(\frac{1}{2}\sqrt{15} + 8\sin^{-1}\frac{1}{4}\right)\right]$$

$$= \left[2\sqrt{3} + \frac{4\pi}{3} - \left(\frac{\sqrt{15}}{2} + 8\sin^{-1}\frac{1}{4}\right)\right] \text{ sq units}$$

Note The area should be same, either by taken horizontal strip or vertical strip.

Area of Region when Curve is Below the X-axis

If the curve $y = f(x)$ lies below the X-axis, then area bounded by the curve $y = f(x)$, X-axis and the lines $x = a$ and $x = b$ comes out to be negative. But only numerical value of the area is taken into consideration.

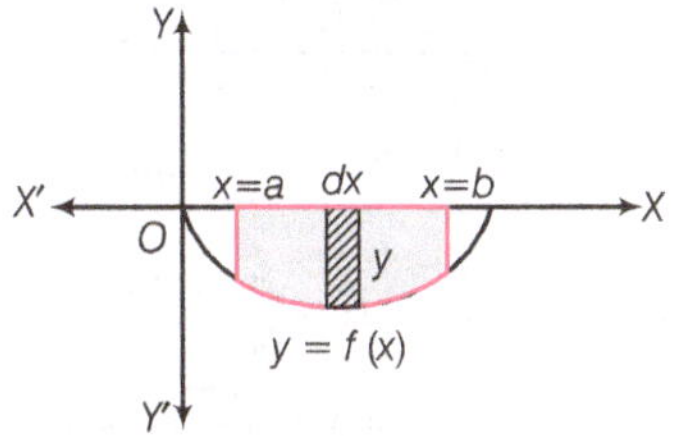

Thus, if the area is negative, then we take its absolute value, i.e. $\left|\int_a^b f(x)\,dx\right|$.

$\therefore$ $$\text{Area} = \left|\int_a^b y\,dx\right| = \left|\int_a^b f(x)\,dx\right|$$

e.g. The area of the region bounded by the line $2x - y = 2$ and lines $x = \frac{1}{4}$ and $x = \frac{3}{4}$ is given by

$$\text{Area} = \left|\int_{1/4}^{3/4} y\,dx\right|$$

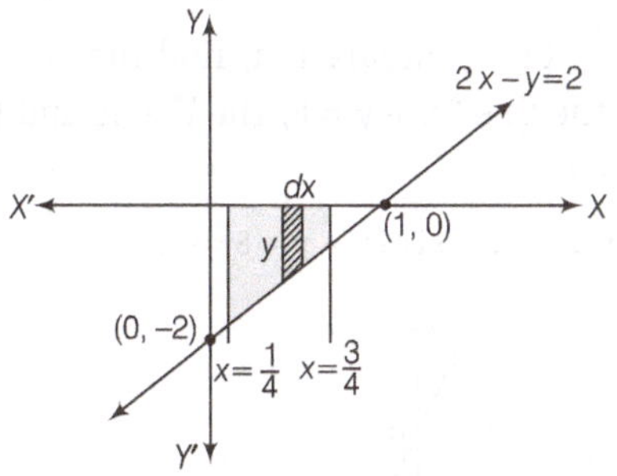

$$= \left|\int_{1/4}^{3/4} (2x-2)\,dx\right| \quad [\because 2x - y = 2 \Rightarrow y = 2x - 2]$$

$$= \left|[x^2 - 2x]_{1/4}^{3/4}\right|$$

$$= \left|\left[\left(\frac{3}{4}\right)^2 - 2\left(\frac{3}{4}\right) - \left\{\left(\frac{1}{4}\right)^2 - 2\left(\frac{1}{4}\right)\right\}\right]\right|$$

$$= \left|\left[\frac{9}{16} - \frac{6}{4} - \left(\frac{1}{16} - \frac{1}{2}\right)\right]\right| = \left|\frac{8}{16} - \frac{4}{4}\right|$$

$$= \left|\frac{8-16}{16}\right| = \frac{8}{16} = \frac{1}{2} \text{ sq unit}$$

Note We take area of elementary strip below the X-axis equal to $-ydx$. By using this, we can calculate the area of the region bounded by the given lines.

$\therefore$ Required area $= \int_{1/4}^{3/4} (-y)dx = \int_{1/4}^{3/4} -(2x-2)dx$

$[\because y = 2x - 2]$

$$= \int_{1/4}^{3/4} (2-2x)dx = [2x - x^2]_{1/4}^{3/4}$$

$$= \left[2\left(\frac{3}{4}\right) - \left(\frac{3}{4}\right)^2\right] - \left[2\left(\frac{1}{4}\right) - \left(\frac{1}{4}\right)^2\right]$$

$$= \left(\frac{3}{2} - \frac{9}{16}\right) - \left(\frac{1}{2} - \frac{1}{16}\right)$$

$$= \left(\frac{2}{2} - \frac{8}{16}\right) = \frac{1}{2} \text{ sq unit}$$

Area of Region when Curve is Above and Below the X-axis

It may happen that some portion of the curve is above the X-axis and some is below the X-axis, which is shown in the figure given below

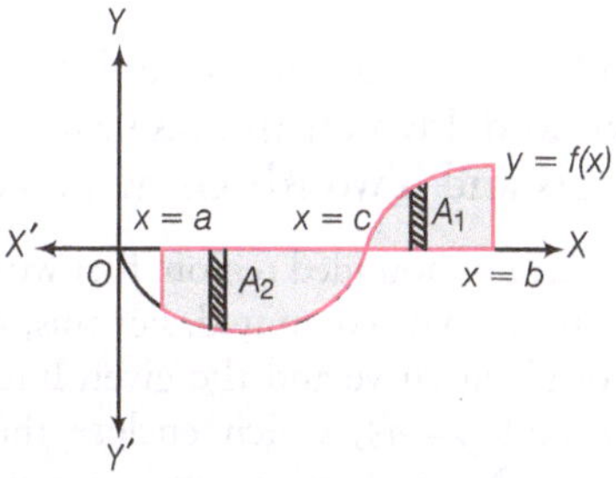

Here, $A_1 > 0$ and $A_2 < 0$. Therefore, the area A bounded by the curve $y = f(x)$, X-axis and the lines $x = a$ and $x = b$ is given by

$$A_2 = -A_2 + A_1 \text{ or } |A_2| + A_1 = \left|\int_a^c f(x)dx\right| + \int_c^b f(x)dx$$

e.g. The area of the region bounded by the line $3x - y = 3$ and lines $x = \frac{1}{2}$ and $x = 2$ is given by

$$\text{Area} = \left|\int_{1/2}^{1} y\,dx\right| + \int_1^2 y\,dx$$

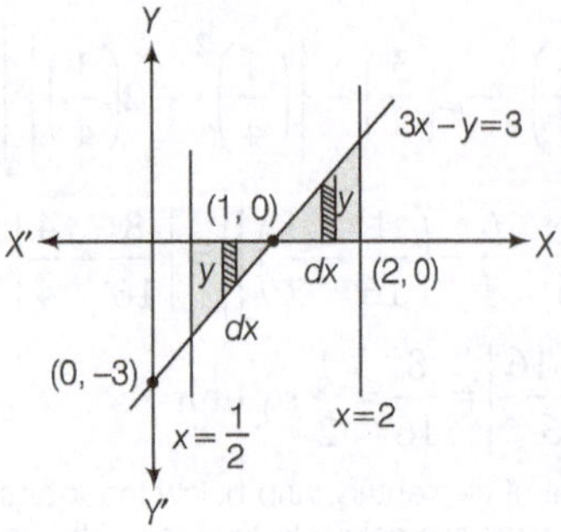

$$= \left|\int_{1/2}^{1}(3x-3)\,dx\right| + \int_{1}^{2}(3x-3)\,dx$$

$$= \left|3\left[\frac{x^2}{2}-x\right]_{1/2}^{1}\right| + 3\left[\frac{x^2}{2}-x\right]_{1}^{2}$$

$$= 3\left|\left[\frac{1}{2}-1-\left(\frac{1}{8}-\frac{1}{2}\right)\right]\right| + 3\left[\frac{4}{2}-2-\left(\frac{1}{2}-1\right)\right]$$

$$= 3\left|\left[-\frac{1}{2}+\frac{3}{8}\right]\right| + 3\left[0+\frac{1}{2}\right]$$

$$= 3\left|-\frac{1}{8}\right| + \frac{3}{2} = \frac{3}{8}+\frac{3}{2}$$

$$= \frac{3+12}{8}$$

$$= \frac{15}{8} \text{ sq units}$$

Note Area of any bounded region cannot be negative.

Working Rule to Find the Area Bounded by a Curve, X-axis and Two Ordinates ($x = a$, $x = b$) or a Curve, Y-axis and Two Abscissae ($y=c$, $y=d$)

For finding the area of bounded region, first we identify the region, whose area is to be computed. For this, we draw the rough sketch of given curve and the given lines $x=a$ and $x=b$ (or $y=c$ and $y=d$), which enclose the area with X-axis (or Y-axis). Now, there are two cases arise

Case I If the bounded area included between two ordinates $x=a$ and $x=b$ and lies above X-axis, then construct an arbitrary vertical strip of height y and width dx.

$\therefore$ Required area $= \int_a^b y\,dx$

If the bounded area lies below the X-axis, then

Required area $= \left|\int_a^b y\,dx\right|$

Case II If the bounded area lies to the right of Y-axis and included between two abscissae $y=c$ and $y=d$, then construct an arbitrary horizontal strip of length x and width dy.

$\therefore$ Required area $= \int_c^d x\,dy$

If the bounded area lies to the left of Y-axis, then

Required area $= \left|\int_c^d x\,dy\right|$

Example 1 Find the area of the region bounded by the parabola $y^2 = 4ax$, its axis and two ordinates $x = 4$ and $x = 9$ in first quadrant.

Sol. Given equation of parabola is $y^2 = 4ax$, its axis is $Y = 0$ and vertex is (0, 0). Also, given ordinates $x = 4$ and $x = 9$. The bounded region in I quadrant is $ABCDA$.

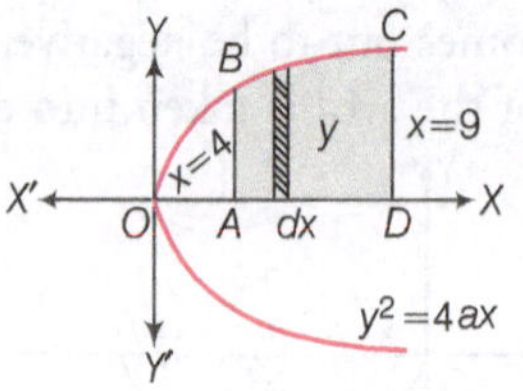

$\therefore$ Required area $= \int_4^9 y\,dx = \int_4^9 \sqrt{4ax}\,dx$

[$\because y^2 = 4ax \Rightarrow y = \sqrt{4ax}$, as y is in I quadrant]

$$= 2\sqrt{a}\int_4^9 \sqrt{x}\,dx = 2\sqrt{a}\left[\frac{x^{3/2}}{3/2}\right]_4^9$$

$$= 2\sqrt{a} \times \frac{2}{3}[(9)^{3/2} - (4)^{3/2}]$$

$$= \frac{4}{3}\sqrt{a}\,[(3^2)^{3/2} - (2^2)^{3/2}]$$

$$= \frac{4}{3}\sqrt{a}\,[27-8]$$

$$= \frac{4}{3}\sqrt{a}\,(19) = \frac{76}{3}\sqrt{a} \text{ sq units}$$

Example 2 Using integration, find the area of region bounded by the line $2x + y = 8$, the Y-axis and the lines $y = 2$ and $y = 4$.

Sol. The given line AB is $2x + y = 8 \Rightarrow x = 4 - \frac{1}{2}y$

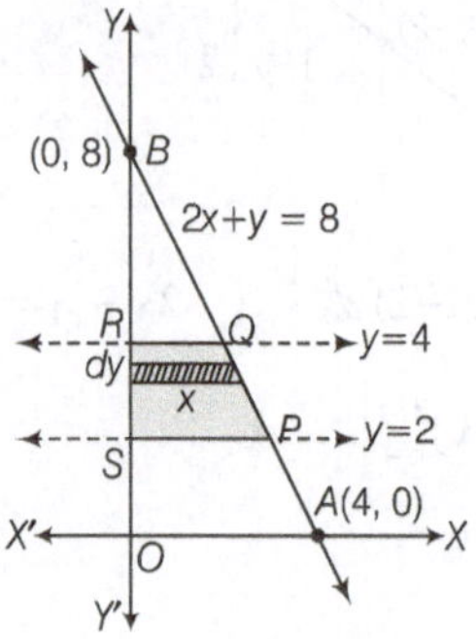

Required area = Area of region $PQRSP$

$= $ Area between the line $x = 4 - \frac{1}{2}y$, the Y-axis and the lines $y = 2$ and $y = 4$

$$= \int_2^4 x\,dy = \int_2^4 \left(4 - \frac{1}{2}y\right) dy$$

$$= \left[4y - \frac{y^2}{4}\right]_2^4 = (16-4)-(8-1)$$

$$= 12 - 7 = 5 \text{ sq units}$$

Note Sometimes, lines $x = a$ and $x = b$ (or $y = c$ and $y = d$) are not given to us, then we find the intersection points of curve and axes. If we get the intersection of curve with both axes, then we can consider either vertical strips or horizontal strips for calculating the area of the region.

Example 3 Find the area of the region bounded by the ellipse $\frac{x^2}{9} + \frac{y^2}{4} = 1$ in fourth quadrant.

Sol. Given equation of ellipse is $\frac{x^2}{9} + \frac{y^2}{4} = 1$ ...(i)

We know that the standard equation of ellipse is

$$\frac{x^2}{a^2} + \frac{y^2}{b^2} = 1 \quad \text{...(ii)}$$

On comparing Eqs. (i) and (ii), we get

$$a^2 = 9 \text{ and } b^2 = 4$$

$\Rightarrow \quad a = 3$ and $b = 2$

Here, we see that $a > b$, so the horizontal ellipse will be formed.

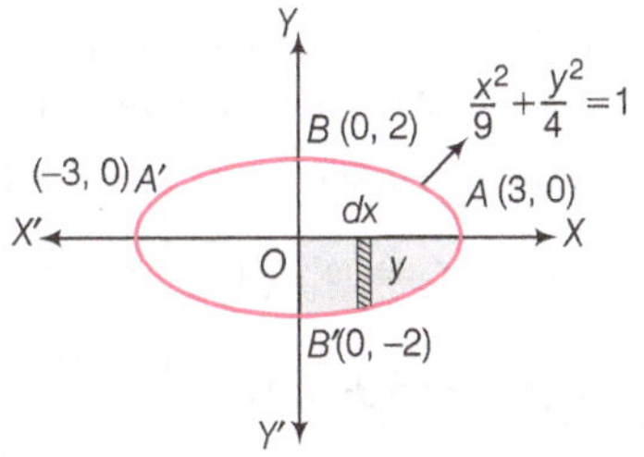

Now, required area = Area of region in IV quadrant

$= $ Area of region $OAB'O$

$$= \left|\int_0^3 y\,dx\right| = \left|\int_0^3 -\frac{2\sqrt{9-x^2}}{3}\,dx\right|$$

$$\left[\because \frac{y^2}{4} = 1 - \frac{x^2}{9} \Rightarrow y = \pm\frac{2\sqrt{9-x^2}}{3}\right]$$

[$\because$ portion of the curve lies below the X-axis, so y will be negative]

$$= \frac{2}{3}\left|-\left[\frac{x}{2}\sqrt{9-x^2} + \frac{9}{2}\sin^{-1}\left(\frac{x}{3}\right)\right]_0^3\right|$$

$$\left[\because \int\sqrt{a^2-x^2}\,dx = \frac{x}{2}\sqrt{a^2-x^2} + \frac{a^2}{2}\sin^{-1}\left(\frac{x}{a}\right)\right]$$

$$= \frac{2}{3}\left|-\left[\frac{3}{2}\sqrt{9-9} + \frac{9}{2}\sin^{-1}\frac{3}{3} - 0 - \frac{9}{2}\sin^{-1}(0)\right]\right|$$

$$= \frac{2}{3}\left|-\left[0 + \frac{9}{2}\times\frac{\pi}{2} - 0\right]\right| = \frac{2}{3}\left|-\frac{9\pi}{4}\right|$$

$$= \frac{2}{3}\times\frac{9\pi}{4} = \frac{3\pi}{2} \text{ sq units}$$

Example 4 Find the area bounded by the line $y = x$, the X-axis and the lines $x = -1$ and $x = 2$.

Sol. We know that $y = x$ is the line passing through the origin and making angle of 45° with the X-axis as shown in the given figure.

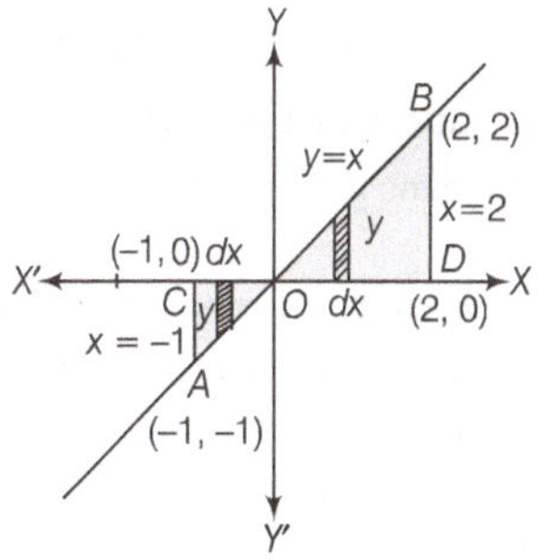

Now, we have to find the area of the shaded region.

$\therefore$ Required area = Area of $OACO$ + Area of $OBDO$

$$= \left|\int_{-1}^0 y\,dx\right| + \int_0^2 y\,dx$$

[$\because$ area $OACO$ is below the X-axis, so we take its absolute value]

$$= \left|\int_{-1}^0 x\,dx\right| + \int_0^2 x\,dx = \left|\left[\frac{x^2}{2}\right]_{-1}^0\right| + \left[\frac{x^2}{2}\right]_0^2$$

$$= \left|\left[0 - \frac{1}{2}\right]\right| + \left[\frac{4}{2} - 0\right]$$

$$= \frac{1}{2} + \frac{4}{2} = \frac{5}{2} \text{ sq units}$$

Area of Symmetrical Region

Sometimes, the bounded region, for which we have to calculate area, is symmetrical about X-axis (i.e. symmetric in I and IV or in II and III quadrants) or Y-axis (i.e. symmetric in I and II or in III and IV quadrants) or both X-axis and Y-axis (i.e. symmetric in all quadrants) or origin (i.e. symmetric in I and III or in II and IV quadrants). Then, first we calculate the area of bounded region in one quadrant and then multiply this area by number of quadrants in which region is symmetrical.

Example 5 Sketch the region $\{(x, y) : y = \sqrt{4 - x^2}\}$ and X-axis. Find the area of the region using integration. **[NCERT Exemplar]**

Sol. Given region is $\{(x, y) : y = \sqrt{4 - x^2}\}$ and X-axis.

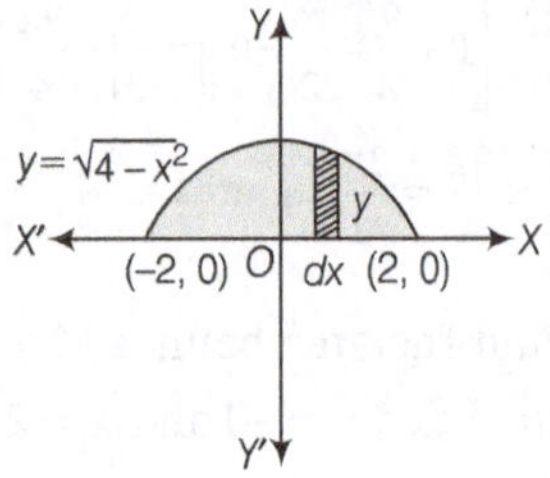

We have, $y = \sqrt{4 - x^2}$

$\Rightarrow \quad y^2 = 4 - x^2 \Rightarrow x^2 + y^2 = 4$

This represent the equation of circle having centre (0, 0) and radius 2. But original equation is $y = \sqrt{4 - x^2}$, so y is positive. It means that, we have to take a curve above the X-axis.

Thus, only semi-circle is formed above the X-axis.

Since, the region is symmetrical about Y-axis.

$\therefore$ Area of shaded region,

$$A = 2\int_0^2 y\,dx = 2\int_0^2 \sqrt{4 - x^2}\,dx = 2\int_0^2 \sqrt{2^2 - x^2}\,dx$$

$$= 2\left[\frac{x}{2}\sqrt{2^2 - x^2} + \frac{2^2}{2}\cdot\sin^{-1}\frac{x}{2}\right]_0^2$$

$$\left[\because \int\sqrt{a^2 - x^2}\,dx = \frac{x}{2}\sqrt{a^2 - x^2} + \frac{a^2}{2}\sin^{-1}\left(\frac{x}{a}\right) + C\right]$$

$$= 2\left[\frac{2}{2}\cdot 0 + 2\cdot\frac{\pi}{2} - \frac{0}{2}\cdot 2 - 2\sin^{-1}(0)\right]$$

$$= 2\left[2\cdot\frac{\pi}{2} - 0\right] = 2\pi \text{ sq units}$$

Example 6 Using integration, find the area enclosed by the circle $x^2 + y^2 = a^2$.

Sol. Given equation of circle is $x^2 + y^2 = a^2$, its centre is (0, 0) and radius is a. It cuts the X-axis at $A(a, 0)$ and Y-axis at $B(0, a)$. Also, it is symmetrical about X and Y-axes both.

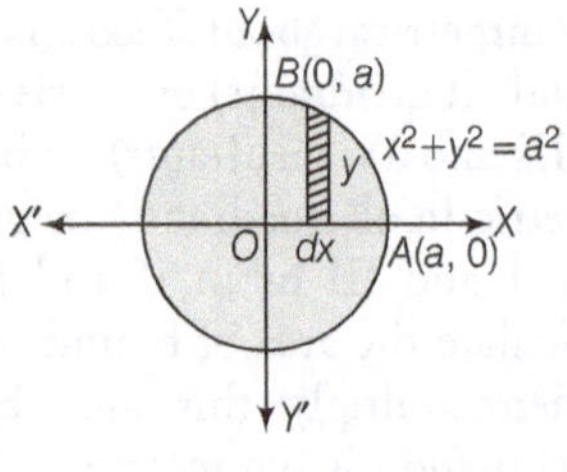

Clearly, area of region in I quadrant

$$= \int_0^a y\,dx = \int_0^a \sqrt{a^2 - x^2}\,dx \text{ [consider vertical strip]}$$

$$\left[\because x^2 + y^2 = a^2 \Rightarrow y = \sqrt{a^2 - x^2}, \text{ as } y \text{ is in I quadrant}\right]$$

$$= \left[\frac{x}{2}\sqrt{a^2 - x^2} + \frac{a^2}{2}\sin^{-1}\frac{x}{a}\right]_0^a$$

$$= \left[\left(\frac{a}{2}\times 0 + \frac{a^2}{2}\sin^{-1}1\right) - 0\right] = \frac{a^2}{2}\left(\frac{\pi}{2}\right) = \frac{\pi a^2}{4}$$

$$\left[\because \sin^{-1}(1) = \frac{\pi}{2}\right]$$

Now, required area = 4 × Area of region in I quadrant

$$= 4 \times \frac{\pi a^2}{4} = \pi a^2 \text{ sq units}$$

[$\because$ region is symmetrical in all quadrants]

Example 7 Find the area bounded by the curve $x = 4 - y^2$ and the Y-axis.

Sol. We have, $x = 4 - y^2$

$\Rightarrow \quad y^2 = -x + 4 \Rightarrow y^2 = -(x - 4)$

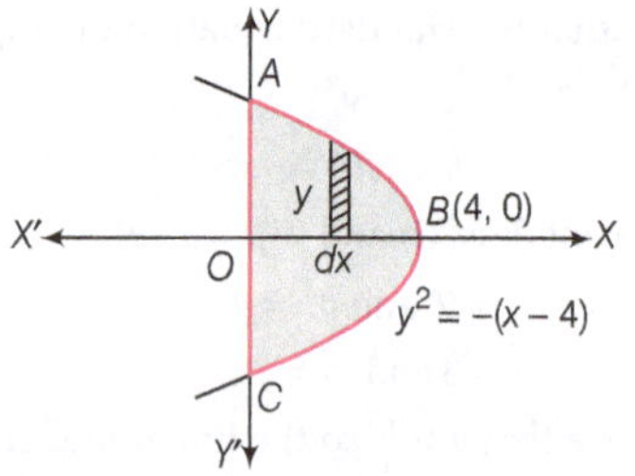

which is the parabola of the form $Y^2 = -4AX$.

Its vertex is (4, 0) and it is symmetrical about X-axis.

$\therefore$ Required area = Area of shaded region

$$= 2 \text{ (Area of region } OABO) = 2\int_0^4 y\,dx = 2\int_0^4 \sqrt{4 - x}\,dx$$

$$\left[\because x = 4 - y^2 \Rightarrow y = \sqrt{4 - x}, \text{ as } y \text{ is in I quadrant}\right]$$

$$= 2\int_0^4 (4 - x)^{1/2}\,dx = 2\left[\frac{-(4 - x)^{3/2}}{3/2}\right]_0^4$$

$$= -2\times\frac{2}{3}[(4 - x)^{3/2}]_0^4$$

$$= -\frac{4}{3}[(4 - 4)^{3/2} - (4 - 0)^{3/2}]$$

$$= -\frac{4}{3}[0 - (4)^{3/2}] = \frac{4}{3}\times(4)^{3/2}$$

$$= \frac{4}{3}\times(2^2)^{3/2}$$

$$= \frac{4}{3}\times 8 = \frac{32}{3} \text{ sq units}$$

Area of Region Bounded by a Curve and a Line

To find the area of the region bounded by a line and a circle, a line and a parabola, a line and an ellipse, we use the following steps

I. First, we **draw the rough sketch** of given curves and identify the region for which we have to find the area.

II. Find the intersection point (or points) of curve and line.

III. Draw perpendicular lines from the intersection points of line and curve to X-axis (or Y-axis).

If these perpendicular lines divide the region (whose area is to be determined) into two (or more) parts, then take two (or more) vertical strips (or horizontal strips), otherwise take one vertical strip (or horizontal strip).

IV. Now, find the area of region by using the suitable formula, i.e.

For one vertical strip Area $= \int_{x=a}^{b} y\, dx$, where y is height of the vertical strip.

For two vertical strips

Area $= \int_{x=a}^{c} y_1\, dx + \int_{x=c}^{b} y_2\, dx$, where y_1 and y_2 represent the heights of vertical strips.

or

For one horizontal strip Area $= \int_{c}^{d} x\, dy$, where x is the length of the horizontal strip.

For two horizontal strips Area $= \int_{c}^{e} x_1 dy + \int_{e}^{d} x_2 dy$, where x_1 and x_2 represent the lengths of the horizontal strips.

Example 8 Using integration, find the area bounded by the curve $y^2 = 4ax$ and the line $x = a$. **[ISC 2024]**

Sol. Shaded part of the following figure shows area enclosed by curve $y^2 = 4ax$ and the line $x = a$.

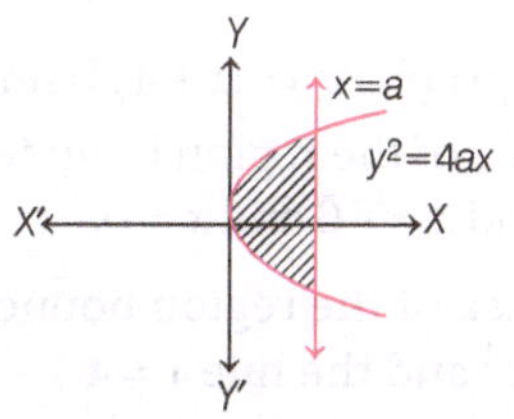

Thus, the required area $= 2\int_{x=0}^{x=a} y dx = 2\int_0^a \sqrt{4ax}\, dx$

$$= 4\sqrt{a}\int_0^a \sqrt{x}\, dx$$

$$= 4\sqrt{a}\cdot\left[\frac{x^{3/2}}{3/2}\right]_0^a$$

$$= 4\sqrt{a} \times \frac{2}{3}[a^{3/2} - 0^{3/2}]$$

$$= \frac{8\sqrt{a}}{3}\cdot a^{3/2}$$

$$= \frac{8}{3}a^2 \text{ sq units}$$

Example 9 Find the area of region in the first quadrant enclosed by the X-axis, the line $y = x$ and the circle $x^2 + y^2 = 32$.

Sol. We have, circle $x^2 + y^2 = 32$

having centre (0, 0) and radius $4\sqrt{2}$ ...(i)

and the line, $y = x$ ...(ii)

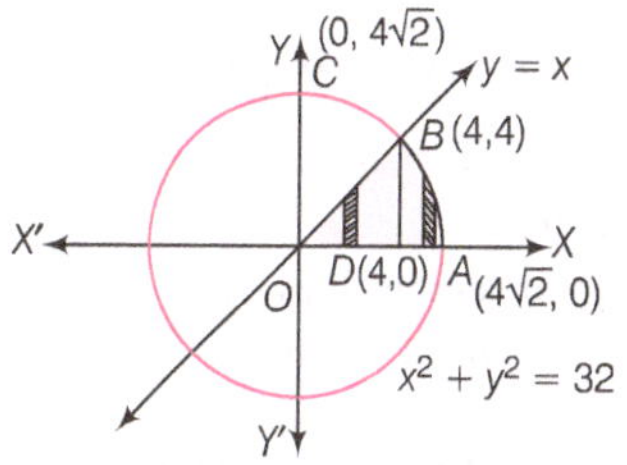

It is clear from the figure that, required region is $OABO$.

On putting the value of y from Eq. (ii) in Eq. (i), we get

$$x^2 + x^2 = 32 \Rightarrow 2x^2 = 32$$

$$\Rightarrow \quad x^2 = \frac{32}{2} = 16 \Rightarrow x = \pm 4$$

From Eq. (ii), we get $y = \pm 4$

Thus, the line and circle intersect at two points (4, 4) and (− 4, − 4).

So, the coordinates of B are (4, 4) [since, it is in I quadrant].

Also, circle cuts the X-axis at $A\,(4\sqrt{2}, 0)$ and Y-axis at C $(0, 4\sqrt{2})$ in I quadrant. [$\because 4\sqrt{2}$ is radius of a circle]

Here, we have to draw two vertical strips, as perpendicular line drawn from intersection point to the X-axis, divides the region into two parts. Now, first strip is drawn in region $ODBO$ and then limit is taken from 0 to 4. Second strip is drawn in region $DABD$ and then limit is taken from 4 to $4\sqrt{2}$.

Now, area of region $ODBO = \int_0^4 y\, dx$, where y is the height of vertical strip

$$= \int_0^4 x\,dx = \left[\frac{x^2}{2}\right]_0^4 = \frac{(4)^2}{2} - 0 = 8 \text{ sq units}$$

and area of region $DABD = \int_4^{4\sqrt{2}} y\,dx$, where y is the height of vertical strip in this region

$$= \int_4^{4\sqrt{2}} \sqrt{32 - x^2}\,dx = \int_4^{4\sqrt{2}} \sqrt{(4\sqrt{2})^2 - x^2}\,dx$$

$$= \left[\frac{x}{2}\sqrt{(4\sqrt{2})^2 - x^2} + \frac{(4\sqrt{2})^2}{2} \times \sin^{-1}\left(\frac{x}{4\sqrt{2}}\right)\right]_4^{4\sqrt{2}}$$

$$\left[\because \int \sqrt{a^2 - x^2}\,dx = \frac{x}{2}\sqrt{a^2 - x^2} + \frac{a^2}{2}\sin^{-1}\left(\frac{x}{a}\right) + C\right]$$

$$= \left[\left\{\frac{4\sqrt{2}}{2}\sqrt{(4\sqrt{2})^2 - (4\sqrt{2})^2} + \frac{32}{2}\sin^{-1}\left(\frac{4\sqrt{2}}{4\sqrt{2}}\right)\right\} - \left\{\frac{4}{2}\sqrt{(4\sqrt{2})^2 - (4)^2} + \frac{32}{2}\sin^{-1}\left(\frac{4}{4\sqrt{2}}\right)\right\}\right]$$

$$= 2\sqrt{2} \times 0 + 16\sin^{-1}(1) - 2\sqrt{32 - 16} - 16\sin^{-1}\left(\frac{1}{\sqrt{2}}\right)$$

$$= 16 \cdot \left(\frac{\pi}{2}\right) - 2\sqrt{16} - 16 \cdot \left(\frac{\pi}{4}\right)$$

$$= 8\pi - 8 - 4\pi = 4\pi - 8$$

$\therefore$ Required area

= Area of region $ODBO$ + Area of region $DABD$

$= 8 + 4\pi - 8 = 4\pi$ sq units

Example 10 Find the area of the region $\{(x, y) : 0 \le y \le x^2 + 1, 0 \le y \le x + 1, 0 \le x \le 2\}$. **[NCERT]**

Sol. Given equations of curve and lines are

$$y = x^2 + 1 \quad \text{or} \quad x^2 = y - 1 \qquad \text{...(i)}$$

$$y = x + 1 \qquad \text{...(ii)}$$

and $\quad x = 2 \qquad$ ...(iii)

Here, Eq. (i) represents a parabola with vertex $A(0, 1)$ and axis along the positive direction of Y-axis.

Eq. (ii) represents a line which intersects the coordinate axes at $(0, 1)$ and $(-1, 0)$.

Eq. (iii) represents a line which is perpendicular to X-axis.

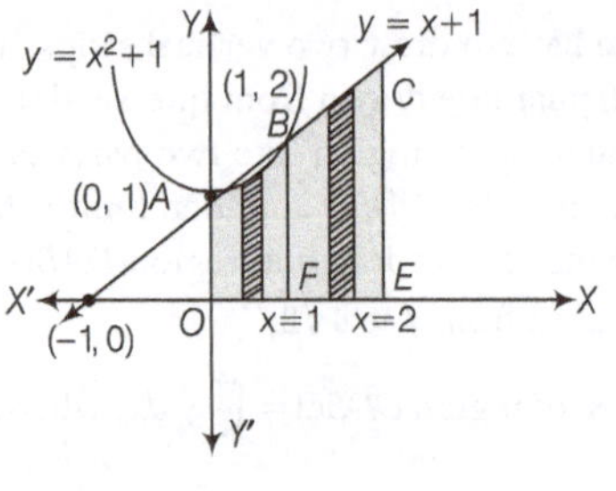

As $0 \le y \le x^2 + 1$, therefore it represents the area below the parabola and above the X-axis.

Similarly, $0 \le y \le x + 1$ represents the area below the line AB and above X-axis and $0 \le x \le 2$ represents the area between the parallel lines $x = 0$ and $x = 2$.

$\therefore$ The region common to $\left.\begin{array}{l} 0 \le y \le x^2 + 1 \\ 0 \le y \le x + 1 \\ 0 \le x \le 2 \end{array}\right\}$ is shown as shaded region $OABCEFO$.

Now, solving Eqs. (i) and (ii), we get

$$x^2 + 1 = x + 1 \Rightarrow x^2 - x = 0$$

$$\Rightarrow \quad x(x - 1) = 0 \Rightarrow x = 0, 1$$

When $x = 0$, then $y = 0 + 1 = 1$. [using Eq. (ii)]

When $x = 1$, then $y = 1 + 1 = 2$. [using Eq. (ii)]

So, the points of intersection are $A(0, 1)$ and $B(1, 2)$.

$\therefore$ Required area = Area of shaded region $OABCEFO$

= Area of region $OABFO$ + Area of region $FECBF$

$$= \int_0^1 y(\text{parabola})\,dx + \int_1^2 y(\text{line})\,dx$$

$$= \int_0^1 (x^2 + 1)\,dx + \int_1^2 (x + 1)\,dx$$

$$= \left[\frac{x^3}{3} + x\right]_0^1 + \left[\frac{x^2}{2} + x\right]_1^2$$

$$= \left[\left(\frac{1}{3} + 1\right) - 0\right] + \left[\left(\frac{4}{2} + 2\right) - \left(\frac{1}{2} + 1\right)\right]$$

$$= \frac{4}{3} + \left[4 - \frac{3}{2}\right] = \frac{4}{3} + \frac{5}{2}$$

$$= \frac{8 + 15}{6} = \frac{23}{6} \text{ sq units}$$

Topic Practice 1

Short Answer Type Questions

4 Marks

1 Draw a rough sketch of the curve and find the area of the region bounded by curve $y^2 = 8x$ and the line $x = 2$. **[ISC 2018]**

2 Sketch the graph of $y = |x + 4|$. Using integration, find the area of the region bounded by the curve $y = |x + 4|$ and $x = -6$ and $x = 0$. **[ISC 2018]**

3 Find the area of the region bounded by the curve $y = x^2$ and the line $y = 4$. **[NCERT]**

Long Answer Type Questions

6 Marks

4 Find the area of the region bounded by $y^2 = 9x$, $x = 2, x = 4$ and the X-axis in the first quadrant. **[NCERT]**

5 Find the area of the region bounded by the curves $x = 4y - y^2$ and the Y-axis. **[ISC 2012]**

6 Draw a rough sketch of the curve $y = x^2 - 5x + 6$ and find the area bounded by curve and the X-axis. **[ISC 2010]**

7 Draw a rough sketch of the curve $x^2 + y = 9$ and find the area enclosed by the curves, the X-axis and the lines $x + 1 = 0$ and $x - 2 = 0$. **[ISC 2009]**

8 Draw a rough sketch of the curve $y^2 + 1 = x, x \le 2$. Find the area enclosed by the curve and the line $x = 2$. **[ISC 2008]**

9 Sketch and shade the area of the region lying in first quadrant and bounded by $y = 9x^2$, $x = 0$, $y = 1$ and $y = 4$. Find the area of the shaded region. **[ISC 2004]**

10 Show that the area enclosed between the X-axis and the curve $a^2y = x^2 (x + a)$ is $a^2/12$. **[ISC 2003]**

11 Find the area under the curve $y = \sqrt{3x + 4}$ between $x = 0$, $x = 4$ and the X-axis.

12 Draw a rough sketch of the curve $y = \sqrt{x-1}$ in the interval [1, 5]. Find the area under the curve and the lines $x = 1$ and $x = 5$. **[NCERT Exemplar]**

13 Find the area of the smaller part of the circle $x^2 + y^2 = a^2$ cut-off by the line $x = \frac{a}{\sqrt{2}}$. **[NCERT]**

14 Find the area of the minor segment of the circle $x^2 + y^2 = a^2$ cut-off by the line $x = \frac{a}{2}$. **[NCERT Exemplar]**

15 Find the area of the parabola $y^2 = 4ax$ bounded by its latusrectum. **[NCERT]**

16 Find the area of the region bounded by $y = -1$, $y = 2$, $x = y^3$ and $x = 0$.

17 Find the area of the region bounded by the line $y = 3x + 2$, the X-axis and the ordinates $x = -1$ and $x = 1$. **[NCERT]**

18 Draw a rough sketch of the given curve $y = 1 + |x + 1|$, $x = -3$, $x = 3$ and $y = 0$ and find the area of the region bounded by them, using integration. **[NCERT Exemplar]**

Hints & Solutions

1. Given curve $y^2 = 8x$ and line $x = 2$.

The graph of curve $y^2 = 8x$ are given below.

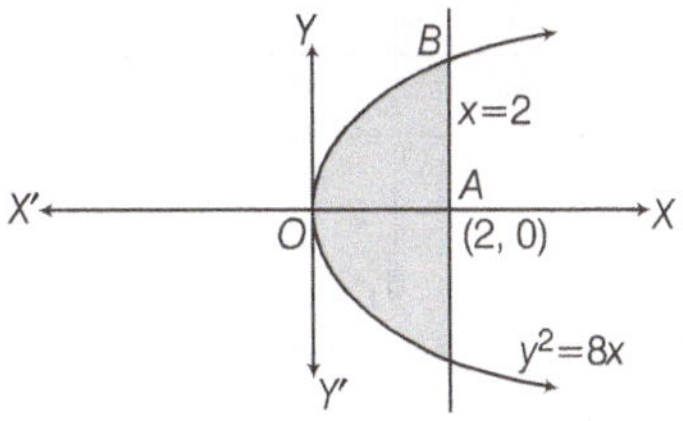

[2]

Area of region bounded by the curve $y^2 = 8x$ and $x = 2$
= 2 (area of region $OABO$)

$$= 2\int_0^2 y\,dx = 2\int_0^2 \sqrt{8x}\,dx$$

[$\because$ parabola is symmetrical about X-axis]

$$= 2\cdot 2\sqrt{2}\int_0^2 \sqrt{x}\,dx = 4\sqrt{2}\left[\frac{2}{3}(x)^{\frac{3}{2}}\right]_0^2$$

$$= \frac{8\sqrt{2}}{3}((2)^{3/2} - 0)$$

$$= \frac{8\sqrt{2}}{3} \times 2\sqrt{2} = \frac{32}{3} \text{ sq units}$$ [2]

2. Given, $y = |x + 4|$

$$\Rightarrow \quad y = \begin{cases} -(x+4), & x < -4 \\ x + 4 & x \ge -4 \end{cases}$$

Graph of $y = |x + 4|$ is given below

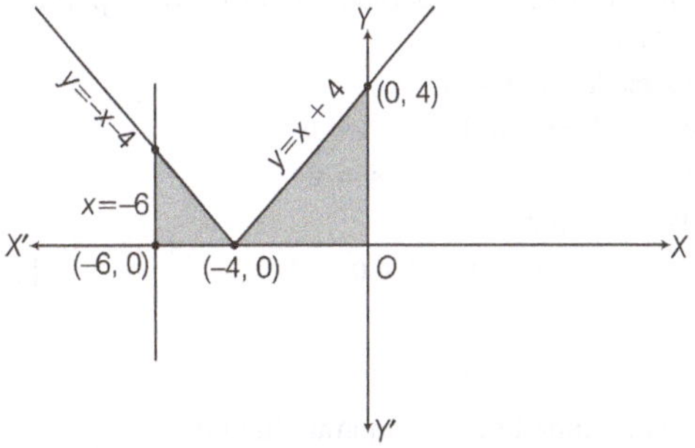

[2]

Area of shaded region $= \int_{-6}^{-4} y_1 dx + \int_{-4}^{0} y_2 dx$

[where, $y_1 = -x - 4$ and $y_2 = x + 4$]

$$\therefore A = \int_{-6}^{-4} -(x+4)dx + \int_{-4}^{0} (x+4)dx$$

$$= -\left[\frac{x^2}{2}+4x\right]_{-6}^{-4} + \left[\frac{x^2}{2}+4x\right]_{-4}^{0}$$

$$= -\left[\left(\frac{16}{2}-16\right)-\left(\frac{36}{2}-24\right)\right]+\left[0-\left(\frac{16}{2}\right)+16\right]$$

$$= -8+16+18-24-8+16 = 10 \text{ sq units}$$ [2]

3. **Hint** Required area = 2 (Area of region *OABO*) $= 2\int_0^4 x\,dy$

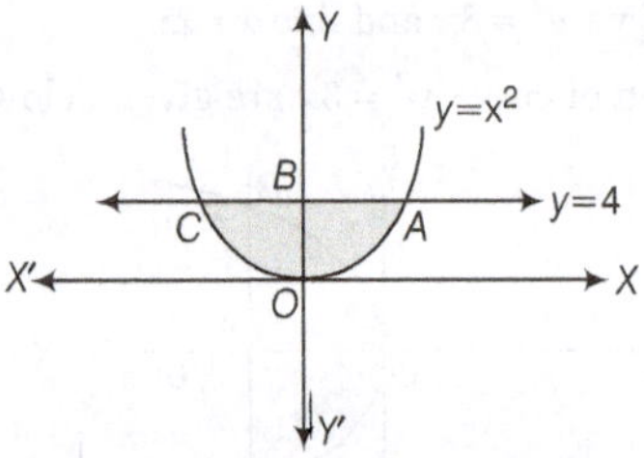

$\left[\textbf{Ans. } \frac{32}{3} \text{sq units}\right]$

4. Similar as Example 1. [**Ans.** $4(4-\sqrt{2})$ sq units]

5. Given curve is $x = 4y - y^2$

$\Rightarrow \quad x = -(y^2 - 4y)$ ...(i)

$\Rightarrow \quad x = -(y^2 - 4y + 4) + 4$

$\Rightarrow \quad x = -(y-2)^2 + 4$

$(y-2)^2 = 4 - x = -(x-4)$

Let $y - 2 = Y$ and $(x-4) = X$

Then, $Y^2 = -X$

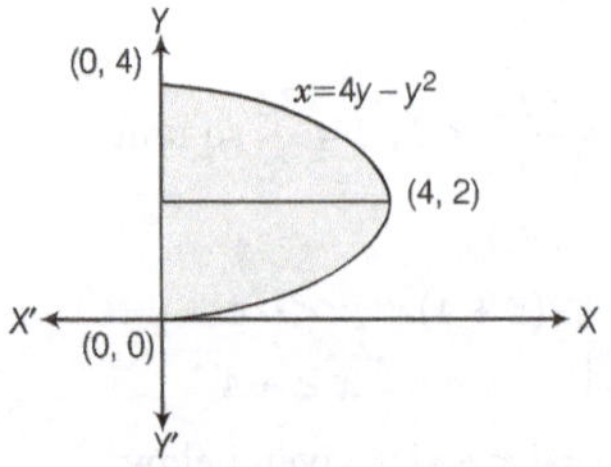

which represents a parabola whose axis is parallel to *X*-axis. [2]

Vertex $X = 0,\ Y = 0$

i.e. $x - 4 = 0$ and $y - 2 = 0$

$\Rightarrow \quad x = 4$ and $y = 2$

Also, at *Y*-axis,

$(y-2)^2 = 4 - 0$ $[\because x = 0]$

$\Rightarrow \quad y - 2 = \pm 2$

$y = 4, 0$ [2]

Area bounded between parabola and *Y*-axis

$$= \int_0^4 x\,dy = \int_0^4 (4y - y^2)\,dy \quad \text{[from Eq. (i)]}$$

$$= \left[\frac{4y^2}{2} - \frac{y^3}{3}\right]_0^4 = \left[2y^2 - \frac{y^3}{3}\right]_0^4$$

$$= \left[32 - \frac{64}{3} - 0\right]$$

$$= \frac{96-64}{3} = \frac{32}{3} \text{ sq units}$$ [2]

6. Given curve is $y = x^2 - 5x + 6$

$\Rightarrow \quad y = x^2 - 3x - 2x + 6 = x(x-3) - 2(x-3)$

$\Rightarrow \quad y = (x-3)(x-2)$

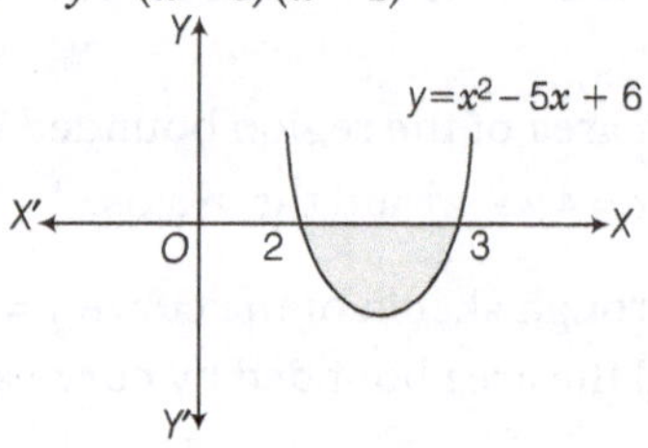

[2]

We know that, at *X*-axis, $y = 0$

$\therefore \quad 0 = (x-3)(x-2) \Rightarrow x - 3 = 0$ or $x - 2 = 0$

$\Rightarrow \quad x = 3$ or 2

$\therefore$ Required area $= \left|\int_2^3 y\,dx\right|$ [2]

$$= \left|\int_2^3 -(x^2 - 5x + 6)\,dx\right|$$

$$= \left|-\left[\frac{x^3}{3} - \frac{5x^2}{2} + 6x\right]_2^3\right|$$

$$= \left|-\left(\frac{27}{3} - \frac{45}{2} + 18 - \frac{8}{3} + 10 - 12\right)\right|$$

$$= \left|-\left(9 - \frac{45}{2} - \frac{8}{3} + 16\right)\right|$$

$$= \left|-\left(\frac{150-135-16}{6}\right)\right|$$

$$= \left|\frac{-(150-151)}{6}\right| = \frac{1}{6} \text{ sq unit}$$ [2]

7. Given curves are $x^2 + y = 9$, $x + 1 = 0$ and $x - 2 = 0$.

Now, $x^2 = -(y-9)$

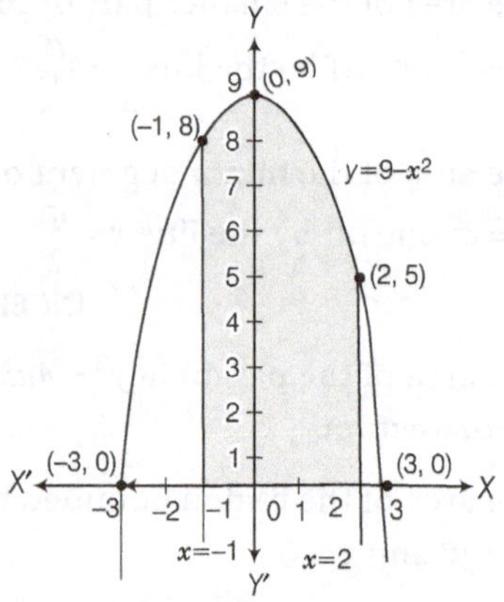

[2]

This represents a parabola having vertex (0, 9) and open downwards.

$\therefore$ Required area $= \int_{-1}^{2} y\,dx = \int_{-1}^{2} (9 - x^2)\,dx$

$$= \left[9x - \frac{x^3}{3}\right]_{-1}^{2} = \left(18 - \frac{8}{3}\right) - \left(-9 + \frac{1}{3}\right)$$

$$= 27 - \frac{8}{3} - \frac{1}{3} = 27 - 3$$

$$= 24 \text{ sq units}$$ [4]

8. Given curves are

$$y^2 + 1 = x,\ x \le 2 \quad \text{...(i)}$$

and $$x = 2 \quad \text{...(ii)}$$

Now, $y^2 = x - 1 \Rightarrow y = \pm\sqrt{x-1}$ ...(iii)

which is defined only when $x - 1 \ge 0$ or $x \ge 1$

$$y^2 = x - 1$$

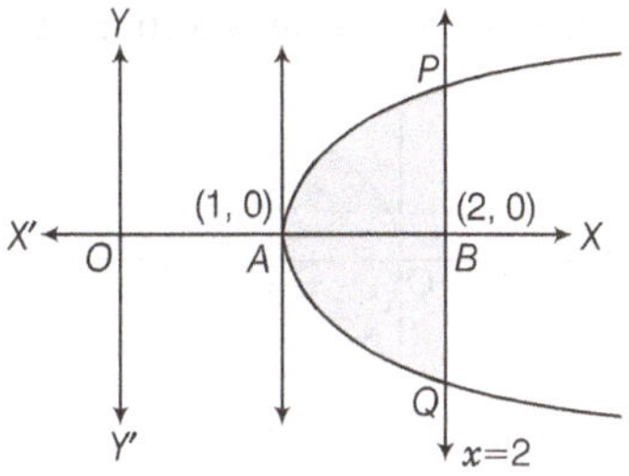

[2]

Now, $y^2 = x - 1$ is a right open parabola with vertex (1, 0).

$\therefore$ Required area = 2 (Area of curve *ABP*)

$$= 2\int_1^2 y\,dx = 2\int_1^2 \sqrt{x-1}\,dx \quad \text{[from Eq. (iii)]}$$

Put $x - 1 = t^2 \Rightarrow dx = 2t\,dt$

Upper limit, when $x = 2$, then $t = 1$

Lower limit, when $x = 1$, then $t = 0$

$\therefore$ Required area $= 4\int_0^1 t \cdot t\,dt = 4\int_0^1 t^2\,dt$

$$= 4\left[\frac{t^3}{3}\right]_0^1 = 4\left[\frac{1}{3} - 0\right] = \frac{4}{3} \text{ sq units}$$ [4]

9. Given curve is $y = 9x^2$

$\Rightarrow \quad x^2 = \frac{y}{9}$, which represents a parabola.

Now, at $x = 0,\ y = 0$

At $y = 1,\ x = \pm\sqrt{\frac{1}{9}} = \pm\frac{1}{3}$

At $y = 4,\ x = \pm\sqrt{\frac{4}{9}} = \pm\frac{2}{3}$

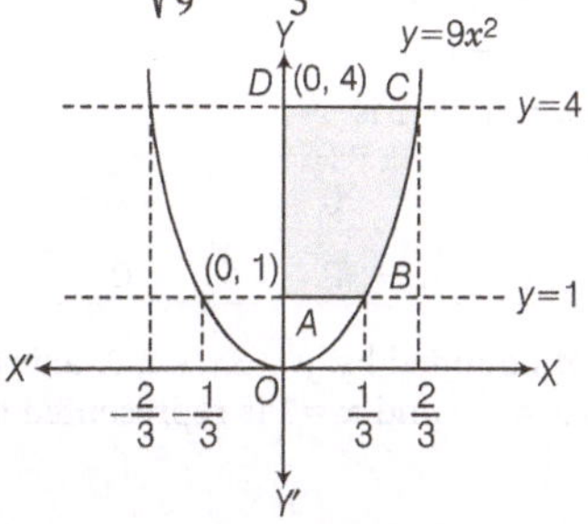

[2]

$\therefore$ Required area = Area of shaded region (*ABCDA*)

$$= \int_1^4 x\,dy \text{ (for parabola)} = \int_1^4 \frac{y^{1/2}}{3}\,dy = \frac{1}{3}\left(\frac{y^{3/2}}{3/2}\right)_1^4$$

$$= \frac{2}{9}(4^{3/2} - 1) = \frac{2}{9}(8 - 1)$$

$$= \frac{14}{9} \text{ sq units}$$ [4]

10. Given curve is $a^2 y = x^2(x + a)$ ...(i)

At *X*-axis, $y = 0$

Then, $x^2(x + a) = 0 \Rightarrow x = 0$ or $x = -a$

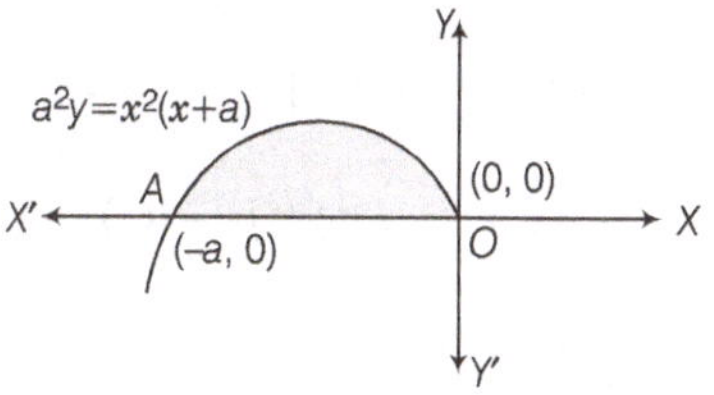

[2]

$\therefore$ Required area $= \int_{-a}^{0} y\,dx$

$$= \int_{-a}^{0}\left(\frac{x^3 + ax^2}{a^2}\right)dx = \frac{1}{a^2}\left[\frac{x^4}{4} + \frac{ax^3}{3}\right]_{-a}^{0}$$

$$= \frac{1}{a^2}\left[0 - \frac{a^4}{4} + \frac{a^4}{3}\right] = \frac{1}{a^2}\left[\frac{(-3+4)}{12}a^4\right]$$

$$= \frac{1}{a^2}\left[\frac{a^4}{12}\right] = \frac{a^2}{12} \text{ sq units}$$ [4]

11. Given curve is $y = \sqrt{3x + 4}$

On squaring both sides, we get

$$y^2 = 3x + 4$$

$$\Rightarrow \quad y^2 = 3\left(x + \frac{4}{3}\right)$$

$$\Rightarrow \quad y^2 = 3\left[x - \left(\frac{-4}{3}\right)\right]$$

which is the equation of the parabola of the form $Y^2 = 4AX$, whose vertex is $\left(-\frac{4}{3}, 0\right)$ and symmetrical about *X*-axis.

As $y = \sqrt{3x + 4}$ is a positive square root, so we take a upper part of the parabola, $y^2 = 3x + 4$ [1]

The area of the region bounded by the curve $y = \sqrt{3x+4}$ between $x = 0$, $x = 4$ and the *X*-axis, is the area shown in the figure given below

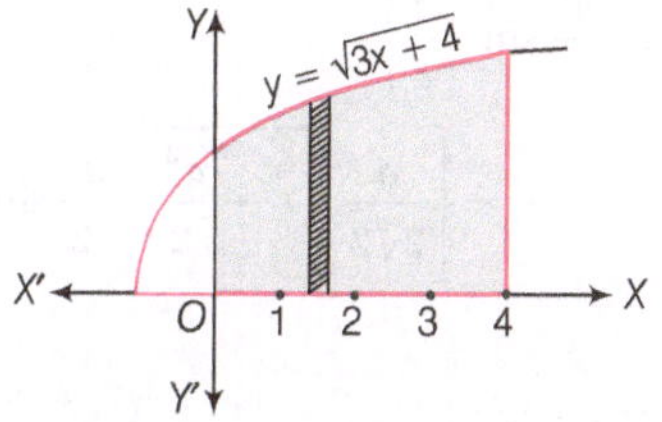

[1]

$\therefore$ Required area $= \int_0^4 y\,dx = \int_0^4 (\sqrt{3x+4})\,dx$ [1]

$$= \int_0^4 (3x+4)^{1/2}\,dx = \left[\frac{(3x+4)^{3/2}}{\frac{3}{2}\cdot 3}\right]_0^4$$ [1]

$$\left[\because \int (ax+b)^n\,dx = \frac{(ax+b)^{n+1}}{a(n+1)}\right]$$

$$= \frac{2}{9}[(12+4)^{3/2} - (4)^{3/2}]$$

$$= \frac{2}{9}[(16)^{3/2} - (4)^{3/2}]$$ [1]

$$= \frac{2}{9}[(2^4)^{3/2} - (2^2)^{3/2}] = \frac{2}{9}[(2)^6 - (2)^3]$$

$$= \frac{2}{9}(64-8)$$

$$= \frac{2}{9}\times 56 = \frac{112}{9} \text{ sq units}$$ [1]

12. Solve as Question 11. $\left[\textbf{Ans. } \frac{16}{3} \text{ sq units}\right]$

13. Given equations of circle and line are

$$x^2 + y^2 = a^2 \quad \text{...(i)}$$

and $$x = \frac{a}{\sqrt{2}} \quad \text{...(ii)}$$

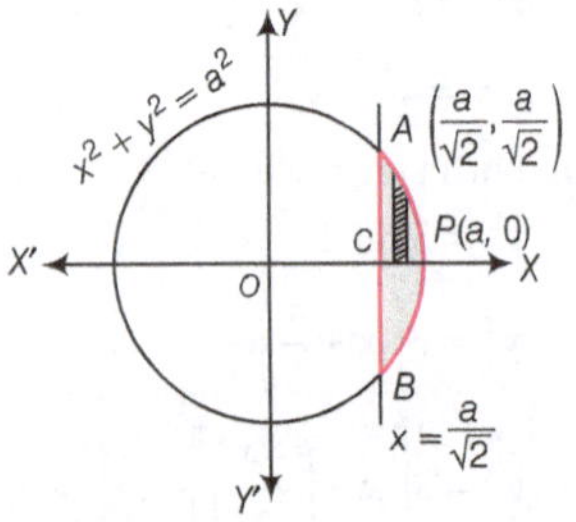

[2]

Clearly, required region is *APBCA*, which is symmetrical about *X*-axis. and the *x*-coordinate of point of intersection curve and line is $\frac{a}{\sqrt{2}}$. [1]

Now, required area = Area of region *APBCA*

= 2 (Area of region *APCA*)

$$= 2\int_{a/\sqrt{2}}^{a} y\,dx = 2\int_{a/\sqrt{2}}^{a} \sqrt{a^2-x^2}\,dx$$

$$= 2\left[\frac{x}{2}\sqrt{a^2-x^2} + \frac{a^2}{2}\sin^{-1}\frac{x}{a}\right]_{\frac{a}{\sqrt{2}}}^{a}$$ [1]

$$= 2\left[\left(0 + \frac{a^2}{2}\sin^{-1}\frac{a}{a}\right) - \left\{\frac{a}{2\sqrt{2}}\sqrt{a^2 - \frac{a^2}{2}} + \frac{a^2}{2}\sin^{-1}\left(\frac{a}{\sqrt{2}}\cdot\frac{1}{a}\right)\right\}\right]$$

$$= 2\left[\left(\frac{a^2}{2}\sin^{-1}(1)\right) - \frac{a}{2\sqrt{2}}\sqrt{\frac{a^2}{2}} - \frac{a^2}{2}\sin^{-1}\frac{1}{\sqrt{2}}\right]$$ [1]

$$= 2\left[\frac{a^2}{2}\cdot\frac{\pi}{2} - \frac{a}{2\sqrt{2}}\cdot\frac{a}{\sqrt{2}} - \frac{a^2}{2}\cdot\frac{\pi}{4}\right] = 2\left[\frac{\pi a^2}{4} - \frac{a^2}{4} - \frac{a^2\pi}{8}\right]$$

$$= \frac{\pi a^2}{2} - \frac{a^2}{2} - \frac{\pi a^2}{4} = \frac{2\pi a^2 - 2a^2 - \pi a^2}{4}$$

$$= \frac{\pi a^2 - 2a^2}{4} = \frac{a^2(\pi-2)}{4} \text{ sq units}$$ [1]

14. Solve as Question 13. $\left[\textbf{Ans. } \frac{a^2}{12}(4\pi - 3\sqrt{3}) \text{ sq units}\right]$

15. **Hint** The equation of the latus rectum LSL' is $x = a$

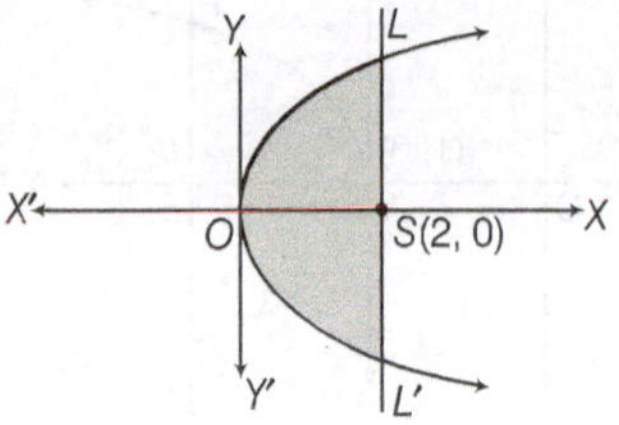

$\therefore$ The required of shaded region $= 2\int_0^a y\,dx$

$\left[\textbf{Ans. } \frac{8}{3}a^2 \text{ sq units}\right]$

16. **Hint** Required area $= \int_0^2 y^3\,dx + \left|\int_{-1}^0 y^3\,dx\right|$

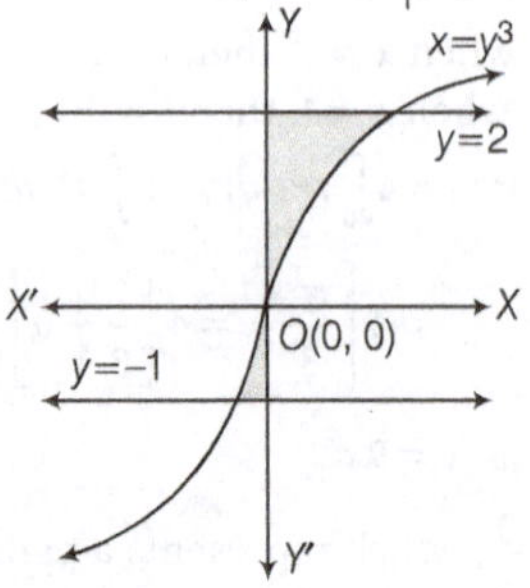

$\left[\textbf{Ans. } \frac{17}{4} \text{ sq units}\right]$

17. Given lines are $y = 3x + 2$ ...(i)

$y = 0$ [*X*-axis] ...(ii)

$x = -1$ ...(iii)

and $x = 1$ ...(iv)

Table for $y = 3x + 2$ is

x	0	−2/3
y	2	0

[1]

The region bounded by $y = 3x + 2$, *X*-axis and the ordinates $x = -1$ and $x = 1$ is represented by the shaded portion.

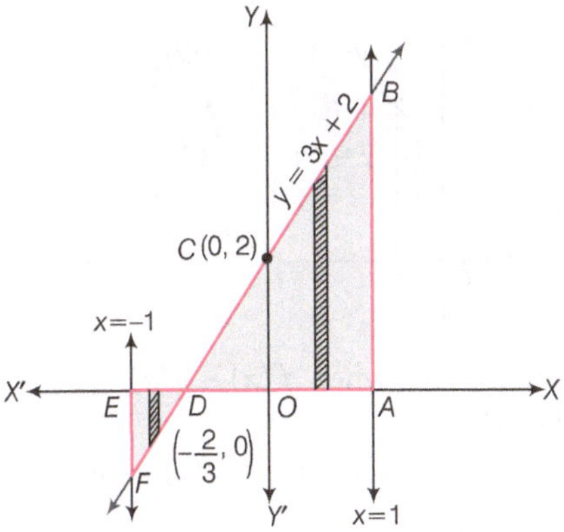

[2]

∴ Required area

= Area of region $EFDE$ + Area of region $ABDA$

$$= \left|\int_{-1}^{-2/3} y_1 dx\right| + \int_{-2/3}^{1} y_2\, dx \quad [1]$$

$$= \left|\int_{-1}^{-2/3} (3x+2)\, dx\right| + \int_{-2/3}^{1} (3x+2)\, dx$$

[∵ in region $EFDE$, the graph is below the X-axis, so its bounded area comes out to be negative, therefore we take the absolute value]

$$= \left|\left[\frac{3x^2}{2} + 2x\right]_{-1}^{-2/3}\right| + \left[\frac{3x^2}{2} + 2x\right]_{-2/3}^{1} \quad [1]$$

$$= \left|\left\{\frac{3}{2}\left(\frac{4}{9}\right) - \frac{4}{3}\right\} - \left(\frac{3}{2} - 2\right)\right| + \left[\left(\frac{3}{2} + 2\right) - \left\{\frac{3}{2}\left(\frac{4}{9}\right) - \frac{4}{3}\right\}\right]$$

$$= \left|\frac{2}{3} - \frac{4}{3} + \frac{1}{2}\right| + \left[\frac{7}{2} - \frac{2}{3} + \frac{4}{3}\right]$$

$$= \left|\frac{4 - 8 + 3}{6}\right| + \left[\frac{21 - 4 + 8}{6}\right]$$

$$= \left|\frac{-1}{6}\right| + \frac{25}{6}$$

$$= \frac{1}{6} + \frac{25}{6} = \frac{26}{6} = \frac{13}{3} \text{ sq units} \quad [1]$$

18. We have, $y = 1 + |x + 1|$

$$= \begin{cases} 1 + (x+1), & x \ge -1 \\ 1 - (x+1), & x < -1 \end{cases} = \begin{cases} 2 + x, & x \ge -1 \\ -x, & x < -1 \end{cases} \quad [1]$$

The graph of above curve is given below

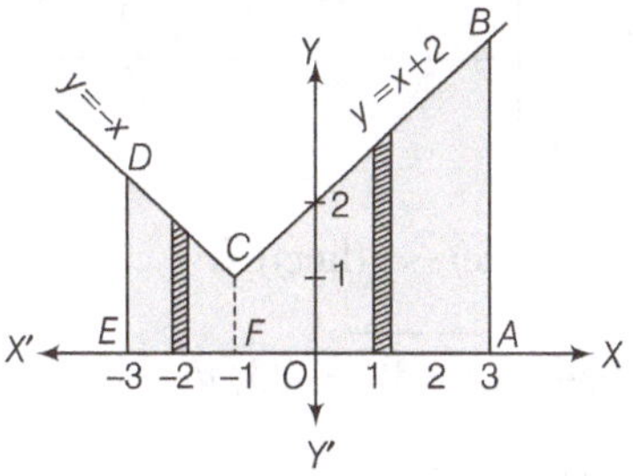

[2]

∴ Required area = Area of shaded region $FCDE$ + Area of shaded region $ABCF$

$$= \int_{-3}^{-1} y_1\, dx + \int_{-1}^{3} y_2\, dx$$

$$= \int_{-3}^{-1} -x\, dx + \int_{-1}^{3} (x+2)\, dx \quad [1]$$

$$= -\left[\frac{x^2}{2}\right]_{-3}^{-1} + \left[\frac{x^2}{2} + 2x\right]_{-1}^{3} \quad [1]$$

$$= -\left[\frac{1}{2} - \frac{9}{2}\right] + \left[\frac{9}{2} + 6 - \left(\frac{1}{2} - 2\right)\right]$$

$$= -\left[\frac{-8}{2}\right] + \frac{8}{2} + 8 = 4 + 4 + 8$$

$$= 16 \text{ sq units} \quad [1]$$

TOPIC 02 Area between Two Curves

We know that integration is the act of calculating the area by cutting the region into a large number of small strips of elementary area and then adding up these elementary areas. Here, we wish to find the area of region bounded by two curves using integration.

Area between Two Curves

(One Below the Other)

Suppose two curves are given by $y = f(x)$ and $y = g(x)$ and their points of intersection are given by $x = a$ and $x = b$ (obtained by taking common values of y from given equation of two curves), then for finding area between these two curves, we have two conditions

When $f(x) \ge g(x)$ in $[a, b]$

Suppose $f(x) \ge g(x)$ in $[a, b]$, then take a vertical strip whose width is dx and length is $f(x) - g(x)$. Then, elementary area, $dA = [f(x) - g(x)]\, dx$ and the total area,

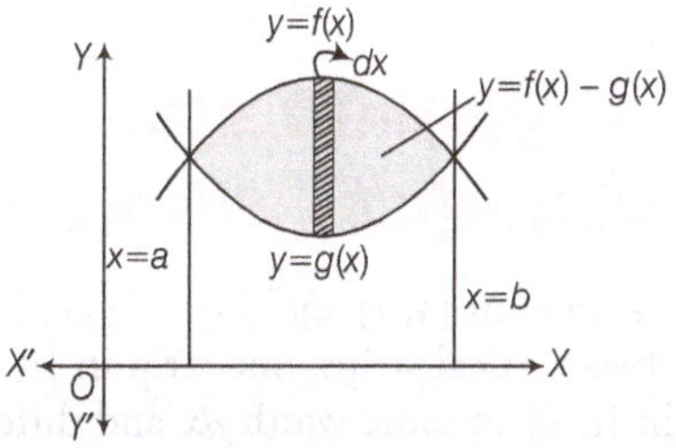

$$A = \int_a^b [f(x) - g(x)]\, dx \text{ or } A = \int_a^b f(x)\, dx - \int_a^b g(x)\, dx$$

e.g. The area of region bounded by the curves $(x-3)^2 + y^2 = 4$ and $y = \sqrt{3}$ between the lines $x = 2$ and $x = 4$ is given by

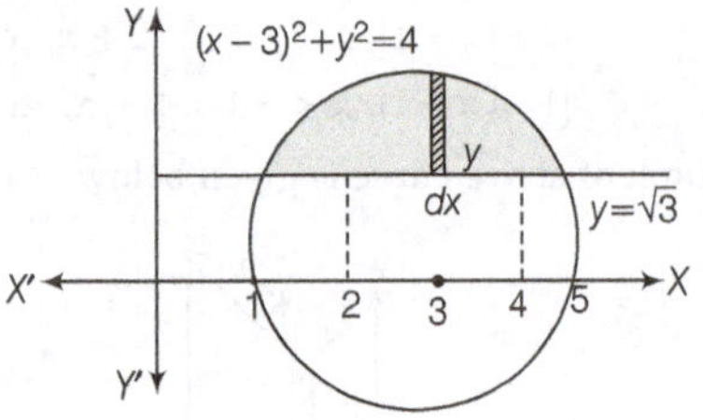

$$\text{Area} = \int_2^4 [y\,(\text{circle}) - y\,(\text{line})]\, dx$$

$$= \int_2^4 (\sqrt{4-(x-3)^2} - \sqrt{3})\, dx$$

$$= \left[\frac{(x-3)}{2}\sqrt{4-(x-3)^2} + \frac{4}{2}\sin^{-1}\frac{(x-3)}{2} - \sqrt{3}x\right]_2^4$$

$$= \left[\frac{1}{2}\sqrt{4-1} + \frac{4}{2}\sin^{-1}\left(\frac{1}{2}\right) - 4\sqrt{3} - \left(\frac{-1}{2}\sqrt{4-1} + 2\sin^{-1}\left(\frac{-1}{2}\right) - 2\sqrt{3}\right)\right]$$

$$= \left[\frac{\sqrt{3}}{2} + 2\times\frac{\pi}{6} - 4\sqrt{3} - \left(-\frac{\sqrt{3}}{2} - 2\times\frac{\pi}{6} - 2\sqrt{3}\right)\right]$$

$$= \left[-2\sqrt{3} + \frac{2\pi}{3}\right] \text{ sq units}$$

Note If two curves $x = f(y)$ and $x = g(y)$ are such that $g(y) \le f(y)$, then area bounded by the two curves $x = f(y)$ and $x = g(y)$ between the lines $y = c$ and $y = d$, is given by

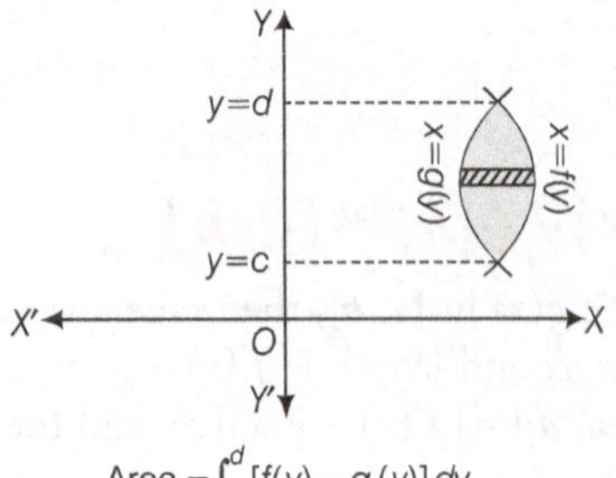

$$\text{Area} = \int_c^d [f(y) - g(y)]\, dy$$

When $f(x) \ge g(x)$ in $[a, c]$ and $0 \le f(x) \le g(x)$ in $[c, b]$, where $a < c < b$

Suppose $f(x) \ge g(x)$ in $[a, c]$ and $f(x) \le g(x)$ in $[c, b]$, then we take two vertical strips, one strip in $[a, c]$ and second strip in $[c, b]$ of same width dx and different height $f(x) - g(x)$ and $g(x) - f(x)$.

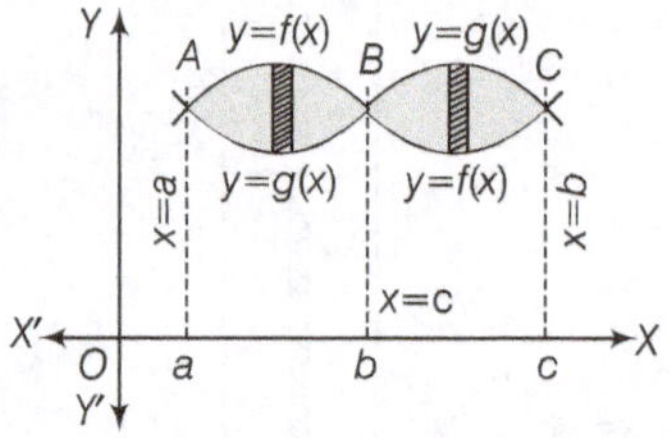

Then, elementary area when $f(x) \ge g(x)$
$= [f(x) - g(x)]\, dx$

and elementary area when $f(x) \le g(x) = [g(x) - f(x)]\, dx$

Hence, total area is given by

$$A = \int_a^c [f(x) - g(x)]\, dx + \int_c^b [g(x) - f(x)]\, dx$$

Working Rule to Find the Area between Two Curves

Suppose two curves $y = f(x)$ and $y = g(x)$ are given to us, then for finding the area of region between (or bounded by) two curves, we use the following steps

I. First, draw the rough sketches of both given curves and identify the region bounded by them.

II. Find the intersection points of both curves.

III. Take the limit for bounded region and draw the vertical strips (one or two).

IV. Now, find the area by using suitable formula.

Example 1 Using integration, find the area of the region bounded by the curve $y^2 = 4x$ and $x^2 = 4y$.

[ISC 2024]

Sol. We have two parabolas,

$$y^2 = 4x \text{ and } x^2 = 4y$$

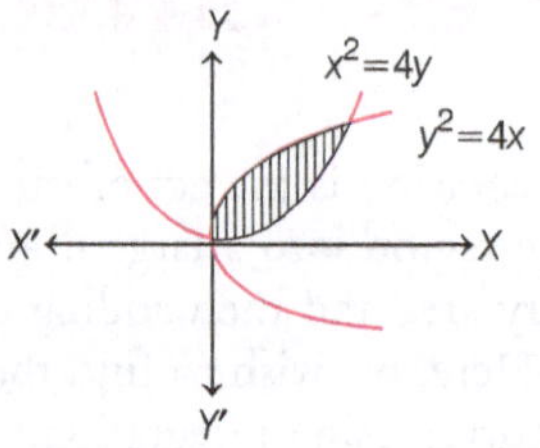

Since, $y^2 = 4x$

$\Rightarrow \left(\frac{x^2}{4}\right)^2 = 4x \qquad \left[\because \frac{x^2}{4} = y\right]$

$\Rightarrow \frac{x^4}{16} = 4x$

$\Rightarrow x^4 - 64x = 0$

$\Rightarrow x(x^3 - 64) = 0$

$\Rightarrow \quad x = 0, x^3 = 64$

$\Rightarrow \quad x = 0, x = 4$

When $x = 0$, then $y = 0$

When $x = 4$, then $y = 4$

$\therefore$ Required area $= \int_{x=0}^{x=4} [y(\text{parabola } y^2 = 4x) - y(\text{parabola } 4y = x^2)]\,dx$

$$= \int_0^4 \left[\sqrt{4x} - \frac{x^2}{4}\right] dx$$

$$= \int_0^4 \left[2\sqrt{x} - \frac{x^2}{4}\right] dx$$

$$= \left[2 \cdot \frac{2}{3} \cdot x^{3/2}\right]_0^4 - \frac{1}{4}\left[\frac{x^3}{3}\right]_0^4$$

$$= \frac{4}{3}[4^{3/2} - 0] - \frac{1}{12}[4^3 - 0]$$

$$= \frac{4}{3}[8 - 0] - \frac{1}{12}[64 - 0]$$

$$= \frac{32}{3} - \frac{64}{12} = \frac{16}{3} \text{ sq units}$$

Example 2 Using integration, find the area enclosed by the parabola $4y = 3x^2$ and the line $2y = 3x + 12$. **[NCERT]**

Or

Find the area enclosed between the parabola $4y = 3x^2$ and the straight line $3x - 2y + 12 = 0$.

Sol. Given equation of parabola is $4y = 3x^2$ ...(i)

and the given line is $2y = 3x + 12$ ...(ii)

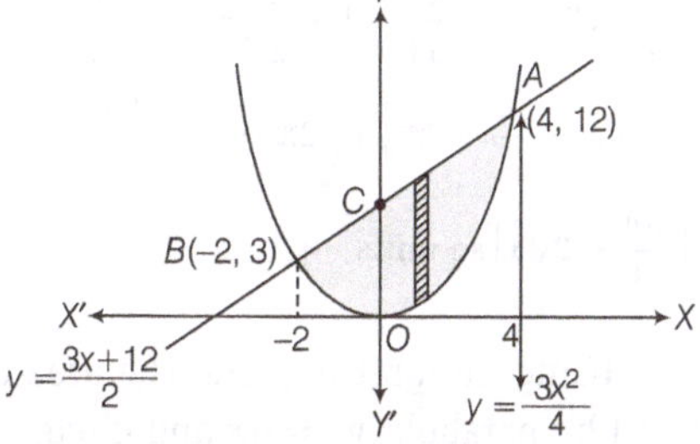

It is clear from the figure that the required region is *AOBCA*.

Now, the point of intersection of given curve and line is given by

$$2(3x + 12) = 3x^2$$

[eliminating y between Eqs. (i) and (ii)]

$\Rightarrow \quad 3x^2 - 6x - 24 = 0$

$\Rightarrow \quad x^2 - 2x - 8 = 0$

$\Rightarrow \quad (x-4)(x+2) = 0$

$\Rightarrow \quad x = 4, -2$

When $x = 4$, then $y = \frac{3 \times 4 + 12}{2} = 12$,

When $x = -2$, then $y = \frac{3 \times (-2) + 12}{2} = 3$.

So, the points of intersection are $A(4, 12)$ and $B(-2, 3)$.

$\therefore$ Required area = Area of shaded portion *AOBCA*

$$= \int_{-2}^{4} [y(\text{line}) - y(\text{parabola})]\,dx$$

$$= \int_{-2}^{4} \left(\frac{3x + 12}{2} - \frac{3x^2}{4}\right) dx$$

$$= \left[\frac{1}{2}\left(\frac{3x^2}{2} + 12x\right) - \frac{3x^3}{4 \times 3}\right]_{-2}^{4}$$

$$= \left[\frac{3x^2}{4} + 6x - \frac{x^3}{4}\right]_{-2}^{4}$$

$$= \left\{\frac{3 \times 4^2}{4} + 6 \times 4 - \frac{4^3}{4}\right\} - \left\{\frac{3 \times (-2)^2}{4} + 6 \times (-2) - \frac{(-2)^3}{4}\right\}$$

$$= 12 + 24 - 16 - 3 + 12 - 2 = 27 \text{ sq units}$$

Example 3 Find the area of the region bounded by the curves $y = x^2 + 2$, $y = x$, $x = 0$ and $x = 3$.

Sol. Given equations of curves are

$y = x^2 + 2$ or $x^2 = y - 2$ ...(i)

$y = x$ ...(ii)

$x = 0$ ...(iii)

and $x = 3$ ...(iv)

Eq. (i) represents a parabola of the form $X^2 = 4aY$ with vertex at (0, 2) and axis along positive direction of Y-axis.

Eq. (ii) represent a line which intersect the coordinate axes at (0, 0).

Eqs. (iii) and (iv) represent the lines perpendicular to the X-axis.

The graph of given curves is shown below

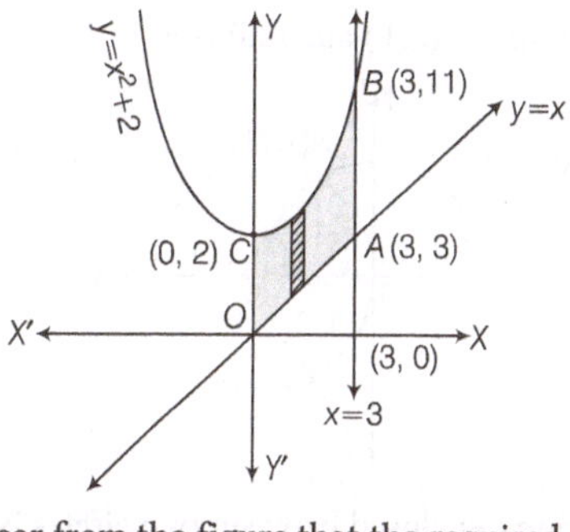

It is clear from the figure that the required region is *OABCO*.

Note that the line $x = 3$ intersects $y = x$ at (3, 3) and $y = x^2 + 2$ at (3, 11).

$\therefore$ Required area = Area of shaded portion *OABCO*

$$= \int_0^3 [y_2\,(\text{parabola}) - y_1\,(\text{line})]\,dx$$

$$= \int_0^3 (x^2 + 2 - x)dx = \left[\frac{x^3}{3} - \frac{x^2}{2} + 2x\right]_0^3$$

$$= \frac{27}{3} - \frac{9}{2} + 6 = 9 + 6 - \frac{9}{2} = 15 - \frac{9}{2}$$

$$= \frac{30 - 9}{2} = \frac{21}{2} \text{ sq units}$$

Hence, the required area is $\frac{21}{2}$ sq units.

Area Bounded by Two Curves and Axis

Area bounded by the two curves $y = f(x)$ and $y = g(x)$ and X-axis, between the lines $x = a$ and $x = b$ is given by

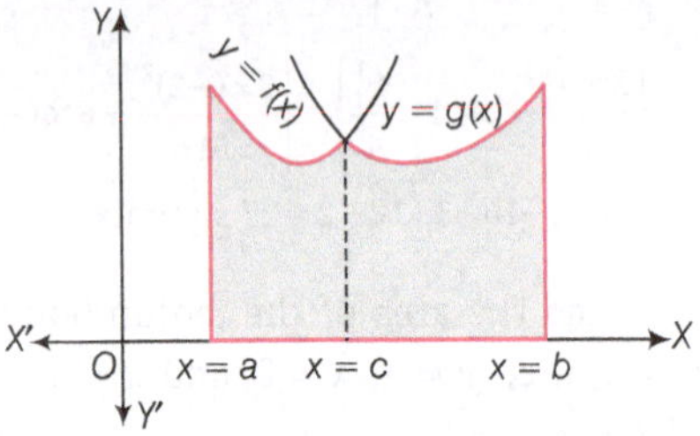

$$\text{Area} = \int_a^c f(x)dx + \int_c^b g(x)\, dx$$

where, c is abscissa of intersecting point of $f(x)$ and $g(x)$.

Example 4 Find the area of the region enclosed between the two circles $x^2 + y^2 = 4$ and $(x - 2)^2 + y^2 = 4$.

Sol. Given circles are

$$x^2 + y^2 = 4 \quad \text{...(i)}$$

whose centre is origin and radius is 2;

and $$(x - 2)^2 + y^2 = 4 \quad \text{...(ii)}$$

whose centre is (2, 0) and radius is 2.

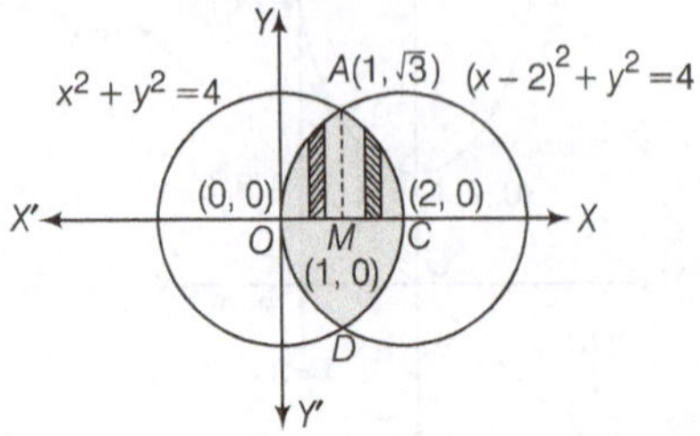

Here, region enclosed between two circles is $OACDO$, which is symmetrical about X-axis.

Now, from Eqs. (i) and (ii), we get

$$(x - 2)^2 + y^2 = x^2 + y^2$$

$$\Rightarrow x^2 + 4 - 4x + y^2 = x^2 + y^2$$

$$\Rightarrow 4 - 4x = 0 \Rightarrow x = 1$$

From Eq. (i), we get

$$y^2 = 4 - x^2 = 4 - 1 = 3 \Rightarrow y = \pm\sqrt{3}$$

So, the points of intersection are $A(1, \sqrt{3})$ and $D(1, -\sqrt{3})$.

Here, we will draw two vertical strips [one for circle (i) and other for circle (ii)].

$\therefore$ Required area = Area of region $OACDO$

= 2 × Area of region $OACO$

= 2 [Area of region $OAMO$ + Area of region $AMCA$]

$$= 2\left[\int_0^1 y\,(\text{circle (ii)})\,dx + \int_1^2 y\,(\text{circle (i)})\,dx\right]$$

$$= 2\left[\int_0^1 \sqrt{4 - (x - 2)^2}\,dx + \int_1^2 \sqrt{4 - x^2}\,dx\right]$$

$$\left[\begin{array}{l}\text{from Eq. (i), } y^2 = 4 - x^2 \Rightarrow y = \sqrt{4 - x^2} \\ \text{and from Eq. (ii), } y^2 = 4 - (x - 2)^2 \\ \qquad \Rightarrow y = \sqrt{4 - (x - 2)^2}\end{array}\right]$$

$$= 2\left[\frac{(x - 2)}{2}\sqrt{4 - (x - 2)^2} + \frac{4}{2}\sin^{-1}\left(\frac{x - 2}{2}\right)\right]_0^1 + 2\left[\frac{x}{2}\sqrt{4 - x^2} + \frac{4}{2}\sin^{-1}\frac{x}{2}\right]_1^2$$

$$= \left[(x - 2)\sqrt{4 - (x - 2)^2} + 4\sin^{-1}\left(\frac{x - 2}{2}\right)\right]_0^1 + \left[x\sqrt{4 - x^2} + 4\sin^{-1}\frac{x}{2}\right]_1^2$$

$$= \left[\left\{-\sqrt{3} + 4\sin^{-1}\left(\frac{-1}{2}\right)\right\} - 0 - 4\sin^{-1}(-1)\right] + \left[0 + 4\sin^{-1}1 - \sqrt{3} - 4\sin^{-1}\frac{1}{2}\right]$$

$$= \left[\left\{-\sqrt{3} - 4 \times \frac{\pi}{6}\right\} + 4 \times \frac{\pi}{2}\right] + \left[4 \times \frac{\pi}{2} - \sqrt{3} - 4 \times \frac{\pi}{6}\right]$$

$$= \left(-\sqrt{3} - \frac{2\pi}{3} + 2\pi\right) + \left(2\pi - \sqrt{3} - \frac{2\pi}{3}\right)$$

$$= \left(\frac{8\pi}{3} - 2\sqrt{3}\right) \text{ sq units}$$

Example 5 Using integration, find the area of the region bounded by parabola $y^2 = 4x$ and circle $4x^2 + 4y^2 = 9$.

Or

Using integration, find the area of the region

$$\{(x, y) : y^2 \le 4x, 4x^2 + 4y^2 \le 9\}. \quad \textbf{[NCERT]}$$

Sol. Given curves are $y^2 = 4x$ ...(i)

and $4x^2 + 4y^2 = 9$

$$\Rightarrow x^2 + y^2 = \frac{9}{4} \quad \text{...(ii)}$$

Here, Eq. (i) represents a parabola having vertex (0, 0) and axis along X-axis.

Also, Eq. (ii) represents a circle with centre (0, 0) and radius $\frac{3}{2}$.

So, the region bounded by them is *OABCO*. Also, it is symmetrical about *X*-axis.

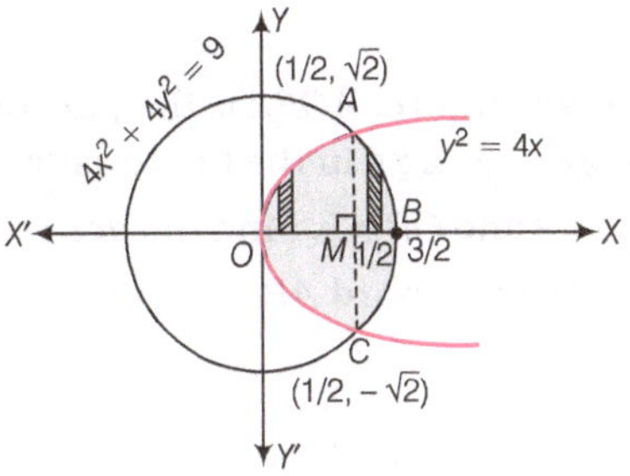

For the points of intersection of circle and parabola, put the value of y^2 from Eq. (i) in Eq. (ii),

i.e. $x^2 + 4x = \frac{9}{4} \Rightarrow 4x^2 + 16x = 9$

$\Rightarrow \quad 4x^2 + 16x - 9 = 0 \Rightarrow 4x^2 + 18x - 2x - 9 = 0$

$\Rightarrow \quad 2x(2x + 9) - 1(2x + 9) = 0 \Rightarrow (2x - 1)(2x + 9) = 0$

$\Rightarrow \quad x = \frac{1}{2}$ or $x = -\frac{9}{2}$

Now, $x = \frac{-9}{2}$ is rejected, because it does not satisfy Eq. (i).

$\therefore \quad x = \frac{1}{2}$

When $x = \frac{1}{2}$, then from Eq. (i), we get

$$y^2 = 4x \Rightarrow y = \pm\sqrt{4x} = \pm 2\sqrt{\frac{1}{2}} = \pm\sqrt{2}$$

So, the points of intersection of the curves are $A\left(\frac{1}{2}, \sqrt{2}\right)$ and $C\left(\frac{1}{2}, -\sqrt{2}\right)$.

$\therefore$ Required area = Area of shaded region *OABCO*

= 2 (Area of shaded region *OABMO*)

= 2 (Area of shaded region *OAMO* + Area of shaded region *ABMA*)

[here, we draw two vertical strips]

$$= 2\left[\int_0^{1/2} y\,(\text{parabola})\,dx + \int_{1/2}^{3/2} y(\text{circle})\,dx\right]$$

$$= 2\left[\int_0^{1/2} \sqrt{4x}\,dx + \int_{1/2}^{3/2} \sqrt{\frac{9}{4} - x^2}\,dx\right]$$

$$\left[\because y^2 = 4x \Rightarrow y = \sqrt{4x} \text{ and } 4x^2 + 4y^2 = 9 \Rightarrow y = \sqrt{\frac{9}{4} - x^2}\right]$$

$$= 2\left[2\int_0^{1/2} \sqrt{x}\,dx + \int_{1/2}^{3/2} \sqrt{\left(\frac{3}{2}\right)^2 - x^2}\,dx\right]$$

$$= 2\left[2\left[\frac{x^{3/2}}{3/2}\right]_0^{1/2} + \left\{\left(\frac{x}{2}\right)\sqrt{\frac{9}{4} - x^2} + \frac{9}{4 \cdot 2}\sin^{-1}\frac{x}{\left(\frac{3}{2}\right)}\right\}_{1/2}^{3/2}\right]$$

$$\left[\because \int \sqrt{a^2 - x^2}\,dx = \frac{x}{2}\sqrt{a^2 - x^2} + \left(\frac{a^2}{2}\right)\sin^{-1}\left(\frac{x}{a}\right)\right]$$

$$= 2\left[\frac{2 \cdot 2}{3}[x^{3/2}]_0^{1/2} + \left[\frac{x}{2}\sqrt{\frac{9}{4} - x^2} + \frac{9}{8}\sin^{-1}\left(\frac{2}{3}x\right)\right]_{1/2}^{3/2}\right]$$

$$= 2\left[\frac{4}{3}\left(\frac{1}{2}\right)^{3/2} + 0 + \frac{9}{8}\sin^{-1}\left(\frac{2}{3} \cdot \frac{3}{2}\right) - \left\{\frac{1}{4}\sqrt{\frac{9}{4} - \frac{1}{4}} + \frac{9}{8}\sin^{-1}\left(\frac{2}{3} \cdot \frac{1}{2}\right)\right\}\right]$$

$$= 2\left[\frac{4}{3} \cdot \frac{1}{(2)^{3/2}} + \frac{9}{8}\sin^{-1}(1) - \frac{1}{4}\sqrt{\frac{8}{4}} - \frac{9}{8}\sin^{-1}\left(\frac{1}{3}\right)\right]$$

$$= 2\left[\frac{4}{3 \cdot 2\sqrt{2}} + \frac{9}{8} \cdot \frac{\pi}{2} - \frac{1}{4}\sqrt{2} - \frac{9}{8}\sin^{-1}\left(\frac{1}{3}\right)\right]$$

$$= 2\left[\frac{2}{3\sqrt{2}} + \frac{9\pi}{16} - \frac{\sqrt{2}}{4} - \frac{9}{8}\sin^{-1}\left(\frac{1}{3}\right)\right]$$

$$= 2\left[\frac{\sqrt{2}}{3} - \frac{\sqrt{2}}{4} + \frac{9\pi}{16} - \frac{9}{8}\sin^{-1}\left(\frac{1}{3}\right)\right]$$

$$= 2\left[\frac{4\sqrt{2} - 3\sqrt{2}}{12} + \frac{9\pi}{16} - \frac{9}{8}\sin^{-1}\left(\frac{1}{3}\right)\right]$$

$$= 2\left[\frac{\sqrt{2}}{12} + \frac{9\pi}{16} - \frac{9}{8}\sin^{-1}\left(\frac{1}{3}\right)\right]$$

$$= \left[\frac{\sqrt{2}}{6} + \frac{9\pi}{8} - \frac{9}{4}\sin^{-1}\left(\frac{1}{3}\right)\right] \text{ sq units}$$

Example 6 Using the method of integration, find the area of the triangular region whose vertices are (2, – 2), (4, 3) and (1, 2).

Sol. Let $P(2, -2)$, $Q(4, 3)$ and $R(1, 2)$ be the vertices of a ΔPQR.

Now, the equation of line *PQ* passing through the points $P(2, -2)$ and $Q(4, 3)$ is given by

$$y + 2 = \frac{3 + 2}{4 - 2}(x - 2)$$

$$\left[\because \text{equation of line passing through } (x_1, y_1) \text{ and } (x_2, y_2) \text{ is } y - y_1 = \frac{y_2 - y_1}{x_2 - x_1}(x - x_1)\right]$$

$$\Rightarrow \quad y + 2 = \frac{5}{2}(x - 2) \Rightarrow y = \frac{5}{2}(x - 2) - 2 \Rightarrow y = \frac{5x - 14}{2}$$

Similarly, equation of line QR passing through points $Q(4, 3)$ and $R(1, 2)$ is

$$y - 3 = \frac{2-3}{1-4}(x-4)$$

$$\Rightarrow \quad y - 3 = \frac{-1}{-3}(x-4)$$

$$\Rightarrow \quad y = \frac{x-4}{3} + 3 \quad \Rightarrow \quad y = \frac{x+5}{3}$$

and equation of a line RP passing through the points $R(1, 2)$ and $P(2, -2)$ is

$$y - 2 = \frac{-2-2}{2-1}(x-1) \Rightarrow y - 2 = -\frac{4}{1}(x-1)$$

$$\Rightarrow \quad y = -4x + 4 + 2 \Rightarrow y = -4x + 6$$

Now, plot all the lines, which is shown below

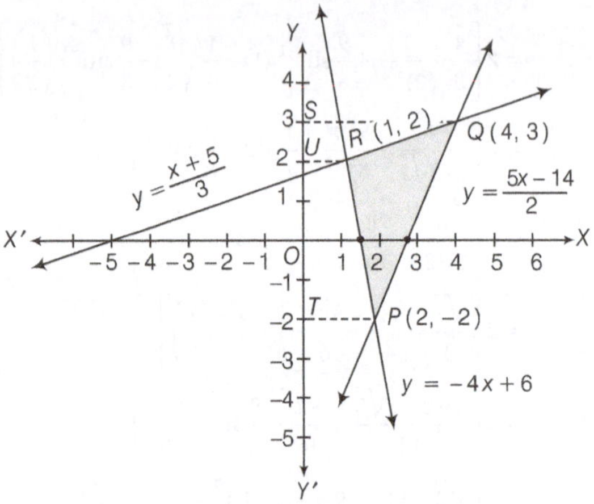

∴ Area of triangular region PQR

= Area of region $PQST$ − Area of region $SQRU$ − Area of region $PRUT$

$$= \int_{-2}^{3} x(\text{Straight line } PQ)\, dy - \int_{2}^{3} x\,(\text{Straight line } QR)\, dy - \int_{-2}^{2} x(\text{Straight line } PR\, dy$$

$$= \int_{-2}^{3}\left(\frac{2y}{5} + \frac{14}{5}\right)dy - \int_{2}^{3}(3y-5)\,dy - \int_{-2}^{2}\left(\frac{6-y}{4}\right)dy$$

$$= \left[\frac{2}{5} \times \frac{y^2}{2} + \frac{14}{5}y\right]_{-2}^{3} - \left[\frac{3y^2}{2} - 5y\right]_{2}^{3} - \frac{1}{4}\left[6y - \frac{y^2}{2}\right]_{-2}^{2}$$

$$= \left[\frac{3^2}{5} + \frac{42}{5} - \left(\frac{4}{5} - \frac{28}{5}\right)\right] - \left[\frac{27}{2} - 15 - (6 - 10)\right] - \frac{1}{4}[12 - 2 - (-12 - 2)]$$

$$= \left(\frac{51}{5} + \frac{24}{5}\right) - \left(\frac{27}{2} - 11\right) - \frac{1}{4}(24)$$

$$= 15 - \frac{5}{2} - 6$$

$$= 9 - \frac{5}{2} = \frac{13}{2} \text{ sq units}$$

Hence, the required area is $\frac{13}{2}$ sq units.

Topic Practice 2

Long Answer Type Questions

(6 Marks)

1 In the given figure, $AOBA$ is the part of the ellipse $9x^2 + y^2 = 36$ in the first quadrant, such that $OA = 2$ and $OB = 6$. Find the area between the arc AB and chord AB. **[NCERT]**

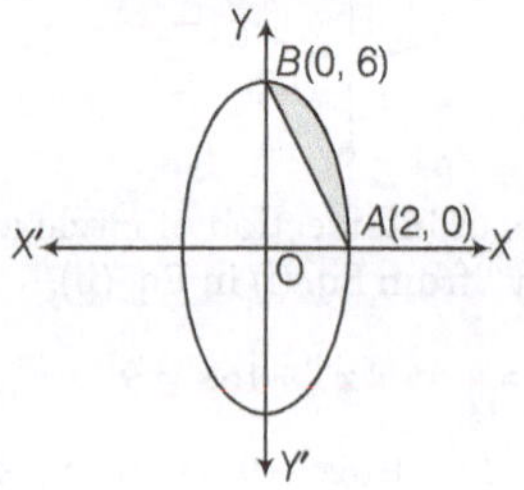

2 Find the area bounded by the curves $y = x$ and $y = x^3$.

3 Find the area enclosed between the parabola $y^2 = 4ax$ and the line $y = mx$. **[NCERT]**

4 Using integration, find the area of the region bounded by the curves $y = x^2$ and $y = x$.

5 Find the area of the region included between the parabola $y^2 = 2x$ and the straight line $x - y = 4$. **[NCERT Exemplar]**

6 Find the area of the region bounded by parabolas $y^2 = 4ax$ and $x^2 = 4ay$ by considering vertical strip.

7 If the area enclosed between the curves $y = ax^2$ and $x = ay^2 (a > 0)$ is 1 sq unit, then find the value of a.

8 Draw a rough sketch and find the area bounded by the curve $x^2 = y$ and $x + y = 2$. **[ISC 2019]**

9 Find the area bounded by the curves $y = 2x - x^2$ and the line $y = x$. **[ISC 2013]**

10 Find the smaller area enclosed by the circle $x^2 + y^2 = 4$ and the line $x + y = 2$. **[ISC 2015]**

11 Find the area of the region bounded by the curves $y = 6x - x^2$ and $y = x^2 - 2x$. **[ISC 2016]**

12 Draw a rough sketch of the curves $y^2 = x$ and $y^2 = 4 - 3x$ and find the area enclosed between them. **[ISC 2020]**

13 Draw a rough sketch of the curve $y = (x-1)^2$ and $y = |x-1|$. Hence, find the area of the region bounded by these curves. **[ISC 2011]**

14 Using integration, find the area of the region enclosed between the circles $x^2 + y^2 = 1$ and $(x-1)^2 + y^2 = 1$. **[NCERT]**

15 Using integration, find the area of the region lying above X-axis and included between the circle $x^2 + y^2 = 8x$, the parabola $y^2 = 4x$ and X-axis.

16 Using integration, find the area of the region $\{(x, y): y^2 \geq ax, x^2 + y^2 \leq 2ax, a > 0\}$.

17 Draw a rough sketch of the region $\{(x, y): y^2 \leq 6ax \text{ and } x^2 + y^2 \leq 16a^2\}$. Also, find the area of the region sketched using method of integration. **[NCERT Exemplar]**

18 Using integration, find the area of the region common to the circle $x^2 + y^2 = 16$ and the parabola $y^2 = 6x$.

19 Using integration, find the area of the region bounded by the triangle, whose vertices are $(-1, 2)$, $(1, 5)$ and $(3, 4)$.

20 Using integration, find the area of the region bounded by the triangle, whose vertices are $(-1, 0)$, $(1, 3)$ and $(3, 2)$. **[NCERT]**

21 Find the area bounded by the lines $y = 4x + 5$, $y = 5 - x$ and $4y = x + 5$. **[NCERT Exemplar]**

Hints & Solutions

1. Given equation of ellipse is $9x^2 + y^2 = 36$

which can be expressed as $\frac{x^2}{4} + \frac{y^2}{36} = 1$

$$\Rightarrow \quad \frac{x^2}{2^2} + \frac{y^2}{6^2} = 1 \Rightarrow \frac{y^2}{6^2} = 1 - \frac{x^2}{2^2}$$

$$\Rightarrow \quad y^2 = 6^2\left(\frac{4-x^2}{2^2}\right)$$

$$\Rightarrow \quad y = 6\sqrt{\frac{4-x^2}{2^2}} \Rightarrow y = 3\sqrt{4-x^2} \quad \text{...(i)}$$

[considering y in I quadrant] [1]

Now, equation of chord AB is $y - 0 = \frac{6-0}{0-2}(x-2)$

$\left[\because \text{equation of line passing through two points is } y - y_1 = \frac{y_2 - y_1}{x_2 - x_1}(x - x_1)\right]$

$$\Rightarrow \quad y = -3(x-2) = -3x + 6 \quad \text{...(ii)} \; [1]$$

$\therefore$ Required area = Area of shaded region

$$= \int_0^2 [y\,(\text{ellipsee}) - y\,(\text{chord})]dx \quad [1]$$

$$= \int_0^2 \left[3\sqrt{4-x^2} - (-3x+6)\right]dx \quad [1]$$

$$= 3\int_0^2 \sqrt{4-x^2}\,dx - \int_0^2 (6-3x)dx$$

$$= 3\left[\frac{x}{2}\sqrt{4-x^2} + \frac{4}{2}\sin^{-1}\left(\frac{x}{2}\right)\right]_0^2 - \left[6x - \frac{3x^2}{2}\right]_0^2 \quad [1]$$

$$= 3[0 + 2\sin^{-1}(1) - 0] - [12 - 3 \times 2 - 0]$$

$$= 6\sin^{-1}(1) - 6 = 6 \times \frac{\pi}{2} - 6 = 3\pi - 6 \text{ sq units} \quad [1]$$

2. Given equations of curves are $y = x^3$ ...(i)

and $y = x$ ...(ii)

The graph of above curves is shown below

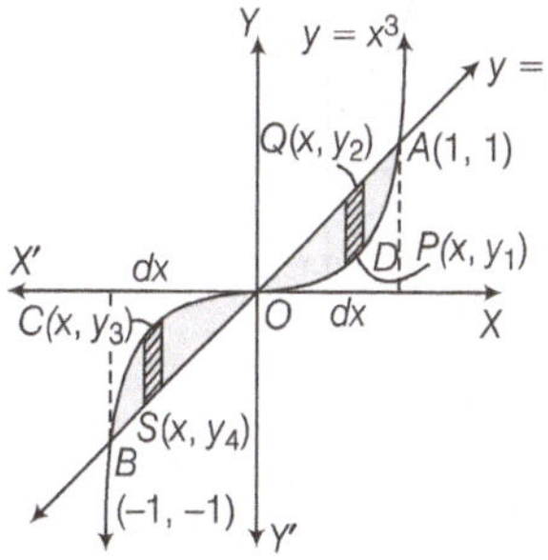

It is clear from the graph that the required region is the shaded region. [2]

Now, for point of intersection of line and curve, put $y = x$ in Eq. (i).

i.e. $x = x^3 \Rightarrow x - x^3 = 0$

$\Rightarrow \quad x(1 - x^2) = 0 \Rightarrow x = 0, x^2 = 1 \Rightarrow x = 0, x = \pm 1$

When $x = 0$, then $y = 0$ [using Eq. (ii)]

When $x = 1$, then $y = 1$. [using Eq. (ii)]

When $x = -1$, then $y = -1$ [using Eq. (ii)]

Thus, the points of intersection are O (0, 0), $A(1, 1)$ and $B(-1, -1)$.

$\therefore$ Required area = Area of shaded portion

= Area of region $ODAO$ + Area of region $OBCO$ [1]

$$= \int_0^1 (y_2 - y_1)dx + \left|\int_{-1}^0 (y_4 - y_3)dx\right| \quad [1]$$

$$= \int_0^1 (x - x^3)dx + \left|\int_{-1}^0 (x - x^3)\,dx\right|$$

$$= \left[\frac{x^2}{2} - \frac{x^4}{4}\right]_0^1 + \left|\left[\frac{x^2}{2} - \frac{x^4}{4}\right]_{-1}^0\right| = \left[\frac{1}{2} - \frac{1}{4}\right] + \left|\left[\frac{-1}{2} + \frac{1}{4}\right]\right|$$

$$= \frac{1}{4} + \left|\frac{-1}{4}\right|$$

$$= \frac{1}{4} + \frac{1}{4} = \frac{2}{4} = \frac{1}{2} \text{ sq unit} \quad [2]$$

3. **Hint** Area of shaded region $= \int_0^{4a/m^2} (\sqrt{4ax} - mx)\,dx$

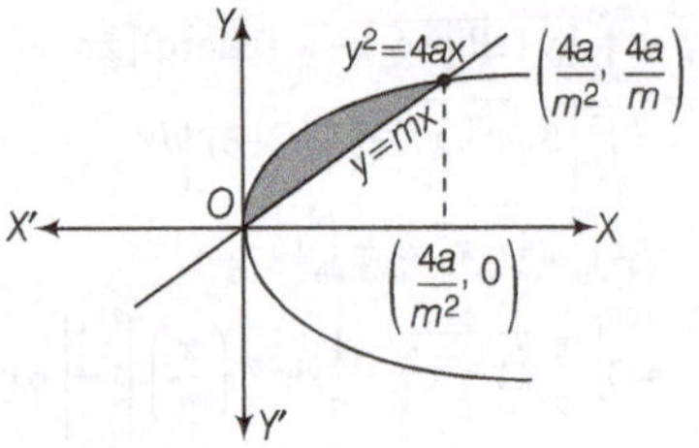

$\left[\textbf{Ans. } \frac{8a^2}{3m^3} \text{ sq units}\right]$

4. **Hint** Required area $= \int_0^1 [x - (x^2)]dx$

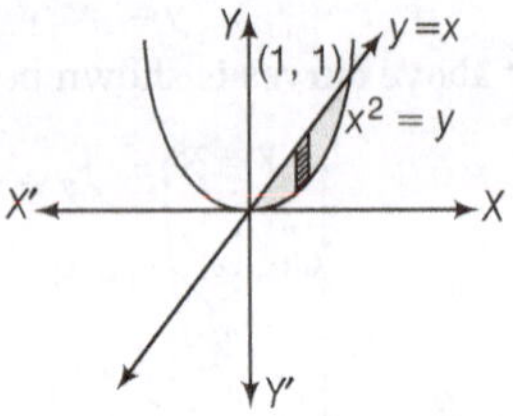

$\left[\textbf{Ans. } \frac{1}{6} \text{ sq unit}\right]$

5. **Hint** Area $= \int_{-2}^{4} \left[(y+4) - \left(\frac{y^2}{2}\right)\right] dy$

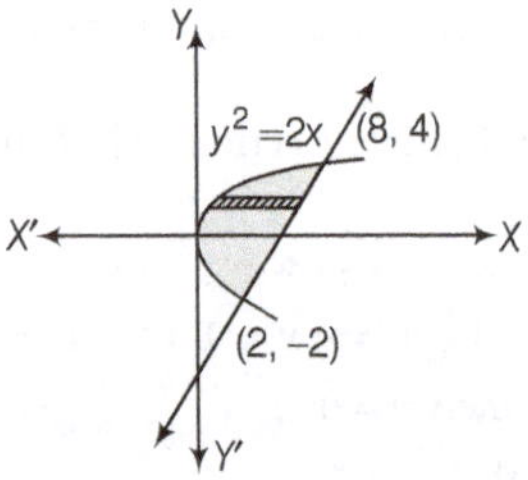

[**Ans.** 18 sq units]

6. Similar as Example 1. $\left[\textbf{Ans. } \frac{16}{3}a^2 \text{ sq units}\right]$

7. Similar as Example 1. $\left[\textbf{Ans. } \frac{1}{\sqrt{3}}\right]$

8. Similar as Example 2. [**Ans.** 6 sq units]

9. Given curves are $y = 2x - x^2$ ...(i)

and $y = x$ ...(ii)

From Eqs. (i) and (ii),

$x = 2x - x^2 \Rightarrow x^2 = x$

$(x-1)x = 0 \Rightarrow x = 0, 1$

When $x = 0$, then $y = 0$

When $x = 1$, then $y = 1$

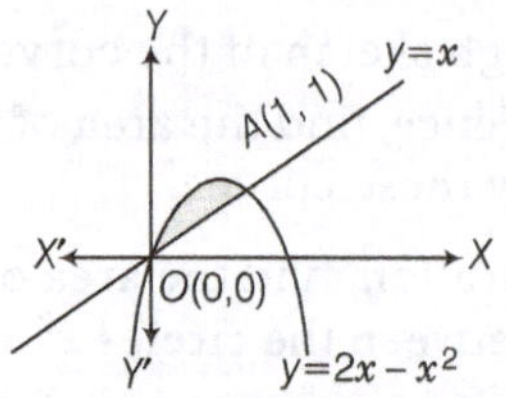

[2]

$\therefore$ The point of intersection of two curves are $O(0,0)$ and $A(1,1)$.

Required area $= \int_0^1 [y\,dx \text{ (From parabola)} - y\,dx \text{(From line)}]\,dx$

$= \int_0^1 (2x - x^2 - x)\,dx$

$= \int_0^1 (x - x^2)\,dx = \left[\frac{x^2}{2} - \frac{x^3}{3}\right]_0^1$

$= \left(\frac{1}{2} - \frac{1}{3} - 0\right) = \frac{3-2}{6} = \frac{1}{6}$ sq unit [4]

10. **Hint** Required area $= \int_0^2 [\sqrt{4 - x^2} - (2 - x)]\,dx$

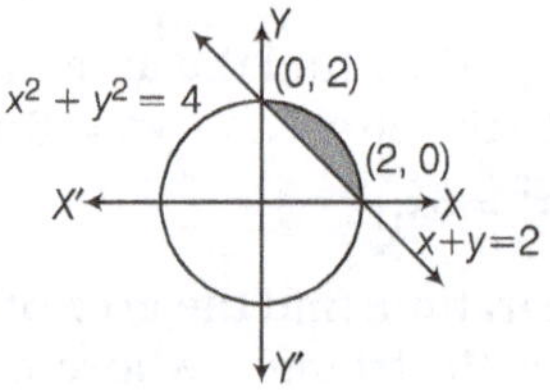

[**Ans.** $(\pi - 2)$ sq units]

11. Given curves are $y = 6x - x^2$ ...(i)

and $y = x^2 - 2x$ ...(ii)

Eq. (i) can be written as

$x^2 - 6x + 9 = -y + 9$

$\Rightarrow (x-3)^2 = -(y-9)$, which represents a downward parabola with vertex at (3, 9). Now, Eq. (ii) can be written as $(x^2+1)^2 = y+1$, which represents an upward parabola with vertex at (1, – 1). [2]

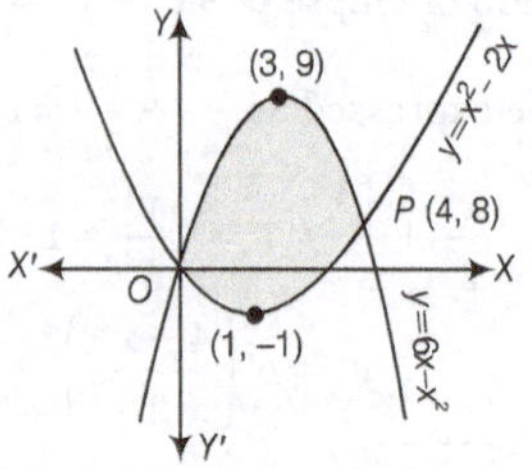

On solving Eqs. (i) and (ii), we get

$6x - x^2 = x^2 - 2x \Rightarrow 2x^2 - 8x = 0$

$\Rightarrow x(x-4) = 0 \Rightarrow x = 0, x = 4$

So, the points of intersection are $O(0, 0)$ and $P(4, 8)$. [2]

$\therefore$ Required area = Area of the shaded region

$= \int_0^4 [(6x - x^2) - (x^2 - 2x)]\,dx$

$$= \int_0^4 (8x - 2x^2)\, dx = \left[8 \cdot \frac{x^2}{2} - 2 \cdot \frac{x^3}{3}\right]_0^4$$

$$= \left(64 - \frac{128}{3}\right) - 0 = \frac{64}{3} \text{ sq units} \quad [2]$$

12. Given the curve $y^2 = x$ and $y^2 = 4 - 3x$

The graph of given curves are

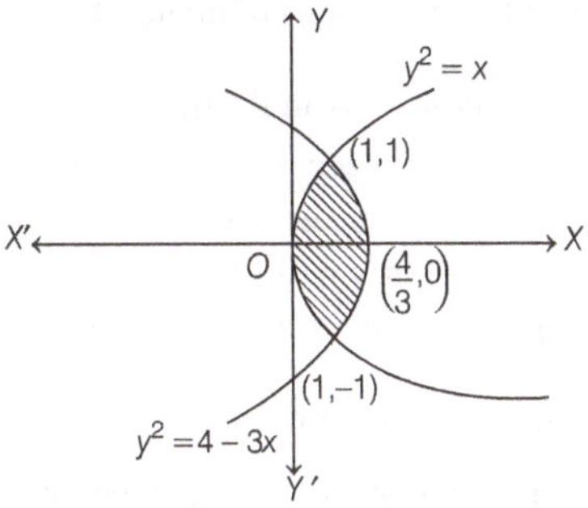

The intersection point of curve $y^2 = x$ and $y^2 = 4 - 3x$ is (1, 1) and (1, – 1).

$\therefore$ Area of shaded region is

$$= 2\left[\int_0^1 \sqrt{x}\, dx + \int_1^{4/3} \sqrt{4 - 3x}\, dx\right]$$

$$= 2\left[\left[\frac{x^{3/2}}{3/2}\right]_0^1 + \left(-\frac{1}{3}\left[\frac{(4 - 3x)^{3/2}}{3/2}\right]_1^{4/3}\right)\right]$$

$$= 2\left[\frac{2}{3}(1 - 0) - \frac{2}{9}\left(\left(4 - 3 \times \frac{4}{3}\right)^{3/2} - (4 - 3)^{3/2}\right)\right]$$

$$= 2\left[\frac{2}{3} - \frac{2}{9}(0 - 1)\right]$$

$$= 2\left(\frac{2}{3} + \frac{2}{9}\right) = 2\left(\frac{6 + 2}{9}\right) = \frac{16}{9}$$

$$= \frac{16}{9} \text{ sq units}$$

$\therefore$ Area enclosed between curves is $\frac{16}{9}$ sq units.

13. Given curves are $y = (x - 1)^2$ ...(i)

and $y = |x - 1|$ ...(ii)

$$= \begin{cases} x - 1, & x \geq 1 \\ -x + 1, & x < 1 \end{cases}$$

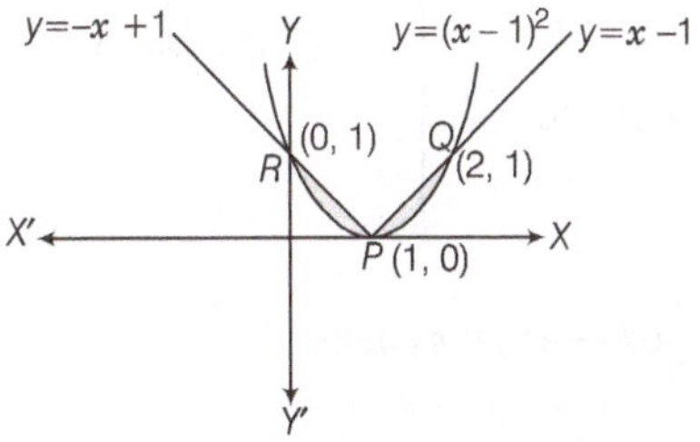

[2]

Now, from $y = (x - 1)^2$ and $y = x - 1$, $(x - 1) = (x - 1)^2$

$\Rightarrow \quad (x - 1)^2 - (x - 1) = 0$

$\Rightarrow \quad (x - 1)(x - 1 - 1) = 0$

$\Rightarrow \quad (x - 2)(x - 1) = 0$

$\Rightarrow \quad x = 2 \text{ or } 1$

When $x = 2$, then $y = (2 - 1)^2 = 1$ [1]

When $x = 1$, then $y = (1 - 1)^2 = 0$

Thus, the points of intersection are $P(1, 0)$ and $Q(2, 1)$.

From the equations

$$y = (x - 1)^2 \text{ and } y = -x + 1$$

$$(x - 1)^2 = -x + 1 \Rightarrow x^2 - 2x + 1 = -x + 1$$

$\Rightarrow \quad x^2 - x = 0 \Rightarrow x(x - 1) = 0$

$\Rightarrow \quad x = 0 \text{ or } 1$

When $x = 0$, then $y = (0 - 1)^2 = 1$ [1]

When $x = 1$, then $y = (1 - 1)^2 = 0$

Thus, the points of intersection are $R(0, 1)$ and $P(1, 0)$.

$\therefore$ Required area

$$= \text{Area of curve } PRP + \text{Area of curve } PQP$$

$$= \int_0^1 [-x + 1 - (x - 1)^2]\, dx + \int_1^2 [(x - 1) - (x - 1)^2] dx$$

$$= \int_0^1 (-x + 1 - x^2 + 2x - 1)\, dx + \int_1^2 (x - 1 - x^2 + 2x - 1)\, dx$$

$$= \int_0^1 (x - x^2)\, dx + \int_1^2 (-x^2 + 3x - 2)\, dx$$

$$= \left[\frac{x^2}{2} - \frac{x^3}{3}\right]_0^1 + \left[-\frac{x^3}{3} + \frac{3x^2}{2} - 2x\right]_1^2$$

$$= \left[\frac{1}{2} - \frac{1}{3} + 0\right] + \left[-\frac{8}{3} + \frac{12}{2} - 4 + \frac{1}{3} - \frac{3}{2} + 2\right]$$

$$= \frac{1}{6} + \left(-\frac{8}{3} + 4 + \frac{1}{3} - \frac{3}{2}\right)$$

$$= \frac{1}{6} + \frac{-16 + 24 + 2 - 9}{6}$$

$$= \frac{1}{6} + \frac{1}{6} = \frac{1}{3} \text{ sq unit} \quad [2]$$

14. Similar as Example 4. $\left[\textbf{Ans.} \left(\frac{2\pi}{3} - \frac{\sqrt{3}}{2}\right) \text{sq units}\right]$

15. Given equation of circle $x^2 + y^2 = 8x$ can be written as

$$x^2 + y^2 - 8x = 0$$

$\Rightarrow \quad (x - 4)^2 + y^2 - 16 = 0$

$\Rightarrow \quad (x - 4)^2 + y^2 = 16$ ...(i)

$\Rightarrow \quad y = \sqrt{16 - (x - 4)^2}$

Eq. (i) is a circle with centre (4, 0) and radius 4.

Given equation of parabola is

$y^2 = 4x \Rightarrow y = \sqrt{4x}$ ...(ii) [1]

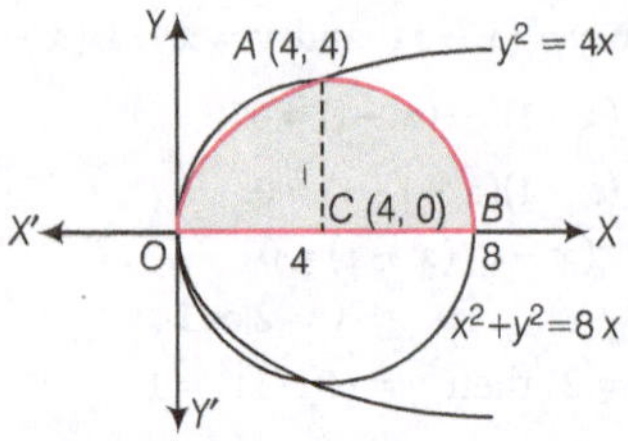

It is clear from the figure that the required region is OABO.

For the points of intersection of circle and parabola, put $y^2 = 4x$ in Eq. (i).

i.e. $(x-4)^2 + 4x = 16$ [1]

$\Rightarrow x^2 + 16 - 8x + 4x = 16 \Rightarrow x^2 - 4x = 0$

$\Rightarrow x(x-4) = 0 \Rightarrow x = 0, 4$

When $x = 0$, then $y = \sqrt{4x} = \sqrt{4 \cdot 0} = 0$.

When $x = 4$, then $y = \sqrt{4x} = \sqrt{4 \cdot 4} = 4$

So, the points of intersection are (0, 0) and (4, 4). [1]

$\therefore$ Required area = Area of shaded region OABCO

= Area of shaded region OACO

+ Area of shaded region ABCA

$= \int_0^4 y \text{ (parabola) } dx + \int_4^8 y \text{ (circle) } dx$ [1]

$= \int_0^4 \sqrt{4x}\, dx + \int_4^8 \sqrt{16-(x-4)^2}\, dx$

$= 2\int_0^4 \sqrt{x}\, dx + \int_4^8 \sqrt{16-(x-4)^2}\, dx$ [1]

$= 2\left[\frac{x^{3/2}}{3/2}\right]_0^4 + \left[\frac{(x-4)}{2}\sqrt{16-(x-4)^2} + \frac{16}{2}\sin^{-1}\left(\frac{x-4}{4}\right)\right]_4^8$

$\left[\because \int \sqrt{a^2-x^2}\,dx = \frac{x}{2}\sqrt{a^2-x^2} + \frac{a^2}{2}\sin^{-1}\left(\frac{x}{a}\right)\right]$

$= \frac{2 \cdot 2}{3}[(4)^{3/2} - 0] + \left[0 + 8\sin^{-1}\left(\frac{4}{4}\right) - (0+0)\right]$

$= \frac{4}{3}(4)^{3/2} + [8\sin^{-1}(1)]$

$= \frac{4}{3} \times 8 + 8 \times \frac{\pi}{2} = \left(\frac{32}{3} + 4\pi\right)$ sq units

Hence, the required area is $\left(\frac{32}{3} + 4\pi\right)$ sq units. [1]

16. Given equation of curves are

$x^2 + y^2 = 2ax$ ...(i)

and $y^2 = ax$ ...(ii)

Eq. (i) can be rewritten as $x^2 + y^2 - 2ax = 0$

$\Rightarrow (x-a)^2 + y^2 = a^2$, which represents a circle with centre $(a, 0)$ and radius a.

Eq. (ii) represents a parabola with vertex (0, 0) and open right hand side. [1]

Clearly, required area = Area of shaded region

= 2 (Area of shaded region in first quadrant) ...(iii) [1]

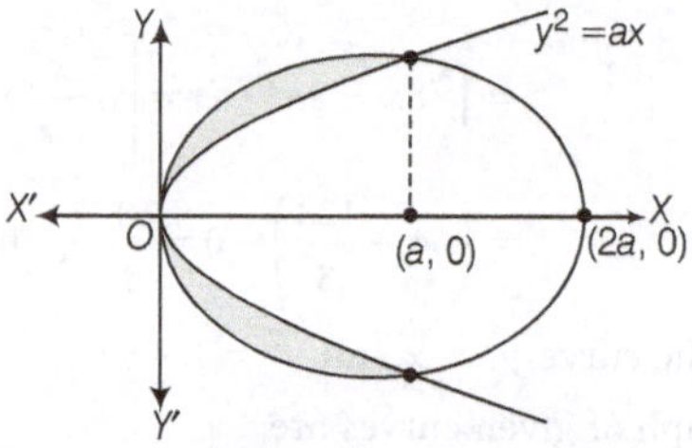

[1]

Now, let us find the points of intersection of Eqs. (i) and (ii).

On substituting $y^2 = ax$ in Eq. (i), we get

$x^2 + ax = 2ax \Rightarrow x^2 - ax = 0$

$\Rightarrow x(x-a) = 0 \Rightarrow x = 0$ or $x = a$

From Eq. (ii), we get $y = 0$ or $y = \pm a$

Thus, the points of intersection are $(0, 0)$ (a, a) and $(a, -a)$ [1]

Now, from Eq. (iii), required area

$= 2\left(\int_0^a y(\text{circle})dx - \int_0^a y(\text{parabola})dx\right)$

$= 2\left(\int_0^a \sqrt{a^2-(x-a)^2}\,dx - \int_0^a \sqrt{ax}\,dx\right)$ [1]

$= 2\left\{\left[\frac{(x-a)}{2}\sqrt{a^2-(x-a)^2} + \frac{a^2}{2}\sin^{-1}\left(\frac{x-a}{a}\right)\right]_0^a - \frac{2}{3}\sqrt{a}\left[x^{\frac{3}{2}}\right]_0^a\right\}$

$= 2\left\{\left[0 + \frac{a^2}{2}\sin^{-1}(0) - \left(\frac{-a}{2} \times 0 + \frac{a^2}{2}\sin^{-1}(-1)\right)\right] - \frac{2}{3}\sqrt{a}\,[a\sqrt{a} - 0]\right\}$

$= 2\left[\frac{a^2}{2}\sin^{-1}(1) - \frac{2}{3}a^2\right] = 2\left[\frac{a^2}{2} \cdot \frac{\pi}{2} - \frac{2}{3}a^2\right] = \left(\frac{\pi}{2} - \frac{4}{3}\right)a^2$ [1]

17. Hint Required area

$= 2\left[\int_0^{2a} \sqrt{6ax}\,dx + \int_{2a}^{4a} \sqrt{16a^2 - x^2}\,dx\right]$

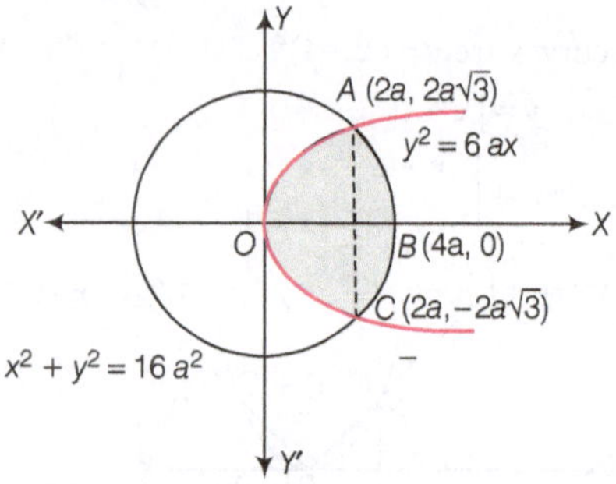

$\left[\textbf{Ans. } \frac{4}{3}(\sqrt{3} + 4\pi)a^2 \text{ sq units}\right]$

18. Similar as Example 5. $\left[\textbf{Ans. } \frac{4}{3}(\sqrt{3}+4\pi) \text{ sq units}\right]$

19. Let $A(-1, 2)$, $B(1, 5)$ and $C(3, 4)$ be the vertices of ΔABC. Equation of line AB passing through the points $A(-1, 2)$ and $B(1, 5)$ is

$$(y-2) = \frac{5-2}{1+1}(x+1)$$

$\left[\because \text{ equation of a line passing through two points is } y - y_1 = \frac{y_2 - y_1}{x_2 - x_1}(x - x_1)\right]$

$$\Rightarrow \quad y - 2 = \frac{3}{2}(x+1)$$

$$\Rightarrow \quad 2y - 3x = 7 \quad \text{...(i)} \quad [1]$$

Equation of line BC passing through the points $B(1, 5)$ and $C(3, 4)$ is given by

$$y - 5 = \frac{4-5}{3-1}(x-1)$$

$$\Rightarrow \quad y - 5 = \frac{-1}{2}(x-1)$$

$$\Rightarrow \quad 2y - 10 = -x + 1$$

$$\Rightarrow \quad 2y + x = 11 \quad \text{...(ii)} \quad [1/2]$$

and the equation of line CA passing through the points $C(3, 4)$ and $A(-1, 2)$ is given by

$$y - 4 = \frac{2-4}{-1-3}(x-3)$$

$$\Rightarrow \quad y - 4 = \frac{-2}{-4}(x-3)$$

$$\Rightarrow \quad -4y + 16 = -2x + 6$$

$$\Rightarrow \quad -4y + 2x = -10$$

$$\Rightarrow \quad 4y - 2x = 10 \quad \text{...(iii)} \quad [1/2]$$

On plotting the points on the graph, we get ΔABC.

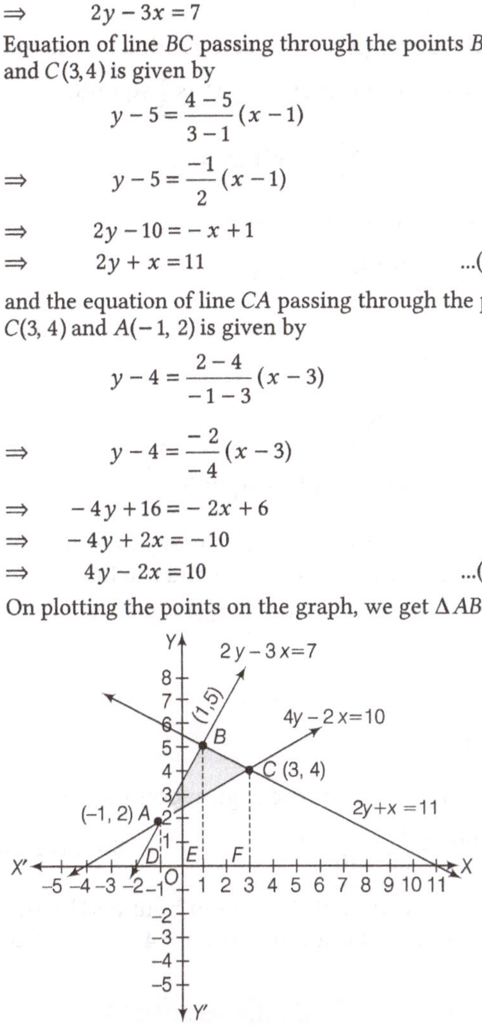

[1]

$\therefore$ Area of triangular region ABC

= Area of trapezium $ABEDA$ + Area of trapezium $BCFEB$ – Area of trapezium $DACFD$ [1]

$$= \int_{-1}^{1} y \,[\text{from line (i)}]\, dx + \int_{1}^{3} y\,[\text{from line (ii)}]\, dx - \int_{-1}^{3} y\,[\text{from line (iii)}]\, dx$$

$$= \int_{-1}^{1}\left[\frac{3x+7}{2}\right]dx + \int_{1}^{3}\left[\frac{11-x}{2}\right]dx - \int_{-1}^{3}\left[\frac{10+2x}{4}\right]dx$$

$$= \left[\frac{3}{2}\cdot\frac{x^2}{2} + \frac{7}{2}x\right]_{-1}^{1} + \left[\frac{11}{2}x - \frac{x^2}{4}\right]_{1}^{3} - \left[\frac{5}{2}x + \frac{x^2}{4}\right]_{-1}^{3} \quad [1]$$

$$= \left[\frac{3}{4} + \frac{7}{2} - \frac{3}{4} + \frac{7}{2}\right] + \left[\frac{33}{2} - \frac{9}{4} - \frac{11}{2} + \frac{1}{4}\right] - \left[\frac{15}{2} + \frac{9}{4} + \frac{5}{2} - \frac{1}{4}\right]$$

$$= 7 + 9 - 12 = 4 \text{ sq units}$$

Hence, the required area is 4 sq units. [1]

20. Solve as Question 19. [**Ans.** 4 sq units]

21. Given equations of lines are

$$y = 4x + 5 \quad \text{...(i)}$$

$$y = 5 - x \quad \text{...(ii)}$$

$$\text{and} \quad 4y = x + 5 \quad \text{...(iii)}$$

On solving Eqs. (i) and (ii), we get

$$4x + 5 = 5 - x$$

$$\Rightarrow \quad x = 0$$

On solving Eqs. (i) and (iii), we get

$$4(4x+5) = x + 5$$

$$\Rightarrow \quad 16x + 20 = x + 5$$

$$\Rightarrow \quad 15x = -15$$

$$\Rightarrow \quad x = -1$$

On solving Eqs. (ii) and (iii), we get

$$4(5-x) = x + 5$$

$$\Rightarrow \quad 20 - 4x = x + 5$$

$$\Rightarrow \quad x = 3$$

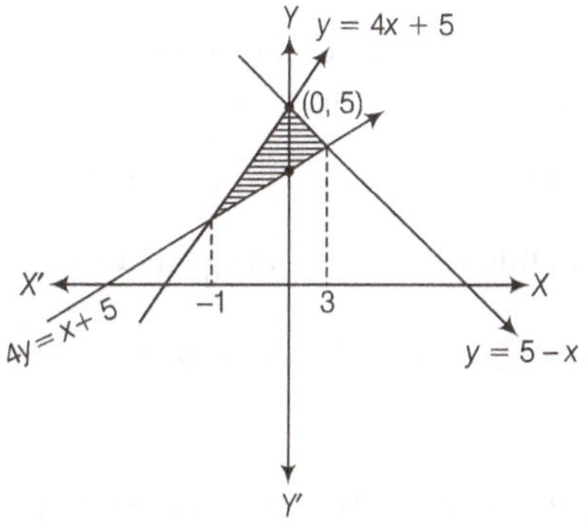

$\therefore$ Required area

$$= \int_{-1}^{0}(4x+5)dx + \int_{0}^{3}(5-x)dx - \frac{1}{4}\int_{-1}^{3}(x+5)dx$$

$$= \left[\frac{4x^2}{2} + 5x\right]_{-1}^{0} + \left[5x - \frac{x^2}{2}\right]_{0}^{3} - \frac{1}{4}\left[\frac{x^2}{2} + 5x\right]_{-1}^{3}$$

$$= [0 - 2 + 5] + \left[15 - \frac{9}{2} - 0\right] - \frac{1}{4}\left[\frac{9}{2} + 15 - \frac{1}{2} + 5\right]$$

$$= 3 + \frac{21}{2} - \frac{1}{4}\cdot 24 = -3 + \frac{21}{2} = \frac{15}{2} \text{ sq units}$$

Chapter Practice

Multiple Choice Type Questions

1 Mark

1 Area of the region bounded by the curve $y=|x+1|+1, x=-3, x=3$ and $y=0$ is

(a) 8 sq units (b) 16 sq units
(c) 32 sq units (d) None of these

2 The area of the region bounded by the circle $x^2+y^2=1$ is

(a) π (b) 2π
(c) 3π (d) π^2

3 If a curve $y=a\sqrt{x}+bx$ passes through the point (1, 2) and the area bounded by the curve, line $x=4$ and X-axis is 8 sq units, then

(a) $a=3, b=-1$ (b) $a=3, b=1$
(c) $a=-3, b=1$ (d) $a=-3, b=-1$

4 The area of region bounded by the curve $y^2=4x$ and the line $x=4$

(a) $\frac{60}{3}$ sq units (b) 16 sq units
(c) $\frac{64}{5}$ sq units (d) $\frac{64}{3}$ sq units

5 The area of the region bounded by two parabolas $y=x^2$ and $y^2=x$ is

(a) $\frac{1}{3}$ sq unit (b) $\frac{2}{3}$ sq unit
(c) $\frac{4}{3}$ sq units (d) $\frac{5}{3}$ sq units

Assertion-Reason Type Questions

1 Mark

Directions (Q. Nos. 6-9) *In the questions given below are two statements labelled as Assertion (A) and Reason (R). In the context of the two statements, which one of the following is correct?*

(a) Both A and R are correct; R is the correct explanation of A
(b) Both A and R are correct; R is not the correct explanation of A
(c) A is correct; R is incorrect
(d) R is correct; A is incorrect

6 **Assertion (A)** The area bounded by $y^2=4x$ and $y=x$ is $\frac{8}{3}$ sq units.

Reason (R) The area bounded by $y^2=4ax$ and $y=mx$ is $\frac{8a^2}{3m^3}$ sq units.

7 **Assertion (A)** The area bounded by the line $y=x$ and the curve $y=x^3$ is $\frac{1}{2}$ sq unit.

Reason (R) $\int_0^1 (x-x^3)\,dx=\frac{1}{4}$.

8 **Assertion (A)** The area bounded by the curve $\frac{x^2}{9}+\frac{y^2}{16}$ is 12π sq units.

Reason (R) The standard form of ellipse is $\frac{x^2}{a^2}+\frac{y^2}{b^2}=1$.

9 **Assertion (A)** The area bounded by the curves $y=\sqrt{x}$ and $y=x$ is $\frac{1}{6}$ sq unit.

Reason (R) The area of the region bounded by the curves $f(x)$ and $g(x)$ and the lines $x=a$ and $x=b$ is given by $A=\int_a^b [f(x)-g(x)]dx$.

Short Answer Type Questions

4 Marks

10 Find the area of the region bounded by the ellipse $\frac{x^2}{25}+\frac{y^2}{16}=1$. **[NCERT Exemplar]**

11 Find the area of the region bounded by the curve $x^2=4y$ and the line $x=4y-2$. **[ISC 2023]**

Long Answer Type Questions

6 Marks

12 Draw a rough sketch of the curve $y^2=4x$ and find the area of the region enclosed by the curve and the line $y=x$. **[ISC 2017]**

13 Find the area bounded by the curve $y^2 = 4a^2(x-1)$ and the lines $x = 1$ and $y = 4a$.
[**Hint** Required region is the shaded region]

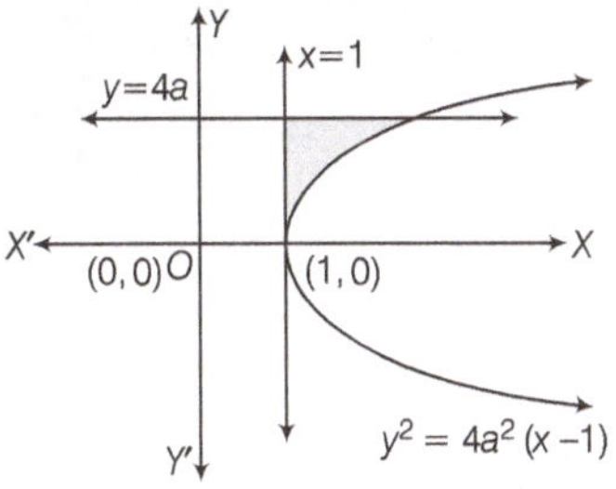

14 Find the area of the region bounded by $x^2 = 4y$, $y = 2$, $y = 4$ and the Y-axis in the first quadrant. **[NCERT]**

15 Find the area bounded by the curve $y = x^3$, the X-axis and the ordinates $x = -2$ and $x = 1$. **[NCERT]**

16 The area between $x = y^2$ and $x = 4$ is divided into two equal parts by the line $x = a$. Find the value of a. **[NCERT]**

17 Find the area bounded by the ellipse $\frac{x^2}{a^2} + \frac{y^2}{b^2} = 1$ and the coordinates $x = 0$ and $x = ae$, where $b^2 = a^2(1-e^2)$ and $e < 1$. **[NCERT]**

18 Sketch the graph of $y = |x+3|$ and evaluate the area under the curve $y = |x+3|$ above X-axis and between $x = -6$ to $x = 0$.

19 Find the area of the smaller region bounded by the ellipse $\frac{x^2}{a^2} + \frac{y^2}{b^2} = 1$ and the line $\frac{x}{a} + \frac{y}{b} = 1$. **[NCERT]**

20 Find the area of the smaller region bounded by the ellipse $\frac{x^2}{16} + \frac{y^2}{9} = 1$ and the straight line $8x + 3y = 12$.

21 Find the area bounded by the curves $y = \sqrt{x}$, $x = 2y + 3$ in the first quadrant and X-axis. **[NCERT Exemplar]**

22 Find the area of the region

$$\{(x, y) : (x^2 + y^2) \le 1 \le x + y\}.$$

23 Find the area of the region $\{(x, y) : x^2 + y^2 \le 2ax, y^2 \ge ax; x, y \ge 0\}$.

24 Find the area of region bounded by the curve $y = x^3$, $y = x + 6$ and $x = 0$. **[NCERT Exemplar]**

25 Find the area of the circle $4x^2 + 4y^2 = 9$, which is interior to the parabola $x^2 = 4y$. **[NCERT]**

26 Using integration, find the area of triangular region, whose vertices are (1, 0), (2, 2) and (3, 1). **[NCERT]**

27 Using integration, find the area of region bounded by the triangle whose vertices are (−2, 1), (0, 4) and (2, 3).

28 Using integration, find the area of triangular region ABC, whose sides have the equations $y = 2x + 1$, $y = 3x + 1$ and $x = 4$. **[NCERT]**

Answers

1. (b)
2. (a)
3. (a)
4. (d)
5. (a)
6. (a)
7. (a)
8. (b)
9. (b)
10. 20π sq units
11. $\frac{9}{8}$ sq units
12. $\frac{8}{3}$ sq units
13. $\frac{16a}{3}$ sq units
14. $\frac{8}{3}[4-\sqrt{2}]$ sq units
15. $\frac{17}{4}$ sq units
16. $a = (4)^{2/3}$
17. $ab[e\sqrt{1-e^2} + \sin^{-1}(e)]$ sq units
18. 9 sq units
19. $\frac{ab}{4}(\pi - 2)$ sq units
20. $(3\pi - 6)$ sq units
21. 9 sq units
22. $\left(\frac{\pi}{4} - \frac{1}{2}\right)$ sq units
23. $\left(\frac{\pi a^2}{4} - \frac{2}{3}a^2\right)$ sq units
24. 10 sq units
25. $\frac{\sqrt{2}}{6} + \frac{9}{4}\sin^{-1}\left(\frac{2\sqrt{2}}{3}\right)$ sq units
26. $\frac{3}{2}$ sq units
27. 4 sq units
28. 8 sq units

CHAPTER 16

Application of Calculus in Commerce & Economics

In calculus, we have learnt that when y is a function of x, then $\frac{dy}{dx}$ represent the instantaneous rate of change of y w.r.t. x. In commerce and economics we come across many such variables where one variable is a function of other, e.g. Demand of quantity can be treated as a function of price. Calculus helps us in finding the rate at which one such quantity changes w.r.t. the other. It also helps in finding maximum profit or minimum cost, etc.

- Basic Functions
- Maximization and Minimization, Applications of Integration

TOPIC 01 Basic Functions

In this topic, we will define some functions which are basic in commerce and economics.

Cost Function

The cost function or total cost function written as $C(x)$, is the total cost of producing x units of a product. It consists of two parts.

(i) **Fixed Cost** (F) The fixed cost consists of all types of costs which do not change with the level of production. e.g. The rent of the premises, the insurance, taxes, etc.

(ii) **Variable Cost** $V(x)$ The variable cost is the sum of all costs that are dependent on the level of production. e.g. The cost of material, casual labour cost, cost of packaging, etc.

Thus, the cost function is $C(x) = F + V(x)$

e.g. If $C(x) = p + qx^2$, then the fixed cost $= C(0) = p$ and the variable cost $= qx^2$.

Graph of Cost Function and Its Interpretation

In the figure, production level is measured along the X-axis and the cost is measured along the Y-axis.

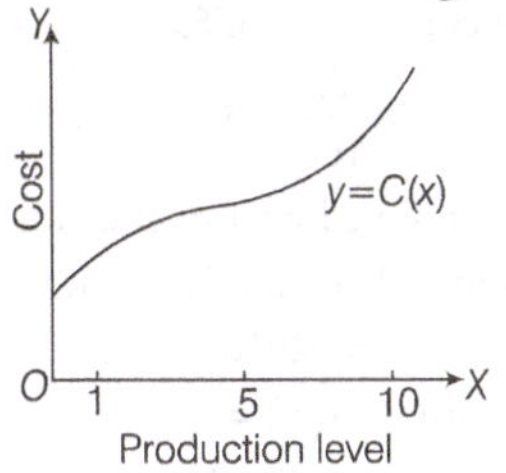

Note that fixed cost is constant at any level of production while the variable cost is increasing with the increase in level of production, which reflect the behaviour of cost function.

Demand Function

The demand of a product depends on various factors such as choice of customer, quality, price, income, etc. But to understand the demand function easily, we will consider the relationship between demand and price only, assuming all other factors as constant.

If 'p' is the price per unit of a certain product and x is the number of units demanded, then we can write the demand function as $x = f(p)$

Graph of Demand Function and Its Interpretation

In the adjoining figure, price is measured along the X-axis and the quantity demanded is measured along the Y-axis.

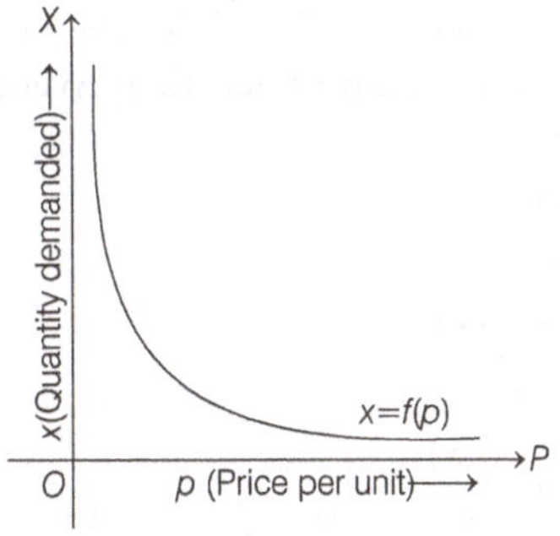

Note that demand curve is decreasing, because demand decreases as the price increases.

Note If the price of the item depends upon the demand of the item, then the demand function is given by $p = g(x)$.

Revenue Function

Revenue is the amount received from the sales of goods. It completely depends upon the selling price of the product and the number of units sold.

If x is the number of units of certain product sold at a rate of ₹ 'p' per unit, then the amount received from the sale of x units of a product is the total revenue.

Thus, if R represents the total revenue, then $R = p \cdot x$

Thus, revenue function $R(x) = p \cdot x = x \cdot p(x)$,

where $x > 0$, $p > 0$.

The graphs of revenue function is shown below

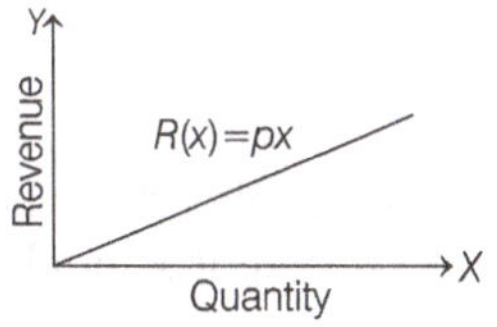

Fig. (i)

[In purely competitive environment]

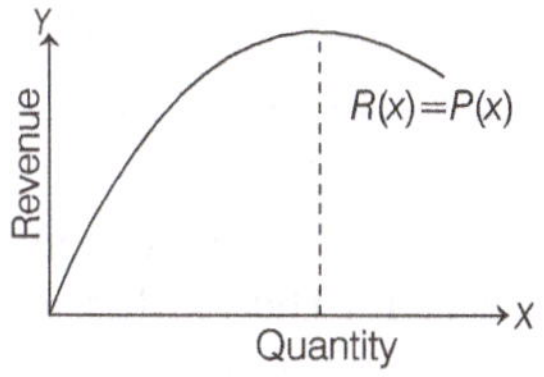

Fig. (ii)

[In monopolistic environment]

In Fig. (i), revenue rises but a constant rate because price is constant.

In Fig. (ii), initially revenue rises but at a decreasing rate. It is maximum at the some level of output but after this starts falling, as more is sold at lower price.

Note

(i) In a **purely competitive environment,** price is determined by market not by the producer. So, price is independent of the level of output x. Thus, in this environment price (p) is constant.

(ii) In a **monopolistic environment,** the price of commodity depends upon the number of items produced and sold. Generally, price decreases with the increase in output x.

Profit Function

The profit is calculated by subtracting the total cost from the total revenue obtained by selling x units of a product. Thus, if $P(x)$ is the profit function, then

$$P(x) = R(x) - C(x)$$

Breakeven Point

The breakeven point is that point, where total revenue equals to total cost incurred i.e. $R(x) = C(x)$. At breakeven point, a company begins to earn a profit.

Graphically, the breakeven point is the intersection of total revenue $R(x)$ and the total cost $C(x)$ curves, as shown in the figure.

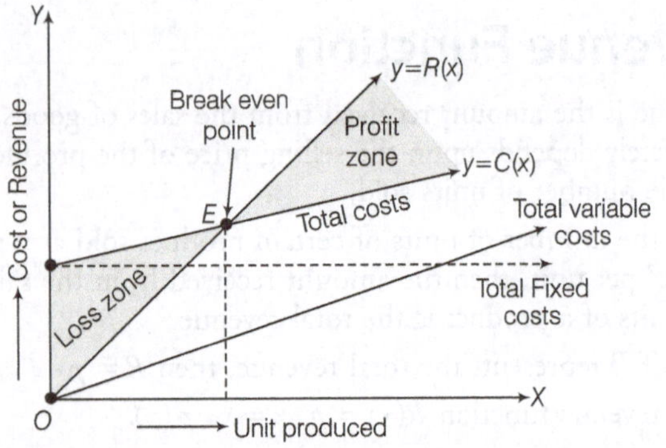

To the left of point 'E' cost is more than revenue, so the firm suffers a loss. Further, to the right of point 'E', revenue exceeds cost, so the firm makes profit.

Note At breakeven point $P(x) = 0$.

Example 1 A television manufacturer finds that the total cost for the production and marketing of x number of television sets is $C(x) = 300x^2 + 4200x + 13500$. Each product is sold for ₹ 8400. Determine the breakeven points **[ISC 2006]**

Sol. Given, the total cost function of the products (x units)

$$C(x) = 300x^2 + 4200x + 13500$$

Each product is sold at ₹ 8400.

So, revenue function of x units product,

$$R(x) = 8400 \times x = 8400x$$

For breakeven point, $R(x) = C(x)$

$\therefore \quad 8400x = 300x^2 + 4200x + 13500$

$\Rightarrow \quad 300x^2 + 4200x - 8400x + 13500 = 0$

$\Rightarrow \quad 300x^2 - 4200x + 13500 = 0$

$\Rightarrow \quad 100(3x^2 - 42x + 135) = 0$

$\Rightarrow \quad 3x^2 - 42x + 135 = 0$

$\Rightarrow \quad 3x^2 - 27x - 15x + 135 = 0$

$\Rightarrow \quad 3x(x - 9) - 15(x - 9) = 0$

$\Rightarrow \quad (3x - 15)(x - 9) = 0$

$\Rightarrow \quad (3x - 15) = 0$ or $(x - 9) = 0$

$\Rightarrow \quad x = \frac{15}{3}$ or $x = 9$

$\therefore \quad x = 5$ or $x = 9$

Hence, the breakeven point will be 5 or 9.

Example 2 A company produces a commodity with ₹ 24000 as fixed cost. The variable cost, estimated to be 25% of the total revenue received on selling the product, is at the rate of ₹ 8 per unit. Find the break-even point. **[ISC 2019]**

Sol. Given, fixed cost of the commodity = ₹ 24000

Let the number of units produced by company be x and p be the price per unit.

Then, total revenue $R = xp = ₹\, 8x$

Since, the variable cost is 25% of the total revenue.

Thus, variable cost = 25% of $8x$

$$= \frac{25}{100} \times 8x = \frac{1}{4} \times 8x = ₹\, 2x$$

Total cost $C(x)$ = Fixed cost of the commodity + Variable cost of the commodity $= 24000 + 2x$

For breakeven point, $R(x) = C(x)$

$\Rightarrow \quad 8x = 24000 + 2x$ $\quad [\because R(x) = 8x$ and $C(x) = 24000 + 2x]$

$\Rightarrow \quad 8x - 2x = 24000$

$\Rightarrow \quad 6x = 24000$

$\therefore \quad x = \frac{24000}{6} = 4000$

Hence, the break-even point is 4000.

Average and Marginal Functions

If two quantities x and y are related by $y = f(x)$, then the average function is defined as $\frac{f(x)}{x}$ and the marginal function is defined as the instantaneous rate of change of y with respect to x. i.e. Marginal function is $\frac{dy}{dx}$, i.e. $\frac{d}{dx}(f(x))$.

Average Cost Function

The Average Cost (AC) or Average Total Cost (ATC) represents the cost per unit. So, if $C(x)$ be the total cost of producing x units of a product, then Average Cost (AC) is given by

$$AC = \frac{C(x)}{x} = \frac{F + V(x)}{x} = \frac{F}{x} + \frac{V(x)}{x}$$

= AFC (Average Fixed Cost) + AVC (Average Variable Cost)

where, F = Fixed cost and $V(x)$ = Variable cost

Graph of Average Cost Function and Its Interpretation

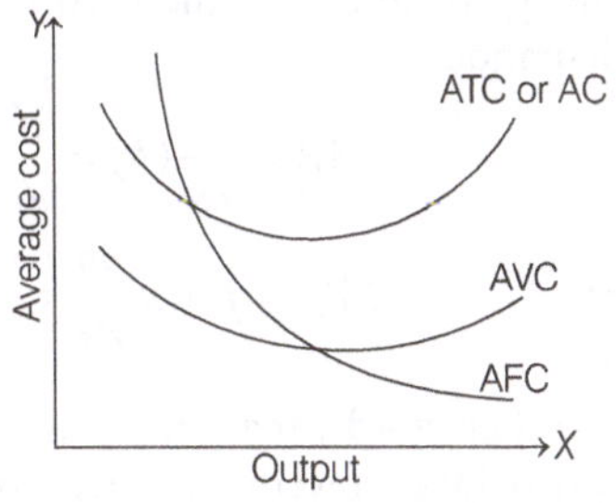

The behaviour of the Average Total Cost (ATC) depends upon the behaviour of the Average Fixed Cost (AFC) and Average Variable Cost (AVC). Initially average total cost is high as both the average fixed cost and average variable cost are high at low levels of output. As the level of output increases ATC falls sharply as both AFC and AVC curves fall.

When AVC curve begins to rise, AFC curve still continues to fall. The ATC curve continues to fall, because the fall in AFC curve out weighs the rise in AVC curve.

When AFC = AVC, then ATC reaches its minimum point. Futher, if output increases then rise in AVC more than offsets the fall in AFC. As a result of this ATC rises. That is why, ATC or AC curve is always U-shaped.

Marginal Cost Function

The marginal cost, denoted by MC, is defined as the rate of change of $C(x)$ w.r.t. x, i.e. $MC(x) = \frac{d}{dx} C(x)$. In other words, MC is interpreted as the approximate cost of one additional unit of output.

Marginal Average Cost (MAC)

If C is the total cost of producing x units of a product, then $AC = \frac{C}{x}$ and Marginal Average Cost (MAC) is defined as the rate of change of Average Cost (AC) w.r.t. x.

$$\therefore \quad \text{MAC} = \frac{d}{dx}(\text{AC})$$

Graph of Marginal Cost Function and Its Interpretation

Geometrically, marginal cost is also U-shaped curve which shows MC declines sharply, reaches a minimum, and then rises sharply.

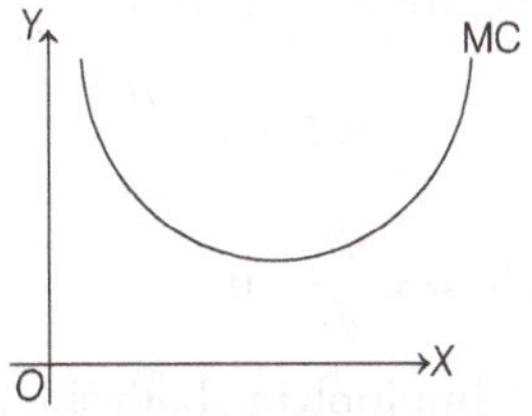

Note Marginal cost also gives the slope of cost curve.

Relation between AC and MC

We know that, $\text{AC} = \frac{C}{x}$

$$\therefore \quad \frac{d}{dx}(\text{AC}) = \frac{x \cdot \frac{dC}{dx} - C \cdot 1}{x^2}$$

$$\Rightarrow \quad \frac{d}{dx}(\text{AC}) = \frac{1}{x}\left(\frac{dC}{dx} - \frac{C}{x}\right)$$

$$\Rightarrow \quad \frac{d}{dx}(\text{AC}) = \frac{1}{x}(\text{MC} - \text{AC}) \qquad \text{...(i)}$$

Now, in Eq. (i), if MC > AC, then $\frac{d}{dx}(\text{AC}) > 0 \Rightarrow$ AC increases with increase in x.

If MC = AC, then $\frac{d}{dx}(\text{AC}) = 0 \Rightarrow$ AC remain constant at all level of production.

If MC > AC, then $\frac{d}{dx}(\text{AC}) \quad 0 \Rightarrow$ AC decreases with increase in x.

Note $\frac{d}{dx}$(AC) is nothing but the marginal average cost (MAC).

Example 3 Given the total cost function for x units of a commodity as $C(x) = \frac{1}{3}x^3 + 3x^2 - 16x + 2$. Find

(i) Marginal cost function.

(ii) Average cost function. **[ISC 2018]**

Sol. Given, $C(x) = \frac{1}{3}x^3 + 3x^2 - 16x + 2$

(i) Marginal Cost (MC) $= \frac{dC}{dx}$

$$= \frac{d}{dx}\left(\frac{1}{3}x^3 + 3x^2 - 16x + 2\right)$$

$$= x^2 + 6x - 16$$

(ii) Average Cost (AC) $= \frac{C}{x} = \frac{\frac{1}{3}x^3 + 3x^2 - 16x + 2}{x}$

$$= \frac{x^2}{3} + 3x - 16 + \frac{2}{x}$$

Example 4 The average cost function associated with producing and marketing x units of an item is given by $AC = x + 5 + \frac{36}{x}$.

(a) Find the total cost function.

(b) Find the range of values of x for which average cost is increasing. **[ISC 2024]**

Sol. Given, average cost function is

$$(\text{AC}) = x + 5 + \frac{36}{x}$$

(a) We know that,

$$\text{Average Cost (AC)} = \frac{\text{Cost function}}{x}$$

$$\Rightarrow \quad C = x(\text{AC})$$

$$\Rightarrow \quad C = x\left(x + 5 + \frac{36}{x}\right),$$

$$\Rightarrow \quad C = x^2 + 5x + 36$$

Thus, the total cost function is $x^2 + 5x + 36$.

(b) Condition for increasing of AC,

$$\frac{d}{dx}(\text{AC}) > 0 \Rightarrow \frac{d}{dx}\left(x + 5 + \frac{36}{x}\right) > 0$$

$$\Rightarrow \quad 1 - \frac{36}{x^2} > 0 \Rightarrow \frac{x^2 - 36}{x^2} > 0$$

$$\Rightarrow \quad (x^2 - 6^2) > 0$$

$$\Rightarrow (x + 6)(x - 6) > 0 \qquad [\because a^2 - b^2 = (a+b)(a-b)]$$

$$\therefore \quad x < -6 \text{ or } x > 6$$

So, the average cost function increases, when $x \in (6, \infty)$.

Average Revenue Function

If R is the revenue obtained by selling x units of the product at a price 'p' per unit, then the term Average Revenue means the revenue per unit, and is written as AR.

$$\text{AR} = \frac{R}{x}$$

But $\quad R = p \cdot x$

$$\text{AR} = \frac{p \cdot x}{x} = p$$

Hence, average revenue is the same as price per unit.

Graph of Average Revenue Function and Its Interpretation

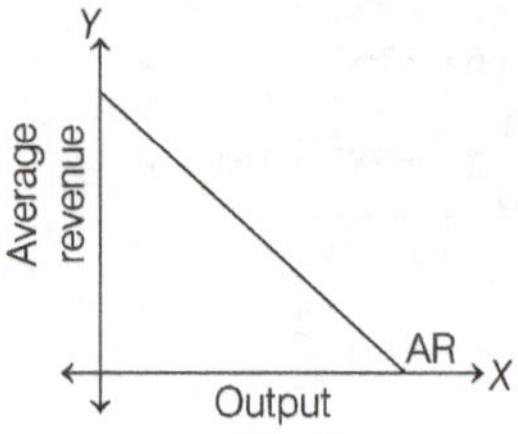

Fig. (i)
[In monopolistic environment]

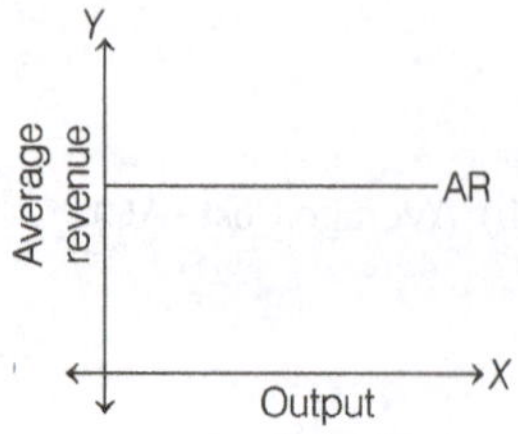

Fig. (ii)
[In purely competitive environment]

(i) As AR equal to the price per unit, therefore AR curve falls if more is produced. This makes the AR curve downward sloping throughout.

(ii) As price is unchanged, therefore AR curve is always parallel to the X-axis.

Marginal Revenue Function

The marginal revenue (MR) is defined as the rate of change of total revenue with respect to the quantity demanded

i.e. $$\text{MR} = \frac{d}{dx}(R) = \frac{d}{dx}(p \cdot x) \qquad [\because R = px]$$

$$\Rightarrow \quad \text{MR} = p + x\frac{dp}{dx} = p\left(1 + \frac{x}{p} \cdot \frac{dp}{dx}\right)$$

In other words, marginal revenue is interpreted as the approximate revenue received from producing and selling one additional unit of product.

Graph of Marginal Revenue and Its Interpretation

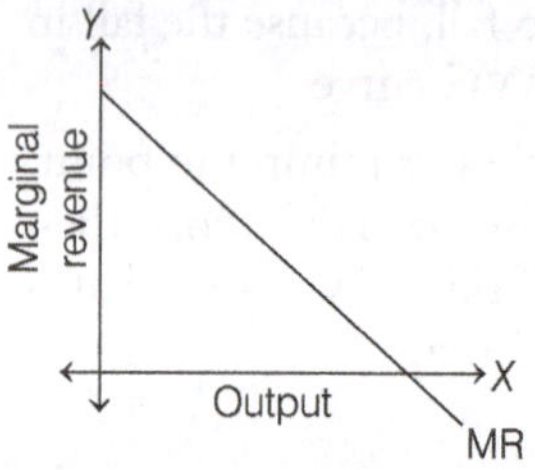

Fig. (i)
[In monopolistic environment]

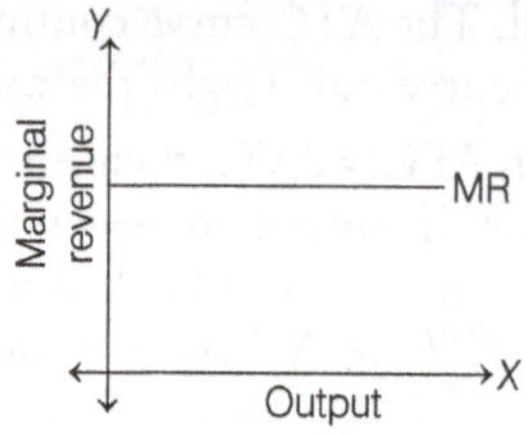

Fig. (ii)
[In purely competitive environment]

(i) Marginal revenue falls as output is increased, and become negative after an output level.

(ii) When price is constant, then

$\text{MR} = \frac{d}{dx}(P \cdot x) = P\frac{d}{dx}(x) = P$, constant and equal to AR. Thus, MR curve is also parallel to the X-axis and coincides with the AR curve.

Note Marginal revenue also gives the slope of revenue curve.

Relation between AR and MR

(i) In perfect competition market, AR and MR are equal and constant at all level of sales.

(ii) In monopolistic market, we know $\frac{dP}{dx} < 0$

[$\because$ price decreases with the increase in x]

Also, we have $\text{MR} = \frac{d}{dx}(R(x)) = \frac{d}{dx}(P \cdot x)$

$$= P + x \cdot \frac{dP}{dx} \qquad \text{...(i)}$$

Now, $\frac{dP}{dx} < 0 \Rightarrow x\frac{dP}{dx} < 0$

[multiplying both sides by x and $x \geq 0$]

$$\Rightarrow \quad P + x\frac{dP}{dx} < P \quad \text{[adding } P \text{ on both sides]}$$

$$\Rightarrow \quad \text{MR} \quad P \quad \text{[from Eq. (i)]}$$

$$\Rightarrow \quad \text{MR} < \text{AR} \quad [\because P = \text{AR}]$$

Example 5 The demand for a certain product is represented by the equation $p = 500 + 25x - \frac{x^2}{3}$ in rupees where x is the number of units and p is the price per unit. Find

(i) marginal revenue function.

(ii) the marginal revenue when 10 units are sold. **[ISC 2017]**

Sol. Given, $p = 500 + 25x - \frac{x^2}{3}$

Clearly, total revenue

$$R(x) = px = \left(500 + 25x - \frac{x^2}{3}\right)x$$

$$= 500x + 25x^2 - \frac{x^3}{3}$$

(i) We know that,

$$\text{Marginal revenue} = \frac{dR}{dx} = 500 + 50x - x^2$$

(ii) Marginal revenue at $x = 10$, is given by

$$\left(\frac{dR}{dx}\right)_{x=10} = 500 + 50(10) - (10)^2$$

$$= 500 + 500 - 100 = 900$$

Example 6 The total revenue received from the sale of x units of a products is given by $R(x) = 12x + 2x^2 + 6$. Find

(i) the average revenue.

(ii) the marginal revenue.

(iii) marginal revenue at $x = 50$.

(iv) the actual revenue from selling 51st item.

Sol. (i) Average Revenue (AR) $= \frac{12x + 2x^2 + 6}{x} = 12 + 2x + \frac{6}{x}$

(ii) Marginal Revenue (MR) $= \frac{d}{dx}(R) = 12 + 4x$

(iii) $[\text{MR}]_{x=50} = 12 + 4(50) = 212$

(iv) Actual revenue received on selling 51st item

$$= R(51) - R(50)$$

$$= [12(51) + 2(51)^2 + 6] - [12(50) + 2(50)^2 + 6]$$

$$= 12(51 - 50) + 2[51^2 - 50^2]$$

$$= 12 + 2 \times 101$$

$$= 12 + 202 = 214$$

Topic Practice 1

Very Short Answer Type Questions

(2 Marks)

1 Find the profit function and hence find the breakeven points when $C(x) = 35000 + 500x$ and $R(x) = 5000x - 100x^2$.

2 The price of a commodity is fixed at ₹ 55 and its cost function is $C(x) = 30x + 250$. Determine (i) the breakeven point (ii) the profit when 6 items are sold.

3 The cost function of a firm is given by $C = 2x^2 + x - 5$. Find

(i) the average cost

(ii) the marginal cost, when $x = 4$ and interpret it.

4 The total cost function for a company is given by $C(x) = \frac{3}{4}x^2 - 7x + 27$. Find the level of output for which $=$.

5 The demand function of a monopolist is given by $P = 1500 - 2x - x^2$. Find (i) the revenue function, (ii) the marginal revenue function.

Short Answer Type Questions

(4 Marks)

6 For a new product, a manufacturer spends ₹ 100000 on the infrastructure and the variable cost is estimated as ₹ 150 per unit of the product. The sale price per unit was fixed at ₹ 200. Find

(i) cost function.

(ii) revenue function.

(iii) profit function.

(iv) the breakeven point.

7 A company produces a commodity with ₹ 24000 fixed cost. The variable cost is estimated to be 25% of the total revenue recovered on selling the product at a rate of ₹ 8 per unit. Find the following.

(i) Cost function.

(ii) Revenue function.

(iii) Breakeven point. **[ISC 2013]**

8 A manufacturing company finds that the daily cost of producing x item of a product is given by $C(x) = 210x + 7000$.

(i) If each item is sold for ₹ 350, find the minimum number that must be produced and sold daily to ensure no loss.

(ii) If the selling price is increased by ₹ 35 per piece, what would be the breakeven point.

(iii) Calculate $C(5) - C(4)$ and interpret it.

9 If total cost function is given by $C = a + bx + cx^2$, where x is the quantity of output. Show that

$$\frac{d}{dx}(\text{AC}) = \frac{1}{x}(\text{MC} - \text{AC})$$

where, MC is the marginal cost and AC is the average cost. **[ISC 2012]**

10 If cost of producing 100 units of a commodity is ₹ 250 and cost of producing 200 units is ₹ 300. Assuming that AVC is constant, find the cost function.

11 Find the relationship between the slopes of marginal revenue curve and the average revenue curve, for the demand function $x = \frac{b-p}{a}$, where x denotes the number of units sold at the price p per unit.

Long Answer Type Questions

6 Marks

12 A company is selling a certain product. The demand function of the product is linear. The company can sell 2000 units, when the price is ₹ 8 per unit and when the price is ₹ 4 per unit, it can sell 3000 units. Determine

(i) the demand function.

(ii) the total revenue function. **[ISC 2005]**

13 Given that the total cost function for x units of a commodity is $C(x) = \frac{x^3}{3} + 3x^2 - 7x + 16$.

(i) Find the Marginal Cost (MC).

(ii) Find the Average Cost (AC).

(iii) Prove that

Marginal Average Cost

$$(\text{MAC}) = \frac{x(\text{MC}) - C(x)}{x^2}.$$

[ISC 2011]

14 The average cost function associated with producing and marketing x units of an item is given by $\text{AC} = 2x - 11 + \frac{50}{x}$. Find

(i) the total cost function and marginal cost function.

(ii) the range of values of the output x, for which AC is increasing. **[ISC 2018; 2008]**

15 If the total cost function C of a product is given by $C = 2x\left(\frac{x+7}{x+5}\right) + 7$. Prove that the marginal cost falls continuously as the output increases.

Hints & Solutions

1. **Hint** (i) Profit function $P(x) = R(x) - C(x)$

(ii) For breakeven point put $P(x) = 0$

[**Ans.** $P(x) = 4500x - 100x^2 - 35000$ and breakeven values are 10 or 35]

2. **Hint** (i) $R(x) =$ (price) (demand) $= 55x$

(ii) $P(x) = R(x) - C(x)$

(iii) For breakeven point put $P(x) = 0$.

(iv) The profit when 6 items are sold is given by putting $x = 6$ in $P(x)$.

[**Ans.** (i) 10 (ii) 0]

3. We have, $C(x) = 2x^2 + x - 5$

Clearly, $= \frac{C(x)}{x} = \frac{2x^2 + x - 5}{x} = 2x + 1 - \frac{5}{x}$

and $\text{MC} = \frac{d}{dx}[C(x)] = \frac{d}{dx}(2x^2 + x - 5) = 4x + 1$ [1]

Now, when $x = 4$, then $= 16 + 1 = 17$

This means that when we increase the output from 4 to 5 units, the additional cost incurred is ₹ 17. [1]

4. We have, $C(x) = \frac{3}{4}x^2 - 7x + 27$

Clearly, $\text{AC} = \frac{3}{4}x - 7 + \frac{27}{x}$ and $\text{MC} = \frac{3}{2}x - 7$ [1]

Now, consider AC = MC, then

$$\frac{3}{4}x - 7 + \frac{27}{x} = \frac{3}{2}x - 7$$

$$\Rightarrow \quad \frac{3}{4}x - \frac{3}{2}x = -\frac{27}{x}$$

$$\Rightarrow \quad -\frac{3}{4}x = -\frac{27}{x}$$

$$\Rightarrow \quad x^2 = 4 \times 9 = 36$$ [1]

$$\Rightarrow \quad x = 6$$

5. **Hint** (i) $R(x) = p \cdot x$

(ii) $\text{MR} = \frac{d}{dx}(R(x))$

[**Ans.** (i) $1500x - 2x^2 - x^3$ (ii) $1500 - 4x - 3x^2$]

6. (i) Let x be the number of units produced and sold, then cost function $C(x)$ = Fixed cost + Variable cost

$$= 100000 + 150x \quad [1]$$

(ii) Revenue function $= px = 200x$ [1]

(iii) Profit function $P(x) = R(x) - C(x)$

$$= 200x - (100000 + 150x) \quad [1]$$
$$= 50x - 100000$$

(iv) At breakeven point $P(x) = 0$

$$50x = 100000 = 0 \Rightarrow x = \frac{100000}{50} = 2000$$

Hence, $x = 2000$ is the breakeven point, i.e. when 200 units of the product are produced and sold, there will be no profit or loss. [1]

7. Given, fixed cost of the commodity = ₹ 24000

Let the number of units produced by company be x.

$\therefore$ Revenue function, $R = xp =$ ₹ $8x$ [1/2]

Since, the variable cost is 25% of the total revenue.

Thus, variable cost = 25% of $8x$

$$= \frac{25}{100} \times 8x = \frac{1}{4} \times 8x = ₹\ 2x \quad [1]$$

(i) Cost function, $C(x)$ = Fixed cost of the commodity + Variable cost of the commodity

$$= 24000 + 2x$$

(ii) Revenue function, $R(x) = 8x$ [1]

(iii) For breakeven point, $R(x) = C(x)$

$$\Rightarrow \quad 8x = 24000 + 2x \quad [1/2]$$
$$[\because R(x) = 8x \text{ and } C(x) = 24000 + 2x]$$
$$\Rightarrow \quad 8x - 2x = 24000 \Rightarrow 6x = 24000$$
$$\therefore \quad x = \frac{24000}{6} = 4000$$

Hence, the breakeven point is 4000. [1]

8. (i) We have, $R(x) = 350x$ and $C(x) = 210x + 7000$

$$\therefore \quad P(x) = 350x - 210x - 7000 \quad [1/2]$$
$$= 140x - 7000$$

For no loss, $P(x) = 0$

$$\Rightarrow \quad 140x - 7000 = 0 \text{ or } x = 50$$

Hence, to ensure no loss, the company must produce and sell at least 50 items daily. [1]

(ii) When selling price is increased by ₹ 35 per unit, then

$$R(x) = (350 + 35)x = 385x$$
$$\therefore \quad P(x) = 385x - (210x + 7000) = 175x - 7000 \quad [1]$$

At breakeven point, $P(x) = 0$

$$\Rightarrow \quad 175x - 7000 = 0$$
$$\therefore \quad x = \frac{7000}{175} = 40 \quad [1/2]$$

(iii) $C(5) - C(4) = (210 \times 5 + 7000) - (210 \times 4 + 7000)$

$$= 210(5 - 4) = 210$$

This shows the exact amount of increase in cost when production is increased from 4 units to 5 units. [1]

9. Given, the total cost function is

$$C(x) = a + bx + cx^2$$

We know that,

$$\text{Average Cost} = \frac{\text{Cost function}}{x} \Rightarrow \text{AC} = \frac{C}{x}$$

$$\Rightarrow \quad \text{AC} = \frac{a + bx + cx^2}{x} \quad [\because C = a + bx + cx^2]$$

$$\Rightarrow \quad \text{AC} = \frac{a}{x} + \frac{bx}{x} + \frac{cx^2}{x}$$

$$\Rightarrow \quad \text{AC} = \frac{a}{x} + b + cx \quad \text{...(i) [1]}$$

Also, marginal cost function $= \frac{d}{dx}$(cost function)

$$\Rightarrow \quad \text{MC} = \frac{dC}{dx} = \frac{d}{dx}(a + bx + cx^2)$$
$$[\because C = a + bx + cx^2]$$

$$\Rightarrow \quad \text{MC} = b + 2cx \quad [1]$$

On differentiating Eq. (i) w.r.t. x, we get

$$\frac{d}{dx}(AC) = \frac{d}{dx}\left(\frac{a}{x} + b + cx\right) = \frac{-a}{x^2} + c \quad \text{...(ii)}$$

Now, $\text{MC} - \text{AC} = b + 2cx - \left(\frac{a}{x} + b + cx\right)$ [1/2]

$$\Rightarrow \quad \text{MC} - \text{AC} = b + 2cx - \frac{a}{x} - b - cx \quad \text{...(iii)}$$

On dividing Eq. (iii) by x, we get

$$\frac{\text{MC} - \text{AC}}{x} = \frac{b + 2cx - \frac{a}{x} - b - cx}{x} \quad [1/2]$$

$$\Rightarrow \frac{1}{x}(\text{MC} - \text{AC}) = \frac{1}{x}\left(cx - \frac{a}{x}\right) = c - \frac{a}{x^2} \quad \text{...(iv) [1/2]}$$

From Eqs. (ii) and (iv), we get

$$\frac{d}{dx}(\text{AC}) = \frac{1}{x}(\text{MC} - \text{AC})$$ **Hence proved.** [1/2]

10. Let a denotes the fixed cost (F) and b denote the Average Variable Cost (AVC)

Since, $\quad \text{AVC} = \frac{V(x)}{x}$

$$\therefore \quad b = \frac{V(x)}{x} \quad [1]$$
$$\Rightarrow \quad V(x) = bx$$

Now, total cost function

$$C(x) = F + V(x) = a + bx. \quad \text{...(i) [1]}$$

Given that, $C(x) = 250$ when $x = 100$

and $\quad C(x) = 300$, when $x = 200$

$$\therefore \quad a + 100b = 250 \quad \text{...(ii)}$$
$$\text{and} \quad a + 200b = 300 \quad \text{...(iii)}$$

On subtracting Eq. (ii) from Eq. (iii), we get [1]

$$100b = 50 \Rightarrow b = \frac{1}{2}$$

On putting $b = \frac{1}{2}$ in Eq. (ii), we get

$$a + 50 = 250 \Rightarrow a = 200$$

From Eq. (i), we get $C(x) = 200 + \frac{x}{2}$ [1]

11. We have, $x = \frac{b-P}{a} \Rightarrow ax = b - P \Rightarrow P = b - ax$

Now, revenue function, $R(x) = Px = (b - ax)x = bx - ax^2$

Clearly, Average Revenue (AR $= \frac{R(x)}{x} = b - ax$ [1]

and Marginal Revenue MR $= \frac{d}{dx}(R(x))$

$$= \frac{d}{dx}(bx - ax^2) = b - 2ax$$

Now, slope of (AR) curve $= \frac{d}{dx}(\text{AR})$ [1]

$$= \frac{d}{dx}(b - ax) = -a \quad ...(i)$$

and slope of MR curve $= \frac{d}{dx}(\quad = \frac{d}{dx}(b - 2ax)$

$$= -2a \quad ...(ii) \; [1]$$

From Eqs. (i) and (ii), we can see that Slope of MR curve is twice the slope of (AR) curve. [1]

12. Let the demand function $f(x)$ be $ax + b$ for ₹ x per unit price. [1]

If the company sell 2000 units for ₹ 8 per unit, then equation will be

$$2000 = 8a + b \quad ...(i)$$

If the company sell 3000 units for ₹ 4 per unit, then equation will be

$$3000 = 4a + b \quad ...(ii)$$

On subtracting Eq. (ii) from Eq. (i), we get [1]

$$\begin{array}{r} 2000 = 8a + b \\ 3000 = 4a + b \\ - \quad - \quad - \\ \hline -1000 = 4a \end{array}$$

$\Rightarrow \quad 4a = -1000$

$\therefore \quad a = \frac{-1000}{4} = -250$ [1]

Now, put the value of $a = -250$ in Eq. (i), we get

$$2000 = 8 \times (-250) + b \Rightarrow 2000 = -2000 + b$$

$\Rightarrow \quad b = 2000 + 2000 = 4000$ [1]

Now, putting the values of a and b in equation of demand function, we get

Demand function, $f(x) = -250x + 4000$

[$\because f(x) = ax + b$]

(ii) Now, total revenue function, [1]

$$R(x) = \text{Demand function} \times x$$
$$= f(x) \times x = (4000 - 250x)\,x$$
$$= 4000x - 250x^2 \quad [1]$$

13. Given, the total cost function of the commodity (for x unit) is

$$C(x) = \frac{x^3}{3} + 3x^2 - 7x + 16 \quad [1/2]$$

(i) Marginal Cost (MC) $= \frac{dC}{dx}$

[cost function of commodity]

$$= \frac{d}{dx}\left(\frac{1}{3}x^3 + 3x^2 - 7x + 16\right)$$
$$= \frac{3}{3}x^2 + 2 \times 3x - 7$$
$$= x^2 + 6x - 7 \quad [1]$$

(ii) Average Cost (AC) $= \frac{\text{Cost function of commodity}}{x}$

$$= \frac{C}{x} = \frac{\frac{x^3}{3} + 3x^2 - 7x + 16}{x}$$
$$= \frac{\frac{x^3}{3}}{x} + \frac{3x^2}{x} - \frac{7x}{x} + \frac{16}{x}$$
$$= \frac{x^2}{3} + 3x - 7 + \frac{16}{x} \quad [1]$$

(iii) Marginal Average Cost (MAC)

$$= \frac{d(\text{AC})}{dx} = \frac{d}{dx}\left(\frac{1}{3}x^2 + 3x - 7 + \frac{16}{x}\right)$$
$$= 2 \times \frac{1}{3}x + 3 - \frac{16}{x^2}$$
$$= \frac{2}{3}x + 3 - \frac{16}{x^2} \quad ...(i)$$

Now, $\frac{x\,(\text{MC}) - C(x)}{x^2}$ [1]

$$= \frac{x(x^2 + 6x - 7) - \left(\frac{1}{3}x^3 + 3x^2 - 7x + 16\right)}{x^2}$$
$$= \frac{x^3 + 6x^2 - 7x - \frac{x^3}{3} - 3x^2 + 7x - 16}{x^2} \quad [1]$$
$$= \frac{\frac{2}{3}x^3 + 3x^2 - 16}{x^2} = \frac{\frac{2}{3}x^3}{x^2} + \frac{3x^2}{x^2} - \frac{16}{x^2}$$

$$\Rightarrow \quad \frac{x\,(\text{MC}) - C(x)}{x^2} = \frac{2}{3}x + 3 - \frac{16}{x^2} \quad ...(ii)$$

Hence, Marginal Average Cost

$$(\text{MAC}) = \frac{x(\text{MC}) - C(x)}{x^2}$$

$\therefore$ [From Eqs. (i) and (ii)] [1/2]

14. **Hint** Similar as Example 4.

[**Ans.** (i) $C(x) = 2x^2 - 11x + 50$; MC $= 4x - 11$ (ii) $(5, \infty)$]

15. We have, $C(x) = 2x\left(\frac{x+7}{x+5}\right) + 7$

which can be rewritten as

$$C(x) = 2\left(\frac{x^2+7x}{x+5}\right) + 7 \qquad [1]$$

Now, differentiating both sides w.r.t. x, we get

$$\frac{dC}{dx} = 2\left[\frac{(x+5)(2x+7) - (x^2+7x)\cdot 1}{(x+5)^2}\right] + 0$$

$$= 2\left[\frac{2x^2+17x+35-x^2-7x}{(x+5)^2}\right] \qquad [1]$$

$$= 2\left[\frac{x^2+10x+35}{(x+5)^2}\right] \qquad [1]$$

$$= 2\left[\frac{(x+5)^2+10}{(x+5)^2}\right] \qquad [1]$$

$$\therefore \quad MC = 2\left[1 + \frac{10}{(x+5)^2}\right]$$

Now, to show that MC falls continuously with increase in x, we need to show that $\frac{d}{dx}(MC) \quad 0, \forall\, x \geq 0.$ [1]

Here, $\frac{d}{dx}(MC) = 2\left[0 + \frac{10(-2)}{(x+5)^3}\right]$

$$= -\frac{40}{(x+5)^3} < 0, \text{ for all } x \geq 0.$$

Hence, the marginal cost falls continuously as the output increases. [1]

TOPIC 02 Maximization and Minimization, Applications of Integration

Minimization of AC and MC Functions

In commerce and Economics, it is very important to find the level of output for which the average cost and marginal cost is minimum. This can be calculated using the concept of maxima and minima.

Following steps are used to find the optimal level of output.

For Minimization of AC

***Step* I** First, find $\frac{d}{dx}$(AC).

***Step* II** Put $\frac{d}{dx}$(AC) = 0 and solve for x.

***Step* III** Now, find $\frac{d^2}{dx^2}$(AC).

***Step* IV** The value of x for which $\frac{d^2}{dx^2}$(AC) > 0, is the required value.

Similar, steps can be defined for minimization of MC

Example 1 The cost of manufacturing of certain items consists of ₹ 1600 as overheads, ₹ 30 per item as the cost of the material and the labour cost ₹ $\frac{x^2}{100}$ for x items produced. How many items must be produced to have a minimum average cost? **[ISC 2009]**

Sol. Given, cost of manufacturing of the items (for overheads) is ₹ 1600.

Cost of material per item is ₹ 30.

Labour cost of x items $= \frac{x^2}{100}$

Thus, the total cost of manufacturing of x items is

$C(x)$ = Cost of material of x items + Labour cost of x items + Overheads

$$\therefore \quad C(x) = \frac{x^2}{100} + 30x + 1600$$

We know that,

$$\text{Average cost (AC)} = \frac{\text{Total cost}}{x}$$

$$= \frac{C}{x} = \frac{x^2/100 + 30x + 1600}{x} = \frac{x}{100} + 30 + \frac{1600}{x}$$

For minimum average cost, $\frac{d^2}{dx^2}\text{AC} > 0$

Now, $\frac{d}{dx}(\text{AC}) = \frac{d}{dx}\left(\frac{x}{100} + 30 + \frac{1600}{x}\right)$

$$= \frac{1}{100} + \left(-\frac{1600}{x^2}\right) = \frac{1}{100} - \frac{1600}{x^2} \qquad \text{...(i)}$$

Put $\frac{d}{dx}(\text{AC}) = 0 \Rightarrow \frac{1}{100} - \frac{1600}{x^2} = 0$

$$\Rightarrow \quad \frac{1600}{x^2} = \frac{1}{100} \Rightarrow x^2 = 160000$$

$$\therefore \quad x = \pm 400$$

Now, again differentiating Eq. (i) w.r.t. x, we get

$$\frac{d^2}{dx^2}(\text{AC}) = \frac{3200}{x^3}$$

$\because \quad \frac{d^2}{dx^2}(\text{AC}) > 0$

At $x = 400$, $\frac{d^2}{dx^2}(\text{AC}) = \frac{3200}{(400)^3} > 0$

Hence, for minimum average cost, 400 items should be produced.

Example 2 The cost function of a product is given by $C(x) = \frac{x^3}{3} - 45x^2 - 900x + 36$, where x is the number of units produced. How many units should be produced to minimise the marginal cost? **(ISC 2019)**

Sol. Given cost function is

$$C(x) = \frac{x^3}{3} - 45x^2 - 900x + 36$$

$\therefore$ Marginal Cost, MC $= \frac{dC}{dx}$

$$= \frac{d}{dx}\left(\frac{x^3}{3} - 45x^2 - 900x + 36\right)$$

$$= \frac{3x^2}{3} - 90x - 900$$

$\Rightarrow \quad \text{MC} = x^2 - 90x - 900 \quad \ldots(\text{i})$

On differentiating Eq. (i) w.r.t. x, we get

$$\frac{d(\text{MC})}{dx} = 2x - 90 \text{ and } \frac{d^2(\text{MC})}{dx^2} = 2$$

For minimum marginal cost, put $\frac{d(\text{MC})}{dx} = 0$

$\Rightarrow \quad 2x - 90 = 0 \Rightarrow x = 45$

At $x = 45$, $\frac{d^2(\text{MC})}{dx^2} = 2 > 0$

Hence, it produce 45 units, to minimise the marginal cost.

Maximization of Revenue and Profit

In Commerce and Economics, it is also important to find the level of output for which the total revenue and profit is maximum. This can also be done using the concept of maxima and minima.

Following steps are used to find the optimal level of output.

For Maximization of $R(x)$ (Revenue Function)

In this method, we use the following steps

***Step* I** First, find $\frac{d}{dx}(R(x))$.

***Step* II** Put $\frac{d}{dx}(R(x)) = 0$ and solve for x.

***Step* III** Now, find $\frac{d^2}{dx^2}(R(x))$.

***Step* IV** The value of x for which $\frac{d^2}{dx^2}(R(x)) < 0$, is the required value.

Similar steps can be defined for maximization of profit function, $P(x)$.

Example 3 The demand function is $x = \frac{24 - 2p}{3}$, where x is the number of units demanded and p is the price per unit.

(i) Find the revenue function R in terms of p.

(ii) Find the price and the number of units demanded for which the revenue is maximum. **[ISC 2016]**

Sol. (i) Given, demand function, $x = \frac{24 - 2p}{3}$

$\therefore$ Revenue function, $R(p)$

= Demand function × Per unit price

$$= \frac{24 - 2p}{3} \times p = \frac{(24 - 2p)\,p}{3}$$

(ii) For revenue to be maximum, put $\frac{dR(p)}{dp} = 0$

$$\therefore \quad \frac{d}{dp}\left[\frac{(24 - 2p)\,p}{3}\right] = 0 \Rightarrow \frac{d}{dp}\left[\frac{24p - 2p^2}{3}\right] = 0$$

$$\Rightarrow \quad \frac{1}{3}(24 - 4p) = 0 \Rightarrow p = 6$$

Now, $\frac{d^2R}{dp^2} = -\frac{4}{3} < 0$

$\therefore$ Revenue is maximum when $p =$ ₹ 6.

Hence, the number of units demanded for maximum revenue is $x = \frac{24 - 2 \times 6}{3} = \frac{12}{3} = 4$ units.

Example 4 A firm has the cost function, $C = \frac{x^3}{3} - 7x^2 + 111x + 50$ and demand function, $x = 100 - p$.

(i) Write the total revenue in terms of x.

(ii) Formulate the total profit function P in terms of x.

(iii) Find the profit maximising level of output x. **[ISC 2014]**

Sol. Given, cost function, $C = \frac{x^3}{3} - 7x^2 + 111x + 50$

and demand function, $x = 100 - p$

We know that,

(i) Revenue function, $R = xp$

From equation of demand function,

$$x = 100 - p$$

$$\therefore \quad p = 100 - x$$

Now, we put the value of $p = 100 - x$ in equation of revenue function, we get

$$R = x(100 - x)$$

$$\Rightarrow \quad R = 100x - x^2$$

(ii) Also, profit function

$$P(x) = \text{Revenue} - \text{Cost}$$

$$= 100x - x^2 - \left(\frac{x^3}{3} - 7x^2 + 111x + 50\right)$$

$$= 100x - x^2 - \frac{x^3}{3} + 7x^2 - 111x - 50$$

$$= \frac{-x^3}{3} + 6x^2 - 11x - 50$$

Hence, profit function, $P(x) = \frac{-x^3}{3} + 6x^2 - 11x - 50$

(iii) For the profit maximising level of output x, $\frac{dP}{dx} = 0$

$$\therefore \quad \frac{d(P)}{d(x)} = 0$$

$$\Rightarrow \quad \frac{d}{dx}\left(\frac{-x^3}{3} + 6x^2 - 11x - 50\right) = 0$$

$$\Rightarrow \quad \frac{-3x^2}{3} + 2 \times 6x - 11 = 0$$

$$\Rightarrow \quad -x^2 + 12x - 11 = 0$$

$$\Rightarrow \quad -(x^2 - 12x + 11) = 0$$

$$\Rightarrow \quad x^2 - 12x + 11 = 0$$

$$\Rightarrow \quad x^2 - 11x - x + 11 = 0$$

$$\Rightarrow \quad x(x - 11) - 1(x - 11) = 0$$

$$\Rightarrow \quad (x - 1)(x - 11) = 0$$

$$\Rightarrow \quad x - 1 = 0 \text{ or } x - 11 = 0$$

$$\therefore \quad x = 1 \text{ or } x = 11$$

Now, $\frac{d^2P}{dx^2} = \frac{d}{dx}\left(\frac{dP}{dx}\right) = \frac{d}{dx}(-x^2 + 12x - 11)$

$$= -2x + 12$$

At $x = 1$, $\frac{d^2P}{dx^2} = -2 \times 1 + 12 = -2 + 12 = 10 > 0$

At $x = 11$, $\frac{d^2P}{dx^2} = -2 \times 11 + 12 = -22 + 12 = -10 < 0$

Hence, at $x = 11$, the profit will be maximum.

Applications of Integration

Integration is used to find the cost function when the marginal cost is given and to find revenue function when marginal revenue is given.

Determination of Cost Function

Let C denotes the total cost and $\text{MC} = \frac{dC}{dx}$ is the marginal cost, then we can write $C = C(x)$ $= \int (\text{MC})\, dx + k$, where k is the constant of integration, k, being the constant, is the fixed cost.

Example 5 The marginal cost function of producing x units of a product is given by $\text{MC} = \frac{x}{\sqrt{x^2 + 2500}}$. Find the total cost function and the average cost function if the fixed cost is ₹ 1000.

Sol. We have, $\text{MC} = \frac{x}{\sqrt{x^2 + 2500}}$

$$\therefore \quad C(x) = \int \frac{x}{\sqrt{x^2 + 2500}}\, dx + k$$

Put $x^2 + 2500 = t^2 \Rightarrow x\, dx = t\, dt \Rightarrow C(x) = \int \frac{t\,dt}{t} + k$

$$C(x) = \int dt + k = t + k = \sqrt{x^2 + 2500} + k$$

Given that, when $x = 0$, $C(x) = ₹\ 1000$

$$\therefore \quad 1000 = \sqrt{2500} + k = 50 + k \Rightarrow k = 950$$

Thus, $C(x) = \sqrt{x^2 + 2500} + 950$

and $\quad \text{AC} = \sqrt{1 + \frac{2500}{x^2}} + \frac{950}{x} \quad \left[\because \text{AC} = \frac{C}{x}\right]$

Determination of Total Revenue Function

Let $R(x)$ denotes the total revenue function and $\text{MR} = \frac{d}{dx}[R(x)]$ is the marginal revenue function.

$\therefore R(x) = \int (\text{MR}\ dx + k$, where k is the constant of integration.

Note

(i) When $R(x)$ is known, the demand function can be found by $p = \frac{R(x)}{x}$.

(ii) When $x = 0$, then $R = 0$.

(iii) Total revenue from the sale of m units $= \int_0^m (\text{MR})dx$

Example 6 The revenue function is given by $R(x) = 100x - x^2 - x^3$. Find

(i) the demand function.

(ii) marginal revenue function. **[ISC 2020]**

Sol. Given, $R(x) = 100x - x^2 - x^3$

(i) Demand function $p = \frac{R(x)}{x}$

$$= \frac{100x - x^2 - x^3}{x} = 100 - x - x^2$$

(ii) Marginal revenue function $= \frac{d(R(x))}{dx}$

$$= \frac{d(100x - x^2 - x^3)}{dx} = 100 - 2x - 3x^2$$

Topic Practice 2

Very Short Answer Type Questions

2 Marks

1 If marginal cost function of manufacturing x units of a product is $5 + 16x - 3x^2$ and total cost of producing 5 items is ₹ 500, then find the total cost function.

2 The marginal revenue function of a commodity is given as $MR = 12 - 3x^2 + 4x$. Find the total revenue from the sale of 4 units.

3 The marginal revenue function of a product is given by $MR = \frac{6}{(x-3)^2} - 4$.

Find the total revenue function and the corresponding demand function.

Short Answer Type Questions

4 Marks

4 The manufacturing cost of an item consists of ₹ 6000 as over heads, material cost ₹ 5 per unit and labour cost ₹ $\frac{x^2}{60}$ for x units produced. Find how many units must be produced so that the average cost is minimum.

5 The demand function for a manufacturer's product is $x = 70 - 5p$, where x is the number of units and 'p' is the price per unit. At what value of x will there be maximum revenue? What is the maximum revenue?

6 (a) A product can be manufactured at a total cost $C(x) = \frac{x^2}{100} + 100x + 40$, where x is the number of units produced. The price at which each unit can be sold is given by $P = \left(200 - \frac{x}{400}\right)$. Determine the production level x at which the profit is maximum. What is the price per unit and total profit at the level of production? **[ISC 2018]**

7 The marginal cost of a product is a constant multiple of number of units (x) produced. Find the total cost and the average cost function, if the fixed cost is ₹ 2000 and cost of producing 20 units is ₹ 3000.

8 Find the total revenue from the sale of 2000 pens if the marginal revenue function $R(x)$ is given by $R'(x) = \frac{x}{2000} + 3.50$, where x denotes the number of units sold.

9 A manufacturer's marginal cost function is $\frac{500}{\sqrt{2x+25}}$. Find the cost involved to increase production from 100 units to 300 units. **[ISC 2018]**

Long Answer Type Questions

6 Marks

10 Let the cost function of a firm be given by the equation $C = 300x - 10x^2 + \frac{1}{3}x^3$, where C stands for cost and x for output. Calculate

(i) Output, at which the marginal cost is minimum. Also, calculate the minimum marginal cost.

(ii) Output, at which the average cost is minimum.

(iii) Output, at which the average cost is equal to the marginal cost.

11 A company charges ₹ 700 for a ratio set on an order of 60 or less sets. The charge is reduced by ₹ 10 per set for each set ordered in excess of 60. Find the largest size order company should allow so as to receive a maximum revenue.

12 The marginal revenue function of a firm is given by $MR = 25e^{-\frac{x}{400}}\left(1 - \frac{x}{400}\right)$, show that the corresponding demand function is $P = 25e^{-\frac{x}{400}}$, where P is the price and x is quantity.

Hints & Solutions

1. We have, MC $x) = 5 + 16x - 3x^2$

$\Rightarrow \quad \frac{d}{dx} C(x) = 5 + 16x - 3x^2$

Now, $C(x) = \int MC(x)\,dx + k$

$= \int (5 + 16x - 3x^2)\,dx + k$

$= 5x + 8x^2 - x^3 + k$ [1]

Since, $C(x) = 500$ when $x = 5$

$\therefore \quad 500 = 25 + 200 - 125 + k \Rightarrow k = 400$

Thus, $C(x) = 5x + 8x^2 - x^3 + 400$ [1]

2. We have, $MR(x) = 12 - 3x^2 + 4x$

$\therefore \quad R(x) = \int MR\,dx + k$

$\Rightarrow \quad R(x) = \int (12 - 3x^2 + 4x)\,dx + k$ [1/2]

$= 12x - x^3 + 2x^2 + k$ [1]

We know that, $R = 0$ when $x = 0$

$\therefore \quad k = 0$

Thus, $R(x) = 12x - x^3 + 2x^2$ [1/2]

Now, the total revenue from the sale of 4 units is given by $R(4) = 48 - 64 + 32 = 80 - 64 = 16$.

3. **Hint** Similar as Example 6.

$\left[\textbf{Ans. } R = -\frac{6}{x-3} - 4x - 2 \text{ and } P = \frac{2}{3-x} - 4\right]$

4. **Hint** Similar as Example 1. [**Ans.** 600 units]

5. Demand function is given as $x = 70 - 5p$, which can be rewritten as $p = \frac{70 - x}{5}$ [1]

Now, $R(x) = p \cdot x = \frac{70x - x^2}{5}$ [1]

$\Rightarrow \quad \frac{d}{dx}[R(x)] = \frac{1}{5}[70 - 2x]$

Put $\frac{d}{dx}[R(x)] = 0$, which gives $x = 35$

Now, $\frac{d^2}{dx^2}[R(x)] = \frac{1}{5}(-2) < 0 \,\forall\, x$

$\therefore$ For maximum revenue, $x = 35$

and maximum revenue is given by $R(35)$ [1]

$= ₹\,\frac{70(35) - (35)^2}{5} = ₹\,245$ [1]

6. Given, total cost $C(x) = \frac{x^2}{100} + 100x + 40$

Price of each unit can be sold $P = 200 - \frac{x}{400}$

Price of x unit sold

$\Rightarrow \quad R(x) = px = 200x - \frac{x^2}{400}$ [1]

Profit $P(x) = R(x) - C(x)$

$= 200x - \frac{x^2}{400} - \frac{x^2}{100} - 100x - 40$

$\Rightarrow \quad P(x) = -\frac{x^2}{80} + 100x - 40$ [1]

On differentiating w.r.t. x, we get

$P'(x) = -\frac{2x}{80} + 100 = -\frac{x}{40} + 100$

For maxima or minima, put $P'(x) = 0$

$\Rightarrow \quad -\frac{x}{40} + 100 = 0 \Rightarrow x = 4000$

Now, $\quad P''(x) = -\frac{1}{40} < 0$

Hence, $P(x)$ is maximum when $x = 4000$.

Total profit at $x = 4000$, [1]

$P(4000) = \frac{-(4000)^2}{80} + 100(4000) - 40$

$= -200000 + 400000 - 40 = 199960$

Hence, the total profit is ₹ 199960. [1]

7. Let MC $= kx$, where k is a constant.

Then, $C(x) = \int (MC)\,dx + k'$

where, k' is a constant of integration.

$\Rightarrow \quad C(x) = \int (kx)\,dx + k'$ [1]

$= k\int x\,dx + k' = k \cdot \frac{x^2}{2} + k'$ [1]

Since, $C(0) = 2000$

$\therefore \quad k' = 2000$

Also, given that, $C(20) = 3000$ [1/2]

$\therefore \quad 3000 = k \cdot \frac{400}{2} + 2000$

$\Rightarrow \quad 200k = 1000$ [1/2]

$\Rightarrow \quad k = 5$

Thus, $\quad C(x) = \frac{5x^2}{2} + 2000$

and $\quad AC(x) = \frac{5x}{2} + \frac{2000}{x}$ [1]

8. We have, $MR = R'(x) = \frac{x}{2000} + 3.5$ [1/2]

Clearly, total revenue from the sale of 2000 pens

$= \int_0^{2000} (MR)\,dx$ [1½]

$= \int_0^{2000} \left(\frac{x}{2000} + 3.5\right) dx$ [1/2]

$= \left[\frac{x^2}{4000} + 3.5x\right]_0^{2000}$ [1]

$= (1000 + 7000) - 0 = ₹\,8000$ [1/2]

9. Given, Marginal Cost (MC) $= \dfrac{500}{\sqrt{2x+25}}$

We know that, MC $= \dfrac{dC}{dx}$

$\therefore \quad \dfrac{dC}{dx} = \dfrac{500}{\sqrt{2x+25}} \Rightarrow dC = \dfrac{500}{\sqrt{2x+25}}dx$ [1]

Cost involved to increase production from 100 units to 300 units is given by $\int_{100}^{300} \dfrac{500}{\sqrt{2x+25}}\, dx$

$= \dfrac{500 \times (2x+25)^{1/2}}{1/2} \times \dfrac{1}{2}$ [2]

$= 500\,[\sqrt{(2x+25)}]_{100}^{300}$

$= 500(\sqrt{625} - \sqrt{225})$

$= 500(25-15) =$ ₹5000 [1]

10. We have, $\quad C = 300x - 10x^2 + \dfrac{1}{3}x^3$ ...(i)

$\therefore$ Average cost (AC) $= \dfrac{C}{x} = 300 - 10x + \dfrac{1}{3}x^2$ ...(ii)

and marginal cost (MC) $= \dfrac{dC}{dx} = 300 - 20x + x^2$ ...(ii)

(i) $\dfrac{d(\text{MC})}{dx} = \dfrac{d}{dx}(300 - 20x + x^2)$

$= -20 + 2x$ and $\dfrac{d^2(\text{MC})}{dx^2} = 2$

For MC to be minimum, put $\dfrac{d(\text{MC})}{dx} = 0$ [1]

$\Rightarrow \quad -20 + 2x \Rightarrow x = 10$

Also, $\left(\dfrac{d^2(\text{MC})}{dx^2}\right)_{x=10} = 2 > 0$

So, the output for the marginal cost to be minimum is 10 units. [1]

Also, from Eq. (iii), Minimum marginal cost

$= (\text{MC})_{x=10} = 300 - 20 \times 10 + 10^2$

$= 300 - 200 + 100 = 200$ [1/2]

(ii) $\dfrac{d(\text{AC})}{dx} = \dfrac{d}{dx}\left(300 - 10x + \dfrac{1}{3}x^2\right) = -10 + \dfrac{2}{3}x$

and $\dfrac{d^2A}{dx^2} = \dfrac{2}{3}$ [1]

For average cost to be minimum, put $\dfrac{dA}{dx} = 0$

$\Rightarrow \quad -10 + \dfrac{2}{3}x = 0 \Rightarrow x = 15$

Also, $\left(\dfrac{d^2A}{dx^2}\right)_{\text{at } x=15} = \dfrac{2}{3} > 0$

So, the output level for average cost to be minimum is 15 units. [1]

(iii) AC = MC, i.e. $300 - 10x + \dfrac{1}{3}x^2 = 300 - 20x + x^2$

$\Rightarrow \quad \dfrac{2}{3}x^2 - 10x = 0 \Rightarrow x = 0$ or $x = 15$ [1]

But x cannot be zero, therefore $x = 15$ is the level of output at which marginal cost becomes equal to the average cost. [1/2]

11. Let x be the number of sets ordered in excess of 60. Then, total number of sets ordered $= (60 + x)$ [1]

Price per set = ₹$(700 - 10x)$

Total revenue $R = (60 + x)(700 - 10x)$ [1]

Now, $\dfrac{dR}{dx} = (60 + x)(-10) + (700 - 10x) \cdot 1$

$= -600 - 10x + 700 - 10x = 100 - 20x$ [1]

Put $\dfrac{dR}{dx} = 0 \Rightarrow x = 5$

Also, $\dfrac{d^2R}{dx^2} = -20 < 0$ for $x = 5$ [2]

$\therefore$ For maximum revenue, largest size of order

$= (60 + 5)$ sets $= 65$ sets [1]

12. We have, MR $= 25\, e^{-\frac{x}{400}}\left(1 - \dfrac{x}{400}\right)$

$\therefore \quad R(x) = \int 25\, e^{-\frac{x}{400}}\left(1 - \dfrac{x}{400}\right) dx + k$

$= 25 \int e^{-\frac{x}{400}}\left(1 - \dfrac{x}{400}\right) dx + k$

Now, by integrating by parts, we get

$$R(x) = 25\left[\left(1 - \frac{x}{400}\right) \cdot \frac{e^{-\frac{x}{400}}}{\left(-\frac{1}{400}\right)} - \int \left(-\frac{1}{400}\right) \cdot \frac{e^{-\frac{x}{400}}}{\left(-\frac{1}{400}\right)} dx\right] + k$$

$$= 25\left[-\left(1 - \frac{x}{400}\right) \cdot 400\, e^{-\frac{x}{400}} - \int e^{-\frac{x}{400}} dx\right] + k \quad [2]$$

$$= 25\left[-\left(1 - \frac{x}{400}\right) \cdot 400\, e^{-\frac{x}{400}} - \frac{e^{-\frac{x}{400}}}{\left(-\frac{1}{400}\right)}\right] + k$$

$$= 25 e^{-\frac{x}{400}}[-400 + x + 400] + k$$

$$= 25x\, e^{-\frac{x}{400}} + k \quad [1]$$

We know that, $R = 0$ when $x = 0$

$\therefore \quad k = 0$ [1]

Thus, $\quad R(x) = 25x\, e^{-\frac{x}{400}}$

and the corresponding demand function is given by [1]

$$P = \frac{R}{x} = \frac{25x\, e^{-\frac{x}{400}}}{x} = 25\, e^{-\frac{x}{400}}$$

Hence proved. [1]

Chapter Practice

Multiple Choice Type Questions

1 Mark

1 A company sells hand towels at ₹100 per unit. The fixed cost for the company to manufacture hand towels is ₹ 35000 and variable cost is estimated to be 30% of total revenue. What will be the total cost function for manufacturing hand towels? **[ISC 2024]**

(a) $35000 + 3x$ (b) $35000 + 30x$
(c) $35000 + 100x$ (d) $35000 + 10x$

2 The average cost function associated with producing and marketing x units of an item is given by $AC = 4x - 11 + \frac{25}{x}$. What will be the total cost function?

(a) $C(x) = 4 - \frac{11}{x} + \frac{50}{x^2}$ (b) $C(x) = 4 - \frac{50}{x^2}$
(c) $C(x) = 4x - 11$ (d) $C(x) = 4x^2 - 11x + 25$

3 If the demand function is given by $p(x) = 1500 - 2x - x^2$, then find the marginal revenue when $x = 10$. **[ISC 2023]**

(a) 1160 (b) 1600
(c) 1100 (d) 1200

4 The demand function for a certain commodity is given by $p = 1000 - 15x - x^2, 0 < x < 25$. What is the total revenue from the scale of 5 units?

(a) 900 (b) 1000
(c) 4500 (d) 5000

Assertion-Reason Type Questions

1 Mark

Directions (Q. Nos. 5-8) *In the questions given below are two statements labelled as Assertion (A) and Reason (R). In the context of the two statements, which one of the following is correct?*

(a) Both A and R are correct; R is the correct explanation of A
(b) Both A and R are correct; R is not the correct explanation of A
(c) A is correct; R is incorrect
(d) R is correct; A is incorrect

5 Assertion (A) The profit function is calculated by subtracting the total cost from the revenue obtained by selling x units of a product i.e. $P(x) = R(x) - C(x)$

Reason (R) The breakeven point is that point, where total revenue equals to total cost incurred i.e. $R(x) = C(x)$.

6 Assertion (A) The fixed cost of a product is ₹ 7500 and the variable cost is ₹ 500 per unit. If the demand function $p(x) = 2500 - 100x$, then the breakeven points will be 5 or 15.

Reason (R) The breakeven point is that point where total revenue equals to total cost incurred i.e. $R(x) = C(x)$.

7 Assertion (A) The total cost function for x units of a product is $C(x) = x^3 + 4x^2 - 8x + 2$. Then, the average cost function will be $x^2 + 4x - 8 + \frac{2}{x}$.

Reason (R) If $C(x)$ is the total cost of producing x units of a product, then the average cost is given by $AC = \frac{C(x)}{x}$.

8 Assertion (A) The demand function for a certain product is represented by the equation $p = 300 + 24x - \frac{x^2}{3}$ in rupees where x is the number of units and p is the price per unit. Then, the marginal revenue function is $300 + 48x - x^2$.

Reason (R) The marginal revenue (MR) is the rate of change of total revenue with respect to the quantity demanded

i.e. $MR = \frac{d}{dx}(R) = \frac{d}{dx}(p \cdot x)$.

Very Short Answer Type Questions

2 Marks

9 A manufacturer can sell x items of commodity at price of ₹ $(330 - x)$ each. Find the revenue function. If the cost of producing x items is ₹ $(x^2 + 10x + 12)$, determine the profit function.

10 The fixed cost of a new product is ₹ 30000 and the variable cost per unit is ₹ 800. If the demand function is $P(x) = 4500 - 100x$, find the breakeven values. [ISC 2023]

11 The total cost $C(x)$ of a company is given as $C(x) = 1000 + 25x + 2x^2$, where x is the output. Determine
(i) average cost.
(ii) marginal cost.
(iii) marginal cost when $x = 15$.

12 The demand function for a product is given as $P = 30 + 2x - 5x^2$, where x is the number of units demanded and P is the price per unit. Find
(i) Total Revenue.
(ii) Marginal Revenue.
(iii) MR when $x = 3$.

13 The demand function for a product is given by $P = \frac{5}{x+3}$. Show that the marginal revenue function is a decreasing function.

14 The marginal revenue function for a firm is given by $\text{MR} = \frac{2}{x+3} - \frac{2x}{(x+3)^2} + 5$. Show that the demand function is $P = \frac{2}{x+3} + 5$.

Short Answer Type Questions

4 Marks

15 A company produced a commodity with ₹20000 fixed costs. The variable cost estimated to 35% of the total revenue when it is sold at a rate of ₹ 6 per unit. Find the total revenue, total cost and profit function of revenue when it is sold.

16 The average cost function (AC) for a product is given by $\text{AC} = x + 5 + \frac{36}{x}$, where x is the output. Find the output for which AC is increasing and the output for which AC is decreasing with increasing output. Also find the total cost C and the marginal cost MC.

17 In a factory it is found that the number of units (x) produced in a day depends upon the number of workers (n) and is obtained by the relation $x = 5n/\sqrt{n+5}$. The demand function of the product is $p = 2/x + x$.
Determine the marginal revenue when $n = 20$.

18 If $C = 0.01x^2 + 5x + 100$ is the cost function for x items of a product. At what level of production average cost is minimum? What is the minimum average cost?

19 A firm produces x units of output per week at a total cost of ₹$\frac{x^3}{3} - x^2 + 5x + 3$, find the output levels at which the marginal cost and average variable cost attain their respective minima.

20 The demand function for a product marketed by a company is $p = \frac{80 - x}{4}$, where x is the number of units and p is the price per unit. At what value of x will there be maximum revenue? What is the maximum revenue?

21 A firm has found from past experience that its profit in terms of number of units x produced, is given by $P(x) = -\frac{x^3}{3} + 729x + 2700, 0 \le x \le 35$.
Compute
(i) the value of x that maximizes the profit.
(ii) the profit per unit of the product, when this maximum level is achieved.

22 The marginal cost (MC) of a product is given to be a constant multiple of number of units (x) produced. Find the total cost function, if fixed cost is ₹ 5000 and the cost of producing 50 units is ₹ 5625.

23 If the marginal revenue function is $\text{MR} = \frac{4}{(2x+3)^2} - 1$, find the total revenue and the demand function.

24 A manufacture's marginal revenue function is given by $\text{MR} = 275 - x - 0.3x^2$. Find the increase in the manufacturer's total revenue if the production is increased from 10 to 20 units.

Long Answer Type Questions

6 Marks

25 The demand function of a product for a manufacturer is $p(x) = ax + b$. He knows that he can sell 1250 units when the price is ₹ 5 per unit and he can sell 1500 units at a price of ₹ 4 per unit. Find the total, average and marginal revenue functions. Also find the price per unit when the marginal revenue is zero.

26 A company charges ₹ 15000 for a refrigerator on orders of 20 or less refrigerators. The charge is reduced on every set by ₹ 100 per piece for each piece ordered in excess of 20. Find the largest size order the company should allow so as to receive a maximum revenue.

27 Given that the marginal cost MC and the average cost AC of a product are directly proportional to each other, find the total cost function so that the cost of producing 2 units is ₹ 8 and of producing 4 units is ₹ 64.

Case-Based Type Question

6 Marks

28 A mobile phone manufacturer finds that the total cost for the production and marketing of x number of mobile phones is

$$C(x) = 100x - 10x^2 + \frac{1}{3}x^3.$$

Calculate

(i) Output, at which the marginal cost is minimum.

(ii) Output, at which the average cost is minimum.

(iii) Output, at which the average cost is equal to the marginal cost.

Answers

1. (b)	**2.** (d)	**3.** (a)	**4.** (c)
5. (b)	**6.** (a)	**7.** (a)	**8.** (a)

9. $R(x) = 330x - x^2$; $P(x) = 320x - 12 - 2x^2$

10. 12 units, 25 units

11. (i) $\frac{1000}{x} + 25 + 2x$ (ii) $25 + 4x$ (iii) 85

12. (i) $30x + 2x^2 - 5x^3$ (ii) $30 + 4x - 15x^2$ (iii) 177

15. $R(x) = 6x$, $C(x) = 2000 + \frac{21x}{10}$, $P(x) = \frac{39x}{10} - 20000$

16. $x > 6$, $0 < x < 6$, $x^2 + 5x + 36$, $2x + 5$

17. 40

18. 100; ₹ 7

19. MC is minimum at $x = 1$ and AVC is minimum at $x = \frac{2}{3}$.

20. 40; 400

21. (i) 27 (ii) ₹ 586

22. $C = \frac{x^2}{4} + 5000$

23. $R = \frac{4x}{6x+9} - x$, $P = \frac{4}{6x+9} - 1$

24. ₹ 1900

25. $R = 10x - \frac{x^2}{250}$; $= 10 - \frac{x}{250}$, MR $= 10 - \frac{x}{125}$; ₹ 5 per unit

26. 85

27. $C(x) = x^3$

28. (i) $x = 10$ (ii) $x = 15$ (iii) $x = 0$, $x = 15$

CHAPTER 17

Linear Regression

- Definition of Regression
- Scatter Diagram
- Line of Regression

In class XI, we have learnt about correlation, which measures and analyses the degree to which the two variables fluctuate with reference to each other.

After knowing the relationship between two variables we may be interested in estimating (predicting) the value of one variable given the value of another. This can be done by regression analysis, as it reveals average relationship between two variables and this makes possible estimation or prediction.

Definition of Regression

Regression is the measure of the average relationship between two or more variables in terms of the original units of the data.

In other words, the statistical method which helps in estimating or predicting the value of one variable for a given value of the related variable is called the **regression**.

Difference between Correlation and Regression Analysis

There are two major difference given as follows

(i) Correlation coefficient is the measure of degree of relationship between variables where as regression analysis study the nature of relationship between the variables.

(ii) By using correlation, we cannot predict the value of one variable from that of the other variable, but through regression analysis we can do this.

Scatter Diagram

It is the simplest method of the diagrammatic representation of bivariate data. Let (x_i, y_i), $i = 1, 2, 3, \ldots, n$ be a bivariate distribution. Let the values of the variables x and y be plotted along the X-axis and Y-axis on a suitable scale. Then, corresponding to every ordered pair, there corresponds a point or dot in the XY-plane. The diagram of dots so obtained is called **scatter diagram**.

e.g. Let us draw a scatter diagram for the observations (2, 8), (3, 7), (4, 6), (5, 5), (6, 4), (7, 3), (8, 2)

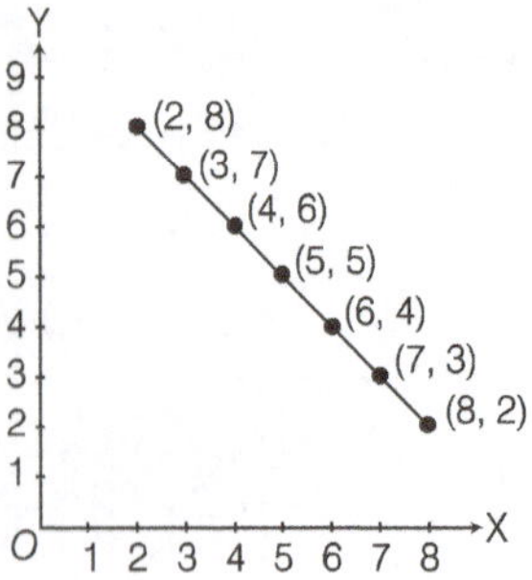

Note Data connecting two variables are known as **bivariate data**.

Line of Regression

If the data $(x_1, y_1), (x_2, y_2), \ldots, (x_n, y_n)$ is plotted on a scatter diagram, then visualising a smooth curve approximating the data is called **curve fitting**. The main purpose of curve fitting is to estimate one of the variable (the dependent variable) from the other (the independent variable). It is shown in the following diagram.

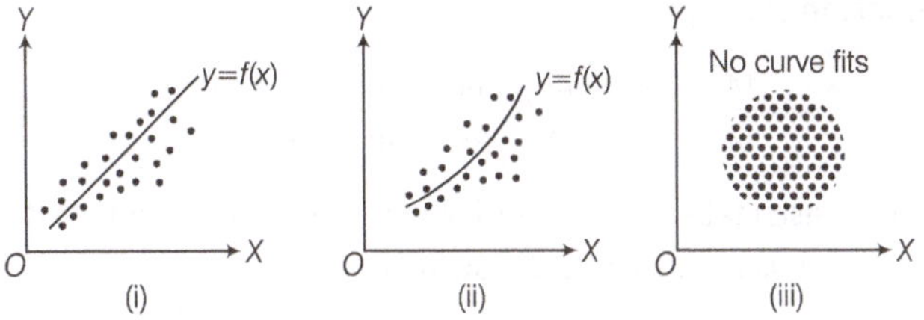

In the diagrams (i) and (ii), curve $y = f(x)$ is called the **curve of regression** and when the curve is a straight line, then it is called a **line of regression** and the regression is said to be **linear**.

Lines of Regression of *x* on *y* and *y* on *x*

In the case of two variables x and y, we have two regression lines, namely, the regression line of x on y and the regression line of y on x. The regression line of y on x is represented by $y = a + bx$ and it gives the most probable values of y for given values of x. Similarly, the regression line of x on y is represented by $x = a + by$ and it gives the most probable values of x for given value of y.

Method of Least Squares

It is the best method of fitting a curve approximating a given set of data points. According to this method, out of all curves approximating a given set of data points, the curve having the property that $d_1^2 + d_2^2 + \ldots + d_n^2$ is minimum is the best fitting curve.

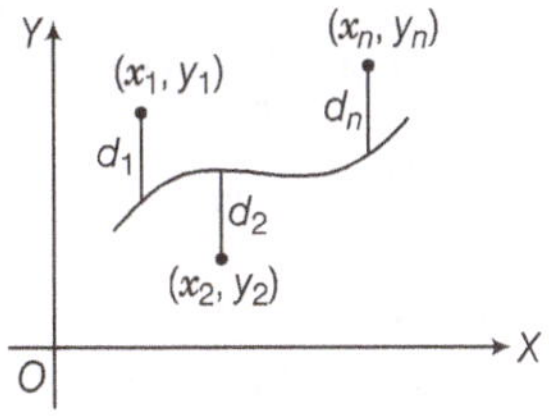

Lines of Best Fit

If the line of regression is so chosen that $d_1^2 + d_2^2 + \ldots + d_n^2$ is minimum, then it is called the **line of best fit** and it gives the best estimate.

Let $y = a + bx$ be the equation of the line of regression of y on x approximating the set of points $(x_1, y_1), (x_2, y_2), \ldots, (x_n, y_n)$.

To find the line of best fit, we need to determine the constants a and b.

Using a bit of calculus, it can be shown that the line of best fit should satisfy the following equations

$$\Sigma y = na + b\Sigma x \quad \ldots(i)$$

$$\Sigma xy = a\Sigma x + b\Sigma x^2 \quad \text{[normal equations]} \ldots(ii)$$

On solving above equations simultaneously, we can determine the constants a and b.

On solving Eqs. (i) and (ii), we get

$$b = \frac{n\,\Sigma xy - (\Sigma x)(\Sigma y)}{n\,\Sigma x^2 - (\Sigma x)^2} \quad \ldots(iii)$$

and from Eq. (i), we get $\bar{y} = a + b\bar{x} \Rightarrow a = \bar{y} - b\bar{x}$ ...(iv)

Now, $y = a + bx$ can be written as

$$y = \bar{y} - b\bar{x} + bx \quad \text{[using Eq. (iv)]}$$

or $(y - \bar{y}) = b(x - \bar{x})$ ...(v)

which is required equation of regression line of y on x

where, $b = \dfrac{n\Sigma xy - (\Sigma x)(\Sigma y)}{n\Sigma x^2 - (\Sigma x)^2}$

Note that b is slope of the Eq. (v).

It is also called the **regression coefficient** of y on x and denoted b_{yx}. So, $b_{yx} = \dfrac{n\Sigma xy - (\Sigma x)(\Sigma y)}{n\Sigma x^2 - (\Sigma x)^2}$

Similarly, regression coefficient of x on y is denoted by b_{xy} and defined by $b_{xy} = \dfrac{n\,\Sigma xy - (\Sigma x)(\Sigma y)}{n\,\Sigma y^2 - (\Sigma y)^2}$

and equation of the regression line of x on y is

$$x - \bar{x} = b_{xy}(y - \bar{y}).$$

Note (i) It is clear that both the lines passes through the point $(\bar{x}, \bar{y})$.

(ii) (a) If x and y are small numbers, then we generally use

$$b_{yx} = \frac{\Sigma xy - \frac{1}{n}\Sigma x \Sigma y}{\Sigma x^2 - \frac{1}{n}(\Sigma x)^2}$$

(b) If $x - \bar{x}$, $y - \bar{y}$ are small fraction less numbers, then we use

$$b_{yx} = \frac{\Sigma(x - \bar{x})(y - \bar{y})}{\Sigma(x - \bar{x})^2}.$$

Otherwise, we use assumed means A and B and

$u = x - A$, $v = y - B$, so that $b_{yx} = \dfrac{\Sigma uv - \frac{1}{n}\Sigma u \Sigma v}{\Sigma u^2 - \frac{1}{n}(\Sigma u)^2}$

(iii) Similarly, the regression coefficient of x on y is given by

$$b_{xy} = \frac{\Sigma xy - \frac{1}{n}\Sigma x \Sigma y}{\Sigma y^2 - \frac{1}{n}(\Sigma y)^2} = \frac{\Sigma(x - \bar{x})(y - \bar{y})}{\Sigma(y - \bar{y})^2} = \frac{\Sigma uv - \frac{1}{n}\Sigma u \Sigma v}{\Sigma v^2 - \frac{1}{n}(\Sigma v)^2}$$

Example 1 Find the line of regression of y on x from the following table.

x	1	2	3	4	5
y	7	6	5	4	3

Hence estimate the value of y when $x = 6$. **[ISC 2018]**

Sol. Let us construct the following table

x	y	x^2	xy
1	7	1	7
2	6	4	12
3	5	9	15
4	4	16	16
5	3	25	15
$\Sigma x = 15$	$\Sigma y = 25$	$\Sigma x^2 = 55$	$\Sigma xy = 65$

Here, $\bar{x} = \frac{\Sigma x}{n} = \frac{15}{5} = 3$ and $\bar{y} = \frac{\Sigma y}{n} = \frac{25}{5} = 5$

Regression coefficient of y on x, i.e. $b_{yx} = \dfrac{\Sigma xy - \dfrac{\Sigma x \cdot \Sigma y}{n}}{\Sigma x^2 - \dfrac{(\Sigma x)^2}{n}}$

$$\Rightarrow \quad b_{yx} = \frac{65 - \dfrac{15 \times 25}{5}}{55 - \dfrac{(15)^2}{5}} = \frac{65 - 75}{55 - 45} = \frac{-10}{10} = -1$$

Equation of line regression of y on x is

$$y - \bar{y} = b_{yx}(x - \bar{x}) \Rightarrow y - 5 = -1(x - 3)$$

$$\Rightarrow \quad y - 5 = -x + 3 \Rightarrow x + y = 8$$

Clearly, when $x = 6$, then $y = 8 - 6 = 2$.

Thus, the estimated value of y is 2.

Alternate Method (It is easier to solve this problem by using normal equations)

Assume that line of best fit (i.e. regression line of y on x) is $y = a + bx$

Then, the normal equations are

$$\Sigma y = na + b\Sigma x \quad \text{...(i)}$$

and $$\Sigma xy = a\Sigma x + b\Sigma x^2 \quad \text{...(ii)}$$

Now, construct the following table

x	y	xy	x^2
1	7	7	1
2	6	12	4
3	5	15	9
4	4	16	16
5	3	15	25
$\Sigma x = 15$	$\Sigma y = 25$	$\Sigma xy = 65$	$\Sigma x^2 = 55$

On substituting these values in Eqs. (i) and (ii), we get

$$25 = 5a + 15b, \text{ i.e. } a + 3b = 5,$$

$$65 = 15a + 55b, \text{ i.e. } 3a + 11b = 13$$

On solving these equations, we get $a = 8$, $b = -1$

Hence, the line of best fit is

$$y = a + bx = 8 - x$$

i.e. $y = -x + 8$

When $x = 6$ estimated values of $y = -6 + 8 = 2$

Example 2 Find the line of best fit for the following data, treating x as dependent variable (regression equation x on y).

x	14	12	13	14	16	10	13	12
y	14	23	17	24	18	25	23	24

Hence, estimate the value of x when $y = 16$. **[ISC 2017]**

Sol. Let us construct the following table.

x	x^2	y	y^2	xy
14	196	14	196	196
12	144	23	529	276
13	169	17	289	221
14	196	24	576	336
16	256	18	324	288
10	100	25	625	250
13	169	23	529	299
12	144	24	576	288
$\Sigma x = 104$	$\Sigma x^2 = 1374$	$\Sigma y = 168$	$\Sigma y^2 = 3644$	$\Sigma xy = 2154$

Here, $\bar{x} = \frac{\Sigma x}{n} = \frac{104}{8} = 13$ and $\bar{y} = \frac{\Sigma y}{n} = \frac{168}{8} = 21$

Regression line of x on y is

$x - \bar{x} = b_{xy}(y - \bar{y})$, where

$$b_{xy} = \frac{\Sigma xy - \frac{1}{n}\Sigma x \cdot \Sigma y}{\Sigma y^2 - \frac{1}{n}(\Sigma y)^2}$$

$$= \frac{2154 - \frac{1}{8} \times 104 \times 168}{3644 - \frac{1}{8} \times (168)^2} = \frac{2154 - 104 \times 21}{3644 - 168 \times 21}$$

$$= \frac{-30}{116} = -0.25862$$

$\therefore$ Regression line of x on y is

$$x - 13 = -0.25862\,(y - 21)$$

$$\Rightarrow \quad x = -0.25862y + 5.43102 + 13$$

$$\Rightarrow \quad x = -0.25862y + 18.43102$$

When $y = 16$, then $x = 14.2931$.

Example 3 Given that the observations are (9, – 4), (10, – 3), (11, – 1), (12, 0), (13, 1), (14, 3), (15, 5), (16, 8). Find the two lines of regression and estimate the value of y, when $x = 13.5$. **[ISC 2015]**

Sol. Let us construct the following table for given data

x	y	x^2	y^2	xy
9	– 4	81	16	– 36
10	– 3	100	9	– 30
11	– 1	121	1	– 11
12	0	144	0	0
13	1	169	1	13
14	3	196	9	42
15	5	225	25	75
16	8	256	64	128
$\Sigma x = 100$	9	1292	125	181

Here, $n = 8$, $\Sigma x = 100$, $\Sigma y = 9$, $\Sigma x^2 = 1292$, $\Sigma y^2 = 125$ and $\Sigma xy = 181$

Now, mean of x, $\bar{x} = \frac{\Sigma x}{n} = \frac{100}{8} = 12.5$

and mean of y, $\bar{y} = \frac{\Sigma y}{n} = \frac{9}{8}$

Regression coefficients of y on x is

$$b_{yx} = \frac{\Sigma xy - \frac{1}{n}\Sigma x \cdot \Sigma y}{\Sigma x^2 - \frac{1}{n}(\Sigma x)^2} = \frac{181 - \frac{1}{8}(100 \times 9)}{1292 - \frac{1}{8}(100)^2} = \frac{181 - \frac{900}{8}}{1292 - \frac{10000}{8}}$$

$$= \frac{1448 - 900}{10336 - 10000} = \frac{548}{336} = \frac{137}{84}$$

and regression coefficients of x on y is

$$b_{xy} = \frac{\Sigma xy - \frac{1}{n}\Sigma x \Sigma y}{\Sigma y^2 - \frac{1}{n}(\Sigma y)^2}$$

$$= \frac{181 - \frac{1}{8}(100 \times 9)}{125 - \frac{1}{8}(9)^2} = \frac{1448 - 900}{1000 - 81} = \frac{548}{919}$$

$\therefore$ Regression line of x on y is $x - \bar{x} = b_{xy}(y - \bar{y})$

$\therefore$ $$(x - 12.5) = \frac{548}{919}\left(y - \frac{9}{8}\right)$$

$\Rightarrow$ $919x - 11487.5 = 548y - 616.5$

$\Rightarrow$ $919x - 548y = 10871$

and regression line of y on x is

$$y - \bar{y} = b_{yx}(x - \bar{x})$$

$\therefore$ $$y - \frac{9}{8} = \frac{137}{84}(x - 12.5)$$

$\Rightarrow$ $$84\left(y - \frac{9}{8}\right) = 137x - 1712.5$$

$\Rightarrow$ $84y - 94.5 = 137x - 1712.5$

$\Rightarrow$ $137x - 84y = 1618$

Since, the regression line of y on x is

$$137x - 84y = 1618$$

For $x = 13.5$, $137 \times 13.5 - 84y = 1618$

$\Rightarrow$ $84y = 1849.5 - 1618$

$\Rightarrow$ $84y = 231.5 \Rightarrow y = 2.76$

Example 4 Find the equation of the regression line of y on x, if the observations (x, y) are as follows (1, 4), (2, 8), (3, 2) (4, 12), (5, 10), (6, 14), (7, 16), (8, 6), (9, 18)

Also, find the estimated value of y when $x = 14$. **[ISC 2019]**

Sol. Let us construct the following table for given data

x	y	x^2	y^2	xy
1	4	1	16	4
2	8	4	64	16
3	2	9	4	6
4	12	16	144	48
5	10	25	100	50
6	14	36	196	84
7	16	49	256	112
8	6	64	36	48
9	18	81	324	162
$\Sigma x = 45$	$\Sigma y = 90$	$\Sigma x^2 = 285$	$\Sigma y^2 = 1140$	$\Sigma xy = 530$

Here, $n = 9$

$\therefore$ $$\bar{x} = \frac{\Sigma x}{n} = \frac{45}{9} = 5$$

and $$\bar{y} = \frac{\Sigma y}{y} = \frac{90}{9} = 10$$

$\therefore$ Regression coefficient of y on x is

$$b_{yx} = \frac{\Sigma xy - \frac{1}{n}\Sigma x \, \Sigma y}{\Sigma x^2 - \frac{1}{n}(\Sigma x)^2}$$

$$= \frac{530 - \frac{1}{9} \times 45 \times 90}{285 - \frac{1}{9} \times (45)^2}$$

$$= \frac{530 - 450}{285 - 225} = \frac{80}{60} = \frac{4}{3}$$

Now, regression equation of y on x is

$$(y - \bar{y}) = b_{yx}(x - \bar{x})$$

$\because$ $$y - 10 = \frac{4}{3}(x - 5)$$

$\Rightarrow$ $4x - 3y + 10 = 0$

Now, estimated value of y when $x = 14$ is

$$4 \times 14 - 3y + 10 = 0$$

$\Rightarrow$ $3y = 56 + 10$

$\Rightarrow$ $y = \frac{66}{3}$

$\Rightarrow$ $y = 22$

Example 5 The data for marks in Physics and History obtained by ten students are given below

Marks in Physics	15	12	8	8	7	7	7	6	5	3
Marks in History	10	25	17	11	13	17	20	13	9	15

Using this data

(i) Find the line of regression in which Physics is taken as the independent variable.

(ii) A candidate had scored 10 marks in Physics but was absent from the history test. Estimate his probable score for the letter test. **[ISC 2008]**

Sol. Let the marks obtained in Physics and History are x and y, respectively. Now, taking assumed mean $a = 8$ and $b = 15$, we construct the following table as follows

x	$u = x - 8$	u^2	y	$v = y - 15$	v^2	uv
15	7	49	10	−5	25	−35
12	4	16	25	10	100	40
8	0	0	17	2	4	0
8	0	0	11	−4	16	0
7	−1	1	13	−2	4	2
7	−1	1	17	2	4	−2
7	−1	1	20	5	25	−5
6	−2	4	13	−2	4	4
5	−3	9	9	−6	36	18
3	−5	25	15	0	0	0
Total	−2	106		0	218	22

(i) Since, Physics is taken as independent variable, so we consider regression line of y on x.

We know that,

$$b_{yx} = \frac{\Sigma uv - \frac{1}{n}\Sigma u \Sigma v}{\Sigma u^2 - \frac{1}{n}(\Sigma u)^2} = \frac{22 - \frac{1}{10} \times (-2) \times 0}{106 - \frac{1}{10}(-2)^2}$$

$$= \frac{220}{1060 - 4} = \frac{220}{1056} = \frac{5}{24}.$$

$$\therefore \quad \bar{x} = a + \frac{\Sigma u}{n} = 8 + \frac{(-2)}{10} = 8 - \frac{1}{5} = \frac{39}{5}$$

$$\text{and} \quad \bar{y} = b + \frac{\Sigma u}{n} = 15 + \frac{0}{10} = 15 + 0 = 15.$$

Also, the regression line of y on x is

$$y - \bar{y} = b_{yx}(x - \bar{x})$$

$$\Rightarrow \quad y - 15 = \frac{5}{24}\left(x - \frac{39}{5}\right)$$

$$\Rightarrow \quad y - 15 = \frac{5x}{24} - \frac{39}{24}$$

$$\Rightarrow \quad 24y - 360 = 5x - 39$$

$$\Rightarrow \quad 24y = 5x + 321$$

Hence, the required line of regression is

$$24y = 5x + 321$$

(ii) When a student scored 10 marks in Physics, i.e. when $x = 10$, the probable score in history in a letter test is given by

$$24y = 5 \times 10 + 321$$

$$\Rightarrow \quad 24y = 371$$

$$\Rightarrow \quad y = \frac{371}{24} = 15.49$$

$$= 15.5 \text{ (approx.)}$$

Hence, the required probable score is 15.5 marks.

Relation between Regression Coefficient and Correlation Coefficient

We know that, $$b_{yx} = \frac{n\,\Sigma xy - \Sigma x \,\Sigma y}{n\,\Sigma x^2 - (\Sigma x)^2} = \frac{\Sigma xy - \frac{1}{n}\Sigma x\,\Sigma y}{\Sigma x^2 - \frac{1}{n}(\Sigma x)^2}$$

$$= \frac{\text{Cov}(x, y)}{\text{Var}(x)} = \frac{\text{Cov}(x, y)}{\sigma_x^2}$$

where, σ_x is the standard deviation of x-variate.

$$\Rightarrow \quad b_{yx} = \frac{\text{Cov}(x, y)}{\sigma_x \cdot \sigma_y} \cdot \frac{\sigma_y}{\sigma_x}$$

$$\Rightarrow \quad b_{yx} = r \cdot \frac{\sigma_y}{\sigma_x} \quad \ldots\text{(i)}$$

where, r is the correlation coefficient.

$$\text{Similarly,} \quad b_{xy} = r \cdot \frac{\sigma_x}{\sigma_y} \quad \ldots\text{(ii)}$$

Now, from Eqs. (i) and (ii), we get

$$b_{yx} \cdot b_{xy} = r\frac{\sigma_y}{\sigma_x} \cdot r\frac{\sigma_x}{\sigma_y}$$

$$\Rightarrow \quad r^2 = b_{yx} \cdot b_{xy} \Rightarrow r \text{ or } \rho(x, y) = \sqrt{b_{yx} \cdot b_{xy}}$$

i.e. correlation coefficients is the geometric mean of regression coefficients.

Note (i) Both the regression coefficients must have same sign.

(ii) The correlation coefficients will have the same sign as that of regression coefficients, i.e. b_{yx} and b_{xy} have the same sign as that of r.

(iii) If $r = 0$, then the lines of regression are parallel to the coordinate axes and so perpendicular to each other.

Example 6 In a bivariate distribution, it was found $\sigma_x = 3$, the regression line of y on x is $8x - 10y + 66 = 0$ while regression line of x on y is $40x - 18y - 214 = 0$. Calculate $\bar{x}, \bar{y}, \rho(x, y)$, Cov (x, y) and σ_y.

Sol. We know that $(\bar{x}, \bar{y})$ is always passes through regression lines.

We have, $8x - 10y + 66 = 0$ ...(i)

$40x - 18y - 214 = 0$ ...(ii)

On solving Eqs. (i) and (ii), we get

$\therefore \quad \bar{x} = 13$ and $\bar{y} = 17$

Now, from Eq. (i), we get

$$y = \frac{8}{10}x + \frac{66}{10} = 0.8x + 6.6$$

$\therefore \quad b_{yx} =$ slope of this line $= 0.8$

From Eq. (ii), we get

$$x = \frac{18}{40}y + \frac{214}{40} = 0.45y + 7.85$$

$\therefore \quad b_{xy} =$ slope of this line $= 0.45$

$\therefore \quad r^2 = b_{xy} \cdot b_{yx} = (0.45)(0.8) = 0.36$

$\therefore \quad r = \rho(x, y) = \sqrt{0.36} = 0.6$

[$\because r$ has same sign as b_{yx}]

Now, $b_{yx} = \dfrac{\text{cov}(x, y)}{\sigma_x^2}$

$\therefore$ Cov $(x, y) = b_{yx} \cdot \sigma_x^2 = (0.8)(3)^2 = 7.2$

To calculate σ_y, we use $b_{xy} = \dfrac{\text{Cov}(x, y)}{\sigma_y^2}$

$$\Rightarrow \quad 0.45 = \frac{7.2}{\sigma_y^2} \Rightarrow \sigma_y^2 = \frac{7.2}{0.45} = 16 \Rightarrow \sigma_y = 4.$$

Example 7 By using the data $\bar{x} = 25, \bar{y} = 30$, $b_{yx} = 1.6$ and $b_{xy} = 0.4$, find

(i) the regression equation y on x.

(ii) what is the most likely value of y when $x = 60$?

(iii) what is the coefficient of correlation between x and y?

[ISC 2017]

Sol. We have, $\bar{x} = 25, \bar{y} = 30, b_{yx} = 1.6$ and $b_{xy} = 0.4$

(i) The regression equation y on x is

$$y - \bar{y} = b_{yx}(x - \bar{x})$$

$\Rightarrow \quad y - 30 = 1.6(x - 25) \quad \Rightarrow y = 1.6x - 40 + 30$

$\Rightarrow \quad y = 1.6x - 10$

(ii) When $x = 60$, then

$$y = 1.6 \times 60 - 10 = 96 - 10 = 86$$

(iii) Coefficient of correlation between x and y

$$= \sqrt{b_{xy} \times b_{yx}} = \sqrt{0.4 \times 1.6} = \sqrt{0.64} = 0.8$$

[$\because$ coefficient of correlation has the same sign as regression coefficients]

Example 8 You are given the following data

	x	y
Arithmetic mean	36	85
Standard deviation	11	8

Correlation coefficient between x and y is 0.66. Find

(i) the two regression coefficients

(ii) the two regression equations

(iii) the most likely value of y when $x = 10$.

Sol. From given table, we have

$$\bar{x} = 36, \bar{y} = 85, \sigma_x = 11, \sigma_y = 8, r = 0.66$$

(i) We know that

$$b_{yx} = r \cdot \frac{\sigma_y}{\sigma_x} = 0.66 \times \frac{8}{11} = 0.48,$$

$$b_{xy} = r \cdot \frac{\sigma_x}{\sigma_y} = 0.66 \times \frac{11}{8} = 0.9075$$

(ii) We know that,

Regression equation of y on x is

$$y - \bar{y} = b_{yx}(x - \bar{x})$$

$\therefore \quad y - 85 = 0.48(x - 36)$

$\Rightarrow \quad y = 0.48x + 67.72$

and also regression equation of x on y is

$$x - \bar{x} = b_{xy}(y - \bar{y})$$

$\therefore \quad x - 36 = 0.9075(y - 85)$

$\Rightarrow \quad x = 0.9075y - 41.41$

(iii) Putting $x = 10$ in $y = 0.48x + 67.72$, we get

$$y = 0.48 \times 10 + 67.72 = 72.52$$

Thus, when $x = 10$, the most likely value of y is 72.52.

Example 9 The following table shows the Mean, the Standard Deviation and the coefficient of correlation of two variables x and y.

Series	x	y
Mean	8	6
Standard deviation	12	4
Coefficient of correlation	0.6	

Calculate

(a) the regression coefficient b_{xy} and b_{yx}

(b) the probable value of y when $x = 20$

[ISC 2023]

Sol. (a) Given, $\bar{x} = 8, \bar{y} = 6, \sigma_x = 12, \sigma_y = 4$ and $r = 0.6$

$$\therefore \quad b_{xy} = r \cdot \frac{\sigma_y}{\sigma_x} = 0.6 \times \frac{4}{12} = 0.2$$

$$\therefore \quad b_{yx} = r \cdot \frac{\sigma_x}{\sigma_y} = 0.6 \times \frac{12}{4} = 1.8$$

(b) Regression equation of y on x is

$$y - \bar{y} = b_{yx}(x - \bar{x})$$

$$y - 6 = 1.8(x - 8)$$

$$\Rightarrow \quad y = 1.8x - 14.4 + 6 \Rightarrow y = 1.8x - 8.4$$

Putting $x = 20$, we get

$$y = 1.8(20) - 8.4 = 36 - 8.4 = 27.6$$

Example 10 Find the regression coefficients b_{yx}, b_{xy} and correlation coefficient 'r' for the following data (2, 8), (6, 8), (4, 5), (7, 6), (5, 2). **[ISC 2020]**

Sol. Given data (2, 8), (6, 8), (4, 5), (7, 6) (5, 2)

We construct the following table

	x	y	x^2	y^2	xy
	2	8	4	64	16
	6	8	36	64	48
	4	5	16	25	20
	7	6	49	36	42
	5	2	25	4	10
Total	24	29	130	193	136

$$b_{yx} = \frac{\Sigma xy - \frac{1}{n}\Sigma x \Sigma y}{\Sigma x^2 - \frac{1}{n}(\Sigma x)^2} = \frac{136 - \frac{1}{5} \times 24 \times 29}{130 - \frac{1}{5}(24)^2}$$

$$= \frac{136 - 139.2}{130 - 115.2} = \frac{-3.2}{14.8} = \frac{-8}{37}$$

$$b_{yx} = \frac{\Sigma xy - \frac{1}{n}\Sigma x \; \Sigma y}{\Sigma y^2 - \frac{1}{n}(\Sigma y)^2}$$

$$= \frac{136 - \frac{1}{5}(24)(29)}{193 - \frac{1}{5}(29)^2} = \frac{136 - 139.2}{193 - 168.2}$$

$$= \frac{-3.2}{24.8} = \frac{-4}{31}$$

$$r = \sqrt{b_{yx} \times b_{xy}} = \sqrt{-\frac{8}{37} \times \frac{-4}{31}}$$

$$= \sqrt{\frac{32}{1147}} = 0.167$$

Example 11 From the following data find the coefficient of correlation and obtain the two regression equations.

x	1	2	3	4	5	6	7	8	9
y	9	8	10	12	11	13	14	16	15

Sol. We construct follow table as

x	$d_x = x - \bar{x}$ $(\bar{x} = 5)$	d_x^2	y	$d_y = y - \bar{y}$ $(\bar{y} = 12)$	d_y^2	$d_x \cdot d_y$
1	−4	16	9	−3	9	12
2	−3	9	8	−4	16	12
3	−2	4	10	−2	4	4
4	−1	1	12	0	0	0
5	0	0	11	−1	1	0
6	1	1	13	1	1	1
7	2	4	14	2	4	4
8	3	9	16	4	16	12
9	4	16	15	3	9	12
$\Sigma x = 45$		$\Sigma d_x^2 = 60$	$\Sigma y = 108$		$\Sigma d_y^2 = 60$	$\Sigma(d_x \cdot d_y) = 57$

Here, mean $\bar{x} = \frac{\Sigma x}{n} = \frac{45}{9} = 5$ and $\bar{y} = \frac{\Sigma y}{n} = \frac{108}{9} = 12$

Now, regression coefficients $b_{yx} = \frac{\Sigma(d_x \cdot d_y)}{\Sigma d_x^2} = \frac{57}{60} = 0.95$

and $b_{xy} = \frac{\Sigma d_x \cdot d_y}{\Sigma d_y^2} = \frac{57}{60} = 0.95$

Regression equation of y on x is $y - \bar{y} = b_{yx}(x - \bar{x})$

$$\Rightarrow \quad y - 12 = 0.95(x - 5)$$

$$\Rightarrow \quad y - 12 = 0.95x - 4.75$$

$$\Rightarrow \quad y = 0.95x - 4.75 + 12$$

$$\Rightarrow \quad y = 0.95x + 7.25$$

And also regression equation of x on y is

$$x - \bar{x} = b_{xy}(y - \bar{y})$$

$$\Rightarrow \quad x - 5 = 0.95(y - 12)$$

$$\Rightarrow \quad x - 5 = 0.95x - 11.4$$

$$\Rightarrow \quad x = 0.95x - 6.4$$

$\therefore$ Coefficient of correlation $= \sqrt{b_{yx} \times b_{xy}}$

$$= \sqrt{0.95 \times 0.95} = 0.95$$

Example 12 If the regression equation of x on y is given by $mx - y + 10 = 0$ and the equation of y on x is given by $-2x + 5y = 14$, determine the value of 'm' if the coefficient of correlation between x and y is $1/\sqrt{10}$. **[ISC 2010]**

Sol. Given regression equation of x on y is

$$mx - y + 10 = 0 \quad \text{...(i)}$$

and regression equation of y on x is

$$-2x + 5y = 14 \quad \text{...(ii)}$$

Also, given $r(x, y) = \frac{1}{\sqrt{10}}$

Now, Eq. (i) can be rewritten as

$$x = \frac{1}{m}(y - 10)$$

$\therefore$ Regression coefficient of x on y is

$$b_{xy} = \frac{1}{m}$$

Now, Eq. (ii) can be rewritten as

$$y = \frac{2}{5}x + \frac{14}{5}$$

$\therefore$ Regression coefficient of y on x is $b_{yx} = \frac{2}{5}$

$\because \quad r^2 = b_{yx} \times b_{yx}$

$$\therefore \quad \left(\frac{1}{\sqrt{10}}\right)^2 = \frac{1}{m} \times \frac{2}{5} \Rightarrow \frac{1}{10} = \frac{2}{5m} \Rightarrow m = \frac{20}{5} = 4$$

Example 13 The following results were obtained with respect to two variables x and y.

$$\Sigma x = 30, \Sigma y = 42, \Sigma xy = 199,$$
$$\Sigma x^2 = 184, \Sigma y^2 = 318 \text{ and } n = 6$$

Find the following.

(i) The regression coefficients
(ii) Correlation coefficient between x and y
(iii) Regression equation of y on x
(iv) The likely value of y when $x = 10$ **[ISC 2012]**

Sol. (i) We have, $\Sigma x = 30, \ \Sigma y = 42, \Sigma xy = 199,$

$$\Sigma x^2 = 184, \ \Sigma y^2 = 318 \text{ and } n = 6$$

$\therefore$ Regression coefficient of x on y is

$$b_{xy} = \frac{\Sigma xy - \frac{\Sigma x \cdot \Sigma y}{n}}{\Sigma y^2 - \frac{(\Sigma y)^2}{n}} = \frac{199 - \frac{30 \times 42}{6}}{318 - \frac{42 \times 42}{6}}$$

$$= \frac{199 - 210}{318 - 294} = -\frac{11}{24} = -0.458$$

and regression coefficient of y on x is

$$b_{yx} = \frac{\Sigma xy - \frac{\Sigma x \ \Sigma y}{n}}{\Sigma x^2 - \frac{(\Sigma x)^2}{n}} = \frac{199 - 210}{184 - \frac{900}{6}}$$

$$= \frac{199 - 210}{184 - 150} = \frac{-11}{34} = -0.324$$

(ii) Since, b_{yx} and b_{xy} both are negative, so r also be negative.

$$\therefore \quad r = -\sqrt{b_{yx} \times b_{xy}} = -\sqrt{-\frac{11}{24} \times \frac{(-11)}{34}}$$

$$= -\frac{11}{\sqrt{24 \times 34}} = -\frac{11}{\sqrt{816}} = -\frac{11}{28.6} = -0.38$$

(iii) Regression equation of y on x is $y - \bar{y} = b_{yx}(x - \bar{x})$.

Now, mean, $\bar{x} = \frac{\Sigma x}{n} = \frac{30}{6} = 5, \ \bar{y} = \frac{\Sigma y}{n} = \frac{42}{6} = 7$

Also, $\quad b_{yx} = -\frac{11}{34}$

Regression equation of y on x is

$$y - 7 = -\frac{11}{34}(x - 5)$$

$$\Rightarrow \quad 34y - 238 = -11x + 55$$

$$\Rightarrow \quad 11x + 34y - 293 = 0 \quad \text{...(i)}$$

(iv) When $x = 10$

Then, from Eq. (i), $11 \times 10 + 34y - 293 = 0$

$$\Rightarrow \quad 34y = 293 - 110$$

$$\Rightarrow \quad 34y = 183$$

$$\Rightarrow \quad y = \frac{183}{34} = 5.382$$

Hence, the likely value of y, when $x = 10$ is 5.382.

Example 14 For the bivariate data, you are given the following information.

$\Sigma (x - 28) = 77, \ \Sigma (x - 28)^2 = 1363, \ \Sigma (y - 33) = 46,$
$\Sigma (y - 33)^2 = 552, \ \Sigma (x - 28)(y - 33) = 579$ and $n = 10$

Find

(i) the regression coefficient b_{xy} and b_{yx}.
(ii) the two lines of regressions.
(iii) the coefficient of correlation between x and y.

Sol. Let $u = x - 28$ and $v = y - 33$.

Here, x is deviated from 28, i.e. $a = 28$

and also y is deviated from 33, i.e. $b = 33$.

$$\therefore \quad \Sigma u = 77, \Sigma v = 46, \Sigma u^2 = 1363, \Sigma v^2 = 552$$

$$\Sigma uv = 579 \text{ and } n = 10.$$

$\therefore$ Mean of $x = \bar{x} = a + \frac{\Sigma u}{n} = 28 + \frac{77}{10}$

$$= 28 + 7.7 = 35.7$$

and mean of $y = \bar{y} = b + \frac{\Sigma v}{n} = 33 + \frac{46}{10}$

$$= 33 + 4.6 = 37.6$$

(i) We know that, regression coefficient

$$b_{xy} = \frac{\Sigma uv - \frac{\Sigma u \cdot \Sigma v}{n}}{\Sigma v^2 - \frac{(\Sigma v)^2}{n}} = \frac{579 - \frac{77 \times 46}{10}}{552 - \frac{46 \times 46}{10}}$$

$$= \frac{5790 - 3542}{5520 - 2116} = \frac{2248}{3404} = 0.66$$

and $\quad b_{yx} = \frac{\Sigma uv - \frac{\Sigma u \cdot \Sigma v}{n}}{\Sigma u^2 - \frac{(\Sigma u)^2}{n}} = \frac{579 - \frac{77 \times 46}{10}}{1363 - \frac{77 \times 77}{10}}$

$$= \frac{5790 - 3542}{13630 - 5929} = \frac{2248}{7701} = 0.29$$

(ii) Regression equation of y on x is $y - \bar{y} = b_{yx}(x - \bar{x})$

$\Rightarrow \quad y - 37.6 = 0.29(x - 35.7)$

$\Rightarrow \quad y = 0.29x - 10.35 + 37.6$

$\Rightarrow \quad y = 0.29x + 27.25$

$\therefore$ Regression equation of x on y is $x - \bar{x} = b_{xy}(y - \bar{y})$

$\Rightarrow \quad x - 35.7 = 0.66(y - 37.6)$

$\Rightarrow \quad x = 0.66y - 24.82 + 35.7$

$\Rightarrow \quad x = 0.6y + 10.88$

(iii) Since both b_{xy} and b_{yx} are positive, therefore correlation coefficient (r) also be positive.

$\therefore \quad r = \sqrt{b_{xy} \times b_{yx}} = \sqrt{0.66 \times 0.29} = \sqrt{0.1914} = 0.44$

Properties of Regression Coefficients and Regression Lines

(i) $b_{yx} \cdot b_{xy} = r^2$, where $0 \le r^2 \le 1$ and $0 \le b_{yx} \cdot b_{xy} \le 1$.

(ii) Both the regression coefficients cannot be greater than unity.

(iii) Arithmetic mean of two regression coefficients is either equal to or greater than the **correlation coefficient.**

i.e. $\dfrac{b_{yx} + b_{xy}}{2} \ge r$

(iv) The two regression lines coincide if and only if there is perfect linear relation between x and y.

i.e. $\rho(x, y) = r = \pm 1$

Identification of Regression Equations

Suppose two equations $a_1x + b_1y + c_1 = 0$ and $a_2x + b_2y + c_2 = 0$ are given and we have to identify the regression line of y on x or x on y, we use the following steps

***Step* I** First, we consider any one of the equations say first, i.e., $a_1x + b_1y + c_1 = 0$ as y on x and other equation say second, i.e. $a_2x + b_2y + c_2 = 0$ as x on y.

***Step* II** Adjust the first equation y on x such that y should be on left side with coefficient 1 and rest of the terms be on right side $\left(\text{i.e. } y = -\dfrac{a_1}{b_1}x - \dfrac{c_1}{b_1}\right)$. The coefficient of x will considered as regression coefficient y on x, i.e. $b_{yx} = \dfrac{-a_1}{b_1}$. Similarly, for another equation x on y, adjust the equation as $x = -\dfrac{b_2}{a_2}y - \dfrac{c_2}{a_2}$. The coefficient of y will give regression coefficient of x on y, i.e. $b_{xy} = \dfrac{-b_2}{a_2}$.

***Step* III** If b_{xy} and b_{yx} are not of same sign, then we can not determine the regression line. If they have the same sign, then determine correlation coefficient by using the formula.

$$r^2 = b_{yx} \times b_{xy},\ 0 \le b_{yx} \times b_{xy} \le 1$$

***Step* IV** $r^2 \in [0, 1]$, then our consideration is true, otherwise we have to change the considering equations.

Example 15 If the regression coefficient of y on x is 2.4 and that of x on y is 0.6. To check the statement is true or false and also give the reason.

Sol. We have, $b_{yx} = 2.4$ and $b_{xy} = 0.6$

Now, $\quad r^2 = b_{yx} \times b_{xy} = 2.4 \times 0.6 = 1.44 > 1$

Since, r^2 must be ≤ 1.

Therefore, the given statement is false.

Example 16 Out of the two regression lines $x + 2y - 5 = 0$ and $2x + 3y = 8$, find the line of regression of y on x. **[ISC 2023]**

Sol. Assuming $x + 2y - 5 = 0$ to be regression line of y on x

$$2y = -x + 5 \Rightarrow y = -\frac{1}{2}x + \frac{5}{2}$$

$\Rightarrow \quad b_{yx} = -\dfrac{1}{2}$

Then, $2x + 3y = 8$ is regression line of x on y.

$\therefore \quad 2x = -3y + 8 \Rightarrow x = \dfrac{-3}{2}y + \dfrac{8}{2}$

$\Rightarrow \quad b_{xy} = \dfrac{-3}{2}$

Now, $b_{yx} \cdot b_{xy} = \left(-\dfrac{1}{2}\right)\left(\dfrac{-3}{2}\right) = \dfrac{3}{4} < 1$

$\therefore$ Regression line of y on x is $x + 2y - 5 = 0$.

Example 17 If the two regression lines of a bivariate distribution are $4x - 5y + 33 = 0$ and $20x - 9y - 107 = 0$,

(i) calculate $\bar{x}$ and $\bar{y}$, the arithmetic means of x and y, respectively.

(ii) estimate the value of x, when $y = 7$. **[ISC 2009]**

(iii) find the variance of y when $\sigma_x = 3$.

Sol. (i) Given two regression lines are

$$4x - 5y = -33 \quad \text{...(i)}$$

and $$20x - 9y = 107 \quad \text{...(ii)}$$

On multiplying Eq. (i) by 20 and Eq. (ii) by 4 and then subtracting Eq. (ii) from Eq. (i),we get

$$80x - 100y = -660$$
$$80x - 36y = 428$$
$$\underline{- \quad + \quad -}$$
$$-64y = -1088$$

$\Rightarrow$ $y = 17$

Put $y = 17$ in Eq. (i), we get

$$4x - 5 \times 17 = -33$$

$\Rightarrow$ $4x = -33 + 85$

$\Rightarrow$ $x = \frac{52}{4} = 13$

We know that two lines of regression intersect each other at mean of x and y.

$\therefore$ $\bar{x} = 13$ and $\bar{y} = 17$

Let us consider the equation y on x is

$$4x - 5y + 33 = 0$$

$\Rightarrow$ $5y = 4x + 33$

$\Rightarrow$ $y = \frac{4}{5}x + \frac{33}{5} \quad \text{...(iii)}$

$\therefore$ Regression coefficient of y on x is

$$b_{yx} = \frac{4}{5}$$

and consider x on y is

$$20x - 9y = 107$$

$\Rightarrow$ $20x = 9y + 107$

$\Rightarrow$ $x = \frac{9}{20}y + \frac{107}{20} \quad \text{...(iv)}$

$\therefore$ Regression coefficient of x on y is

$$b_{xy} = \frac{9}{20}$$

Now, to check whether the consideration is true or false.

Here, $r^2 = b_{yx} \times b_{xy}$

$$= \frac{4}{5} \times \frac{9}{20} = \frac{9}{25} \in [0, 1]$$

Hence, our consideration is true.

(ii) To estimate the value of x, put $y = 7$ in Eq. (iv), we get

$$x = \frac{9}{20} \times (7) + \frac{107}{20}$$
$$= 3.15 + 5.35$$
$$= 8.5$$

(iii) Since, $b_{yx} = r\frac{\sigma_y}{\sigma_x}$

$\therefore$ $\frac{4}{5} = \frac{3}{5} \cdot \frac{\sigma y}{3}$ $\quad [\sigma_x = 3]$

$\Rightarrow$ $\sigma_y = 4$

Hence, the variance of y is 16.

Chapter Practice

Multiple Choice Type Questions

(1 Mark)

1 For a bivariate data set on (x, y), if the means, standard deviations and correlation coefficient are $\bar{x} = 1.0$, $\bar{y} = 2.0$, $\sigma_x = 3.0$, $\sigma_y = 9.0$, $r = 0.8$. Then, the regression line of y on x is

(a) $y = 1 + 2.4(x - 1)$ (b) $y = 2 + 0.27(x - 1)$
(c) $y = 2 + 2.4(x - 1)$ (d) $y = 1 + 0.27(x - 2)$

2 If the correlation coefficient of two sets of variables (X, Y) is $\frac{-3}{4}$, which one of the following statements is true for the same set of variables? **[ISC 2024]**

(a) Only one of the two regression lines has a negative coefficient.
(b) Both regression coefficients are positive.
(c) Both regression coefficients are negative.
(d) One of the lines of regression is parallel to the X-axis.

3 If the two regression coefficients are 0.8 and 0.2, then the value of coefficients of correlation r will be **[ISC 2023]**

(a) ± 0.4 (b) ± 0.16
(c) 0.4 (d) 0.16

4 Which of the following is incorrect?

(a) $b_{yx} \cdot b_{xy} = r^2$, where $0 \le r^2 \le 1$ and $0 \le b_{yx} \cdot b_{xy} \le 1$.
(b) The regression coefficients can be greater than unity.
(c) Arithmetic mean of two regression coefficients is either equal to or greater than the correlation coefficient.
(d) The two regression lines coincide if an only if there is perfect linear r.

Assertion-Reason Type Questions

(1 Mark)

Directions (Q. Nos. 5-8) *In the questions given below are two statements labelled as Assertion (A) and Reason (R). In the context of the two statements, which one of the following is correct?*

(a) Both A and R are correct; R is the correct explanation of A
(b) Both A and R are correct; R is not the correct explanation of A
(c) A is correct; R is incorrect
(d) R is correct; A is incorrect

5 **Assertion** (A) We cannot find out the regression of x on y from that of y on x.

Reason (R) In one equation x is dependent variable and y is independent where in other equation y is dependent variable and x is independent.

6 **Assertion** (A) Two regression lines are represented by $x + 2y + 5 = 0$ and $4x + y - 5 = 0$. Then, the line of regression y on x is $x + 2y + 5 = 0$.

Reason (R) $b_{yx} \cdot b_{xy} = r^2$, where $0 \le r^2 \le 1$ and $0 \le b_{yx} \cdot b_{xy} \le 1$.

7 **Assertion** (A) If the regression coefficient of y on x is 2.5 and that of x on y is 0.5.

Reason (R) The regression coefficients cannot be greater than unity.

8 **Assertion** (A) Correlation coefficient is the geometric mean of regression coefficients.

Reason (R) Arithmetic mean of two regression coefficients is either equal to or greater than the correlation coefficient.

Very Short Answer Type Questions

(2 Marks)

9 Compute b_{yx} for the following data.

$$\{(x, y) : (5, 2), (7, 4), (8, 3), (4, 2), (6, 4)\}$$

10 If the two coefficients of regression are -0.6 and -1.4, then find the coefficient of correlation.

11 If $r = 0$, then show that the two lines of regression are parallel to the axes.

12 Find the regression coefficients b_{yx} and b_{xy} of y on x and x on y respectively, if standard

deviations of x and y are 4 and 3 respectively and coefficients of correlation between x and y is 0.8.

13 From the following data, calculate
(i) correlation coefficient.
(ii) standard deviation of $Y(\sigma_y)$
$$x = 0.85y,\ y = 0.89x,\ \sigma_x = 3.$$

14 Two regression lines are represented by $4x + 10y = 9$ and $6x + 3y = 4$. Find the line of regression of y on x. **[ISC 2013]**

15 Is the following statement true? Give reasons.
$40x - 18y = 5$ and $8x - 10y + 6 = 0$ are respectively the regression equations of y on x and x on y.

16 Find the coefficient of correlation from the regression lines $x - 2y + 3 = 0$ and $4x - 5y + 1 = 0$. **[ISC 2018]**

17 Given two lines of regression $x + 3y = 11$, $2x + y = 7$, find the coefficient of correlation between x and y.

18 The two lines of regressions are $4x + 2y - 3 = 0$ and $3x + 6y + 5 = 0$. Find the correlation coefficient between x and y. **[ISC 2015]**

Short Answer Type Questions

4 Marks

19 Find the equations of two lines of regression for the data

x	1	2	3	4	5
y	7	6	5	4	3

and hence find an estimate of y for $x = 3.5$ from the appropriate line of regression.

20 Show that if five students get respectively 1, 2, 3, 4, 5 marks (X) out of 10 in subject A, and 3, 3, 5, 7, 6 marks (Y) out of 10 in subject B, the regression equation of y on x can be written as $y = 1.8 + x$.

21 If x and y are a pair of correlated variables. Ten observations of their values (x_i, y_i) have the following results.
$$\Sigma x_i = 55,\ \Sigma y_i = 55,\ \Sigma x_i y_i = 350,\ \Sigma x_i^2 = 385$$
Predict the value of y when the value of x is 6.

22 For the bivariate data, you are given the following information $\Sigma(x - 89) = 0$, $\Sigma(x - 89)^2 = 5770$, $\Sigma(y - 71) = 0$, $\Sigma(y - 71)^2 = 2958$, $\Sigma(x - 89)(y - 71) = 3470$ and $n = 10$. Find
(i) the regression coefficient b_{xy} and b_{yx}.
(ii) the two lines of regressions.

23 The correlation coefficient between x and y is 0.60. If the variance of x is 2.25, the variance of y is 4.00, mean of x is 10 and mean of y is 20, find the equation of the regression lines of
(i) y on x. (ii) x on y.

24 If $\bar{x} = 18$, $\bar{y} = 100$, $\sigma_x = 14$, $\sigma_y = 20$ and $r(X, Y) = 0.8$, Find the regression lines. Estimate the value of y, when $x = 70$ and that of x, when $y = 90$.

25 The two lines of regressions are $x + 2y - 5 = 0$ and $2x + 3y - 8 = 0$ and the variance of x is 12. Find the variance of y and the coefficient of correlation. **[ISC 2016]**

26 For the given lines of regression, $3x - 2y = 5$ and $x - 4y = 7$, find
(i) regression coefficients b_{yx} and b_{xy}.
(ii) coefficient of correlation $r(x, y)$. **[ISC 2014]**

27 *XYZ* company plans to advertise some vacancies. The Manager is asked to suggest the monthly salary for these vacancies based on the years of experience. To do so, the Manager studies the years of service and the monthly salary drawn by the existing employees in the company. **[ISC 2024]**

Following is the data that the Manager refers to

Years of service (X)	11	7	9	5	8	6	10
Monthly salary (in ₹ 1000) (Y)	10	8	6	5	9	7	11

(a) Find the regression equation of monthly salary on the years of service.
(b) If a person with 13 years of experience applies for a job in this company, what monthly salary will be suggested by the Manager?

28 The line of regression of marks in Statistics (X) and marks in Accountancy (Y) for a class of 50 students is $3y - 5x + 180 = 0$. The average score in Accountancy is 44 and the variance of marks in Statistics is $\left(\frac{9}{16}\right)$th of variance of marks in Accountancy. **[ISC 2024]**
(a) Find the average score in Statistics
(b) Find the coefficient of correlation between marks in Statistics and marks in Accountancy.

Long Answer Type Questions

6 Marks

29 Given the observations (10, –5), (10, –3), (11, –2), (11, 0), (12, 1), (15, 6), (16, 4), (11, –2), predict the value of Y corresponding to the value 14 of X and predict the value of X when the value of Y is 3.

30 Find the equations of the two lines of regression for the following observations

(3, 6), (4, 5), (5, 4), (6, 3), (7, 2).

Find an estimate of y for $x = 2.5$. [ISC 2010]

31 Fit a least square line to the data in the following table using.

(i) x as the independent variable.

(ii) y as the independent variable.

Find y when $x = 5$ and also find x when $y = 7$.

x	3	5	6	8	9	11
y	2	3	4	6	5	8

32 The marks obtained by 10 candidates in English and Mathematics are given below.

Marks in English	20	13	18	21	11	12	17	14	19	15
Marks in Mathematics	17	12	23	25	14	8	19	21	22	19

Estimate the probable score for Mathematics, if the marks obtained in English are 24. [ISC 2016]

33 Find two regression equation from the following data.

x	38	48	43	40	41
y	31	38	43	33	35

34 Using the following data, determine the estimated value of x, when $y = 22$ with the help of suitable regression line.

x	4	5	8	9	11	12	14
y	16	10	8	7	6	5	4

35 The coefficient of correlation between the values denoted by X and Y is 0.5. The mean of X is 3 and that of Y is 5. Their standard deviations are 5 and 4 respectively. Find

(i) the two lines of regression.

(ii) the expected value of Y, when X is given 14.

(iii) the expected value of X, when X is given 9.

[ISC 2014]

Answers

1. (c) **2.** (c) **3.** (a) **4.** (b)

5. (a) **6.** (a) **7.** (d) **8.** (b)

9. 0.4 **10.** – 0.916 **12.** 0.6, 1.07 **13.** (i) 0.869 (ii) 3.067

14. $4x + 10y = 9$ **15.** The statement is false, because $b_{yx} \cdot b_{xy} > 1$. **16.** 0.790

17. – 0.408 **18.** $\frac{-1}{2}$ **19.** $x + y = 8$, $x + y = 8$; 4.5

21. 5.79 **22.** (i) 1.17 (ii) 0.60 **23.** (i) $y = 0.8x + 12$ (ii) $x = 0.45y + 1$

24. $y = 1.143x + 79.43$, $x = 0.56y - 38$, when $x = 70$, $y = 159.44$ and when $y = 90$, $x = 12.4$

25. 4, $\frac{-\sqrt{3}}{2}$ **26.** (i) $b_{yx} = \frac{1}{4}$, $b_{xy} = \frac{2}{3}$ (ii) $\frac{1}{\sqrt{6}}$ **27.** (a) $\hat{y} = 0.75x + 2$ (b) ₹ 11750 **28.** (a) 62.4, (b) 0.8

29. 2.875 and 13.778 **30.** 6.5 **31.** $x = 5$, $y = 3.22$ and $x = 10.03$, $y = 7$

32. 27.12 **33.** $x = 0.52y + 23.18$, $y = 0.79x + 2.69$ **34.** $98x = 1530 - 81y$, $-\frac{18}{7}$

35. (i) $Y = 0.4x + 3.8$, $X = 0.625y - 0.125$ (ii) 9.4 (iii) 5.5

CHAPTER

18

Linear Programming

The term 'Programming' means 'Planning' and it refers to a particular plan of action from amongst several alternatives for maximising or minimising a function under given restrictions, such as maximising profit or minimising cost, etc. The term 'linear' means that all the mathematical relations used in the problem are linear. Thus, linear programming is a technique for resource utilisation, that indicates how the available resources can be used in the best effective way to achieve the desired objective.

TOPIC 01 Linear Programming Problem and Its Graphical Solution

Linear Inequalities

An inequality or inequation is said to be linear, if each variable occurs in first degree only and there is no term involving the product of the variables.

e.g. $ax + b \leq 0$, $ax + by + c > 0$, $ax \leq 4$, etc.

(i) **Linear Inequality in One Variable** A linear inequality or inequation, which has only one variable, is called linear inequality or inequation in one variable. e.g. $ax + b < 0$, where $a \neq 0$.

(ii) **Linear Inequality in Two Variables** A linear inequality, which have only two variables, is called linear inequality in two variables. e.g. $3x + 11y \leq 0, 4t + 3s > 0$.

Solution of a Linear Inequality in Two Variables by Graphical Method

Suppose, given linear inequality is $ax + by \leq c$ or $ax + by \geq c$ or $ax + by < c$ or $ax + by > c$, then to find its solution by graphical method, we use the following steps

I. Consider the equation $ax + by = c$ in place of given inequality, which represents a straight line in XY-plane.

II. Put $x = 0$ in the equation obtained in step I to get the point, where the line meets Y-axis. Similarly, put $y = 0$ to obtain a point, where the line meets X-axis.

III. If the inequality is of the form $<$ or $>$, then draw dotted line joining the points obtained in step II, to indicate that the points on the line are excluded from the solution set. Otherwise, mark it by thick or dark line to indicate that the points on this line are included in the solution set.

IV. Take any point {preferable origin, i.e. (0, 0)} not lying on the line and check whether this satisfies the given linear inequality or not.

V. If the inequality is satisfied, then shade that portion of the plane, which contains the chosen point. Otherwise, shade that portion, which does not contain the chosen point.

Thus, shaded region obtained in Step V, represents the required solution set.

Note (i) If it is not possible to find the intersection points of line with axes, then to draw the line find any two points on it.

(ii) The solution region of a system of linear inequalities is the region which satisfies all the given inequalities in the system simultaneously.

Example 1 Solve the inequality $y + 8 \geq 2x$ by graphical method.

Sol. Given inequality is $y + 8 \geq 2x$.

In equation form, it can be written as $y + 8 = 2x$

Table for line $y + 8 = 2x$ is

x	0	4
y	−8	0

Clearly, the points of intersection with X and Y-axes are $A(4, 0)$ and $B(0, -8)$, respectively.

On plotting $A(4, 0)$ and $B(0, -8)$ on graph paper and then joining them by a dark line, we get the line AB.

[∵ given inequality has sign '≥', so we join then by a draw dark line].

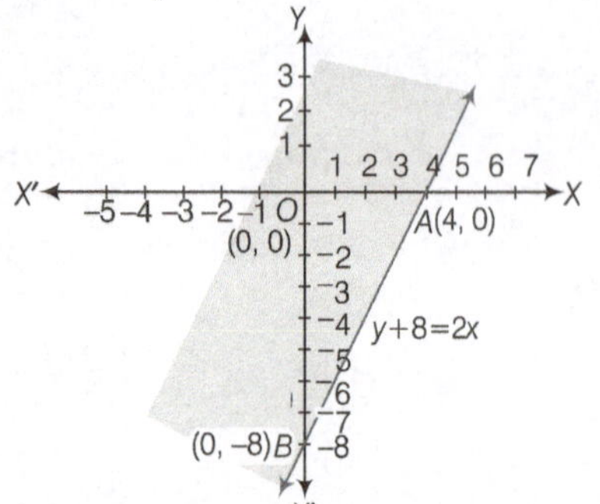

Now, putting $x = y = 0$ in $y + 8 \geq 2x$, we get

$0 + 8 \geq 2(0) \Rightarrow 8 \geq 0$, which is true.

So, shade the region containing (0, 0), i.e. the region above the line AB.

Hence, the shaded region containing origin, is the required solution set.

Linear Programming Problem (LPP)

A linear programming problem is one which is concerned with finding the optimal value (maximum or minimum value) of a linear function of several variables, subject to the constraints that the variables are non-negative and satisfy a set of linear inequalities.

Mathematical Form of LPP

The general mathematical form of a linear programming problem may be written as follows

Maximise or Minimise, $Z = c_1x + c_2y$, subject to constraints are $a_1x + b_1y \leq d_1$, $a_2x + b_2y \leq d_2$, etc., and non-negative restrictions are $x \geq 0$, $y \geq 0$.

Some Important Terms Related to LPP

There are various terms related to a linear programming problem, which are define as below

(i) **Constraints** The linear inequations or inequalities or restrictions on the variables of a linear programming problem, are called constraints. The conditions $x \geq 0$, $y \geq 0$ are called **non-negative restrictions.**

(ii) **Optimisation Problem** A problem which seeks to maximise or minimise a linear function subject to certain constraints, determined by a set of linear inequalities, is called an optimisation problem. Linear programming problems are special type of optimisation problems.

(iii) **Objective Function** A linear function of two or more variables which has to be maximised or minimised under the given restrictions is called an objective function. The variables used in the objective function are called **decision variables.**

(iv) **Optimal Value** The maximum or minimum value of an objective function is known as the optimal value of LPP.

(v) **Feasible and Infeasible Region** The common region determined by all the constraints including non-negative constraints $x, y \geq 0$ of a linear programming problem is called the feasible region or solution region. Each point in this region represents a feasible choice. The region other than feasible region is called an infeasible region.

(vi) **Bounded and Unbounded Region** A feasible region of a system of linear inequalities is said to be bounded, if it can be enclosed within a circle. Otherwise, it is said to be unbounded region, i.e. the feasible region does extend infinitely in any direction.

(vii) **Feasible and Infeasible Solution** Points within and on the boundary of the feasible region, represents feasible solution of the constraints. Any point outside the feasible region is called an infeasible solution.

(viii) **Optimal Feasible Solution** A feasible solution at which the objective function has optimal value (maximum or minimum), is called the optimal solution or optimal feasible solution of the linear programming problem.

(ix) **Optimisation Technique** The process of obtaining the optimal solution of the linear programming problem is called optimisation technique.

Advantages of Linear Programming

(i) Linear programming helps in attaining the optimum use of productive resources.

(ii) It is used in almost all areas of human life, for e.g. determining the shortest routes for travelling, finding the best investment plane, choosing the best crop etc. So that the profit is maximum or cost is minimum.

(iii) It improves the quality of decision.

(iv) Its not only consider internal factors like machine, budget, manpower, storage etc., but also external factors like market demand, purchasing power of the customer etc.

Limitations of Linear Programming

(i) A primary requirement of linear programming is that the objective function and every constraint must be linear. But in real life situations, several business and industrial problems are non-linear in nature.

(ii) It deals with optimising a single objective only.

(iii) Factors such as uncertainty, weather conditions etc. are not taken into consideration.

Some Important Theorems

We know that every point in the feasible region will satisfy all the constraints given in the LPP and non-negative restrictions. Also, a feasible region contains infinitely many points. So, it is not easy to find a point that gives a maximum or minimum value of objective function. To handle this situation, we use the following theorems:

Theorem 1 Let R be the feasible region (convex polygon) for a linear programming problem and $Z = ax + by$ be the objective function. When Z has an optimal value (maximum or minimum), where the variables x and y are subject to constraints described by linear inequalities, this optimal value must occur at a corner point (vertex) of the feasible region. (A corner point of a feasible region is a point of intersection of two boundary lines in the region)

Theorem 2 Let R be the feasible region for a linear programming problem and $Z = ax + by$ be the objective function. If R is bounded, then the objective function Z has both a maximum and minimum value on R and each of these occurs at a corner point (vertex) of R.

Note (i) If R is unbounded, then a maximum or minimum value of the objective function may not exist. However, if it exists, it must occur at a corner point of R.

(ii) A polygon is said to be convex polygon, if the line joining any two of its points lies completely in the region. Figures (i) and (ii) are convex polygon but Figure (iii) is not a convex polygon.

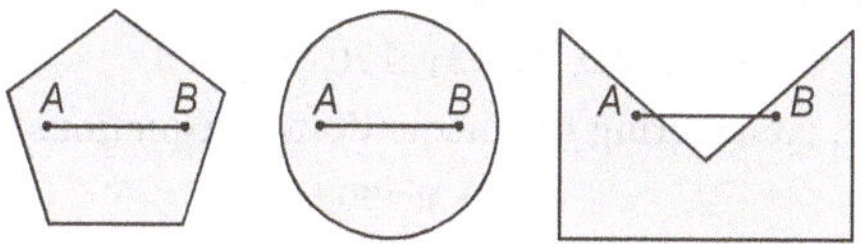

(i) (ii) (iii)

Graphical Method for Solving Linear Programming Problem (LPP)

The graphical method is suitable for solving linear programming problems containing two variables only. This method of solving linear programming problem is referred as corner point method.

The process of this method is as follows

1. Find the feasible region of the LPP and determine its corner points (vertices) either by inspection or by solving the two equations of the lines intersecting at that point.
2. Find the value of objective function $Z = ax + by$ at each corner point. Let M and m respectively, denote the largest and the smallest values at these points.
   (i) When the feasible region is **bounded**, then M and m are the maximum and minimum values of Z.

(ii) When the feasible region is **unbounded**, then

(a) M is the maximum value of Z, if the open half plane determined by $ax + by > M$ has no point in common with the feasible region. Otherwise, Z has no maximum value.

(b) m is the minimum value of Z, if the open half plane determined by $ax + by < m$ has no point in common with the feasible region. Otherwise, Z has no minimum value.

Note (i) A half plane (if a line divides XY-plane into two parts, then each part is known as half plane) in XY-plane is called an open half plane, if the line separating the plane is not included in the half plane.

(ii) It two corner points of the feasible region are both optimal solution of the same type, i.e. both produce the same maximum or minimum, then any point on the line segment joining these two points is also an optimal solution of the same type.

Example 2 Solve the following linear programming problem graphically.

Maximise $Z = 34x + 45y$

subject to constraints $x + y \le 300$, $2x + 3y \le 70$; $x, y \ge 0$

Sol. We have the following LPP

Maximise $Z = 34x + 45y$

subject to the constraints

$$x + y \le 300,\ 2x + 3y \le 70;\ x,\ y \ge 0$$

Now, considering the inequations as equations, we get

$$x + y = 300 \quad \text{...(i)}$$

and $$2x + 3y = 70 \quad \text{...(ii)}$$

Table for line $x + y = 300$ is

x	0	300
y	300	0

So, the line is passing through the points (0,300) and (300,0).

On putting (0,0) in the inequality $x + y \le 300$, we get

$0 + 0 \le 300$, which is true.

So, the half plane is towards the origin.

Table for line $2x + 3y = 70$ is

x	35	0
y	0	70/3

So, the line is passing through the points (35, 0) and (0, 70/3).

On putting (0, 0) in the inequality $2x + 3y \le 70$, we get

$0 + 0 \le 70$, which is true.

So, the half plane is towards the origin.

Also, $x, y \ge 0$, implies that the region lies in the 1st quadrant.

The graphical representation of the system of inequations is as given below.

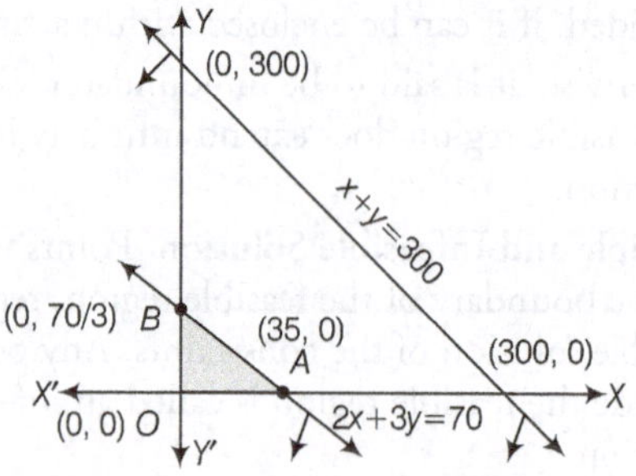

Clearly, the feasible region is $OABO$, where the corner points are $O(0,0)$, $A(35,0)$ and $B(0, 70/3)$.

Now, the values of Z at corner points are as follow

Corner points	$Z = 34x + 45y$
$O(0,0)$	$Z = 0 + 0 = 0$
$A(35,0)$	$Z = 34 \times 35 + 45 \times 0 = 1190$
$B(0,70/3)$	$Z = 34 \times 0 + 45 \times \frac{70}{3} = 1050$

Hence, the maximum value of Z is 1190 at (35, 0).

Example 3 Solve the following problem graphically.

Minimise and maximise $Z = 3x + 9y$,

subject to constraints

$x + 3y \le 60,\ x + y \ge 10,\ x \le y;\ x \ge 0,\ y \ge 0$ **[NCERT]**

Sol. Given objective function is maximise and minimise

$Z = 3x + 9y$

subject to constraints

$$x + 3y \le 60 \quad \text{...(i)}$$

$$x + y \ge 10 \quad \text{...(ii)}$$

$$x \le y \quad \text{...(iii)}$$

and $$x \ge 0,\ y \ge 0 \quad \text{...(iv)}$$

Table for line $x + 3y = 60$ is

x	60	0
y	0	20

So, the line $x + 3y = 60$ is passing through (60, 0) and (0, 20).

On putting (0, 0) in the inequality $x + 3y \le 60$, we get

$0 + 0 \le 60$, which is true.

So, the half plane is towards the origin.

Table for line $x + y = 10$ is

x	10	0
y	0	10

So, the line $x + y = 10$ is passing through (10, 0) and (0, 10).

On putting (0, 0) in the inequality $x + y \geq 10$, we get

$$0 + 0 \geq 10, \text{ which is not true.}$$

So, the half plane is away from the origin.

Table for line $x = y$ is

x	0	5
y	0	5

So, the line $x = y$ is passing through (0, 0) and (5, 5).

On putting (0, 4) is the inequality $x \leq y$, we get

$$0 \leq 4, \text{ which is true.}$$

So, the half plane is towards the Y-axis.

Also, $x \geq 0$ and $y \geq 0$, implies that the region lies in the I quadrant.

On drawing these lines on graph paper, we get the following graph

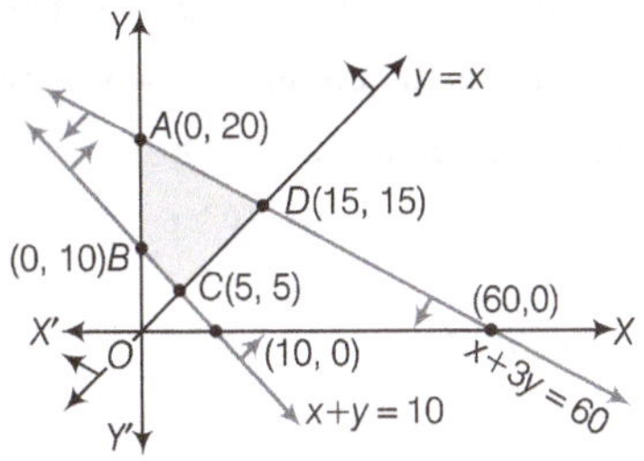

Now, shading the common region, we get the feasible region $ABCDA$.

The intersection point of lines corresponding to inequations (i) and (iii) is D (15, 15) and corresponding to inequations (ii) and (iii) is C(5, 5).

Thus, the corner points of feasible region are A(0, 20), B(0, 10), C(5, 5) and D(15, 15).

The values of Z at corner points are given below

Corner points	$Z = 3x + 9y$
$A(0, 20)$	$Z = 3(0) + 9(20) = 180$
$B(0, 10)$	$Z = 3(0) + 9(10) = 90$
$C(5, 5)$	$Z = 3(5) + 9(5) = 60$
$D(15, 15)$	$Z = 3(15) + 9(15) = 180$

Here, minimum value of Z is 60 which occur at point C(5, 5) and maximum value of Z is 180 which occur at two points A(0, 20) and D(15, 15). So, each point on the line segment AD will give the maximum value of Z.

Example 4 Solve the following linear programming problem graphically. **[ISC 2023]**

Maximise $Z = 5x + 2y$ subject to

$x - 2y \leq 2,\ 3x + 2y \leq 12,\ -3x + 2y \leq 3,\ x \geq 0,\ y \geq 0$

Sol. We have, Maximize $Z = 5x + 2y$

Subject to constraints,

$$x - 2y \leq 2 \quad \text{...(i)}$$

$$3x + 2y \leq 12 \quad \text{...(ii)}$$

$$-3x + 2y \leq 3 \quad \text{...(iii)}$$

and $$x \geq 0,\ y \geq 0 \quad \text{...(iv)}$$

Given constraints can be written in equation form as

$$x - 2y = 2 \quad \text{...(v)}$$

$$3x + 2y = 12 \quad \text{...(vi)}$$

$$-3x + 2y = 3 \quad \text{...(vii)}$$

and $$x = 0,\ y = 0 \quad \text{...(viii)}$$

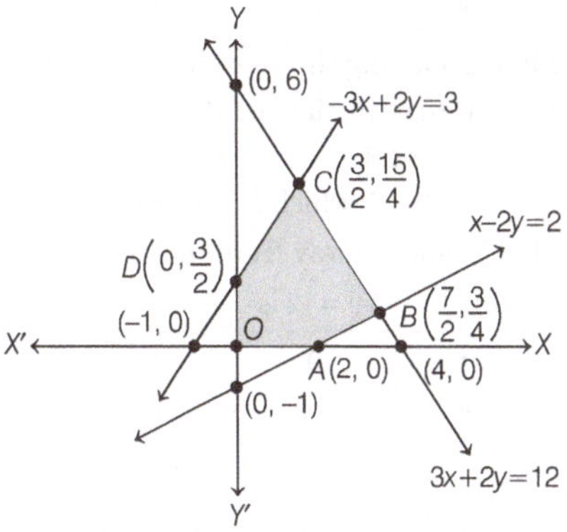

The corner points of the feasible region are

$O(0, 0)$, $A(2, 0)$, $B\left(\frac{7}{2}, \frac{3}{4}\right)$, $C\left(\frac{3}{2}, \frac{15}{4}\right)$ and $D\left(0, \frac{3}{2}\right)$

Corner points	$Z = 5x + 2y$
$O(0, 0)$	0
$A(2, 0)$	10
$B\left(\frac{7}{2}, \frac{3}{4}\right)$	19 (Maximum)
$C\left(\frac{3}{2}, \frac{15}{4}\right)$	15
$D\left(0, \frac{3}{2}\right)$	3

Hence, maximum value of Z is 19 at $B\left(\frac{7}{2}, \frac{3}{4}\right)$.

Example 5 Determine graphically the minimum value of the objective function $Z = -50x + 20y$, subject to constraints $2x - y \geq -5$, $3x + y \geq 3$, $2x - 3y \leq 12$ and $x \geq 0$, $y \geq 0$.

Sol. Given objective function is Minimise $Z = -50x + 20y$

subject to constraints, $2x - y \geq -5$ ...(i)

$$3x + y \geq 3 \quad \text{...(ii)}$$

$$2x - 3y \leq 12 \quad \text{...(iii)}$$

and $$x \geq 0,\ y \geq 0 \quad \text{...(iv)}$$

Table for line $2x - y = -5$ is

x	$-5/2$	0
y	0	5

So, the line is passing through the points $\left(\frac{-5}{2}, 0\right)$ and (0, 5).

On putting (0, 0) in the inequality $2x - y \geq -5$, we get

$$0 - 0 \geq -5 \Rightarrow 0 \geq -5, \text{ which is true.}$$

So, the half plane is towards the origin.

Table for line $3x + y = 3$ is

x	0	1
y	3	0

So, the line is passing through the points (0, 3) and (1, 0).

On putting (0, 0) in the inequality $3x + y \geq 3$, we get

$$0 + 0 \geq 3$$

$\Rightarrow$ $0 \geq 3$, which is not true.

So, the half plane is away from the origin.

Table for line $2x - 3y = 12$ is

x	0	6
y	−4	0

So, the line is passing through (0, − 4) and (6, 0).

On putting (0, 0) in the inequality $2x - 3y \leq 12$, we get

$$0 - 0 \leq 12 \Rightarrow 0 \leq 12, \text{ which is true.}$$

So, the half plane is towards the origin.

Also, $x \geq 0$ and $y \geq 0$, implies that the region lies in the I quadrant.

On drawing the graph we get that the feasible region is *ABCD*, which is unbounded.

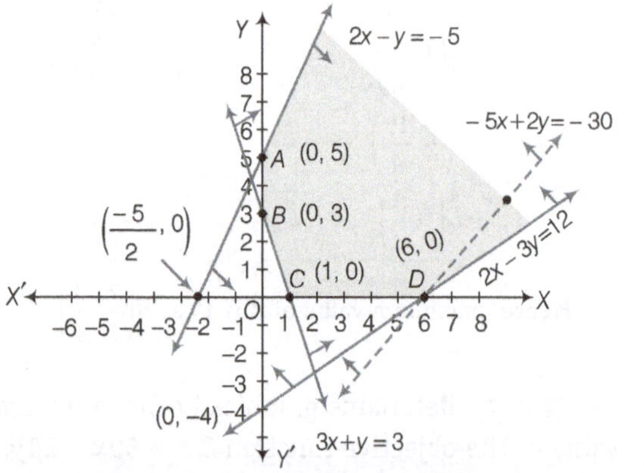

The corner points of feasible region are $A(0, 5)$, $B(0, 3)$, $C(1, 0)$ and $D(6, 0)$.

The value of Z at corner points are given below

Corner points	$Z = -50x + 20y$
$A(0, 5)$	$Z = -50(0) + 20(5) = 100$
$B(0, 3)$	$Z = -50(0) + 20(3) = 60$
$C(1, 0)$	$Z = -50(1) + 20(0) = -50$
$D(6, 0)$	$Z = -50(6) + 20(0) = -300$ (minimum)

Here, feasible region is unbounded so the minimum value of z may or may not be exist.

Now, let us draw the half plane corresponding to the inequation

$$-50x + 20y < -300 \text{ or } -5x + 2y < -30$$

Here, we see that half plane determined by $-5x + 2y < -30$ has a point in common with the feasible region. Hence, no minimum value exists.

Example 6 Minimise $Z = x + 2y$, subject to constraints $2x + y \geq 3$, $x + 2y \geq 6$ and $x, y \geq 0$.

(i) Show that the minimum of Z occurs at more than two points.

(ii) Also, check whether the point $P(5, 2)$ lies inside the shaded portion, if it lies inside the shaded region, then find the distance between the origin and point. **[NCERT]**

Sol. (i) Our problem is to minimise, $Z = x + 2y$ ...(i)

subject to constraints, $2x + y \geq 3$ ...(ii)

$x + 2y \geq 6$ ...(iii)

and $x \geq 0, y \geq 0$ ...(iv)

Table for line $2x + y = 3$ is

x	0	3/2
y	3	0

So, line is passing through the points (0,3) and $\left(\frac{3}{2}, 0\right)$.

On putting (0, 0) in the inequality $2x + y \geq 3$, we get

$$2 \times 0 + 0 \geq 3 \Rightarrow 0 \geq 3, \text{ which is not true.}$$

So, the half plane is away from the origin.

Table for line $x + 2y = 6$ is

x	0	6
y	3	0

So, line is passing through the points (0,3) and (6, 0).

On putting (0, 0) in the inequality $x + 2y \geq 6$, we get

$$0 + 2 \times 0 \geq 6 \Rightarrow 0 \geq 6, \text{ which is not true.}$$

So, the half plane is away from the origin.

Also, $x \geq 0$ and $y \geq 0$, implies that the region lies in the I quadrant. The intersection point of the lines $x + 2y = 6$ and $2x + y = 3$ is $B(0, 3)$.

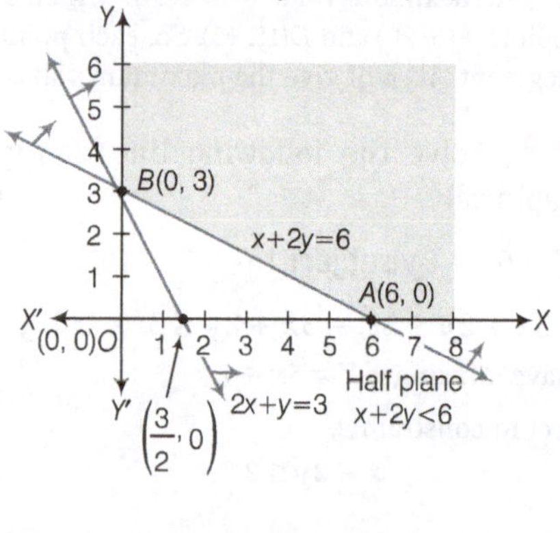

The corner points of the feasible region are $A(6, 0)$ and $B(0, 3)$.

The values of Z at the corner points are given below

Corner points	$Z = x + 2y$
$A(6, 0)$	$Z = 6+2\times0 = 6$
$B(0, 3)$	$Z = 0+2\times3 = 6$

As the feasible region is unbounded, therefore 6 may or may not be the minimum value of Z. For this we will draw the half plane corresponding to the inequality $x + 2y < 6$ and check whether the resulting half plane has points in common with a feasible region or not. It can be seen that the feasible region has no common point with $x + 2y < 6$.

Therefore, the minimum value of Z is 6.

Note that the minimum value of Z occurs at more than 2 points. [$\because$ value of Z is minimum at every point on the line segment AB]

(ii) Let $f(x, y) = x + 2y - 6$

At point $P(5, 2)$, $f(5, 2) = 5 + 2\times2 - 6 = 3 > 0$

So, point lies inside the shaded region.

Now, distance between O and P

$$= \sqrt{(5-0)^2 + (2-0)^2} = \sqrt{25+4} = \sqrt{29} = 5.39$$

Topic Practice 1

Short Answer Type Questions

(4 Marks)

Directions (Q. Nos. 1-7) *Solve the following linear programming problems graphically.*

1 Maximise $Z = 2x + 3y$

subject to constraints $x + 2y \le 10, 2x + y \le 14$ and $x \ge 0,\ y \ge 0$

2 Minimise $Z = x + y$

subject to constraints $3x + 2y \ge 12, x + 3y \ge 11$ and $x \ge 0, y \ge 0$

3 Maximise $Z = x + y$

subject to constraints $x - y \le -1, -x + y \le 0$ and $x, y \ge 0$

4 Maximise $Z = -x + 2y$, subject to constraints are $x \ge 3, x + y \ge 5, x + 2y \ge 6$ and $x, y \ge 0$. **[NCERT]**

5 Minimise $Z = 6x + 3y$

subject to the constraints

$4x + y \ge 80,\ x + 5y \ge 115,\ 3x + 2y \le 150,\ x \ge 0,\ y \ge 0.$

6 Maximise $Z = 105x + 90y$ graphically under the following constraints.

$x + y \le 50, 2x + y \le 80,\ x \ge 20$ and $x \ge 0,\ y \ge 0$

7 Maximise $Z = 7x + 10y$

subject to the constraints

$4x + 6y \le 240, 6x + 3y \le 240, x \ge 10$

and $x \ge 0, y \ge 0$

8 In the given figure, the feasible region for a LPP is shown. Determine the maximum and minimum value of $Z = x + 2y$. **[NCERT Exemplar]**

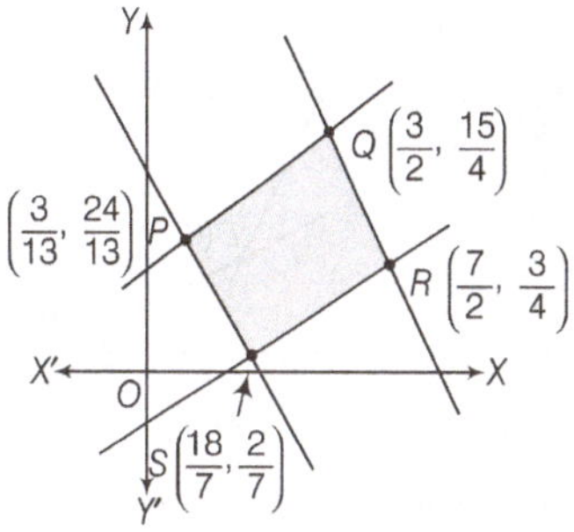

9 The corner points of the feasible region determined by the system of linear constraints are (0, 3), (1, 1) and (3, 0). Let $Z = px + qy$, where $p, q > 0$. Find the condition in p and q, so that the minimum of Z occurs at (3, 0) and (1, 1). **[NCERT Exemplar]**

10 Solve the following LPP graphically.

Maximise $Z = 3x + 2y$, subject to constraints are $x + 2y \le 10, 3x + y \le 15$ and $x \ge 0, y \ge 0$.

Also, determine the area of the feasible region.

Hints & Solutions

1. Given, maximise $Z = 2x + 3y$

subject to constraints

$x + 2y \le 10$ ...(i)

$2x + y \le 14$ ...(ii)

and $x \ge 0, y \ge 0$ ...(iii)

Table for line $x + 2y = 10$ is

x	0	4	10
y	5	3	0

So, the line is passing through the points (0, 5), (4, 3) and (10, 0). [1]

On putting (0, 0) in the inequality $x + 2y \le 10$, we get $0 + 0 \le 10$, which is true.

So, the half plane is towards the origin.
Table for line $2x + y = 14$ is

x	4	6	7
y	6	2	0

So, the line is passing through the points (4, 6), (6, 2) and (7, 0).
On putting (0, 0) in the inequality $2x + y \le 14$, we get $0 + 0 \le 14$, which is true.
So, the half plane is towards the origin.
Also, $x \ge 0$ and $y \ge 0$ implies that the region lies in I quadrant.
On shading the common region, we get the feasible region *OABCO*. **[1]**

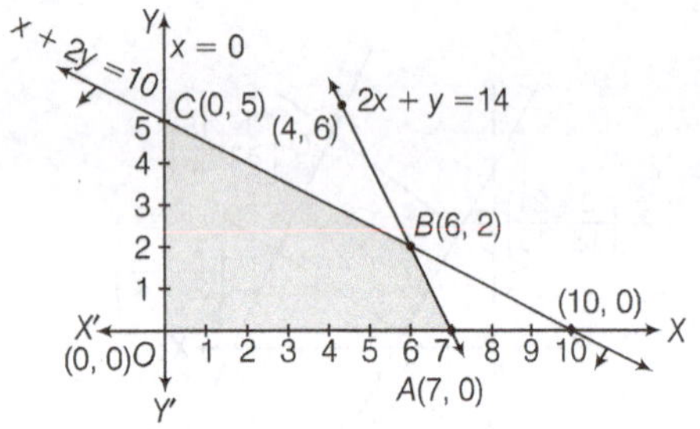

[1]

The intersection point of lines corresponding to inequations (i) and (ii) is $B(6, 2)$.
Thus, the corner points of the feasible region are $O(0, 0)$, $A(7, 0)$, $B(6, 2)$ and $C(0, 5)$
The values of Z at corner points are given below

Corner points	$Z = 2x + 3y$
$O(0, 0)$	$Z = 2 \times 0 + 3 \times 0 = 0$
$A(7, 0)$	$Z = 2 \times 7 + 3 \times 0 = 14$
$B(6, 2)$	$Z = 2 \times 6 + 3 \times 2 = 18$
$C(0, 5)$	$Z = 2 \times 0 + 3 \times 5 = 15$

Clearly, the maximum value of Z is 18, which occurs at the point $B(6, 2)$. **[1]**

2. Given, minimise $Z = x + y$
subject to constraints

$$3x + 2y \ge 12 \quad \text{...(i)}$$
$$x + 3y \ge 11 \quad \text{...(ii)}$$
and $$x \ge 0, y \ge 0 \quad \text{...(iii)}$$

Table for line $3x + 2y = 12$ is

x	0	4
y	6	0

So, the line $3x + 2y = 12$ is passing through the points (0, 6) and (4, 0).
On putting (0, 0) in the inequality $3x + 2y \ge 12$, we get
$0 + 0 \ge 12$, which is not true.
So, the half plane is away from the origin. **[1]**
Table for line $x + 3y = 11$ is

x	2	11
y	3	0

So, the line $x + 3y = 11$ is passing through the points (2, 3) and (11, 0). **[1]**
On putting (0, 0) in the inequality $x + 3y \ge 11$, we get
$0 + 0 \ge 11$, which is not true.
So, the half plane is away from the origin.
Also, $x \ge 0$ and $y \ge 0$, implies that the region lies in I quadrant.

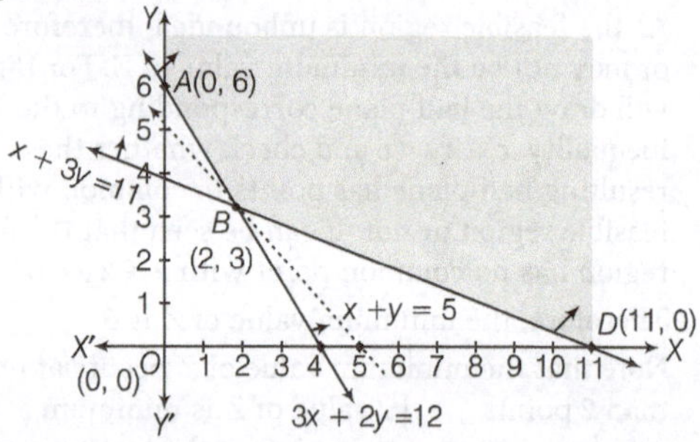

[1]

The intersection point of lines corresponding to inequations (i) and (ii) is $B(2, 3)$.
The shaded region *ABD* represents the feasible region.
The corner points of the feasible region are $A(0, 6)$, $B(2, 3)$ and $D(11, 0)$.
The values of Z at corner points are given below

Corner points	$Z = x + y$	
$A(0, 6)$	$Z = 0 + 6 = 6$	
$B(2, 3)$	$Z = 2 + 3 = 5$	(minimum)
$D(11, 0)$	$Z = 11 + 0 = 11$	

As the feasible region is unbounded, therefore 5 may or may not be the minimum value of Z. For this, we draw the half plane corresponding to the inequality $x + y < 5$ and check whether the resulting half plane has points in common with a feasible region or not. It can be seen that the feasible region has no common point with $x + y < 5$.
Therefore, the minimum value of Z is 5 at $B(2, 3)$. **[1]**

3. Our problem is to maximise $Z = x + y$ ...(i)
subject to constraints, $x - y \le -1$ ...(ii)
$$-x + y \le 0 \quad \text{...(iii)}$$
and $$x \ge 0, y \ge 0 \quad \text{...(iv)}$$

Table for line $x - y = -1$ is

x	0	-1
y	1	0

So, the line $x - y = -1$ is passing through the points (0, 1) and $(-1, 0)$. On putting (0, 0) in the inequality $x - y \le -1$, we get $0 - 0 \le -1 \Rightarrow 0 \le -1$, which is not true.
So, the half plane is away from the origin. **[1]**
Table for line $-x + y = 0$ is

x	0	1
y	0	1

So, the line $-x+y=0$ is passing through the points (0, 0) and (1, 1).

On putting (2, 0) in the inequality $-x+y \le 0$, we get

$$-2+0 \le 0 \Rightarrow -2 \le 0, \text{ which is true.}$$

So, the half plane is towards the X-axis.

Also, $x, y \ge 0$, implies that the region lies in the I quadrant. **[1]**

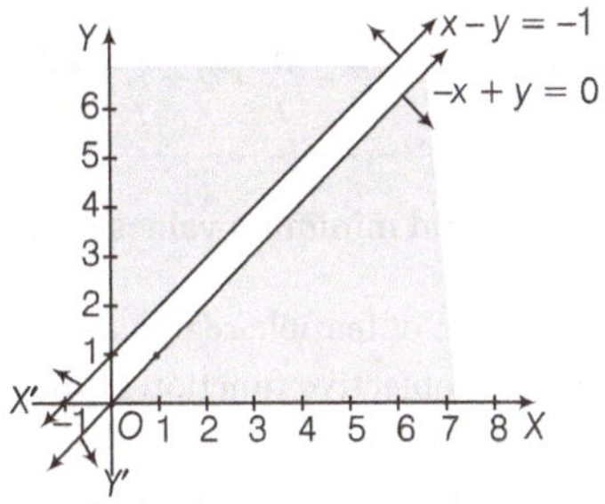

[1]

From the above graph it is clearly shown that there is no common region.

Thus, there is no feasible region and hence Z has no maximum value. [1]

Note If there is no common region i.e. no feasible region exists, then we can not determine the minimum/maximum value.

4. Our problem is to maximise $Z=-x+2y$ ...(i)

subject to constraints

$x \ge 3$ ...(ii)

$x+y \ge 5$ ...(iii)

$x+2y \ge 6$ ...(iv)

and $x \ge 0, \ y \ge 0$ ...(v)

Table for line $x+y=5$ is

x	0	5
y	5	0

So, the line is passing through the points (0, 5) and (5, 0).

On putting (0, 0) in the inequality $x+y \ge 5$, we get

$$0+0 \ge 5$$

$\Rightarrow \quad 0 \ge 5$, which is not true.

So, the half plane is away from the origin.

Table for line $x+2y=6$ is

x	0	6
y	3	0

[1]

So, the line is passing through the points (0,3) and (6,0).

On putting (0, 0) in the inequality $x+2y \ge 6$, we get

$$0+2\times 0 \ge 6 \Rightarrow 0 \ge 6, \text{ which is not true.}$$

So, the half plane is away from the origin.

Also, $x \ge 3$, represent the region lying on the right side of $x=3$.

Since, $x \ge 0, y \ge 0$, the region lies in the I quadrant. [1]

It can be seen that the feasible region is unbounded.

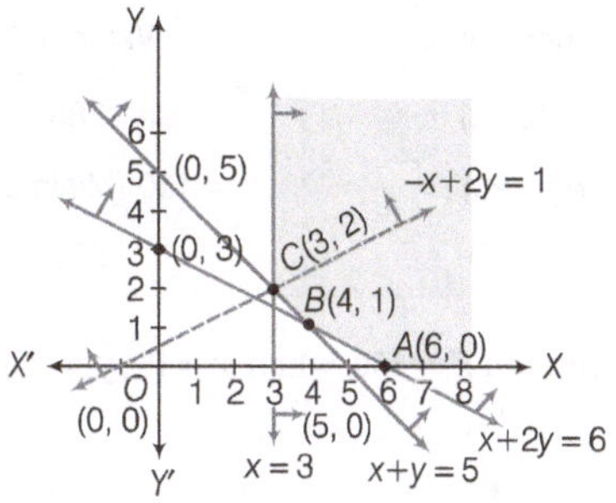

[1]

The points of intersection of lines $x=3$ and $x+y=5$ is $C(3, 2)$ and lines $x+2y=6$ and $x+y=5$ is $B(4, 1)$.

Thus, the corner points of the feasible region are $A(6, 0)$, $B(4, 1)$ and $C(3, 2)$. The values of Z at corner points are given below

Corner points	$Z=-x+2y$
$A(6, 0)$	$Z=-6+2\times 0=-6$
$B(4, 1)$	$Z=-4+2\times 1=-2$
$C(3, 2)$	$Z=-3+2\times 2=1$ (maximum)

As the feasible region is unbounded, therefore $Z=1$ may or may not be the maximum value. For this, we draw the half plane corresponding to the inequality $-x+2y>1$ and check whether the resulting half plane has points in common with the feasible region or not. The feasible region have points in common with the $-x+2y>1$. Therefore, $Z=1$ is not the maximum value. Hence, Z has no maximum value. [1]

5. Hint

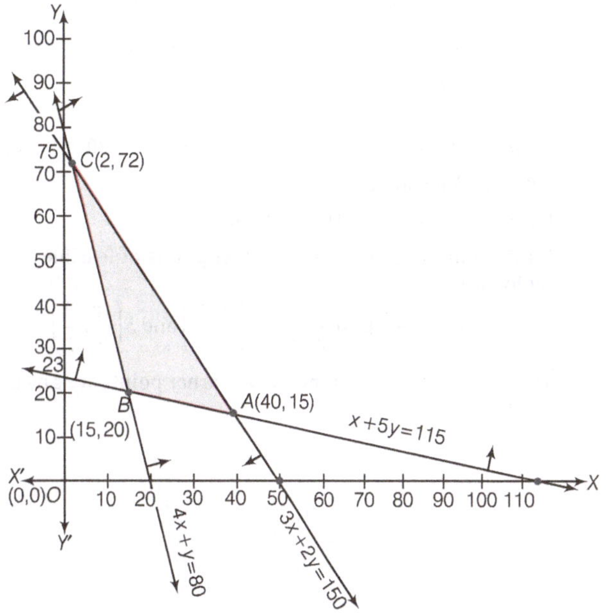

Corner points	Value of Z
A(40, 15)	285
B(15, 20)	150 (Minimum)
C(2, 72)	228

[**Ans.** Minimum $Z = 150$, when $x = 15$, $y = 20$]

6. Hint

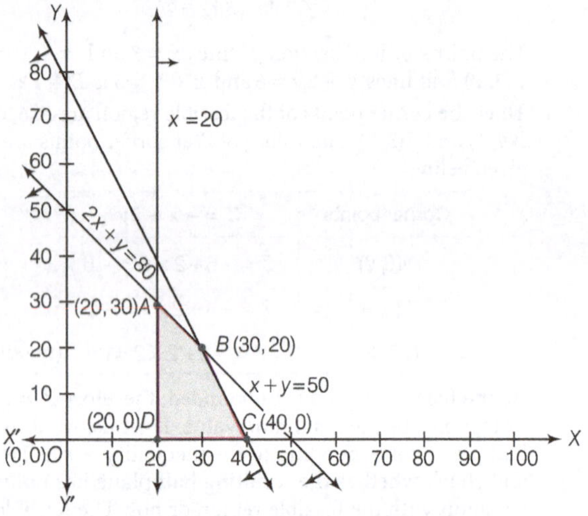

Corner points	Value of Z
D(20, 0)	2100
C(40, 0)	4200
B(30, 20)	4950 (Maximum)
A(20, 30)	4800

[**Ans.** Maximum value of Z is 4950, when $x = 30$, $y = 20$]

7. Solve as Question 6.

[**Ans.** Maximum $Z = 410$ at (30, 20)]

8. Hint From the given figure, corner points of feasible region are

$$P\left(\frac{3}{13}, \frac{24}{13}\right), Q\left(\frac{3}{2}, \frac{15}{4}\right), R\left(\frac{7}{2}, \frac{3}{4}\right) \text{ and } S\left(\frac{18}{7}, \frac{2}{7}\right).$$

The value of objective function at corner points are given below

Corner points	$Z = x + 2y$
$P\left(\frac{3}{13}, \frac{24}{13}\right)$	$Z = \frac{3}{13} + 2 \times \frac{24}{13} = \frac{51}{13}$
$Q\left(\frac{3}{2}, \frac{15}{4}\right)$	$Z = \frac{3}{2} + 2 \times \frac{15}{4} = \frac{6+30}{4} = \frac{36}{4} = 9$
$R\left(\frac{7}{2}, \frac{3}{4}\right)$	$Z = \frac{7}{2} + 2 \times \frac{3}{4} = \frac{10}{2} = 5$
$S\left(\frac{18}{7}, \frac{2}{7}\right)$	$Z = \frac{18}{7} + 2 \times \frac{2}{7} = \frac{22}{7} = 3\frac{1}{7}$

[**Ans.** Maximum and minimum values of Z are 9 and $3\frac{1}{7}$]

9. Given corner points of feasible region are (0, 3), (1, 1) and (3, 0). The value of objective function at these corner points are given below [1]

Corner points	$Z = px + qy$
(0, 3)	$Z = p \times 0 + q \times 3 = 3q$
(1, 1)	$Z = p \times 1 + q \times 1 = p + q$
(3, 0)	$Z = p \times 3 + q \times 0 = 3p$

[2]

Also, given that the minimum of Z occurs at (3, 0) and (1, 1).

$\therefore \; 3p = p + q$

$\Rightarrow \; 2p = q$, which is the required condition. [1]

10. Our problem is to maximise $Z = 3x + 2y$ ...(i)

subject to constraints,

$$x + 2y \le 10 \quad \text{...(ii)}$$
$$3x + y \le 15 \quad \text{...(iii)}$$
and $$x \ge 0, \; y \ge 0 \quad \text{...(iv)}$$

Table for line $x + 2y = 10$ is

x	0	4
y	5	3

So, the line is passing through the points (0, 5) and (4, 3).

On putting (0, 0) in the inequality $x + 2y \le 10$, we get

$$0 + 2 \times 0 \le 10$$

$\Rightarrow 0 \le 10$, which is true.

So, the half plane is towards the origin. [1]

Table for line $3x + y = 15$ is

x	4	5
y	3	0

So, the line is passing through the points (4, 3) and (5, 0).

On putting (0, 0) in the inequality $3x + y \le 15$, we get

$3 \times 0 + 0 \le 15 \Rightarrow 0 \le 15$, which is true.

So, the half plane is towards the origin. [1]

Also, $x, y \ge 0$, implies that the region lies in the I quadrant.

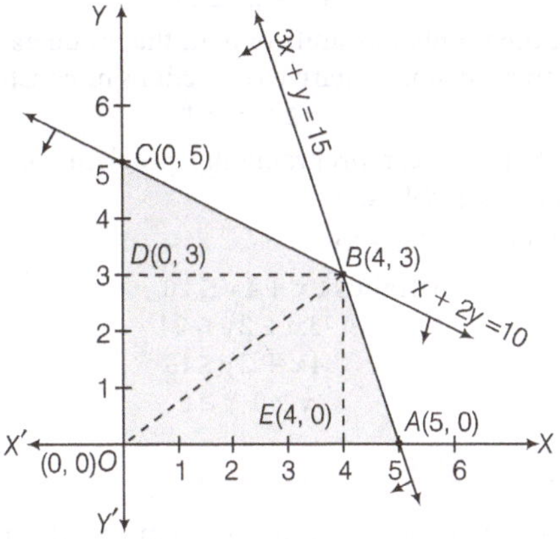

On solving equations $x + 2y = 10$ and $3x + y = 15$, we get $x = 4$ and $y = 3$

So, the intersection point B is (4, 3).

∴ Clearly, feasible region is $OABCO$. [1]

The corner points of the feasible region are $O(0, 0)$, $A(5, 0)$, $B(4, 3)$ and $C(0, 5)$.

The values of Z at the corner points are given below

Corner points	$Z = 3x + 2y$
$O(0, 0)$	$Z = 3 \times 0 + 2 \times 0 = 0$
$A(5, 0)$	$Z = 3 \times 5 + 2 \times 0 = 15$
$B(4, 3)$	$Z = 3 \times 4 + 2 \times 3 = 18$
$C(0, 5)$	$Z = 3 \times 0 + 2 \times 5 = 10$

Clearly, the maximum value of Z is 18 which occurs at the point $B(4, 3)$.

Now, area of feasible region

$= \text{Area of } \Delta BOC + \text{Area of } \Delta OAB$

$= \frac{1}{2} \times OC \times BD + \frac{1}{2} \times OA \times BE$

$= \frac{1}{2} \times 5 \times 4 + \frac{1}{2} \times 5 \times 3$

$= 10 + \frac{15}{2} = 10 + 7.5$

$= 17.5$ sq units [1]

TOPIC 02 Mathematical Formulation and Different Types of LPP

Different Areas of Applications of LPP

Linear programming technique is very useful in solving the problems pertaining to number of areas. Some of them are as follow

(i) **Manufacturing Problems** In manufacturing problems, we have to determine the number of units of different products which should be produced and sold by a firm, when each product requires a fixed manpower, machine hours, labour hour per unit of product, warehouse space per unit of the output, etc, in order to make maximum profit.

(ii) **Investment Problems** In investment problems, we have to determine the amount to be invested in a number of securities giving fixed income, to maximise the return.

(iii) **Diet Problems** In diet problems, we have to determine the amount of different kinds of foods which should be included in a diet, so as to minimise the cost of the desired diet.

(iv) **Transportation Problems** In transportation problems, we have to determine a transportation schedule in order to minimise the cost of transporting a product from plants/factories situated at different locations to different markets.

(v) **Blending Problems** In blending problems, we have to determine the optimum amount of various constituents used in producing a set of products when optimum quantity of each product is to be produced.

(vi) **Advertising Media Selection Problems** In advertising media problems, we have to determine the optimum allocation of advertisements in different media in order to maximise the total number of effective customers.

Mathematical Formulation of LPP

Formulation of the problem is the process of transforming the verbal description of a decision problem into a mathematical form. There is no particular method to formulate linear programming problem but following steps will be helpful in the formulation of linear programming problems.

I. Identify the decision variables of the problem, i.e. identify the unknown quantities, whose values are to be determined and denote them by x, y, etc.

II. Identify the objective function to be optimised (maximised or minimised) and express it as a linear function of the decision variables obtained in step I.

III. Identify the set of constraints in terms of decision variables and express them as linear inequations or equations.

IV. State the non-negative restrictions, so that negative values of the decision variables do not have any valid physical interpretation.

Thus, objective function, the set of constraints and the non-negative restrictions or constraints together form the linear programming problem.

Example 1 A factory produces two products P_1 and P_2. Each of the product P_1 requires 2 h for moulding, 3 h for grinding and 4 h for polishing and each of the product P_2 requires 4 h for moulding, 2 h for grinding and 2 h for polishing.
The factory has moulding machine available for 20 h, grinding machine for 24 h and polishing machine for 13 h. The profit is ₹ 5 per unit of P_1 and ₹ 3 per unit of P_2 and the factory can sell all that it produces.
Formulate the problem as a linear programming problem to maximise the profit.

Sol. Here, two unknown quantities are number of units of products P_1 and P_2. So, let decision variables be x and y, where x represents number of units of product P_1 and y represents number of units of product P_2 which are to be produced.

Now, as the profit is ₹ 5 per unit of P_1 and ₹ 3 per unit of P_2.

∴ Objective function is maximise, $Z = 5x + 3y$

The factory has moulding machine available for 20 h and product P_1 requires 2 h, product P_2 requires 4 h for moulding. So, first constraint is

$$2x + 4y \le 20$$

The factory has grinding machine available for 24 h and product P_1 requires 3 h, product P_2 requires 2 h for grinding.

So, second constraint is

$$3x + 2y \le 24$$

The factory has polishing machine available for 13 h and product P_1 requires 4 h, product P_2 requires 2 h for polishing. So, third constraint is

$$4x + 2y \le 13$$

Also, the number of units of both the products cannot be negative. So, non-negative restrictions or constraints are

$$x \ge 0, y \ge 0$$

Hence, the linear programming problem for the given problem is as follows:

Maximise $Z = 5x + 3y$

Subject to constraints $2x + 4y \le 20$

$3x + 2y \le 24$

$4x + 2y \le 13$

and $x \ge 0, y \ge 0$

Working Rule to Solve LPP

To solve a linear programming problem, we use the following steps

I. Firstly, write the given LPP in mathematical form by using mathematical formulation (if not given in mathematical form).

II. Consider all constraints as linear equations.

III. Draw the graph of each linear equation obtained in Step II and find their intersection points (if any).

IV. Shade the common region of all the linear inequalities, i.e. find feasible region and check that feasible region is bounded or unbounded.

V. Now, find the corner points of feasible region and calculate the value of objective function at each corner point.

VI. (a) If region is bounded, then maximum (say M) or minimum (say m) value is the required maximum or minimum value of the objective function.

(b) If region is unbounded, then maximum (say M) or minimum (say m) value, may or may not be the required maximum or minimum values of the objective function. In this case, we go to next step.

VII. Suppose the given objective function is $Z = ax + by$. Draw the graph of inequality $ax + by > M$ (for maximum value) or $ax + by < m$ (for minimum value). If open half plane obtained by these inequalities has no point in common with the feasible region obtained in Step IV, then M or m is the required maximum or minimum value. Otherwise, objective function has no maximum or no minimum value.

Different Types of Linear Programming Problems

Some important types of linear programming problems are given below. To solve such problems, we first formulate the mathematical form of LPP and then solve them by using previous method, i.e. corner point method.

Diet Problems

Example 2 A dietician wishes to mix two types of foods f_1 and f_2 in such a way that the vitamin contents of the mixture contain atleast 6 units of vitamin A and 8 units of vitamin B.

Food f_1 contains 2 units/kg of vitamin A and 3 units/kg of vitamin B while food f_2 contains 3 units/kg of vitamin A and 2 units/kg of vitamin B. Food f_1 costs ₹ 50 per kg and food f_2 costs ₹ 75 per kg. Formulate the problem as an LPP to minimise the cost of mixture and solve it graphically.

Sol. Let the mixture contains x kg of food f_1 and y kg of food f_2.

Here, cost of food f_1 = ₹ 50 per kg and cost of food f_2 = ₹ 75 per kg and we have to minimise the cost of mixture.

So, the objective function is Minimise $Z = 50x + 75y$

Here, food f_1 contains 2 units/kg and food f_2 contains 3 units/kg of vitamin A. Also, mixture contains atleast 6 units of vitamin A. So, first constraint is $2x + 3y \ge 6$.

Similarly, food f_1 contains 3 units/kg and food f_2 contains 2 units/kg of vitamin B. Also, mixture contains atleast 8 units of vitamin B. So, second constraint is $3x + 2y \ge 8$.

Also, volume of foods f_1 and f_2 cannot be negative, so $x \ge 0$, $y \ge 0$. Thus, linear constraints are $2x + 3y \ge 6$, $3x + 2y \ge 8$ and $x, y \ge 0$.

Consider, the constraints as linear equations

$$2x + 3y = 6 \quad \text{...(i)}$$
$$3x + 2y = 8 \quad \text{...(ii)}$$
and $$x = 0, y = 0 \quad \text{...(iii)}$$

Table for line $2x + 3y = 6$ is

x	0	3
y	2	0

So, line is passing through the points (0, 2) and (3, 0).

On putting (0, 0) in the inequality $2x + 3y \ge 6$, we get

$2(0) + 3(0) \ge 6$

$\Rightarrow \quad 0 \ge 6$, which is not true.

So, the half plane is away from the origin.

Table for line $3x + 2y = 8$ is

x	0	8/3
y	4	0

So, line is passing through the points (0, 4) and $\left(\frac{8}{3}, 0\right)$.

On putting (0, 0) in the inequality $3x + 2y \ge 8$, we get

$3(0) + 2(0) \ge 8$

$\Rightarrow \quad 0 \ge 8$, which is not true.

So, the half plane is away from the origin.

Also, $x \ge 0$, $y \ge 0$, implies that the region lies in I quadrant.

On plotting these lines, we get the following graph.

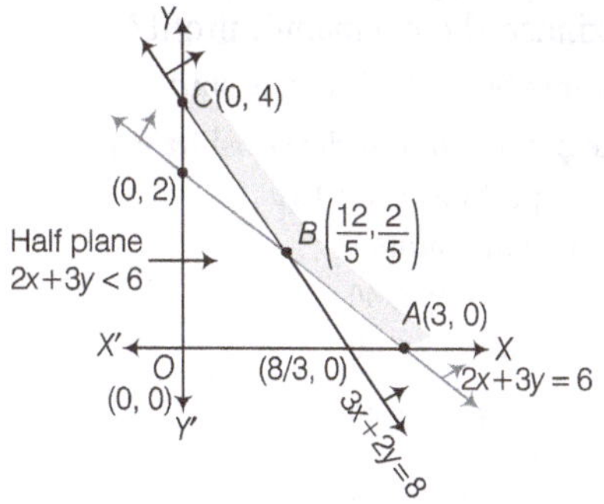

The intersection point of lines (i) and (ii) is $B\left(\frac{12}{5}, \frac{2}{5}\right)$.

Clearly, the shaded region is a feasible region, which is unbounded.

Now, the corner points are A (3, 0), $B\left(\frac{12}{5}, \frac{2}{5}\right)$ and C (0, 4).

The values of Z at the corner points are given below

Corner points	$Z = 50x + 75y$
$A(3, 0)$	$Z = 50(3) + 75(0) = 150$
$B\left(\frac{12}{5}, \frac{2}{5}\right)$	$Z = 50\left(\frac{12}{5}\right) + 75\left(\frac{2}{5}\right) = 150$
$C(0, 4)$	$Z = 50(0) + 75(4) = 300$

As the feasible region is unbounded, therefore 150 may or may not be the minimum value of Z. For this, we draw a graph of inequality $50x + 75y < 150$ or $2x + 3y < 6$ and check whether the resulting half plane has points in common with the feasible region or not. It can be seen that the feasible region has no common point with $2x + 3y < 6$.

Hence, minimum cost of the mixture will be ₹ 150 at each point of the line segment joining the points $A(3, 0)$ and $B\left(\frac{12}{5}, \frac{2}{5}\right)$.

Manufacturing Problems

Example 3 A company uses three machines to manufacture two types of shirts, half sleeves and full sleeves. The number of hours required per week on machine M_1, M_2 and M_3 for one shirt of each type is given in the following table

	M_1	M_2	M_3
Half sleeves	1	2	8/5
Full sleeves	2	1	8/5

None of the machines can be in operations for more than 40 h/week. The profit on each half sleeve shirt is ₹ 1 and the profit on each full sleeve shirt is ₹ 1.50. How many of each type of shirts should be made per week to maximise the company's profit? **[ISC 2020]**

Sol. Let the number of half sleeves shirt $= x$

and the number of full sleeves shirt $= y$

Maximise profit $Z = x + 1.5y$

Subject to constraints

$$x + 2y \le 40$$
$$2x + y \le 40$$
$$\frac{8}{5}x + \frac{8}{5}y \le 40$$
$$\Rightarrow \quad x + y \le 25$$
$$x,\ y \ge 0$$

We draw the line $x + 2y = 40$, $2x + y = 40$, $x + y = 25$

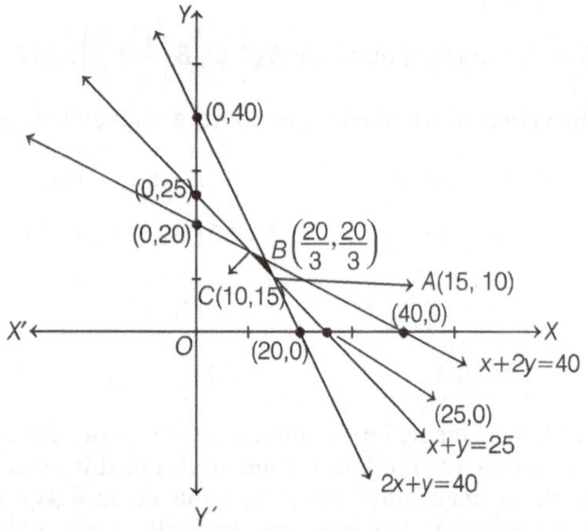

Clearly, the shaded region is a feasible region which is bounded.

Now, the corner point $A(15, 10)$, $B\left(\frac{20}{3}, \frac{20}{3}\right)$, $C(10,15)$.

The value of Z of the corner points

Corner points	$Z = x + 1.5y$
$A(15, 10)$	$15 + 15 = 30$
$B\left(\frac{20}{3}, \frac{20}{3}\right)$	$\frac{20}{3} + \frac{30}{3} = \frac{50}{3}$
$C(10, 15)$	$10 + 22.5 = 32.5$ (Maximum)

Here, maximum value of $Z = 32.5$ at $x = 10,\ y = 15$

$\therefore$ Number of half sleeves shirt $= 10$

Number of full sleeves shirt $= 15$

Allocation Problems

Example 4 An aeroplane can carry a maximum of 200 passengers. A profit of ₹ m is made on each executive class ticket and a profit of ₹ n is made on each economy class ticket, where m and n are obtained on multiplying first term and common ratio by 100 of the geometric series 10,60,360,... times. The airline reserves atleast 20 seats for executive class. However, atleast 4 times as many passengers prefer to travel by economy class than by the executive class. Determine, how many tickets of each type must be sold in order to maximise the profit for the airline. What is the maximum profit?

Sol. Given geometric series is 10, 60, 360, ...

Here, first term $(a) = 10$ and common ratio $(r) = \frac{60}{10} = 6$

According to the given condition,

$m = a \times 100$ and $n = r \times 100$

$\therefore \quad m = 10 \times 100$ and $n = 6 \times 100$

$\Rightarrow \quad m = 1000$ and $n = 600$

Let x be the number of passengers travel by executive class and y be the number of passengers travel by economy class.

We can construct the following table

Class	Number of tickets	Profit (in ₹)
Executive	x	$1000x$
Economy	y	$600y$
Total	$x + y$	$1000x + 600y$

So, our problem is to maximise

$$Z = 1000x + 600y \quad \text{...(i)}$$

subject to constraints

$$x + y \le 200 \quad \text{...(ii)}$$
$$x \ge 20 \quad \text{...(iii)}$$
$$y - 4x \ge 0 \text{ or } y \ge 4x \quad \text{...(iv)}$$
$$\text{and} \quad x \ge 0,\ y \ge 0 \quad \text{...(v)}$$

Table for line $x + y = 200$ is

x	0	200
y	200	0

So, line is passing through the points (0, 200) and (200, 0).

On putting (0, 0) in the inequality $x + y \le 200$, we get

$0 + 0 \le 200$

$\Rightarrow \quad 0 \le 200$, which is true.

So, the half plane is towards the origin.

Table for line $y = 4x$ is

x	0	20
y	0	80

So, line is passing through the points (0, 0) and (20, 80).

On putting (10, 0) in the inequality $y \ge 4x$, we get

$0 \ge 4 \times 10$

$\Rightarrow$ $0 \geq 40$, which is not true.

So, the half plane is towards Y-axis.

Now, draw the graph of the line $x = 20$.

On putting (0, 0) in the inequality $x \geq 20$, we get

$0 \geq 20$, which is not true.

So, the half plane is away from the origin.

Also, $x, y \geq 0$, implies that the region lies in the I quadrant.

On finding the points of intersection of lines, corresponding to inequalities (ii), (iii) and (iv), we get $A(20, 80)$, $B(40, 160)$ and $C(20, 180)$.

Clearly, feasible region is $ABCA$.

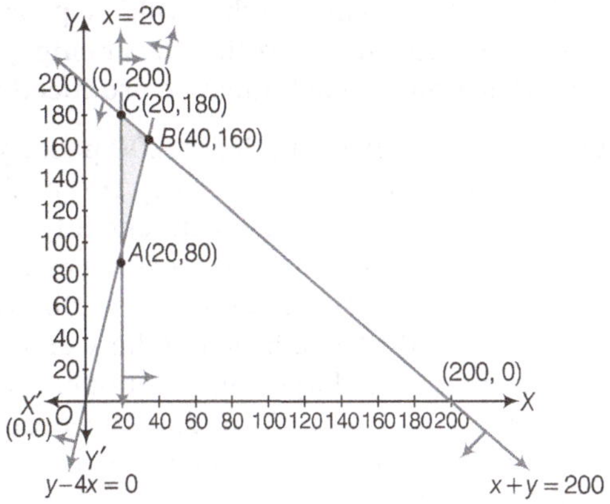

The corner points of the feasible region are $A(20, 80)$, $B(40, 160)$ and $C(20, 180)$.

The value of Z at the corner points are given below

Corner points	$Z = 1000x + 600y$
$A(20, 80)$	$Z = 1000 \times 20 + 600 \times 80 = 68000$
$B(40, 160)$	$Z = 1000 \times 40 + 600 \times 160 = 136000$
$C(20, 180)$	$Z = 1000 \times 20 + 600 \times 180 = 128000$

Thus, the maximum value of Z is 136000 at $B(40, 160)$. Hence, 40 tickets of executive class and 160 tickets of economy class should be sold to maximise the profit and the maximum profit is ₹ 136000.

Transportation Problems

Example 5 There is a factory located at each of the two places P and Q. From these locations, certain commodity is delivered to each of the three depots situated at A, B and C.

The weekly requirements of the depots are respectively 5, 5 and 4 units of the commodity while the production capacity of the factory at P and Q are respectively 8 and 6 units. The cost of transportation per unit is given below

From \ To	Cost (in ₹) A	B	C
P	16	10	15
Q	10	12	10

How many units should be transported from each factory to each depot in order that the transportation cost is minimum? What will be the minimum transportation cost?

Sol. Let the unit supplied from P to A be x and the unit supplied from P to B be y.

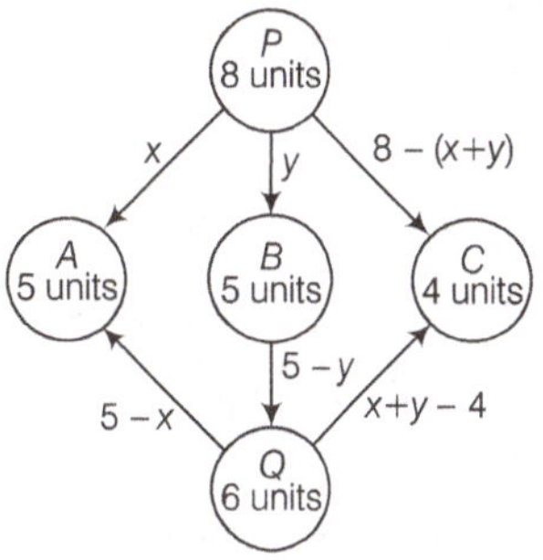

Then, the unit supplied from P to C is $8-(x+y)$, the unit supplied from Q to A is $5-x$, the unit supplied from Q to B is $5-y$ and the unit supplied from Q to C is $x+y-4$.

$\therefore$ The objective function is to

$$\text{Minimise } Z = 16x + 10y + 15(8 - x - y) + 10(5 - x) + 12(5 - y) + 10(x + y - 4)$$
$$= 16x + 10y + 120 - 15x - 15y + 50 - 10x + 60 - 12y + 10x + 10y - 40$$
$$= x - 7y + 190$$

subject to constraints are

$$x + y \leq 8, x + y \geq 4, \ x \leq 5, \ y \leq 5 \text{ and } x, \ y \geq 0$$

Consider the constraints as linear equations

$$x + y = 8 \quad \text{...(i)}$$
$$x + y = 4 \quad \text{...(ii)}$$
$$x = 5, \ y = 5 \quad \text{...(iii)}$$
and $$x = 0, \ y = 0 \quad \text{...(iv)}$$

Table for line $x + y = 8$ is

x	0	8
y	8	0

So, line is passing through the points (0, 8) and (8, 0).

On putting (0, 0) in the inequality $x + y \leq 8$, we get $0 + 0 \leq 8 \Rightarrow 0 \leq 8$, which is true.

So, the half plane is towards the origin.

Table for line $x + y = 4$ is

x	0	4
y	4	0

So, line is passing through the points (0, 4) and (4, 0).

On putting (0, 0) in the inequality $x + y \geq 4$, we get $0 + 0 \geq 4 \Rightarrow 0 \geq 4$, which is not true.

So, the half plane is away from the origin.
Draw the graph of the lines $x = 5$ and $y = 5$, which is perpendicular to X and Y-axes. Clearly the half plane $x \le 5$ and $y \le 5$ is towards Y-axis and X-axis, respectively. Also, $x, y \ge 0$, implies that the region lies in the I quadrant.
The points of intersection of lines (i), (ii) and (iii) are $C(5, 3)$ and $D(3, 5)$.
The graphical representation of these lines is given below

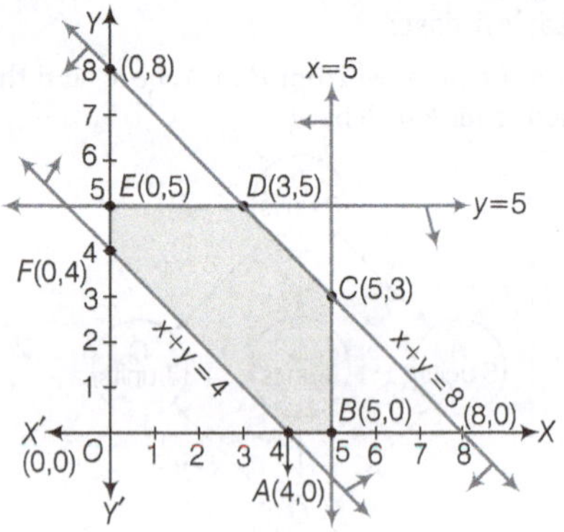

The shaded region in the graph represents the feasible region $ABCDEFA$ and its corner points are $A(4, 0)$, $B(5, 0)$, $C(5, 3)$, $D(3, 5)$, $E(0, 5)$ and $F(0, 4)$.
The values of Z at the corner points are given below

Corner points	$Z = x - 7y + 190$
$A(4, 0)$	$Z = 4 - 7(0) + 190 = 194$
$B(5, 0)$	$Z = 5 - 7(0) + 190 = 195$
$C(5, 3)$	$Z = 5 - 7(3) + 190 = 174$
$D(3, 5)$	$Z = 3 - 7(5) + 190 = 158$
$E(0, 5)$	$Z = 0 - 7(5) + 190 = 155$
$F(0, 4)$	$Z = 0 - 7(4) + 190 = 162$

Thus, Z is minimum at $x = 0$ and $y = 5$ and minimum value of Z is 155.
Hence, the optimal transportation strategy will be deliver to 0, 5 and 3 units from the factory at P and 5, 0 and 1 units from the factory at Q to the depots at A, B and C, respectively. Also, the minimum transportation cost will be ₹ 155.

Topic Practice 2

Very Short Answer Type Questions

(2 Marks)

1 Two tailors A and B earn ₹ 300 and ₹ 400 per day, respectively. A can stitch 6 shirts and 4 pairs of trousers while B can stitch 10 shirts and 4 pairs of trousers per day. To find how many days should each of them work and if it is desired to produce at least 60 shirts and 32 pairs of trousers at a minimum labour cost, formulate this as an LPP.

2 A small firm manufactures necklaces and bracelets. The total number of necklaces and bracelets that it can handle per day is at most 24. It takes one hour to make a bracelet and half an hour to make a necklace. The maximum number of hours available per day is 16. If the profit on a necklace is ₹ 100 and that on a bracelet is ₹300. Formulate linear programming problem for finding how many, each should be produced daily to maximise the profit, if it is being given that atleast one of each must be produced?

3 A firm has to transport atleast 1200 packages daily using large vans which carry 200 packages each and small vans which can take 80 packages each. The cost for engaging each large van is ₹ 400 and each small van is ₹ 200. Not more than ₹ 3000 is to be spent daily on the job and the number of large vans cannot exceed the number of small vans. Formulate this problem as an LPP given that the objective is to minimise cost.

4 An aeroplane can carry a maximum of 250 passengers. A profit of ₹ 1500 is made on each executive class ticket and a profit of ₹ 1000 is made on each economy class ticket. The airline reserves atleast 25 seats for executive class. However, atleast 3 times as many passengers prefer to travel by economy class than by executive class.

Frame the linear programming problem to determine how many tickets of each type must be sold in order to maximise the profit for the airline?

Long Answer Type Questions

(6 Marks)

5 A housewife wishes to mix together two kinds of foods X and Y in such a way that the mixture contains atleast 10 units of vitamin A, 12 units of vitamin B and 8 units of vitamin C. The vitamin contents of 1kg of food is given below

	Vitamin A	Vitamin B	Vitamin C
Food X	1	2	3
Food Y	2	2	1

1 kg of food X cost ₹ 6 and 1 kg of food Y cost ₹ 10. Then, find the least cost of the mixture which will produce the diet.

6 A dietician wishes to mix two kinds of food X and Y in such a way that the mixture contains at least 10 units of vitamin A, 12 units of vitamin B and 8 units of vitamin C. The vitamin contents of 1 kg food is given below

Food	Vitamin A	Vitamin B	Vitamin C
X	1 unit	2 units	3 units
Y	2 units	2 units	1 unit

1 kg food of X costs ₹ 24 and 1 kg food of Y costs ₹ 36. Using linear programming, find the least cost of the total mixture which will contain the required vitamins. **[ISC 2015]**

7 A new cereal formed of a mixture of bran and rice contains atleast 88 g of protein and atleast 36 mg of iron. Knowing that bran contains 80 g of protein and 40 mg of iron per kilogram and the rice contains, 100 g of protein and 30 mg of iron per kilogram, then find the minimum cost of producing a kilogram of this new cereal, if bran costs ₹ 28 per kg and rice costs ₹ 25 per kg. **[ISC 2009]**

8 A company manufactures two types of products A and B. Each unit of A requires 3 g of nickel and 1 g of chromium, while each unit of B requires 1 g of nickel and 2 g of chromium. The firm can produce 9 g of nickel and 8 g of chromium. The profit is ₹ 40 on each unit of product of type A and ₹ 50 on each unit of type B. How many units of each type should the company manufacture so as to earn maximum profit? Use linear programming to find the solution. **[ISC 2016]**

9 A company produces two types of items, P and Q. Manufacturing of both items requires the metals gold and copper. Each unit of item P requires 3 g of gold and 1 g of copper while that of item Q requires 1 g of gold and 2 g of copper. The company has 9 g of gold and 8 g of copper in its store. If each unit of item P makes a profit of ₹ 50 and each unit of item Q makes a profit of ₹ 60, determine the number of units of each item that the company should produce to maximise profit. What is the maximum profit? **[ISC 2010]**

10 A manufacturing company makes two types of teaching aids A and B of Mathematics for Class X. Each type of A requires 9 labour hours of fabricating and 1 labour hour for finishing. Each type of B requires 12 labour hours for fabricating and 3 labour hours for finishing. For fabricating and finishing, the maximum labour hours available per week are 180 and 30, respectively. The company makes a profit of ₹ 80 on each piece of type A and ₹ 120 on each piece of type B. How many pieces of type A and type B should be manufactured per week to get a maximum profit? Formulate this as linear programming problem and solve it. Identity the feasible region from the rough sketch. **[ISC 2018]**

11 A company manufactures two types of toys A and B. A toy of type A requires 5 min for cutting and 10 min for assembling. A toy of type B requires 8 min for cutting and 8 min for assembling. There are 3 h available for cutting and 4 h available for assembling the toys in a day. The profit is ₹ 50 each on a toy of type A and ₹ 60 each on a toy of type B. How many toys of each type should company manufacture in a day to maximise the profit? Use linear programming to find the solution. **[ISC 2014]**

12 A company manufactures three kinds of calculators: A, B and C in its two factories I and II. The company has got an order for manufacturing atleast 6400 calculators of kind A, 4000 of kind B and 4800 of kind C. The daily output of factory I is of 50 calculators of kind A, 50 calculators of kind B and 30 calculators of kind C. The daily output of factory II is 40 calculators of kind A, 20 of kind B and 40 of kind C. The cost per day to run factory I is ₹ 12000 and of factory II is ₹ 15000. How many days do the two factories have to be in operation to produce the order with the minimum cost? Formulate this problem as an LPP and solve it graphically.

13 A factory makes tennis rackets and cricket bats. A tennis racket takes 1.5 h of machine time and 3 h of craftman's time in its making, while a cricket bat takes 3 h of machine time and 1 h of craftman's time. In a day, the factory has the availability of not more than 42 h of machine time and 24 h of craftman's time.
If the profits on a racket and a bat are ₹ 20 and ₹ 10 respectively, then find the number of tennis rackets and cricket bats that the factory must manufacture to earn the maximum profit. Make it as an LPP and solve it graphically. **[NCERT]**

14 A carpenter has 90, 80 and 50 running feet respectively of teak wood, plywood and rosewood which is used to produce product A and product B. Each unit of product A requires 2, 1 and 1 running feet and each unit of product B requires 1, 2 and 1 running feet of teak wood, plywood and rosewood respectively. If product A is sold for ₹ 48 per unit and product B is sold for ₹ 40 per unit, how many units of product A and product B should be produced and sold by the carpenter, in order to obtain the maximum gross income?

Formulate the above as a linear programming problem and solve it, indicating clearly the feasible region in the graph. **[ISC 2024]**

15 A dealer in rural area wishes to purchase a number of sewing machines. He has only ₹ 5760 to invest and has space for atmost 20 items for storage. An electronic sewing machine cost him ₹ 360 and a manually operated sewing machine ₹ 240. He can sell an electronic sewing machine at a profit of ₹ 22 and a manually operated sewing machine at a profit of ₹ 18. Assuming that he can sell all the items that he can buy, how should he invest his money in order to maximise his profit? Make it as an LPP and solve it graphically.

16 A farmer has a supply of chemical fertilizer of type A which contains 10% nitrogen and 6% phosphoric acid and of type B which contains 5% nitrogen and 10% phosphoric acid. After soil test, it is found that at least 7 kg of nitrogen and same quantity of phosphoric acid is required for a good crop. The fertilizer of type A costs ₹ 5.00 per kg and the type B costs ₹ 8.00 per kg. Using linear programming, find how many kilograms of each type of the fertilizer should be bought to meet the requirement and for the cost to be minimum. Find the feasible region in the graph. **[ISC 2017]**

17 A mill owner buys two types of machines A and B for his mill. Machine A occupies 1000 sq m of area and requires 12 men to operate it, while machine B occupies 1200 sq m of area and requires 8 men to operate it. The owner has 7600 sq m of area available and 72 men to operate the machines. If machine A produces 50 units and machine B produces 40 units daily, how many machines of each type should he buy to maximize the daily output? Use linear programming to find the solution. **[ISC 2013]**

18 Two tailors P and Q earn ₹ 150 and ₹ 200 per day respectively. P can stitch 6 shirts and 4 trousers a day, while Q can stitch 10 shirts and 4 trousers per day. How many days should each work to produce atleast 60 shirts and 32 trousers at minimum labour cost? **[ISC 2012]**

19 A manufacturer manufactures two types of tea cups, A and B. Three machines are needed for manufacturing the tea cups. The time in minutes required for manufacturing each cup on the machines is given below

Type of cup	Time (in min)		
	Machine I	Machine II	Machine III
A	12	18	6
B	6	0	9

Each machine is available for a maximum of six hours per day. If the profit on each cup of type A is ₹ 1.50 and that on each cup of type B is ₹ 1.00, find the number of cups of each type that should be manufactured in a day to get maximum profit. **[ISC 2011]**

20 Two godowns A and B have a grain storage capacity of 100 quintals and 50 quintals, respectively. They supply it to 3 ration shops D, E and F, whose requirements are 60, 50 and 40 quintals, respectively. The cost of transportation per quintal from godowns to the shops are given in the following table

From \ To	Transportation cost per quintal (in ₹)	
	A	B
D	6.00	4.00
E	3.00	2.00
F	2.50	3.00

How should the supplies be transported in order that the transportation cost is minimum? **[NCERT]**

Hints & Solutions

1. Suppose tailor A work for x days and tailor B work for y days.
The given data can be written in the tabular form as follows

Tailor	Number of shirts	Number of trousers	Cost/day
A	6	4	₹ 300
B	10	4	₹ 400
Minimum requirement	60	32	

[1]

Required linear programming problem is
$\text{Min}(Z) = 300x + 400y$
subject to constraints

$$6x + 10y \geq 60,$$
$$4x + 4y \geq 32$$
and $\quad x \geq 0,\ y \geq 0$ [1]

2. Let x necklaces and y bracelets manufactured by small firm.

Item	Number	Manufactures times (in hours)	Profit (in ₹)
Necklaces	x	$x/2$	$100x$
Bracelets	y	y	$300y$
Total	$x + y$	$\frac{x}{2} + y$	$100x + 300y$
Availability	24	16	

[1]

Our problem is to maximise $Z = 100x + 300y$
subject to constraints are
$$x + y \leq 24,$$
$$\frac{x}{2} + y \leq 16$$
and $\quad x \geq 1,\ y \geq 1$ [1]

3. Let the number of large vans $= x$
and number of small vans $= y$
Minimise cost $Z = 400x + 200y$ [1/2]
subject to constraints
$$200x + 80y \geq 1200 \text{ or } 5x + 2y \geq 30,$$
$$400x + 200y \leq 3000 \text{ or } 2x + y \leq 15,$$
$x < y$ and $x \geq 0,\ y \geq 0$ [1½]

4. Let the number of executive class tickets be x and economy class tickets be y.
$\therefore$ LPP is maximise profit $P = 1500x + 1000y$ [1]
subject to constraints $x + y \leq 250,\ x \geq 25,\ y \geq 3x$ and $x,\ y \geq 0$. [1]

5. Let the quantity of food X be x kg and the quantity of food Y be y kg.
$\therefore$ The objective function is to minimise $Z = 6x + 10y$.
subject to constraints,
$$x + 2y \geq 10 \quad \text{...(i)}$$
$$2x + 2y \geq 12 \quad \text{...(ii)}$$
$$3x + y \geq 8 \quad \text{...(iii)}$$
and $\quad x,\ y \geq 0$ ...(iv)

Table for line $x + 2y = 10$ is

x	0	10
y	5	0

So, line is passing through the points (0, 5) and (10, 0). [1]
On putting (0, 0) in the inequality $x + 2y \geq 10$, we get
$0 + 2(0) \geq 10 \Rightarrow 0 \geq 10$, which is not true.
So, the half plane is away from the origin.
Table for line $2x + 2y = 12$ is

x	0	6
y	6	0

So, line is passing through the points (0, 6) and (6, 0).
On putting (0, 0) in the inequality $2x + 2y \geq 12$, we get
$2(0) + 2(0) \geq 12$
$\Rightarrow \quad 0 \geq 12$, which is not true.
So, the half plane is away from the origin. [1]
Table for line $3x + y = 8$ is

x	0	8/3
y	8	0

So, line is passing through the points (0, 8) and (8/3, 0)
On putting (0, 0) in the inequality $3x + y \geq 8$, we get
$3(0) + 0 \geq 8 \Rightarrow 0 \geq 8$, which is not true.
So, the half plane is away from the origin.
Also, $x, y \geq 0$, implies that the region lies in the I quadrant.

The points of intersection of lines corresponding to inequations (i), (ii) and (iii) are $B(2, 4)$ and $C(1, 5)$. [1]
The graphical representation of these lines is given below

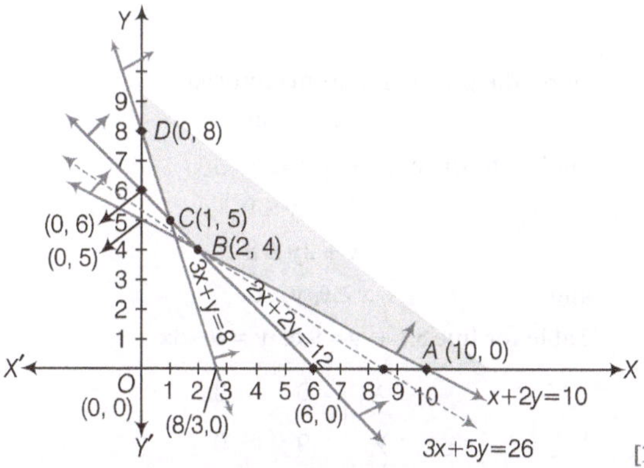

[1]

The shaded region in the graph represents the feasible region and its corner points are $A\ (10, 0)$, $B\ (2, 4)$, $C\ (1, 5)$ and $D\ (0, 8)$.

The values of Z at corner points are given below

Corner points	$Z = 6x + 10y$
$A\ (10, 0)$	$Z = 6\,(10) + 10\,(0) = 60$
$B\ (2, 4)$	$Z = 6\,(2) + 10\,(4) = 52$
$C\ (1, 5)$	$Z = 6\,(1) + 10\,(5) = 56$
$D\ (0, 8)$	$Z = 6\,(0) + 10\,(8) = 80$

Note that Z is minimum at $x = 2$ and $y = 4$ and mimimum value of Z is ₹ 52. [1]

But as the feasible region is unbounded, therefore 52 may or may not be the minimum value of Z.

For this, we draw a dotted graph of the inequality $6x + 10y < 52$ or $3x + 5y < 26$ and check whether the resulting half plane has points in common with the feasible region or not.

It can be seen that the feasible region has no common point with $3x + 5y < 26$.

Therefore, the minimum value of Z is 52 at $B\ (2, 4)$.

Hence, the mixture should contain 2 kg of food X and 4 kg of food Y. The minimum cost of the mixture is ₹ 52. [1]

6. Similar as Question 5. **Ans.** ₹ 192

7. **Hint** Minimise $Z = 28x + 25y$

subject to constraints are

$80x + 100y \geq 88,\ 40x + 30y \geq 36,\ x + y = 1$ and $x, y \geq 0$

[**Ans.** Bran = 0.6 kg, Rice = 0.4 kg; Minimum cost is ₹ 26.8]

8. Let the company manufactures x units of product A and y units of product B.

Let us construct the following table

Type	Unit	Nickel (in g)	Chromium (in g)	Profit
A	x	$3x$	x	$40x$
B	y	y	$2y$	$50y$
Total	$x + y$	$3x + y$	$x + 2y$	$40x + 50y$
Availability		9	8	

[1]

Here, the profit is to be maximised

i.e. $$Z = 40x + 50y \quad \text{...(i)}$$

Subject to the constraints are

$$3x + y \leq 9 \quad \text{...(ii)}$$

$$x + 2y \leq 8 \quad \text{...(iii)}$$

and $$x \geq 0,\ y \geq 0 \quad \text{...(iv)}$$

Table for line $3x + y = 9$ or $y = 9 - 3x$

x	0	3
y	9	0

[1]

On putting (0, 0) in the inequality

$3x + y \leq 9$, we get $0 + 0 \leq 9$

$\Rightarrow$ $0 \leq 9$, which is true.

So, the half plane is towards the origin.

Table for line $x + 2y = 8$ or $y = \dfrac{8 - x}{2}$

x	0	8
y	4	0

On putting (0, 0) in the inequality [1]

$x + 2y \leq 8$, we get $0 + 0 \leq 8$

$\Rightarrow$ $0 \leq 8$, which is true.

So, the half plane is towards the origin.

Since, $x,\ y \geq 0$

So, the feasible region lies in the first quadrant.

On solving equations $3x + y = 9$ and $x + 2y = 8$, we get $B(2, 3)$.

Clearly, the feasible region is $OABCO$.

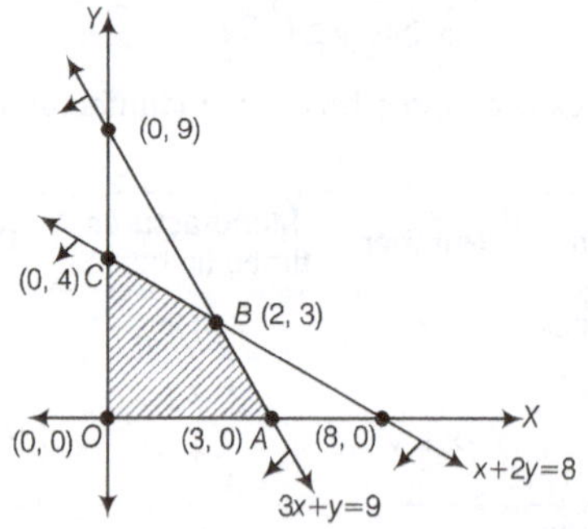

[1]

The corner points of the feasible region are $O(0, 0)$, $A(3, 0)$, $B(2, 3)$ and $C(0, 4)$. Now, the values of Z at these points are as follows [1]

Corner point	$Z = 40x + 50y$
$O(0, 0)$	$Z = 40(0) + 50(0) = 0$
$A(3, 0)$	$Z = 40(3) + 50(0) = 120$
$B(2, 3)$	$Z = 40(2) + 50(3) = 230$ (Maximum)
$C(0, 4)$	$Z = 40(0) + 50(4) = 200$

Thus, the maximum value of Z is ₹ 230 at $B(2, 3)$. Hence, 2 units of type A and 3 units of type B should be produced, to get the maximum profit of ₹ 230. [1]

9. Similar as Question 8.

Maximise, $Z = 50x + 60y$

Subject to the constraints are $3x + y \leq 9,\ x + 2y \leq 8$ and $x \geq 0,\ y \geq 0$.

[**Ans.** The profit of the company is maximum of ₹ 280 when company produce 2 items of type P and 3 items of type Q.]

10. Let the number of pieces of two types of teaching aids A and B be x and y, respectively.
Let us construct the following table

Items	Number of pieces	Time on fabricating (in hours)	Time on finishing (in hours)	Profit (in ₹)
A	x	$9x$	x	$80x$
B	y	$12y$	$3y$	$120y$
Total	$x+y$	$9x+12y$	$x+3y$	$80x+120y$
Availability		180	30	

The profit on type A is ₹ 80 and on type B is ₹ 120.
Our objective is to maximise, [1]

$$Z = 80x + 120y \quad \text{...(i)}$$

subject to constraints,

$$9x + 12y \le 180 \text{ or } 3x + 4y \le 60 \quad \text{...(ii)}$$

$$x + 3y \le 30 \quad \text{...(iii)}$$

and $x \ge 0,\ y \ge 0$ ...(iv)

Table for line $9x + 12y = 180$ is ...(v)

x	0	20
y	15	0

So, line is passing through the points (0, 15) and (20, 0).
On putting (0, 0) in the inequality $9x + 12y \le 180$, we get

$9(0) + 12(0) \le 180$

$\Rightarrow$ $0 \le 180$, which is true.

So, the half plane is towards the origin.
Table for line $x + 3y = 30$ is

x	0	30
y	10	0

[1]

So, line is passing through the points (0, 10) and (30, 0).
On putting (0, 0) in the inequality $x + 3y \le 30$, we get

$0 + 3(0) \le 30$

$\Rightarrow$ $0 \le 30$, which is true.

So, the half plane is towards the origin.
Also, $x \ge 0$ and $y \ge 0$, implies that the region lies in the I quadrant.
On solving $3x + 4y = 60$ and $x + 3y = 30$, we get the point of intersection $B(12, 6)$. [1]
The graphical representation of the lines is given below

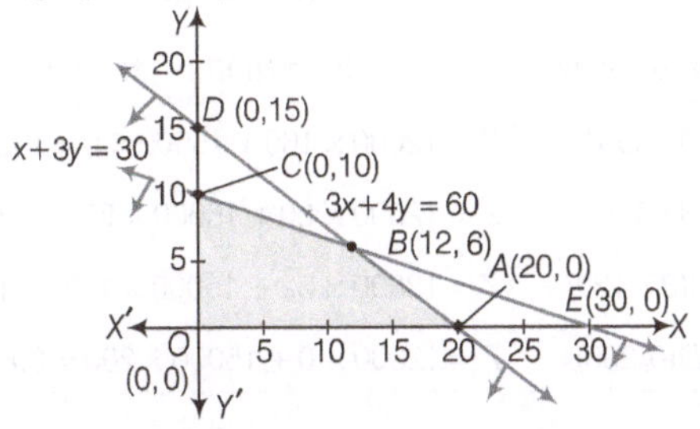

Clearly, feasible region is $OABCO$. [2]
The corner points of the feasible region are $O(0, 0)$, $A(20, 0)$, $B(12, 6)$ and $C(0, 10)$.

Corner points	$Z = 80x + 120y$
$O(0, 0)$	$Z = 80(0) + 120(0) = 0$
$A(20, 0)$	$Z = 80(20) + 120(0) = 1600$
$B(12, 6)$	$Z = 80(12) + 120(6) = 1680$
$C(0, 10)$	$Z = 80(0) + 120(10) = 1200$

Thus, the maximum value of Z is ₹ 1680.
The manufacturer should produce 12 pieces of type A and 6 pieces of type B to earn maximum profit of ₹ 1680. [1]

11. Let x toys of type A and y toys of type B be manufactured.
Since, the profit is to be maximised.
$\therefore$ Maximise profit $(P) = 50x + 60y$ ...(i)
Let us arrange the given data in the following table

Types of toys	Total number	Required time for cutting	Required time for assembling	Profit
A	x	$5x$ min	$10x$ min	₹ $50x$
B	y	$8y$ min	$8y$ min	₹ $60y$
Total		$(5x + 8y)$ min	$(10x + 8y)$ min	₹ $(50x + 60y)$

[1]

Given, total time for cutting ≤ 180 min
and total time for assembling ≤ 240 min

$\therefore$ $5x + 8y \le 180$ ...(ii)

and $10x + 8y \le 240$

or $2(5x + 4y) \le 2(120)$ ...(iii)

and $x \ge 0,\ y \ge 0$ ...(iv)

Table for graph of the line $5x + 8y = 180$.

x	0	36
y	45/2	0

Put (0,0) in the inequality $5x + 8y \le 180$, we get
$0 + 0 \le 180$, which is true. [1]
So, the half plane is towards the origin.
Table for graph of the line $5x + 4y = 120$.

x	0	24
y	30	0

Put (0, 0) in the inequality $5x + 4y \le 120$, we get
$0 + 0 \le 120$, which is true.
So, the half plane is towards the origin.
Also, $x \ge 0$, $y \ge 0$, implies that the feasible region lies in the first qradrant. [1]
The point of intersection of lines corresponding to inequalities (ii) and (iii) is E (12, 15).

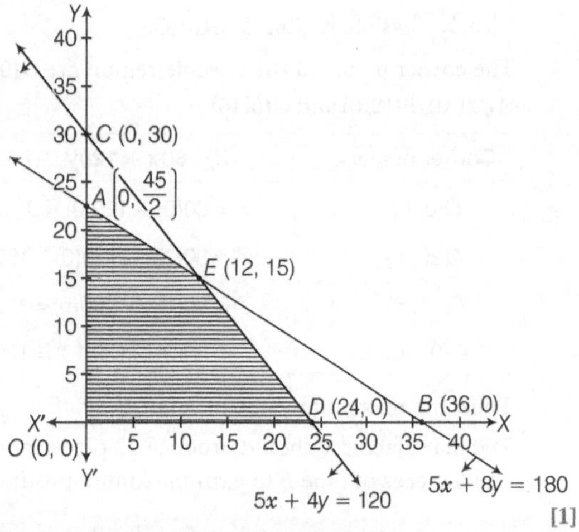

[1]

The shaded region represents the feasible region and its corner points are $O(0,0)$, $A\left(0, \frac{45}{2}\right)$, $D(24, 0)$ and $E(12, 15)$.

Corner points	$P = 50x + 60y$
O (0,0)	$P = 50\times0 + 60\times0 = 0$
A (0, 45/2)	$P = 50\times0 + 60\times\frac{45}{2}$ $= 30\times45 = 1350$
D (24, 0)	$P = 50\times24 + 60\times0$ $= 50\times24 = 1200$
E (12, 15)	$P = 50\times12 + 60\times15$ $= 600 + 900 = 1500$

[1]

Hence, the maximum profit of the company is ₹1500 for manufacturing 12 toys of type A and 15 toys of type B. [1]

12. Let factory I run x days and factory II run y days.

Total cost (in ₹) $= 12000x + 15000y$

Then, minimise $Z = 12000x + 15000y$

subject to constraints are

$50x + 40y \geq 6400$ or $5x + 4y \geq 640$ ...(i)

$50x + 20y \geq 4000$ or $5x + 2y \geq 400$ ...(ii)

$30x + 40y \geq 4800$ or $3x + 4y \geq 480$ ...(iii)

and $x \geq 0,\ y \geq 0$ ...(iv)

Table for line $5x + 4y = 640$ is

x	128	0
y	0	160

So, the line is passing through the points (128, 0) and (0, 160). [1]

On putting (0, 0) in the inequality $5x + 4y \geq 640$, we get

$5(0) + (0) \geq 640$, which is not true.

So, the half plane is away from the origin.

Table for line $5x + 2y = 400$ is

x	80	0
y	0	200

So, the line is passing through the points (80, 0) and (0, 200).

On putting (0, 0) in the inequality $5x + 2y \geq 400$, we get

$5(0) + 2(0) \geq 400$, which is not true.

So, the half plane is away from the origin.

Table for line $3x + 4y = 480$ is

x	160	0
y	0	120

[1]

So, the line is passing through the points (160, 0) and (0, 120).

On putting (0, 0) in the inequality $3x + 4y \geq 480$, we get

$0 + 0 \geq 480$, which is not true.

So, the half plane is away from the origin.

Also, $x \geq 0$ and $y \geq 0$, implies the feasible region lies in the I quadrant.

The point of intersection of lines corresponding to (i) and (iii) is B (80, 60) and corresponding to (i) and (ii) is C(32, 120). [1]

The above Eqs. (i), (ii), (iii) and (iv) can be represented graphically as

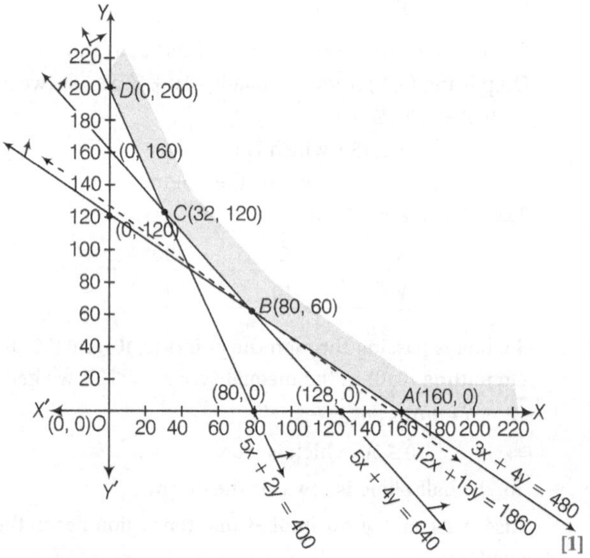

[1]

Clearly, feasible region is $ABCD$ (shaded region), where corner points are $A(160, 0)$, $B(80, 60)$, $C(32, 120)$ and $D(0, 200)$.

The values of Z at corner points are given below

Corner points	$Z = 12000x + 15000y$
A(160, 0)	$Z = 12000\times160 + 15000\times0 = 1920000$
B(80, 60)	$Z = 12000\times80 + 15000\times60 = 1860000$
C(32, 120)	$Z = 12000\times32 + 15000\times120 = 2184000$
D(0, 200)	$Z = 12000\times0 + 15000\times200 = 3000000$

[1]

In the above table, we find that minimum value of Z is 1860000 occur at the point $B(80, 60)$.

But we cannot say that it is a minimum value of Z as region is unbounded.

Therefore, we have to draw the graph of the inequality

$$12000x + 15000y < 1860000$$

or $$12x + 15y < 1860$$

or $$\frac{x}{155} + \frac{y}{124} < 1$$

Now, check whether the resulting open half plane has any point common with feasible region. From figure, we see that it has no point in common.

Thus, the minimum value of Z is ₹ 1860000 attained at the point $B(80, 60)$.

Hence, factory I should run for 80 days and factory II should run for 60 days. [1]

13. Hint Maximise $Z = 20x + 10y$,

subject to constraints are

$1.5x + 3y \leq 42,\ 3x + y \leq 24$ and $x, y \geq 0$

[**Ans.** For maximum profit of ₹ 200, 4 tennis rackets and 12 cricket bats must be produced]

14. Let x units of product A and y units of product B will be produced.

Type	Number	Teak wood	Plywood	Rosewood
A	x	$2x$	$1x$	$1x$
B	y	$1y$	$2y$	$1y$

$\therefore$ The objective function is to maximise

$$Z = 48x + 40y$$

Subject to constrains are

$$2x + y \leq 90 \Rightarrow x + 2y \leq 80$$

$$x + y \leq 50 \text{ and } x,\ y \geq 0$$

Consider the constraints as linear equations

$$2x + y = 90 \quad \text{...(i)}$$

$$x + 2y = 80 \quad \text{...(ii)}$$

$$x + y = 50 \quad \text{...(iii)}$$

and $$x = y = 0 \quad \text{...(iv)}$$

Table for line $2x + y = 90$ is

x	0	45
y	90	0

So, line is passing through the points (0, 90) and (45, 0).

On putting (0, 0) in the inequality $2x + y \leq 90$, we get $0 + 0 \leq 90$, which is true.

So, the half plane is towards the origin.

Table for line $x + 2y = 80$ is

x	0	80
y	40	0

So, line is passing through the points (0, 40) and (80, 0).

On putting (0, 0) in the inequality $x + 2y \leq 80$, we get $0 + 0 \leq 80$, which is true

So, the half plane is towards the origin.

Table for line $x + y = 50$ is

x	0	50
y	50	0

So, line is passing through the points (0, 50) and (50, 0).

On putting (0, 0) in the inequality $x + y \leq 50$, we get

$$0 + 0 \leq 50$$

$$\Rightarrow \quad 0 \leq 50, \text{ which is true.}$$

So, the half plane is towards the origin.

Also, $x, y \geq 0$, implies the feasible region lies in the I quadrant.

Now, the point of intersection of lines (i) and (iii); (ii) and (iii), are respectively, $C(40, 10)$ and $B(20, 30)$.

The graphical representation of these lines is given below

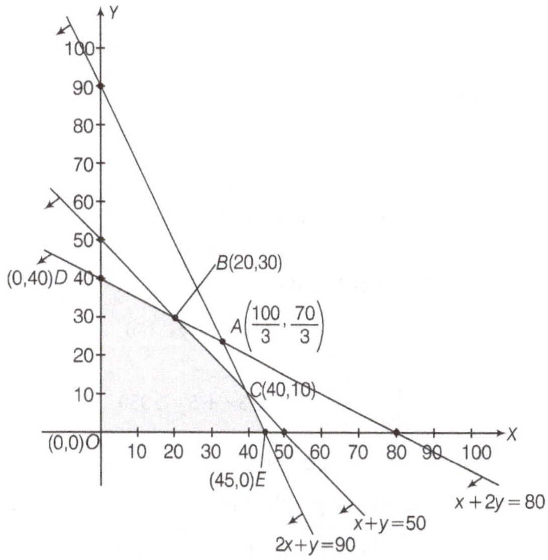

The shaded region $OECBDO$ represents the feasible region and its.

Corner points are $O(0, 0)$, $B(20, 30)$, $C(40, 10)$, $D(0, 40)$ and $E(45, 0)$.

The values of Z at the corner points are given below

Corner points	$Z = 48x + 40y$
$O(0,0)$	$Z = 48 \times 0 + 40 \times 0 = 0$
$B(20,30)$	$Z = 48 \times 20 + 40 \times 30 = 2160$
$C(40,10)$	$Z = 48 \times 40 + 40 \times 10 = 2320$
$D(0,40)$	$Z = 48 \times 0 + 40 \times 40 = 1600$
$E(45,0)$	$Z = 48 \times 45 + 40 \times 0 = 2160$

Thus, Z is maximum at $x = 40$, $y = 10$ and maximum value of z is 2320.
Hence, the product A produce 40 quantity and product B produce 10 quantity to obtain maximum gross income.

15. **Hint** Maximise profit $Z = 22x + 18y$
subject to constraints are

$$360x + 240y \le 5760,\ x + y \le 20 \text{ and } x, y \ge 0$$

[**Ans.** Dealer should purchase 8 electronic sewing machine and 12 manually operated sewing machine. Maximum profit = ₹ 392]

16. Let the farmer uses x kg of type A fertilizer and y kg of type B fertilizer. Then, we have the following table

Type	Quantity (in kg)	Nitrogen	Phosphoric acid	Cost in (₹)
A	x	$\frac{10}{100}x = \frac{1}{10}x$	$\frac{6}{100}x$	$5x$
B	y	$\frac{5}{100}y = \frac{1}{20}y$	$\frac{10}{100}y$	$8y$
Total	$x + y$	$\frac{x}{10} + \frac{y}{20}$	$\frac{6x}{100} + \frac{10y}{100}$	$5x + 8y$
Requirement (in kg)		7	7	

[2]

Total cost of fertilizers $= 5x + 8y$
Here, we have to minimise the cost
i.e. $Z = 5x + 8y$ ...(i)
Subject to constraints

$$\frac{x}{10} + \frac{y}{20} \ge 7 \Leftrightarrow 2x + y \ge 140 \quad ...(ii)$$

$$\frac{6x}{100} + \frac{10y}{100} \ge 7 \Leftrightarrow 3x + 5y \ge 350 \quad ...(iii)$$

and $x \ge 0,\ y \ge 0$ ...(iv)

Firstly, draw the graph of the line $2x + y = 140$.

x	0	70
y	140	0

[1]

Putting (0, 0) in the inequality $2x + y \ge 140$, we get

$$2 \times 0 + 0 \ge 140$$

$\Rightarrow$ $0 \ge 140$, which is false.
So, the half plane is away from the origin.
Since, $x, y \ge 0$, so the feasible region lies in the first quadrant.
Secondly, draw the graph of the line $3x + 5y = 350$.

x	0	350/3
y	70	0

Putting (0, 0) in the inequality $3x + 5y \ge 350$, we get

$$3 \times 0 + 5 \times 0 \ge 350$$

$\Rightarrow$ $0 \ge 350$, which is false.
So, the half plane is away from the origin.
On solving the equations $2x + y = 140$ and $3x + 5y = 350$, we get $B(50, 40)$.

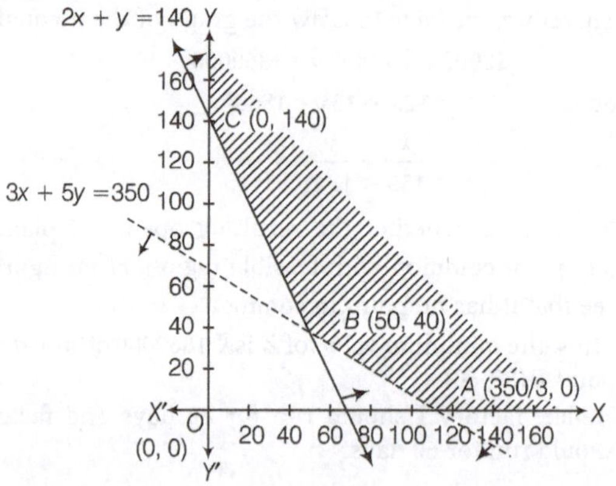

[1]

It can be seen that the feasible region is unbounded. [1]
The corner points of the feasible region are $A\left(\frac{350}{3}, 0\right)$, $B(50, 40)$ and $C(0, 140)$. The values of Z at these points are as follows

Corner points	$Z = 5x + 8y$
$A\left(\frac{350}{3}, 0\right)$	$Z = 5\left(\frac{350}{3}\right) + 8(0) = \frac{1750}{3} \approx 583$
$B(50, 40)$	$Z = 5(50) + 8(40) = 570$ (Minimum)
$C(0, 140)$	$Z = 5(0) + 8(140) = 1120.$

As the feasible region is unbounded therefore, 570 may or may not be the minimum value of Z. For this, we draw a graph of the inequality, $5x + 8y < 570$ and check, whether the resulting half plane has points in common with the feasible region or not.
It can be seen that the feasible region has no common point with $5x + 8y < 570$.
Therefore, 50 kg of fertilizer A and 40 kg of fertilizer B should be used to minimize the cost. The minimum cost is ₹570. [1]

17. Let the total number of type A machines is x and the total number of type B machines is y.
Since, the daily output is to be maximised.
$\therefore$ Maximise $Z = 50x + 40y$ ...(i)
Subject to the constraints are

$$1000x + 1200y \le 7600 \text{ or } 5x + 6y \le 38 \quad ...(ii)$$

$$12x + 8y \le 72 \text{ or } 3x + 2y \le 18 \quad ...(iii)$$

$$x \ge 0 \text{ and } y \ge 0 \quad ...(iv)$$

Table for graph of line $5x + 6y = 38$ is

x	0	38/5
y	19/3	0

[1]

Put (0, 0) in the ineqality $5x + 6y \le 38$, we get

$0 + 0 \le 38 \Rightarrow 0 \le 38$ [which is true]

So, the half plane is towards the origin.

Table for graph of line $3x + 2y = 18$

x	0	6
y	9	0

Put (0, 0) in the inequality $3x + 2y \le 18$, we get

$0 + 0 \le 18$

$\Rightarrow$ $0 \le 18$ [which is true]

So, the half plane is towards the origin. [1]

Also, $x \ge 0$, $y > 0$, implies that the feasible region lies in the first quadrant.

The point of intersection of lines corresponding to (ii) and (iii) is $B(4, 3)$.

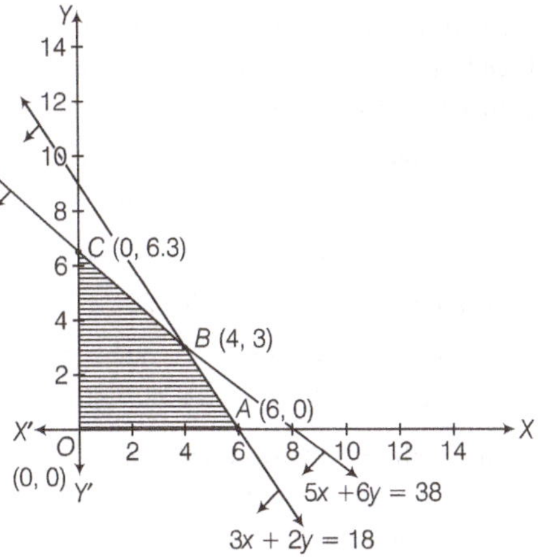

[1]

The shaded region represents a bounded feasible region and its corner point are $O(0,0)$, $A(6, 0)$, $B(4, 3)$, $C(0, 6.3)$.

Corner points	$Z = 50x + 40y$
O (0,0)	$Z = 50 \times 0 + 40 \times 0 = 0$
A (6, 0)	$Z = 50 \times 6 + 40 \times 0 = 300$
B(4, 3)	$Z = 50 \times 4 + 40 \times 3$ $= 200 + 120 = 320$
C (0,6.3)	$Z = 50 \times 0 + 40 \times 6.3 = 252$

[2]

Hence, maximum daily output is 320, which will be achieved, when 4 machines of type A and 3 machines of type B are bought. [1]

18. Let the tailor P works for x days, while tailor Q works for y days.

Since, the cost is to be minimised

$\therefore$ Minimise $Z = 150x + 200y$ ...(i)

Subject to the constraints are $6x + 10y \ge 60$

or $3x + 5y \ge 30$ ...(ii)

$4x + 4y \ge 32$ or $x + y \ge 8$ ...(iii)

$x \ge 0, y \ge 0$ ...(iv)

Table for graph of line $3x + 5y = 30$ is

x	0	10
y	6	0

[1]

Put (0, 0) in the inequality $3x + 5y \ge 30$, we get

$0 + 0 \ge 30 \Rightarrow 0 \ge 30$, which is false.

So, the half plane is away from the origin.

Table for graph of the line $x + y = 8$ is

x	0	8
y	8	0

Put (0, 0) in the inequality $x + y \ge 8$, we get

$0 + 0 \ge 8 \Rightarrow 0 \ge 8$, which is false.

So, the half plane is away from the origin.

Also, $x \ge 0$, $y \ge 0$, implies that the feasible region lies in the first quadrant. The intersection point of lines corresponding to (ii) and (ii) is $B(5,3)$. [1]

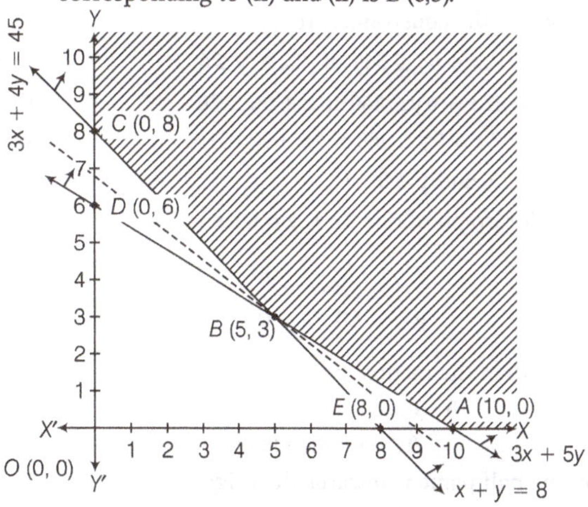

[2]

The shaded region represents an unbounded feasible region and its corner points are $A(10,0)$, $B(5,3)$ and $C(0,8)$.

Corner points	$Z = 150x + 200y$
A (10, 0)	$Z = 150 \times 10 + 200 \times 0 = 1500$
B (5, 3)	$Z = 150 \times 5 + 200 \times 3$ $= 750 + 600 = 1350$
C (0, 8)	$Z = 150 \times 0 + 200 \times 8 = 1600$

[1]

The cost is minimum at $B(5, 3)$.

But the feasible region is unbounded, therefore 1350 may or may not be the minimum value of Z.

Now, we draw the graph of the inequality $150x + 200y < 1350$, i.e. $3x + 4y < 27$ and check whether the open half plane has points in common with feasible region or not. From the graph, we see that the open half plane $3x + 4y < 45$ has no points in common with the feasible region.

So, the minimum value of Z is 1350 at $B(5,3)$.

Hence,tailor P should works for 5 days and tailor Q should work for 3 days to minimise the labour cost. [1]

19. Let the manufacturer makes x cups of type A and y cups of type B. Let us construct the following table

Types of Cups	Number of Cups	Time on machine I (in min)	Time on machine II (in min)	Time on machine III (in min)	Profit (in ₹)
A	x	$12x$	$18x$	$6x$	$7.50x$
B	y	$6y$	$0y$	$9y$	$5y$
Total	$x+y$	$12x+6y$	$18x+0y$	$6x+9y$	$7.50x+5y$
Maximum time available		$6\times60=360$	$6\times60=360$	$6\times60=360$	

Since, the profit is to be maximised.

$\therefore$ Maximise, $Z=1.5x+y$ ...(i)

Subject to the constraints are

$12x+6y\le360$ or $2x+y\le60$ ...(ii)

$18x+0y\le360$ or $x+0y\le20$ ...(iii)

$6x+9y\le360$ or $2x+3y\le120$ ...(iv)

and $x\ge0$ and $y\ge0$

Table for graph of line $2x+y=60$ is

x	0	30
y	60	0

Put (0, 0) in the inequality $2x+y\le60$, we get

$0+0\le60$

$\Rightarrow$ $0\le60$, which is true.

So, the half plane is towards the origin. [1]

Table for graph of line $x+0y=20$ is

	20	20
	0	3

Put (0, 0) in the inequality $x+0y\le20$, we get

$0+0\le20$

$\Rightarrow$ $0\le20$, which is true.

So, the half plane is towards the origin.

Table for graph of the line $2x+3y=120$ is

x	0	60
y	40	0

Put (0, 0) in the inequality $2x+3y\le120$, we get

$0+0\le120\Rightarrow0\le120$, which is true.

So, the half plane is towards the origin. [1]

Also, $x\ge0$, $y\ge0$, so the feasible region lies in the first quadrant.

The points of intersection of lines corresponding to (ii) and (iii), (ii) and (iv) are B(20, 20) and C(15, 30).

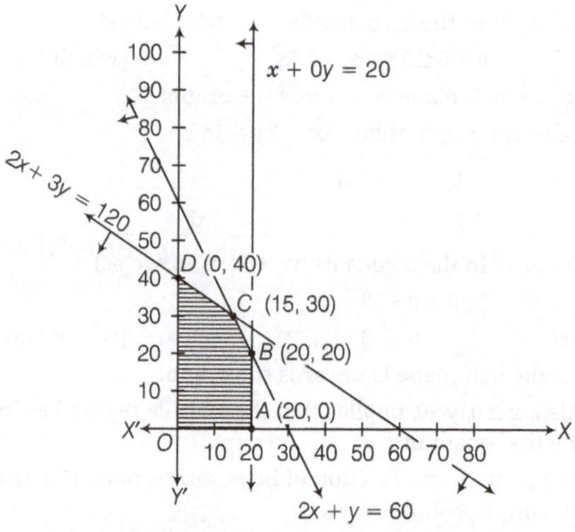

The shaded region represents the feasible region $OABCDO$ and the corner points are $O(0,0)$, $A(20,0)$, $B(20,20)$, $C(15,30)$ and $D(0,40)$. [1]

Corner points	$Z=1.5x+y$
O(0, 0)	$Z=1.5\times0+0=0$
A(20, 0)	$Z=1.5\times20+0=30$
B(20, 20)	$Z=1.5\times20+20=50$
C(15, 30)	$Z=15\times1.5+30\times1=52.50$
D(0, 40)	$Z=1.5\times0+40=40$

[1]

Maximum profit = ₹52.50 at C(15,30).

$\therefore$ Type $A=15$ cups, Type $B=30$ cups should be manufactured in a day to maximise the profit. [1]

20. Let godown A supplies x and y quintals of grain to the shops D and E, respectively.

Then, $(100-x-y)$ will be supplied to shop F.

The requirement at shop D is 60 quintals, since x quintals are transported from godown A.

Therefore, the remaining $(60-x)$ quintals are transported from godown B. Similarly, $(50-y)$ quintals and $40-(100-x-y)=(x+y-60)$ quintals will be transported from godown B to shops E and F, respectively. The given problem can be represented diagrammatically as follows [1]

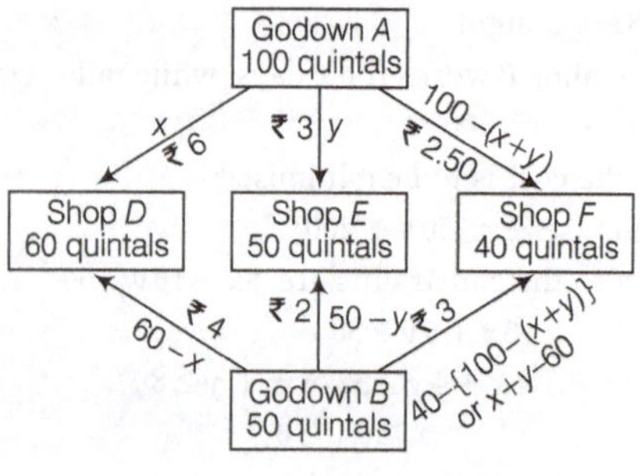

Let Z be the total cost of transportation, then

$$Z = 6x + 3y + 2.50(100 - x - y) + 4(60 - x) + 2(50 - y) + 3[(x + y) - 60]$$

$$= 6x + 3y + 250 - 2.50x - 2.50y + 240 - 4x + 100 - 2y + 3x + 3y - 180$$

$$= 2.50x + 1.50y + 410 \quad \text{...(i)} \ [1]$$

subject to constraints

$$60 - x \geq 0 \quad \text{or} \quad x \leq 60 \quad \text{... (ii)}$$

$$50 - y \geq 0 \quad \text{or} \quad y \leq 50 \quad \text{... (iii)}$$

$$100 - (x + y) \geq 0 \quad \text{or} \quad x + y \leq 100 \quad \text{... (iv)}$$

$$x + y - 60 \geq 0 \quad \text{or} \quad x + y \geq 60 \quad \text{... (v)}$$

and $x \geq 0, y \geq 0$ ... (vi)

Table for line $x + y = 100$ is

x	100	0
y	0	100

So, line is passing through the points (100, 0) and (0, 100).
On putting (0, 0) in the inequality $x + y \leq 100$, we get

$0 + 0 \leq 100$

$\Rightarrow$ $0 \leq 100$, which is true. [1]

So, the half plane is towards the origin.
Table for line $x + y = 60$ is

x	0	60
y	60	0

So, line is passing through the points (0, 60) and (60, 0).

On putting (0, 0) in the inequality $x + y \geq 60$, we get

$0 + 0 \geq 60$

$\Rightarrow$ $0 \geq 60$, which is not true.

So, the half plane is away from the origin. [1]

Now, draw the graph of lines $x = 60$ and $y = 50$, which is perpendicular to X and Y-axes, respectively.

Clearly, the half planes $x \leq 60$ and $y \leq 50$ is towards Y and X-axes, respectively.

Also, $x, y \geq 0$, implies that the region lies in the I quadrant.

The points of intersection of lines corresponding to inequalities (ii), (iii), (iv) and (v) are $A(60, 0)$, $B(60, 40)$, $C(50, 50)$ and $D(10, 50)$.

The graphical representation of these lines is given below

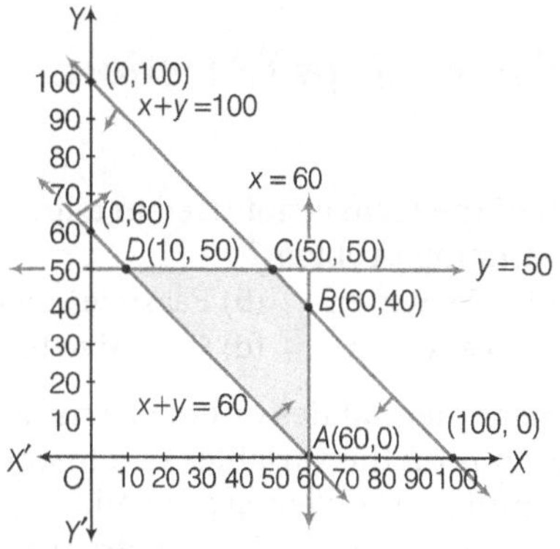

[1]

The shaded region in the graph represents the feasible region and its corner points are $A(60, 0)$, $B(60, 40)$, $C(50, 50)$ and $D(10, 50)$.

The values of Z at the corner points are given below

Corner points	$Z = 2.5x + 1.5y + 410$
$A(60, 0)$	$Z = 2.5(60) + 1.5(0) + 410 = 560$
$B(60, 40)$	$Z = 2.5(60) + 1.5(40) + 410 = 620$
$C(50, 50)$	$Z = 2.5(50) + 1.5(50) + 410 = 610$
$D(10, 50)$	$Z = 2.5(10) + 1.5(50) + 410 = 510$

The minimum value of Z is 510 at $D(10, 50)$.

Thus, the amount of grain transported from A to D, E and F is 10 quintals, 50 quintals and 40 quintals, respectively and from B to D, E and F is 50 quintals, 0 quintal and 0 quintal, respectively. The minimum cost is ₹ 510. [1]

Chapter Practice

Multiple Choice Type Questions

1 Mark

1 Which of the term is not used in a linear programming problem?
(a) Optimal solution (b) Feasible solution
(c) Concave region (d) Objective function

2 The linear inequalities or equations or restrictions on the variables of a linear programming problem are called
(a) linear relations (b) constraints
(c) functions (d) objective functions

3 The objective function of an LPP is
(a) a constraint
(b) a function to be optimised
(c) a relation between the variables
(d) None of the above

4 The corner points of the feasible region in the graphical representation of a linear programming problem are (2, 72), (15, 20) and (40, 15). If $Z = 18x + 9y$ be the objective function, then
(a) Z is maximum at (2, 72), minimum at (15, 20)
(b) Z is maximum at (15, 20), minimum at (40, 15)
(c) Z is maximum at (40, 15), minimum at (15, 20)
(d) Z is maximum at (40, 15), minimum at (2, 72)

5 The solution set of the inequation $3x + 5y < 7$ is
(a) whole XY-plane except the points lying on the line $3x + 5y = 7$
(b) whole XY-plane along with the points lying on the line $3x + 5y = 7$
(c) open half plane containing the origin except the points of line $3x + 5y = 7$
(d) open half plane not containing the origin

Assertion-Reason Type Questions

1 Mark

Directions (Q. Nos. 6-8) Consider the graph of constraints stated as linear inequalities as below

$5x + y \leq 100$ ...(i)
$x + y \leq 60$ ...(ii)
$x \geq 0$ ...(iii)
$y \geq 0$ ...(iv)

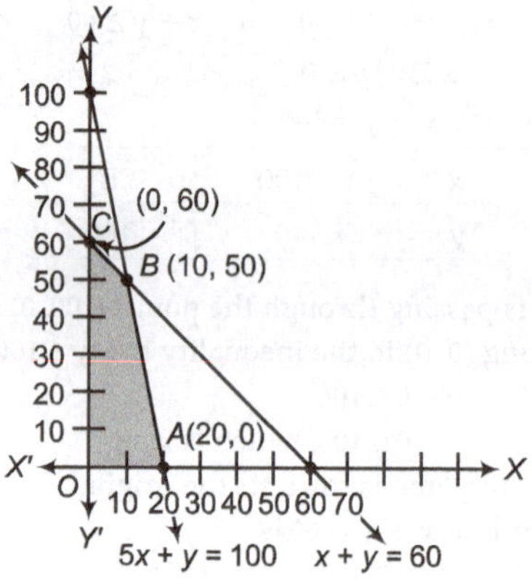

On the basis of above information, the questions given below has two statements labelled as Assertion (A) and Reason (R). In the context of the two statements, which one of the following is correct?

(a) Both A and R are correct; R is the correct explanation of A
(b) Both A and R are correct; R is not the correct explanation of A
(c) A is correct; R is incorrect
(d) R is correct; A is incorrect

6 **Assertion (A)** The points (10, 50), (0, 60) or (20, 0) are feasible solutions.

Reason (R) Points within and on the boundary of the feasible region represent feasible solutions of the constraints.

7 **Assertion (A)** The objective function $Z = -50x + 20y$
Subject to the constraints

$$2x - y \geq -5$$
$$3x + y \geq 3$$
$$2x - 3y \leq 12$$
$$x \geq 0, y \geq 0$$

in the feasible region has no minimum value.

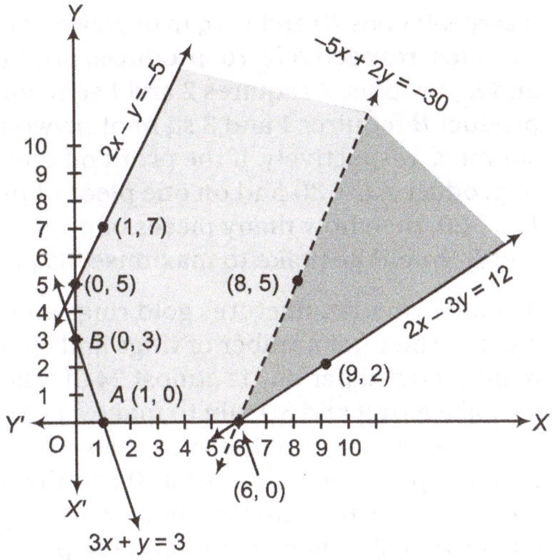

Reason (R) If the open half plane determined by $ax + by < m$, where m is the minimum value of Z, has a point in common with feasible region, then Z has no minimum value.

8 **Assertion (A)** The maximum value of

$$Z = 11x + 7y$$

Subject to the constraints

$$2x + y \le 6, x \le 2 \text{ and } x \ge 0, y \ge 0$$

in the feasible region occurs at the corner point (0, 6).

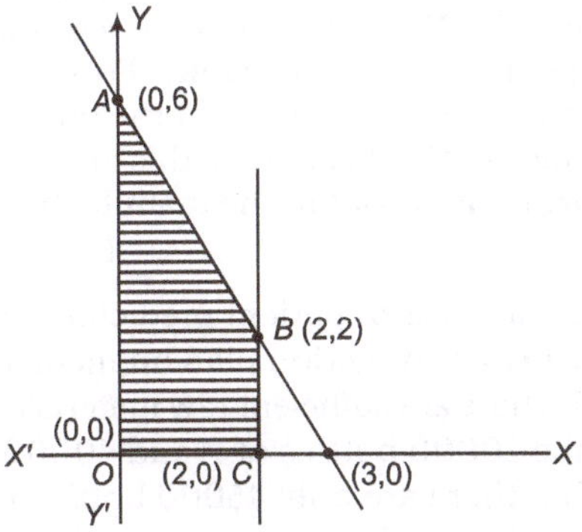

Reason (R) If the feasible region of the given LPP is bounded, then the maximum and minimum value of the objective function occurs at corner points.

Very Short Answer Type Questions

2 Marks

9 A diet for a sick person must contain atleast 4000 units of vitamins, 50 units of minerals and 1400 calories. Two foods A and B are available at a cost of ₹ 4 and ₹ 3 per unit, respectively. Food A contains 200 units of vitamins, 1 unit of minerals and 40 calories. Food B contains 100 units of vitamins, 2 units of minerals and 40 calories. Express this problem as a linear programming problem.

10 A man rides his motorcycle at the speed of 50 km/h. He has to spend ₹ 2 per km on petrol. If he rides it at a faster speed of 80 km/h, the petrol cost increases to ₹ 3 per km. He has atmost ₹ 120 to spend on petrol and one hour time. He wishes to find the maximum distance that he can travel. Express this problem as a linear programming problem. **[NCERT Exemplar]**

11 Feasible region (shaded) for an LPP is shown in the following figure, Maximise $Z = 5x + 7y$. **[NCERT Exemplar]**

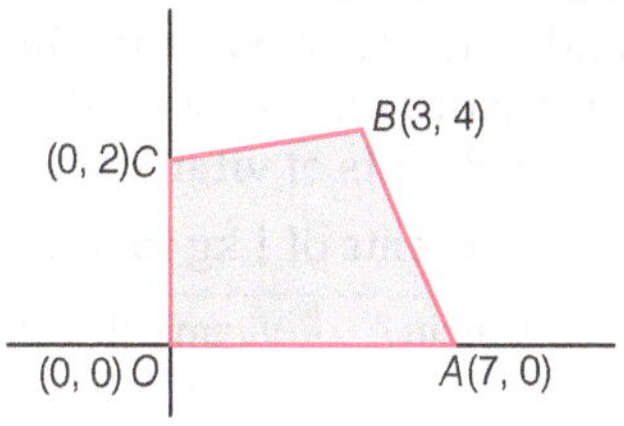

Short Answer Type Questions

4 Marks

Directions (Q. Nos. 12-15) *Solve the following LPP graphically.*

12 Maximise $Z = 3x + 2y$, subject to constraints are $x + y \ge 8$, $3x + 5y \le 15$ and $x, y \ge 0$.

13 Maximise $Z = 3x + 4y$, subject to constraints are $x + y \le 1$; $x \ge 0, y \ge 0$. **[NCERT Exemplar]**

14 Minimise $Z = 2x + 4y$, subject to constraints are $x + y \ge 8, x + 4y \ge 12, x \ge 3, y \ge 2$ and $x, y \ge 0$.

15 Maximise and minimise $Z = 3x - 4y$, subject to constraints are $x - 2y \le 0, -3x + y \le 4, x - y \le 6$ and $x, y \ge 0$. **[NCERT Exemplar]**

16 Aman has ₹ 1500 to purchase rice and wheat for his grocery shop. Each sack of rice and wheat costs ₹ 180 and ₹ 120 respectively. He can store a maximum number of 10 bags in his shop.
He will earn a profit of ₹ 11 per bag of rice and ₹ 9 per bag of wheat. **[ISC 2024]**

(i) Formulate a linear programming problem to maximise Aman's profit.

(ii) Calculate the maximum profit.

Long Answer Type Questions

(6 Marks)

17 A dietician has to develop a special diet using two foods P and Q. Each packet (containing 30 g) of food P contains 12 units of calcium, 4 units of iron, 6 units of cholesterol and 6 units of vitamin A. Each packet of the same quantity of food Q contains 3 units of calcium, 20 units of iron, 4 units of cholesterol and 3 units of vitamin A.

The diet requires atleast 240 units of calcium, atleast 460 units of iron and atmost 300 units of cholesterol. How many packets of each food should be used to minimise the amount of vitamin A in the diet? What is the minimum amount of vitamin A? [NCERT]

18 A dietician wishes to mix together two kinds of foods X and Y in such a way that the mixture contains atleast 10 units of vitamin A, 12 units of vitamin B and 8 units of vitamin C.

The vitamin contents of 1 kg food is given below

Food	Vitamin A	Vitamin B	Vitamin C
X	1	2	3
Y	2	2	1

1 kg of food X costs of ₹ 16 and 1 kg of food Y costs ₹ 20. Find the least cost of the mixture, which will produce the required diet? [NCERT]

19 A firm deals with two kinds of fruit juice. These are mixed and two mixtures are sold as soft drink A and B. 1 tin of A requires 4 of pineapple and 1 of orange juice. 1 tin of B requires 2 of pineapple and 3 of orange juice. The firm has only 46 of pineapple juice and 24 of orange juice. Each tin of A and B are sold at a profit of ₹ 4 and ₹ 3, respectively. How many tins of each type should the firm produce to maximise the profit? Solve the problem graphically.

20 One kind of cake requires 200 g of flour and 25 g of fat and another kind of cake requires 100 g of flour and 50 g of fat. Find the maximum number of cakes which can be made from 5 kg of flour and 1 kg of fat assuming that there is no shortage of other ingredients used in making the cakes. Formulate the above as a linear programming problem and solve it graphically. [NCERT]

21 A carpenter has 20 and 15 sq m of plywood and sunmica, respectively. He produces products A and B. Product A requires 2 and 1 sq m and product B requires 1 and 3 sq m of plywood and sunmica, respectively. If the profit on one piece of product A is ₹ 30 and on one piece of product B is ₹ 20, then how many pieces of products A and B should he make to maximise his profit?

22 A small firm manufactures gold rings and chains. The total number of rings and chains manufactured per day is atmost 24. It takes 1h to make a ring and 30 min to make a chain. The maximum number of hours available per day is 16. If the profit on a ring is ₹ 300 and that on a chain is ₹ 190, then find the number of rings and chains that should be manufactured per day, so as to earn the maximum profit, make it as an LPP and solve it graphically.

23 A company manufactures two types of screws A and B. All the screws have to pass through a threading machine and a slotting machine. A box of type A screws requires 2 min on the threading machine and 3 min on the slotting machine. A box of type B screws requires 8 min on the threading machine and 2 min on the slotting machine. In a week, each machine is available for 60 h.

On selling these screws, the company gets a profits of ₹ 100 per box on type A screws and ₹ 170 per box on type B screws. Formulate this problem as an LPP given that the objective is to maximise profit. Also, solve this and determine the maximum profit to the manufacturer. [NCERT Exemplar]

24 A manufacturer of patient medicines is preparing a production plan on medicines A and B. There are sufficient raw materials available to make 20000 bottles of A and 40000 bottles of B, but there are only 45000 bottles into which either of the medicines can be put.

Further, it takes 3 h to prepare enough material to fill 1000 bottles of A, it takes 1 h to prepare enough material to fill 1000 bottles of B and there are 66 h available for this operation. The profit is ₹ 8 per bottle for A and ₹ 7 per bottle for B. How should the manufacturer schedule his production in order to maximise his profit?

25 A manufacturer produces nuts and bolts. It takes 1 h of work on machine A and 3 h on machine B to produce a package of nuts.

While it takes 3 h on machine A and 1 h on machine B to produce a package of bolts. He earns a profit of ₹ 17.50 per package on nuts and ₹ 7 per package on bolts.

How many packages of each should be produced each day so as to maximise his profits, if he operates his machines for atmost 12 h a day? Formulate above as an linear programming problem and solve it graphically.

26 A manufacturer makes two types A and B of tea cups. Three machines are needed for this purpose and the time (in minutes) required for each cup on the machine is given below

Type	Machines		
	I	II	III
A	4	6	2
B	2	0	3

Each machine is available for a maximum of 2 h per day. The profit on each cup of type A is ₹ 6 and that on each cup of type B is ₹ 5. Show that 15 tea cups of type A and 30 of type B should be manufactured in a day to get the maximum profit.

27 A merchant plans to sell two types of personal computers, a desktop model and a portable model that will cost ₹ 25000 and ₹ 40000, respectively. He estimates that the total monthly demand of computers will not exceed 250 units. Determine the number of units of each type of computers which the merchant should stock to get maximum profit, if he does not want to invest more than ₹ 70 lakh and his profit on the desktop model is ₹ 4500 and on the portable model is ₹ 5000. Make it as an LPP and solve it graphically. **[NCERT]**

28 An aeroplane can carry a maximum of 200 passengers. A profit of ₹ 400 is made on each first class ticket and a profit of ₹ 300 is made on each economy class ticket. The airline reserves atleast 20 seats for first class.

However, atleast 4 times as many passengers prefer to travel by economy class to the first class. Determine, how many each type of tickets must be sold in order to maximise the profit for the airline. What is the maximum profit?

29 A farmer mixes two brands P and Q of cattle feed. Brand P, costing ₹ 250 per bag, contains 3 units of nutritional element A, 2.5 units of elements B and 2 units of element C.

Brand Q, costing ₹ 200 per bag, contains 1.5 units of nutritional element A, 11.25 units of element B and 3 units of element C. The minimum requirements of nutrients A, B and C are 18 units, 45 units and 24 units, respectively. Determine the number of bags of each brand which should be mixed in order to produce a mixture having a minimum cost per bag? What is the minimum cost of the mixture per bag? **[NCERT]**

30 A retired person wants to invest an amount of ₹ 50000. His broker recommends investing in two type of bonds 'A' and 'B' yielding 10% and 9% return respectively on the invested amount.

He decides to invest atleast ₹ 20000 in bond 'A' and atleast ₹ 10000 in bond 'B'. He also wants to invest atleast as much in bond 'A' as in bond 'B'. Solve this linear programming problem graphically to maximise his returns.

31 Anil wants to invests atmost ₹ 12000 in bonds A and B. According to the rules, he has to invests atleast ₹ 2000 in bond A and atleast ₹ 4000 in bond B. If the rate of interest on bond A is 8% per annum and on bond B is 10% per annum, then how should he invests his money for maximum interest? Solve the problem graphically.

32 A library has to accommodate two different types of books on a shelf. The books are 6 cm and 4 cm thick and weight 1 kg and $1\frac{1}{2}$ kg each, respectively. The shelf is 96 cm long and atmost can support a weight of 21 kg. How should the shelf be filled with the books of two types in order to include the greatest number of books? Make it as an LPP and solve it graphically.

Answers

1. (c) 2. (b) 3. (b) 4. (c) 5. (c) 6. (a) 7. (a) 8. (a)

9. Minimise $Z = 4x + 3y$, subject to constraints $200x + 100y \geq 4000$, $x + 2y \geq 50$, $40x + 40y \geq 1400$ and $x \geq 0$, $y \geq 0$.
10. Maximise $Z = x + y$, subject to constraints are $2x + 3y \leq 120$, $8x + 5y \leq 400$ and $x \geq 0$, $y \geq 0$.
11. $Z = 43$ at (3, 4).
12. There is no feasible region, so no maximum value exist.
13. Maximum value of Z is 4 at (0, 1).
14. Minimum value of $Z = 16$ at $x = 4$, $y = 2$
15. Maximum value = 12 and no minimum value exist.
16. Maximum value of $Z = 100$ at (5, 5)
17. 15 packets of food P and 20 packets of food Q should be used to minimise the amount of vitamin A. The minimum amount of vitamin A is 150 units.
18. Mixture contains 2 kg of food X and 4 kg of food Y, Minimum cost = ₹ 112
19. For maximise the profit, the firm should produce 9 tins of drink A and 5 tins of drink B and the maximum profit will be ₹ 51.
20. Number of first kind cake = 20, number of second kind cake = 10, maximum number of cakes = 30.
21. He should make 9 pieces of product A and 2 pieces of product B to maximise the profit.
22. 8 rings and 16 chains
23. Maximise $Z = 100x + 170y$ subject to $3x + 2y \leq 3600$, $x + 4y \leq 1800$, $x \geq 0$, $y \geq 0$.
    The maximum profit to the manufacturer is ₹ 138600.
24. 10500 bottles of type A, 34500 bottles of type B; maximum profit = ₹ 325500
25. Number of packages of nuts produce = 3, number of package of bolts produce = 3, maximum profit = ₹ 73.50
27. The profit is maximum, i.e. ₹ 1150000, when 200 desktop computers and 50 portable computers are stocked.
28. First class ticket = 40 and economy class ticket = 160; maximum profit = ₹64000
29. 3 bags of brand P and 6 bags of brand Q should be used in the mixture to minimise the cost to ₹ 1950.
30. To get maximum returns, he has to invest ₹25000 to each bond A and B.
31. He should invests ₹ 2000 for bond A and ₹ 10000 for bond B for finding maximum interest of ₹ 1160.
32. 12 and 6

ISC
EXAMINATION PAPER 2025

ISC Examination Paper 2025

A Highly Simulated Sample Question Paper for ISC Class XII

MATHEMATICS (Fully Solved)

GENERAL INSTRUCTIONS

1. The Question Paper consists of three sections A, B and C.
2. Candidates are required to attempt all questions from ***Section A*** and all questions either from ***Section B*** or ***Section C***.
3. ***Section A*** Internal choice has been provided in two questions of two marks each, two questions of four marks each and two questions of six marks each.
4. ***Section B*** Internal choice has been provided in one question of two marks and one question of four marks.
5. ***Section C*** Internal choice has been provided in one question of two marks and one question of four marks.
6. All working, including rough work, should be done on the same sheet as, and adjacent to the rest of the answer.
7. The intended marks for questions or parts of questions are given in brackets [ ].
8. Mathematical tables and graph papers are provided.

Time : 3 Hours ***Max. Marks : 80***

Section A (65 Marks)

1. In subparts (i) to (xi), choose the correct options and in subparts (xii) to (xv), answer the questions as instructed. **[15]**

(i) If $A = \begin{bmatrix} 0 & a \\ 0 & 0 \end{bmatrix}$ then A^{16} is

(a) unit matrix (b) null matrix
(c) diagonal matrix (d) skew-symmetric matrix

(ii) Which of the following is a homogeneous differential equation?

(a) $(4x^2 + 6y + 5)\, dy - (3y^2 + 2x + 4)\, dx = 0$
(b) $(xy)\, dx - (x^3 + y^3)\, dy = 0$
(c) $(x^3 + 2y^2)\, dx + 2xy\, dy = 0$
(d) $y^2 dx + (x^2 - xy - y^2)\, dy = 0$

(iii) Consider the graph of the function $f(x)$ shown below

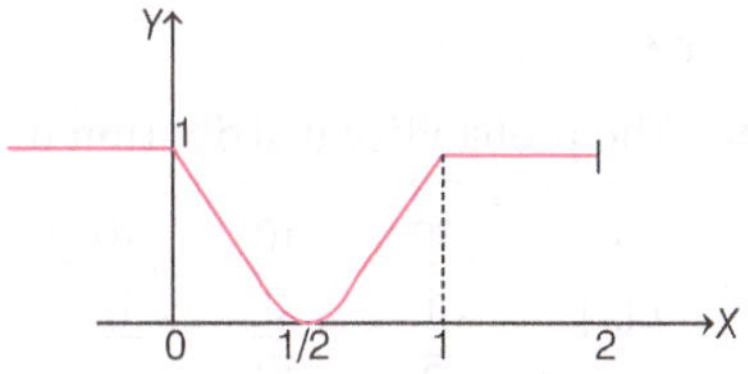

Statement I The function $f(x)$ is increasing in $\left(\frac{1}{2}, 2\right)$.

Statement II The function $f(x)$ is strictly increasing in $\left(\frac{1}{2}, 1\right)$.

Which of the following is correct with respect to the above statements?

(a) Statement I is true and Statement II is false.

(b) Statement II is true and Statement I is false.

(c) Both the statements are true.

(d) Both the statements are false.

(iv) $\int_0^1 \frac{x^4 - 1}{x^2 + 1} dx$ is equal to

(a) $\frac{2}{3}$ (b) $\frac{1}{3}$ (c) $\frac{-2}{3}$ (d) 0

(v) **Assertion** Consider the two events A and B such that $n(A) = n(B)$ and $P\left(\frac{A}{B}\right) = P\left(\frac{B}{A}\right)$.

Reason The events A and B are mutually exclusive.

(a) Both Assertion and Reason are true and Reason is the correct explanation for Assertion.

(b) Both Assertion and Reason are true but Reason is not the correct explanation for Assertion.

(c) Assertion is true and Reason is false.

(d) Assertion is false and Reason is true.

(vi) The existence of unique solution of the system of equations $x + y = \lambda$ and $5x + ky = 2$ depends on

(a) λ only (b) $\frac{\lambda}{k} = 1$ (c) Both k and λ (d) k only

(vii) A cylindrical popcorn tub of radius 10 cm is being filled with popcorns at the rate of 314 cm^3 per minute. The level of the popcorns in the tub is increasing at the rate of

(a) 1 cm/min (b) 0.1 cm/min (c) 1.1 cm/min (d) 0.5 cm/min

(viii) If $f(x) = \begin{cases} x + 2, & x < 0 \\ -x^2 - 2, & 0 \le x < 1 \\ x, & x \ge 1 \end{cases}$ then the number of point(s) of discontinuity of $f(x)$, is/are

(a) 1 (b) 3 (c) 2 (d) 0

(ix) **Assertion** If set A has m elements, set B has n elements and $n < m$ then the number of one-one function(s) from $A \to B$ is zero.

Reason A function $f : A \to B$ is defined only if all elements in set A have an image in set B.

(a) Both Assertion and Reason are true and Reason is the correct explanation for Assertion.

(b) Both Assertion and Reason are true but Reason is not the correct explanation for Assertion.

(c) Assertion is true and Reason is false.

(d) Assertion is false and Reason is true.

(x) Let X be a discrete random variable. The probability distribution of X is given below.

X	30	10	−10
$P(X)$	$\frac{1}{5}$	$\frac{3}{10}$	$\frac{1}{2}$

Then, $E(X)$ will be

(a) 1 (b) 4 (c) 2 (d) 30

(xi) **Statement I** If A is an invertible matrix then $(A^2)^{-1} = (A^{-1})^2$.

Statement II If A is an invertible matrix then $|A^{-1}| = |A|^{-1}$.

(a) Statement I is true and Statement II is false.
(b) Statement II is true and Statement I is false.
(c) Both the statements are true.
(d) Both the statements are false.

(xii) Write the smallest equivalence relation from the set A to set A, where $A = \{1, 2, 3\}$.

(xiii) For what value of x, is $A = \begin{bmatrix} 0 & 1 & -2 \\ -1 & 0 & 3 \\ x & -3 & 0 \end{bmatrix}$ a skew-symmetric matrix?

(xiv) Three critics review a book. Odds in favour of the book are 5 : 2, 4 : 3 and 3 : 4 respectively for the three critics. Find the probability that all critics are in favour of the book.

(xv) Evaluate $\int \frac{5}{\sqrt{2x+7}}\, dx$

2. Find the point on the curve $y = 2x^2 - 6x - 4$ at which the tangent is parallel to the X-axis. [2]

3. Find the value of $\tan^{-1} x - \cot^{-1} x$ if $(\tan^{-1} x)^2 - (\cot^{-1} x)^2 = \frac{5\pi}{8}$. [2]

4. (i) If $x^y = e^{x-y}$, prove that $\frac{dy}{dx} = \frac{\log x}{(1+\log x)^2}$. [2]

Or

(ii) If $f(x) = \log(1+x) + \frac{1}{1+x}$, show that $f(x)$ attains its minimum value at $x = 0$. [2]

5. Three shopkeepers Gaurav, Rizwan and Jacob use carry bags made of polythene, handmade paper and newspaper. The number of polythene bags, handmade bags and newspaper bags used by Gaurav, Rizwan and Jacob are (20, 30, 40), (30, 40, 20) and (40, 20, 30), respectively. One polythene bag costs ₹1, one handmade bag is for ₹5 and one newspaper bag costs ₹2. Gaurav, Rizwan and Jacob spend ₹A, ₹B and ₹C respectively on these carry bags.

Using the concepts of matrices and determinants, answer the following questions

(i) Represent the above information in matrix form.

(ii) Find the values of ₹A, ₹B and ₹C. [2]

6. (i) Differentiate $\sin^{-1}\left(\frac{2^{x+1}\, 3^x}{1+(36)^x}\right)$ with respect to x. [2]

Or

(ii) Show that $\tan^{-1} x + \tan^{-1} y = C$ is the general solution of the differential equation

$(1+x^2)\, dy + (1+y^2)\, dx = 0$. [2]

7. If $x + y + z = 0$ then show that $\begin{vmatrix} 1 & 1 & 1 \\ x & y & z \\ x^3 & y^3 & z^3 \end{vmatrix} = 0$, using properties of determinant. **[4]**

8. (i) Evaluate $\int \frac{\cos x}{3\cos x - 5}\, dx$ **[4]**

Or

(ii) Evaluate $\int (\log x)^2\, dx$ **[4]**

9. (i) If $x = \tan\left(\frac{1}{a}\log y\right)$ then show that $(1 + x^2)\frac{d^2y}{dx^2} + (2x - a)\frac{dy}{dx} = 0$. **[4]**

Or

(ii) The graph of $f(x) = -x^3 + 27x - 2$ is given below. **[4]**

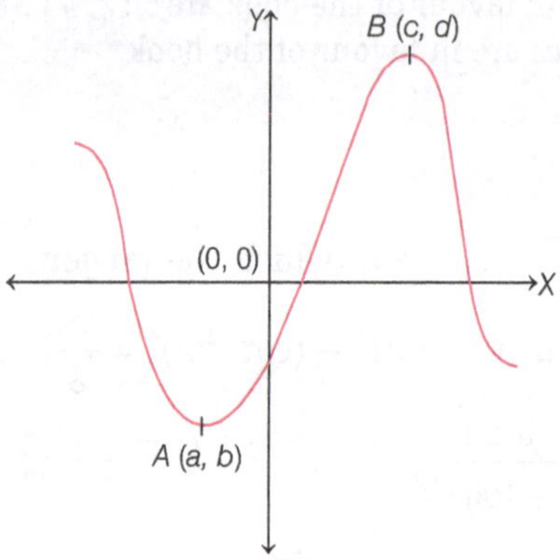

(a) Find the slope of the above graph.

(b) Find the coordinates of turning points A and B.

(c) Evaluate $f''(-2)$, $f(0)$ and $f'(3)$ and arrange them in ascending order.

10. Pia, Sia and Dia displayed their paintings in an art exhibition. The three artists displayed 15, 5 and 10 of their paintings, respectively. A person bought three paintings from the exhibition.

(i) Find the probability that he bought one painting from each of them.

(ii) Find the probability that he bought all the three paintings from the same person. **[4]**

11. (i) Prove $\int_{\frac{\pi}{4}}^{\frac{3\pi}{4}} \frac{x\, dx}{1 + \sin x} = (\sqrt{2} - 1)\pi$ **[6]**

Or (ii) Evaluate $\int \frac{x^2}{(x-1)^2(x^2+1)}\, dx$ **[6]**

12. (i) Solve the differential equation $(x + 5y^2)\frac{dy}{dx} = y$ when $x = 2$ and $y = 1$. **[6]**

Or

(ii) Find the particular solution of the differential equation $(x^2 - 2y^2)\, dx + 2xy\, dy = 0$, when $x = 1$ and $y = 1$. **[6]**

13. Observe the two graphs, Graph 1 and Graph 2 given below and answer the questions that follow.

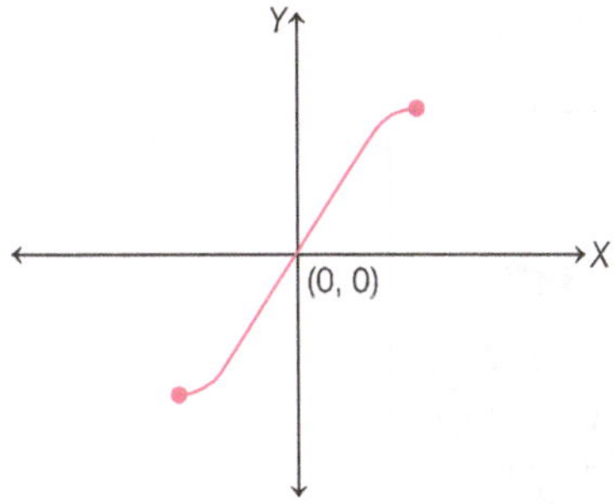

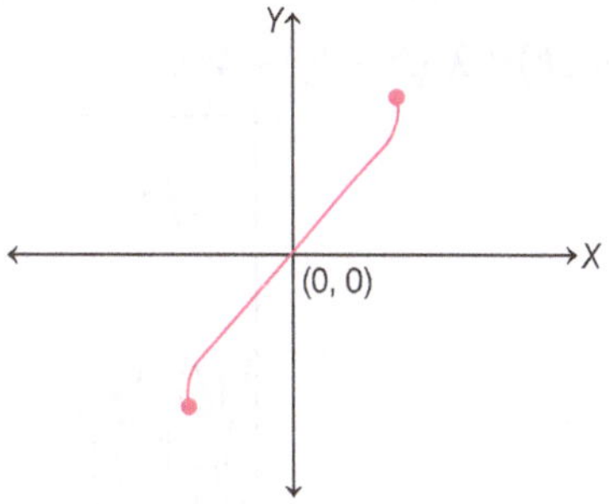

(i) Which one of the graphs represents $y = \sin^{-1} x$?

(ii) Write the domain and range of $y = \sin^{-1} x$.

(iii) Prove that $\sin^{-1}\frac{1}{\sqrt{5}} + \sin^{-1}\frac{2}{\sqrt{5}} = \frac{\pi}{2}$.

(iv) Find the value of $\tan^{-1}\left[2\sin\left(2\cos^{-1}\frac{\sqrt{3}}{2}\right)\right]$.

[6]

14. An international conference takes place in a metropolitan city. International leaders, scientists and industrialists participate in it.

The organisers of the conference appoint three agencies namely X, Y and Z for the security of the participants. The track record of the success of X, Y and Z in providing security services is 99%, 98.5% and 98%, respectively. The organisers assign the responsibility of ensuring the security of 1000 people to agency X, 2000 people to agency Y and 3000 people to agency Z.

At the end of the conference, one participant goes missing from the conference room.

What is the probability that the missing participant was placed under the responsibility of the security agency X? [6]

Section B (15 Marks)

15. In subparts (i) and (ii), choose the correct options and in subparts (iii) and (iv), answer the questions as instructed.

(i) **Assertion** $(\vec{a} + \vec{b})^2 + (\vec{b} - \vec{a})^2 = 2(\vec{a}^2 + \vec{b}^2)$

Reason Dot product of any two vectors is commutative.

(a) Both Assertion and Reason are true and Reason is the correct explanation for Assertion.
(b) Both Assertion and Reason are true but Reason is not the correct explanation for Assertion.
(c) Assertion is true and Reason is false.
(d) Assertion is false and Reason is true. [1]

(ii) The angle between the two planes $x + y + 2z = 9$ and $2x - y + z = 15$ is [1]

(a) $\frac{\pi}{2}$ (b) $\frac{\pi}{3}$ (c) π (d) $\frac{3\pi}{4}$

(iii) Show that points $P(-2, 3, 5)$, $Q(1, 2, 3)$ and $R(7, 0, -1)$ are collinear. [1]

(iv) Two honeybees are flying parallel to each other in the garden to collect the nectar. The path traced by the bees is given in the form of a straight line. The equation of the path traced by one honeybee is $\vec{r} = (\hat{i} + 2\hat{i} + 3\hat{k}) + \lambda\,(2\hat{i} + 3\hat{j} + 4\hat{k})$.

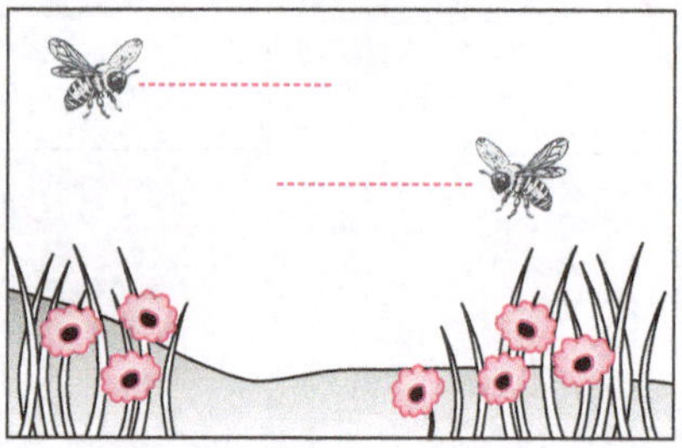

(a) Write the above mentioned equation in cartesian form. [1]

(b) Find the equation of the path traced by the other honeybee passing through the point (2, 4, 5). [1]

16. (i) Find the equation of the plane passing through the points (2, 2, − 1), (3, 4, 2) and (7, 0, 6). [2]

Or

(ii) Find the equation of the plane passing through the points (2, 3, 1), (4, −5, 3) and parallel to X-axis. [2]

17. Consider the position vectors of A, B and C as $\vec{OA} = 2\hat{i} - 2\hat{j} + \hat{k}$, $\vec{OB} = \hat{i} + 2\hat{j} - 2\hat{k}$ and $\vec{OC} = 2\hat{i} - \hat{j} + 4\hat{k}$.

(i) Calculate $\vec{AB}$ and $\vec{BC}$.

(ii) Find the projection of $\vec{AB}$ on $\vec{BC}$.

(iii) Find the area of the ΔABC whose sides are $\vec{AB}$ and $\vec{BC}$. [4]

18. (i) The equation $y = 4 - x^2$ represents a parabola.

(a) Make a rough sketch of the graph of the given function.

(b) Determine the area enclosed between the curve, the X-axis, the lines $x = 0$ and $x = 2$.

(c) Hence, find the area bounded by the parabola and the X-axis. [4]

Or

(ii) A farmer has a field bounded by three lines $x + 2y = 2$, $y - x = 1$, $2x + y = 7$. Using integration, find the area of the region bounded by these lines. [4]

Section C (15 Marks)

19. In subparts (i) and (ii), choose the correct options and in subpart (iii), answer the questions as instructed.

(i) The total revenue received from the sale of x units of a product is $R(x) = 36x + 3x^2 + 5$. Then, the actual revenue for selling the 10th item will be [1]

(a) 27 (b) 90 (c) 93 (d) 33

(ii) Read the following statements and choose the correct option.

(I) The correlation coefficient and the regression coefficients are of the same sign.

(II) The correlation coefficient is the arithmetic mean between the regression coefficients.

(III) The product of two regression coefficients is always equal to 1.

(IV) Both the regression coefficients cannot be numerically greater than unity.

(a) Only (IV) is correct.

(b) Only (I) and (II) are correct.

(c) Only (I) and (IV) are correct.

(d) Only (III) and (IV) are correct. **[1]**

(iii) Consider the following data:

x	1	2	3	6
y	6	5	4	1
$x-\bar{x}$				
$y-\bar{y}$				

(a) Calculate $\bar{x}$ and $\bar{y}$. (b) Complete the table. (c) Calculate b_{xy}. **[1 + 1 + 1]**

20. (i) Find the regression line of best fit from the following data.

$\Sigma x = 24$, $\Sigma y = 44$, $\Sigma xy = 306$, $\Sigma x^2 = 164$, $\Sigma y^2 = 576$, $n = 4$ **[2]**

Or

(ii) Two lines of regression are given as $4x + 3y + 7 = 0$ and $3x + 4y + 8 = 0$. Identify the line of regression of x on y. **[2]**

21. (i) A utensil manufacturer produces x dinner sets per week and sells each set at ₹p, where $x = \frac{600 - p}{8}$.

The cost of production of x sets is ₹$x^2 + 78x + 2000$.

(a) Write the revenue function.

(b) Write the profit function.

(c) Calculate the number of dinner sets to be produced and sold per week to ensure maximum profit. **[4]**

Or (ii) The average cost of producing x units of commodity is given by $AC = \frac{x^2}{200} - \frac{x}{50} - 30 + \frac{5000}{x}$.

(a) Find the cost function.

(b) Find the marginal cost function.

(c) Find the marginal average cost function.

(d) Verify that $\frac{d}{dx}(AC) = \frac{MC - AC}{x}$. **[4]**

22. Two different types of books have to be stacked in the shelf of a library. The first type of book weighs 1 kg and has a thickness of 6 cm. The second type of book weighs 1.5 kg and has a thickness of 4 cm. The shelf is 96 cm long and can support a maximum weight of 21 kg.

How should both the types of books be placed in the shelf to include the maximum number of books? Formulate a LPP and solve it graphically. **[4]**

SOLUTIONS

1. (i) (b) We have, $A = \begin{bmatrix} 0 & a \\ 0 & 0 \end{bmatrix}$

Now, $A^2 = A \cdot A$

$$= \begin{bmatrix} 0 & a \\ 0 & 0 \end{bmatrix}\begin{bmatrix} 0 & a \\ 0 & 0 \end{bmatrix}$$

$$= \begin{bmatrix} 0+0 & 0+0 \\ 0+0 & 0+0 \end{bmatrix} = \begin{bmatrix} 0 & 0 \\ 0 & 0 \end{bmatrix}$$

$\therefore$ A^2 is a null matrix.

Since, A^2 is a null matrix. So, any higher power of A will also be a null matrix.

$\therefore$ $A^{16} = (A^2)^8$

$$= \begin{bmatrix} 0 & 0 \\ 0 & 0 \end{bmatrix}^8 = \begin{bmatrix} 0 & 0 \\ 0 & 0 \end{bmatrix}$$

So, A^{16} is a null matrix.

(ii) (d) From option (a), we have,

$$(4x^2 + 6y + 5)\,dy - (3y^2 + 2x + 4)\,dx = 0$$

$$\Rightarrow \quad \frac{dy}{dx} = \frac{3y^2 + 2x + 4}{4x^2 + 6y + 5}$$

It is not a homogeneous differential equation because degree of numerator and denominator are not same.

From option (b), we have, $(xy)\,dx - (x^3 + y^3)\,dy = 0$

$$\Rightarrow \quad \frac{dy}{dx} = \frac{xy}{x^3 + y^3}$$

It is not a homogeneous differential equation because degree of numerator and denominator are not same.

From option(c), we have, $(x^3 + 2y^2)\,dx + 2xy\,dy = 0$

$$\Rightarrow \quad \frac{dy}{dx} = -\left(\frac{x^3 + 2y^2}{2xy}\right)$$

It is not a homogeneous differential equation because degree of numerator and denominator are not same.

From option (d), we have, $y^2 dx + (x^2 - xy - y^2)\,dy = 0$

$$\Rightarrow \quad \frac{dy}{dx} = -\frac{y^2}{x^2 - xy - y^2}$$

It is a homogeneous differential equation because degree of numerator and denominator are same.

(iii) (b) From the graph, it is clear that $f(x)$ is strictly increasing in $\left(\frac{1}{2}, 1\right)$.

So, Statement I is false and Statement II is true.

(iv) (c) Let $I = \int_0^1 \frac{x^4 - 1^4}{x^2 + 1}\,dx$

$$= \int_0^1 \frac{(x^2)^2 - (1^2)^2}{x^2 + 1}\,dx = \int_0^1 \frac{(x^2 + 1)(x^2 - 1)}{x^2 + 1}\,dx$$

$$= \int_0^1 (x^2 - 1)\,dx = \left[\frac{x^3}{3} - x\right]_0^1$$

$$= \frac{1^3}{3} - 1 - (0 - 0) = \frac{1}{3} - 1 = -\frac{2}{3}$$

(v) (c) **Assertion** $P\left(\frac{A}{B}\right) = \frac{P(A \cap B)}{P(B)}$

and $P\left(\frac{B}{A}\right) = \frac{P(B \cap A)}{P(A)}$

Now, we have, $P\left(\frac{A}{B}\right) = P\left(\frac{B}{A}\right)$

$$\Rightarrow \quad \frac{P(A \cap B)}{P(B)} = \frac{P(B \cap A)}{P(A)}$$

$$\Rightarrow \quad \frac{P(A \cap B)}{P(B)} = \frac{P(A \cap B)}{P(A)}$$

$[\because P(A \cap B) = P(B \cap A)]$

$$\Rightarrow \quad P(A) = P(B)$$

$$\Rightarrow \quad \frac{n(A)}{n(S)} = \frac{n(B)}{n(S)}$$

$\Rightarrow$ $n(A) = n(B)$ which is given.

$\therefore$ Assertion is true.

Reason If A and B are mutually exclusive then $P(A \cap B) = 0$.

If $P(A \cap B) = 0$ then $P\left(\frac{A}{B}\right) = \frac{0}{P(B)} = 0$

and $P\left(\frac{B}{A}\right) = \frac{0}{P(A)} = 0$

Thus, $P\left(\frac{A}{B}\right) = P\left(\frac{B}{A}\right) = 0$

However, this does not mean that events A and B have to be mutually exclusive for $P\left(\frac{A}{B}\right) = P\left(\frac{B}{A}\right)$ to hold true.

As shown in Assertion, $P\left(\frac{A}{B}\right) = P\left(\frac{B}{A}\right)$

if $P(A) = P(B)$ which means $n(A) = n(B)$.

$\therefore$ Reason is false.

(vi) (d) The given system of equations is

$$x + y = \lambda \text{ and } 5x + ky = 2.$$

The given system of equations can be written in matrix form as $AX = B$,

where $A = \begin{bmatrix} 1 & 1 \\ 5 & k \end{bmatrix}$, $X = \begin{bmatrix} x \\ y \end{bmatrix}$ and $B = \begin{bmatrix} \lambda \\ 2 \end{bmatrix}$

We know that the system of equations has a unique solution if the determinant of the matrix is non-zero.

$$\therefore \quad |A| \neq 0$$

$$\Rightarrow \quad \begin{vmatrix} 1 & 1 \\ 5 & k \end{vmatrix} \neq 0$$

$$\Rightarrow \quad k - 5 \neq 0$$

$$\Rightarrow \quad k \neq 5$$

So, the existence of unique solution depends on the value of k.

(vii) (a) Let r be radius, h be the height and V be the volume of the cylindrical popcorn.

$$\therefore \quad r = 10\text{cm}, \ \frac{dV}{dt} = 314 \text{ cm}^3/\text{min}$$

Now, $V = \pi r^2 h = \pi (10)^2 h = 100\pi h$

On differentiating both sides w.r.t. t, we get

$$\frac{dV}{dt} = 100\pi \frac{dh}{dt}$$

$$\Rightarrow \quad 314 = 100\pi \frac{dh}{dt}$$

$$\Rightarrow \quad \frac{dh}{dt} = \frac{314}{100\pi} = \frac{314}{100 \times 3.14}$$

$$\Rightarrow \quad \frac{dh}{dt} = 1$$

So, the level of the popcorns in the tub is increasing at the rate of 1 cm/min.

(viii) (c) We have,

$$f(x) = \begin{cases} x+2, & x<0 \\ -x^2-2, & 0 \le x < 1 \\ x, & x \ge 1 \end{cases}$$

At $x = 0$,

$$\text{LHL} = \lim_{x \to 0^-} f(x) = \lim_{h \to 0} f(0-h)$$

$$= \lim_{h \to 0} f(-h)$$

$$= \lim_{h \to 0} -h + 2 = -0 + 2 = 2$$

$$\text{RHL} = \lim_{x \to 0^+} f(x) = \lim_{h \to 0} f(0+h)$$

$$= \lim_{h \to 0} f(h)$$

$$= \lim_{h \to 0} -(h)^2 - 2 = 0 - 2 = -2$$

$\because$ LHL $\neq$ RHL

$\therefore$ $f(x)$ is discontinuous at $x = 0$.

At $x = 1$,

$$\text{LHL} = \lim_{x \to 1^-} f(x) = \lim_{h \to 0} f(1-h)$$

$$= \lim_{h \to 0} -(1-h)^2 - 2$$

$$= -(1-0)^2 - 2 = -1 - 2 = -3$$

$$\text{RHL} = \lim_{x \to 1^+} f(x) = \lim_{h \to 0} f(1+h)$$

$$= \lim_{h \to 0} f(1+h) = 1 + 0 = 1$$

$\because$ LHL $\neq$ RHL

$\therefore$ $f(x)$ is discontinuous at $x = 0$.

So, the number of points of discontinuity of $f(x)$ is 2.

(ix) (b) If A has n elements, B has m elements and $n < m$ then the number of one-one function from A to B is zero because if $n < m$, it is impossible to map each element of A to distinct element of B.

Clearly, Reason is true.

Hence, both Assertion and Reason are true but Reason is not the correct explanation for Assertion.

(x) (b) We know that $E(X) = \Sigma x_i p_i$

$$= 30 \times \frac{1}{5} + 10 \times \frac{3}{10} + (-10) \times \frac{1}{2}$$

$$= 6 + 3 - 5 = 4$$

(xi) (c) **Statement I** $(A^2)^{-1} = (A \cdot A)^{-1}$

$$= A^{-1} \cdot A^{-1} \qquad [\because (AB)^{-1} = B^{-1}A^{-1}]$$

$$= (A^{-1})^2$$

$\therefore$ Statement I is true.

Statement II We know that $AA^{-1} = I$

$$\Rightarrow \quad |AA^{-1}| = |I|$$

$$\Rightarrow \quad |A||A^{-1}| = 1 \qquad [\because |AB| = |A||B| \text{ and } |I| = 1]$$

$$\Rightarrow \quad |A^{-1}| = \frac{1}{|A|}$$

$$\Rightarrow \quad |A^{-1}| = |A|^{-1}$$

$\therefore$ Statement II is true.

(xii) We have, $A = \{1, 2, 3\}$

The smallest equivalence relation from the set A to set A is $R = \{(1, 1), (2, 2), (3, 3)\}$.

(xiii) We have, $A = \begin{bmatrix} 0 & 1 & -2 \\ -1 & 0 & 3 \\ x & -3 & 0 \end{bmatrix}$

$$\therefore \quad A' = \begin{bmatrix} 0 & -1 & x \\ 1 & 0 & -3 \\ -2 & 3 & 0 \end{bmatrix}$$

and $-A = \begin{bmatrix} 0 & -1 & 2 \\ 1 & 0 & -3 \\ -x & 3 & 0 \end{bmatrix}$

Since, A is a skew-symmetric matrix.

$$\therefore \quad A' = -A$$

$$\Rightarrow \begin{bmatrix} 0 & -1 & x \\ 1 & 0 & -3 \\ -2 & 3 & 0 \end{bmatrix} = \begin{bmatrix} 0 & -1 & 2 \\ 1 & 0 & -3 \\ -x & 3 & 0 \end{bmatrix}$$

On equating the corresponding element, we get

$$x = 2$$

(xiv) Let A, B and C denote the events that the book be favoured by the first, second and third critic, respectively.

$$\therefore \quad P(A) = \frac{5}{2+5} = \frac{5}{7},$$

$$P(B) = \frac{4}{4+3} = \frac{4}{7}$$

and $P(C) = \frac{3}{3+4} = \frac{3}{7}$

$\therefore$ Required probability

$$= \frac{5}{7} \times \frac{4}{7} \times \frac{3}{7} = \frac{60}{343}$$

(xv) Let $I = \int \frac{5}{\sqrt{2x+7}} dx$

Put $2x + 7 = t \Rightarrow 2 = \frac{dt}{dx}$

$$\Rightarrow \quad dx = \frac{dt}{2}$$

$\therefore \quad I = \int \frac{5}{\sqrt{t}} \times \frac{dt}{2} = \frac{5}{2} \int t^{-\frac{1}{2}} dt$

$= \frac{5}{2} \frac{t^{\frac{1}{2}}}{\frac{1}{2}} + C \qquad \left[\because \int x^n dx = \frac{x^{n+1}}{n+1} + C \right]$

$= 5\sqrt{t} + C = 5\sqrt{2x+7} + C$

2. We have,

$y = 2x^2 - 6x - 4 \qquad \ldots \text{(i)}$

On differentiating both sides w.r.t. x, we get

$$\frac{dy}{dx} = 4x - 6$$

$\therefore$ Slope of tangent is $4x - 6$.

Since, the tangent is parallel to X-axis.

$\therefore \quad \frac{dy}{dx} = 0$

$\Rightarrow \quad 4x - 6 = 0$

$\Rightarrow \quad 4x = 6$

$\Rightarrow \quad x = \frac{3}{2}$

On putting the value of x in Eq. (i), we get

$$y = 2\left(\frac{3}{2}\right)^2 - 6\left(\frac{3}{2}\right) - 4$$

$$= 2 \times \frac{9}{4} - 9 - 4$$

$\Rightarrow \quad y = \frac{9}{2} - 13 = -\frac{17}{2}$

So, the point on the curve $y = 2x^2 - 6x - 4$ at which the tangent is parallel to X-axis is $\left(\frac{3}{2}, -\frac{17}{2}\right)$.

3. We have,

$$(\tan^{-1} x)^2 - (\cot^{-1} x)^2 = \frac{5\pi}{8}$$

$\Rightarrow \quad (\tan^{-1} x + \cot^{-1} x)(\tan^{-1} x - \cot^{-1} x) = \frac{5\pi}{8}$

$[\because a^2 - b^2 = (a+b)(a-b)]$

$\Rightarrow \quad \frac{\pi}{2}(\tan^{-1} x - \cot^{-1} x) = \frac{5\pi}{8}$

$\left[\because \tan^{-1}\theta + \cot^{-1}\theta = \frac{\pi}{2}\right]$

$\Rightarrow \quad \tan^{-1} x - \cot^{-1} x = \frac{5\pi}{8} \times \frac{2}{\pi} = \frac{5}{4}$

4. (i) We have, $x^y = e^{x-y}$

On taking log both sides, we get

$$\log x^y = \log e^{x-y}$$

$\Rightarrow \quad y \cdot \log x = (x-y) \log e$

$[\because \log a^b = b \cdot \log a]$

$\Rightarrow \quad y \cdot \log x = x - y \qquad \ldots \text{(i)}$

On differentiating both sides w.r.t. x, we get

$$\frac{dy}{dx} \log x + y \times \frac{1}{x} = 1 - \frac{dy}{dx}$$

$\Rightarrow \quad \frac{dy}{dx} \log x + \frac{dy}{dx} = 1 - \frac{y}{x}$

$\Rightarrow \quad \frac{dy}{dx}(\log x + 1) = \frac{x-y}{x}$

$\Rightarrow \quad \frac{dy}{dx}(\log x + 1) = \frac{y \log x}{x} \qquad$ [from Eq. (i)]

$\Rightarrow \quad \frac{dy}{dx} = \frac{y \log x}{x(\log x + 1)}$

$\Rightarrow \quad \frac{dy}{dx} = \frac{\log x}{(1 + \log x)^2} \qquad$ **Hence proved.**

$\left[\text{from Eq. (i), } \frac{y}{x} = \frac{1}{1 + \log x}\right]$

Or

(ii) We have,

$$f(x) = \log(1+x) + \frac{1}{1+x} \qquad \ldots \text{(i)}$$

On differentiating both sides w.r.t. x, we get

$$f'(x) = \frac{1}{1+x} - \frac{1}{(1+x)^2}$$

Again, on differentiating both sides w.r.t. x, we get

$$f''(x) = \frac{-1}{(1+x)^2} + \frac{2}{(1+x)^3}$$

For maxima or minima, put $f'(x) = 0$

$\Rightarrow \quad \frac{1}{1+x} - \frac{1}{(1+x)^2} = 0$

$\Rightarrow \quad \frac{1}{1+x} = \frac{1}{(1+x)^2}$

$\Rightarrow \quad 1 = \frac{1}{1+x}$

$\Rightarrow \quad 1 + x = 1$

$\Rightarrow \quad x = 0$

Now, $f''(0) = \frac{-1}{(1+0)^2} + \frac{2}{(1+0)^3} = \frac{-1}{1} + \frac{2}{1}$

$= 1 > 0$

So, $f(x)$ attains its minimum value at $x = 0$. **Hence proved.**

5. (i) Let the matrix M represent the bags used and the matrix N represent the costs.

$\therefore \quad M = \begin{bmatrix} 20 & 30 & 40 \\ 30 & 40 & 20 \\ 40 & 20 & 30 \end{bmatrix}$ and $N = \begin{bmatrix} 1 \\ 5 \\ 2 \end{bmatrix}$

(ii) Now, $MN = \begin{bmatrix} 20 & 30 & 40 \\ 30 & 40 & 20 \\ 40 & 20 & 30 \end{bmatrix} \begin{bmatrix} 1 \\ 5 \\ 2 \end{bmatrix}$

$\Rightarrow \quad \begin{bmatrix} A \\ B \\ C \end{bmatrix} = \begin{bmatrix} 20 + 150 + 80 \\ 30 + 200 + 40 \\ 40 + 100 + 60 \end{bmatrix} = \begin{bmatrix} 250 \\ 270 \\ 200 \end{bmatrix}$

Since, matrices are equal.

So, their corresponding elements are also equal.

$\therefore \quad A = ₹250, B = ₹270$ and $C = ₹200$

6. (i) Let $y = \sin^{-1}\left(\dfrac{2^{x+1}\cdot 3^x}{1+36^x}\right)$

$$= \sin^{-1}\left(\frac{2^x\cdot 2\cdot 3^x}{1+(6^2)^x}\right) = \sin^{-1}\left(\frac{2\cdot 6^x}{1+(6^x)^2}\right)$$

Put $6^x = \tan\theta$

$\Rightarrow \quad \theta = \tan^{-1}(6^x)$

$\therefore \quad y = \sin^{-1}\left(\dfrac{2\cdot\tan\theta}{1+\tan^2\theta}\right)$

$\Rightarrow \quad y = \sin^{-1}(\sin 2\theta) \quad \left[\because \sin 2x = \dfrac{2\tan x}{1+\tan^2 x}\right]$

$\Rightarrow \quad y = 2\theta$

$\Rightarrow \quad y = 2\tan^{-1}(6^x)$

On differentiating both sides w.r.t. x, we get

$$\frac{dy}{dx} = \frac{2}{(1+(6^x)^2)} \times \frac{d}{dx}(6^x)$$

$$= \frac{2}{1+(6^2)^x} \times 6^x \log 6$$

$$= \frac{2\times 2^x \times 3^x \log 6}{1+(36)^x}$$

$$= \frac{2^{x+1}\, 3^x \log 6}{1+(36)^x}$$

OR

(ii) Given equation is

$$\tan^{-1}x + \tan^{-1}y = C$$

On differentiating both sides w.r.t. x, we get

$$\frac{1}{1+x^2} + \frac{1}{1+y^2}\frac{dy}{dx} = 0$$

$\Rightarrow \quad \dfrac{dy}{dx}\left(\dfrac{1}{1+y^2}\right) = -\dfrac{1}{1+x^2}$

$\Rightarrow \quad (1+x^2)\,dy = -(1+y^2)\,dx$

$\Rightarrow \quad (1+x^2)\,dy + (1+y^2)\,dx = 0$

So, $\tan^{-1}x + \tan^{-1}y = C$ is the general solution of the differential equation $(1+x^2)\,dy + (1+y^2)\,dx = 0$.

Hence Proved

7. We have, $x + y + z = 0$

$$\text{LHS} = \begin{vmatrix} 1 & 1 & 1 \\ x & y & z \\ x^3 & y^3 & z^3 \end{vmatrix}$$

Applying $C_1 \to C_1 - C_2$ and $C_2 \to C_2 - C_3$, we get

$$= \begin{vmatrix} 0 & 0 & 1 \\ x-y & y-z & z \\ x^3-y^3 & y^3-z^3 & z^3 \end{vmatrix}$$

$$= \begin{vmatrix} 0 & 0 & 1 \\ x-y & y-z & z \\ (x-y)(x^2+xy+y^2) & (y-z)(y^2+yz+z^2) & z^3 \end{vmatrix}$$

On taking common $(x-y)$ from C_1 and $(y-z)$from C_2, we get

$$(x-y)(y-z)\begin{vmatrix} 0 & 0 & 1 \\ 1 & 1 & z \\ x^2+xy+y^2 & y^2+yz+z^2 & z^3 \end{vmatrix}$$

Expanding along R_1, we get

$(x-y)(y-z)\,[1\,(y^2+yz+z^2) - (x^2+xy+y^2)]$

$= (x-y)(y-z)\,[y^2+yz+z^2-x^2-xy-y^2]$

$= (x-y)(y-z)\,[(yz-xy)+(z^2-x^2)]$

$= (x-y)(y-z)\,[y(z-x)+(z-x)(z+x)]$

$= (x-y)(y-z)\,[(z-x)(x+y+z)]$

$= (x-y)(y-z)(z-x)\times 0 \quad [\because x+y+z=0]$

$= 0 = \text{RHS}$

Hence proved.

8. (i) Let $I = \displaystyle\int \frac{\cos x}{3\cos x - 5}\,dx$

$$= \frac{1}{3}\int \frac{3\cos x}{3\cos x - 5}\,dx = \frac{1}{3}\int \frac{3\cos x - 5 + 5}{3\cos x - 5}\,dx$$

$$= \frac{1}{3}\int \frac{3\cos x - 5}{3\cos x - 5}\,dx + \frac{1}{3}\int \frac{5}{3\cos x - 5}\,dx$$

$$= \frac{1}{3}\int 1\,dx + \frac{5}{3}\int \frac{1}{3\left(\dfrac{1-\tan^2\frac{x}{2}}{1+\tan^2\frac{x}{2}}\right) - 5}\,dx$$

$$= \frac{x}{3} + \frac{5}{3}\int \frac{1}{\dfrac{3 - 3\tan^2\frac{x}{2} - 5 - 5\tan^2\frac{x}{2}}{1+\tan^2\frac{x}{2}}}\,dx$$

$$= \frac{x}{3} + \frac{5}{3}\int \frac{\sec^2\frac{x}{2}}{-2-8\tan^2\frac{x}{2}}\,dx$$

$$= \frac{x}{3} - \frac{5}{6}\int \frac{\sec^2\frac{x}{2}}{1+4\tan^2\frac{x}{2}}\,dx$$

Put $\tan\dfrac{x}{2} = t$

$\Rightarrow \quad \sec^2\dfrac{x}{2} \times \dfrac{1}{2} = \dfrac{dt}{dx} \Rightarrow \sec^2\dfrac{x}{2}\,dx = 2dt$

$\therefore \quad I = \dfrac{x}{3} - \dfrac{5}{6}\displaystyle\int \frac{2}{1+4t^2}\,dt$

$$= \frac{x}{3} - \frac{5\times 2}{6\times 4}\int \frac{1}{\left(\frac{1}{2}\right)^2 + t^2}\,dt$$

$$= \frac{x}{3} - \frac{5}{12} \times \frac{1}{\frac{1}{2}}\tan^{-1}\left(\frac{t}{\frac{1}{2}}\right) + C$$

$$\left[\because \int \frac{1}{a^2+x^2}\,dx = \frac{1}{a}\tan^{-1}\frac{x}{a} + C\right]$$

$$= \frac{x}{3} - \frac{5}{6}\tan^{-1}\left(2\tan\frac{x}{2}\right) + C$$

OR

(ii) Let $I = \int \underset{\text{I}}{(\log x)^2} \cdot \underset{\text{II}}{1}\, dx$

$= (\log x)^2 \int 1 dx - \int \left[\frac{d}{dx}(\log x)^2 \int 1 dx\right] dx$ [integration by parts]

$= x \cdot (\log x)^2 - \int 2 \cdot \log x \times \frac{1}{x} \times x\, dx$

$= x \cdot (\log x)^2 - 2\int \underset{\text{I}}{\log x} \cdot \underset{\text{II}}{1}\, dx$

$= x(\log x)^2 - 2\left[\log x \int 1 dx - \int\left(\frac{d}{dx}\log x \int 1 dx\right) dx\right]$

$= x(\log x)^2 - 2\left[x \log x - \int \frac{1}{x} \times x\, dx\right]$

$= x(\log x)^2 - 2\,[x \log x - \int 1 dx]$

$= x(\log x)^2 - 2\,[x \log x - x] + C$

$= x(\log x)^2 - 2x \log x + 2x + C$

$= x(\log x)^2 + 2x(1 - \log x) + C$

9. (i) We have, $x = \tan\left(\frac{1}{a}\log y\right)$

$\Rightarrow \quad \tan^{-1} x = \frac{1}{a}\log y$

$\Rightarrow \quad a \tan^{-1} x = \log y$

On differentiating both sides w.r.t. x, we get

$$\frac{a}{1 + x^2} = \frac{1}{y}\frac{dy}{dx}$$

$\Rightarrow \quad \frac{dy}{dx} = \frac{ay}{1 + x^2}$

$\Rightarrow \quad (1 + x^2)\frac{dy}{dx} = ay$

Again, on differentiating both sides w.r.t. x, we get

$$(1 + x^2)\frac{d^2y}{dx^2} + \frac{dy}{dx}(0 + 2x) = a\frac{dy}{dx}$$

$\Rightarrow \quad (1 + x^2)\frac{d^2y}{dx^2} + 2x\frac{dy}{dx} - a\frac{dy}{dx} = 0$

$\Rightarrow \quad (1 + x^2)\frac{d^2y}{dx^2} + (2x - a)\frac{dy}{dx} = 0$

OR

(ii) (a) We have,

$$f(x) = -x^3 + 27x - 2$$

On differentiating both sides w.r.t. x, we get

$$f'(x) = -3x^2 + 27 \quad \ldots(i)$$

$\therefore$ The slope of the given graph is $-3x^2 + 27$

(b) For the turning point, put $f'(x) = 0$

$\Rightarrow \quad -3x^2 + 27 = 0$

$\Rightarrow \quad 3x^2 = 27$

$\Rightarrow \quad x^2 = 9$

$\Rightarrow \quad x = \pm 3$

On putting $x = 3$ into $f(x)$, we get

$f(3) = -(3)^3 + 27 \times 3 - 2$

$= -27 + 81 - 2 = 52$

and on putting $x = -3$ into $f(x)$, we get

$f(-3) = -(-3)^3 + 27 \times (-3) - 2$

$= 27 - 81 - 2 = -56.$

So, point A is $(-3, -56)$ and point B is $(3, 52)$.

(c) We have, $f'(x) = -3x^2 + 27$

On differentiating both sides w.r.t. x, we get

$f''(x) = -6x$

$\therefore \quad f''(-2) = -6 \times (-2) = 12$

Now, $\quad f(0) = -(0)^3 + 27 \times 0 - 2 = -2$

and $\quad f'(3) = -3(3)^2 + 27$

$= -27 + 27 = 0$

Hence, ascending order of $f''(-2)$, $f(0)$ and $f'(3)$ is $f(0) < f'(3) < f''(-2)$.

10. Given, number of paintings Pia has = 15,

number of paintings Sia has = 5

and number of paintings Dia has = 10

$\therefore$ Total number of paintings = 15 + 5 + 10 = 30

Total number of ways to select 3 paintings from 30 paintings

$$= {}^{30}C_3 = \frac{30 \times 29 \times 28}{3 \times 2 \times 1}$$

$= 4060$

(i) Number of ways to select 1 painting from Pia $= {}^{15}C_1 = 15,$

number of ways to select 1 painting from Sia $= {}^{5}C_1 = 5$

and number of ways to select 1 painting from Dia $= {}^{10}C_1 = 10$

$\therefore$ Number of ways to select 1 painting from each artist $= 15 \times 5 \times 10 = 750$

$\therefore \quad$ Required probability $= \frac{750}{4060} = \frac{75}{406}$

(ii) Number of ways to select 3 paintings from Pia

$$= {}^{15}C_3 = \frac{15 \times 14 \times 13}{3 \times 2 \times 1} = 455,$$

number of ways to select 3 paintings from Sia

$$= {}^{5}C_3 = \frac{5 \times 4 \times 3}{3 \times 2} = 10$$

and number of ways to select 3 paintings from Dia

$$= {}^{10}C_3 = \frac{10 \times 9 \times 8}{3 \times 2 \times 1} = 120$$

$\therefore$ Number of ways to select all three paintings from the same artist

$= 455 + 10 + 120 = 585$

$\therefore$ Required probability

$$= \frac{585}{4060} = \frac{117}{812}$$

11. (i) Let $I = \int_{\pi/4}^{3\pi/4} \frac{x}{1+\sin x} dx$ ...(i)

$$= \int_{\pi/4}^{3\pi/4} \frac{\left(\frac{3\pi}{4}+\frac{\pi}{4}-x\right)}{1+\sin\left(\frac{3\pi}{4}+\frac{\pi}{4}-x\right)} dx$$

$$\left[\because \int_a^b f(x)\,dx = \int_a^b f(a+b-x)\,dx\right]$$

$$= \int_{\pi/4}^{3\pi/4} \frac{\pi - x}{1+\sin(\pi - x)} dx$$

$$= \int_{\pi/4}^{3\pi/4} \frac{\pi - x}{1+\sin x} dx \quad \text{...(ii)}$$

On adding Eqs. (i) and (ii), we get

$$2I = \int_{\pi/4}^{3\pi/4} \frac{x}{1+\sin x} dx + \int_{\pi/4}^{3\pi/4} \frac{\pi - x}{1+\sin x} dx$$

$$= \int_{\pi/4}^{3\pi/4} \frac{x}{1+\sin x} dx + \int_{\pi/4}^{3\pi/4} \frac{\pi}{1+\sin x} dx - \int_{\pi/4}^{3\pi/4} \frac{x}{1+\sin x} dx$$

$$= \pi \int_{\pi/4}^{3\pi/4} \frac{1}{1+\sin x} dx$$

$$\Rightarrow \quad I = \frac{\pi}{2} \int_{\pi/4}^{3\pi/4} \left(\frac{1}{1+\sin x} \times \frac{1-\sin x}{1-\sin x}\right) dx$$

$$\Rightarrow \quad I = \frac{\pi}{2} \int_{\pi/4}^{3\pi/4} \frac{1-\sin x}{1-\sin^2 x} dx = \frac{\pi}{2} \int_{\pi/4}^{3\pi/4} \frac{1-\sin x}{\cos^2 x} dx$$

$$= \frac{\pi}{2} \int_{\pi/4}^{3\pi/4} \left(\sec^2 x - \frac{\sin x}{\cos^2 x}\right) dx$$

$$I = \frac{\pi}{2} \int_{\pi/4}^{3\pi/4} \sec^2 x\,dx - \frac{\pi}{2} \int_{\pi/4}^{3\pi/4} \frac{\sin x}{\cos^2 x} dx$$

Put $\cos x = t$

$$\Rightarrow \quad -\sin x = \frac{dt}{dx}$$

$$\Rightarrow \quad \sin x dx = -dt$$

Lower limit When $x = \frac{\pi}{4}$ then $t = \cos \frac{\pi}{4} = \frac{1}{\sqrt{2}}$

Upper limit When $x = \frac{3\pi}{4}$ then $t = -\frac{1}{\sqrt{2}}$

$$\therefore \quad I = \frac{\pi}{2} [\tan x]_{\pi/4}^{3\pi/4} - \frac{\pi}{2} \int_{1/\sqrt{2}}^{-1/\sqrt{2}} \frac{-dt}{t^2}$$

$$= \frac{\pi}{2}\left[\tan\frac{3\pi}{4} - \tan\frac{\pi}{4}\right] + \frac{\pi}{2}\left[-\frac{1}{t}\right]_{1/\sqrt{2}}^{-1/\sqrt{2}}$$

$$= \frac{\pi}{2}[-1-1] - \frac{\pi}{2}[-\sqrt{2}-\sqrt{2}]$$

$$= -\frac{2\pi}{2} + \frac{\pi}{2} \times 2\sqrt{2}$$

$$= -\pi + \pi\sqrt{2} = \pi(\sqrt{2}-1)$$ **Hence Proved**

OR

(ii) Let $I = \int \frac{x^2}{(x-1)^2 (x^2+1)} dx$

Here, integrand is a proper rational function.

So, by the form of partial fraction, we get

$$\frac{x^2}{(x-1)^2 (x^2+1)} = \frac{A}{x-1} + \frac{B}{(x-1)^2} + \frac{Cx+D}{x^2+1}$$

$$\Rightarrow x^2 = A(x-1)(x^2+1) + B(x^2+1) + (Cx+D)(x-1)^2 \quad \text{...(i)}$$

On putting $x = 1$ in Eq. (i), we get

$$1^2 = A(0)(1^2+1) + B(1^2+1) + (C(1)+D)(0)$$

$$\Rightarrow \quad 1 = 2B \Rightarrow \quad B = \frac{1}{2}$$

On putting $x = 0$ Eq. (i), we get

$$0 = A(-1)(1) + B(1) + (0+D)(-1)^2$$

$$\Rightarrow \quad 0 = -A + B + D$$

$$\Rightarrow \quad D - A = -B$$

$$\Rightarrow \quad D - A = -\frac{1}{2} \quad \text{...(ii)}$$

On putting $x = -1$ in Eq. (i), we get

$$(-1)^2 = A(-1-1)((-1)^2+1) + B((-1)^2+1) + (C(-1)+D)(-1-1)^2$$

$$\Rightarrow \quad 1 = -2A(2) + 2B + (-C+D)(4)$$

$$\Rightarrow \quad 1 = -4A + 2B - 4C + 4D$$

$$\Rightarrow \quad 1 = -4A + 2 \times \frac{1}{2} - 4C + 4D$$

$$\Rightarrow \quad 4(D-A) - 4C = 0 \quad \text{...(iii)}$$

On putting $x = 2$ in Eq. (i), we get

$$2^2 = A(2-1)(2^2+1) + B(2^2+1) + (2C+D)(2-1)^2$$

$$\Rightarrow \quad 4 = 5A + 5B + 2C + D$$

$$\Rightarrow \quad 4 = 5A + 5 \times \frac{1}{2} + 2C + D$$

$$\Rightarrow \quad 4 - \frac{5}{2} = 5A + 2C + D$$

$$\Rightarrow \quad \frac{3}{2} = 5A + 2C + D \quad \text{...(iv)}$$

On solving Eqs. (ii) and (iii), we get

$$C = -\frac{1}{2}$$

On putting the value of C in Eqs. (iii) and (iv), we get

$$4(D-A)-4\times\left(-\frac{1}{2}\right)=0$$

$\Rightarrow \quad 4D-4A+2=0$

$\Rightarrow \quad 2D-2A=-1 \quad \ldots(v)$

and $\quad \frac{3}{2}=5A+2\left(-\frac{1}{2}\right)+D$

$\Rightarrow \quad 5A+D=\frac{3}{2}+1=\frac{5}{2}$

$\Rightarrow \quad 10A+2D=5 \quad \ldots(vi)$

On solving Eqs. (v) and (vi), we get

$$A=\frac{1}{2}, D=0$$

Now,

$$\frac{x^2}{(x-1)^2(x^2+1)}=\frac{\frac{1}{2}}{x-1}+\frac{\frac{1}{2}}{(x-1)^2}+\frac{-\frac{1}{2}x+0}{x^2+1}$$

$\therefore \quad I=\int\frac{x^2}{(x-1)(x^2+1)}dx=\frac{1}{2}\int\frac{1}{x-1}dx$

$$+\frac{1}{2}\int\frac{1}{(x-1)^2}dx-\frac{1}{2}\int\frac{x}{x^2+1}dx$$

$$=\frac{1}{2}\int\frac{1}{x-1}dx+\frac{1}{2}\int(x-1)^{-2}dx-\frac{1}{4}\int\frac{2x}{x^2+1}dx$$

$$=\frac{1}{2}\log|x-1|+\frac{1}{2}\left(\frac{(x-1)^{-1}}{-1}\right)-\frac{1}{4}\log|x^2+1|+C$$

$$=\frac{1}{2}\log|x-1|-\frac{1}{2(x-1)}-\frac{1}{4}\log|x^2+1|+C$$

12. (i) Given differential equation is

$$(x+5y^2)\frac{dy}{dx}=y$$

$\Rightarrow \quad \frac{dx}{dy}=\frac{x+5y^2}{y}$

$\Rightarrow \quad \frac{dx}{dy}=\frac{x}{y}+5y$

$\Rightarrow \quad \frac{dx}{dy}-\frac{x}{y}=5y$

On comparing above equation with linear differential equation $\frac{dx}{dy}+Px=Q$, we get

$$P=-\frac{1}{y} \text{ and } Q=5y$$

$\therefore \quad \text{IF}=e^{\int P dy}=e^{-\int\frac{1}{y}dy}$

$$=e^{-\log|y|}=e^{\log\frac{1}{|y|}}=\frac{1}{y}$$

The solution is $x\times\text{IF}=\int(Q\times\text{IF})\,dy+C$

$\Rightarrow \quad \frac{x}{y}=\int\frac{5y}{y}dy+C$

$\Rightarrow \quad \frac{x}{y}=5\int dy+C$

$\Rightarrow \quad \frac{x}{y}=5y+C$

$\Rightarrow \quad x=5y^2+yC \quad \ldots(i)$

Also given, $x=2$ and $y=1$, therefore from Eq. (i), we get

$$2=5(1)^2+C$$

$\Rightarrow \quad C=2-5=-3$

On putting the value of C in Eq. (i), we get

$$x=5y^2-3y,$$

which is the required solution.

OR

(ii) Given, $(x^2-2y^2)dx+2xy\,dy=0$

$\Rightarrow \quad 2xy\,dy=-(x^2-2y^2)dx$

$\Rightarrow \quad \frac{dy}{dx}=\frac{2y^2-x^2}{2xy},$

which is a homogeneous differential equation.

Put $y=vx$

$\Rightarrow \quad \frac{dy}{dx}=v+x\frac{dv}{dx}$

$\therefore \quad v+x\frac{dv}{dx}=\frac{2v^2x^2-x^2}{2x\,vx}$

$$=\frac{2v^2-1}{2v}$$

$\Rightarrow \quad x\frac{dv}{dx}=\frac{2v^2-1}{2v}-v$

$\Rightarrow \quad x\frac{dv}{dx}=\frac{2v^2-1-2v^2}{2v}$

$\Rightarrow \quad x\frac{dv}{dx}=-\frac{1}{2v}$

$\Rightarrow \quad 2v\,dv=-\frac{1}{x}dx$

On integrating both sides, we get

$$\int 2v\,dv=\int-\frac{1}{x}dx$$

$\Rightarrow \quad v^2=-\log|x|+C$

$\Rightarrow \quad \frac{y^2}{x^2}=-\log|x|+C \quad \left[\because v=\frac{y}{x}\right]$

$\Rightarrow \quad y^2=x^2(-\log|x|+C) \quad \ldots(i)$

Also given, when $x=2$ and $y=1$, therefore from Eq. (i), we get

$$1=4(-\log 1+C)$$

$\Rightarrow \quad C=\frac{1}{4}$

On putting the value of C in Eq. (i), we get

$$y^2=x^2\left(\frac{1}{4}-\log x\right),$$

which is the required solution.

13. (i) Graph 2 represents $y=\sin^{-1}x$.

(ii) Domain of $y=\sin^{-1}x$ is $[-1, 1]$.

Range of $y=\sin^{-1}x$ is $\left[-\frac{\pi}{2},\frac{\pi}{2}\right]$.

(iii) LHS $= \sin^{-1}\frac{1}{\sqrt{5}} + \sin^{-1}\frac{2}{\sqrt{5}}$

$$= \sin^{-1}\left[\frac{1}{\sqrt{5}}\sqrt{1-\left(\frac{2}{\sqrt{5}}\right)^2} + \frac{2}{\sqrt{5}}\sqrt{1-\left(\frac{1}{\sqrt{5}}\right)^2}\right]$$

$[\because \sin^{-1}x + \sin^{-1}y = \sin^{-1}[x\sqrt{1-y^2} + y\sqrt{1-x^2}]$

$$= \sin^{-1}\left[\frac{1}{\sqrt{5}}\sqrt{\frac{5-4}{5}} + \frac{2}{\sqrt{5}}\sqrt{\frac{5-1}{5}}\right]$$

$$= \sin^{-1}\left[\frac{1}{\sqrt{5}} \times \frac{1}{\sqrt{5}} + \frac{2}{\sqrt{5}} \times \frac{2}{\sqrt{5}}\right]$$

$$= \sin^{-1}\left[\frac{1}{5} + \frac{4}{5}\right] = \sin^{-1}(1)$$

$$= \sin^{-1}\left(\sin\frac{\pi}{2}\right) = \frac{\pi}{2} = \text{RHS}$$

Hence proved.

(iv) We have, $\tan^{-1}\left[2\sin\left(2\cos^{-1}\frac{\sqrt{3}}{2}\right)\right]$

$$= \tan^{-1}\left[2\sin\left(2\cos^{-1}\left(\cos\frac{\pi}{6}\right)\right)\right]$$

$$= \tan^{-1}\left[2\sin\left(2 \times \frac{\pi}{6}\right)\right]$$

$$= \tan^{-1}\left[2\sin\frac{\pi}{3}\right]$$

$$= \tan^{-1}\left(2 \times \frac{\sqrt{3}}{2}\right) = \tan^{-1}(\sqrt{3})$$

$$= \tan^{-1}\left(\tan\frac{\pi}{3}\right) = \frac{\pi}{3}$$

14. Let X, Y and Z be the events that the missing person was the responsibility of agencies X, Y and Z respectively and A be the event that a person is missing.

$$P(X) = \frac{1000}{1000 + 2000 + 3000} = \frac{1000}{6000} = \frac{1}{6},$$

$$P(Y) = \frac{2000}{6000} = \frac{1}{3}$$

and $P(Z) = \frac{3000}{6000} = \frac{1}{2}$

Also, $P(A/X) = 1 - \frac{99}{100}$

$= 1 - 0.99 = 0.01,$

$P(A/Y) = 1 - \frac{98.5}{100}$

$= 1 - 0.985 = 0.015$

and $P(A/Z) = 1 - \frac{98}{100}$

$= 1 - 0.98 = 0.02$

$\therefore$ Required probability $= P(X/A)$

$$= \frac{P(X)\,P(A/X)}{P(X)\,P(A/X) + P(Y)\,P(A/Y) + P(Z)\,P(A/Z)}$$

$$= \frac{\frac{1}{6} \times 0.01}{\frac{1}{6} \times 0.01 + \frac{1}{3} \times 0.015 + \frac{1}{2} \times 0.02}$$

$$= \frac{0.00167}{0.00167 + 0.005 + 0.01} = \frac{0.00167}{0.01667}$$

$= 0.1001$

Section B

15. (i) (a) We have,

$$(\vec{a} + \vec{b})^2 + (\vec{b} - \vec{a})^2 = 2(\vec{a}^2 + \vec{b}^2)$$

$$\text{LHS} = (\vec{a} + \vec{b})^2 + (\vec{b} - \vec{a})^2$$

$$= (\vec{a}^2 + 2\vec{a}\cdot\vec{b} + \vec{b}^2) + (\vec{b}^2 - 2\vec{b}\cdot\vec{a} + \vec{a}^2)$$

$$= 2\vec{a}^2 + 2\vec{b}^2 + 2\vec{a}\cdot\vec{b} - 2\vec{a}\cdot\vec{b} \quad [\because \vec{a}\cdot\vec{b} = \vec{b}\cdot\vec{a}]$$

$$= 2(\vec{a}^2 + \vec{b}^2) = \text{RHS}$$

Thus, Assertion is true.

We know that dot product of any two vectors is commutative.

Hence, both Assertion and Reason are true and Reason is the correct explanation for Assertion.

(ii) (b) Given equations of planes are

$x + y + 2z - 9 = 0$ and $2x - y + z - 15 = 0$

On comparing with $a_1x + b_1y + c_1z + d_1 = 0$

and $a_2x + b_2y + c_2z + d = 0$, we get

$a_1 = 1, b_1 = 1, c_1 = 2$

and $a_2 = 2, b_2 = -1, c_2 = 1$

Now, the angle between two planes is given by

$$\theta = \cos^{-1}\left|\frac{a_1a_2 + b_1b_2 + c_1c_2}{\sqrt{a_1^2 + b_1^2 + c_1^2}\sqrt{a_2^2 + b_2^2 + c_2^2}}\right|$$

$$= \cos^{-1}\left|\frac{1 \times 2 + 1 \times (-1) + 2 \times 1}{\sqrt{1 + 1 + (2)^2}\sqrt{(2)^2 + 1 + 1}}\right|$$

$$= \cos^{-1}\left|\frac{2 - 1 + 2}{\sqrt{6}\sqrt{6}}\right|$$

$$= \cos^{-1}\left(\frac{3}{6}\right)$$

$$= \cos^{-1}\left(\frac{1}{2}\right) = \frac{\pi}{3}$$

(iii) Given points are $P(-2, 3, 5)$, $Q(1, 2, 3)$ and $R(7, 0, -1)$.

Direction ratios of line joining P and Q are $(1 - (-2), 2 - 3, 3 - 5)$ i.e. $(3, -1, -2)$.

Direction ratios of line joining Q and R are $(7 - 1, 0 - 2, -1 - 3)$ i.e. $(6, -2, -4)$.

Now, ratios of direction ratios of PQ and QR are

$\frac{3}{6}, \frac{-1}{-2}, \frac{-2}{-4}$ i.e. $\frac{1}{2}, \frac{1}{2}, \frac{1}{2}$

Thus, the direction ratios of PQ and QR are proportional. So, PQ is parallel to QR but Q is common to both PQ and QR. Hence, P, Q and R are collinear points.

(iv) (a) The given vector equation of the path traced by one honeybee is

$$\vec{r} = (\hat{i} + 2\hat{j} + 3\hat{k}) + \lambda(2\hat{i} + 3\hat{j} + 4\hat{k})$$

Let $\vec{r} = x\hat{i} + y\hat{j} + z\hat{k}$

Then,

$$x\hat{i} + y\hat{j} + z\hat{k} = (\hat{i} + 2\hat{j} + 3\hat{k}) + \lambda(2\hat{i} + 3\hat{j} + 4\hat{k})$$

$$\Rightarrow x\hat{i} + y\hat{j} + z\hat{k} = (1 + 2\lambda)\hat{i} + (2 + 3\lambda)\hat{j} + (3 + 4\lambda)\hat{k}$$

On comparing the coefficients of $\hat{i}\ \hat{j}$ and $\hat{k}$, we get

$$x = 1 + 2\lambda,\ y = 2 + 3\lambda,\ z = 3 + 4\lambda$$

$$\Rightarrow \quad \lambda = \frac{x-1}{2}, \lambda = \frac{y-2}{3}, \lambda = \frac{z-3}{4}$$

$$\therefore \quad \frac{x-1}{2} = \frac{y-2}{3} = \frac{z-3}{4} = \lambda$$

Thus, the required cartesian equation of the given line is

$$\frac{x-1}{2} = \frac{y-2}{3} = \frac{z-3}{4}$$

(b) Since, the other honeybee flies parallel to the first one. So, it has the same direction ratios i.e. 2, 3, 4.

$\therefore$ The equation of the line passing through the point (2, 4, 5) with direction ratios 2, 3 and 4 is

$$\frac{x-2}{2} = \frac{y-4}{3} = \frac{z-5}{4}$$

Hence, the equation of the path traced by the other honeybee is $\frac{x-2}{2} = \frac{y-4}{3} = \frac{z-5}{4}$.

16. (i) Let the three points be $A(2, 2, -1)$, $B(3, 4, 2)$ and $C(7, 0, 6)$.

Now, direction ratios of AB are (1, 2, 3) and direction ratios of BC are (4, –4, 4).

$\because$ Direction ratios of AB and BC are not proportional.

$\therefore$ The points are non collinear.

We know that, the cartesian equation of plane passing through three points $A(x_1, y_1, z_1)$, $B(x_2, y_2, z_2)$ and $C(x_3, y_3, z_3)$ is given by

$$\begin{vmatrix} x - x_1 & y - y_1 & z - z_1 \\ x_2 - x_1 & y_2 - y_1 & z_2 - z_1 \\ x_3 - x_1 & y_3 - y_1 & z_3 - z_1 \end{vmatrix} = 0$$

$$\therefore \begin{vmatrix} x-2 & y-2 & z+1 \\ 3-2 & 4-2 & 2+1 \\ 7-2 & 0-2 & 6+1 \end{vmatrix} = 0$$

$$\Rightarrow \begin{vmatrix} x-2 & y-2 & z+1 \\ 1 & 2 & 3 \\ 5 & -2 & 7 \end{vmatrix} = 0$$

Expanding along R_1, we get

$$(x-2)(14+6) - (y-2)(7-15) + (z+1)(-2-10) = 0$$

$$\Rightarrow \quad 20(x-2) + 8(y-2) - 12(z+1) = 0$$

$$\Rightarrow \quad 5(x-2) + 2(y-2) - 3(z+1) = 0$$

$$\Rightarrow \quad 5x - 10 + 2y - 4 - 3z - 3 = 0$$

$$\Rightarrow \quad 5x + 2y - 3z = 17,$$

which is the required equation of the plane in cartesian form.

OR

(ii) The equation of plane passing through (2, 3, 1) is

$$a(x-2) + b(y-3) + c(z-1) = 0 \quad \ldots\text{(i)}$$

This plane also passes through (4, –5, 3).

So, $a(4-2) + b(-5-3) + c(3-1) = 0$

$$\Rightarrow \quad 2a - 8b + 2c = 0 \quad \ldots\text{(ii)}$$

Also given plane (i) is parallel to X-axis.

It means the, plane (i) is perpendicular to the YZ-plane whose equation is $x = 0$.

$$\therefore \quad a(1) + b(0) + c(0) = 0 \quad \ldots\text{(iii)}$$

$$[\because a_1a_2 + b_1b_2 + c_1c_2 = 0]$$

On solving Eqs. (i), (ii) and (iii), we get

$$\begin{vmatrix} x-2 & y-3 & z-1 \\ 2 & -8 & 2 \\ 1 & 0 & 0 \end{vmatrix} = 0$$

$$\Rightarrow \quad 0 - 0 + 2(y-3) + 8(z-1)) = 0$$

$$\Rightarrow \quad 2y - 6 + 8z - 8 = 0$$

$$\Rightarrow \quad 2y + 8z - 14 = 0$$

$$\Rightarrow \quad y + 4z - 7 = 0,$$

which is the required equation of plane.

17. Given position vectors of A, B and C are

$$\vec{OA} = 2\hat{i} - 2\hat{j} + \hat{k}, \vec{OB} = \hat{i} + 2\hat{j} - 2\hat{k}$$

and $\vec{OC} = 2\hat{i} - \hat{j} + 4\hat{k}$

(i) Here, $\vec{AB} = \vec{OB} - \vec{OA}$

$$= (\hat{i} + 2\hat{j} - 2\hat{k}) - (2\hat{i} - 2\hat{j} + \hat{k})$$

$$= -\hat{i} + 4\hat{j} - 3\hat{k}$$

and $\vec{BC} = \vec{OC} - \vec{OB}$

$$= (2\hat{i} - \hat{j} + 4\hat{k}) - (\hat{i} + 2\hat{j} - 2\hat{k})$$

$$= \hat{i} - 3\hat{j} + 6\hat{k}$$

(ii) Projection of $\vec{AB}$ on $\vec{BC}$ is given by

$$\frac{\vec{AB} \cdot \vec{BC}}{|\vec{BC}|}$$

$$= \frac{(-\hat{i} + 4\hat{j} - 3\hat{k}) \cdot (\hat{i} - 3\hat{j} + 6\hat{k})}{\sqrt{1^2 + (-3)^2 + 6^2}}$$

$$= \frac{-1 - 12 - 18}{\sqrt{1 + 9 + 36}} = \frac{-31}{\sqrt{46}}$$

(iii) Area of ΔABC, whose sides are $\vec{AB}$ and $\vec{BC}$ is given by

$$= \frac{1}{2}|\vec{AB} \times \vec{BC}|$$

Now, $$\vec{AB} \times \vec{BC} = \begin{vmatrix} \hat{i} & \hat{j} & \hat{k} \\ -1 & 4 & -3 \\ 1 & -3 & 6 \end{vmatrix}$$

$$= \hat{i}(24 - 9) - \hat{j}(-6 + 3) + \hat{k}(3 - 4)$$

$$= 15\hat{i} + 3\hat{j} - \hat{k}$$

$$|\vec{AB} \times \vec{AC}| = \sqrt{(15)^2 + (3)^2 + (-1)^2}$$

$$= \sqrt{225 + 9 + 1} = \sqrt{235}$$

$$\therefore \text{Area of } \Delta ABC = \frac{1}{2} \times \sqrt{235} = \frac{\sqrt{235}}{2} \text{ sq. units}$$

18. (i) (a) Given equation is $y = 4 - x^2$

$\Rightarrow \quad x^2 = 4 - y$

$\Rightarrow \quad x^2 = -(y - 4)$

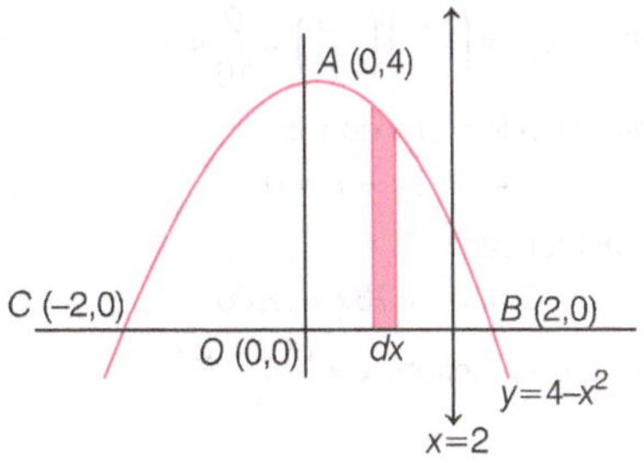

which is the parabola of the form $X^2 = -4AY$.

Its vertex is (0, 4) and it is symmetrical about X-axis.

(b) Area enclosed between the curve, X-axis, the lines $x = 0$ and $x = 2$

$= \text{Area of region } OABO$

$$= \int_0^2 y\,dx = \int_0^2 (4 - x^2)\,dx$$

$$= \left[4x - \frac{x^3}{3}\right]_0^2 = \left[4(2) - \frac{2^3}{3}\right] - \left[4(0) - \frac{0}{3}\right]$$

$$= 8 - \frac{8}{3} = \frac{24 - 8}{3} = \frac{16}{3} \text{ sq. units}$$

(c) Area bounded by the parabola and the X-axis

$= \text{Area of region } CABC$

$= 2(\text{Area of region } OABO)$

$$= 2 \times \frac{16}{3} = \frac{32}{3} \text{ sq. units}$$

OR

(ii) Given equations of lines are

$x + 2y = 2 \quad \ldots(\text{i})$

$y - x = 1 \quad \ldots(\text{ii})$

$2x + y = 7 \quad \ldots(\text{iii})$

Table for line (i) is

x	0	2
y	1	0

So, line (i) passes through the points (0, 1) and (2, 0).

Table for line (ii) is

x	0	–1
y	1	0

So, line (ii) passes through the points (0, 1) and (–1, 0).

Table for line (iii) is

x	0	3.5
y	7	0

So, line (iii) passes through the points (0, 7) and (3.5, 0).

On plotting these lines, we get the following graph.

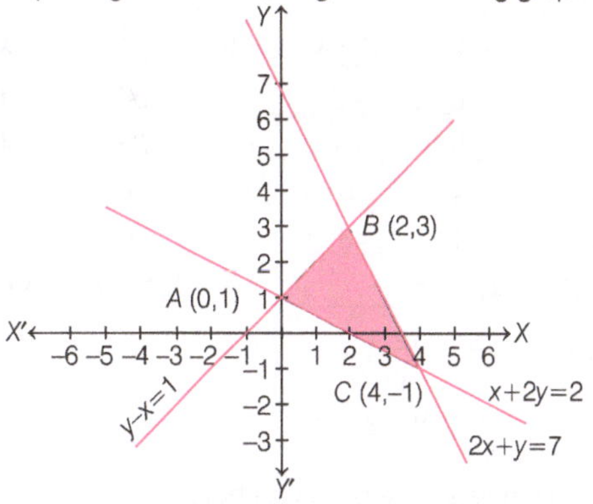

On solving the lines (ii) and (iii) and lines (i) and (iii), we get the intersection point $B(2, 3)$ and $C(4, -1)$, respectively.

$\therefore$ Required area

$$= \int_{-1}^{3} x_{BC}\,dy - \int_{-1}^{1} x_{AC}\,dy - \int_{1}^{3} x_{AB}\,dy$$

$$= \frac{1}{2}\int_{-1}^{3}(7 - y)\,dy - \int_{-1}^{1}(2 - 2y)\,dy - \int_{1}^{3}(y - 1)\,dy$$

$$= \frac{1}{2}\left[7y - \frac{y^2}{2}\right]_{-1}^{3} - 2\left[y - \frac{y^2}{2}\right]_{-1}^{1} - \left[\frac{y^2}{2} - y\right]_{1}^{3}$$

$$= \frac{1}{2}\left[\left(21 - \frac{9}{2}\right) - \left(-7 - \frac{1}{2}\right)\right]$$

$$-2\left[\left(1 - \frac{1}{2}\right) - \left(-1 - \frac{1}{2}\right)\right] - \left[\left(\frac{9}{2} - 3\right) - \left(\frac{1}{2} - 1\right)\right]$$

$$= \frac{1}{2}\left(\frac{33}{2} + \frac{15}{2}\right) - 2\left(\frac{1}{2} + \frac{3}{2}\right) - \left(\frac{3}{2} + \frac{1}{2}\right)$$

$$= \frac{1}{2} \times 24 - 2 \times 2 - 2$$

$= 12 - 4 - 2 = 6$ sq. units

Section C

19. (i) (c) Given, $R(x) = 36x + 3x^2 + 5$

Actual revenue received on selling 10th item

$= R(10) - R(9)$

$= [36(10) + 3(10)^2 + 5] - [36(9) + 3(9)^2 + 5]$

$= 36(10 - 9) + 3(10^2 - 9^2) = 36 + 3 \times 19$

$= 36 + 57 = 93$

(ii) (c) **Statement I** The correlation coefficients will have the same sign as that of regression coefficients i.e. b_{yx} and b_{xy} have the same sign as that of r. Thus, Statement I is correct.

Statement II The correlation coefficient is the geometric mean of regression coefficients. Thus, Statement II is incorrect.

Statement III The product of two regression coefficients is equal to the square of the correlation coefficient, which lies between 0 and 1. Thus, Statement III is incorrect.

Statement IV Both the regression coefficients cannot be greater than unity because their product cannot exceeds one. Thus, Statement IV is correct.

(iii) Let us construct the following table.

x	y	$x-\bar{x}$	$y-\bar{y}$	y^2	xy
1	6	−2	2	36	6
2	5	−1	1	25	10
3	4	0	0	16	12
6	1	3	−3	1	6
$\Sigma x=12$	$\Sigma y=16$			$\Sigma y^2=78$	$\Sigma xy=34$

(a) Here, $\bar{x}=\frac{\Sigma x}{n}=\frac{12}{4}=3$

and $\bar{y}=\frac{\Sigma y}{n}=\frac{16}{4}=4$

(b) The complete table is shown above.

(c) $$b_{xy}=\frac{\Sigma xy-\frac{1}{n}\Sigma x\cdot\Sigma y}{\Sigma y^2-\frac{1}{n}(\Sigma y)^2}=\frac{34-\frac{1}{4}\times 12\times 16}{78-\frac{1}{4}\times 16\times 16}=\frac{34-48}{78-64}=\frac{-14}{14}=-1$$

20. (i) We have, $\Sigma x=24$, $\Sigma y=44$, $\Sigma xy=306$, $\Sigma x^2=164$, $\Sigma y^2=576$, $n=4$

Now, regression of y on x is

$$b_{yx}=\frac{\Sigma xy-\frac{\Sigma x\,\Sigma y}{n}}{\Sigma x^2-\frac{(\Sigma x)^2}{n}}=\frac{306-\frac{24\times 44}{4}}{164-\frac{24\times 24}{4}}=\frac{306-264}{164-144}=\frac{42}{20}=2.1$$

Now, mean, $\bar{x}=\frac{\Sigma x}{n}=\frac{24}{4}=6$

and $\bar{y}=\frac{\Sigma y}{n}=\frac{44}{4}=11$

$\therefore$ Regression equation of y on x is

$$y-\bar{y}=b_{yx}(x-\bar{x})$$
$\Rightarrow$ $y-11=2.1(x-6)$
$\Rightarrow$ $y-11=2.1x-12.6$
$\Rightarrow$ $2.1x-y-1.6=0$

OR

(ii) Assuming $4x+3y+7=0$ to be regression of x on y

$\therefore$ $4x=-3y-7$

$\Rightarrow$ $x=-\frac{3}{4}y-\frac{7}{4}$

$\Rightarrow$ $b_{xy}=-\frac{3}{4}$

Then, $3x+4y+8=0$ is regression line of y on x.

$\therefore$ $4y=-3x-8$

$\Rightarrow$ $y=-\frac{3}{4}x-\frac{8}{4}$

$\Rightarrow$ $b_{yx}=\frac{-3}{4}$

Now, $b_{xy}\cdot b_{yx}=\left(\frac{-3}{4}\right)\left(\frac{-3}{4}\right)=\frac{9}{16}<1$

$\therefore$ Regression line of x on y is

$$4x+3y+7=0.$$

21. (i) Given, cost function,

$$C=x^2+78x+2000$$

and demand function, $x=\frac{600-p}{8}$

(a) We know that

revenue function, $R=xp$

From equation of demand function,

$$x=\frac{600-p}{8}$$

$\therefore$ $p=600-8x$

Now, we put $p=600-8x$ in equation of revenue function, we get

$$R=x(600-8x)$$
$\Rightarrow$ $R=600x-8x^2$

(b) Also, profit function,

$$P(x)=\text{Revenue}-\text{Cost}$$
$$=(600x-8x^2)-(x^2+78x+2000)$$
$$=600x-8x^2-x^2-78x-2000$$
$$=-9x^2+522x-2000$$

(c) For the profit maximising level of output x, $\frac{dP}{dx}=0$.

$\therefore$ $\frac{d(P)}{dx}=0$

$\Rightarrow$ $\frac{d}{dx}(-9x^2+522x-2000)=0$

$\Rightarrow$ $-18x+522=0$

$\Rightarrow$ $18x=522$

$\Rightarrow$ $x=29$

Now, $\frac{d^2P}{dx^2}=\frac{d}{dx}\left(\frac{dP}{dx}\right)=\frac{d}{dx}(-18x+522)$

$$=-18<0$$

Hence, the number of dinner sets to maximise profit is 29.

OR

(ii) Given, average cost function is

$$AC=\frac{x^2}{200}-\frac{x}{50}-30+\frac{5000}{x} \quad \ldots(i)$$

(a) We know that

Average cost (AC) $=\frac{\text{Cost function }(C)}{x}$

$\Rightarrow$ $C=x(AC)$

$\Rightarrow$ $C=x\left(\frac{x^2}{200}-\frac{x}{50}-30+\frac{5000}{x}\right)$

$\Rightarrow$ $C=\frac{x^3}{200}-\frac{x^2}{50}-30x+5000 \quad \ldots(ii)$

(b) Marginal cost (MC) $= \frac{dC}{dx}$

$$= \frac{d}{dx}\left(\frac{x^3}{200} - \frac{x^2}{50} - 30x + 5000\right)$$

$$= \frac{3x^2}{200} - \frac{2x}{50} - 30$$

$$MC = \frac{3x^2}{200} - \frac{x}{25} - 30 \quad \ldots(iii)$$

(c) Marginal average cost (MAC)

$$= \frac{d}{dx}(AC)$$

$$= \frac{d}{dx}\left(\frac{x^2}{200} - \frac{x}{50} - 30 + \frac{5000}{x}\right)$$

$$= \frac{2x}{200} - \frac{1}{50} - \frac{5000}{x^2}$$

$$\Rightarrow \quad MAC = \frac{x}{100} - \frac{1}{50} - \frac{5000}{x^2} \quad \ldots(iv)$$

(d) We have to verify $\frac{d}{dx}(AC) = \frac{MC - AC}{x}$

$$LHS = \frac{d}{dx}(AC) = \frac{x}{100} - \frac{1}{50} - \frac{5000}{x^2}$$

[from Eq. (iv)]

$$RHS = \frac{MC - AC}{x}$$

$$= \frac{\left(\frac{3x^2}{200} - \frac{x}{25} - 30\right) - \left(\frac{x^2}{200} - \frac{x}{50} - 30 + \frac{5000}{x}\right)}{x}$$

[from q.s (i) and (iii)]

$$= \frac{1}{x}\left[\frac{3x^2}{200} - \frac{x^2}{200} - \frac{x}{25} + \frac{x}{50} - 30 + 30 - \frac{5000}{x}\right]$$

$$= \frac{1}{x}\left[\frac{2x^2}{200} - \frac{x}{50} - \frac{5000}{x}\right]$$

$$= \frac{x}{100} - \frac{1}{50} - \frac{5000}{x^2}$$

Thus, LHS = RHS **Hence verified.**

22. Let x and y be the numbers of books of the first and second type, respectively.

So, our problem is to maximise

$$Z = x + y \quad \ldots(i)$$

Subject to constraints,

$$x + 1.5y \le 21 \quad \ldots(ii)$$

$$6x + 4y \le 96 \quad \ldots(iii)$$

$$\text{and } x \ge 0, \; y \ge 0 \quad \ldots(iv)$$

Table for line $x + 1.5y = 21$ is

x	0	21
y	14	0

So, line is passing through the points (0, 14) and (21, 0).

On putting (0, 0) in the inequality $x + 1.5y \le 21$, we get

$0 + 0 \le 21$

$\Rightarrow 0 \le 21$, which is true.

So, the half plane is towards the origin.

Table for line $6x + 4y = 96$

x	0	16
y	24	0

So, line is passing through the points (0, 24) and (16, 0).

On putting (0, 0) in the inequality

$6x + 4y \le 96$ we get

$0 + 0 \le 96$

$\Rightarrow \quad 0 \le 96$ which is true.

So, the half plane is towards the origin.

On plotting these lines, we get the following graph

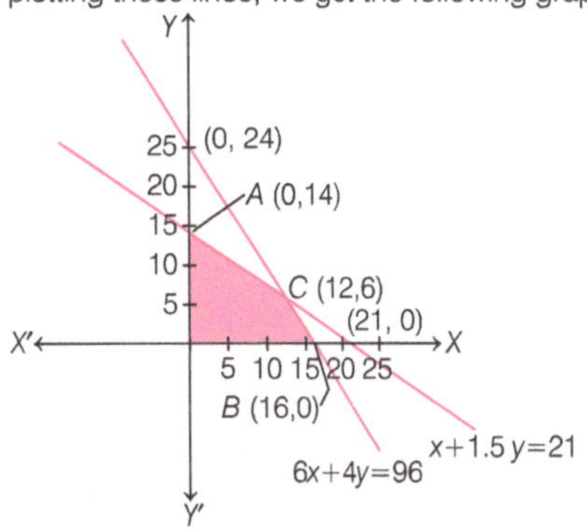

The intersection point of lines (ii) and (iii) is $C(12, 6)$.

Clearly, the feasible region is $OBCAO$, where the corner points are $O(0, 0)$, $B(16, 0)$, $C(12, 6)$ and $A(0, 14)$.

Now, the value of Z at corner points are as follow.

Corner points	$Z = x + y$
$O(0, 0)$	$Z = 0 + 0 = 0$
$A(0, 14)$	$Z = 0 + 14 = 14$
$B(16, 0)$	$Z = 16 + 0 = 16$
$C(12, 6)$	$Z = 12 + 6 = 18$ (Maximum)

The maximum value of Z is 18 at (12, 6).

Hence, the maximum number of books to be placed by placing 12 books of first type and 6 books of second type.

ISC
SPECIMEN PAPER

ISC Specimen Paper

MATHEMATICS

Class 12

General Instructions

1. This Question Paper consists of three sections A, B and C.
2. Candidates are required to attempt all questions from Section A and all questions either from Section B Or Section C.
3. **Section A** Internal choice has been provided in two questions of 2 marks each, two questions of 4 marks each and two questions of 6 marks each.
4. **Section B** Internal choice has been provided in one question of 2 marks and one question of 4 marks.
5. **Section C** Internal choice has been provided in one question of 2 marks and one question of 4 marks.
6. All working, including rough work, should be done on the same sheet as and adjacent to the rest of the answer.
7. The intended marks for questions or parts of questions are given in brackets [].
8. Mathematical tables and graph papers are provided.

Time : 3 Hrs.

Max. Marks : 80

Section A (65 Marks)

1. In subparts (i) to (xi) choose the correct options and in subparts (xii) to (xv), answer the questions as instructed.

(i) A matrix which is both symmetric and skew-symmetric matrix is a/ an • *Understanding*

(a) triangular matrix

(b) identity matrix

(c) diagonal matrix

(d) null matrix

(ii) The value of $\int a^x \cdot e^x dx$ equals • *Recall* [1]

(a) $(a^x \cdot \log_e a)e^x + c$ (b) $\frac{a^x \cdot e^x}{\log_e(ae)} + c$

(c) $\frac{a^x \cdot e^x}{\log_{ae} e} + c$ (d) $\log_e(ae)(ae)^x + c$

(iii) The trigonometric equation $\tan^{-1} x = 3\tan^{-1} a$ has solution for • *Application* [1]

(a) $|a| \le \frac{1}{\sqrt{3}}$

(b) $|a| > \frac{1}{\sqrt{3}}$

(c) $|a| < \frac{1}{\sqrt{3}}$

(d) all real value of a.

(iv) **Assertion** Degree of the differential equation $a\left(\frac{dy}{dx}\right)^2 + b\frac{dx}{dy} = c$, is 3.

Reason If each term involving derivatives of a differential equation is a polynomial (or can be expressed as polynomial), then highest exponent of the highest order derivative is called the degree of the differential equation. • *Analysis* [1]

Which of the following is correct?

(a) Both Assertion and Reason are true and Reason is the correct explanation for Assertion.

(b) Both Assertion and Reason are true but Reason is not the correct explanation for Assertion.

(c) Assertion is true and Reason is false.

(d Assertion is false and Reason is true.

(v) Five numbers x_1, x_2, x_3, x_4 and x_5 are randomly selected from the numbers 1, 2, 3, ..., 18 and are arranged in the increasing order such that $x_1 < x_2 < x_3 < x_4 < x_5$. What is the probability that $x_2 = 7$ and $x_4 = 11$? • *Application* [1]

(a) $\frac{26}{51}$ (b) $\frac{3}{104}$

(c) $\frac{1}{68}$ (d) $\frac{1}{34}$

(vi) If $\begin{vmatrix} a & b & c \\ m & n & p \\ x & y & z \end{vmatrix} = k$, then what is the value of $\begin{vmatrix} 6a & 2b & 2c \\ 3m & n & p \\ 3x & y & z \end{vmatrix}$? • *Understanding* [1]

(a) $\frac{k}{6}$ (b) $2k$ (c) $3k$ (d) $6k$

(vii) Consider the graph $y = x^{\frac{1}{3}}$

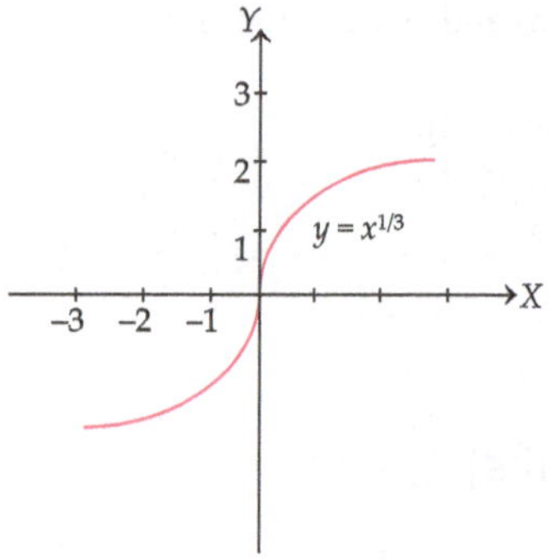

Statement I The above graph is continuous at $x = 0$.

Statement II The above graph is differentiable at $x = 0$ • *Application* [1]

Which of the following is correct?

(a) Statement I is true and Statement II is false.

(b) Statement II is true and Statement I is false.

(c) Both the statements are true.

(d) Both the statements are false.

(viii) The value of $\frac{dy}{dx}$, if $y = |x-1| + |x-4|$ at $x = 3$ is

(a) -2 (b) 0 (c) 2 (d) 4

(ix) **Statement I** The intersection of two equivalence relations is always an equivalence relation.

Statement II The Union of two equivalence relations is always an equivalence relation. • *Understanding* [1]

Which one of the following is correct?

(a) Statement I implies Statement II.

(b) Statement II implies Statement I.

(c) Statement I is true only if Statement II is true.

(d) Statement I and II are independent of each other.

(x) In a third order matrix a_{ij} denotes the element of the ith row and the jth column.

$$A = a_{ij} = \begin{cases} 0, & \text{for } i = j \\ 1, & \text{for } i > j \\ -1, & \text{for } i < j \end{cases}$$

Assertion Matrix A is not invertible.

Reason Determinant of $A = 0$

Which of the following is correct? • *Application* [1]

(a) Both Assertion and Reason are true and Reason is the correct explanation for Assertion.

(b) Both Assertion and Reason are true but Reason is not the correct explanation for Assertion.

(c) Assertion is true and Reason is false.

(d) Assertion is false and Reason is true.

(xi) Given two events A and B such that $P\left(\frac{A}{B}\right) = 0.25$ and $P(A \cap B) = 0.12$. The value of $P(A \cap B')$ is • *Understanding* [1]

(a) 0.36 (b) 0.48 (c) 0.88 (d) 0.036

(xii) The value of the determinant of a matrix A of order 3 is 3. If C is the matrix of co-factors of the matrix A, then what is the value of determinant of C^2? • *Analysis* [1]

(xiii) If a relation R on the set $\{a, b, c\}$ defined by $R = \{(b, b)\}$, then classify the relation. • *Understanding* [1]

(xiv)

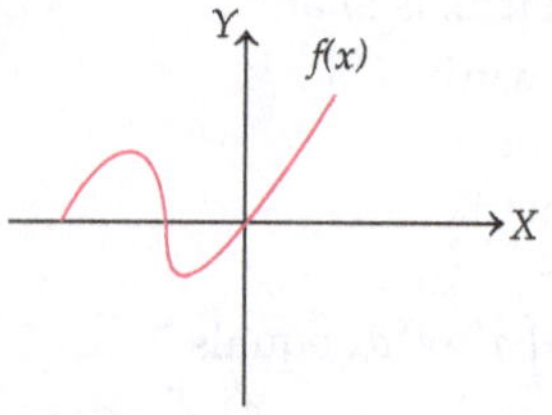

The given function $f : R \to R$ is not onto function. Give reason. • *Understanding* [1]

(xv) There are three machines and 2 of them are faulty. They are tested one by one in a random order till both the faulty machines are identified. What is the probability that only two tests are needed to identify the faulty machines? • *Application* [1]

2. (i) If $x^y = y^x$, then find $\frac{dy}{dx}$. • *Understanding* [2]

Or

(ii) Find the interval in which the function $f(x) = x^2e^{-x}$ is strictly increasing or decreasing. • *Understanding* [2]

3. Evaluate $\int_0^{\sqrt{2}} [x^2]dx$ • *Evaluate* [2]

4. Find the equation to the tangent at (0, 0) on the curve $y = 4x^2 - 2x^3$. • *Analysis* [2]

5. (i) Evaluate $\int \frac{2x^3 - 1}{x^4 + x} dx$ • *Evaluate* [2]

Or

(ii) Evaluate $\int e^x \operatorname{cosec} x(1 - \cot x)dx$ • *Evaluate* [2]

6. Find the value of $\tan^{-1}\left(\frac{x}{y}\right) + \tan^{-1}\left(\frac{y-x}{y+x}\right)$ • *Application* [2]

7. Solve $\sin^{-1}(x) + \sin^{-1}(1-x) = \cos^{-1} x$ • *Application* [4]

8. Evaluate $\int \sqrt{\sec\frac{x}{2} - 1}\, dx$ • *Application* [4]

9. (i) A kite is being pulled down by a string that goes through a ring on the ground 8 m away from the person pulling it. If the string is pulled in at 1 m per second, how fast is the kite coming down when it is 15 m high? • *Application* [4]

Or

(ii) If $y = (x + \sqrt{a^2 + x^2})^m$, prove that

$$(a^2 + x^2)\frac{d^2y}{dx^2} + x\frac{dy}{dx} - m^2y = 0$$ • *Analysis* [4]

10. (i) Three friends go to a restaurant to have pizza. They decide who will pay for the pizza by tossing a coin. It is decided that each one of them will toss a coin and if one person gets a different result (heads or tails) than the other two, that person would pay. If all three get the same result (all heads or all tails), they will toss again until they get a different result. • *Analysis* [4]

(a) What is the probability that all three friends will get the same result (all heads or all tails) in one round of tossing?

(b) What is the probability that they will get a different result in one round of tossing?

(c) What is the probability that they will need exactly four rounds of tossing to determine who would pay?

Or

(ii) Students of under graduation submitted a case study on 'Understanding the Probability of Left-Handedness in Children Based on Parental Handedness'.

Following recent studies suggest that roughly 12% of the world population is left-handed. Depending on the parents' handedness, the chances of having a left-handed child vary as follows:

Scenario A

Both parents are left-handed, with a 24% chance of the child being left-handed.

Scenario B

The father is right-handed and the mother is left-handed, with a 22% chance of child being left-handed.

Scenario C

The father is left-handed and the mother is right-handed, with a 17% chance of child being left-handed.

Scenario D

Both parents are right-handed, with a 9% chance of having a left-handed child.

Assuming that scenarios A, B, C and D are equally likely and L denotes the event that the child is left-handed, answer the following questions.

(a) What is the overall probability that a randomly selected child is left-handed?

(b) Given that exactly one parent is left-handed, what is the probability that a randomly selected child is left-handed?

(c) If a child is left-handed, what is the probability that both parents are left-handed?

11. To raise money for an orphanage, students of three schools *A*, *B* and *C* organised an exhibition in their residential colony, where they sold paper bags, scrap books and pastel sheets made by using recycled paper. Students of school *A* sold 30 paper bags, 20 scrap books and 10 pastel sheets and raised ₹ 410. Students of school *B* sold 20 paper bags, 10 scrap books and 20 pastel sheets and raised ₹ 290.

Students of school C sold 20 paper bags, 20 scrap books and 20 pastel sheets and raised ₹ 440.

Answer the following question.

(i) Translate the problem into a system of equations.

(ii) Solve the system of equation by using matrix method.

(iii) Hence, find the cost of one paper bag, one scrap book and one pastel sheet.

• *Application* [6]

12. (i) Solve the differential equation.

$$(xdy - ydx)y \sin\left(\frac{y}{x}\right) = (ydx + xdy)\, x \cos\left(\frac{y}{x}\right).$$

Find the particular solution satisfying the condition that $y = \pi$ when $x = 1$.

• *Application* [6]

Or

(ii) Evaluate $\int_0^{\pi} (\sin^4 x + \cos^4 x)dx$ and hence evaluate $\int_{-2\pi}^{2\pi} \frac{\sin^4 x + \cos^4 x}{1 + e^x}\, dx.$

• *Evaluate*

13. (i) A cone of maximum volume is inscribed in a given sphere. Then, prove that ratio of the height of the cone to the diameter of the sphere is equal to 2 / 3.

• *Application*

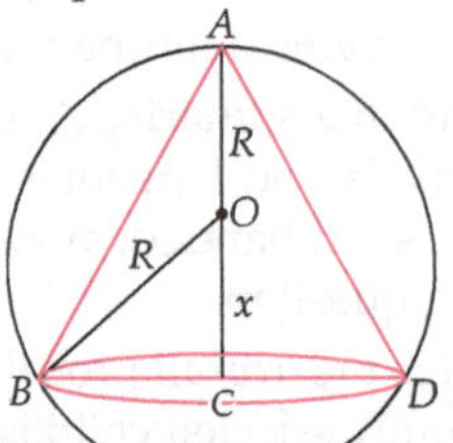

Or (ii) A given quantity of metal is to be cast into a solid half circular cylinder with a rectangular base and semi-circular ends. If the total surface area is minimum, then prove that the ratio of the length of cylinder to the diameter of semi-circular ends is $\pi : \pi + 2$.

• *Application*

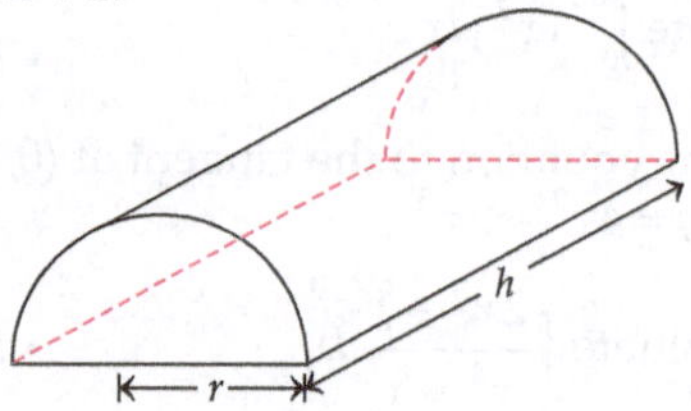

14. Kiran plays a game of throwing a fair die 3 times but to quit as and when she gets a six. Kiran gets + 1 point for a six and − 1 for any other number.

• *Analysis* [6]

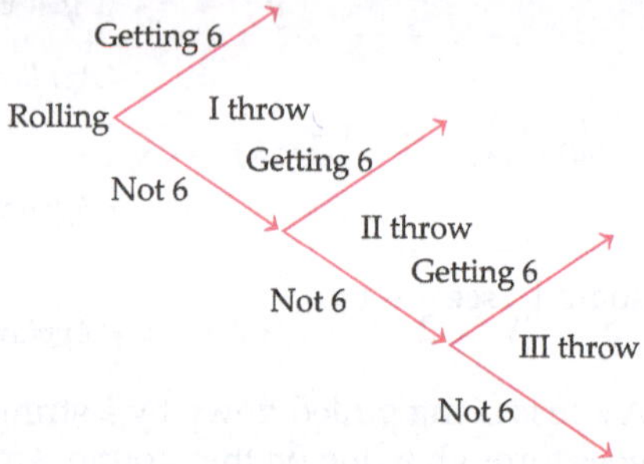

(i) If X denotes the random variable 'points earned' then what are the possible values X can take?

(ii) Find the probability distribution of this random variable X.

(iii) Find the expected value of the points she gets.

Section B (15 Marks)

15. In subparts (i) and (iii) choose the correct options and in subparts (iv) to (v), answer the questions as instructed.

(i) Consider the following statements and choose the correct option.

Statement I If $\vec{a}$ and $\vec{b}$ represent two adjacent sides of a parallelogram, then the diagonals are represented by $\vec{a} + \vec{b}$ and F$\vec{a} - \vec{b}$.

Statement II If $\vec{a}$ and $\vec{b}$ represents two diagonals of a parallelogram, then the adjacent sides are represented by $2(\vec{a} + \vec{b})$ and $2(\vec{a} - \vec{b})$.

• *Recall*

Which of the following is correct?

(a) Only Statement I

(b) Only Statement II

(c) Both Statements I and II

(d) Neither Statement I nor Statement II

(ii) The distance of the plane through (1, 1, 1) and perpendicular to the line $\frac{x-1}{3} = \frac{y-1}{0} = \frac{z-1}{4}$ from the origin is

• *Application*

(a) $\frac{3}{4}$ (b) $\frac{4}{3}$

(c) $\frac{7}{5}$ (d) 1

(iii) If the direction cosines of a line are $<\frac{1}{c}, \frac{1}{c}, \frac{1}{c}>$, then • *Understanding*

(a) $c > 0$

(b) $0 < c < 1$

(c) $c = \pm\sqrt{3}$

(d) $c > 2$

(iv) If $\hat{a}$ is a unit vector perpendicular to $\vec{b}$ and $(\vec{a} + 2\vec{b})\cdot(3\vec{a} - \vec{b}) = -5$, find $|\vec{b}|$ • *Understanding*

(v) Shown below is a cuboid. Find $\overrightarrow{BA} \cdot \overrightarrow{BC}$

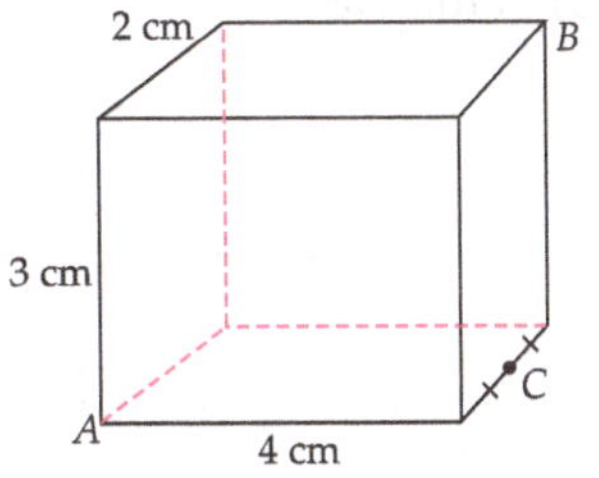

16. (i) Find a vector of magnitude 9 units and perpendicular to the vectors $\vec{a} = 4\hat{i} - \hat{j} + \hat{k}$ and $\vec{b} = -2\hat{i} + \hat{j} - 2\hat{k}$ • *Application*

Or

(ii) What are the values of x for which the angle between the vectors? $2x^2\hat{i} + 3x\hat{j} + \hat{k}$ and $\hat{i} - 2\hat{j} + x^2\hat{k}$ is obtuse? • *Application*

17. (i) Show that the line whose vector equation is $\vec{r} = (2\hat{i} - 2\hat{j} + 3\hat{k}) + \lambda(\hat{i} - \hat{j} + 4\hat{k})$ is parallel to the plane whose vector equation is $\vec{r}\cdot(\hat{i} + 5\hat{j} + \hat{k}) = 5$. Also, find the distance between them. • *Application*

Or

(ii) Find the equation of the plane containing the line $\frac{x}{-2} = \frac{y-1}{3} = \frac{1-z}{1}$ and the point $(-1, 0, 2)$. • *Application*

18. (i) Sketch the region enclosed bounded by the curve, $y = x|x|$ and the coordinates $x = -1$ and $x = 1$.

(ii) Evaluate $\int_0^1 x^2 dx$.

(iii) Hence, find the area bounded by the curve, $y = x|x|$ and the coordinates $x = -1$ and $x = 1$.

Section C (15 Marks)

19. In subparts (i) and (ii) choose the correct options and in subparts (iii) to (v), answer the questions as instructed.

(i) Which condition is true if Average Cost (AC) is constant at all levels of out put • *Recall*

(a) $MC > AC$ (b) $MC = AC$

(c) $MC < AC$ (d) $MC = \frac{1}{2}AC$

(ii) Read the following statements and choose the correct option.

(I) If $r = 0$, then regression lines are not defined.

(II) If $r = 0$, then regression lines are parallel.

(III) If $r = 0$, then regression lines are perpendicular.

(IV) If $r = \pm 1$, then regression lines coincide. • *Recall*

Which of the following is correct?

(a) Only IV is correct.

(b) Only I and II are correct.

(c) Only I and IV are correct.

(d) Only III and IV are correct.

(iii) Mean of $x = 53$, mean of $y = 28$, regression coefficient of y on $x = -1\cdot2$, regression coefficient of x on $y = -0.3$. Find coefficient of correlation (r). • *Understanding*

(iv) The total revenue received from the sale of x unit of a product is given by $R(x) = 3x^2 + 36x + 5$. Find the marginal revenue when $x = 5$. • *Understanding*

(v) A manufacturing company finds that the daily cost of producing x item of product is given by $C(x) = 210x + 7000$. Find the minimum number that must be produced and sold daily, if each item is sold for ₹ 280. • *Understanding*

20. (i) The cost function of a commodity is $C(x) = 200 + 20x - \frac{1}{2}x^2$ (in rupees). Find the range where AC falls. • *Application* [2]

Or

(ii) The demand function of a monopoly is given by $x = 100 - 4p$. Find the quantity at which the MR will be zero. • *Application*

21. (i) A survey of 50 families to study the relationships between expenditure on accommodation in (₹ x) and expenditure on food and entertainment (₹ y) gave the following results.

$\Sigma x = 8500, \Sigma y = 9600, \sigma_x = 60, \sigma_y = 20, r = 0.6$

Estimate the expenditure on food and entertainment when expenditure on accommodation is ₹ 200. • *Application*

Or

(ii) The random variables have regression lines $3x + 2y - 26 = 0$ and $6x + y - 31 = 0$

Calculate

(a) Mean value of x and y.

(b) Coefficient of correlations. • *Application*

22. A linear programming problem is given by $Z = px + qy$ where $p, q > 0$ subject to the constraints: • *Analysis* [4]

$x + y \le 60, 5x + y \le 100, x \ge 0$ and $y \ge 0$

(i) Solve graphically to find the corner points of the feasible region.

(ii) If $Z = px + qy$ is maximum at (0, 60) and (10, 50), find the relation of p and q.

Also mention the number of optimal solution(s) in this case.

SOLUTIONS

1. (i) (d) Let A be a matrix.

$\because A$ is symmetric,

$\Rightarrow \quad A = A^T \quad$ ...(i)

and A is skew-symmetric

$\Rightarrow \quad A = - A^T \quad$ ...(ii)

On adding Eqs. (i) and (ii), we get

$\Rightarrow \quad A + A = A^T - A^T$

$\Rightarrow \quad 2A = O \Rightarrow A = O$

which is null matrix.

(ii) (b) Let $I = \int \underset{\text{I}}{a^x} \cdot \underset{\text{II}}{e^x} \, dx \quad$ ...(i)

On integrating by parts, we get

$$I = a^x \int e^x dx - \int \left(\frac{d}{dx} a^x \cdot \int e^x dx \right) dx + C$$

$$= a^x \cdot e^x - \int a^x \log_e a \cdot e^x \cdot dx + C$$

$$= a^x e^x - \log_e a \cdot \int a^x \cdot e^x \, dx + C$$

From Eq. (i), we get

$$I = a^x e^x - \log_e a \cdot I + C$$

$$(1 + \log_e a) I = a^x e^x + C$$

$$\therefore \quad I = \frac{a^x e^x}{1 + \log_e a} + C$$

$$= \frac{a^x e^x}{\log_e e + \log_e a} + C \quad [\because \log_e e = 1]$$

$$= \frac{a^x e^x}{\log_e (ae)} + C$$

$[\because \log m + \log n = \log mn]$

(iii) (c) We have, $\tan^{-1} x = 3 \tan^{-1} a$

We know that

$$3 \tan^{-1} \theta = \tan^{-1} \left(\frac{3\theta - \theta^3}{1 - 3\theta^2} \right)$$

$$\therefore \quad \tan^{-1} x = \tan^{-1} \left(\frac{3a - a^3}{1 - 3a^2} \right)$$

$$\Rightarrow \quad x = \frac{3a - a^3}{1 - 3a^2}$$

For the tangent inverse function to be defined, the argument must be real.

So, $\quad 1 - 3a^2 \ne 0$

$\Rightarrow \quad 1 \ne 3a^2$

$\Rightarrow \quad a^2 \ne \frac{1}{3}$

$\Rightarrow \quad |a| \ne \frac{1}{\sqrt{3}}$

So, the solution is valid for $|a| < \frac{1}{\sqrt{3}}$.

(iv) (d) **Assertion** (A) The given differential equation

$$a \left(\frac{dy}{dx} \right)^2 + b \left(\frac{dy}{dx} \right) = C$$

The power of the heighest order derivative = 2

$\therefore$ The degree of the given differential equation is 2.

So, Assertion is false and reason is true.

(v) (c) Given, five numbers x_1, x_2, x_3, x_4 and x_5 randomly selected from the numbers 1, 2, 3, ..., 18.

$\therefore$ Total number of ways to choose 5 numbers out of

$$18 = {}^{18}C_5$$

$$= \frac{18!}{5! \, 13!}$$

$$= \frac{18 \times 17 \times 16 \times 15 \times 14}{5 \times 4 \times 3 \times 2}$$

$$= 18 \times 17 \times 2 \times 14$$

These number arranged in the increasing pattern

$x_1 < x_2 < x_3 < x_4 < x_5$,

On fixing $x_2 = 7$ and $x_4 = 11$

Then, number of ways of choosing x_1 from (1, 2, ..., 6) = 6 ways.

Number of ways choosing x_3 from {8, 9, 10} = 3 ways.
and number of ways of choosing x_5 from {12, 13, ..., 18} = 7 ways

Now, the number of favourable outcomes

$$= 6 \times 3 \times 7$$
$$= 126 \text{ ways}$$

$\therefore$ Required probability

$$= \frac{\text{Number of favourable outcomes}}{\text{Total number of outcomes}}$$
$$= \frac{126}{18 \times 17 \times 2 \times 14} = \frac{1}{17 \times 2 \times 2} = \frac{1}{68}$$

Hence, the probability that $x_2 = 7$ and $x_4 = 11$ is $\frac{1}{68}$.

(vi) (d) Given, $\begin{vmatrix} a & b & c \\ m & n & p \\ x & y & z \end{vmatrix} = k$ ...(i)

Then, $\Delta = \begin{vmatrix} 6a & 2b & 2c \\ 3m & n & p \\ 3x & y & z \end{vmatrix}$

On taking 2 as common from first row, we get

$$\Delta = 2\begin{vmatrix} 3a & b & c \\ 3m & n & p \\ 3x & y & z \end{vmatrix}$$

Now, taking 3 as common from first "Column" we get

$$\Delta = 2 \times 3\begin{vmatrix} a & b & c \\ m & n & p \\ x & y & z \end{vmatrix}$$

$$\Delta = 6k \quad \text{[using Eq. (i)]}$$

Hence, $\begin{vmatrix} 6a & 2b & 2c \\ 3m & n & p \\ 3x & y & z \end{vmatrix} = 6k$

(vii) (a) Given, $y = x^{\frac{1}{3}}$

To check the continuity at $x = 0$, we find

$$\text{LHL} = \lim_{x \to 0^-} f(x) = \lim_{h \to 0} f(0 - h)$$
$$= \lim_{h \to 0} (-h)^{1/3} = 0$$
$$\text{RHL} = \lim_{x \to 0^+} f(x) = \lim_{h \to 0} f(0 + h)$$
$$= \lim_{h \to 0} h^{1/3} = 0$$
$$f(0) = 0$$

Here, LHL = RHL = $f(0)$

Hence, $f(x) = x^{\frac{1}{3}}$ is continuous at $x = 0$.

Now, $y = x^{\frac{1}{3}}$

On differentiating w.r.t. x, we get

$$\frac{dy}{dx} = \frac{1}{3}x^{-\frac{2}{3}}$$

at $x = 0$,

$$\left.\frac{dy}{dx}\right|_{x=0} = \left.\frac{1}{3x^{\frac{2}{3}}}\right|_{x=0}$$

which is not define.

Hence, the function is not differentiable at $x = 0$.

(viii) (b) We have, $y = |x - 1| + |x - 4|$

for $x = 3$, $y = (x - 1) - (x - 4)$

$$y = x - 1 - x + 4$$
$$\Rightarrow \quad y = 3$$

On differentiating w.r.t. x, we get

$$\frac{dy}{dx} = \frac{d}{dx}(3) = 0 \qquad \left[\because \frac{d}{dx}(\text{constant}) = 0\right]$$

(ix) (c) **Statement I** An equivalence relation on a set is a relation which is reflexive, symmetric and transitive.

Reflexivity Let R and S be two equivalence relations on set A, then for any $a \in A$, $(a, a) \in R$ and $(a, a) \in S$. Thus, $(a, a) \in R \cap S$. Therefore, $R \cap S$ is reflexive.

Symmetry If $(a,b) \in R \cap S \Rightarrow (a, b) \in R$ and $(a,b) \in S$. Since, R and S are symmetric, therefore $(b, a) \in R$ and $(b, a) \in S$.

$$\Rightarrow \quad (b, a) \in R \cap S$$

Therefore, $R \cap S$ is symmetric.

Transitivity If $(a,b) \in R \cap S$ and $(b,c) \in R \cap S$, then $(a,b) \in R$, $(a, b) \in S$ and $(b,c) \in R$, $(b, c) \in S$

$\Rightarrow (a,c) \in R$ and $(a,c) \in S$

$\Rightarrow (a,c) \in R \cap S$

Therefore, $R \cap S$ is transitive.

Thus, the intersection of two equivalence relation is also an equivalence relation. So, Statement I is true.

The union of two equivalence relations is not necessarily an equivalence relation.

If the union of two equivalence relations is an equivalence relation, then intersection also will be an equivalence relation.

So, Statement I is true only if Statement II is true.

(x) (a) Given a_{ij} denotes the elements of ith row and j^{th} column.

and $\quad A = a_{ij} = \begin{cases} 0 & \text{for } i = j \\ 1 & \text{for } i > j \\ -1 & \text{for } i < j \end{cases}$

Let $A = \begin{bmatrix} a_{11} & a_{12} & a_{13} \\ a_{21} & a_{22} & a_{23} \\ a_{31} & a_{32} & a_{33} \end{bmatrix}$

Then, $A = \begin{bmatrix} 0 & -1 & -1 \\ 1 & 0 & -1 \\ 1 & 1 & 0 \end{bmatrix}$

$\because \quad |A| = \begin{vmatrix} 0 & -1 & -1 \\ 1 & 0 & -1 \\ 1 & 1 & 0 \end{vmatrix}$

$= 0(0+1) + 1(0+1) - 1(1-0)$

$= 0 + 1 - 1 = 0$

So, A is not invertible.

and Reason is the correct explanation of A.

(xi) (a) Given, $P\left(\frac{A}{B}\right) = 0.25$ and $P(A \cap B) = 0.12$

$\because \quad P\left(\frac{A}{B}\right) = \frac{P(A \cap B)}{P(A)}$

$\Rightarrow \quad P(A) = \frac{P(A \cap B)}{P\left(\frac{A}{B}\right)} = \frac{0.12}{0.25} = 0.48$

Now, we know that

$P(A) = P(A \cap B) + P(A \cap B')$

$\Rightarrow P(A \cap B') = P(A) - P(A \cap B)$

$= 0.48 - 0.12 = 0.36$

Hence, $P(A \cap B') = 0.36$

(xii) Given, $|A| = 3$

$\because \quad C = (\text{adj } A)^T$

$\Rightarrow \quad |C| = |(\text{adj } A)^T| = |\text{adj } A| = |A|^{3-1}$

[$\because |\text{adj } A| = |A|^{n-1}$, where n is the order of A]

$= 3^{3-1} = 3^2 = 9$

Hence, $|C^2| = |C| \cdot |C| = 9 \times 9 = 81$

(xiii) Given, R is a relation on set $\{a, b, c\}$ and $R = \{(b, b)\}$

Reflexivity Since, $(a, a) \notin R$ and $(c, c) \notin R$, therefore the relation R is not reflexive.

Symmetry If a relation is symmetric, then $(a, b) \in R \Rightarrow (b, a) \in R$.

Here, $(b, b) \in R$, so it is symmetric.

Transitivity R is not transitive.

Hence, the relation R is symmetric but not reflexive and transitive.

(xiv) Given function, $f: R \to R$.

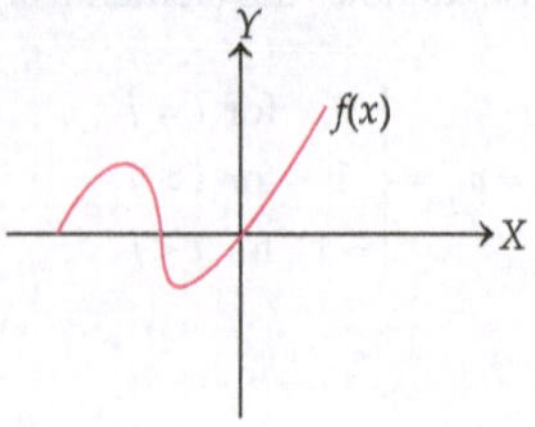

Since, each line in co-domain of the function parallel to X-axis, does not cuts the graph of function at least one point, therefore $f(x)$ is not an onto function.

(xv) Given, total number of machines = 3

Number of faulty machines = 2

Number of good machines = 3 − 2 = 1

Two test will be required and outcome will be first machine is faulty and second is good or both machines are faulty.

$\therefore$ Probability that only two tests are needed

$= \frac{2}{3} \times \frac{1}{2} + \frac{2}{3} \times \frac{1}{2} = \frac{1}{3} + \frac{1}{3}$

$= \frac{2}{3}$

2. (i) We have, $x^y = y^x$

On taking log both sides, we get

$y \log x = x \log y$

On differentiating both sides, we get

$\frac{d}{dx}(y \log x) = \frac{d}{dx}(x \log y)$

$\Rightarrow \quad y \cdot \frac{1}{x} + \log x \frac{dy}{dx} = x \cdot \frac{1}{y}\frac{dy}{dx} + \log y$

$\Rightarrow \quad \frac{dy}{dx}\left(\log x - \frac{x}{y}\right) = \log y - \frac{y}{x}$

$\therefore \quad \frac{dy}{dx} = \frac{\log y - \frac{y}{x}}{\log x - \frac{x}{y}}$

Or

(ii) We have, $f(x) = x^2 e^{-x}$

On differentiating both sides, we get

$f'(x) = -x^2 e^{-x} + e^{-x} \cdot 2x$

$= e^{-x}(-x)[x - 2] = -e^{-x}[x(x-2)]$

$\because e^x$ is always positive.

$\therefore \; x(x-2) = 0 \Rightarrow x = 0$ or $x = 2$

For strictly decreasing function, $f'(x) < 0$

$\Rightarrow x < 0$ or $x > 2$

$\therefore \; x \in (-\infty, 0) \cup (2, \infty)$

For strictly increasing function,

$f'(x) > 0 \Rightarrow 0 < x < 2 \Rightarrow x \in (0, 2)$

$\therefore f(x)$ is strictly increasing in $(0, 2)$ and strictly decreasing in $(-\infty, 0) \cup (2, \infty)$.

3. Let $I = \int_0^{\sqrt{2}} [x^2]\, dx$

We know that if $n \le x < n + 1$ for any integer n, then $[x] = n$

$\therefore \int_0^{\sqrt{2}} [x^2]\, dx = \int_0^1 0\, dx + \int_1^{\sqrt{2}} 1\, dx = (x)_1^{\sqrt{2}} = \sqrt{2} - 1$

4. Given, the equation of the curve is $y = 4x^2 - 2x^3$

On differentiating w.r.t. x, we get

$$\frac{dy}{dx} = 8x - 6x^2 = 2x(4 - 3x)$$

Slope of the tangent to the curve at origin.

$$m = \left(\frac{dy}{dx}\right)_{(0,0)} = 0$$

Now, the equation of tangent to the curve at $(0, 0)$ is

$$y - y_1 = m(x - x_1)$$

$$\Rightarrow \quad y - 0 = 0(x - 0)$$

$$\Rightarrow \quad y = 0$$

Hence, X-axis is the tangent to the curve.

5. (i) Let $I = \int \frac{2x^3 - 1}{x^4 + x} dx$

On dividing both numerator and denominator by x^2, we get

$$= \int \frac{\left(2x - \frac{1}{x^2}\right)}{x^2 + \frac{1}{x}} dx$$

On putting $x^2 + \frac{1}{x} = t, \Rightarrow \left(2x - \frac{1}{x^2}\right)dx = dt$

We get, $\quad I = \int \frac{1}{t} dt = \ln|t| + C$

$$\therefore \quad I = \ln\left|x^2 + \frac{1}{x}\right| + C$$

Or

(ii) Let $I = \int e^x \operatorname{cosec} x(1 - \cot x)dx$

$$= \int e^x(\operatorname{cosec} x - \operatorname{cosec} x \cdot \cot x)dx$$

$$= \int e^x(\operatorname{cosec} x + (-\operatorname{cosec} x \cdot \cot x)dx$$

$$\therefore \quad I = e^x \operatorname{cosec} x + C$$

$$\left[\because \int e^x(f(x) + f'(x))\, dx = e^x f(x) + C\right]$$

6. We have, $\tan^{-1}\left(\frac{x}{y}\right) + \tan^{-1}\left(\frac{y - x}{y + x}\right)$

$$= \tan^{-1}\left(\frac{x}{y}\right) + \tan^{-1}\left(\frac{1 - \frac{x}{y}}{1 + \frac{x}{y}}\right)$$

$$= \tan^{-1}\left(\frac{x}{y}\right) + \tan^{-1}(1) - \tan^{-1}\left(\frac{x}{y}\right)$$

$$\left[\because \tan^{-1} a - \tan^{-1} b = \tan^{-1}\left(\frac{a - b}{1 + ab}\right)\right]$$

$$= \tan^{-1}(1) = \frac{\pi}{4}$$

7. We have, $\sin^{-1}(x) + \sin^{-1}(1 - x) = \cos^{-1} x$

$$\Rightarrow \sin^{-1}(x) + \sin^{-1}(1 - x) = \frac{\pi}{2} - \sin^{-1} x,$$

$$\left[\because \cos^{-1} a + \sin^{-1} a = \frac{\pi}{2}\right]$$

$$\Rightarrow \quad \sin^{-1}(1 - x) = \frac{\pi}{2} - 2\sin^{-1} x$$

$$\Rightarrow \quad (1 - x) = \sin\left(\frac{\pi}{2} - 2\sin^{-1} x\right)$$

$$\Rightarrow \quad (1 - x) = \cos(2\sin^{-1} x)$$

$$\left[\because \sin\left(\frac{\pi}{2} - \theta\right) = \cos\theta\right]$$

$$\Rightarrow \quad (1 - x) = \cos(\cos^{-1}(1 - 2x^2))$$

$$[\because 2\sin^{-1} a = \cos^{-1}(1 - 2a^2)]$$

$$\Rightarrow \quad (1 - x) = 1 - 2x^2$$

$$\Rightarrow \quad 2x^2 - x = 0 \Rightarrow x(2x - 1) = 0$$

$$\therefore \quad x = 0, \frac{1}{2}$$

8. Let $I = \int \sqrt{\sec\frac{x}{2} - 1}\, dx$

$$= \int \sqrt{\frac{1 - \cos\frac{x}{2}}{\cos\frac{x}{2}}}\, dx$$

$$= \int \sqrt{\frac{\left(1 - \cos\frac{x}{2}\right)\left(1 + \cos\frac{x}{2}\right)}{\cos\frac{x}{2}\left(1 + \cos\frac{x}{2}\right)}}\, dx$$

$$= \int \frac{\sin\frac{x}{2}}{\sqrt{\cos^2\frac{x}{2} + \cos\frac{x}{2}}}\, dx$$

Put $\cos\frac{x}{2} = t$

$$\Rightarrow -\sin\frac{x}{2} \cdot \frac{1}{2} dx = dt$$

$$\Rightarrow \sin\frac{x}{2} \cdot dx = -2dt$$

Then, $\quad I = -2\int \frac{dt}{\sqrt{t^2 + t}} = -2\int \frac{dt}{\sqrt{\left(t + \frac{1}{2}\right)^2 - \left(\frac{1}{2}\right)^2}}$

$$= -2\log_e\left|\left(t + \frac{1}{2}\right) + \sqrt{t^2 + t}\right| + C$$

$$= -2\log_e\left|\left(\cos\frac{x}{2} + \frac{1}{2}\right) + \sqrt{\cos^2\frac{x}{2} + \cos\frac{x}{2}}\right| + C$$

$$\left[\because t = \cos\frac{x}{2}\right]$$

9. (i) Let $y(t)$ be the height of the kite at time t, x be the horizontal distance between the person and the ring on the ground, which is given as 8 m and $s(t)$ be the length of the string between the kite and the ring at time t.

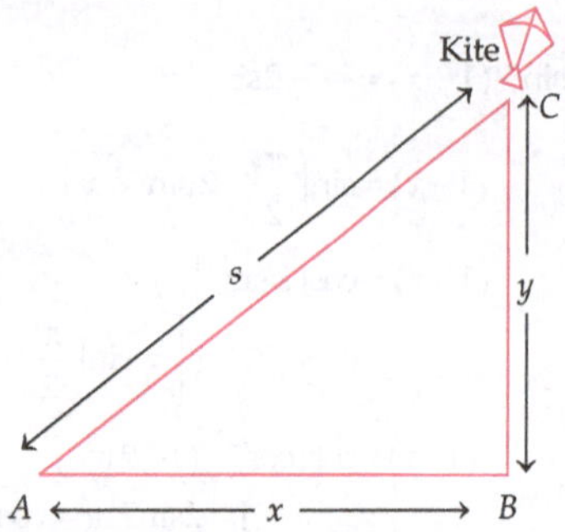

Given, $\frac{ds}{dt} = -1$ m/sec

In ΔABC, using Pythagoras theorem,

$$s^2 = x^2 + y^2$$

$$\Rightarrow \quad s^2 = 8^2 + y^2 \quad \text{...(i)}$$

On differentiating w.r.t t, we get

$$2s\frac{ds}{dt} = 2y\frac{dy}{dt}$$

$$\Rightarrow \quad s\frac{ds}{dt} = y\frac{dy}{dt} \quad \text{...(ii)}$$

From Eq. (i), when $y = 15$, we get

$$s^2 = 8^2 + 15^2$$

$$= 64 + 225 = 289$$

$$\Rightarrow \quad s = 17\text{ m}$$

Now, from Eq. (ii), putting $\frac{ds}{dt} = -1$ m/sec,

$s = 17$ m and $y = 15$, we get

$$17(-1) = 15\frac{dy}{dt}$$

$$\therefore \quad \frac{dy}{dt} = -\frac{17}{15}\text{ m/sec}$$

Hence, the kite is coming down at $\frac{17}{15}$ m/sec.

Or

(ii) We have, $y = (x + \sqrt{a^2 + x^2})^m$ ...(i)

On differentiating w.r.t. x, we get

$$\frac{dy}{dx} = m(x + \sqrt{a^2 + x^2})^{m-1} \cdot \left(1 + \frac{2x}{2\sqrt{a^2 + x^2}}\right)$$

$$\Rightarrow \frac{dy}{dx} = m(x + \sqrt{a^2 + x^2})^{m-1} \cdot \left(\frac{x + \sqrt{a^2 + x^2}}{\sqrt{a^2 + x^2}}\right) \quad \text{...(ii)}$$

$$\frac{dy}{dx} = \frac{m(x + \sqrt{a^2 + x^2})^m}{\sqrt{a^2 + x^2}}$$

$$\Rightarrow \quad \sqrt{a^2 + x^2} \cdot \frac{dy}{dx} = my$$

On squaring both sides, we get

$$\Rightarrow \quad (a^2 + x^2)\left(\frac{dy}{dx}\right)^2 = m^2y^2$$

Again, differentiating w.r.t. x, we get

$$2x \cdot \left(\frac{dy}{dx}\right)^2 + (a^2 + x^2) \cdot 2 \cdot \frac{dy}{dx}\frac{d^2y}{dx^2} = 2m^2y \cdot \frac{dy}{dx}$$

On dividing by $2 \cdot \frac{dy}{dx}$ both sides, we get

$$x \cdot \frac{dy}{dx} + (a^2 + x^2) \cdot \frac{d^2y}{dx^2} = m^2y$$

$$\therefore \quad (a^2 + x^2)\frac{d^2y}{dx^2} + x\frac{dy}{dx} - m^2y = 0$$ **Hence proved.**

10. Total number of possible outcomes, when a coin tossed three times $= 2^3 = 8$.

$S = \{HHH, HHT, HTT, HTH, TTH, THT, THH, TTT\}$

(a) If all three friends will get the same result, then

$S_1 = \{HHH, TTT\}$

Number of favourable outcomes = 2

$\therefore$ Probability that all three friends will get same result.

i.e. P(no odd person)

$$= \frac{\text{Number of favourable outcomes}}{\text{Total number of outcomes}}$$

$$= \frac{2}{8} = \frac{1}{4}$$

(b) Probability that they will get a different result in one round of tossing $= 1 - P$(no odd person)

$$= 1 - \frac{1}{4} = \frac{3}{4}$$

(c) Probability that they will need exactly four rounds of tossing to determine who would pay

$= P$(no odd person) $\times P$(no odd person) $\times P$(no odd person) $\times P$(odd person)

$$= \frac{1}{4} \times \frac{1}{4} \times \frac{1}{4} \times \frac{3}{4} = \frac{3}{256}$$

Or

(ii) Let us define the events,

L = The event that the child is left-handed.

A = If both parents are left-handed with a 24% chance of the child being left handed.

B = If father is right-handed and the mother is left-handed with a 22% chance of child being left handed.

C = If father is left-handed and mother is right-handed with a 17% chance of child being left-handed.

D = Both parents are right-handed with a 9% chance of having a left handed-child.

Given that the events A, B, C and D are equally likely.

Therefore, $P(A) = P(B) = P(C) = P(D) = \frac{1}{4}$.

Now, $P\left(\frac{L}{A}\right) = \frac{24}{100} = 0.24$, $P\left(\frac{L}{B}\right) = \frac{22}{100} = 0.22$,

$P\left(\frac{L}{C}\right) = \frac{17}{100} = 0.17$ and $P\left(\frac{L}{D}\right) = \frac{9}{100} = 0.09$

(a) Probability that a randomly selected child is left-handed

$$= P(A) \times P\left(\frac{L}{A}\right) + P(B) \times P\left(\frac{L}{B}\right) + P(C) \times P\left(\frac{L}{C}\right) + P(D) \times P\left(\frac{L}{D}\right)$$

$$= \frac{1}{4} \times \frac{24}{100} + \frac{1}{4} \times \frac{22}{100} + \frac{1}{4} \times \frac{17}{100} + \frac{1}{4} \times \frac{9}{100}$$

$$= \frac{1}{4} \times \frac{72}{100} = \frac{18}{100} = 0.18$$

(b) The probability that a randomly selected child is left-handed given that exactly one of the parents is left handed $= P\left(\frac{L}{B}\right) + P\left(\frac{L}{C}\right)$

$$= \frac{22}{100} + \frac{17}{100}$$

$$= \frac{39}{100} = 0.39$$

(c) If a child is left handed, then the probability that both parents are left handed

$$P\left(\frac{A}{L}\right) = \frac{P(A) \times P\left(\frac{L}{A}\right)}{P(A) \times P\left(\frac{L}{A}\right) + P(B) \times P\left(\frac{L}{B}\right) + P(C) \times P\left(\frac{L}{C}\right) + P(D) \times P\left(\frac{L}{D}\right)}$$

$$= \frac{\frac{1}{4} \times \frac{24}{100}}{\frac{1}{4} \times \frac{72}{100}} \quad \text{[using part (i)]}$$

$$= \frac{24}{72} = \frac{1}{3}$$

11. Let x, y and z be the cost of one paper bag, one scrapbook and one pastel sheet respectively.

	Paper bags	Scrap books	Pastel sheets	Fund raised
School A	30	20	10	₹ 410
School B	20	10	20	₹ 290
School C	20	20	20	₹ 440

(i) Now, setting up the above information into a system of equations.

$$30x + 20y + 10z = 410$$
$$20x + 10y + 20z = 290$$
$$20x + 20y + 20z = 440$$

(ii) We have, $30x + 20y + 10z = 410$

$$20x + 10y + 20z = 290$$
$$20x + 20y + 20z = 440$$

Rewrite the system in matrix form $MX = N$ ...(i)

where $M = \begin{bmatrix} 30 & 20 & 10 \\ 20 & 10 & 20 \\ 20 & 20 & 20 \end{bmatrix}$, $X = \begin{bmatrix} x \\ y \\ z \end{bmatrix}$ and $N = \begin{bmatrix} 410 \\ 290 \\ 440 \end{bmatrix}$

$$\because |M| = \begin{vmatrix} 30 & 20 & 10 \\ 20 & 10 & 20 \\ 20 & 20 & 20 \end{vmatrix}$$

$$= 30(200 - 400) - 20(400 - 400) + 10(400 - 200)$$
$$= 30 \times (-200) + 10 \times 200$$
$$= -6000 + 2000 = -4000 \neq 0$$

$\therefore M^{-1}$ exists.

The cofactors of matrix M are

$M_{11} = -200$, $M_{12} = 0$, $M_{13} = 200$

$M_{21} = -200$, $M_{22} = 400$, $M_{23} = -200$

$M_{31} = 300$, $M_{32} = -400$, $M_{33} = -100$

$$\because \text{adj}(M) = \begin{bmatrix} -200 & 0 & 200 \\ -200 & 400 & -200 \\ 300 & -400 & -100 \end{bmatrix}^T$$

$$= \begin{bmatrix} -200 & -200 & 300 \\ 0 & 400 & -400 \\ 200 & -200 & -100 \end{bmatrix}$$

$$\therefore \quad M^{-1} = \frac{1}{|M|} \text{adj}(M)$$

$$= \frac{-1}{4000} \begin{bmatrix} -200 & -200 & 300 \\ 0 & 400 & -400 \\ 200 & -200 & -100 \end{bmatrix}$$

Now, from Eq. (i), we get $X = M^{-1}N$

$$= -\frac{1}{4000} \begin{bmatrix} -200 & -200 & 300 \\ 0 & 400 & -400 \\ 200 & -200 & -100 \end{bmatrix} \begin{bmatrix} 410 \\ 290 \\ 440 \end{bmatrix}$$

$$= -\frac{1}{40} \begin{bmatrix} -2 & -2 & 3 \\ 0 & 4 & -4 \\ 2 & -2 & -1 \end{bmatrix} \begin{bmatrix} 410 \\ 290 \\ 440 \end{bmatrix}$$

$$= -\frac{1}{4} \begin{bmatrix} -2 & -2 & 3 \\ 0 & 4 & -4 \\ 2 & -2 & -1 \end{bmatrix} \begin{bmatrix} 41 \\ 29 \\ 44 \end{bmatrix}$$

$$= -\frac{1}{4}\begin{bmatrix} -82-58+132 \\ 0+116-176 \\ 82-58-44 \end{bmatrix} = -\frac{1}{4}\begin{bmatrix} -8 \\ -60 \\ -20 \end{bmatrix} = \begin{bmatrix} 2 \\ 15 \\ 5 \end{bmatrix}$$

Hence, $x = 2$, $y = 15$ and $z = 5$

(iii) The cost of one paper bag is ₹ 2,
the cost of one scrap book is ₹ 15,
and the cost of one pastel sheet is ₹ 5.

12. (i) **Method 1**

We have,

$$(xdy - ydx)y\sin\left(\frac{y}{x}\right) = (ydx + xdy)x\cos\left(\frac{y}{x}\right).$$

$$\Rightarrow \frac{dy}{dx} = \frac{(xy)\cos\left(\frac{y}{x}\right) + y^2\sin\left(\frac{y}{x}\right)}{(xy)\sin\left(\frac{y}{x}\right) - x^2\cos\left(\frac{y}{x}\right)}$$

$$\Rightarrow \frac{dy}{dx} = \frac{1+\left(\frac{y}{x}\right)\tan\left(\frac{y}{x}\right)}{\tan\left(\frac{y}{x}\right) - \frac{1}{\left(\frac{y}{x}\right)}},$$

which is homogenous differential equation of type $\frac{dy}{dx} = f\left(\frac{y}{x}\right)$.

Let $y = vx \Rightarrow \frac{dy}{dx} = v + x\frac{dv}{dx}$

$$\Rightarrow \quad v + x\frac{dv}{dx} = \frac{1+v\tan v}{\tan v - \frac{1}{v}}$$

$$\Rightarrow \left(\tan v - \frac{1}{v}\right)dv = 2\frac{dx}{x},$$

which is variable separable form where variables are v and x.

On integrating both sides, we get

$$\Rightarrow \quad \int\left(\tan v - \frac{1}{v}\right)dv = 2\int\frac{dx}{x}$$

$$\Rightarrow \log|\sec v| - \log|v| = 2\log|x| + \log c$$

$$\Rightarrow \quad \log|\sec v| = \log|v\cdot x^2\cdot c|$$

$$\Rightarrow \quad \sec v = cx^2 v$$

$$\Rightarrow \quad \sec\left(\frac{y}{x}\right) = c(xy)$$

Given that $y = \pi$ when $x = 1$

Then, $\sec\pi = c\pi$

$$\Rightarrow \quad c = -\frac{1}{\pi}$$

Hence, required particular solution is

$$\sec\left(\frac{y}{x}\right) = -\frac{1}{\pi}(xy)$$

Alternate

The given differential equation is

$$(xdy - ydx)\,y\sin\left(\frac{y}{x}\right) = (ydx + xdy)\,x\cos\left(\frac{y}{x}\right).$$

$$\Rightarrow (xdy - ydx)\frac{\sin\left(\frac{y}{x}\right)}{\cos\left(\frac{y}{x}\right)} = \frac{(ydx + xdy)x}{y}$$

On dividing both sides by x^2, we get

$$\Rightarrow \frac{(xdy - ydx)}{x^2}\tan\left(\frac{y}{x}\right) = \frac{(ydx + xdy)x}{x^2y}$$

$$\Rightarrow \frac{(xdy - ydx)}{x^2}\tan\left(\frac{y}{x}\right) = \frac{(ydx + xdy)}{xy}$$

$$\Rightarrow \tan\left(\frac{y}{x}\right)d\left(\frac{y}{x}\right) = \frac{d(xy)}{xy}$$

which is variable separable form where variables are $\frac{y}{x}$ and xy.

On integrating both sides, we get

$$\Rightarrow \quad \int\tan\frac{y}{x}\cdot d\left(\frac{y}{x}\right) = \int\frac{d(xy)}{xy}$$

$$\Rightarrow \quad \log\left|\sec\left(\frac{y}{x}\right)\right| = \log(xy) + \log c$$

$$\Rightarrow \quad \sec\left(\frac{y}{x}\right) = c(xy)$$

Given that $y = \pi$ when $x = 1$

So that $c = -\frac{1}{\pi}$.

Hence, required particular solution is

$$\sec\left(\frac{y}{x}\right) = -\frac{1}{\pi}(xy).$$

Or

(ii) We have, $\int_0^{\pi}(\sin^4 x + \cos^4 x)dx$

$$\left[\because \sin^4 x + \cos^4 x = 1 - \frac{1}{2}\sin^2 2x = \frac{1}{4}(3 + \cos 4x)\right]$$

$$\therefore \int_0^{\pi}(\sin^4 x + \cos^4 x)dx = \frac{1}{4}\int_0^{\pi}(3 + \cos 4x)dx$$

$$= \frac{1}{4}\left[3x + \frac{\sin 4x}{4}\right]_0^{\pi} = \frac{3\pi}{4}$$

Let $$I = \int_{-2\pi}^{2\pi}\frac{\sin^4 x + \cos^4 x}{1+e^x}dx \quad \text{...(i)}$$

$$= \int_{-2\pi}^{2\pi}\frac{\sin^4(-x) + \cos^4(-x)}{1+e^{-x}}dx$$

$$\left[\because \int_a^b f(x)dx = \int_a^b f(a+b-x)dx\right]$$

$$= \int_{-2\pi}^{2\pi}\frac{\sin^4 x + \cos^4 x}{1+e^{-x}}dx$$

$$I = \int_{-2\pi}^{2\pi}\frac{e^x(\sin^4 x + \cos^4 x)}{1+e^x}dx \quad \text{...(ii)}$$

On adding Eqs. (i) and (ii), we get

$$I+I=\int_{-2\pi}^{2\pi}\frac{\sin^4 x+\cos^4 x}{1+e^x}dx + \int_{-2\pi}^{2\pi}\frac{e^x(\sin^4 x+\cos^4 x)}{1+e^x}dx$$

$$\therefore 2I=\int_{-2\pi}^{2\pi}(\sin^4 x+\cos^4 x)dx$$

$$=2\int_0^{2\pi}(\sin^4 x+\cos^4 x)dx$$

$$\left[\because \int_{-a}^{a} f(x)dx = 2\int_0^a f(x)dx, \text{ if } f(-x)=f(x)\right]$$

$$\therefore I=\int_0^{2\pi}(\sin^4 x+\cos^4 x)dx$$

$$=2\int_0^{\pi}(\sin^4 x+\cos^4 x)dx$$

$$\left[\because \int_0^{2a} f(x)dx = 2\int_0^a f(x)dx, \text{ if } f(2a-x)=f(x)\right]$$

$$=2\cdot\frac{3\pi}{4}=\frac{3\pi}{2} \quad \left[\because \int_0^{\pi}(\sin^4 x+\cos^4 x)\,dx=\frac{3\pi}{4}\right]$$

13. (i) Given radius of sphere be R.

Let radius and height of cone be r and h.

Then, height of cone, $h=R+x$

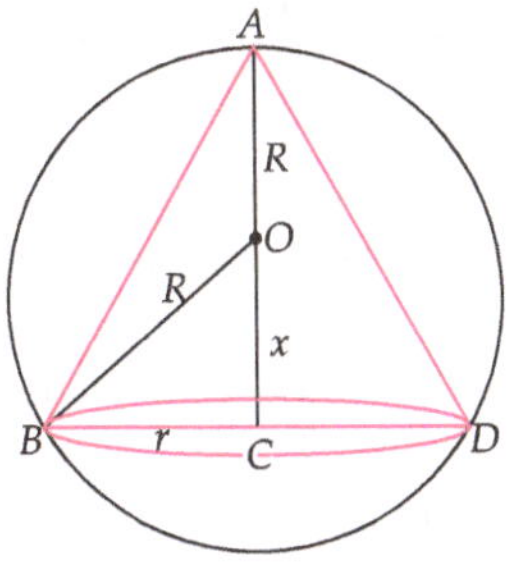

From the diagram

In ΔOCB, $r^2+x^2=R^2$ ...(i) [using Pythagoras theorem]

Volume of cone, $V=\frac{1}{3}\pi r^2 h=\frac{1}{3}\pi r^2(R+x)$

$$=\frac{1}{3}\pi(R+x)(R^2-x^2)$$ [from Eq. (i)]

$$\frac{dV}{dx}=\frac{1}{3}\pi[(R^2-x^2)(1)+(R+x)(-2x)]$$

$$\frac{dV}{dx}=\frac{1}{3}\pi(R+x)(R-3x)$$

and $$\frac{d^2V}{dx^2}=\frac{1}{3}\pi\,[1(R-3x)+(R+x)(-3)]$$

$$=\frac{1}{3}\pi\,(-2R-6x)$$

For maxima and minima, $\frac{dV}{dx}=0$

$$\Rightarrow \quad \frac{1}{3}\pi\,(R+x)(R-3x)=0$$

$$\Rightarrow R=3x \text{ or } x=\frac{R}{3}$$

Now, applying the second derivative test, we have

$$\frac{d^2V}{dx^2}=\frac{1}{3}\pi[-2R-6x]<0, \text{ at } x=\frac{R}{3}$$

Volume is maximum at $x=\frac{R}{3}$

Height of cone, $h=R+x=R+\frac{R}{3}=\frac{4R}{3}$

$\therefore$ Ratio of height of cone to diameter of sphere

$$=\frac{h}{2R}=\frac{\frac{4R}{3}}{2R}=\frac{2}{3}$$

Or

(ii) Given r and h be the radius and height of the cylinder, respectively. (from figure)

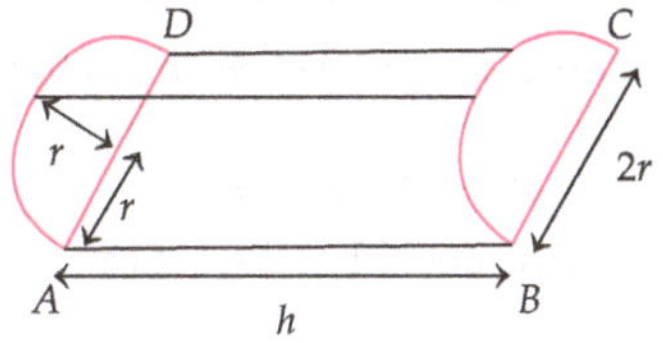

Volume of half cylinder $=\frac{1}{2}\pi r^2 h=V$

$$\Rightarrow \quad h=\frac{2V}{\pi r^2}$$

and total surface area $S=\pi r^2+\pi rh+2rh$

$$=\pi r^2+\pi r\cdot\frac{2V}{\pi r^2}+2r\cdot\frac{2V}{\pi r^2}$$

$$=\pi r^2+\frac{1}{r}\left(2V+\frac{4V}{\pi}\right)$$

On differentiating two times w.r.t. r, we get

$$\frac{dS}{dr}=2\pi r-\frac{1}{r^2}\left(2V+\frac{4V}{\pi}\right)$$

and $$\frac{d^2S}{dr^2}=2\pi+\frac{2}{r^3}\left(2V+\frac{4V}{\pi}\right)$$

For maximum and minimum, $\frac{dS}{dr}=0$

$$\Rightarrow \quad 2\pi r-\frac{1}{r^2}\left(2V+\frac{4V}{\pi}\right)=0$$

$$\Rightarrow \quad 2\pi r=\frac{1}{r^2}\left(2V+\frac{4V}{\pi}\right)$$

$$\Rightarrow \quad \pi r^3=V\left(\frac{\pi+2}{\pi}\right)$$

$$\Rightarrow \quad r^3=\frac{V}{\pi}\left(\frac{\pi+2}{\pi}\right)$$

At $r^3=\frac{V}{\pi}\left(\frac{\pi+2}{\pi}\right)$,

$$\frac{d^2S}{dr^2}=2\pi+\frac{2}{r^3}\left(2V+\frac{4}{\pi}\right)>0$$

$\therefore$ Surface area is minimum.

Now, on putting the value of V in Eq. (i), we get

$$\pi r^3 = \frac{1}{2}\pi r^2 h \cdot \frac{\pi + 2}{\pi} \Rightarrow \frac{2r}{h} = \frac{\pi + 2}{\pi}$$

Hence, ratio of the length of cylinder to the diameter of semi-circular ends is $\pi : \pi + 2$.

14. The random variable X denotes the points earned by Kiran. The possible values of X depends on the outcomes of the die rolls.

(i) If Kiran get a six on the first throw, then

$X = 1$ [∵ she gets + 1for the six]

If Kiran does not get a six on the first throw but get a six on the second throw, then

$X = -1 + 1 = 0$

If Kiran does not get a six on the first two throws but gets a six on the third throw, then

$$X = -1 - 1 + 1 = -1$$

If Kiran does not get a six on any of the three throws.

$$X = -1 - 1 - 1 = -3$$

Therefore, the possible values X can take are

$$X = 1, 0, -1, -3$$

(ii) Probability that Kiran does not get a six on any of the three throws, then

$$P(X = -3) = \frac{5}{6} \times \frac{5}{6} \times \frac{5}{6} = \frac{125}{216}$$

Probability that Kiran gets a six on the third thrown, then

$$P(X = -1) = \frac{5}{6} \times \frac{5}{6} \times \frac{1}{6} = \frac{25}{216}$$

Probability that Kiran gets a six on the second thrown, then

$$P(X = 0) = \frac{5}{6} \times \frac{1}{6} = \frac{5}{36}$$

Probability that Kiran gets a six on the first throw, then

$$P(X = 1) = \frac{1}{6}$$

Hence, required probability distribution

X	-3	-1	0	1
$P(X)$	$\frac{125}{216}$	$\frac{25}{216}$	$\frac{5}{36}$	$\frac{1}{6}$

(iii) Required expected value $= \Sigma P_i X_i = (-3)\left(\frac{125}{216}\right) + (-1)\left(\frac{25}{216}\right) + 0 + \left(\frac{1}{6}\right)$

$$= -\frac{91}{54} = -1\frac{37}{54} \approx -1.69$$

15. (i) (a) **Statement I** If $\vec{a}$ and $\vec{b}$ represent two adjacent sides of a parallelogram, then the diagonals are represented as

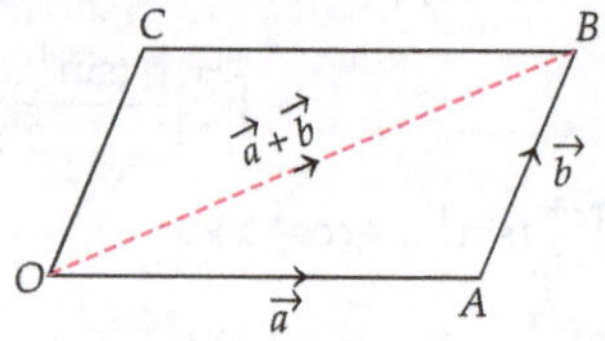

Here, the diagonals $\overrightarrow{OB} = \vec{a} + \vec{b}$

and diagonal $\overrightarrow{AC} = \vec{a} - \vec{b}$

So, Statement I is correct.

Statement II We know that the diagonals of a parallelogram intersects each other at the mid point.

Therefore, the sides of the parallelogram are actually represented by $\frac{1}{2}(\vec{a} + \vec{b})$ and $\frac{1}{2}(\vec{a} - \vec{b})$.

So, Statement II is incorrect.

(ii) (c) Given, plane passes through the point $P \equiv (1, 1, 1)$ and the equation of line is

$$\frac{x-1}{3} = \frac{y-1}{0} = \frac{z-1}{4}$$

Since, the line is perpendicular to the plane, therefore the normal of the plane is parallel to the line.

⇒ The direction ratios of the plane = The direction ratios of the line = (3, 0, 4)

The equation of plane

$$a(x - x_1) + b(y - y_1) + c(z - z_1) = 0$$

$$\Rightarrow \quad 3(x - 1) + 0(y - 1) + 4(z - 1) = 0$$

$$\Rightarrow \quad 3x - 3 + 4z - 4 = 0$$

$$\Rightarrow \quad 3x - 4z - 7 = 0$$

The distance of the plane from the origin

$$d = \left|\frac{3 \times 0 + 4 \times 0 - 7}{\sqrt{3^2 + 4^2}}\right|$$

$$d = \left|\frac{-7}{\sqrt{25}}\right| = \left|\frac{-7}{5}\right| = \frac{7}{5} \text{ units}$$

(iii) (c) Given, the direction cosines of the line are $< \frac{1}{c}, \frac{1}{c}, \frac{1}{c} >$.

We know that

$$l^2 + m^2 + n^2 = 1$$

$$\Rightarrow \quad \left(\frac{1}{c}\right)^2 + \left(\frac{1}{c}\right)^2 + \left(\frac{1}{c}\right)^2 = 1$$

$\Rightarrow \quad \frac{3}{c^2} = 1 \Rightarrow c^2 = 3$

$\therefore \quad c = |\sqrt{3}| \Rightarrow c = \pm\sqrt{3}$

(iv) Given, $\hat{a}$ is a unit vector

$\Rightarrow \quad |\hat{a}| = 1$

and $\vec{a}$ is perpendicular to $\vec{b}$

$\Rightarrow \quad \vec{a} \cdot \vec{b} = 0$

$\because \quad (\vec{a} + 2\vec{b}) \cdot (3\vec{a} - \vec{b}) = -5$

$\because 3|\vec{a}|^2 - \vec{a} \cdot \vec{b} + 6\vec{b} \cdot \vec{a} - 2|\vec{b}|^2 = -5$

$\Rightarrow \quad 3 - 2|\vec{b}|^2 = -5$

$[\because \vec{a} \cdot \vec{b} = \vec{b} \cdot \vec{a} = 0]$

$\Rightarrow \quad 8 = 2|\vec{b}|^2 \Rightarrow |\vec{b}|^2 = 4$

$\therefore \quad |\vec{b}| = 2$

(v) Placing the coordinate axes as illustrated, coordinates of A are (2, 0, 0), B are (0, 4, 3) and C are (1, 4, 0).

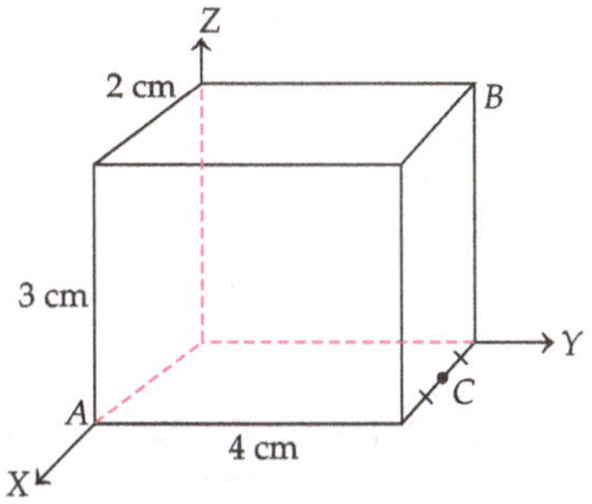

$\therefore \quad \overrightarrow{BA} = \overrightarrow{OA} - \overrightarrow{OB} = 2\hat{i} - 4\hat{j} - 3\hat{k}$

and $\overrightarrow{BC} = \overrightarrow{OC} - \overrightarrow{OB} = \hat{i} - 3\hat{k}$

Now, $\overrightarrow{BA} \cdot \overrightarrow{BC} = (2\hat{i} - 4\hat{j} - 3\hat{k}) \cdot (\hat{i} - 3\hat{k}) = 2 + 9 = 11$

16. (i) Given, $\vec{a} = 4\hat{i} - \hat{j} + \hat{k}$ and $\vec{b} = -2\hat{i} + \hat{j} - 2\hat{k}$

$$\vec{a} \times \vec{b} = \begin{vmatrix} \hat{i} & \hat{j} & \hat{k} \\ 4 & -1 & 1 \\ -2 & 1 & -2 \end{vmatrix}$$

$= \hat{i}(2-1) - \hat{j}(-8+2) + \hat{k}(4-2)$

$= \hat{i} + 6\hat{j} + 2\hat{k}$

and $|\vec{a} \times \vec{b}| = \sqrt{(1)^2 + 6^2 + 2^2} = \sqrt{41}$

A vector of magnitude 9 units and perpendicular to the vectors $\vec{a}$ and $\vec{b}$ is $9\left(\frac{\vec{a} \times \vec{b}}{|\vec{a} \times \vec{b}|}\right)$

Hence, required vector is $\frac{9}{\sqrt{41}}(\hat{i} + 6\hat{j} + 2\hat{k})$.

Or

(ii) Let $\vec{a} = 2x^2\hat{i} + 3x\hat{j} + \hat{k}$

and $\vec{b} = \hat{i} - 2\hat{j} + x^2\hat{k}$

$\because$ Angle between the vectors is obtuse

$\Rightarrow \quad \cos\theta < 0$

$\Rightarrow \quad \frac{\vec{a} \cdot \vec{b}}{|\vec{a}||\vec{b}|} < 0$

$\Rightarrow \quad \vec{a} \cdot \vec{b} < 0$

$\Rightarrow \quad 2x^2 - 6x + x^2 < 0$

$\Rightarrow \quad 3x(x-2) < 0$

$\therefore 0 < x < 2$ i.e. $x \in (0, 2)$

17. Given equation of line is

$\vec{r} = (2\hat{i} - 2\hat{j} + 3\hat{k}) + \lambda(\hat{i} - \hat{j} + 4\hat{k})$.

Position vector of the point on the line is $2\hat{i} - 2\hat{j} + 3\hat{k}$

and direction vector, $\vec{d} = \hat{i} - \hat{j} + 4\hat{k}$

Given plane is $\vec{r} \cdot (\hat{i} + 5\hat{j} + \hat{k}) - 5 = 0$.

$\therefore$ Normal vector of the plane is $\vec{n} = \hat{i} + 5\hat{j} + \hat{k}$

If straight line and plane are parallel to each other, then direction vector of line and normal vector of the plane are perpendicular to each other.

Now, $\vec{n} \cdot \vec{d} = (\hat{i} - \hat{j} + 4\hat{k})(\hat{i} + 5\hat{j} + \hat{k}) = 1 - 5 + 4 = 0$

$\Rightarrow$ They are perpendicular to each other.

$\therefore$ Straight line and plane are parallel to each other.

$\therefore$ Required distance $= \frac{(2\hat{i} - 2\hat{j} + 3\hat{k}) \cdot (\hat{i} + 5\hat{j} + \hat{k}) - 5}{\sqrt{1 + 25 + 1}}$

$= \frac{10}{\sqrt{27}} = \frac{10}{3\sqrt{3}}$ units

Or

(ii) Let the equation of the plane be $a(x - x_1) + b(y - y_1) + c(z - z_1) = 0$, which is passing through $(-1, 0, 2)$.

$\therefore \quad a(x+1) + b(y-0) + c(z-2) = 0$ ...(i)

Given line $\frac{x-0}{-2} = \frac{y-1}{3} = \frac{z-1}{-1}$ is passing through the point (0, 1, 1) and having direction ratios $<-2, 3, -1>$

Since, the plane contains the line and the point, then

$a(1) + b(1) + c(1-2) = 0$

$\Rightarrow \quad a + b - c = 0$ ...(ii)

Also, the line and normal to the plane are perpendicular

$\therefore \quad -2a + 3b - c = 0$ ...(iii)

On solving Eqs. (ii) and (iii), we get

$$\frac{a}{\begin{vmatrix} 1 & -1 \\ 3 & -1 \end{vmatrix}} = \frac{b}{\begin{vmatrix} -1 & 1 \\ -1 & -2 \end{vmatrix}} = \frac{c}{\begin{vmatrix} 1 & 1 \\ -2 & 3 \end{vmatrix}}$$

$$\frac{a}{2} = \frac{b}{3} = \frac{c}{5} = k \text{ (say)}$$

Hence, required equation of the plane is

$$2(x+1) + 3(y-0) + 5(z-2) = 0$$

or $\quad 2x + 3y + 5z - 8 = 0$

18. (i) Given, the equation of the curve is $y = x|x|$.

$$\therefore \begin{cases} -x^2, & x < 0 \\ x^2, & x \geq 0 \end{cases}$$

Hence, sketch of the region enclosed bounded by the curve, $y = x|x|$ and the ordinates $x = -1$ and $x = 1$ is as follows.

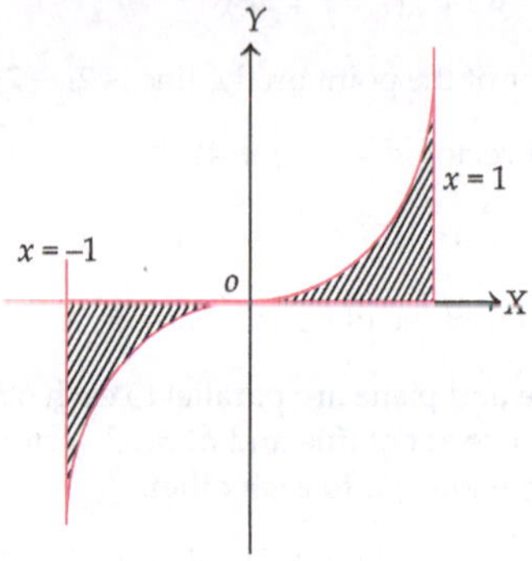

(ii) $\int_0^1 x^2 dx = \left[\frac{x^3}{3}\right]_0^1 = \frac{1}{3}$

(iii) Area of the shaded region $= 2\times$ Area of shaded region is Ist quadratnt $= 2\int_0^1 x^2 dx = \frac{2}{3}$ sq units

19. (i) (b) If the average cost (AC) is constant at all level of output, it means that the marginal cost (MC) is equal to the average cost (AC).

So, MC = AC

(ii) (d) If $r = 0$, then the regression lines are perpendicular to each other and if $r = \pm 1$, then regression lines are coincide.

Hence, only III and IV statements are correct.

(iii) Given, $\bar{x} = 53$, $\bar{y} = 28$, $b_{yx} = -1.2$ and $b_{xy} = -0.3$

We know that $r^2 = b_{yx} \times b_{xy} = (-1.2) \times (-0.3) = 0.36$

$\Rightarrow \quad r = -0.6$

[b_{xy} and b_{yx} both are negative]

(iv) Given, $\quad R(x) = 36x + 3x^2 + 5$

$\Rightarrow \quad MR = \frac{d}{dx}(36x + 3x^2 + 5) = 36 + 6x$

$\therefore \; MR(x = 5) = 66$

(v) Given, $C(x) = 210x + 7000$ and $R(x) = 280x$

Minimum number must be produced and sold daily when $R(x) = C(x)$

$\Rightarrow \quad 210x + 7000 = 280x$

$\Rightarrow \quad 70x = 7000$

$\Rightarrow \quad x = 100$

Hence, minimum number that must be produced and sold is 100.

20. (i) Given, $C(x) = 200 + 20x - \frac{1}{2}x^2$

We know that average cost

$$AC = \frac{C(x)}{x}$$

$$\Rightarrow \quad AC = \frac{200}{x} + 20 - \frac{1}{2}x$$

To find AC falls,

$$\frac{d}{dx}(AC) = \frac{d}{dx}\left(\frac{200}{x} + 20 - \frac{1}{2}x\right)$$

$$= -\frac{200}{x^2} - \frac{1}{2} = -\left(\frac{200}{x^2} + \frac{1}{2}\right) < 0, \quad \forall\, x > 0.$$

Hence, AC falls continuously.

Or

(ii) Given, $x = 100 - 4p$

$$\Rightarrow \quad p = \frac{100 - x}{4}$$

$\therefore$ Revenue, $\quad R(x) = px = \frac{100x - x^2}{4}$

Then, $\quad MR = \frac{d}{dx}(Rx) = \frac{d}{dx}\left(\frac{100x - x^2}{4}\right) = \frac{100 - 2x}{4}$

$\because \quad MR = 0$

$$\frac{100 - 2x}{4} = 0 \Rightarrow 100 = 2x$$

$\therefore \quad x = 50$

21. (i) Given,

Number of families, $n = 50$

Expenditure on accommodation = ₹ x

Expenditure on food and entertainment = ₹ y

$\Sigma x = 8500$, $\Sigma y = 9600$

$\sigma_x = 60$, $\sigma_y = 20$ and $r = 0.6$.

Now, $\quad \bar{x} = \frac{\Sigma x}{n} = \frac{8500}{50} = 170,$

$$\bar{y} = \frac{\Sigma y}{n} = \frac{9600}{50} = 192,$$

and $b_{yx} = r\frac{\sigma_y}{\sigma_x} = 0.6 \times \frac{20}{60} = 0.2$

Regression equation y on x is

$$y - \bar{y} = b_{yx}(x - \bar{x})$$

$$y - 192 = 0.2(x - 170)$$

$$\Rightarrow \quad y - 192 = 0.2x - 34$$

$\Rightarrow \quad y = 0.2x + 158$

When $\quad x = 200$

Then, $\quad y = 0.2(200) + 158 = 198$

$\therefore$ Expenditure on food and entertainment is ₹ 198.

Or

(ii) (a) Given, linear regression $3x + 2y - 26 = 0$ ...(i)

and $\quad 6x + y - 31 = 0$ ...(ii)

Let $\bar{x}$ and $\bar{y}$ be the mean value of x and y.

Then, $(\bar{x}, \bar{y})$ satisfies the Eqs. (i) and (ii), we get

$3\bar{x} + 2\bar{y} - 26 = 0$ ...(iii)

$6\bar{x} + \bar{y} - 31 = 0$ ...(iv)

By cross-multiplication method, we get

$$\frac{\bar{x}}{\begin{matrix} 2 & -26 \\ 1 & -31 \end{matrix}} = \frac{\bar{y}}{\begin{matrix} -26 & 3 \\ -31 & 6 \end{matrix}} = \frac{1}{\begin{matrix} 3 & 2 \\ 6 & 1 \end{matrix}}$$

$$\Rightarrow \quad \frac{\bar{x}}{-36} = \frac{\bar{y}}{-63} = \frac{1}{-9}$$

or $\quad \dfrac{\bar{x}}{4} = \dfrac{\bar{y}}{7} = \dfrac{1}{1}$

$\Rightarrow \bar{x} = 4$ and $\bar{y} = 7$

Hence, the mean values of x and y are 4 and 7.

(b) We have,

$3x + 2y - 26 = 0$ ...(i)

$6x + y - 31 = 0$ ...(ii)

From Eq. (i)

$2y = -3x + 26$

$y = -\dfrac{3}{2}x + 13$

$\therefore \quad b_{xy} = -\dfrac{3}{2}$

From Eq. (ii), we get

$6x = -y + 31$

$\Rightarrow \quad x = \dfrac{-1}{6}y + \dfrac{31}{6}$

$\Rightarrow \quad x = \dfrac{-1}{6}y + \dfrac{31}{6}$

$\therefore \quad b_{yx} = \dfrac{-1}{6}$

Now, $\quad r^2 = b_{yx} \times b_{xy}$

$$= \left(-\frac{3}{2}\right) \times \left(\frac{-1}{6}\right) = \frac{1}{4}$$

$\therefore \quad r^2 = \dfrac{1}{4}$

$\Rightarrow \quad r = \dfrac{\pm 1}{2}$

We know that b_{yx}, b_{xy} and r have same sign, therefore $r = -\dfrac{1}{2}$.

22. Given, $Z = px + qy, \quad p, q > 0$

Subject to constraints $x + y \leq 60$

$5x + y \leq 100$

and $x, y \geq 0$

Table for $x + y = 60$ is ...(i)

x	0	60
y	60	0

The line passes through the points (0, 60) and (60, 0).

At (0, 0),

$0 + 0 \leq 60$

$\Rightarrow \quad 0 \leq 6$ (true)

So, the half plane lies towards the origin.

Table for $5x + y = 100$ is ...(ii)

x	0	20
y	100	0

The line passes through the points (0, 100) and (20, 0).

At (0, 0),

$0 + 0 \leq 100$

$\Rightarrow \quad 0 \leq 100$ (true)

So, the half plane lies towards the origin.

On solving Eqs. (i) and (ii), we get

$x = 10$ and $y = 50$

On plating the graph, we get the feasible region $ABCD$ as shown below

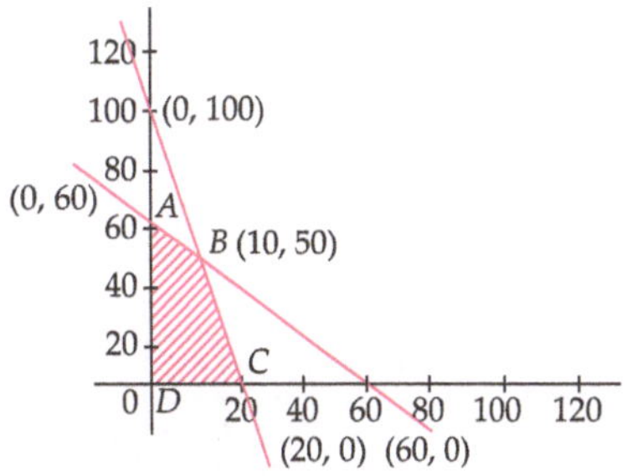

Thus, the corner points of the feasible region are $A(0, 60)$, $B(10, 50)$, $C(20, 0)$ and $D(0, 0)$.

(ii) We have, $Z = px + qy$

Given, Z is maximum at (0, 60) and (10, 50)

$\therefore \quad 0 \cdot p + 60 \cdot q = 10 \cdot p + 50 \cdot q$

$\Rightarrow \quad 10p = 10q$

$\Rightarrow \quad p = q$

which is the required relation. Also, there can be infinite number of optimal solutions.

3 SAMPLE QUESTION PAPERS

SAMPLE QUESTION PAPER 1

A Highly Simulated Sample Question Paper for ISC Class XII

MATHEMATICS (Unsolved)

General Instructions

1. This Question Paper consists of three sections A, B and C.
2. Candidates are required to attempt all questions from Section A and all questions either from Section B Or Section C.
3. **Section A** Internal choice has been provided in two questions of 2 marks each, two questions of 4 marks each and two questions of 6 marks each.
4. **Section B** Internal choice has been provided in one question of 2 marks and one question of 4 marks.
5. **Section C** Internal choice has been provided in one question of 2 marks and one question of 4 marks.
6. All working, including rough work, should be done on the same sheet as and adjacent to the rest of the answer.
7. The intended marks for questions or parts of questions are given in brackets [].
8. Mathematical tables and graph papers are provided.

Time : 3 Hrs.

Max. Marks : 80

Section A (65 Marks)

1. In sub-parts (i) to (xi) choose the correct option and in sub-parts (xii) to (xv), answer the questions as instructed. **[15]**

(i) Let $A = \{3, 5\}$. Then, number of reflexive relations on A is • *Understanding*

(a) 2 (b) 4 (c) 0 (d) 8

(ii) **Statement I** If $y = \sin(x^2 + 5)$, then the value of $\frac{dy}{dx}$ is $2x\cos(x^2 + 5)$.

Statement II If $y = \log x + \frac{1}{x}$, then the value of $\frac{dy}{dx}$ is $\frac{1}{x} + \frac{1}{x^2}$. • *Analysis*

(a) Statement I is true and Statement II is false.
(b) Statement II is true and Statement I is false.
(c) Both the statement are true.
(d) Both the statement are false.

(iii) **Assertion** (A) The function $f : R \to R$ given by $f(x) = x^3$ is injective.

Reason (R) The function $f : X \to Y$ is injective, if $f(x) = f(y) \Rightarrow x = y$ for all $x, y \in X$. • *Analysis*

(a) Both Assertion and Reason are true and Reason is the correct explanation for Assertion.
(b) Both Assertion and Reason are true but Reason is not the correct explanation for Assertion.
(c) Assertion is true and Reason is false.
(d) Assertion is false and Reason is true.

(iv) What positive value of x makes the following pair of determinants equal? • *Understanding*

$$\begin{vmatrix} 2x & 3 \\ 5 & x \end{vmatrix}, \begin{vmatrix} 16 & 3 \\ 5 & 2 \end{vmatrix}$$

(a) 2 (b) 3 (c) 4 (d) 5

(v) If $A = \begin{bmatrix} 1 & 1 & -1 \\ 2 & 0 & 3 \\ 3 & -1 & 2 \end{bmatrix}, B = \begin{bmatrix} 1 & 3 \\ 0 & 2 \\ -1 & 4 \end{bmatrix}$ and $C = \begin{bmatrix} 1 & 2 & 3 & -4 \\ 2 & 0 & -2 & 1 \end{bmatrix}$, then value of $A(BC)$ is • *Understanding*

(a) $\begin{bmatrix} 4 & 4 & 4 & -7 \\ 35 & -2 & -39 & 22 \\ 31 & 2 & -27 & 11 \end{bmatrix}$ (b) $\begin{bmatrix} 4 & 5 & 5 & -6 \\ 25 & -1 & -38 & 11 \\ 30 & 1 & -22 & 10 \end{bmatrix}$

(c) $\begin{bmatrix} 4 & 4 & -1 \\ 35 & -2 & -39 \\ 31 & 2 & -27 \end{bmatrix}$ (d) None of these

(vi) If $A = \begin{bmatrix} 0 & 2 \\ 3 & -4 \end{bmatrix}$ and $KA = \begin{bmatrix} 0 & 3a \\ 2b & 24 \end{bmatrix}$, then the values of K, a, b are respectively. • *Evaluation*

(a) $-6, -12, -18$ (b) $-6, 4, 9$ (c) $-6, -4, -9$ (d) $-6, 12, 18$

(vii) **Statement I** A balloon, which always remains spherical, has a variable radius. The rate, at which its volume is increasing with the radius when the radius is 10 cm, is $400\,\pi\,\text{cm}^3/\text{cm}$.

Statement II Rate of change of volume (v) of balloon with respect to radius (r) is $\frac{dv}{dr} = \left(\frac{2}{3}\pi\right)\cdot 3r^2$ • *Analysis & Application*

(a) Both the statements are correct
(b) Both the statements are incorrect
(c) Statement I is correct, and Statement II is false
(d) Statement I is incorrect, and Statement II is correct

(viii) **Assertion** (A) The value of $\sin^{-1}\left(\cos\frac{33\pi}{5}\right)$ is $\frac{-\pi}{10}$.

Reason (R) The principal value branch of $\sin^{-1} x$ is $[0, \pi]$. • *Analysis*

(a) Both Assertion and Reason are true and Reason is the correct explanation for Assertion.
(b) Both Assertion and Reason are true but Reason is not the correct explanation for Assertion.
(c) Assertion is true and Reason is false.
(d) Assertion is false and Reason is true.

(ix) The curve $y = x^{1/5}$ has at (0, 0). • *Analysis*

(a) a vertical tangent (Parallel to Y-axis) (b) a horizontal tangent (Parallel to X-axis)
(c) Both (a) and (b) (d) None of these

(x) If a coin is tossed 8 times, then probability of atleast 6 heads is • *Understanding*

(a) $\frac{47}{256}$ (b) $\frac{87}{256}$ (c) $\frac{37}{256}$ (d) $\frac{57}{256}$

(xi) If $\int(\cot x - \operatorname{cosec}^2 x)e^x\,dx = e^x f(x) + C$, then $f(x)$ will be • *Evaluation*

(a) $\cot x + \operatorname{cosec} x$ (b) $\cot^2 x$ (c) $\cot x$ (d) $\operatorname{cosec} x$

(xii) For what value of λ, the matrix $\begin{bmatrix} 1 & \lambda & 0 \\ 3 & -1 & 2 \\ 4 & 1 & 5 \end{bmatrix}$ is singular?

• *Evaluation*

(xiii) Find the solution of the differential equation $\frac{dy}{dx} - \frac{y}{x} = x^2 + 1$.

• *Application*

(xiv) If A and B are two events such that $P(A) = \frac{1}{2}$, $P(B) = \frac{1}{3}$ and $P(A \cap B) = \frac{1}{4}$, then find $P(\bar{A} / B)$

• *Evaluation*

(xv) An urn contains 10 black and 5 white balls. Two balls are drawn from the urn one after the other without replacement. What is the probability that both drawn balls are black?

• *Analysis*

2. Examine the differentiability of $f(x) = \begin{cases} 1 + x & \text{if } x \le 2 \\ 5 - x & \text{if } x > 2 \end{cases}$ at $x = 2$.

• *Evaluation* [2]

3. Let $f : N \to R$ be a function defined as $f(x) = 4x^2 + 12x + 15$. Show that $f : N \to S$, where S is range of f, is invertible. Find the inverse of f.

• *Analysis* [2]

4. (i) Differentiate $(\sin x)^{\log x}$ w.r.t. $\sin x$.

• *Application* [2]

Or

(ii) Find $\frac{dy}{dx}$, if $y = \sin^{-1} [x \sqrt{1-x} - \sqrt{x} \sqrt{1-x^2}]$. Also, find the value of dy/dx at $x = 1/2$.

• *Evaluation* [2]

5. Let $y = x\frac{dy}{dx} + \sqrt{1 + \left(\frac{dy}{dx}\right)^2}$ be a differential equation, then find

• *Understanding*

(i) order of the differential equation

(ii) the sum of the order and degree of the differential equation. [2]

6. (i) If $\int_0^a \frac{1}{4+x^2} dx = \frac{\pi}{8}$, then find the value of a.

• *Evaluation* [2]

Or

(ii) Evaluate $\int_0^1 x \cdot \sqrt{\frac{1+x^2}{1+x^2}} dx$.

• *Evaluation* [2]

7. Show that $\sin^{-1}\frac{12}{13} + \cos^{-1}\frac{4}{5} + \tan^{-1}\frac{63}{16} = \pi$.

• *Understanding*[4]

8. Find the least value of a such that the function f given by $f(x) = x^2 + ax + 1$ is strictly increasing on [1, 2].

• *Evaluation*[4]

Or

Find the equation of the tangent and normal to the curve $\frac{x^2}{a^2} - \frac{y^2}{b^2} = 1$ at the point $(\sqrt{2}a, b)$.

• *Application*[4]

9. (i) If $\begin{bmatrix} x^2 & 3 & 4 \\ 1 & 9 & 8 \end{bmatrix} + \begin{bmatrix} -3x & 1 & -5 \\ -3 & -2 & -6 \end{bmatrix} = \begin{bmatrix} 4 & 4 & 1 \\ -2 & 7 & 2 \end{bmatrix}$, then find the value of x.

• *Evaluation* [4]

Or

(ii) If $2\begin{bmatrix} x & z \\ y & t \end{bmatrix} + 3\begin{bmatrix} 1 & -1 \\ 0 & 2 \end{bmatrix} = 3\begin{bmatrix} 3 & 5 \\ 4 & 6 \end{bmatrix}$ then find the value of

• *Evaluation*

(a) x (b) $y + z$ (c) t [4]

10. In a school, Madam Sharma explains the additive property of definite integration which is as follows:

$$\int_a^b f(x)\,dx = \int_a^{c_1} f(x)\,dx + \int_{c_1}^{c_2} f(x)\,dx + \ldots + \int_{c_n}^{b} f(x)\,dx$$

where, $a < c_1 < c_2 \ldots < c_n < b$

After explaining it, she asks some questions to her class which are as follows. Now, answer these questions.

(i) Find the value of $\int_1^4 f(x)\,dx$, where $f(x) = \begin{cases} 7x+3, & 1 \le x \le 3 \\ 8x, & 3 \le x \le 4 \end{cases}$. [2]

(ii) Find the value of $\int_0^2 2x[x]\,dx$.

• *Evaluation* [2]

11. (i) Evaluate $\int \frac{x}{(x^2+1)(x-1)}\,dx$.

• *Evaluation* [6]

Or

(ii) Evaluate $\int_e^{e^{2x}} \sin x\,dx$

• *Evaluation* [6]

12. (i) A given right circular cone has volume p and the largest right circular cylinder that can be inscribed in the cone has a volume q. Find the ratio of p and q. • *Application* [6]

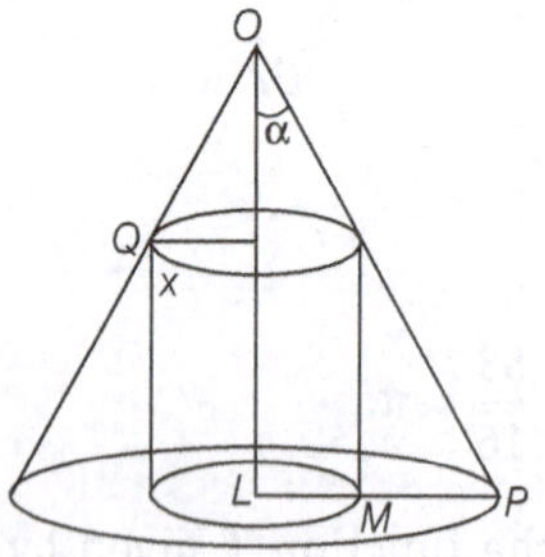

Or

(ii) Show that the semi-vertical angle of a right circular cone of given total suraace and maximum volume is $\sin^{-1}\frac{1}{3}$.

• *Application* [6]

13. A LML scooter company has two plants to manufacture. Plant I manufactures 70% of the scooters and Plant II manufactures 30%. At Plant I, 80% of the scooters are rated as of standard quality and at Plant II, 90% of the scooters are rated as of standard quality. A scooter is chosen at random and is found to be of standard quality. • *Evaluation*

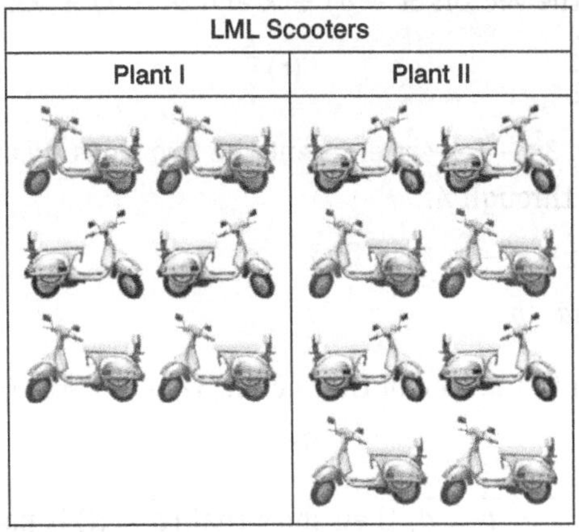

(i) Find the probability that the chosen scooter is not of standard quality, which is not manufacturing in Plant II. [1]

(ii) Find the probability that the chosen scooter is manufacturing either of any plant. [1]

(iii) Find the probability that the chosen scooter is not manufacturing by any of the plant. [2]

(iv) Find the probability that the chosen scooter is of standard quality. [2]

14. Serum institute of India uses three types of gradients namely G_1, G_2 and G_3 for manufacturing the type of vaccines, that are mRNA, mDNA and qHPV. • *Analysis & Application*

The gradients requirement (in kg) for each type of vaccine are given below.

	mRNA	mDNA	qHPV
G_1	1	1	1
G_2	2	5	7
G_3	2	1	+ 1

It is found that 9 kg of G_1, 52 kg of G_2 and 3 kg of G_3 are available to make all three vaccines. Represent it algebraically and find the number of mRNA, mDNA and qHPV vaccines produced using matrix method. [6]

Section B (15 Marks)

15. In sub-parts (i) and (ii) choose the correct options and in sub-parts (iii) and (iv), answer the questions as instructed.

(i) **Assertion** (A) : The angle between vectors $\vec{a}$ and $\vec{b}$ having the same length $\sqrt{2}$ and scalar product -1 is $\frac{2\pi}{3}$.

(a) Both Assertion and Reason are true and Reason is the correct explanation for Assertion.
(b) Both Assertion and Reason are true but Reason is not the correct explanation for Assertion.
(c) Assertion is true and Reason is false.
(d) Assertion is false and Reason is true. [1]

(ii) The value of λ for which the vectors $3\hat{i} - 6\hat{j} + \hat{k}$ and $2\hat{i} - 4\hat{j} + \lambda\hat{k}$ are parallel, is • *Evaluation* [1]

(a) $\frac{2}{3}$ (b) $\frac{3}{2}$ (c) $\frac{5}{2}$ (d) $\frac{2}{5}$

(iii) The two vectors $\hat{j} + \hat{k}$ and $3\hat{i} - \hat{j} + 4\hat{k}$ represent the two sides AB and AC, respectively of ΔABC. Find the length of the median through A. • *Understanding* [1]

(iv) If $\vec{a} = \hat{i} + \hat{j} + 2\hat{k}$ and $\vec{b} = 3\hat{i} + 2\hat{j} - \hat{k}$, then find • *Evaluation* [2]

(a) $\vec{a} + 2\vec{b}$ (b) $3\vec{a} - \vec{b}$

16. (i) Find a unit vector parallel to the sum of the vectors, (2, – 1, 1) and (3, 1, – 5). • *Understanding* [2]

Or

(ii) If $\vec{a} \times \vec{b} = \vec{c} \times \vec{b}$ and $\vec{a} \times \vec{c} = \vec{b} \times \vec{d}$, then show that $(\vec{a} - \vec{d})$ is parallel to $(\vec{b} - \vec{c})$. It is being given that $\vec{a} \neq \vec{d}$ and $\vec{b} \neq \vec{c}$. • *Analysis* [2]

17. Consider the area of the region enclosed between the two circles $x^2 + y^2 = 4$ and $(x - 2)^2 + y^2 = 4$.

(i) Find the points of intersection. • *Understanding* [1]

(ii) Set up the integration for the bounded region. • *Analysis* [1]

(iii) Find the area of the bounded region. • *Understanding* [2]

18. (i) Find the angle between the plane whose vector equations are $\vec{r} \cdot (2\hat{i} + 2\hat{j} - 3\hat{k}) = 5$ and $\vec{r} \cdot (3\hat{i} - 3\hat{j} + 5\hat{k}) = 3$. • *Evaluation* [4]

Or

(ii) Find the vector equation of the plane that contains the lines $\vec{r} \cdot (\hat{i} + \hat{j}) + \lambda(\hat{i} + 2\hat{j} - \hat{k})$ and $\vec{r} \cdot (\hat{i} + \hat{j}) + \mu(-\hat{i} + \hat{j} - 2\hat{k})$. Also, find the length of the perpendicular drawn from the point (2, 1, 4) to the plane thus obtained. • *Analysis* [4]

Section C (15 Marks)

19. In sub-parts (i) and (ii) choose the correct options and in sub-parts (iii), answer the questions as instructed.

(i) The demand function of a monopolist is given by $P = 15000 - 2x - x^2$, then revenue function is • *Understanding* [1]

(a) $15000x + 2x^2 + x$ (b) $15000x - 2x^2 - x^3$
(c) $50x + 2x^2 + x$ (d) $15000 - 2x - x^3$

(ii) Read the following statements and choose the correct option. • *Analysis*

I If C is the total cost of producing x units of a product, then Marginal Average cost (NAC) $= \frac{C}{x}$

II The sum of all costs that are dependent on the level of production is called fixed cost.

III In perfect competition market average revenue and marginal revenue are equal.

IV If $MC > AC$, then $\frac{d}{dx}(AC) = 0 \Rightarrow AC$ decreases with increase in x.

(a) Only (IV) is correct.
(b) Only I and II are correct.
(c) Only I and IV are correct.
(d) Only III and IV are correct. [1]

(iii) The total revenue received from the sale of x units of a products is given by $R(x) = 12x + 2x^2 + 6$. Find

(a) the average revenue.
(b) the marginal revenue.
(c) marginal revenue at $x = 50$. [1]

20. (i) The marginal cost of production of a commodity is $30 + 2x$. It is known that fixed costs are ₹ 120. Find

(a) the total cost of producing 100 units
(b) the cost of increasing output from 100 to 200 units. • *Application* [2]

Or

(ii) The cost of manufacturing x units of a commodity is $27 + 15x + 3x^2$.

(a) Find the output for which AC is (i) decreasing (ii) increasing. • *Analysis* [2]
(b) Find the output where AC = MC.

21. (i) By using the data $\bar{x} = 25$, $\bar{y} = 30$, $b_{yx} = 1.6$ and $b_{xy} = 0.4$, find • *Understanding*

(a) what is the coefficient of correlation between x and y?
(b) the regression equation y on x.
(c) what is the most likely value of y when $x = 60$? [4]

Or

(ii) The following results were obtained with respect to two variable x and y.

$\Sigma x = 30$, $\Sigma y = 42$, $\Sigma xy = 199$,

$\Sigma x^2 = 184$, $\Sigma y^2 = 318$ and $n = 6$

Find the following. • *Understanding* [4]

(a) The regression coefficients
(b) Correlation coefficient between x and y
(c) Regression equation of y on x
(d) The likely value of y when $x = 10$

22. A dietician has to develop a special diet using two foods P and Q. Each packet (containing 30 g) of food P contains 12 units of calcium, 4 units of iron, 6 units of cholesterol and 6 units of vitamin A. Each packet of the same quantity of food Q contains 3 units of calcium, 20 units of iron, 4 units of cholesterol and 3 units of vitamin A. The diet requires atleast 240 units of calcium, atleast 460 units of iron and atmost 300 units of cholesterol. How many packets of each food should be used to minimise the amount of vitamin A in the diet? What is the minimum amount of vitamin A? • *Application* [4]

Answers

1. (i) (b) (ii) (a) (iii) (a) (iv) (c) (v) (a) (vi) (c)
(vii) (b) (viii) (c) (ix) (a) (x) (c) (xi) (c) (xii) −1
(xiii) $y = \frac{x^2}{2} + \log x + C$ (ix) $\frac{1}{4}$ (xv) $\frac{3}{7}$

3. $f^{-1}(y) = \frac{\sqrt{y-6}-3}{2}$ **4.** (i) $(\sin x)^{\log x}\left[\cot x \log x + \log \frac{\sin x}{x}\right]$

or (ii) $\frac{1}{\sqrt{1-x^2}} - \frac{1}{2\sqrt{x-x^2}}, \frac{2}{\sqrt{3}} - 1$ **5.**(i) 1 (ii) 3 **6.** (i) 2 or (ii) $\frac{\pi}{4} + \frac{1}{2}$

8. (i) −2 or (ii) $\sqrt{2}bx - ay - ab = 0, ax + \sqrt{2}\, by - \sqrt{2}(a^2 + b^2) = 0$

9. (i) −1 ,4 or (ii) (a) 3, (b) 15, (c) 6

10. (i) 62 (ii) 3 **11.** (i) $\frac{1}{2}\log|x-1| - \frac{1}{4}\log|x^2+1| + \frac{1}{2}\tan^{-1} x + C$ or (ii) $\frac{1}{5}e^{2x}(2\sin x - \cos x) + C$

12. (i) 9 : 4 **13.** (i) $\frac{1}{10}$ (ii) 1 (iii) 0 (iv) $\frac{83}{100}$

14. mRNA = 1 kg, mDNA = 20.5 kg, qHPV = 5.5 kg **15.** (i) (a) (ii) (a) (iii) $\frac{\sqrt{34}}{2}$ units (iv) (a) $7\hat{i} + 5\hat{j}$

(b) $\hat{j} + 7\hat{k}$ **16.** (i) $\pm\frac{(5\hat{i} - 4\hat{k})}{\sqrt{41}}$ **17.** (i) $(1, \sqrt{3})$ and $(1, -\sqrt{3})$ (ii) $2\left[\int_0^1 \sqrt{4-(x-2)^2} + \int_1^2 \sqrt{4-x^2}\,dx\right]$

(iii) $\left(\frac{8\pi}{3} - 2\sqrt{3}\right)$ sq units **18.** (i) $\cos^{-1}\left(\frac{15}{\sqrt{731}}\right)$ or (ii) $r\cdot(-\hat{i} + \hat{j} + \hat{k}) = 0, \sqrt{3}$

19. (i) (b) (ii) (d) (iii) (a) $12 + 2x + \frac{6}{x}$ (b) $12 + 4x$ (c) 212 **20.** (i) (a) ₹ 13120 (b) ₹ 33000

or (ii) (a) $0 < x < 3$ (ii) $x > 3$ (b) $x = 3$ **21.** (i) (a) 0-8 (b) $y = 1.6x - 10$ (c) 86

or (ii) (a) −0.458, −0.324 (b) −0.38 (c) $11x + 34y - 293 = 0$ (d) 5.382

22. 15 packets of food P and 20 packets of food Q. Minimum amount of vitamin A = 150 units.

SAMPLE QUESTION PAPER 2

A Highly Simulated Sample Question Paper for ISC Class XII

MATHEMATICS (Unsolved)

General Instructions

1. This Question Paper consists of three sections A, B and C.
2. Candidates are required to attempt all questions from Section A and all questions either from Section B Or Section C.
3. **Section A** Internal choice has been provided in two questions of 2 marks each, two questions of 4 marks each and two questions of 6 marks each.
4. **Section B** Internal choice has been provided in one question of 2 marks and one question of 4 marks.
5. **Section C** Internal choice has been provided in one question of 2 marks and one question of 4 marks.
6. All working, including rough work, should be done on the same sheet as and adjacent to the rest of the answer.
7. The intended marks for questions or parts of questions are given in brackets [].
8. Mathematical tables and graph papers are provided.

Time : 3 Hrs.

Max. Marks : 80

Section A (65 Marks)

1. In sub-parts (i) to (xi) choose the correct option and in sub-parts (xii) to (xv), answer the questions as instructed. **[15×1 = 15]**

(i) Let R be a relation in the set N given by $R = \{(a, b) : a = b - 2, b > 6\}$. Then, the correct option is

• *Analsysis*

(a) $(2, 4) \in R$ (b) $(3, 8) \in R$ (c) $(6, 8) \in R$ (d) $(8, 7) \in R$

(ii) A relation f from C to R is defined by $x f y \Leftrightarrow |x| = y$, then the correct option is • *Analsysis*

(a) $(2 + i)f3$ (b) $3f(-3)$ (c) $if1$ (d) $(2 + 3i) f 13$

(iii) **Assertion** (A) Maximum value of $(\cos^{-1} x)^2$ is π^2.

Reason (R) Range of the principal value branch of $\cos^{-1} x$ is $\left[\frac{-\pi}{2}, \frac{\pi}{2}\right]$.

• *Analsysis*

(a) Both Assertion and Reason are correct and Reason is the correct explanation of Assertion.
(b) Both Assertion and Reason are correct but Reason is not the correct explanation of Assertion.
(c) Assertion is correct but Reason is incorrect.
(d) Assertion is incorrect but Reason is correct.

(iv) If $A = \begin{bmatrix} 0 & b & -2 \\ 3 & 1 & 3 \\ 2a & 3 & -1 \end{bmatrix}$ is symmetric matrix, then the values of a and b are

• *Understanding*

(a) −1, 3 (b) 1, 3 (c) 3, 1 (d) 4, 1

(v) **Statement I** If A is a non-singular square matrix of order 3×3, then $|\text{adj}(A)| = |A|^2$.

Statement II If B is a square matrix of order n, then $|kB| = k^{n-1}|B|$, where $n = 1, 2, 3$........

• ***Analysis & Understanding***

(a) Statement I is true and Statement II is false.
(b) Statement II is true and Statement I is false.
(c) Both the statements are true.
(d) Both the statement are false.

(vi) If the matrix A is both symmetric and skew-symmetric, then • ***Understanding***

(a) A is a diagonal matrix (b) A is a zero matrix
(c) A is a square matrix (d) None of these

(vii) Let $f(x)$ be a polynomial function of degree 6 such that $\frac{d}{dx}[f(x)] = (x-1)^3 (x-3)^2$, then

Assertion (A) $f(x)$ has a minimum at $x = 1$.

Reason (R) When $\frac{d}{dx}(f(x)) < 0, \forall x \in (a-h, a)$ and $\frac{d}{dx}[f(x)] > 0, \forall x \in (a, a+h)$; where '$h$' is an infinitesimally small positive quantity, then $f(x)$ has a minimum at $x = a$, provided $f(x)$ is continuous at $x = a$. • ***Analysis***

(a) Both (A) and (R) are true and (R) is the correct explanation of (A).
(b) Both (A) and (R) are true, but (R) is not the correct explanation of (A).
(c) (A) is true and (R) is false.
(d) (A) is false, but (R) is true.

(viii) If $f: R \to R$ be defined by $f(x) = 2x + \cos x$, then f • ***Understanding***

(a) has a minimum at $x = \pi$ (b) has a maximum at $x = 0$
(c) is a decreasing function (d) is increasing function

(ix) The area of greatest rectangle that can be inscribed in an ellipse $\frac{x^2}{a^2} + \frac{y^2}{b^2} = 1$, is • ***Application***

(a) ab sq units (b) $\frac{ab}{2}$ sq units (c) $2ab$ sq units (d) $3ab$ sq units

(x) P speaks truth in 70% of cases and Q in 80% of the cases. Then, percent of cases are they likely to agree in stating the same fact • ***Understanding***

(a) 56% (b) 60% (c) 62% (d) 64%

(xi) **Statement I** The function $f: R \to R$ defined by $f(x) = 4x + 7$ is one-one.

Statement II A function $g: X \to Y$ is an into function if there exists one element in Y, which have no pre-image in X. • ***Analysis & Understanding***

(a) Statement I is true and Statement II is false.
(b) Statement II is true and Statement I is false.
(c) Both the statement are true.
(d) Both the statement are false.

(xii) Solve the differential equation $\frac{dy}{dx} = (1 + x^2)(1 + y^2)$ • ***Application***

(xiii) If $P(A) = \frac{7}{13}$ and $P(B) = \frac{9}{13}$ and $P(A \cap B) = \frac{4}{13}$, then find

(a) $P(\bar{A}/B)$ (b) $P(\bar{A}/\bar{B})$ • ***Evaluation***

(xiv) If A is a matrix of order 2×2, then find the value of $(A^3)^{-1}$. • *Evaluation*

(xv) A card is drawn from a well-shuffled deck of 52 cards. Find the probability of getting an ace card. • *Understanding*

2. Evaluate $\lim_{x\to\pi/4}(\tan x-1)\sec 2x$. • *Evaluation* [2]

3. Let $f: N\to Y$ be a function defined as $f(x)=4x+3$, where $y=\{y\in N:\ y=4x+3 \text{ for some } x\in N\}$. Show that f is invertible. Also, find the inverse. • *Analysis* [2]

4. (i) Differentiate $\sin^2 x$ w.r.t. $e^{\cos x}$. • *Application* [2]

Or

(ii) If the following function is differentiable at $x=2$, then find the values of a and b.

$$f(x)=\begin{cases} x^2, & \text{if } x\le 2\\ ax+b, & \text{if } x>2\end{cases}$$

• *Evaluation* [2]

5. Find $\dfrac{dy}{dx}$ if • *Application* [2]

(i) $y=\cos^{-1}\left(\dfrac{1-x^2}{1+x^2}\right)$ (ii) $y=\tan^{-1}\left(\dfrac{2x}{1-x^2}\right)$

6. (i) Evaluate $\displaystyle\int\frac{x^2-1}{x^9+x^2+1}dx$. • *Evaluation* [2]

Or

(ii) Evaluate $\displaystyle\int_{-\pi/2}^{\pi/2}\sin^2 x\,dx$. • *Evaluation* [2]

7. Solve the differential equation $x\dfrac{dy}{dx}=y+\sqrt{x^2+y^2},\ x>0$. • *Application* [4]

8. Prove that $\tan\left\{\dfrac{\pi}{4}+\dfrac{1}{2}\cos^{-1}\left(\dfrac{a}{b}\right)\right\}+\tan\left\{\dfrac{\pi}{4}-\dfrac{1}{2}\cos^{-1}\left(\dfrac{a}{b}\right)\right\}=\dfrac{2b}{a}$. • *Understanding* [4]

Or

Solve for x, $\tan^{-1}\left(\dfrac{2x}{1-x^2}\right)+\cot^{-1}\left(\dfrac{1-x^2}{2x}\right)=\dfrac{\pi}{3},\ -1<x<1$. • *Evaluation* [4]

9. (i) Evaluate $\displaystyle\int e^x\left(\frac{1-\sin x}{1+\cos x}\right)dx$. • *Evaluation* [4]

Or

(ii) Evaluate (a) $\displaystyle\int_0^{\pi} x\log|\sin x|\,dx$. • *Evaluation* [4]

(b) $\displaystyle\int_0^{\pi/4}\sqrt{1+\sin 2x}\,dx$

10. Mohan, Ravi and Rahul donates some stationary items to the children who belongs to the poor family.

The table shows the data.

	Pen	Bag	Stationary box
Mohan	2	3	4
Ravi	1	1	2
Rahul	3	2	1

It is found that Mohan, Ravi and Rahul spend ₹ 29, ₹ 13 and ₹ 16, respectively.
Use the above information. Answer the following questions

(i) Set the system of simultaneous equations.

(ii) Solve the system by matrix method. • *Analysis* [4]

11. (i) Evaluate $\int \frac{1-x^2}{x-2x^2}\, dx.$ • *Evaluation* [6]

Or

(ii) Evaluate $\int_0^{\frac{\pi}{2}} |\cos x - \sin x|\, dx.$ • *Evaluation* [6]

12. Let $f(x)$ be a function defined in $1 \le x < \infty$ by $f(x) = \begin{cases} 2-x & \text{for } 1 \le x \le 2 \\ 3x - x^2 & \text{for } x \quad 2 \end{cases}$.

Find the interval for x in which two function $f(x)$ is continuous. • *Understanding & Evaluation* [6]

Or

Let $f(x) = \begin{cases} \dfrac{1-\cos 4x}{x^2} & \text{if } x > 0 \\ a & \text{if } x = 0 \\ \dfrac{\sqrt{x}}{\sqrt{16+\sqrt{x}}-4} & \text{if } x > 0 \end{cases}$ for what value of a, f is continuous at $x = 0$?

• *Evaluation* [6]

13. Suppose we have four boxes. A, B, C and D containing coloured marbles as given below:

Box	Marble Colour		
	Red	White	Black
A	1	6	3
B	6	2	2
C	8	1	1
D	0	6	4

One of the boxes has been selected at random and a single marble is drawn from it.

If the marble is red, what is the probability that it was drawn from • *Analysis & Evaluation* [6]

(a) box A? (b) box B? (c) box C? (d) Not box A.

14. Five bad oranges are accidently mixed with 20 good ones. If four oranges are drawn one by one successively with replacement, then

(i) find the probability distribution of number of bad oranges drawn.

(ii) find the mean.

(iii) find $P(2 < X < 5)$ • *Understanding & Evaluation* [6]

Section B (15 Marks)

15. In sub-parts (i) and (ii) choose the correct options and in sub-parts (iii) and (iv), answer the questions as instructed.

(i) **Assertion** (A) The angle between vectors $\vec{a}$ and $\vec{b}$ having the same length $\sqrt{2}$ and scalar product -1 is $\frac{2\pi}{3}$.

Reason (R) The angle between two vectors $\vec{a}$ and $\vec{b}$ is $\theta = \cos^{-1}\left(\frac{\vec{a}\cdot\vec{b}}{|\vec{a}||\vec{b}|}\right)$. • *Analysis* [1]

(a) Both Assertion and Reason are true and Reason is the correct explanation for Assertion.
(b) Both Assertion and Reason are true but Reason is not the correct explanation for Assertion.
(c) Assertion is true and Reason is false.
(d) Assertion is false and Reason is true.

(ii) The reflection of the point (α, β, γ) in the XY-plane is • *Understanding* [1]

(a) $(\alpha, \beta, 0)$ (b) $(0, 0, \gamma)$ (c) $(-\alpha, -\beta, \gamma)$ (d) $(\alpha, \beta, -\gamma)$

(iii) P and Q are two points with position vectors $3\vec{a} - 2\vec{b}$ and $\vec{a} + \vec{b}$ respectively. Write the position vector of a point R which divides the line segment PQ externally in the ratio 2 : 1. • *Analysis & Understanding* [1]

(iv) If the lines $\frac{x-1}{-2} = \frac{y-4}{3p} = \frac{z-3}{4}$ and $\frac{x-2}{4p} = \frac{y-5}{2} = \frac{z-1}{-7}$ are perpendicular to each other, then

(a) find the value of P. • *Evaluation & Understanding* [1]

(b) write the vector equations of these lines [1]

16. (i) Find the area of parallelogram determined by the vectors $\hat{i} + 2\hat{j} + 3\hat{k}$ and $3\hat{i} - 2\hat{j} + \hat{k}$. • *Evaluation* [2]

Or

(ii) Using vectors, find the area of triangle whose vertices are $A(1, 2, 3)$, $B(2, -1, 4)$ and $C(4, 5, -1)$. • *Evaluation* [2]

17. Consider the region in the first quadrant enclosed by the Y-axis, the line $y = x$ and the circle $x^2 + y^2 = 32$ using integration. • *Analysis & Evaluation*

(i) find the point of intersection [1]

(ii) set up the integration for the region [1]

(iii) find the area of bounded region [2]

18. (i) Find the distance of a point $(2, 2, -1)$ from the plane

(a) $\vec{r}\cdot(3\hat{i} - 3\hat{j} + 5\hat{k}) = 7$ (b) $3x - 3y + 5z = 7$ • *Evaluation* [4]

Or

(ii) Find the coordinates of the foot of the perpendicular drawn from the origin to the plane $2x + 3y + 4z - 12 = 0$. • *Application & Evaluation* [4]

Section C (15 Marks)

19. In sub-parts (i) and (ii) choose the correct options and in sub-part (iii), answer the questions as instructed.

(i) The cost function of a firm is given by $C(x) = 2x^2 + x - 5$, then the marginal cost when $x = 4$ is

(a) ₹ 15 (b) ₹ 16 (c) ₹ 17 (d) ₹ 18 • *Evaluation* [1]

(ii) Read the following statements and choose the correct option.

I. The equation of the regression line of x on y is represented by $x - \bar{x} = b_{xy}(y - \bar{y})$.

II. If $\bar{x} = 25, \bar{y} = 30, b_{yx} = -1.6$ and $b_{xy} = 0.4$ then the regression equation y or x is $y = 1.4x - 10$.

III. Both the regression coefficient must have different sign.

IV. Coefficient of correlation between x and y is given by $\sqrt{b_{xy} \times b_{yx}}$. • *Analysis* [1]

(a) Only (IV) is correct. (b) Only (I) and (II) are correct.

(c) Only (I) and (IV) are correct. (d) Only (III) and (IV) are correct.

(iii) The cost function $C(x)$ of a firm is given by $C(x) = 2x^2 - 4x + 5$. Find • *Understanding & Evaluation*

(a) the average cost function. (b) the average cost.

(c) the marginal cost when $x = 10$. [1 + 1 + 1 = 3]

20. (i) Find the correlation coefficient between x and y from the following data.

$\Sigma x = 40, \Sigma y = 50, \Sigma xy = 220, \Sigma x^2 = 200, \Sigma y^2 = 262, n = 10.$ • *Understanding & Evaluation* [2]

Or (ii) From the following information

$\Sigma(x - 58) = 46, \Sigma(x - 58)^2 = 3086, \Sigma(y - 58) = 9, \Sigma(y - 58)^2 = 483, (x - 58)(y - 58) = 1095, n = 7.$ [2]

Find the equations of two lines of regression. Also find the coefficient of correlation between x and y.

• *Understanding & Evaluation*

21. (i) A dietician wishes to mix two types of food in such a way that the vitamin contents of the mixture contain atleast 8 units of vitamin A and 10 units of vitamin C. Food I contains 2 units/kg of vitamin A and 1 unit/kg of vitamin C. Food II contains 1 unit/kg of vitamin A and 2 units/kg of vitamin C. It costs ₹ 50 per kg to purchase food I and ₹ 70 per kg to purchase food II.

(a) Formulate this is as Linear programming problem and solve it. Identify the feasible region from the rough sketch. • *Analysis & Application*

(b) Determine the minimum cost of such a mixture.

(c) Identify the feasible region from the rough sketch. [4]

Or (ii) A library has to accommodate two different types of books on a shelf. The books are 6 cm and 4 cm thick and weight 1 kg and $1\frac{1}{2}$ each, respectively. The shelf is 96 cm long and atmost can support a weight of 21 kg. • *Understanding & Evaluation* [4]

(a) How should the shelf to filled with the books of two types in order to include the greatest number of books.

(b) Formulate this is a linear programming problem.

(c) Solve the formed LPP graphically and find the maximum number of books.

(d) Find the number of books of both different types.

22. Given the total cost function for x units of a commodity as

$C(x) = \frac{1}{3}x^3 + x^2 - 8x + 5$, find the marginal cost function and average cost function. Also find the slope of average cost function. • *Analysis & Application* [4]

Answers

1. (i) (a) (ii) (c) (iii) (c) (iv) (a) (v) (a) (vi) (b) (vii) (a) (viii) (d) (ix) (c) (x) (c)

(xi) (c) (xii) $\tan^{-1} y = x + \frac{x^3}{3} + C$ (xiii) (a) $\frac{5}{9}$ (b) $\frac{1}{4}$ (xiv) $(A^{-1})^3$ (xv) $\frac{1}{13}$

2. -1 **3.** $f^{-1}(x) = \frac{x-3}{4}$ 4. (i) $\frac{-2\cos x}{e^{\cos x}}$ **Or** (ii) $a = 4, b = -4$

5. (i) $\frac{2}{1+x^2}$ (ii) $\frac{2}{1+x^2}$ **6.** (i) $\frac{1}{2}\log\left|\frac{x^2+1-x}{x^2+1+x}\right| + C$ **Or** (ii) $\frac{\pi}{2}$

7. $y + \sqrt{x^2+y^2} = Cx^2$

8. $2-\sqrt{3}$

9. (i) $-e^x \cot\frac{x}{2} + C$ **Or** (ii) (a) $\frac{\pi^2}{2}\log\left(\frac{1}{2}\right)$ (b) 1

10. (i) $2x+3y+4z=29, x+y+2z=13, 3x+2y+z=16$, (ii) $x=2, y=3, z=4$

12. $x \in [1,\infty) - \{2\}$ or $a = 8$

13. (a) $\frac{1}{15}$ (b) $\frac{2}{5}$ (c) $\frac{8}{15}$ (d) $\frac{14}{15}$

11. (i) $\frac{x}{2} + \frac{1}{8}\log|x-2x^2| - \frac{7}{16}\log\left|\frac{2x-1}{2x}\right| + C$ **Or** (ii) $2(\sqrt{2}-1)$

14.

X	0	1	2	3	4
P (X)	$\frac{256}{625}$	$\frac{256}{625}$	$\frac{96}{625}$	$\frac{16}{625}$	$\frac{1}{625}$

Mean $= \frac{4}{5}$, (v) $\frac{17}{625}$

15. (i) (a) (ii) (d) (iii) $4\hat{b} - \hat{a}$ (iv) (a) $p = -14$ (b) $\vec{r} = (\hat{i} + 4\hat{j} + 3\hat{k}) + \lambda(-2\hat{i} + 3P\hat{j} + 4\hat{k})$ and $\vec{r} = (2\hat{i} + 5\hat{j} + \hat{k}) + \lambda(4p\hat{i} + 2\hat{j} - 7\hat{k})$

16. (i) $8\sqrt{3}$ sq. units **Or** (ii) $\frac{5a}{2}$

17. (i) (4, 4) (ii) $\int_0^4 x\,dx - \int_0^4 \sqrt{32-x^2}\,dx$ (iii) 4π

18. (i) (a) $\frac{12}{\sqrt{43}}$ units (b) $\frac{12}{\sqrt{43}}$ units **Or** (ii) $\left(\frac{24}{29}, \frac{36}{29}, \frac{48}{29}\right)$

19. (i) (c) (ii) (c) (iii) (a) $A(x) = 2x - 4 + \frac{5}{x}$ (b) 16.5 (c) 36

20. (i) 0.91 **Or** (ii) y on x : $y - 59.29 = 0.37$; x on y : $x = -65.69 + 2.197y$ and coefficient of correlation $r = 0.904$

21. (i) (a) [Minimise $Z = 50x + 70y$, Subject to constraints : $2x + y \geq 8$, $2x + 2y \geq 10$ and $x, y \geq 0$], 2 kg of food I, 4 kg of food II;

(b) Minimum cost = ₹ 380 **Or** (ii) (a) LPP is $Z_{max} = x + y$, subject to constraints $6x + 4y \leq 96$, $x + \frac{3}{2}y \leq 21$ and $x, y \geq 0$

(b) 18 (c) 12 and 6

22. $MC = x^2 + 2x - 8$, $AC = \frac{1}{3}x^2 + x - 8 + \frac{5}{x}$ and slope $\frac{d}{dx}(AC) = \frac{2}{3}x + 1 - \frac{5}{x^2}$

SAMPLE QUESTION PAPER 3

A Highly Simulated Sample Question Paper for ISC Class XII

MATHEMATICS (Unsolved)

General Instructions

1. This Question Paper consists of three sections A, B and C.
2. Candidates are required to attempt all questions from Section A and all questions either from Section B Or Section C.
3. **Section A** Internal choice has been provided in two questions of 2 marks each, two questions of 4 marks each and two questions of 6 marks each.
4. **Section B** Internal choice has been provided in one question of 2 marks and one question of 4 marks.
5. **Section C** Internal choice has been provided in one question of 2 marks and one question of 4 marks.
6. All working, including rough work, should be done on the same sheet as and adjacent to the rest of the answer.
7. The intended marks for questions or parts of questions are given in brackets [].
8. Mathematical tables and graph papers are provided.

Time : 3 Hrs.

Max. Marks : 80

Section A (65 Marks)

1. In sub-parts (i) to (xi) choose the correct option and in sub-parts (xii) to (xv), answer the questions as instructed.

× =

(i) **Statement I** The value of integral $\int \frac{e^{\tan^{-1} x}}{1+x^2} dx$ is $e^{\tan^{-1} x} + C$.

Statement II The value of integral $\int e^x (\sin x + \cos x) dx$ is $e^x \sin x + C$. • *Analysis*

(a) Statement I is true and Statement II is false.
(b) Statement II is true and Statement I is false.
(c) Both the statements are true.
(d) Both the statements are false.

(ii) Let $A = \{1, 2, 3, \dots n\}$ and $B = \{a, b\}$. Then, the number of surjection from A into B is • *Understanding*

(a) ${}^nP_n$ (b) $2^n - 2$
(c) $2^n - 1$ (d) None of these

(iii) **Assertion** (A) The relation R in the set $A = \{1, 2, 3, 4, 5, 6\}$ defined as $R = \{(x, y) : y$ is divisible by $x\}$ is not an equivalence relation.

Reason (R) The relation R will be an equivalence relation, if it is reflexive, symmetric and transitive. • *Analysis*

(a) Both A and R are correct; R is the correct explanation of A
(b) Both A and R are correct; R is not the correct explanation of A
(c) A is correct; R is incorrect
(d) R is correct; A is incorrect

(iv) If $A = \begin{bmatrix} 2 & 3 \\ 1 & 2 \end{bmatrix}$, $B = \begin{bmatrix} 1 & 3 & 2 \\ 4 & 3 & 1 \end{bmatrix}$, $C = \begin{bmatrix} 1 \\ 2 \end{bmatrix}$ and $D = \begin{bmatrix} 4 & 6 & 8 \\ 5 & 7 & 9 \end{bmatrix}$, then which of the sum is defined?
• ***Understanding***

(a) $A + B$ (b) $C + D$ (c) $B + C$ (d) $B + D$

(v) **Assertion** (A) $\int_{-\pi}^{\pi} x\tan^2 x\, dx = 0$

Reason (R) If $f(x)$ is an even function then $\int_{-a}^{a} f(x)dx = 2\int_{0}^{a} f(x)dx$.
• ***Analysis***

(a) Both Assertion and Reason are true and Reason is the correct explanation for Assertion.
(b) Both Assertion and Reason are true but Reason is not the correct explanation for Assertion.
(c) Assertion is true and Reason is false.
(d) Assertion is false and Reason is true.

(vi) The values of k, if the area of a triangle is 4 sq units and vertices are $(k, 0)$, $(4, 0)$ and $(0, 2)$ are
• ***Evaluation***

(a) 0, 6 (b) 0, 7 (c) 0, 8 (d) 0, 9

(vii) Let $A = \begin{bmatrix} 1 & 2 & 4 \\ 2 & 3 & -1 \\ 4 & -1 & 5 \end{bmatrix}$ and $B = \begin{bmatrix} 0 & 1 & -2 \\ -1 & 0 & 3 \\ 2 & -3 & 0 \end{bmatrix}$ be two matrices. Then, consider the following statements.
• ***Analysis & Understanding***

Statement I A is symmetric matrix.

Statement II B is skew-symmetric matrix.

(a) Both the statements are correct (b) Both the statements are incorrect
(c) Statement I is correct, and Statement II is false
(d) Statement I is incorrect, and Statement II is correct

(viii) The function $f(x) = x^x$ has a stationary point at
• ***Understanding***

(a) $x = c$ (b) $x = \frac{1}{e}$ (c) $x = 1$ (d) $x = \sqrt{e}$

(ix) At $x = \frac{5\pi}{6}$, $f(x) = 2\sin 3x + 3\cos 3x$ is
• ***Understanding***

(a) maximum (b) minimum (c) zero (d) neither maximum nor minimum

(x) Rajeev appears for an interview for two posts A and B for which selection is independent. The probability of his selection for post A is 1/5 and for post B is 1/6. He prepare well for two posts by getting all the possible informations. What is the probability that he is selected for atleast one of the post?
• ***Understanding & Evaluation***

(a) $\frac{1}{3}$ (b) $\frac{2}{3}$ (c) $\frac{3}{4}$ (d) $\frac{5}{7}$

(xi) If $\begin{vmatrix} 2x & 5 \\ 8 & x \end{vmatrix} = \begin{vmatrix} 6 & -2 \\ 7 & 3 \end{vmatrix}$, then the value of x is
• ***Evaluation***

(a) 6 (b) 4 (c) ± 6 (d) ± 4

(xii) Find wheather the function $f : Z \to Z$, defined by $f(x) = x^2 + 5$, $\forall\ x \in Z$ is one-one or not.
• ***Understanding***

(xiii) Find the order and degree of the given differential equation.

$$x\left(\frac{d^3y}{dx^3}\right)^2+\left(\frac{dy}{dx}\right)^4+y^2=e^{-x}$$

• *Understanding & Evaluation*

(xiv) A die is tossed thrice, find the probability of getting an even number atleast once. • *Understanding*

(xv) Evaluate $P(A \cup B)$, if $2P(A)=P(B)=\frac{5}{13}$ and $P\left(\frac{A}{B}\right)=\frac{2}{5}$.

• *Evaluation*

2. Find the relationship between a and b so that the function of defined by $f(x)=\begin{cases}ax+1 & \text{if } x\le 3\\ bx+3 & \text{if } x>3\end{cases}$ is continuous at $x=3$ • *Understanding* [2]

3. Show that the function $f: R \to \{x \in R : -1<x<1\}$ defined by $f(x)=\frac{x}{1+|x|}$, where $x \in R$ is one-one and onto function. • *Understanding* [2]

4. (i) Differentiate the equation $y=e^{\sin x}+(\tan x)^x$ w.r.t. x. • *Application* [2]

Or (ii) If $y=\log\sqrt{\frac{1+\sin^2 x}{1-\sin x}}$, then find $\frac{dy}{dx}$.

• *Application* [2]

5. Solve the following differential equations.

(i) $\frac{dy}{dx}=\frac{x+1}{y+2}$ (ii) $\frac{dy}{dx}=\frac{1}{\sin y}$

• *Application and Evaluation* [2]

6. (i) Evaluate $\int\frac{dx}{5+4\cos x}$.

• *Evaluation* [2]

Or (ii) Evaluate $\int\frac{\sin 2x}{(1+\sin x)(2+\sin x)}dx$.

• *Evaluation* [2]

7. Prove that $\cos^{-1}(x)+\cos^{-1}\left\{\frac{x}{2}+\frac{\sqrt{3-3x^2}}{2}\right\}=\frac{\pi}{3}$.

• *Understanding* [4]

8. If $x=a\left(\cos\theta+\log\tan\left(\frac{\theta}{2}\right)\right)$ and $y=a\sin\theta$, then find the value of $\frac{dy}{dx}$ at $\theta=\frac{\pi}{4}$.

• *Understanding & Evaluation* [4]

Or Differentiate $\tan^{-1}(\sec x+\tan x)$ w.r.t. x. • *Application & Evaluation* [4]

9. (i) Evaluate $\int\frac{dx}{(x-1)\sqrt{2x+3}}$.

• *Evaluation* [4]

Or (ii) If $\int_1^k(3x^2+2x+1)dx=11$, then find

• *Understanding & Evaluation*

[1 + 2 + 1 = 4]

(a) the value of k. (b) $\int_1^{2k}(3x^2+2x+1)\,dx$ (c) $\int_0^k(3x^2+2x+1)\,dx$

10. Coloured balls are distributed in four boxes as shown in following table.

Box	Colours			
	Black	White	Red	Blue
I	3	4	5	6
II	2	2	2	2
III	1	2	3	1
IV	4	3	1	5

A box selected at random and then a ball is randomly drawn from the selected box. If the colour of the ball is black, then • *Analysis & Evaluation*

(i) what is the probability that ball drawn is from the Box III. **[2]**

(ii) What is the probability that ball drawn is from the Box IV. **[2]**

11. (i) Evaluate $\int_0^3 f(x)\,dx$, where $f(x) = |x| + |x-1| + |x-2|$.

• *Evaluation* **[6]**

Or (ii) Evaluate $\int_0^{\pi/2} [2\log(\sin x) - \log(\sin 2x)]\,dx$

• *Evaluation* **[6]**

12. (i) An open box with a square base is to be made out of a given quantity of metal sheet of area c^2. Show that maximum volume of the box is $c^3/6\sqrt{3}$. • *Application* **[6]**

Or (ii) Find the intervals in which $f(x) = \sin 3x - \cos 3x,\ 0 < x < \pi$, is strictly increasing or strictly decreasing. • *Analysis & Application* **[6]**

13. The table gives the probability distribution of a random variable X.

X	1	2	3	4	5
$P(X = x)$	0.2	0.1	0.3	0.3	P

• *Understanding & Evaluation*

(i) Evaluate $P(2 < x < 5)$

(ii) Find $P(x \le 2)$

(iii) Find P.

(iv) Find the mean of X. **[1 + 1 + 2 + 2 = 6]**

14. A manufacturer produces three models of toys in the form of bikes say X, Y and Z per week. The manufacturer needs per unit man hour, handling and marketing cost and profit per unit.

For each type of bike, requirement is given below. • *Analysis & Evaluation*

Models	X	Y	Z
Per unit man hour	10	5	4
Handling and Marketing cost	20	30	40
Profit per unit	40	10	70

It is found that 212 men hour available per week, total fund for these purpose is ₹ 920 per week and he gain total profit in a week is ₹ 810.

Using the above information, answer the following questions.

(i) Express the data in the table above in the form of a set of simultaneous equations.

(ii) Solve the set of equations by matrix method.

(iii) Hence, find the number of bikes X, Y and Z. **[6]**

Section B (15 Marks)

15. In sub-parts (i) and (ii) choose the correct options and in sub-parts (iii) and (iv), answer the questions as instructed.

(i) **Assertion** (A) The projection of the vector $\vec{a} = 2\hat{i} + 3\hat{j} + 2\hat{k}$ on the vector $\vec{b} = \hat{i} + 2\hat{j} + \hat{k}$ is $\frac{5}{3}\sqrt{6}$.

Reason (R) The projection of vector $\vec{a}$ on vector $\vec{b}$ is $\frac{1}{|\vec{a}|}(\vec{a} \cdot \vec{b})$

• *Analysis*

(a) Both Assertion and Reason are true and Reason is the explanation for Assertion.
(b) Both Assertion and Reason are true but Reason is not the correct explanation for Assertion.
(c) Assertion is true and Reason is false.
(d) Assertion is false and Reason is true. [1]

(ii) If the plane $2x - 3y + 6z - 11 = 0$ makes an angle $\sin^{-1} \alpha$ with X-axis, then the value of α is

• *Evaluation* [1]

(a) $\frac{\sqrt{3}}{2}$ (b) $\frac{\sqrt{2}}{3}$ (c) $\frac{2}{7}$ (d) $\frac{3}{7}$

(iii) Find $|\vec{a} - \vec{b}|$, if two vectors $\vec{a}$ and $\vec{b}$ are such that $|\vec{a}| = 2$, $|\vec{b}| = 3$ and $\vec{a} \cdot \vec{b} = 4$. • *Evaluation* [1]

(iv) If $\vec{a} = \hat{i} + \hat{j} + \hat{k}$, $\vec{b} = 4\hat{i} - 2\hat{j} + 3\hat{k}$ and $\vec{c} = \hat{i} - 2\hat{j} + \hat{k}$, then find • *Understanding & Evaluation*

(a) a vector of magnitude 6 units, which is parallel to the vector $2\vec{a} - \vec{b} + 3\vec{c}$. [1]

(b) the value of $\vec{a} \cdot \vec{b} - \vec{a} \cdot \vec{c}$ [1]

16. (i) Find the equation of the plane passing through the point $(-1, -1, 2)$ and perpendicular to the planes $3x + 2y - 3z = 1$ and $5x - 4y + z = 5$. • *Understanding & Evaluation* [2]

Or (ii) Find the length and foot of the perpendicular drawn from the point $(2, -1, 5)$ to the line $\frac{x-11}{10} = \frac{y+2}{-4} = \frac{z+8}{-11}$.

• *Understanding & Evaluation* [2]

17. Consider the area of the region included between the parabola $y^2 = x$ and the line $x + y = 2$ and the X-axis. • *Application & Evaluation*

(i) Find the point(s) of intersection. [1]

(ii) Set up the integration for bounded region (Do not solve). [1]

(iii) Find the area of the bounded region. [2]

18. (i) If $\vec{a} = 3\hat{i} - 2\hat{j} + \hat{k}$ and $\vec{b} = 2\hat{i} - 4\hat{j} - 3\hat{k}$, then find • *Understanding & Evaluation*

(a) $\vec{a} + \vec{b}$ [1]

(b) $|\vec{a} - 2\vec{b}|$ [2]

(c) $\vec{a} \cdot \vec{b}$ [1]

Or

(ii) Find the projection of the vector $4\hat{i} - 3\hat{j} + \hat{k}$ on the line joining the points $(2, 3, -1)$ and $(-2, -4, 3)$.

• *Application & Evaluation* [4]

Section C (15 Marks)

19. In sub-parts (i) and (ii) choose the correct options and in sub-parts (iii), answer the questions as instructed.

(i) The total revenue received from the sale of x units of a products is given by $R(x) = 12x + 2x^2 + 6$, then marginal revenue at $x = 50$ is • *Understanding* [1]

(a) 212 (b) 210 (c) 214 (d) 216

(ii) Read the following statements and choose the correct option.

I. Marginal cost is interpreted as the approximate cost of one additional unit of output.

II. The break even point is that point, where total revenue is greater than total cost incurred.

III. If $MC > AC$, then $\frac{d}{dx}(AC) > 0$

$\Rightarrow AC$ decreases with increase in x.

IV. The profit is calculated by subtracting the total cost from the total revenue obtained by selling x units of a product.

(a) Only IV is correct.
(b) Only I and II are correct.
(c) Only I and IV are correct.
(d) Only III and IV are correct. • *Analysis* [1]

(iii) The total cost $C(x)$ of a firm is $C(x) = 0.0005x^3 - 0.7x^2 - 30x + 3000$ where x is the output. Determine

(a) Average Cost (AC). (b) Marginal Cost (MC).

(c) Average cost (AC) at $x = 100$. • *Understanding* [1 + 1 + 1 = 3]

20. (i) The rate of change of total cost (y) of a commodity per unit change of output (x) is called the marginal cost of the commodity. If there exists a relation between y and x in the form $y = 3x\left(\frac{x+7}{x+5}\right) + 5$, prove that the marginal cost falls continuously as the output increases. • *Application* [2]

Or

(ii) Find the profit function and hence find the breakeven points when $C(x) = 35000 + 500x$ and $R(x) = 5000x - 100x^2$ • *Understanding & Evaluation* [2]

21. (i) You are given the following data

	x	y
Arithmetic mean	36	85
Standard deviation	11	8

Correlation coefficient between x and y is 0.66. Find • *Analysis & Evaluation*

(a) the two regression coefficients. [1]

(b) the two regression equations. [2]

(c) the most likely value of y when $x = 10$. [1]

Or

(ii) Given two regression lines $4x + 3y + 7 = 0$ and $3x + 4y + 8 = 0$, determine

• ***Understanding & Evaluation***

(a) the regression line of y on x. [1]

(b) the regression line of x on y. [1]

(c) b_{yx} [1]

(d) b_{xy} [1]

22. A merchant plans to sell two types of personal computers, a desktop model and a portable model that will cost ₹ 25000 and ₹ 40000, respectively. He estimates that the total monthly demand of computers will not exceed 250 units. Find the number of units of each type of computers which the merchant should stock to get maximum profit, if he does not want to invest more than ₹ 70 lakh and his profit on the desktop model is ₹ 4500 and on the portable model is ₹ 5000. Make an LPP and solve it graphically.

• ***Analysis & Application* [4]**

ANSWERS

1. (i) (c) (ii) (b) (iii) (a) (iv) (d) (v) (b) (vi) (c) (vii) (b) (viii) (b) (ix) (d) (x) (a) (xi) (c)
(xii) f is not one-one (xiii) order = 3, degree = 2 (xiv) $\frac{7}{8}$ (xv) $\frac{11}{26}$

2. $a = b + \frac{2}{3}$ **4.** (i) $e^{\sin x}\cdot \cos x + (\tan x)^x[\log \tan x + 2x \operatorname{cosec} x]$ or (ii) $\frac{1}{2}\left[\frac{\sin 2x}{1+\sin^2 x} + \frac{\cos x}{1-\sin x}\right]$

5. (i) $\frac{y^2}{2} + 2y = \frac{x^2}{2} + x + C$ (ii) $-\cos y = x + C$

6. (i) $\frac{2}{3}\tan^{-1}\left(\frac{\tan\frac{x}{2}}{3}\right) + C$ or (ii) $-2\log[1 + \sin x] + 4\log(2 + \sin x) + C$

8. 1 or $\frac{1}{2}$ **9.** (i) $\frac{1}{\sqrt{5}}\log\left|\frac{\sqrt{2x+3}-\sqrt{5}}{\sqrt{2x+3}+\sqrt{5}}\right| + C$ or (ii) (a) 2 (b) 81 (c) 3

10. (i) $\frac{156}{947}$ (ii) $\frac{336}{947}$ **11.** (i) $\frac{19}{2}$ or (ii) $-\frac{\pi}{2}\log 2$

12. (ii) Strictly in $\left(0, \frac{\pi}{4}\right)$ and $\left(\frac{7\pi}{12}, \frac{11\pi}{12}\right)$, Strictly decreasing in $\left(\frac{\pi}{4}, \frac{7\pi}{12}\right)$ and $\left(\frac{11\pi}{12}, \pi\right)$

13. (i) 0.6 (ii) 0.3 (iii) 0.1 (iv) 3

14. $x = 10$, $y = 20$ and $z = 3$ **15.** (i) (c) (ii) (c) (iii) $\sqrt{5}$ (iv) (a) $\pm 2(\hat{i} - 2\hat{j} + 2\hat{k})$ (b) 5

16. (i) $5x + 9y + 11z = 8$ or (ii) Foot of the perpendicular = (1, 2, 3), Length of the perpendicular = $\sqrt{14}$ units.

17. (i) (1, 1), (4, −2) (ii) $\int_0^1 \sqrt{x}\,dx + \int_1^2 (2 - x)\,dx$ (iii) $\frac{7}{6}$ sq units **18.** (i) (a) $5\hat{i} - 6\hat{j} - 2\hat{k}$ (b) $\sqrt{86}$ (c) 11 *or* (ii) 1

19. (i) (a) (ii) (c) (iii) (a) $0.0005x^2 - 0.7x - 30 + \frac{3000}{x}$ (b) $0.0015x^2 - 1.4x - 30$ (c) −35

20. (ii) $P(x) = 4500x - 100x^2 - 35000$ and breakeven values are 10 or 35.

21. (i) (a) 0.48, 0.9075 (b) $y = 0.48x + 67.72$, $x = 0.9075y - 41.14$ (c) 72.52 *or* (ii) (a) $3x + 4y + 8 = 0$
(b) $4x + 3y + 7 = 0$ (c) $\frac{-3}{4}$ (d) $\frac{-3}{4}$

22. Maximum profit is ₹ 1150000 at (200, 50).